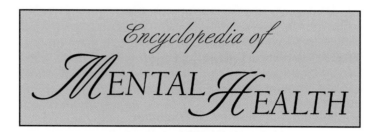

Encyclopedia of
ENTAL EALTH

Volume 3   O–Z, Index

Editor-in-Chief

Howard S. Friedman
University of California, Riverside

Executive Advisory Board

Nancy E. Adler
University of California, San Francisco

Ross D. Parke
University of California, Riverside

Christopher Peterson
University of Michigan, Ann Arbor

Robert Rosenthal
Harvard University

Ralf Schwarzer
Freie Universität Berlin

Roxane Cohen Silver
University of California, Irvine

David Spiegel
Stanford University School of Medicine

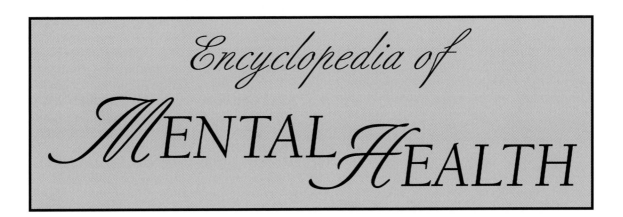

Encyclopedia of *Mental Health*

Volume 3 O–Z, Index

Editor-in-Chief

HOWARD S. FRIEDMAN

Department of Psychology
University of California, Riverside

ACADEMIC PRESS

SAN DIEGO   LONDON   BOSTON   NEW YORK   SYDNEY   TOKYO   TORONTO

Copyright © 1998 by ACADEMIC PRESS

Academic Press
a division of Harcourt Brace & Company
525 B Street, Suite 1900, San Diego, California 92101-4495, USA
http://www.apnet.com

Academic Press Limited
24-28 Oval Road, London NW1 7DX, UK
http://www.hbuk.co.uk/ap/

Library of Congress Card Catalog Number: 98-84208

International Standard Book Number: 0-12-226675-7 (set)
International Standard Book Number: 0-12-226676-5 (volume 1)
International Standard Book Number: 0-12-226677-3 (volume 2)
International Standard Book Number: 0-12-226678-1 (volume 3)

PRINTED IN THE UNITED STATES OF AMERICA
99 00 01 02 03 MM 9 8 7 6 5 4 3 2

Contents

R

S

VOLUME II

Contents

How to Use the Encyclopedia

The *Encyclopedia of Mental Health* is intended for use by students, research professionals, and practicing clinicians. Articles have been chosen to reflect major disciplines in the study of mental health, common topics of research by professionals in this domain, and areas of public interest and concern. Each article serves as a comprehensive overview of a given area, providing both breadth of coverage for students, and depth of coverage for research and clinical professionals. We have designed the encyclopedia with the following features for maximum accessibility for all readers.

Articles in the encyclopedia are arranged alphabetically by subject. Complete tables of contents appear in all volumes. The index is located in Volume 3. Because the reader's topic of interest may be listed under a broader article title, we encourage use of the Index for access to a subject area, rather than use of the Table of Contents alone. For instance, the topic area of recovered/repressed memories is covered under the article title "Standards for Psychotherapy." Because a topic of study in mental health is often applicable to more than one article, the Index provides a complete listing of where a subject is covered and in what context. As an example, the topic of aging and mental health is covered in a number of articles including "Aging and Mental Health," "Assessment of Mental Health in Older Adults," and "Emotion and Aging."

Each article contains an outline, a glossary, cross-references, and a bibliography. The outline allows a quick scan of the major areas discussed within each article. The glossary contains terms that may be unfamiliar to the reader, with each term defined *in the context of its use in that article*. Thus, a term may appear in the glossary for another article defined in a slightly different manner or with a subtle nuance specific to that article. For clarity, we have allowed these differences in definition to remain so that the terms are defined relative to the context of the particular article.

The articles have been cross-referenced to other related articles in the encyclopedia. Cross-references are found at the first or predominant mention of a subject area covered elsewhere in the encyclopedia. Cross-references will always appear at the end of a paragraph. Where multiple cross-references apply to a single paragraph, the cross-references are listed in alphabetical order. We encourage readers to use the cross-references to locate other encyclopedia articles that will provide more detailed information about a subject.

The Bibliography lists recent secondary sources to aid the reader in locating more detailed or technical information. Review articles and research articles that are considered of primary importance to the understanding of a given subject area are also listed. Bibliographies are not intended to provide a full reference listing of all material covered in the context of a given article, but are provided as guides to further reading.

Obesity

Michael A. Friedman and Kelly D. Brownell

Yale University

Binge Eating An episode in which an individual eats a large amount of food and experiences a feeling of loss of control.

Body Mass Index (BMI) A common measurement of obesity, BMI is expressed as weight in kilograms per height in meters squared.

Cognitive–Behavioral Therapy An approach to the treatment of obesity that attempts to modify eating habits, physical activity, and attitudes about eating, shape, and weight in order to produce weight loss.

Dieting Readiness How motivated a client is at a particular time to change attitudes and behaviors necessary to lose weight.

Obesity A term used to describe an excess of body fat, as opposed to overweight, which refers to weight in excess of some standard. It is common for the terms to be used interchangeably. While there is debate about the level at which health risk increases, government standards suggest that weight is associated with elevated risk for chronic disease (e.g., heart disease, diabetes, hypertension) as Body Mass Index (see definition) exceeds 27 kg/m² (approximately 20% overweight). Standards have not been set to establish health risk at rising levels of body fat.

Reasonable Weight An amount of weight that can be lost and maintained over time, typically 5 to 10% of original body weight.

OBESITY is a prevalent and serious problem. Approximately one-third of the American population is sufficiently overweight to be at increased health risk, and the prevalence has risen by 8% in the last decade. Risk for obesity is increased among minorities or low socioeconomic status populations. Obesity also becomes more common with increased age, particularly among women. When these factors converge, as in the case of African American women ages 45 to 75 years, the prevalence rate of obesity is as high as 60%.

The health care costs associated with obesity are approximately $46 billion yearly. Obesity is associated with increased risk for hypertension, diabetes, and cardiovascular disease. Further, the risk may increase with as little as 5% overweight. These effects are mediated in part by body fat distribution. Specifically, fat found in the upper body, particularly in the intraabdominal cavity, carries greater risk than does fat stored in the lower body.

I. PSYCHOSOCIAL CONSEQUENCES OF OBESITY

A. Social Stigma of Obesity

Cultural norms emphasize a thin body ideal, in which individuals should be thin, physically fit, and have bodies contoured in specific ways. As a result, vast numbers of individuals are dieting, buying exercise equipment, and undergoing plastic surgery in an effort to achieve this physical ideal. The drive for this lean aesthetic ideal is supported by a dieting industry valued at more than $30 billion per year that supplies diet books, programs, videos, foods, pills, and devices to help individuals shape their bodies. [*See* DIETING.]

Current culture not only condemns obese individuals for their physical appearance, but also blames them for their condition. Our culture emphasizes personal responsibility for many aspects of living, including the control of weight and shape. Further, there is a prevailing cultural belief that the body is infinitely malleable and that the rewards of looking good are believed to be so vast as to justify enormous cost and effort. In addition, there is a psychological tendency to blame the victims of medical or physical problems. [*See* EATING AND BODY WEIGHT: PHYSIOLOGICAL CONTROLS.]

As a result of these cultural assumptions, obese individuals face widespread bias, and have been described as "lazy," "stupid," "cheats," and "ugly." Further, obese individuals are subject to discrimination in employment, housing, and college admissions.

B. Psychological Consequences of Obesity

When considering the stigma associated with their condition, it is logical to assume that obese persons would be at risk for suffering severe psychological distress. However, studies investigating the psychological correlates of obesity that have compared the psychological functioning of obese and nonobese individuals have produced inconsistent results. Specifically, while some studies show that obese individuals demonstrate more psychological problems than nonobese individuals, other studies find no differences between these two groups, and still others find that obese individuals demonstrate fewer psychological problems than normal weight individuals. These inconsistent results have led to several broad conclusions, the most important being that obesity is not associated with general psychological problems. Comparing obese individuals as a whole to nonobese individuals assumes that the obese population is homogeneous and could be identified by a single psychological characteristic. In fact, obesity is strikingly heterogeneous with respect to etiology and response to treatment.

Friedman and Brownell have suggested a new approach to address the heterogeneity among the obese population. They suggest that studies comparing obese to nonobese individuals represent only a first generation of research in the field. A new conceptual approach suggests that some obese individuals suffer negative psychological consequences while others do not, and that the goal of future research should be to identify the factors that are related to psychological suffering. They propose a second and third generation of research that would identify factors likely to place an overweight individual at risk for psychological problems, such as gender, dieting frequency, binge eating, weight cycling, and early age of onset of obesity (see Fig. 1).

II. ETIOLOGY OF OBESITY

A. Historical Overview

Divergent theoretical explanations of etiology have been proposed over the past 40 years. While these theories differ in their conception of etiology, they all share the common error of attempting to explain the onset of obesity with a single cause. For example, in the 1950s, psychoanalytic theorists believed that obesity was the result of a fundamental personality problem in which obese individuals acted out unconscious conflicts. Subsequently, behavior therapists in the 1960s argued that overeating was a learned disorder that could be explained by the principles of conditioning. In the 1970s and 1980s, physiologists demonstrated in laboratory animals that weight was influenced by a complex interaction of neural, hormonal, and metabolic factors that may have a genetic origin. A flurry of studies on the genetics of obesity began in the 1980s, concluding now that genetic factors can account for from 10 to 70% of the variance of the body mass index (BMI). The distribution of body fat in either the upper or lower body has also been shown to be heritable. Consequently, it is clear that obesity is a strikingly heterogeneous disorder with respect to etiology, and that many risk factors may contribute to its onset individually or in combination.

B. Risks to Population

The fact that the prevalence of obesity has risen since the early 1900s despite stable or even declining caloric

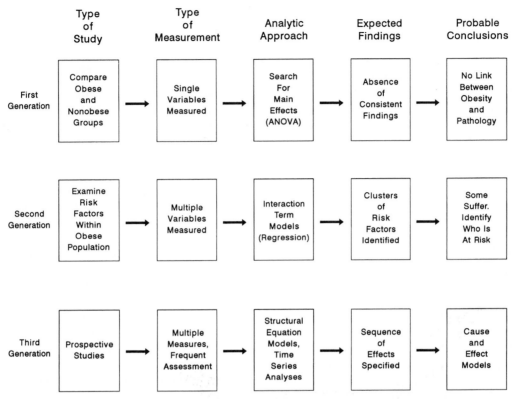

Figure 1 Schematic conceptualization showing three generations of research on the psychological correlates of obesity. The likely conclusions reached in any generation depend in part on the design of the studies, choice of measures, and analytic approach. The field currently is in the early stages of the second generation. (From M. A. Friedman, & K. D. Brownell (1995). *Psychological Bulletin, 117,* 4. Copyright 1995 by the American Psychological Association. Reprinted with permission.)

intake suggests the role of decreased physical activity, consumption of a diet higher in fat, and specific food-intake patterns. Daily energy expenditure has decreased over the past 200 years as our nation has changed from an agricultural, to an industrial, and now to an information economy. For example, from 1965 to 1977 alone, daily energy expenditure was thought to have dropped by nearly 200 kcal daily. However, while daily energy expenditure has decreased, consumption of dietary fat has increased dramatically. Since 1910, the percentage of calories consumed from fat increased from 32% to 34%, whereas that from carbohydrate declined from 57% to 46%. Since dietary fat is converted with approximately 25% greater efficiency than is carbohydrate, a person will gain more weight when consuming fat than when consuming the same number of calories from carbohydrates.

This increase in fat intake can be explained in part by our shopping and eating habits. Food choice is influenced by a multibillion dollar advertising industry that focuses particularly on impulse items (i.e., salty snacks, sweets, and frozen desserts) that are high in fat and sugar and bring retailers their greatest profits. In addition, our nation is eating out more. For example, in 1985, 88% of women ate away from home at least 1 day in 4, as compared with half that frequency just 8 years earlier.

C. Biological Risks to Individuals

Resting metabolic rate (RMR), the energy required to maintain vital bodily functions, including respiration, heart rate, and blood pressure, may differ by as much as 1000 kcal a day in obese women of approximately the same age, weight, and height. In addition, while mildly obese individuals usually have normal fat cell number, the cells are increased in size and weight (i.e., hypertrophy). Fat cell number apparently increases, however, once the individual doubles a normal fat mass. RMR and fat cell number and size have also been found to have a significant genetic component.

The common methodologies for studying the heritability of human traits have now been applied to obesity. These include family aggregation studies, adoption studies, the comparison of monozygotic and dizygotic twins, and the comparison of twins reared apart with twins reared together. The studies are consistent in showing a significant contribution to body weight, body fat distribution, and resting metabolic rate. It is clear, therefore, that excess body weight is, at the very least, made possible by genetics, and in some cases may be largely determined by genetics.

D. Behavioral Risks to Individuals

Obesity also results from overeating. While common wisdom would hold this statement to be obviously true, this explanation was attacked in the 1970s by nearly 20 studies that found that obese individuals reported consuming no more calories than their lean counterparts. Further, studies using direct observation of food consumption revealed no differences between obese and nonobese subjects. However, these studies were limited by reliance on self-report or observation of obese persons in public places. Recent studies using more sophisticated metabolic measures do in fact show increased eating in overweight individuals.

III. TREATMENT OF OBESITY

With multiple etiologies for obesity it is logical that multiple treatments may be necessary. This leads to a model of treatment in which practitioners would have at their disposal treatments with varying effects and methods of action. Different approaches would be applied to different individuals, or combinations of approaches applied to a single individual, depending on etiology of the weight problem and its expression (e.g., increased appetite, diminished satiety, low levels of exercise, binge eating, emotional eating). We approach a new generation of research that may allow the field to place such a model into action. With this in mind, it is instructive to examine what is currently known about specific treatments.

A. Medical Treatments

1. Pharmacological Treatments

Research on pharmacology for obesity has spanned 4 decades. The early part of this history involved amphetamines. The goal was to provide quick, short-term weight loss to individuals with more resistant cases of obesity. The logic was that once weight loss was achieved, the patient would maintain the lower weight by avoiding the problems that would again produce obesity. However, amphetamines produced dangerous side effects, particularly because of their high potential for abuse and dependence, and they were prescribed for individuals at relatively low weights. Amphetamines are no longer considered an appropriate or safe treatment for obesity.

Currently, there are two major pharmacologic treatments in use for the treatment of obesity, with two others likely to receive FDA approval. The first is a combination of the drug phentermine and fenfluramine, commonly known as the "phen-fen" combination. Phentermine is an anorexiant agent that reduces net energy intake by slowing the central nervous system (CNS) stimulant activity. The main antiobesity effect of fenfluramine is also appetite suppression, but it tends to have slightly depressant CNS effects. One recent study by Weintraub and colleagues suggested that a combination of medications that have relatively different modes of action may be effective in reducing and maintaining a lower weight for a long duration with an acceptable level of side effects. These investigators found that in a small group of subjects prescribed this combination for several years, weight loss averaged about 30 pounds.

Another drug that has been utilized in the treatment of obesity is dexfenfluramine. Dexfenfluramine stimulates the release of serotonin and inhibits all reuptake, thereby increasing serotonin concentrations in the synaptic cleft. The precise causal chain leading from increased CNS serotonin levels to appetite suppression is unknown. Immediate effects of improved glycemic control and lowering of blood pressure, independent of weight loss, have been observed. Dexfenfluramine, while used widely in Europe, was not approved for use in the United States until the spring of 1996. It produces weight losses of 7 to 12% of initial body weight, but there is no evidence of maintenance once the drug is discontinued.

Major concerns have been raised with the safety of these drugs. Concerns with risk of primary pulmonary hypertension in individuals using the fenfluramine–phentermine combination intensified with publication of a report in the *New England Journal of Medicine* in 1996. This report suggested that the risk of this often deadly disease was increased 23-fold in individuals taking these drugs for more than three months. Some experts noted that the disease, while very serious, was rare and that even a 23-fold increase represents relatively few cases; hence the cost–benefit of using the medications would still be positive.

Even greater alarm occurred in the Fall of 1997 with the publication of a review of studies on brain serotonin neurotoxicity and primary pulmonary hypertension from fenfluramine and dexfenfluramine, and with the release of a report from the Mayo Clinic on valvular heart disease (sometimes necessitating open-heart surgery) associated with use of the fenfluramine-phentermine combination. There was an immediate drop of at least 50% in prescriptions being written for these drugs.

A drug with approval pending before the FDA is sibutramine. Sibutramine was originally investigated as an antidepressant agent. While sibutramine does not have a sedative side effect, a small but statistically significant rise in blood pressure and heart rate may occur. This drug appears to produce a slightly greater loss than dexfenfluramine (7–15% of initial weight), and is not thought to increase risk for primary pulmonary hypertension or valvular heart disease, although further tests on these issues will probably be done in the near future.

Another drug under consideration for approval by the FDA is orlistat, a lipase inhibitor, which blocks absorption of dietary fat. Weight losses from this medication appear to be somewhat less than those from the centrally acting drugs discussed above, but there do not appear to be concerns about primary pulmonary hypertension or valvular heart disease. At the time of this writing, there are reports that the manufacturer of orlistat has delayed the request for approval from the FDA to further investigate reports of breast neoplasms occurring in women on the drug.

To say that the pharmaceutical market for obesity is labile is nearly understatement. It is likely that safe and effective drugs will be developed at some point. The question is whether consumers and health care professionals will generalize from problems with some to all medications. Given the staggering prevalence of obesity, and the massive costs to both society and affected individuals, any treatment that offers help is welcome, but only if the benefits are considerable and the risks low.

2. Surgery for Pronounced Obesity

As was the case with pharmacological agents, early methods of surgical interventions for obesity had serious complications. Intestinal bypass surgery was the first such procedure. This involved surgery to bypass part of the small intestine to decrease the absorptive surface area. The rationale was that excess consumed energy would pass unabsorbed into the stools, enabling patients to maintain their eating habits. Intestinal bypass also influenced ingestive behavior through mechanisms involving the release of gastrointestinal "satiety" peptides from the small intestines, toxins from bacterial overgrowth, and undetermined factors. However, numerous complications of intestinal bypass, most preventable, and the development of gastric operations as alternative procedures, led to the virtual discontinuation of the intestinal bypass after 1980.

There are two forms of purely restrictive gastric procedures currently in use: vertical stapled gastroplasty with banded outlet, and circumgastric banding. Both function by limiting the capacity of the stomach, and by delaying the emptying of solids through the banded opening. These operations do not restrict the intake of caloric liquids or semisolids unless solid food is already filling or obstructing the upper stomach. There are limitations to purely restrictive operations. They can be defeated by the soft calorie syndrome (eating many calories in soft foods) or by the expansion of the pouch, and many patients are unwilling or unable to accept the constraints on their eating behavior.

In a review of the literature, Kral suggests that expected weight loss after surgical procedures can range from 40 to 60% of excess weight. Current patient mortality with the surgical treatment of obesity in competent hands is less than 0.5%. When considering epidemiological data demonstrating that the mortality (3 to 12 times normal) of severe obesity not treated or treated nonsurgically exceeds operative mortality, the gastric procedures can be defended. Research suggests that surgery for morbidly obese patients results in an improved quality of life to the majority of patients who undergo the procedure and who with few exceptions, would elect to have it done again, if necessary. Surgery is reserved for only those individuals with morbid obesity (at least double ideal body weight) who have failed with less aggressive treatments.

B. Behavioral and Dietary Interventions

1. Cognitive–Behavioral Treatment

Cognitive–behavioral treatments attempt to modify eating habits, physical activity, and attitudes about eating, shape, and weight in order to produce weight loss. The goal is to reduce overall caloric consumption and to increase energy expenditure through increased exercise. There has been extensive research evaluating the efficacy of cognitive–behavioral programs. Since the field began in the 1970s, the average weight loss has more than doubled. The average weight loss during an initial program is approximately 0.5 kg per week. This is similar to the loss per week in earlier studies, but treatments have been extended from 8 to 10 weeks to 16 to 20 weeks. Further, attrition has stayed low and stable (10–15%). However, long-term outcomes of treatment are discouraging. While approximately 60 to 70% of the weight loss is likely to be maintained for a year following treatment, longer follow-up periods of 3 and 5 years show return to baseline weights. [*See* BEHAVIOR THERAPY; COGNITIVE THERAPY.]

2. Very Low-Calorie Diet

Very low-calorie diets (VLCD) seek to maximize weight loss by keeping calorie intake as low as possible while preserving adequate nutrition. Nutrition is provided through powdered supplements or small amounts of food. VLCDs have been defined in several ways. What is considered a VLCD has ranged from 400 to 800 kilocalories daily intake. Atkinson suggested that a VLCD be defined in terms of the energy requirements of the individual and that it provide 10 kilocalories per kilogram of ideal body weight. VLCDs are prescribed only to individuals who are a minimum of 30% overweight, because mildly obese patients do not retain body protein as do heavier in-

dividuals during severe caloric restriction. Excessive losses of bodily protein may be associated with serious complications.

In a review of the literature, Wadden found that as in the case of cognitive-behavioral treatments, VLCDs typically produce substantial short-term weight loss. Weight losses average from 15 to 20 kg for 12 weeks of treatment, with larger losses for longer treatment. These reductions are also associated with marked improvements in health and psychological status. However, follow-up studies are highly variable, with some showing high rates of regain, and others showing maintenance of as much as 67% of the original weight loss at one year. Patients treated by VLCDs regain 35 to 50% of their lost weight in the year following treatment, even when they receive a program of lifestyle modification, and long-term studies show that patients gain increasing amounts of weight over time.

IV. INTERPRETING AVAILABLE DATA ON WEIGHT LOSS

There has been significant debate as to the costs and benefits of undertaking weight loss attempts. A central argument of the recent antidieting movement is that all diets fail, and that attempts at long-term weight loss are futile. This perspective has its roots in earlier reports that only 5% of people could lose weight and keep it off, as well as more recent data showing poor long-term results from clinical treatment trials of obesity.

Brownell and Rodin suggest that the claim that all weight loss attempts fail can be challenged based on the nature of the current research. First, available data are from highly select samples. Virtually all data on weight loss and maintenance are from clinical trials conducted in university settings. The vast majority of individuals who attempt to lose weight do so on their own, with books, magazines, or diets given them by others, or by joining exercise programs, or enrolling in commercial or self-help programs. Individuals who participate in university-based weight loss programs are more likely to be binge eaters, which is a poor prognostic indicator for the treatment of obesity. Binge eaters are more likely to be overweight, and are likely to have more psychopathology than are dieters in general.

Further, there is evidence that not all attempts at

weight loss fail. Although there are reports of poor long-term results, there are recent studies showing more favorable results. There are also reports of smaller but perhaps important weight losses from population and community studies found. From these data, it would appear that some people, even in professional programs, do lose weight and maintain.

Also, there is now considerable evidence that small weight losses can produce important medical improvements in blood pressure, blood glucose control, and blood lipids and lipoproteins. The possibility also exists that smaller losses will be more easily maintained. Therefore, it may be a mistake to dismiss small losses. It may be preferable to ask whether risk has been reduced than whether goal weight has been achieved.

In addition, a problem arises in interpreting data when individuals lose weight but then return to baseline weight. While this can be considered an undesirable outcome, what must also be considered, however, is what an individual would weigh if weight loss was not attempted. Data suggest that most people gain weight with time, especially obese persons. Hence, long-term results must be considered in light of weight gain as the logical reference point.

Finally, nearly all data used to address the issue of whether weight loss attempts are effective are from clinical studies with obese persons. Because many dieting individuals are not obese, the normal weight population must be studied to develop a clear picture of the effects of dieting. Two population surveys have found that nonobese individuals who have dieted report losses of from 8 to 12 pounds for their most recent effort. This may be significant for persons with small or moderate amounts to lose. Hence, the point at which a weight loss effort is "successful" and a given weight loss is "significant" must be evaluated when considering the broad population of individuals who attempt to lose weight. Based on the existing evidence, Brownell and Rodin concluded that it is important to avoid broad, sweeping statements about the effectiveness of weight loss attempts, because the conclusions that can be drawn from current research are limited.

V. NEW DEVELOPMENTS IN TREATMENT

There has been growing concern that professionals have little to offer the obese patient. This is evident from articles in the media and even from a panel of esteemed obesity experts from the Institute of Medicine:

> Many programs and services exist to help individuals achieve weight control. But the limited studies paint a grim picture; those who complete weight loss programs lose approximately 10% of their body weight, only to regain two thirds of it back within one year and almost all of it back within five years.

In response to this concern, different uses of familiar methods have been proposed (e.g., chronic pharmacotherapy), as well as the testing of methods designed specifically for the maintenance of weight loss. However, some authors have called for a complete abandonment of dieting and attempts at weight loss. We believe that the concern with treatment failure, combined with the rising prevalence of obesity, argue for new conceptual approaches to intervention.

A. Dieting Readiness

We feel that clients enter treatment with different levels of "readiness" to engage in behaviors associated with treatment. Losing weight and sustaining behavior changes over the long term can be challenging under any circumstances, but can be particularly daunting for a person who is not highly committed or motivated, or who has significant life circumstances likely to interfere. While all individuals present for treatment to lose weight, the degree to which an individual is committed or motivated to begin a program varies across individuals. When approaching the treatment of an obese individual, it is important to identify how motivated the client is to change attitudes and behaviors.

We do not view the client's motivation as dichotomous (i.e., the client as either motivated or not motivated). Rather, we view the motivation associated with treatment as a continuous *process*. This approach suggests that throughout a treatment, an individual passes through different stages of change that are associated with different levels of motivation. Prochaska suggested that the process of change consists of five stages: precontemplation, contemplation, preparation, action, and maintenance. Each stage is associated with different cognitive and behavioral processes. For example, individuals in the contemplation stage may not be considering change or may deny a problem. In our experience, people beginning a weight loss program are in the action stage with respect to diet, but widely varying stages with respect to exercise. It is important for the therapist to determine what stage of change the client is in when presenting for treatment, and to monitor the client's stage throughout treatment. Conceptualizing the client's stage of change will have implications for the interventions which would be most appropriate with the client. Measures of dieting readiness and stages of change have been developed, and work is underway to test whether these are overlapping constructs. Such work is necessary to determine who is most suitable for treatment.

B. Reasonable Weight

Based on arbitrary and demanding cultural ideals of beauty, and "ideal weights" from height–weight tables, individuals begin weight loss programs with unrealistic expectations of how much weight they might lose. Most individuals enter weight loss programs in pursuit of a specific goal weight. The goal weight is nearly always far in excess of typical weight losses, setting up a cycle of large ideal/actual discrepancies, negative mood, distorted cognitions, and even more strict goals. Recent studies of cognitive-behavioral programs that have a strong focus on enhancing maintenance of weight loss indicate that reductions of 10% of initial body weight can be sustained for a 1-year follow-up-period, but the same is not true of a 20% weight loss. One study reported that subjects on a very low-calorie diet who lost an average of 21.5 kg regained approximately half the weight in the ensuing year, despite being provided 39 weight loss maintenance sessions. In contrast, a group losing 11.9 kg on a moderate diet maintained the full weight loss a year later. Three studies by Perri and colleagues found similarly that subjects who lost an average of 8 to 12 kg maintained their full weight loss for one year if provided regular contact with a practitioner. The larger losses that people seek and expect, therefore, are rarely attained.

There is empirical support from a literature demonstrating impressive medical gains with modest weight losses and from treatment studies showing that losses of 10% of initial body weight are maintained for at least 1 year, but that larger losses are not. As a result, a new alternative to goal setting in weight loss programs suggests that if an individual attempts to achieve smaller weight loss goals, as opposed to traditional goals based on aesthetic or health ideals, these weight losses will be better maintained, will have more positive psychological effects, and will lead to greater improvement in risk factors.

C. Treatment Matching

Advances in treating obesity have been made by searching for individual treatments that provide an increment in weight loss beyond the prevailing standard. Underlying this approach is the assumption that obese persons comprise a homogeneous population that can be treated effectively by one superior treatment. However, many treatments are available, and it is not clear that across the obese population, any one treatment is superior. It is therefore possible to hypothesize that the effect of various treatments is not consistent across individuals. As Brownell and Wadden have argued: "The challenge is no longer to conduct only parametric studies to determine if one approach is superior to another, but to develop criteria to match the needs of individuals."

While several possible approaches are available for matching individuals to treatment, none has yet been validated by experimental studies. A scheme roposed by Brownell and Wadden is shown in Fig. 2.

This is a conceptual approach in which three possible matching processes are integrated into a scheme in which a classification decision is made first, followed by a stepped-care decision, then a matching decision. The classification decision is based on percentage overweight and helps narrow the range of approaches that would be relevant to the individual. For instance, a person who is massively overweight would not likely respond to a self-directed program and might need something more intensive. Conversely, a person who is mildly overweight would not be appropriate for surgery.

The second level is based on a stepped-care approach. After a range of approaches has been established by the classification decision, approaches or programs may be ranked according to cost, intrusiveness, side effects (in the case of medication), risk, and other factors used to make a cost-effectiveness judgment. The third step is a matching decision based on the personal needs of the individual. Issues such as probable response to group versus individual treatments, the need for supervised exercise, and the de-

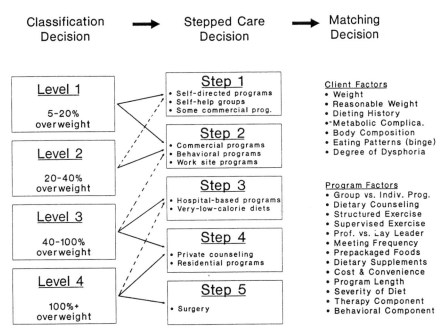

Figure 2 A conceptual scheme showing the three-stage process in selecting a treatment for an individual. The first step, the classification decision, divides individuals according to percentage overweight into four levels. This level dictates which of the five steps would be reasonable in the second stage, the stepped-care decision. This indicates that the least intensive, costly, and risky approach will be used from among alternative treatments. The third stage, the matching decisions, is used to make the final selection of a program, and is based on a combination of client and program variables. The dashed lines with arrows between the classification and stepped-care stages show the lowest level of treatment that may be beneficial, but more intensive treatment is usually necessary for people at the specified weight level. (From K. D. Brownell & T. A. Wadden (1991). *Behavior Therapy, 22,* p. 162. Copyright 1991 by the Association for Advancement of Behavior Therapy. Reprinted with permission.)

gree to which the diet needs to be structured may be considered.

Thus far, very little work has been conducted on matching, so at present specific matching criteria cannot be specified. In an attempt to determine if a consensus would exist among experts on which treatments would be most appropriate, Schwartz and Brownell conducted a survey of leaders in the obesity field. The leaders were provided a list of approaches to weight loss (e.g., self-help programs, commercial programs, very low calorie diets, surgery). There was a diversity of responses obtained in the survey, suggesting that while a matching approach would be essential, there is little available data to guide a researcher or clinician in the matching process. They identified an array of factors that may be critical in the matching process, such as degree of obesity, weight

loss history, medical profile, and level of eating and general psychopathology (see Table I).

D. Treatment of Binge Eating

Obese binge eaters represent a distinct clinical subtype among the obese population that deserves special consideration when approaching treatment. Stunkard first identified a pattern among obese individuals of eating large amounts of food accompanied by a feeling of loss of control. More recently, Spitzer and colleagues argued that this phenomenon represents a distinct disorder, Binge Eating Disorder (BED). Recent estimates of a national probability sample of U.S. women suggest that the lifetime prevalence of BED across all weight categories was estimated to be 1.6%. However, the rate of binge eating increases

Table 1 Most Frequently Cited Indicators for Different Approaches to Weight Loss

Category, indicator, and no. of experts responding	% experts listing this indicator
Dieting on one's own (*n* = 24)	
Client's weight status is in the mild-to-moderate range	63
Client is not a weight cycler; first weight loss	42
Client has no weight-related medical complications	38
Client has a history of success with this approach	25
Client has no history of or current eating disorder	25
Client has good social support already in place	25
Twelve-Step program (*n* = 22)	
Client's comfort with addiction model, spiritual element	45
Client desires social support	41
Client has no weight-related medical complications	27
Client is a binge eater	27
Client's weight status is in the moderate range	14
Exercise program (*n* = 24)	
Clients at all weight levels should exercise	79
Client is free of medical contraindications to exercise	63
Client has a history of exercising	13
Client is male	13
Client's weight status is in the mild range	8
Commercial program with group support (*n* = 23)	
Client's weight status	39
Indication: mild	13
Indication: moderate	9
Contraindication: moderate to morbid	17
Client's weight loss history regarding this approach	35
Client has not tried it before	22
Client has had success in the past with it	13
Client desires social support	30
Client has no weight-related medical complications	30
Client is female	17
Client has no history of or current eating disorder	17
Commercial program with food provided (*n* = 24)	
Client is nonresponsive to less structured programs	33
Client's weight status	29
Indication: mild	4
Indication: moderate	17
Contraindication: mild	4
Contraindication: moderate to morbid	13
Client desires prepared meals	17
Client desires structure	21
Client has sufficient economic resources available	21
University behavioral program (*n* = 22)	
Client's weight status	41
Indication: mild	9
Indication: moderate	32
Contraindication: mild	5
Contraindication: morbid	18
Client is nonresponsive to self-help and lay programs	27
Client meets criteria for a psychiatric diagnosis	32
Indication:	18
Contraindication	14

Table I *Continued*

Category, indicator, and no. of experts responding	% experts listing this indicator
Client has an obesity-related medical condition	27
Indication	9
Contraindication	18
Client meets criteria for an eating disorder	9
Very-low-calorie diet (*n* = 24)	
Client's weight status is in the moderate-morbid range	67
Client has an obesity-related medical condition	42
Client is free of medical contraindications for a very-low-calorie diet	42
Client has no substance abuse, eating, or mood disorders	42
Client is willing to make long-term behavior changes	21
Client is nonresponsive to moderate calorie diets	21
Private counseling (*n* = 23)	
Client meets criteria for an Axis I or Axis II diagnosis	70
Client meets criteria for an eating disorder	22
Client has sufficient economic resources available	17
Client has previously lost weight and relapsed	9
Client's weight status is in the moderate range	4
Residential program (*n* = 24)	
Client's weight status	46
Indication: mild	8
Indication: moderate	13
Indication: severe	21
Contraindication: mild	8
Contraindication: morbid	8
Client has sufficient economic resources available	46
Client has sufficient time available	29
Client desires a "jump start" for diet and exercise	25
Client is nonresponsive to less expensive efforts	25
Medication (*n* = 23)	
Client is nonresponsive to behavioral approaches	35
Client is free of medical contraindications	30
Client's weight status is in the moderate-to-morbid range	22
Client is willing to make long-term behavior chanages	17
Client is maintaining a weight loss	13
Surgery (*n* = 23)	
Client's weight status is in the massive-to-morbid range	74
Client has an obesity-related medical condition	43
Client is nonresponsive to all conservative approaches	39
Client does not have a severe Axis I or Axis II disorder	35
Client is willing to make long-term behavior changes	26

From Schwartz and Brownell (1995). Matching individuals to weight loss treatments: A survey of obesity experts. *Journal of Consulting and Clinical Psychology, 63*(1), 149–153. Copyright 1995 by the American Psychological Association.

with increasing weight, and the prevalence of BED in obese persons in the general community is approximately 2%. Further, BED is particularly common in obese persons seeking treatment, with from 25% to 50% having this problem.

Comparisons of obese binge eaters versus obese nonbingers suggest that binge eaters eat more than nonbinge eaters, and choose a greater percentage of calories from fat. Obese binge eaters presenting for weight loss treatment have higher levels of psychopathology, particularly affective disorders, than do nonbinge-eating obese persons also seeking treatment. Further, binge eating tends to be associated with poor response to obesity treatments. However, studies have found no differences between BED and non-BED subjects on metabolic variables such as blood glucose, blood lipids, and resting metabolic rate, after controlling for BMI and age. In addition, studies of body image among binge eaters have produced mixed results.

One possible approach with this population is that binge eaters require treatment for their disordered eating prior to or during a weight loss program. No studies have tested this assumption but several promising treatments for binge eating have been derived from work on bulimia nervosa, namely cognitive–behavior therapy and interpersonal psychotherapy. Cognitive–behavioral approaches target dysfunctional attitudes about weight and shape and aim to create more structured eating from the chaos of binges. Interpersonal psychotherapy does not deal with the core symptoms of the eating disorder per se, but focuses instead on key relationships in the client's life.

Studies by Wilfley and colleagues have found that essentially equivalent reductions in binge eating have been produced by these two fundamentally different approaches. This raises several important possibilities. First, eating-disordered symptoms may arise from different causes. Second, binge eating may be a reflection of other pathology, perhaps as a "secondary symptom." Third, matching individuals to treatments may prove to be part of treating obese binge eaters. Research is now underway to examine matching factors, but criteria for matching are not yet available. One might speculate that individuals with serious relationship disturbances, which would include those with one of the personality disorders, might require interpersonal psychotherapy, whereas symptom-focused cognitive-behavioral therapy may be more effective with others.

VI. PREVENTION AND SOCIAL POLICY

Because obesity is a problem with serious public health consequences, growing prevalence, and resistance to treatment, bold new initiatives must be considered if any progress is to be made. Even with interventions that are potentially available to the population as med-

ications, detailed life-style counseling is also necessary. This may limit the number of people who can be treated, so even in the face of safe and effective treatments, the obesity problem is likely to remain massive.

An alternative is to move from a medical to a public health model. The fundamental difference between the models is one of curing a person with a disease versus minimizing the public health impact of a disease. To minimize impact, which may mean deceasing prevalence, it is often more cost-effective to prevent a disease than to treat its victims (immunizations are an example). The obvious question, then, is whether obesity can be prevented.

There has been some discussion in the literature of applying public health models to obesity. The focus, however, has been to propose ways for traditional cognitive–behavioral concepts to be applied in a more cost-effective fashion, through channels such as schools, work sites, the media, or large-scale community programs. Such approaches have had modest success and do not offer the prospect of having any appreciable effect on the obesity problem.

A. Social Policy, the Cost of Food, and Advertising

It has been proposed recently that social policy be considered as a means for better confronting the obesity problem. The basic thesis is that Americans are exposed to a toxic food environment, with vast segments of the population having unprecedented access to high-fat, high-calorie foods at low cost that are advertised heavily (and in some cases deceptively), and that the environment conspires to discourage physical activity. If one considers food a potentially harmful substance that is similar in danger to tobacco or alcohol, and a potentially valuable substance if used correctly, public policy interventions follow naturally. Diet contributes to disease and disability to a similar degree as does smoking and more than does alcohol.

Let us begin with advertising. The average American child sees 10,000 food advertisements each year on television. Fully 95% of these are for sugared cereals, candy, soft drinks, and fast food. This may have a powerful and toxic effect. As a society we ban advertising for cigarettes and alcohol aimed at children, so is it logical to consider a similar stance with food advertising. One public policy intervention would be to regulate such advertising in hopes that demand for and consumption of food with poor nutrient density would decline.

Another approach would be target food availability by altering its cost. Taxes have been shown to have a significant and now predictable effect on the sales of cigarettes and alcohol (as prices increase, use declines). If the sales of healthy foods could be subsidized and sales of poor foods taxed, the relative use of the foods might shift. Similarly, tax incentives for employers to provide exercise facilities, the use of public funds to build bicycle paths and recreational facilities, and other regulatory means for encouraging physical activity should have an effect on weight in the population.

We hasten to note that such an approach has not been tested, so only speculation on its effects is possible. We also emphasize that the obesity problem is alarming and is getting worse, so every means of intervention must be considered. Thus far, experts in the obesity field have not turned their attention to research on public policy. Such a turn is clearly indicated. The potential could be considerable.

VII. SUMMARY

Obesity is growing in prevalence. It takes an enormous toll on the nation's health, and because of the severe bias against obesity, prejudice and discrimination are common. Unlike most diseases, there are many etiologic paths to obesity, with biology, psychology, and the environment all implicated. Research on the genetics of body weight regulation may help remove some of the blame others express toward overweight people, it may help curb society's preoccupation with thinness and the tendency to equate appearance with personal value, and most importantly, it may diminish the self-hatred so many overweight individuals experience.

With a disease showing complicated and varied etiology, it is not reasonable to expect that any single treatment will prevail over all others. Instead, matching individuals to treatments turns the attention to the best fit of an individual with an approach. There are positive signs that the field is considering this concept of matching, so our hope is that in a relatively short time, matching criteria will be identified from research. While it is true that no existing treatment produces reduction to ideal weight and maintenance in the majority of people treated, many approaches show some success, especially with initial weight loss, so there is cause to be optimistic. If the goal of obesity treatment changes from risk elimination to risk reduction, reasonable weight losses can become the focus and better long-term results are likely.

Public policy interventions have been discussed only recently in the obesity field. There is a near-total absence of empirical information to justify some of the ideas proposed here and elsewhere (regulating food advertising, subsidizing healthy foods and taxing poor foods), but these may ultimately be more successful in curtailing the obesity problem than are additional efforts at treatment.

ACKNOWLEDGMENTS

Work on this article was supported in part by a fellowship from the Jenny Craig Foundation. Some sections of the article were adapted from information in a paper by Brownell and Wadden (1992) and a chapter by Brownell and O'Neil (1993).

BIBLIOGRAPHY

Allison, D. B. (Ed.). (1995). *Handbook of assessment methods for eating behaviors and weight-related problems.* London: Sage Publications.

Bjorntorp, P., & Brodoff, B. N. (Eds.). (1992). *Obesity.* New York: J. B. Lippincott Company.

Brownell, K. D., & Fairburn, C. G. (Eds.). *Eating disorders and obesity: A comprehensive handbook.* New York: Guilford.

Brownell, K. D., & Wadden, T. A. (1992). Etiology and treatment of obesity: Understanding a serious, prevalent, and refractory disorder. *Journal of Consulting and Clinical Psychology, 60,* 505–517.

Friedman, M. A., & Brownell, K. D. (1995). Psychological correlates of obesity: Moving to the next research generation. *Psychological Bulletin, 117,* 3–20.

Obsessive-Compulsive Disorder

Randy O. Frost

Smith College

Gail Steketee

Boston University

I. Diagnosis and Symptoms
II. Family and Patient Characteristics
III. Theory and Treatment
IV. Future Directions

Compulsions Behaviors or mental acts one feels driven to perform in response to an obsession or according to certain rules.
DSM-III *Diagnostic and Statistical Manual of Mental Disorders—Third Edition,* published by the American Psychiatric Association.
DSM-IV *Diagnostic and Statistical Manual of Mental Disorders—Fourth Edition,* published by the American Psychiatric Association.
Obsessions Repetitive, unwelcome, and intrusive thoughts, images, or impulses that are inappropriate and cause distress.
Schizotypal Personality Disorder A personality disorder characterized by social and interpersonal deficits as well as by cognitive or perceptual distortions.
Tourette's Syndrome An Axis I disorder characterized by multiple motor and vocal tics.
(YBOCS) *Yale-Brown Obsessive-Compulsive Scale* An assessment interview used in most current obsessive-compulsive disorder treatment outcome studies.

OBSESSIVE-COMPULSIVE DISORDER (OCD) is an Axis I Anxiety Disorder in the American Psychiatric Association's (APA) *Diagnostic and Statistical Manual of Mental Disorders—Fourth Edition* (DSM-IV). The primary diagnostic criteria are the existence

of obsessions or compulsions, some degree of recognition of the irrationality of the behavior, and significant interference with everyday functioning. This article provides an up-to-date summary of the state of knowledge regarding obsessive-compulsive disorder.

I. DIAGNOSIS AND SYMPTOMS

Obsessions are recurring and persistent thoughts, images, or impulses that are experienced as intrusive, distressing, and, at least at times, unreasonable. Responding to these experiences, the individual may "neutralize" them, using some ritualistic thought or action, or attempt to ignore or suppress them. These repeated behaviors or mental acts are undertaken to relieve anxiety provoked by the obsessions and are called compulsions. Compulsions are usually applied rigidly or excessively. From the patient's perspective, they restore safety or prevent a dreaded event. The intent of the compulsion is often hidden from the casual observer or even close family members. These symptoms consume at least an hour a day and interfere with the person's normal activities. The symptoms of OCD are relatively common in the general population, but are not usually severe enough or do not interfere enough to meet diagnostic criteria. The content of clinical obsessive intrusions differs little from ordinary intrusive thoughts experienced by most people, but the former provoke much more anxiety and are more difficult to dismiss.

The content of obsessions and compulsions vary considerably from patient to patient, sharing only the

15

disturbing nature of the intrusions and the ritualistic efforts to neutralize the obsessions. Often, patients report more than one type of obsession and ritual, and sometimes the content of the obsession or compulsion changes (e.g., cleaning to checking). The most common compulsions are checking rituals, which are usually designed to prevent catastrophes like fire, burglary, causing someone harm, or embarrassing oneself. Also common are washing rituals, which serve to remove "contamination" or "dirt" and thereby prevent a feared disaster (e.g., disease). Other common compulsions include repeating compulsions or magical rituals in which ordinary actions (such as crossing a threshold or lifting an object) are repeated to prevent harm from occurring (e.g., a loved one dying in an accident). Less common are ordering rituals, which involve arranging objects to produce symmetry or balance, and hoarding, the acquisition of and failure to discard seemingly useless objects like old magazines and receipts or empty containers.

The APA's DSM-III defined obsessive-compulsive disorder (OCD) not only by the obsessions and compulsions, but by patients' recognition of the irrationality of obsessions. Individuals who did not recognize the irrationality of their thoughts were considered either psychotic or "overvalued" in their ideas about the obsessions. Recent research demonstrates that patients vary on this characteristic from complete awareness to complete lack of awareness of the rationality of the symptoms, with most having at least some insight. This criterion has changed somewhat in DSM-IV in that patients must have insight at least at some point in the disorder. DSM-IV added a category of "poor insight" for patients with OCD who do not recognize the unreasonableness of their behavior.

Diagnostically, obsessions can be distinguished from symptoms of generalized anxiety disorder and hypochondriasis in that they are mental experiences that are not merely excessive worries about real-life problems (e.g., finances, family well-being, health, etc.). Also, obsessions are different in character from the guilty or depressive ruminations characteristic of people with major depression. Preoccupations with food, alcohol, drugs, gambling, and buying are readily distinguishable from obsessive fears of contamination, causing harm, preventing danger, and other anxiety-provoking concerns and rituals. The former symptoms are all appetitive preoccupations, while obsessive fears generally involve avoidance or escape responses.

A. Epidemiology and Clinical Course

Epidemiological studies of community samples estimate the annual and lifetime prevalence rates to be considerably higher than previously thought (annual, 0.8 to 2.3%; lifetime, 1.9 to 3.3%). Prevalence rates in this range have been replicated in a variety of studies throughout the world. While some studies have shown a slightly higher percentage of women than men with OCD, other studies have failed to find this difference. When examining childhood onset of OCD, however, males outnumber females by up to 2 to 1. For males, the mean age of onset is 14 to 19 years, while for females it is 21.7 to 22.0 years. Most patients develop symptoms before age 25 (65%), and only a small number (15%) develop symptoms after age 35. Patients typically wait 7 to 8 years after the onset of symptoms before seeking treatment. While 40% of those with OCD can identify no clear precipitant, some research suggests that changes in life roles and demands (i.e., pregnancy, childbirth, etc.) may be precipitants.

Recent prospective studies of the course of OCD indicate that despite significant advances in treatment, most OCD patients (at least 75%) remain at least partially symptomatic over the long term. Between 43% and 75% of treated patients remain at least partially improved 2 to 5 years after treatment. Despite limited research on prediction of treatment outcome, mild or atypical symptoms, a short duration of symptoms, and a good premorbid personality appear to predict a good outcome. On the other hand, early onset in males, symmetry or exactness-related symptoms, symptoms of hopelessness, delusions or hallucinations, a family history of OCD, and the presence of tics suggest a poor prognosis.

There is some indication that the expression of OCD symptomatology is at least partially influenced by cultural factors. Similarities exist between OCD rituals and religious or cultural rituals, and certain religious practices are associated with OCD symptomatology. Culture-specific beliefs, as illustrated by *koro* (a fear of penile shrinkage found exclusively in Chinese cultures), also suggest the influence culture has on the expression of OCD symptoms. However, while these cultural variables may influence the symptom expression in OCD, there is little evidence to suggest they contribute to the development of the disorder. There is also little evidence to suggest that race or socioeconomic status are associated with OCD, although at least one study suggests that African-Americans may present with more severe OCD symptomatology. Given the lack of research in this area, however, any such conclusions must be tentative. Furthermore, different patterns of help-seeking among minority populations may mask potential differences between minority and nonminority groups. [*See* Epidemiology: Psychiatric.]

B. Comorbidity

Comorbidity of OCD with other disorders is as high as 60% or more. Anxiety disorders, depression, alcohol abuse (dependence), eating disorders, Tourette's syndrome, body dysmorphic disorder, hypochondriasis, and schizophrenia have all been found to be associated with OCD. Comorbidity with anxiety disorders is quite high, ranging from 25 to 60%, with the highest frequencies for specific phobias, followed by social phobia and panic disorder. Comorbidity and family study data have led some to suggest that OCD patients share a general genetic vulnerability with anxiety disorders. [*See* Anxiety.]

There may be a shared vulnerability for various forms of depression as well, with studies indicating concurrent prevalence rates of 12 to 80%. At least one third of patients with OCD report histories of clinical depression, although 25 to 33% do not report depression. An important question concerning the relationship of OCD and depression is whether the depression that accompanies OCD is primary or secondary. The majority of patients report an onset of depressive symptoms that occurred after the onset of OCD, and several investigators have found that successful treatment of OCD resulted in the reduction of depressive symptoms. [*See* Depression.]

Despite a wide range in the degree of insight shown by OCD patients, OCD is relatively rarely accompanied by schizophrenia, although some research suggests a link. Patients with OCD may have more schizotypal traits and less cognitive inhibition than other anxiety disorder patients, similar to schizotypal and schizophrenic patients. Further research is necessary to test the hypothesis that obsessional thoughts (like schizophrenic thoughts) result from a failure in the cognitive inhibition of associations to ongoing stimulation. [*See* Schizophrenia.]

Some impulse control disorders overlap with OCD and, consequently, they have been labeled as OC Spectrum Disorders. Tourette's, Sydenham's chorea, and other tic disorders have shown an association with OCD. One form of Tourette's may be OCD-related and some OCD cases are Tourette's-related. This has led to speculation that OCD and Tourette's may be different expressions of a similar underlying genetic abnormality, for example, of the basal ganglia-frontal cortex pathway. Some investigators report associations between OCD and kleptomania, as well as exhibitionism. These reports are suggestive enough to warrant closer examination of a possible link with obsessive and compulsive symptoms. [*See* Impulse Control.]

As mentioned earlier, if the content of obsessions or compulsions concerns primary symptoms of eating disorders, body dysmorphic disorder, or hypochondriasis, a diagnosis of OCD is ruled out. In each of these cases, similarity of symptoms, comorbidity evidence, and response to treatment suggest that these disorders are closely related to OCD. Some have even suggested that they are actually forms of OCD.

Studies of comorbidity of OCD with Axis II disorders reveal that over one half of patients with OCD have at least one diagnosable personality disorder (PD). Unfortunately, the evidence fails to provide any clear indication of which co-occur most frequently. Despite its name, obsessive-compulsive personality disorder is no more closely related to OCD than avoidant, dependent, histrionic, or several other personality disorders. One observation from this literature deserves comment. Antisocial personality disorder often has the smallest overlap with OCD, which may reflect the importance of beliefs about excessive responsibility in patients with OCD. Questions remain about the role of personality disorders in OCD, as some evidence suggests that PD symptoms decline with successful treatment of OCD.

II. FAMILY AND PATIENT CHARACTERISTICS

A. Family Factors

Although marital satisfaction among OCD patients resembles that of the general population, OCD patients (especially males who have an early onset) have higher celibacy rates than the general population. When OCD symptoms occur within a family context, family members often involve themselves in the rituals or avoidance behaviors of the patients. In families where households are restructured to adapt to OCD symptoms, greater family dysfunction and negative attitudes toward the patient have been observed.

A number of parental characteristics have been hypothesized to play a role in the development of OCD. The parents of OCD cleaners are hypothesized to be overcontrolling and overprotective and may model excessive cleaning behaviors. Parents of checkers are hypothesized to set higher standards for their children, to be overcontrolling and overcritical, as well as modeling meticulousness. Numerous cases report similar characteristics in the parents of OCD patients, including demanding or critical attitudes, overprotectiveness, perfectionism, and rejecting attitudes. Despite the frequency with which these characteristics have been informally observed, systematic research comparing parents of OCD patients and controls has been limited. A small number of controlled studies on this issue support the existence of these characteristics in the parents of OCD patients. In particular, parents of OCD patients and/or subclinical obsessive compulsives have been found to be overprotective, critical, perfectionistic, and risk aversive. In addition, the families of OCD patients show higher levels of expressed emotion (criticism and overinvolvement) than families of controls.

Clinical observation and preliminary evidence on these issues suggest that the parents of people who develop OCD are more likely to show a constellation of behaviors, including perfectionism, overprotectiveness, overcritical and demanding attitudes, and high levels of risk avoidance. Further research must establish that these characteristics are more prominent in the families of OCD patients than in controls; then, the question of their role in the development of the disorder can be addressed.

B. Cognitive Characteristics

Patients with OCD display a number of cognitive characteristics to a greater degree than other people. International experts have identified at least six such characteristics as being very important in OCD. These include overestimation of risk, excessive responsibility, controllability, overimportance of thoughts, intolerance of ambiguity, and perfectionism.

In the early 1970s, it was first noted that patients with OCD exaggerate the probability and severity of negative outcomes. Clinical and empirical studies indicate that people with OCD are risk-aversive, that is, they are less likely to engage in behavior that they consider risky. Threat overestimation can be defined as the exaggeration of the probability or severity of harm believed to result from or follow intrusive internal experiences.

A second widely noted cognitive characteristic is an exaggerated sense of responsibility for harm that might befall oneself or others. Some investigators have argued that exaggerated responsibility is central to OCD. According to recent work on this issue by Salkovskis and others, obsessional responsibility refers to the belief that one has power to bring about or prevent subjectively crucial negative outcomes that may be actual (having real consequences) and/or moral.

In normal cognitive processing, irrelevant and intrusive thoughts are simply ignored, whereas in cognitive processing by people with OCD these thoughts are attended to, believed important, and attempts to suppress them are undertaken. Efforts at suppression typically provoke a paradoxical increase in the intrusions and associated discomfort. When efforts to suppress these thoughts fail, sensitization and vigilance to similar thoughts occurs, and this process escalates into an obsessional pattern. Individuals with OCD appear to have a need for control, which can be defined as an overvaluation of the importance of exerting complete control over intrusive thoughts, images, and impulses, and the belief that this is possible and desirable. Such efforts at control are hypothesized to be evident in hypervigilance for mental events, in a moral attitude toward control as a virtue, and in feared psychological and behavioral consequences of the failure to control thoughts.

People with OCD may believe that simply having an unwanted, objectionable thought is morally equivalent to engaging in the objectionable act, a form of moral "thought–action fusion." Furthermore, when OCD patients imagine negative events, they may come to believe that the events are more likely to actually occur. Recent research on thought–action fusion supports the importance of this construct. Overimportance of thoughts can be defined as a belief that the mere presence of an intrusive thought gives it significance.

Related to this concept are possible problems that people with OCD have with Cartesian reasoning and magical thinking.

Doubt about the veracity of one's experience and the need for absolute certainty are commonly noted features of OCD. Some suggest that doubt stems from a belief that every situation has a perfect solution and the person with OCD will not feel comfortable unless that perfect solution is found. Others have suggested that because of their need for certainty, OCD patients repeat actions in an attempt to achieve perfect certainty. Such doubt may be central to the indecision seen in people with obsessive-compulsive tendencies. Intolerance for ambiguity is evident in obsessional beliefs about the necessity of being certain, about poor capacity to cope with unpredictable change, and about inadequate functioning in situations that are inherently ambiguous.

Perfectionism has been closely linked to OCD in both theory and clinical descriptions of the disorder. Recent research has found higher levels of perfectionism among OCD-diagnosed populations, as well as nonclinical populations, that exhibit obsessive-compulsive tendencies. Although it appears that high levels of perfectionism also characterize other disorders (e.g., social phobia, depression, and eating disorders), it appears to be important in shaping the course of OCD, and consequently international experts consider it a key cognitive component.

C. Information Processing in OCD

Several information processing capabilities, including memory, categorization, and attention, have been hypothesized to distinguish OCD patients from nonpatients. Four types of memory deficits have been hypothesized: (a) memory for actions, (b) general memory, (c) confidence in memory, and (d) reality monitoring (distinguishing actual from imagined actions). Among subclinical compulsive checkers, several studies reported deficits in memory for actions performed. Among clinical patients, this finding is less consistent, however, with one study supportive and another failing to replicate. Similar findings have emerged for general memory deficits. Nonclinical subjects showed poorer overall memory functioning, whereas findings for clinical patients were mixed, although most studies reported poorer memory func-

tioning, especially with regard to visual memory. One consistent finding in this literature has been the lowered confidence in memory capacity shown by OCD subjects. No reality-monitoring deficits have been found.

Related to memory dysfunction in OCD, some argue that OCD patients also fail to categorize and integrate information properly. They categorize in an underinclusive way, such that many small categories are generated with narrow boundaries and overspecified rules for category membership. Some clinical, as well as empirical, research supports this hypothesis. Because of a failure to recognize proper category boundaries, OCD patients create artificial structures that become rituals to determine the proper end of a sequence of behaviors.

A related hypothesis suggests that OCD patients fail to adequately inhibit irrelevant stimuli during normal processing, interfering with their focus on relevant stimuli. Consequently, processing ordinary information requires more conscious effort and active suppression of irrelevant or unwanted thoughts. A similar attention or cognitive inhibition deficit is hypothesized to characterize schizophrenia and schizotypal personality disorder. Several studies support this hypothesis having used a negative priming paradigm.

Another approach to studying attentional processes in OCD involves the use of the Stroop Color Word test. Subjects watch fearful and nonfearful words presented in different colors and are asked to name the color of the word. Fearful word meanings should be harder to inhibit and naming the color in which they are printed should take longer. Indeed, some studies have found that OCD washers take longer to name contamination words than neutral words, and that non-OCD patients do not. In other studies, OCD subjects have been found to attend selectively to negative OC-related words (e.g., disease, disaster) but to not show an attentional bias toward positive words (e.g., clean, precise). In another test of attentional processing, it has also been reported that after successful treatment, OCD patients no longer showed attentional bias toward contamination items in a dichotic listening task.

The research on memory and OCD provides some confirmation of deficits in memory for actions, general memory, decreased confidence in memory functioning, problems with overspecification in categorization, and problems in inhibiting attention to irrelevant information and in attending to relevant information. The findings fail to support any difficulties in distinguishing actual from imagined actions. Specific causes for these deficits will require further research.

III. THEORY AND TREATMENT

This section reviews the three major theoretical models for the development and maintenance of OCD and the treatment methods derived from these models, and summarizes evidence for the effectiveness of these treatments.

A. Behavioral Models

Early behavioral treatments for OCD (thought stopping, aversion therapy) were based on contingent reinforcement and punishment models and worked for only a limited number of patients. Efforts to use conditioning models alone (e.g., systematic desensitization) improved the situation only slightly. In the early 1970s, a refinement in the conditioning model led to the development of a more promising treatment. Exposure and response prevention (ERP), the standard and most effective of the behavioral techniques, is derived from the two-stage theory of fear and avoidance.

The first part of the two-stage theory posits that an otherwise neutral event acquires the capacity to provoke fear because of its pairing with an aversive stimulus, much as a dog phobia might develop in someone who has been bitten. While this can account for the onset of a number of cases, there is evidence that it does not account for all. Many patients cannot recall conditioning experiences associated with symptom onset. Also, although onset often follows stressful life events, it rarely does so immediately, as would be expected by the traumatic onset theory. Modifications of the acquisition portion of the two-stage theory suggest that stressful events sensitize some individuals to cues that have an innate tendency to elicit fear, were learned during early traumatic experiences, or have special cultural significance. Observational or informational learning also seems to account for the onset of some cases of OCD, particularly when patients report that their symptoms resemble their parents' behavior.

In the second stage of this model, compulsions or escape/avoidance behaviors provide relief from the obsessional anxiety or discomfort. This relief negatively reinforces the compulsions. Thus, the frequency of compulsive actions increases in future situations, which triggers an obsessional concern. Both external cues (objects or situations) and internal triggers (thoughts, images, or impulses) serve as fear stimuli and can produce obsessional discomfort. Many of these cues or triggers cannot be avoided (e.g., closing the front door when leaving the house). Therefore, the passive avoidance which allows phobics to manage their fears is often insufficient to control anxiety for those with OCD. More active strategies like compulsive behaviors are needed to prevent harm or restore a feeling of safety.

Substantial evidence supports a behavioral account of OCD in which obsessions increase discomfort and compulsions reduce it. Obsessive thoughts increase heart rate and skin conductance more than normal thoughts, and contact with contaminants increases subjective and physiological anxiety reactions. In most instances, compulsions reduce anxiety in the short run. Although this model clearly accounts for the maintenance of OCD symptoms, it does not adequately account for many instances of onset, and expansion of this theory is necessary.

B. Behavioral Treatments

Treatment strategies based on the behavioral model attempt to disconnect obsessions from the associated discomfort and to eliminate rituals that prevent habituation of obsessional fears. Behavioral treatment for obsessions and compulsions involves exposure to overt and covert cues that provoke obsessions, followed by prevention of the compulsion. Because compulsions interfere with habituation of the negative mood generated by obsessions, blocking the rituals prevents the premature reduction of fear. This program of ERP has been widely studied and has been found to be highly effective.

Exposure and response prevention was developed by British researchers in the early 1970s to treat hospital patients who feared contamination and performed washing rituals. In the first attempt to use ERP, daily direct contact with contaminants and complete prevention of compulsions (turning off the plumbing in patients' rooms, having nurses observe all washing) resulted in 10 of 15 patients being much improved or symptom-free, and the remaining 5 being moderately improved. After 5 to 6 years, only 2 patients relapsed. Since then, approximately 30 open trials and controlled studies, representing more than 600 patients with OCD, have reported good outcomes with ERP and its variants.

Numerous studies have shown that using from 10 to 20 sessions of ERP produces significant improvement in symptoms. After ERP, approximately 55% can be labeled "much" or "very much" improved, indicating that target symptoms improved by more than half; approximately 85% show at least some degree of improvement. Improvement rates remain high at follow-up, with 50% of patients still in the "much" or "very much" improved categories and 75% in the "improved" category.

With regard to the amount of symptom improvement, the average degree of benefit from ERP ranges from 40 to 75%. At follow-ups ranging from 3 months to 6 years, treatment gains remain high, in the 45 to 70% range for target symptoms. The degree of benefit and the consistency of ERP results from multiple treatment sites and countries are quite impressive and clearly indicate that exposure and response prevention is an effective intervention.

Support for the behavioral model from which ERP is derived can be found in studies examining the separate effects of exposure and response prevention on obsessions and compulsions. According to behavioral theory, exposure should reduce anxiety associated with obsessions, while response prevention should influence rituals more than obsessions. Several case series provide support for these hypotheses. When delivered independently, exposure reduces subjective anxiety more than rituals, although both decline. Response prevention reduces rituals more than it does obsessions. When exposure and response prevention are both given, patients show maximum improvement in symptoms.

Foa and Kozak suggested that ERP allows for the processing of emotional information which is prevented by compulsions. Compulsions circumvent this processing by allowing the patient to escape from a fearful situation before they have had a chance to habituate to it. These theorists hypothesize that fear-related memories are stored in fear structures that are activated by exposure to a fear stimulus. In the case of OCD, this may include any stimulus that prompts an obsession. Fear activated by exposure will dissipate unless neutralized by a compulsion. Exposure and response prevention activate the fear structure causing the patient to experience anxiety. When the ritual is prevented, habituation of anxiety will eventually occur. If habituation occurs within a session, then the fear structure is weakened and initial response to exposure should be lower at subsequent sessions. The new emotional information processed within such a session contains information about habituation, coping with anxiety, and so on, which is incompatible with a "fear" structure and therefore weakens the OC fear. Several parts of this process have been supported by research. As predicted by this model, attention-focusing instructions are associated with more anxiety during exposure and better habituation, whereas distracting instructions reduce initial anxiety and subsequent habituation, leading to poorer outcome. Therefore, standard clinical practice should focus attention on the exposure situation and avoid distracting conversation that might interfere with the processing of fearful information.

Traditional ERP has been supplemented by varying the procedure to enhance benefits and reduce the cost of the treatment. Several investigations have found that imagery-based exposure is as effective as in vivo exposure. Furthermore, some evidence suggests that imaginal exposure may work better for patients with checking compulsions, perhaps because their fears can be more easily accessed by imagery. Other variants that have shown some promise include the use of therapist modeling and varying the duration of treatment and the spacing of ERP sessions. Additionally, several studies have found that self-controlled treatment is as effective as therapist directed, and may produce more durable gains. Recently, a number of self-help books have been published with background information and instructions to help in setting up self-directed ERP. Preliminary findings from one study suggest that using self-help texts can lead to significant improvement. Although it may be too early to tell whether completely self-directed ERP is effective, it may represent a significant development in the treatment of ERP.

Another recent advance in the application of modified versions of ERP is group administration. Only one controlled trial of group ERP has been reported in the literature, however. This study compared group ERP, with or without imagined exposure, to comparable individual treatment and to an individual relaxation control treatment. After 12 weeks, both exposure treatment conditions showed significant improvement in OCD symptoms, while the control group did not. Average posttest Yale-Brown OC Scale (YBOCS) scores fell below the clinical range. The group treatment led to changes comparable to those of individual therapy, although group benefits occurred somewhat more slowly. This study demonstrates the potential for group administration of ERP.

Several researchers have suggested the use of support groups for patients and family members. Some have used open-ended monthly group meetings for family members and patients to discuss the effect of OCD on the family and to plan coping strategies and rehearse behavioral exercises. Other reports have outlined psychoeducational groups for families that include sessions on diagnosis, assessment, theories of OCD, behavioral treatment, medications, and prevention of relapse. Goals for such groups include improving self-esteem, sharing feelings and experiences, accepting patients' realistic limitations, and learning strategies for coping with OCD symptoms. Most of these studies reported high participant satisfaction, but no outcome data.

Further developments along these lines include using family members as treatment assistants. Evidence that spouse assistance in exposure treatment improves outcome, at least in the short run, has been reported by some investigators, although more research is needed to clarify the amount of added benefit over individual treatment. It appears that involving spouses and other family members in ERP leads to significant gains in OCD symptoms, mood state, and social and occupational functioning compared with unassisted treatment. Furthermore, family-treated patients continue to improve after treatment. Some studies suggest that nonanxious, consistent family members are more successful in providing support and supervision than anxious and inconsistent members, especially those who engage in argument and ridicule. Similar programs that teach relatives to reduce their involvement in rituals and to encourage self-exposure in noncritical ways have been found to be successful. Symptom decreases of 45% at discharge and 60% at 6-month follow-up indicate good success with family member involvement. Substantial reductions in YBOCS scores among patients in multiple family therapy groups that included spouses/partners, parents, and other relatives have been reported. The reductions are still significant 1 year later.

Research on predictors of success with ERP has failed to reveal consistent trends. Sex, age of onset, symptom severity, and duration have generally not been found to predict success in ERP. However, severity of avoidance behavior may be associated with poor ERP outcome. Some research also suggests that comorbid personality disorders, especially schizotypal personality disorder, are associated with poorer outcome in ERP. Greater insight regarding obsessions has been associated with positive ERP outcome in some studies, but not in others.

The studies on group, self-directed, and family-assisted behavioral treatments guide the way for the future of OCD treatment. Cost-effective applications of the behavioral treatments known to work for OCD are sorely needed. Further research in these areas is vital.

C. Cognitive Models

Models emphasizing the appraisal of threat form the backdrop for most of the cognitive theories of OCD. These models involve a two-step process. Identification of a potentially harmful situation (primary appraisal) creates an initial state of apprehension, and a secondary appraisal (of one's ability to cope with the threat) determines whether the anxiety will rise or decline. As noted earlier in discussing cognitive characteristics of OCD, obsessive-compulsive patients are thought to make abnormally high estimates of the probability of bad things happening to them. That is, they anticipate danger or misfortune more readily than nonobsessionals and may believe in the need to be concerned about danger and to dwell on its possible occurrence in order to protect themselves. This overestimation of threat is part of an inaccurate appraisal process which contributes to the development of OCD. From a cognitive perspective, several types of beliefs or assumptions contribute to inaccurate appraisal. These include beliefs described by rational emotive therapists (RET) and by other cognitive theorists. Perfectionistic beliefs may take the form that one should be thoroughly competent, adequate, and achieving in all possible respects (i.e., perfect) to consider oneself worthwhile and to avoid criticism, and that perfect solutions to all problems are available and should be found. Other hypothesized OCD beliefs include the notion that making mistakes or failing to reach one's ideals is unacceptable and should result in punishment, that one has the power to prevent disastrous outcomes by magical rituals, and that certain thoughts and feelings are unacceptable. Related to the cognitive features described earlier is the need for certainty to avoid criticism and reduce risk. Coping with threats generated by these beliefs is thought to be difficult for people with OCD. These early theories are similar with respect to the role and content of specific irrational beliefs, although they have been largely subsumed by more recent cognitive theorizing.

The most prominent cognitive theory of OCD was proposed by Salkovskis in 1985. He drew heavily from Beck's cognitive theory of emotional disorders. Salkovskis noted that extensive research shows that intrusive cognitions are normal phenomena experienced by more than 90% of the population. What distinguishes people with OCD is not the experience of intrusive thoughts, but the way in which their occurrence and content are interpreted. People with OCD give special importance to their intrusions, whereas people not suffering from OCD simply ignore them. According to Salkovskis, the reaction to negative intrusive experiences in people with OCD depends on a set of underlying beliefs. These beliefs are characterized by an exaggerated sense that one is responsible for harm to oneself or to others and that one must act to prevent it. The OCD patient seeks to reduce the discomfort produced by these thoughts by engaging in neutralization (i.e., compulsion, suppression, or avoidance). The first step in the process is an appraisal of an intrusive thought as an indication that they are in some way responsible for harm or its prevention. In the second step, this appraisal elicits neutralizing behavior (overt or covert). If negative appraisal occurs without the appraisal of responsibility, neutralization will not take place and the result will be anxiety and/or depression, but not OCD. Thus, the core assumption of this model is that OCD symptoms are efforts to neutralize or ameliorate the appraisal of responsibility for harm.

Neutralization includes overt behaviors (washing, checking, etc.) as well as mental events, attempts to put things right, thought suppression, and reassurance seeking. Salkovskis suggests that neutralization effectively reduces the level of perceived responsibility in the short run, but increases the probability of intrusive thoughts in the longer term.

Research on the nature and measurement of obsessional responsibility, as well as experimental manipulations of responsibility, lend support to this theory, but there have been suggestions for modification. It has been proposed that in this theory, more emphasis should be given to dysfunctional beliefs about controlling thoughts and the costs of not doing so, as well as to the effect of depression in impairing the ability to control thoughts. Theorists also suggest that neutralization may develop only when other thought control efforts fail.

An alternate cognitive theory of OCD proposed recently is quite different from the appraisal model that has characterized previous cognitive theories. This model focuses on the inference process. It suggests that people with OCD do not react to an actual feared stimulus nor to its perceived consequences. Instead, they react to what they imagine might be there despite a lack of sensory evidence to support the belief. In this model, a faulty inference process is responsible for OCD beliefs. Rather than forming an hypothesis about an obsessional fear (the table is dirty) and testing it (feeling the table), the person with OCD changes the evidence to fit the hypothesis (the table must be dirty because I can imagine it dirty). The rituals are attempts to change this "fictional narrative" by changing what is real. The reliance on superstition, or on magical or pseudoscientific justifications for obsessional beliefs also reflects attempts to make the reality fit the fiction. This theory is quite interesting and deserves further research.

Although early cognitive treatments for OCD were not derived from these cognitive conceptualizations, more recently developed treatments have been. In particular, the use of rational emotive therapy (RET) and Beckian cognitive therapy tailored specifically for OCD have been investigated. Although still in the early stages of testing, these treatments show great promise.

D. Cognitive Treatments

Some investigators have observed cognitive changes after ERP treatment, especially with respect to the overestimation of risk. They suggest that ERP may reduce the overestimation of risk experienced by people with OCD. If exposure-based treatments can change cognitions associated with OCD, and if, as is suggested by the cognitive theories just reviewed, these cognitions are important components of the disorder, then perhaps other ways of changing cognitions exist. The assumption underlying cognitive therapy is that changing cognitions will lead to reductions in OCD symptomatology. Early studies of the effects of cognitive therapy on OCD were hampered by the fact that the therapies were generic and not specifically tied to OCD cognitions. Not surprisingly, these treatments were not very successful. Subsequent studies in which the cognitive therapy was tailored to OCD have met with considerably more success.

Several studies have compared RET focusing on OCD beliefs with self-controlled ERP. Both treatments led to substantial improvement in patient symptoms and RET was superior to ERP in improving mood. In subsequent studies, comparable improvement for RET and ERP treatments was seen among patients randomly assigned to treatment type and RET was also associated with a greater decline in irrational beliefs.

The other cognitive treatment model used in treating OCD is Beck's cognitive model, in which faulty beliefs are identified, examined, and challenged. Case studies of the application of this type of therapy have been promising. Alternating cognitive therapy with response prevention resulted in improvement in a suicidal adolescent who previously refused exposure. Others have reported that this form of cognitive therapy altered unrealistic beliefs in a case with overvalued ideas. Furthermore, another investigation found that this type of therapy—focusing on excessive responsibility and without ERP—proved successful in treating four patients with checking rituals.

The application of this model to OCD has been described by clinical researchers in the Netherlands and in Quebec, Canada. These researchers reported on two controlled trials that used this approach. The first of these studies compared cognitive therapy with exposure only in the context of behavioral experiments to an exposure-alone group. Both treatments resulted in substantially improved symptoms at posttest and follow-up. There was a trend for more favorable outcome for cognitive therapy, but the results were comparable to findings reported by others using ERP. A second study found cognitive therapy plus exposure significantly better than a waiting-list control for 29 obsessional ruminators. The treatment was successful for 85% of the patients and the gains were maintained at 1-year follow-up.

Although to date only a small number of studies have been completed, cognitive therapy for OCD shows clear promise with or without ERP. It may also help in the reduction of relapse after treatment. In order for cognitive therapy to develop, however, research must identify which cognitions to target and how best to measure them. Research on the six cognitive characteristics associated with OCD identified by international experts in the field is an obvious place to start this process. [*See* COGNITIVE THERAPY.]

E. Biological Models

The discovery of the effectiveness of serotonin reuptake inhibitors (SRIs) in treating OCD produced a surge of speculation and theory about a biological basis for the disorder. Positron-emission tomography (PET) and related technology have generated dramatic advances in our knowledge of the biology of OCD. Two types of explanations have emerged. Neuropharmacological explanations have focused on the role of the serotonergic transmission system, and neuroanatomical explanations have concentrated on the orbitofrontal cortex, the basal ganglia, and their connections. These two types of explanations are by no means mutually exclusive.

Studies of the effects of administering SRIs as a treatment for OCD constitute the most consistent evidence for a neurochemical explanation. The evidence clearly shows that treatment with SRIs reduces OCD symptoms (see the following treatment section). Although this provides strong evidence for the role of serotonin in the biology of OCD, drug response studies are not the best source of evidence for neurochemical processes.

Direct evidence of the role of serotonin in OCD comes from two types of studies. First, concentrations of known metabolites of serotonin (5-hydroxyindole-acetic acid: 5-HIAA) in the blood or cerebrospinal fluid provide peripheral markers of serotonin in the brain. Administration of serotonin agonists provoke serotonergic responses in people whose serotonergic system is dysregulated. These pharmacologic challenge studies provide a second direct way of testing the role of serotonin in OCD. Unfortunately, peripheral marker studies have been inconsistent in establishing the role of serotonin function in OCD. It is possible that compensatory mechanisms in the body mask peripheral markers that would indicate serotonin dysregulation. Although the effectiveness of SRIs in treating OCD suggest that patients suffer from a functional deficit in serotonin, surprisingly, pharmacologic challenge studies have suggested the opposite. Administration of serotonin agonists produce exacerbated OCD symptoms, suggesting that OCD patients have heightened sensitivity to serotonergic stimulation. Furthermore, administration of serotonin receptor antagonists reverses this effect. There is some inconsistency in the findings of these challenge studies, however. Neuroendocrine responses to pharmacologic challenge suggest a hyposensitivity, whereas behavioral responses suggest a hypersensitivity. This suggests that dysregulation of the serotonergic system is probable, but the nature of the dysregulation is not clear. A number of investigators suggest taking multiple transmitter systems into account in developing a more complex model of OCD.

The basal ganglia, frontal cortex, and the limbic structures which connect them have been the focus of anatomical models of OCD. The basal ganglia assist in the regulation of movement and cognitive functioning. Within the basal ganglia, the three structures that make up the corpus striatum (caudate nucleus, putamen, and globus pallidus) have been the focus of attention with respect to OCD. The volume of the caudate nucleus appears to be smaller in OCD patients than in controls, as measured by computerized tomography (CT) studies. Increased metabolic activity has also been observed in the caudate nucleus of OCD patients during rest. Other PET scan studies have found increased metabolic activity in the striatum during exposure among OCD cleaners, but reduced metabolic activity among OCD checkers. The latter finding may reflect the ability of checkers to engage in covert neutralization during the PET scan procedure. In any case, there is clear evidence of a striatal abnormality in OCD, but whether it is primary or secondary is not clear.

On the basis of evidence for basal ganglia involvement, some investigators postulate that OCD is a basal ganglia disorder. The function of the basal ganglia is to detect stimuli that activate fixed-action patterns and to allow their release. These fixed-action patterns are innate species-specific responses that are motor programs for action and take the form of grooming and safety rituals. The basal ganglia stores these programs and provides a gating mechanism for their release. In OCD patients, basal ganglia dysfunction allows the inappropriate release of fixed-action patterns (i.e., compulsive rituals).

Neuropsychological testing and electroencephalo-gram (EEG) studies suggest that deficits in frontal lobe functioning also play a role in OCD. In addition, PET scan studies and single-photon-emission computed tomography (SPECT) studies have shown increased metabolic activity in the frontal cortex of OCD patients compared with controls. Increased metabolic activity in response to provocative stimulation (obsessional rumination) has been found in OCD patients and in normal controls. This suggests that the mental activity associated with obsessional thinking can be localized in the frontal lobe. Furthermore, elevations in metabolic activity in the frontal lobes are no longer present after successful treatment with medication or behavior therapy. Based on this evidence and that of basal ganglia involvement, in 1992, Insel suggested a hyperactive cortical-striatal-thalamic-cortical circuit in OCD. According to this theory, the caudate nucleus sends erroneous inhibitory signals to the globus pallidus. As a result, the globus pallidus fails to inhibit the thalamus from sending signals to the cortex. Thus, the cortex receives signals that it would not have received if the circuit operated normally. Further erroneous signals from the caudate nucleus inhibit the interruption of the circuit and messages continue to reverberate.

Baxter and colleagues suggested that the gating and screening activities of the striatum fail to inhibit impulses or thoughts that "leak" into consciousness and are experienced as obsessions. Fixed-action patterns (obsessions) occur automatically in response to obsessions and require effortful suppression and/or neutralization. This produces hyperactivity in the basal ganglia and frontal lobes. Similar models postulate a problem with the "comparator mechanism" in the limbic system or in the basal ganglia which matches sensory information with what is anticipated. When a mismatch occurs, arousal and corrective procedures are undertaken. A defective comparator mechanism might result in faulty evaluation of sensory input (i.e., hands feel dirty when they are not) and ineffective corrective action (washing hands to remove dirt that is not there). The dirt can only be felt but not removed.

There is strong evidence for frontal-striatal circuit involvement in OCD. The etiologic significance of this circuit is unclear, however. It may cause the disorder or may simply be the biological expression of it. Future research along these lines will clarify the mechanisms and roles of biochemical substances and structures in OCD.

Studies of genetic involvement in OCD have been inconsistent. Those using strict diagnostic criteria to define concordance have found only weak or inconsistent evidence for genetic transmission. Studies using subclinical OCD symptoms to establish concordance have found strong evidence of genetic involvement in OCD. However, some have suggested that what is transmitted is a diathesis for anxiety disorders rather than OCD specifically. Also along these lines, some researchers suggest that at least a subtype of OCD and Gilles de la Tourette's syndrome are different phenotypic expressions of a common underlying genotype.

F. Biological Treatments for OCD

A substantial number of clinical and placebo controlled trials have now been conducted with the serotonin reuptake inhibitors, including clomipramine (Anafranil), fluvoxamine (Luvox), fluoxetine (Prozac), and sertraline (Zoloft). Qualitative and quantitative reviews of the treatment outcome literature generally conclude that all SRIs are effective in the treatment of OCD. Recent studies have also shown promise for a newer SRI, paroxetine (Paxil). At least moderate improvement occurs with SRIs in 55 to 70% of previously untreated patients. Although these drugs are also considered antidepressants, the SRIs appear to work for OCD patients whether or not they are depressed.

Meta-analytic comparisons among the SRIs show a preference for clomipramine, although at least one such study was equivocal on this issue. More large-scale direct comparisons of treatment efficacy are needed before drawing conclusions regarding differential effectiveness of these drugs. More research is also needed on the effects of method of administration. Intravenously administered clomipramine may work significantly faster than oral administration, as has been seen in several clinical series, and it may be effective for patients who do not respond to standard treatment. Dosage ranges have been partly tested for fluoxetine, with higher doses (up to 60 mg) producing better results, but additional research is needed to identify optimal dosage ranges for the SRIs.

Despite the effectiveness of SRIs in the treatment of OCD, there are some drawbacks to their use. Patients treated with SRIs show only a modest (30 to 60%) reduction in their symptoms, and a significant number (30% or more) show no improvement at all. While the side effects of newer SRIs are less severe than those of tricyclic antidepressants and clomipramine, they still represent a problem. The major side effects include sedation, sexual dysfunction, and weight changes. Although many patients may be willing to tolerate the side effects for the symptom relief they provide, these side effects can be a major cause of treatment dropout. Unfortunately, few studies report dropout or noncompliance rates for SRIs. In recent reports, from 10 to 27% of patients drop out of SRI treatment. Little information is available regarding relapse rates for the SRIs. Cessation of SRIs resulted in 89% and 90% relapse, respectively, in two studies. Relapse during continued SRI treatment has ranged from 18 to 23%.

Predictors of treatment response have been examined in a recent multicenter trial of more than 500 patients. Only age of onset predicted outcome. Later age of onset was associated with better response to SRIs. Other research suggests that patients with schizotypal personality disorder respond poorly to SRI treatment for OCD. There is some evidence that augmenting SRI treatment with neuroleptics may benefit those patients with schizotypal personality disorder and comorbid tic disorders.

The development of sophisticated instrumentation, more precise lesion placement, and the increasing safety record make psychosurgery a viable treatment option for patients who have failed to respond to multiple medication trials and behavior therapy. Four types of such surgery are in use: cingulotomy, capsulotomy, limbic leucotomy, and subcaudate tractotomy. Few studies of psychosurgery outcome for patients who have failed to respond to medication or behavior therapy exist. One such study reported that 45% of cingulotomy patients who had failed at adequate trials of medication and behavior therapy were at least partial treatment responders. Reviews of the available literature have recommended cingulotomy as the first choice for psychosurgery with these patients. A newer method of psychosurgery, gamma knife, may also show promise for intractable OCD.

Few studies offer a direct comparison of behavior therapy, SRIs, or a combination of the two. The first such comparison, in the early 1980s, found greater average improvement with exposure treatment compared with clomipramine. In a later study, 75 to 80% of ERP patients improved compared with 22 to 23% of clomipramine patients. The combination of clomipramine and ERP resulted in more subjects in the "much" improved category after 1 year (73%). Others have reported a slight advantage for the combination of fluoxetine and behavior therapy at 6 months, but after 1 year the effects are minimal. Preliminary results from a multicenter trial suggests that ERP alone may be more effective than clomipramine and the combination of clomipramine and ERP.

Reviews of combined ERP and SRI efficacy are hampered by the small number of studies using both treatments and by the inconsistencies in outcome measures. Nonetheless, they provide some pertinent information. In a comprehensive 1993 review, Abel concludes that ERP is more effective than clomipramine, especially in the treatment of rituals. For patients with severe depression, obsessions only, and overvalued ideas about obsessions, however, clomipramine appears to be more effective. While SRIs have the advantage of less time and effort by therapist and patient, ERP has fewer dropouts, side effects, and risks, and better maintenance. Meta-analytic reviews have provided additional information about comparative efficacy. These reviews have found behavioral and pharmacologic treatments equivalent, or that ERP alone and ERP in combination with medication were both more effective than SRIs alone, according to self-report measures. No differences among the treatments have been observed when assessor-rated measures were used. So far, no studies examining the efficacy of SRIs compared to or combined with cognitive treatments have been reported.

IV. FUTURE DIRECTIONS

Although our knowledge of the nature and treatment of this disorder is far greater than it was a decade ago, there remain significant gaps. For example, the level of insight into obsessions varies both between and within OCD patients. It is not yet understood how insight influences treatment or whether some treatments (e.g., cognitive therapy) can change insight. In addition to level of insight, other issues remain unsolved. A number of other disorders appear to be closely associated with OCD, including hypochondriasis, eating disorders, impulsive disorders, and more. Research is needed to identify the core overlapping features of these disorders.

There may be some utility to identifying subtypes of OCD. One subtype may be those with early onset (especially males), tics, and/or schizotypal traits. These patients have been found to respond poorly to treatment. Similarly, identification of cultural influences on symptomatology and treatment response is needed. The influence of family members on the maintenance of OCD symptoms also remains largely unexplored. Efforts to incorporate family members into the treatment process must be guided by such research.

Attempts to develop cognitive treatments for OCD developed out of the realization of the importance of belief structures and cognitive processing in the disorder. Progress in this endeavor depends on the conceptualization and measurement of these phenomena. Thoughtful progression from conceptual models to treatment strategies is needed to ensure that newly developed treatments will be effective. Cooperative investigation offers the potential for speeding this process along.

BIBLIOGRAPHY

Abel, J. L. (1993). Exposure with response prevention and serotonergic antidepressants in the treatment of obsessive compulsive disorder: A review and implications for interdisciplinary treatment. *Behaviour Research and Therapy, 31,* 463–478.

Baxter, L., Schwartz, J., Guze, B., Bergman, K., & Szuba, M. (1990). PET imagining in obsessive-compulsive disorder with and without depression. *Journal of Clinical Psychiatry, 51,* 61–69.

Foa, E. B., & Kozak, M. (1986). Emotional processing of fear: Exposure to corrective information. *Psychological Bulletin, 99,* 20–35.

Foa, E. B., & Wilson, R. (1991). *Stop obsessing: How to overcome your obsessions and compulsions.* New York: Bantam Books.

Freeston, M., Rhéaume, J., & Ladouceur, R. (1996). Correcting faulty appraisals of obsessional thoughts. *Behaviour Research and Therapy, 34,* 433–446.

Insel, T. (1992). Toward a neuroanatomy of obsessive compulsive disorder. *Archives of General Psychiatry, 49,* 739–744.

Salkovskis, P. M. (1985). Obsessional-compulsive problems: A cognitive-behavioral analysis. *Behaviour Research and Therapy, 23,* 571–583.

Steketee, G. (1993). *Treatments of obsessive compulsive disorder.* New York: Guilford Press.

Steketee, G., & White, K. (1990). *When once is not enough.* Oakland, CA: New Harbinger.

van Oppen, P., & Arntz, A. (1994). Cognitive therapy for obsessive-compulsive disorder. *Behaviour Research and Therapy, 32,* 79–87.

Optimal Development from an Eriksonian Perspective

James E. Marcia

Simon Fraser University

Dialetical Based upon the concept that an integrating idea (synthesis) emerges out of the thorough exploration of two opposing ideas (thesis and antitheses).

Ego Psychoanalytic Theory An extension of classical psychoanalytic theory that emphasizes processes of adaptation to the environment as contrasted with a more intrapsychic focus.

Epigenetic Sequence The patterns for psychological development that will be manifested given an average expectable environment.

Psychosexual Stages of Development Course of personality development postulated by Freud, based upon successive predominance of body zones (e.g., oral, anal, etc.).

Psychosocial Stages of Development A course of personality development outlined by Erikson, based upon somatic aspects of persons (beginning with Freudian psychosexual stages and extending throughout the life cycle) and the psychological consequences of a particular society's response to the needs and abilities of the growing individual (e.g., Basic Trust–Mistrust, Integrity–Despair, etc.).

"Virtues" The ego qualities hypothesized to arise from the resolution of Eriksonian psychosocial stages.

ERIK ERIKSON has formulated a theory of psychosocial development that encompasses the entire life cycle. His stages of ego growth parallel and then extend beyond the classical psychoanalytic psychosexual stages of childhood into late adulthood and old age. Each developmental period contributes an ego strength whose formation is based upon the individual's somatic state, previous psychosocial development, and social context. The overall nature of psychosocial development and the specific resolutional patterns of different chronological eras are presented in this article.

I. THEORETICAL ORIGINS OF ERIKSON'S THEORY

Erik Erikson was a psychoanalyst, born in Germany, who did most of his clinical and theoretical work in the United States. He was trained initially as an artist and subsequently worked at Dorothy Burlingham's school in Vienna where he came into contact with Anna and Sigmund Freud. Erikson was one of a number of theorists (e.g., Hartmann, Rapaport, Kris, Lowenstein) who considered themselves ego psychoanalysts. They built upon Freud's earlier work on unconscious processes by emphasizing the importance of the ego's adaptation to external reality. Accepting Freud's descriptions of a dynamic intrapsychic world dominated by impulse and control, they traced the impact of this interior struggle on the ways in which the individual copes with society. They also described the impact of society's positive and negative effects on the individual. Whereas Freud considered the development of adaptive skills to be the result of conflict between individual desires and social constraints, the ego psychoanalytic theorists posited additional developmental achievements that were conflict-free. This new emphasis on adaptation, rather than on inner compromise alone, led to a more finely differentiated view of both social contexts and ego development than had been afforded by classical analytic theory. Erikson was the most specific of these theorists in delineating different stages of ego growth and describing various social contexts as promoting or inhibiting ego development. Hence, to Freud's description of personality as the result of struggle between impulse and control, the ego psychoanalytic theorists added the notions of built-in stages of growth, more or less independent of conflict, as well as the importance of differing social conditions affecting positively and negatively these developing ego strengths.

II. STAGE RESOLUTION AS BALANCE AND INTEGRATION

Freud's conception of healthy personality functioning had largely to do with balance: balance between desire and expression, between restraint and release, between social demands and individual gratification. The hallmark of maturity was the ability to engage in relatively conflict-free love and work, to maintain one's passion within the bounds of rationality, to be moral without being moralistic, to be able to tolerate with mere unhappiness the inevitable losses and disappointments in life without descending into the misery of despair. Erikson would disagree with none of the above; rather, he would expand the possibilities for human development beyond mere balance. Because he saw ego growth as humans' epigenetic heritage, given any one of a number of average expectable environments, he added certain ego qualities, and even their related "virtues," to the Freudian achievement of a balanced life. These ego qualities will be de-

scribed below. It is important to note that Erikson's earlier developmental periods can probably be best described in terms of a "balance" of qualities, similar in *form* to the possibilities for positive personality development envisioned by Freud. However, this form of resolution likely differs beginning with late adolescence, a period considered more terminally than developmentally important by Freud. From late adolescence on, stage resolution assumes more the nature of an integration of opposites, of a synthetic resolution of an essentially dialectical problem. Development beyond childhood, for Erikson and psychosocial researchers building upon his work, is a matter of construction and integration. The discussion of this issue will be taken up again after the nature of ego development, illustrated in the chart of psychosocial periods, is described (see Fig. 1). I shall discuss first the formal qualities of the diagram and then fill in the content of the stages.

III. SOME IMPLICATIONS OF THE FORM OF THE PSYCHOSOCIAL CHART

The vertical axis of the diagram consists of life periods from infancy through old age. The diagonal boxes are the major stages of ego growth related to these chronological periods. This structure implies that the developing ego qualities are age-linked. That is, there is something about, say, the period of infancy that predisposes the development of Basic Trust, or about old age that enables Integrity. Whether or not these are the most relevant chronological periods and whether there should be more or fewer stages, each with their own psychosocial resolution, has been a recently disputed question. In particular, because of extended adolescence and because of an extended life span, some theorists have recently suggested that both the adolescent and the middle-age periods be subdivided. However, the bulk of the research that has been done to date has used the age periods as given in the chart. Rather than using actual chronological dates (e.g., young adulthood from ages 20 to 28), Erikson has preferred to let the definition of a developmental epoch rest with a particular culture and with that culture's timetable for requirements and permissions. For example, adolescence in Western societies, partially because of the time necessary

Identity issue at Integrity Stage

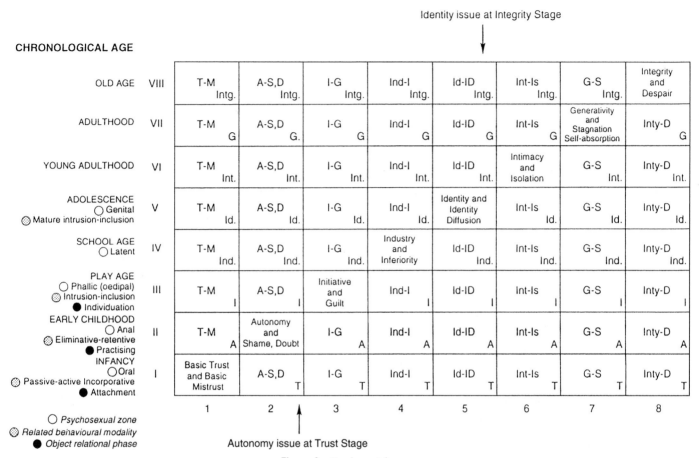

CHRONOLOGICAL AGE

		1	2	3	4	5	6	7	8
OLD AGE	VIII	T-M Intg.	A-S,D Intg.	I-G Intg.	Ind-I Intg.	Id-ID Intg.	Int-Is Intg.	G-S Intg.	Integrity and Despair
ADULTHOOD	VII	T-M G	A-S,D G.	I-G G	Ind-I G	Id-ID G	Int-Is G	Generativity and Stagnation Self-absorption	Inty-D G
YOUNG ADULTHOOD	VI	T-M Int.	A-S,D Int.	I-G Int.	Ind-I Int.	Id-ID Int.	Intimacy and Isolation	G-S Int.	Inty-D Int.
ADOLESCENCE ○ Genital ◎ Mature intrusion-inclusion	V	T-M Id.	A-S,D Id.	I-G Id.	Ind-I Id.	Identity and Identity Diffusion	Int-Is Id.	G-S Id.	Inty-D Id.
SCHOOL AGE ○ Latent	IV	T-M Ind.	A-S,D Ind.	I-G Ind.	Industry and Inferiority	Id-ID Ind.	Int-Is Ind.	G-S Ind.	Inty-D Ind.
PLAY AGE ○ Phallic (oedipal) ◎ Intrusion-inclusion ● Individuation	III	T-M I	A-S,D I	Initiative and Guilt	Ind-I I	Id-ID I	Int-Is I	G-S I	Inty-D I
EARLY CHILDHOOD ○ Anal ◎ Eliminative-retentive ● Practising	II	T-M A	Autonomy and Shame, Doubt	I-G A	Ind-I A	Id-ID A	Int-Is A	G-S A	Inty-D A
INFANCY ○ Oral ◎ Passive-active Incorporative ● Attachment	I	Basic Trust and Basic Mistrust	A-S,D T	I-G T	Ind-I T	Id-ID T	Int-Is T	G-S T	Inty-D T

○ *Psychosexual zone*
◎ *Related behavioural modality*
● *Object relational phase*

Autonomy issue at Trust Stage

Figure 1 Psychosocial stages.

for technological training in those societies, is more protracted than adolescence in developing countries. Similarly, "old age" in some cultures may begin at age 50, in others at age 70.

The psychosexual stages (oral, anal, etc.) are also included on the chart. Again, this is because, especially in early development, Erikson's psychosocial stages rest upon Freud's psychosexual stages. And these stages, defined as they are by body zones, furnish an indication of the prototypical situations within which ego development takes place. In both Erikson's writings and in the description that follows, there is a harmony between the classical and the ego psychoanalytic. For example, if one were to discuss the development of Initiative and Guilt without mentioning the oedipal drama one would miss the psychosexual heart of the matter.

Erikson's original version of the psychosocial developmental chart listed the stage resolutions as being in an antagonistic relationship; that is, Autonomy *versus* Shame, Doubt. He then explained in a description of the diagram that his intention was not an "either-or" resolution but a kind of balance of qualities, tilted toward the positive pole. Because I think that the "versus" obscures this, and especially because it violates the synthetic nature of stage resolution at adolescent and postadolescent periods, I have cast the stages as more equally valanced in resolution by using the word "and" rather than "versus"; for example, Initiative and Guilt, rather than Initiative versus Guilt. Although this may seem a small issue, it is an important one in two senses. When we have done research within the theory, it has been important to consider whether one is expected to develop, say, *just* Intimacy at young adulthood, or some synthesis involving both Intimacy *and* Isolation, with a predominant emphasis on the former. Also, when speaking of optimum development, the "versus" description of stage resolution suggests that at, say, middle age, one *should* be only Generative, with as little Stagnation or Self-Absorption as possible. However, it is the creative synthesis of the positive and negative poles that makes for the most lively, and livable, resolution. Even at earlier stages, it is crucial that some sense of the negative alternatives also be incorporated into the personality; realistic Mistrust, Shame, Doubt, Guilt, and Inferiority are, themselves, significant developmental achievements.

Only somewhat less important than the diagonal of the 8 major stage-specific resolutions, is the fact that the full diagram consists of 64, not just 8, squares. That is, each stage has its preparatory predecessors in the form of partial resolutions occurring before that stage's ascendancy. As well, each stage, once its ascendancy has been reached and the psychosocial issues resolved, contributes its strength to the resolution of succeeding stages. There is, for example, an Intimacy aspect (probably relating to friendship) of Industry–Inferiority resolution during school age that is preparatory for resolution of the Intimacy–Isolation issue during young adulthood. And on the future, contributory, side, the major resolution of that Intimacy–Isolation issue at young adulthood furnishes a necessary strength to Generativity development in middle age and to Integrity at old age. The most crucial contribution of a particular stage resolution is assumed to the stage immediately succeeding it.

The occurrence of every stage, in either preparatory or contributory form, at every age period, allows for some issues to be resolved "prematurely"; for example, the school-age child dying of cancer facing Integrity–Despair; the teenage parent dealing simultaneously with Identity, Intimacy, and Generativity. More importantly, the recurrence of every stage at every age suggests both the possibility for, and the topical sequence of, remediation of previously unresolved, or incompletely resolved, stages. Some adolescents, for example, who are struggling with identity problems, may be involved only with that issue, previous psychosocial stages having been primarily positively resolved. If they seek help, they are likely to be candidates for brief counseling rather than intensive psychotherapy. Other adolescents presenting with

identity problems may, in fact, be confronting issues going as far back as Basic Trust–Mistrust. In those cases, one can assume difficulty with all of the stages succeeding Trust, and intervention in the form of psychotherapy then takes on a much more structural (structure-building, structure-repairing) nature.

IV. GENERAL CHARACTERISTICS OF PSYCHOSOCIAL STAGE RESOLUTION

The elements to be taken into consideration in the resolution of any psychosocial stage are: somatic, societal, and psychological. Each stage is assumed to be built, epigenetically, on the physical characteristics of a person at a particular age. There are certain physiological needs and capabilities at each of the chronological periods noted in the diagram. These are reflected in the early stages by the delineation of the classical psychoanalytic body "zones" (e.g., oral) and the more ego-oriented behavioral "modes" (e.g., active and passive incorporation). The "zones" refer primarily to somatic needs; the "modes" indicate rudimentary patterns of behavior developed in reference to the "zones." Especially in the first three stages, body zones (oral, anal, sexual [phallic, clitoral]) are foci for much of the developmental drama played out between child and caretakers. These zones are considered as both actual and as metaphorical. "Orality," for example, refers both to the stimulation of the mucous membrane linings of the mouth as well as to a general pattern of "incorporation" through all body (and mind) receptive mechanisms.

In terms of more generalized needs and abilities, the infant, for example, needs dependable care, and comes equipped both reflex responses and a capacity for rapid learning. The adolescent, because of the changes of puberty and the development of higher levels of operational thought, needs a defining context that recognizes the transition from childhood to adulthood, and is capable of dedicated work, high levels of cognition, and adultlike sexuality. Each age, then, has somatic features that involve both needs and capabilities—even old age, in which the dwindling physical capacities almost force psychological, some would say as well spiritual, development.

Recalling the earlier statement concerning ego psychoanalysts' interest in adaptation, it is not only individuals who adapt to social environments but societal milieux, over time, that adapt to individuals as well. Social institutions (e.g., elementary school, marriage contracts) as well as institutionalized social practices (e.g., infant care techniques, child socialization mores) have developed with reference to their constituents' differing physical needs and abilities at different ages. There are events at each age period that are prototypical, that is, both actual as well as metaphorical, of the main issue of that stage (as these stages are construed). In order, these would be: Infancy: feeding, weaning; Early Childhood: toilet training; Play age: oedipal issues; School age: education; Adolescence: self/social definition; Early Adulthood: mating; Middle Age: parenting; Old Age: physical decline and psychological/spiritual growth. The age-specific events listed are not necessarily the only contexts in which the psychosocial issue can be resolved. For example, although sexual intercourse (mating) may be the prototypical situation for Intimacy, it is not the necessary condition. And, for many, it can even be irrelevant. However, it can be useful as both an occasion for and as a metaphor for Intimacy (i.e., tender and loving concern for the other in depth). It is also useful to tie psychosocial development to some concrete physical events. One can certainly be Generative, for example, without having children, but nothing challenges that development quite as much as parenting one's own early adolescent child.

The social institutions relevant to each of the psychosocial stages provide the more or less nutritional contexts which will influence the forms that the development of ego qualities will take. Some examples of such "institutions" which differ from culture to culture are the "rules" for marital relationships, provisions for the elderly, toilet training of children, and so on. The particular practices employed by the culture are guided by that culture's values and desired outcomes for its members. Hence, although all cultures must provide institutional contexts for such basic human events as birth, impulse control, education and training, mating, parenting, and aging, these contexts take culturally diverse forms; according to a particular society, they make differing demands and offer differing rewards. The optimum situation exists when the societal demands and rewards mesh "well enough" with individuals' capabilities and needs. "Well enough," here, refers to the ego psychoanalytic concept of "average expectable environment"—an environment sufficient to yield a primarily posi-

tive psychosocial resolution of the life-cycle stages in most of its members. This is a tautological definition. A better one cannot be supplied until measures for the resolution of individual stages have been well-developed, a taxonomy of environments formulated, and a linkage established between specific environments and the resolution of particular psychosocial issues. There are enough data available now on identity development, at least, to begin the task of environmental specification.

Out of the interaction between individual needs and capabilities and societal rewards and demands emerge the psychological stages that are noted in the chart as psychosocial stage outcomes. These stages have both antecedents and consequences. Identity structure may be assumed to change across the life cycle in a manner consistent with Piaget's description of cognitive development; that is, via the processes of assimilation, disequilibration, and accommodation. Integrity may be considered to be the final form that the Identity structure assumes in old age.

Erikson's theory differs from Freud's in that the psychological emerges not just from the societal via the familial, but more directly from the societal. This is reflected in the view that personality development is seen as continuing throughout the life cycle, with the possibility of major shifts occurring at adolescence. The societal is important enough to influence not just the relative balance among impulse, restraint, and sanction, but to give behavior its final acceptable form. For Erikson, the social becomes qualitatively, not just quantitatively, embedded in the psyche. In his studies of famous figures such as Gandhi and Luther, he proposes a new type of psychological analysis called psychohistory. This is the study of the interplay between social/economic/historical conditions and individual developmental stages, which yields particular personality types in different historical ages within defining cultural contexts.

To summarize, the stages of psychosocial growth to be described below result from ways in which developmentally differential individual needs and abilities are socialized at differing life-cycle periods. The importance of these life-cycle periods, their sequence, and even their definition as periods, may be culturally determined; although it is difficult to imagine that Identity and Trust, say, would not be important in any culture, and that Identity would precede Trust in any culture. However, since all stages of Erikson's theory have not been adequately scientifically validated even in the cultural context in which they arose, let alone cross-culturally, the theory's cross-cultural accuracy remains an open question. The most widely researched construct from Erikson's theory, Identity (as assessed within the identity status paradigm), has been found to be applicable in the United States, Canada, United Kingdom, Holland, Iran, Norway, France, Germany, Poland, Portugal, Kuwait, Nigeria, South Africa, Israel, Mexico, India, Taiwan, and Japan. The psychosocial periods are not stages in the strict cognitive developmental sense that each is a necessary precursor to the next. The fact that all occur, in a sense, simultaneously, belies that. They are stages in the sense that there is a presumed succession of issues and that the resolution of each is important for the resolution of its successor.

V. PSYCHOSOCIAL STAGE OUTCOMES

A. Basic Trust and Mistrust

Basic Trust refers to the infant's sense of the essential all-rightness of the self in the world. It is difficult to convey in words what is sensed primarily on a body level and only represented cognitively, so far as we know, in the vaguest sense. But, perhaps just because this optimistic sense is so vague and pervasive, it is crucial to all further development. Basic Trust involves an expectation that no uncomfortable state will last too long. States that must, at first, be felt as a totality of awfulness are followed by states of relief and even euphoria if they are responded to by caretakers who are reasonably well attuned to the infant. The hourly, daily succession of these states establishes a rhythmic pattern of uncomfortable arousal and pleasurable relief, interspersed with periods of just "being," and exploring the world via incorporating it, not just through the mouth in feeding, but through the skin and eyes and ears.

Some Mistrust accumulates as distressing states are not met when they arise, a not uncommon occurrence. This can be kept within reasonable limits if painful arousal is not allowed too frequently to mount beyond the infant's tolerance capacity. In optimal individual-environmental meshing (and at infancy it is the environment, not the individual, that undergoes the major adaptation), instances of "hits" (the right stuff at the right time) outnumber significantly the

number of "misses" (no stuff, or the wrong stuff, or the wrong time). However, if painful stimulation is permitted to overwhelm the infant too often, the expectation, based, again, on an hourly, daily succession of such unassuaged uncomfortable states, is either of a succession of painful periods followed by oblivion (sleep), or of intermittent, unpredictable occasions of soothing. In this case, a predominant sense of basic Mistrust emerges.

While some Mistrust is both inevitable and adaptively useful, too much establishes a pessimistic expectation concerning oneself (a sense of inner badness) and the world of relationships (as uncaring or malevolent) that pervades the successive life-cycle stages. A sense of Basic Trust, on the other hand, bequeaths a psychological legacy of optimism to successive psychosocial stages: a sense that one's needs will not mount to intolerable heights (a sense of inner positive dependability) because a beneficent world (predictable and caring) will intervene in time—that, overall, there is a dependable rhythm establishable between oneself and caring others, that one is fundamentally safe inside one's own skin and within the world.

The sense of Basic Trust is a global feeling about oneself and the world; it rests on top, as it were, of the sensori-motor cognitive development described by Piaget and the state of secure attachment described by investigators such as Bowlby, Mahler, and Stern. The cognitive and emotional-interpersonal development outlined by these theorists provides the necessary infrastructure for acquiring an overall sense of Basic Trust balanced by judicious Mistrust. The "virtue" of this stage is Hope.

B. Autonomy and Shame, Doubt

The central issue of early childhood is will. Although will became an issue in the earlier oral period around weaning, this is an event more imposed upon the child than negotiated with caretakers. Toilet training is a different matter. Here the child is being asked to modify what is essentially pleasurable to him/her in both process and content in order to meet demands of the parent. (Parent, here, can refer to other socializing adults.) This process can be a matter of willing acquiescence and joyful pride in accomplishing a pleasing performance, or it can degenerate into a demeaning struggle in which the child's will is eventually broken by a superior force. If the parent is sufficiently attuned to the child's needs and abilities, toilet training can be a cooperative joint project. If not, either the dominant power ("unjustly") prevails, or the child is eventually shamed into compliance at preschool. Which of these alternatives prevails depends, ultimately, upon the parents' attitudes toward their *own* impulses and the degree of tolerant control they exercise over themselves. How the parents view their own desires determines how they will treat their children's. Of course, toilet training is not the only arena in which conflict between the child's will and the parents' will is at issue; locomotion is another. The pride that parents take in children's first steps soon gives way to alarm and a succession of "no, no's" when perambulation leads to peril. Again, the issue is: whose will is going to prevail and by what means?

The defiant "no's" of the 2-year-old, accompanied as they are by all of the passion that the toddler's body can muster, are less related to any particular activity at hand than to the sheer exercise of willfulness. It is in the testing of this willfulness against clearly superior parental power that a sense of justice either is or is not forged. If the small person's will is harshly broken or is treated with ridicule, then pervasive feelings of Shame and Doubt are the consequences. Shame is the sense that what issues from inside oneself is dirty and disgusting, that it is difficult or impossible for one to express inner contents without suffering belittlement or punishment. There is a residing fear that if one acts on one's own will, one can never get it right. To paraphrase Erikson, Doubt refers to the lingering knowledge that one possesses the potential for Shame, a "backside," and that one has to be extremely cautious lest one be caught with one's pants down. The common expression, "covering your ass," refers to this self-protective reaction to the fear of accidental exposure. To the individual constricted by Doubt, it is important to determine exactly where the proper lines are and to color precisely within them. Clearly, Shame and Doubt are early adversaries of later creativity.

Optimum development consists neither of shameless defiance nor of crippling doubt, but of a sense of Autonomy wherein the child learns that her/his will can be successfully integrated with that of powerful, but loving, caretakers so that each is satisfied. Adults learn to be attuned to the child's needs for "going" and to make demands within the child's cognitive and muscular capabilities. The child learns that adult demands can be met successfully with only some sacri-

fice of volition and that rewards for such compromise and good performance are quick and dependable in coming. Healthy Autonomy has some components of realistic Shame (one's "big" will does not make one "big") and Doubt (one cannot do everything that one wills). Yet, predominantly, there is a lasting sense that what one wills is, or can become, in accord with the wills of essentially caring, although sometimes restricting, others. While it is not the case that "anything goes," "going" itself, especially if realistically self-restrained, is valued. The virtue of this stage is a relatively free sense of Will.

C. Initiative and Guilt

Whereas Autonomy referred to sheer willingness, Initiative, at play age, refers to the harnessing of that will to the planning and accomplishment of specific projects. The prototypical arenas for the establishment of Autonomy were toilet training and toddling; for Initiative they are parents and play. Because of growing cognitive capacities, the awareness dawns on the child that having a parent all to oneself would be a major acquisition. Consider that the 5-year old lives in a world of knees where parents are not young or middle-aged adults with all their failings and foibles, but gods and goddesses who can mete out, apparently at their whim, rich rewards or terrible punishments. Learning to please or placate these delightful or demonic giants is a project well worth the undertaking.

Play is children's developmental work at this period, and Initiative refers to the ability to formulate a plan (for a game, a picture, a song, getting a parent's attention) and carry it through. The most common danger is that the child will develop a sense of Guilt over either the ends or the means of such projects. Guilt is a kind of internalized sense of Shame and Doubt carried over from the previous stage. Rather than fearing ridicule or punishment from others external to the self, these praisers and persecutors now take up residence within oneself, so that it is in the internal mirror of one's own conscience that one's acts and wishes are reflected and evaluated. Children (and adults) hobbled by excessive Guilt may always need someone else's permission to proceed with a project, and may even need to punish themselves while achieving their goals. A less common danger is that the child will succeed too well in the oedipal project and, in fact, secure for her/himself the almost undivided attention of the desired parent. This establishes unrealistic expectations for what is going to befall most children as they enter adult relationships later in life. Incompletely resolved oedipal situations can also lead to a caricature of Initiative wherein every interpersonal situation encountered is turned into an oedipal project, so that the world is experienced as full of threatening rivals to be defeated and desirable persons to be won; one's life becomes a continuing drama of competition and seduction. A *realistic* sense of Guilt helps to forestall the interpersonal carnage that is attendant on such an approach to relationships. As in the preceding stage where the child had to cope with the limits to "going," here he/she begins to develop an appreciation of his/her abilities (and limitations) in "getting" and "making." The virtue of this stage, emerging from the balance of Initiative and Guilt, is a sense of relatively untrammeled Purpose.

D. Industry and Inferiority

Having learned the rudiments of relationship within the familial context, the school-age child is ready to "take it on the road"; that is, to enter the world of education outside of home. Every society trains its young in the technologies necessary to be a productive member, whether these be basket making, food growing, hunting, reading and writing, or even computer literacy. It is in the context of such "schooling" that the child develops a sense of her/himself as a worker. The "play" world of the previous stage gives way to a more "work"-oriented world. And the child hopefully acquires the sense that working is worthwhile, that sustained effort at meaningful tasks is going to be rewarded.

The danger is that, in this setting of peers and teachers, the child will be made to feel Inferior, that there is little or nothing that he/she can do right, no matter how hard he/she tries. Some children react to this feeling of Inferiority by giving up; others "try too hard," not knowing when to stop. A sense of Industry involves the feeling that perseverance at valued tasks is advantageous and that it is also all right to quit sometimes. It is with this stage that we begin to have empirically developed measures of the psychosocial stages. The empirically determined aspects of Industry are a realistic attention span, task perseverance, the ability to discriminate among effort, ability, and performance, and a feeling that work is worthwhile and

that one is a worthy worker. The associated virtue of this stage is Competence.

E. Identity and Identity Diffusion[1]

The beginning of childhood's end in early adolescence sees the young person hopefully having accrued all of the psychosocial raw material needed for achieving Freud's vision of optimum development: the ability to love (Basic Trust and Initiative) and to work (Initiative and Industry). Until this period in the life cycle, the individual has made a number of part-identifications; that is, he or she has identified with some aspects of other people and with some aspects of the self, and has been generally content with playing different roles at different times without much concern for integration. The physiological, sexual, cognitive, and social-expectational changes attendant upon puberty and subsequent adolescence have two effects: they disequilibrate the fairly structured life of the latency-aged child; and they require an accommodation in the form of a new integration of physique, sexuality, ideology, abilities, personal needs, and perceived social demands.

Early adolescence, from about puberty to age 16, may be considered as a primarily "de-structuring" period. Middle adolescence, from about age 15 to age 19, is a "re-structuring" phase, a time during which an identity is being constructed. During these two periods, parents without a strong sense of their own identity are especially vulnerable to adolescents' disconfirmation of them as the adolescents strive to define themselves, to forge their own identities, often in opposition.[2] Late adolescence, about 18 to 22, is the developmental interval within which the newly constructed identity is consolidated and tried out in the world. Identity formation becomes paramount during this life-cycle era because the individual is required to make a transition in both physical and social position from child to adult, from receiver to provider. Our research indicates that two processes are important in

---

[1] Diffusion is Erikson's initial term; he subsequently changed it to "Confusion." Diffusion has been retained for two reasons: most of the research done on identity development has used this term; and it is likely an underlying structural diffusion of identity that produces the feelings of confusion.

[2] These time periods are highly approximate. Those suggested here apply to the much lengthier adolescence found in technologically sophisticated cultures.

identity formation: the *exploration* of alternative beliefs, values, and occupational goals; and a subsequent *commitment* to a selected set of alternatives.

Once formed, an identity furnishes the person with a historical sense of who they have been (continuity), an existentially meaningful sense of who they are now (differentiation), and a teleological sense of who they might, in the future, become (direction). Experientially, identity refers to an inner sense of who one, most essentially, is—independent of the separate roles one plays or the varied perceptions others have of oneself. Identity is not the sum of one's previous identifications or abilities or beliefs; it is the *integration* of these.

Not all persons construct an identity. Some merely carry over into adult form the identity conferred upon them as children. This "foreclosed" identity can be a serviceable one if the person remains in the same social context throughout their life. However, when the context changes, the person must either abandon the formerly serviceable identity or rigidly, and nonadaptively remain fixed in place. For those attempting to change a foreclosed identity at mid-life or later, the process is especially painful because this new identity must be formed under conditions considerably less supportive than existed during the optimal developmental period of adolescence. The other situation in which identity is not constructed is the case of the "diffused" identity wherein no alternatives are chosen and identity exploration becomes mere wandering. Here, the person becomes an easy target for identity-conferring cults (or charismatic individuals), or drifts into adulthood, sailing rudderless with the strongest prevailing breezes. The development of an identity furnishes the individual with the virtue of Fidelity.

F. Intimacy and Isolation

Having determined who one is, and is to be, during the previous adolescent period, the young adult now faces the task of sharing this newly minted identity with at least one other person. Intimacy refers to a relationship characterized by depth of expression of feeling, care, and concern for the other, and commitment. The risk is that in sharing oneself deeply with another, one risks losing oneself unless one's new identity is sufficiently strongly flexible to permit it to be temporarily lost in merger and then recovered. Similar to the earlier stages with their proto-typical somatic events of nursing—weaning, toilet training—locomotion, and parental sexual possession, this stage's prototypical situation is sexual intercourse. The opportunity to merge deeply and caringly, to "lose oneself in the other," furnished by intercourse is a kind of model for a psychological relationship in which one can suspend temporarily self-concern and self-protection, and attend to another.

Clearly, sexual intercourse is neither a necessary or sufficient condition for Intimacy. In fact, the most technically proficient intercourse, if it is merely "performed," can be one of life's more isolating experiences. Rather, Intimacy refers to a psychological relationship, which usually does—but may not—have a physical component. The lines from a now somewhat dated Simon and Garfunkel song, "I am a rock, I am an island . . . I touch no one and no one touches me," describe the position of the Isolate. In the best outcome, Intimacy is integrated with Isolation, so that one develops one's own style of being Intimate—Isolate, of maintaining a sense of separate self while cherishing the mutuality of deep contact with at least one other.

There are a number of intermediate Intimacy—Isolation patterns that have been defined by research. One of the most common of these is the Pseudo-Intimate in which the individual is in a societally recognized context for Intimacy, say marriage, but the content of the relationship is superficial and routine, devoid of deep contact. Commitment is superimposed on the relationship rather than emerging organically from it. Our research has indicated that women and men differ developmentally in the timing of Intimacy development. Because of their greater concern with relationship establishment and maintenance, Intimacy issues become central earlier for women than for men, and their Identity tends to include somewhat more Intimacy aspects. Hence, although Identity development appears to precede Intimacy development for most men, Intimacy and Identity formation are more often found to codevelop for women. For both sexes, there appears to be a strong relationship between Identity and Intimacy formation. This stage's virtue is Love.

G. Generativity and Stagnation, Self-Absorption

Middle age sees the development of a predominant concern with caring for the life cycles of others. The prototypical situation for this is the generation of one's own children; yet, Generativity applies as well to care for any of one's valued creations, to one's relationship to the next generation as a mentor, and to contributions to one's community in the form of establishing contexts for the growth of others. In addition, one finds one's caring directed to those older than oneself in the life cycle, frequently to one's own parents as they become less capable of caring for themselves. The alternative of Stagnation suggests a kind of lying fallow, which if continued too long, becomes sterility. The other "negative" possibility, Self-Absorption, involves treating oneself as one's one and only beloved child. On the other hand, as with the other psychosocial stages beginning with Identity, Generativity involves not just a balance, but an integration of care for other and care for self.

The Generative trap is that the better one becomes at it, the greater the expectations of others, and of oneself, for continued self-giving. Hence, an important aspect of authentic Generativity is a generative approach to oneself as well as to others. Clearly, this involves an element of Self-Absorption. As well, continued Generativity in one direction can degenerate into drivenness and "burnout." Thus, periods of Stagnation may be important in leading to a renewed Generativity.

Our research has suggested that there are different styles of Generativity based upon inclusivity and involvement. Inclusivity refers to the bandwidth of one's care: Who qualifies? Just one's "own kind" or a broader spectrum of the next generation? Involvement refers to the extent of investment one makes in care-giving activity. Two examples of styles of Pseudo-Generativity are Agentic and Communal. The Agentic person is engaged in fostering the growth of others, but only so long as they are instrumental in aiding the Agentic person in the attainment of his/her own personal goals. The Communal individual is involved in the nurturance of others, but the continuance of this activity is contingent upon fairly regular expressions of gratitude on the part of the object of care. In both cases, the ultimate focus of generativity is more on the giver than on the recipient; and the care ceases when the giver is no longer the central beneficiary. Generativity, in its most highly developed form, is independent of immediate results. Generative activity is predicated upon the benefits for generations to come, on the concern for life cycles of "children" not yet born.

The Generative individual is engaged presently and for the future with "growing" things: persons, projects, communities. This stage's virtue is Care.

H. Integrity and Despair

Erikson's theory is unique (save for Jung's) among psychodynamic approaches to personality in that it posits a stage of ego growth even at the end of the life cycle. Again, the body is involved; but this time in a more minor key. The physical issue now is the experience of physical decline as an omen of dying and death. The individual stands at the terminal phase of his/her one and only life cycle. Pain and loss vie with psychological strength and wisdom. Integrity implies a sense of wholeness and completeness even, especially, in the face of disintegration. Only when the whole of the life cycle has been completed, when each stage has been satisfactorily resolved, can the developed parts be fit together in an integral way. This involves some withdrawal from the Generative preoccupations of the previous period, some ceasing to "do," in order to "be," and to reflect on the meaning of what one has done.

Integrity, while referring somewhat to authenticity, has more to do with wholeness. Can the parts fit together? Is there too much missing? Too many risks untaken? In understanding Despair, the words of Ibsen, interpreted as the inner self-reproaches of an aging Peer Gynt come to mind:

> We are thoughts, you should have formed us . . . We are watchwords, you should have proclaimed us . . . We are tears that were never shed; we might have melted the ice spears that wounded you . . . We are deeds, you should have performed us; doubts that strangle have crippled and bent us . . . We are songs, you should have sung us; a thousand times you curbed and suppressed us. In the depths of your heart we have lain and waited . . . We were never called forth— now we are poison in your throat. (Ibsen, H., 1966)

Yet, there is no possibility of Integrity without an awareness of Despair. We have tried to capture this in our research that outlines different patterns of Integrity resolution based upon commitment (to values and beliefs), continuity (from beliefs to actions), and comprehensiveness (solidarity with humankind). One of these, called Pseudointegrated, refers to persons who maintain a cheerful, but brittle, facade by means of "uplifting" slogans and bromides. Another pattern, Nonexploratory, is composed of individuals who simply go on being who they have always been with little or no reflection on the history of their lives or the meanings of those lives in other than familiar and unexamined terms. Interestingly, Integrity resolution seems related to Identity resolution. Perhaps this is because both have a structure-like quality; both refer to an integration of previously developed parts into a new whole.

An important shift to universality occurs with Integrity development, a shift that has been going on at least since adolescence. This is reflected in the change of referent for the pronoun "we" from I-and-my-peer group—at adolescence, to my-partner-and-I—at young adulthood, to our family (biological or professional)—at middle age, to all of humankind—past, present, and future—at old age. The final virtue is Wisdom—in Erikson's words: "detached concern with life itself in the face of death itself."

VI. GENERATIONAL MUTUALITY AND SUMMARY

The foregoing description of the psychosocial stages of development focuses on the individual moving through the life cycle. But, in fact, the psychosocial stages reflect interpersonal interdependency. While young children and adolescents require "good enough" parental figures in order to resolve positively their ego growth issues, parents, likewise, depend upon those for whom they care for the confirmation of their Generativity. For example, a teacher, engaged in promoting a sense of Industry in her/his students, looks to their confirmatory responses for her/his sense of Identity and Generativity. The partner looks to the significant other for confirmation of Intimacy. The elder looks to the culture for some validation (and sometimes forgiveness) for his/her life cycle commitments to persons, ideas, and achievements.

The picture of optimal development offered by Erikson is neither as pessimistic as Freud's nor as optimistic as, say Rogers' or Maslow's. What he posits is the successive formation of ego strengths that are more or less guaranteed given an average expectable environment. Even the less-than-optimal Identity, Intimacy, Generativity, and Integrity statuses that we have outlined have their strengths. Only the most negative alternatives bode ill for development; and, even then, the more positive resolutions must encompass some aspects of these negative alternatives. Our research indicates that only about 10% of our samples (from adolescence through old age) fall at the maladaptive poles. The characteristics ("virtues") associated with the psychosocial stage resolutions such as hope, will, purpose, competence, fidelity, love, care, and wisdom are not foreign to any peoples in any cultures at any time. The only developmental heroics involved are the heroics of everyday life.

BIBLIOGRAPHY

Bradley, C. L., & Marcia, J. E. (in press). Generativity-Stagnation: A five category model. *Journal of Personality*.

Erikson, E. H. (1980). *Identity and the life cycle: A reissue*. New York: Norton.

Hearn, S., Glenham, M., Strayer, J., Koopman, R., & Marcia, J. E. Integrity, Identity, and beyond: Development of a measure of Erikson's eighth stage. Manuscript submitted for publication.

Ibsen, H. (1966). *Peer Gynt: A dramatic poem*. (Translation by Peter Watts.) London: Penguin.

Kowaz, A. M., & Marcia, J. E. (1991). Development and validation of a measure of Eriksonian Industry. *Journal of Personality and Social Psychology, 60*, 390–397.

Marcia, J. E., Waterman, A. S., Matteson, D. R., Archer, S. A., & Orlofsky, J. L. (1993). *Ego identity: A handbook for psychosocial research*. New York: Springer-Verlag.

Optimism, Motivation, and Mental Health

Charles S. Carver
University of Miami

Stacie M. Spencer
University of Pittsburgh

Michael F. Scheier
Carnegie Mellon University

I. Contemporary Models of Motivation
II. Effects of Optimism
III. Becoming an Optimist

Disengagement   Giving up on the attempt to attain a goal.
Expectancy   Belief about the likelihood that a given outcome or event will occur.
Explanatory Style   A person's characteristic pattern of causal explanations for the occurrence of bad (or good) events.
Optimism   A generalized expectancy for positive outcomes in one's future.
Self-Efficacy Expectancy   A person's expectancy of being able to perform a particular behavior.
Self-Regulation   Matching behavior to goals that one has taken up by monitoring and adjusting the behavior as needed.

OPTIMISM versus pessimism is having the expectation of good versus bad outcomes for one's future. This article focuses on how this variable, as a quality of personality, relates to mental health. Contemporary work on optimism is rooted deeply in broader views of human motivation and action. Accordingly, we begin this discussion by briefly describing these models of motives and behavior. As we do so, we place optimism within the context of these models. We then present portions of the substantial body of evidence of the benefits of optimism (or, conversely, evidence of the detriments of pessimism) and turn to paths that seem to link optimism to those positive out-

comes. We conclude with a brief discussion of potential therapeutic implications of these findings.

I. CONTEMPORARY MODELS OF MOTIVATION

To understand the dynamics of optimism and pessimism and how these qualities of personality influence human experience, it is useful to step back and consider how contemporary theorists conceptualize the nature of motivation. A common view in today's personality and social psychology is that human behavior is organized around the pursuit of goals. Goal constructs are given a variety of labels by different theorists, and there are minor conceptual differences among the constructs, but at present what is most important is what they have in common. Goals are values that people take as either desirable or undesirable (what one might think of as "antigoals" or "repellers"). People try to fit their behaviors (or indeed their very selves) to values that they see as desirable, and they try to keep away from values or qualities that they see as undesirable.

Motivation, in this view, is partly a matter of identifying and taking on goals and regulating one's actions with respect to the goals that one takes up. Thus, these models are sometimes referred to categorically as *self-regulatory* models. There are many distinctions that can be made among the goals that serve as the focal point of these motivational processes. Some goals are abstract (to be a responsible or honest person) or broad in scope (to create financial security, to extend your musical talents as far as possible, to maintain good health). Other goals are more concrete and yet still involve multiple steps or phases (to complete a college course, to buy groceries for the coming week, to get to work on time). Other goals are far smaller and more restricted in scale (to pick up a coffee cup, to close and lock the door). In many goal-based models of motivation, it is either explicit or implicit that people attain high-level, abstract goals through the process of attaining lower-level, concrete goals.

We should also perhaps be explicit in noting that these theories of motivation as self-regulation also assume that the goal concept applies to virtually all areas of human endeavor. Thus, the goal of having a close intimate relationship, or of spending time with a friend, fits this picture just as easily as does the goal of preparing a report or scoring well on an exam.

A. Meeting Adversity: Persistence and Giving Up

Goal-based views of motivation typically have at least one more facet that is critical to their function as models of behavior. That is, the description to this point has included no mention of adversity, of difficulty encountered in the attempt to move toward one's desired ends (or away from antigoals). Sometimes people do meet impediments in their efforts toward goal attainment. When this happens, what follows?

The answer given most commonly by motive theorists today is that what happens next depends on whether the person feels the obstacle can be overcome, the difficulty resolved, the problem either circumvented or bulldozed. When people expect to succeed (given the opportunity for further effort), they tend to keep trying, and sometimes they even enhance their efforts. When people believe that success is out of reach, there is a tendency to withdraw effort, even to give up completely the attempt to reach the goal. These motive models of behavior thus rely in part on an assumption about people's expectancies regarding the goal whose attainment is being threatened. Favorable expectancies lead to continued or renewed efforts; unfavorable expectancies lead to a tendency toward giving up.

The idea that expectancies influence behavior,

though important, is not entirely new. It traces to previous generations of cognitively based motive theories. Nevertheless, this disjunction between efforts and giving up, which reflects variations in expectancies from confident to doubtful, represents a prime element in most of today's self-regulatory motive theories.

The fact that people's goals vary in specificity—from the very general, to domain relevant, to very specific—suggests that people have a comparable range of variation in expectancies. To put it differently, people can be confident or doubtful about having a good life, about performing well in evaluative circumstances, about winning a particular tennis match, about finding healthy food for dinner, or about tying their shoes. Which of these expectancies matter? Probably all of them do. Expectancy-based theories tend to hold that behavior is predicted best from expectancies when the level of specificity of the expectancy matches the level of specificity of the behavior. Sometimes it is argued that prediction is best when a combination of several levels of specificity are taken into account. However, many outcomes in life have multiple causes, and people often face situations they have never experienced before or situations that unfold and change over time. It has been suggested that in circumstances such as these, generalized expectations are particularly useful in predicting behavior and emotions.

B. Theoretical Variants

As has been implicit in our discussion thus far, we are describing here not a single specific theory, but rather a family of motive theories that share certain assumptions (those just outlined) but differ in other respects. Our own approach to conceptualizing and studying optimism adds little to what we have said so far. Expectancies that are generalized—expectancies that pertain more or less to the person's entire life space—are what we think of when we use the terms optimism and pessimism.

Some variants on this conceptualization emphasize roles played by additional variables that have not yet been introduced into the discussion. For example, a theory developed by Abramson, Seligman, Peterson, and their collaborators includes the assumption that expectancies for the future derive from attributions about the causes of events in the past. If attributions or explanations for past failures in some domain focus on causes that are stable, the person's expectancy for the future in that domain will be unfavorable, because the cause is seen as relatively permanent and thus likely to remain in force. If attributions for past failures focus on cases that are *unstable,* then the outlook for the future may be brighter, because the cause may no longer be in force. Although attributions can be specific to a particular area of action (e.g., playing tennis) or to a moderately broad domain (e.g., performance in evaluative situations), they are usually treated at an even broader level. That is, it is often assumed that people have "explanatory styles," which bear on the person's whole life space. The theory that is identified with the term explanatory style holds that optimism and pessimism are defined by adaptive patterns of explanation versus problematic patterns of explanation.

Another member of this family is the model of self-efficacy developed by Bandura. Bandura distinguishes between the perceived likelihood that a particular behavior will produce a desired outcome (outcome expectancies) and the individual's expectancy of being able to perform that behavior (self-efficacy expectancies). Both outcome and self-efficacy expectancies contribute to the prediction of behavior and affect, but the theory places much greater emphasis on the role of perceived efficacy. That is, not knowing what behavior to do can stall task-directed efforts, but people sometimes stall and stop trying even when they *do* know what to do. The problem is doubt about being able to do the behavior.

High perceived self-efficacy leads to greater effort and perseverance in the face of difficulty, whereas low self-efficacy is associated with giving up, more distress, and greater autonomic arousal. Although self-efficacy was originally conceptualized very narrowly (pertaining to specific behaviors rather than to broad domains of behavior), the principle has been relaxed in recent years. There is now a developing literature on generalized self-efficacy, the broad sense of confidence of being able to create positive events in one's life. This concept remains somewhat more specific than optimism, in that it focuses so closely on the causal role played by the self. Nevertheless, it is quite similar to optimism in its predictions and in its presumed methods of operation.

C. Placing Optimism in the Context of Self-Regulatory Motive Models

The theoretical models reviewed in this section share several important elements. The critical common theme at present is an emphasis on the importance of people's expectations as a determinant of their actions and subjective experiences. This emphasis provides a sound logical basis for conceptualizing optimism. Optimism is the expectation that one will experience good outcomes in life, even in the face of adversity. Pessimism is the expectation that one will have bad outcomes and that adversity will not be overcome. Each of the theories of this family has led to its own research literature, all of which can be thought of as shedding light on the nature and function of optimism and pessimism. Generally speaking, theorists are most likely to use the labels optimism and pessimism when referring to generalized expectancies, but these labels are sometimes used in reference to specific expectancies.

The literatures in question are large and space constraints prevent us from surveying all of their facets here. In what follows, we focus mostly on the literature of optimism as conceptualized and operationalized by Scheier and Carver in 1985, that is, in terms of generalized expectancies for the future. The explanatory style literature is presented somewhat more briefly. The literature on generalized self-efficacy is not addressed in detail.

D. Assessment of Optimism

Another issue that should be mentioned briefly concerns the assessment of optimism and pessimism. Different researchers measure optimism with different measurement tactics. In the Scheier–Carver framework, optimism is measured with the Life Orientation Test (LOT). The LOT includes eight scored items and four filler items. Half the scored items are phrased optimistically (e.g., "I'm always optimistic about my future") and half are phrased pessimistically (e.g., "I hardly ever expect things to go my way"). Each item is a statement about life in general. Respondents indicate the extent to which they agree with each statement. Pessimistically phrased items are reverse scored and summed with the optimistic items, with higher scores indicating more optimism. The LOT has recently undergone a revision that focuses its content more closely on expectancies, as opposed to qualities that are related to, but distinguishable from, expectancies. The revision also has the effect of reducing the number of scored items to six.

Other researchers measure optimism with different techniques. A measure called the Generalized Expectancy for Success Scale (GESS) asks respondents to rate their expectations in each of a wide array of life domains. Responses to these various domains are summed, yielding an index of expectancies about life in general. This approach, while intuitively plausible, differs in strategy from the approach behind the LOT. Each LOT item is general in form; thus the sense of generality is embedded in each item. In the GESS, in contrast, the sense of generality accrues from the merging of responses across diverse items. Are these approaches ultimately equivalent? Apparently not entirely so, because correlations between the two measures tend to be moderate in strength. It is unclear why the association is not stronger; this is a question that will have to be addressed in future work.

The literature of explanatory style uses a measure that differs in important ways from both of the previous scales. The Attributional Style Questionnaire (ASQ) asks respondents to imagine each of a series of events (good and bad) as happening to them. For each event, they are to write down the event's most likely cause. They then are asked to rate that cause on a number of dimensions, including locus (internal vs. external), stability (stable vs. variable), and globality (specific vs. global in applicability). From these ratings come a number of indices of attributional style. As in the GESS, the sense of generality in the ASQ comes from the accumulation of ratings across several distinct events. Once again, although the logic behind the measure is reasonable, there is some question about the equivalence of this measure with other measures of optimism, because the correlations between measures are not terribly high.

The explanatory style literature also includes the use of another measure, which differs substantially from any of the scales described thus far. This final measure is a content analysis of verbal material that has been generated by a person. Rather than ask a person what he or she is like, this method just requires people to talk or write for a while. Eventually the person talks about an event and its causes, thereby providing information for scoring attributions. This method also allows researchers to assess the optimistic or pessimistic explanatory tendencies of people who never planned to be research participants, even the tendencies of historical figures. This technique thus is very broad in its applicability.

II. EFFECTS OF OPTIMISM

Research on optimism and pessimism has examined a fairly wide variety of questions. The studies can be roughly divided into those that focus on behavioral tendencies (and the outcome consequences of those behavioral tendencies) and those that focus primarily on feelings. A few studies have also examined pathways by which these feelings come to exist and be maintained. We examine these groups of studies in the following sections.

A. Persistence and Giving Up

The motive model that underlies this research holds that optimistic people will continue to struggle toward their goals, even if progress is difficult or slow, and that pessimistic people are more likely to withdraw their effort and disengage themselves from the goals under the same circumstances. This conceptual dichotomy—extensive efforts versus giving up the struggle—provides the basis for a number of more specific predictions.

For example, imagine that you have a job in a highly competitive line of work, such as sales. Such work can be frustrating, because you often meet with failure. That is, potential customers sometimes decide not to buy your product or decide to buy from someone else. To be effective in this line of work requires persistence under conditions of adversity. There is evidence that optimists (defined in terms of explanatory style) are more likely to display this kind of effort, as reflected in their sales levels over a 2-year period. Optimists are also less likely to quit their jobs during the first year than pessimists.

Another example of optimistic persistence comes from a literature on maintaining physical health. Having good health is a goal that most people have. Theory suggests that optimists should work harder than pessimists to attain and maintain that goal. This implies that optimists may be more likely than pessimists to engage in health-promoting behaviors and less likely to engage in risk behaviors.

One study examining the possibility of differences in health promotion followed a group of heart patients who were participating in a cardiac rehabilitation program. Optimism among participants was related to greater success in lowering levels of saturated fat, body fat, and global coronary risk. Optimism was also related to increases in level of exercise across the rehabilitation period. Another study followed coronary artery bypass patients for 5 years after their surgery and investigated their lifestyles at that point. This study found that optimists were more likely than pessimists to take vitamins, to eat low-fat lunches, and to enroll in a cardiac rehabilitation program.

Heart disease is not the only aspect of health that is responsive to people's behavior, and it is not the only aspect of health-related behavior that has been related to optimism. Another obvious health risk that is related to people's behavior is HIV infection. By avoiding certain sexual practices (e.g., sex with unfamiliar partners), people reduce their risk of infection. One study of HIV-negative gay men revealed that optimists reported having fewer anonymous sexual partners than did pessimists. This suggests that optimists were making efforts to reduce their risk, thereby safeguarding their health. [See HIV/AIDS.]

Taken together, the available studies suggest that optimism is associated with behaviors aimed at promoting health and reducing health risk. Very recent research suggests that optimists display a pattern of attending selectively to risks that are both applicable to them and also related to serious health problems. If the health problem is minor, or is unlikely to bear on them personally, optimists do not display this heightened vigilance. Only when it matters does the effect emerge.

We said earlier that optimism should be related to goal-directed efforts and pessimism should lead to tendencies to give up. Thus far, we have focused primarily on persistence. What about giving up? Several kinds of health-relevant behaviors can be viewed as reflecting this giving-up tendency. One such behavior is drinking alcohol. Excessive alcohol consumption is often seen as taking place to escape from one's problems. If so, it follows from the motive theories with which we started that pessimists should be more vulnerable than otherwise comparable optimists to engage in this pattern of alcohol abuse.

At least two studies have yielded findings that fit this picture. One was a study of women with a family history of alcoholism. This study found that pessimists were more likely than their optimistic counterparts to report having drinking problems. Indeed, pessimists in this sample who reported having few uplifts in their lives were the most likely of the sample to describe themselves as heavy drinkers. Another study of drinking examined people who had been treated for alcohol abuse and who were now entering an aftercare program. This study found that pessimists were more likely to drop out of the aftercare program and to return to drinking than optimists. These two studies converge in showing that pessimists display one form of disengagement—alcohol consumption—more than optimists. [See ALCOHOL PROBLEMS.]

People can give up on goals in many ways. Alcohol dulls awareness of failures and problems. People can turn their backs on their problems by distracting themselves with other activities. Even sleeping can sometimes serve the purpose of escaping from situations that one does not want to face. Sometimes, though, giving up is far more complete than this. Sometimes people give up not just on specific goals, but on all the goals that make up their lives. In such an extreme case, suicide may be the result. Are some people more vulnerable to this event than others? Yes. It is commonly assumed that depression is the best indicator of suicide risk. But at least one study has found that pessimism was a stronger indicator of this act, the ultimate total disengagement from life.

B. Emotional Consequences of Optimism and Pessimism

People's behavioral responses to adversity or difficulty are important, but behavior is not the only response that people are having in these situations. They are also experiencing emotions. Difficulties elicit a mixture of feelings, and the balance among these feelings seems to be related to optimism. Again, the predictions are easily derived from theory. Optimists expect to have positive outcomes, even when things are presently difficult. This confidence should be related to a more positive mix of feelings. Pessimists expect negative outcomes. This doubt should be related to more intense negative feelings—anxiety, guilt, anger, sadness, or despair.

Over the past decade, a great many studies have examined the relationship between optimism and distress in people facing difficulty or adversity. The range of stressors involved in this research is enormous. Studies have examined the experiences of students entering college, employees of businesses, survivors of missile attacks, survivors of earthquakes, and even the experience of being a rescue worker cleaning up after a plane crash. Other studies have examined the responses of people caring for cancer patients, patients with Alzheimer's disease, and patients with rheumatoid arthritis. Studies have also examined the experiences of people dealing with medical procedures such as abortion, attempts at in vitro fertilization, childbirth, coronary artery bypass surgery, and bone marrow transplant. Still others have examined how people deal with the diagnosis of cancer, HIV infection, and progression of AIDS. Thus, many of these studies focus on people who are undergoing serious life crises, rather than just dealing with the ordinary problems of daily life. [See STRESS.]

There are many studies in this group, some of which are more limited than others. In many cases, the researchers examined subjects' responses to a difficult event, but measured this response at only one time point. What is known from these studies is that pessimists experienced more distress after the event in question. What is *not* known is whether the pessimists in these studies might have had more distress even before the event. It is far more useful to examine people repeatedly to see how their distress shifts over time and events. It is sometimes impossible to recruit participants before the event one is interested in (e.g., because it is hard to know when an earthquake will occur, it is hard to recruit people 2 weeks before the earthquake). But even in cases of that sort, it is useful to examine the process of adaptation to the event across an extended period. Some of the studies that make up this literature on stress and mental health did take this form, and we will emphasize these studies in our discussion here.

One early study of the effect of optimism examined the development of dysphoria after childbirth, which is a moderately common occurrence. Women in this study completed the LOT and a depression scale in their third trimester of pregnancy. They completed the depression scale again 3 weeks after giving birth. Optimism was related to lower levels of prebirth dysphoria; optimism also predicted lower levels of postpartum dysphoria, even when controlling for prebirth depression levels. Thus optimism appeared to confer a resistance to the development of depressive symptoms in postpartum women.

Other research has investigated the reactions of men who were undergoing and recovering from coronary artery bypass surgery. Patients completed questionnaires at three time points: the day before surgery, 6 to 8 days postsurgery, and 6 months postsurgery. Questionnaires assessed optimism (by the LOT), mood, levels of fatigue, pain, morale, coping strategies, and expectancies for short-term recovery. Before surgery, optimists reported lower levels of hosility and depression than did pessimists. A week after surgery, optimists reported feeling more relief and happiness, greater satisfaction with their medical care, and greater satisfaction with the emotional support they had received from friends. Six months after surgery, optimists reported higher quality of life than pessimists. In a follow-up of the same patients 5 years after surgery, optimists continued to experience greater subjective well-being and general quality of life compared with pessimists. All of these differences remained significant when medical factors were statistically controlled.

Another study on the relationship between optimism and quality of life after coronary artery bypass surgery measured several other variables, including specific expectancies related to the procedure. Subjects were assessed 1 month before surgery and 8 months after surgery. Analysis revealed that generalized optimism was negatively related to presurgical distress. Of greater importance, optimism was also positively related to postsurgical life satisfaction, even when taking into account presurgical levels of life satisfaction. Further analysis, which included the specific expectancy index as well as LOT scores, revealed that the specific expectancy took over the predictive role when both were included. In this study, then, generalized optimism seemed to influence patients' life satisfaction through the path of the specific optimism.

Optimism has also been studied in the context of other kinds of health crises. One study examined the effect of optimism on psychological adaptation to treatment for early-stage breast cancer. Although cancer poses a threat to health, treatment for early-stage cancer is relatively effective and prognosis for survival is generally good. Patients in this study were interviewed six times: at the time of diagnosis, the day before surgery, 7 to 10 days after surgery, and 3, 6, and 12 months later. Optimism was assessed (using the LOT) at the time of diagnosis and was used to predict distress levels at subsequent time points. [See CANCER.]

Optimism inversely predicted distress over time, above and beyond the effect of relevant medical variables and also beyond the effects of earlier measures of distress. The prediction of distress shortly after surgery (7 to 10 days) was only marginal when these controls were included, but the prediction of distress at 3, 6, and 12 months after surgery was significant even with the controls. Thus, optimism predicted resilience to distress in this study through the first 12 months after surgery.

Another medical situation that has been studied in this way is people's adaptation to a failed attempt at in vitro fertilization. Approximately 8 weeks before the fertilization attempt, the researchers measured optimism, specific expectancies for fertilization success, coping strategies, physical and emotional status, and the impact of the infertility on subjects' lives. Two weeks after notification of a negative pregnancy test, distress (measured with a structured interview and by a depression checklist) and self-esteem were assessed by telephone. Neither demographics, obstetric history, marital adjustment, nor effect of infertility on subjects' lives predicted Time-2 distress when Time-1 distress was controlled. However, optimism was negatively related to Time-2 distress. Indeed, controlling for Time-1 distress, optimism was the strongest predictor of Time-2 distress.

Yet another recent study examined the influence of optimism on adjustment to abortion. One hour before an abortion, women completed measures of optimism, self-esteem, self-mastery, self-efficacy, and depression. Depression and psychological adjustment were assessed 30 minutes after the abortion and again 3 weeks later. Optimists had less preabortion depression, better postabortion adjustment, and better 3-week adjustment than did pessimists. The author of this study concluded that optimism is related to psychological adjustment directly and also indirectly through a sense of self-efficacy.

Not only does optimism have a positive effect on the psychological well-being of people undergoing medical treatments, it also influences the psychological well-being of caregivers of patients. One project supporting this conclusion studied a group of cancer patients and their caregivers and found that caregivers' optimism related to a number of caregiver well-being variables. Higher optimism was associated with lower symptoms of depression, less impact of caregiving on physical health, and less impact on caregivers'

daily schedules. Optimists also reported less change in impact on their schedules and less change in health between two time points. Caregiver optimism proved to be independent of patient variables in predicting caregiver reactions to the burdens of caring for a family member with cancer.

Although most of the evidence for the relationship between optimism and psychological well-being has come from populations facing health threats, there is also evidence from samples of students adjusting to their first semester of college. Optimism, self-esteem, and a number of other variables were assessed when the students first arrived on campus. Measures of psychological and physical well-being were obtained at the end of the semester. Analysis revealed that higher levels of optimism upon entering college were associated with lower levels of psychological distress at the end of the semester. The relationship was independent of effects due to self-esteem, locus of control, desire for control, and baseline levels of mood. [*See* SELF-ESTEEM.]

Another, more recent study of adjustment to college life included some additional variables. This project assessed most variables both at the beginning of the semester and at the end of the semester (rather than just at the end), and looked at changes in these measures over time. The data revealed that optimists became less stressed, less depressed, less lonely, and more socially supported over the semester, compared with their pessimistic counterparts.

C. Coping as a Potential Mediator

As the evidence reviewed in the previous section makes clear, optimists experience less distress than do pessimists when dealing with difficulties in their lives. Is this just a matter of optimists being more cheerful than pessimists? Apparently not, because these differences often appear even when statistical controls are incorporated for previous level of distress. Thee must be other explanations. Do optimists do anything in particular to cope that helps them adapt better than pessimists? Many researchers are now investigating this possibility as a potential mechanism through which optimism confers psychological benefits.

In considering coping, we return again to the self-regulation model of behavior. As noted, this model suggests that optimists should respond to adversity with persistence. They should immerse themselves in active attempts to change challenging or threatening situations when possible and to deal actively with the psychological reverberations of threats that are unavoidable. One would also expect them to solicit support from friends and family when they need it. In contrast, pessimists should respond to adversity by becoming mired in their distress, by trying to push the experience away from them rather than taking it on as a challenge, and even succumbing to the desire to disengage from the adjustment process.

Differences in coping methods used by optimists and pessimists have been found in a number of studies. One early project asked undergraduates to recall the most stressful event that had happened to them during the previous month and complete a checklist of coping responses with respect to that event. Optimism correlated positively with problem-focused coping, especially when the stressful situation was perceived to be controllable. Optimism was also positively related to the use of positive reframing and (when the situation was perceived to be uncontrollable) with the attempt to accept the reality of the situation. In contrast, optimism correlated negatively with the use of denial and the attempt to distance oneself from the problem. These findings provided the first indication that optimists are not limited to problem-focused coping. They also use a host of emotion-focused coping techniques, including striving to accept the reality of difficult situations and putting the situations in the best possible light. These findings hint that optimists may enjoy a coping advantage over pessimists even in situations that cannot be changed.

Other research has studied differences in dispositional coping styles reported by optimists and pessimists. As with situational coping responses, optimists reported a dispositional tendency to rely on active, problem-focused coping, and to plan carefully when confronting stressful events. Pessimism was associated with the dispositional tendency to disengage from the goal or goals with which the stressor is interfering. While optimists reported a tendency to accept the reality of stressful events, they were also likely to try to construe negative situations as positive and to learn something from the situation. In contrast, pessimists reported the use of overt denial and substance abuse, strategies that lessen their awareness of the problem. Thus, optimists appear to be active copers and pessimists appear to be avoidant copers.

Other projects have studied the relationship between optimism and coping strategies in the work environment. This research found that optimists used more problem-focused coping than pessimists (self-control, directed problem solving, and positive reinterpretation). Pessimists used more emotion focused coping (including both the use of social support and the avoidance of being with people, and self-indulgent escapism such as sleeping, eating, and drinking). Another study focused on executive women. This study found that optimistic executives appraised and evaluated daily hassles differently from pessimistic executive women. Optimistic women expected gain or growth from stressful events and reported coping indicative of acceptance, expressiveness, and tension reduction. They also reported using their social support in stressful circumstances rather than withdrawing, distancing, or engaging in self-blame.

Several studies described earlier also provide evidence of a relationship between optimism and coping, and between coping and mental health. One study of coronary artery bypass surgery assessed the use of attentional-cognitive strategies as ways of dealing with the experience. Before surgery, optimists were more likely than pessimists to report that they were making plans for their future and setting goals for their recovery. Optimists also tended to report being less focused on the negative aspects of their experience (their distress emotions and physical symptoms) than pessimists. Once the surgery was past, optimists were more likely than pessimists to report seeking out and requesting information about what the physician would be requiring of them in the months ahead. Optimists were also less likely to report trying to suppress thoughts about their physical symptoms. Results from path analyses suggested that the impact of optimism on quality of life 6 months postsurgery was due to the indirect effect of differences in coping.

In the study of adaptation to failed in vitro fertilization described earlier, the researchers did not find a relationship between optimism and instrumental coping. They did find, however, that pessimism was related to escape as a coping strategy. Escape, in turn, was related to distress after the fertilization failure. Furthermore, optimists reported feeling that they benefited to some degree from the experience of failed in vitro fertilization (e.g., becoming closer to their spouse).

The study of AIDS patients described earlier also provides information regarding coping. In general, optimism was associated with active coping strategies.

Optimism predicted positive attitudes and tendencies to plan for recovery, seek information, and reframe bad situations so as to see their most positive aspects. Optimists made less use of fatalism, self-blame, and escapism, and did not focus on the negative aspects of the situation or try to suppress thoughts about their symptoms. Optimists also appeared to accept situations they could not change, rather than trying to escape those situations.

Several studies have examined the relationship between optimism and coping among cancer patients. One study followed women who were scheduled for breast biopsy. Optimism, coping, and mood were assessed the day before biopsy and (for women who received a cancer diagnosis) again 24 hours before surgery and 3 weeks after surgery. Women with a benign diagnosis completed a second assessment that corresponded to either the second or the third assessment of the cancer group. Pessimistic women in this study used more cognitive avoidance in coping with the upcoming diagnostic procedure for cancer than did optimists. This avoidance contributed significantly to negative affect prior to biopsy. Indeed, cognitive avoidance proved to be a mediator of the effect of optimism on prebiopsy negative affect. Cognitive avoidance prebiopsy also predicted postbiopsy distress among women with positive diagnoses.

Another study of cancer patients examined the ways women cope with treatment for early stage breast cancer during the first year after treatment. Optimism, coping (with the diagnosis of cancer), and mood were assessed the day before surgery. Coping and mood were also assessed 10 days postsurgery, and 3, 6, and 12 months postsurgery. Both before and after surgery, optimism was associated with a pattern of reported coping tactics that revolved around accepting the reality of the situation, placing as positive a light on the situation as possible, trying to relieve the situation with humor, and (at presurgery only) taking active steps to do whatever there was to be done. Pessimism was associated with denial and behavioral disengagement (giving up) at each measurement point.

The coping tactics that were related to optimism and pessimism were also strongly related to the distress that subjects reported. Positive reframing, acceptance, and the use of humor were all related inversely to self-reports of distress, both before surgery and after. Denial and behavioral disengagment were positively related to distress at all measurement points.

At the 6-month point, a new association emerged such that distress was positively related to another kind of avoidance coping: self-distraction. Not unexpectedly, given the pattern of the correlations, further analyses revealed that the effect of optimism on distress was largely indirect through coping, particularly at postsurgery.

Other studies have assessed the mediational role of coping in the relationship between optimism and psychological well-being. In one of the college adaptation studies described earlier, optimistic students were more likely than pessimistic students to engage in active coping and less likely to engage in avoidance coping. Avoidance coping was negatively associated with adjustment and active coping was positively associated with adjustment. The paths from optimism to well-being through coping were significant. Thus, as in the health studies, the beneficial effects of optimism in this context seemed to be operating at least in part through the differences in coping.

In sum, these studies indicate that optimists differ from pessimists both in their stable coping tendencies and in the kinds of coping responses that they spontaneously generate when confronting stressful situations. Optimists also differ from pessimists in the manner in which they cope with serious disease and with concerns about specific health threats. In general, findings from this research suggest that optimists tend to use more problem-focused coping strategies than do pessimists. When problem-focused coping is not a possibility, optimists turn to adaptive emotion-focused coping strategies such as acceptance, use of humor, and positive reframing. Pessimists tend to cope through overt denial and by mentally and behaviorally disengaging from the goals with which the stressor is interfering.

It is particularly noteworthy that optimists turn toward acceptance in uncontrollable situations, whereas pessimists are more tied to the use of denial. Although both tactics reflect emotion-focused coping, there are important qualitative differences between them that may, in turn, be associated with different qualities of outcomes. More concretely, denial (the refusal to accept the reality of the situation) means attempting to adhere to a world view that is no longer valid. In contrast, acceptance implies a restructuring of one's experience so as to come to grips with the reality of the situation one confronts. Acceptance thus may involve a deeper set of processes, in which the person actively works through the experience, attempting to integrate it into an evolving world view. The active attempt to come to terms with problems may confer special benefits to acceptance. It has been speculated that acceptance serves the critical purpose of keeping the person goal-engaged, and indeed "life-engaged." [*See* Coping with Stress.]

D. Is Optimism Always Good?

As this review has made clear by now, there is a good deal of evidence that people who are optimistic about life experience less distress, cope in more effective ways, and in many cases have better behavioral outcomes than do people who are more pessimistic. We should raise one more question, however, before turning to the next topic. The question is whether optimism is always beneficial, or whether this is true only under certain conditions.

Several people have argued that optimism may not always be a good thing. The argument is essentially that by expecting things to go well, optimists cause themselves to be unprepared for catastrophically bad events, should such events occur. The pessimist, in contrast, expects things to go bad eventually and is less shattered when the catastrophe comes. Is there merit to this argument?

This is a difficult question to answer with certainty, in part because most studies reviewed here have examined the experiences of people who were experiencing generally good outcomes. The cancer patients were early-stage patients with good prognosis. The bypass patients were undergoing a difficult surgery, but were then on their way to recovery with an objectively positive outlook. Even the HIV studies have focused on people whose disease is not advanced. Would the picture be different if the cancers were terminal, if the bypass surgeries had been unsuccessful at improving quality of life, or if the AIDS patients were nearing death?

The available evidence, such as it is, suggests that the answer is no, that optimists are resilient in the face of crisis in spite of the fact that the event contradicts their world view, and that they respond better to crisis than their pessimistic counterparts for whom the crisis is belief-confirming. We should acknowledge, however, that there is not a great deal of evidence on this question. This question will certainly be one of the focuses for future research.

III. BECOMING AN OPTIMIST

Given the evidence of the powerful impact an optimistic outlook has on psychological well-being, several other questions arise. Where does optimism come from? How can it be fostered in children? Can even an adult pessimist become an optimist?

A. Origins of Optimism

The origins of optimism as a psychological construct were presented earlier in this chapter in terms of contemporary theories of motivation. Regardless of the construct's conceptual origins, there are many ways to think about optimism as a quality of personality. For example, it is well known that many aspects of personality are genetically influenced. Is optimism one of these qualities? The answer appears to be yes. According to twin studies, optimism, whether assessed in terms of generalized expectancies or in terms of explanatory style, appears to be genetically influenced.

As is always the case in considering genetic influence, there is some question about whether this quality of personality is *itself* heritable or whether it displays genetic influence because it is closely related to (or even derived from) some biologically based aspect of temperament. There is, after all, evidence that optimism is related both to the temperament of neuroticism (negative emotionality) and to the temperament of extraversion. Both of these temperamental dispositions have long been known to be genetically influenced. Although it appears to be the case that optimism and pessimism are distinguishable from both neuroticism and extraversion, it may be that the heritability of optimism is a product of these associations.

Another potential influence on the development of an optimistic versus pessimistic outlook is early childhood experience. A variety of psychological theories suggest that early childhood is an important time. Erikson's well-known theory of personality development holds that the infant who experiences the social world as predictable develops a sense of "basic trust," whereas the infant who experiences the world as unpredictable develops a sense of "basic mistrust." These qualities are not so different from optimism and pessimism. Recent discussions of attachment in infancy similarly hold that attachment varies from secure to insecure (with variations in insecurity). Indeed, it has also been suggested that adults display the same manifestations of security versus insecurity in relationships, possibly as a direct outgrowth of these childhood experiences. It may be important in this regard that security in adult relationships is related to optimism. Perhaps, then, optimism derives in part from the early childhood experience of secure attachment to a caregiver.

These sources of information are suggestive, but at present are limited. The origin of optimism is another question that doubtlessly will receive further research attention in the future.

B. Cognitive-Behavioral Therapies: Turning Pessimists into Optimists

Regardless of the origins of this quality of personality, another important question can be raised about it. Can a person who lacks optimism acquire it? Even biologically based temperaments are malleable. Even if optimism does have genetic roots, should it not be possible in principle to bend a pessimist in the direction of greater optimism?

The answer to this question is yes, albeit a somewhat cautious yes. That is, it seems clear that change in an optimistic direction is possible. However, there remain questions about how large a change can be reasonably expected and how permanent the change will be. There also remain questions about whether an induced optimistic view on life will act in the same way—have the same beneficial effects—as a naturally occurring optimistic view.

There are many ways to try to turn a pessimist into an optimist. The most straightforward approach seems to be the group of intervention techniques known collectively as cognitive-behavioral therapies. Indeed, turning (either generalized or focused) pessimists into optimists would seem to be an apt characterization of the main point of these therapies.

The first applications of cognitive therapies were to problems such as depression and anxiety. The logic behind the therapies was that people with these problems make a variety of unduly negative cognitive distortions of reality. These unrealistically negative cognitions (e.g., I can't do anything right) cause negative affect (e.g., dysphoria, anxiety) and also set the person up to behave maladaptively (e.g., by not trying). In cases such as this, the dysfunctional cognition distortions closely resemble what we would imagine to be the interior monologue of the pessimist.

If inappropriately negative cognitions and self-statements define the nature of the problem, the goal of the cognitive therapies is to change the cognitions, to make them more positive, and to thereby diminish distress and allow more adaptive behaviors to emerge. Many techniques have been devised for producing these changes. In general, this approach to therapy begins by having the person pay close attention to his or her experience to identify points where distress arises and the cognitions associated with (or immediately preceding) these points. The idea is to give the person a better awareness of what are now automatic thoughts. In many cases, the cognitions in question will turn out to be pessimistic beliefs. Once the beliefs have been isolated, they can be challenged and changed. (This attempt to deal with pessimistic beliefs by shifting them has an interesting resemblance to positive reframing, which was described earlier as a useful coping strategy.) [See COGNITIVE THERAPY.]

In the broad view, a fundamental goal of cognitive-behavioral therapies is to change pessimistic expectations to more optimistic expectations. Any technique that has this consequence would be considered useful. Sometimes this change can be induced through environmental enrichment aimed at decreasing the likelihood of bad outcomes and increasing the likelihood of good outcomes. For example, a pessimist might be trained to monitor and attend to positive events rather than negative events, might be instructed to increase pleasant activities, or to develop positive future expectancies by means of imagery.

Another method often used is personal efficacy training (illustrating once again what can be a thin line between efficacy and optimism). The focus of such procedures is on increasing specific kinds of competence or control (e.g., by assertiveness training or social skill training). However, the specific techniques often address thoughts and behaviors that relate to a more general sense of pessimism. For example, problem-solving training, teaching people to select and define obtainable subgoals, and decision-making training all improve the ways in which a person handles a wide range of everyday situations.

Although the development of positive expectations is an important goal of these therapies, it is also important to recognize that it can be counterproductive to try to substitute immediately an unquestioning optimism for an existing doubt. Sometimes the reason for pessimism is that people have unrealistically high aspirations or expectations for themselves. They demand perfection in themselves, hardly ever find it, and as a result develop doubts about their adequacy. This tendency has to be countered by establishing more realistic goals and identifying which situations must be accepted rather than changed. The person must learn to relinquish unattainable goals and set alternative goals to replace those that cannot be attained.

ACKNOWLEDGMENTS

Preparation of this chapter was facilitated by support from the National Cancer Institute (CA64710 and CA64711) and the National Heart, Lung, and Blood Institute (HL44436).

BIBLIOGRAPHY

Bandura, A. (1995). *Self-efficacy: The exercise of control.* New York: Freeman.

Gollwitzer, P. M., & Bargh, J. A. (Eds.). (1996). *The psychology of action: Linking cognition and motivation to behavior.* New York: Guilford.

Pervin, L. (Ed.). (1989). *The goal concept in personality and social psychology.* Hillsdale, NJ: Lawrence Erlbaum.

Peterson, C., & Bossio, L. M. (1991). *Health and optimism: New research on the relationship between positive thinking and well-being.* New York: Free Press.

Scheier, M. F., & Carver, C. S. (1992). Effects of optimism on psychological and physical well-being: Theoretical overview and empirical update. *Cognitive Therapy and Research, 16,* 201–228.

Seligman, M. E. P. (1991). *Learned optimism.* New York: Knopf.

Organizational and Occupational Psychiatry

Len Sperry

Medical College of Wisconsin

Corporate Therapy   The provision of clinically oriented organizational interventions by a clinician or consultant that can be focused on the individual, the team or work group, or the entire organization. Work-focused psychotherapy is an individual intervention that is similar to but different from personal counseling or psychotherapy.

Executive Consultation   A type of organizational consultation in which the focus is the individual executive and the service provided can range from psychiatric evaluation, to counseling and coaching, to developing mental health policy.

Occupational and Organizational Psychiatry   The study of adaptation of the individual to the workplace, with emphasis on the psychopathology brought to and resulting from the work setting, as well as of organizational factors that stimulate healthy behavior and functioning.

Occupational Mental Health   An umbrella designation for all professional mental health services provided in the corporate setting by a variety of professionals, including occupational and organizational psychiatrists, organizational psychologists, occupational clinical psychologists, and occupational health nurses.

Occupational Stress   A perceived substantial imbalance between work demands and the worker's response capability, where failure to meet the demand has significant consequences, including manifestation of physiological, psychological, or behavioral symptoms; also called work or job stress.

Organizational Consultation   The process by which a consultant, acting internally or externally to the organization, provides technical, diagnostic, or facilitative assistance to achieve specific, planned change goals within the organization that will affect individuals and work teams within the organization.

Psychiatric Disability Evaluation   A specialized psychiatric evaluation to determine whether an individual is unable to engage in gainful employment by reason of mental impairment, for example, a psychiatric disorder or other severe stress reaction. A related evaluation task is a psychiatric fitness for duty evaluation to determine an individual's capacity for performing an assigned job within certain required standards.

ORGANIZATIONAL AND OCCUPATIONAL PSYCHIATRY is the topic of this article's overview. It discusses the relationship of work to health and psychological well being, summarizes the history and recent rediscovery of the field, and describes four areas of professional practice within the field.

53

I. WORK AND ORGANIZATIONAL AND OCCUPATIONAL PSYCHIATRY

Organizational and occupational psychiatry—previously called industrial psychiatry and, alternately, workplace or corporate psychiatry—has long recognized the interconnectedness of the love and work dimensions in an individual's life. Most mental health professionals believe that work is central to personal identity, and many would agree with Sigmund Freud's observation that love and work are the two basic criteria for mental health. However, until recently, very few mental health professionals reflected these beliefs in their clinical practice. Today, however, these beliefs have profound implications for the practice of mental health, as work is becoming more central to the lives of most individuals.

The link between work and mental health has been increasingly articulated. In fact, work is now thought to be more basic to survival and self-esteem than love and friendship. Research indicates that job satisfaction is highly correlated with positive mental health, and incapacity to work correlates with poor mental health. Recently, the phenomenon of "occupational happiness" has been described along with the personal and workplace influences that facilitate or hinder it. Within the past decade, the workplace has become a new venue for psychiatric interventions. This has resulted largely from the increasing recognition of work as a critical variable in mental health. Job satisfaction and occupational happiness is influenced by multiple factors beyond holding a specific job.

Economic and cultural factors prominently affect the work experience. For instance, in *The Overworked American,* Schor reported that in 1991 the average American worked the equivalent of 1 month longer than his or her counterpart in 1970. If this trend continues, it is estimated that in 20 years the average employee will work 60 hours a week, 50 weeks a year. This increase in working hours—particularly for the hourly wage earner—reflects current wages. In 1991, individuals must work about 200 additional hours per year to maintain their 1973 standard of living. Although the wages of professional and managerial jobs have risen proportionally in the last two decades, so has the pressure to work more hours and to endure enormous stresses. [*See* STRESS.]

The United Nations' International Labor Office has dubbed occupational stress the "twentieth century disease." Perhaps the most compelling way of describing occupational stress is in terms of the demand/control research reported by Karasek and Theorell in their book, *Healthy Work: Stress, Productivity, and the Reconstruction of the Working Life.* Basically, this line of research suggests that high job demands combined with low decisional control over one's job is predictive of high job strain and occupational stress. Data from studies of more than 5000 American and Swedish males indicate that workers at the lowest level of employment, measured in terms of their ability to control their own jobs, were 5 times more likely to develop heart disease than workers in the highest level of the workplace hierarchy, who had the greatest control over their jobs. Curiously, there are differential rates of heart disease, hypertension, and other medical and psychiatric illnesses among executives, depending on their level of demand/control. Thus, even when the psychological demands of a job are exceedingly high, senior executives tend to have fewer medical and psychiatric illnesses than junior executives, because the senior executives have considerably more control over their job context, that is, how and when they will plan and execute their work job tasks, take coffee breaks and vacations, and so on, than their more junior colleagues.

Not surprisingly, the incidence of stress disability claims has skyrocketed in the past decade and has now replaced lower back pain as the most common disability claim. Furthermore, it should be noted that work has become the locus of many American lives. Not only vacations, but hobbies, pastimes, and most daily functions are primarily planned around one's work schedule. In addition, one's love and friendship needs are more likely to be met in the work environment than anywhere else. The intense impact that certain jobs and careers can have on individuals, couples, or their families has been described as the "work-centered individual, couple, or family."

II. BRIEF HISTORY OF ORGANIZATIONAL AND OCCUPATIONAL PSYCHIATRY

A journal article appearing in 1917 on psychiatric symptoms in jobless men probably represents the first publication in organizational and occupational psychiatry. In 1922, the Metropolitan Life Insurance Company employed a full-time psychiatrist, while 2 years later, a mental health service was begun at Macy's department store in New York City. Following that auspicious first decade of what was then called industrial psychiatry, the stature of organizational and occupational psychiatry has alternately risen and regressed.

Psychiatrists were the dominant force in the field of occupational mental health from the 1920s until the early 1980s. In large part they provided clinical services such as psychiatric evaluation, inpatient hospitalization, medication monitoring, and substance abuse treatment, as well as psychiatric disability evaluations and psychiatric fitness for duty evaluations of "troubled employees." Most functioned as internal consultants, in that they were paid employees of large corporations and often held titles such as medical director or vice-president for medical services. A smaller number functioned as external consultants providing similar services but to more than one smaller corporation. Occasionally, such a psychiatrist might engage in executive consultation or even organizational consultation activities, but this tended to be rare.

During the late 1970s and early 1980s, increasing numbers of other mental health professionals streamed into the field because of the widespread expansion of substance abuse programs and Employee Assistance Programs (EAP). Most of these professionals provided clinical services to the "troubled employee," particularly in newly formed EAPs. Because general psychiatrists had little motivation for involvement in EAPs and because the number of organizational and occupational psychiatrists was relatively small, nonmedical mental health professionals quickly assumed ascendancy and leadership for much of occupational mental health. Other mental health professionals, particularly psychologists with training or interest in organizational development, engaged in various types of organizational consultation activities. Since the 1980s, organizational and occupational psychiatrists have broadened their focus beyond the troubled individual employee and have also addressed the psychological concerns of work teams, corporate divisions, and the whole organization. Nevertheless, the number of psychiatrists interested and involved in work-related issues has remained quite small.

Perhaps the major reason why only a relatively small number of psychiatrists have been attracted to organizational and occupational psychiatry is that the work dimension has not yet been taken very seriously by psychiatry. A review of psychiatry textbooks reflects this attitude. While several pages are devoted to love-related topics, at the most only a few focus on work and occupational issues. Assessing work history and evaluating work-related disability were rarely, if ever, included in psychiatric training. This attitude of benign neglect toward the work dimensions is rooted in the profession's ambivalence and cultural beliefs. The profession's ambivalence is reflected in the American Psychiatric Association's (APA) establishing, then disbanding, and only recently reestablishing committees on industrial and occupational psychiatry. Culturally, both American employers and employees had tended to view work life and personal life as strictly separate domains. Family and personal problems were considered private matters which were not supposed to "spill over" into the employee's work life. In short, love and work had been viewed as separate realities, and psychiatry was decidedly enamored of the love dimension.

Very recently, organizational and occupational psychiatry has experienced a renaissance or rediscovery of sorts with the reestablishment of the APA Committee on Occupational Psychiatry in 1986, the founding of the Academy of Organizational and Occupational Psychiatry in 1990, and the updating of its mission and the renaming of the Group for the Advancement of Psychiatry (GAP) Committee on Psychiatry in Industry to the Committee on Occupational Psychiatry in early 1993. Membership in the Academy of Organizational and Occupational Psychiatry has increased dramatically since its founding. Members include psychiatrists experienced as internal or external consultants to corporations, or in managed care settings, universities, government, or the military, as well as psychiatrists looking for an alternative to traditional clinical practice or to the direction health care appears to be taking. The demand for quality psychiatric consultative and clinical services to work in organizations largely accounts for these developments. The academy was established, primarily, to provide access to various educational and training opportunities, as well as to develop a referral network. Furthermore, an increasing number of articles, research reports, and books on various aspects of organizational and occupational psychiatry have been published in the past few years.

III. WORK-RELATED DISORDERS

The amount of epidemiological data on psychiatric disorders associated with the workplace is quite limited. Data from the Equitable Life Insurance EAP indicate that anxiety disorders are the most common presentation (25%), followed by depression (20%), stress-related disorders (15%), substance abuse disorders (15%), and marital, family, and financial issues (accounting for the remaining 25%). Other data suggest that affective disorders, anxiety disorders, psychotic disorders and personality disorders are the most common psychiatric presentations in blue-collar workers. [See ANXIETY; DEPRESSION; SUBSTANCE ABUSE.]

In the 1990 report of their epidemiological study of impairment in executives, Bromet et al. found that the lifetime and 1-year prevalence rates for major depression in men were 23% and 9%, respectively, with rates of 36% and 17%, respectively, for women. Lifetime and 1-year prevalence rates for alcohol abuse or substance dependence were 16% and 4%, respectively, for men, and 9% and 4%, respectively, for women. In his 1988 book, Speller offers no incidence or prevalence rates but lists alcoholism, substance abuse, depression, and bipolar disorder as common forms of impairment among executives. [See ALCOHOL PROBLEMS.]

Emotional crises in the workplace are becoming increasingly common. These crises can include (a) traumatic disasters such as fires, earthquakes, and tornadoes, toxic spills, and serious accidents; (b) aggression, including both threats and physical acts; (c) substance abuse and dependence, causing an unsafe/disruptive workplace; and (d) depression and suicidal and parasuicidal behavior.

Lowman, in *Counseling and Psychotherapy of Work Dysfunctions*, has developed a taxonomy for the diagnosis of work-related dysfunctions and disorders. He describes psychological problems associated with overcommitment and burnout, undercommitment and fears of success or failure, work-related depressive and anxiety disorders, as well as personality disorders in work settings. He describes the use of spe-

cific psychotherapeutic and other tailored treatment interventions for these dysfunctions and disorders. [See BURNOUT.]

Sperry, in *Corporate Therapy and Consulting*, details a "taxonomy of organizational and work dysfunctions" and provides case definitions for 54 discrete entities. Two main categories are delineated: dysfunctional organizational work context and dysfunctional work capacity. Nine categories articulate dysfunctional work contexts: the strategy/structure mismatch, structural problems, environmental problems, job design problems, restructuring problems, problematic work culture, dysfunctional interpersonal and team relations, defective supervision, and authority problems and issues. Four categories pertain to dysfunction of work capacity: undercommitment and overcommitment patterns, problematic work–personality styles, life-role conflicts, and other work difficulties or disorders.

Unfortunately, no psychiatric diagnostic or nosological systems for work disorders have been published. The *Diagnostic and Statistical Manual of Mental Disorders—Fourth Edition* (DSM-IV) includes only a designation for work dysfunctions. It is a V-code, labeled as "Occupational Problem" and coded as V62.2. Finally, as research on organizational dysfunctioning and work-related dysfunctions and disorders progresses, it is hoped that an empirically based taxonomy of such conditions will be available to guide assessment and intervention.

IV. AREAS OF PROFESSIONAL PRACTICE

There are five main areas of practice in organizational and occupational psychiatry: direct clinical services, psychiatric disability and fitness for duty evaluations, consultation, corporate therapy, and applied research. This section briefly describes these areas.

A. Clinical Services

A variety of direct organizational and occupational psychiatry clinical services can be competently provided by most psychiatrists and other mental health professionals. These include inpatient hospitalization, impaired professionals programs, substance abuse treatment, work-focused psychotherapy, and a variety of other psychiatric interventions to both hourly employees and management. Referral is often made by the corporate medical director or EAP personnel. These clinical services may be provided on-site or in the psychiatrist's office. Because corporate executives are unlikely to use their firm's EAP, they are usually referred to outside clinicians for individual psychotherapy, couples therapy, psychiatric evaluation, or medication evaluation and management.

B. Psychiatric Disability and Fitness for Duty Evaluation

One of the most common occupational psychiatry services involves psychiatric disability evaluations and psychiatric fitness for duty evaluations. Because these two types of evaluations continue to be a mainstay of organizational and occupational psychiatry, the components of both will be described in some detail.

A detailed work history is an essential component of any psychiatric disability or fitness for duty evaluation. Open-ended statements such as, "Tell me about your job" or "I'll begin by asking you about where you've worked," are useful ways of beginning the evaluation. If the alleged injuries are physical with a secondary mental component, the worker is encouraged to describe his or her injuries, including any treatment and the impact of the treatment. Direct inquiry into the emotional component is made by the psychiatrist, allowing the worker to comment spontaneously. Obtaining a clear longitudinal history of the worker's emotional symptoms can then be elicited, noting their emergence and any waxing and waning in the course of the symptom complex.

Specific details of a worker's job must be elicited. These include a description of the job components and the worker's attitude toward work. The psychiatrist notes the relative ease or difficulty the worker has in doing the work. If the worker describes difficulties in supervisory or peer relationships, a detailed description of these difficulties is obtained. Specific attention to the worker's affect in describing the alleged difficulties is noted. The evaluator needs to distinguish current symptoms from symptoms and adjustment present during earlier phases of the symptom complex. A detailed account of the worker's daily life is often quite telling, in that the patient may inadvertently disclose a higher level of functioning than the impression he or

she may directly convey. Finally, eliciting the worker's own theory or explanation about how such difficulties emerged can be highly relevant and suggestive of secondary gain factors.

Six elements are typically included in a written report of a psychiatric disability or fitness for duty evaluation. First, the reasons and questions that initiated the referral are specified along with a summary of conclusions drawn from a review of the worker's records. Second, the worker's presenting problems and concerns are noted along with a description of the worker's lifestyle and any current treatments. Third, a summary is made of significant data regarding the individual's occupational, medico-surgical-psychiatric, and developmental-familial-socioeconomic history. Fourth, pertinent findings from the psychiatric evaluation and work history are included. Fifth, the evaluator's case formulation, including diagnosis and prognosis, are recorded, along with, sixth, specific suggestions for additional investigation and/or referral, placement, or treatments.

C. Consultation

Perhaps the most common form of consultation practice with employees is case management. The organizational and occupational psychiatrist evaluates the employee, plans and coordinates appropriate treatment and referral if necessary, and sees to it that necessary information about the employee's health and work status is conveyed to the appropriate parties. Periodically, the psychiatrist reviews progress and follows up as necessary.

Another common form of consultation involves executives. The psychiatrist may be asked to evaluate a candidate for an executive position, advise a chief executive officer or vice-president on motivating, promoting, or firing a staff member, or serve as a sounding board, advisor, or medical expert regarding any number of personal or professional concerns of an executive. The consultant may also be engaged to provide or arrange for an executive seminar on any number of health and mental health topics. As business increasingly embraces the concept of work teams, the consultant is being called on to work with project and management teams to increase their effectiveness by means of team building, communications training, and cultural diversity training. Psychiatrists are also being engaged to assist with organization-wide issues. These include diagnosing complex organizational problems and modifying corporate culture.

D. Corporate Therapy

Today, because of the many changes in the landscape of mental health practice, as well as the fallout from corporate downsizing, organizations are finding their consultation needs are changing and mental health professionals are increasingly becoming involved with such consultation needs. Clinical training is quite useful in addressing many of these consultation needs. Nevertheless, clinical training cannot address all of a corporation's consultation needs, nor does it provide a sufficient basis for functioning as an organizational consultant. Still, the mental health professional's clinical perspective is invaluable in providing a specialized type of consultation to individuals with work-related issues and to the organizations for which they work.

The application of a clinical perspective to organizational concerns and issues has a long and venerable history in both organizational and occupational psychiatry as well as in occupational clinical psychology. Both have traditionally emphasized mental health issues and have focused on the troubled employee. Harry Levinson was one of the first psychologists to advocate the role of what he called the "clinician-consultant" to be distinct from the role of the traditional organizational consultant. For Levinson, the clinician providing consultation to an organization needs diagnostic and intervention methods for organizational work akin to the diagnostic and intervention methods used in working with individual clients and patients. His clinical approach to organizational issues contrasts markedly with the traditional consultation approach practiced by nonclinical consultants.

Organizational consultants are a varied lot, representing training and development specialists, human resources specialists, management consultants, and industrial/organizational psychologists. More specifically, industrial/organizational psychologists typically practice as consultants to private and public organizations, including consulting firms. Those in consulting firms serving large corporations tend to focus the majority of their consulting efforts on employee selection, organizational development, performance appraisal, and employee and managerial assessment.

Because they are not trained as clinicians, it is not surprising that only a small percentage of their consultation time is spent on clinical issues or personal counseling.

Whereas the organizational consultant principally focuses on organizational troubles, the clinician-consultant focuses more on troubled employees. Corporate therapy is a clinically oriented form of consultation that uses clinical-organizational interventions and focuses on troubled employees and executives and the troubled or troubling organization in which they work.

Clinical-organizational interventions are different from traditional clinical interventions and from traditional organizational interventions. Traditionally, the clinician typically did initial evaluations and individual psychotherapy—and sometimes couples, family, and group therapy—while the consultant typically did executive coaching and consultation, career counseling, and some type of team and/or organizational interventions. Clinical-organizational interventions include outplacement counseling and consultation, work-focused psychotherapy, conflict resolution with work teams and family businesses, crisis intervention consultation, merger syndrome consultation, and violence prevention consultation.

In short, despite the changing nature of consultation needs, traditional organizational consultation interventions will still be necessary and useful. However, the demand for clinical-organizational interventions—and the clinician-consultants who can provide them—will continue to increase. Accordingly, mental health professionals with additional training and experience, who want to base their careers in the corporate arena, should be able to provide a unique and necessary professional service.

E. Applied Research in Organizational and Occupational Psychiatry

The workplace provides numerous opportunities for doing applied research on factors affecting employee health and well-being as well as research on dysfunction. These include epidemiological studies of psychopathology and stress-related disorders and conditions and their determinants. Organizational and occupational psychiatrists can also specialize in developing integrated health and mental health care tracking systems to ensure continuity and quality of care and initiating surveillance systems to track highly vulnerable individuals and stressful areas of the corporation.

V. CONCLUSIONS

With the rise of the work-centered couple and family, the downsizing and reengineering of corporate America, and the stressors engendered by these changes, it is becoming increasingly likely that mental health professionals will, of necessity, become more involved in work-related issues and organizational concerns. It is therefore incumbent on mental health professionals to become more sensitized to such work-related issues. The use of the occupational or work history in the context of an initial evaluation is particularly valuable in increasing the mental health professional's sensitivity to and recognition of work-related issues. Continuing efforts to develop a taxonomy of work dysfunctions and disorders, as well as treatment interventions tailored to them, will likewise increase the professional's capacity to deal with a vast array of work-related issues.

BIBLIOGRAPHY

Bromet, E., Parkinson, D., & Curtis, C. et al. (1990). Epidemiology of depression and alcohol abuse/dependence in a managerial and professional workforce. *Journal of Occupational Medicine, 32,* 989–995.

Crandall, R., & Perrewe, P. (Eds.). (1995). *Occupational stress: A handbook.* Washington, DC: Taylor & Francis.

Group for the Advancement of Psychiatry: Committee on Occupational Psychiatry (1993). *An introduction to occupational psychiatry* (Report No. 138). Washington, DC: American Psychiatric Press.

Karasek, R., & Theorell, T. (1990). *Healthy work: Stress, productivity, and the reconstruction of the working life.* New York: Basic Books.

Lowman, R. (1993). *Counseling and psychotherapy of work dysfunctions.* Washington, DC: American Psychological Association Books.

Schor, J. (1991). *The overworked American: The unexpected decline in leisure.* New York: Basic Books.

Speller, J. (1988). *Executives in crisis: Recognizing and managing the alcoholic, drug-addicted or mentally ill executive.* San Francisco: Jossey-Bass.

Sperry, L. (1993). *Psychiatric consultation in the workplace.* Washington, DC: American Psychiatric Press.

Sperry, L. (1996). *Corporate therapy and consultation.* New York: Brunner-Mazel.

P

Pain

Dennis C. Turk and Akiko Okifuji

University of Washington School of Medicine

Chronic Pain Pain that persists months beyond the usual course of an acute disease or reasonable time for an injury to heal, or that is associated with a chronic pathologic process that causes continuous pain, or the pain recurs at intervals for months or years.

Cognitive-Behavioral Model of Chronic Pain A model conceptualizing chronic pain as a complex perceptual phenomenon in which a person's thoughts, expectations, beliefs, feelings, and behaviors reciprocally interact with nociceptive stimuli.

Coping Cognitive and behavioral efforts to manage specific external and/or internal demands that are appraised as taxing or exceeding the resources of the person.

Disability A diminished capacity for daily and occupational activities.

Nociception A sensory process involving the activation of sensory transduction in nerves that conveys information about tissue damage. This information may be perceived as pain.

Pain Unpleasant sensory and emotional experience associated with actual or potential tissue damage or described in terms of such damage.

Pain-Prone Personality Hypothesized personality style, with which an individual is predisposed to develop pain.

Pain Behaviors Overt behaviors that express the presence of pain, suffering, and distress, such as limping, sighing, avoiding physical activities, and taking medications.

Physical Impairment An anatomical, pathological, or physiological abnormality of structure or function, resulting in loss of normal bodily ability.

Somatogenic-Psychogenic Dichotomy Dualistic views of chronic pain in which the presence and degree of pain can be explained either by physical pathology or psychological problems.

PAIN is a universal human experience, all of us encounter pain at some point in our lives. Pain may be functional, serving as an alarm signaling that there is a problem requiring attention. In most of these instances pain is usually short-lived with no significant impact, either remitting spontaneously with reduced activity, healing, or well controlled by over-the-counter medications. When pain persists medical attention is often sought. In fact, pain is the second most common reason for visiting physicians after upper respiratory infections.

I. INTRODUCTION

In many cases, pain symptoms can be treated successfully by physicians using conventional medical, pharmacological, or surgical interventions. For a significant proportion of patients, however, pain is recalcitrant to even the most advanced therapeutic approaches. For some people with headaches, sickle cell disease, or temporomandibular disorders, pain recurs periodically. Individuals with these conditions suffer from episodic pain, often severe enough to disrupt their daily routines. In many circumstances, the pathophysiology underlying pain episodes is ambiguous. Thus, unlike acute pain, in chronic and episodic pain the adaptive functions of pain are not clear.

Pain may also be unremitting, extending for long periods of time, often years. Unlike those who have recurrent pain, people with chronic pain suffer 24 hours a day, 365 days a year, although the severity may fluctuate. It is estimated that more than 50 million Americans have some form of persistent or recurrent pain problems. Individuals who are afflicted with chronic pain are often compelled to modify all aspects of their lives. Loss of gainful employment is common. Chronic pain can be quite costly due to disability cost, reduced productivity, and health care expenditures. It is estimated, for example, that approximately $300,000 (in 1992 dollars) are lost to permanent disability for each disabled individual with work-related, back pain.

In the case of chronic pain, in addition to limitations in physical activities, people experience alterations in family roles and responsibilities, and social activities are curtailed. Thus, it is hardly surprising that pain and disability are frequently accompanied by profound emotional distress for both patients and their significant others.

Chronic pain may or may not be associated with identifiable organic pathology. For example, in chronic illnesses such as cancer and rheumatoid arthritis the physical basis for reports of pain is well documented. There are millions of individuals, however, who suffer from chronic pain with no identifiable organic pathology. For example, in up to 85% of people who report back pain there is no identifiable source of the symptom. Duration and intensity of chronic pain in these cases are generally beyond what is expected from the condition that initiated the pain, and conventional medical and surgical treatments have proved to be largely ineffective. In a recent study, for example, Franklin and colleagues reported that most patients (67.7%) who were treated with lumbar surgery for back pain reported their pain was worse and 55.8%

indicated that the quality of their lives was no better following surgery than it was prior to surgery.

Given the recent advancement in biomedical technology, it may seem surprising that the mechanisms of so many types of pain are poorly understood and that treatments are often inadequate. The reasons for this troubling state of affairs may lie in the multifactorial nature of pain. It is common to consider pain as synonymous with nociception. A clear distinction, however, must be made between nociception and pain. Nociception is a sensory event, involving peripheral sensory stimulation that *may* be perceived as pain. On the other hand, the experience of pain involves cognitive processes such as conscious awareness, attention and appraisal. According to the International Association for the Study of Pain, pain is defined as "an unpleasant sensory *and* emotional experience associated with actual or potential tissue damage or described in terms of such damage" (italics added). Pain is a consequence of one's interpretation of a sensory event, not the sensory stimulation alone. Thus, pain may best be conceptualized as a perceptual process. A better understanding of pain requires careful examination of various components—psychological as well as physical.

This chapter provides an overview of our current understanding of pain. We will focus upon chronic pain, due to the magnitude of problems, costs in care and disability, and difficulties associated with treating these conditions. We will first review the common conceptualization of pain and then we will describe psychological factors that have been associated with pain. We will discuss chronic pain from the psychiatric perspective, reviewing the diagnostic entities that imply underlying pathology of chronic pain as well as common comorbid psychiatric disorders. Finally, various assessment and treatment strategies developed from behavioral and cognitive–behavioral perspectives will be reviewed.

II. CONCEPTUALIZATIONS OF PAIN

It is important to review the different conceptualizations of pain because how one thinks about the phenomenon will influence the manner in which patients are assessed and treated. In general, two perspectives have characterized the thinking about pain: unidimensional models focusing on either physical or psychological causation and multidimensional models that attempt to integrate physical and psychological components of the pain experience.

A. Unidimensional Models of Pain

Conceptualization of pain has been historically dominated by mind–body dualism.

1. Somatogenic Perspective

At one extreme of the dualistic view, an isomorphic relationship between pain and physiological pathology is assumed. In this somatogenic model, the severity of pain should be explained by the degree of physical abnormality. Thus, pain should be alleviated when the abnormality is identified, removed, or corrected, or the pain pathways are blocked pharmacologically or surgically severed. As noted earlier, however, there is no identifiable pathology in many types of pain. The failure of the somatogenic model to account for the report and extent of pain in the absence of physical pathology, the absence of reported pain in the presence of demonstrable pathology, and the differential response by individuals to the same degree of structural abnormalities and identical treatment has prompted a move to the other pole of the mind–body dichotomy. That is, if individuals' pain complaints are not congruent with physical pathology, their pain complaints are assumed either to be psychological in origin (psychogenic) or driven by the motivation to receive secondary gain (e.g., attention, financial compensation, avoidance of undesirable activities).

2. Psychogenic Perspective

As an extension of the psychogenic pole of the dichotomy of chronic pain, Blumer and Heibronn in 1982 proposed that intractable pain is attributable to a psychological predisposition of afflicted individuals. The proposed predisposition, "pain-prone personality," is characterized by tendency to use denial and repression as primary defense mechanisms when stress is encountered. According to this view, those individuals with the pain-prone personality are at high risk for developing chronic pain as a mean of expressing psychological distress. The assumptions and logic of this model, however, have been seriously challenged. [*See* STRESS.]

If one views pain in the absence of adequate physical causes as primarily the result of psychological processes, the assessment should focus on evaluation of personality characteristics and early experiences. Traditional psychological assessment instruments such as the Minnesota Multiphasic Personality Inventory (MMPI) are frequently used, despite the fact that such instruments were never standardized on medical patients. The validity of the results from these questionnaires is questionable since medical patients' responses may be biased by the fact that have a physical disorder and consume medication. Long-term activity restrictions and effects of medications may also affect their responses.

3. Motivational Perspective

For many third-party payers, symptoms in the absence of objective physical pathology are taken as an indication of motivational factors for symptom reporting—"secondary gains." For many patients chronic pain occurs subsequent to a work-related injury or vehicular accident. These individuals commonly have legal and financial issues enmeshed with their situation. The assumption that pain complaints are driven by financial incentives has resulted in a number of attempts to identify malingerers using physical performance tests, psychological tests, and surreptitious observation. It should be noted, however, that there has been no evidence that persistent pain complaints, even in the absence of identifiable pathology, are motivated by financial gain. Research by Mendelson tends to indicate that persistent pain complaints are "not cured by verdict."

4. Operant Perspective

Suffering associated with pain can be expressed in various ways, including verbal complaints, motor behaviors (e.g., limping), and help-seeking behaviors (e.g., medication consumption). These overt actions are termed "pain behaviors." These behaviors may serve a communicative function informing others that one is suffering from pain. In acute pain, overt pain behaviors are most likely to result from reflexive avoidance of pain and to protect oneself from aggravating the condition. On the other hand, in chronic pain there is generally only a modest relationship between pain reports and exhibition of pain behaviors, suggesting that there are factors other than nociceptive stimuli that contribute to the exhibition of pain behavior. This discrepancy may be explained by operant learning process. Pain behaviors may have been acquired as reflexive responses during the acute stage; however, they may be maintained through contingent reinforcement. Positive reinforcement, such as sympathetic attention and negative reinforcement to avoid exacerbation of pain, has been considered a mechanism underlying the maintenance of pain behaviors.

Pain behaviors may be functional in acute pain, protecting patients from aggravating the condition. However, the persistence of pain behaviors can be detrimental. For example, avoidance of physical activity may lead to physical deconditioning, contributing to increased muscle weakness and greater sensitivity to pain.

Past research has demonstrated that sympathetic and supportive responses from others tend to be associated with increased frequency of pain behaviors. For example, frequency of pain behaviors has been shown to be related positively to patients' perception of how supportive their significant others are. Similarly, patients whose spouses are perceived to be solicitous tend to exhibit pain behaviors at greater frequency compared to those whose spouses are not solicitous. Solicitous behaviors by significant others seem to be temporally related to pain behaviors by patients.

Although operant factors may play an important role in the maintenance of disability, the model has been criticized at two levels. First, it fails to integrate factors other than reinforcement, such as sensory, emotional, and cognitive factors, when considering the overall pain experience. Secondly, the assumption that pain behaviors are acquired, maintained, and extinguished only through environmental reinforcement contingencies may need to be reconsidered. For example physical pathology, self-efficacy beliefs, and depression have been reported to be related to pain behaviors.

Recently, Turk and Okifuji (1997) directly evaluated the contributions of various factors to frequency of pain behaviors and found that the biomedical findings and observed physical functioning accounted for a significant amount of variance in pain behavior. Interestingly, the operant factor, specifically positive reinforcement from others, was not related to pain behavior after controlling for the biomedical and physical factors. However, each of the cognitive factors, de-

pression, and perceived disability added a significant amount of variance beyond the biomedical, physical, and operant factors.

Pain behaviors have been conventionally considered as maladaptive manifestations of pain, guided by an incentive for secondary gain or avoidance of physical activity. However, pain behaviors may be functional if indeed the behaviors protect patients from further injury or exacerbation of pain. Thus, these results suggest that determination of whether overt pain behavior in a given patient is functional or maladaptive needs to be based upon careful assessment of various factors associated with his or her pain condition and the antecedent and consequent events.

Accumulating evidence from empirical studies suggest that chronic pain, regardless of the presence of accountable pathology, cannot be fully understood on a basis of any of the unidimensional models. For example, although there are many who complain of back pain in the absence of physical pathology, there are asymptomatic individuals who show significant abnormalities. Similarly, the presence and severity of pain associated with cancer may vary with the diagnosis itself, suggesting that factors other than disease-related or treatment-related pathology are involved in defining the pain experience in cancer patients. Thus, although the unidimensional models reviewed may not be totally incorrect, they are nonetheless incomplete. [See CANCER.]

B. Multidimensional Models

Failure to understand and to adequately treat pain based on a purely physiological, emotional, motivational, or operant perspective has suggested the need for an alternative, more comprehensive model. There are two complementary models that have contributed to understanding of the complexity of pain: the gate control model and the cognitive–behavioral model.

1. Gate Control Model

The gate control theory was proposed by Melzack and Wall to integrate physical and psychological factors regarding pain experience, with three dimensions incorporated: sensory-discriminative, motivational-affective, and cognitive-evaluative. The gate control theory has had a substantial impact by moving the conceptualization of pain from unidimensional models to a multidimensional model in which psychological factors play a significant role. The theory is, however, silent regarding the role of operant factors in the pain experience.

2. Cognitive-Behavioral Model

The most important focus of the cognitive-behavioral model is patients' own subjective perspectives and feelings about their pain conditions. The model assumes that although a nociceptive event has likely preceded pain, how patients perceive the nociceptive event forms a total pain experience by interacting with the sensory event. For example, negative and pessimistic views by individuals about their pain condition and their capabilities for managing pain and stress are likely to potentiate their emotional distress and sense of disability. Similarly, if one expects to experience pain (e.g., "I was injured, I must be hurting."), attention to one's sensory events may become pronounced, and as a consequence, relatively subtle sensory information may be interpreted as being painful.

The cognitive–behavioral model also acknowledges the effects of physiological factors and the environment on behaviors and of behaviors on thoughts and feelings. Demonstration of symptoms to family and health care providers is influenced by how patients view their pain problem and, of course, physical pathology. Patients communicate with others about their pain conditions according to what they believe to be true about the severity and controllability of the condition.

Treatment plans and implementation can be strongly influenced by how patients present their complaints. How family members and others, including health care professionals, treat patients may also be affected by how patients communicate with them about the pain conditions. Thus, assessment and treatment of pain from the cognitive–behavioral perspective require addressing a broader range of issues because cognitive, behavioral, environmental, affective, and physiological factors form a complex interaction defining the idiosyncratic pain experience for each patient.

The basic assumption of the cognitive–behavioral model is that patients are not passive entities who simply react reflexively to nociception, but are actively engaging themselves in defining the experience. Based upon past learning and medical history, individuals develop schemas, subjective representations of illness and symptoms. The schema becomes a reference guide with which individuals process a new sensory stimulus.

Beliefs about the meaning of pain and one's ability to function despite pain are important aspects of the schema about pain. When confronted with pain, patients draw causal, covariational, and consequential inferences about their symptoms based upon their own schematic references. For example, if the schema includes a strong belief that any physical activities must be ceased when experiencing pain and that pain is an acceptable justification for neglecting domestic and occupational responsibilities, poor adjustment and coping are likely to result. In the following sections, we will review some specific thoughts and beliefs that have been demonstrated as important in the chronic pain experience.

III. COGNITIVE FACTORS

A. Self-Efficacy Beliefs

One's beliefs about the effectiveness of his or her coping skills and about whether he or she can execute such skills ("self-efficacy beliefs") are essential for adaptive coping with pain. It has been suggested that individuals' choice of action and the amount of effort to be spent for the action are largely determined by the self-efficacy beliefs. In several studies, pain tolerance was shown to be related to how much subjects believed that they could tolerate pain. Similarly, clinical studies have demonstrated the importance of self-efficacy beliefs in emotional functioning, treatment, and disability.

Self-efficacy beliefs may be acquired or strengthened after successful performance or when one vicariously observes such performance in someone else. For example, Dolce and colleagues demonstrated that the enhancement of patients' self-efficacy beliefs occurred in accordance with the increased amount of their actual physical performance. Cioffi hypothesized that at least four psychological processes may account for the impact of self-efficacy beliefs in pain. A self-efficacious person may (1) have decreased levels of anxiety and arousal leading to less potentially distressing physical feedback while engaging in physical tasks; (2) use distraction; (3) be stoic; and (4) interpret sensations as less distressing (altered interpretation).

B. Beliefs about Controllability

The cognitive–behavioral model suggests that behavior and emotion do not result from objective characteristics of an event alone, but rather are strongly influenced by subjective appraisals of the event. Thus, how patients view their pain and their plight is likely to impact levels of suffering and disability.

Chronic pain patients commonly believe that their pain is uncontrollable. Such beliefs appear to directly impact functioning and mood as well as influence patients' willingness to engage in coping efforts. Patients who believe that their pain is uncontrollable tend to rate their coping strategies as ineffective. Thus, not only can the belief of uncontrollability affect pain perception, it may reinforce the experience of demoralization and inactivity, and result in an overreaction to nociceptive stimulation.

C. Cognitive Errors

Cognitive errors are beliefs about oneself and situations that are distorted in a way that emphasizes negative aspects and imply pessimistic sequels. Endorsement of such cognitive errors tends to increase emotional distress. Maladaptive cognitions are commonly observed among chronic pain patients with "medically incongruent" signs, suggesting that maladaptive thoughts may adversely affect pain experience. Cognitive errors and distortions have been shown to be associated with depression, increased pain severity, and greater disability.

D. Catastrophizing

One type of cognitive error is labelled as "catastrophizing." Catastrophizing has been reported to be associated with decreased pain tolerance in laboratory settings, elevated pain reporting in clinical settings, and poor outcome for rehabilitation.

IV. AFFECTIVE FACTORS

Emotional distress is commonly associated with chronic pain. There has been a considerable debate over which—pain or affective distress—precedes the other. As noted earlier, the psychogenic model emphasizes the importance of underlying psychological distress being manifested as physical pain. There have been reports showing the positive relationship between psychological distress and pain. Parker and associates argued that emotional inhibited individuals tend to describe their emotionally distress in terms of physical pain. A recent prospective study conducted by Dworkin and colleagues demonstrated that herpes zoster patients who reported persistent pain (i.e., longer than 3 months) tended to show higher levels of depressive symptoms at the onset of illness compared with those who did not develop chronic pain, suggesting that depression may contribute to the transition from acute to persistent pain.

Others have hypothesized that biochemical abnormalities are the underlying mechanisms for both pain and depression. Similarly, Beutler and associates suggest that there are psychological and biological predispositions that place individuals at risk for both depression and chronic pain. At this time, however, there is no empirical support for these hypotheses.

Another important factor in the development of affective distress in chronic pain is chronicity of the conditions. Garron and Leavitt reported that psychopathological patterns tended to increase with duration of pain. A group of "new" chronic pain patients (i.e., pain duration of 6 months or less) did not show elevated psychopathological tendencies. Using a 2-latent variable, cross-lagged design, Brown has demonstrated that pain severity predicted subsequent development of depressive symptoms. It is thus possible that psychological difficulties in chronic pain result not necessarily from preexisting or predisposition to psychopathology but from long-term suffering associated with the condition.

Interestingly, the association between the severity of depression and pain varies across studies; positive correlations between those two variables have been reported by some studies but not by others. Rudy, Kerns, and Turk hypothesized that the presence of cognitive mediators may explain the variability. They empirically tested the pain–depression relationship with patients' perception of the degree of life interference and patients' sense of control over life as mediators. Although there was a modest significant association between pain and depression, the association disappeared when the cognitive mediators were entered in the model. Subsequent studies have replicated these results to support cognitive mediation of the pain–depression relationship.

A. Cognitive Factors Influencing Physiology and Biochemistry Relevant to Chronic Pain

It is well known that cognitive activity can influence physiological activity. Induced perspiration and hot flushes while thinking about something embarrassing and increased heart rate while imagining something exciting are but two examples of how thinking can influence our physiological activities. Several early studies demonstrated the effects of cognition on physiological state. These studies showed elevated physiological reactivity when subjects thought about painful stimuli or imaged taking part in a pain-induction task.

Subsequent studies have confirmed that unpleasant cognitive activities tend to increase muscle tension. Elevated electromyographic (EMG) reactivity in the affected bodily areas has been observed when discussing recent stressful events, engaging in stressful imagery, and facing an interpersonally conflictual situation. Chronic pain patients also exhibit slow recovery from reactive muscle tension but only in the affected bodily areas. These studies suggest that a lack of or deficiency in coping resources for dealing with stress may place an individual at risk for excessive sympathetic arousal and muscle tension, further predisposing him or her to experience spasms and pain.

Cognitive activities may also have a direct effect on the brain biochemistry. For example, opioid-mediated hypoalgesia was observed when individuals' sense of control was compromised due to uncontrollability of stressor. Similarly, the analgesic effects of increased self-efficacy belief following training could be blocked by naloxone, suggesting the mediating role of endogenous opioid release in the effects of cognitive coping skills on pain perception.

V. PSYCHIATRIC DIAGNOSES AND CHRONIC PAIN

Epidemiological research suggests that psychiatric disorders are very prevalent among chronic pain patients. For example, approximately one-third of patients with chronic low-back pain meet lifetime diagnosis and over 50% meet at least one co-occurring psychiatric diagnosis. In a study by Fishbain and colleagues, more than 90% of the patients meet at least one Axis I disorder. There are a number of specific diagnostic entities that seem to be commonly observed among chronic pain patients.

A. Psychiatric Diagnoses of Pain Disorders

In the most recent diagnostic manual for psychiatric disorders (*Diagnostic and Statistical Manual of Mental Disorders,* Fourth Edition: *DSM-IV,* American Psychiatric Association, 1994), two types of pain disorders are listed as mental disorders: pain disorder associated with psychological factors and pain disorder associated with both psychological factors and a general medical condition.

A somewhat presumptuous assumption underlying the pain disorder diagnoses is that the "true" physical etiology of chronic pain is always identifiable. Typically, psychological factors are considered as significant only if physical pathology is unable to explain the presence and extent of pain complaints—the mind–body dualistic perspective. However, as we have noted, chronic and recurrent pain, due to their multifactorial nature, cannot be conceptualized without considering its relevance to the psychological factors. Thus, virtually all patients who have chronic or recurrent pain can be diagnosed with a psychiatric diagnosis of pain disorder with or without the presence of a general medical condition that might cause the pain. However, the rationale for defining chronic pain as a mental disorder and the treatment implications for providing such a diagnosis are not clearly stated.

B. Other Psychiatric Diagnosis Concerning the Origin of Pain

There are other psychiatric diagnoses that should be considered when patients' complaints are believed be originated in motivations to be ill or psychological distress expressed in a somatic way. However, the prevalence of these disorders in chronic pain is quite low.

- *Factitious disorders* are characterized by physical or psychological symptoms that are intentionally produced. It is hypothesized that individuals with the factitious disorders have a psychological need to be "ill" in the absence of external incentives (e.g., financial gain).
- *Hypochondriasis* is characterized with preoccupation with one's bodily symptoms and signs due to

fear or belief of having a serious disease. Various tests and physical examinations are commonly conducted for individuals with hypochondriasis but the results are usually negative.

- *Conversion disorder* is characterized by an alteration or loss of physical functioning due to psychological needs. Even though the clinical manifestation suggests physical illness, symptoms are generally incongruent with physical findings. However, conversion disorder is not intentionally produced as is the case in malingering.
- *Malingering* is characterized by exaggerated or fabricated symptom reporting, however, unlike the factitious disorders, is generally associated with external incentives such as avoiding occupational responsibility and obtaining disability benefits. Malingering is not attributed to a mental disturbance but rather to a personal motivation that is highly congruent to one's environmental circumstance.

C. Psychiatric Comorbidity in Chronic Pain

There are several psychiatric disorders commonly diagnosed in chronic pain patients. Since patients' comorbid psychiatric conditions may influence treatment plans, psychological evaluation of chronic pain patients should include assessment of the following disorders:

- *Psychological factors affecting a physical condition* are diagnosed when a temporal relationship exists between the environmental conditions and an identifiable physical condition. Unlike the pain disorders or conversion disorders, no psychogenic assumption is made; thus, individuals are diagnosed with the psychological factor affecting a physical condition when psychological factors are judged to be contributory to any physical problems.
- *Adjustment disorders* are reactive, psychological maladaptation to an identifiable stressor. Adjustment disorders are diagnosed when one's reaction to the stressor is excessive in terms of the level of functional impairment. Adjustment disorders are divided into types with specific features in moods (e.g., adjustment disorder with depressive moods) or functional symptoms (adjustment disorder with physical complaints).

- *Depressive disorders* may be the most prevalent psychiatric diagnoses among chronic pain patients. It is estimated that from 10 to 90% of chronic pain patients can be diagnosed with depression. Degrees of depressive symptomatology, often measured with self-report inventories (e.g., Beck Depression Inventory, Center of Epidemiological Study-Depression Scale) are significantly higher among chronic pain patients compared to healthy individuals.
  An important assessment issue regarding depression in chronic pain is the overlap of somatic symptoms between the two conditions. Symptoms such as sleep disturbance and fatigue may be attributable to either or both conditions. Thus it is possible that the presence or severity of depression may be inflated because patients endorse somatic symptoms that they experience due to the pain conditions. Several studies have suggested that standard cutoff points of the depression inventories, which had been determined with psychiatric or community samples, may not be useful in determining clinically significant depressive levels. [*See* Depression.]
- *Substance abuse,* the chronic use of excessive alcohol, opioid, or sedative-hypnotic medications is relatively common among chronic pain patients. Fishbain and colleagues reported that co-occurring alcohol abuse and drug dependence were diagnosed in 4.3% and 10.6% of their chronic pain patients, respectively. One study reported life-time prevalence of alcohol abuse in 65% of male chronic low-back patients, whereas 39% of the age-matched and socioeconomic status-matched control males met the lifetime diagnosis of alcohol abuse.
  There seem to be several possible mechanisms underlying substance abuse in chronic pain patients. For example, patients' substance abuse may have preceded their pain problem, and patients use pain as a rationalization for drinking or taking medications. Alternatively, it is possible that withdrawal symptoms from abstinence are misinterpreted as pain. Thirdly, substance abuse may exist independently of their pain status. Finally, substance abuse may be a consequence of overprescribing by physicians. Determination of the nature of the relationship between substance abuse and chronic pain should be derived from careful review of history and the usual pattern that has evolved since the pain onset. [*See* Substance Abuse.]

- *Personality Disorders:* The relatively low reliability of the diagnostic criteria makes it difficult to explicate the prevalence of personality disorders in chronic pain patients. Generally, however, a long-term personality dysfunction seems relatively common in chronic pain patients. Reich and colleagues reported 37% of the prevalence rate for the Axis II diagnoses in their sample. Fishbain and colleagues reported that 58% of their sample was diagnosed with at least one personality disorder. Dependent, passive-aggressive, and histrionic personality disorders were most commonly diagnosed. However, Atkinson and colleagues found comparable rates of the antisocial personality disorder between the male chronic pain patients and the matched healthy control males (21% and 18%, respectively). [*See* PERSONALITY.]

VI. PSYCHOLOGICAL ASSESSMENT OF CHRONIC PAIN

Due to the complex, multifactorial nature, optimal evaluations for chronic pain involve not only an examination of biomedical aspects of the pain condition but also comprehensive assessment of psychological factors related to the condition. It has been suggested that the biomedical and psychosocial aspects of pain operate independently; thus, a comprehensive psychological evaluation of chronic pain should include understanding the phenomenology of chronic pain, regardless of the presence of identifiable physical pathology.

The primary purposes of a psychological evaluation are to:

- provide pertinent information on aspects of a patient's psychosocial history and current situation that may be relevant to the pain problems;
- determine psychological and behavioral factors contributing to pain, disability, and distress;
- determine appropriate treatment targets and strategies.

On the other hand, it is inappropriate to use psychological evaluations to determine whether the etiology of pain is psychogenic, to identify malingers, or to justify refusal to treat difficult patients.

From the cognitive–behavioral perspective, it is important to assess how patients perceive their pain conditions, for example, regarding the etiology and modifying factors for their pain, their beliefs about how pain affects quality of life, and their coping strategies and their beliefs about the efficacy of those strategies. In addition, patients' mood, the nature of their interpersonal relationships, and changes in their social, occupational, and physical activities may also be helpful in understanding the impact of chronic pain on their current psychological functioning. Psychopathology, either preexisting, reactive to pain, or co-occurring, should be carefully assessed for optimal treatment planning. Table I provides a list of example questions that may help organize a clinical interview.

Table I Issues to Be Addressed in a Psychological Evaluation

- Patient's perspectives on the onset and history of the problem.
- Patient's concerns and worry about the problem (e.g., re-injury, paralysis).
- Patient's perspectives on the health care system and how the problem has been assessed and treated.
- Behavioral antecedents that are consistently associated with elevated pain levels.
- Thoughts and feelings that precede, accompany, and follow exacerbation of pain.
- Problems that have arisen due to the pain problem.
- How the patient expresses pain.
- How others react to patient's pain and disability.
- Patient's view on the effects of the pain problem on others.
- Activity patterns.
- History of pain and other chronic conditions.
- Relationship with significant others, including sexual functioning.
- Current or recent life stresses.
- Vocational history and goals for return to work.
- Job satisfaction.
- Compensation–litigation status.
- Benefits and secondary gains from having pain and disability.
- Past and current alcohol and medication use.
- Mental status examination, including anxiety and depression.
- What the patient has tried to do alleviate the pain.
- Psychological moderators of the pain condition.
- Inconsistencies and incongruities between patient report and behavior, or between patient and significant other reports.
- Patient's and significant other's goals for treatment.

A. Preparing Patients for a Psychological Evaluation

Chronic pain patients are often unwilling to accept referral to a psychologist, and it is worth spending time preparing patients for a psychological evaluation. For many patients, a psychological referral implies that the clinician believes that their pain is not "real," that they are psychiatrically disturbed, and that no medical remedy can be provided for their pain problems. Some patients may feel compelled to "prove" that their pain is "real" by exaggerating their pain and disability because they fear that no one believes their complaints. Some may have difficulty understanding the relevance of a psychological evaluation in treating their pain. It is not uncommon to see patients react rather defensively when a referral to a psychologist is suggested. The defensiveness may be expressed in various ways, some with hostility, others with reticence.

When making a referral to a psychologist, even when no overt resistance is apparent, clear rationale for the referral should be provided to patients, including why a psychological evaluation is recommended, the specific nature of referral questions, how the results will be used, and who will have access to them. Acknowledging that the patient's pain is real and the devastating effects of chronic pain on important aspects of patients' lives can be helpful in reducing resistance and can add further justification for the psychological referral. Patients are generally willing to acknowledge that pain has caused various life difficulties. Discussion of the importance of addressing stress and coping should alleviate misunderstanding that patients may have regarding psychological evaluations.

VII. TREATMENT

A number of nonmedical treatment modalities have been used based on the conceptualization of pain. We will provide a brief discussion of some of the most frequently used. For more detailed description of these strategies, see Gatchel and Turk's recent volume.

A. Operant Conditioning

Psychological intervention using the operant paradigm involves specific targets (overt behavior) that can be increased or decreased by reinforcement. Pain behaviors (e.g., attention-seeking behaviors, "down time") are subjected to no positive consequences whereas "well-behaviors" are encouraged and rewarded. The method is often used for tapering inappropriate medication use. The reinforcing property of medications is diminished by altering medication schedules from an "as needed" basis to an interval basis. Thus, the medication schedule becomes time contingent, rather than pain contingent.

Operant treatment may be most effective when implemented in inpatient settings because they allow maximum control over the environmental contingencies. Family involvement is generally recommended in order to transfer the contingency plans from the hospital to the home environment. Although the operant treatment is effective in increasing physical activity in the short-term, failure to provide patients with intrinsic reinforcement or providing any coping strategies that they might use to control the pain may inhibit motivation, maintenance, and generalization. It may be more appropriate to incorporate operant factors within a more comprehensive treatment program.

B. Cognitive Restructuring

As noted earlier, cognitive activities such as maladaptive thoughts, beliefs, and expectancies are important determinants of pain experience. Most of the cognitive activities have become an automatic process and we may not be conscious of the effects of our thoughts on our mood, behavior, the environment, our physiology, and the pain experience. Cognitive restructuring is designed to help patients identify and modify maladaptive thoughts. In order to accomplish these patients may be asked to write down (1) the nature of a situation in which their pain seems particularly elevated, (2) their level of emotional and physiological arousal, and (3) thoughts they had and the impact of the thoughts on pain perception and emotions.

A list of common maladaptive thoughts observed in chronic pain patients is included in Table II. Once patients' thought patterns are identified, more adaptive thoughts are introduced to help patients modify their maladaptive appraisals, beliefs, and attitudes. Alternative thoughts should emphasize adaptive ways of thinking and responding to minimize stress and dysfunction. Patients are generally instructed to prac-

Table II Examples of Common Cognitive Errors

- **Overgeneralization:** Extrapolation from the occurrence of a specific event or situation to a large range of possible situations. *"This coping strategy didn't work; nothing will ever work for me."*
- **Catastrophyzing:** Focusing exclusively on the worst possibility regardless of its likelihood of occurrence. *"My back pain means my body is degenerating and falling apart."*
- **All-or-none thinking:** Considering only the extreme "best" or "worst" interpretation of a situation without regard to the full range of alternatives. *"If pain is not completely gone, I cannot do anything right."*
- **Jumping to conclusions:** Accepting an arbitrary interpretation without a rational evaluation of its likelihood. *"The doctor didn't return my call today. He thinks I am a hopeless case."*
- **Selective attention:** Selectively attending to negative aspects of a situation while ignoring any positive factors. *"Physical exercises only make my pain worse."*
- **Negative predictions:** Assuming the worst. *"I know I will not get better even with all these therapies and everyone will dislike me for that."*
- **Mind-reading:** Make arbitrary assumptions about others without finding out what others are thinking. *"My husband does not talk to me about my pain because he doesn't care about me."*

tice identifying and modifying maladaptive thoughts outside of clinics and their progress is reviewed during therapy sessions.

Patients are often taught problem-solving skills. The six steps of the problem-solving strategy (i.e., problem identification, goal selection, generation of alternatives, decision making, implementation, and evaluation) can be introduced. Patients are informed that although there may not be a perfect solution, some solutions are more effective or adaptive than others. Problem-solving skills can be applied to specific situations that tend to trigger pain as well as the problems that are created by persistent pain. An important goal is to convey the message that the problems are manageable and that the patients can learn how to deal with these successfully and thereby foster their self-efficacy beliefs.

C. Self-Management Strategies

Treatment that emphasizes self-management strategies generally aims at enhancing patients' adaptive coping with the pain conditions and the problems cre-

ated by persistent pain, specifically to resume a productive and enjoyable life despite pain. Adaptive coping requires patients to be aware that they can use skills to cope and be able to execute those skills as necessary. Some of the self-management strategies are related to the former part (thought-based: covert coping) whereas there are several skill-based training techniques (e.g., relaxation training, biofeedback: overt coping) that can be helpful in better managing pain.

Past research has suggested that there is no one specific coping skill that best manages pain and disability. It is generally recommended that chronic pain patients be taught various types of coping skills that patients can select from among.

D. Relaxation and Biofeedback

Relaxation is a method to manipulate levels of autonomic nervous system activity. Generally, relaxation involves two steps: (1) awareness of maladaptive physiological activity (e.g., ability to discriminate muscle tension and relaxation) and (2) modification of the maladaptive autonomic activity. Because many types of pain have musculoskeletal or neuromuscular components, learning to manage muscle tension can be effective for several reasons. First, relaxation can have a direct impact on pain perception by minimizing pain due to a muscle spasm or controlling other mechanisms related to pain. In addition, relaxation training is known to manage various types of emotional distress, especially anxiety. Once mastered, patients can use the relaxation technique to better cope with negative feelings associated with episodes of persistent pain. Since relaxation requires patients to focus on various muscle groups, the technique may act as a distraction, taking patients' attention away from persistent pain. Relaxation also has the potential to provide patients with a sense of control over their bodies and consequently their pain.

Biofeedback procedures help patients not only accurately perceive their physiological state but also voluntarily modify the physiological state. In general, electrophysiologic devices are used to measure specific physiological output, and auditory or visual signals are provided for patients to exercise voluntary control. In chronic pain, electromyographic (EMG) and thermal biofeedback procedures are commonly employed. The former helps patients to identify and signal maladaptive autonomic activity and the latter is frequently used for treating migraine headaches, in which peripheral blood flow is manipulated via skin temperature. [See BIOFEEDBACK.]

The mechanisms by which biofeedback is effective are not well understood. As biofeedback has been originally designed for reduction of maladaptive physiological responses, it is plausible that the efficacy of biofeedback is based upon direct impact of physiological manipulation on pain conditions. However, research has demonstrated that biofeedback could be beneficial to pain patients in the absence of actual changes in their physiological states. An alternative explanation is that biofeedback may help patients to increase a sense of control by altering physiological activity, patients may feel that they have some control over their pain and symptoms.

VIII. CONCLUDING COMMENTS

In this article, we reviewed the most common unidimensional and multidimensional models of pain. Common comorbid psychiatric diagnoses were described. A number of psychological factors associated with pain perception and response were listed. We also outlined the assessment and treatment methods that follow from the different perspectives.

Although pain is generally considered a physical phenomenon, pain involves various cognitive, affective, and behavioral factors. These psychological factors are important in not only determining the perception of pain, but also defining disability and the general well-being of patients. It should be clear from the review that pain has three main components: physical, psychosocial, and behavioral, each interacting with the other to define the unique pain experience. Because pain experience is subjective and idiosyncratic, it cannot be understood without evaluating how patients perceive and appraise their pain conditions. A total clinical picture includes how patients view their plight, and by understanding the phenomenology of chronic pain, effective treatment can be planned to alleviate persistent and disabling pain and disability.

BIBLIOGRAPHY

Atkinson, J. H., Slater, M. A., Patterson, T. L., Grant, I., & Garfin, S. R. (1991). Prevalence, onset, and risk of psychiatric disorders in men with chronic low back pain: A controlled study. *Pain, 45,* 111–121.

Beutler, L. E., Engel, D., Oró-Beutler, M. E., Daldrup, R., & Meredith, K. (1986). Inability to express intense affect: A common link between depression and pain? *Journal of Consulting and Clinical Psychology, 54,* 752–759.

Blumer, D., & Heibronn, M. (1982). Chronic pain as a variant of depressive disease: The pain-prone disorder. *Journal of Nervous and Mental Disease, 170,* 381–406.

Brown, G. K. (1990). A causal analysis of chronic pain and depression. *Journal of Abnormal Psychology, 99,* 127–137.

Cioffi, D. (1991). Beyond attentional strategies: A cognitive-perceptual model of somatic interpretation. *Psychological Bulletin, 109,* 25–41.

Dolce, J. J., Crocker, M. F., Moletteire, C., & Doleys, D. M. (1986). Exercise quotas, anticipatory concern and self-efficacy expectancies in chronic pain: A preliminary report. *Pain, 24,* 365–375.

Dworkin, R. H., Harstein, G., Rosner, H. L., Walther, R. R., Sweeney, E. W., Brand, L. (1992). A high-risk method for studying psychological antecedents of chronic pain: The prospective investigation of herpes zoster. *Journal of Abnormal Psychology, 101,* 200–205.

Fishbain, D. A., Goldberg, M., Meagher, B. R., Steele, R., & Rosomoff, H. (1986). Male and female chronic pain patients categorized by DSM-III psychiatric diagnostic criteria. *Pain, 26,* 181–197.

Franklin, G. M., Haug, J., Heyer, N. J., McKeffrey, S. P., & Picciano, J. F. (1994). Outcome of lumber fusion in Washington state workers' compensation. *Spine, 19,* 1897–1904.

Garron, D. C., & Leavitt, F. (1983). Chronic low back pain and depression. *Journal of Clinical Psychology, 39,* 486–493.

Gatchel, R. J., & Turk, D. C. (Eds.) (1996). *Psychological approaches to pain management: A practitioner's handbook.* New York: Guilford Press.

Melzack, R., & Wall, P. D. (1965). Pain mechanisms: A new theory. *Science, 50,* 971–979.

Mendelson, G. (1982). Not "cured by a verdict". *Medical Journal of Australia, 2,* 132–134.

Parker, J. C., Doerfler, L. A., Tatten, H. A., & Hewett, J. E. (1983). Psychological factors that influence self-reported pain. *Journal of Clinical Psychology, 39,* 22–25.

Reich, J., Tupen, J. P., & Abramowitz, S. I. (1983). Psychiatric diagnosis of chronic pain patients. *American Journal of Psychiatry, 140,* 1495–1498.

Rudy, T. E., Kerns, R. D., & Turk, D. C. (1988). Chronic pain and depression: Toward a cognitive–behavioral mediation model. *Pain, 35,* 129–140.

Turk, D. C., & Okifuji, A. (1997). Evaluating the role of physical, operant, cognitive, and affective factors in pain behavior in chronic pain patients. *Behavior Modification, 21,* 259–280.

Panic Attacks

Richard J. McNally

Harvard University

Anxiety Neurosis   A *DSM-II* diagnosis characterized by chronic, excessive anxiety not triggered by specific phobic stimuli.

Anxiety Sensitivity   Refers to fears of anxiety-related symptoms that are based on beliefs that these symptoms have harmful consequences.

Diagnostic and Statistical Manual of Mental Disorders (DSM)   The manual that describes diagnostic criteria for diagnosing mental disorders. The fourth edition (*DSM-IV*) appeared in 1994.

Epidemiologic Catchment Area (ECA) Study   The largest house-to-house survey of mental disorders ever conducted in the United States. Interviewers evaluated more than 18,000 adults in five geographical areas (Los Angeles, North Carolina Piedmont region, St. Louis, New Haven, Baltimore) to estimate the prevalence of *DSM-III* mental disorders.

First-Degree Relatives   First-degree relatives are one's parents, siblings, and children. If a disorder is influenced by genetic variables, it ought to occur more often among first-degree relatives of a person with the disorder than among more distant relatives of this person.

Hyperventilation   Occurs when minute ventilation exceeds metabolic needs (i.e., more carbon dioxide is exhaled than is produced by cellular metabolism). Minute ventilation is the product of respiration rate and tidal volume (i.e., amount of air inhaled per breath).

Incidence   The rate of new cases of a disorder that appear during a certain time period (e.g., annual incidence).

Interoceptive Conditioning   A form of Pavlovian (classical) conditioning in which the conditioned stimuli arise within the body (e.g., an increase in heart rate) rather than outside the body (e.g., a flashing light, a tone).

Prevalence   The percentage of a population that has a disorder during a certain time period (e.g., annual prevalence, lifetime prevalence).

PANIC ATTACKS are discrete episodes of terror that begin suddenly and are associated with intense physiological symptoms (e.g., breathlessness, rapid heart rate, dizziness) and thoughts that one is about to die, lose self-control, or "go crazy."

I. HISTORY OF THE CONCEPT OF PANIC ATTACK

In 1959, research psychiatrist Donald F. Klein was studying imipramine, a new drug synthesized by a minor alteration in the chemical structure of the "major tranquilizer" chlorpromazine. Researchers hoped that imipramine, like chlorpromazine, would help people with schizophrenia, whose psychotic symptoms were at that time believed to result from excessive anxiety. Unfortunately, imipramine did not attenuate delusions or hallucinations, but it did alleviate depressive symptoms in schizophrenic patients, and its mood-improving effects were notably dramatic in patients suffering from severe depression.

As evidence for the antidepressant effects accumulated, Klein and his associates struggled to treat a group of highly anxious inpatients who had been diagnosed as "schizophrenic" but who exhibited neither delusions nor hallucinations. Not only had they failed to respond to sedatives and to psychotherapy, their anxiety was not reduced by chlorpromazine. These results were puzzling in light of prevailing theory: chlorpromazine helped typical schizophrenics whose psychotic symptoms supposedly resulted from extreme anxiety, yet it failed to help an atypical group of schizophrenics who were very anxious, but who were not psychotic.

Klein's decision to prescribe imipramine for these atypical schizophrenics was born of frustration. Other approaches had failed, and the new drug was known to be safe and to have some anxiety-reducing properties. However, after taking imipramine for several weeks, the patients maintained that the drug was ineffective because it failed to attenuate their chronic anxiety. Their psychotherapist concurred, but the nursing staff did not. Before taking imipramine, these patients had been rushing to the nursing station several times a day, terrified, and exclaiming that they were dying. The nurses would reassure them that they were not dying, and their terror would pass after about 20 minutes or so. Despite their claims of lack of improvement, patients were no longer experiencing these terrifying episodes of suddenly feeling on the brink of death. Also, once their sudden, unpredictable episodes of terror (i.e., panic attacks) had ceased, patients became increasingly comfortable, moving freely throughout the hospital unaccompanied by others.

Based on these observations, Klein inferred that imipramine was effective against acute panic attacks, but not against chronic anxiety. Indeed, their chronic anxiety was itself the consequence of panic; they lived in dread of these recurrent episodes of terror. These observations also suggested a qualitative distinction between episodic panic attacks and chronic anticipatory anxiety. Klein reasoned that the effects of imipramine would make no sense if panic were just an extreme form of anxiety. Indeed, why should a drug be effective against the severe form of a disease, but not against its mild form? This paradox would disappear if panic and anxiety arose from different underlying processes rather than being two points on a quantitative continuum of severity. As Klein observed, such apparent paradoxes are common in nonpsychiatric medicine. Bacterial pneumonia and the common cold are respiratory disorders that share many symptoms, and although the former might be mistaken for a severe form of the latter, antibiotics are effective against bacterial pneumonia but are useless against the common cold. Therefore, reasoned Klein, just as bacterial pneumonia does not lie on a continuum of severity with the common cold, panic is not merely a severe form of ordinary anxiety. [See ANXIETY.]

Klein's experience with imipramine not only motivated his distinction between panic and anxiety, it also led him to conclude that agoraphobia was chiefly a consequence of panic attacks. (The "schizophrenic" patients who first responded to imipramine would now be diagnosed as having "panic disorder with agoraphobia" because they fearfully avoided many activities in addition to having panic attacks.) Traditional views conceptualized agoraphobia as a fear of open or public places. But it became apparent that the motivation for avoidance was fear of panicking in situations where escape was not easy or help readily available.

Klein subsequently delineated three types of panic attack. Spontaneous panic attacks are sudden, unexpected surges of terror accompanied by intense (especially cardiorespiratory) symptoms. Spontaneous panics are often accompanied by catastrophic thoughts that one is about to die, "go crazy," or lose self-control. From the perspective of the panicker, the attacks seem to "come out of the blue," uncaused by any obvious environmental precipitant. "Spontaneous" does not imply "uncaused"; it implies only the absence of external triggers, not the absence of neurobiological dysregulation. Spontaneous panics are akin to other conditions in medicine that erupt without clear-cut external provocation, like paroxysmal tachycardia, migraine, and vertigo (i.e., rotational dizziness) arising from inner ear disease.

Stimulus-bound panics refer to the sudden surge of

intense fear experienced by people with specific phobias (e.g., of animals, of heights) when they encounter, or anticipate encountering, their feared object. These episodes are similar to spontaneous attacks except that the panicker is aware of the external precipitant and is less likely to misinterpret the attacks as a sign of impending insanity. [*See* PHOBIAS.]

Situationally predisposed panics occur in some situations more than in others, but are not inevitably or immediately triggered by these external stimuli. For example, people with agoraphobia often panic while in crowded stores, but crowded stores do not inevitably trigger panic with the same predictability that snakes trigger panic in people with snake phobia.

Klein's work greatly influenced the inclusion of panic disorder as a diagnostic category in the third edition of the *Diagnostic and statistical manual of mental disorders* (*DSM-III*), which appeared in 1980. Based partly on his work, *DSM-III* postulated two types of anxiety neurosis. One type was characterized by repeated spontaneous panic attacks (panic disorder), and the other was characterized by chronic high levels of anxiety that did not erupt into panic attacks (generalized anxiety disorder). In the revised version of *DSM-III* (*DSM-III-R*), which appeared in 1987, panic disorder was coded as either panic disorder without agoraphobia or panic disorder with agoraphobia. This important change acknowledged the consensus view among American psychopathologists that although some people with panic disorder do not extensively avoid situations and activities, when people *do* develop agoraphobia, their avoidance almost always develops as a consequence of panic disorder. Some people, however, develop agoraphobia after having experienced episodes of intense symptoms that do not qualify as full-blown panic attacks (e.g., sudden bouts of dizziness).

Because research has indicated that spontaneous panic attacks occasionally occur in people with other disorders (e.g., social phobia, major depressive disorder), *DSM-IV* defines panic attacks separately from panic disorder. That is, recurrent spontaneous panics are insufficient for the diagnosis of panic *disorder*: the person must also alter his or her life to accommodate the attacks, develop a chronic fear of the attacks, or both.

According to current *DSM-IV* criteria, panic attacks are discrete periods of intense fear or discomfort that begin suddenly and reach peak intensity within 10 minutes. (Most research studies, however, indicate that panic attacks usually reach peak intensity well before 10 minutes have elapsed, and often seem to peak almost instantly.) To qualify as a panic attack, an episode of sudden-onset fear must be accompanied by at least four of the following symptoms: (1) palpitations, pounding heart, or accelerated heart rate; (2) sweating; (3) trembling or shaking; (4) sensations of shortness of breath or smothering; (5) feeling of choking; (6) chest pain or discomfort; (7) nausea or abdominal distress; (8) feeling dizzy, unsteady, lightheaded, or faint; (9) derealization (feelings of unreality) or depersonalization (being detached from oneself); (10) fear of losing control or going crazy; (11) fear of dying; (12) paresthesias (numbness or tingling sensations); and (13) chills or hot flushes. Rapid-onset attacks of fear that are characterized by fewer than four of these symptoms are called "limited-symptom attacks."

DSM-IV distinguishes three types of panic attack that are approximately equivalent to Klein's spontaneous, stimulus bound, and situationally predisposed panics. Unexpected (uncued) panic attacks are not triggered by any obvious external stimulus, and seem to occur "out of the blue" for no apparent reason.

Situationally bound (cued) panic attacks are triggered by an encounter with a feared (phobic) stimulus or in anticipation of such an encounter. For example, a person with a snake phobia will typically experience a situationally bound panic upon encountering a snake in the woods.

Finally, situationally predisposed panic attacks are triggered by encounters with feared situational stimuli, but are not invariably triggered by such encounters. For example, a person with a fear of driving automobiles will tend to experience panic attacks more often while driving than while doing other things, but driving does not invariably cause panics.

II. ASSESSING PANIC ATTACKS

Most research on spontaneous panic attacks has been based on the patients' retrospective self-report. Patients are often asked to recall their most recent, most severe, or most typical attack, and then indicate the presence and severity of the *DSM* symptoms on some scale. Regrettably, these ratings are subject to unintentional distortion. Research suggests that atypically intense, and therefore memorable, attacks are often described as "typical," and patients often overestimate the frequency and severity of their attacks when asked about them days or weeks later.

To circumvent this problem, clinical researchers now have patients prospectively self-monitor their attacks and record them in structured diaries designed for this purpose shortly after the attack occurs.

Because classic panic attacks occur unpredictably, they have rarely been captured in the psychophysiology laboratory. Indeed, most laboratory research on panic involves attacks provoked by biological challenges (see below). Nevertheless, about 20 unexpected attacks have been recorded while patients were undergoing various assessments while wired for psychophysiologic assessments. These recorded episodes have indicated that panics do, indeed, begin abruptly, as patients say, and are marked by increases in heart rate, skin conductance (i.e., sweating), facial muscle tension, and hyperventilation.

III. PANIC ATTACK VARIANTS

During the mid-1980s, researchers noted that about one-third of the young adult (nonclinical) population reported having experienced a "panic attack" during the previous year. These nonclinical panic attacks seemed to suggest that a phenomenon so common might not be indicative of psychopathology. Subsequent studies revealed, however, that most of these attacks were not especially severe and nor were many the spontaneous, unexpected attacks that characterize panic disorder. Consensus now holds that between 2% and 7% of the general young adult population experiences at least one spontaneous panic attack that meets *DSM* criteria each year. Occasional panic attacks may presage the development of panic disorder in people who also have elevated anxiety sensitivity.

Researchers have described the seemingly oxymoronic condition of nonfearful panic attacks among cardiology patients seeking help for unexplained chest pain. These individuals complain of sudden rushes of somatic symptoms identical to those of panic attacks, but do not experience fearful thoughts about imminent death and so forth. Comparisons between typical panickers and nonfearful panickers on variables such

as age of onset, average number of symptoms per attack, duration of disorder, depressive, agoraphobic symptoms, and so forth indicate that the two groups are nearly indistinguishable except for the fact that typical panickers experience terror during their attacks, whereas nonfearful panickers do not. Nonfearful panic indicates that sudden rushes of autonomic symptoms are not equivalent to panic attacks, thereby raising the possibility that a person's interpretation of the symptoms as threatening may partly determine whether they experience the episode as terrifying.

Although panic attacks most often occur during the daytime, they can also erupt while the person is sleeping. Nocturnal (or sleep) panics are characterized by abrupt awakening, terror, and intense physiological arousal. Because nocturnal attacks emerge during non-REM (rapid-eye-movement) sleep, they are rarely preceded by dreams (which occur during REM sleep). Most attacks occur during the transition from stage 2 to stage 3 sleep (i.e., as the person is going into a deeper stage of sleep). About 5% of college students report having had a nocturnal panic at some point in their lives, and about 69% of panic disorder patients have had at least one nocturnal panic. It is very unusual for a person with panic disorder to have only nocturnal panics, but those who experience nocturnal panics tend to experience more daytime panics as well. [*See* Sleep.]

There are similarities and differences between nocturnal panics and night terrors (also known as *pavor nocturnus* in children and *incubus* in adults). Both erupt during non-REM sleep; both are rarely preceded by dreams; and both are marked by abrupt awakenings, terror, and autonomic arousal. Yet night terrors are more common in children than in adults, and emerge after a sustained period of very deep (stage 4) sleep. Panic attacks, including nocturnal ones, are more common in adults than in children. Furthermore, night terrors begin with a blood-curdling scream, yet the person who experiences a night terror rarely remembers the episode, and easily returns to sleep. Also, a person experiencing a night terror may become combative or run out of the house. In contrast, nocturnal panickers vividly remember their attacks, and often experience difficulty returning to sleep.

The causes of nocturnal attacks are unknown. One possibility is that physiological irregularities waken the person who then panics in response to perplexing symptoms like breathlessness, racing heart, and so forth. Another possibility is that the psychobiological substrate of the emotion of fear does, indeed, begin while the person is sleeping, consistent with patients' reports that they awoke already in the midst of fear.

IV. THE DEVELOPMENT OF PANIC DISORDER AND AGORAPHOBIA

Panic attacks usually start in late adolescence or in early adulthood; they rarely begin before puberty or late in life. They typically emerge during periods of life stress such as after the death of a loved one, in anticipation of a major life event (e.g., wedding), after losing a job, and so forth. Occasional panic attacks are not uncommon in the general population, but if individuals become persistently fearful of them or alter their lives in response to them, panic disorder is diagnosed.

The vast majority of people who develop agoraphobia do so as a consequence of their fear of panic attacks. It is very unusual for someone to become agoraphobic without first having had panic attacks. Rarely, clinicians encounter people who appear to have agoraphobia without a history of panic. But close inspection of these cases reveals that such patients fear other forms of sudden bodily incapacitation that do not qualify as panic per se (e.g., diarrhea, migraine headaches).

Some panickers become agoraphobic within days of their first attack; others become increasingly agoraphobic over weeks, months, and years; and still others never become agoraphobic. Researchers have studied what factors predict which panickers develop agoraphobia by comparing panickers with and without agoraphobia. Avoiders and nonavoiders do not differ in their age of onset or duration of panic disorder, and there are few differences in the severity of the attacks themselves: agoraphobic panickers do not seem to have worse attacks than nonagoraphobic panickers. There are no differences in the frequency of attacks. The best predictors of avoidance are cognitive. Predictors of agoraphobic avoidance include expectations of panicking in certain situations, perceived negative consequences of panic, fears of dying or going crazy during attacks, and lack of confidence in one's ability to cope with panic.

V. EPIDEMIOLOGY

Epidemiology is the study of the distribution and determinants of disease in the population. Interviewing more than 18,000 American adults, the Epidemiologic Catchment Area (ECA) team endeavored to determine the prevalence and incidence of panic disorder and other mental disorders. The ECA data indicated that the annual prevalence rate of *DSM-III* panic disorder (without agoraphobia) was 1.2% in women and 0.6% in men, and the lifetime prevalence was 2.1% in women and 1.0% in men. Panic disorder was most common among people aged 30 to 44 years, and least common in people older than 65 years old. People with panic disorder sought the services of mental health professionals more than people with any other disorder, including alcoholism and schizophrenia.

The ECA team reported annual prevalence rates for *DSM-III* agoraphobia of 5.9% for women and 2.1% for men. Surprisingly, however, the ECA team reported that only 7% of the subjects diagnosed with agoraphobia also had panic disorder. This result was dramatically at variance with the observations of clinicians who rarely see agoraphobics without panic disorder. Subsequent reexamination of the "agoraphobia without panic" cases strongly suggested that the ECA team had inadvertently classified many cases of specific phobias (e.g., of flying, driving, crossing bridges) as instances of agoraphobia.

The ECA researchers estimated the annual incidence of panic disorder 2.4 new cases per 1000 persons per year. The estimated incidence of a severe panic attack was 9 per 1000 persons per year.

The ECA team found that 20% of people with panic disorder reported having attempted suicide at some point in their lives. This finding was surprising because panic patients often fear dying in the midst of their attacks, and most studies on patients with the disorder indicate that they are not at high risk for attempting suicide. A reanalysis of the ECA data suggested that the presence of comorbid disorders that independently increase risk for suicide attempt (e.g., schizophrenia, alcoholism, depression) may have been the basis for the apparent connection between panic disorder and suicide attempts. Nevertheless, the presence of panic disorder in a person with, say, depression provides no guarantee that the person will not attempt suicide.

The National Comorbidity Survey (NCS), a nationwide *DSM-III-R* assessment of mental disorders, revealed a lifetime prevalence rate for panic disorder of 3.5%; 1.5% of the respondents had panic disorder at the point of the survey. The NCS indicated that 1.5% of the population develops panic disorder with agoraphobia at some point in their lives; 0.7% had it at the time of the survey. As in the ECA study, the rate was about twice as high for women as for men. The NCS team also found that those with less than a high school education were more than 10 times as likely to have panic disorder as those who had graduated from college. Because income level, unlike education, was unrelated to risk for panic disorder, the NCS team suggested that lower cognitive ability may be linked to panic. Race/ethnicity was unrelated to panic disorder. Being married (or living with someone) and being employed was associated with reduced risk. [*See* EPIDEMIOLOGY: PSYCHIATRIC.]

VI. BIOLOGICAL ASPECTS OF PANIC

One early hypothesis was that chronic hyperventilators are prone to panic because they are more likely than other people to experience hyperventilation-induced sensations (e.g., dizziness) that may frighten them, causing further overbreathing, greater fear, and so forth until full-blown panic results.

However, most subsequent research indicates that panic patients are usually not chronic hyperventilators. But excessive ventilation is a common accompaniment of panic attacks and can worsen the symptoms associated with panic. Therefore, hyperventilation does not seem to cause panic attacks, but it does seem to intensify attacks that do occur.

An important tool for studying panic in the laboratory has been the biological challenge test. Biological challenge tests produce intense bodily sensations, and incite panic attacks far more often in panic patients than in patients with other disorders or in healthy subjects. They are designed to stress specific neurobiological systems, and if panic occurs, then dysfunction in the stress system may constitute a vulnerability to naturally occurring panic attacks. A purpose of this research is to identify procedures that will reliably initiate attacks in the laboratory that strongly resemble spontaneous panic attacks. These procedures, in turn, enable researchers to investigate the mechanisms of panic in controlled experimental situations.

However, panic attacks occurring in response to biological challenges have been interpreted in two principal ways. One interpretation holds that challenges directly incite panic by exacerbating a neurobiological dysfunction. The other interpretation holds that they incite attacks merely by generating intense bodily sensations that these patients are prone to fear.

Several challenges have been used. Infusion of sodium lactate occasions panic in about 67% of panic patients, but in only about 13% of healthy control subjects. Controversy persists about whether the response of panic patients differs qualitatively from that of control subjects. For example, panic patients often are more anxious and more physiologically aroused than control subjects before the infusion begins. That is, the reactivity of panic patients is often not greater than that of control subjects (i.e., the magnitude of change is not greater), but patients begin the challenge at a higher baseline level of arousal and anxiety.

Some psychopathologists believe that dysregulation in the noradrenergic system is involved in the genesis of panic attacks. This hypothesis stems partly from the phenomenology of panic itself. Panic attacks are characterized by symptoms indicative of massive autonomic arousal associated with norepinephrine surges, thereby implying an instability in the noradrenergic system. Consistent with this possibility, oral (or infused) yohimbine challenges, which stimulate noradrenergic activity, produce panic in about 63% of panic patients and in about 7% of control subjects.

Carbon dioxide inhalations have also been used as biological challenge tests. One hypothesis is that panic disorder patients are characterized by hypersensitive carbon dioxide receptors in the brainstem such that increases in central carbon dioxide produce an excessive ventilatory response that can initiate panic attacks. A related hypothesis is that panic is attributable to a pathologically low threshold for firing of an evolved suffocation alarm. That is, carbon dioxide receptors in the brainstem may respond to relatively low increases in carbon dioxide as if the person is suffocating. When this alarm fires, the person begins hyperventilating and experiences the terror appropriate to one who cannot breathe. Physiological evidence in support of carbon dioxide receptor hypersensitivity is mixed. In some studies, panic patients have exhibited excessively vigorous ventilatory responses to carbon dioxide inhalation, whereas in others they have not.

Panic disorder appears to run in families, suggesting the possibility of a genetic vulnerability. It is unclear whether this vulnerability is for panic attacks per se, for overactive physiological responding, or for personality traits that may predispose people to react fearfully to bodily symptoms.

Rates of panic disorder are higher in the first-degree relatives of patients with panic disorder (17.3%) than in the first-degree relatives of healthy control subjects (1.8%). Estimates of the heritability of panic attacks and panic disorder vary depending on the population from which the subjects are drawn. In one study involving patients, 31% of the identical twins with panic attacks had a co-twin with panic attacks as well, whereas none of the fraternal twins with panic attacks had a co-twin with panic attacks. In one population study, 23.9% of the identical twins were concordant for panic disorder as compared to 10.9% of the fraternal twins when a psychiatrist made the diagnosis based on the collected data, but the respective concordance rates were nearly identical (14.5% vs. 14.6%) when a computer algorithm evaluated the data. [*See* GENETIC CONTRIBUTORS TO MENTAL HEALTH.]

VII. PSYCHOLOGICAL ASPECTS OF PANIC

Psychological theorists hold that physiological symptoms are insufficient to produce the experience of panic. For panic qua panic to occur, the person must react to these bodily sensations with fear. Responding to one's own bodily sensations as if they were phobic stimuli, panickers worsen these symptoms, and thereby amplify their terror. Moreover, only those people who dread these symptoms will qualify for panic disorder. According to psychological theorists, panic disorder is in large part a "fear of fear" itself.

There have been several versions of the fear-of-fear hypothesis of panic disorder. One view holds that Pavlovian interoceptive conditioning figures in development of panic disorder. Initial panic attacks establish certain bodily sensations (e.g., heart palpitations, breathlessness) as conditioned stimuli that evoke subsequent panic attacks.

Another view holds that panic attacks occur because individuals catastrophically misinterpret certain benign bodily sensations as harbingers of imminent psychological or physical disaster. Thus, a person might misinterpret palpitations as an impending heart attack, become more anxious, and thereby intensifying these sensations until they culminate into a panic attack. According to this view, catastrophic misinterpretations of bodily sensations are necessary for a panic attack to occur.

A third approach emphasizes that not everyone is equally likely to respond fearfully to their own bodily sensations. People who hold mistaken beliefs about rapid heartbeats, dizziness, and so forth are presumably more likely than other people to react fearfully when these sensations occur. This notion is embodied in the anxiety sensitivity hypothesis. Anxiety sensitivity is an individual difference variable that may constitute a cognitive risk factor for panic disorder. It is conceptually and empirically distinguishable from trait anxiety. Trait anxiety refers to a proneness to react fearfully to a wide range of potential stressors, whereas anxiety sensitivity refers to the specific tendency to react fearfully to bodily sensations associated with anxiety. Importantly, people with elevated scores on the Anxiety Sensitivity Index (ASI)—a questionnaire measure of this variable—respond just like panic patients to biological challenges (e.g., carbon dioxide inhalation) even if they have no history of panic attacks or panic disorder. These studies imply that a fearful response to challenge is a marker for the fear of symptoms rather than a marker for panic disorder per se. Longitudinal research indicates that people with elevated ASI scores are at enhanced risk for developing panic and other anxiety disorders.

Implicit in the fear-of-fear construals of panic is the notion that people prone to experience panic attacks process arousal-related information differently than do people who are not prone to experience panic attacks. That is, people with panic disorder seem characterized by cognitive biases favoring the interpretation of threat. A growing body of experimental research indicates that panickers are characterized by interpretive, attentional, and memory biases favoring threat. For example, when asked to provide explanations for ambiguous scenarios (e.g., "You feel discomfort in your chest area. Why?"), panic patients are prone to interpret them in a catastrophic manner (e.g., reacting to chest discomfort as indicative of heart attack rather than indigestion).

Panic patients are also characterized by attentional

biases favoring threat, as evinced by their responses on "emotional Stroop" tasks. In these tasks, subjects are shown words of positive, neutral, and negative emotional significance, and are asked to name the colors in which the words appear (on a computer screen) while ignoring the meanings of the words. Delays in color-naming occur when the meaning of the word captures the subject's attention despite the subject's effort to attend to the color of the word. In one experiment, panic patients exhibited delayed color naming for words related to fear (e.g., *panic*), bodily sensations (e.g., *breathless*), and catastrophe (e.g., *insane*). In another experiment, they exhibited greater interference for catastrophe words than for positive words of equivalent but opposite valence (e.g., *carefree*). These studies suggest that panic disorder is characterized by biases for selectively attending to threat cues.

Finally, other studies have shown that panic patients exhibit superior memory for words related to anxiety and threat. This memory bias for threat appears enhanced when patients are in a state of physiological arousal. Taken together, these results suggest that threat-related material may have preferential access to conscious mentation in these patients.

VIII. PSYCHOPHARMACOLOGIC TREATMENTS FOR PANIC

As noted earlier, the tricyclic antidepressant, imipramine, was the first compound shown effective against panic attacks. Patients need not be depressed for this drug to work against panic. The effects of imipramine are potentiated by combining it with exposure in vivo, a behavior therapy method (see below).

Unfortunately, a substantial minority of panic patients fail to tolerate the side effects of imipramine, which include increased heart rate and jitteriness. Some clinicians suggest slowly increasing dosage until a therapeutic effects are reached as a means of managing side effects.

High-potency benzodiazepines, such as alprazolam, have been used to treat panic disorder. Their side effects are less disagreeable, and these medications begin to exert their antipanic effects within days of commencing treatment in contrast to imipramine, which often takes weeks before benefits begin to appear. Disadvantages of these compounds include their capacity to induce pharmacologic and psychological depen-

dence; panic patients often find it difficult to cease taking alprazolam. This can pose a problem for women who wish to become pregnant, and therefore need to be free of alprazolam. Moreover, cessation of these compounds often results in the return of panic attacks, and sometimes these rebound panics are more intense than the attacks that had been occurring before the patient began taking alprazolam. Some evidence suggests that panic patients with agoraphobia who undergo otherwise effective in vivo exposure treatments do worse at follow-up if they had been taking alprazolam than if they had been taking placebo.

The selective serotonin reuptake inhibitors (SSRIs) have been widely prescribed for many psychiatric conditions in recent years. Originally developed as antidepressants, SSRIs, such as fluoxetine, have been recently used as antipanic agents. Indeed, the study reporting the most impressive evidence for the pharmacologic treatment of panic disorder tested the SSRI fluvoxamine. Although controlled research on the treatment of panic disorder with SSRIs has only recently begun, the consensus among psychopharmacologists is that SSRIs are the drug treatment of choice for panic disorder. The SSRIs appear to have more tolerable side effects than tricyclic antidepressants and they appear to be less likely to produce dependence than high-potency benzodiazepines. Limited data also suggest that relapse upon drug discontinuation may be less likely than relapse following discontinuation of alprazolam and similar compounds. [*See* PSYCHOPHARMACOLOGY.]

IX. PSYCHOLOGICAL TREATMENTS FOR PANIC

Despite differences in emphasis, most cognitive-behavior therapists treat panic as follows. Early sessions usually are designed to reduce the patient's anxiety sensitivity by providing the patient with basic information about panic attacks that counteracts the patient's catastrophizing tendencies. For example, one approach emphasizes that panic attacks reflect an adaptive, evolved fight-or-flight response that fires at inappropriate times. Under this view, panic attacks are not dangerous events but rather reflect an evolved mechanism for protecting against danger. Patients are also shown how they may inadvertently maintain their disorder by hypervigilantly monitoring their bodies for feared sensations and then misinterpreting them as harbingers of harm. [*See* BEHAVIOR THERAPY; COGNITIVE THERAPY.]

Some clinicians next train patients to use symptom (or panic) management techniques. These include respiratory control procedures for counteracting patients' tendencies to hyperventilate during panic attacks (and thus worsening them). Patients are taught to breathe by using their abdomen rather than just their upper chest, and are taught to breathe at a comfortable pace instead of gasping for air and making things worse. They are taught to breathe through the nose, not the mouth, as an additional means of counteracting hyperventilation. Patients are taught a technique called applied relaxation as another means of managing symptoms. This method first involves teaching them how to tense and relax different muscle groups in the clinic and to detect signs of tension. They are then given practice in applying these procedures while they engage in everyday activities. It is unclear whether these methods are effective because they blunt symptoms during episodes of panic, or whether they enhance the patient's sense of restoring control.

Inspired by the notion that panic attacks are akin to conditioned responses to the phobic stimuli of one's own bodily sensations, clinicians structure interoceptive exposure exercises. Interoceptive exposure refers to graduated, structured induction of feared bodily sensations done in a fashion so as to reduce the patient's fear of the sensations. Patients may be asked to run up stairs to increase heart rate, to breathe through a straw to increase breathlessness, and so forth. The rationale is that structured exposure to harmless bodily sensations reduces the patient's fear of them.

Just as the fear-of-fear hypothesis inspired the development of interoceptive exposure, so has the catastrophic misinterpretation hypothesis inspired cognitive techniques for refuting patient's beliefs about the harmfulness of bodily sensations. These beliefs are treated as experimental hypotheses, and therapists work with patients to evaluate the evidence for and against their catastrophic hypotheses and noncatastrophic alternative interpretations of bodily sensations. This approach entails the conducting of behavioral experiments. If, for example, a patient hypothesizes that dizziness leads one to collapse, the therapist might have the patient hyperventilate while sitting and then have the patient stand up quickly. The failure of the patient to collapse disconfirms the cata-

strophic hypothesis while confirming the noncatastrophic alternative that intense lightheadedness may produce unsteadiness, but not collapse. The basic notion behind these experiments is that patients often engage in subtle avoidance behavior in the midst of panic attacks that prevents their catastrophic beliefs from being tested and refuted. Thus, if patients always sit down when becoming dizzy and panicky, they will never learn that their feared catastrophe of collapse never occurs. The object of cognitive therapy is to provide these instructive learning experiences.

Finally, most patients with panic disorder have developed varying degrees of agoraphobic avoidance behavior. Although few become entirely housebound, most have restricted their lives to a considerable extent. Therefore, patients are urged to undertake in vivo (i.e., real-life) exposure exercises whereby they practice entering previously avoided situations and engaging in previously avoided activities. The general rule is for patients to remain in these situations until their discomfort has diminished. Although it was once believed that exiting a feared situation in the midst of a panic would automatically worsen the patient's fear and avoidance, subsequent research has indicated that this is not necessarily true. Even if a patient leaves the feared situation, no lasting exacerbation of fear seems to occur if the patient reenters the situation soon afterward.

The chief goal is to ensure that patients regularly practice engaging in feared activities. It is not essential that the therapist accompany the patient on these forays, but for highly avoidant patients, it is often helpful.

Most early psychological research on the treatment of panic disorder and agoraphobia concentrated on the reduction of fear and avoidance via exposure therapies. Although in vivo exposure does not directly target panic, catastrophic misinterpretations, and so forth, it has been shown to reduce (but not always to eliminate) panic attacks. Some studies have shown that the combination of imipramine and exposure is better than either alone, whereas adding alprazolam to exposure seems to reduce the effectiveness of the latter. There are no data on combined SSRI and behavioral treatment.

During the past several years, researchers have tested the efficacy of the cognitive-behavioral approach described above. This strategy eliminates panic attacks in approximately 80% to 90% of patients, and most retain their gains at follow-ups of 1 to 2 years posttreatment. Indeed, the percentages of patients who are panic-free at posttreatment are comparable and often higher than the percentages of panic-free patients who receive medication. Moreover, rates of relapse are lower after cognitive-behavior therapy than after drug treatment, probably because patients have learned not to react fearfully to bodily sensations and have therefore learned how not to let fear spiral into panic.

Moreover, cost-effectiveness analyses have confirmed that cognitive-behavioral treatment for panic is not only at least as effective in the short term as drug treatment, it is less expensive in the long term, and it does not generate side effects or pharmacologic dependence.

X. CONCLUSIONS

Although most researchers agree that panic attacks constitute emotional phenomena distinct from anxiety, there is no consensus about their cause. Biological researchers have identified several possible pathways that may give rise to unusual bodily sensations (e.g., noradrenergic overreactivity, carbon dioxide hypersensitivity), it is unlikely that one physiologic cause is the source of sensations in all patients. More likely,

several different biological abnormalities produce the sensations that patients fear.

Most data indicate that surges of sensations do not produce the emotional phenomenon of panic unless the person reacts to them as threatening stimuli. Taken together, the data suggest that panic disorder comprises abnormalities in both biology and cognition. Fortunately, effective treatments, both pharmacologic and cognitive-behavioral, are available.

BIBLIOGRAPHY

Barlow, D. H., & Craske, M. G. (1989). *Mastery of your anxiety and panic.* Albany, NY: Graywind.

Clark, D. M. (1986). A cognitive approach to panic. *Behav. Res. Ther., 24,* 461–470.

Eaton, W. W., Kessler, R. C., Wittchen, H. U., & Magee, W. J. (1994). Panic and panic disorder in the United States. *Am. J. Psychiat., 151,* 413–420.

Gould, R. A., Otto, M. W., & Pollack, M. H. (1995). Meta-analysis of treatment outcome for panic disorder. *Clin. Psychol. Rev., 15,* 819–844.

Klein, D. F. (1981). Anxiety reconceptualized. In D. F. Klein & J. G. Rabkin (Eds.), *Anxiety: New research and changing concepts* (pp. 235–263). New York: Raven Press.

Margraf, J., Barlow, D. H., Clark, D. M., & Telch, M. J. (1993). Psychological treatment of panic: Work in progress on outcome, active ingredients, and follow-up. *Behav. Res. Ther., 31,* 1–8.

McNally, R. J. (1994). *Panic disorder: A critical analysis.* New York: Guilford Press.

Paranoia

Allan Fenigstein
Kenyon College

Delusions   Faulty interpretations of reality that cannot be shaken, despite clear evidence to the contrary, and that are not shared by other members of the community.

Ideas of Reference   The misperception of oneself as the target of others' thoughts and actions; for example, a person seeing others laughing might relate the event to himself, and see himself as the target of their laughter.

Paranoia   A disordered mode of thought that is dominated by a pervasive, exaggerated, and unwarranted suspiciousness and mistrust of people, and a corresponding tendency to interpret the actions of others as deliberately threatening or demeaning.

Paranoid Illumination   The point at which the paranoid realizes that he has been singled out for mistreatment, and others are working against him; suddenly, everything begins to make sense.

Projection   A psychological defense often associated with paranoid thinking, in which the individual attributes one's own unacceptable motives or characteristics to others.

Pseudo-Community   A delusional system in which the paranoid organizes a variety of unrelated persons into a structured group whose primary purpose is to engage in a conspiracy against him.

Self-Focus   A behavioral style characteristic of paranoia, in which the individual is especially prone to be aware of himself as an object of attention to others.

Therapeutic Alliance   A tactic frequently used in treating paranoids, in which the therapist acknowledges the patient's delusional beliefs as understandable, in an attempt to build trust.

PARANOIA, although originally referring (in Greek) to almost any kind of mental aberration or bizarre thinking, is currently used to describe a disordered mode of thought that is dominated by an intense, irrational, but persistent mistrust or suspicion of people and a corresponding tendency to interpret the actions of others as deliberately threatening or demeaning. Because of the general expectation that others are against them or are somehow trying to exploit them, paranoid persons tend to be guarded, secretive, and ever vigilant, constantly looking for signs of disloyalty or malevolence in their associates. These expectations are easily confirmed: the hypersensitivity of paranoids turns minor slights into major insults, and even innocuous events are misinterpreted as harmful or vindictive. As a result, a pernicious cycle is set in motion whereby expectations of treachery and hostility often serve to elicit such reactions from others, thus confirming and justifying the paranoid's initial suspicion and animosity. Of all psychological disturbances, paranoia is among the least understood and most difficult to treat.

I. PARANOID SYNDROMES

Paranoid features are found in a variety of different psychological conditions. Although these conditions are often regarded as distinct, the criteria for distinction are not entirely clear and the practical utility of the distinction, in terms of etiology or treatment implications, has not been established. Thus, it may be useful to consider the different paranoid disorders as related syndromes existing along a continuum which varies in terms of the frequency and severity of paranoid thoughts, the degree to which reality is allowed to influence perceptions, and the extent to which functioning is impaired. The continuum extends from paranoid personality disorder, which is nondelusional, but where suspicion and its sequelae occur so regularly that work and family life are often disrupted; to delusional (paranoid) disorder, involving a chronic, dysfunctional delusional system, although apart from the delusion, reality testing is good and behavior is not obviously odd; and finally, to paranoid schizophrenia, a severe, incapacitating psychosis, involving a serious loss of contact with reality in which all thought is affected by the delusion.

A. Delusional (Paranoid) Disorder

The cardinal feature of this disorder is the presence of a delusion that is so systematic, logically developed, well-organized, and resistant to contradictory evidence, that others are often convinced by it. Delusions are faulty interpretations of reality that cannot be shaken, despite clear evidence to the contrary. Although the delusions in this disorder are nonbizarre (unlike those found in paranoid schizophrenia) and involve situations that may occur in real life, in fact they have no basis in reality, and are not shared by others in the culture. Delusional systems are usually idiosyncratic, but some themes or combination of themes are more frequently seen than others, and psychiatric diagnosis of this disorder is now specified by the predominant theme of the delusions present.

Delusions of persecution, in which the paranoid believes that "others are out to get me," are the most common form of this disorder. While those with a paranoid personality disorder may be suspicious that colleagues are talking about them behind their backs, persons with delusional disorder may go one step further and suspect others of participating in elaborate master plots to persecute them. They often believe that they are being poisoned, drugged, spied upon, or are the targets of conspiracies to ruin their reputations. Many of them tend to be inveterate "injustice-

detectors," inclined to take retributive actions of one sort or another, and are constantly embroiled in litigation or letter writing campaigns, in an attempt to redress imagined injustices.

Persons with delusions of grandiosity have an exaggerated sense of their own importance. In some cases, these beliefs are related to persecutory delusions, in that the paranoid eventually comes to feel that all the attention he's receiving is indicative of his superiority or unique abilities. Such exalted ideas usually center around messianic missions, extremist political movements, or remarkable inventions. Persons suffering from delusions of grandeur often feel that they have been endowed with special gifts or powers and, if allowed to exercise these abilities, they could cure diseases, banish poverty, or ensure world peace. When these efforts are ignored or thwarted, as they almost inevitably are, the paranoid may become convinced of a conspiracy directed against him.

Another theme frequently seen is that of delusional jealousy, in which any sign—even an apparent wrong number on the phone or a short delay in returning home—is summoned up as evidence that a spouse is being unfaithful. When the jealousy becomes irrationally pathological, and the paranoid becomes convinced beyond all reason that his spouse is cheating and plotting against him in an attempt to humiliate him, he may become violently dangerous.

An erotic delusion (also known as erotomania) is based on the belief that one is romantically loved by another, usually someone of higher status or a well-known public figure, although the other, presumably, cannot acknowledge it openly. Because of unrealistic expectations about the likelihood of living with the celebrity, these delusions often result in stalking or harassment of famous persons through incessant phone calls, letters, visits, and surveillance. When their love is not returned, these delusional individuals feel a sense of betrayal that may turn to rage and hatred. Although this disorder has been reported most often in women, it occurs in men as well (perhaps the best example being John Hinckley, whose erotomanic delusions involving the actress Jodie Foster led to his attempted assassination of then-President Ronald Reagan).

Those with somatic delusions are convinced that there is something very wrong with their bodies—that they emit foul odors, or have bugs crawling inside of them, or are misshapen. These delusions often result in an avoidance of others, except for physicians who, despite being accused of conspiring to deny the problem, are consulted continuously regarding the imagined condition.

The thinking and behavior of these individuals tend to become organized around the delusional theme in the form of a pathological "paranoid construction" that, for all its distortion of reality and loss of critical judgment, provides a sense of identity, importance, and meaning not otherwise available. The meaningfulness of delusions is also suggested by the fact that they often reflect the person's position in the social universe: Women and married men are most likely to have delusions with sexual content; foreign immigrants are most prone to have persecutory delusions; and people from higher socioeconomic levels are the most likely to have delusions of grandeur.

Once the basic delusion is accepted, other aspects of behavior, including emotional responses, may be described as appropriate and more or less conventional. Delusionally disordered persons do not suffer hallucinations or indications of other mental disorders, and their personalities do not change drastically; there are few exacerbations or remissions. There is a relatively high level of cognitive integration skills in areas that do not impinge on the delusional thought structure. Despite their mistrust, defensiveness, and fear of being exploited, they can sometimes function adequately, especially when their suspicions are limited to one specific area; for example, if they suspect poisoners everywhere, they may be satisfied if they can prepare all their own food. Their lives may be very limited and isolated, but they are just as likely to be regarded as harmless cranks than as someone requiring the help of a mental health professional.

Sometimes, however, the consequences of the delusions are debilitating and not so easy to manage; for example, a person suffering from delusions of persecution may assault an imagined persecutor or spend a fortune fleeing enemies and pursuing redress for imagined wrongs. In other instances, the disorder may be dangerous. In particular, paranoid delusional disorder may be overrepresented among fanatical reformers and self-styled prophets and cult leaders. These individuals may be especially attracted to an enterprise that encourages blaming others, regarding themselves as a victim, and putting themselves at the center of things. Especially in times of social cataclysm or uncertainty, their grandiosity and moralistic tendencies, as well as the logical and compelling presentation of their messi-

anic or political delusions, can often attract disciples. In addition, their garrison mentality is quite capable of provoking events which then serve to confirm their apocalyptic prophecies.

Much of the difficulty involved in diagnosing paranoid disorders is because of the slipperiness of the concept of delusion. Even in the real world, it is not always possible to determine the truth or falsity of an idea: Does the government keep track of unsuspecting individuals? Is our air and water filled with unseen toxins? Does our boss really have our best interests in mind? Some ideas that are patently false are held with sincere conviction by many; and even when an idea is held as preposterous by the majority, that majority may be wrong. How, then, do we evaluate the irrationality of an idea, or decide whether clearly eccentric and convoluted thinking merits the designation "delusional?" Although it may be difficult to distinguish reality from illusion, particularly when the belief system develops around a potentially real injustice, other indications may be diagnostically helpful. An inability to see facts in any other light or to place them in an appropriate context, a glaring lack of evidence for far-reaching conclusions, and a hostile, suspicious, and uncommunicative attitude when delusional ideas are questioned usually provides clues of pathology.

B. Paranoid Personality Disorder

Anyone starting in a new situation or relationship may be cautious and somewhat guarded until they learn that their fears are unwarranted. Those with paranoid personality disorder cannot abandon those concerns. Although not of sufficient severity to be considered delusional, theirs is a rigid and maladaptive pattern of thinking, feeling, and behavior, usually beginning by early adulthood, that is built upon mistrust, vigilance, and hostility. The conviction that others "have it in for them" represents their most basic and unrelenting belief; they feel constantly mistreated, and have a high capacity for annoying and provoking others.

Seeing the world as a threatening place, these individuals are preoccupied with hidden motives and the fear that someone may deceive or exploit them. They are inordinately quick to take offense, slow to forgive, and ready to counterattack at the first sign of imagined criticism, even in their personal relationships. Disordered paranoid personalities see references to themselves in everything that happens. If people are seen talking, the paranoid knows they are talking about him. If someone else gets a promotion, that person's advancement is seen as a deliberate attempt to humiliate him and downgrade his achievements. Even offers of help and concern are taken as implied criticisms of weakness or as subtle manipulations of indebtedness. The constant suspicions and accusations eventually strain interpersonal relations to the point where these individuals are in continual conflict with spouses, friends, and legal authorities.

Given their hypersensitivity, any speck of evidence that seems to confirm their suspicions is blown out of proportion, and any indication to the contrary is ignored or misinterpreted. Trivial incidents become accumulated and unconnected "facts" are fit together to create false, but unshakeable beliefs regarding their mistreatment. Because of their conviction that others are undermining their efforts or ruining their achievements, they tend to see themselves as blameless, instead finding fault for their own mistakes and failures in others, even to the point of ascribing evil motives to others.

Those with disordered paranoid personalities also tend to overvalue their abilities, and have an inflated sense of their rationality and objectivity, making it extraordinarily difficult for them either to question their own beliefs or to accept or even appreciate another's point of view. Unable to recognize the possibility of genuine dissent, simple disagreement by others becomes a sign of disloyalty. The resulting obstinacy, defensiveness, and self-righteousness exasperates and infuriates others, and elicits responses that exacerbate the conflict and confirm the original paranoid expectations.

In addition to being argumentative and uncompromising, paranoids appear cold and aloof, and emotionally cut off from others. They avoid intimacy, partly because they fear betrayal, partly in an attempt to maintain total control over their affairs, and partly because of profound deficits in their capacity for joy, warmth, and nurturance. The resulting social isolation, by limiting the opportunity to check social reality and learn from others, only reinforces their egocentric perspective.

Compared to some other paranoid pathologies, those with disordered personalities tend not to progressively worsen, but rather reach a certain level of severity and stay there. They show considerably less disorganization of personality, and they do not develop the kind of systematic and well-defined delusions found in delusional disorders. However, the proverbial kernel of truth is often greater in the suspicions of disordered paranoid personalities than in those with delusional disorders; their accusations have more plausibility and their paranoid attitudes are more diffuse. Because of the complexity and pervasiveness of personality disorders, these individuals may have more impoverished lives, although some do manage to function adequately in society, often by carving out a social niche in which a moralistic and punitive style is acceptable or at least tolerated.

C. Paranoid Schizophrenia

This major mental illness is one of the most common types of psychotic disorders. Paranoid schizophrenics may be distinguished from those with delusional disorder on the basis of the extreme bizarreness of their paranoid delusions, such as the belief that their thoughts or actions are being controlled by external forces, and by the presence of hallucinations (e.g., hearing voices) and other indications of a serious break with reality. The delusions of schizophrenics are not organized and systematic, but fragmentary and unconnected. Although these individuals may be suspicious and very much threatened by outside influences, their reaction, unlike that of the disordered paranoid personality, is usually hesitant and confused; their anger has no concentrated intensity. The behavioral, cognitive, and perceptual disorders of paranoid schizophrenics are so dysfunctional that performance on the job or at home almost invariably deteriorates, and emotional expressiveness becomes severely diminished.

These individuals commonly suffer from delusions of persecution, wherein they are convinced that they are constantly being watched or followed, and that strangers or government operatives or even alien beings are plotting against them with fantastic machines, undetectable poisons, or extraordinary mental powers. Of course, given the exceptional cunning and duplicity of these diabolical forces, virtually anything—a look, a sound, a bodily sensation, for that matter, even the absence of anything, a particularly shrewd maneuver—is seen as confirmation of one's suspicions. When the schizophrenic experiences the "paranoid illumination," and recognizes that all this overwhelming evidence fits together, the sense of his own visibility and vulnerability is profoundly increased, as is the tendency to misperceive himself as the target of other people's stares, comments, and laughter. In some cases, persecutory beliefs are accompanied by delusions of grandeur: that they are the target of these forces is only because they are special or powerful or dangerous. They may recognize that others reject them and their message, but they interpret these negative reactions as persecution based on jealousy, hostility, or enemy conspiracies.

Some paranoid schizophrenics avoid detection for long periods because their extreme suspiciousness encourages them to keep their "precious knowledge" secret. Moreover, although these individuals are deeply disturbed and are subject to intense panic (given their sense of imminent danger) and extreme excitement (over their irrational "discoveries"), many of them are not overtly bizarre or belligerent. [*See* Schizophrenia.]

D. Other Paranoid Disorders

Some paranoid thinking manifests itself in a less persistent form. Acute paranoid disorder, in which delusions develop quickly and last only a few months, sometimes appear after a sudden, stressful social change, such as emigration, prison, induction into military service, or even leaving a family home. Although these conditions are multifaceted, they all are associated with extreme social isolation, unfamiliarity with the appropriate customs and rules of behavior, a sense of vulnerability to exploitation, and a general loss of control over life, psychological factors which may play an important, albeit temporary, role in inducing episodes of paranoia.

Paranoid symptoms may also be a byproduct of physical illness, organic brain disease, or drug intoxication. Among organic illnesses, hypothyroidism, multiple sclerosis, Huntington's disease, and epileptic disorders, as well as Alzheimer's disease and other forms of dementia, are common causes of paranoia. In some people, alcohol stimulates a paranoid reaction even in small doses, and paranoia is a common feature of alcohol hallucinosis and alcohol withdrawal delirium. Chronic abuse of drugs, such as amphetamines, cocaine, marijuana, PCP, LSD, or other stimulants or psychedelic compounds, may produce some of the symptoms of paranoid personality disorder, and in high doses, may cause an acute psychosis that is almost indistinguishable from paranoid schizophrenia. These drugs may also exacerbate symptoms in persons already suffering from a paranoid disorder. [*See* Dementia; Substance Abuse.]

II. PREVALENCE

It is difficult to estimate the frequency of paranoia in the general population because many paranoids function well enough in society to avoid coming to the attention of professionals, and because their suspiciousness and intellectual arrogance usually prevent them from volunteering for treatment. While clinical diagnoses of paranoid disorders are rare, a more realistic picture of its actual occurrence is suggested by the many exploited inventors, morbidly jealous spouses, persecuted workers, fanatic reformers, and self-styled prophets who are often able to maintain themselves in the community without their paranoid condition being formally recognized.

Estimates of prevalence are further complicated by the fact that almost everyone engages in paranoid thinking at one time or another. Most people can think of an occasion when they thought that they were being watched or talked about, or felt as if everything was going against them, or were suspicious of someone else's motives without adequate proof that such things had actually occurred. Recent studies have shown that for a significant number of people, these paranoid beliefs represent a relatively stable personality pattern. Such paranoid personalities—although characterized by suspiciousness, self-centeredness, scapegoating tendencies, and a generally hostile attitude—apparently are capable of functioning reasonably well in society.

III. CAUSES OF PARANOIA

A. Biological Bases

1. Genetic Contribution

Although there is little research on the role of heredity in causing paranoia, there is some evidence from twin studies indicating that paranoid symptoms in schizophrenia may be genetically influenced. In addition, family studies suggest that features of the paranoid personality disorder occur disproportionately more often in families with members who have either delusional disorders or paranoid schizophrenia, suggesting that these syndromes may be genetically related. [*See* GE-NETIC CONTRIBUTORS TO MENTAL HEALTH.]

2. Biochemistry

No identifiable biochemical substrate or demonstrable neuropathology relates specifically to paranoid thought or delusions; that is, there is no brain system whose dysfunction would specifically produce the psychological characteristics associated with paranoia. Although the abuse of drugs, such as amphetamines, may lead to paranoid symptoms, thus suggesting a possible biochemical pathway, no such pathway has been identified; whatever drug effects have been found may be psychologically, and not biochemically, mediated.

B. Psychological Bases

In the absence of a clear organic basis or effective drug treatment for paranoia, most researchers have sought to identify the psychological mechanisms that explain how paranoid ideas become fixed in the mind.

I. Psychodynamic Theory

Of all psychological theories, Freud's is perhaps the best known, although it is increasingly challenged. He believed that paranoia was a form of repressed homosexual love. According to Freud, paranoia arises, at least in men, when a child's homosexual feelings for his father are preserved but driven into the unconscious, from which they re-emerge during an adult emotional crisis, converted into suspicions and delusions by projection—the attribution of one's own unacknowledged wishes and impulses to another person. That is, before reaching consciousness, the impulses undergo some kind of transformation that disguise their homosexual origin; for example, a man suffering from paranoid jealousy, unable to acknowledge that he himself loves another man, projects that feeling onto his wife and becomes convinced that it is his wife who loves the man.

Although Freud's theory of unconscious homosexuality has been largely discredited, projection is still recognized as a basic mechanism used by paranoids to defend against their feelings. Paranoids will explain their sense of helplessness by pointing to the control exerted by others; or self-critical ideas are transformed into the belief that others are criticizing them. Viewing others as hostile not only justifies the paranoid's feeling of being threatened, it may actually elicit the other's anger,

thus confirming the paranoid's original assumption. As a result, paranoids are left feeling weakly vulnerable, but morally righteous. [*See* DEFENSE MECHANISMS.]

2. Faulty Development

Rather than emphasizing unconscious dynamics, other approaches have viewed paranoid thinking as the outcome of a complex interaction of personality traits, social skills, and environmental events, some of which may be traced to early family dynamics. Paranoids, even as children, were often described as aloof, suspicious, secretive, stubborn, and resentful of punishment. Rarely was there a history of normal play with other children, or good socialization with warm, affectionate relationships. Their family background was often authoritarian, and excessively dominating and critical. Paranoid persons may dread being watched and judged because, it has been suggested, that reminds them of their parents, who were distant, demanding, and capricious.

This inadequate socialization may have kept them from learning to understand others' motives and points of view which, in turn, may have led to a pattern of suspicious misinterpretation of unintentional slights. Social relationships tended to be suffused with hostile, domineering attitudes that drove others away. These inevitable social failures further undermined self-esteem and led to deeper social isolation and mistrust. In essence, these individuals emerged from childhood with deeply internalized struggles involving issues of hostility, victimization, power, submission, weakness, and humiliation. In later development, these early trends merged to create self-important, egocentric, and arrogant individuals, who maintained their unrealistic self-image and a sense of control by projecting blame for their problems onto others, and seeing weaknesses in others that they could not acknowledge in themselves. Their suspicion and hypersensitivity were made even more problematic by their utter inability to see things from any viewpoint but their own.

3. The Paranoid "Illumination" and the Paranoid Pseudo-Community

Other theorists have focused, not on early family history, but on the later emergence of a fixed, unyielding paranoid belief system. Given the paranoid's rigidity, self-importance, and suspiciousness, he is likely to become a target of actual discrimination and mistreatment; and ever alert to such occurrences, the paranoid is likely to find abundant "proof," both real and imagined, of persecution. The cycle of misunderstanding is then perpetuated by the paranoid's subsequent responses. The belief that others are plotting against him results in hostile, defensive behavior. This in turn elicits the others' anger and irritability in response to the paranoid's apparently unprovoked hostility, thus confirming the paranoid's original suspicion that they are out to get him. This cycle of aggression and counter-aggression has also been offered as one explanation for the greater prevalence of paranoia among males than females. The paranoid's inability to consider the others' perspective—that the other may be operating out of defensiveness against the paranoid's antagonism and belligerence—only exacerbates the conflict. [*See* AGGRESSION.]

As failures and seeming betrayals mount, the paranoid, to avoid self-devaluation, searches for "logical" explanations. He becomes more vigilant in his scrutiny of the environment, looking for hidden meanings and asking leading questions. Eventually, a meaningful picture, in the form of the "paranoid illumination," crystallizes and everything begins to make sense: he has been singled out for some obscure reason, and others are working against him. Failure is not because of any inferiority on his part, but rather because of some conspiracy or plot directed at him. With this as his fundamental defensive premise, he proceeds to distort and falsify the facts to fit the premise, and gradually develops a logical, fixed delusional system, referred to as the "pseudocommunity," in which the paranoid organizes surrounding people (real and imaginary) into a structured group whose purpose is centered on his victimization. As each additional experience is misconstrued and interpreted in light of the delusional idea, more and more events, persons, and experiences become effectively incorporated into the delusional system. Because the delusion meaningfully integrates all the vague, disturbing, amorphous, and unrelated "facts" of his existence, the paranoid is unwilling to accept any other explanation and is impervious to reason or logic; any questioning of the delusion only convinces him that the interrogator has sold out to the enemy.

4. Anomalous Perceptions

Another theory offers the intriguing hypothesis that delusions are the result of a cognitive attempt to account for aberrant or anomalous sensory experiences. For example, research has shown that persons with visual or hearing loss—because of both heightened suspiciousness and an attempt to deny the loss—may conclude that others are conspiring to conceal things from them. The experience of many elderly people, who are a high risk group for paranoia, provides a particularly good example of this phenomena. These individuals, because of physical disability or social isolation, often feel especially vulnerable. These realistic feelings may be converted to paranoia by an unacknowledged loss of hearing. That is, an awareness of oneself as a potential victim of greedy relatives or petty criminals, together with an increased sense that others are whispering, may contribute to a growing suspicion that others are whispering about them, or harassing them, or perhaps planning to steal from them. When the others angrily deny the accusation, that only reinforces the conspiratorial delusion, and intensifies the cycle of hostility and suspicion.

The occurrence of paranoia in those with degenerative brain disorders, such as Alzheimer's disease, may be explained through a similar process. These diseases commonly involve a disruption of memory that victims may be unwilling to acknowledge. As a result, failures of memory become an anomalous experience that needs to be explained. For example, not being able to locate one's keys is transformed into the belief that someone else has stolen or misplaced them. This suspicion may then be incorporated with actual perceptions, such as seeing one's child speaking to the doctor, to produce the conviction that others are conspiring to confuse the patient in order to put them away. [*See* ALZHEIMER'S DISEASE.]

The general hypothesis that anomalous experience may be the basis for paranoia assumes that the process by which delusional beliefs are formed is very similar to the process that operates in the formation of normal beliefs; that is, delusions are not the result of a disturbed thought process, but arise because of abnormal sensory or perceptual experiences. Anomalous experiences demand an explanation, and in the course of developing hypotheses and testing them through observations, the delusional insight is confirmed through selective evidence. This explanation offers relief in the form of removing uncertainty, and the relief in turn works against abandonment of the explanation.

5. Stress

A related explanation may account for the often observed association between paranoia and stressors such as social isolation, economic deprivation, and abrupt situational changes. These conditions generally involve feelings of confusion, vulnerability, and a loss of control, suggesting that, in some ways, paranoid thought may serve to impose meaning and control in an otherwise uncertain and threatening environment. The paranoid belief that others are responsible for one's own misfortune, although threatening and irrational, may still be preferable to the belief that one is responsible for one's own misfortune or that such misfortune is a purely random event. In this regard, it is possible that the paranoid thinking which often develops as a result of acute drug intoxication (for example, amphetamine abuse), or aging (and its concomitant sensory loss and social isolation), or degenerative brain disorders (such as Alzheimer's disease) may be mediated by the confusion and vulnerability often found in these conditions. [See STRESS.]

6. Biases in Information Processing

Some of the approaches discussed thus far have emphasized the fact that, apart from the paranoid construction itself, the cognitive functioning of paranoids is essentially intact. In fact, given their delusional system, paranoid reactions are not unlike the biased tendencies of many individuals with strong belief systems, who are likely to exaggerate, distort, or selectively focus on events which are consistent with their beliefs. Once the paranoid suspects that others are working against him, he starts carefully noting the slightest signs pointing in the direction of his suspicions, and ignores all evidence to the contrary. With this frame of reference, it is quite easy, especially in a highly competitive, somewhat ruthless world, for any event, no matter how innocuous, to be selectively incorporated into the delusion. This, in turn, leads to a vicious cycle: suspicion, distrust, and criticism of others drives people away, keeps them in continual friction with others, and generates new incidents for the paranoid to magnify. [See INFORMATION PROCESSING AND CLINICAL PSYCHOLOGY.]

Although these information processing biases serve to maintain the paranoid's beliefs once they are established, they do not address the question of the origin of paranoid beliefs. The essence of paranoia is a malfunctioning of the capacity to assign meanings and understand causes for events. Ordinarily, these cognitive processes operate in a reasonably logical and objective fashion. In paranoia, such objective assessments are overwhelmed by judgments and interpretations that

bear little relation to what actually happened, but instead are perverted in accord with the paranoid's own concerns and interests. The persistent misperception of oneself as the target of others' thoughts and actions, referred to as an idea or delusion of reference, is the hallmark characteristic of almost all forms of paranoid thought. Even when there is no basis for making any connection, paranoids tend to perceive others' behavior as if it is more relevant to the self than is actually the case as, for example, when the laughter of others is assumed to be self-directed, or the appearance of a stranger on the street is taken to mean that one is being watched or plotted against. Why does the paranoid consistently feel singled out or targeted by others?

a. Paranoia and Self-Focus Part of the answer may lie in the characterization of paranoia as a very self-focused style of functioning. Recent studies have suggested that self-awareness, or the ability of an individual to recognize itself as an object of attention, heightens the tendency to engage in paranoid inferences. In essence, to see oneself as an object of attention, particularly to others, leaves a person susceptible to the paranoid idea that he is being targeted by others. Apparently, as a result of recognizing the self as an object of attention, the self is more likely to be interjected into the interpretation of others' behavior, thus transforming insignificant and irrelevant events into ones that appear to have personal relevance for the self. Self-focus not only relates directly to paranoid ideas of reference, it has important implications for other critical aspects of paranoid thought.

b. Personalism and Intent Unfortunate things happen to everyone, and usually they are dismissed as random or chance events. But paranoids rarely accept the idea that bad things just happen; instead they are likely to believe that it is someone else's doing. Why? Because events that are taken personally or are seen as uniquely targeted toward the self, are more likely to be understood in terms of others' personal characteristics or intentions. For the paranoid, the negative event itself is evidence for others' malevolent intentions toward them. Eventually, the accumulation of such events constitutes evidence for a fundamentally irrational view of the world as a hostile and threatening place. Once the assumption of ubiquitous danger is accepted, the other manifestations of paranoia become comprehensible: suspicion and guardedness; selective attention and memory for signs of trickery or exploitation; misinterpretation of apparently harmless events as malevolent; and blaming others for all of one's difficulties. Moreover, when negative events are seen not as fortuitous occurrences, but as personally intended by others, hostilities become intensified and enemies are found everywhere.

c. Egocentricity

One of the critical elements of paranoid thinking is the utter inability to understand the motivations and perspectives of others. Not only are paranoids more likely to misinterpret the other's behavior, they are less likely to correct that misinterpretation by altering their point of view. The narrowness and rigidity of paranoid thought—the failure to examine events critically or in a broader context, the ability to fit anything into one's belief system, the unwillingness to consider ever changing one's mind—is, in large part, the result of being locked into one's own perspective. Although social isolation may account, in part, for this deficit in role taking, self-focused attention may also contribute to the self-centeredness of paranoids. Attention directed toward the self interferes with the ability to take the role of another or appreciate the existence of alternative perspectives. As a result, paranoids are likely to assume that others share their own view of events, and fail to appreciate the way in which their own actions are viewed by others. Thus, in a typical encounter, they are unlikely to consider how their own behavior provokes the hostility of others, but instead are likely to see themselves as the innocent victim of the other's hostility. Self-focus may also play a role in the egocentric tendency of paranoids to project their own characteristics onto others.

IV. TREATMENT OF PARANOIA

Treatment of paranoia is extraordinarily difficult for a number of reasons. First, little is known about the causes that presumably are to be treated. Second, it is difficult for the paranoid to recognize a problem when he is locked into his own perspective and is reluctant to accept another's viewpoint. Finally, it is nearly impossible for therapists to penetrate the barrier of suspiciousness. For all these reasons, paranoids are generally unlikely and unwilling to enter therapy; and once in therapy, their wariness often leads them to sabotage treatment, or break it off prematurely. Paranoids also generally refuse to take responsibility for their treatment, because the only problems they see

are those created by the people intent upon harming them. In addition, the disclosure of personal information or other aspects of therapy may represent a loss of control, especially to male paranoids.

Mistrust obviously serves to undermine the therapeutic relationship. Any expression of friendliness or concern by the therapist is likely to arouse suspicion or be taken as confirmation that others are trying to humiliate them. Any questions or suggestions are likely to be seen as criticisms or attacks. Even if therapy improves other aspects of the paranoid's functioning, their delusional system is so strenuously defended, and so easily confirmed by "clues" detected in the therapeutic situation, that it often remains intact, yielding a highly unfavorable prognosis for complete recovery.

Because of the paranoid patient's guardedness and insistence on their own correctness, an effective therapeutic approach usually focuses on trust building rather than direct confrontation of the delusional beliefs. Perhaps the most powerful strategy is to establish rapport by forming a "therapeutic alliance" in which the therapist recognizes whatever kernel of trust exists in a paranoid system, and acknowledges the delusional beliefs as powerful, convincing, and understandable. The therapist can then try to identify the ways in which these beliefs may interfere with the patient's goals or create frustration for others as well as for the patient. The patient's paranoid reactions have usually driven others away or incited them to counterattack, heightening the cycle of suspicion and hostility. The therapist can sometimes bring about change by providing a different, empathic response that serves as a model of nonparanoid behavior. The task is then to help the paranoid become more competent at discriminating real threats from perceived ones, and the final step is the development of more adaptive responses to real or even ambiguous threats.

Behavioral theory assumes that paranoids have learned to be hypersensitive to the judgments of others and, as a result, they behave in ways that invite just the sort of reaction they anticipate and fear. As others begin to avoid them, they become socially isolated and develop increasingly elaborate suspicions that maintain the isolation. Behavior therapy tries to break the cycle by first using relaxation and anxiety management to teach the patient to be less sensitive to criticism, and then improving social skills by training the patient to act in ways that will not invite attack or avoidance. The patient can also be given help with recognition and avoidance of situations that produce or increase delusions. Paranoid thinking can in some cases be altered by aversive conditioning or the removal of factors that reinforce maladaptive behavior. [*See* Behavior Therapy.]

This article has been reprinted from the *Encyclopedia of Human Behavior, Volume 3.*

BIBLIOGRAPHY

Akhtar, S. (1990). Paranoid personality disorder: A synthesis of developmental, dynamic, and descriptive features. *Am. J. Psychother.* **44,** 5–25.

Bentall, R. P., Kaney, S., & Dewey, M. E. (1991). Paranoia and social reasoning: An attribution theory analysis. *Br. J. Clin. Psychol.* **30,** 13–23.

Cameron, N. (1943). The development of paranoic thinking. *Psychol. Rev.* **50,** 219–233.

Fenigstein, A., & Vanable, P. A. (1992). Paranoia and self-consciousness. *J. Pers. Soc. Psychol.* **62,** 129–138.

Kaney, S., & Bentall, R. P. (1989). Persecutory delusions and attributional style. *Br. J. Med. Psychol.* **62,** 191–198.

Magaro, P. A. (1980). "Cognition in Schizophrenia and Paranoia: The Interpretation of Cognitive Processes." Erlbaum, Hillsdale, NJ.

Maher, B. A. (1988). Anomalous experience and delusional thinking: The logic of explanations. In "Delusional Beliefs" (T. F. Oltmanns and B. A. Maher, Eds.), Wiley, New York.

Shapiro, D. (1965). "Neurotic Styles." Basic Books, New York.

Williams, J. G. (1988). Cognitive intervention for a paranoid personality disorder. *Psychotherapy* **25,** 570–575.

Zimbardo, P. G., Andersen, S. M., & Kabat, L. G. (1981). Induced hearing deficit generates experimental paranoia. *Science* **212,** 1529–1531.

Parenting

Marc H. Bornstein

National Institute of Child Health and Human Development

Childhood The period before birth until the attainment of maturity or majority status in a society, which may be age restricted (18 years), or physically or psychologically defined (menstruation).

Compensatory Care Caregiving that (for whatever antecedent cause) returns a child to accepted states of health or development.

Didactic Caregiving Strategies parents use to stimulate children to engage and understand the environment and to enter the world of learning. Didactics include introducing, mediating, and interpreting the external world; teaching, describing, and demonstrating; provoking or providing opportunities to observe, to imitate, and to learn.

Material Caregiving The ways in which parents provision, organize, and arrange the child's physical world, especially the home and local environment. Adults are responsible for the number and variety of inanimate objects (toys, books, tools) available to the child, the level of ambient stimulation, the limits on physical freedom, and the overall safety and physical dimensions of children's experiences.

Nurturant Caregiving Meeting the biological, physical, and health requirements of childhood. Parents are responsible for promoting children's wellness and preventing their illness. Parents in virtually all higher species nurture their young, providing sustenance, routine care, protection, supervision, grooming, comfort, and the like. Nurturance is prerequisite to children's survival and well-being.

Social Caregiving The behaviors parents use to engage children and manage their interpersonal exchanges. Rocking, kissing, tactile comforting, smiling, vocalizing, and playful face-to-face contact are illustrative of parent–child interpersonal interactions designed to make a child feel valued, accepted, and approved of as a person. Social caregiving also includes helping children to regulate their own affect and emotions, and encompasses planning family activities and assigning duties to family members, and monitoring and managing children's interpersonal relationships with others, such as relatives, nonfamilial caregivers, and peers.

Specificity Specific experiences parents provide children at specific times exert specific effects over specific aspects of child growth in specific ways as opposed to overall level of parental stimulation directly affecting children's overall level of functioning.

Stimulating Care Caregiving that normally serves to promote child health and development.

Transaction Experiences shape the characteristics of an individual through time just as, reciprocally, the characteristics of an individual shape experiences. Parent and child bring distinctive characteristics to, and parent and child alike are believed to change as a result of, their mutual interactions.

PARENTING It is the principal and continuing task of parents in each generation to prepare children of the next generation for the physical, economic, and psychosocial situations in which they must survive and thrive. Parents are the "final common pathway" to childhood oversight and caregiving, development and stature, adjustment and success. Parenting combines shared cultural constructions with direct experiences with children and with specific tasks. Human beings appear to possess some intuitive knowledge about parenting; that is, some characteristics of parenting may be a part of our biological makeup. Human beings also acquire additional understandings of parenting simply by living in a culture: Generational, social, and media images of parenting, children, and family life—handed down or ready-made—play significant roles in helping people form their parenting beliefs and guide their parenting behaviors. Notably, parents from different cultures differ in the ages they expect children to reach different milestones or acquire various competencies, and they differ in their opinions about the significance of specific competencies for their children's successes. Direct experiences with children and the self-constructive aspects of parenting are equally important factors in the formulation of parenting attitudes and actions. Parenting has intrinsic positives for parents. Parenting entails responsibilities in its purview. Parents vary in their parenting. The nature and dimensions of parenting per se, conditions of parenting, and recurrent themes in parenting as well as prerequisites for parenting, present-day problems of parenting, and parenting programs are addressed in this article.

I. THE PROPER PLACE OF PARENTS IN THE CHILD'S WORLD

States Parties agree that the education of the child shall be directed to:

(a) The development of the child's personality, talents and mental and physical abilities to their fullest potential; . . .

(c) The development of respect for the child's parents, his or her own cultural identity, language and values, for the national values of the country in which the child is living, the country from which he or she may originate, and for civilizations different from his or her own;

Article 29
Convention on the Rights of the Child

Parents create people. It is the principal and continuing task of parents in each generation to prepare chil-

dren of the next generation for the physical, economic, and psychosocial situations in which they must survive and thrive. Many factors influence the development of children, but parents are the "final common pathway" to childhood oversight and caregiving, development and stature, adjustment and success. Childhood is the phase of the life cycle when parenting is believed to exert its most significant and salient influences: Not only is the sheer amount of interaction between parent and child greatest then, but children may be particularly susceptible and responsive to parent-provided experiences. Indeed, the opportunity of enhanced parental influence and prolonged childhood learning is thought to be the evolutionary reason for the extended duration of human childhood.

Yet, as the twentieth century closes, parenting is under "friendly fire" on account of strong secular and historical trends operating in modern society. These advancing forces include industrialization, urbanization, widespread poverty, the decline in fertility and family size, increasing population growth and density, longevity and mortality patterns, and the changing constellation of the family structure itself. Migration, both rural-to-urban and international, has also altered the family, sometimes separating male from female partners or one generation from another. Likewise, the growth of maternal employment reflects an increasingly erosive issue for parenting: The second half of the twentieth century has witnessed an impressive increase in the number of women working in the paid labor force (both as a proportion of the total labor force and as a proportion of women 15 years of age and older). Women's labor force participation peaks between 25 and 44 years, which is also the period when women normally experience demanding childcare responsibilities. These diverse factors contribute to the single most significant change in family structure that has occurred in the last quarter century, the great number of female-headed households. In addition to these several social processes, cultural phenomena that impact the family include changing belief systems, religious transformations, and social values. Finally, society at large is also witnessing the emergence of striking permutations on the theme of parenting: rising single parenthood, divorced and blended families, lesbian and gay parents, teen versus fifties first-time moms and dads.

In short, the family generally, and parenting specifically, are today in an agitated state of question, flux, and redefinition. Societywide changes have exerted many unfortunately debilitative influences on parenting, interaction patterns between parents and children, and consequently on children and their development. In response, organizations at all levels of society increasingly feel the necessity to intercede in childrearing, that is to right some of society's ills through family intervention. This trend too leads away from a focus on parents as the proximal protectors, providers, and proponents of their own progeny. Yet, parents are children's primary advocates and their frontline defense. They are the corps available in the greatest numbers to lobby and labor for children, and they have earliest and continuing access to children. Insofar as parents can be enlisted and empowered to provide children with environments and experiences that optimize child development, after-the-fact remediation is obviated: An ounce of proper parenting reduces the need for cure with children. Historians of family life contend that parents in early times cared for but resisted emotional investment in young children, a circumstance that persists today mostly where especially dire circumstances prevail. Parents have generally improved in their orientation to and treatment of the young because parents seem to have, through successive generations, developed in their ability to identify and empathize with the special qualities of childhood. In short, few sentient parents *want* to abrogate childrearing responsibilities. Quite the opposite, virtually all parents respond to the natural inclination to *want only the best* for their children.

Significantly, contemporary family research teaches that parenting combines shared cultural constructions with direct experiences with children and with specific tasks. Adults already know (or think they know) something about parenting by the time they first become parents. Human beings appear to possess some intuitive knowledge about parenting; that is, some characteristics of parenting may be "wired" into our biological makeup. For example, parents speak to babies even though they know that babies cannot understand language and will not respond, and parents even speak to babies in a special speech register. Human beings also acquire additional understandings of parenting simply by living in a culture: Generational, social, and media images of parenting, children, and family life—handed down or ready-made—play significant roles in helping people form their parenting beliefs and guide their parenting behaviors. Thus, par-

ents from different cultures differ in the ages they expect children to reach different milestones or acquire various competencies, and they differ in their opinions about the significance of specific competencies for their children's success in social adjustment. Direct experiences with children and the self-constructive aspects of parenting are equally important factors in the formulation of parenting attitudes and actions. On the one hand, the family life of the later born child is not the same as that of the firstborn child for many reasons, some of which have to do with parents' changing experiences of parenting. On the other, achieving successful parenting implies psychological understanding and interpretation and the confidence to enact culturally defined programs. One important consequence of this emerging complex view of the origins and conduct of parenting is that parenting can be influenced and modified through education and cultural climate.

This article undertakes a review of several key topics in *parenting* normal (not clinical) populations. They include the positives of parenting for parents, the purview of parenting, who parents, persistent versus protean aspects of parenting, prerequisites for parenting, present-day problems of parenting, as well as parenting programs. The article is concerned less with child outcomes of parenting, and more with the nature and dimensions of parenting per se, conditions of parenting, and recurrent themes in parenting.

Parenting is a principal reason why individuals are who they are, and are often so different from one another. Most contemporary research about parenting is of Western origin. Much less is currently known scientifically about non-Western families, children, and parents. Indeed, to paraphrase one critic, three different cultural limitations have constrained the scope of understanding parenting: a narrow subject data base, a biased sampling of world cultures in its authorship, and a corresponding bias in the audience to which it is addressed. Moreover, for good or ill, researchers in many cultures have been schooled almost exclusively in the framework of Western social science. Therefore, many thinkers about parenting use (if not embrace) similar concepts and paradigms. Of course, projecting Western ideas onto the behavior and experience of peoples developing within different cultural contexts is problematic. Adults in different cultures adopt some different orientations to parenting. Indeed, at the very heart of the concept culture is the expectation that different peoples possess different values, beliefs, and motives, and behave in different ways. This article presents a synopsis of theory, data, and principles about parenting derived from the body of available Western research. The categories and determinations of parenting represented are, therefore, weighted by a Western orientation. Some may apply outside the context in which they were derived; others may not "travel" so well. An issue for the reader to bear in mind is the cultural generalizability versus the cultural specificity of principles of parenting. However, parents in different cultures also show some striking similarities in interacting with their children. Such similarity could reflect an inherent truism of caregiving, or the historical convergence of parenting styles, or the increasing prevalence of homogeneous childrearing patterns through migration or dissemination via mass media. In the end, different peoples (presumably) wish to promote similar general competencies in their young, and they may do so in some manifestly similar ways. Others appear to do so in different ways, however. Significantly, specific patterns of childrearing are adapted to each specific culture's settings and needs.

II. POSITIVES OF PARENTING FOR PARENTS

1. States Parties recognize the right of the child to the enjoyment of the highest attainable standard of health and to facilities for the treatment of illness and rehabilitation of health.

(d) To ensure appropriate pre-natal and post-natal health care for mothers;

(e) To ensure that all segments of society, in particular parents and children, are informed, have access to education and are supported in the use of basic knowledge of child health and nutrition, the advantages of breast-feeding, hygiene and environmental sanitation and the prevention of accidents;

(f) To develop preventive health care, guidance for parents and family planning education and services.

Article 24
Convention of the Rights of the Child

Adults are motivated by a strong self-interest to be good parents. Parenting has its own intrinsic privileges and profits. Becoming a parent enhances a person's psychological development, self-confidence, and sense of well-being. Parenting children augments adult self-esteem and fulfillment and gives adults ample opportunity to test and display diverse competencies. Parents can also find interest and derive much pleasure in

their relationships and activities with their children. Furthermore, parenting translates into a constellation of new adult trusts and often affords a unique view of the "larger picture" of life. At the very least, these observations hold for the educated, affluent, and less stressed among parents. But, sociobiological theories of human evolution assert that *all* individuals are compelled to see their childbearing and childrearing succeed on the argument that it is in that way that their genes continue.

Becoming or being a parent means having new and vital responsibilities to oneself as well as to others. When women are inadequately nourished, for example, their health and social development may be compromised, *and* their ability to bear healthy children is threatened. Malnourished women fall ill more often, *and* they have smaller babies. Where birth rates are high, infant and child mortality is also high, thereby increasing the stress on women's bodies and trapping them and their children in a cycle of poor health and nutrition.

Parents everywhere appear, at least at first, to be highly motivated to carry out the many tasks associated with the parenting role, and children likewise reciprocate the investment of their parents. *Children influence their parents just as parents influence their children.* Parents recognize and appreciate the human beings in their care. From infancy, children also show that they recognize and prefer the sights, sounds, and smells of their caregivers, and over the course of just the first year of life children develop deep and life-long attachments to their parents. The parent–child relationship is a two-way street from which parents and children alike may benefit.

III. THE PURVIEW OF PARENTING

1. States Parties recognize the right of every child to a standard of living adequate for the child's physical, mental, spiritual, moral and social development.

2. The parent(s) or others responsible for the child have the primary responsibility to secure, within their abilities and financial capabilities, the conditions of living necessary for the child's development.

Article 27
Convention on the Rights of the Child

Parenting children is a 168-hour-a-week job. That is because young human children are totally dependent on their parents for survival. Childhood is also a period normally attended to and invested in by parents the world over. Parenting responsibilities are greatest during childhood; reciprocally, at least the youngest children depend on caregiving, their ability to cope alone is minimal, and they seem to profit most from parent care.

During the early course of life span, the child transforms from an immature being unable to move his or her limbs in a coordinated manner to a more mature one who controls complicated sequences of muscle contractions and flections in order to walk, reach, or grasp; and from one who can only cry or babble to one who makes needs and desires abundantly clear with articulate language. Childhood is the time when people first make sense of and understand objects in the world, forge their first social bonds, and first learn how to express and read basic human emotions. In childhood, individual personalities and social styles also first develop. Parents escort children through all these dramatic "firsts." Not surprisingly, all of these developmental dynamics are closely tracked by parents, all are shaped by parents, and all, in turn, shape parenting. Moreover, influences of these developments reverberate through the balance of childhood: In the short-term, a history of shared work and play activities with parents is positively linked to the child's smooth transition into school, and parents' involvement with their children's school-related tasks relates positively to their children's school performance. In the view of some social theorists, the child's first observations of parents and first relationships with parents set the tone and style for all of the child's later social relationships.

Human children do not and cannot grow up as solitary individuals; parenting constitutes an initial and all-encompassing ecology of child development. In effect, adult or other more mature caregivers are responsible for determining most, if not all, of young children's earliest experiences. Mothers and fathers as well as other caregivers (including siblings and other family members as well as children's nonfamilial daycare providers) guide the development of their children via many direct and indirect means. *Direct effects* are of two kinds: genetic and experiential. Biological parents endow a significant and pervasive *genetic makeup* to their children . . . with its beneficial or other consequences. Although genes certainly contribute to children's proclivities and abilities in many different domains of growth and development, all

prominent theories of development put *experience* in the world as either the principal source of individual growth or as a major contributing component. It falls mostly to parents and caregivers to provide and to shape their children's experiences; parents directly influence child development both by the beliefs they hold and by the behaviors they exhibit.

Parents' and caregivers' *beliefs* constitute a significant force at work in the development of children. Whether they are perceptions about, attitudes toward, or knowledge of parenting, parenting beliefs are generally recognized to play telling parts in the development of children. Seeing oneself in a particular way vis-à-vis children may lead to certain affect, thinking, and behavior in childrearing situations. Seeing childhood in a particular way functions likewise: Parents who believe that they can or cannot affect their children's temperament, intelligence, or what have you modify their parenting accordingly. Finally, seeing one's own children in a particular way can have similar consequences: Difficult children may solicit avoidance from their parents, but parents who regard their children as being difficult are also less likely to pay attention or respond to their children's overtures. In turn, inattentiveness and nonresponsiveness inhibit child growth. In this way, parental perceptions themselves foster temperamental difficulty because they lead adults to treat children more negatively. Significantly, parents in different cultures possess different beliefs about the meaning and significance of their own parenting behaviors as well as the behaviors and development of their children, and parents act on these culturally defined beliefs about children, as much as they do on their own experiences with children.

Perhaps most salient in the phenomenology of childhood, however, are parents' or caregivers' *behaviors,* the tangible experiences these individuals provide. Until the time that children participate in informal or formal social learning situations outside the family, like play groups and school, virtually all of their worldly experiences stem directly from interactions they have within the family. In this context, at least in Western cultures, two adult caregiving figures—mom and dad—are normally responsible for determining the constellation of their children's life experiences. This situation can be constructed as a "vertical" social relationship. That is, initially there is asymmetry in parent and child contributions: Responsibility for development in early childhood lies unambiguously with parents. The individuals hold unequal power and authority vis-à-vis one another and their interactions tend to be complementary and asymmetrical. Nonetheless, some are "horizontal" meaning they are more egalitarian, cooperative, symmetrical, and collaborative. Middle childhood youngsters and adolescents play increasingly active and anticipatory roles in vertical interactions with parents, and they also engage more and more often in horizontal interactions with peers. In early childhood, displays of affection and compromise illustrate reciprocity between parent and child; in adolescence, joint decision making is an important horizontal component of the relationship. Horizontal interactions can have beneficial effects in, for example, promoting autonomy and an all-important sense of self in the child. Departures from the normal vertical relationship can have adverse consequences, however, in that an overly egalitarian parent–child relationship denies the child the nurturance, knowledge, and limit-setting that are requisite to successful socialization.

The mechanisms of socialization of children are several and worthy of note. Parents may hold certain beliefs, communicate them to and expect them from their offspring. Parents may model specific behaviors, possibly leading to the expression of those behaviors by children as the result of their children's observations and practice. Parents may promote behaviors in children as well, as for example through praise or reward of actions they appreciate. So, consider, adolescents' actions with their peers. Parents might influence their children's peer relationships directly by expressing attitudes, or based on the social responses children observe in their parents, children develop representations or expectations of how others will treat them and behave in accordance with those expectations. Parents might also directly intervene in their children's behaviors with peers or teach peer interaction strategies. Or, parents may affect their children's interactions indirectly by structuring peer–peer availability and activities.

The contents of parent–child interactions are dynamic, varied, and in some measure discretionary. However, a small number of central domains of parental caregiving and interactions have been identified as a prominent common "core" of the childcare repertoire. Nurturant, material, social, and didactic caregiving constitute perhaps universal categories, even if their instantiation or emphases in different locales or cultures vary. These categories apply to childhood and to normal caregiving in the West; they can be expected to vary with age, context, and place of residence. Components of the taxonomy are conceptually and operationally distinct, but in practice caregiver–child interactions are intricate and multidimensional, and caregivers regularly engage in combinations of them. For their part, human children are reared in, influenced by, and adapted to a physical and social ecology commonly characterized by the elements of this taxonomy. This taxonomy incorporates *stimulating care,* that is, types of caregiving that normally serve to promote child health and development, as well as *compensatory care,* that is, types of caregiving that (for whatever antecedent cause) return a child to accepted states of health or development.

A. Domains of Parenting

1. *Nurturant caregiving* meets the biological, physical, and health requirements of childhood. Child mortality is a perennial individual family as well as cultural concern, and parents are responsible for promoting children's wellness and preventing their illness. Parents in virtually all higher species nurture their young, providing sustenance, routine care, protection, supervision, grooming, comfort, and the like. Parents are supposed to shield children from risks and stressors. Nurturance is prerequisite to children's survival and well-being.

2. *Material caregiving* includes the ways in which parents provision, organize, and arrange the child's physical world, especially the home and local environment. Adults are responsible for the number and variety of inanimate objects (toys, books, tools) available to the child, the level of ambient stimulation, the limits on physical freedom, and the overall safety and physical dimensions of children's experiences. Notably, the amount of time that children normally spend interacting with the inanimate environment exceeds the time they spend in direct social interaction with parents.

3. *Social caregiving* includes the variety of visual, verbal, affective, and physical behaviors parents use to engage children and manage their interpersonal exchanges. Rocking, kissing, tactile comforting, smiling, vocalizing, and playful face-to-face contact are illustrative of parent–child interpersonal interactions. Through positive feedback, openness and negotiation,

listening, and emotional closeness, parents make a child feel valued, accepted, and approved of as a person. Parental displays of physical warmth peak in early childhood and decline thereafter to be replaced by alternative displays of affection as children grow. Social caregiving includes helping children to regulate their own affect and emotions. It also encompasses planning family activities and assigning duties to family members, and monitoring and managing children's interpersonal relationships with others, including relatives, nonfamilial caregivers, and peers. Parents play key roles in mediating young children's entry into wider social relationships and influencing the affective responses, communicative styles, and interpersonal repertoires which their children bring to forming meaningful and sustained relationships and associations with others. Furthermore, parents can be sources of emotional and social support to children in coping with risky or threatening situations.

4. *Didactic caregiving* consists of the variety of strategies parents use to stimulate children to engage and understand the environment and to enter the world of learning. Didactics include introducing, mediating, and interpreting the external world; teaching, describing, and demonstrating; as well as provoking or providing opportunities to observe, to imitate, and to learn.

Taken as a totality, this constellation of caregiving categories constitutes a varied and demanding set of tasks. Even when they come from socioeconomically homogeneous groups or from the same culture, adults differ considerably in terms of how they esteem and engage in components of this caregiving repertoire and in how successful they may be in executing different components. However, individual style is rather consistent, and individual parents do not vary much from day to day. Over longer periods, of course, parenting may change, and it adapts in response to children's development.

Research into parenting has also identified typologies of parenting styles, the most common of which are authoritative, authoritarian, indulgent-permissive, and indifferent-involved. These styles vary along global dimensions of parental warmth and control, and different parenting styles reflect combinations of high or low levels of these dimensions. For children in the middle class, for example, the authoritative style (combining high levels of warmth with moderate to high levels of discipline and control) is associated with achievement of social competence and overall adaptation when compared to other parenting styles, such as authoritarian parenting (containing high levels of control, but little warmth or responsiveness to children's needs), which has generally been associated with poor developmental outcomes in children. In other social classes or other ethnic groups, other patterns may obtain. For example, examination of adolescents' academic performance and reports of parenting shows that adolescents from European-American and Hispanic-American homes who report having experienced authoritative parenting in growing up perform well academically, and better than those coming from nonauthoritative households. However, school performance is similar for authoritatively and for nonauthoritatively reared Asian Americans and African Americans. Furthermore, ethnographic observations suggest that authoritarian parenting may be adaptive in some situations. Caucasian parents in different income groups who engage in intrusive and controlling behaviors typically score high on scales of authoritarian parenting. However, work among low-income African-American families suggests that a style of interaction that is very directive is adaptive, and is not harsh control. That is, an authoritarian style may constitute an appropriate adjustment in circumstances (e.g., certain inner-city neighborhoods) where it is a parent's job to impress upon the child the necessity of following rules. Indeed, authoritarian parenting in some contexts may achieve the same ultimate function—successful social adaptation—that authoritative parenting serves in other contexts.

Caregiving behaviors and styles constitute some direct experience effects of parenting. *Indirect effects* are more subtle and less noticeable than direct effects, but perhaps no less meaningful. Parents influence their children by virtue of their influence on each other, for example. Primary among this type of effect are marital support and communication. Parents' attitudes about themselves, their spouse, and their marriages can modify the quality of their interactions with their children and, in turn, their children's adjustment and development. Parents in disagreement, for example, are likely to convey confusing messages to their children, have less time for and become less involved in their children's lives, and engage in more hostile relationships with their children. Parents who feel negatively about their marriage (as those who feel negatively about themselves) tend to act with their children in inattentive and nonresponsive ways. By contrast, those who report having supportive relationships with "secondary parents" (husbands, lovers, or grandparents) are more attentive and sensitively responsive to their children. Marital distress may lead fathers to withdraw from active parenting. [See MARITAL HEALTH.]

B. Principles of Parenting

Whether direct or indirect, parental influences on children operate on two noteworthy principles.

1. The *specificity principle* states that specific experiences parents provide children at specific times exert specific effects over specific aspects of child growth in specific ways. It is probably not the case that overall level of parental stimulation directly affects children's overall level of functioning: Simply providing an adequate financial base, a big house, or the like does not guarantee or even speak to the child's development of an empathic personality, linguistic competence, or other desirable capacity.

2. The *transaction principle* asserts that experiences shape the characteristics of an individual through time just as, reciprocally, the characteristics of an individual shape his or her experiences. Thus, children influence which experiences they will be exposed to as well as how they interpret those experiences and, so, how those experiences might affect them. Child and parent bring distinctive characteristics to, and child and parent alike are believed to change as a result of, their mutual interactions; both parent and child then enter future interactions as "different" individuals.

In short, in parenting children and in child development, specific parent-provided experiences at specific times affect specific aspects of the child's growth in specific ways *and* specific child abilities and proclivities affect specific experiences and specific aspects of development just as specific patterns and practices of parenting do.

Parenting is central to childhood, to child development, and to society's long-term investment in children. Parents are fundamentally invested in young children: their survival, their socialization, and their education. So, we are motivated to know about the meaning and importance of parenting as much for itself as out of the desire to improve the lives of children.

Parenting portends much about the later life of children *and* parents.

IV. WHO PARENTS

2. States Parties shall respect the rights and duties of the parents and, when applicable, legal guardians, to provide direction to the child in the exercise of his or her right in a manner consistent with the evolving capacities of the child.
                                    Article 14
                Convention on the Rights of the Child

1. Parties shall use their best efforts to ensure recognition of the principle that both parents have common responsibilities for the upbringing and development of the child. Parents or, as the case may be, legal guardians, have primary responsibility for the upbringing and development of the child. The best interests of the child will be their basic concern.
                                    Article 18
                Convention on the Rights of the Child

Cultures distribute the tasks of caregiving in different ways. In the minds of many, *mother* is unique, the role of mother universal, and motherhood unequivocally principal in the development of children. Mother is the traditional caregiver to young children. In the minds of others, pluralistic caregiving arrangements are much more common and, on this account, much more significant in the lives of children. In many places around the globe, young children spend much or most of their time under the care of significant others, including siblings, other relatives, or nonfamilial caregivers.

In the West, mothers normally play the central part in guiding children's development in the nuclear family, even if historically fathers' social and legal claims and responsibilities on children were preeminent. Cross-cultural surveys attest to the primacy of biological mothers in all forms of caregiving, and theorists, researchers, and clinicians have typically concerned themselves with mothering, rather than parenting, in recognition of this fact. Fathers are neither inept nor uninterested in caregiving, however. In actuality, in the West mothers and fathers interact with and care for their children in complementary ways; that is, they tend to share the labors of caregiving and engage children by emphasizing different types of interactions. Mothers are more likely to kiss, hug, talk to, smile at, tend, and hold their young, whereas fathers are identified with tactile and physical playful interactions. Mothers and fathers also normally differ in degree of responsibility they take for management of different family tasks. Time budget constraints and variation in parental interests and abilities may cause mothers and fathers to devote different amounts of time and resources to their children across different domains, such as school, sports, or household responsibilities.

Western industrialized nations have witnessed some increases in the amount of time *fathers* spend with their children; in everyday life, however, fathers still assume little responsibility for childcare and rearing, and fathers are primarily helpers. Modern fatherhood appears to have "two faces": On the one hand, fathers seem to be increasing their involvement and moving toward more equal participation with their wives in the care and rearing of children. On the other hand, extended absence, nonpayment of child support, and denial of paternity are all too common and point to a substantially less-desirable side of contemporary fatherhood. When mothers earn a larger percentage of total family income, their decision-making power tends to be greater, and the nutritional status of their children better. Regardless of absolute income level, however, the more of his total income a father contributes to the family, the better the nutritional status of his children, suggesting perhaps that a very important piece of family business is for fathers to feel committed to their children's welfare. Men generally have fewer opportunities to acquire and practice skills that are central to caregiving and therefore may benefit from social support more than mothers. Because the paternal role is somewhat less well articulated and defined than is the maternal role, maternal support helps to crystallize appropriate paternal behavior. Beside the increasing number of single-parent fathers, fathers' indirect impact on children includes the various ways in which they modify and mediate mother–child relationships; in turn, women affect their children indirectly through their husbands by modifying both the quantity and the quality of father–child interactions.

Today, many individuals—other than mother and father—also "parent" young children. Indeed, direct childcare by a biological parent has been historically more the exception than the rule. Sources of nonparental childcare can be divided roughly into four types.

1. The first (and unfortunately not infrequent) childcare arrangement used throughout the world, in spite of the hazards involved, is *nonexistent childcare.* Children are simply unattended while the mother or father is otherwise occupied.

2. Second is childcare provided by other members of the mother's *household* or *kin group*. Siblings (or other available older children) typically display features of both vertical adult-child (nurturant) and horizontal peer-child (play) systems of caregiving. (In Western and industrialized societies, siblings are seldom entrusted with much responsibility for parenting children per se, however; rather, older children normally engage in activities preparatory to their own maturity.) Other members of the kin group ordinarily recruited for childcare responsibilities include grandparents, aunts, and the like.

Children also commonly encounter a social caregiving world that extends beyond the immediate family. In different cultures, children are tended by nonparental careproviders—nurses and sitters, daycare providers and metaplot. In some societies, multiple caregiving of children is natural: Usually, these include women who provide care in their own homes, in the child's own home, or in formal daycare settings of some sort.

3. The third source of nonparental care involves reciprocal exchanges of childcare or other services among members of a *residential group,* usually without any financial compensation.

4. The fourth type is a combination of *formal and informal care services,* where childcare is provided for a fee at home (either the home of the child or the provider) or in an institutional setting. [*See* CHILD CARE PROVIDERS.]

Siblings, grandparents, and various nonparents play salient roles in contemporary childcare, offering degrees of nurturing, material, social, and didactic caregiving that vary depending on a variety of factors about the childcare provider, including age, gender, age gap, quality of attachment, personality, and so forth. Often the child's caregivers behave in a complementary fashion to one another, dividing the full labor of child caregiving by individually emphasizing different parenting responsibilities and functions. The implications of diverse patterns of early "parenting" relationships for children's development are still unclear. It is a curious and sad fact that superb parenting work is often low in value and remuneration for most people in all cultures, yet the outcome for succeeding generations is unquestionable.

V. PARENTING: PERSISTENT YET PROTEAN

. . . the family, as the fundamental group of society and the natural environment for the growth and well-being of all its members and particularly children, should be afforded the necessary protection and assistance so that it can fully assume its responsibilities within the community . . .

Preamble
Convention on the Rights of the Child

2. The parent(s) or others responsible for the child have the primary responsibility to secure, within their abilities and financial capacities, the conditions of living necessary for the child's development.

Article 27
Convention on the Rights of the Child

Parenting is a peculiar kind of life job, marked by challenging demands, changing and ambiguous criteria, and frequent evaluations. Successful parenting entails both *affective components*—commitment, empathy, and positive regard for children—as well as *cognitive components*—the how, what, and why of caring for children. The path to achieving satisfaction and success in parenting is not linear or incremental, but tends to be winding and cyclic. Moreover, different tasks are more or less salient and challenging at different times in the course of childrearing. Parenting is a process that formally begins during pregnancy, but continues through the balance of life span: Practically speaking, *once a parent, always a parent.* No matter when parenting takes place, however, the different categories in the taxonomy of caregiving and different styles of parenting seem consistently important. Consider two functions, surveillance and responsiveness in social caregiving, as examples. Parents need to keep track of and tend to their children to be effective at parenting, and they need to let their children know that they and the child alike coexist in a loving and trusting relationship.

Some features of parenting and of parent–child relationships are constant, but others vary, insofar as they are linked, for example, to distinctive changes in childhood or to different places. The primary foci of parenting in the early months of an infant's life are to establish successful routine interactions, clear patterns of communication, and dependable emotional attachments. The tasks of nurturing and guiding toddlers over the threshold of mobility and language acquisition present a different set of challenges. A wealth of language nurturance seems requisite to ease the child into a print-dominated society that demands composition and reading skills at high levels. Children quickly become capable of learning family and community standards for proper and desirable behavior. In most cultures, socialization pressures begin in earnest during the second or third years of life, when children show increasing abilities to reason in terms of abstract representations of objects and events and begin to organize tasks more maturely and on their own. Middle childhood already sees sons and daughters spending less time in the company of adults and family members, relative to peers and other adults outside of the family. Children thus enter ever wider social worlds through time and increasingly determine their own contacts and experiences with others outside of parents. The roles and responsibilities of parents change with them.

Families are social systems marked by strong forms of interdependence among all members and by the kaleidoscopic redistribution of forces associated with responsibilities and functions of family members through time. On *interdependence*: To understand the responsibilities and functions of one member of a family, the complementary responsibilities and functions of other family members also need to be recognized. All family members—mothers, fathers, and children as well as other interested parties—influence each other both directly and indirectly. When one member of the family changes, all members of the family are potentially affected. Furthermore, all families are embedded in, interact with, influence, and are themselves affected by larger social systems. These include both formal and informal support systems, extended families, community ties such as friends and neighbors, work sites, social, educational, and medical institutions, as well as the culture at large. On *redistribution of forces*: Parents change in their persons and positions, and children constantly develop. Moreover, each influences the other so that elements of who we were yesterday, who we are today, and who we will be tomorrow are in constant transformation. To fathom the nature of parenting and parent–child relationships within families, therefore, calls for a *multivariate* and *dynamic* approach. Only multiple levels of analysis of diverse key concepts can capture the individual, dyadic, and family unit aspects of coordinated operation within the family and reflect the embeddedness of the family within the variety of relevant extrafamilial systems. The dynamic aspect involves the many different developmental trajectories of related individuals that unfold through time. Therefore, multivariate and dynamic estimates are simultaneously required for understanding the nature of parenting. [*See* FAMILY SYSTEMS.]

Parents and children stimulate and provide feedback to—they mutually influence—one another. In order to maintain appropriate influence and guidance, parents must effectively adjust their interactions, cognitions, emotions, affections, and strategies for exerting influence to the age-graded activities and experiences of children, including cognitive competencies, transitions in social contexts, relationships, and responsibilities, vulnerability to stress, altered functions of the self, and self-regulation. Not only are their children growing and developing, of course, but parents themselves also grow and develop during their adult years.

In general it can be said that parents face a continuous onrush of transitions in children's physical maturity, cognitive capabilities, emotional adjustments, social access to new settings, opportunities, and demands, and diversity of relationships with others. Parents must meet these challenges with adaptive executive processes of control, foster self-management and responsibility, facilitate children's positive relationships outside of the family, and maintain productive contacts with children's out-of-home settings, such as schools.

VI. PREREQUISITES FOR PARENTING

2. States Parties shall respect the rights and duties of the parents and, when applicable, legal guardians, to provide direction to the child in the exercise of his or her right in a manner consistent with the evolving capacities of the child.
Article 14
Convention of the Rights of the Child

Each day more than three-quarters of a million adults around the world experience the joys and heartaches, challenges and rewards of becoming new parents. Despite the fact that most people become parents and everyone who ever lived has had parents, *parenting* remains a somewhat mystifying subject about which almost everyone has opinions, but about which few people agree. (Freud listed bringing up children as one of the three "impossible professions"—the other two being governing nations and psychoanalysis.) What factors make parents the kind of parents they are?

The origins of variation in maternal and paternal beliefs and behaviors are extremely complex, but certain factors seem to be of paramount importance: (1) biological determinants; (2) personality characteristics; (3) actual or perceived characteristics of children; and (4) contextual influences, including social situational factors, family background, socioeconomic status, and culture.

1. First, basic physiology is mobilized to support parenting, and several aspects of parenting initially arise out of *biological processes* associated with pregnancy and parturition. For example, pregnancy in human beings causes the release of certain hormones thought to be involved in the development of protective, nurturant, and responsive feelings toward offspring. Prenatal biological events—parental age, diet, and stress, as well as other factors such as contraction of disease, exposure to environmental toxins, and even birth anesthetics—affect postnatal parenting as well as child development.

2. Second, parenting calls upon enduring *personality characteristics,* including intelligence, traits and attitudes toward the parenting role, motivation to become involved with children, and childcare and childrearing knowledge and skills. Some personality characteristics that favor good parenting include well-being, empathic awareness, predictability, responsiveness, and emotional availability. More educated parents promote the authoritative style of childrearing. Perceived self-efficacy is likely to affect parenting positively because parents who feel effective vis-à-vis their children are motivated to engage in further interaction with their children, which in turn provides them with additional opportunities to understand and interact positively and appropriately with their children. The more rewarding their interactions, the more motivated parents may be to seek "quality" interactions again. Negative characteristics of personality, whether transient or permanent, are likely to affect parenting adversely: Notable examples are self-centeredness and depression. [*See* PERSONALITY.]

3. Third, *characteristics of children* influence parenting and, in turn, child development. These characteristics may be obvious (gender or physical appearance), or they may be subtle (temperament). All can affect the job parents do. The nature of childhood is change, and significant normative developments in childhood also influence parenting. With infants, parents take primary responsibility for pro-

viding for needs and maintaining homeostatic balance, by warmth, nourishment, diapering, and regulating. During the preschool years, children develop rapidly in motor, cognitive, and socioemotional capacities, and later still extra-familial influences from peers and teachers come into play. These developmental changes place new demands on parents and require adjustments in parenting skills. Gaining the ability to stand upright and walk signal moments of substantial change in the child vis-à-vis parents; during adolescence, parent–child relationships become more peer-like. Every child also develops at his or her own rate. The age at which individual children achieve a given developmental milestone (puberty) varies enormously, just as children of a given age vary dramatically among themselves on nearly every index of development. Understanding and responding to dynamic developmental change in the context of individual variation among children challenge and shape parenting.

4. Biology, personality, and child characteristics constitute salient factors that influence parenting from the start. Beyond these, *contextual factors* motivate and help to define the behaviors and beliefs of parents. Social support, social class, and cultural worldview encourage divergent patterns of parenting perceptions and practices. In some places, children are reared in extended families in which care is provided by many relatives; in others, mothers and babies are isolated from almost all other social contexts. In some childcare settings, fathers are treated as irrelevant social objects; in others, fathers assume complex responsibilities for their children. In the West, well-supported mothers are less restrictive and punitive with their children than are less well-supported mothers, and frequency of contact with significant others improves the quality of parent–child relationships as well as parents' sense of their own efficacy and competence. The ways in which spouses provide support and show respect for each other in parenting, how they work together as a co-parenting team, may have either positive or negative consequences for their children. Community and friendship supports benefit mothers, but (in Western cultures at least) intimate support from husbands has the most general positive consequences for maternal competence, family dynamics, and child outcomes. Socioeconomic status also exerts differential effects on parenting: Mothers in different SES groups behave similarly in certain parenting domains, however SES—through differential provisions in the

environment and education of parents—also orders home circumstances and other attitudes and actions of parents toward children. In different cultures, higher compared to lower SES parents typically provide children with more opportunities for variety in daily stimulation, more appropriate play materials, and more total stimulation, especially language. Finally, cross-cultural comparisons show that virtually all aspects of parenting children—whether beliefs or behaviors—can be shaped by cultural habits. Culture influences some parenting patterns and practices (and, in turn, child development) from a very early age through such persuasive factors as when and how parents care for children and which behaviors parents appreciate and emphasize. Inasmuch as culture is organized information, parenting consists of mechanisms for transmitting that information, and childhood consists of processing that information. Both parent and child then "select, edit, and refashion" cultural information. So, minimally, enculturation involves bidirectional processes in which adult and child play active roles.

These several forces on the origins of parenting may engender similarities or differences in parenting. No doubt, there are culture-specific as well as culture-general parenting practices. Despite different cultural perspectives, a "common core" of primary family experiences underwrites the possibility of meaningful cross-cultural comparisons of parenting. Some authorities espouse the universalist position, that certain beliefs and behaviors in parenting recur across (even very different) cultures, on account of common determinants of parenting in factors indigenous to children and their biology. For example, by virtue of their helplessness or "babyish" characteristics, which are universal, infants may elicit universal patterns of caregiving from their parents. Others argue that universal characteristics of parenting may be instinctual to a "parenting stage" in the human life cycle, and are not necessarily provoked by a particular stimulus, even the child. On this argument, it is in the nature of being a parent to optimize the development and probability of success of one's offspring, possibly to ensure the success of one's own genes. A third set of explanations for the universalist position points to the environment as cause. Insofar as certain economic or ecological factors are shared, they may collectively press for parents to think and behave in similar ways. The late twentieth century has witnessed a worldwide pattern of change toward urbanization, modernization, media homogeneity, and Westernization that cumulatively contribute to breaking down traditionally differentiated cultural patterns. There are special and exacting constraints and demands on parenting children, and opportunistically these may be more universal than not.

Some attitudes and actions of parents are culturally unique and specifically contextualized. The arguments marshaled by culture-specifists to assert this view are in principle the same kind as invoked by culture-universalists. Certain culturally consistent biological characteristics of children, such as constitutionally based unique features of temperament, could promote parental attitudes and activities that vary systematically, even across cultures. Adults in different cultures could parent differently because of their own unique biological characteristics, as for example, differential threshold sensitivity or attention to child signals. Finally, ecological or economic conditions specific to a given social or cultural setting might promote parental attitudes and activities specific to that setting, ones differentially geared to optimize adjustment and adaptation in offspring to the unique circumstances of the local situation. Prominent aspects might include parental employment, neighborhood quality, access to recreational and health care facilities, and the like.

VII. PRESENT-DAY PROBLEMS AND PROGRAMS IN PARENTING

1. In all actions concerning children, whether undertaken by public or private social welfare institutions, courts of law, administrative authorities or legislative bodies, the best interests of the child shall be a primary consideration.

2. States Parties undertake to ensure the child such protection and care as is necessary for his or her well-being, taking into account the rights and duties of his or her parents, legal guardians, or other individuals legally responsible for him or her, and, to this end, shall take all appropriate legislative and administrative measures.

3. States Parties shall ensure that the institutions, services and facilities responsible for the care or protection of children shall conform with the standards established by competent authorities, particularly in the areas of safety, health, in the number and suitability of their staff, as well as competent supervision.

Article 3
Convention on the Rights of the Child

2. For the purpose of guaranteeing and promoting the rights set forth in the present Convention, States Parties shall render appropriate assistance to parents and legal guardians in the performance of their child-rearing responsibilities and shall ensure the development of institutions, facilities and services for the care of children.

Article 18
Convention on the Rights of the Child

In everyday life, parenting children, young or old, does not always go well and right. Infanticide was practiced historically, and although it is very rare today, it is not unknown. Numerous risks alter postnatal parenting and compromise the innocent child. Increasing numbers of births worldwide occur to single or teenage mothers; many children live in poverty; children are common victims of abuse and neglect; babies are born drug addicted; many children are not fully immunized. For these and other reasons, contemporary parenting has witnessed an explosive growth in information and support programs.

Once upon a time, parenting was a seemingly simple thing: Mothers mothered. Fathers fathered. Today, parenting has many motives, many meanings, and many manifestations. Parenting is viewed as immensely time consuming and effortful. Parenting a young child is akin to trying to hit a moving target, the everchanging child developing in fits and starts at his or her own pace. Furthermore, a multitude of factors—biopsychological, dyadic, contextual—contributes to an unrelenting flood of decisions that surround parenting.

Recognizing this complexity is important to informing people's thinking about parenting, especially information-hungry parents. The time available for families for nurturing children has diminished, and economic pressures on families often cause children to receive inadequate care and to be placed in nonfamilial environments at ever earlier times in their lives. Much more is known today about the patterns and critical periods of early learning and the quality of environments beneficial to young children's development. Thus, the need for a range of support from child development programs and activities is no longer questioned. Children are reared in families, but also in childcare programs, schools, and communities. Caregivers in these settings are responsible for meeting children's developmental needs and also for preparing them for a future in society. Belief in the potential of the early years as a time when families can aid the developmental and educational processes of children is strong. In the early years (from birth through the lower primary grades), children's physical, emotional, and social learning requirements can be managed better by parents with supportive efforts from professionals. Parent programs can make a significant contribution to the child's growth, learning, and development as well as to the family's functioning. Moreover, as a consequence of contemporary social and cultural changes, notably female employment, a demand for high-quality community-based childcare services has burgeoned. The best programs educate parents and other caregivers in ways that enhance their care of and interaction with the child and enrich the child's environment.

The family is the principal source of care and development of the child. However, substantial variation exists among parents in terms of effectiveness of interactions. For example, some parental teaching styles, language interactions, and cognitive expectations appear to be less conducive to providing "optimal learning environments" for children. Thus, for those who want it, the primary socializing function of the family can be profitably supplemented with child-rearing information and guidance. Reciprocally, the ability of the family to care for and educate the child is weakened by stresses and can be strengthened by supports from neighbors, friends, relatives, social groups, and relevant professionals. Relations between parental behavior and child adjustment are complex. Some reside in the child, including, for example, early childhood temperament. But others lie in parents or in parent-provided experiences, such as parental psychopathology, exposure to stressful life events, and a negative family environment, all of which have come to be viewed as important sources of influence in the development of problems in children. Furthermore, if benefits to the child provided by experiences in child development or parenting programs are to be maintained over time, people at home must take part. Parental involvement remains the indispensable ingredient for sustaining the accomplishments of extrafamilial childhood education programs. The responsibility for determining the child's best interest rests first and foremost with parents. Therefore, the doctrine of parental rights must remain a fundamental premise of parent education efforts. Educators may involve themselves in helping parents and future parents in family care and education skills.

Parent service programs are typically available from a wide range of professionals and paraprofessionals either for an individual or for the entire family; they usually involve psychological support and information about parenting and child development; and they normally focus on social, psychological, educational, or health needs. Such programs are diverse in their theoretical and conceptual frameworks, the populations they serve, the scope of service, and the types of intervention activity they advocate depending on the needs and cultural context.

The development of parenting programs is guided by several assumptions: (1) Parents are usually the most consistent and caring people in the lives of their children. (2) If parents are provided with knowledge, skills, and support, they can respond more positively and effectively to their children. (3) Parents' own emotional and physical needs must be met if they are to respond positively and effectively to their children. Parenting programs are guided by beliefs that emphasize the importance of addressing family needs when serving individual children, recognizing the family as a social system, and considering environmental and cultural influences when evaluating family needs and resources.

Some Basic Parenting Tools

Certain tools can help to address these parenting requirements successfully. They include knowledge of child development, observing skills, strategies for problem prevention and discipline, supports for cognition and language and emotional and social development, and the personal sources of support.

1. *Knowledge about child development.* Parents benefit from knowledge of how children develop. Children's normative patterns and stages of physical, verbal, cognitive, emotional, and social development, as well as their nutritional and health needs at different stages, should be part of the knowledge base for parenthood. Knowledge of children's emotional needs and typical early social-emotional behaviors may promote positive responses and forestall inappropriate responses to children's expressed emotions and behaviors. Understanding the patterns and processes of early cognitive development, for example, will help parents to develop more realistic expectations of the stages of child development and the requisite skills for children's achieving more mature competencies.

2. *Observing skills.* Parents need to know how to observe young children. Child watching can help one understand a child's level of development in relation to what one would like the child to learn or accomplish. Parents need information and observation skills to help them discover the match between their child's ability or readiness and ways and means to help their child achieve developmental goals. These capacities also allow parents to spot potential trouble early. Such awareness helps parents handle a child's daily frustrations more skillfully.

3. *Strategies for problem prevention and discipline.* Parents need insights for managing their children's behaviors. Knowledge and skills regarding alternative methods of discipline and problem avoidance are basic. Knowing how to implement a variety of positive rewards can help a child more fully enjoy and appreciate the exploration and struggles required in mastering new skills.

4. *Supports for cognition and language, emotion and social development.* The parent who has learned to speak and read to a child and to present the child with appealing solvable problems will enrich the actions a child carries out and the feelings a child expresses. Knowing how to take advantage of settings, routines, and activities at hand to create learning and problem-solving opportunities as well as turning household objects into learning materials for children's exploration both enhance parenting. The development of emotion regulation suggests that individual differences in children's socioemotional development relates to the affective quality of parent–child relationships.

5. *Personal sources of support.* Parents need patience and flexibility, they need to be goal oriented, and they must command an ability to extract pleasure from their encounters with children. Parents need to understand the tremendous impact they have on their children's lives through their attention, expressed pleasure, listening, and interest. These activities nourish a child's growing sense of self, just as food nourishes a child's growing body.

The general orientation of parent support programs is to help families to provide stable, nurturing, and healthy environments for children. Parents come to feel that they are not rearing their children in isolation, that there are people in programs to which they can turn for information and for a shared sense of

the challenges and satisfactions surrounding child and family development. Childcare programs exemplify a main source of parental support. Families may rely on early child development programs for a variety of types of child and family assistance, health care guidelines, and advice on child learning and behavior.

Positive programs for parents are guided by beliefs in the consummate role of families in the rearing of their own children and the importance of family participation in defining its own priorities and identifying appropriate intervention strategies. Families are best served when they are helped to enhance their own skills, rather than when decisions are made and solutions implemented for them. Interventions need to be sensitive to sociocultural diversity in families in terms of values and beliefs, and they need to build on the strengths of the family. Because individuals who share sociocultural similarities can still differ significantly in goals, values, and resources, each family must be responded to according to its unique characteristics including age, gender, and ethnicity.

Parents ultimately benefit from more information about who can provide what kinds of supports to families, when, and where, in the most sensitive and appropriate ways. Some practitioners have argued that the central responsibility for a family lies with the family, and that it is outside the purview of government or other institutions to intervene. However, public and private responsibility are not dichotomous, but rather a continuum exists in which families that need support can receive it in different ways. The degree to which the formal structures in a community should provide these supports depends on the characteristics, desires, and current circumstances of the individual family.

The costs of inadequate parenting are high. Children lacking appropriate care are exposed more frequently to a cluster of risk factors including illness, poor nutrition, family stress, and unstimulating environments. Children need to receive deep psychological messages about how special and precious each one is. Maternal depression, violence in the family, and just feeding and clothing a child will not produce the kind of person who will nurture well in the next generation. The long-term costs of failures can be measured in terms of school dropout, unemployment, delinquency, and the intergenerational perpetuation of poverty. On the other hand, parenting competently provides a window of opportunity, offering an element of hope: Even small positive changes in the child's environment can accrue to generate long-term benefits. Thus, the increasing childcare needs resulting from changes in family structures and women's work patterns, for example, combined with recognition of the developmental needs of the child, provide a powerful argument for governments, communities, employers, and families to identify appropriate and affordable solutions to the provision of valuable and effective parenting programs.

VIII. PARENTS: A POSTSCRIPT

. . . in the Universal Declaration of Human Rights, the United Nations has proclaimed that childhood is entitled to special care and assistance . . .

Preamble
Convention on the Rights of the Child

Parents intend much in their interactions with their children: They promote their children's mental development through the structures they create and the meanings they place on those structures, and they foster their children's emotional regulation, development of self, and social awareness of meaningful relationships and experiences outside of the family through the models they portray and the values they display. The complex of parent behaviors with children is divisible into domains and styles, and parents tend to show interest and consistency over time in their parenting. A parent's job is to facilitate a child's self-confidence, capacity for intimacy, achievement motivation, pleasure in play and work, friendships with peers, and early and continued academic success and fulfillment.

A full understanding of what it means to parent a child, however, depends on the ecology in which that parenting takes place. Within-family experiences exercise a major impact during the early years of life. The nuclear family triad—mother, father, child—constitutes the crucible within which young children initially grow and develop. Young children also naturally form relationships with siblings and grandparents, and children have significant experiences outside the family—often through enrollment in alternative care settings—and the nature and effects of out-of-home care experiences vary depending on type and quality, as well as the individual characteristics of children, their families, and those institutions. Family consti-

tution, social class, and cultural variation affect patterns of childrearing and exert salient influences on the ways in which young children are reared and what is expected of them as they grow. These early relationships with mothers, fathers, siblings, and others all ensure that the "parenting" that children experience is rich and multifaceted.

The characteristics developed and acquired in early childhood may be formative and fundamental in the sense that they endure or (at least) constitute features that later developments or experiences in maturity build on or modify. Of course, human development is too subtle, dynamic, and intricate to admit that parental caregiving alone determines the course and outcome of ontogeny; stature in adulthood is shaped by individuals themselves and by experiences that take place after childhood. That is, parenting the child does not fix the route or terminus of development. But it makes sense that effects have causes and that the start exerts an impact on the end. Hence, the enormity and enduring significance of parents on their young.

ACKNOWLEDGMENTS

Portions of this article appear as "Parenting Young Children" in the UNICEF *Child in Focus* series.

BIBLIOGRAPHY

Baumrind, D. (1989). Rearing competent children. In W. Damon (Ed.), *Child development today and tomorrow* (pp. 349–378). San Francisco: Jossey-Bass.

Belsky, J. (1984). The determinants of parenting: A process model. *Child Development, 55*, 83–96.

Bornstein, M. H. (1989). *Maternal responsiveness: Characteristics and consequences.* San Francisco: Jossey-Bass.

Bornstein, M. H. (Ed.). (1991). *Cultural approaches to parenting.* Hillsdale, NJ: Lawrence Erlbaum Associates.

Bornstein, M. H. (Ed.). (1995). *Handbook of parenting* (Vols. 1–4). Mahwah, NJ: Lawrence Erlbaum Associates.

Bronfenbrenner, U., & Crouter, A. C. (1983). The evolution of environmental models in developmental research. In W. Kessen (Ed.), P. H. Mussen (Series Ed.), *Handbook of child psychology: Vol. 1. History, theory, and methods* (pp. 357–414). New York: Wiley.

Elder, G. H., Modell, P. J., & Parke, R. D. (1993). *Children in time and place: Developmental and historical insights.* New York: Cambridge University Press.

Goodnow, J. J., & Collins, W. A. (1990). *Development according* to parents. *The nature, sources, and consequences of parents' ideas.* Hove, UK: Erlbaum.

Gottfried, A. E., & Gottfried, A. W. (Eds.). (1988). *Maternal employment and children's development: Longitudinal research.* New York: Plenum.

Harkness, S., & Super, C. M. (Eds.). (1996). *Parents cultural belief systems: Their origins, expressions, and consequences.* New York: Guilford Press.

Maccoby, E. E., & Martin, J. A. (1983). Socialization in the context of the family: Parent-child interaction. In E. M. Hetherington (Ed.), P. H. Mussen (Series Ed.), *Handbook of child psychology: Vol. 4. Socialization, personality, and social development* (pp. 1–101). New York: Wiley.

Minuchin, P. (1985). Families and individual development: Provocations from the field of family therapy. *Child Development, 56,* 289–302.

Sigel, I., McGillicuddy-deLisi, A., & Goodnow, J. J. (Eds.). (1992). *Parental belief systems.* Hillsdale, NJ: Erlbaum.

United Nations General Assembly. (1990). *Convention on the rights of the child.* New York, NY: United Nations Children's Fund.

Personality

Theodore Millon

Harvard Medical School and University of Miami

Roger D. Davis

Institute for Advanced Studies in Personology and Psychopathology

Adaptive Modes An organism's life-style within its environment, either passive accommodation to what is offered, or active transformation of the environment for its own needs and desires.

Existential Aims Goals to which all organisms aspire, the enhancement and preservation of life, experienced subjectively as pleasure and pain.

Persona Greek origin of the term personality, representing the theatrical mask worn by ancient dramatic players.

Replication Strategies The orientation of an organism toward the care of its young, expressed in personality in the more male strategy of the perpetuation of self, or the more female strategy of the nurturance of others.

Principles of health and abnormal **PERSONALITY** functioning may be derived from a number of classical perspectives on the field, including the psychoanalytic, interpersonal, cognitive, biophysical, and statistical. Some framework is needed to integrate these diverse views. Evolutionary theory is discussed as a contemporary means from which to derive the essential polarities for a theory of healthy and abnormal personality. Healthy and abnormal personality are then discussed in terms of a three-stage model based in evolutionary theory.

I. WHAT IS PERSONALITY?

The meaning of the term personality has changed across history. Its origin derives from the Greek term *persona*, the theatrical mask worn by dramatic players. Here it suggests an affectation or pretense, that is, the possession of traits other than those that actually characterized the individual behind the mask. In time, however, the term *persona* lost its connotation of pretense and illusion, and began to represent, not the mask, but the apparent, explicit, and manifest features of the real person. The third and final meaning that *personality* has acquired goes "beneath" surface impressions in order to highlight the inner, less revealed, and hidden psychological qualities of the individual. Thus, historically the meaning of the term shifted from external illusion to surface reality, and finally to opaque or veiled inner traits. This last meaning comes closest to contemporary use, Personality is seen today as a complex and highly contextualized pattern of deeply embedded psychological characteristics or dispositions that express themselves automatically in most areas of functioning. Intrinsic and pervasive, personality is composed of traits that emerge from the interaction of each person's unique biological matrix and experiential history.

II. PERSPECTIVES ON PERSONALITY

Personality may be viewed from many different perspectives. Classical psychoanalytic theorists, for example, hold that personality is the expression of the vicissitudes of drives, while cognitive theorists hold that beliefs are central. Both reflect fundamental approaches to personality, and both reflect a defining characteristic of the construct—that personality regards the entire matrix of the person. The problem when attempting to coordinate such diverse perspectives on personality is how to do so in a logical way that is consonant with the intrinsic organismic integrity of personality itself. Various perspectives on personality are reviewed below.

A. Intrapsychic Formulations

Psychoanalytic theorists stress the importance of early childhood experiences, believing that it is these that dispose the individual to lifelong patterns of pathological adaptation. In what has been termed the psychogenetic hypothesis, early events establish deeply ingrained defensive systems that lead the individual to react to new situations as if they were duplicates of what occurred in childhood. These anticipatory defensive styles persist throughout life and result in progressive maladaptations or personality disorders. For the most part, these causes remain out of awareness, kept unconscious owing to their potentially troublesome character, notably the memories and impulses they contain and the primitive nature with which defenses and emotions are expressed. Central to the analytic viewpoint is the concept of psychic conflict. In this notion, behavior is seen to result from competing desires and their prohibitions that, through compromise and defensive maneuver, express themselves overtly.

Sigmund Freud, Karl Abraham, and Wilhelm Reich (1933) laid the foundation of the psychoanalytic character typology in the first third of the century. These categories were conceived initially as a product of frustrations or indulgences of instinctual or libidinous drives, especially in conjunction with specific psychosexual stages of maturation. Since the essentials of this typology may be traced to Freud, it may be of value to note alternative formulations he proposed at different times as potential schemas for personality, that is, schemas based on conceptions other than psychosexual theory.

Freud wrote in 1915 what many consider to be his most seminal papers, those on metapsychology and, in particular, the section entitled "Instincts and Their Vicissitudes." Speculations that foreshadowed several concepts developed more fully later were presented in this paper. Particularly notable is a framework that Freud proposed as central to the understanding of personality functioning; unfortunately, this framework was never fully developed as a system for personality dynamics, as Freud appears to have intended. His conception was formulated as follows:

> . . . Our mental life as a whole is governed by three polarities, namely, the following antitheses:
> Subject (ego)-Object (external world),
> Pleasure-Pain, and
> Active-Passive.

> The three polarities within the mind are connected with one another in various highly significant ways (pp. 76–77).

> We may sum up by saying that the essential feature in the vicissitudes undergone by instincts is their subjection to the influences of the three great polarities that govern mental life. Of these three polarities we might describe that of activity-passivity as the biological, that of the ego-external world as the real, and finally that of pleasure-pain as the economic respectively (1915/1925, p. 83).

At another time in his exploration of personality dimensions, Freud speculated that character classification might best be based on his threefold structural distinction of id, ego, and superego. Thus, in 1932 he sought to devise character types in accord with which intrapsychic structure was dominant. First, he proposed an "erotic" type whose life is governed by the instinctual demands of the id; second, in what he termed the "narcissistic" type, are found persons so dominated by the ego that neither other persons nor the demands of id or superego can affect them; third, he suggested a "compulsive" type whose life is regulated by the strictness of the superego such that all other functions are dominated; and last, Freud identified a series of mixed types in which combinations of two of the three intrapsychic structures outweigh the third. Freud's compulsive character type has been well represented in the literature, but only in the past 10 years have his proposals for a narcissistic personality disorder gained attention.

Freud's 1908 paper planted the seeds for psychoanalytic character types. Freud's primary interest at that time was not in tracing the formation of character structure but rather in discovering the derivatives of instincts as they evolve during particular psychosexual stages. Although Freud noted that developmental conflicts give rise to broadly generalized defensive tendencies, these were noted only incidentally, written largely as minor digressions from the main point of his early papers; unlike Karl Abraham, he did not focus on character structure derivatives but attempted to identify the psychosexual roots of specific and narrowly circumscribed symptoms, such as compulsions or conversions.

Despite the decline in the status and centrality of psychoanalysis over the past 20 or 30 years, adherents of this school of thought have continued to be highly productive and insightful. Of special significance have been contributions by ego-analytic theorists, the British object-relations school, as well as proposals from a number of contemporary thinkers.

Among psychoanalytic scholars, Fenichel is particularly impressive. In 1945, Fenichel classified character traits into "sublimation" and "reactive" types, depending on whether normally maturing instinctual energies were compatible with the ego, and thereby fashioned into conflict-free or neutral patterns (sublimation) or whether they were "dammed up" by the aims of the ego and "countermanded" by conflict-resolving defensive measures (reactive). In making this distinction Fenichel was the first to recognize that instinctual energy can develop into character forms free of conflict resolution. Although Fenichel considered the sublimation character traits to be as deeply ingrained as the reactive types, he viewed them to be nonpathological and, hence, paid little attention to the diverse forms into which they might take shape. In this regard, he failed to recognize the possibility that pathological personality traits could arise from conflict-free sources, that is, simply result from deficient or other inappropriate experiences that set the stage for maladaptive learning. Instead, Fenichel limited his attention to reactive characters, differentiating them into "avoidance" and "oppositional" types, each representative of a major form of defensive control. Fenichel died without being fully satisfied with his classification schema.

Other thinkers, notably Hartmann, Rapaport, and Erikson, also recognized that the origins of character may be found in instinctual energies that are independent of conflicts and their resolutions. To both Hartmann and Rapaport, the ego and id instincts derived from a common matrix of biological potentials, differentiating into separable energies for adaptive functioning. Termed "autonomous apparatuses," these ego potentials were seen as "preadapted to handle average expectable environments." Erikson extended the notion of autonomous apparatuses by stating that character development emerges out of three interwoven roots: Instinctual energies, the ma-turational capacities of the ego, and the external standards that society provides at each developmental stage.

Several major thinkers from Great Britain began to formulate new directions for psychoanalytic theory in the 1940s and 1950s. Perhaps most inventive of these was Melanie Klein, one of the originators of child psychoanalysis. It was her view that fantasy was a major primitive ability; furthermore, that these fantasies exhibit a regular developmental sequence that reflects the infant's relationship with its mother. The key element of Klein's object-relations theory is the view that the mind is composed of preformed internal representations of the infant's external relationships, that is, to its "objects." This contrasted with Freud's view that the mind possesses instinctual urges that are object-seeking, but are not preformed in their character; in this formulation, objects become part of the mind only secondarily. Klein believed that the mind possessed "prewired" fantasies, implying unlearned knowledge that gave shape to and prepared the child for subsequent experiences.

Similar conceptions to those of Klein may be found in the early writings of Jung and, subsequently, in a number of her followers, such as Fairbairn, Winnicott, and Guntrip. For example, Jung attributed the existence of instinctive object relationships to constitutionally derived archetypes that are then projected upon the external world. Fairbairn, in this vein, proposed "infantile endopsychic objects," that is, universal pristine images in the unconscious of children. Fairbairn asserted that these objects may fail to mature unless the child obtains satisfying experiences with their real world counterparts. Deprivation of these instinctively sought-for relationships would result in a loss of social capacities or in the aversion to social contacts, each of which may become a forerunner of later personality disorders.

Although numerous analytic theorists have contributed in recent years to the study of character, the work of Otto Kernberg deserves special note. Taking steps to develop a new characterology, Kernberg constructed a useful framework for organizing established types in terms of their level of severity. Breaking away from a rigid adherence to the psychosexual model, Kernberg proposed another dimension as primary, that of structural organization. Coordinating character types in accord with severity and structural organization led Kernberg to speak of "higher, intermediate and lower levels" of character pathology; both intermediate and lower levels are referred to as "borderline" personality organizations. To illustrate his ordering of types, Kernberg assigns most hysterical, obsessive-compulsive, and depressive personalities to the higher level. At the intermediate level of organization Kernberg locates the "infantile" and most narcissistic personalities. Last, clear-cut antisocial personalities are classified as distinctly of a lower borderline organization. Despite having been strongly influenced by the major ego and object-relations theorists, and despite the innovative nature of his proposals, Kernberg has remained anchored to the view that all pathological character types are inevitably "reactive" in their formation rather than potentially conflict-free in their origins. Nevertheless, many of Kernberg's proposals are innovative and insightful.

In the 1970s Kohut developed an influential variant of analytic theory that furnished a special role for the self-construct as the major organizer of psychological development. For Kohut, self-psychology was the proper next step following the earlier orientations of id-psychology and ego-psychology. Kohut's primary focus was on the development of self from its infantile state of fragility and fragmentation to that of a stable and cohesive adult structure. Disagreeing with classical analytic views concerning the role of conflicts as central to pathology, Kohut asserted that most disorders stemmed from deficits in the structure of the self. Owing to failures in empathic mothering, aspects of the self remain fragile and enfeebled, resulting in a variety of "narcissistically injured" personality disorders. Paying special attention to the importance of empathic responsiveness as a foundation for effective psychotherapy, Kohut added a new group of populations treatable by psychoanalytic methods. [*See* PSYCHOANALYSIS.]

B. Interpersonal Formulations

A person's style of relating to others also is noted essentially at the "behavioral" data level, and may be captured in a number of ways, such as how his or her actions impact on others, intended or otherwise, the attitudes that underlie, prompt, and give shape to these actions, the methods by which he or she engages others to meet his or her needs, or his or her way of coping with social tensions and conflicts. Extrapolating from these observations, the clinician may construct an image of how the patient functions in relation to others, be it antagonistically, respectfully, aversively, secretively, and so on.

The interpersonal approach has its origins in the seminal contributions of Harry Stack Sullivan. Sullivan differed from Freud in locating the source of pathology not exclusively within the individual's own head, but in terms of disordered interpersonal interactions and communication patterns. While biographies of Sullivan invariably document his own personal struggles, it is said that he had an amazingly high success rate in the treatment of schizophrenics.

The tradition that Sullivan started has been developed in many directions. Timothy Leary's 1957 work summarized the "Interpersonal Circumplex," developed some years earlier. According to its most basic conception, each person constricts the response repertoire of others in order to evoke specifically those responses that confirm or validate our perceptions of ourselves and the world. Interpersonal interactions are viewed as being either hierarchical (dominance versus submission) or communal (love versus hate). These form the two axes of the circle. The circumplex is a powerful conception of personality because it specifies ways in which personality may be either healthy or abnormal, and links these to a geometric model. Healthy or flexible styles appear as balanced or circular patterns concentric with the circle. Such individuals possess a full range of styles by which to relate to others, and are able to confirm and be confirmed, regardless of other personality styles. Personality pathology is expressed geometrically through distortions of this healthy circular and concentric pattern. Some individuals, for example, may be highly shifted along one axis. To the extent that an individual's pattern approaches the periphery of the circle, the personality style may be assumed to be increasing intense. To the extent that a particular segment of the circle dominates the whole, the personality style may be assumed to be increasingly narrow or rigid in its range of coping maneuvers, interpersonal behaviors, and role characteristics. Thus, the geometric representation of personality allows deficiencies to be described specifically, and suggests directions in which alternative ways of interacting with others might be practiced in order to move the individual in the direction of greater health (Benjamin, 1993).

C. Cognitive Formulations

How the individual perceives events, focuses attention, processes information, organizes thoughts, and communicates reactions and ideas to others represent data at a "phenomenological" level, and are among the most useful indices to the clinician of the patient's distinctive way of functioning. By synthesizing these characteristics or symptoms, it may be possible to identify indications of what may be termed an impoverished style, or distracted thinking, or cognitive flightiness, or constricted thought, and so on.

In 1990, Aaron Beck formulated a cognitive model of personality anchored to evolution. He speculates on how the prototypes of personality may be derived from the phylogenetic heritage of our species. Various genetically determined strategies are seen to have facilitated survival and reproduction through natural selection. Derivatives of these evolutionary strategies may be identified, according to Beck, in exaggerated form among the Axis I clinical syndromes, and less dramatically among the personality disorders. Each of these strategies possess a cognitive dimension, embedded in relatively stable structures called "schemas." These select and organize incoming experiences, translating them into habitual emotional and behavioral strategies. By assigning meanings to events, cognitive schemas start a chain reaction that culminates in overt patterns of behavior that we know as personality traits. Dysfunctional and distorting schemas give rise to maladaptive strategies that, in turn, make the individual susceptible to repetitive and pervasive life difficulties. The dependent personality, for example, is hypersensitive to the possibility of a loss of love and help. These highly personalized cognitive schemas displace and perhaps inhibit other schemas that may be more adaptive or more appropriate for a given situation. As a result, they introduce a persistent and systematic bias into the individual's processing machinery.

Beck recognizes the presence of both overdeveloped and underdeveloped cognitive assumptions. Thus, dependent personalities quickly activate widely generalized and erroneous cognitive expectancies of personal loss. Other personalities exhibit comparatively underdeveloped cognitive schemas. The antisocial, for example, has an underdeveloped disposition to find reasons to be responsible or to feel guilt for their behavioral deficiencies, whereas obsessive-compulsives are disposed to judge themselves responsible and guilt-ridden. They show a marked underdevelopment in the inclination to interpret events spontaneously, creatively, and playfully. In contrast, healthy personalities do not hold such beliefs that distort their perceptions, and ultimately, their interactions and behavior. [See COGNITIVE THERAPY; OBSESSIVE–COMPULSIVE DISORDER.]

D. Biophysical Formulations

Few observables are clinically more relevant from the biophysical level of data than the predominant character of an individual's affect and the intensity and frequency with which it is expressed. The "meaning" of extreme emotions is easy to decode. This is not so with the more subtle moods and feelings that insidiously and repetitively pervade ongoing relationships and experiences. Not only are the expressive features of mood and drive conveyed by terms such as distraught, labile, fickle, or hostile communicated via self-report, they are revealed as well, albeit indirectly, in the patient's level of activity, speech quality, and physical appearance.

Drawing upon genetic and neurobiologic substrates, Cloninger proposed a complex theory based on the interrelationship of several heritable trait dispositions: novelty seeking, harm avoidance, and reward dependence. Specifically, novelty seeking is hypothesized to dispose the individual toward exhilaration or excitement in response to novel stimuli, which leads to the pursuit of potential rewards as well as an active avoidance of both monotony and punishment. Harm avoidance reflects a disposition to respond strongly to aversive stimuli, leading the individual to inhibit behaviors to avoid punishment, novelty, and frustrations. Thirdly, reward dependence is hypothesized as a tendency to respond to signals of reward (e.g., verbal signals of social approval), and to resist extinction of behaviors previously associated with rewards or relief from punishment. Extending the theme of novelty seeking, for example, individuals with this disposition, but average on the other two dimensions, would be characterized as impulsive, exploratory, excitable, quick tempered, and extravagant, likely to seek out new interests, but inclined to neglect details and to become quickly distracted or bored. Anchored fundamentally to the dopamine neuromodulator, individuals who might be low in this neurobiologic substrate (e.g., under average in novelty seeking) are likely to be characterized as slow to engage in new interests, preoccupied with narrow details, and inclined to be reflective, rigid, stoic, slow-tempered, orderly, and persistent. Each is viewed as being associated with a different neurotransmitter system: novelty seeking with the dopaminergic system, harm avoidance with the serotonergic system, and reward dependence with the noradrenergic system. These heritable traits interact to shape the development of personality by influencing learning experiences, information processing, mood reactions, and general adaptation. Depending upon the combinations of these three core dimensions, individuals will be inclined to develop particular patterns of behavior and personality styles. In 1993, Cloninger, Svrakic, and Przybeck extended the original model to include a fourth dimension, labeled persistence, and three dimensions of character, as they put it, that mature in adulthood and influence personal and social effectiveness as well as the acquisition of self-concepts. Each aspect of self-concept corresponds to the three character dimensions. Unfortunately, the recent expansion of the original neurobiologic temperament model appears to weaken the strength of the original model by adding character themes that are culturally bound and philosophically tenuous constructs.

Another original thinker in the biophysical domain of personality is Larry Siever. In many regards, Siever's proposals concerning the temperamental underpinning of personality dispositions and disorders can be traced back through history to the humoral thesis of Hippocrates. However, the specificity and clarity of Siever's reasoning shows how advanced this ancient notion of temperament has become. Although not intended to accommodate all of the particulars and complexities of the many varieties of personality disorders in the current classification system, it provides a means for integrating the clinical characteristics of several of these disorders and their possible psychobiologic and developmental roots.

Siever develops a dimensional model that has major Axis I syndromes at one extreme and milder personality inclinations at the other end. He proposes four major predispositions: cognitive/perceptual organization, impulsivity/aggression, affective instability, and anxiety/inhibition. For example, schizophrenic disorders are seen as disturbances of a cognitive/percep-

tual nature, exhibited in thought disorders, psychotic symptoms, and social isolation; the schizotypal disorder would serve as the prototype among the personality types. Disorders of impulsivity/aggression are hypothesized as resulting in poor impulse control, particularly as seen in aggressive actions. In the more distinct Axis I forms, Siever suggests its presence in explosive disorders, pathologic gambling, or kleptomania. When this dimension is more pervasive and chronic, as in Axis II, the predisposition may be seen in persistent self-destructive behaviors, such as in Axis II borderline and antisocial personality disorders. Problems of affective instability are most clearly observed in the intensity and dysregulation of mood disorders. Where this inclination is more sustained over time, it may interfere with the development of stable relationships and self-image, as may be seen manifested in borderline or histrionic personality disorders. Lastly, the anxiety/inhibition dimension appears to be related to the Axis I Anxiety disorders (e.g., social phobia, compulsive rituals); when present at a low threshold over extended periods of development, we may observe a resulting avoidant, compulsive, or dependent Axis II personality disorder. [See ANXIETY; IMPULSE CONTROL; MOOD DISORDERS.]

E. Statistical Formulations

Factor analysis is an inductive statistical method for uncovering dimensions that account for the intercorrelations between numerous variables. Perhaps the most sophisticated investigator of the factorial structure of personality and pathology is W. John Livesley and his associates. Drawing initially on descriptive characterizations found in a wide range of personality-oriented texts and articles, these authors generated a set of 100 separate traits for the personality disorders. Factor analysis was used to reduce these to a more manageable set of dimensions: identity disturbance, rejection, restricted expression, compulsive behaviors, perceptual-cognitive distortion, insecure attachment, interpersonal disesteem, diffidence, intimacy, avoidance, narcissism, passive oppositionality, stimulus-seeking, social apprehension, and conduct problems. According to Livesley, these components provide a readily interpretable and clinically meaningful structure that is consistent with a number of the *DSM* personality disorders. As he sees it, the obsessive-compulsive and narcissistic personality disorders are clearly represented by a single component. Others are represented by combinations of several dimensions. For example, dependent personality disorder is represented by insecure attachment and diffidence, whereas antisocial personality disorder is best represented by conduct problems and interpersonal disesteem.

While Livesley is perhaps the most sophisticated, the most vigorous exponents of the statistical approach to personality follow the Five-Factor Model, most notably Costa and McCrae, and more recently Widiger. The Five-Factor Model derives its data primarily from studies of folk lexicals, that is, the codification of descriptive words found in the language of lay persons. Although disagreements exist regarding the labels to be used to represent the five factors, there is sufficient commonality from one context and culture to another to view them as highly reliable. These factors have been termed: Factor 1, neuroticism, reflecting chronic levels of emotional instability and susceptibility to psychological distress; Factor 2, extraversion, signifying a disposition to interpersonal interactions, activity and stimulus seeking, as well as a capacity for joy; Factor 3, openness to experience, seen typically in an appreciation for new experiences, a willingness to entertain novel ideas, as well as curiousness and imaginativeness; Factor 4, agreeableness, representing those who are disposed to be good-natured, trusting, helpful, and altruistic; and Factor 5, conscientiousness, signifying a high degree of organization, reliability, persistence, ambitiousness, and control.

Although there have been serious critiques of this model, both in its assumptions and empirical support, it does provide an interesting schema of factorial traits that may serve to characterize the *DSM* personality disorders. For example, histrionic and schizoid disorders appear to fall on opposite extremes of the extraversion factor. Agreeableness may be seen among dependents and compulsives, whereas deficits in agreeableness are likely to be found among antisocials and paranoids. Low scores on conscientiousness appear to be consistently associated with antisocial and passive-aggressive (negativistic) personality disorders. And neuroticism seems especially notable among borderlines. The FFM has proven to be extremely robust across numerous factor solutions, is found in a number of cultures and languages, appears stable across observers, and correlates well with a variety of non-factorially based clinical measures.

III. PERSONALITY AS A PSYCHOLOGICAL PARALLEL TO THE IMMUNE SYSTEM

The perspectives we have described above illustrate the many views that may be taken on personality. All of these are likely to be valid to some extent. In fact, we can think of personality as a system in which the various elements from these perspectives interact to form the whole person. A systems conception of personality breaks the long-entrenched habit of conceiving personality types as internally homogeneous "substances" that fill the "vessel" of the person. Instead, personality may be seen as a multifaceted matrix anchored across all of the traditional approaches to its subject matter.

The misconception of personality-as-substance is particularly troublesome in the area of personality pathology, where personality disorders are often viewed as diseases, that is, as essentially some foreign entity or lesion that intrudes insidiously within the person to undermine so-called normal functions. The archaic notion that all mental disorders represent external intrusions or internal disease processes is an offshoot of prescientific ideas such as demons or spirits that ostensibly possess or cast spells on the person. The role of infectious agents and anatomical lesions in physical medicine has reawakened this archaic view. Such misconception is an appealing simplification to the layman, who can attribute irrationalities or abnormal behaviors to some intrusive or upsetting agent. In addition, it appeals to less-sophisticated clinicians, by supporting the belief that the insidious intruder can be identified, hunted down, and destroyed.

Such naive notions carry little weight among advanced medical and behavioral scientists. Given our increasing awareness of the complex nature of both health and disease, we now recognize, for example, that most disorders, both physical and psychological, result from a dynamic and changing interplay between individuals' capacities to cope and the environment within which they live. It is the patients' overall constitutional makeup that serves as a substrate that inclines them to resist or to succumb to potentially troublesome environmental forces. To illustrate: While infectious viruses and bacteria flourish within the environment, it is the person's immunologic defenses that determine whether or not such microbes will take hold, spread, and, ultimately, result in illness. Individuals with robust immune activity counteract the usual infectious microbes with ease, whereas those with weakened immune capacities are vulnerable, fail to handle "intrusions," and succumb.

Psychological health and pathology should be conceived as reflecting the same interactive pattern between person and environment. Here, however, it is not the individual's physical immunologic defenses but rather the basic personality pattern—that is, coping skills and adaptive flexibilities—that determine whether the person will master or succumb to the psychosocial environment. Just as physical ill health is likely to be less a matter of some alien virus than it is a dysfunction in the body's capacity to deal with infectious agents, so too is psychological ill health likely to be less a product of some single intrusive psychic stressor than it is a dysfunction in the personality's capacity to cope with life's difficulties. Viewed this way, the structure and characteristics of personality, normal or abnormal, become the foundation for the individual's capacity to function in a mentally healthy or ill way.

IV. AN EVOLUTIONARY MODEL OF OPTIMALITY AND ABNORMALITY IN PERSONALITY

If human beings are intrinsically contextualized systems, how is a taxonomy of personality, normal and abnormal, to be derived? Healthy and abnormal aspects of personality could be discussed through any one of the perspectives presented above. Such an approach, however, would be necessary, but not sufficient, since it would simply conceptualize the whole in terms of one or more of its parts. Obviously, any approach that is to be necessary and sufficient cannot commit the same error, that of attempting to get all of personality into what is but a single viewpoint within psychology. Instead, what is required are a set of scientific, rational principles that not only supply content to a personality theory, but also transcend the particularism of any single domain or perspective.

Evolution provides a set of an organizing principles for studying both health and pathology of personality. Owing to the mathematical and deductive insights of our colleagues in physics, we have a deeper and clearer sense of the early evolution and structural relations among matter and energy. So too has knowledge progressed in our studies of physical chemistry, microbiology, evolutionary theory, population biology, ecology, and ethology. The relationship between

evolutionary principles and psychology, however, represents a newer area that has been less investigated. It is clear that each evolved species displays commonalities in its adaptive or survival style. Within each species, however, there are differences in style and differences in the success with which its various members adapt to the diverse and changing environments they face. In these simplest of terms, personality would be conceived as representing the more-or-less distinctive style of adaptive functioning that an organism of a particular species exhibits as it relates to its typical range of environments. "Disorders" of personality, so formulated, would represent particular styles of maladaptive functioning that can be traced to deficiencies, imbalances, or conflicts in a species' capacity to relate to the environments it faces.

To provide a conceptual background from these sciences, and to furnish a rough model concerning the styles of personality, normal and abnormal, four spheres in which evolutionary and ecological principles can be applied are labeled as existence, adaptation, replication, and abstraction. The first relates to the serendipitous transformation of random or less organized states into those possessing distinct structures of greater organization; the second refers to homeostatic processes employed to sustain survival in open ecosystems; the third pertains to reproductive styles that maximize the diversification and selection of ecologically effective attributes; and the fourth concerns the emergence of competencies that foster anticipatory planning and reasoned decision making. These first three spheres parallel the "three great polarities of mental life" noted by Freud. Unfortunately, Freud failed to capitalize on them as a basis for formulating personality types. Preoccupied with discovering the symptom derivatives of instincts as they unfold during psychosexual development, Freud showed little interest at the time in constructing a typology of character structures. Although he failed to pursue their potentials, the ingredients he formulated for his tripartite polarity schema were drawn on by his disciples for many decades to come, seen prominently in the recent growth of "ego psychology," "self-psychology," and "object relations" theory.

A. Existential Aims: The Life Enhancement-Life Preservation Polarity

Every system can be conceptualized on its own terms, as a closed system, existing in and of itself. The most basic of all motivations, that of existence, has a two-fold aspect. The first pertains to the enrichment or enhancement of life, that is, creating or strengthening ecologically survivable organisms. The second is the preservation of life, that is, creating survivability and security by avoiding events that might terminate it. Although the authors disagree with Freud's concept of a death instinct (Thanatos), we believe he was essentially correct in recognizing that a balanced yet fundamental biological bipolarity exists in nature, a bipolarity that has its parallel in the physical world. As Freud wrote in *An Outline of Psychoanalysis* in 1940 (one of his last works), "The analogy of our two basic instincts extends from the sphere of living things to the pair of opposing forces—attraction and repulsion—which rule the inorganic world." Among humans, the former may be seen in life-enhancing acts that enrich existence by what are experientially recorded as "pleasurable" events (positive reinforcers), the latter in life-preserving behaviors oriented to achieve security by repelling or avoiding events that are experientially characterized as "painful" (negative reinforcers).

For all organic systems, existence is literally a to-be or not-to-be issue. In the inorganic world, "to be" is essentially a matter of possessing qualities that distinguish a phenomenon from its surrounding field, that is, of not being in a state of entropy. Among organic beings, "to be" is a matter of possessing the properties of life as well as being located in ecosystems that facilitate processes that enhance and preserve life, maintaining the integrity of the organism within its surrounding field. In the phenomenological or experiential world of sentient organisms, events that extend life and preserve it correspond to metaphorical terms such as pleasure and pain, that is, recognizing and pursuing life-enriching motivations and rewards, on the one hand, and recognizing and eschewing life-threatening emotions and sensations, on the other.

1. Life Preservation:
Avoiding Danger and Threat

What criteria for healthy personality may be deduced from this first dimension of life? One might assume that a criterion based on the avoidance of psychic or physical pain would be sufficiently self-evident not to require specification. As is well known, debates have arisen in the literature as to whether mental health/normality reflects the absence of mental disorder, being merely the reverse side of the mental illness or abnormality coin. That there is a relationship between health and disease cannot be questioned; the two are intimately connected, conceptually and physically. On the other hand, to define health solely as the absence of disorder will not suffice. As a single criterion among several, however, features of behavior and experience that signify both the lack of (for example, anxiety, depression) and an aversion to (for example, threats to safety and security) pain in its many and diverse forms provide a necessary foundation upon which other, more positively constructed criteria may rest. Substantively, positive normality must comprise elements beyond mere nonnormality or abnormality. And despite the complexities and inconsistencies of personality, from a definitional point of view normality does preclude nonnormality.

Notable here are the contributions of Abraham Maslow, particularly his hierarchic listing of "needs." Best known are the five fundamental needs that lead to self-actualization, the first two of which relate to our evolutionary criterion of life preservation. Included in the first group are physiological needs such as air, water, food, and sleep, qualities of the ecosystem essential for survival. Next, and equally necessary to avoid danger and threat, are what Maslow terms the safety needs, including the freedom from jeopardy, the security of physical protection and psychic stability, as well as the presence of social order and interpersonal predictability.

Many pathologies of personality can be traced to aberrations in meeting this first criterion of normality. For example, among those termed avoidant personalities there exists an excessive preoccupation with threats to psychic security, an expectation of and hyperalertness to signs of potential rejection that leads these persons to disengage from everyday relationships and pleasures. Other personalities engage in excessive risk taking, a proclivity to chance hazards that endanger life and liberty. Such a pattern is characteristic of those labeled antisocial personalities. Here there is little of the caution and prudence expected in the normality criterion of avoiding danger and threat; rather, we observe its opposite, a rash willingness to put one's safety in jeopardy, to play with fire and throw caution to the wind.

2. Life Enhancement:
Seeking Rewarding Experiences

At the other end of the "existence polarity" are attitudes and behaviors designed to foster and enrich life, to generate joy, pleasure, contentment, fulfillment, and thereby strengthen the capacity of the individual to remain vital and competent physically and psychically. This criterion asserts that existence/survival calls for more than life preservation alone; beyond pain avoidance is the enhancement of life.

This idea asks us to go at least one step further than Freud's notion that life's motivation consists wholly of "reducing tensions" (that is, avoiding or minimizing pain), maintaining thereby a steady state, if you will, a homeostatic balance and inner stability. In accord with our view of evolution's polarities, we would assert that normal humans are driven also by the desire to enrich their lives, to seek invigorating sensations and challenges, to venture and explore, all to the end of increasing the replicability of both the individual and the species.

The view that there exists an organismic striving to expand one's inherent potentialities (as well as those of one's kind and species) has been implicit in the literature for ages. Regarding the key instrumental role of "the pleasures," Spencer wrote, well more than a century ago in 1870, that "pleasures are the correlatives of actions conducive to [organismic] welfare . . . the incentives to life supporting acts." That "the pleasures" may be both sign and vehicle for this realization was recorded even in the ancient writings of the Talmud, which states that "everyone will have to justify himself in the life hereafter for every failure to enjoy a legitimately offered pleasure in this world."

Turning to more recent psychological formulations, both Carl Rogers and Abraham Maslow have proposed concepts akin to the criterion of enhancing and enriching life. In his notion of "openness to experience," Rogers asserts that the fully functioning person has no aspect of his or her nature closed off. Such individuals are not only receptive to the experiences that life offers but are able also to use them in expanding all of life's emotions, as well as being open to all forms of personal expression. Along a similar vein, Maslow speaks of the ability to maintain a freshness to experience, to keep up one's capacity to appreciate relationships and events. No matter how often events or persons are encountered, one is neither sated nor bored but is disposed to view them with an ongoing sense of "awe and wonder."

Failure to enrich one's own life is seen clearly in the schizoid and avoidant personalities. In the former there is a marked hedonic deficiency, stemming either from an inherent deficit in affective substrates or the failure of stimulative experience to develop either or both attachment behaviors or affective capacity. Among those designated avoidant personalities, constitutional sensitivities or abusive life experiences have led to an intense attentional sensitivity to psychic pain and a consequent distrust in either the genuineness or durability of the "pleasures," such that these individuals can no longer permit themselves to experience them. Both of these personalities tend to be withdrawn and isolated, joyless and grim, neither seeking nor sharing in the rewards of life.

B. Adaptive Modes: The Accommodation-Modification Polarity

The second basic polar distinction relates to what are here termed the modes of adaptation; it is also framed as a two-part polarity. One may best be characterized as the mode of ecologic accommodation, signifying inclinations to passively "fit in," to locate and remain securely anchored in a niche, subject to the vagaries and unpredictabilities of the environment, all acceded to with one crucial proviso: that the elements comprising the surroundings will furnish both the nourishment and the protection needed to sustain existence. Although based on a somewhat simplistic bifurcation among adaptive strategies, this *passive* accommodating mode is one of the two fundamental methods that living organisms have evolved as a means of survival. It represents the core process employed in the evolution of what has come to be designated as the plant kingdom, a stationary, rooted, yet essentially pliant and dependent survival mode. By contrast, the other of the two major modes of adaptation is seen in the lifestyle of the animal kingdom. Here we observe a primary inclination toward ecologic modification, an *active* tendency to change or rearrange the elements comprising the larger milieu, to intrude upon otherwise quiescent settings, a versatility in shifting from one niche to another as unpredictability arises, a mobile and interventional mode that actively stirs, maneuvers, yields, and, at the human level, substantially transforms the environment to meet its own survival aims. This second, accommodating–modifying, polarity differs from the first, enhancing–preserving, in that it characterizes how that which now exists endures. Both passive and active modes have proven impressively capable of nourishing and preserving life. Whether the polarity sketched is phrased in terms of accommodating versus modifying, passivity versus activity, or plant versus animal, it represents, at the most basic level, the two fundamental modes that organisms have evolved to sustain their existence.

One interesting expression of this polarity lies in the distinction between mechanistic and organismic theories of human behavior, which parallel the passive and active modes, respectively. Whether from without (environmental pressures) or from within (biologic drives or unconscious determinants), more-or-less traditional and mechanistic theories assert that humans are subjected to and have minimal control over forces that compel them to behave as they do. By contrast, organismic theories, reflecting the views of more contemporary thinkers and cultures, dismiss the attitude that humans are essentially passive robots reacting to external and largely unknown promptings. Rather, they propose that humans actively determine the course of their own behaviors, that they confront life's opportunities and dilemmas, choose what will be done, and even initiate actions that alter the very character of their environments. Both views in our judgment are correct in part; humans are at times actors and at other times reactors. Moreover, it is our contention that important individual differences of personologic significance are to be found along this activity-passivity dimension. No individual is one or the other, but both in varying proportions, a difference relevant to the assessment of personality styles.

Descending now from lofty theoretical concerns to the level of the individual, those who are passively oriented are often reflective and deliberate, but may possess few overt strategies to gain their ends. They display a seeming inertness, a phlegmatic quality, a tendency toward acquiescence, a restrained attitude in which they initiate little to modify events, waiting for the circumstances of their environment to take their course before making accommodations. Some may be temperamentally ill-equipped to rouse or assert themselves; perhaps past experience has deprived them of opportunities to acquire a range of competencies or confidence in their ability to master the events of their environment; equally possible is a naive confidence that things will come their way with little or no effort on their part. From a variety of diverse sources, then, those at the passive end of the polarity appear to merely sustain their existence, engaging in few direct instrumental activities to intercede in life events or to generate change. They seem suspended, quiescent,

placid, immobile, restrained, listless, waiting for things to happen and reacting to them only after they occur.

In contrast, individuals at the active end of the polarity are best characterized by their alertness, vigilance, liveliness, vigor, forcefulness, stimulus-seeking energy, and drive. Some plan strategies and scan alternatives to circumvent obstacles or avoid the distress of punishment, rejection, and anxiety. Others are impulsive, precipitate, excitable, rash, and hasty, seeking to elicit pleasures and rewards. Although specific goals vary and change from time to time, actively aroused individuals seek to alter their lives, to intrude on passing events by energetically and busily modifying the circumstances of their environment.

Normal or optimal functioning, at least among humans, appears to call for a flexibility that interweaves both polar extremes. In the first evolutionary stage, that relating to existence, behaviors encouraging both life enhancement (pleasure) and life preservation (pain avoidance) are likely to be more successful in achieving survival than actions limited to one or the other alone. Similarly, regarding adaptation, modes of functioning that exhibit both ecologic accommodation and ecologic modification are likely to be more successful than either by itself. Normality again requires a synchronous and coordinated personal style that weaves a balanced answer to the question of whether one should accept what the fates have brought forth or take the initiative in altering the circumstances of one's life.

1. Ecological Accommodation: Abiding Hospitable Realities

On first reflection, it would seem to be less than optimal to submit meekly to what life presents, to adjust obligingly to destiny. Crucial to this adaptive course is the capacity of the surroundings to provide nourishment and protection requisite to the individual life. Whether this capacity is adequate and likely to endure is of course a matter of judgment, but if the events of life have been and continue to be caring and giving, is it not perhaps wisest, from an evolutionary perspective, to accept this good fortune and "let matters be"? This accommodating or passive life philosophy has worked extremely well in sustaining and fostering those complex organisms that comprise the plant kingdom. Hence passivity, the yielding and adapting to environmental forces, is in itself not only unproblematic but, where events and circumstances provide the "pleasures" or enrichment of life and protect against their "pains," positively adaptive and constructive.

Once again we find a precedent for this position in the writings of humanistic psychology. Maslow stated that "self-actualized" individuals accept their nature as it is, despite personal weaknesses and imperfections. Comfortable with themselves and the world around them, they do not seek to change "the water because it is wet, or the rocks because they are hard." They have learned to accept the natural order of things, and need not hide behind false masks or transform others to fit "distorted needs." Accepting themselves without shame or apology, they are equally at peace with the shortcomings of those with whom they live and relate.

Failure in respecting the accommodating/abiding criterion is seen in the histrionic personality. Their persistent and unrelenting manipulation of events is designed to maximize the receipt of attention and favors as well as to avoid social disinterest and disapproval. They show an insatiable if not indiscriminate search for stimulation and approval. Their clever and often artful social behaviors may give the appearance of an inner confidence and self-assurance, but beneath this guise lies a fear that a failure on their part to ensure the receipt of attention will, in short order, result in indifference or rejection, and hence their desperate need for reassurance and repeated signs of approval. Tribute and affection must constantly be replenished and are sought from every interpersonal source. As they are quickly bored and sated, they keep stirring up things, becoming enthusiastic about one activity and then another. There is a restless stimulus-seeking quality in which they cannot leave well enough alone.

At the other end of the polarity are personality disorders that exhibit an excess of passivity, failing thereby to give direction to their own lives. Several personality disorders demonstrate this passive style, although their passivity derives from and is expressed in appreciably different ways. For dependents, passivity stems from deficits in self-confidence and competence, leading to deficits in initiative and autonomous skills as well as a tendency to wait passively while others assume leadership and guide them. Passivity among obsessive-compulsive personalities stems from their fear of acting independently, owing to intrapsychic resolutions they have made to quell hidden thoughts and emotions generated by their intense self-

other ambivalence. Dreading the possibility of making mistakes or engaging in disapproved behaviors, they become indecisive, immobilized, restrained, and passive. High on pain and low on both pleasure and self, masochistic personalities operate on the assumption that they dare not expect nor deserve to have life go their way; giving up any efforts to achieve a life that accords with their "true" desires, they passively submit to others' wishes, acquiescently accepting their fate. Finally, narcissists, especially high on self and low on others, benignly assume that "good things" will come their way with little or no effort on their part; this passive exploitation of others is a consequence of the unexplored confidence that underlies their self-centered presumptions.

2. Ecologic Modification: Mastering the Environment

The active end of the bipolarity signifies the taking of initiative in altering and shaping life's events. As stated previously, such persons are best characterized by their alertness, vigilance, liveliness, vigor, and forcefulness, their stimulus-seeking energy and drive. There are many theoretical precedents that express the active or modifying end of the "adaptational" polarity. One is White's concept of "effectance," an intrinsic motive that prompts the individual to impose his or her own desires upon the environment. De Charms elaborated this same theme through his idea of the person as either "Origin" or "Pawn," constructs that parallel the active and passive, respectively. According to this author, "An Origin is a person who perceives his behavior as determined by his own choosing; a Pawn is a person who perceives his behavior as determined by external forces beyond his control." In a similar vein, Fromm proposed in 1955 a need on the part of man to rise above the roles of passive creatures in an accidental and random world. To him, humans are driven to transcend their status as created beings, and instead seek to become creators themselves, actively shaping their own destiny. By generating their own purposes, humans provide themselves with a true basis of freedom.

C. Replicatory Strategies: The Nurturing-Individuating Polarity

Although less profound than the first polarity, which represents the enhancement of order (existence-life-pleasure) and the prevention of disorder (nonexistence-death-pain), or the second polarity, which differentiates the adaptive modes, accommodation (plant-passive) versus those of modification (animal-active), the third polarity, based on distinctions in reproductive strategies (gene replication), is no less fundamental; it contrasts the maximization of reproductive propagation (male-self) from that of the maximization of reproductive nurturance (female-other).

Evolutionary biologists have recorded marked differences among species in both the cycle and pattern of their reproductive behaviors. Of special interest is the extreme diversity among and within species in the number of offspring spawned and the consequent nurturing and protective investment of the parents in the survival of their progeny. Designated the r-strategy and K-strategy in population biology, the former seeks to produce a vast number of offspring that are then given but minimal attention in terms of their survival; the latter is typified by the production of a few offspring that are then nurtured assiduously to adulthood. Oysters, which generate some 500 million eggs annually, exemplify the r-strategy; the K-strategy is found among the great apes, which produce only one offspring every 5 or 6 years.

The distinction between r- and K-strategies may be made within a species, as well. Human females typically produce about 400 eggs in a lifetime, of which no more than 20 to 25 can mature into viable infants. The energy investment expended in gestation, nurturing, and caring for each child, both before and during the years following birth, is extraordinary. Not only is the female required to devote much of her energies to bring the fetus to full term, but during this period she cannot be fertilized again; in contrast, the male is free to mate with numerous females. And should her child fail to survive, the waste in physical and emotional exertion is not only enormous, but amounts to a substantial portion of the mother's lifetime reproductive potential. There appears to be good reason, therefore, to encourage a protective and caring inclination on the part of the female, as evident in a sensitivity to cues of distress and a willingness to persist in attending to the needs and nurturing of her offspring.

In contrast, the male discharges tens of millions of sperm when mating. On fertilization, his physical and emotional commitment can end with minimal consequences. Although the protective and food-gathering efforts of the male may be lost by an early abandonment of a mother and an offspring or two, much more

may be gained by investing energies in pursuits that achieve the wide reproductive spread of his genes. Relative to the female of the species, whose best strategy appears to be the care and comfort of child and kin, that is, the K-strategy, the male is likely to be reproductively more prolific by maximizing self-propagation, that is, adopting the r-strategy. To focus primarily on self-replication may diminish the survival probabilities of a few of a male's progeny, but this occasional reproductive loss may be well compensated for by mating with multiple females and thereby producing multiple offspring.

In sum, males tend to be self-oriented owing to the fact that competition for reproductive resources maximizes the replicatory advantages of their genes. Conversely, females tend to be other-oriented owing to the fact that their competence in nurturing and protecting their limited progeny maximizes the replicatory advantages of their genes. The consequences of the male's r-strategy are a broad range of what may be seen as self-advancing as opposed to other-promoting behaviors, such as acting in an egotistic, insensitive, inconsiderate, uncaring, and noncommunicative manner. Male relationships thereby exhibit a "vertical" or hierarchical quality, one characterized by dominance of self over others. In contrast, females are more disposed to be other-promoting, affiliative, intimate, empathic, protective, and solicitous. Female relationships demonstrate a horizontal or even reverse hierarchical quality, one founded on equalitarian transactions, or even priority given to others.

As before, both of the following criteria are necessary to normality; there is no necessary opposition between the two. Humans can be both self-actualizing and other-encouraging, although most persons are likely to be biased toward one or the other side. Again, a coordinated balance is the key.

I. Progeny Nurturance: Constructively Loving Others

As described earlier, recombinant replication achieved by sexual mating entails a balanced though asymmetric parental investment in both the genesis and nurturance of offspring.

Numerous eloquent passages have been written that relate to the self-other polarity. The three addressed here are from Maslow, Allport, and Fromm. According to Maslow, once basic safety and security needs are met, need for belonging and love emerge. Here intimate and caring relationships with significant others are established in which giving love is just as important as receiving it. Noting the difficulty in satisfying these needs in our unstable and changing modern world, Maslow saw here a basis for family therapy and for more communal life-styles. One of Allport's criteria of a mature personality, by which he meant a warm relating of self to others, refers to an individual's ability to display intimacy and love for a parent, child, spouse, or close friend. Because of this authentic oneness with the other, there is a deep and genuine concern for his or her welfare. Finally, beyond one's intimate family and friends, there exists an extension of warmth in the mature person to humankind at large, an understanding of the human condition and a kinship with all peoples. Fromm felt that human beings have become aware of the growing loss of their ties with nature as well as with each other, and feel increasingly separate and alone. Accordingly, it is necessary to pursue new ties with others to replace those that have been lost or can no longer be depended on. To counter the loss of communion with nature, Fromm felt that health requires a brotherliness with mankind, a sense of involvement, concern, and relatedness with the world.

The pathological consequences of failing to embrace the more nurturant and other-oriented aspects of this polarity are seen most clearly in the antisocial and narcissistic personality disorders. Both exhibit an imbalance through their primary reliance on self rather than others. In the narcissistic personality, development reflects a self-image of superior worth, often learned in response to admiring and doting parents. Self-rewards are highly gratifying if all that is valued is the self. Displaying manifest confidence, arrogance, and an exploitative egocentricity in social contexts, the individual "already" has all that is important, the self. Often, they blithely assume that others will recognize their specialness, and maintain an air of arrogant self-assurance that allows them to exploit others to their own advantage, without much thought or even conscious intent. Their sublime confidence that things will work out well provides them with little incentive to engage in the reciprocal give and take of social life.

Related through the focus on self, but more active in orientation is the antisocial personality. These individuals act to counter the expectation of pain at the hand of others by engaging in duplicitous or illegal behaviors through which others can be exploited for self-gain. Skeptical regarding the motives of others, they desire autonomy and wish revenge for what are felt as past injustices. Many are irresponsible and impulsive, dispositions justified through the unreliable and disloyal actions of others. Insensitivity and ruthlessness with others are the primary means they have learned to head off abuse and victimization.

2. Individual Propagation: Actualizing Self

Throughout this article we have drawn on the humanistic construct of self-actualization. Carl Jung noted that any imposed "collective standard is a serious check to individuality," injurious to the vitality of the person, a form of "artificial stunting." Kurt Goldstein was perhaps the first to use the concept under review here in a modern sense. As he phrased it, "There is only one motive by which human activity is set going: the tendency to actualize oneself."

The early views of Jung and Goldstein have been enriched by later theorists, notably Fromm, Perls, Rogers, and Maslow. Following the views of his forerunners, Maslow stated that self-actualization is the "supreme development" and use of all our abilities, ultimately becoming what we have the potential to become. Noting that self-actualists often require detachment and solitude, Maslow asserted that such persons are strongly self-centered and self-directed, make up their own mind and reach their own decisions, without the need to gain social approval. Similarly, Carl Rogers posited a single, overreaching motive for the normal or healthy person—maintaining, actualizing, and enhancing one's potential. Such a goal is identical to maintaining a homeostatic balance or a high degree of ease and comfort, but reflects the desire to move forward in becoming what is intrinsic to self and to enhance further that which one has already become. Believing that humans have an innate urge to create, Rogers stated that the most creative product of all is one's own self.

A failure in the achievement of self-actualization, a giving up of self to gain the approbation of others, is seen in the dependent personalities. These individuals have learned that feeling good, secure, confident, and so on—that is, those feelings associated with pleasure or the avoidance of pain—is provided almost exclusively through their relationship with others. Behaviorally, these persons learn early that rewarding experiences cannot be readily achieved alone. Instead, such experiences are better secured by appealing to others as their source of nurturance and security. Often, they wait passively for others to take the initiative in providing safety and sustenance, searching for relationships in which others reliably furnish affection, protection, and leadership. Lacking both initiative and autonomy, they assume a dependent role in interpersonal relations, accepting what kindness and support they may find and willingly submitting to the wishes of others in order to maintain nurturance and security.

As we have seen, exact specification of the essential dimensions of health and abnormality in personality is a difficult undertaking, one complicated by the complexity of personality itself, and by the variety of perspectives that exist on the field. While any of these might form a useful point of departure in describing personality, they cannot be regarded as endpoints. A modern, evolutionary perspective on personality seeks to synthesize these views on a scientific basis, enabling health and pathology to be conceptualized through personality as the specific adaptational or immunologic component of the mental sphere.

BIBLIOGRAPHY

Beck, A. T., & Freeman, A. (1990). *Cognitive therapy of personality disorders.* New York: Guilford.

Benjamin, L. S. (1993). *Interpersonal diagnosis and treatment of personality disorders.* New York: Guilford Press.

Cloninger, C. R. (1987). A systematic method for clinical description and classification of personality variants. *Archives of General Psychiatry, 44,* 573–588.

Costa, P. T., & Widiger, T. (Eds.). (1993). *Personality disorders and the five-factor model of personality.* Washington, DC: American Psychological Association.

Kernberg, O. F. (1984). *Severe personality disorders.* New Haven: Yale University Press.

Millon, T. (1990). *Toward a new personology: An evolutionary model.* New York: Wiley-Interscience.

Millon, T., & Davis, R. D. (1996). *Disorders of personality: DSM-IV and beyond.* New York: Wiley-Interscience.

Siever, L. J., & Davis, K. L. (1991). A psychobiological perspective on the personality disorders. *American Journal of Psychiatry, 148,* 1647–1658.

Personality Assessment

Paul T. Costa, Jr., and Robert R. McCrae

National Institutes of Health

Five-Factor Model An organization of personality traits in terms of the broad factors of neuroticism versus emotional stability, extraversion, openness to experience, agreeableness, and conscientiousness.
Objective Test An assessment device that can be scored clerically, without the need for clinical interpretation.
Projective Technique A method of assessment in which responses to ambiguous stimuli (e.g., inkblots) are thought to reveal aspects of the respondent's personality.
Reliability The consistency with which an assessment instrument gives the same results.
Validity The accuracy with which an assessment instrument measures its intended construct.

The term personality is used by different theorists in widely different ways, and the practice of **PERSONALITY ASSESSMENT** is correspondingly varied. Nevertheless, most definitions of personality refer to features that characterize an individual and distinguish him or her from others, and most assessment procedures attempt to measure these features, usually in comparison to the average person. Different approaches to personality assessment differ in the variables they measure, in the source of information about the individual, and in the way information is evaluated. This article reviews the most common approaches to personality assessment (projective techniques, self-report questionnaires, observer ratings, and laboratory measures) and their status in contemporary psychological science and practice.

Personality variables are pervasive and enduring, and thus can be expected to have an impact on a variety of areas in the individual's life—for example, the prototypic extrovert has a wide circle of friends, speaks out in class, does well in enterprising occupations, enjoys competitive sports, and has an optimistic outlook in life. In consequence, personality assessment is important in many applied areas. Psychiatrists who need to diagnose psychopathology, counselors who want to suggest meaningful vocational choices, and physicians concerned with behavioral health risk factors may all turn to personality assessment. Personality variables are important in forensic, developmental, educational, social, industrial, and clinical psychology, as well as personality psychology, the discipline which seeks a scientific understanding of personality itself. For all these purposes, accurate assessment of personality is crucial.

Personality is also of great importance to laypersons in everyday life and in such significant decisions as whom to vote for or marry. Lay evaluations of personality are in some respects unscientific and susceptible to many biases; in other respects they are extremely sophisticated interpretations of observed behavior. Much (though not all) of personality assessment consists of knowing how to systematize the information laypersons have about themselves and each other in order to capitalize on the strengths and reduce the limitations of lay perceptions of personality.

The scientific study of individual differences in personality can be traced to the work of Sir Francis Galton in the 1880s, and it has occupied many of the brightest minds in psychology since. During the 1950s and 1960s, personality assessment underwent a period of crisis, based in part on humanistic objections to the depersonalizing labeling that much assessment seemed to foster, and in part on real (although exaggerated) technical problems with assessment instruments. Considerable progress has been made in the past 30 years in both personality theory and test construction, and today personality assessment is once again assuming a central role in psychology. [*See* PERSONALITY.]

I. ASSESSMENT METHODS AND INSTRUMENTS

A. Projective Techniques

The single most influential theory of personality is psychoanalysis, a complex system developed by Sigmund Freud and elaborated by a host of his followers. Briefly, psychoanalysis sees human personality as the result of conflict between the individual's sexual and aggressive impulses and society's demand for their control. In the course of early development, people evolve characteristic ways of resolving these conflicts which guide their adult behavior, particularly their interpersonal relationships. Because the underlying conflicts are psychologically painful and threatening, both the impulses and the defenses against them are repressed from consciousness. From this perspective, individuals never really know themselves and hide their most important features from those around them.

Thus, psychoanalytic theory poses formidable problems for personality assessment. The central information is not merely unavailable; it is systematically distorted. The analyst must make elaborate inferences on the basis of free associations, dreams, and slips of the tongue. But patients may not recall dreams or make revealing slips, and psychoanalysts need a dependable source of information that can be gathered as needed. Projective tests were designed to fill this need.

Rorschach's inkblots are a series of 10 cards shown to the patient or subject, who is asked to explain what he or she sees in them. The basic premise is that these abstract blots, having no meaning of their own, will act as a screen onto which the inner conflicts, impulses, and emotions of the patient will be projected. They will of course still be disguised—otherwise they would be censored by the patient's defenses—but they can be interpreted by the knowledgeable analyst just as an X-ray can be read by a skilled radiologist.

The projective technique is an ingenious approach to the problem of assessing unconscious conflicts, and the window it promises into the depths of the mind is extremely appealing. The Rorschach continues to be one of the most widely used instruments in personality assessment, and dozens of variations (including the Holtzman Inkblot Technique) and scoring systems have been developed.

It is therefore more than a little unfortunate that the scientific basis of these instruments—and of psychoanalysis itself—is highly questionable. Different interpreters draw very different conclusions from the same set of responses, and few rigorous studies have demonstrated that inkblot scores predict important external criteria. While clinical psychologists still rely heavily on the Rorschach, academic personality researchers have almost entirely abandoned it. A search of abstracts in the personality research field's most important publication, the *Journal of Personality and Social Psychology,* showed that of over 4000 articles appearing between 1974 and 1992, only four studies employed the Rorschach. (Rorschach studies do still appear regularly in more clinically oriented journals.)

All projective techniques use responses to relatively unstructured, ambiguous stimuli on the assumption that these will elicit spontaneous expressions of psychologically important features. This general approach to assessment is not limited to psychoanalytic theories of personality, but can also be applied to better supported theories about needs, motives, or traits. The Thematic Apperception Test, or TAT, shows a series of drawings about which individuals are asked to tell stories. The responses can be scored in a relatively straightforward fashion—for example, a story about overcoming obstacles in pursuit of a goal is scored as evidence of a need for achievement—and when so scored they typically show somewhat better evidence of scientific validity.

Note that these approaches do not assume that the characteristics they assess are repressed. When asked, people who tell stories about achievement or intimacy often report that they are high in achievement striving or nurturance. These projective tests apparently do not reveal a level of personality from which self-reports are excluded. [*See* PSYCHOANALYSIS.]

B. Objective Tests: Self-Reports

Projective tests are usually contrasted with *objective tests,* typically questionnaires in which subjects are asked to describe themselves by answering a series of questions. For example, a measure of conscientiousness may ask 10 questions such as "Do you always keep your desk clean?" and "Are you devoted to your work?" The test is considered objective because it can be scored directly, without the need for clinical interpretation: The number of conscientiousness items to which an individual responds *true* is that individual's score, and higher scores indicate higher levels of conscientiousness.

That basic paradigm—asking a standard set of questions and scoring responses with a predetermined key—has been used in thousands of assessment applications. Intelligence tests, vocational interest inventories, mood indicators, and measures of psychopathology as well as personality scales have adopted this model. Its scientific appeal lies in the fact that it can be repeated at different times and with different subjects, and consequently its accuracy can be evaluated. A whole branch of statistics, *psychometrics,* has been developed to analyze responses, both for what they tell us about the individual and for what they tell us about the quality of the test. Psychometric analyses provide information that can allow researchers to improve the quality of the test by changing the questions or the response format or the interpretation of the results.

If psychoanalysis formed the theoretical basis of projective tests, then trait psychology must be considered the basis of objective personality tests. Briefly, trait psychologies hold that individuals differ in a number of important ways that are usually thought to be continuously and normally distributed. Just as a few people are short, a few tall, and most average in height, so some people may be very agreeable, some very antagonistic, and most intermediate along this psychological dimension. Unlike moods, traits are enduring dispositions; and unlike specific habits, they are general and pervasive patterns of thoughts, feelings, and actions. Scores on trait measures should therefore be relatively constant, and scale items measuring different aspects of the

trait should go together. These theoretical premises are the basis of the psychometric requirements of retest reliability and internal consistency in personality scales.

Among the most important personality questionnaires in current use are the Minnesota Multiphasic Personality Inventory (MMPI), developed in the 1940s to measure aspects of psychopathology; the Sixteen Personality Factor Questionnaire and the Eysenck Personality Questionnaire, representing the personality theories of Raymond B. Cattell and Hans J. Eysenck, respectively; the Myers-Briggs Type Indicator, which is based on C. J. Jung's theory of psychological types; the California Psychological Inventory, a set of scales intended to tap folk concepts, the personality constructs used in everyday life; and the Personality Research Form, a psychometrically sophisticated measure of needs or motives. The NEO Personality Inventory is a more recent addition, based on new discoveries about the basic dimensions of personality. In addition to these omnibus inventories which all measure a variety of traits, there are a number of individual scales that are widely used in personality research, such as the self-monitoring scale and the locus of control scale.

C. Objective Tests: Observer Ratings

The vast majority of personality assessments are made on the basis of either projective tests or self-reports, but observer ratings provide a powerful alternative that is increasingly used in both research and clinical contexts. The clinical interview is a kind of observer rating, because the clinician not only asks questions, but also observes the reactions of the patient to the interview process. With a few exceptions (such as the Structured Interview for the Type A Behavior Pattern), these observations are not standardized, and thus they share with projective tests potential problems of unreliability.

There are, however, assessment methods that are both objective and observer based. These methods apply the same psychometric principles used in self-report questionnaires to ratings from informants. One simple and effective way to do this is by rephrasing questions in the third person. Instead of asking the individual, "Are you devoted to your work?" we could ask her spouse, "Is she devoted to her work?" One advantage of observer ratings is that we are not limited to a single respondent. It is possible to obtain ratings from friends, relatives, and neighbors, and there is evidence that aggregating or averaging several ratings yields better information on the individual.

Ranking methods provide an alternative to observer rating questionnaires. In these methods, all the members of a group rank each other on a series of characteristics. For example, all the members of a fraternity may be asked to decide which fraternity members are most and least *talkative,* and rank order all the other members between them. In the assessment center method, a group of expert raters (typically psychologists) interacts with a group of subjects over a period of a few days, observing them in both standardized and unstructured situations. They then make personality ratings, perhaps by checking descriptive adjectives.

The advantages of these different forms of gathering information from observers are still debated, as are the relative merits of self-reports versus observer ratings. Fortunately, however, many recent studies have shown general agreement between many different objective methods of assessing personality. This consensual validation of observations about personality traits forms an essential basis for scientific personality psychology.

D. Objective Tests: Laboratory Procedures

Researchers dedicated to objectivity have often hoped that personality could be assessed by laboratory tests that did not depend on the judgments of individuals. Quantity of salivation in response to a drop of lemon juice, perspiration as measured by the galvanic skin response, and dilation of the pupil have all been proposed as measures of personality attributes. This approach to personality assessment has been of limited value; physiological responses typically have shown only modest and inconsistent relations to personality variables.

Yet accumulating evidence on the heritability of most personality traits suggests that there is some genetic and presumably physiological basis for many traits. Increasing sophistication in our understanding of the brain and new techniques such as magnetic resonance imaging may one day lead to discoveries about personality/brain relations with implications for assessment. At present, however, our best source of

information about personality is the individual and those who know him or her well. [*See* BEHAVIORAL GENETICS.]

II. EVALUATING ASSESSMENT METHODS

A. Reliability and Validity

Although well-constructed objective measures of personality are valuable scientific tools, it should not be assumed that all objective measures are well-constructed. Psychometricians have, however, established a series of criteria by which scales can be evaluated. It is traditional to divide these into *reliability* criteria and *validity* criteria, although the distinction between the two is somewhat artificial. In essence, both require that the scale perform in ways that are consistent with its intended theoretical interpretation.

The two most common forms of reliability are *internal consistency* and *retest reliability*. If each of the items in a scale is considered to be an indicator of the same underlying trait, it seems reasonable to require that they all agree with each other. Cronbach's coefficient α is a commonly used measure of this internal consistency of scale items. Internal consistency can be increased by discarding items that show limited agreement with other items, or by adding more items of the same kind (longer scales are more reliable because the errors introduced by individual items tend to cancel each other out in the long run).

For narrow constructs, the higher the internal consistency, the better. For broad constructs, however, higher internal consistency is not necessarily better because it may be purchased with a loss of generality. For example, a measure of general psychological distress that consisted of the items, "I am fearful," "I am nervous," and "I am anxious" would probably have high internal consistency, but it would offer a very narrow measure of distress focused exclusively on anxiety. Depression, frustration, shame, and other aspects of psychological distress are omitted. By including items to measure them, we would probably produce a scale with lower internal consistency but higher fidelity to the broad theoretical construct of psychological distress.

Test–retest reliability refers to the reproducibility of scores on different occasions. We would not expect major changes in personality over a 2-week period, so if individuals score very differently when they complete the questionnaire twice over this interval, it suggests that there are problems with the test.

In essence, questions about reliability ask whether the scale elicits responses that are consistent across items and across time. Without some minimum of reliability, it is hard to argue that the scale measures anything meaningful, so reliability is often taken as a prerequisite to validity. *Validity* refers to the degree to which a scale actually measures the construct it is intended to measure. A spelling test might have excellent internal consistency and retest reliability, but no validity at all if it were intended to be used as a measure of extraversion.

The central problem in establishing the validity of a test is that we rarely have completely satisfactory external criteria. A good measure of agreeableness–antagonism would separate agreeable from antagonistic people, but—without giving the test—how do we know who is agreeable and who is antagonistic? No single answer is usually sufficient, so we rely on a pattern of evidence in evaluating the construct validity of a scale. We may correlate it with other scales that measure similar constructs, (e.g., scales measuring trust and altruism), or we may see if it distinguishes between known groups that should differ on the dimension (e.g., social workers versus convicted felons), or we may compare self-reports with ratings on the same scale made by spouses or peers.

All of these studies would give information on the convergent validity of the scale, but they would not necessarily speak to its *discriminant validity*. The criterion of discriminant validity requires that scales be *un*related to scales which measure theoretically different constructs. If a test is designed to measure agreeableness, it should not be strongly related to intelligence, because intelligence is theoretically independent of agreeableness. In order to establish discriminant validity, a scale must be related to a series of other measures, especially those with which it is apt to be confounded. The strongest designs for construct validity usually require that multiple methods be used for assessing multiple traits, and that stronger correlations be seen for measures of the same trait obtained from different methods than for measures of different traits obtained from the same method.

Table I gives an example of convergent and discriminant validity across instruments and observers. Five basic dimensions of personality—neuroticism, extroversion, openness to experience, agreeableness, and conscientiousness—are measured by self-reports on adjective rating scales, and by peer ratings on a questionnaire measure, the NEO Personality Inventory. The convergent correlations (given in boldface) show substantial agreement—far greater agreement than would be expected by chance. By contrast, the discriminant correlations (e.g., between peer-rated neuroticism and self-reported openness to experience) are much smaller and generally do not exceed chance. Such data provide evidence that both instruments measure the intended constructs with considerable success.

Table I Convergent and Discriminant Validity of Measures of Five Basic Dimensions of Personality

Mean peer rated NEO personality inventory domains	Self-reported adjective factors				
	N	E	O	A	C
Neuroticism (N)	**.44*****	−.03	.00	−.03	−.15*
Extroversion (E)	.06	**.45*****	.16**	.00	.06
Openness to experience (O)	.07	.08	**.45*****	.13*	−.07
Agreeableness (A)	−.06	−.11	−.15*	**.45*****	−.10
Conscientiousness (C)	−.11	−.05	−.10	−.09	**.39*****

Note. N = 267. Convergent correlations are given in boldface. Adapted from McCrae and Costa (1987). *J. Pers. Soc. Psychol.* **52**, 81–90.

*$p < .05$.   **$p < .01$.   ***$p < .001$.

B. Sources of Error and Bias; Response Styles

Most personality questionnaires consist of a series of statements that the respondent must answer either *true* or *false* or rate on a scale (e.g., from *strongly disagree* to *strongly agree*). As anyone who has taken such a test knows, the items are often ambiguous and sometimes of dubious relevance. The question, "Are you devoted to your work?" might be interpreted in several ways. Some respondents might compare their devotion to work with their commitment to family. Some might compare their own devotion to that of their co-workers. Retired or unemployed respondents might not know how to respond. Even with the sincerest cooperation, respondents may not give the response the test developer intended.

Further, some respondents may not be sincerely cooperative. They may respond carelessly or at random simply to be finished with the task. Or they may wish to present a flattering picture of themselves to the tester. One of the most troubling discoveries of personality psychology was that laypeople are exquisitely sensitive to the social desirability of items and can, if so instructed, fake most personality tests.

Another common problem is acquiescent responding. It was discovered long ago that individuals differ in the tendency to agree with statements, regardless of content. So-called yea-sayers interpret items in ways that allow them to endorse most of them; nay-sayers find something in most items to which they object. If all the items are keyed in the same direction—that is, if *true* or *agree* responses are always indicative of the trait—then scale scores will confound measurement of the trait with measurement of acquiescent tendencies. Two such scales might show a positive correlation even if they measured very different traits, because both might also measure acquiescent tendencies.

This particular response style can be controlled quite effectively by creating scales with balanced keying: Half the items are scored in the positive direction, half in the negative. For example, we might measure conscientiousness by including the item "I often fail to keep my promises," and giving points for conscientiousness if the respondent *disagrees*. In responses to a balanced scale, acquiescent tendencies cancel themselves out, leaving a purer measure of the trait.

Similar strategies have been developed for dealing with other response styles. For example, random responding can be detected by including a set of items that virtually no one would endorse if they were paying attention and cooperating (e.g., "I keep an elephant in my basement"). Endorsing several such items would suggest random responding, and test results should be considered invalid. Cooperative respondents, however, may find the inclusion of such "trick questions" offensive. An alternative way of detecting one common form of random responding is by looking for a string of identical responses on an answer sheet, which may indicate thoughtless, repetitive responding merely intended to finish the questionnaire. This is an unobtrusive measure of random responding.

The greatest attention has been paid to the problem of socially desirable responding. Many scales have been devised in the hopes that they could identify individuals who responded on the basis of the desirability of an item rather than its accuracy as a description of their personality. Researchers routinely include such scales in construct validity studies to estimate the discriminant validity of the scales of interest from socially desirable response tendencies. Unfortunately, however, no good measure of desirable responding per se has yet been developed, and most research suggests that attempts to correct for social desirability do more harm than good.

The root of the problem is that statements have both substantive and evaluative meanings. Anyone who wished to appear in a good light would endorse the item "I always try to do my best"—but so would highly conscientious individuals who are scrupulously honest in their responses. It is impossible to determine from the response alone whether the individual really has desirable characteristics or is presenting a falsely favorable picture of him- or herself.

Two general strategies appear to be useful for dealing with this problem. First, in most cases it appears that respondents are more truthful than psychologists anticipated. Even though they *can* endorse desirable items when instructed to do so, test takers normally do not, when asked to be honest and accurate. Research volunteers have little incentive to distort their responses, and clients in counseling and psychotherapy should be convinced by the assessor that accurate responding will be in their best interest. Mutual respect and trust between test administrators and test takers is usually the best basis for assuring valid results.

However, in some cases there may be good reasons for mistrusting self-reports. The responses of prison inmates who describe themselves as saints when being evaluated for parole should be regarded with considerable skepticism. In these cases, the most appropriate tactic may be to obtain observer ratings from knowledgeable and impartial informants. The current availability of validated observer-rating questionnaires (such as Form R of the NEO Personality Inventory) makes that approach feasible.

None of these approaches to scale construction or administration eliminates all the limitations of personality assessment by questionnaire. The inevitable ambiguity of items and respondents' imperfect knowledge of themselves or the individuals they rate mean than personality measures lack the precision that we admire in the physical sciences. The data in Table I show that our assessments are on the right track, but they can also be interpreted to show that our measurements are far from perfect. Both self-reports and observer ratings are useful tools that give valuable information about personality, and either is acceptable for use in research on groups. For the intensive understanding of the individual (e.g., in psychotherapy), it is desirable to obtain both self-reports and informant ratings, and all inferences about personality traits should be considered provisional, subject to revision or refinement as new information becomes available.

C. Content and Comprehensiveness in Personality Questionnaires

Psychometric theory gives general guidelines for constructing and evaluating measures of psychological characteristics, but it gives little guidance about *what* should be measured. For decades, one of the central problems in personality psychology was the proliferation of hundreds of scales measuring aspects of personality that some researcher or theorist thought important in understanding human beings. Many of the most eminent personality psychologists were those who offered a system, a model of personality structure that specified the most important aspects of personality and thus brought some kind of order to the chaos of competing ideas.

Factor analysis has frequently been used as the statistical technique for studying personality structure. Factor analysis is a mathematical procedure which condenses the information about intercorrelations among many variables by detecting groups of variables that covary separately from other groups. These groups of variables define a factor, a dimension along which individuals can be ranked. For example, the individual traits of trust, straightforwardness, altruism, compliance, modesty, and tender-mindedness covary to define the broad dimension of agreeableness.

In the days before computers, a factor analysis might consume months of computational labor, and it is not surprising that early factor analysts tended to defend whatever structure they first uncovered. As a result, for many decades disputes raged about whether there were 2 basic factors, or 3, or 5, or 10, or 16. Failure to resolve this issue lowered the credibility of the field, and paralyzed much personality research: How could we study personality and aging, say, unless we knew which aspects of personality we needed to measure as individuals aged?

In 1961 two Air Force psychologists, Ernest Tupes and Raymond Christal, factored data from several different studies and concluded that five, and only five, major factors seemed to recur. Their work was largely ignored during the next 20 years, but around 1980 interest in the five-factor model revived. Initially, these five factors were seen as the basic dimensions underlying trait adjective terms used by laypersons and encoded in the natural language—terms such as *nervous, enthusiastic, original, accommodating,* and *careful.* Questionnaire measures, including the NEO Personality Inventory, were then developed to measure these five factors (see Table I for names of the factors). Subsequent research showed that the same five factors were also found in most of the theoretically based questionnaires that had previously been constructed. For example, the four scales of the Myers-Briggs Type Indicator correspond to four of the five factors (introversion–extroversion to extroversion, sensation–intuition to openness, thinking–feeling to agreeableness, and perception–judgment to conscientiousness).

The same basic dimensions have been recovered in cross-cultural analyses of personality (including studies conducted in Hebrew, German, and Chinese), in self-reports and observer ratings, in men and women, and in young, middle-aged, and older adults. Although disagreements remain over the precise nature and scope of the factors, there is a general consensus that these five represent basic and universal features of personality. (Intelligence, another fundamental dimension of individual differences, is generally considered to be outside the realm of personality proper.) The five-factor model thus provides a general answer to the question of what personality traits should be measured: A comprehensive assessment must include measures of all five factors.

However, the five factors themselves are too broad to give a detailed picture of the individual. Anxiety and depression are both aspects of neuroticism, and in general, people who are anxious also tend to be depressed. But some anxious people are not depressed, and some depressed people are not anxious, and it is extremely important to clinical psychologists to determine whether a patient is anxious, depressed, or both. A global measure of neuroticism would not provide that information; instead, more specific scales are needed to provide the details. The same could be said for all five factors. [See ANXIETY; DEPRESSION.]

While most personality psychologists see the need for assessment of personality at this more specific level, there is no consensus about which specific traits should be measured, or even how to go about identifying the most important specific traits. Advocates of circumflex models suggest that we expand the five-factor model by measuring traits that represent combinations of pairs of factors. For example, friendliness is related to both extraversion and agreeableness, so it might merit separate assessment.

Other researchers believe that there are a large number of important traits—perhaps 100 or more—that should be separately analyzed; the five-factor model could then be used primarily to organize the results. In the Revised NEO Personality Inventory, 30 separate traits identified from an analysis of the psychological literature are measured by facet scales, and global domain scales are formed by summing groups of six of them, as shown in Table II. This scheme encourages hierarchical personality assessment at both the more specific and more general levels.

III. PERSONALITY ASSESSMENT AND PERSONALITY THEORY

Human beings have always tried to understand themselves and the people around them; scientific psychology has made real, if slow, progress in this endeavor over the past century. Theories of test construction and validation and psychometric techniques have provided the technical basis for developing sound measures, and the five-factor model specifies which aspects of personality should be measured. As usual in science, there is a continuing interaction between theory and measurement: The more we know about human personality, the better our techniques for measuring it, and the better we measure it, the more we are able to refine our theories.

Psychoanalysis, behaviorism, and humanistic psychologies in turn dominated personality psychology, and each led to serious problems for personality assessment. Self-reports about thoughts, feelings, and actions were considered trivial by psychoanalysts, who believed that the important psychological variables were unconscious, and unscientific by behaviorists, who preferred observation of behavior in laboratory settings. Humanistic psychologists sometimes opposed assessment on principle, because they believed that rating individuals on a fixed set of dimensions was depersonalizing.

Table II   Global Domains and Specific Facets in the Revised NEO Personality Inventory

Neuroticism	Extroversion	Openness	Agreeableness	Conscientiousness
Anxiety	Warmth	Fantasy	Trust	Competence
Angry hostility	Gregariousness	Aesthetics	Straightforwardness	Order
Depression	Assertiveness	Feelings	Altruism	Dutifulness
Self-consciousness	Activity	Actions	Compliance	Achievement striving
Impulsiveness	Excitement seeking	Ideas	Modesty	Self-discipline
Vulnerability	Positive emotions	Values	Tender-mindedness	Deliberation

Trait psychology has always coexisted with these other schools, but has rarely been dominant. But personality assessments based on the principles of trait psychology have shown themselves to be scientifically defensible and useful in applied contexts. For these reasons, trait psychology and the five-factor model appear poised to be the dominant paradigm in personality psychology in the next century.

This article has been reprinted from the *Encyclopedia of Human Behavior, Volume 3*.

BIBLIOGRAPHY

Briggs, S. R. (1992). Assessing the five-factor model of personality description. *J. Pers.* **60**, 253–293.
Funder, D. C. (1991). Global traits: A Neo-Allportian approach to personality. *Psychol. Sci.* **2**, 31–39.
Kline, P. (1993). "The Handbook of Psychological Testing." Routledge, New York.
McCrae, R. R., & Costa, P. T., Jr. (1990). "Personality in Adulthood." Guilford, New York.
Wiggins, J. S., & Pincus, A. L. (1992). Personality: Structure and assessment. *Annu. Rev. Psychol.* **43**, 473–504.

Personality Development

Kevin MacDonald

California State University, Long Beach

I. Research on Temperament in Childhood
II. Personality Development in Later Childhood and Adulthood
III. Evolutionary Approaches to Temperament and Personality

Factor Analysis A statistical technique which is used to find clusters of measures which intercorrelate with each other and thus define a dimension of personality or temperament. For example, a personality questionnaire may consist of several items such as "Has many friends," "Enjoys working with others," "Avoids being alone," etc., which correlate together and define a dimension labeled by the researcher as "sociability."

Heritability Individual variation in traits is understood to be the result of both variation in genes between individuals as well as variation in the environments individuals are exposed to. Heritability is the proportion of the variation of the trait which is due to genetic variation.

Personality Dimension Personality is a more inclusive term than temperament (see below). Personality theory attempts to develop a set of individual difference dimensions consisting of all the ways in which individuals differ from each other. Although there has been much research on the biological basis of some personality traits, there is no implication that these traits are biologically influenced, as is the case with temperament. Nor is there any implication that personality dimensions must appear early in life.

Stability A trait is stable if individuals maintain their relative position in a distribution between two points of measurement. For example, the trait of height (or sociability) is stable if individuals measured as relatively tall (or sociable) at one time remain relatively tall (or sociable) when measured at a second time. Notice that stability does not imply that there is no change. Thus, height could be a stable trait because tall individuals measured at age 5 are still relatively tall at age 10, even though all of the children grew substantially during the time interval. In the case of personality, the stability of individual differences is a major issue. However, researchers are also interested whether there are average developmental changes in personality traits over time, so that, for example, individuals become less prone to taking risks in later adulthood than during adolescence.

Temperament Dimension Individual differences which appear early in life, are of a reasonably enduring nature, and underlie the typical manner in which an individual either reacts to stimulation or regulates his or her behavior in order to approach or avoid stimulation. Temperament is thus usually applied to differences in emotion, attention, and activity. These individual differences are viewed as rooted in biological differences between individuals, and are often viewed as influenced by both environmental and genetic sources of variation.

Research on **PERSONALITY DEVELOPMENT** is concerned with individual differences in a wide ranging set of traits which are important in describing and evaluating human social behavior. For example, some people are highly sociable and enjoy interacting with others. They enjoy an occupation in which there is a

Encyclopedia of Mental Health
Volume 3

great deal of contact with other people and they may be more likely to be sought after as friends and associates. Others would find high levels of social interaction to be aversive. They prefer to be alone and could be expected to seek a fairly solitary occupation in which socializing with others is unimportant. Notice that when we say that a person is sociable, we are implicitly saying that the person has a tendency to behave in a sociable manner in a wide range of situations which are conducive to sociability (e.g., parties, attitudes toward meeting new people, etc.), although we certainly do not expect such a person to behave sociably in all situations (e.g., being interrogated by the police). Moreover, we also suppose that if a person is sociable, then he or she will more than likely continue to be sociable for a prolonged period of time. Being sociable is not simply an ephemeral mood, but a relatively stable aspect of one's behavior. If change occurs at all, it is expected to be gradual and over a fairly prolonged period of years, while one's mood can change quite quickly. The extent to which personality changes over time is an important area of developmental research on personality.

In developmental research on children, the field of personality research is closely intertwined with research on temperament. Like personality research, temperament is concerned with individual differences in behavioral tendencies, but there is the understanding that these individual differences are present very early in life. For example, some infants may react with a great deal of distress even at very low levels of stimulation, whereas another infant may react to the same stimulation in a very positive manner, and yet another infant may show very little response at all. [See PERSONALITY.]

For several theorists, there is an explicit understanding not only that temperament traits are influenced by biological systems, but that temperament traits by definition are traits which have a genetic component. Thus, several theorists have defined temperament as including only those traits which show significant heritability (i.e., traits for which individual differences are at least partially due to genetic differences between individuals). For these theorists, infants and children vary on these behavioral traits, and at least some of that variation is due to genetic variation. However, these researchers also accept the idea that not all variation in temperament is due to genetic

variation. Children are exposed to different environments as well, and these different environments are also viewed as influencing the child's temperament. [See BEHAVIORAL GENETICS.]

For many researchers, therefore, temperament research involves understanding the biological basis of a variety of behavioral traits which appear early in life. As in the case of personality, temperament traits are of obvious relevance to social behavior, and they are viewed as fairly stable across time and characteristic of individuals in a wide range of situations. However, it should be noted that there is continuing research, summarized below, on the extent to which temperament and personality traits are stable over time.

The field of temperament research uses several methods for measuring temperament. Temperament traits may be studied at a behavioral level (such as observing individual differences in negative emotional response in a laboratory situation), or they may be studied from a biological perspective (such as attempting to find individual differences in neurotransmitter level associated with negative emotional responding). By far the most widely used technique is parental ratings of the child's behavior in response to questions developed by the researcher. The responses are then subjected to factor analysis in an attempt to discover independent dimensions of temperament. Personality and temperament dimensions are independent of each other in the sense that an individual's status on one dimension is not highly correlated with his or her status on another dimension. Thus, if sociability and emotional reactivity are temperament dimensions, knowing that a person is sociable tells us little or nothing about that person's emotional reactivity.

I. RESEARCH ON TEMPERAMENT IN CHILDHOOD

The field of temperament research is far from settled territory. However, despite continuing lack of agreement on such basic issues as the correct set of temperament dimensions, the following is a set of temperament traits based on a fairly broad convergence of findings obtained by a number of researchers in the field. Moreover, the stability of temperament traits during childhood, and especially during infancy, although significant, is not very robust. Between-age correlations for temperament traits in childhood are in the .3 to .4 range, and therefore explain only 10–25% of the variation. While some of this lack of stability is undoubtedly due to the unreliability of the measurements, the data available at present suggest that there are important environmental influences on temperament in childhood.

A. Reactivity

Children differ in the extent to which they become aroused by particular levels of environmental stimulation. As a general rule, children respond positively to low levels of stimulation. At intermediate levels of stimulation there are also positive responses, but in addition there is the onset of negative, inhibitory responses which result in a tendency to withdraw and function to protect the child from overstimulation. At very high levels of stimulation, the response tends to be overwhelmingly negative and inhibitory and the child withdraws. Individual differences in this system define the temperament trait of reactivity.

Children who are highly reactive respond very strongly to stimulation, and are conceptualized as having a very low threshold for arousal. These children are often viewed as having a weak nervous system in the sense that they are easily overstimulated. In the presence of high levels of stimulation, these high-reactive individuals inhibit their responding and tend to withdraw from the source of stimulation. On the other hand, they respond very intensely to even low levels of stimulation. Low-reactive children, on the other hand, may be said to have a relatively strong nervous system in the sense that they have a relatively high threshold of stimulation and do not become aroused by stimulation which would overwhelm a high-reactive individual. These low-reactive individuals are thus more likely to be found in highly stimulating environments, although at extremely high levels of stimulation, even these individuals begin to inhibit their responding and withdraw from stimulation.

As can be seen in these comments, the concept of reactivity really involves two separate ideas. The first is the idea of threshold of responding (low versus high threshold for arousal) and the second involves the onset of inhibitory (withdrawal) tendencies. There is some evidence that individuals with a low threshold for arousal also tend to show inhibition at relatively

low levels of stimulation. On the other hand, individuals with a high threshold for arousal (relatively insensitive) begin to inhibit their responding only at very intense levels of stimulation.

It should also be noted that there are individual differences in the extent to which individuals show reactivity depending on the modality of the stimulation— the concept of *modality specificity*. Thus, a child may be highly reactive to tactile stimulation, but much less reactive to vestibular stimulation.

The trait of *negative emotionality* is often distinguished as a temperament trait closely linked to reactivity. Children who are high on the trait of negative emotionality are prone to negative emotional response to stimulation (irritability), including distress and anger. Individual differences in negative emotionality can be observed in the newborn period, and there are important cross-cultural differences in this trait beginning during the newborn period, with Chinese-American infants and other Mongoloid infants being less prone to distress than Caucasian-American or African American infants. There is also some evidence for general developmental shifts in negative emotionality, with peaks around age 2 (perhaps accounting for the "terrible twos") and during adolescence. [*See* REACTIVITY.]

B. Positive Emotionality and Sociability

This cluster of traits essentially measures individual differences in behavioral approach. Even in the newborn period there are individual differences in the extent to which infants will approach rewarding stimulation, such as sweet foods or interesting visual patterns. At around 4 weeks of age behavioral approach is accompanied by smiling and other indications of positive affect in both social and nonsocial situations. Children who are high on the trait of positive emotionality are prone to positive emotional response, including smiling, joy, and laughter available in rewarding situations, including the pleasant social interaction sought by sociable children.

As a result, sociability is intimately linked with the trait of positive emotionality. Sociable children tend to seek and enjoy social contact with others. Positive emotionality and sociability may thus be seen as *appetitive* traits in which the child regulates his or her own behavior in a manner which results in positive emotional response. There is some indication of sex differences in behavioral approach tendencies, with boys being more prone to behavioral approach than girls. Later in childhood sociability has been linked to the more general trait of extraversion, and such a relationship continues during adulthood (see below).

C. Behavioral Inhibition

Children who are high on behavioral inhibition respond negatively to new people and other types of novel stimulation. This trait has been subjected to considerable research, and the results will be presented in somewhat greater detail than for the other temperament dimensions. Unlike the other temperament traits discussed here, behavioral inhibition is not observable at birth, but becomes established in the second half of the first year. The predominant emotions of the behavioral inhibition system are fear and anxiety, and children are typically tested for differences in this trait by placing them in unfamiliar situations, and especially with unfamiliar people. Approximately 10–15% of normal, healthy 2-year-old children will react to these unfamiliar situations by becoming quiet, vigilant, and subdued. They cling to their mothers and attempt to withdraw from the novel situation. Longitudinal research indicates considerable stability for this trait: children who were behaviorally inhibited at age 2 also tended to be behaviorally inhibited at age 7½ when placed in a group of other unfamiliar children. During the play sessions the children made few spontaneous comments and tended to remain apart from the group.

Physiological research on behaviorally inhibited children indicates that these children generally have a more responsive sympathetic nervous system. This sympathetic dominance can be seen by the finding that behaviorally inhibited children tend to have a high and stable heart rate in unfamiliar situations, indicating that these children are highly aroused by the unfamiliarity. This sympathetic dominance can also be seen in the tendency for behaviorally inhibited children to have greater muscular tension and arousal, especially in the larynx, as well as greater pupillary dilation. Finally, behaviorally inhibited children have been shown to have higher levels of the stress hormone cortisol. The indications are that behaviorally inhibited children have a very strong emotional response to novel situations, and in particular, they

tend to be highly prone to tension, anxiety, and fear in these situations.

D. Attention Span, Distractibility, and Focused Effort

By 3 months of age there are clear differences in distractibility and persistence among infants as indicated by differences in the length of time infants will attend to visual and auditory stimulation. In early childhood, this trait is manifested in differences in gaze shifting and in duration of orienting toward objects such as toys. This trait is linked to individual differences in the development of effortful, persistent behavior in a pursuit of a goal, since such effortful performance requires inhibiting responses to other stimuli in the environment. There is a general trend in development such that older children have longer attention spans, are less distractible, and are better able to effortfully pursue a goal.

E. Activity

Activity refers to the degree of energy expenditure characteristic of the child. Active children are "on the go," and they tend to engage in frequent and intense bouts of motor activity. Individual differences in activity level can be observed from early infancy and throughout childhood. There is some indication that activity is positively associated with the positive emotionality dimension mentioned above and thus with Factor I on adult personality dimensions described below.

These temperament traits are of great importance in understanding the social development of children. A commonly held view in the area of social development is that children have significant effects on their social and nonsocial environments, and these temperament traits are an important means by which the child affects the world around him or her. Children are viewed as actively influencing the world around them and choosing environments which are conducive to their temperament. For example, a sociable child actively seeks social contact with others and in a sense creates his or her own world. A child who enjoys fast-paced high energy motor activities seeks out opportunities to engage in this type of activity and selects friends who have similar interests.

Moreover, children with different temperaments

evoke different responses from their environment. For example, children with a short attention span have difficulty sustaining the prolonged attention and effort required at school, and this behavior in turn is likely to result in negative responses from teachers. As another example, there is evidence that extremely withdrawn, behaviorally inhibited children can become rejected by the peer group. Children who begin life high on temperamental behavioral inhibition and continue to exhibit this trait tend to be less mature, less assertive, and more compliant or deferential than their more sociable peers, and some extremely withdrawn children tend to be victimized by the peer group.

Finally, despite the conceptualization of temperament as a set of biological systems, there is very good evidence that temperament can be influenced by the environment, especially during infancy and childhood. For example, many premature infants as well as infants whose mothers have taken drugs such as cocaine, are very high on negative emotionality. They are thus very difficult to interact with, and such babies are at significantly higher risk for child abuse, at least partly because their intense negative emotionality is very aversive to caregivers.

II. PERSONALITY DEVELOPMENT IN LATER CHILDHOOD AND ADULTHOOD

One of the unfortunate aspects of writing in the area of personality development and temperament is that, despite some very obvious commonalities, there has been little research which formally establishes the linkages between these areas. Research on adult personality has been dominated by the Five Factor Model of personality. This model has emerged consistently as a result of factor analytic studies of personality questionnaires performed over the last 50 years. In the following, I briefly describe the five factors, link them with the research on temperament in childhood, and provide an overview of the development of these systems in adulthood.

Factor I is generally labeled extraversion. Individuals high on this factor are described as talkative, assertive, active, energetic, outgoing, dominant, forceful, enthusiastic, and adventurous, while individuals who are low in this factor are described as quiet, withdrawn, and retiring. At a more general level, this dimension may be viewed as encompassing individual differences in what may be termed a set of "GO" systems underlying behavioral approach, impulsivity, and attraction to reward, and is therefore linked with the "positive emotionality and sociability" and "activity" dimensions found in temperament studies of childhood.

Although at a general level the GO systems can be viewed as a single dimension, there are a several semi-independent traits characteristic of behavioral approach in addition to sociability as discussed above. For example, sensation seeking is a trait which involves attraction to novelty, danger, and excitement, and is phenotypically and genetically correlated with sociability. The trait of sensation seeking peaks in late adolescence and young adulthood, followed by a gradual decline during adulthood. There is also some evidence to support the view that extraversion and sociability decline in adulthood, although the evidence is mixed and the declines are minor. These trait dimensions have been observed cross-culturally and show an important sex difference: Males tend to be higher in these "GO" trait dimensions.

Factor II is often termed agreeableness or warmth. Individuals high on this trait are described as sympathetic, affectionate, warm, generous, trusting, and unselfish, while those low on this trait are described as cold, unfriendly, hard-hearted, cruel, and stingy. This trait has been hypothesized to underlie the development of close affectional relationships in the family, including especially romantic attachments. This trait is not found among the temperament dimensions of childhood described above, but there is some evidence that individual differences in warmth and affection observable in early parent–child relationships, including secure attachments, are linked with this dimension later in life. There is an important sex difference in this trait throughout development, with females tending to be higher than males. In addition, there is some indication that this trait increases during adult development, concurrent with decreases in aggression and hostility, although the change is minor and there are conflicting data.

Factor III is often termed conscientiousness. Individuals high on this trait are described as thorough, planful, efficient, dependable, reliable, responsible and deliberate, while those low on this dimension are described as careless, disorderly, frivolous, and irresponsible. Individual differences in this trait can be found as early as age 5, and this trait is highly correlated with academic success. While formal research is lacking, this trait has been linked to the temperament trait of attention span and distractibility described above as a temperament trait in infancy and early childhood. Like the other dimensions of personality and temperament described here, the trait is moderately stable through childhood. While we have noted that there is a developmental increase in attention span and persistence during childhood, this trait has not been found to change significantly during adulthood.

Factor IV is often termed neuroticism or emotionality. Individuals on one extreme of this factor are described as tense, anxious, fearful, emotionally unstable, and nervous, while individuals on the other extreme are described as calm, stable and unemotional. This factor appears to be related to both the childhood temperament dimensions of behavioral inhibition (as indicated by the emphasis on fear and anxiety in this dimension) and high reactivity (especially negative emotionality, as indicated by the importance of intense, negative emotional response for this dimension). Based on cross-sectional studies with adults, there are no age differences in neuroticism.

Factor V is often termed intelligence, intellect, or openness to experience. Individuals high on this dimension are intelligent, have a wide range of interests, are curious, open to new experiences, inventive, and original, while those low on this dimension are described as having narrow interests, and commonplace, shallow ideas. Research on this dimension as a personality trait in childhood is lacking (although there is much research on intelligence of children as it relates to academic success), but the trait has been found consistently in studies of adult personality. No age differences in this trait during adulthood have been found. [See INTELLIGENCE AND MENTAL HEALTH.]

III. EVOLUTIONARY APPROACHES TO TEMPERAMENT AND PERSONALITY

The general conclusion is that there is very good evidence for a set of basic personality traits which show some stability beginning in infancy and persisting throughout the lifespan. While stability as assessed by correlations between ages is fairly low during childhood, ranging between .3 and .4 even over a span of a few years, there is considerable evidence that adult personality is quite stable. Several studies have found correlations in the range of .7 to .85 for adult person-

ality over periods as long as 12 years, indicating a very high level of stability indeed. However, despite some evidence for changes in traits related to extraversion and agreeableness, there is relatively little evidence for changes in the average level of personality traits over the lifespan.

While traditional personality and temperament research emphasizes individual differences, recent evolutionary approaches to this field emphasize the idea that these individual differences should be thought of as individual variation in discrete biological systems with particular evolved functions. There is evidence that all of the personality dimensions reviewed here are significantly heritable, indicating that genetic variation is an important source of individual differences for the trait. Moreover, while only the physiological data relevant to behavioral inhibition are reviewed here, there is increasing evidence that all of these personality/temperament systems have important physiological roots.

From an evolutionary perspective, the evolved function of the GO systems described as being central to Factor I in adult personality research is proposed to be that of motivating the individual to actively engage the environment. Individuals high on the GO systems actively seek out rewards and a variety of other sources of environmental stimulation, including other people (sociability). At the extreme end of this dimension, individuals high on this trait engage in high levels of risk-taking and impulsive behavior—what one might term a high-risk evolutionary strategy. On the other hand individuals who are low on this dimension are implicitly adopting a more cautious strategy in which there are lower payoffs as well as lower risks.

The behavioral inhibition system which is central to Factor IV, on the other hand, is proposed to function as a mechanism for protection and the inhibition of behavior in the face of threat. This system is viewed as a biological STOP system which responds to perceived threat with behavioral inhibition and the initiation of fight or flight behaviors.

The proposed evolved function of Factor II (agreeableness) is to provide a mechanism for facilitating close personal relationships within the family. The high level of altruism and generosity characteristic of individuals who are high on this dimension is proposed to function to facilitate transfer of resources within close, intimate human relationships such as family relationships, including care of children.

Finally, the evolutionary functions of Factors III

(conscientiousness) and V (intellect) are perhaps obvious. Both are correlated with academic success, with the former underlying the ability to make effortful, persistent, and careful behavior in pursuit of a goal, and the latter underlying the ability to process information and solve problems creatively.

From the evolutionary perspective, personality dimensions may thus be thought of as discrete, independent systems which are differentially recruited in particular life situations. In a situation of personal threat, personality systems underlying fear and anxiety (Factor II) may predominate, while at a party, sociability and positive emotionality are more likely to be exhibited (Factor I). Individuals thus not only have a characteristic level of a particular personality dimension which is highly stable, at least during adulthood, but are also able to finely tune their behavior in response to particular environmental contingencies, so that a person who is generally low on behavioral inhibition may show fear and anxiety in a situation of extreme threat to his or her interests. An individual's personality is thus flexibly responsive to environmental contingencies rather than uniform across all possible situations.

The basic design of the biological basis of children's (and adults') temperament and personality is finely tuned to be able to both approach the world and engage in enthusiastic interaction with it (the GO systems), but also to be able to inhibit behavior in the face of threat (neuroticism or behavioral inhibition), conscientiously and persistently pursue important goals (conscientiousness), and engage in close, affectionate relationships with others (agreeableness). Evolution, like a good engineer, designed children (and adults) with both a powerful engine (the GO systems) and a good set of brakes and monitoring systems (the STOP system and conscientiousness). All of these systems have important functions, but the field of temperament and personality research shows that there is enormous variation in the power and salience of these traits among individuals.

Clearly evolution did not result in an "optimum" or "ideal" personality profile for all humans. Instead evolution appears to have resulted in a broad range of individual differences in approach and avoidance, affiliation and conscientiousness, and even for such traits as creativity, originality, and intelligence. It is quite possible that this variation in personality and temperament serves to enable humans to occupy a wide range of possible niches and occupations in the human and non-human environment. Several different personality combinations may function equally well in many human environments, while a personality which is ideally suited to one type of environment (working as a military officer) may be poorly suited to another (working in a library). The result is the fascinating kaleidoscope of diversity which is an endless source of fascination to both researchers and laypeople alike.

This article has been reprinted from the *Encyclopedia of Human Behavior, Volume 3.*

BIBLIOGRAPHY

Buss, A. H., & Plomin (1984). "Temperament: Early Developing Personality Traits." Erlbaum, Hillsdale, NJ.

Digman, J. M. (1990). Personality structure: Emergence of five-factor model. *Annu. Rev. Psychol.* **41**, 417–440.

Goldsmith, H. H., Buss, A. H., Plomin, R., Rothbart, M. K., Thomas, A., Chess, S., Hinde, R. A., & McCall, R. (1987). Roundtable: What is temperament? Four approaches. *Child Dev.* **58**, 505–529.

Halverson, C. F., Kohnstamm, G. A., & Martin, R. P. (Eds.) (1994). "The Developing Structure of Temperament and Personality from Infancy to Adulthood." Erlbaum, Hillsdale, NJ.

Kagan, J. (1989). "Unstable Ideas: Temperament, Cognition, and Self." Harvard University Press, Cambridge.

Kohnstamm, G. A., Bates, J. E., & Rothbart, M. K. (Eds.) (1989). "Temperament in Childhood." Wiley, New York.

MacDonald, K. B. (1988). "Social and Personality Development: An Evolutionary Synthesis." Plenum, New York.

McCrae, R. R., & Costa, P. T. (1990). "Personality in Adulthood." Guilford, New York.

Pervin, L. A. (Ed.). (1990). "Handbook of Personality." Guilford, New York.

Rubin, K. H., LeMare, L. J., & Mills, S. (1990). Social withdrawal in childhood. Developmental pathways to peer rejection. In "Peer Rejection in Childhood" (S. R. Asher and J. D. Coie, Eds.), pp. 217–249. Cambridge University Press, New York.

Personality Disorders

Robert G. Meyer

University at Louisville

I. Personality Types and Disorders
II. Treatment Relationships and the
   Personality Disorders
III. Summary

Paranoid Pseudocommunity The conspiracy network of persons a paranoid perceives as against him or her.

Personality Disorder Chronic disruptive adjustment patterns, found as a formal diagnosis on Axis II of the *DSM* system.

Personality Type Patterns of behavior found in normals that operate as a predisposition to a personality disorder.

Underlying Beliefs The cognitive beliefs that help to generate, and maintain, a personality disorder.

PERSONALITY DISORDERS are chronic, cognitive–behavioral patterns, generated from an early age, that the individual has developed in order to cope with his or her particular problems of living. These disorders are not so clearly bizarre as the psychoses, nor do they include the clear anxiety patterns of the neuroses. However, they are severely maladaptive, because (1) the psychopathology is pervasive and thoroughly integrated into the personality, (2) the patterns are chronic and often recognizable by the time of adolescence or earlier, and (3) such persons usually avoid treatment and are difficult to treat if for some reason they do enter treatment. Thus, a personality disorder describes a pattern of behavior, or lack of behavior, that is troublesome to others or whose pleasure sources are socially defined as either harmful or illegal.

I. PERSONALITY TYPES AND DISORDERS

The various personality disorders are generated because they are effective, at least in the short run, in coping with that person's individual environment. Of course, the more distorted or disturbed that environment is, the more likely it is that a distorted coping pattern will emerge and become reinforced. Within this perspective, a personality type (a behavior pattern seen as within the normal range of adjustment) is a way-station on the developmental road toward a full-blown personality disorder. Table I describes common personality types (which we all manifest to some degree), along with the personality disorder they are most likely to develop, if they are exaggerated and crystallized.

The *DSM-IV* personality disorders have traditionally been grouped into three clusters in the *DSM*'s. The first includes the paranoid, schizoid, and schizotypal personality disorders, as these are denoted by peculiar or eccentric behavior. The second cluster focuses on dramatic and emotionally labile behavior: It includes the histrionic, narcissistic, antisocial, and borderline personality disorders. The last cluster, which emphasizes chronic fearfulness and/or avoidance behaviors, includes the avoidant, dependent, obsessive–compulsive, and passive–aggressive personality disorders.

Table I Personality Types and Correlated Traits and Disorders

	Personality Types									
Correlates	Controlling	Aggressive	Confident	Sociable	Cooperative	Sensitive	Respectful	Inhibited	Introverted	Emotional
Typical behaviors	Manipulative demanding	Bold, initiating	Poised, distant	Animated, engaging	Docile, submissive	Erratic, responsive	Organized, formal	Watchful, preoccupied	Passive, quiet	Energetic, engaging
Interpersonal patterns	Authoritarian	Intimidating	Unempathic	Demonstrative	Compliant	Unpredictable	Polite	Shy	Withdrawn	Provocative
Thinking styles	Calculating	Dogmatic	Imaginative	Superficial	Open	Divergent	Respectful	Repressed	Vague	Distracted
Mood-affect expression	Disappointment resentment	Anger, distrust	Calm, unconcerned	Dramatic, labile	Tender, fearful	Pessimistic, hurt	Restrained, content	Uneasy, wary	Bland, coolness	Intense, frenetic
View of self	Unappreciated	Assertive	Self-assured	Charming	Weak	Misunderstood	Reliable	Lonely	Placid	Interesting
Probable personality disorders	Passive-aggressive, sadistic, paranoid	Antisocial, sadistic, paranoid	Narcissistic, paranoid, antisocial	Histrionic, borderline narcissistic	Dependent, compulsive, avoidant	Passive-aggressive, borderline avoidant	Compulsive, paranoid, passive-aggressive	Avoidant, schizotypal, self-defeating	Schizoid, schizotypal, compulsive, avoidant	Borderline schizotypal, histrionic, narcissistic

Source: Adapted in part from T. Millon and G. Everly, 1985, *Personality and Its Disorders*, Wiley, New York.

The following is a discussion of each individual personality disorder, from the perspective of both behavioral patterns and the more recently articulated cognitive patterns.

A. Paranoid Personality Disorder

The paranoid personality disorder can be thought of as anchoring the other end of the continuum of paranoid disorders from the most disturbed and fragmented pattern, paranoid schizophrenia. However, since there is neither thought disorder nor even a well-formed delusional system in the paranoid personality disorder, it is not listed under the *DSM* paranoid disorders and is not a psychotic condition. Like the other personality disorders, it is a chronic, pervasive, and inflexible pattern of behavior that typically has been in evolution since childhood and is already recognizable in adolescence. Modeling of parental or other significant others is possibly even more important in this disorder than in the psychotic paranoid conditions. [*See* Paranoia.]

I. Behavioral Patterns

Paranoid personalities manifest hyperalertness toward the environment and have a chronic mistrust of most people. They see themselves as morally correct, yet vulnerable and envied, and see others as far less than perfect. As a result, their information base is continuously distorted and their affect is constricted. Consequently, they find it difficult to adapt adequately to new situations or relationships, which is paradoxical because of their hyperalertness to their environment. Paradoxically, they will frequently be correct in assuming that other people are against them. Yet the paranoia is usually a disabling overreaction to a low initial level of scrutiny by others.

Unless these individuals have almost absolute trust in another person, they cannot develop intimacy and are continually seeking various ways to be self-sufficient. They avoid the emotional complexities of working out a meaningful relationship and tend to be litigious. For example, they may write negative letters to public figures or bring lawsuits on minimal grounds. It is rare for them to come into therapy without significant coercion from others. The disorder is more common in men.

Both Nero and Robespierre displayed characteristics of the paranoid personality pattern. As with other individuals in this classification, these important historical figures were suspicious and oversensitive about the behavior and intentions of other people. Each was very manipulative in his relationships so that the other person could not gain the advantage. Nero was a Roman emperor during the first century, and Robespierre was a leader of the French Revolution; each man had considerable power over large numbers of people. Unlike most paranoid personalities, therefore, their paranoid reactions had a significant impact on a great many lives; and their delusions or misperceptions may have caused them to unjustifiably imprison or execute many innocent people. Although most paranoid personalities are not dangerous or physically injurious, they are at best perceived as a nuisance, e.g., through perennial complaints and lawsuits against other persons.

In order to relate to, or even treat the paranoid personality, it is essential to gain their trust through empathy, but not through participation in the disorder patterns. It is especially necessary to empathize with and articulate the consequences of such an individual's behavior, such as the sense of being isolated and not understood or the interpersonal rejection that appears unfair to the paranoid.

The underlying beliefs that paranoids often struggle with are (a) I am unique and others are jealous; (b) others will exploit my mistakes; (c) it always pays to be wary, accusatory, and adversarial (some paranoids do make good trial lawyers); (d) people who are trusting or content are fools, i.e., I can't be that way; (e) negative events are generated purposefully by others.

The concept of the paranoid pseudocommunity holds that the paranoid is unable to communicate freely with other persons and has a pattern of finding fault with others as a result of inadequate social development. This inability creates a problem when the paranoid is under stress, because he cannot corroborate his perceptions with those of other persons or cannot assume the perspectives of other individuals. Relying on his own devices, he continues in his misperceptions and reconstructs reality to make it consistent with them. The culmination of this behavior is the paranoid's conception of himself as the center of a community of persons who are in a conspiracy against him. Because the situation does not exist as the paranoid perceives it, he is said to be living in a pseudocommunity.

B. Schizoid Personality Disorder

The essential feature of this disorder is impairment in the ability to form adequate social relationships. As a result, schizoid personalities are shy and socially withdrawn or, as novelist Joan Didion states in *The White Album* (p. 121), "only marginally engaged in the dailiness of life." They have difficulty expressing hostility and have withdrawn from most social contacts. But, unlike agoraphobia, the behavior is ego-syntonic, i.e., the individual is at least minimally comfortable with the behavior.

1. Behavioral Patterns

In contrast to the personalities who relate to the environment, the schizoid personality is particularly characterized by distancing behaviors and alienation. The schizoid individual reacts to disturbing experiences and conflicts by apparent detachment from the environment rather than by manifesting normal coping responses. The schizoid personality is described in *DSM* as shy, oversensitive, seclusive, often eccentric, and likely to avoid close or especially competitive relationships.

Walter Mitty is the schizoid hero of James Thurber's novel and the movie *The Secret Life of Walter Mitty*. Mitty is essentially detached from his environment and is much more absorbed in his elaborate, heroic fantasies. Given the situation of an idle moment or a disturbing experience, he plunges into his imaginings, rather than utilizing normal coping mechanisms. Most schizoid persons are considered to be cold and withdrawn because they do not seem to respond to their environment. Walter Mitty, however, seems more warm and likeable, although no more reachable, than other schizoid personalities.

2. Cognitive Patterns

Like the person with an avoidant personality disorder (discussed later in this article), the schizoid has inadequate interpersonal relations. But unlike one with an avoidant personality disorder, the schizoid does not care, so therapy is quite difficult.

Characteristic underlying cognitive assumptions are (a) any disruption of my emotional routine (however minimal the emotions are) is scary and messy—in that sense they are analogous to the obsessive–compulsive's fear of disruption of external routines; (b) I can survive alone (maybe not optimally, but at least predictably), and need space to do that; (c) it's necessary to be free and independent—other people are like Brer Rabbit's "Tar Baby"; if you relate to them, you get stuck to them.

C. Schizotypal Personality Disorder

The reader is referred to the previous category, the schizoid personality disorder, since many of the features of that disorder are found here. The essential difference is that in addition to the disturbances in social functioning, the schizotypal personality manifests peculiarities in the communication process. Schizotypal individuals are much more likely than the schizoid to show dysphoria and anxiety, and because of the odd thinking patterns, they are more likely to have developed eccentric belief systems and become involved in fringe religious groups. The schizotypal personality is also more likely to be emotionally labile, overtly suspicious, and hostile of others than is the schizoid. Many schizotypal individuals also appear to meet the criteria for the borderline personality disorder. Any therapist's attention must be directed not only toward the interpersonal withdrawal processes, but also to the emergent disturbances in affect and thinking that are common.

D. Histrionic Personality Disorder

These persons seek attention and are overreactive, with the response being expressed more dramatically and intensely than is appropriate—hence, the term "histrionic." This category has traditionally been labeled the "hysterical personality." However, "hysteric" wrongly suggests a disorder that parallels the causes and symptoms of what has been traditionally labeled "hysterical neurosis."

1. Behavioral Patterns

Histrionic personalities may elicit new relationships with relative ease, as they appear to be empathic and socially able. However, they turn out to be temperamentally and emotionally insensitive and have little depth of insight into their own responsibilities in a relationship. Even though they may be flirtatious and seductive sexually, there is little mature response or true sensuality. If one accepts the apparent sexual overture in the behavior, the histrionic individual may act as if insulted or even attacked.

There has been a continuing controversy as to whether this disorder occurs with any frequency in males. But, it is clear that this disorder is found in males, but because the symptoms are a caricature of the traditional role expectations for women, it is more common in women.

An excellent behavioral example of a histrionic personality pattern is seen in the character of Martha in Albee's play *Who's Afraid of Virginia Woolf?* The stormy relationship between Martha and her husband, George, alternating between wild physical and verbal abuse and tender affection, is not fiction created for the stage, as many couples live in what can be termed a "conflict–habituated" marriage. In such a marriage, there is private though sometimes unverbalized acknowledgment by both husband and wife as a rule that incompatibility is pervasive, that conflict is ever-potential, that an atmosphere of tension permeates the relationship—nevertheless, the relationship will continue. It seems likely that at least one of the partners in this kind of marital situation would be labeled as a hysterical personality, and often, as is the case with the character George in *Who's Afraid of Virginia Woolf?*, the other partner is a passive–aggressive personality. Such people do not often seek treatment. Rather, they maintain the core around which the pretense and the conflict revolve, much as Martha and George maintained her fantasied pregnancy as well as their mythical child.

2. Cognitive Patterns

Histrionics quickly avoid blame for any difficulties of interpersonal relationship and, in that sense, show a degree of the projection that is characteristic of paranoid disorders. Common underlying beliefs in histrionics are (a) being responsible or attending to details means the loss of "zest for life"; (b) rejection is disastrous; (c) people won't love me for what I do but what I pretend to be, or what I present to entertain/entice them; (d) being "special" means never having to say "I'm sorry" (or at least I don't have to feel it or mean it).

E. Narcissistic Personality Disorder

This category, which was new in the *DSM-III-R*, centers on individuals who are to a degree products of our modern social-value systems. No doubt, such people have always existed, but it appears that this pattern has become more common recently. It is not a surprising development when there are advertisements about "The Arrogance of Excellence" and self-help seminars unequivocally urging people to live out the axiom "I'm number one" (with little evidence that there is much room for a number two or three close behind). [*See* NARCISSISTIC PERSONALITY DISORDER.]

1. Behavioral Patterns

Narcissistic personalities are "flattery-operated"; more specifically, they manifest an unrealistic sense of self-importance, exhibitionistic attention seeking, inability to take criticism, interpersonal manipulation, and lack of empathy resulting in substantial problems in interpersonal relationships.

Narcissistic personalities are similar to antisocial personalities, except that they are not so aggressive or hostile and their value systems are more asocial and hedonic than antisocial. The prognosis for major change is moderate at best.

In 1984, Otto Kernberg introduced the subdiagnosis of *malignant narcissist*. It was first applied to people like Adolf Hitler and Joseph Stalin, and more recently it has been suggested as fitting Saddam Hussein. The four characteristics of this pattern are (1) a strong suspiciousness, occasionally to the point of paranoia; (2) an extremely inflated sense of self, often grandiose; (3) sadistic cruelty (which in some individuals is turned inward as self-mutilation—"for a higher goal"); and (4) an utter lack of remorse.

There are numerous *productive narcissists* in society. One night while we were on a fishing trip, my friend and I had dinner at a fine Chinese restaurant. The restaurant was named after the owner, an aging but still attractive Chinese woman. The walls were totally covered with formal photographs of her, there was a bulletin board filled with candid shots from throughout her life, the restaurant's cards had a photo of her as a young woman, and you could even purchase postcards with various pictures from her life. A short conversation with her quickly revealed her narcissism, but it should have been evident to any customer. She was not especially offensive (it was a short conversation); however, by narcissistically including her restaurant as a part of her "self," she had turned it into an excellent operation that she groomed as carefully as her hair. Certain media-created stars, "personalities," and politicians are also examples of extreme but at least occasionally productive narcissism.

2. Cognitive Patterns

Underlying beliefs common to this disorder are (a) I am special, unique, elite; (b) I like to challenge or compete with others, but because of both "a" and the fact it is psychologically necessary for me to prevail, I may play by other rules (usually known only to me); (c) any defects I have come from my bad parents and/or background; (d) recognition, admiration, and respect are necessary and others exist to provide it, and indeed, promote it; (e) sharing, serving others, or selfless behaviors are signs of weakness and signal disintegration of my self.

F. Antisocial Personality Disorder

The antisocial personality is an interesting category that deserves special consideration in light of its evolution as a concept. In the early 1800s Prichard suggested the term "moral insanity" or "moral imbecility" to designate persons who did not fit the psychiatric categories of that time. The first reference to the classic notation "psychopathic" occurred in 1891 with the introduction of the label "psychopathic inferiority." This classification was an attempt to place the disorder with other disturbances, such as retardation, that were believed to be congenital. Caesare Lombroso's classic conception of the criminal as showing consistent and significantly different facial characteristics was also a popular view. The *Zeitgeist* of that period therefore maintained that the psychopathic disorder was the result of genetic or hormonal defects rather than learning or environmental factors.

Eventually, the term "psychopathic personality" was used, but in such a way that there was much confusion about the concept. In time the term "sociopathic personality pattern" was also adopted by the American Psychiatric Association for *DSM-I* (to emphasize, now apparently inaccurately, that this pattern is largely a result of social conditioning) and became the broad category under which several problematic social behaviors, such as sexual deviations, alcoholism, and drug addiction, were listed.

Hervey Cleckley, a pioneer in this area, has described the antisocial personality (more specifically, psychopathy) as having a "mask of sanity," or the absence of the usual indicators of insanity. These are persons who discard meaningful relationships, goals, and success for reasons that others cannot understand. Cleckley's list of the following 16 indicators of psychopathy has been influential through the ensuing years:

1. Superficial charm and good "intelligence"
2. Absence of delusions and other signs of irrational "thinking"
3. Absence of "nervousness" or psychoneurotic manifestations
4. Unreliability
5. Untruthfulness and insincerity
6. Lack of remorse or shame
7. Inadequately motivated antisocial behavior
8. Poor judgment and failure to learn by experience
9. Pathologic egocentricity and incapacity for love
10. General poverty in major affective reactions
11. Specific loss of insight
12. Unresponsiveness in general interpersonal relations
13. Fantastic and uninviting behavior, with drink and sometimes without
14. Suicide rarely carried out
15. Sex life impersonal, trivial, and poorly integrated
16. Failure to follow any life plan

There is good evidence that the category of antisocial personality can be further subdivided, e.g., into categories of primary psychopath and secondary psychopath. [See ANTISOCIAL PERSONALITY DISORDER.]

G. Borderline Personality Disorder

At first glance, this disorder may seem to overlap with the schizotypal personality disorder, as both imply an easy transition into a schizophrenic adjustment. However, individuals with borderline personality disorder are neither as consistently withdrawn socially nor as bizarre in symptomatology as are schizotypals, and the borderline diagnosis covaries most commonly in inpatients with a diagnosis of histrionic personality disorder. [See BORDERLINE PERSONALITY DISORDER.]

I. Behavioral Patterns

Though the *DSM* does not specifically mention it, this category seems to be a resurrection of an old term at one time much favored by clinicians: "emotionally unstable personality." Persons in the borderline personality disorder category do show significant emotional instability, are impulsive and unpredictable in behavior, and are irritable and anxious. They also often show "soft" neurological signs, and avoid being alone or experiencing the psychological emptiness or boredom to which they are prone. There is some evidence that as these individuals improve, they show more predictable behavior patterns, yet this is combined with increasingly evident narcissism. Glenn Close's character in the movie "Fatal Attraction" is a good example of this disorder.

2. Cognitive Patterns

Borderlines are intense and labile emotionally and cognitively, and are draining to significant others (and therapists). Yet, paradoxically, they need to understand that they fear facing their own intense negative emotions over time, and so find it hard to grieve the many relationship losses they generate. They maintain a facade of competence and independence, yet desperately want various types of help, and then react negatively when it is not forthcoming.

The following beliefs are common: (a) I'm afraid I'll be alone forever, as no one who really gets to know me will want to love me; (b) If I ignore my own needs, I can entrap some people into relationships, but, since I can't control my feelings, and I need the relationships, I'll be very unhappy; (c) though I need people, they will eventually hurt or reject me, so I must protect myself; (d) I deserve any bad things that happen to me; (e) my misery (and/or "badness") is how people recognize me as a unique self.

H. Avoidant Personality Disorder

These individuals are shy and inhibited interpersonally, yet at the same time desire to have interpersonal relationships, which distinguishes them from those with the schizotypal or schizoid personality disorders. They also do not show the degree of irritability and emotional instability seen in the borderline personality disorder. This is a common secondary diagnosis in inpatient populations.

1. Behavioral Patterns

A major feature of this chronic disorder is an unwillingness to tolerate risks in deepening interpersonal relationships. These persons are extremely sensitive to rejection and seem to need a guarantee ahead of time that a relationship will work out. Naturally, such guarantees are seldom available in healthy relationships. Thus, the friends they manage to make often show a degree of instability or are quite passive.

In many ways, this disorder is close to the anxiety disorders, since there is a degree of anxiety and distress, and low self-esteem is common. However, the behaviors that produce the distress are relatively egosyntonic. Their depression and anxiety are more related to the perceived rejection and criticism of others. This common disorder is seen more often in women. Any disorder in childhood that focuses on shyness predisposes one to the avoidant personality disorder.

2. Cognitive Patterns

Avoidant personalities are extremely sensitive to rejection and seem to need an advance guarantee that a relationship will work out—a relationship with an attached warranty. Thus, they resonate negatively to the refrain from W. B. Yeats: "Only God, my dear / Can love you for yourself alone / and not for your yellow hair."

Other cognitions common to the avoidant personality include (a) if people really got to know me, they would see how inadequate (or odd) I really am, and they would reject me; (b) I am unable to cope with unpleasant people or situations; (c) not thinking about a problem or unpleasant situation or not trying to cope with it may allow it to go away; (d) you'll never leave me because I'll make sure I leave you first; (e) nothing ventured, nothing failed.

I. Dependent Personality Disorder

In one way, dependent personality disorders can be seen as successful avoidant personality disorders. They have achieved a style that elicits the desired relationships, though at the cost of any consistent expression of their own personality. They show elements of agoraphobia, not crystallized, and they lack any real self-confidence. [*See* DEPENDENT PERSONALITY.]

1. Behavioral Patterns

People with the dependent personality disorder have a pervasive need to cling to stronger personalities who are allowed to make a wide range of decisions for them. They are naive and show little initiative. There is some suspiciousness of possible rejection, but not to the degree found in the avoidant personality disorder.

Since this is an exaggeration of the traditional feminine role, it is not surprising that it is far more common in women. If the individual is not in a dependent relationship, anxiety and upset are common. Even if enmeshed in a dependent relationship, there is still residual anxiety over the possibility of being abandoned.

Dependent personalities may be getting many rewards for their behavior, in the midst of the negatives that may have led them into therapy, e.g., abusive relationships. Very often significant others only want very circumscribed changes, so once changes begin, they will likely subvert things. At the same time, the eventual termination of any therapy is always threatening with these clients.

2. Cognitive Patterns

Underlying cognitive systems that are often included are (a) I am perpetually at risk of being alone in a cold and dangerous world; (b) I'm not able to cope with and/or enjoy life without a supportive other; (c) a loss of self is a fair price to pay in order to obtain a relationship with a supportive other, even if they periodically abuse me in some fashion; (d) I need constant access to this other, with as much intimacy as I can elicit, so I'll be as subservient and inoffensive as I need to be.

J. Obsessive–Compulsive Personality Disorder

This disorder is occasionally confused with the obsessive–compulsive disorder (which is an anxiety disorder), but there are significant differences between the two syndromes. First, the obsessive–compulsive personality seldom becomes obsessed about issues. Second, for the obsessive–compulsive personality the term *compulsive* refers to a lifestyle in which compulsive features are pervasive and chronic, but it does *not* refer to a specific behavior such as persistent hand-washing. Third, the person with an obsessive–compulsive personality disorder is not upset, anxious, or distressed about his or her lifestyle, whereas anxiety is generic and often obvious at times in the functioning of the obsessive–compulsive disorder. [*See* Obsessive–Compulsive Disorder.]

1. Behavioral Patterns

According to Sigmund Freud, their essential characteristics are that they are "exceptionally orderly, parsimonious and obstinate." Obsessive–compulsive personalities are preoccupied with rules and duties, are unable to express warmth and caring except in lim-

ited situations, are highly oriented toward a lifestyle marked by productivity and efficiency, are temperamentally and emotionally insensitive, and are generally distant from other individuals. They are inclined to be excessively moralistic, litigious, and hyperalert to criticism and perceived slights from others. They can be described as workaholics without warmth.

The extent to which the ritualistic and conforming behavior is generalized throughout the person's life and, more importantly, the degree to which it is functional must be taken into consideration before a diagnosis is made. For example, a pilot develops rituals for determining that his plane is safe before takeoff. If a part of the ritual is omitted by a copilot, the pilot may experience considerable distress and may actually risk alienation by insisting on the performance of the ritual. The pilot's insistence on carrying out a ritualistic check of the instruments makes him appear obsessive, but it also keeps him alive.

Captain Queeg, in the novel and movie *The Caine Mutiny,* may be regarded as an obsessive–compulsive personality. Queeg continually insisted on order, cleanliness, and obedience; disruption of routine panicked him. However, because Captain Queeg's symptom pattern also included paranoid features, he does not completely fit the obsessive–compulsive category.

2. Cognitive Patterns

It is true that a degree of compulsivity is effective, particularly in our society. It becomes a problem when it overwhelms the rest of the personality. Paradoxically, obsessive–compulsives are often indecisive in their thinking and poor planners of their time, a result of their narrow focus and concern with precision, even when precision may be irrelevant.

Typical underlying beliefs such as (a) to err, or worse, to fail, is anxiety-provoking, will allow others to criticize me, and makes me feel less than a whole person; (b) to lose control is anxiety-provoking; (c) my obsessiveness and/or compulsivity are powerful enough to avoid errors, failure, or finding myself with nothing to do, yet; (d) as regards meaningful decisions, rather than "Better to have tried and failed than to never have tried at all," my motto is "Better to have not tried at all, than to have tried and failed"; (e) details are important, i.e., if you can see trees, no need to look for the forest; (f) I am responsible for myself and others; (g) I hate others when they don't follow "the rules," i.e., my rules, and especially if they get by with it.

K. Passive–Aggressive Personality Disorder

Most parents have had the experience of a child pushing them to the limit of their control and then backing off. Like that child, the passive–aggressive becomes acutely sensitive to such limits and is consistently able to go so far but no further. When this pattern becomes an integral part of a social and vocational lifestyle, a passive–aggressive personality disorder exists. Although these patterns are commonly modeled and learned in childhood, such a family usually reaches a state of mutual détente. The pattern then causes severe problems when it is transferred into any new intimate, consistent contact relationship, such as marriage.

1. Behavioral Patterns

The passive–aggressive pattern is characterized by pouting, procrastination, stubbornness, or intentional inefficiency that is designed to frustrate other people. The essential condition in this category is that there is a social context in which something has been requested from the individual exhibiting passive–aggressive behavior. The individual is apparently capable of complying with what is requested but does nothing. This inaction results in severe frustration for the observer rather than for the passive–aggressive individual. Typically, there is no overt opposition from the individual such as a blatant refusal to comply. Rather, there is an apparently cooperative attitude but no resulting action. For example, there may be stubborn insistence on procedural detail that effectively renders any actual achievement impossible. The classic example of this behavior pattern is seen in the character of Schweik in *The Good Soldier Schweik* (Hasek, 1930), the model for the cartoon character Beetle Bailey, who managed to infuriate his military commanders by carrying out each order to the ultimate detail, thereby revealing its absurdity.

The passive–aggressive personality disorder often takes the standards and the belief system of significant others and turns them around to immobilize the others effectively. The strategy (which is not thought to be a conscious behavior) is to present the "enemy" (often a person depended on) with a choice that forces one either to capitulate or to violate an individual belief system. That person is thus immobilized, with no adequate reason to justify retaliation.

2. Cognitive Patterns

The automatic thought "I don't have to get there on time—nobody can tell me what to do" is common to passive–aggressives. Thus, they are inclined to be late for payments, sessions, etc., so clear contracts with detailed consequences are necessary.

Passive–aggressives are also often late within a much longer perspective—the developmental tasks of life, e.g., establishing a career, or getting married or having children. This stems not only from their sense "You (in this case, society) can't make me do it . . ." but also from an inability to tie responsibilities to time, and the fact that responsibility per se is often aversive because it is interpreted as a "society should." Analogously, there is often a passive refusal to accept the discipline and sacrifice needed to develop either vocational or interpersonal "careers." Attaining the required credentials and "putting in your time" in order to attain the payoff of an accrual process is seen as too restricting and demanding.

In addition to the beliefs embedded in the prior points, beliefs common in the passive–aggressive are (a) I know I can really be self-sufficient, but I apparently do need others, at least now, and I resent that; (b) any control by others is aversive; (c) while I apparently have to accept some subjugation of my desires and/or loss of control, they'll pay a price for making me do so; (d) if the conditions were right (and/or I really tried), I would be outstanding; (e) following rules, expectations, deadlines, etc., makes me less of a whole person; (f) no one, including me, really deserves to have authority.

L. Sadistic Personality Disorder

The term "sadistic personality disorder" does not officially appear in the *DSM*'s, though it was made available in an Appendix of the *DSM-III-R* as an optional diagnosis for clinicians to add when they find it helpful. In any case, the concept has a long history. Kernberg (1984) terms the sadistic personality the "malignant narcissistic" and places it between the antisocial and the narcissistic personalities on this continuum. The personality might also be thought of as an antisocial pattern, though with better socialization and a more prominent quality of revenge. See the prior description of those disorders for the relevant cognitive patterns, as they are an amalgam of those two, combined with the cognitive schemata "Not only does pain in others not generate empathic emotions, it may result in pleasure or an enhanced sense of self for me."

The *DSM* criteria were (1) uses violence or cruelty to establish a dominance relationship; (2) demeans or humiliates people in the presence of others; (3) takes pleasure in physical or psychological suffering of other humans or animals; (4) has, with unusual harshness, disciplined someone under his or her control; (5) has lied with the goal of inflicting pain or harm; (6) uses intimidation, or even terror, to get others to do what he or she wants; (7) restricts the autonomy of someone with whom he or she has a close relationship; or (8) is fascinated by weapons, martial arts, injury, torture, or violence in general. The dominant trend is a love of cruelty and an absence of remorse.

There is a noteworthy distinction between sadism, which is a paraphilia and the sadistic personality disorder. While sadistic sexual patterns are common in the sadistic personality disorder, it is not a necessary part of the pattern. In essence, the sadistic personality disorder is marked by a very assertive lifestyle based on power motives, commonly accompanied by gender dominance, the inflicting of pain for pleasure, and extreme aggression with or without sexual motivation. Yet, the sadistic behavior is well rationalized, and the individual may even present a very self-righteous air.

II. TREATMENT RELATIONSHIPS AND THE PERSONALITY DISORDERS

Modern theorists point out that treating the personality disorders, particularly those with antisocial, narcissistic, or borderline components, requires a rethinking of what are often termed transference issues. They note that such individuals often elicit an "objective counter-transference." This is usually a response of anger and frustration, even hate, but in some cases can be a type of protective affection.

The important point is to recognize that these emotional reactions of the therapist are reasonable, and based on good data. This is in contrast to the traditional conception of the therapist's reactions to neurot-

ics. In the latter instance, such feelings would be seen as indicative of emotional blocks in the therapist, which would signal a need for more analysis for the therapist and/or a transfer of the patient to another therapist.

However, in the "objective counter-transference" to the personality disordered client, the therapist needs to (a) recognize and "metabolize" such feelings, i.e., not act out toward the client in response to such feelings; (b) gradually let the client know that such reactions are occurring; (c) relate them to the eliciting behaviors; and (d) thus let the client know they can and are being controlled. Therefore, rather than allowing the client to project "onto" the therapist, as with a neurotic type in more classical analysis, this type of client is allowed to project "into" the therapist. Most such clients seem to use this as a means of communication, as well as control, almost as if it is the only way another can ever know the level of pain they went through.

III. SUMMARY

Personality or character disorders, unlike other mental disorders, are manifested primarily in a social context. They are more like "us," and we would rather not think so. These disorders trouble society, over time, more than they trouble the individual. Rarely do such individuals experience the crippling anxiety that is characteristic of the neuroses, the loss of functioning due to thought disorder characteristic of the schizophrenic process, the incapacity of organic brain syndromes, or the consistently manifested extremes of mood found in the affective disorders. Instead, one finds an apparently intact organism, with little evident symptomatology, whom is unable to organize his or her behavior and relate interpersonally in an effective manner. These disorders present a life-long problem for the individual, the treater, and society as a whole.

This article has been reprinted with updated references to *DSM-IV* from the *Encyclopedia of Human Behavior, Volume 3.*

BIBLIOGRAPHY

Beck, A., Freeman, A., *et al.* (1990). "Cognitive Therapy of Personality Disorders." Guilford, New York.
Cleckley, H. (1982). "The Mask of Sanity," 5th ed. Mosby, St. Louis.
Kernberg, O. (1984). "Severe Personality Disorders: Psychotherapeutic Strategies." Yale University Press, New Haven.

Meyer, R. (1993). "The Clinician's Handbook," 3rd ed. Allyn and Bacon, Boston.

Meyer, R. (1992). "Abnormal Behavior and the Criminal Justice System." Lexington Books, Lexington, MA.

Millon, T. (1981). "Disorders of Personality. DSM-III Axis II." Wiley, New York.

Oates, W. (1987). "Behind the Masks." Westminster, Philadelphia.

Turkat, D. (1990). "The Personality Disorders." Pergamon, New York.

Widiger, T., & Frances, A. (1985). The DSM-III personality disorders: Perspectives from psychology. *Arch. Gen. Psych.*, **42**, 615–623.

Phobias

George A. Clum

Virginia Polytechnic Institute and State University

Greg A. R. Febbraro

Medical University of South Carolina

Atypical Depression Depression that is not related to a stressful event and does not meet criterion for a major depressive disorder.

Cognitive Symptoms Specific thoughts or patterns of thoughts found to characterize certain mental disorders.

Comorbidity Coexistence, in the same individual, of more than one diagnosable psychiatric disorder.

Epidemiology The study of rates of an illness in different groups within a population.

Etiology An approach to understanding the cause of a phenomenon.

Obsessive-Compulsive Disorder A mental disorder characterized by the persistent intrusion of thoughts, images, or behaviors.

Physiological Arousal Response of increased activation of the organism characterized by such things as increases in heart rate, respiration, and muscle tension.

Prognosis The future course of a disorder.

PHOBIA derives from the Greek word *phobos*, meaning "fear." Phobias are persistent, excessive fear responses to objects or situations that are for most people neutral or only mildly anxiety-arousing. Phobias typically involve fears of the commonplace situations involved in life and, if the feared situation is frequently encountered, can interfere greatly in the general conduct of life. The current classification of phobias includes three types: specific phobia, social phobia, and agoraphobia. They tend to occur frequently, as approximately one in seven adults will experience a phobia at some point in their lives. While we think of the various types of phobias as separate entities, it is not uncommon for a given person to experience more than one type of phobia at the same time. Similarly, individuals who develop phobias are likely to experience other types of mental disorders, among them depression, and other anxiety disorders such as obsessive-compulsive disorder and generalized anxiety disorder. Phobic disorders, in addition to being relatively common, often have a profound effect on the lives of individuals who suffer with them.

In this article, each of the three types of phobias will be examined. A definition of each type will be provided, followed by an examination of the associated features of the disorder, its typical course and prognosis. Several causal models of each phobia group will be evaluated, followed by a discussion of therapeutic approaches.

I. SPECIFIC PHOBIA

A. Definition

The *Diagnostic and Statistical Manual of Mental Disorders,* Fourth Edition, (*DSM-IV,* the primary source in the United States for defining the various mental disorders) defines specific phobias as irrational and persistent fears of certain objects or animals. Specific phobias have historically been known as "simple phobias," "monosymptomatic phobias," or "focal phobias." The phenomenon of specific phobias has been described for centuries. Hippocrates, for example, described a man displaying an irrational fear of bridges. Detailed discussions of phobic symptoms can be found in the writings of seventeenth- and eighteenth-century authors such as Descartes, Le Camus, and Sauvages. [*See* DSM-IV.]

DSM-IV identifies three central features of specific phobias: (1) fear is directed at a limited set of stimuli; (2) confrontation with these stimuli elicits fear and avoidance behavior; and (3) the fear is unreasonable and excessive to a degree that it interferes with daily life. In addition, the fear persists over an extended period of time.

With the publication of *DSM-IV,* specific phobias were for the first time differentiated into four highly prevalent types: (1) animal type (e.g., spider phobia); (2) natural environment type (e.g., height phobia); (3) blood-injection-injury type (e.g., dental phobia); and (4) situational type (e.g., claustrophobia). In addition, *DSM-IV* introduces an "other type" that includes phobias of specific situations not covered above—choking phobia, for example. The validity of such distinctions is supported by data showing that these types tend to differ with respect to age of onset, familial aggregation, and physiological responses to the phobic stimulus.

B. Clinical Features

1. Symptoms and Epidemiology

When not confronting the feared object, individuals with specific phobias are not different from nonphobic individuals in their level of physiological arousal. When confronting the feared situation, however, phobic individuals reported a number of common anxiety-related somatic symptoms such as heart palpitations, trembling, and sweating. In addition, individuals with specific phobias demonstrate similar increases in indices of arousal upon exposure to cues associated with their phobia. Thus, a person with a fear of spiders might become fearful when looking at a picture of a spider or when entering a dusty place where spiders may be present. In addition to physiological arousal, phobic individuals also show increases in subjective level of fear and in their tendency to avoid the phobic object. However, this consistency is not always present as phobic individuals

may manifest increases in one or two of these domains and not the other(s).

Blood-injection-injury phobics are characterized by a unique physiological response to their fear cues. These individuals exhibit an initial increase in heart rate and blood pressure, as do most other phobics, followed by a dramatic drop on these measures, often resulting in fainting.

Not much is known about the cognitive symptoms in individuals with specific phobias due to an assumption that any thoughts individuals with specific phobias might have would be related to the feared object. Furthermore, cognitions have not been considered to be important in the etiology of specific phobias. This view—that cognitions are unimportant in the development of specific phobias—is changing. For example, 37% of individuals exposed to a phobic stimulus reported being equally or more concerned with their physical sensations than with the stimulus itself. In addition, many claustrophobics report thoughts of being trapped, suffocating, and losing control, thoughts characteristic of individuals who experience panic attacks.

It was found in a recent national survey of mental disorders that 11.3% of the population will have a specific phobia in their lifetime. Situational and environmental phobias are the most common (13% of the population), followed by animal phobias (8%), and blood-injection-injury phobias (3%).

Women are twice as likely as men to be diagnosed with a specific phobia. This is especially true for animal phobias and situational and environmental phobias, but less so for blood-injection-injury phobias.

2. Course/Prognosis and Comorbidity Issues

Specific phobias develop at different points in the life cycle. Animal phobias develop earliest (average age around 7 years), followed by blood phobias (average age around 9 years), dental phobias (average age around 12 years), and claustrophobia (average age around 20 years). The differences in age of onset among the specific phobias suggest that different causal factors are at work in their development.

The heterogeneity of the diagnostic group is further evidenced when one examines claustrophobia. Claustrophobia may well be descriptively and functionally a less constricting form of agoraphobia, a disorder described later. Support for a link between claustrophobia and agoraphobia comes from (1) a similar age of onset with both developing around 20 years of age; (2) a similar mode of acquisition, with agoraphobia (81% of the time) and claustrophobia (69% of the time) developing after experiencing a stressful event; and (3) the co-occurrence in claustrophobia of uncued/unexpected panic attacks, worry about becoming anxious and panicky, fear of bodily symptoms of arousal (e.g., "fear of fear"), and unpredictability of the fear response in claustrophobic situations, all of which are features of Panic Disorder with Agoraphobia. In contrast, other specific phobias have an earlier age at onset, are less likely to be acquired after experiencing a traumatic event, and are more consistently associated with fear of specific situations than of internal anxiety symptoms.

The natural course of specific phobias is usually chronic and can be characterized by the persistence of mild rather than severe symptoms of anxiety over time. Only 16% of individuals with specific phobias have a complete remission of symptoms over a follow-up period of 7 years. While specific phobias appear to occur frequently in the general population, few sufferers seek treatment, even though this problem may seriously threaten their social or occupational functioning and in spite of the fact that treatment can be highly successful.

C. Etiology

I. Genetic Factors

The genetic hypothesis contends that a predisposition to develop specific phobias is inherited. Evidence indicates there is a consistent, modest contribution of genetic factors to the development of specific phobias. Furthermore, the genetic factors underlying specific fears appear to be of a general nature, such that what is inherited is a trait that predisposes to anxiety in general rather than inheritance of a specific fear. In some cases, the predisposition is expressed as a specific phobia; in other cases, the complaints may take the form of, for example, social phobia or agoraphobia. However, blood-injection-injury phobia may represent an exception to this pattern. Evidence suggests that in blood-injection-injury phobia, the genetic contribution is much stronger than in other phobias and that what is inherited is the specific vulnerability to develop this phobia. [See GENETIC CONTRIBUTORS TO MENTAL HEALTH.]

2. Biological Factors

The preparedness hypothesis suggests specific phobias are an example of evolution-prepared learning. The concept of "preparedness" refers to the observation that anxiety responses are more easily learned to some stimuli than to others and that the ease of learning in any one instance varies from species to species. Most specific phobias involve stimuli that over the course of evolution might have been dangerous to man (e.g., snakes, heights) and are still reacted to as though intrinsically dangerous. Several human and animal studies have tested the preparedness hypothesis under laboratory conditions and found evidence to support it. In one such study, it was found that when conditioned responses to evolution-relevant cues are acquired, they continue to persist much longer than conditioned responses to evolution-neutral cues. A number of studies on monkeys lend further support to the preparedness hypothesis. In these studies, observer monkeys acquired an extremely persistent fear of snakes after they watched model monkeys reacting fearfully to snakes. In contrast, observer monkeys failed to acquire a fear of flowers after they had seen models exhibiting identical fear responses when presented with flowers. These various research studies provide support for the contention that fear responses to some stimuli are much easier to acquire if fear responses to these stimuli were adaptive to our ancestors' survival.

The "Preparedness" hypothesis specifies that learning a phobic response will occur more easily for some stimuli than for others. An association with a negative unconditioned stimulus is still, however, required. An alternative, nonassociative hypothesis is that certain stimuli are hard-wired to produce fear, that is, they elicit a fear response without a previous negative experience with the stimulus. Darwin noted, after observing his 2-year-old's nonfearful response to caged animals, that fears are inherited effects of real dangers. When Darwin tried to control his fear response to the strike of a puff adder seated behind a solid glass barrier, he was unable to restrain his automatic recoil from the barrier. Perhaps the best evidence for the biological basis of fear comes from examining the responses of infant rhesus monkeys. Shown slides of monkeys in various poses, these monkeys displayed clear fear responses when shown pictures of threatening, but not of nonthreatening, monkeys. Because these infant monkeys were reared in isolation, they could not have learned this fearful response by experiencing trauma themselves or by watching other monkeys display a fear response. Similar nonlearned fearful responses in human children develop at specific periods in the developmental cycle. Thus, human infants display a fear of strangers from around 4 to 9 months of age, peaking at 12.5 months. Human infants, after they develop locomotion, also display a fear of falling when placed on the edge of an apparatus that looks like a visual cliff. Infants will crawl away from mothers who call to them from across the cliff even after patting the surface to assure themselves of its solidity. Such data indicate that for at least some stimuli there is a built-in readiness to experience fear in their presence.

There are critics of the biological hypothesis. These critics point out that the results of these studies are open to alternative interpretations. One such interpretation is that the tendency for learned responses to some stimuli to persist might be the product of expectancies rooted in culture rather than genes. Such an explanation fails to account for the automatic fear response of infants and of monkeys raised in isolation to specific fear stimuli.

3. Associative Learning

Classical conditioning is a process by which different stimuli, which occur at the same time, come to be associated. The earliest demonstration that humans could learn a fear response via classical conditioning occurred in 1920 when Watson and Rayner produced a fearful response in an 11-month-old infant named Albert. Watson observed that Albert's response to a white laboratory rat was initially positive—Albert smiled and played with the animal. Subsequently, whenever the rat was present, a loud noise was sounded that startled Albert. The rat, through repeated presentations with the noise, came to be associated with the noise. This association of an initially neutral stimulus (rat) with an aversive unconditioned stimulus (UCS = loud noise) resulted in a conditioned fear response (CR) when only the rat was presented. For some time after this demonstration it was thought that all phobic reactions were obtained via aversive conditioning as in the "Little Albert" study.

The classical conditioning model of phobias explains why people react with subjective and physiological fear when they are exposed to a learned phobic stimulus. However, it does not account for the persistent avoidance behavior phobics display. A

two-stage model explaining the development of the fear response and avoidance behavior was subsequently developed. Classical conditioning explained the learned fear response in the first stage, while instrumental conditioning explained the learned avoidance response in the second stage. Instrumental conditioning in this case refers to the reinforcement of the avoidance response produced by the decrease in anxiety. During classical conditioning, the pairing of a neutral CS and an aversive UCS results in a conditioned fear response to the CS. During instrumental learning, the person learns that the fear response to the CS can be reduced by escaping or avoiding the CS. The reduction in fear levels that follows avoidance reinforces this behavior (a process termed negative reinforcement) and, in time, avoidance behavior becomes an integral part of the phobia. This two-stage theory has been well-documented in the laboratory. However, the two-stage theory has several limitations. First, the conditioning approach fails to explain why specific fears are nonrandomly distributed, that is, why some individuals are more likely to develop phobias than are others. Second, individuals do not always acquire phobias as a result of confronting an aversive stimulus and pairing it with a neutral stimulus. Individuals who have specific phobias, for example, frequently are unable to remember a traumatic event during which they learned to fear the stimulus. Lastly, fearful behavior that is produced via classical conditioning in the laboratory requires repeated pairings of the unconditional and neutral stimuli, a circumstance inconsistent with reports of how specific phobias develop.

Because of the failure of classical conditioning to explain how most specific fears developed, Rachman proposed two additional pathways: (1) vicarious learning (i.e., learning to fear by watching someone else act fearfully toward a stimulus) and (2) acquisition of negative information and the aforementioned associative learning. All three of these explanations for the development of specific fears have in common a cognitive expectancy of threat that is connected to the feared stimulus. People essentially learn through direct or indirect experience that some stimuli pose a threat to them and that fear is proportional to the likelihood and severity of that threat. The vicarious learning hypothesis has been supported by both animal and human laboratory studies that show individuals react fearfully after watching others act fearfully. Negative information provided by significant others, such as parents, or through the media of books or television may give rise to fear of stimuli that are subjects of the negative information.

Support for the three modes of fear acquisition comes from studies that ask individuals with specific phobias to identify what they believe caused their disorder. A proportion of phobic individuals report their phobias began suddenly, following a fear-producing encounter with the stimulus, while a smaller proportion report their fear began when they viewed someone respond fearfully or learned indirectly of the potential danger associated with the object. These three avenues for acquiring phobias through learning occur with different frequencies in the four subtypes of specific phobias. Animal phobics and blood-injection-injury phobics more often ascribe their fears to seeing others respond fearfully and to negative information that do claustrophobics. In contrast, the associative learning pathway is more pronounced in claustrophobia than in animal phobia, blood-injection-injury or height phobia. The acquisition of a fear through modeling or negative information is associated with phobias with an early age of onset. It is also likely that the acquisition of a specific phobia is overdetermined, that is, individuals who acquire a phobia often report negative learning experiences of more than one variety. There are even indications that subjects with "mixed" pathways (e.g., conditioning and modeling) have higher levels of fear.

4. Treatment

It is generally accepted that the most successful treatments for specific phobias employ a reconditioning paradigm. In specific phobias, neutral stimuli such as animals, storms, or blood have become associated with an anxiety response, whether through direct association, vicarious learning, or anxiety-producing information. Presenting the phobic stimulus to the sufferer in the absence of a reinforcing or unconditioned stimulus leads to reductions in the fear response to the stimulus. This has been accomplished using a variety of treatment approaches, including systematic desensitization—both imaginal and "in vivo," that is, in "real life"—and vicarious learning techniques.

Systematic desensitization refers to a process in which the phobic stimuli are arranged in hierarchical fashion from least anxiety-producing to most anxiety-producing, and these stimuli are systematically paired

with a response incompatible with anxiety. Taking as an example an individual with a spider phobia, an item low on the hierarchy might be a picture of a small spider, while an item high on the hierarchy might be holding a jar containing a live tarantula. After constructing the hierarchy, the phobic individual would then be taught a method of inducing relaxation. The final step would involve the phobic individual sequentially confronting items in the hierarchy while remaining relaxed. Phobic items are presented repeatedly until the sufferer reports little or no anxiety when presented with the phobic cue. When this level of comfort is reached, the sufferer proceeds to the next item on the hierarchy until he is able to tolerate all phobic stimuli on the hierarchy with a minimal level of anxiety. In one version of this approach, all the stimuli are presented imaginally, while in another version the sufferer is exposed to the fearful stimuli in vivo. The in vivo approach has been found very successful with improvement rates in excess of 85%.

Vicarious learning techniques are used adjunctively to the above two approaches as well as alone. Vicarious learning is a phenomenon by which organisms learn a response by watching the emotional responses of others to these same stimuli. Children whose parents exhibit fearless responses to a variety of situations are themselves likely to show low fear responses to the same situations. On the other hand, children who observe their parents or peers responding fearfully to certain situations are themselves likely to respond fearfully to these same situations. Used therapeutically, vicarious learning involves corrective information, for example, "the spider is not harmful," skills on how to handle the feared object, and exposure to models who respond positively to the phobic stimuli. The sufferer is then encouraged to expose himself to the previously feared situations.

Interestingly, individuals with blood-injury phobias can also be treated with exposure techniques, but in this case the phobic stimulus is paired with a muscle-tensing response that is incompatible with the drop in blood pressure characterizing this group of phobias. When this procedure is carried out repeatedly, both the fear of blood-injury and the drop in blood pressure experienced at the sight of blood diminish.

All the above treatment techniques involve learning a new and incompatible response in place of the fearful response to the phobic stimulus. The process by which the new learning takes place is still a matter of some debate. One explanation is a simple reconditioning model in which either the old fearful response to the phobic stimulus is changed by prolonged exposure without the reinforcement provided by the presence of an aversive stimulus, or a new relaxation response is learned in the presence of the phobic stimulus. Another explanation is provided by the information-processing theory of fear reduction. In this model, phobic knowledge that exists in the brain consists of both stimulus (such as images associated with the phobic object) and response propositions, including the behavioral, verbal, and physiological reactions to the phobic object. Change is thought to occur when the individual processes the phobic stimulus and the response to that stimulus thoroughly, thereby altering the fearful images and anxious responses associated with that stimulus.

II. SOCIAL PHOBIA

A. Definition

Although fears in the presence of others have been described for centuries and have been addressed in the mental health literature since at least 1970, social phobia was not considered a diagnosable entity until the publication of the third *Diagnostic and Statistical Manual of Mental Disorders,* published in 1980. *DSM-IV* (the current system) identifies the essential feature of Social Phobia (also referred to as Social Anxiety Disorder) as a marked and persistent fear of social or performance situations in which embarrassment may occur. Social phobics fear and/or avoid a variety of situations in which they would be required to interact with others or to perform a task in front of other people. Typical social phobia situations include speaking, eating, or writing in public, using public bathrooms, and attending parties or interviews. In addition, a common fear of social phobics is that other individuals will identify and ridicule their anxiety in social situations. When a person fears a broad spectrum of social situations, it is referred to as Social Phobia, Generalized subtype, whereas fear of one or a few social situations is referred to as Social Phobia, Specific subtype. Individuals with social phobia are aware that their fears and social isolation are unreasonable

and excessive, but they feel unable to control these feelings. [*See* SHYNESS.]

B. Clinical Features: Symptomatology and Epidemiology

As in specific phobia, the anxiety of social phobics is stimulus-bound, that is, it occurs only in the presence of the feared situation or when anticipating that situation. When in or anticipating a potentially embarrassing situation, the individual with social phobia experiences profound anxiety, accompanied by a variety of somatic symptoms including palpitations, muscle tension, nausea, and blurred vision. The person with a social phobia experiences symptoms that underscore the fear of public scrutiny, including symptoms such as trembling, shaking, blushing, twitching, and sweating.

Social phobics also experience more negative self-evaluative thoughts and fewer positive thoughts prior to and during social situations than do individuals who do not experience anxiety. Not only do individuals with social phobia experience more negative arousal symptoms compared to nonphobic individuals, social phobics also perform less well in social situations and systematically underestimate their performance. Judging from their response to social situations, social phobics have a variety of information that serves to underpin their fears.

Social anxiety and reports of shyness in the general population are relatively common, occurring in about 40% of college students. Furthermore, social anxiety is a common accompaniment of all anxiety disorders. The most recent National Comorbidity Survey found a given individual had a 13% chance of developing a social phobia in his/her lifetime.

The distinction between generalized and specific social phobia is a useful one. Individuals with generalized social phobia have a fear of and will avoid a wide variety of interpersonal and performance situations. These may include formal speaking to a group, informal interactions such as going to parties or meeting strangers, assertive interactions and being observed by others. Individuals with specific social phobia typically are afraid only in performance situations or in a limited number of interpersonal situations. Most individuals with social phobia experience anxiety in two or more different social situations. A lack of social skills has been found in the generalized type, with increases in subjective feelings of anxiety being found in the specific type. Individuals with generalized social phobia reported themselves as more shy and, especially for males, less likely to date during the late adolescent period. Differences between the two types are also indicated by treatment studies that attempt to match treatment type to type of social phobia, a distinction discussed further in the section on treatment of social phobias.

Unlike agoraphobia and specific phobia, social phobia has repeatedly been found to have an essentially equal sex distribution or even a slight tendency to affect males more than females. A similar sex distribution has been found among socially anxious college students.

C. Course/Prognosis and Comorbidity Issues

The consensus among individuals who study anxiety disorders is that social phobia typically begins in late childhood or early adolescence, with fewer individuals developing the disorder in early childhood. Onset is generally gradual and, clinically, most social phobics report they cannot specifically remember the beginning of their symptoms. Some social phobics report specific stressful experiences prior to the onset of the disorder. The course of social phobia is often continuous, with duration frequently being lifelong. Social phobia may fluctuate in severity or remit during adulthood, and severity of impairment may fluctuate with life stressors and demands. Social phobia is much more serious and disabling than previously thought and can have severe functional consequences. More than 50% of individuals diagnosed with social phobia are unable to complete high school, more than 70% of these individuals are in the lowest two socioeconomic quartiles, and 22% of individuals with pure social phobia receive welfare. The majority of individuals with social phobia are unmarried. It is clear from the prevailing information that social phobia is a severe illness with numerous social consequences.

In addition to the social and occupational consequences of social phobia, almost 19% of individuals with social phobia are likely to abuse alcohol, while 13% will likely develop some type of drug abuse. In addition, social phobia is also commonly associated with major depression (16.6%), dysthymia (chronic low-grade depression) (12.5), obsessive-compulsive disorder (11.1%), and anxiety disorders such as panic disorder (4.7), agoraphobia (4.9%), and specific phobia (59%). In the majority of cases, the onset of social phobia precedes the onset of the second psychiatric disorder, with the exception of specific phobias, by many years. Social phobia, generalized subtype, is viewed as being more severe than social phobia, specific subtype, and thus is associated with more frequent comorbidity.

D. Etiology

1. Genetic

It is likely there is a genetic predisposition to developing social anxiety and shyness. The rate for social phobia in first-degree relatives (parents, children, siblings) of individuals with pure social phobia is 16%, compared to 5% in individuals selected randomly from the population. Identical twins were also found to have a higher rate of social phobia (49%) if their cotwin had the disorder than did fraternal twins whose cotwin had the disorder (30%). Such findings have been reported by several different investigators, even when controlling for gender in various studies. It has been estimated that genetic factors account for 30% of the vulnerability for social phobia.

2. Biological Factors

Little research has been conducted on the biological causes of social phobia. One line of research has examined biological differences between anxiety in social phobics and other anxiety disorders. When in social situations perceived as evaluative, 50% of individuals with social phobia symptoms experience a surge of epinephrine (a drug secreted in your body to prepare you for an emergency), distinguishing them from panic attacks in which an adrenaline surge is not regularly seen. Another line of investigation has assessed the relationship between sensitivity to social disapproval and neurotransmitters (chemicals necessary for efficient transmission of nerve signals). These studies have revealed a connection between depletion of specific neurotransmitters and mood responses to social approval and disapproval. The possibility exists that this transmission system is poorly regulated in social phobics and those with atypical depression. Both these groups overreact to criticism or rejection, and greatly benefit from a group of anti-depressant drugs—monoamino oxidase inhibitors—that reduce their sensitivity to rejection and also inhibit the metabolism of specific neurotransmitters.

3. Environmental Factors

In addition to direct conditioning experiences, social phobics report parental behavior that tends to foster dependency and insecurity. Social phobics compared to nonphobic normals perceive their parents as overprotective and low in emotional support. Other research has replicated these findings and additionally found social phobics rated their parents as rejecting. These parental patterns could account for general feelings of insecurity, typical of most individuals who experience anxiety. Other research compared social phobics to agoraphobics. Social phobics reported their parents isolated them from social experiences, overemphasized the opinions of others, and de-emphasized socializing with others as a family. These additional patterns in the parents of social phobics could account for the specific manifestation of anxiety found in these individuals.

4. Psychological Factors

Four types of concerns have been identified among social phobics: (1) perceptions of autonomic arousal; (2) concern with others' awareness; (3) feelings of social inadequacy; and (4) fear of negative evaluation. Of these, the last three have all been identified as important causal and/or maintaining factors in social phobia.

Awareness of others' perceptions was one of the earliest areas to be investigated in social phobia. Research studies substantiated increased public self-consciousness in socially anxious individuals accompanied by a fear of negative evaluation. Increases in self-consciousness led to increased autonomic arousal.

Social phobics believe that compared to others they are deficient in social skills. They combine a belief that others hold high expectations for their performance with the perception of their own inadequacy. Consequently, they anticipate negative evaluations and are predisposed to interpret neutral feedback or even moderately positive feedback in negative terms. This bias in the manner in which information is processed by socially anxious individuals tends to maintain these perceptions as socially phobic individuals tend to "find" the behaviors in others for which they search. When asked to recall their past evaluations, they are more likely to recall negative feedback than are non-socially anxious individuals.

E. Therapy

1. Psychological Approaches

Psychological treatment approaches are both effective and often preferred to medications by people who experience side effects from medications. Relapse rates for social phobics treated by specialized psychological treatments tend to be lower than for those treated with medications.

Specific psychological techniques can be linked to the symptoms and characteristics of social phobias. Aspects of successful interactions that cut across a variety of approaches can be identified. These common elements constitute the basic ingredients of a successful approach. They include:

1. Education regarding the defining characteristics and treatment of the disorder. Social phobics are frequently ashamed of their problem, believe their problem to be unique, and thus have not discussed it with others. Informing such individuals that much is known about the problem and that many people share the problem is very reassuring and anxiety-reducing.

2. Anxiety-reduction techniques such as relaxation training and diaphragmatic breathing (breathing that begins in the diaphragm) can be used to diminish the anticipatory anxiety as well as anxiety within the phobic situation itself. Social phobics experience heightened arousal manifested in a variety of somatic experiences of anxiety. Anxiety-reduction techniques are effective in dealing with these symptoms and in restoring confidence in the ability to decrease arousal in phobic situations.

3. Cognitive-retraining techniques deal with the exaggerated beliefs of being humiliated or ridiculed for having anxiety symptoms. Techniques that challenge such beliefs, invite the sufferer to test his beliefs against reality, and even dismiss or reframe the perceived negative evaluations of others are a critical element of therapy.

4. Training in social interaction techniques and social skills is important for individuals with generalized

social phobia. Sufferers of the generalized form are deficient in assertiveness techniques, in techniques for starting a conversation or engaging a stranger, as well as techniques for deepening intimacy. Training in the use of such approaches and practice with them serves to improve social skills and increase their confidence in the ability to engage in these behaviors.

5. Graduated exposure to the feared situation. It is in this context alone that the social phobic learns to apply the above techniques in real-life situations. Such self-exposure increases the belief that the feared situation can be faced and that the sufferer can reduce the anxiety and cognitions and engage actively in social situations.

2. Pharmacological Approaches

The use of pharmacologic interventions in the treatment of social phobics has been relatively rare until recent times. Some drugs have achieved a high rate of acceptability, in part because of their effectiveness and in part because of their low rate of side effects.

Beta-adrenergic blockers—beta blockers—have been widely accepted as a treatment for performance anxiety. Fast-acting and with a relatively short presence in the body, beta blockers are used by seasoned performers and amateurs facing their first public appearance as a way of reducing the physiological accompaniments of anxiety. Side effects from using these drugs are negligible. The effectiveness of beta blockers appears to be restricted to social phobics with specific fears such as stage fright. Generalized social phobias are less likely to be helped by this group of medications, perhaps because of the failure of these drugs to reduce the negative cognitions associated with this disorder.

A second class of drugs—an antidepressant group known as monoamino oxidase inhibitors (MAOIs)—have the highest success rates in the treatment of social phobia. This class of drugs was initially found to be effective with a type of depression characterized by interpersonal sensitivity. They were then tried on social phobics who, as previously discussed, also display a high level of interpersonal sensitivity. This class of drugs is successful with both specific and generalized social phobics, and also has beneficial effects for a variety of disorders that frequently co-occur with social phobia, including panic disorder, obsessive-compulsive disorder, and depression. The principal drawback of the MAOIs is that severe side effects are likely to occur, including hypertensive crisis, unless the individual taking the drug eliminates from his diet foods that contain tyramine (including cheeses, wines, beers, and some brans). For this reason, the use of MAOIs in the treatment of social phobia has been restricted.

A new class of antidepressant medication called selective serotonin reuptake inhibitors (SSRIs) has also been used in the treatment of both specific and generalized social phobias. This class of drugs has been found effective with the advantage that the individual taking these drugs experiences few side effects. Because of the frequency with which this class of drugs is well-tolerated, it may well be the first choice of pharmacologic interventions. The level of effectiveness is high even when the social phobia is accompanied by other anxiety disorders or depression, all of which are also responsive to this class of medications.

III. AGORAPHOBIA

A. Definition

The term agoraphobia, which literally means "fear of the marketplace," was initially used by Westphal in 1871 to reflect the frequent observation that individuals with this problem were afraid of venturing into public places. The diagnosis requires the existence of two primary features: (1) anxiety about being in places or situations from which escape might be difficult (or embarrassing) or in which help might not be available, and (2) avoidance of these situations, enduring them with marked distress or fear of having panic symptoms, or requiring the presence of a companion before entering the phobic situation.

The agoraphobic individual fears the onset of panic attacks (a discrete period of intense fear or discomfort that develops abruptly and reaches its peak within 10 minutes) or panic symptoms and avoids situations associated with such attacks. Four feared situations typically yield the avoidance behavior that occurs in agoraphobia: (1) situations, typically social, from which escape might be difficult, including restaurants, shopping malls, hairdressers, dentist chairs, and so on; (2) travelling where escape is difficult, including strange cities, bridges, tunnels, planes; (3) traveling away from home; and (4) being home alone. The common feature of these situations is the fear of being unable to obtain help in the event of a panic attack, or the possibility of embarrassment if one obtained help. This response has been referred to as the fear of fear.

B. Clinical Features: Symptomatology and Epidemiology

The chief feature of agoraphobia is escape from or avoidance of situations where panic symptoms might occur. While agoraphobia is frequently accompanied by or preceded by panic attacks, many agoraphobics are unable to recall a distinct panic episode prior to developing avoidance behavior. In these individuals, limited-symptom panic attacks (attacks where fewer than four symptoms are present) or fears of putting themselves at risk by leaving their safe base appear to underlie the avoidance behavior. Thoughts of dying, losing control, becoming seriously ill, going insane, or acting in an embarrassing fashion are likely to precede the avoidance behavior.

Recent evidence indicates that the lifetime prevalence for agoraphobia is 6.7%. Agoraphobia tends to develop later in life than specific or social phobias and occurs more than twice as frequently in women as in men. Individuals who are agoraphobic tend to have lower income and education levels, are frequently unemployed, and are more likely to live with someone other than a spouse. It is unknown whether agoraphobics, because of their illness, drift into these less productive circumstances or whether the stress of these circumstances produces agoraphobia. When individuals with agoraphobia are studied in the general community, they are often found to have at least one additional diagnosis, with major depressive disorder, specific phobia, and panic disorder among the most likely of these. While a number of mental disorders tend to co-occur with agoraphobia, it is often less related to substance abuse or dependence, indicating that agoraphobics tend not to medicate themselves with alcohol or street drugs. When unaccompanied by another disorder, agoraphobics tend to perceive little role impairment, which may account for the finding that only about one-fourth of these individuals seek help even when their agoraphobic avoidance is extensive. Having another diagnosable mental illness, and especially the existence of panic attacks, significantly increases the likelihood that agoraphobics perceive

themselves as being impaired socially or occupationally, with as many as 70% of these individuals reporting that they have sought help for their problem.

C. Course and Prognosis

Agoraphobia develops from young adulthood through middle life with few instances of agoraphobia beginning in late life. The average age for the onset of this disorder is between 25 and 29. Panic attacks, which frequently are the precursor of agoraphobia, often begin with the onset of puberty. These findings indicate there is a lag between the onset of panic attacks and the development of avoidance behavior.

When agoraphobia is accompanied by panic disorder, long-term outcome is poor. Studies up to 20 years in length reveal 50% of untreated individuals with this problem experience significant social and occupational impairment, with 80% at least occasionally symptomatic. A variety of additional problems either co-occur with this disorder or develop in response to it, including increased depression, suicidality, sexual and marital problems, tranquilizer addiction, unemployment, and financial difficulties. Treatment using one of several recognized approaches improves the long-term adjustment, although a significant portion of sufferers who receive treatment continue to experience symptoms or, in fact, relapse to the level of adjustment prior to treatment. Individuals who at the conclusion of treatment continue to experience occasional panic attacks, or who remain avoidant, are more likely to experience a relapse to their previous level of functioning. Likewise, individuals who experience low levels of social support, problems in their marital relationship, or significant stressors after treatment is completed are likely to suffer a relapse.

D. Causal Factors

Agoraphobia is best viewed as the endpoint of a series of factors that contribute to the development of this disorder. Genetic factors produce a biological vulnerability that then interacts with stressors and other environmental factors that in turn increase the likelihood one will develop panic disorder and agoraphobia. A strong genetic and biological vulnerability will require fewer environmental factors to produce agoraphobia, while a weak genetic and biological vulnerability will require more and stronger environmental factors before agoraphobia develops.

E. Heredity

There is a demonstrable link between genetic factors and the development of panic disorder, a frequent precursor of agoraphobia. First-degree relatives of individuals with panic disorder are approximately seven times more likely to be diagnosed as panic disordered than are first-degree relatives of individuals with no panic disorder. Similarly, identical twins are twice as likely to share a common diagnosis of anxiety disorder than are fraternal twins, although they are unlikely to share the same diagnosis for the specific type of anxiety disorder. If one twin has a diagnosis of agoraphobia with panic attacks, their identical cotwin is likely to experience panic attacks as well, while their fraternal cotwin is not.

It appears from the limited research in this area that a biological vulnerability exists for panic attacks but not necessarily agoraphobia. A stronger genetic relationship is likely to exist for anxiety problems in general such that what is inherited is a vulnerability to develop anxiety.

F. Biological Factors

If genetic factors play a role in the development of panic, the question remains as to what type of vulnerability is inherited. One possibility is that panic disorder may involve a deficit in the metabolism of factors that inhibit the transmission of anxiety messages in the brain, while another possibility is that there is an increased sensitivity to certain substances. If the latter is true, the introduction of these substances to the bodies of individuals with panic disorder and agoraphobia should produce symptoms of panic, while this response would not be expected in individuals without panic attacks.

These differences in sensitivity to certain substances have been demonstrated in a wide variety of studies. Panic disordered agoraphobics have been shown more sensitive to sodium lactate, adrenalin, caffeine, and hyperventilation. The first of these—sodium lactate—is similar to lactic acid, a substance that increases naturally in the body in response to

physical exercise. It is known that agoraphobic individuals possess a sensitivity to increases in physiological arousal such as increased heart rate, respiration, and sweating, body changes common to both exercise and panic attacks. Panic attacks, therefore, may be an alarm reaction to detected physiological changes produced by increases in lactic acid. People suffering from panic disorder show this increased sensitivity by developing panic attacks when injected with sodium lactate, while people who do not have this problem do not show this sensitivity. Similarly, panic-disordered agoraphobics respond with panic attack symptoms when administered a standard hyperventilation procedure, when they drink caffeine, or when they are injected with adrenalin. This response is not typically seen in nonpanickers, thus supporting the biological vulnerability hypothesis.

The finding that panic-disordered agoraphobics have an increased sensitivity to symptoms of physiological arousal may help explain why there is an increase vulnerability to panic in individuals with certain cardiovascular problems. One such line of evidence has shown that individuals with mitral valve prolapse syndrome (MVPS), a problem characterized by chest pain, difficulty in breathing, dizziness, fatigue, and tachycardia are at risk for developing panic disorder. Individuals who experience such symptoms and are psychologically sensitized to them may come to fear them and develop catastrophic cognitions when they occur—the previously identified "fear of fear."

Further evidence for the role of biological factors comes from panic-disordered individuals who report fluctuations in the frequency and severity of attacks they experience. Recent findings in women indicate increases in panic attacks of as much as 100% occur during the premenstrual period, while there is no change in the degree of anticipatory anxiety or avoidance behavior at these times. Again, the biological contribution is more apparent for panic attacks than for agoraphobia.

G. Psychological Factors

The childhood backgrounds of agoraphobics suggest family experiences play a role in the development of this problem. Lack of maternal care and a general lack of social support, coupled with high intrafamily conflict, have been linked to the development of agoraphobia in adulthood. This deficiency in a warm, supportive parent–child relationship and frequent punishment and criticism produce individuals who view themselves as incompetent and unable to handle challenging situations. This self-view in turn leads to withdrawal and avoidance when faced with challenging situations as an adult.

As many as 80% of agoraphobics report the onset of their panic symptoms was preceded by identifiable stressors or a period of prolonged stress. Interpersonal problems is a frequent precipitant of agoraphobia in adults. Rejection or loss have been reported by a majority of sufferers able to identify a precipitant. Also implicated are marital conflicts in which persons fail to assert themselves, or when they do assert themselves are threatened with loss of the relationship. Loss by death, divorce, or separation, either of a family member or a friend, has been reported as a factor that has led to the development of agoraphobia. The combination of low support and high conflict in childhood and threatened or actual loss of interpersonal relationships in adulthood produces a unique psychological vulnerability to agoraphobia.

Some people who have panic attacks do not become agoraphobic. Women, who tend to value social relationships more than men do, may be uniquely vulnerable to losing such relationships, a fact that may help explain why so many more women with panic than men with panic develop agoraphobia. Two additional factors are predictive of who among panic-disordered individuals develops agoraphobia—how panickers think about their attacks, and how they cope with them. Those panickers who develop agoraphobia believe there is a connection between the situations they avoid and the likelihood they will suffer panic attacks in those situations, while nonavoiders are less likely to make such links. Further, individuals who become agoraphobic believe that if they do have a panic attack, there will be nothing they can do to control it—the absence of a belief known as self-efficacy. The belief that coping strategies are available that will help control panic attacks is also associated with lower levels of avoidance. The use of coping strategies such as seeking out social support, reasoning out what is happening, controlling one's breathing and relaxing one's muscles are specific strategies linked to lower levels of avoidance, while wishful thinking is a strategy linked to higher levels of avoidance.

IV. PANIC DISORDER AND AGORAPHOBIA

A. Psychological Approaches

Psychological treatments for this disorder target each of the disorder's components—the panic attacks, anticipatory anxiety, and agoraphobic avoidance. Panic attacks themselves are comprised of several features, each of which is targeted within the treatment program. These features include physiological arousal symptoms and catastrophic cognitions. In addition, panic attacks develop from a baseline of chronically high anxiety and are preceded by high levels of anticipatory anxiety when sufferers face situations where panic attacks have previously occurred. Panic sufferers typically have little information about their problem and considerable misinformation. The first phase of treatment aims at providing an understanding of the disorder as well as factors that may have caused it and serve to maintain it. Subsequently, techniques that reduce the chronically high baseline anxiety—such as applied relaxation—are taught to the panicker with instructions to frequently practice them. Reducing the level of generalized anxiety decreases the frequency of panic attacks but only infrequently eliminates them completely.

Strategies for dealing with both the physiological and cognitive components of the panic attacks themselves have the greatest positive effects. The physiological symptoms are reduced by using a variety of coping strategies, including diaphragmatic breathing, distraction strategies, and social support strategies. Catastrophic cognitions, which are interpretations of the symptoms and inaccurate predictions of the likely consequences of the symptoms, are reduced by providing accurate information and by teaching the sufferer ways of challenging the negative thoughts. Because one of the principal symptoms that occurs during panic attacks is confusion of thought, and because the panic sufferer does not believe in his ability to use these techniques during the panic attack itself, the techniques are practiced in contexts similar to those experienced during an actual panic attack. As the sufferer gains confidence in the new coping strategies, he is encouraged to enter previously avoided situations and to practice strategies for dealing with attacks prior to entering the phobic situation and when in the situation itself. Mastery of the panic attacks is accompanied by a decrease in anticipatory anxiety and a willingness to enter phobic situations. As the phobic situations are entered absent the panic attacks, the agoraphobia decreases.

B. Pharmacologic Treatments

A variety of classes of psychotropic medications have been evaluated as treatments for panic disorder and agoraphobia. These include (1) three classes of antidepressants—tricyclics, MAO inhibitors, and the SSRIs; (2) two classes of benzodiazepines—low-potency benzodiazepines such as valium and librium, and high-potency benzodiazepines such as alprazolam; and (3) beta-blockers. Both low-potency benzodiazepines and beta-blockers have limited effectiveness with panic attacks and are used infrequently in the treatment of this disorder.

All three types of antidepressants have been studied as treatments for panic attacks. Tricyclics and MAO inhibitors are moderately effective in reducing panic attacks, but each is often accompanied by significant side effects. One principal side effect is an initial increase in paniclike symptoms, a response that leads from 30 to 40% of individuals given these drugs to discontinue their use. Similar problems are encountered with the SSRIs, but less frequently. Another problem occurs when panic sufferers attempt to discontinue their use of these drugs: panic attacks frequently return and the individual is faced with a choice between relapse of panic symptoms or remaining on the medication indefinitely.

High-potency benzodiazepines such as alprozalam are the pharmacologic treatment of choice for panic disorder and agoraphobia. Side effects are few, and approximately 80% of those on a therapeutic dose experience an elimination of their panic attacks. As with the antidepressants, however, stopping use of this drug is frequently accompanied by a return of panic attacks.

A comparison of the best psychological intervention with the antidepressants and high-potency benzodiazepines on the three criteria of treatment dropout, treatment improvement, and treatment relapse seems to favor the psychological approach. Antidepressants produce an unfavorable side effect profile with numerous treatment dropouts. Relapse rates are high after discontinuing treatment. Treatment success rates are comparable for the best psychological treatments and high-potency benzodiazepines—approximately 80% are significantly improved. Relapse rates after concluding treatment are considerably higher for the high-potency benzodiazepines than for the best psychological treatment, however, thus favoring the psychological approach. Another avenue is to combine pharmacologic and psychological treatments. This approach produces treatment improvement rates similar to the best psychological approach alone. Other considerations may lead to choosing this alternative, however, such as the necessity to produce a quick reduction in panic attacks.

In typical clinical practice, panic-disordered and agoraphobic individuals are treated with a combination of medications and psychological interventions. There is some evidence that drugs interfere with the beneficial effects of psychotherapy techniques that involve exposure to phobic stimuli. The individual's choice of what approach to use—drugs or psychotherapy—often comes down to biases and expectations that exist prior to seeking help. Some who choose drugs do not want to spend the time or make the effort required by psychological treatments. Others do not want the stigma or side effects associated with the use of drugs. Future intervention strategies may take into consideration these basic attitudes and best available treatments in recommending a course of therapeutic action. [See Panic Attacks.]

BIBLIOGRAPHY

American Psychiatric Association (1994). *Diagnostic and statistical manual of mental disorders* (4th Ed.). Washington, CD: Author.

Clum, G. A. (1989). *Coping with panic: A drug-free approach for dealing with anxiety attacks.* Pacific Grove, CA: Brooks-Cole Publishing Co.

Markway, B. (1992). *Dying of embarrassment: Help for social anxiety and social phobia.* Oakland, CA: New Harbinger.

Rosenbaum, J. F., Pollock, R. A., Otto, M. W., & Pollock, M. H. (1995). Integrated treatment of panic disorder. *Bulletin of the Meninger Clinic, 59*, A4–A27.

Sheehan, D. (1983). *The anxiety disease.* New York: Charles Scribner's Sons.

Physical Activity and Mental Health

Rod K. Dishman

The University of Georgia

Anxiety Disorders Phobia, intense fear of an object; Panic, intense fear of unknown source; Obsessive-Compulsive, repetitive acts or rituals to relieve anxiety; Generalized, excessive worry about two or more life events. Signs or symptoms: motor tension, hyperactivity of the autonomic nervous system, (e.g., shortness of breath, heart palpitations, dry mouth, dizziness, flushes or chills), hypervigilance, easily startled, irritability, feeling on edge.

Depression Disorders The loss of pleasure or feelings of despair. Results from loss or arises spontaneously. Signs or symptoms of Major Depression: marked weight loss or gain, insomnia or hypersomnia, motor agitation or retardation, easy fatigue, guilt, confusion, suicidal thoughts or attempts.

Effect Size The magnitude of the outcome of an experimental manipulation, usually expressed as a standard score [e.g., (experimental mean-control mean)/standard deviation].

Physical Activity Locomotion by skeletal muscle action that expends energy during leisure time, including planned exercise.

Quantitative Review A method of synthesizing a research literature by cumulating effect sizes or relative risks. Differs from a narrative critique of each study's results based on statistical hypothesis-testing that depends on sample size.

Relative Risk The ratio of the two rates (i.e., proportions) of disease in two groups. If the disease rates are 20% in an inactive group and 10% in an active group, the relative risk for inactivity is 2.0, or conversely, the relative risk for activity is 0.50.

Self-Esteem That aspect of self-concept, image of the self, that provides a feeling of value or worth. A general indicator of psychological adjustment.

Sleep A state of reversible unconsciousness characterized by little movement and reduced responses to external stimuli. Stages of sleep are defined by their depth and by periodic features of electrical potentials measured from the brain cortex and from eye and chin muscles.

This chapter clarifies the evidence about **PHYSICAL ACTIVITY AND MENTAL HEALTH** by summarizing population-based studies and experiments designed to determine whether physical activity affects mental health in positive or negative ways. The topics are limited to areas in which enough controlled studies have been reported to permit conclusions or pose testable hypotheses for future studies. Included are depression, anxiety, self-esteem, sleep, and abusive exercise. Other emotional and cognitive responses to physical activity may influence the quality of life among people with normal psychological health, but the focus here is on mental health problems that are prevalent in the United States (U.S.). (~20–35% lifetime prevalence among adults) and contribute directly to human suffering and escalating health care costs. Competitive athletics are excluded, with the exception of overtraining/staleness among athletes, characterized by worsened mental health and performance after heavy endurance training.

I. CONSENSUS OR CONUNDRUM?

An international consensus among exercise scientists in 1992 concluded that studies show acute exercise is associated with reduced state anxiety and that chronic exercise and/or physical fitness are associated with reduced trait anxiety and depression. Similar conclusions were reached in 1984 by a panel convened by the National Institute of Mental Health. Skeptical reviews of the studies have criticized investigators' predominant use of quasi-experimental designs with nonclinical samples and their reliance on self-ratings of anxiety and depression by the subjects without verification by clinical diagnosis or biological signs indicative of depression or anxiety. The U.S. Preventive Services Task Force of the U.S. Office of Disease Prevention and Health Promotion concluded in 1989 that the quality of the available evidence showing exercise reduces depression and anxiety was poor and that the role of exercise in the primary prevention of mental health problems was poorly understood. The Task Force concluded that the strongest evidence about exercise came from studies of self-esteem. Although the quantitative effect of exercise on self-esteem is moderately large, particularly for children ($\sim\frac{1}{2}$ standard deviation), it varies according to several moderating features of children and physical activity. For example, larger effects have been reported for aerobic fitness training compared with sports. However, it is not established that exercise, moreso than the social context of exercise settings, is directly responsible for increased self-esteem. A recent experiment indicated that a regular exercise program increased the self-esteem of young adults only when they were told they were in a study of exercise and psychological well-being. Subjects not informed about the study's purpose had no increase in self-esteem despite an increase in fitness similar to that of their peers who were informed about the study's purpose.

Quantitative reviews of the literature have discounted that the effects of exercise on depression and anxiety are influenced by the quality of the research.

Nonetheless, important factors moderating the effects of exercise such as the type of subjects, research design, and the measurement both of physical activity and mental health have been viewed independently, not as they interact. Scrutiny of exercise studies indicates that most of the literature concerning the influence of exercise on depression, anxiety, and self-esteem has design and methodology flaws that preclude firm generalizations to clinical groups or a population base and limit conclusions of a true and independent effect of physical exertion, rather than changes dependent upon subjects' expectations of benefits, selection bias, or social interaction. Physical activity and exertion seldom have been quantified accurately (i.e., self-reports or indirect physiological measures have been used without adjusting for measurement error), thus preventing a complete or biologically interpretable description of dose-response relationships in many studies. A minority of studies have examined clearly defined clinical groups, and only a few studies have used clinical diagnostic criteria or Research Diagnostic Criteria for defining anxiety and depression. Usually it has not been possible to determine that studies examining the association of physical activity or fitness with physiological responses at rest or after nonexercise stress employed methods consistent with uniform standards for psychophysiological research. [*See* ANXIETY; DEPRESSION.]

Quantitative reviews of studies in the area have focused on different features of the studies, used different criteria for combining studies, used different methods, and not surprisingly reached some different conclusions about the circumstances that result in a positive impact of physical activity on mental health. This sometimes has been the result of low statistical power for estimating a population effect of physical activity or for detecting heterogeneous effects among moderating features of the studies. Common sense dictates that the amount, type, and context of exercise will interact with participants' health and activity history to determine in what ways depression, anxiety, self-esteem, sleep, and other aspects of mental health may change after physical activity.

II. THE SCIENTIFIC STANDARD

To help reconcile differing conclusions in previous reviews about the effects of physical activity on depres-

Table I Criteria for Judging the Scientific Strength of Evidence for Cause-and-Effect Used in Epidemiological Research

[1] Strength of association:	The lower the disease rate among active people relative to inactive people, the more likely physical activity protects against disease. A halving of the rate of disease is an acceptable standard in a population study. In a secondary prevention study, effect sizes of 0.20, 0.50, and 0.80 standard deviation are often viewed as small, moderate, and large, respectively.
[2] Temporal sequence:	The measurement of physical activity must precede the onset of disease with sufficient time for healthful biological adaptations.
[3] Consistency:	The association of increased activity with reduced disease should appear in different regions and types of people, using different methods of study.
[4] Independence:	The reduced disease among physically active people is not explained by disproportionately higher occurrence of other causes of the disease among the physically inactive (e.g. age, family history, co-existing health problems, poor social support).
[5] Dose-Response gradient:	Increasing levels of physical activity should correspond with decreased levels of disease in a linear or curvilinear manner.
[6] Alterability:	Naturally occurring increases in physical activity are followed by a reduced rate of disease.
[7] Plausibility:	Explanations for reduced disease with increased physical activity are coherent with existing theory or knowledge about the etiology of the disease and about biological adaptations that occur with physical activity.
[8] Experimental confirmation:	Controlled experiments confirm that increasing physical activity prevents or reduces the disease.

sion and anxiety, criteria from epidemiology for judging the strength of causal evidence can be employed. The criteria presented in Table I are used to determine cause-and-effect in a population, but they also apply to clinical studies. Each criterion has an analogous application to the concepts of internal validity (study outcomes are explained best by the experimental manipulation) and external validity (study outcomes generalize to other people or settings) commonly applied to small clinical and nonclinical experiments. Since there are few population studies of physical activity that have examined self-esteem or sleep, studies on these topics are reviewed separately according to the standards of internal and external validity.

A. Depression and Anxiety

About a dozen population-based studies and 100 small sample studies agree that exercise is associated with a moderate reduction in self-rated depression (relative risk of ~0.33–0.75 and effect size ~0.50 SD, respectively), and about 150 small sample studies show a small-to-moderate reduction in self-ratings of generalized anxiety (~0.25 to 0.60 SD) after exercise. Most of the population-based and the experimental studies show the appropriate temporal sequence for a possible causal effect of exercise. The focus here is on the criteria of consistency, dose-response, and

plausibility. These areas are crucial for judging the scientific acceptability of evidence and for guiding the professional application of physical activity toward improving mental health.

Four population studies completed between 1971 and 1984 provided the first published data showing a cross-sectional association between self-reported activity and depressive symptoms. The National Health and Nutrition Examination Survey I (NHANES I; N = 6913 individuals ages 25–74) and the National Survey of Personal Health Practices and Consequences (NSPHPC I; 3025 individuals ages 20–64 years) were administered in the United States. The 1978–1979 Canada Health Survey (CHS; N = 23,791 individuals ages 15 years and over) and the 1981 Canada Fitness Survey (CFS; N = 22,250 individuals ages 10 years and older) were administered in Canada. Ordinal activity groups were formed from self-reports of types, frequencies, and amounts of physical activity. Constructs such as general well-being (e.g., energy levels, freedom from worry, satisfaction with life), somatic symptoms associated with anxiety and depression (e.g., sweaty hands, loss of appetite, morning tiredness, etc.) and positive and negative mood states, including a standardized depression scale, were assessed. An age variable was created by dichotomizing those less than 40 into a "young" group and the rest into an "elderly" group.

Twenty-five of 32 statistical tests showed that the various mental health measures differed across the physical activity groups. The differences were most clear for women and people over age 40, but none represented strong effects. Evidence for the independence of the effect of physical activity was limited to adjustments for socioeconomic status (SES) and self-rated physical health status. Since the measurement of physical activity did not precede the measurement of mental health, the temporal sequence required for a possible causal effect of activity on reduced depression or anxiety was not present. There was not a dose-dependent association between increasing levels of activity and decreasing levels of depressive symptoms. In the NHANES study, depressive symptoms were most frequent when the level of activity was classified as none-or-low, but symptoms were not decreased further when activity increased from the moderate to the high physical activity category. Likewise in the Canada Health Survey and the Canada Fitness Survey, individuals were protected from symptoms of depression and anxiety if their daily leisure energy expenditure approximated at least 1 kcal/kg of body weight/day, which is a low level of activity (e.g., about 20 minutes of walking). There was no further reduction in relative risk across an activity gradient from 1 to 5 kcal/kg of body weight/day.

The first prospective study of the relationship between physical activity and symptoms of depression used a follow-up to the original NHANES study. From 1982 to 1984, 3059 individuals who had participated in the NHANES study in 1975 were again surveyed. Subjects who reported health conditions that limited physical activity (e.g., strokes, heart attacks) were excluded from the study. The final sample size was 1497 subjects. Separate analyses created physical activity categories based on recreational activity or nonrecreational activity. After age, education, income, employment status, and chronic conditions were statistically controlled in the cross-sectional analysis, both little-or-no recreational and little-or-no nonrecreational activity was associated with a higher frequency of self-rated depressive symptoms (in Blacks and Whites). The 8-year prevalence rate of high depression scores among sedentary White women who were not depressed at the outset of the study was about twice that among those engaging in little or no recreational physical activity compared to those with much-or-moderate recreational activity. White men who

were depressed and inactive at the outset of the study were 12 times more likely to be depressed after 8 years than those who were initially depressed but physically active. This observation was unchanged by adjustments for age, education, chronic illness and SES. There was no dose-dependent relationship between physical activity and reduced depression. Results were only partly consistent across gender and race, although most of the sample was White.

A report from the Alameda County Study near Oakland, California, stratified samples of non-depressed adults prospectively in 1965, 1974 and 1983. Physical activity was estimated by a question about self-reported frequency of participation (i.e., never, sometimes, often) in the categories of either active sports, swimming, walking, "doing exercises," or gardening. Depression symptoms were determined by questionnaire. There was increased risk for future depression among inactive people who were not depressed in 1965. The increased risk for depression among the inactive was not altered much when adjustments were made for age and other psychosocial predictors of depression that included: education, physical disability, chronic conditions, physical symptoms, perceived health, social isolation, feelings of autonomy, and five stressful life events (moving, job loss, separation or divorce, death of spouse, and financial difficulties). The relative risk for low activity vs high activity was about 1.7 for both men and women. Associations between changes in activity between 1965 and 1983 and symptoms of depression in 1983 suggested that the risk of depression was alterable by increasing exercise, but this association was not independent of the other risk factors for depression. Also, high levels of activity conferred no more protective effect on depression than did moderate levels of activity.

Prospective results from self-reports by about 10,000 Harvard male alumni studied from the mid-1960s through 1977 showed results similar to those in the Alameda County study. Alumni spending 3 or more hours per week playing sports during their leisure time had a 17% age-adjusted reduction in the risk of developing physician-diagnosed depression when compared with their less active peers over 12 years of followup. The relative risk for depression was 28% lower among those who expended 2500 or more kcals per week walking, climbing, or playing sports.

A report from Germany was the first study that used a standardized psychiatric interview that was conducted in the homes of 1536 randomly selected residents (15 years of age and older) of three rural communities in Upper Bavaria. Statistical adjustments were made to equate physical activity groups on physical illness, sex, age, and social class. In a cross-sectional analysis, the relative risk for several types of depressive disorders meeting an International Classification of Diseases diagnostic category was 3.15 for persons who stated that they currently did not exercise for sports compared with those who stated that currently they regularly exercised for sports. Those who reported occasional exercise for sports had a similar rate of depression compared with the regularly active group. However in a 5-year followup interview of depressive symptoms conducted with 87% of the original sample, low physical activity reported at the time of the cross-sectional analysis did not confer increased risk for developing depression 5 years later.

A recent reanalysis of data from 1317 adults who participated in both the NHANES I and the NHANES I Epidemiologic Followup study combined recreational and nonrecreational physical activity into a single index; subjects then were categorized as low, moderately, and highly active. Relative risk for elevated scores on self-rated depression in the prospective analysis was about 2.0 among the low-to-moderately active groups compared to the highly active, regardless of smoking status and independent of age, gender, education, alcohol use, and self-rated health. Troubling for a clear interpretation of the results was the high prevalence of highly active people (69%) and the low prevalence of lowly active people (6%); the best estimates of leisure physical activity in the U.S. population are that from 10 to 25% of the adult population is highly active and about 60% is lowly active. Hence, either the NHANES followup sample did not represent the U.S. population or the measure definition of physical activity employed was inaccurate.

B. Consistency

It is important to consider whether the effects of exercise hold across gender, race/ethnicity, and age both to establish the scientific consistency of the effects and for practical reasons of implementing physical activity optimally within segments of the public. Most studies were not designed to compare demographic groups on their depression or anxiety after exercise and were limited to ages younger than 55 years, or arbitrarily

used middle age (e.g., 40 or 45 years) as a criterion for aging effects. There have been fewer controlled studies of children or people over age 65, although their mental health outcomes after exercise are about the same as for people of middle age. Quantitative reviews have reported statistically similar reductions in depression for men and women (0.82 ± 1.09 vs. 0.45 ± 0.86 standard deviations) that were inversely related to increasing age. In contrast, exercise was inversely associated with depression symptoms independently of age in two community-based studies and one national sample. Cross-sectional population studies in the United States and Canada showed that sedentary leisure time was associated with increased depression in different ways for men and women when they were grouped above or below 40 years of age. Nonetheless, both men and women who were sedentary had increased relative risk for developing depression symptoms during an 8-year followup of the U.S. study.

Quantitative reviews concluded that age did not moderate reductions in self-ratings of state anxiety and trait anxiety. Neither men nor women had reduced state anxiety in one review, but the small number of studies reviewed led to low statistical power, and it appears that sampling errors prevented powerful tests of age in both analyses. Another quantitative review found that state anxiety was reduced after exercise among men but not women. Reductions in physiological variables measured in unstressful conditions were significant for subjects under 45 years but not over 45 years.

Although sociocultural factors may differently influence the ways in which people of various ages, gender, education, race, or ethnicity perceive exercise, its outcomes, and its context, the current evidence does not permit conclusions about whether the association of exercise with depression or anxiety is consistent across demographic groups. [*See* EXERCISE AND MENTAL HEALTH.]

C. Dose Dependence

Determining whether there are dose-dependent gradients between exercise and depression or anxiety addresses a criterion for establishing cause and effect. It also is necessary for recommending to people the types and amounts of exercise that will optimize healthful adaptations. Among the handful of the aforementioned population studies, only data from the Harvard

Alumni suggested a dose-dependent reduction in depression with increasing exercise. This occurred after 2500 kcal of weekly expenditure, which apparently exceeded the range of physical activity measured in the other population studies. The significance of this finding for public health is limited because fewer than 10% of U.S. adults currently engage in this much leisure time physical activity (e.g., 30 minutes of constant cycling, fast walking, or jogging expend ~200–300 calories for most adults). The absence of a consistent dose-gradient decrease in symptoms of depression or anxiety with increasing levels of physical activity suggests that the observed associations may be primarily due to increased symptoms with inactivity, and not due to positive effects of high physical activity levels on lowering depression or anxiety scores.

Despite biological reasons to expect that the effects of physical activity on depression and anxiety will vary according to exercise intensity (e.g., body temperature, endocrine and metabolic responses, as well as perceived exertion, increase with exercise intensity and are influenced by exercise history), results from experiments do not show dose-dependent reductions in depression and anxiety with increasing exercise intensity (see Fig. 1). Also, there are too few studies conducted to permit a statistically powerful quantitative analysis of the effects of exercise that concomitantly examines intensity and duration. It appears that exercise lasting up to about 30 minutes generally is associated with the largest reductions (~0.40–75 standard deviation) in self-rated state anxiety and resting measures of electromyographic and brain electrocortical activity (see Fig. 2). There are few studies of short durations (e.g. ~5–10 minutes) or intermittent sessions. A few studies have specifically contrasted different intensities or durations of exercise on anxiety, but they confounded intensity and duration and used only slightly different intensities or used intensities too high and durations too short for most practical applications of physical activity.

Studies of the intensity of chronic exercise on depression or anxiety confounded each intensity with a different mode of exercise and with psychotherapy or pharmacotherapy. With the exception of one report, studies examining dose-response effects of acute exercise on state anxiety did not equate total caloric expenditure between exercise conditions of varying intensity and duration. Thus, effects of physical activity that result from different energy expenditures may be falsely attributed to varying intensity or duration of

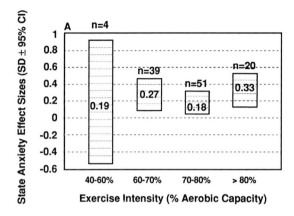

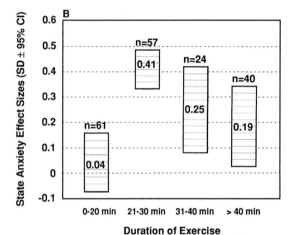

Figure 1   Moderating effects of exercise intensity (panel A) and duration (panel B) on reductions in self-rated state anxiety. The reduction for durations of 21–30 min were larger than for durations up to 20 min. Reductions did not differ among exercise intensities. Adapted from Petruzzello et al., 1991.

activity. Substantial reductions (~1.0–2.0 standard deviation) in trait anxiety and depression reportedly require about 4 to 5 months of exercise training (see Fig. 3). However, most studies report that changes in self-ratings of self-esteem and depression after exercise training occur independently of increases in aerobic capacity.

D. Biological Plausibility

Because exercise often involves social interaction, it has been hypothesized that the antianxiety and antidepressant effects of physical activity may stem from improved opportunities for social interaction. Exercise also may reduce anxiety and depression through

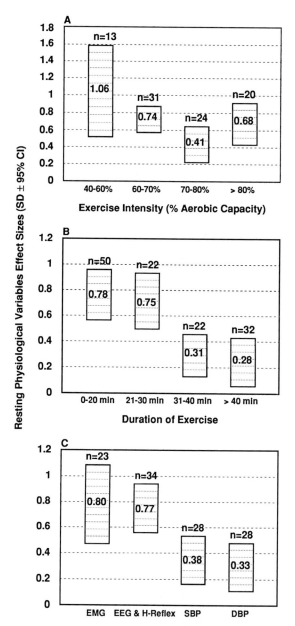

Figure 2 Moderating effects of exercise intensity (panel A), duration (panel B), and type of measure on reductions in physiological variables that can be correlates of anxiety. Reductions for intensities from 40–60% were larger than for intensities between 70–80%. Reductions for durations of less than 20 min were larger than for durations from 31–40 min. Reductions in neurological measures (EMG, EEG, and H-Reflex) were larger than reductions in blood pressures. Adapted from Petruzzello et al., 1991.

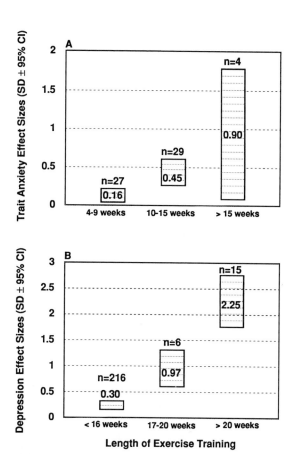

Figure 3 Moderating effects of the length of exercise training on reductions in self-rated trait anxiety (panel A) and depression (panel B). The reduction in trait anxiety was greater after 15 wk compared to 4–9 weeks. The reduction in depression after 20 wk was greater than periods less than 20 weeks. Adapted from Petruzzello et. al., 1991, and North et al., 1990.

cognitive mechanisms. Cognitively based explanations include distraction from worries or symptoms and increased perceptions of the self, including self-

esteem or self-efficacy. A sedentary person experiencing improved fitness can have an increased sense of mastery over physical tasks and greater confidence that such physical tasks can be completed. If this confidence generalizes beyond exercise settings, as some evidence suggests, improvements in physical self-esteem might reduce anxiety and depression or enhance positive moods. None of the social-cognitive explanations have received strong experimental tests. Moreover, none of them would be unique to physical activity compared with other approaches for enhancing mental health. Physical activity is unique among most mental health interventions because it evokes marked changes in several biological systems that support mental health. Biologically based hypotheses for explaining reduced depression or anxiety after exercise include: thermogenesis, brain blood flow, endorphins, autonomic nervous system changes, brain norepinephrine, brain serotonin and hypothalamic-pituitary-adrenal cortex charges.. The latter four hypotheses will be covered in more detail because they are better understood.

1. Thermogenesis

It is plausible that the thermogenic hypothesis that reduced anxiety after exercise is dependent on the increased body temperature typical of moderate to heavy exertion, but the handful of studies testing the idea have not supported it. Generally, changes in anxiety after acute exercise have not corresponded with manipulations of body temperature before or during exercise. However, the studies that simulated natural exercise did a poor job controlling temperature during exercise or used inadequate nonexercise control conditions, while a study that effectively controlled temperature during exercise did so in an unnatural exercise setting (i.e., underwater cycling).

2. Brain Blood Flow

The hypothesis that increased brain blood flow during acute exercise can explain changes in mood or anxiety has not been developed in a way consistent with current evidence from physiology. Brain blood flow and metabolism are increased by various stressors in humans and rats, but the effects of exercise are unclear. Both animal and human studies using indirect estimates of blood flow suggest that cerebral flow is increased during acute exercise, but studies have not examined regional distribution consistent with altered metabolism in brain areas most associated with emotion such as the frontal cortex or limbic areas. Studies of dogs and miniature pigs have used radio-labeled microspheres that lodge in the microvasculature in order to measure brain blood flow during exercise. The studies suggest that increased flow to the cerebellum, motor-sensory cortex and spinal cord, presumably resulting from locomotion, accounts for the increased brain blood flow during exercise. One study in humans showed increased uptake of glucose from the blood, a response closely associated with increased blood flow, in the visual cortex after exercise.

3. Endorphins

The hypothesis that endorphins influence mood or anxiety following exercise remains plausible, but it has been perpetuated without consideration of evidence from exercise physiology. Plasma β-endorphin (an opiate-like peptide) originates from the pituitary gland and is reliably elevated after vigorous exercise. A plausible link between plasma levels of β-endorphin or enkephalins and mood or analgesic responses to acute exercise is not established. In nearly all studies, general opioid antagonists have not blocked mood changes after exercise. The influence of blood β-endorphin on brain is limited by the blood-brain barrier to peptides at the body temperatures characteristic of typical exercise. Although studies with rats and mice show increased levels of endorphin or receptor binding in brain after acute exercise, the effects of the level on behavior, emotion, or physiology are unknown. The effects of exercise on brain opioid-peptide activity after exercise are not known for humans. While opioid-mediated analgesia could indirectly influence mood, exercise-induced analgesia has not been shown in humans by convincing experimental evidence. Peripheral endorphin activity during acute exercise inhibits catecholamine influences on cardiovascular, respiratory and endocrine responses during exercise, but its direct influence on mood is implausible at present.

4. Autonomic Nervous System

The sympathetic nervous system (SNS) is dysregulated in both depression and anxiety disorders and may adapt positively to physical activity. Norepinephrine (NE) is the main nerve chemical of the SNS, and it modulates a wide range of functions in the central nervous system, including behavior during threat, pituitary hormonal release, cardiovascular function, sleep, and analgesic responses. The cell bodies for synthesizing brain NE are mainly located centrally in brain neurons in the pons (locus coeruleus; LC), which has ascending and descending tracts to other brain and spine structures, and peripherally in post-ganglionic areas of the thoracic and the upper lumbar spine and in chromaffin cells of the adrenal medulla (see Figs. 4 and 5). A large number of brain NE neurons also lie outside the LC and are located throughout the lateral ventral tegmental fields. Fibers from these neurons intermingle with the LC neurons.

Norepinephrine is synthesized in cell bodies from tyrosine taken up from blood. The rate of synthesis of NE varies with the degree of sympathetic nerve activity and its associated changes in the activity of tyrosine hydroxylase, the rate-limiting enzyme in NE synthesis (see Fig. 6). If NE is not taken back into the

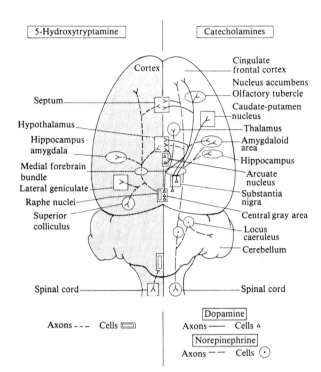

5-Hydroxytryptamine | Catecholamines

Cortex

Cingulate frontal cortex
Nucleus accumbens
Olfactory tubercle
Caudate-putamen nucleus
Thalamus
Amygdaloid area
Hippocampus
Arcuate nucleus
Substantia nigra
Central gray area
Locus caeruleus
Cerebellum

Septum
Hypothalamus
Hippocampus amygdala
Medial forebrain bundle
Lateral geniculate
Raphe nuclei
Superior colliculus

Spinal cord — — Spinal cord

Axons - - - Cells ▭

Dopamine
Axons —— Cells △
Norepinephrine
Axons — — Cells ⊙

Figure 4 Monamine neural pathways in the rat brain from the dorsal view. The serotoninergic, i.e., 5-hydroxytryptamine, system is on the left. The noradrenergic and dopaminergic systems are on the right. Reprinted with permission from Elliot, G.R. et al. Indoleamines and other neuroregulators. In *Psychopharmacology: from theory to practice*. J. D. Barchas et al., (Eds.). (1977). New York: Oxford University Press, pp. 33–50. Copyright Oxford University Press, 1977.

presynaptic neuron and bound in storage vesicles, it is metabolized by the enzymes monoamine oxidase (MAO) and catechol-o-methyl transferase (COMT). The major metabolites of NE are 3,4 dihydroxy phenylglycol (DOPEG), inside the neuron, and 3-methoxy-4-hydroxy phenylglycol (MHPG), outside the neuron. The action of NE is mediated by two types of adrenergic receptors, alpha-receptors and beta-receptors, which have been further subdivided into alpha-1 and alpha-2 and beta-1 and beta-2. When beta-1 receptors bind with NE there is a stimulation of the enzyme adenylate cyclase by a stimulatory G protein and a subsequent rise in the level of intracellular cyclic AMP which acts as a second messenger for neural transmission via phosphorylation. Beta-2 receptors have high affinity for epinephrine and in the brain are primarily associated with glial cells rather than NE nerve transmission. Alpha-2 receptor binding with NE is associ-

ated with an inhibition of NE synthesis and nerve activity. Presynaptic alpha-2 autoreceptors decrease NE neuron activity and the synthesis of NE by a G protein inhibition of tyrosine hydroxylase. When alpha-1 receptors are bound with NE, activity of the second-messenger phosphoinositide system is increased. The phosphorylation of regulatory proteins that control ion channels and neural conductance/resistance consequent to receptor-second messenger coupling plays the major role in brain NE activity.

In humans, changes in brain NE activity after acute physical activity have been estimated by measuring MHPG levels in urine, plasma, or CSF. Studies of urinary MHPG after a single session of physical activity found increased MHPG excretion or no change. There were methodological problems with these studies. Sample sizes were small and patients with very different types of depression were in the exercise condition. Also, exercise levels were not quantified relative to fitness, or very low levels of physical activity were used in some studies. Studies of acute physical activity and MHPG in nondepressed subjects typically quantified the exercise, and some studies reported exercise intensity relative to fitness. Again, the findings were mixed. Plasma MHPG typically was increased, but urinary MHPG remained unchanged. The relative contributions of NE from peripheral sympathetic nerves was not determined in these studies. At rest from 20 to 60% of MHPG in peripheral blood or urine comes from metabolism of brain NE. However, the increase in blood levels of NE during exercise comes mainly from sympathetic nerves innervating the heart, with some coming from the exercising skeletal muscles. A few studies of acute exercise have reported increases in blood levels of sulphated subtractions of MHPG, believed to originate from the brain in rats and possibly in humans. However, the relevance of increased MHPG sulfate in blood plasma after acute exercise is unclear for depression or anxiety. Most studies of acute exercise and MHPG did not assess mood.

Animal studies show that exercise training increased tyrosine hydoxylase activity in the adrenal gland and liver (indicative of increased synthesis of NE), but decreased tyrosine hydroxylase activity and NE turnover (i.e., storage of newly synthesized NE) in the heart. Changes in the synthesis or turnover of NE in the brain after exercise has not been reported. Human studies indicate that exercise training does not alter plasma levels of NE or muscle sympathetic nerve

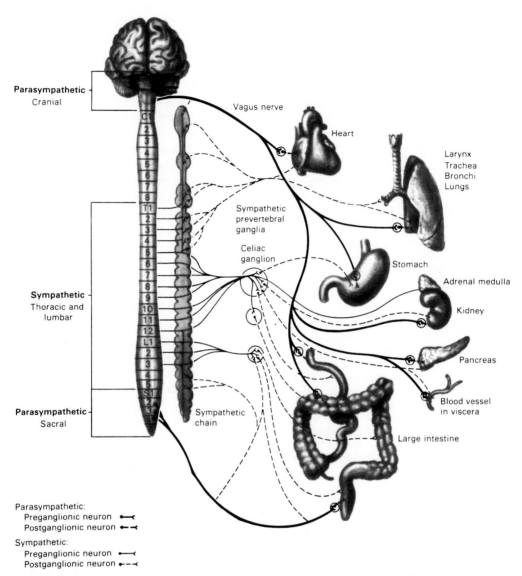

Figure 5 The autonomic nervous system. Source: Adapted from Carlson, N.R. (1986). *Physiology of behavior.* (p. 117). Boston: Allyn & Bacon, Inc. Copyright Allyn & Bacon, 1986

activity measured under resting conditions. Among exercise-trained men, plasma NE levels are lower at a given absolute exercise intensity, unchanged at the same intensity relativized to maximal aerobic capacity, but higher than normal at maximal exercise. Nonetheless, studies consistently have found that aerobic fitness does not attenuate plasma or urine levels of catecholamines measured during mild laboratory mental stressors. Sympathetic nerve discharge was not measured in those studies. Because levels of circulating catecholamines can rise as a result of reduced clearance

from the blood, in addition to release from sympathetic nerves or the adrenal gland, it is premature to conclude that fitness or physical activity has no effect on sympathetic nervous system responses during mental stress. Moreover, a cross-stressor adaptation from exercise training to non-exercise stress may be delimited to intense exercise (i.e., 60–90% aerobic capacity) and to intense mental stressors that result in blood levels of NE (1800 pg/ml) and epinephrine (50–100 pg/ml) high enough to initiate systemic physiological activation. It is also necessary to measure cardiac vagal

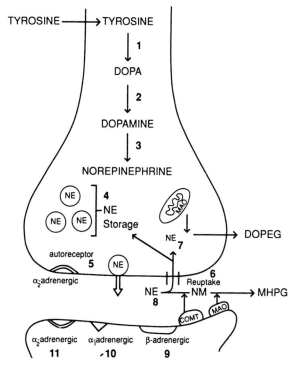

Figure 6 The synthesis of NE. Source: Dunn & Dishman (1991). Exercise and the neurobiology of depression. *Exercise and Sport Sciences Reviews*, *19*, p.53. Copyright American College of Sports Medicine.

primary-adrenal cortical responses to stressors are associated with menstrual status, but how exercise and fitness moderates estrous-dependent autonomic or endocrine responses in women during stress is not known. [*See* Catecholamines and Behavior.]

Hypotheses for a presumed reduction in physiological responsiveness to stressors among physically active or fit people generally have not been tested using direct measures. Despite some evidence that acute exercise temporarily alters brain electrocortical activity and somatosensory neuromuscular reflexes, the studies did not examine the responses under anxiety-provoking conditions and most did not report corresponding changes in moods. Nonetheless, hyper-responsiveness of the cardiovascular system at rest and during provocation (e.g., increased heart rate and blood pressure) is a prominent feature of anxiety disorders including generalized anxiety and panic. Because chronic physical activity can lead to decreased cardiac sympathetic nerve activity and increased cardiac vagal tone (the vagus nerve slows heart rate) at rest, there is interest in the role of physical activity in altering autonomic balance during anxiety-provoking stress. But, contrary to one quantitative review, such an effect of physical activity or fitness on reducing responses to stress is not established,

A down-regulation (reduced number or sensitivity) of β-receptors on the heart after chronic physical activity reported in some studies would help explain reduced heart rate and systolic blood pressure by attenuating the effect of NE on cardiac output. Drugs that block β-receptors, thus downregulating the NE receptor-effector system, reduce anxiety, and they reduce heart rate responsiveness to psychosocial stressors. Endurance trained athletes have higher than normal β-adrenoreceptor density on lymphocytes (a type of white blood cell), and a session of prolonged physical activity at high intensity is accompanied by increased β-adrenoreceptor density on lymphocytes. However, lymphocyte adrenoreceptors are β_2 types with high affinity for epinephrine, like those found in skeletal and smooth muscle, the liver and peripheral sympathetic tissue. It is unclear whether they provide an index of peripheral SNS receptors, but they do not provide a measure of brain NE activity.

5. Brain Norepinephrine

Established neurobiological models of depression and anxiety provide hypotheses about plausible mecha-

tone or activity during mental stressors in order to interpret fully the contribution of sympathetic activity to autonomic balance and the regulation of cardiovascular responses during stress.

Studies have not adequately examined how age and gender affect the above conclusions. Catecholamine responses are less adaptable to stress with advancing age. Exercise training reduces adrenal tyrosine hydroxylase, as well as the messenger RNA for tyrosine hydroxylase in young adult female rats, but the effects are not seen in senescent rats. Those results may not generalize to humans. Plasma NE responses to submaximal exercise and to mental stress have been reported to be higher in older men. However, a recent study compared young and old men of similar aerobic fitness ($\dot{V}O_{2peak}$) showed no difference in plasma NE or epinephrine during ~20 min of vigorous cycling at 75% $\dot{V}O_{2peak}$. Thus, age differences in the responsiveness of the sympatho-adrenalmedullary system may be moderated by aerobic fitness. There is some evidence that mood and catecholamine or hypothalamic-

nisms whereby exercise might influence some signs and symptoms by re-regulating the brain monoamine systems of NE and serotonin, as well as the hypothalamic-pituitary-adrenal axis.

The most commonly prescribed antidepressant drugs upregulate CNS alpha-adrenergic and serotonergic receptors, and downregulate (and/or desensitize the post-synaptic second messenger) beta-adrenergic receptors. An early study of activity wheel running in rats showed no change in brain beta-adrenergic receptor density. Recently, we found that both activity wheel running and treadmill exercise training increased levels of norepinephrine in the brain frontal cortex of young adult male rats that had been treated as neonates with clomipramine, a serotonin reuptake inhibitor that causes adult-onset depression in the rat. Only the activity wheel animals had increased serotonin metabolism, a therapeutic decrease in β-adrenoreceptors that was equal to the effect of the antidepressant drug imipramine, and improved sexual behavior (another sign of an antidepressant effect by the wheel running).

We also found that treadmill exercise training and chronic activity wheel running increased NE levels in the pons-medulla, the site of most NE cell bodies, while treadmill training increased metabolites of NE in ascending areas of the frontal cortex and hippocampus (brain areas containing nuclei that integrate behaviors related to anxiety and depression). Similarly, we have seen that sedentary rats have lower NE levels in locus coeruleus, hippocampus, and central amygdala following footshock or immobilization stress compared with sedentary unstressed rats and rats that ran each day on an activity wheel. Activity wheel runners were quicker than sedentary animals to escape the footshock, suggesting they were less depressed or anxious.

6. Brain Serotonin

Francis Chaouloff, a French psychopharmacologist, conducted a series of studies of the effects of acute running on synthesis and metabolism of serotonin (5-hydroxytryptamine; 5-HT) in various brain regions. In the brain, serotonin synthesis is rate limited by the enzyme tryptophan hydroxylase but is directly dependent on the supply of tryptophan to the brain following increased levels of free (i.e., not albumin-bound) tryptophan in the plasma. Tryptophan is the only amino acid that is protein-bound in plasma. It competes with free fatty acids for binding with albumin, so lipolysis, which increases free fatty acids, during

exercise leads to increased free tryptophan. Tryptophan also competes with branched chain amino acids, including glutamate, for entry into the brain blood supply. Thus, decreases in other amino acids during prolonged exercise (i.e., >2 hours) may help increase brain uptake of tryptophan. Chaouloff's work with rats shows that acute treadmill running is usually accompanied by large increases in brain tryptophan and increased serotonin metabolism.

Studies are needed to determine whether physical activity increases the activity of rate-limiting enzymes for the synthesis of NE or 5-HT in the brain. Pharmacologic studies have shown that changes in receptor sensitivity can occur independently of changes in receptor density. Thus, exercise studies are needed of second-messenger systems including those linked to adenylate cyclase (5-HT$_{1A}$, α_2 and β receptors) and phosphoinositide (α_1, 5-HT$_2$) as well as intracellular transport of potassium and sodium. Plausible biological explanations for stimulation of the brain NE and 5-HT systems by exercise are needed. Sensory afferent fibers from locomotory muscle to the locus coeruleus, influences of locomotory muscle metabolism on central neurotransmitters, and motoric/limbic interactions are plausible explanations that are untested at this time.

7. Hypothalamic-Pituitary-Adrenal (HPA) Cortex

Most studies of physiological responses to stress after exercise training have been limited to cardiovascular and sympathetic/sympathoadrenal medullary responses. It is important to also understand the hypothalamic-pituitary-adrenal (HPA) cortical axis after exercise training because it is involved in models of the pathogenesis of cardiovascular disease, anxiety disorders, and major depression. Moderate exercise training results in a diminished HPA response during the same absolute exercise intensity, but heavy exercise training can be associated with abnormal HPA responses under resting conditions.

Another approach to understanding the effects of physical activity on the HPA examines the magnitude and recovery of increases in HPA hormone levels elicited by standardized stressors other than exercise. Studies using this approach with humans have yielded conflicting results partly because they did not compare acute responses to exercise with responses to other stressors that are familiar versus novel, or did not consider influences on exercise responses exerted by reproductive hormones known to influence physiological responses to nonexercise stressors, despite evidence of such an interaction in highly trained women.

We have found that treadmill exercise training of female rats treated with estrogen was accompanied by attenuated adrenocorticotrophic hormone (ACTH) and corticosterone responses to treadmill running but a hyperresponsiveness of ACTH to immobilization or footshock. Whether this hyperresponsiveness of ACTH is a healthful adaptation and whether it is due to increased corticotropin releasing hormone (CRH) or other factors that release ACTH is not known. The latter seems likely since treadmill exercise training in male rats is accompanied by reduced ACTH after immobilization stress with no change in brain CRH. Altered CRH activity with exercise would be particulary relevant for anxiety and depression, since CRH increases activity of the locus coeruleus. We have not observed changes in ACTH in response to footshock after chronic activity wheel running, which is a voluntary circadian activity.

III. SELF-ESTEEM

Depression and anxiety often are associated with low self-esteem, the evaluative aspect of self-concept. Physical self-esteem is one part of general self-esteem, and it includes self-perceptions about sport compe-

tence, physical condition, body attractiveness, and strength. Because body image is related to general self-concept, an increase in body image or physical skills can contribute to general self-esteem in individuals for whom physical attributes are highly valued relative to other aspects of self-concept. Both increases and decreases in self-esteem can also occur without actual changes in fitness or ability depending on whether reinforcing feedback of a positive or negative nature is provided in the exercise setting. The greatest gains in self-esteem can be expected for individuals with low initial levels and for whom physical attributes are valued as a part of general self-concept.

One quantitative review of studies reported that the typical effect on self-esteem in children after a physical activity program was about one-half standard deviation. However, the effects differed according to attributes of the children or features of the physical activity setting, although variability of the mean effects for the different attributes and features was not reported. Larger effects occurred (1) for children with disabling conditions (e.g., mental retardation or obesity) compared with normal children, (2) under clinically oriented rather than typical classroom conditions, or (3) using fitness activities (running or weight training) rather than sport skills or creative movement. These findings suggest that fitness activities can increase self-esteem moreso than competitive sport for most children (see Fig. 7). [*See* SELF-ESTEEM.]

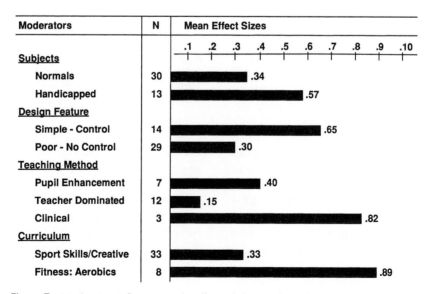

Figure 7 Moderating influences on the effects of chronic physical activity on self-esteem in children. Adapted from Gruber, 1986.

IV. SLEEP

About a third of the adult population will experience insomnia. However, only about 5% to 20% of people who suffer sleep disturbances will seek help from a primary care physician. About half who seek treatment will receive a drug prescription, usually a hypnotic or a benzodiazepine. Many who do not seek treatment purchase over-the-counter sleep aids. Because drugs often do not address the source of the sleep problem and can increase risk for mortality, exercise is a frequently mentioned component of good sleep hygiene.

Sleep is measured by describing changes in action potentials on the brain cortex, the chin musculature, and eye movements. Sleep is delineated into periods of rapid eye movement (REM) sleep and four stages of non-REM sleep with decreasing activation of brain and skeletal muscle. Brain electroencephalography (EEG) shows that during sleep, activity of the brain cortex fluctuates along a continuum from synchronous, low-frequency (1 wave period per second is 1 Hz), high-amplitude activity to asynchronous, high-frequency, low-amplitude activity. This continuum can be delineated by corresponding periods of delta (0.5–3 Hz), theta (3.5–7.5 Hz), alpha (8–12 Hz), and beta (13–30 Hz) activity. Alpha activity is commonly described by relaxed wakefulness. Sleep progresses from drowsiness to Stage 1, marked by theta activity. Stage 2 occurs later, denoted by theta activity, sleep spindles (short bursts of 12–14 Hz), and K complexes (sudden sharp spikes). Spindles occur several times a minute throughout Stages 1–4, while K complexes occur only in stage 2. Stage 3 begins later, characterized by delta activity. Increasing delta activity denotes Stage 4, or deep sleep. REM sleep typically begins about 45 minutes after the onset of stage 4 sleep, denoted by beta activity, rapid eye movements and little skeletal muscle activity. During the night, a normal sleeper (8 hours) will have four or five sleep cycles each lasting 90 minutes and consisting of from 20 to 30 minutes of REM sleep. Meajsures used to describe sleep include the time spent in: Stage 2, Stages 3 and 4 (Stages 3 and 4 combined equal slow-wave sleep; SWS), REM, REM latency, wakefulness after sleep onset (WASO), sleep onset latency (SOL), and total sleep time (TST) (see Fig. 8).

Convincing studies using standard polysomnography to measure sleep after chronic exercise with ini-

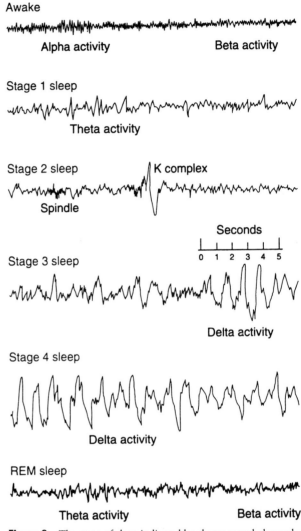

Figure 8 The stage of sleep indicated by electroencephalography (EEG). From Horne, J. A. (1988). *Why We Sleep: The Functions of Sleep in Humans and Other Mammals.* Oxford, England: Oxford University Press. Copyright Oxford University Press, 1988.

tially sedentary people who are poor sleepers have not been conducted. However, a few recent studies of people with insomnia have shown improved sleep based on subjects' reports of improved sleep. The small number of studies on chronic physical activity in normal sleepers indicate small-to-moderate effects of increased SWS and TST, with decreased SOL, WASO, and REM sleep. The question of mechanisms whereby exercise may facilitate sleep remains unresolved. One study of highly fit women who were normal sleepers reported that increased SWS after acute

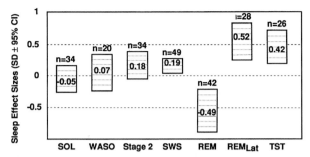

Figure 9 Effects of acute exercise on sleep variables among normal sleepers. SOL (sleep onset latency); WASO (wakefulness after sleep onset); SWS (slow wave sleep); REM (rapid eye movement); REM$_{LAT}$ (REM latency); TST (total sleep time). Adapted from Youngstedt, O'Connor, & Dishman, 1997.

exercise depends on body heating during exercise. Other possible but unconfirmed explanations include body restitution, energy conservation, anxiety reduction, and increased secretion of melatonin, which helps regulate circadian sleep.

Our recent quantitative review of the effects of an exercise session on sleep found increases in total sleep time, slow wave sleep, and REM latency, with a decrease in REM (see Fig. 9). The effects ranged from about .20 to .50 standard deviation, which are small-to-moderately large effects statistically, but which equate to only a few minutes of sleep in each stage, well within normal night-to-night variation. Contrary to previous results, exercise that was associated with a high heat load did not increase SWS above the average effect of exercise, but high heat load was associated with increased wakefulness after sleep onset. A long duration (~2 hr) of exercise was associated with larger increases in total sleep time and larger decreases in REM, but this is of little practical importance for most people, who exercise from 20 to 45 minutes each session. The subjects studied were good sleepers, so the effects of exercise gauged by our analysis of studies may be underestimates of the potential efficacy of exercise among people with sleep disorders, who have been understudied. [*See* SLEEP.]

V. ABUSIVE EXERCISE

A maximal exercise bout can be followed by a small and temporary increase in state anxiety. However, there are few scientific studies testing whether extreme amounts of physical activity, or its social context, increase anxiety or depression to an extent that is clinically meaningful. Bill Morgan of the University of Wisconsin first proposed that increased anxiety and depression are defining features of the staleness syndrome that frequently occurs with overtraining in endurance sports; a paradoxical dose-response gradient with heavy chronic physical exertion. Some evidence shows that increased negative moods with overtraining in athletes can be accompanied by altered hypothalamic-pituitary-adrenal cortical responses consistent with those typically observed in patients diagnosed with major depression. However, the incidence and prevalence rates, risk factors, and the etiology of increased anxiety and depression due to overtraining are not established according to epidemiological or medical traditions, and the volume of exercise training that precedes athletic staleness far exceeds the amount engaged in by the vast majority of leisure-time exercisers.

Clinical parallels, including elevated anxiety and depression, also have been drawn between highly committed runners and patients diagnosed as suffering from anorexia nervosa. There is some concern by mental health professionals that the disciplined training and social milieu in sports that emphasize a lean body composition and dietary restriction promote the development of eating problems or add to existing eating problems. Despite recognition of abusive exercise nearly 20 years ago, it is still not known whether excessive exercise and disordered eating share a common course that is motivated by common goals and followed by common medical outcomes. Results from about 50 studies on the topic are inconclusive because the studies were correlational, generally not controlling for subject selection biases, and lacked standard definitions and measures validated for abusive exercise. Anorexics often augment food restriction by hyperactivity, but their aerobic fitness ($\dot{V}O_2$ peak) is well below average compared with the above-average aerobic fitness of habitual runners and overtrained athletes. In addition, cross-sectional studies have not revealed a common psychopathology between obligatory (i.e., excessively committed) runners and anorexic patients.

Researchers who have inferred that sport participation increases risk for disordered eating have typically sampled small groups of athletes without control for how different sports, regions, levels of competition, behaviors of coaches or teammates, eating or activity histories, and socioeconomic backgrounds of the athletes affect eating problems. Comparisons of the rates of disordered eating, or risk factors, among sports or athletes are not meaningful when other influences on eating behaviors such as age, personal and family history, personality, or socioeconomic status are not first equated between the groups being compared. This is a fundamental principle for determining the causes of a disease that has been ignored by researchers in this area. Athletes' risk profiles have not been evaluated against those for nonathletes from the same academic, socioeconomic, or psychological background. Studies that have compared habitual exercisers from a population base with anorexic or bulimic patients have not quantified the physical activity differences assumed to exist between the two groups. These scientific failures prevent conclusions that differences or similarities in eating behaviors or attitudes seen between athletes and patients diagnosed with eating disorders resulted from involvement in sport or exercise rather than from attributes that existed prior to people becoming anorexic, bulimic, athletic, or physically active during leisure. The predictive validity (i.e., specificity and sensitivity) of questionnaires for detecting eating disorders among athletes is unknown.

There are case reports of excessive involvement or dependence with leisure exercise training. Bill Morgan first described eight cases of "running addiction," when commitment to running exceeded prior commitments to work, family, social relations, and medical advice. Similar cases have been labeled as positive addiction, runner's gluttony, fitness fanaticism, athlete's neurosis, obligatory running, and exercise abuse. However, little is understood about the origins, diagnostic validity, or the mental health impact of abusive exercise. The population prevalance of abusive exercise is unknown. The prevalence rates for anorexia and bulimia in the U.S., are about 1 and 4%, respectively, at any time, while only about 10 to 20% of U.S. adults are active enough to increase fitness. Thus, abusive exercise likely has very low prevalence, representing a problem for clinical medicine rather than a problem for public health. The potential risk that sedentariness poses for increased depression or anxiety in the U.S. population clearly represents a greater concern for public health than does the potential mental health risk of abusive exercise. [*See* ANOREXIA NERVOSA AND BULIMIA NERVOSA.]

VI. CONCLUSION

On balance, research studies show that small-to-moderate decreases in self-rated depression and anxiety accompany acute and chronic exercise. The internal and external validity of most of the studies are weak judged by the standards of natural science. Other research traditions such as case history and qualitative ethnography have not been used much. A few population studies using cross-sectional and prospective designs have reported moderately higher proportions of self-rated depression symptoms among sedentary men and women. The population studies of exercise and depression demonstrated some independence of the exercise effects, and some consistency across gender, age, and race. However, very few studies examined cultural aspects of physical activity and mental health. The experimental studies that focused on children or older adults are difficult to summarize because of their many design and measurement problems. Generally, the mental health benefits of physical activity did not depend upon the intensity of physical activity. Nonetheless, studies usually did a poor job quantifying the intensity of physical activity. The few experiments on large numbers of adults did not confirm that independent reductions in depression or anxiety occurred after chronic exercise; sometimes reductions early in an exercise program did not last after a few months of the program. Experiments with small numbers of subjects also show small-to-moderate increases in self-esteem in children and adults and small effects of acute exercise on the sleep of normal sleepers.

The mechanisms for explaining how physical activity reduces self-rated depression or generalized anxiety are unknown. Plausible social-cognitive explanations include distraction, self-perceptions of control, and social interactions. Plausible biological mechanisms include changes in body temperature, brain blood flow, endorphins, the autonomic nervous system, brain norepinephrine, brain serotonin, and the hypothalamic-pituitary-adrenal cortical axis.

In many instances, increased aerobic fitness does not appear necessary for reductions in depression, generalized anxiety, or self-esteem. However, better experimental tests of the dose-response gradient effects of exercise and better tests of biological models that explain such effects are needed to demonstrate that physical activity directly and independently alters depression, anxiety, self-esteem, and sleep. Studies of a dose–response relationship between depression, anxiety, or self-esteem with physical activities that increase aspects of physical fitness other than aerobic capacity, such as muscular strength, have been grossly understudied. Although evidence does not indicate that the mental health benefits of physical activity depend upon a dose-dependent relationship, recommendations by the American College of Sports Medicine (ACSM) for exercise that increases or maintains fitness among healthy adults offer prudent guidelines for a graduated exercise program that can enhance mental health among people who have no other medical contraindications for physical exertion. The ACSM recommendations include: [aerobics, resistance training, and stretching; 20–60 minutes daily; 3–5 days each week; at 45–85% of physical capacity or at a level of exertion perceived as somewhat hard]. People who do not desire to exercise for the purpose of marked gains in fitness may benefit from a complementary recommendation from the ACSM and the U.S. Centers for Disease Control and Prevention that people engage in moderate intensity physical activity (e.g., walking) for 30 minutes each day, possibly accumulated in multiple sessions, most days of the week.

Despite physical activity's potential efficacy for promoting mental health, its overall effectiveness is limited by the low proportion of the U.S. population that participates regularly. Only from 10 to 20% of the population is active at levels known to increase fitness, while 25 to 60% can be regarded as sedentary, depending on the strictness of the definition used. The rest are sporadically active, with a mean dropout rate from exercise programs of nearly 50% in both healthy and patient groups. These statistics from studies of the U.S. population generally reflect the activity patterns in several other industrialized nations that have a national surveillance system for physical activity. Interventions based on behavior modification can increase physical activity participation, and participation rates in exercise programs with depressed or anxious patients has been as high or higher in some studies as the compliance rates among patients treated with psychotherapy and pharmacotherapy. Nonetheless, achiev-

ing the potential effectiveness of physical activity for enhancing mental health will require the promotion of physical activity in the population.

ACKNOWLEDGMENTS

Thanks to William P. Morgan, Patrick J. O'Connor and Jack Raglin for their helpful comments.

BIBLIOGRAPHY

Calfas, K. J., & Taylor, W. C. (1994). Effects of physical activity on psychological variables in adolescents. *Pediatric Exercise Science, 6*, 406–423.

Chaouloff, F. (1997). Effects of acute physical exercise on central serotonergic systems. *Medicine and Science in Sports and Exercise, 29*, 58–62.

Dishman, R. K. (1997). Brain monoamines, exercise and behavioral stress: animal models. *Medicine and Science in Sports and Exercise, 28*, 63–74.

Dishman, R. K. (1995). Physical activity and public health: Mental health. *Quest: The Academy Papers*, American Academy of Kinesiology and Physical Education, 47, 362–385.

Dishman, R. K., & Buckworth, J. (1996). Increasing physical activity: a quantitative synthesis. *Medicine and Science in Sports and Exercise, 28*, 706–719.

Dunn, A. L., & Dishman, R. K. (1991). Exercise and the neurobiology of depression. *Exercise and Sport Sciences Reviews, 19*, 41–98.

Gruber, J. (1986). Physical activity and self-esteem development in children: A meta-analysis. In G.A. Stull and H.M. Eckhardt (Eds.) *Effects of Physical Activity on Children: Papers of the American Academy of Physical Education, 19*, (pp. 30–48). Champaign, IL: Human Kinetics Publishers.

Hoffman, P. (1997). The endorphin hypothesis. In W. P. Morgan (Ed.), *Physical activity and mental health* (pp. 163–177). Washington, DC: Taylor & Francis Publishers.

King, A. C., Oman, R. F., Brassington, G. S., Bliwise, D., & Haskell, W. L. (1997). Moderate intensity exercise and self-rated quality of sleep in older adults: a randomized controlled trial. *JAMA, 227*, 32–37.

McDonald, D. G., & Hodgdon, J. A. (1991). *Psychological effects of aerobic fitness training: Research and theory.* New York: Springer-Verlag.

Morgan, W. P. (1979). Negative addiction in runners. *Physician and Sportsmedicine, 7(2)*, 57–70.

Morgan, W. P. (1997). *Physical activity and mental health.* Washington, DC: Taylor & Francis Publishers.

Morgan, W. P. (1994). Physical activity, fitness, and depression. In, C. Bouchard, R. J. Shephard, & T. Stephens (Eds.), *Physical activity, fitness and health* (pp. 851–867). Champaign, IL: Human Kinetics Publishers.

Morgan, W. P., Brown, D. R., Raglin, J. S., O'Connor, P. J., & Ellickson, K. A. (1987). Psychological monitoring of overtraining and staleness. *British Journal of Sports Medicine, 21,* 107–114.

North, T. C., McCullagh, P., & Tran, Z. V. (1990). Effects of exercise on depression. *Exercise and Sport Sciences Reviews, 18,* 379–415.

O'Connor, P. J., Aenchbacher, L. E., & Dishman, R. K. (1993). Physical activity and depression in the elderly. *Journal of Aging and Physical Activity, 1,* 34–58.

Peronnet, F., & Szabo, A. (1993). Sympathetic response to acute psychosocial stressors in humans: linkage to physical exercise and training. In, P. Seraganian (Ed.), *Exercise psychology: the influence of physical exercise on psychological processes.* (pp. 172–217). New York: John Wiley.

Petruzzello, S. J., Landers, D. M., Hatfield, B. D., Kubitz, K. A., & Salazar, W. (1991). A meta-analysis on the anxiety-reducing effects of acute and chronic exercise: Outcomes and mechanisms. *Sports Medicine, 11,* 143–182.

Singh, N. A., Clements, K. M. & Fiatrone, M. A. (1997). A randomized controlled trial of the effects of exercise on sleep. *Sleep, 20,* 40–46.

Sonstroem, R. J. (1998). The physical self-concept: Measurement and external validity. *Exercise and Sport Sciences Reviews, 26,* in press.

Sothmann, M. S., Buckworth, J., Claytor, R. P. Cox, R. H. White-Welkley, J. E., & Dishman, R. K. (1996). Exercise training and the cross-stressor adaptation hypothesis. *Exercise and Sport Sciences Reviews, 24,* 267–287.

Youngstedt, S. D., O'Connor, P. J., & Dishman, R. K. (1997). The effects of acute exercise on sleep: a quantitative synthesis. *Sleep, 20,* 203–214.

Play

Cindy Dell Clark

DePaul University

Peggy J. Miller

University of Illinois at Urbana-Champaign

Catharsis Process by which unresolved emotional distress is relieved and resolved, in a distanced or removed context.

Constructive Play Play using objects or materials to make something.

Functional Play Play through which children gain sensorimotor practice, or engage in repetitive actions with or without an object.

Language Play Play in which children transform and practice linguistic forms, including sounds, words, and sentences, as well as narratives.

Metacommunication Communication between players during sociodramatic play that serves to negotiate and mutually maintain the play frame.

Play Frame Parameters for sociodramatic play, as negotiated between players, regarding roles to be played, actions, and objects used for representative purposes.

Rough-and-Tumble Play Vigorous physical play, which is friendly in intent, but that might involve mock fighting, chasing, pushing, throwing, and similar physical mock aggression.

Sociodramatic Play Social pretend play, in which children enact dramatic roles and fantasy scenarios.

Childhood **PLAY**, a phenomenon at once seemingly nonessential and yet potentially advantageous, is a subject which has eluded easy definition by social scientists. Recognized mainly through contrast with other orientations or states, play does not rest in a single form of action. Play comes in many forms, ranging from pretending with props (sociodramatic play) to building with blocks (constructive play) to mock-wrestling and chasing (rough-and-tumble play). Play, as a disposition, closely resembles yet differs from the related behavior of exploration, which (unlike play) is a behavior focused on acquiring knowledge about an object. Play shares many elements with other human activities, as well, including story telling and ritual. In attempting to set apart the defining features of play, a plausible approach has been to assess a behavior according to multiple criteria: the more criteria applicable to a behavior, the more it can be argued to constitute play. Criteria for defining play are laid out in Table I, which also gives an example of a behavior that qualifies as meeting each criterion. These criteria include: *nonliterality* (an "as if" stance toward reality, that allows for transformations in meanings and actions); *intrinsic motivation* (an activity pursued for its own sake, rather than for external motivation); *positive affect* (enjoyment); and *process-flexibility* (free,

Table I Defining Criteria of Play

Criterion	Definition	Example
Nonliterality	Transforms meanings and actions, taking an "as if" stance toward reality.	The child holds a hand to her ear and says "ring, ring," as if calling someone on the telephone.
Intrinsic motivation	Activity done for its own sake, rather than externally motivated.	The child rides a tricycle purely for the fun of it, rather than to get somewhere.
Positive affect	Enjoyment or pleasure.	The child squeals with glee while descending the slide.
Process flexibility	Flexible use of an object, as means, rather than action directed by the object.	The child freely tries many variations (of their own choosing) for using a Frisbee: throwing it, spinning it, using it as a hat, carrying marbles on it, throwing things at it as a target, and/or jumping on it.

flexible use of an object, as means, rather than action constrained by the object). Play, then, can be seen as multifaceted yet singularly remarkable conduct.

I. INTRODUCTION: THEORIES OF PLAY

This article will focus on play among children, although other age groups (and even nonhuman species) also play. Childhood play has been widely studied, perhaps because it is often outwardly observable (on playgrounds, in schools, at home, etc.). Play among children has caught the attention of a broad range of theorists, empirical researchers, and clinicians—with each contributing much to our knowledge of play.

Early theorists of play (prior to World War I) based their ideas on "armchair" reflections about play, rather than empirical observation. An example of such a theory is the *surplus energy theory* of play, traced back to eighteenth-century German poet Friedrich Schiller. The surplus energy theory posited that each organism generates a certain amount of energy to meet the needs of survival. Any excess energy builds up pressure, and is released through play. Another such classical theorist of play was philosopher Karl Groos, who believed that play served as *practice* for young, partially formed organisms who needed to perfect their survival skills. Both practice theory and surplus energy theory have a commonsense appeal to many modern-day observers of play. For instance, when children take on the roles of parents in pretend play, they seem to be practicing the social behaviors of those future roles—as stated by practice theory. When preschoolers go outside to

the playground at recess (after a morning of sedentary activity), they release much physical energy—as predicted by surplus energy theory.

Contemporary thinking about play is greatly influenced by more recent theorists, including Sigmund Freud, Jean Piaget, and Lev Semyonovich Vygotsky. Each of these theorists represents a particular way of thinking about play. The modern theories of play nevertheless share an implicit assumption that play is beneficial, in the sense that it contributes in a positive way to a child's development. Whether considering a child's emotional well-being, their cognitive and language abilities, or their social understanding and functioning, *play has been argued by modern theorists to serve childhood mastery through the transformation of themes within a nonliteral domain.* By representing issues and events through the symbolism of play, children come to master those issues. The importance of play as a domain, according to modern theories, is closely tied to its developmental significance as a way to build competence and mastery.

Sigmund Freud believed that play was important to children's emotional mastery. In his book *Beyond the Pleasure Principle* Freud asserted that play could have a cathartic effect for children, allowing children to vent and discharge their negative feelings associated with traumatic events. Through play, children can temporarily suspend reality and even switch roles, such as when (in play) a child pretends to subject another being (such as a doll) to the same negative treatment they themselves received earlier. For example, a child who receives daily injections of insulin for diabetes might pretend to give the same shot to their playmate or stuffed animal, as a form of catharsis.

This promotes mental health by providing a means to discharge negative feelings.

Other theorists have built upon Freud's psychoanalytic theories, including modern practitioners of child therapy who have used play therapy in a clinical context. Eric Erikson, in his classic work *Childhood and Society,* asserted that play provides a kind of "harbor," a domain returned to by a child in need of self-healing. This healing is possible because, through play, the child can create model situations and master these situations through experiment and planning. For example, a child traumatized by an outer event (such as a flood) may repeatedly reenact the event in play scenarios (by pretending to drown a doll). Melanie Klein, in her book *The Psychoanalysis of Children,* proposed that play was useful to children because it allowed them to express complex thoughts and affects that they were not yet able to verbalize. To Klein, play was the child's natural medium of expression. Adults with conflicted emotions may "talk it out" to find resolution, but children must "play it out." Therapist and theorist D. W. Winnicott discussed his view of play and playthings in his book *Playing and Reality.* According to Winnicott, the capacity to play is rooted in a sense of trust, tracing back to the mother–baby relationship. Out of this trust comes a special state of "near-withdrawal," within which objects or phenomena from external reality are endowed with "dream feeling and meaning." Playing involves a paradoxical interplay between the subjective inner world and the objectively perceived, outer world. Cultural experience (such as experience with literature and the arts), according to Winnicott, is a derivative of play, occupying the same intermediate space between the subjective-inner and objective-outer world.

Theorist Jean Piaget placed cognitive functioning at the forefront of his theories of play. Piaget viewed learning as a balance between two complementary forces: assimilation (modifying reality to fit one's cognitive structures) and accommodation (changing one's cognitive structures to conform with reality). As Piaget discussed in *Play, Dreams and Imitation,* he viewed play as an unbalanced state in which assimilation dominates over accommodation. This state, while not invoking new learning, was seen as useful for practicing and consolidating recently acquired cognitive skills (such as the skill of using one thing to represent another).

Lev Vygotsky, a Russian psychologist, treated play as having an even more central role in cognitive development. In the process of creating an imaginary situation that reproduces the real situation, for purposes of play, the child develops abilities of abstract representational thought. That is, children grow able to think about meanings abstractly, as they gain experience in using substitute objects (such as a stick) to stand for other things (such as a horse). Vygotsky acknowledged affective, as well as cognitive, aspects to play. Children acted out, through play, desires that could neither be fulfilled nor forgotten, according to Vygotsky.

Across these theoretical approaches, play constitutes a system of communication in which meaning can be reconfronted and remade, perhaps with an outcome of emotional, cognitive, or social mastery. This approach to play, specifically as it relates to cognitive growth, has stimulated an impressive amount of contemporary empirical research on play among psychologists, as will be seen from the research reviewed in the next section. Much of this psychological research has focused on sociodramatic, or pretend play, in which children enact dramatic roles and fantasy scenarios. During recent years, research on pretend play has also begun to examine play's social dimensions.

II. CHILDHOOD PLAY: DEVELOPMENTAL PROGRESSION

Before discussing the developmental pattern by which pretend play transforms across childhood, it is relevant to delineate various forms of play, drawing from knowledge of researchers working in the contemporary Euro-American cultural context. In addition to *sociodramatic or pretend play,* play also takes other forms. *Constructive play* refers to play using objects (blocks, Legos, etc.) or materials (such as clay or construction paper) to make something. *Language play* occurs when children play with and practice linguistic forms, during the course of learning language. For example, a toddler might engage in playful monologue before going to sleep, or upon waking up. *Rough-and-tumble play* is the vigorous physical play that occurs with mock fighting and chasing, when the participants are friendly in intent yet wrestle, leg play, tickle, throw, push, clasp and pursue one another. *Functional play* involves sensorimotor practice or playful repetition (with or without an object) such as gathering and dumping, or running and jumping.

Newborn infants, who enter the world with reflexive behavior but no knowledge of their environment, gain information about their world largely through their playful interactions with people and objects. Much of this interaction is at first visual and manipulative, but at about the end of the first year of life pretend play is added to the repertoire. Jean Piaget (as reported in *Play, Dreams and Imitation in Childhood*) observed his daughter (at age 15 months) to grab hold of a fringed cloth, which resembled her fringed pillow, and to suck her thumb and lie down as she would usually do with her pillow. Her laughter during this act, and her occasional blinking (as if to close her eyes) signaled the playful nature of her actions. Similarly, infants from varied cultures have been shown to produce pretend gestures beginning at about 12 or 13 months of age.

Beyond infancy, the development of pretend play has been well documented, to include three parallel trends that develop into the pretend play seen by approximately 3 years of age. These trends include decentration, decontextualization, and integration, patterns of behavior documented by Larry Fenson and collaborators. *Decentration* is the process by which play comes to be less exclusively self-referential and comes to be more inclusive of the perspective of others. *Decontextualization* refers to a shift from very realistic substitute objects to less realistic substitute objects, including (ultimately) a totally imagined object. *Integration* encompasses a shift from a single action during play to more varied actions, done in sequence. (Illustrative behaviors that move through each of these developmental patterns are given in Table II.)

The simultaneous development of decentration, decontextualization, and integration comes together in sociodramatic or social pretend play, prominent as a form of play in 3- to 6-year-olds. In this social form of play, children pretend with others and develop numerous skills. Skills exercised are both inherent to the activity of play, and drawn from experience outside the contest of play. For example, children enact social roles familiar from other contexts in sociodramatic play, which requires and indicates awareness of others as well as a knowledge of role-appropriate actions, attributes, and relationships. Moreover, social pretend play draws upon and practices skills of communication that are needed within the context of play. Children use verbal discourse to negotiate the parameters of the play drama, including the events to be reenacted (for example, a trip to a fast-food restaurant), the ongoing action sequence (driving to the restaurant, and ordering), and object transformations (which objects will represent the car, or the drive-up window). These agreed-upon parameters of the play drama are referred to, by play researchers, as the *play frame*. When children interact during pretend play, some of their discourse will occur within the play frame, that is, as a fantasy character within the dramatic frame. Other discourse will take place outside the drama, between players, as they negotiate the assignment of roles, the actions to be executed, and so on. The latter conversation outside the play frame is referred to as *metacommunication,* or as the *participation framework,* by investigators of children's play discourse. An example of a brief pretend play episode, indicating which actions are within or outside of the play frame, is given in Table III.

Based on a body of research looking at individual differences in pretend play, early social pretense has been found to significantly correlate with a child's developing understanding of other people's beliefs and feelings. Pretend play links to social understanding among preschoolers, reflecting the social dimension of play.

Table II Developmental Progression in Pretend Play

	Level 1	Level 2	Level 3
Decentration	Child pretends to drink from cup.	Child pretends to feed doll from empty cup.	Child makes doll feed itself from empty cup.
Decontextualization	Child uses empty cup to drink.	Child uses an object such as a hollow block to drink.	Child gestures as if to drink from an imaginary cup.
Integration	Child pretends to feed stuffed bear.	Child feeds one stuffed bear, then another.	Child feeds stuffed bear, then puts bear to bed, then reads it a story.

Table III Play Discourse—Example

Action	Mary (M), age 38 months	Boy partner (B)
M: sits on sofa with doll singing to it.		
B: reaches for baby bottle.	No, that's the bottle for the baby/	
M: with B watching, takes off doll's bonnet.	Does she look pretty when she takes it off?/	No/
M: readjusts bonnet.	She looks prettier/now does she look pretty?/	

Unshaded area: within play frame **Shaded area:** outside play frame (metacommunication)

Adapted from: Miller, P., & Garvey, C. (1984). Mother-baby role play: Its origins in social support. In I. Bretherton (Ed.), *Symbolic play: The development of social understanding*, pp. 112–113. New York: Academic Press.

Piaget theorized that when children reached the stage of concrete operational development (at approximately age 7) pretend play would decrease, to be replaced by games having rules. In other words, Piaget expected pretend play to be an inverted U-shaped function, increasing in frequency over ages 3 to 6 years, and then beginning a decline. Research on middle-class children from intact families has generally supported the rising incidence of sociodramatic pretend play (as a proportion of all play) from 3 years to approximately 6 or 7 years. Sociodramatic play drops off during the late kindergarten and early elementary years, as games-with-rules and solitary pretense apparently increase.

Sociodramatic play sometimes involves the taking of fictional roles, such as individuals with proper names in stories coming from books, television, or oral tradition. Apart from sociodramatic play, stories in and of themselves sometimes are transformed through language in language play, perhaps as a coping tool for reintegration of distressing circumstances. This use of narratives for emotional coping was implicated by Bruno Bettelheim in his treatise on fairy tales, *The Uses of Enchantment*. Empirical case studies have shown that characters in a story can be appropriated through a process of personalization and identification, as children interact with a story and transform its events. Sometimes, children concentrate on a portion of the story with which they identify, as has been reported in a number of case studies of individual children.

One vivid example involved a dying boy who became deeply involved in the classic children's novel *Charlotte's Web* (in which the main character, Charlotte, dies), reported in Bluebond-Langner's work *The Private Worlds of Dying Children*. Numerous books by Vivian Paley (including *Superheroes in the Doll Corner*) report how kindergarten children change around the events in a story to suit themselves.

Such attachment to and use of stories lies at the core of the therapeutic method known as bibliotherapy. Bibliotherapy combines the domains of literature and therapy, by presenting a child with books chosen to closely relate to a current problem, under the guidance of a therapist.

Bibliotherapy, a technique used with adults and children alike, reminds us that the capacities developed in childhood play do not necessarily atrophy and disappear, but instead may be used in other domains as children mature into adulthood. As already mentioned, D. W. Winnicott theorized that cultural experience in adulthood (art, literature, religious experience, and so on) rests on developmental precedents inherent in play.

III. CHILDHOOD PLAY: SOCIOCULTURAL CONTEXTS

Childhood play does not occur in a vacuum. Play takes place in a distinctive physical and social ecology. In a middle-class American cultural context, pretend play is often mediated by available environments (such as playgrounds) or available objects (such as toys).

In a 1993 study by Wendy Haight and Peggy Miller (reported in *Pretending At Home: Early Development in a Sociocultural Context*), it was found that a sample of middle-class American preschoolers consistently had access to a large quantity of child-scaled replica toys. Further, mothers actively incorporated these toys into pretend play with their youngsters as early as 1 year of age. Mothers elaborated upon and prompted children's pretending. Mothers also engaged directly in pretend interactions with their children, serving as children's primary play partners through 3 years of age. At 4 years of age, pretend play seemed to be shifting to the peer domain, as children pretended with siblings and friends. Interestingly, replica objects remained the favored play props in play with peers. This study illustrates that children, in the course of self-directing their play, borrow suggestions and encouragement from the social environment.

Some studies indicate that American children from lower social class backgrounds engage in less pretend play than other children, when studied in schools or laboratories. Intervention studies among disadvantaged American children, aimed at correcting this presumed "play deficit," stimulated children to play in preschool classrooms. Anthropologist of play Helen Schwartzmen offered the criticism in her 1978 book *Transformations* that the presumed "play deficit" may be an artifact of the testing context; Schwartzman questioned whether investigators mistook a differing play style (i.e. non-middle class) for a play deficit. Schwartzman emphasized the importance of studying disadvantaged children on their home turf, urging researchers to investigate alternate expressions of imagination that lower-class children might display.

Recent cross-cultural research shows that sociodramatic play occurs infrequently in some non-Euro-American societies. Mayan adults, it has been reported by Suzanne Gaskins (1996), generally do not recognize play as a valuable activity for children. Preschool Mayan children spend some time in pretend play—although they have access to few props for such play. Mayan infants engage in some object play, but do not seem to use objects to master the environment or to mediate social interactions. Language play is also less frequent among Mayan children.

The social interaction involved in metacommunication about play may also reflect the sociocultural context, in which aggressive versus cooperative behavior may be differentially valued. May Martini (1994), in an ethnographic study of peer interactions among Polynesian Marquesan 2 to 5 year olds, found that these children avoided extensive one-to-one negotiations in their metacommunications about play. In order to maintain consensus (and avoid one-to-one negotiations), they engaged in play activities that were familiar to all players, with little change or elaboration made to play events. Marquesan children also avoided leadership roles, by playing games where all participants did the same actions at the same time. Relative to Marquesan children, American children had a relative "cooperation deficit," since their play involved more one-to-one negotiation and individual innovation, at the expense of consensus.

The assumption that play is necessary for a child's healthy functioning, then, must be assessed within the sociocultural confines of a child's own environment. Cultural circumstances vary in many respects: the value placed on childhood fantasy play by adults, the cultural norms for interaction (and thereby norms for play metacommunication), as well as the role of objects and physical environments in play.

Yet neither is culture all-determining, it should be added. Individual differences occur within a culture, in children's fantasy predisposition or play style. Children in social environments without toys may devise their own play materials using discarded items and places (such as abandoned buildings) to play. A collection of photographs and recollections compiled in 1990 by folklorists Amanda Dargan and Steven Zeitlin vividly depicts how generations of urban children transformed junk into toys and incorporated fire hydrants, lampposts, stoops, rooftops, walls and vacant lots into their play. Dargan and Zeitlin (p. 69) quoted one man, born in 1894, who said: "On our East Side, suffocated with miles of tenements, an open space was a fairy gift to children . . . My gang seized upon one of these Delancey Street lofts, and turned it, with the power of imagination, into a vast western plain. We buried pirate treasure there, and built snow forts . . . We dug caves, and with Peary (sic) explored the North Pole."

Brian Sutton-Smith (author of *Toys As Culture*) has asserted that toys occupy a central place in the play life of contemporary American children, in part because this suits the individualistic, materialistic orientation of modern-day industrial society. At an earlier historical period, toys were less important to American children. Healthy functioning in play is best understood while keeping in mind the sociocultural context of a given time or place.

IV. GENDER DIFFERENCES IN CHILDHOOD PLAY

Gender, along with age, is remarkably predictive of a child's behavior; play is no exception. A consensus of contemporary American research points to differences between boys and girls in some aspects of play. Preschool boys display more rough-and-tumble play than do girls. Preschool boys are more vigorous, aggressive, and active than are girls, in indoor and outdoor play environments, covering more space than girls in the process. In social play, preschoolers show a tendency to interact more with same-sex play partners. When given the option to choose roles for pretend play, preschoolers usually prefer roles that are stereotyped as sex-appropriate. In role play, preschool girls show more nurturant behavior than boys. Male preschoolers tend to avoid playing with girl-stereotyped toys; interestingly, however, girls use toys stereotyped for both genders, to some extent.

Gender segregation is also a fact of life on elementary school playgrounds. Sociologist Barrie Thorne, in her 1994 book *Gender Play,* has described how school-age boys and girls mark boundaries on the playground (and elsewhere) between boys and girls, boundaries that are then crossed, undermined, and challenged. Through their play across the years of childhood, girls and boys exercise (and at times challenge) a degree of sexual self-stereotyping.

Parental influences on children's play also vary by gender. Observational research has found that play with cross-gender stereotyped toys is discouraged during play with mothers and fathers, to a great extent. Parents purchase toys and possessions largely along gender-stereotyped lines, as illustrated in Table IV. For example, parents of boys purchase more toys that replicate violent or aggressive behavior (such as military toys). In the study by Haight and Miller mentioned earlier, preschool-aged girls played with dolls, boys played with action figures, and both genders played with stuffed animals.

Peers also tend to reinforce gender-linked social standards for play and toy use, through the means of acceptance or ostracism, particularly for boys. Cross-

Table IV Types of Bedroom Content

Boys have more . . .	Girls have more . . .
Vehicles	Dolls
Education materials	Dollhouses
Art materials	Domestic toys
Sports equipment	Floral print decorations
Machines	Ruffle decorations
Military toys	
Toys encouraging away-from-home activities	Toys encouraging at-home activities

Adapted from: Reingold, H., & Cook, K. (1975). The content of boys' and girls' rooms as an index of parents' behavior. *Child Development, 46,* 920–927.

gender play is more likely to occur away from a watchful peer group.

Overall, both the metacommunication about play (feedback from parents and peers about play activities) and the content of play (roles acted, objects chosen, and actions taken) serve to shape and practice gender norms. Play, then, forms an impressive model of and model for social behavior, with regard to the dimension of gender.

V. PLAY AS HEALING

Other sections of this article have already alluded to the value of play as a healing or coping activity; play also is inherent to the well known and widely practiced clinical method, play therapy. Play has proven helpful to children under stress, such as when facing a stressful illness or another emotional challenge. The use of play as a form of healing can be discussed in two major contexts: (1) in the formal context of play therapy and (2) without any therapeutic intervention, as a self-generated activity of the child outside a therapeutic setting.

Psychotherapy with children was attempted by Sigmund Freud with his young patient, Little Hans; but it was Anna Freud who pioneered the use of play in therapy, beginning in the 1920s. Anna Freud used toys and games as a way to build a relationship with her child patients. Child psychoanalyst Melanie Klein proposed the use of play as a direct substitute for verbalizations. In her play therapy, Klein viewed play as the child's natural means of expression. Play therapist David Levy further contributed to the advancement of play therapy, by specifically structuring the play session (through selection of available toys) to facilitate the child's cathartic release of a traumatic emotional event.

From these historical roots in the 1920s and 1930s, play therapy has grown into a mainstream means of clinical intervention with children. Within the context of therapy, play has multiple purposes. Play serves as the vehicle of communication between therapist and child. Additionally, play is intended to help create a corrective experience to relieve emotional distress for the child, and to resolve issues that stand in the way of normal development. Play therapy also may introduce the child to new forms of beneficial play behavior that will be carried into the child's life outside the therapy.

Despite the impressively wide application of play therapy, relatively little scientific research has been conducted that elucidates the process of change for the child. Published investigations of play therapy have tended to be theoretical in nature, or oriented to clinical case studies.

Apart from play therapy, play has also been documented to have a helpful impact on children in nonclinical, naturalistic settings as they cope with the everyday emotional issues that are part of "normal" development. For instance, as mentioned earlier, the self-initiated use of stories to express and resolve emotional issues has been reported in ethnographic studies and in case studies of individual children.

Remarkably, the use of play as a means of emotional expression and coping may even occur under extreme and tragic circumstances. Historian George Eisen has recorded that children played amidst the camp life of the Holocaust, rebounding (at least initially) from the stress and absurdity of their circumstances through play. In their 1992 work about children who are growing up in urban war zones, Garbarino, Dubrow, Kostelny, and Pardo found that play can help children cope with the trauma that comes from living with chronic community violence. Garbarino and his coauthors stated that teachers can support these children by creating environments that encourage children to tell their stories in and on their own terms, even though this potentially may be upsetting to teachers. Teachers, these investigators acknowledge, need strong support in this difficult task.

In sum, it appears that play need not be guided by an adult (therapist, parent or teacher) in order to provide transformative value to children confronting the stress of everyday development under "ordinary" circumstances. Adult support is more likely to be needed when children face extraordinary circumstances. With or without clinical supervision, play seems to provide a child-manageable domain for raising and addressing unresolved issues. Further investigation is worthwhile, however, of the underlying process by which emotional resolution takes place.

VI. CONCLUSION

From a child's point of view, the intrinsic motivation of play (for sheer enjoyment) argues strongly for the worth of play, well apart from incidental gain. By virtue of being a self-motivated (or "autotelic") activity,

play has often been compared to M. Csikszentmihalyi's concept of "flow," a dynamic mental state in which inherent enjoyment is achieved, without interference of anxiety or boredom. In "flow" the rewards are intrinsic to the activity and the motivation emerges out of the activity, rather than being extrinsic. In and of itself, this is a positive mental state. Play is a fundamentally self-motivating and self-sustaining enterprise. [See INTRINSIC MOTIVATION AND GOALS.]

Yet in another sense, play is a productive enterprise as well, in the sense of facilitating gain for the child. The child practices and attains greater social, emotional, and cognitive mastery through play, according to a broad consensus of theory and research.

Play, then, represents a conundrum or paradox. Play seems purposeless or even frivolous, yet in many circumstances it has been shown to have profoundly serious potential. For instance, play allows a child to approach and express feelings that, when not masked by the "disguise" of play (or play therapy), seem inexpressible. In turn, pretend play also constitutes an anomalous state: literal reality is suspended, and yet commanding knowledge of ordinary social reality (to perform roles, to enact dramas, as well as to socially manage the play process) is required.

Much about play is not yet fully understood. To comprehend the role of play in healing, more systematic understanding of how affective transformation occurs through play is needed. Knowing more about the role of sociocultural context as a force in shaping the nature and importance of play in natural settings could also enlighten our understanding of the "workings" of play. Play, still in many ways an ambiguous and enigmatic activity, likely holds dynamic forces that could clarify what we know about human meaning and development.

BIBLIOGRAPHY

Block, M., & Pellegrini, A. (1989). *The ecological context of children's play.* Norwood, NJ: Ablex.

Bretherton, I. (1984). *Symbolic play: The development of social understanding.* Orlando, FL: Academic Press.

Dargan, A., & Zeitlin, S. (1990). *City play.* New Brunswick, NJ: Rutgers University Press.

Gabarino, J., Dubrow, N., Kostelny, K., & Pardo, C. (1992). *Children in danger: Coping with the consequences of community violence.* San Francisco: Jossey-Bass.

Gaskins, S. (1996). How Mayan parental theories come into play. In S. Harkness & C. Super (Eds.), *Parents' cultural belief sys-*

tems: Their origins, expressions, and consequences, pp. 345–363. New York: Guilford Press.

Haight, W. L., & Miller, P. J. (1993). *Pretending at home: Early development in a sociocultural context.* Albany, NY: State University of New York Press.

Martini, M. (1994). Peer interactions in Polynesia: A view from the Marquesas. In J. Roopnarine, J. Johnson, & F. Hooper (Eds.), *Children's play in diverse cultures,* pp. 73–103. Albany, NY: State University of New York Press.

O'Connor, K. (1991). *The play therapy primer: An integration of theories and techniques.* New York: John Wiley.

Rubin, K., Fein, G., & Vandenberg, B. (1983). Play. In E. M. Hetherington (Ed.), *Handbook of Child Psychology: Socialization, Personality and Social Development* (Vol. IV), pp. 693–774. New York: John Wiley.

Schwartzman, H. (1978). *Transformations: The anthropology of children's play.* New York: Plenum Press.

Singer, D. G., & Singer, J. L. (1990). *The house of make-believe: Play and the development of imagination.* Cambridge MA: Harvard University Press.

Thorne, B. (1994). *Gender play: Girls and boys in school.* New Brunswick, NJ: Rutgers University Press.

Positive Illusions

Shelley E. Taylor

University of California, Los Angeles

Dispositional Optimism Global expectations, relatively stable across time and context, that one will experience generally good as opposed to bad outcomes in life.

Illusion of Control The perception of oneself as having more control over environmental occurrences than is actually the case.

Mental Health Those qualities thought to be essential to healthy psychological and social functioning, including the ability to be happy or contented; the ability to form and maintain social relationships; the ability to change and grow and to deal effectively with stress; and the ability to engage in creative and productive work.

Positive Illusions Perceptions of one's personal characteristics, one's degree of control over the environment, and a view of the future that are more positive than objective estimates suggest is realistic.

Self-Aggrandizement The tendency to regard oneself in more positive and less negative terms than is actually the case or than one regards other people.

Unrealistic Optimism The perception that the future will be better, especially for oneself, than is objectively probable.

POSITIVE ILLUSIONS about oneself are both highly prevalent in normal thought and predictive of the criteria traditionally associated with mental health. These positive illusions consist of three mildly self-aggrandizing biases: people view themselves in unrealistically positive terms; they believe they have greater control over environmental events than is actually the case; and they hold views of the future that are more rosy than reasonable estimates can justify.

I. THE MENTALLY HEALTHY PERSON

The significance of positive illusions and their apparent beneficial effects stems from the challenge they pose to traditional models of mental health. Many decades of psychological wisdom have established contact with reality as one of the hallmarks of the mentally healthy person. In this view, the well-adjusted person is thought to engage in accurate reality testing, whereas the individual whose vision is clouded by illusion is regarded as vulnerable to mental illness. In an early distillation of dominant views of mental health, Marie Jahoda noted that the majority of theories considered contact with reality to be a critical component. This theme is prominent in the writings of Gordon Allport, Erik Erikson, Erik Fromm, and Abraham Maslow, among others. For example, Maslow argued that healthy people accept themselves with all of their discrepancies from their ideal image, acknowledging their frailties and weaknesses willingly, if without satisfaction. The criterion that the mentally healthy person perceives reality accurately has been incorporated into more recent textbooks on adjustment used to train psychologists and other mental health experts. Theory and research on positive illusions, in contrast, suggests that accurate perceptions of oneself, the world, and the future are not essential to mental health; moreover, mildly positive distortions of one's personal characteristics, one's degree of control over the environment, and one's estimate of one's personal future may well be more psychologically adaptive than accurate perceptions.

In making the case that positive illusions are associated with mental health, it is important to have an appropriate definition of that construct. Fortunately, the literature on mental health and on adjustment provides a reasonably consistent set of criteria that appear to mark the mentally healthy individual. The ability to be happy or relatively contented has been a central criterion of mental health, adopted by a broad range of personality theorists, clinicians, and researchers. The ability to develop caring relationships with others, likewise, has been regarded as an essential task of the mentally healthy adult, one that has emerged as increasingly important, as evidence for the beneficial health and mental health of social support and social relationships accumulates. The ability to grow from change and to cope with the inevitable stresses of life has increasingly been studied as an important task, inasmuch as exposure to stressful life events is an inevitable consequence of the human condition that people incorporate and transcend or succumb to, both mentally and physically. Finally, the ability to engage in creative and productive work and to maintain motivation, persistence, and performance in the face of impediments and setbacks, is regarded to be an important component of the mentally healthy life-style. In evaluating the evidence for positive illusions and their beneficial effects, then, these agreed-upon characteristics of mentally healthy functioning will be adopted as criteria.

II. SELF-AGGRANDIZING SELF-PERCEPTIONS

People consistently regard themselves more positively and less negatively than they regard others. This ro-

bust finding has been identified in populations ranging from college students evaluating themselves in comparison to their fellow students to individuals facing acute or chronic health threats, who evaluate themselves more favorably than other patients with the same diseases. The ways in which people adopt and maintain these self-aggrandizing self-perceptions are manifold. People choose evaluative dimensions on which they are certain to appear more advantaged, they define attributes in idiosyncratic ways that emphasize their personal strengths, and they select worse-off comparison individuals or groups that guarantee a favorable self–other comparison. For example, one heart patient may see himself as better off than fellow heart patients because he is more affluent, he is able to speak openly about his problems, and "all those other people" have more advanced heart disease than he has; another heart patient may see himself as better off than his fellow heart patients because he has many friends, he is participating actively in rehabilitation, and he did not die from a heart attack, as many heart patients do. Thus, each of these individuals may feel confident about his advantaged status by virtue of the attributes on which he evaluates himself and the group of individuals with whom he compares himself.

Such self-serving cognitive machinations would seem amusing, or perhaps troubling, were it not for the fact that they appear to be reliably associated with psychological well-being. In terms of the first criterion of mental health, the ability to be happy or contented, feeling good about oneself through self-aggrandizing self-perceptions clearly fosters a sense of contentment. In addition, people who feel good about themselves are more certain about their self-appraisals and seem to have a clear sense of what their personal characteristics are. The self-ratings of people who perceive themselves positively fluctuate less over time than is true of people who think poorly of themselves. And, people who think well about themselves have more internally consistent self-perceptions than people who think poorly of themselves. A lack of firm self-knowledge may leave people who think poorly of themselves at the mercy of daily events, and this vulnerability appears to be reflected in high emotional reactivity. Research by Brown and his associates found that people who thought poorly of themselves actually suffered adverse health effects when they experienced positive, pleasant life events, apparently because they saw those events as incongruous with their personal characteristics. In contrast, people with higher self-esteem were healthier when life treated them well. In summary, people who think well of themselves have stable and favorable views, which seem to protect them from emotional upheaval that might otherwise arise from the stress of daily life. [*See* Happiness: Subjective Well-Being.]

Evidence from studies of reactions to extreme health events also suggests that positive self-perceptions may aid coping. Research by Taylor and her associates suggests that the perception that one is healthier or coping more successfully than other patients similar to oneself is not only highly prevalent among individuals coping with major health threats, but it is also associated with reduced distress. Thus, in addition to buffering people against the normal stressors of daily life, positive self-perceptions appear to be helpful when people encounter more traumatic life events as well. [*See* Coping with Stress.]

People with favorable self-perceptions of their ability are also more likely to attain success on work-related tasks than people who hold more modest perceptions. As Bandura argues, accurate appraisals of one's own abilities can be self-limiting. The fact that people overestimate their capabilities is a benefit, because it leads them to expend the effort needed to improve and to overcome obstacles. Thus, for example, each of the hypothetical heart patients noted earlier, feeling confident of his advantaged status, may try harder to ensure that his coping and rehabilitation are successful.

Viewing oneself in more positive terms than one views others appears to confer particular advantages in childhood. Psychologists have argued that overly optimistic assessments of one's abilities are beneficial during early childhood, because they facilitate the acquisition of language and the development of problem-solving and motor skills. As Stipek argued in a 1984 paper, because children hold somewhat grandiose self-perceptions and are unrealistically optimistic about their likely success in the future, they are more likely to attempt new tasks, to persist in the face of setbacks, and to master materials and undertakings that initially seem too difficult. To the extent that this is true, skill acquisition should be greater among those with more positive self-perceptions and greater optimism about their abilities. [*See* Optimism, Motivation, and Mental Health.]

To summarize, the perception that most people hold of themselves is not as well balanced as traditional models of mental health have suggested. Rather than being attentive to both favorable and unfavorable aspects of themselves, normal people appear to be quite cognizant of their strengths and assets and less aware of their weaknesses and faults. These self-portrayals have been regarded as illusory because most people see themselves as better than the average person, and most people see themselves as better off than other people see them. By contrast, people who are low in self-esteem, moderately depressed, or both, are more negative in their self-perceptions and may actually be more balanced in their self-perceptions as well.

Are self-aggrandizing self-perceptions always beneficial, and are they more beneficial, the more positive they become? The answer to these questions appears to be no. Taylor and her associates have documented that typically self-aggrandizing self-perceptions remain within a fairly narrow range, representing modest exaggerations of talents that actually exist with concomitant downplaying of personal weaknesses. At this modest level, they appear to be highly adaptive. However, at the extreme, such self-perceptions may interfere with adequate functioning, making people unaware of or unable to deal with information about their weaknesses or personal liabilities. In addition, research suggests that high self-esteem individuals sometimes take more risks than individuals low in self-esteem, and sometimes risk-taking may backfire, setting people up for failure. Under some circumstances, individuals high in self-esteem may lash out at others whom they regard as criticizing or disrespecting them. On balance, however, mildly inflated self-perceptions appear to be adaptive from the standpoint of the criteria normally associated with mental health. [*See* Self-Esteem.]

III. THE ILLUSION OF CONTROL

Most individuals appear to be less than realistic in their beliefs about the degree to which they can exert personal control over environmental occurrences. Psychological theorists have long maintained that a sense of personal control is integral to the self-concept and self-esteem. This theme has been central to the writings of social psychologists such as Fritz Heider, developmental psychologists such as Robert White, social learning theorists including Albert Bandura, and psychoanalytic theorists such as Fenichel and Hendrick. Such beliefs, however, are often greater than can be justified, but nonetheless, appear to be associated with adaptive functioning under both normal and stressful circumstances. A substantial amount of experimental literature indicates that an illusion of control helps people to adjust to forthcoming laboratory stressors. Experiments conducted in medical settings demonstrate that people who believe they have control during stressful procedures cope better than those undergoing the same procedures, but without control-enhancing interventions. These effects emerge on a broad range of physiological, health-related, and affective measures, and occur when "control" is largely perceived, rather than actual. Feelings of control that are self-generated in response to stressful occurrences, such as chronic disease, are also associated with better adjustment.

The form that the illusion of control assumes is important. Except for some laboratory investigations that may have low generalizability to real situations, there is little evidence that believing one can control external events is adaptive if no control exists. Typically, the illusion of control is not held about occurrences that are completely uncontrollable, such as whether one causes the sun to come up in the morning, but rather involves mild distortions of the degree of control that actually exists in many settings. Moreover, there is some evidence that perceptions of control, and specifically, what aspects of a situation are controllable, shift in response to feedback about the success of one's efforts. For example, individuals with advanced cancer or HIV disease may initially believe that they can exert direct control over their illness and help to bring about a cure. But as evidence accumulates to suggest that these perceptions are ill-founded, perceptions of control may shift to arenas in which some semblance of control actually remains, such as the ability to control symptoms or daily activities.

It has been argued that mildly and severely depressed individuals are less vulnerable to the illusion of control, and instead make more accurate estimates of their degree of personal control than do nondepressed individuals. Indeed, research on depressive accuracy has been plentiful in the last two decades. At present, however, the balance of evidence suggests that depressed people are sometimes accurate in their perceptions of the degree to which they can control what goes

on around them, and at other times they are overly negative. [See DEPRESSION.]

In summary, a mild illusion of control often exists in normal individuals, and it appears generally to be associated with good psychological adjustment. There are many reasons why an illusion of control might exist and why it might be adaptive for psychological and social functioning. When individuals believe that their efforts at personal control are likely to be successful, they will try harder, performing more effectively and increasing the likelihood that they can attain their goals. As in the case of self-aggrandizing self-perceptions, research suggests that a sense of control may be especially important in childhood. For example, consistent differences between mastery-oriented children and helpless children have been found, such that mastery-oriented children (i.e., those with a sense of control over tasks) remember their successes better, are more likely to see success as indicative of their personal ability, expect personal success in the future, and are less daunted by failure. Indeed, the desire to control and manipulate the world appears to emerge at a remarkably early age. Within weeks after birth, infants actively explore the environment, responding to a new stimulus with rapt attention and babbling. The infant seems to be primed to master new experiences, seeking a sense of competence. An exaggerated sense of control may be an essential ingredient of this intrinsic need to control and manipulate the world.

IV. UNREALISTIC OPTIMISM

Most children and adults are optimistic. Although such perceptions have become more muted in recent years, especially when they concern economic success, research suggests that most people believe that the present is better than the past and that the future will be better. As an example, when asked what they thought was possible for themselves in the future, college students reported more than four times as many positive as negative possibilities. Typically, people overestimate the likelihood that they will experience a wide variety of pleasant events, such as liking their first job, getting a good salary, or having a gifted child, in comparison to their perceptions of other people attaining these same outcomes. Because not everyone's future can be rosier than that of their peers, the optimism that individuals display appears to be illusory.

Over a wide variety of tasks, people's predictions of what will occur correspond closely to what they would like to see happen or what is socially desirable, but not very closely to what is objectively likely. Both children and adults overestimate the degree to which they will do well on future tasks, and such overestimations increase, the more personally important that task is. Typically, people see themselves as less vulnerable than others to a broad array of future risks and negative life events. In addition, a mounting literature on dispositional optimism indicates the adaptive significance of a pervasive and stable positive outlook on life.

Unrealistic optimism appears to be healthy from the standpoint of the traditional criteria of mental health. It enhances positive mood, it is associated with a high motivation to engage in productive work and, as a dispositional construct, it is associated with the ability to cope more successfully and recover more quickly from some health-related stressors. Inasmuch as optimistic people are better liked by others and are more desirable interaction partners, unrealistic optimism may contribute to the development of social relationships as well.

V. POSITIVE ILLUSIONS AND TRAUMA

The positive illusions of self-aggrandizing self-perceptions, an illusion of control, and unrealistic optimism may be particularly helpful for enabling people to combat the major stressful events or traumas of life. A trauma may be defined as a disruptive negative event that produces life disturbance and at least temporary aberrations in psychological functioning, marked by anxiety, depression, and other negative emotional states. Research on positive illusions began with studies of people adjusting to traumatic events, especially catastrophic health events, such as breast cancer, heart disease, and AIDS.

In an early interview study with breast cancer patients, Taylor and her associates found that women adjusting to the altered circumstances of their lives often voiced the belief that their lives had been changed in many ways for the better by the breast cancer experience. This was true of more than two-thirds of the

women interviewed, and included patients with both good and poor prognoses. They spoke, in particular, of reordering their priorities, spending time on important relationships, and devoting less attention to such mundane activities as household chores and yard work. Many of the women asserted that they had a high degree of personal control over the cancer, despite the fact that there is little evidence for the validity of such beliefs. Many of the women had overly optimistic assessments of the likelihood of their survival, and voiced the belief that they had beaten the cancer, although from the chart records, it was clear that many of them would die.

Relating these positive but false beliefs to a measure of psychological adjustment revealed that such beliefs were associated with good, rather than poor, adjustment. Thus, for example, the belief that one could personally exert control over one's cancer was associated with good psychological adjustment, and this belief was held by more than half of the breast cancer patients studied. Adjustment measures included clinical psychologists' ratings of patients' adjustment, oncologists' ratings of adjustment, and several standardized measures of psychological functioning.

Subsequent work by Taylor and her associates with heart patients, cancer patients, and people living with AIDS, among others, revealed that the majority of people in these circumstances reacted to them by developing perceptions of themselves as physically better off and as coping more successfully than other patients like themselves. When individuals who had sustained these diseases were asked to report on the changes they had experienced in their lives as a result of the illness, positive changes in the self were among the most common changes reported. These changes often reflected the belief that the event had revealed or evoked personal qualities that were either previously latent or nonexistent, such as an increased understanding of others, increased tolerance, and an enhanced meaning of life. Most also felt they had at least some control over their disease. In addition, in several of the studies, patients expressed unrealistic optimism that the future would remain or unfold in a positive direction, and that they would be able to manage their health effectively in the future.

These investigations suggest that when people experience personal tragedies or setbacks, they respond with cognitively adaptive efforts that may enable them to return to or exceed their previous level of psychological functioning. The themes around which such adaptations occur include a search for meaning in the experience, an effort to regain a sense of mastery, and an attempt to restore a positive sense of self. Of course, not all of the beliefs that people develop in the wake of life-threatening diseases are illusory, and indeed, there is nothing intrinsic to such experiences that necessitates that all their effects be adverse. Nonetheless, the illusory component of the adaptive beliefs is clearly intriguing, because it conflicts so sharply with the existing literature on mental health.

Emerging research suggests that positive beliefs may serve people well, even when their circumstances subsequently deteriorate. For example, research has shown that people infected with HIV who were dispositionally optimistic remained optimistic and better adjusted than individuals who were less optimistic, even after their health deteriorated and they were diagnosed with AIDS. Optimists are more flexible in their use of coping strategies than are pessimists, and they may therefore be better able to shift to strategies that will help them deal with a new and worsened reality. Thus, although additional research on this important question is required, it does not appear at present that positive illusions set people up for disappointment when their illusions are disconfirmed by subsequent events. This is important knowledge for examining adjustment to traumatic events, because disconfirmation of positive illusions, such as the belief that one is cured or faith in one's ability to personally control one's disease, may often occur.

VI. POSITIVE ILLUSIONS AND DEFENSE MECHANISMS

On the surface, positive illusions may appear to be repression cast in a positive light. Repression is the involuntary exclusion from consciousness of cognitions whose admission would be painful for the individual. Because repression can lead to the appearance of low anxiety, that "everything is fine," it may mirror the kinds of positive, upbeat beliefs represented by positive illusions. Yet the liabilities of the repressive style have been fairly well documented. Repression has been linked to self-deception and to the use of maladaptive avoidant coping strategies in the face of threat. Moreover, although repressors give the appearance of being low in anxiety, they show high scores on indirect measures of defensiveness. Repressors tend to respond to threat with perceptual avoidance, which leads them to ignore or restrict their attention in response to threat. This restriction of attention may have the beneficial effect of minimizing the distress they experience, but it may interfere with their ability to gain valuable information about the stressful events they are going through. Thus, while there may be short-term benefits to this repressive style in terms of distress management, over time, the repressive style is likely to be unsuccessful, as chronically stressful events continue. Repression may also be associated with immunocompromise and increase the likelihood of certain kinds of cancers. Overall, then, this repressive approach to stressful events appears to be maladaptive.

Are people with positive illusions simply repressors in another guise? Research on the coping strategies of individuals with positive illusions suggests that exactly the opposite condition may obtain. People who hold positive beliefs about themselves, their degree of personal control, and the likelihood of a positive future, appear to use active coping strategies and positive reappraisal, both when they are anticipating stressful events that have not yet occurred and when they are managing stressful events that are actually taking place. People high in optimism, for example, are more rather than less likely to attend to personally threatening information and to undertake efforts to offset the implications of that information, precisely because they are confident in their abilities to succeed. People high in perceived self-efficacy are also less likely to appraise events as threatening or negative, and as a consequence, they are more likely to make active efforts to manage them. There is evidence that people high in perceived self-efficacy or feelings of control are better able to distinguish controllable from uncontrollable events, and thus, may be better able than those without such beliefs to deploy their actions effectively. Individuals who are optimistic appraise their circumstances more favorably, a generalization demonstrated in a variety of medical patient groups, including coronary artery bypass patients, heart disease patients, women awaiting abortion, and men at risk for AIDS. The fact that positive illusions are associated with active coping strategies is important, because it indicates that such illusions are not simply wish-fulfilling beliefs that numb people into inaction or indications of a repressive coping style, but rather, constitute positive assessments that lead to favorable appraisals of one's ability to respond actively to stress.

VII. RECONCILING ILLUSION AND REALITY

Evidence regarding the existence and adaptiveness of positive illusions is quite plentiful. Nonetheless, this point raises a potential problem with respect to mental health: if people hold mildly positive distortions of themselves, the world, and the future, how do they effectively make use of negative information that should be incorporated into their self-perceptions, beliefs, and decisions. That is, if people ignore, minimize, or explain away negative feedback, might they not keep themselves oblivious to important sources of negative feedback and thereby set themselves up for disappointment, faulty decision making, and the pursuit of activities that are ill-advised?

A first response to such a conundrum is to point out that positive illusions are typically modest. They depart only somewhat from objective or consensual indicators of personal attributes, degree of personal control, and the likelihood of a beneficent future. Moreover, positive illusions show a quite high degree of relative accuracy. Although an individual's self-perceptions may be mildly inflated, the individual will nontheless have a quite accurate sense of what his or her talents and shortcomings are. Relative accuracy may be sufficient for making effective use of feedback from one's environment. In addition, although the social environment, which includes family, friends, and acquaintances, may tolerate a modest degree of exaggerated self-perception, it is unlikely to tolerate major departures from reality, and thus, social feedback may also keep positive illusions within a narrow range.

There also appear to be times when people are more honest with themselves, during which they recognize and incorporate negative feedback into their self-perceptions and future plans. Research that distinguishes between deliberation and implementation suggests the conditions under which this may be true. Deliberation is that period of time when people debate their potential goals and actions. It typically involves careful appraisal of potentially competing goals, the weighing of pros and cons with respect to each goal, and a consideration of the feasibility of different goals. Deliberation is the kind of activity people engage in

when deciding whether to leave one job for another, whether to get a divorce or start a relationship, and the like. By contrast, implementation refers to the mindset that occurs when people are attempting to bring about personal goals. It is characterized by mustering motivation, resources, and beliefs in service of an already decided-upon goal or sequence of actions. It leads people in the direction of emotions, actions, and beliefs that favor goal achievement.

Deliberation appears to be a time when people's illusions about themselves, the world, and the future are abated or temporarily suspended in favor of more realistic processing of information. Implementation, by contrast, appears to be a time when people's positive illusions about themselves, the world, and the future, are actually exaggerated in service of goal-directed activity. When people are induced to think about an unresolved personal issue and are thus put into a deliberative mindset, they show very little evidence of positive illusion. By contrast, when people are induced to plan to bring about a specific goal that they have already selected, they show substantial evidence of positive illusion.

Investigations like these provide evidence for the idea that people experience time-outs from positive illusions during which they are more honest with themselves and more readily acknowledge their limitations and shortcomings. As such, these studies help resolve the paradox, "How are people able to function effectively in the world if their perceptions of themselves, the world, and the future are mildly positively distorted?" Specifically, such studies suggest that, at the point when people are making life choices that will determine their subsequent actions, they show relatively realistic thinking, but when they arrive at the point of needing to implement those same goals and decisions, they show more evidence of positive illusions.

VIII. WHO DEMONSTRATES POSITIVE ILLUSIONS?

As just noted, positive illusions appear to be characteristic of normal individuals, and they appear as well to be associated with the criteria normally indicative of mental health. In addition, they appear to have particular significance in enabling people to shore up their self-perceptions and views of personal control in the future in the face of traumatic events. The question remains whether only certain kinds of people with certain personal qualities are able to hold these positive illusions or to develop them in response to traumatic events, or whether they are more general characteristics of the human psyche. Or to put the issue another way, can positive illusions be thought of in a traitlike manner and are there individual differences associated with their development in response to stress? [*See* INDIVIDUAL DIFFERENCES IN MENTAL HEALTH.]

Research evidence suggests that most people may have the capacity to hold or develop positive illusions. Some of the research investigations just described, such as those involving college students evaluating their personal qualities in comparison to other college students, have shown that upward of 94% of the students demonstrate positive illusions. However, it is also possible to create circumstances in which almost no one demonstrates positive illusions, such as asking individuals under stress to deliberate about important life decisions and then to rate their personal qualities. Research like this suggests that positive illusions are more statelike than they are traitlike, given the substantial importance of environmental circumstances in influencing their manifestation. With this context in mind, however, it is clear that certain kinds of individuals may develop positive illusions more and in response to a broader array of circumstances than others. Individuals high in self-esteem can be expected to develop positive illusions, whereas individuals prone to depression or high in negative affectivity are less likely to do so.

There may also be cultural limitations on the form, content, and strength of positive illusions. Although positive illusions that center around self-aggrandizement, a sense of personal control, and unrealistic optimism about one's own future may be associated with mental health in Western cultures, they may not be in Eastern cultures and possibly some Latin cultures. The evidence that positive illusions about one's personal qualities may not be universal exists at two levels. First, these individual illusions prevalent in Western cultures are substantially muted or even reversed in non-Western populations, and as such, they are unlikely to be predictive of mental health. Moreover, it is becoming clear that the very nature of the self-concept, which positive illusions are thought to serve, is shaped in meaningful ways by the culture in which it is socialized. Thus, although the tasks of mental health—feeling good about oneself, developing positive social relationships, engaging in productive and creative work, combating stress effectively—would seem to have some cultural universality, the pathways for meeting those needs may be more varied.

It is possible that positive illusions exist in these other societies, but that the form they assume is culturally quite different. Whereas in Western societies, the individual is valued as an independent, active agent, in Eastern societies, interdependence, or the importance of the social group to individual functioning, is emphasized. Thus, in Western societies, one might expect to see positive illusions centering around self-perceptions, perceptions of control, and optimism about one's personal future, but in collectivist societies, one might instead find aggrandizement of the social group or larger culture, an exaggerated sense of the group's power, and unrealistic optimism about the group's ability to forestall subsequent negative events as more characteristic of shared positive illusions. The illusions that one is able to develop and sustain about the social group and its ability to protect the self from harm may also serve some of the same psychological functions that positive illusions centering around self-aggrandizement appear to serve in the West. A sense of meaning and comfort may be conferred by positive illusions about one's social group or culture. These issues are likely to occupy research attention in the future.

IX. POSITIVE ILLUSIONS, MENTAL HEALTH, AND PHYSICAL HEALTH

Increasingly, mental health experts are recognizing the significance of mental health for physical health. Negative emotions, such as depression, anxiety, and hostility, appear to play a role in health risks, including all-cause mortality and CHD risk. These relations do not appear to be due to behavioral changes associated with affective disorders, such as increased smoking or alcohol consumption, but rather, appear to be due to physiological changes associated with chronic problems in the management of affect.

Major depression, depressive symptoms, anxiety, and past depression have all been related to the likelihood of cardiac events, and depression is a risk factor for mortality following a heart attack, independent of disease severity. Both state depression and clinical depression have been related to sustained supressed immunity. Anger, especially cynical hostility, appears to be significant in the development of coronary artery disease and hypertension, at least among some individuals. Negative emotions can be associated with the activation of both the sympathetic adrenomedullary (SAM) system and the hypothalamic-pituitary-adrenocortical (HPA) axis. The former is manifested in increased blood pressure, heart rate, circulating levels of epinephrine and norepinephrine and constriction of peripheral blood vessels, and as such, SAM activation is believed to contribute to the development of coronary artery disease, essential hypertension, and susceptibility to infectious disease. The activation of HPA leads to high circulating levels of corticotrophin-releasing hormone, adrenocorticotrophic hormone, and cortisol, and HPA activation has been linked to atherosclerosis and chronic inflammatory responses, as are found in rheumatoid arthritis and reactivity of the airways among asthmatics. There may also be specific relationships between affective disorders and physical disease pathology. Anxiety appears to be more closely tied to thrombogenic cardiac events, whereas depressive symptoms have been associated with arrhythmias among patients under treatment for heart disease. [*See* ANGER; ANXIETY; HEART DISEASE: PSYCHOLOGICAL PREDICTORS.]

For the most part, this research has concentrated on the contribution of mental disturbance to the development of illness. Less research has focused on the potential facilitative role that positive emotional states may play. Moreover, much of the research has focused only on affective states, such as anxiety or depression, and not on cognitive beliefs that may shore up or, alternatively, undermine both mental and physical health. The positive illusions framework provides a potential basis for examining the contributing role of positive beliefs to health. Evidence suggestive of a facilitative effect of positive beliefs on health has emerged in recent years. A sense of personal control, commitment, and challenge appear to be associated with resilience in the face of stress. One study of business executives under high degrees of stress found that those who scored high on a hardiness measure were less likely to develop physical illnesses than those who scored low on the measure.

The potential relation of positive illusions to health gains additional interest value from the fact that some literature has suggested that realistic acceptance of one's deteriorating condition and eventual death represent psychologically adaptive responses to terminal illness. Such a response is thought to be psychologically adaptive in that it allows people to come to terms with the inevitable, to make final preparations for their departure, and to use the time to say goodbye to family and friends. This perspective is consistent with other models of coping with loss, which generally assume that people achieve a final stage of realistic acceptance. Failure to reach such a final stage is often regarded as a pathological adaptation to the inevitable.

Inasmuch as death would appear to represent a quite dramatic disconfirmation of positive illusions, terminal illness is a potentially important context within which to look at the adaptiveness of positive illusions. In one suggestive study conducted by Taylor and her associates, gay men who were HIV seropositive were evaluated for whether or not they demonstrated unrealistically optimistic beliefs about their likely future health. The study found that, even among these individuals who were facing terminal illness, optimism was associated with better psychological adjustment and with more active coping than were more realistic beliefs. Moreover, this optimism did not compromise health behaviors or risk-related sexual activity. However, these men had not been diagnosed with AIDS. It is possible that a more realistic perspective becomes more psychologically adaptive when one is faced with illness or the more immediate prospect of death. [*See* HIV/AIDS.]

To examine the competing perspectives regarding the psychological adaptiveness and physical health implications of positive illusions, Reed and his associates conducted a longitudinal study of men with AIDS and examined median survival time for participants who were low in realistic acceptance of their situation versus high in realistic acceptance. Those who realistically accepted the likelihood of death were more psychologically distressed and, more important, they died, on average, 9 months earlier than those who held on to the illusion that their situation might improve. The effect was not accounted for by time since diagnosis, self-reported health status, number of CD 4 T lymphocyte cells, psychological distress, initial diagnosing condition, or a variety of health behaviors and demographic factors. In summary, consistent with the positive illusions framework, realistic acceptance was not associated with positive adjustment to the terminal phase of illness, and it predicted a shorter time to death. Moreover, the findings were not accounted for by any documented emotional state such as depression or anxiety, suggesting that it was the contents of the beliefs themselves, a fundamentally cognitive phenomenon involving negative disease-specific expectancies, that led to the shorter terminal phase. A subsequent investigation largely confirmed these findings, and research with cancer patients has uncovered similar findings.

Future research may identify other disease states for which positive illusions or indicators of them are associated both with successful adjustment to the disease and with the course of disease progression. At present, however, several intermediate conclusions appear warranted. First, given the clear relation of mental distress to physical health outcomes, it is important to consider mental health in the context of physical health. Second, those states or personal characteristics that appear to foster mental health may be related to physical health as well. Third, to date, the relation of positive illusions to mental and physical health appears to be consistent, symmetric, and positive. Further evidence relating positive illusions to physical health states may well accumulate.

X. CAN POSITIVE ILLUSIONS BE TAUGHT?

The fact that positive illusions are associated with criteria indicative of mental health and the fact that they are also associated with beneficial physical health outcomes, leads to the question of whether research on positive illusions may be used to develop interventions with individuals attempting to cope with daily life stress, with particular traumatic stressful events, and with health events. Although some fledgling programs are currently being designed to investigate these issues, at present the answer to this question is unknown. Consequently, this avenue is an important direction for additional investigation. It should be noted that cognitive therapy for depression sometimes comes quite close to teaching positive illusions. Inducing people to view the world more positively, to view themselves more positively, and to think more positively about the future, perceptions that are at the core of cognitive therapy for depression, constitute suggestive evidence that such interventions may be beneficial for helping people overcome the dysphoria that is often associated with stress. [*See* Cognitive Therapy.]

BIBLIOGRAPHY

Brown, J. D. (1991). Accuracy and bias in self-knowledge. In C. R. Snyder & D. F. Forsyth (Eds.), *Handbook of social and clinical psychology: The health perspective* (pp. 158–178). New York: Pergamon Press.

Colvin, C. R., & Block, J. (1994). Do positive illusions foster mental health? An examination of the Taylor and Brown formulation. *Psychological Bulletin, 116*, 3–20.

Reed, G. M., Kemeny, M. E., Taylor, S. E., Wang, H.-Y. J., & Visscher, B. R. (1994). "Realistic acceptance" as a predictor of decreased survival time in gay men with AIDS. *Health Psychology, 13*, 299–307.

Ryff, C. D., & Singer, B. (1996). Psychological well-being: Meaning, measurement, and implications for psychotherapy research. *Psychotherapy and Psychosomatics, 65*, 14–23.

Scheier, M. F., & Carver, C. S. (1993). On the power of positive thinking: The benefits of being optimistic. *Current Directions in Psychological Science, 2*, 26–30.

Stipek, D. J. (1984). Young children's performance expectations: Logical analysis or wishful thinking? *Advances in Motivation and Achievement, 3*, 33–56.

Taylor, S. E. (1983). Adjustment to threatening events: A theory of cognitive adaptation. *American Psychologist, 38*, 1161–1173.

Taylor, S. E. (1989). *Positive illusions: Creative self-deception and the healthy mind.* New York: Basic Books.

Taylor, S. E., & Armor, D. A. (1996). Positive illusions and coping with adversity. *Journal of Personality, 64*, 873–898.

Taylor, S. E., & Brown, J. D. (1988). Illusion and well-being: A social psychological perspective on mental health. *Psychological Bulletin, 103*, 193–210.

Taylor, S. E., & Brown, J. D. (1994). Positive illusions and well-being revisited: Separating fact from fiction. *Psychological Bulletin, 116*, 21–27.

Posttraumatic Stress

Lisa H. Jaycox and Edna B. Foa

Allegheny University of the Health Sciences

Arousal Cluster of Posttraumatic Stress Disorder symptoms that includes concentration problems, anger, exaggerated startle response, sleep disturbance, and overalertness.

Avoidance Cluster of Posttraumatic Stress Disorder symptoms that includes behavioral and psychic avoidance, such as avoidance of thoughts, feelings, and reminders of the trauma, emotional numbing, loss of interest in activities, disconnection from others, psychogenic amnesia, and a sense of foreshortened future.

Diagnostic and Statistical Manual of Mental Disorder (DSM) A reference manual used by mental health professionals of descriptions and diagnostic criteria for psychiatric disorders.

Reexperiencing Cluster of Posttraumatic Stress Disorder symptoms that includes experiencing the trauma in the form of nightmares, flashbacks, or intrusive distressing thoughts, or becoming intensely emotionally upset or having physiological arousal on exposure to reminders of the trauma.

Trauma An event, witnessed or experienced, in which there is threat of death, injury, or physical integrity, and during which an individual feels terrified, horrified, or helpless.

POSTTRAUMATIC STRESS is a set of psychological and physical symptoms that follow a traumatic experience. In some cases, these symptoms persist beyond the immediate aftermath of the trauma and develop into Posttraumatic Stress Disorder (PTSD), an anxiety disorder that includes symptoms of arousal, avoidance, and reexperiencing, lasts for more than 1 month, and causes significant impairment in social or occupational functioning. This article discusses the stress symptoms that commonly follow trauma and describes PTSD and its prevalence. The theories underlying the development and maintenance of symptoms are discussed along with the treatments used for PTSD and their efficacy.

I. REACTIONS TO TRAUMATIC EVENTS

Psychologists and physicians have long been interested in vulnerability and resilience factors in reaction to extreme stress. Earlier accounts of posttrauma reactions focused on descriptions of cases. Spurred by inclusion of Posttraumatic Stress Disorder (PTSD) in the psychiatric diagnosis nomenclature in 1980, experimental research has examined many facets of the phenomenon.

In the *Diagnostic and Statistical Manual (DSM-IV)* published by the American Psychiatric Association in 1994, a trauma is defined as an experienced or witnessed event that involves threat of death or serious injury, and which evokes feelings of terror, horror, or helplessness. Thus, events such as anticipated death of a loved one, job loss, or divorce would not qualify as a trauma in this formulation. The *International Classification of Diseases* (*ICD-10*), published by the World Health Organization in 1992, describes a traumatic event as having an exceptionally threatening or catastrophic nature, which would be likely to cause pervasive distress in almost anyone. [*See* DSM-IV.]

The most common traumas studied are combat, sexual assault, sexual abuse in childhood, criminal victimization, torture, accidents, and natural disasters. Larger-scale traumas, such as mass migration, refugee camp experiences, and holocausts, have not yet been thoroughly researched. Clearly, such mass traumas would be expected to have considerable impact on those individuals directly affected as well as on their children, communities, and cultures.

A. Acute Reactions

A number of physical and psychological symptoms are considered common reactions immediately after a traumatic experience. Many trauma victims report being disoriented and anxious after a trauma and have difficulty sleeping and concentrating. Victims are often reluctant to talk about the trauma or deliberately contemplate it; nevertheless the traumatic memory intrudes on their thoughts quite frequently. In recognition of the severe distress and psychological dysfunction that often occur immediately after a trauma, a new diagnostic classification called Acute Stress Disorder (ASD) was adopted in the *DSM-IV* in 1994. The focus of this disorder is on dissociative features, and, consequently, the symptom criteria include at least three of the following: a sense of numbing, detachment, or lack of emotional responsiveness, a reduction in awareness of surroundings (e.g., being in a daze), derealization, depersonalization, and dissociative amnesia. Reexperiencing of the trauma, avoidance, and arousal, as defined in the criteria for PTSD, must also exist. A diagnosis of Acute Stress Disorder is warranted when such symptoms last between 2 days and 1 month, occur within 1 month of the trauma, and interfere significantly with daily functioning.

B. Posttraumatic Stress Disorder

Posttraumatic Stress Disorder, as described in *DSM-IV*, is a set of symptoms that begins after a trauma and persists for at least 1 month. The symptoms fall into three clusters. First, the individual must reexperience the trauma in one of the following ways: nightmares, flashbacks, or intrusive and distressing thoughts about the event; or intense emotional distress or physiological reactivity when reminded of the event. Second, the individual must have three of the following avoidance symptoms: avoidance of thoughts or feelings related to the trauma, avoidance of trauma reminders, psychogenic amnesia, emotional numbing, detachment or estrangement from others, decreased interest in leisure activities, or a sense of foreshortened future. Third, the individual must experience two of the following arousal symptoms: difficulty falling or staying asleep, difficulty concentrating, irritability or outbursts of anger, hypervigilance, or an exaggerated startle response. To meet diagnostic criteria for PTSD, the symptoms must cause significant impairment in daily functioning. These criteria provide a good operational definition of PTSD, as they describe the symptoms seen in most cases. However, the three categories of symptoms are not empirically validated as distinct symptom clusters. For instance, it is not clear that the symptoms of behavioral avoidance and emotional numbing are similar and belong in the same category.

The *ICD-10* criteria for PTSD also include some reexperiencing symptoms (nightmares, flashbacks, distress on exposure to reminders), actual or preferred avoidance of trauma reminders, and either an inability to recall important aspects of the trauma or sustained psychological sensitivity and arousal (sleep disturbance, hypervigilance, difficulty concentrating). These three criteria must all be met within 6 months of the traumatic event for a diagnosis to be given.

Several differences between the two definitions can be identified. First, the *DSM-IV* specifies a minimal number of symptoms that need to be observed to receive the diagnosis, whereas the *ICD-10* leaves more freedom for clinical judgment. The advantage of the former approach is its utility in clearly operationalizing the concept of PTSD. The disadvantage is its rigidity and the possibility that one symptom can determine diagnostic membership. Second, the *ICD-10* does not recognize the numbing symptoms, which together with flashbacks and nightmares are thought to be cardinal features of PTSD. Third, arousal symptoms are optional in the *ICD-10* but are required in the *DSM-IV*. Clinical observation and theoretical accounts of PTSD support the importance of these symptoms and render the *ICD-10* diagnostic criteria less satisfactory.

C. Course of PTSD

The course of PTSD is variable. For the majority of individuals, symptoms begin immediately after the trauma, although some appear to have a delayed reaction. During the first 3 months after the trauma, the individual is said to have acute PTSD, whereas chronic PTSD is defined as symptoms persisting beyond 3 months. Symptoms can fluctuate over time between diagnosis of PTSD, subthreshold symptoms, and few or no symptoms. Recovery is affected by a number of factors, including perception of oneself and one's surroundings, actual social support, life stress, coping style, and personality.

II. MEASURES OF PTSD

A number of measures have been developed to assess PTSD, including clinical interviews and self-report instruments. These measures vary widely in terms of the target symptoms, administration time, and the samples used for ascertaining psychometric properties. Adult assessment tools are reviewed in the next section. Although some measures have also been developed for children, they are outside the scope of this article. [*See* Clinical Assessment.]

A. Interviews

The Structured Clinical Interview for *DSM* (SCID) is believed to be the most widely used diagnostic interview. Its major disadvantage, however, is that it does not provide a measure of symptom severity. Several other interviews that provide information of both diagnostic status and symptom severity are available. Two interviews are becoming quite widely used in PTSD research. The first is the Clinician-Administered PTSD Scale (CAPS) that yields separate scores for frequency and intensity for each symptom. Disadvantages of this interview include a long administration time and validation on military veterans only. The second interview, the PTSD Symptom Scale Interview (PSS-I), includes a combined frequency/severity rating for each of the 17 PTSD symptoms in the *DSM-IV* and thus yields both a diagnosis and a continuous severity rating. Unlike the CAPS, the PSS-I takes only about 15 to 20 minutes to administer and was validated on female assault victims.

B. Self-Report Measures

Several self-report scales have been developed to assess symptoms of PTSD. The first was the Revised Impact of Events Scale (RIES), which yields two factors: intrusion and avoidance. A revised version of the RIES added hyperarousal items, but has shown mixed results in reliability studies and, like its predecessor, does not correspond fully to the *DSM-IV* PTSD symptoms. Two scales, the Mississippi Scale and the Penn Inventory, have excellent psychometric properties in veteran samples but do not provide information about diagnostic status because they do not fully correspond to the *DSM-IV* defining symptoms.

The PTSD Symptom Scale-Self-Report (PSS-SR) and its successor, the PTSD Diagnostic Scale (PDS), provide information about each of the 17 *DSM-IV* symptoms, yielding both diagnostic and severity information. The PDS is the only self-report instrument that assesses *all DSM-IV* criteria, including information about the nature of the traumatic event and the level of functional interference, in addition to information about PTSD diagnosis and symptom severity. It was validated in a sample of victims of a wide range of traumas and evidenced sound psychometric properties, and thus can be used in studies of various trauma populations.

III. PREVALENCE OF PTSD

Lifetime prevalence of PTSD in the general population is estimated at 9%, with up to a third of these cases having chronic PTSD. Among trauma victims, the rate is much higher, estimated at 24%. However, the rates of PTSD tend to vary considerably among different types of trauma. For instance, estimates of the lifetime prevalence of PTSD in Vietnam War veterans range from 27 to 65%; in civilian populations exposed to terrorism and torture, prevalence ranges from 33 to 54%. Between 35% and 94% of victims of violent assaults manifest PTSD. In contrast, accidents and natural disasters appear to produce lower rates of PTSD, 4.6 to 59%, depending on the event studied and the degree of exposure. Even individuals with little or no direct exposure to the trauma can develop PTSD; this phenomenon has been referred to as the "ripples outward" effect. Importantly, certain occupations are at risk for PTSD by virtue of increased probability of repeated direct exposure to trauma; between 9% and 26% of professionals such as police, nurses, and firefighters develop PTSD in reaction to stressors experienced on the job.

Prevalence in certain vulnerable populations is much higher than in the general population, presumably because individuals in these groups have been exposed to more traumatic experiences. These include populations seeking outpatient psychotherapy and those in substance abuse clinics. Women appear to be somewhat more likely than men to develop PTSD after trauma, 10.4% versus 5%, respectively. As noted earlier, the prevalence of emotional difficulties after mass traumas, such as refugee camp experiences or holocausts, has not been systematically studied. [*See* EPIDEMIOLOGY: PSYCHIATRIC.]

IV. VULNERABILITY AND RESILIENCY FACTORS

Factors implicated in posttrauma reactions can be divided into three categories: pretrauma variables, variables related to the trauma itself, and posttrauma variables.

Research on pretrauma demographic variables has not identified reliable predictors of who will develop chronic PTSD with one exception: women are somewhat more likely to manifest PTSD than men after experiencing a similar trauma. In contrast, it appears that poor psychological and social functioning prior to the trauma renders the individual vulnerable to developing chronic symptoms. For instance, prior hospitalization and a history of drug abuse were found to be associated with a more severe posttrauma reaction. Also, a history of traumatic events in childhood or adulthood predicts a more severe response to a new trauma.

The nature of the trauma itself also appears to affect recovery. First, traumas differ in their likelihood of producing PTSD; rape, for example, is more likely to produce persistent symptoms than a natural disaster. Second, given a specific trauma (e.g., rape), injury and perceived threat of death produce more severe and persistent reactions. [*See* RAPE.]

Several posttrauma factors have been found to exacerbate symptoms. It appears that dissociation (emotional numbing, amnesia, depersonalization) shortly after a trauma hinders recovery. Also, on average, assault victims who exhibit more severe initial reactions

to the trauma also show more symptoms later on. Thus, individuals seem to differ in how strongly they are affected by a similar trauma, and their initial reaction is associated with later psychopathology.

Evidence on the role of social support as facilitating or hindering recovery is equivocal. It seems that negative reactions from others, such as blame, increase posttrauma psychopathology, but, unfortunately, positive reactions do not show the expected positive effects. Excessive anger or guilt after the trauma also appears to block readjustment. Additional longitudinal research on the factors that promote resilience to trauma are clearly needed.

V. CONCOMITANT PROBLEMS FOLLOWING TRAUMA

Traumatized individuals not only exhibit ASD or PTSD symptoms, but also depression, substance abuse, anxiety, dissociation, and physical health problems.

The rate of use and abuse of drugs and alcohol, including nicotine, in traumatized individuals is higher than in the general population. There are at least two explanations for this finding. First, traumatized individuals may choose to cope with their symptoms by increasing substance use. Second, substance abuse may increase the risk of being exposed to a traumatic experience. [*See* SUBSTANCE ABUSE.]

Many individuals report symptoms of depression after a traumatic event, such as sadness, lack of energy, diminished interest in leisure activities, hopelessness, sleeplessness, and eating disturbances. Although some of these symptoms overlap with the defining symptoms of PTSD (e.g., markedly diminished interest in activities), the two disorders are separate entities and both can develop independently as a response to a traumatic experience. [*See* DEPRESSION.]

The incidence of comorbid anxiety disorders is also elevated among individuals with PTSD. For example, lifetime comorbidity of panic disorder in Vietnam veterans with PTSD was 21% in females and 8% in males, versus 1.5 to 3.5% in the general population. The lifetime prevalence of obsessive–compulsive disorder was found to be 13% in females and 10% in males, as compared with 2.5% in the general population. [*See* OBSESSIVE–COMPULSIVE DISORDER; PANIC ATTACKS.]

There is a greater frequency of physical health problems among trauma victims than in the general population, especially among those who develop chronic PTSD. Trauma victims have higher rates of gastrointestinal disorders and pelvic or abdominal pain, and visit the doctor more often than the general population. In the aftermath of rape and child sexual abuse, gynecological and psychosexual problems such as vaginal discharge, dysmennorhea, dyspareunia, vaginismus, and pelvic pain have also been noted.

VI. THEORIES ON THE DEVELOPMENT AND MAINTENANCE OF PTSD

Reactions to trauma have long captured the interest of theorists of psychopathology. Janet's 1889 theory of reactions to trauma has influenced both early and contemporary conceptualizations. Janet proposed that when confronted with a traumatic event that besieges the victim with an overabundance of intense thoughts and feelings, too numerous or intense to integrate, some individuals selectively attend away from the trauma to trauma-irrelevant thoughts and feelings. Thus, ideas related to the trauma remain split off or dissociated from normal consciousness and become "fixed." Although out of consciousness, these "fixed ideas" remain part of the victim's ideational content, and therefore continue to exert influence over his or her thought, mood, and behavior in the form of fragmented reliving of the trauma such as visual images, somatic states, emotional conditions, or behavioral reenactment.

A. Psychoanalytic Theories

Freud wrestled with understanding the influence of traumatic experiences on the individual's psyche. In early writings, he was influenced by Janet's theory on the strength of the emotional reactions that are produced by a traumatic experience and that force the victim to become fixated on the trauma. Later, Freud abandoned the dissociation view and proposed that the persistence of trauma reactions reflects an association between the traumatic event and childhood repressed conflicts, ideas, or impulses, and the efforts to prevent conscious awareness of them. He also coined the concept of "repetition compulsion" to explain trauma reexperiencing, proposing that because of the need to keep it away from consciousness, the individual is forced to repeat aspects of the trauma as a

contemporary experience rather than as a memory of it. Influenced by World War I experiences, Freud refocused on the external reality, and, in the spirit of Janet, viewed the emotional upheaval generated by the trauma as the source of traumatic neurosis. He suggested that the intensity of the trauma, the inability to find conscious expressions for it, and the unpreparedness of the individual cause a breach to the stimulus barrier and overwhelm the defense mechanisms. More recent theorists have proposed that the developmental level and ego resources available to the victim are central to the manner in which the trauma is experienced and to the production of symptoms. For instance, a young child, easily overwhelmed and flooded with emotion, may experience complete helplessness in the face of trauma, whereas a mature adult would be more likely to respond through emotional numbing and cognitive constriction. Psychoanalytic theorists and practitioners focus on the need to help the victim acknowledge and bear the trauma and the resulting psychic damage, and develop coping mechanisms such that the memories of the trauma are incorporated into his or her current experience.

B. Cognitive and Behavioral Theories

Several schools of thought inspired cognitive–behavioral theories of PTSD. The first is learning theory, which explains PTSD symptoms in terms of instrumental and classical conditioning. The learning model that most directly influenced cognitive–behavioral treatments (CBT) aimed at anxiety reduction was Mowrer's two-factor theory. First, Mowrer proposed that fear is acquired through classical conditioning, where a neutral stimulus comes to evoke fear through its pairing with an aversive stimulus. Applying this theory to explain PTSD symptoms, neutral stimuli (e.g., supermarket) that were present during the trauma are presumed to acquire the ability to elicit fear through their associations with the danger stimuli (e.g., gun). Through the processes of generalization and second-order conditioning, stimuli similar to those present during the trauma also come to evoke fear. For instance, the stimuli all men, being alone, and the word *rape* can all acquire the capacity to cause anxiety. In Mowrer's second stage, avoidance behavior is established through the process of operant conditioning. That is, an individual learns to reduce trauma-related anxiety through avoidance of, or escape from, the feared stimuli. Escape and avoidance behaviors are negatively reinforced because avoidance diminishes the aversive fear state. [See BEHAVIOR THERAPY.]

Cognitive–behavioral therapy of PTSD has also been influenced by cognitive theory. Cognitive theory assumes that the interpretation of events, rather than events themselves, underlies emotional reactions. Accordingly, an event can be interpreted in different ways and consequently can evoke different emotions. Aaron Beck and colleagues suggest that trauma victims who manifest chronic persistent anxiety are unable to discriminate between safe and unsafe signals, and consequently their thinking is dominated by the perception of danger. They also suggest that traumatic fear can be maintained through a sense of incompetence to handle stressful events.

Other cognitive theorists have postulated that cognitive schemas are disrupted after victimization. A schema is a meaning structure that guides the perception, organization, and interpretation of incoming information. Common to these theories is the supposition that a traumatic experience requires cognitive modification and that such modification is accomplished by assimilation and accommodation. Accordingly, the victim must either assimilate the traumatic experience into preexisting schemas, or, more often, change schemas to accommodate the traumatic experience. In her 1992 book, Janoff-Bulman took the position that people in general hold the assumptions: "the world is benevolent, the world is meaningful, and self is worthy," and these assumptions are incompatible with a traumatic experience. Building on Janoff-Bulman's ideas, other theorists suggest that the following areas are of particular relevance: safety, dependency/trust of self and others, power, esteem, intimacy, and independence.

Coming from the psychoanalytic tradition, Horowitz integrated psychoanalytical and information processing notions in his 1986 book, suggesting that people have a basic need to match trauma-related information with their "inner models based on old information." The process of recovery entails the repeated revision of both trauma-related information and the inner models until they agree, which Horowitz referred to as the "completion tendency."

Foa and Kozak integrated cognitive and learning theories to explain the development and maintenance of pathological anxiety in what they called emotional processing theory. In their 1986 paper, fear is conceived as a cognitive structure or a program for es-

caping danger which includes representations of fear stimuli, fear responses, and their meaning. Pathological fear, they suggested, is distinguished from normal fear in that it includes erroneous associations and evaluations. Emotional processing theory views anxiety disorders as representing distinctive fear structures in memory, and the persistence of anxiety symptoms is conceived as reflecting impairment in emotional processing. Accordingly, PTSD is construed as reflecting a fear memory that contains erroneous associations and evaluations, whereas a normal trauma memory reflects associations and evaluations that better match reality. First, a pathological PTSD structure contains excessive response representations that are reflected in the PTSD symptoms. Second, this structure includes erroneous stimulus–stimulus associations that do not accurately represent the world. For example, the pathological fear structure of a woman who was raped at gunpoint by a bald man would contain an association between "bald men" and "gun." In reality, however, bald men are not more likely to carry guns or to rape than men with a full head of hair. Third, the structure also includes erroneous associations between harmless stimuli such as "bald," "home," "suburbs," and the meaning of "dangerous." Being raped one time while at home in the suburbs does not tangibly increase the chance of encountering violence in that environment. Fourth, the structure includes erroneous associations between harmless stimuli and escape or avoidance responses. For example, the victim who was raped by the bald man would tend to run away from such men. In reality, however, running away from "bald men" is not likely to enhance safety. These erroneous associations would lead to mistakenly interpreting the world as entirely dangerous.

Another set of erroneous associations and evaluations is the interpretation of the victim's response representations. It is thought that the victim's responses during and after the trauma, and in particular the PTSD symptoms, are interpreted to mean self-incompetence. In summary, emotional processing theory hypothesizes that two major pathological concepts underlie PTSD: the world as entirely dangerous, and the self as entirely inept.

C. Psychobiological Approaches

Psychophysiological, neurohormonal, neuroanatomical, and immunological changes have been observed in animals exposed to extreme stress and in trauma victims who developed PTSD (van der Kolk, McFarlane, & Weisaeth, 1996). These changes have been hypothesized to disregulate responses to incoming information and to inhibit successful processing of traumatic memories.

The normal stress response upon exposure to a high-magnitude stressor is a complex neurohormonal response, including the release of catecholamines (e.g., epinephrine and norepinephrine), serotonin, endogenous opioids, and hormones of the hypothalamus, pituitary, or adrenal gland (e.g., cortisol, vasopressin, oxytocin). Normally, the introduction of a stressor produces intense and rapid stress responses, and these dissipate quickly after the removal of the stressor. However, after prolonged exposure to stress, the stress responses become disregulated. [*See* CATECHOLAMINES AND BEHAVIOR; PSYCHONEUROIMMUNOLOGY.]

Theorists propose that PTSD reflects a failure to regulate autonomic reactions to stimuli such that the individual either experiences hyperreactivity or "shutting down" and emotional numbing. Individuals with PTSD show hyperreactivity, as measured by heart rate, skin conductance, and blood pressure, in reaction to reminders of traumatic events. This disregulation of the emotional and physiological responsiveness occurs with specific reminders of the trauma as well as in reaction to intense but neutral stimuli, signifying a loss of stimulus discrimination. In addition, the individual may come to fear his or her emotional reactions because of being able to do little to control them. [*See* REACTIVITY.]

Neurohormonal changes in individuals with PTSD have also been found. First, prolonged stress causes depletion of the noradrenergic system, such that receptors become hypersensitive to any new release of norepinephrine. This noradrenergic hyperreactivity is linked to the increased arousal and startle of PTSD. The high levels of norepinephrine are proposed to inhibit the release of corticotrophin-releasing hormone and thereby inhibit the entire hypothalamic-pituitary-adrenocortical axis. This inhibition, in turn, produces a deficiency in endogenous opioids. Some theories postulate that the reexperiencing symptoms of PTSD cause a burst in the release of endogenous opioids and therefore make up for this deficiency. These endogenous opioids are thought to produce an artificial numbing or calmness, another hallmark of PTSD. Additional theories propose that cortisol responses are lowered in retraumatized individuals and that serotonin levels may decrease in response to prolonged inescapable stress.

In addition to psychophysiological and neurohormonal factors, specific brain abnormalities have recently been detected in individuals with PTSD. One system that is implicated in the disorder is the limbic system, which is thought to function in memory and in emotional reactions to incoming stimuli. One area in the limbic system, the hippocampus, is presumed to record spatial and temporal aspects of experiences in memory. Researchers have noted decreased hippocampal volume in trauma victims with PTSD compared with those without PTSD. One possible explanation for this finding is that individuals with smaller hippocampuses are more likely to develop PTSD; a more likely interpretation of these results is that increased cortisol activity causes shrinkage, because cortisol is toxic to the hippocampus. [*See* LIMBIC SYSTEM.]

A second area in the limbic system, the amygdala, also appears to be altered in individuals with PTSD. The amygdala is thought to assign meaning to incoming stimulation by integrating memory images with emotional experiences associated with those memories, guiding emotional behavior. A single intense stimulation of the amygdala appears to alter the limbic physiology such that a "kindling" effect occurs. That is, the behavior that follows may be predominantly either "fight" or "flight," and a pattern of conditioned behavior is set up such that there is limited processing of incoming information before the response is initiated.

VII. PSYCHOLOGICAL AND PHARMACOLOGICAL INTERVENTIONS

Several psychological interventions have been used with trauma victims, including supportive counseling individually or in groups, brief dynamic psychotherapy, hypnotherapy, pharmacotherapy, and cognitive–behavioral therapy. As recently reviewed by Foa and Meadows, although a variety of psychological interventions are used routinely with trauma victims, controlled outcome studies have tended to focus on cognitive–behavioral treatments such as systematic desensitization, exposure, and anxiety management. Nevertheless, hypnotherapy and psychodynamic therapy have also shown promise in the few studies examining their efficacy.

A. Early Interventions

The popular supposition among trauma theories is that for recovery to occur after a traumatic experience, special processing efforts should take place. This view has prompted the development of early intervention programs. These programs have focused on education, debriefing after trauma, and training professionals at risk (e.g., police). Usually, "critical incident stress debriefing" is conducted in groups, such as emergency workers, and focuses on education about common reactions to traumatic experiences, encouraging trauma victims to process their experiences in a group setting. Although such programs have become routine in many places, little is known about their efficacy. In fact, some experts have raised concerns that such programs could interfere with rather than facilitate the natural recovery process.

The recognition that victims who exhibit severe reactions immediately after the trauma are more likely to develop chronic dysfunction has prompted researchers to implement interventions that aim to prevent chronic PTSD. Foa and colleagues conducted a study to compare PTSD severity of female assault victims, who received a brief prevention program (four individual therapy sessions), to that of victims who underwent an assessment procedure. Victims who received the brief prevention program had less severe PTSD and depressive symptoms 2 months after the assault. Clearly, more studies of this type are needed before confidence in prevention efforts can be established.

B. Cognitive–Behavioral Therapies

Currently, five cognitive–behavioral interventions are in use for PTSD: Prolonged Exposure, cognitive therapy, Stress Inoculation Training, Cognitive Processing Therapy, and Eye Movement Desensitization and Reprocessing.

1. Prolonged Exposure (PE)

This is a set of procedures that involves confrontation with feared stimuli, either in vivo or in imagination. With PTSD, exposure therapy typically includes repeated reliving of the traumatic event in imagination and actual confrontation with feared situations and objects that have been avoided because they are reminders of the trauma but are not intrinsically dangerous.

As discussed earlier, the theoretical basis of PE lies in learning and emotional-processing theories. Foa and Kozak have proposed that successful therapy involves correcting the pathological elements of the fear structure, and that this corrective process is the essence of emotional processing. They further suggest that regardless of the type of therapeutic intervention used, two conditions are required for fear reduction. First, the fear structure must be activated through introduction of fear-relevant information. If the fear structure is not activated (fear is not evoked), the structure would not be available for modification. Second, during exposure, information that is incompatible with the existing pathological elements (e.g., fear reduction) must be provided so that the pathological fear structure can be corrected. Specifically, exposure researchers hypothesize that repeated reliving promotes several cognitive changes. First, it promotes habituation of anxiety associated with the trauma memory, and this habituation disconfirms the victim's erroneous belief that anxiety will stay forever and therefore lead to disastrous consequences. Second, reliving promotes discrimination between "remembering" the trauma and "encountering" it again, thus reinforcing the realization that remembering itself is not dangerous. Third, repeated exposure promotes differentiation between the trauma and similar but safe situations, disconfirming the idea that the world is extremely dangerous. Fourth, it promotes the association between PTSD symptoms and a sense of mastery, rather than incompetence. Finally, repeated recounting of the trauma narrative helps to organize the narrative and thereby to facilitate the integration of the trauma memory.

Several controlled studies on exposure have shown their usefulness in treating PTSD. Whereas studies on veterans showed only modest improvement, two studies with female rape victims showed more improvement. Foa and colleagues found that exposure (imaginal and in vivo) was effective in eliminating PTSD in 55% of rape victims with chronic PTSD compared with 45% of those who received supportive counseling. Superior results were found in a second study: about 70% of victims who received Prolonged Exposure lost their PTSD diagnosis, and none of the women in a wait-list group lost their diagnosis. These treatment effects were maintained at 6-month follow-up.

2. Stress Inoculation Training (SIT)

This intervention consists of training victims to handle anxiety with several skills for anxiety management:

relaxation, thought stopping, assertiveness, cognitive therapy, coping self-statements, and guided imagery. Although the direct goal of anxiety management techniques is to teach patients techniques to manage their anxiety, the successful acquisition of such techniques can have indirect effects on the victim's schemas of self and the world. Specifically, the victim's experience of being able to control the anxiety fosters a more positive self-image and thereby modifies the perception of the world as overwhelmingly dangerous. Several studies point to the efficacy of this program used alone or in combination with other techniques. For example, the two studies on rape victims reported earlier found that SIT significantly reduced PTSD, to a degree comparable to that of exposure.

Researchers believed that if PE and SIT are quite, but not completely, successful in ameliorating PTSD symptoms, a program that combined these two treatments would yield superior results. However, research does not support this view: combined programs were helpful for female assault victims, but not more than exposure or stress inoculation alone.

3. Cognitive Therapy

Cognitive techniques are often incorporated into anxiety management programs that teach patients to examine and change systematically maladaptive thoughts that can lead to negative responses. Cognitive therapy involves the use of discourse, in which the patient is taught to identify the beliefs underlying the fear, to examine whether they are distorted or accurately reflect reality, and to replace mistaken or dysfunctional beliefs with more realistic, functional ideas about the ability of the patient to cope with stress and the dangerousness of the world. One possible benefit of cognitive restructuring is that it addresses directly beliefs underlying emotions other than fear, such as anger and guilt. Early investigations of this technique revealed some promise in the use of this therapy to reduce symptoms of PTSD in rape victims. [*See* Cognitive Therapy.]

4. Cognitive Processing Therapy (CPT)

Another cognitive–behavioral program called Cognitive Processing Therapy is described in Resick and Schnicke's 1992 book. It involves cognitive restructuring and exposure through writing about the trauma. The cognitive therapy is geared toward correcting maladaptive cognitions associated with rape, such as power, safety, and esteem. In one study, on the aver-

age, victims who received CPT reported 40% symptom reduction, and these gains were maintained over time. More studies are needed to establish the efficacy of this relatively new treatment.

5. Eye Movement Desensitization and Reprocessing (EMDR)

This therapy, described by Shapiro in 1995, is a form of exposure with a cognitive emphasis, accompanied by guided eye movements. The studies that have evaluated the efficacy of this treatment produced equivocal results. Some show good results, but others show no improvement. Because these studies have many methodological problems, it is difficult to determine the validity of the findings. Further well-controlled studies are needed before a definite conclusion about the value of EMDR can be made.

C. Pharmacotherapy

Many medications have been used for the treatment of PTSD, but only a few have been systematically studied. Most of these have used male combat veterans, and thus the efficacy of pharmacotherapy for other traumatized populations is largely unknown. Tricyclic antidepressants have been used in an attempt to reduce locus coeruleus overactivity and noradrenergic disregulation found in PTSD, with equivocal results. Amitriptyline and imipramine have shown modest reductions in PTSD symptoms in comparison with placebo in double-blind studies with male veterans. In contrast, desipramine failed to show efficacy. One study of fluoxetine, a selective serotonin reuptake inhibitor used to regulate serotonergic dysfunction in individuals with PTSD, found it to be effective in reducing symptoms of PTSD, especially in trauma victims other than Vietnam veterans.

Other medications that have been tested include anticonvulsants such as carbamazepine and valproic acid; but no double-blind studies have been conducted to date. Beta-adrenergic blockers such as propanolol have shown promise in reducing aggressivity and arousal symptoms in open studies, and alpha$_2$-adrenergic agonists, such as clonidine, appear to be effective through their suppression of locus coeruleus activity.

Finally, benzodiazepines have been widely used to suppress anxiety and are believed to reduce PTSD symptoms by reducing limbic system kindling and reversing neurochemical changes in the locus coeruleus and hypothalamus. However, the rebound anxiety and withdrawal symptoms associated with benzodiazepines can be problematic.

In summary, most of our knowledge about efficacy of pharmacotherapy for PTSD is confounded by the restricted samples used in existing studies. Most were conducted on Vietnam veterans, whose symptoms are particularly resistant to all types of treatments, and therefore the present results may underestimate the efficacy of this treatment. [*See* PSYCHOPHARMACOLOGY.]

D. Hypnotherapy and Psychodynamic Psychotherapy

Hypnotherapy uses heightened concentration and focused attention to facilitate treatment related to trauma. It is based on the supposition that individuals with PTSD are unknowingly entering trance states when they reexperience the trauma and that hypnotherapy can help them learn how to control their trance states and digest the dissociated traumatic experience in a controlled manner. One study found hypnosis to be as effective as psychodynamic psychotherapy and a type of exposure called systematic desensitization. More studies of this technique are needed before conclusions can be drawn about the usefulness of hypnotherapy. [*See* HYPNOSIS AND THE PSYCHOLOGICAL UNCONSCIOUS.]

Psychodynamic psychotherapy has also been used to help individuals recover from trauma. It focuses on intrapsychic conflict about the trauma rather than on resolution of specific symptoms of PTSD. The methods used are in some respects similar to those used in cognitive–behavioral therapy, as these interventions focus on helping the victims process the traumatic experience and on teaching them how to tolerate anxiety. Both individual and group therapies have been used, and some preliminary studies suggest the utility of these interventions.

BIBLIOGRAPHY

American Psychiatric Association. (1994). *Diagnostic and statistical manual* (4th ed.). Washington, DC: American Psychiatric Press.

Davidson, J. R. T., & Foa, E. B. (Eds.). (1993). *Post-traumatic stress disorder: DSM-IV and beyond*. Washington, DC: American Psychiatric Press.

Foa, E. B., & Kozak, M. J. (1986). Emotional processing of fear: Exposure to corrective information. *Psychological Bulletin, 99*, 20–35.

Foa, E. B., & Meadows, E. A. (1997). Psychosocial treatments for post-traumatic stress disorder: A critical review. In J. Spence (Ed.), *Annual review of psychology*. Palo Alto, CA: Annual Reviews, Inc.

Foa, E. B., & Riggs, D. S. (1993). Post-traumatic stress disorder in rape victims. In J. Oldham, M. B. Riba, & A. Tasman (Eds.), *American psychiatric press review of psychiatry* (Vol. 12, pp. 273–303). Washington, DC: American Psychiatric Press.

Horowitz, M. J. (1986). *Stress response syndromes* (2nd edition). Northvale, NJ: Jason Aronson, Inc.

Janet, P. (1889). *L'Automatisme psychologique*. Paris: Felix Alcan. (Reprinted 1973, Paris, Societe Pierre Janet.)

Janoff-Bulman, R. (1992). *Shattered assumptions: Towards a new psychology of trauma*. New York: Free Press.

Kessler, R. C., Sonnega, A., Bromet, E., Hughes, M., & Nelson, C. B. (1995). Post-traumatic stress disorder in the National Comorbidity Survey. *Archives of General Psychiatry, 52*, 1048–1060.

Resick, P. A., & Schnicke, M. K. (1992). *Cognitive processing therapy for sexual assault survivors: A treatment manual*. Newbury Park, CA: Sage.

Shapiro, F. (1995). *Eye movement desensitization and reprocessing: Basic principles, protocols, and procedures*. New York: Guilford Press.

van der Kolk, B. A., McFarlane, A. C., & Weisaeth, L. (Eds.). (1996). *Traumatic stress: The effect of overwhelming experience on mind, body, and society*. New York: Guilford Press.

World Health Organization. (1993). *ICD-10: The ICD-10 classification of mental and behavioural disorders: Diagnostic criteria for research*. Geneva, Switzerland: Author.

Poverty and Mental Health

Judith R. Smith

Fordham University
Teachers College, Columbia University

Andrea Marie Bastiani

Teachers College, Columbia University

Jeanne Brooks-Gunn

Teachers College, Columbia University

Income-to-Needs Ratio A ratio of family income to family size based on the poverty threshold. Poverty is defined as 1.0. Those living in deep poverty are at 50% or less than the poverty line or an income-to-needs of .5. Families who are just above the poverty threshold (between 100% and 150% of the poverty threshold, 1 to 1.5 income-to-needs) are often called the near-poor.

Life Stress A state that occurs when an individual perceives that the demands of a given situation, one that requires adaptation, exceeds their ability to cope with the situation.

Pathways Mechanisms through which variables (such as poverty) indirectly influence (mental health) outcomes.

Poverty Threshold The official U.S. Poverty Threshold is used to determine whether a family is poor or not poor. The threshold was originally developed based on expected food expenditures (thrifty food basket) for families of particular sizes; this number was then multiplied by a factor of three, because, in 1959, food constituted about one third of household expenses. The poverty threshold in the United States is absolute, not relative. Families whose incomes are above the threshold are classified as "not poor," and families below the threshold as "poor," in any given year. Poverty thresholds take into account household size and are adjusted each year for the cost of living.

Risk An individual is said to be at psychological "risk" or in jeopardy of maladjustment when there are environmental, psychological, and/or physical stressors in her or his life.

Social Support Perceived or actual relations/connections at the individual (friends, family, clergy, therapist, etc.) or community level (church, school, social service agency, etc.), seen by the individual as resources for emotional well-being and maintenance.

Socioeconomic Status (SES) A composite index variable, generally demarcated as "high," "middle," or "low," indicating the level of economic resources, occupational status, or prestige within a community, and level of education attained.

POVERTY decreases access to resources that are important for well-being (food, basic health care, quality education, opportunities for leisure or cultural activities) and increases experiences that pose risks to maintaining mental health (family stress, poor quality child care, environmental hazards, unsafe neighborhoods, and criminal victimization). Income level has long been associated with the physical and mental health outcomes of adults. Furthermore, the association between health and income has been found across the income distribution, not solely in comparisons of poor and nonpoor populations. In 1990, Adler and colleagues reviewed studies that demonstrated a graded association between socioeconomic status (SES) and health. Low SES is associated with higher mortality rates, as well as with greater susceptibility to malignant neoplasms, infectious and parasitic diseases, and diseases of the respiratory, digestive, and circulatory system. Low SES is also associated with higher rates of depressive symptoms, as well as clinical depression, increased hostility, and greater exposure to stress, all of which are linked to poor health outcomes. Depression and hostility are linked to risk of coronary health disease. Persons experiencing heightened levels of life stress are at greater risk for gastrointestinal disorders, heart attacks, and susceptibility to infectious disease. Questions that remain, however, include the size and severity of the association between poverty per se and mental health, the potential existence of similar effects in children and adolescents, and the pathways through which income might influence emotional well-being. Mental disorders may result from prolonged exposure to poverty, and they may also cause economic failure and low income. More research is needed to evaluate both of these models.

I. POVERTY AND MENTAL HEALTH

To understand the links between mental health and poverty, one must understand issues related to (a) measurement and incidence of income poverty, (b) consequences of poverty on mental health at each stage of development, (c) pathways by which income might influence mental health outcomes; (d) consequences of mental disorders on earning capacity, and (e) programs and policies that can mediate poverty and the stresses that accompany economic disadvantage.

Measurement of whether or not an individual is "poor" is based on total family income in a given year in relation to the poverty threshold. The United States has an official poverty threshold which takes into account the individual's household size and is adjusted for the cost of living. In 1996, for example, the poverty threshold for a family of three people was a little under $13,000. Families whose incomes are above the threshold are classifed as "not poor," and families below the threshold as "poor." Because the poverty

threshold focuses solely on adequacy of income, key aspects of well-being are omitted and are not a direct measure of how well the basic needs of the individuals in a family are being met. It is therefore subject to misrepresenting economic well-being. On the one hand, the official poverty level excludes noncash assistance, such as food stamps or housing subsidies, which can lead to overcounting the number of people who cannot meet their needs. Yet, because it does not account for the quality of the home and neighborhood in terms of safety, social support, or cognitive stimulation from parents to their children, some families counted as nonpoor will actually be living in conditions that could negatively affect mental health and well-being. The National Research Council's 1995 report proposed a new poverty measure to identify more accurately those living in poverty. The proposed measure would take into account the value of in-kind benefits (i.e., food stamps, housing vouchers) and count net earnings after deducting for taxes and work expenses.

Mental health is defined as the absence of mental illness and the ability to form peer and family relationships, function in school or work, and cope with stress. A developmental perspective conceptualizes the individual's experience of mental health problems on a continuum. On the one end, individuals may experience little or no symptoms of mental illness; on the other, individuals may experience mental health problems so extreme as to warrant clinical diagnosis. Similarly, poverty exerts its influence on the mental health of individuals at both the symptomalogical and clinical levels, and these effects can be seen for children, adolescents, and adults. Diagnostic manuals used by clinicians identify the experience of financial hardship and/or of living in poverty as a severe psychosocial stressor. Clinicians must document the severity of an environmental stressor in relation to the development of a clinical disorder, the recurrence of prior mental illness, or the exacerbation of an already existing disorder.

II. INCIDENCE OF POVERTY

The incidence of poverty varies by age, ethnicity and family structure. Poverty rates for young children in the United States are higher than for any other demographic group. Beginning with the Great Depression and the Social Security Act, and provision of Social Security Insurance for older Americans, the poverty rates for the elderly (who before the 1930s were most at risk for poverty) have fallen sharply. The 1994 rates for people 65 years and over is 11.7%. In contrast, the 1994 poverty rates for children 6 to 17 years old are almost double (21.8%, one in five), and are higher for children under 3 (25%, one in four). Although the official poverty rates for children dropped during the 1960s, they have been increasing since 1971, and the number of poor children under 6 years old increased by more than 60% between 1971 and 1991.

A. Persistence of Poverty

The poverty rates in any given year underestimate the effect of poverty on development because they are only 1-year estimates. The most accurate way to study the effects of poverty on development is to use longitudinal data, which includes detailed demographic information on participants over time. Studies done with longitudinal data show great variation in the number of years a family may live in poverty. Whether an individual or a family was poor for a short or long period of time portrays life circumstances more accurately than merely knowing a single-year accounting of their poverty status.

Research has shown that living in persistent poverty (being poor most of the time) has a much more potent negative effect on cognitive and emotional well-being than transient poverty, especially for children and adolescents. Although few differences have been found between those who are temporarily poor and the population as a whole, significant differences have been found among those who make up the persistently poor: these individuals are predominantly black and live in female-headed households. In a 1994 study of child poverty over the first 6 years of life, Duncan, Brooks-Gunn, and Klebanov used a sample of 568 black and 796 white children in the Panel Study of Income Dynamics (PSID; an ongoing longitudinal survey of 5000 households begun in 1968 by the Survey Research Center of the University of Michigan). They found large differences between blacks and whites in terms of incidence of persistence poverty, although temporary poverty rates were somewhat comparable (27% and 20%, respectively). The row totals of Table 1 show that among ever-poor white children, only one in five was poor for 5 or 6 years (5.6/[5.6 + 20.2]). Yet for ever-poor black children, more than one half were poor all of the time. Across the whole sample, only one white in twenty was poor in at least 5 of the 6 years, whereas 40% of black children were poor for that prolonged period of time. The high rates of persistent poverty among African American children may explain some of the decrements in cognitive

Table 1 Six-Year Family and Neighborhood Poverty Levels for White and Black Children, Ages 0 to 3 in 1980

No. years family was poor	Six-year average fraction of individuals in neighborhood who were poor					
	0–10%	10–20%	20–30%	30–40%	40%+	Total (%)
White (N = 796)						
None	50.6	19.5	3.1	1.0	0.0	74.2
1–4 Years	8.6	9.2	1.8	0.4	0.3	20.2
5–6 Years	1.6	3.0	0.9	0.1	0.0	5.6
White total (%)	60.8	31.7	5.8	1.4	0.3	100.0
Black (N = 568)						
None	4.6	12.4	12.5	2.5	1.5	33.6
1–4 Years	1.7	7.0	10.9	5.4	2.4	27.4
5–6 Years	3.7	13.4	13.8	3.5	4.5	39.0
Black total (%)	10.1	32.8	37.2	11.5	8.5	100.0

Note. From Panel Study of Income Dynamics, "Economic Deprivation and Early Childhood Development," by G. J. Duncan, J. Brooks-Gunn, and P. K. Klebanov, 1994, *Child Development, 65*(2), 296–318.

achievement and the increases in behavior problems found in this population.

B. Neighborhood Poverty

Poverty rates within a neighborhood may influence emotional well-being, as community context can affect child and adult well-being. Adults living in neighborhoods that have no employment opportunities may experience heightened feelings of hopelessness and anxiety. Parents raising children in isolated, dangerous, and deteriorating neighborhoods may have few competent adults to turn to for social support, role modeling, or shared caretaking and monitoring of young children and adolescents. Access to kin networks or supportive neighbors can moderate the stress of an impoverished neighborhood for some families.

The column totals of Table 1 show large ethnic differences in neighborhood-level poverty. Concentrated neighborhood poverty is defined as poverty rates in excess of 40%, with the incidence of concentrated poverty being 20 times higher for blacks than it is for whites (however, it is also important to note that the fraction of black children living in such neighborhoods is only 8.5%). Table 1 also shows that nearly one half of the blacks but fewer than 1 in 10 whites who escape poverty at the family level encounter it (in rates in excess of 20%) in their neighborhoods. The majority of white but only about one in 20 black children escape both family and neighborhood poverty.

Neighborhoods vary widely with respect to the number, density, and quality of institutions, such as public education, health care and housing, level of affluence of residents, level of street violence and physical safety, and accessibility to employment opportunities. Research done in regions of the country that have experienced large-scale shifts in their economic base because of industrial plants closing or farm foreclosures reveals that living in a declining region can demoralize young people, regardless of whether parents are deprived or not.

C. Female-Headed Households and Poverty

The percentage of families headed by a single parent has increased dramatically in the last 30 years in the United States, as well as in all advanced industrial nations. Rising rates of divorce, as well as increasing numbers of never-married women having children are both contributing factors. Specifically, divorce rates in the United States increased from 9 to 21% between 1960 and 1990. Similarly, out-of-wedlock birth rates increased from 5 to 30% between 1960 and 1992. [See DIVORCE.]

Single-parent families are much more likely to be poor than two-parent families. Never-married mothers are often poor as they rely on one income (their own), they are young, and they have relatively low levels of education. Ever-married mothers also are more likely to be poor than are married mothers, as the incomes of divorced mothers drop by over a third after the marital disruption. In 1992, the median income was about $43,000 for all families with children, whereas it was about $13,500 for all single-parent families. The poverty rate for all married-couple families was 8.4% in 1992, in contrast to the poverty rate for all single-parent families which was 45.7%. Poverty rates of single-parent families vary by ethnicity and education. Single-parent families that are also black or Hispanic or that have less than a high school education are much more likely to be poor than single-parent white families or families with parents with higher educational achievement. For some single-parent families, their poverty is caused by the event of becoming a one-parent family. This is true more often for white families. In contrast, many impoverished black single-parent families were poor before the family split up. The higher poverty rates of black single-parent families is explained by lack of education and job opportunities, and by access to lower earnings compared with white families with similar levels of education.

III. ASSOCIATIONS BETWEEN POVERTY AND MENTAL HEALTH IN CHILDHOOD, ADOLESCENCE, AND ADULTHOOD

The effects of income on development are somewhat different depending on the age and life stage of the individual. Each period of development is characterized by somewhat different indicators of emotional health. More is known about the association between income poverty and outcomes related to cognition, school, and work than on emotional health. Research done on the effects of income at each developmental period, show (a) large effects in the young childhood period on intelligence test scores and verbal ability scores, and small or moderate effects on behavior problems; (b) small to moderate effects of income during adolescence on completed schooling; and (c) large effects of income on adult earnings among young adults. What follows is an in-depth review of what is known about the associations of income poverty and mental health at each developmental period.

A. Childhood

Poor children have significantly more mental and physical health problems, academic difficulties, and social difficulties than nonpoor children. Children from poor families are more likely to present serious conduct and discipline problems to their teachers and parents. Survey data reveal that families living in poverty are asked to come in to school for a conference with the teacher or principal almost twice as often as nonpoor families. Similar rates are reported for suspension or expulsion from school for children living in poverty compared with their nonpoor peers.

The measures of children's socioemotional adjustment that are available in large, nationally representative data sets are generally obtained through maternal reports of increased behavior problems or teacher reports of increased behavior problems (lack of impulse control or frustration tolerance, inability to form and maintain peer relationships, or signs of being withdrawn or depressed). Often, the parent- or teacher-report form of Achenbach's Child Behavior Checklist is used, in which adults are asked to rate the extent to which the child they are reporting on has ever exhibited a particular behavior, for example, is cruel to animals, is withdrawn, demands a lot of attention, has temper tantrums, has nightmares, hangs around with others who get in trouble, lies, or cheats. The assessment taps both externalizing and internalizing behaviors. Children with high levels of antisocial behavior are more likely than other children to have later mental health problems.

Associations between heightened behavior problems and poverty have been shown. Figure 1 compares the behavior problems of children from poor

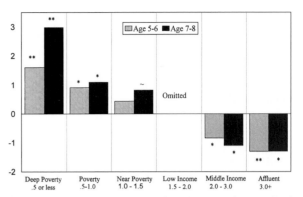

Figure 1 Children's behavior problems by age and income level. From the Center for Young Children and Families. Analyses done with National Longitudinal Survey of Youth (NLSY) mother–child data, cohorts 1986, 1988, 1990, and 1992. Unstandardized regression coefficients, controlling for child's ethnicity, gender, age, birthweight, mother's education, and family structure. Sample includes black and white children: $n = 2,334$ 5 and 6 year olds; $n = 1,917$ 7 and 8 year olds. $*p < .05, **p < .01, ~p < .10$.

and nonpoor families with low-income children using data from the National Longitudinal Survey of Youth (NLSY). Income groups are based on average income-to-needs. The data show the importance of income on children's behavior problems. Children living in deep poverty have behavior problems 1.5 to 3 points higher than children in the low-income group at ages 5 to 6 and 7 to 8 (or one-fourth to one-half of a standard deviation). In addition, children living in affluent families have fewer behavior problems than those in low-income families.

Income effects on behavior problems have also been found in both the Quebec Longitudinal Study and the Ontario Study. The Quebec Study found small to moderate effects for externalizing behaviors (heightened aggression, fighting, and acting out); although no effects of income were found for anxiety and hyperactivity. The Ontario Study found that family income of less than $10,000 was associated with increased morbidity for psychiatric disorder, poor school performance, and social impairment.

B. Adolescence

The transition from childhood to adolescence is marked by numerous changes in the biological, psychological, social, and contextual domains. The consequences of income poverty on adolescent mental health have been documented in studies by Conger and associates which examined the indirect effects on adolescent adjustment of increased parental hostility as a result of living with economic pressures. Outcomes studied were the increased internalizing (depression and anxiety) and externalizing (overt aggression and conduct problems) symptoms.

Risk behaviors such as illicit drug use, smoking tobacco, and alcohol consumption are often exhibited by adolescents. Variations in rates and types of substances used have been associated with different socioeconomic and ethnic groups. Adolescents from more advantaged backgrounds have been identified as those most likely to use the most categories of substances. The substances most frequently used by higher SES youth are marijuana and alcohol. Daily use of any substances, however, is more common in low SES adolescents. In addition, tobacco smoking is more frequent in lower SES adolescents. [See ADOLESCENCE.]

C. Adulthood

The association of cumulative stress from poor social relations, poor health behavior, environmental stress, and poverty are most evident in adulthood. Several researchers have used the term "allostatic load" to denote the ways in which the accumulation of stress translates into physiological stress. Psychopathology is at least 2½ times more prevelant in the lowest social class than in the highest. The relationship between depressive symptomatology and clinical depression with SES has also been well established. Researchers have found that depressive symptoms are more prevalent among women at all income levels, and because of the high prevelance of persistent and deep poverty among single-parent, female-headed minority households, the rates of depressive symptoms in this group are much higher. Depressive symptoms are particularly high among women without confidants, child-rearing assistance, or employment, and for those experiencing chronic stressful conditions, particularly that of living in poverty. [See SOCIO-ECONOMIC STATUS; STRESS.]

Low SES is also commonly listed as a predisposing factor to the development of schizophrenia in clinical manuals. Clinicians and researchers postulate that the reasons for this predisposition may involve one or a combination of the following: the individual's with-drawal from social contact, a lack of upward socioeconomic mobility, and the high stress of living in a financially deprived environment. Homeless schizophrenic men, in particular, are often concurrently diagnosed with substance abuse and antisocial personality disorder. [See ANTISOCIAL PERSONALITY DISORDER; SCHIZOPHRENIA; SUBSTANCE ABUSE.]

IV. PATHWAYS BY WHICH INCOME AFFECTS MENTAL HEALTH

Income poverty has consequences for the mental health of individuals at each developmental stage. A crucial question concerns the pathway by which such effects operate. The processes that link income and mental health outcomes may differ by developmental period. Nutrition, for example, may be a more important pathway in the prenatal/infancy period than later on. Family conflict and harsh parenting may have more influence in early childhood than during infancy, and residential stability and moving might affect children more during the middle school years. However, the research specifying the links within the pathways is still limited. It is also important to recognize that not all people exposed to poverty are impaired by emotional distress or mental disorders. There is growing documentation that many children and adults are resilient and triumph over life's adversities. There are three types of protective factors that can increase an individual's adaptive capacity to cope with stressful life situations: (a) temperament factors, such as activity level, reflectiveness, and cognitive skills; (b) families marked by warmth, cohesion, and the presence of some caring adult who takes responsibility in the absence of responsive parents; and (c) the presence of some source of external support such as a teacher, a neighbor, or even an institutional structure such as a caring agency or a church. In this section, potential pathways are described for each developmental period, keeping in mind the limitations of the work to date.

A. Pathways for Children

I. Nutrition and Health Behavior
The fact that preschool children who live below the poverty threshold are somewhat shorter and weigh

less than children who are above the poverty threshold is believed to be associated with nutrition during the early years. However, no survey data have yet linked poor nutrition to increased behavior problems, although small clinical studies have shown an association between poor diet (as well as malnutrition) and attentional and self-regulatory problems. [*See* FOOD, NUTRITION, AND MENTAL HEALTH.]

The effects of living in extreme poverty on the mental health of children can also be transmitted through unsanitary and unsafe home environments. Exposure to lead and other toxins have been identified in some studies as organic contributors to the development of attention-deficit hyperactivity disorder and autism, as well as to general cognitive and learning difficulties in children. [*See* HEALTHY ENVIRONMENTS.]

2. Parental Interactions with Children

Children are dependent on their parents to provide basic food, shelter, and learning opportunities. A parent's access to adequate economic resources and social support has an impact on their parental abilities. Parents who are poor are likely to be less healthy, both emotionally and physically, than those who are not poor. Parental irritability and depressive symptoms are associated with the emotional and social development of their children. Harsh, punitive, and controlling parenting is associated with low income and with less optimal child outcomes. [*See* PARENTING.]

Although there is no precise standard of an adequate or good enough parent, research has shown that children need parents (or parent figures) who are responsive to the child's verbal and nonverbal needs, provide stable interpersonal relationships that include warmth and affection, hold reasonable expectations for the child's age, provide a variety of learning experiences, and give appropriate monitoring and supervision. The disruption of a secure and stable bond with a parent or substitute caregiver caused by the parent's impaired caregiving abilities associated with the stress of poverty may be one pathway by which the negative effects of poverty are indirectly experienced by the young child.

3. Family Structure

Growing up in a single-parent family has been shown to be a risk factor for heightened behavior problems in children, even when controlling for income and education. Differences in income account for a substantial portion of the differences in well-being between children in one-parent and two-parent households. Children in single-parent families are also disadvantaged in terms of the amount of parental time and supervision available to them in contrast to children living in two-parent families. Adults raising children without a partner or an extensive social support network can experience stress and possible social isolation and depression, which may affect the mental health of all family members. [*See* SOCIAL NETWORKS; SOCIAL SUPPORT.]

4. Substitute Child Care

Children whose families live in strained financial situations cannot afford quality substitute child care. Poor quality child care (untrained providers, low level of stimulation, high staff turnover, and low ratio of staff to children) and unstable child care (number of child care arrangements used by a family within a year) are associated with negative child outcomes. [*See* CHILD CARE PROVIDERS.]

5. Family Turbulence.

Mechanisms by which poverty affects children's mental health have centered on how poverty affects family functioning, that is, increases in family stress, decreases in maternal responsiveness, and increases in marital conflict. Several social problems, including domestic violence, substance abuse, HIV/AIDS, and homelessness, have serious ramifications for children living in families affected by these problems. Families overwhelmed by coping with such problems may not have the resources to attend to a child's need for nurturance, attention, and stability. Family conditions which include abandonment, abuse or neglect, or living with an alcoholic or depressive parent can be risks for developing a mental disorder.

Mothers and children are the fastest growing group of the homeless. Increased levels of behavior problems have been found in these children. Results from a number of studies have shown that homeless children experience higher levels of stress than housed children. The growing epidemic of AIDS and HIV infection also affects children and leaves those with infected or ill parents vulnerable to psychological distress. More frequently than not, the children experience economic hardship in addition to numerous separations from parents, changes in the nature and predictability of parenting behavior, concerns about loss and separation, and disruptions in their daily routine and contact with peers. [*See* HOMELESSNESS.]

B. Pathways for Adolescents

1. Parental Interactions with Adolescents

Conflictual parent–child interactions during adolescence have been shown to be related to economic pressure. Adolescents experience economic pressure through changes in the parent's behavior. Researchers have looked at the effect of income loss through unemployment, underemployment, and unstable work conditions rather than poverty or low income per se. The premise is that income loss and uncertainty lead, in some cases, to family economic pressure, which itself leads to changes in the parent's mood (depression, lability, and irritability). These mood states are associated with marital and family conflict, both of which influence parenting behavior and the strained interactions between adolescents and their parents. Low income (or fluctuation in income) sets off a series of family events—perceived economic pressure, low or labile parental mood, marital conflict, and unresponsive parenting. It has been suggested that conflictual parent–child interactions are the proximal cause of emotional problems in youth and school disengagement.

Family factors that have been linked to living in poverty have also been identified as risk factors for drug abuse. Lack of parental supervision and inconsistent and excessively harsh discipline practices have been linked to income poverty and as a risk factor for drug use.

2. Neighborhood Context

Living in a relatively affluent neighborhood lowers the chances that poor adolescents will experience teen pregnancy or drop out of school. Researchers have hypothesized that youth maladaptive behaviors may be contagious and transmitted through peer processes, particularly in those neighborhoods with extremely high poverty rates. However, the contagion pathway has not yet been demonstrated in all studies for all youth outcomes. Other researchers have found a linear relationship between poverty rates and maladaptive behavior within a neighborhood. Adolescent drug abuse and other antisocial behavior are higher in neighborhoods with high concentrations of poverty. In such neighborhoods, unemployment, poor school situations, isolation, deviant role models, prejudice, and sometimes gang influence may interact with poverty to promote such behaviors.

C. Pathways for Adults

1. Family Relationships

Economic stress causes psychological distress for many adults, and repeated studies have found financial stress as the strongest predictor of depression in men and women, particularly for parents with young children. In addition, married couples living below the poverty line are less likely than those living above to be happily married. Couples suffering from economic hardship may be less satisfied in their marriages because of spousal conflict concerning the spending of limited family resources. Women with three or more children are at most risk for depression. [*See* DEPRESSION.]

2. Employment

Cross-sectional as well as longitudinal studies have demonstrated the positive effect of employment on emotional well-being. Unemployed adults demonstrate lower levels of affective well-being than those who are employed. Studies have been done separately for men and women, as employment has had different meanings for each group at particular historical periods. Men without paid employment have been found to have elevated scores on psychological distress and minor psychiatric morbidity. For women, positive effects of employment on psychological well-being have been found if one controls for the woman's desire to be employed, the quality of her nonoccupational environment (marital status, number of children), and her enjoyment of her employment situation. Employment has been found to be an important source of social connections, particularly for single women with few other resources. The positive effect of paid employment has been found to be stronger in samples of working-class women than in samples of middle-class women (it is possible that the nonwork environment of poorer women is of lower quality, i.e., fewer social supports or less leisure time, so they have more to gain through their paid employment).

A few studies have investigated how the quality

of the job affects mental health. Differentials in job complexity (amount of self-direction compared with amount of routinization or need to follow orders) were associated with feelings of well-being and differentials in parenting behavior. [*See* UNEMPLOYMENT AND MENTAL HEALTH.]

V. PROGRAMS, BENEFITS, AND SERVICES TO ALLEVIATE POVERTY AND SUPPORT MENTAL HEALTH

A broad range of federal and state government programs and policies directly or indirectly provide aid to the poor and comprise what is known as the safety net. The safety net includes (i) means-tested income support programs targeted to those who are poor and who have passed an eligibility test based on poverty or disability status (Temporary Assistance for Needy Families, Supplemental Security Insurance); (ii) social insurance benefits that are income replacement benefits for those with previous labor force experience who can no longer work because of age or disability (old-age social insurance, disability insurance, and unemployment insurance); (iii) in-kind benefits such as food stamps, housing vouchers, or medical care for the poor, near-poor, or elderly (Medicaid, Medicare); (iii) earned income tax credit for low-income workers with dependent children; (iv) service and human capital programs in education (Head Start), training, and employment; and (v) economic development programs aimed at poor neighborhoods and communities. In addition to the public sector, private charity and nonprofit social service agencies provide services and direct aid to the poor.

Macroeconomic trends contribute to the numbers of families who live in poverty or in economic insecurity. America has often been called the land of opportunity. Reality has never quite matched this utopian ideal, but the impressive economic growth that prevailed after World War II until the 1970s did make it easier for opportunity to spread to an increasingly broader group of the population. Economic prosperity in the late 1960s made generous public spending for the War on Poverty a political reality. Yet, in recent years, this trend has not been sustained. In fact, beginning in 1973, economic growth has slowed significantly and there has been a decrease in opportunity

and earnings inequality has increased. Many Americans are no longer able to live up to the American dream of providing a better future for their children and the public will to support the poor has weakened. Those who have been most hurt by declining wages and declining opportunities are the less skilled, the less educated, and younger minority workers. In parallel with the stagnation in wages has been a growing inequality in the distribution of wealth. The United States has the highest division between the rich and poor than any other industrial country.

Starting with the New Deal (President Franklin Delano Roosevelt), the federal government started to take on greater responsibility for creating a safety net which addressed the issue of economic insecurity. President Kennedy's War on Poverty and President Johnson's Great Society included the largest increase in federal expenditures for antipoverty programs. Yet, starting in the 1980s there was a movement to reassert the primacy of the marketplace and reduce the force of federal intervention in the economy in general and in antipoverty policies in particular. Critics of antipoverty efforts from both the right and the left charged that existing programs served the wrong people, served them ineffectively, encouraged bad behavior, were too costly, and did little to alleviate poverty. Despite research that disputed these arguments, radical dismantling of the safety net for poor families was undertaken. The Work Opportunity and Personal Responsibility Reconciliation Act of 1996 was passed with the hope of "ending welfare as we know it." The new bill includes time limits for receiving assistance, allows states rather than the federal government to set eligibility criteria for income support, and includes strict mandates for increased work effort of participants. The new bill emphasizes behavioral requirements for assistance, with a particular emphasis on work behavior. The effect of the new sweeping welfare reform bill is unknown at this time. Critics warn that poverty rates will rise significantly as large numbers of adults and children become ineligible for cash assistance, food stamps and Supplemental Security Insurance. Other researchers suggest that the new welfare reform mandates may lead to decrements in child well-being as a result of fewer economic resources, increased parental employment in unstable menial jobs, poor quality child care, and increased family stress.

Policies to improve the mental health of children, adolescents, and adults must address the structural barriers to economic equality in the United States. Social policies related to child care, child welfare and protective services, adoption, child abuse and neglect, housing, health care financing, and education are all relevant to the creation of programs that can mediate the effects of living in poverty. Social support and family-oriented programs have been shown to reduce the incidence of depressive symptoms in poor mothers and to increase the level of comfort in the parenting role. Long-term and permanent progress against poverty and inequality is possible through programs that make it possible for individuals to acquire sufficient skills and training to become independent and that give them the incentives and hope to make the effort. Income and tax benefits aimed at increasing the family income of poor families are needed, as are early intervention programs aimed at improving the parent/child home learning environment and reducing family stress.

BIBLIOGRAPHY

Achenbach, T. M. (1991). *Manual for the Child Behavior Checklist/4-18 and 1991 Profile*. Burlington, VT: University of Vermont Department of Psychiatry.

Adler, N. E., Boyce, T., Chesney, M. A., Cohen, S., Folkman, S., Kahn, R. L., & Syme, S. L. (1994). Socioeconomic status and health. *American Psychologist, 49*, 15–24.

Belle, D. (1990). Poverty and women's mental health. *American Psychologist, 45*, 385–389.

Brooks-Gunn, J., & Duncan, G. J. (1997). The Effects of Poverty on Children. *Future of Children, 7*, 2, 40–54.

Brooks-Gunn, J., Duncan, G. J., & Aber, J. L. (Eds.). (in press). *Neighborhood poverty: Context and consequences for children*. New York: Russell Sage Foundation.

Chase-Lansdale, L. R. & Brooks-Gunn, J. (1995). *Escape from Poverty: What makes a difference for children*. New York: Cambridge University Press.

Citro, C. & Michael, R. (Eds.). (1994). *Measuring poverty: A new approach*. Washington, DC: National Academy Press.

Conger, R. D., & Elder, G. (1994). *Families in troubled times*. New York: Aldine de Gruyter.

Duncan, G. J., & Brooks-Gunn, J. (Eds.). (1997). *Consequences of Growing up poor*. New York: Russell Sage Foundation.

Duncan, G. J., Brooks-Gunn, J., & Klebanov, P. K. (1994). Economic deprivation and early childhood development. *Child Development, 65*(2) 296–318.

Elder, G. H., Jr. (1974). *Children of the great depression: Social change in life experience*. Chicago: University of Chicago Press.

Elder, G. J., Jr., & Caspi, A. (1988). Economic stress in lives: Developmental perspectives. *Journal of Social Issues, 44*, 25–45.

Garmezy, N. (1993). Children in poverty: Resilience despite risk. *Psychiatry, 56*, 127–136.

Hernandez, D. (1993). *America's children: Resources from family government and the economy*. New York: Russell Sage Foundation.

Huston, A. (Ed.). (1991). *Children in poverty: Child development and public policy*. Cambridge, MA: Cambridge University Press.

McLanahan, S., & Sandefur, G. (1994). *Growing up with a single parent*. Cambridge, MA: Harvard University Press.

Pregnancy and Mental Health

Marci Lobel

State University of New York at Stony Brook

Gestation Period of fetal development from conception through birth, lasting 40 weeks; the period of pregnancy.

Multipara A woman who has delivered one or more viable infants, that is, infants sufficiently developed (usually by 24 weeks of gestation) to survive outside the uterus.

Parity Number of pregnancies that reached viability.

Prenatal Pertaining to pregnancy. Literally, occurring or existing before birth.

Preterm Delivery Delivery prior to 37 weeks of gestation.

Primipara A pregnant woman who has not previously carried a pregnancy to viability.

Women experience a number of physical and life-style changes during **PREGNANCY** that can affect their mental health. This article addresses the major changes that pregnant women undergo, their concerns, the typical emotions that pregnant women experience, and the impact of psychological stress on the health of a pregnant woman and her fetus.

I. INTRODUCTION

The vast majority of women become pregnant and give birth at least once during their lifetime. To many, it is one of the most memorable and important experiences of their life. A study of women 20 years after delivering a baby showed that they had distinct memories of their pregnancy and birth, and retained strong feelings about them. Although pregnancy is a biological process, it also poses substantial life changes that can affect women's emotions, behaviors, and thoughts. Thus, pregnancy offers a rich set of issues for study and is of great interest to psychologists and others concerned about mental health.

Pregnancy is a unique life event. First, it lasts for a fairly lengthy period of time: normal pregnancies are 40 weeks long. Second, it has a predictable end point— birth—although 15 to 20% of recognized pregnancies end earlier in spontaneous abortion, or "miscarriage." Third, many women experience pregnancy more than once, although no pregnancy is the same, psychologically or biologically. Fourth, pregnancy may be associated with happiness and joy, but it may also entail considerable physical, emotional, financial, and interpersonal strain. For all of these reasons, no other major life event is quite like the experience of pregnancy.

II. THE PSYCHOLOGICAL EXPERIENCE OF PREGNANCY

Women's psychological reactions to pregnancy are as diverse as women themselves are. There have been few studies comparing the psychological experiences of pregnant women from various racial and ethnic backgrounds, so we know little about the impact of these factors. However, we do know that characteristics such as women's age, state of health, education, income, occupation, and quality of partner or family support affect the way they experience pregnancy. There are also differences between women having a child for the first time (primiparas) and those who have borne other children (multiparas), and between those who have and have not planned their pregnancy. By comparing the results of studies conducted with different groups of women, it is possible to identify some conditions that are common in *most* pregnancies. By integrating the results of well-conducted scientific research, this section describes the typical psychological experiences of pregnancy.

A. Managing Physical Symptoms

Almost from the beginning of pregnancy, and often until birth, pregnant women are subject to a number of unpleasant physical symptoms. Three-quarters of all pregnant women experience nausea and vomiting, which are most common through the first 5 months. Fatigue is felt by most women in the first and third trimesters. In addition to these discomforts, backaches, heartburn, headaches, indigestion, swollen feet and hands, difficulty breathing, leg cramps, breast tenderness, difficulty sleeping, hemorrhoids, and frequent urination are among the most common symptoms reported by pregnant women. Although they may occur in any normal, healthy pregnancy, occasionally these symptoms signify that a medical problem exists.

In the past, health professionals believed that prenatal physical discomforts, especially nausea and vomiting, were caused by unhappy or ambivalent feelings toward being pregnant. Although evidence overwhelmingly does not support this belief, it is mentioned in some popular books about pregnancy and may therefore lead women to blame themselves or feel guilty over their physical condition.

Physical symptoms may contribute to women's psychological state in pregnancy in other ways, as well. Symptoms are unpredictable and often uncontrollable. Although physical symptoms are usually worst during the first and third trimesters, they may be chronic throughout the entire 9-month period, or arise and disappear at any time. Their intensity may also change from day to day. Also, since some symptoms may indicate important medical problems, women do not always know whether to be concerned or to simply adjust to their physical symptoms. For these reasons,

physical symptoms contribute to a woman's uncertainty about her pregnancy, and cause distress for some. Furthermore, managing such symptoms may require substantial psychological and life-style adjustments, which are addressed more fully below. For example, to cope with nausea, some pregnant women find they must avoid the smell or even the sight of certain foods during the beginning of their pregnancy. This may be particularly difficult for those who are involved in their family's food preparation, or who earn a living working with food.

B. Alterations in Work and Activities

Although many women experience physical discomforts at some time during their pregnancy, pregnancy is not an illness and most pregnant women do not regard themselves as "sick." Under most conditions, it is not necessary for a pregnant woman to curtail her activities at home or at work. For example, she can continue to be employed, care for her family and household, and have sexual relations. Sometimes, such as when a pregnancy is medically complicated or when a woman holds a physically taxing job, a woman and her health care provider may decide that some restrictions of activity are necessary. However, the majority of women continue their pre-pregnant responsibilities, including work outside the home, for most or all of their pregnancy. It is important to note that researchers find no change in women's mental capacity (such as their ability to concentrate or their ability to cope with emotional strains during pregnancy), both of which may be essential in carrying out employment or home responsibilities.

Because of the fatigue and physical discomforts that usually accompany pregnancy, women's total productivity may decline. Studies indicate wide variation in productivity during pregnancy, with many women reporting a decrease, some reporting no change, and few experiencing an increase. Productivity may also change across pregnancy. For example, one study found that women typically experience an improvement in their ability to perform household, childcare, social, and occupational activities from 20 to 30 weeks gestation, but a decrement after 35 weeks. Women in this study felt that pregnancy affected their household responsibilities more than their paid employment.

Many women experience dissatisfaction or worry about their inability to carry out daily activities. In one study, approximately one-quarter of women spontaneously expressed dismay over their slower pace during the last 2 to 6 weeks of pregnancy. In another study, women explained that their physical symptoms, especially fatigue, made it difficult to fulfill their work and household responsibilities, and they often declined social activities in order to rest. Women expressed frustration over having to limit their activities because of low energy, especially in the third trimester.

A number of factors affect whether pregnancy influences a woman's productivity. Women in poor health, and those whose pregnancy is medically complicated are more likely to experience decrements in their productivity. Parity has also been shown to influence women's functioning during pregnancy; not surprisingly, those without children experience fewer changes in their work productivity, and are able to do more than pregnant women with children. Also, women who receive more social support during pregnancy are more productive at work, and report better functioning at home, as well.

There is also much individual variation in sexual activity during pregnancy, since sexuality, like other aspects of women's lives, can be affected by the psychological and physiological changes that accompany pregnancy. On the average, however, studies find that women experience decreased sexual interest and activity in the first trimester of pregnancy, an increase in the second trimester, and a decrease again in the third trimester. A large number of women experience enhanced sexual pleasure during pregnancy compared to other times in their life. Some women who have not experienced orgasm do so for the first time during pregnancy; many women have multiple orgasms during sexual activity in pregnancy. This may be due to the biological changes associated with pregnancy as well as the elimination of concerns over unwanted conception that may inhibit sexual pleasure at other times.

C. Changes in Appearance and Size

Pregnant women undergo a dramatic change in their appearance and size over a short period of time. Since they have little time to adjust to these changes, it is not surprising that many women report feeling clumsy and off-balance. A number of studies find that pregnant women feel ugly, fat, or otherwise unattractive, especially during the latter portion of their pregnancy,

when bodily changes are most prominent. Dissatisfaction with appearance is a central and common component of women's concerns during pregnancy. Furthermore, studies show that pregnant women develop distorted images of their body. As pregnancy progresses, women stand farther away from others, which may result from having an exaggerated perception of their size.

One researcher conducted in-depth interviews throughout pregnancy that provide a detailed picture of pregnant women's concerns about their appearance. In the first trimester, most women were apprehensive and ambivalent about the anticipated changes to their body. Some wanted to camouflage their bodies, but many looked forward to the changes, viewing them both as unique and as a confirmation of their pregnant state. Increased breast size was experienced with greatest enthusiasm, and many women reported that their husbands liked this change.

Positive feelings about their appearance peaked during the second trimester, when women began wearing maternity clothes and their pregnancy became noticeable to others. They reported feelings of pride and a sense of enhanced maturity at this time. However, women also felt increasingly anxious about their physical appearance during the second trimester. In particular, they were concerned about their ability to regain their pre-pregnant appearance, and they felt a sense of shock as their body began to seem alien or unrecognizable.

By the third trimester, women expressed a number of concerns over body changes that they viewed as unsightly: stretch marks, prominent veins, complexion changes, and an increase in body hair were especially troublesome. Typical of women's concerns at this time were thoughts that their internal organs or other parts of their bodies might become damaged, feelings of reduced sexual attractiveness, and worries that they would experience permanent changes in their appearance. They reported feeling a loss of control over their body, increasing conspicuousness, awkwardness, and clumsiness. Some were concerned that their husbands no longer viewed them as attractive.

Pregnant women's reactions to their changing appearance are undoubtedly affected by the value our society places on thinness and youth, which also colors the way that people respond to pregnant women. Many report that friends and even strangers offer unsolicited comments about their growing size. A pregnant woman's belly is also a noticeable sign of her physical maturity. Therefore, pregnant women may not be viewed (and may not view themselves) as sexually appealing as the young, svelte women who grace billboards and magazines. Because the reactions of others have significant influence on women's experiences during pregnancy, the following section describes the manner in which pregnant women are viewed and treated in American society.

D. Reactions from Others

Many signs indicate that pregnant women are viewed with ambivalence. For example, respected images of pregnant women in art, such as the pregnant Madonna or DaVinci's Mona Lisa, suggest that pregnant women are revered. Also, some studies find that a pregnant woman is more likely than a nonpregnant woman to receive assistance in daily life, such as having a door held open for her. Thus, our society views pregnant women as needing and deserving help. However, pregnant women may also be resented or reviled for this same perceived dependence on others. In recent years, some politicians have received support for their attempts to cut social programs that benefit pregnant women, particularly those who are poor, young, or unmarried. Also, pregnant women are not always well treated in public settings, as many bus and subway riders can attest. These examples appear to signal that changes have occurred in society's views of pregnant women. Greater ambivalence toward pregnant women may exist now than at earlier times in history.

Other physical responses to pregnant women also suggest contradictory views of them. One intriguing study found that strangers reacted to a pregnant woman by staring or avoidance. This was especially true for men. Although this study was conducted 20 years ago, pregnant women participating in more recent studies also report being stared at by strangers. These responses, which are similar to those experienced by physically handicapped or disfigured individuals, suggest that pregnancy may be perceived as a social stigma. However, in stark contrast to this perception, pregnant women also report that strangers frequently offer unsolicited advice to them, touch their pregnant bellies, and make comments—often derogatory ones—about their size. Nonpregnant women with other social stigmas such as obesity are rarely,

if ever, subject to such treatment. Thus, contradictory behavioral responses to pregnant women illustrate that they are viewed with a great deal of ambivalence. Such reactions may also explain why pregnant women tend to stand at greater distances from other people, a phenomenon described earlier that is often attributed to pregnant women's distorted body image. Actually, pregnant women may be attempting to avert the negative reactions of others!

Pregnancy is a visible reminder of femininity and sexuality. Yet pregnant women are viewed as motherly, and in some respects, as childlike. The latter may help to explain why pregnant women are often the recipients of unsolicited touch or comments, just as children are treated in our society. Whether pregnant women are perceived as maternal or as childlike, however, most cultures have taboos that forbid sexual attraction to both mothers and children. Thus, there is likely to be great societal ambivalence about the sexual attractiveness of pregnant women. This is well illustrated by the following incident. A few years ago, a popular actress appeared in profile on the cover of a major magazine, pregnant and partially clad. Although the magazine regularly featured revealing photographs of famous women on its cover, this issue was considered too risqué to be distributed without a brown paper wrapping. Only 2 months later, another equally popular but nonpregnant actress was shown on the cover in a sexually provocative pose, wearing nothing other than lingerie. That issue of the magazine was distributed without brown paper wrapping. This example, while somewhat whimsical, demonstrates that the sexual appeal of a pregnant woman may be too "dangerous" or shocking for her to appear in public view.

Perceptions of pregnant women are also affected by socioeconomic status. One researcher examined this by studying the arrangement of maternity clothing in department stores catering to women of different income levels. She found that "high-status stores" usually located maternity clothing near lingerie items. In contrast, in "lower status stores," maternity clothing was located in departments selling uniforms or clothing for large women (i.e., "half-sizes"). These differences may reflect the ways that pregnant women are viewed according to social class. Perhaps more important, these views are likely to be understood by pregnant women and adopted by them. For example, in a separate study by the same researcher, pregnant women of varying social classes were queried about their attitudes toward being pregnant. The differences between women of higher and lower social class closely corresponded to the differences suggested by the placement of maternity clothing across stores: higher class women were more likely to report feeling sexy, attractive, and being treated "specially," whereas working-class women were more likely to say that they felt fat and unattractive. Thus, pregnant women may internalize the attitudes that others hold of them, even when those attitudes are not overtly expressed. These results also show that many societal responses to a pregnant woman may be influenced by the education, occupation, and income of both the woman and the respondent.

III. SPECIFIC CONCERNS DURING PREGNANCY

A handful of studies have examined the issues that most concern women during their pregnancy. Although these studies have identified a range of pregnancy-specific worries or concerns, the following five themes emerge as the most prevalent concerns of pregnant women: physical discomforts, changes in appearance, changes in relationships with others, the labor and delivery, and the baby's health. Concerns over other issues, such as financial resources to pay for medical care and supplies for the baby, may be less common, but do affect individual women.

A. Physical Symptoms and Bodily Changes

Of the five most common concerns, two—physical discomforts and changes in appearance—have already been discussed in previous sections characterizing the psychological experience of pregnancy. Thus it is not surprising that these are central in pregnant women's concerns. As reviewed earlier, physical symptoms are almost ubiquitous in pregnancy and often uncomfortable or painful. They may disrupt a pregnant woman's home or work activities, and raise the specter of damage to a woman or her baby. Bodily changes are often experienced with great reluctance, as they reduce mobility, alter appearance, and influence the ways that women are viewed and treated by others.

B. Labor and Delivery

Pregnant women's worries about labor and delivery comprise another set of common concerns. These concerns, which peak during the third trimester, tend to focus on the possibility of complications, and the certainty that women will experience intense, and often prolonged, pain. A noted pain researcher, reviewing numerous studies of women in labor, concludes that "labor pain is felt universally and is often extremely severe," although there is enormous individual variability. Labor pain has been identified as one of the most extreme forms of pain experienced by human beings. However, popular books written for pregnant women often understate the degree of pain experienced during birth, and may overstate the effectiveness of childbirth preparation in reducing pain. Pregnant women's conversations with those who have given birth are likely to disconfirm the information in such books, and therefore may intensify women's concerns about what to expect during labor and delivery. Having accurate expectations about labor pain is extremely important, however. Studies show that women who are least well-prepared for the intensity of labor pain are the ones who experience the most severe levels of it. [See PAIN.]

Compounding women's uncertainty surrounding birth is the possibility that they will undergo a cesarean delivery, which involves removal of the infant through surgical incisions in the abdomen and uterus. In some cases, complications necessitate delivery by this method, but there is evidence that cesarean deliveries are sometimes performed when not medically necessary. Currently, approximately one-fifth of births in the United States are cesarean deliveries. Women who deliver by this method are significantly more likely to incur infection, injuries, and even death, and they experience more pain, as well as more prolonged and difficult recovery than women who deliver an infant vaginally. Studies show that cesarean delivery also has adverse emotional and psychological impact. Thus there is a strong basis for pregnant women's apprehensions about cesarean delivery.

C. The Baby's Health

An additional set of concerns common in pregnancy pertain to the health of the fetus or newborn. Some studies show that during the first trimester, women worry most about the possibility of miscarriage. After feeling fetal movement (sometimes called "quickening"), which typically occurs by the fifth month, concerns about miscarriage subside, but fears of fetal deformity increase, and persist until birth. Concerns about fetal loss or deformity are especially potent for women who have experienced a prior adverse pregnancy outcome and for those who are at high risk for such an outcome because of a preexisting medical condition (such as diabetes) or a problem (such as bleeding) that arises during their pregnancy. There is also some evidence that prenatal screening tests, which are performed to identify fetal anomalies, can exacerbate women's concerns about the health of their baby. One reason is that simply undergoing such a test focuses a woman's attention on the possibility of fetal loss or impairment; another reason is that these tests and their results are sometimes misconstrued. For example, many women are distressed when they receive "positive" results suggesting the presence of a fetal anomaly, even if follow-up tests with normal findings indicate that the initial result was a "false positive."

D. Relationships with Others

Finally, pregnant women are commonly concerned about the changes that may occur in their relationships with others due to pregnancy and impending motherhood. They are particularly concerned about their relationships with husbands (or other committed partners), and for multiparas, with their other children. Although the importance of a pregnant woman's relationship with her own mother has been emphasized in nonscientific writing on pregnancy, researchers find very little evidence that this relationship is a central consideration of women during their pregnancy. In comparison, many pregnant women voice concerns that their marriage may decline as a result of the changes that they are undergoing. Interestingly, however, several studies find that husbands feel closer to their wives during pregnancy, and both partners experience an increase in marital satisfaction prenatally. Nevertheless, some aspects of the marital relationship invariably decay following birth, particularly when the division of household labor between partners is less equitable than a woman expects it to be. Many studies show that marital satisfaction declines after the birth of a first child. Since pregnant women tend to seek out information about motherhood from

women with children, they may learn about the decline in women's marital satisfaction from these contacts and begin to anticipate problems in their own relationship. They may also plan ways to prevent marital problems. These issues contribute to women's concerns prenatally.

IV. EMOTIONAL STATE IN PREGNANCY

Cartoons, movies, and television shows sometimes depict pregnant women as experiencing extreme mood swings and not in control of their emotions. Is there any scientific basis for such stereotypes? Although there are no large-scale studies that have examined emotions in pregnant women, a number of smaller studies offer findings that can be summarized to describe typical patterns of emotion during pregnancy. For the most part, these studies have focused on levels of anxiety and depression. Unfortunately, we know almost nothing about other emotions during pregnancy, including positive emotions.

Before reviewing the studies of anxiety and depression, an important distinction must be made between *specific fears or concerns* during pregnancy and *general mood or emotion*. As described in the sections above, pregnancy-specific concerns commonly change throughout the 9-month period, and may differ in both content and intensity as pregnancy progresses. For example, women are more fearful about labor and delivery late in pregnancy, and are less troubled by physical symptoms during the second trimester than in the first or third trimester. In contrast, mood or emotion refers to a general feeling state, and is not dependent on specific events or aspects of pregnancy. Thus, the issue is not whether there are changes in women's specific concerns during this period—there are—but whether there are fluctuations in pregnant women's mood.

A. Prenatal Anxiety

Most well-conducted studies of anxiety find a high degree of stability prenatally, with anxiety levels similar to those found in nonpregnant women. In other words, the majority of women do not experience fluctuations in anxiety during pregnancy, and most are within normal levels throughout this 9-month period. However, many of the studies also find substantial individual variation in levels of prenatal anxiety. A minority of women do experience changes across pregnancy, with some becoming highly anxious at times. For example, in one study, more than two-thirds of the participants had stable, low levels of anxiety throughout pregnancy. Sixteen percent became steadily more anxious as pregnancy progressed, 8% became steadily less anxious, and 5% experienced an increase followed by a drop in anxiety. In this study and others, a woman's pattern of prenatal anxiety (stable, increasing, decreasing, or a combination) was not related to her age, level of education, ethnic background, marital status, or other individual characteristics. Thus, there does not appear to be a simple way to identify beforehand the small number of women most likely to become anxious during pregnancy. [*See* ANXIETY.]

B. Prenatal Depression

In comparison to the studies of prenatal anxiety, studies of prenatal depression are less well conducted and their findings are more contradictory. One of the best-conducted of these studies measured levels of depression during the second and third trimesters of pregnancy. Pregnant women in this study were no more likely than a comparison group of nonpregnant women to be clinically depressed, meaning that their depression was not sufficiently high to warrant treatment. The pregnant women did, however, experience *more symptoms* of depression than nonpregnant women (such as feeling hopeless or sad). This indicates that while mood was somewhat impaired among pregnant women in this study, it was not at levels high enough to be considered abnormal. Another study also found that pregnant women were not especially depressed. In a third study, pregnant women were more depressed than nonpregnant women.

Two additional studies, although not scientifically rigorous, found there were changes in depression as pregnancy progressed. The patterns of change in these two studies were exactly opposite, however. In one, depression increased over pregnancy and was highest in the third trimester; in the other study, depression was highest in the first trimester and declined in the third.

Given this contradictory set of findings, it is not possible to definitively conclude whether most women are likely to experience symptoms of depression dur-

ing pregnancy, nor identify the typical time course of these symptoms. However, the preponderance of studies suggest that if women do experience symptoms of depression, they are likely to be within normal ranges, and not require intervention. Of course, this may differ for individual women, some of whom may desire and need help to overcome depressive symptomatology. On the basis of the available research, it is also not possible to predict which women are more likely to become depressed during pregnancy. However, most research suggests that a history of depression is one of the most accurate predictors of later depression, which can be triggered during periods of heightened stress. Therefore, women who experience depressive symptoms *prior* to pregnancy are probably the most likely to become depressed *during* their pregnancy, particularly if the pregnancy adds to preexisting levels of stress. [*See* DEPRESSION.]

Taken together, studies of prenatal anxiety and depression reveal a striking similarity: there is no single, universal emotional response to pregnancy. Regardless of the point during pregnancy when mood is measured, scientists find a wide range of responses, indicating that individual pregnant women differ in how anxious and depressed they feel. Of course, nonpregnant women also differ in levels of anxiety and depression. Presumably, this is because anxiety and depression are emotional responses to life conditions that vary from woman to woman, and also vary over time. Nevertheless, the portrayal of pregnant women as lacking control over wildly fluctuating emotions, seen in some forms of popular culture, appears to be grossly inaccurate for the vast majority of women.

V. STRESS IN PREGNANCY

Although most women are not highly anxious or depressed during pregnancy, some are, often because of stressful conditions in their lives. This makes it important to know whether stress during pregnancy can harm the fetus or result in other problems.

A. Effects on Birth Outcome

Numerous studies have examined the effects of prenatal maternal stress on birth outcomes such as birthweight. Although the findings are not entirely consistent, many of the most scientifically rigorous studies find that stress during pregnancy is associated with worse birth outcomes. For example, women with high stress during pregnancy are more likely to deliver a baby before the full 40 weeks of normal pregnancy, which is called preterm delivery if it occurs prior to 37 weeks of gestation. These babies tend to be smaller and weigh less because they have not had sufficient time in the mother's uterus to complete their growth.

Even if their pregnancy lasts for 40 weeks, women who undergo high stress prenatally are also more likely to deliver a baby of abnormally low weight, which is defined as anything less than 2500 grams. This is equivalent to about 5.5 pounds. Low birthweight is the largest cause of infant mortality. Preterm and low-birthweight survivors are more likely to have medical difficulties, including neurodevelopmental and respiratory complications. Some research shows that later, these children have lower IQ scores and more frequently have trouble in elementary school. Of course, not all low-birthweight and preterm infants have problems later in life. Although they are especially vulnerable at birth and during the first year of life, many of these babies outgrow their medical conditions and develop into normal, healthy children and adults. However, early medical interventions with vulnerable infants are extremely costly and are very disruptive to families.

What type of stress is harmful? All of us experience stress sometimes, as it is unavoidable in modern life. According to studies that I have conducted with other pregnancy researchers, the worst form of prenatal stress involves three components. Pregnant women who have high levels of all three of these components are at greatest risk. The first component involves stressful conditions, such as marital, employment, or financial problems. The second stress component is feeling that one cannot control these problems, feeling overwhelmed, or believing that it is difficult or impossible to manage one's life. The third component of stress involves responses. These include emotional responses (such as anxiety or depression), behavioral responses (such as crying), physical responses (such as trembling), and cognitive responses, which involve problems with thinking (such as impaired memory).

Therefore, according to this approach, women who face difficult conditions during their pregnancy may not incur greater risk if they feel able to manage their lives and are not suffering negative emotions such as anxiety. We have conducted studies to test this approach to stress. As we predicted, the studies show that what women *feel* about their life situation has at least as much impact on their health and the baby's health as what they *objectively experience* during pregnancy. In other words, our research indicates that a pregnant woman who is anxious and feels that her life is very stressful or out of control, even if it does not seem to be stressful to an outside observer, is at increased risk of an adverse birth outcome.

As these examples illustrate, studies of stress in pregnant women also suggest that *chronic* high stress may be more harmful than *occasional* episodes of stress. This means that a woman who undergoes one or a few upsetting life events during her pregnancy is probably not at great risk, especially if she continues healthful practices, receives prenatal care, and is otherwise not experiencing medical complications. Women who have persistently high levels of stress, however, are at increased risk of an adverse birth outcome. [*See* PRENATAL STRESS AND LIFE-SPAN DEVELOPMENT.]

B. Counteracting Stress Effects

Fortunately, not all pregnant women with high levels of stress incur adverse outcomes, even those with chronic stress, or stress from all three of the components described above. One reason is that many women receive social support during pregnancy from their friends, family, and other pregnant women. Social support includes tangible assistance, such as money, food, or help getting things done; emotional assistance, such as listening and affection; and information or advice. Studies of social support during pregnancy show that it contributes to better birth outcomes. Younger women and members of particular ethnic groups derive the greatest benefit of social support during pregnancy, perhaps because they tend to be at high psychosocial and medical risk. Also, studies show that prenatal social support can alleviate some of the harmful effects of high stress on birth outcome. [*See* SOCIAL SUPPORT.]

Another reason why many women do not suffer ill effects of prenatal stress is that they learn to cope well. Coping is defined by psychologists as anything that a person does in an attempt to manage or reduce stress, even if the attempt is not successful. Although few studies have examined coping with stress during pregnancy, some evidence suggests that the most effective way of managing stress prenatally is a type of coping called "positive appraisal." This involves viewing situations in a positive light, or feeling that one will learn something valuable or otherwise benefit from a stressful experience. In the context of pregnancy, someone who copes by positive appraisal might feel that she is lucky to be a woman and able to experience pregnancy, or that having a baby is fulfilling a lifetime dream or goal. In contrast, certain other forms of coping, such as avoiding situations or individuals, appear to be deleterious. In a recent study that members of my research team conducted, pregnant women who coped with stress in this manner became more distressed over time. Coping with problems by using drugs or alcohol was also not successful. Instead, this type of coping heightened distress. Fortunately, few women coped by using drugs or alcohol. Many studies show that substance use is especially dangerous during pregnancy, since a fetus is highly sensitive to toxins in its mother's body. [*See* COPING WITH STRESS; STRESS.]

What should a woman do if she is experiencing stress during her pregnancy? First, she should determine whether it is possible to modify or remove the conditions that are causing her stress. Of course, this cannot always be done, but when it can, women might consider making specific changes. These steps may not only eliminate or reduce sources of stress, they may also imbue a pregnant woman with a greater sense of control over her life, and enhance her pride or self-esteem. Such measures as reassigning household tasks to other family members, or requesting different responsibilities at work, may result in great tangible and psychological benefits.

Second, a pregnant woman can try to prevent some of the adverse medical outcomes associated with high stress by being more vigilant about the health practices that protect against these. Proper nutrition, rest, moderate exercise, restraint from alcohol, tobacco, and drugs, and regular prenatal care have been shown to be essential contributors to healthy birth outcomes.

Finally, a woman who is experiencing high levels of stress during pregnancy can seek help: from her family or friends, her health care provider, her pastor, a social worker or psychologist, or anyone else who is capable of providing assistance. Psychological studies demonstrate the importance of providing precisely the type of help that is needed, and the appropriate amount of help. For example, one recent study found that

pregnant women whose family members provided too much help, or became "enmeshed," delivered infants with significantly lower birthweight. This may have occurred because family overinvolvement can result in a lack of privacy or autonomy that increases a woman's stress. Therefore, it is important that pregnant women receive the right type and amount of help to avert the possibility that help will exacerbate, rather than reduce stress.

VI. CONCLUSIONS

Pregnancy is an important and unique life transition that involves substantial biological, psychological, and interpersonal change. The overwhelming majority of women adjust well to these changes, and complete their pregnancy without emotional or other psychological complications. Most women experience pregnancy as a normal life event.

Pregnancy is not an isolated occurrence which can be separated from other aspects of a woman's life. Accumulated resources and strains from a woman's marriage, finances, family, or work influence the way she experiences pregnancy. Likewise, pregnancy impinges on a woman's other roles. For these reasons, some women experience pregnancy as stressful—either throughout the entire 9-month period or just at limited times. High levels of chronic stress have been shown to have an adverse impact on pregnancy, placing a woman at higher risk of lower birthweight or preterm delivery, for example.

It is evident throughout all of the areas reviewed in this article that there is enormous individual variation in the way that women experience pregnancy. Thus, while it is possible to describe the most common concerns and emotional responses of pregnant women, there is not a single normal way to experience pregnancy. Rather, it is more appropriate to understand pregnancy as involving a potential *range* of concerns and responses, any one of which may or may not be felt by individual women.

Finally, it is important to recognize that pregnancy takes place within a sociocultural milieu that affects women's experiences, and also affects the ways that people treat pregnant women. This topic has not yet been fully explored by researchers, so we currently know very little about the impact of social class, race, ethnicity, or religious background on psychological aspects of pregnancy. From what we do know, however, it is likely that these characteristics add to the variety of ways—all of them normal—that women experience pregnancy.

BIBLIOGRAPHY

DeLuca, R. S., & Lobel, M. (1995). Conception, commitment, and health behavior practices in medically high-risk pregnant women. *Women's Health: Research on Gender, Behavior, and Policy, 1,* 257–271.

Dunkel-Schetter, C., & Lobel, M. (in press). Pregnancy and childbirth. In E. A. Blechman & K. D. Brownell (Eds.), *Behavioral medicine and women: A comprehensive handbook.* New York: Guilford Publications.

Dunkel-Schetter, C., Sagrestano, L. M., Feldman, P., & Killingsworth, C. (1996). Social support and pregnancy: A comprehensive review focusing on ethnicity and culture. In G. R. Pierce, B. R. Sarason, & I. G. Sarason (Eds.), *Handbook of social support and the family* (pp. 375–412). New York: Plenum Press.

Lobel, M. (1994). Conceptualizations, measurement, and effects of prenatal maternal stress on birth outcomes. *Journal of Behavioral Medicine, 17,* 225–272.

Matlin, M. W. (1996). *The psychology of women* (3rd ed.). New York: Harcourt Brace.

Stanton, A. L., & Danoff-Burg, S. (1995). Selected issues in women's reproductive health: Psychological perspectives. In A. L. Stanton & S. J. Gallant (Eds.), *The psychology of women's health* (pp. 261–305). Washington, DC: American Psychological Association.

Premenstrual Syndrome (PMS)

Katharina Dalton

University College Hospital, London, U.K.

Follicular Phase Covers the days from menstruation until ovulation.

Intermenstruum Covers those days of the menstrual cycle that are not included in the paramenstruum.

Luteal Phase The days from ovulation until menstruation.

Menstrual Cycle Measured from the first day of menstruation until the day before the next menstruation.

Paramenstruum The four days immediately before menstruation and the first four days of menstruation.

Premenstruum The days from ovulation until menstruation.

PREMENSTRUAL SYNDROME (PMS) is the recurrence of disabling physical or psychological symptoms occurring in the premenstruum with complete relief in the postmenstruum.

PMS has a precise definition requiring recurrence of the same symptoms at the same phase of the cycle for at least the last three menstrual cycles. The symptoms may last less than 1 day (e.g., epilepsy, migraine,

confusion, or hallucinations), but may not last longer than 14 days, and there must be complete absence of all symptoms for at least 7 days before ovulation. The symptoms should be severely disabling and interfering with work capacity and/or social life, thus excluding the valuable warning symptoms marking the approach of menstruation. Occasionally only one symptom is present, but more frequently the women are polysymptomatic.

I. INTRODUCTION

Before normal bodily functions there are valuable, warning sensations. For instance, these sensations inform the individual when the bladder is full, or when the bowels need emptying. There is a nasal tickling before sneezing, and thirst when dehydrated. In the same way there are valuable, warning sensations before menstruation. These sensations should not be considered premenstrual symptoms, but this does account for the findings of some surveys of an incidence of PMS exceeding 90%. On the other hand there are women whose premenstrual symptoms are disabling, interfering with normal working and social life, they suffer from PMS and are deserving of consideration and treatment.

A normal menstrual cycle varies from 21 to 35 days, and is considered to be regular if variations, cycle to cycle, do not exceed 4 days. Normal menstruation may last from 2 to 8 days, with the bleeding being pink, bright red, or dark brown. The normal age of menarche is from 12 to 14 years, but the age does vary with race, economic, and social factors. Early menarche is usual in the blind, deaf, and congenitally physically handicapped (hydrocephalus, spina bifida, dislocated hip). The normal age of menopause is between 45 and 55 years, therefore if menstruation stops before the age of 45 years, or if bleeding becomes heavy then gynecological examination is indicated. Cyclical symptoms may occur for up to 2 years before the menarche, and up to 2 years after the menopause. Following recovery from the trauma of hysterectomy or bilateral oophorectomy, cyclical symptoms return.

II. SYMPTOMS

There are no unique symptoms; all symptoms also recur in men, children, and postmenopausal women, and almost all organs are involved. The diagnosis depends entirely on the timing and severity of symptoms. Even women with diagnosed PMS may, under certain circumstances, suffer their typical premenstrual symptoms at other times of their menstrual cycle. During pregnancy, when menstruation is temporarily abolished, PMS disappears, and years later the patient will usually recall pregnancy as the time of exceptional good health. However, PMS often returns with increased severity after the pregnancy, especially if complicated by preeclampsia, postnatal depression, or puerperal psychosis. Cyclical symptoms disappear temporarily when ovulation is stopped with estrogen implants, Danazol, or GnHR agonists, but reappear if progestins are used to cause withdrawal bleeding. Cyclical monthly symptoms reappear after recovery from the trauma of hysterectomy or oophorectomy, which may take up to 3 years.

More than 150 symptoms have been described, of which 33% are psychological. These include tension (with the triad of depression, irritability and lethargy), mood swings, anxiety, crying, self-mutilation, as well as psychosis with delusions, hallucinations, and paranoia. Common behavioral symptoms include food cravings, decreased motivation, increased alcohol urges, social isolation, increased libido, insomnia or hypersomnia, clumsiness and forgetfulness. Among the common physical symptoms are headaches, breast tenderness, asthma, sinusitis, epilepsy, skin lesions, conjunctivitis, and joint and muscle pains.

Symptoms never exceed 14 days, but may only last a few hours, for example, panic attacks, psychosis, epilepsy, migraine. Symptoms always increase in severity as menstruation approaches; thus, symptoms that occur a week before the onset of menstruation and then disappear are unlikely to be repeated at the same phase of the cycle month after month. Occasionally, symptoms start during menstruation. This occurs in women who have a slight menstrual bleed for a few days before the full menstrual flow, when symptoms are occurring in the physiological "premenstruum," although recorded as chronological "menstruation." A single severe symptom (e.g., epilepsy, migraine, aggressive outburst, self-mutilation) may occur in the morning, with menstruation starting in the evening, in which case the premenstrual event is recorded as occurring on the first day of menstruation. This is the reason most sociological surveys (accidents, criminal offenses, examination results, hospitalization) compare incidents during the paramenstruum with the other days of the menstrual cycle.

Typically, patients are polysymptomatic, with six or more symptoms recurring during the premenstruum, and with symptoms tending to span more than one medical speciality. Neurologists, rheumatologists, dermatologists, otologists, chest physicians, urologists, and gastroenterologists are also frequently involved. Many workers prefer to limit the initial daily recording to the three priority symptoms, as when those are satisfactorily treated the other minor symptoms tend also to disappear.

Depression is a common PMS symptom, but differs from major depression in that the timing is predictable and shorter, never more than 14 days, and is followed by days of complete normality. It is characterized by weight increase with food cravings and binges, in contrast to the weight loss and diminished appetite of typical depression. Those with PMS have a yearning for sleep and would like to stay in bed all day, as opposed to the early morning waking and restlessness of other depressives, who get up, wander round the house, make tea or even do the housework. Marked irritability and mood swings accompany the depressive days but are absent in the follicular phase. Nulliparous women may have nymphomania during the premenstruum, which differs from the complete loss of libido in other depressions. [See DEPRESSION.]

With PMS irritability there may be loss of self-control resulting in verbal abuse with shouting, yelling, and swearing, as well as violence with banging, slamming, throwing, and hitting. She may become impatient, irrational, illogical, hostile, and paranoidal. Her behavior may lead to criminal offenses for damage to property, grievous bodily harm, or attempted or actual murder. [*See* IMPULSE CONTROL.]

A cry for help during the premenstruum may be an attempted suicide, hoax telephone calls, or arson. PMS-related crimes tend to be committed alone, to the surprise of those near to them at the time; they do not appear to be premeditated; they are without apparent motive; and there is usually no attempt to escape detection. [*See* CRIMINAL BEHAVIOR.]

The headaches tend to be hemicranial or centered in, above, below, or behind one or both eyes, and they may describe the eye as being "stoney hard." Migrainologists recognize "tension headaches" as being occipital, with radiation of pain down the neck and across the shoulders, but this is not the most common type of PMS headache. [*See* HEADACHES.]

III. SIGNS

There are few signs of PMS, although a partner may recognize darkening under and puffiness of the eyes. He is unlikely to recognize excessive weight gain during the premenstruum, unless alerted by the patient, for healthy normal women may also experience weight swings of up to five pounds each cycle.

If one records daily blood pressure readings, there may be paramenstrual swings about 20 mm Hg in both the diastolic and systolic pressure compared with intermenstrual readings, but not reaching hypertensive levels. Those complaining of headaches centered on the eyes may, with daily recording, note an increase in intraocular tension of about 5 mm Hg during the paramenstruum compared with the intramenstruum, occurring both in those whose intraocular tension is normal and those with early or treated glaucoma. There may be proteinuria in catheter specimens of urine during the paramenstruum compared with the intramenstruum. The day-by-day changes in severity of a patient with asthma are easily shown by the peak flow meter. Investigation of these signs in individuals are not always necessary, although they are interesting findings for research.

IV. CHARACTERISTICS

These characteristics of PMS are helpful at the initial screening of women who have not yet started regular recording of symptoms. If present they are accepted in English law as sufficient reason to delay sentencing or court appearances until a positive diagnosis can be made.

PMS women are normal on gynecological examination. They have regular and painless menstruation, with normal loss, normal blood levels of estrogen, follicle stimulating hormone, luteinizing hormone, and prolactin, and do not have infertility problems. Cyclical symptoms may recur for 2 years before menarche, continue for about 2 years after the natural menopause, and also restart up to 3 years after recovery from the trauma of hysterectomy or oophorectomy.

Pain with menstruation is *not* a presenting PMS symptom and always requires further investigation. Common causes of premenstrual and menstrual pain include spasmodic dysmenorrhea, which only occurs in ovulatory cycles and so disappears with the contraceptive pill; endometriosis, which is accompanied by dyspareunia and pain on moving the uterus at vaginal examination; and pelvic inflammatory disease, which causes pain throughout the cycle that is worse in the premenstruum and is usually accompanied by a vaginal discharge. [*See* PAIN.]

PMS tends to start at times of hormonal upheaval—32% at puberty and 33% after pregnancy—while others start on stopping the contraceptive pill, after amenorrhea (e.g., due to anorexia, head injury), after sterilization, and after unilateral oophorectomy. These are also the times when PMS may increase in severity. PMS follows recover from preeclampsia and postnatal depression in 80% of cases. Symptoms are increased at times of stress. One frequently hears a woman describe how she had a difficult time with PMS at puberty, but that it then eased for many years until after a pregnancy, or when she was under stress from an unsatisfactory relationship, a bereavement, redundancy, or a financial problem. [*See* STRESS.]

PMS women have difficulty in tolerating progestin medication, whether administered orally, transdermally, or as long-term injections, in contraceptive pills, or HRT, for progestins lower the blood progesterone level. They have difficulty in tolerating long intervals without food, and easily become shaky, tired, anxious, or aggressive at such times. Symptoms tend to increase if there is sleep deficit, and they are poor jet-lag travelers. While they can tolerate normal alcohol intake during the intermenstruum, they may have uncontrollable alcohol urges premenstrually. Regardless of their poor premenstrual behavior, it is then that their libido is increased and may reach nymphomanic proportions. Monthly weight swings of up to five pounds occur in normal, healthy women, but during their adult years PMS women experience weight swings exceeding 28 pounds between their highest nonpregnant weight and their lowest weight since the age of 16 years.

In common with most hormonal diseases a positive family history is frequent, with three or four generations suffering. This genetic factor has been demonstrated in twin studies, where if one monozygous twin suffers from PMS the other will also be suffering, whereas in female dizygous twins the incidence is similar to that found in sisters. Similarly, adoption studies have shown a statistically significant difference between the low incidence of PMS in mothers of adopted daughters compared with the high incidence in mothers of biological daughters.

Finally, PMS can occur together with any chronic condition (e.g., schizophrenia, Down's syndrome, congenital mental handicap, rheumatoid arthritis, fibromyalgia, bronchitis, tuberculosis), in which case treatment of PMS will only improve premenstrual symptoms and not the underlying condition.

V. DIAGNOSIS

The diagnosis of PMS depends on prospective, daily recording by the patient or responsible person of the days of symptoms and days of menstruation for a minimum of 2 months. This is easier when recording a specific symptom with a marked onset and end (e.g., migraine, new acne papules, epilepsy, sore throat), but it is more difficult when considering symptoms present throughout the cycle and while trying to record an increase or decrease in severity (tiredness, clumsiness, forgetfulness). Ideally, no more than the three most severe symptoms should be recorded; otherwise it makes the patient unduly introspective, or recording is made without full consideration. Therapists, including males working with PMS, should try to record

their symptoms daily for at least 2 months, for only then will they appreciate the difficulties of recording after a late night party, on holiday, or during a stressful event, and they will then understand the need to keep the recording as simple as possible. A simple menstrual chart, which gives the diagnosis of PMS at a glance, is shown in Table I. The patient is advised to keep it by her bed and to mark it with a pen each night before retiring.

Many daily rating scales and visual analog scales have been developed; some demand daily body temperature and body weight, which may be helpful for clinical trials of mild to moderate cases, but will never be completed by desparate women demanding immediate help. Many daily symptom charts list some 30 different symptoms that patients may never have considered, but that they can easily manipulate. Questionnaires are of limited value, as the more often one is used, the less attention the patient pays in completing it. All too often patients completing certain questionnaires tend to confuse menstrual pain with PMS.

In severe cases the partner, or other responsible person, may be able to note the days when symptoms are present. Otherwise it may be necessary to gather particulars of precise dates of specific incidents from other sources such as hospital emergency rooms in cases of suicide attempts or the suturing of slashed wrists; from police in relation to domestic violence or alcohol abuse; from prison for indiscipline, causing a disturbance, or aggressive attacks; from schools or community centers where records are kept of disturbances covering instances of bodily harm or arson attempts; and from college registers showing absences.

No blood tests are diagnostic of PMS. In particular progesterone blood level is of no importance, as progesterone level only rises in the luteal phase in ovular cycles, but PMS also occurs in anovular cycles. Progesterone is secreted in spurts, and is lower after meals. The sex hormone binding globulin (SHBG) level is frequently low in PMS, but the estimation must be done when the patient has been free of all medication (including analgesics, vitamins, minerals, laxatives) for at least 7 days and free of hormone medication (including the pill and HRT) for at least 1 month. Furthermore, it is not reliable in those with thyroid disorder, liver disease, obesity, or hirsuitism, and the blood must be kept frozen until analyzed.

A ferritin estimation is worthwhile and is often sur-

Table I Menstrual Charts

	Jan.	Feb.	Mar.			Oct.	Nov.	Dec.
1					1			
2					2			
3					3			
4					4			
5					5			
6					6			
7	X				7			
8	X				8			
9	X				9			
10	X				10			
11	X	X			11			
12	X	X			12			H
13	X	X			13			H
14	X	X	X		14		H	hM
15	MX	X	X		15		H	M
16	MX	X	X		16		H	M
17	M	X	X		17		MH	M
18	M	X	X		18		Mh	M
19		M	X		19	H	M	M
20		M	X		20	H	M	
21		M	X		21	H	M	
22		M	X		22	H	M	
23			M		23	M	M	
24			M		24	M		
25			M		25	M		
26			M		26	M		
27			M		27	M		
28					28			
29					29			
30					30			
31					31			

X = tension
hH = headache
M = menstruation

prisingly low in PMS patients, who otherwise have a good hemoglobin level and normal hematology. It is a reflection of their iron store, and low levels are found in those who habitually allow their blood glucose levels to drop. Restoring the patient's ferritin level to more than 30 μg/l by giving an iron supplement or improving the diet, will improve their stamina and energy level.

Table II Diagnostic Checklist

	Irrelevant/positive/negative
Hormonal time of onset.	
Hormonal time of increased severity.	
Painless menses (2 -ves if painful).	
Increased libido in premenstruum.	
Pre-eclampsia.	
Postnatal depression.	
Side effect with the pill.	
Adult weight swing exceeding 12 kg.	
Food craving in the premenstruum.	
Alcohol urges in the premenstruum.	
Family history of PMS.	
Total	

$$\% \text{ Score} = \frac{\text{positives} \times 100}{\text{positives} + \text{negatives}}$$

VI. DIAGNOSTIC POINTER CHECKLIST

When a 2-month menstrual record is not immediately available a diagnostic pointer checklist, compiled from the characteristics mentioned earlier, is helpful. Items are scored "positive," "negative," and "irrelevant," while those whose presenting symptom is pain with menstruation, or dysmenorrhea, score two negatives. The total positive scores are multiplied by 100, and divided by the sum of the positives and negatives. Women with a diagnostic pointer scores exceeding 66% are likely to produce a positive menstrual chart after charting for 2 months (Table II).

VII. ETIOLOGY

The many hormonal and chemical interactions, which result in PMS, are not fully understood, although many etiological theories exist. An acceptable etiological theory must be able to explain at the molecular level the following facts known to occur in PMS:

1. Psychological and physical symptoms present in the luteal phase with absence in the follicular phase.
2. Absence of symptoms and general well-being in pregnancy.
3. High incidence after pregnancy, and particularly after postnatal depression.

4. Inability to tolerate progestins, and their failure to relieve PMS.
5. Increased intensity of symptoms at times of stress.
6. Inability to tolerate long food gaps, and symptom relief from the "three hourly starch diet."
7. Relief from high-dose natural progesterone.
8. Symptoms occur in both ovular and anovular cycles.
9. Persistence of symptoms after recovery from the trauma of hysterectomy and oophorectomy.
10. Cyclical symptoms can occur two years before menarche and continue for two years after the natural menopause.

Critical to the diagnosis is the fact that PMS occurs in the luteal phase and not in the follicular phase. Estrogen, measured in picograms, is present in the blood in varying amounts throughout the menstrual cycle. Progesterone is only present in the luteal phase, and is absent in the follicular phase; it is measured in nanograms, which is 1000 times higher than picograms; thus, fluctuations of amplitude of estrogen relative to progesterone are minimal. During pregnancy, when there is a massive increase in progesterone from the placenta, PMS eases and there is a sense of well-being. At labor, when the placenta is also delivered, the progesterone blood level falls abruptly; postnatal blues and a high incidence of postnatal depression follow. The involvement of progesterone in the etiology of PMS is supported by facts 1, 2, and 3.

Molecular biologists in the last decade have further supported the hypothesis that progesterone is involved in PMS by their discovery of progesterone receptors. Progesterone receptors are compounds, found in the hundreds, in those cells that require progesterone. The task of progesterone receptors is to bind to progesterone molecules and to transport the progesterone molecules to the nucleus. Using new technology and animal studies researchers have been able to recognize some of the unique characteristics of progesterone receptors. For instance, after an initial dose of progesterone the receptors become hyposensitive and require a high dose of progesterone to stimulate them again. Progesterone receptors do not accept progestins in the same way as progesterone molecules in the presence of adrenalin, such as occurs at times of stress and at low blood glucose level, for then the progesterone receptors function as corticosterone receptors, correcting the adrenalin balance. Thus, unless current stress can be ameliorated and low blood glucose levels avoided, the administration of progesterone will not help PMS.

Progesterone receptors are widespread throughout the body, with the highest concentration in the limbic area, the center of emotion, which may explain the predominance of psychological symptoms in PMS. Other areas of high concentration of progesterone receptors are the meninges, the nasopharyngeal passages and lungs, eyes, bones, and skin, which would account for headaches, sinusitis, asthma, conjunctivitis, sties, joint and muscle pains, and skin lesions, respectively. It has recently been shown that progesterone receptors are controlled within the cells by a specific stress protein, hsp90. Thus, a fault in the functioning of progesterone receptors, or of the stress proteins controlling them, would explain facts 4, 5, 6, and 7. The function of progesterone receptors in the systemic cells, where PMS symptoms originate, occurs whether or not ovulation is occurring, thus explaining facts 8, 9, and 10.

PMS women do not have hypoglycemia, but a hyperefficient lower controlling mechanism that releases adrenalin whenever the blood glucose level nears the lower optimum level. This adrenalin release mobilizes glucose in cells, which passes into the blood, correcting the low blood glucose level. However, the empty cells soon fill with water, giving the bloatedness and weight gain so familiar to PMS subjects. Adrenalin is the hormone of fight, flight, and fright, which in turns is responsible for the tension and behavioral symptoms.

It is easy to negate the involvement of progesterone in the etiology by recalling that there is no evidence that progesterone blood levels are low in PMS. Recognition of the function of progesterone receptors explains why the blood progesterone level is irrelevant, and also why low-dose progesterone, as used in current double-blind placebo controlled trials is doomed to failure. It is going to be difficult to arrange double-blind controlled trials of high-dose progesterone, which also control for the avoidance of stress and of transient episodes of low blood glucose levels. Both stress and low blood glucose levels stimulate adrenalin and inhibit the action of progesterone receptors.

Progesterone is formed in the adrenals by both sexes and at all ages, and is then converted to estrogens, testosterones, and cortisones. The exact mechanism that controls the menstrual cycle remains unknown. It is though to be in the hypothalamus, at the base of the brain. Zuspan and his colleagues, using a culture of human placental cells, have demonstrated that progesterone has an inhibitory effect on monoamine oxidase activity; in short, progesterone is a natural MAOI antidepressant.

Others have unsuccessfully suggested etiological theories that do not explain the 10 facts enumerated above. These include deficiency of pyridoxine, magnesium, essential fatty acids, dietary irregularities, allergies, and thyroid dysfunction. Most of these studies have been done on LLPPD without consideration of the characteristics of PMS. Ashby and his coworkers noted low serotonin levels in LLPPD, and several reports have appeared of the beneficial effect of the selective serotonin reuptake inhibitors (SSRIs) in PMS. The action of SSRIs on the brain cells is similar to that of progesterone on brain cells, but in other parts of the body progesterone has other effects, such as building up bones, which are not shared by SSRIs.

VIII. TREATMENT

A disease with no universally accepted etiology is always subject to numerous suggested treatments, some that have never been clinically tested and others that rely on symptomatic relief of the common symptoms of PMS. If one accepts the part played by progesterone receptors then the relief of stress and the maintenance of a stable blood sugar level are two imperatives in treatment. [*See* Premenstrual Syndrome Treatment Interventions.]

A. Stress Relief

In the past there may have been family members or religious leaders with whom one could openly discuss the day-to-day problems that cause stress. Today, members of our nuclear societies are often unable to unburden themselves. Counsellors or therapists are needed to help PMS women understand themselves and their problems, while some may need full psychotherapy, either cognitive or behavioral. Abnormal behavior in the premenstruum may be followed by excessive guilt, which is best handled by a therapist. Many benefit from relaxation, stress-relieving, or assertiveness classes. Life-style changes may be needed, through stopping smoking, drugs, or excess alcohol, preventing sleep deficit, and avoiding night work. The woman may need to be advised to change from hormonal contraception, all of which contains progestins, which exacerbates symptoms. Recording of day-to-day symptoms on a menstrual chart should be continued throughout treatment to assess progress. [See BEHAVIOR THERAPY; COGNITIVE THERAPY.]

B. Dietary Advice

Too often one finds women who ensure that their children and partners have regular food while neglecting their own. One English survey found that half of PMS women did not stop for breakfast; in fact, they unknowingly started the day with a blood glucose drop. The "three hourly starch diet" has been found to be the most effective tool in easing PMS in 68% of sufferers. Women are advised to divide their usual day's starch intake (flour, potatoes, rice, rye, oats, and corn) into six or seven portions, and have a starchy snack every 3 hours throughout the day, always within 1 hour of waking and 1 hour of retiring. The diet should be continued throughout the cycle, and other nutrients (especially proteins, fruit, and vegetables), which they normally eat, should be continued. It is worth reminding patients that when they exceed 3 hours on only one occasion it may take up to 7 days before the normal utilization of progesterone can occur. It is a simple multicultural diet, and patients soon get into the habit of always eating little and often. There should be no weight gain if the individual is eating the same amount of starch each day, but in seven portions instead of the more usual three meals. Those who are initially overweight find they lose weight as bloating is eliminated.

Taking a full dietary history is essential before teaching the patient the three hourly starch diet, so any other nutritional deficiencies can be corrected. It should not be necessary to add extra vitamins or minerals, which should be available in the normal diet. In particular, vitamin B6 (pyridoxine) should not be advised now that the possibility of causing pyridoxine overdose neuropathology is recognized. [See FOOD, NUTRITION, AND MENTAL HEALTH.]

C. Symptomatic Treatment

If one premenstrual symptom predominates above all others, particularly in LLPPD where 30% of the symptom may be present throughout the cycle, then individual symptomatic treatment may be preferable. This applies to those likely to benefit from selected antidepressants, anxiolytics, tranquilizers, anticonvulsants, analgesics, or muscle relaxants. It applies even more with respect to physical symptoms, where headaches, asthma, skin lesions, conjunctivitis, and sinusitis are the only PMS symptom. Here, the most effective symptomatic treatment should be used in addition to training the patient on the three hourly starch diet and counseling her on avoiding hormonal contraception. Among the antidepressants most likely to be effective in PMS are the selective serotonin reuptake inhibitors (SSRIs) or the monoamine oxidase inhibitors (MAOIs).

D. Progesterone Therapy

Only a few severe sufferers of PMS require progesterone therapy; the majority will benefit from treatments already suggested. Even if progesterone is needed, the three hourly starch diet is still required.

Progesterone treatment is essentially prophylactic and needs to be started before symptoms develop, so it is usually started 14 days before the next expected menstruation and it is continued until the onset of bleeding. Progesterone cannot be utilized if administered orally or transdermally. The minimal dose is 400 mg suppositories used vaginally or rectally twice daily, but this may be increased to 400 mg used 6 times daily, or progesterone intramuscularly into the buttock in doses of 50 mg or 100 mg daily. It is not possible to overdose with our present methods of administration, which cannot reach the blood progesterone levels found in mid or late pregnancy. There are no interactions with other medications. If vaginal candidiasis is present, symptoms may be exacerbated by progesterone, but today candidiasis can be treated with a single capsule of fluconazole 150 mg given to both the patient and her partner.

There is anecdotal evidence of the effectiveness of progesterone in PMS in the British National Health Service Tribunal on overspending in 1958, and in individual women charged in England with serious crimes, including murder and infanticide, but the only successful double-blind placebo controlled trial was that by Magill in general practice using 400 mg twice daily. All other trials using a lower dose of progesterone have been unsuccessful.

Progesterone can also be used as a contraceptive in cases of severe PMS by starting with a small daily dose of progesterone 100 mg from day 8, raising to the patient's normal progesterone dose on day 14, and continuing until menstruation.

BIBLIOGRAPHY

Dalton, K., & Holton, D. (1994). *PMS: The essential guide to Treatment Options.* London & San Francisco: HarperCollins Publishers.

Dalton, K. (1984). The Premenstrual Syndrome and Progesterone Therapy (2nd ed.). London: W. Heinemann Medical Books, Ltd., and Chicago: Year Book Medical Publishers, Inc.

Smith, S., & Schiff, I. (1993). *Modern management of premenstrual syndrome.* New York and London: Norton Medical Books.

Premenstrual Syndrome Treatment Interventions

Laura Weiss Roberts, Teresita McCarty, and Sally K. Severino

University of New Mexico School of Medicine

Follicular Phase of the Menstrual Cycle The initial portion of the menstrual cycle, starting at the onset of menses until ovulation occurs. The length of the follicular phase is variable.

Hypothalamus and Pituitary Gland Subcortical, midline brain structures that function in the regulation of a number of neuroendocrine systems. Lesions and tumors of the hypothalamus frequently are associated with a broad variety of psychiatric, physical, and behavioral symptoms such as emotional changes (e.g., apathy, sadness, nervousness, irritability, frequent crying), paranoia, abnormal menstrual and thyroid function, and appetite and sleep problems.

Luteal Phase of the Menstrual Cycle The latter portion of the menstrual cycle starting after ovulation until the onset of menses. The phase is about 14 days long and is named after the corpus luteum of the ovary.

Ovaries Paired sexual organs, located in the lower abdomen of women, that serve as the source of ova and secrete a number of steroid hormones necessary for menstruation, ovulation, first trimester pregnancy sustenance, and other aspects of women's sexual health.

Ovulation The point in the menstrual cycle at which the egg, the reproductive germ cell, is released from a mature ovarian follicle.

Premenstrual Dysphoric Disorder (PMDD), formerly Late Luteal Phase Dysphoric Disorder (LLPDD) Terms that refer to that small percentage of women who have premenstrual syndrome with primarily emotional symptoms severe enough to affect their ability to function at home or in the workplace.

Premenstrual Exacerbation Aggravation of such chronic conditions such as asthma, depression, anxiety, eating disorders, substance abuse, headaches, allergies, seizures, or herpes during the premenstrual phase.

Premenstrual Phase, also "Late Luteal Phase" or "Premenstruum" The 5- to 7-day period immediately preceding menses.

Premenstrual Symptoms Those physical, behavioral, or mood changes that appear to change in severity during the late luteal phase of the cycle, do not exist in the same form or severity during the mid or late follicular phase, and disappear or return to their usual level of severity during menses.

Preventive Health Care Clinical care that places an emphasis on the decreased incidence (i.e., number of new cases each year) of disease (primary prevention), the early recognition and eradication of disease (secondary prevention), and the minimization of suffering caused by disease (tertiary prevention).

Uterus The womb, a hollow, muscular organ in women that opens to the vaginal canal and undergoes sequential and cyclic changes (i.e., proliferative, secretory, menstrual) between menarche and menopause. It is the structure in which the fertilized ovum normally becomes embedded and the developing fetus matures before birth.

PREMENSTRUAL SYNDROME (PMS) refers to a condition that some women experience preceding the onset of their monthly menses. It consists of the cyclic recurrence of physical, psychological, and/or behavioral symptoms of sufficient severity that medical treatment is sought. Optimal care for the physical and psychological well-being of women who suffer from PMS is built on an understanding of the developmental aspects of women's sexual health, including biological, psychological, and social/cultural influences.

I. HISTORICAL BACKGROUND

As far back as the time of Hippocrates, physicians have attempted to describe the relationships between menstruation and the subjective experiences, moods, and behavior changes of women. Over the past 24 centuries, "morbid dispositions of the mind" and "madness" in the form of mania, delusions, "nervous excitement," hallucinations, "unreasonable appetites," and suicidal impulses have been attributed to the cyclic menstrual patterns of women. Although much remains to be understood, our clinical and scientific interest in these relationships has grown in modern times. Robert Frank coined the term "premenstrual tension" and offered this remarkable description of the problem in 1931 (p. 1054):

> A feeling of indescribable tension from 10 to 7 days preceding menstruation which, in most instances, continues until . . . menstrual flow occurs. These patients complain of unrest, irritability, "like jumping out of their skin." . . . [T]heir personal suffering is intense.

Premenstrual tension later became known as premenstrual syndrome or PMS. In particular, the work of Katharina Dalton in England, beginning in the 1950s and ongoing today, established PMS as a legitimate health condition of women, worthy of medical attention and scientific investigation (see Premenstrual Syndrome (PMS) by Katharina Dalton). A conference convened by the National Institute of Mental Health in 1983 established diagnostic guidelines for PMS and

affirmed the interest of mental health professionals in the mood symptoms experienced premenstrually by many women. In 1987, Late Luteal Phase Dysphoric Disorder (LLPDD), a more narrowly defined syndrome than PMS, was included as a proposed clinical diagnosis in an appendix of the Diagnostic and Statistical Manual of Mental Disorders (DSM-IIIR). DSM-IV, published in 1994, replaced this terminology and classified Premenstrual Dysphoric Disorder as a clinical diagnosis under the rubric of "Depression Not Otherwise Specified."

After decades of research, PMS remains a puzzle with respect to etiology, physical and psychological correlates, risk and protective factors, and treatment. The true prevalence of PMS remains uncertain, the relative contributions of "nature" and "nurture" to PMS symptomatology have not been determined, and the reasons why only some women develop PMS have not been fully established. We have learned to some extent, however, what PMS is not: PMS is not the result of abnormal menstrual cycles or of abnormal absolute levels of ovarian hormones. It is not solely the result of attributional bias. Moreover, PMS is not a condition relieved uniformly by a single treatment approach such as hormonal therapy or psychiatric medications. After years of inquiry, it appears that PMS is the result of complex interactions among biological, psychological, social, and cultural influences within the lives of women.

For this reason, women's health related to PMS may best be understood from a multidimensional perspective. This article outlines an approach to PMS that focuses on the normal menstrual cycle and the distinct biological, psychological, and social/cultural issues in women's development, and includes a review of the phenomenology of PMS. With this foundation, we describe strategies for restoring mental and physical health related to the menstrual cycle through prevention, accurate diagnosis, and appropriate treatment interventions.

II. NORMAL MENSTRUAL CYCLE

The normal menstrual cycle is an intricately orchestrated, neatly timed physiologic process occurring in women from menarche until menopause. Each cycle revolves around development of an ovarian follicle and the preparation of the uterus, followed by ovula-

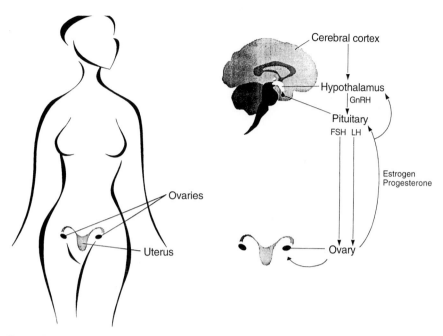

Figure 1 Anatomy and physiology of the menstrual cycle. GnRH, gonadotropin-releasing hormone; FSH, follicle-stimulating hormone; LH, luteinizing hormone. *Illustration by Jim Roberts.*

tion and the transformation of the ovarian follicle into the corpus luteum, which is necessary for sustaining a pregnancy should fertilization and embryo implantation occur. In the absence of pregnancy, the menstrual cycle ordinarily lasts 26 to 32 days (a range of 21 to 36 days), with women between the ages of 20 and 40 having the greatest regularity in cycle length. The menstrual cycle's three distinct phases relate primarily to hormonal changes and events at the hypothalamus and pituitary regions of the brain, the ovary, and the uterus (Figures 1 and 2). The cycle is also influenced by the limbic region of the central nervous system, the adrenal and thyroid glands, the pancreas, and exogenous hormones or medications.

A. Follicular Phase and Ovulation

The follicular phase begins on the first day of menstruation and lasts until approximately Day 14, based on a 28-day cycle. During this phase, a number of ovarian follicles, each typically containing a single ovum, develop under the influence of follicular stimulating hormone (FSH) produced by the anterior pituitary, a deep, midline endocrine organ in the brain. This hormone is produced and delivered in response

to the pulsatile release of a neurohormone, gonadotropin releasing hormone (GnRH), which is produced in the medial basal region of a second brain structure, the hypothalamus. The developing follicles, in turn, produce estrogen, which has three main effects: it dampens the further release of FSH by the anterior pituitary; it, along with GnRH, stimulates the production and gradual release of luteinizing hormone (LH) by the anterior pituitary; and it stimulates the growth of the uterine lining or endometrium. Over the course of 2 weeks, one of the ovarian follicles matures more than the others in that it is larger, has evidence of more mitotic and biosynthetic activity, and has greater vascularization. This "dominant" follicle progresses through three phases (preantral, antral, and preovulatory) and manufactures increasing amounts of estrogen and, to a lesser extent, progesterone. The other follicles gradually and irreversibly decline.

Toward the end of the follicular phase, a rise in progesterone and surges of estrogen, LH, and FSH take place, resulting in ovulation. Estrogen peaks 24 to 36 hours prior to ovulation, whereas LH and FSH peak roughly within 10 to 12 hours of ovulation. Luteinizing hormone stimulates the initiation of oocyte meiosis, leutinizes the granulosa cells of the follicle,

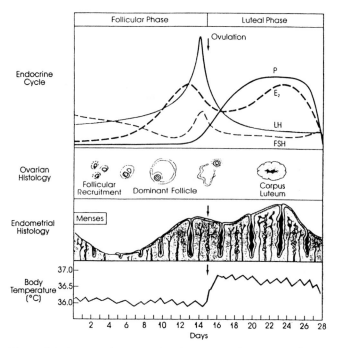

Figure 2 The normal menstrual cycle. Hormonal ovarian, endometrial, and basal body temperature changes throughout the normal menstrual cycle. P, progesterone; E_2, estradiol; LH, luteinizing hormone; FSH, follicle-stimulating hormone. From Carr, B. R., Wilson, J. D. "Disorders of the Ovary and Female Reproductive Tract," in *Harrison's Principles of Internal Medicine,* 13th Edition. Edited by Isselbacher, K. J., Braunwald, E., Wilson, J. D., *et al.,* p. 2022. New York, McGraw-Hill, 1994. Copyright © 1994 McGraw-Hill, Inc. Used with permission.

and promotes progesterone and prostaglandin synthesis within the follicle. Progesterone potentiates estrogen effects and also triggers the FSH surge and activates prostaglandins and enzymes present in the follicle. This allows the follicular wall at the edge of the ovary to rupture. Influenced by hormones and chemicals in the immediate locale, the ovum then detaches from its anchor within the ovarian follicle. The release of the ovum from the ovary, allowing it to travel down one of the two fallopian tubes for possible fertilization, is defined as ovulation.

A number of physical and psychological findings have been noted during the follicular and ovulation phases of the menstrual cycle, including endometrial breakdown and sloughing during the initial 2 to 8 days of the follicular phase (i.e., menses), followed by proliferation, vascularization, and differentiation of the endometrium for implantation; increased production

of thin, relatively alkaline cervical and vaginal mucus in response to raising estrogen levels; an initial sustained decrease in basal body temperature, followed by a temperature rise shortly after ovulation; regular alterations of electrolyte composition of urine and saliva; and a heightened sense of personal well-being, enhanced sensory perceptions, and, perhaps, somewhat improved cognitive task performance throughout the follicular phase.

B. Luteal Phase

The luteal phase occurs after ovulation, spanning approximately Days 15 through 28 of the menstrual cycle. Once the ovum has been released, the ruptured follicle becomes the corpus luteum, or "yellow body," named because of the high concentrations of lipids it contains. Its granulosa cells hypertrophy and produce high amounts of progesterone, estrogen, and androgens necessary for sustaining a pregnancy if fertilization and implantation have occurred. At such concentrations, these hormones serve to decrease GnRH secretion by the hypothalamus. They also stimulate the endometrium to become edematous and to undergo glandular proliferation over the 7 days after ovulation. In addition, progesterone reduces some of the pituitary effects of estrogen by decreasing estrogen receptors in this brain structure.

In the absence of pregnancy, approximately 10 to 14 days after ovulation, the corpus luteum regresses and becomes a fibrotic, hyalinized region of the ovary, called the corpus albicans. Progesterone and estrogen concentrations gradually decrease. These events trigger a number of endometrial responses. Local vasomotor reactions within the spiral arterioles of the uterine lining cause endometrial ischemia. Local prostaglandin synthesis increases, augmenting uterine contractility. Menstruation begins as necrotic tissues slough away and blood from interstitial hemorrhaging enters the uterus. The sustained low levels of estrogen and progesterone stimulate the hypothalamus to release GnRH and the pituitary to secrete FSH and LH, triggering the development of another set of ovarian follicles and setting into motion the next menstrual cycle.

The premenstrual phase spans the 5 to 7 days before menstruation, and thus occurs within the luteal phase of the menstrual cycle. A wide range of symptoms, such as increased fluid retention, fatigue, breast tenderness, headaches or other pain syndromes, mood fluctuations, and subjectively increased appetite, have been associated with this segment of the normal menstrual cycle. Only when it is so severe that patients' daily functioning is affected and health care is formally sought for this problem can the diagnosis of PMS be made.

C. Influences on the Normal Menstrual Cycle

Elements that can modify or disrupt the normal menstrual cycle are many and often interrelated. For example, limbic system neurotransmitters (such as dopamine) appear to inhibit GnRH release by the hypothalamus, whereas norepinephrine stimulates GnRH output. In addition, as the ovarian corpus luteum de-

teriorates, its decrease in estrogen and progesterone production leads to a reduction in hypothalamic endorphin release. This, in turn, triggers greater GnRH, LH, and FSH production and causes follicle maturation early in the next cycle. Psychological and physical stresses may also modify the menstrual cycle through increased secretion of endorphins stimulated by increased corticotropin-releasing hormone (CRH). This leads to a decrease in GnRH release, which interferes with ovulation. Abnormalities in adrenal steroid synthesis or insufficient production of hormones by the thyroid (thyroxin) or the pancreas (insulin) may result in anovulation and infrequent menses, although the mechanisms of action are unknown. Estrogen itself is associated with increased secretion of growth hormone, prolactin, ACTH, and oxytocin controlled in concert by the hypothalamus and the anterior and posterior regions of the pituitary. Genetic syndromes affecting hormone and steroid synthesis or chemical metabolism similarly will influence menstrual cycles. Beyond internal chemical influences, exogenous hormones and medications may induce or prevent ovulation through a number of mechanisms, affecting the length and timing of the menstrual cycle. These richly varied and interconnected processes suggest how women with different central nervous system lesions, life stresses, genetic disorders, endocrine dysfunction, and medical illnesses all may develop interrupted menstrual cycles.

D. Variability in the Normal Menstrual Cycle

The normal menstrual cycle differs between women as well as across an individual woman's lifetime. This variability is shown in many ways: the length of menses (normal range of 2 to 8 days) and the menstrual cycle (normal range of 21 to 36 days); its synchronization with other women in close proximity; symptoms and signs associated with the premenstrual phase and menstruation; the level of interference caused by external factors such as physical illness or extreme exercise; the effects of emotional stress, nutritional deficiencies, medications, and hormonal disruptions; the numbers of follicles that mature during each cycle as a woman ages; and changes that occur at different life stages or with pregnancy and lactation. There is considerable variation that falls within the range of "normal" menstrual cycle experiences. For this reason, recognizing the premenstrual syndrome can be especially challenging. [*See* PREMENSTRUAL SYNDROME (PMS).]

III. DEVELOPMENTAL VIEW OF WOMEN'S HEALTH AND THE MENSTRUAL CYCLE

Development is an orderly pattern of changes within an individual occurring over time, each stage is built upon and shaped by earlier ones. Development is influenced by the unique relationship between an individual's biology and experiences of the self, of others, and of the world. These factors deeply affect personal attributes such as temperament and personality; cognitive capacities including learning, memory, and intelligence; the meanings given to sensations, relationships, and events in life; and one's sense of the self within a specific familial, social, and cultural setting. With each stage of development, aspects of the individual are reconfigured within the current context. Thus, each moment offers indications of both one's distinct personal history and unique adaptation to the present.

A woman's development begins at conception (Table I). The potential for normal female sexual differentiation is genetically determined by the presence of two X chromosomes and the absence of a Y chromosome in the embryo. The actual course of development, however, is affected by a series of critical periods in the subsequent growth of each individual.

During critical periods in the sequence of development, biology and experience work in concert to organize and delimit the "choices" of an organism. The potential for ovaries and female external genitalia is made possible by the XX genotype. Female fetal tissues will not develop into these anatomic structures, however, unless sex hormones are present in specific proportions in the fetal environment at certain times. Abnormal proportions of fetal hormones or chemical exposures may alter subsequent physical development and sexual behavior, as evidenced by animal experiments in which hermaphroditic external genitalia or male-type sexual behaviors have been induced in genotypic females through fetal androgen exposure. In addition to animal models, patients with anomalous sexual development have clearly demonstrated that aspects of sexual differentiation may be irreversibly "settled" in an individual once a critical period

has passed. Analogously, differential androgen production in men and women is implicated in central nervous system sexual differences evident in brain structure, physiology, and vascular patterns. Finally, the clinical observation that mothers, daughters, and sisters often resemble one another with respect to their ages at onset of menarche and at onset of menopause suggests that genetic and other early developmental factors may affect later events of sexual maturation. Further investigation is needed to understand the mechanisms that contribute to critical periods in sexual development.

In infancy and childhood, girls learn through experiencing sensations, through using their muscles, and through relating to others. A girl's sense of herself, her body, and her core gender identity (i.e., the earliest feeling of belonging to one sex) emerges in a familial context of attachment, nurturance, affiliation, intimacy, and identification. Children ideally develop a feeling of fundamental trust through the safety and predictability present in this context; alternatively, they may develop a deep sense of apprehension and vulnerability based on their early experiences. Over time, children become acutely aware of certain social and cultural expectations that may surround gender roles as their bodies grow and mature. Anatomic differences between boys and girls give rise to differences in self-concepts, affirmed or altered by learning and observation. Over time, children also express curiosity and become more comfortable with their anatomic sex. Physical well-being during early childhood may be especially important to later health and illness patterns with respect to recognition of bodily discomfort, interpretations of pain, expression of emotional distress through physical complaints, and external validation or reinforcement of symptomatology.

Puberty marks the beginning of adolescence, bringing with it a number of dramatic physical changes such as breast development, growth of pubic and axillary hair, hip widening, and acne. Menarche normally occurs between the ages of 10 and 16, approximately 2 years after the onset of puberty. Of all of the pubertal changes, the start of menstruation is perhaps the most meaningful event, in that it represents a clear passage into womanhood physically and psychologically. Menarche may be exciting, affirming, frightening, awkward, or all of these and other feelings simultaneously. Although menarche does not itself indicate reproductive maturity, it does signify its future prom-

Table I Menstrual Cycle and Sexual Development of Women throughout the Life Span

Prenatal
- Establishment of sexual genotype (XX or XY) at conception
- Some evidence that genetic factors influence growth, age at menarche, and, possibly, future menstrual characteristics
- Intrauterine environment (e.g., hormones, receptors, timing of exposures) influence anatomical and functional fetal differentiation

Infancy/childhood
- Emergence of core gender identity, i.e., the earliest sense of belonging to one sex, during infancy
- Affiliation, attachment, and identification with parents, other family members, care providers
- Physical growth and development (prepubertal); comfort with one's anatomic sex; emergence of sexual orientation
- Exposure to emotional, familial, cultural, and social expectations related to gender
- Sexual self-stimulation and curiosity, sexual play
- Sense of fundamental safety or vulnerability; potential for sexual abuse and exploitation

Adolescence
- Physical changes associated with puberty, including breast development, growth of pubic and axillary hair, menarche (ages 10–18), hip widening, vaginal discharge, and acne
- Settling into a regular menstrual pattern
- Self-image and body-image changes; for some, risk of eating disorders, other maladaptive patterns
- Gender identity and sexual orientation exploration
- Interest in romantic and sexual relationships and curiosity about sexuality, sexual sensation
- For some, initiation of genital sexual activity, including intercourse
- Learning surrounding emotional and physical intimacy in peer relationships
- Making choices with potentially long-range consequences such as drug use and risky sexual activity
- Forming a value system around personal responsibility, sexuality, relationships, and cultural precepts
- Dealing with potential consequences of initiating sexual relationships, including pregnancy and sexually transmitted diseases
- Making the transition to adulthood and practicing being separate from the family of origin

Young and middle adulthood
- Establishing a regular menstrual pattern
- Active exploration of sexuality in relationships, learning and practicing with enhancement of sexual satisfaction through time
- Coping with physical and emotional risks accompanying sexual activities, including coercion, sexually transmitted diseases, pelvic inflammatory disease, cervical cancer, domestic violence
- Making committed attachments, marriages, partnerships
- Becoming more comfortable with gender identity and sexual orientation
- Dealing with reproduction issues such as contraception, pregnancy, miscarriage, infertility, premature menopause
- Physiological and psychological changes surrounding pregnancy, lactation, and child-rearing, including alterations in libido, energy, physical comfort, desire, self-image, meaning of relationships
- For some, manifesting psychiatric illness such as anxiety, depression, late luteal phase dysphoric disorder, sexual dysfunction, psychosis, substance abuse

Later adulthood
- Physiologic, anatomic, and self-image changes associated with menopause
- Maintenance of menstruation by means of exogenous hormones
- Facing transitions in relationships, including children moving away, divorce, death of parents
- Dealing with medical illness, medications, and surgery (including hysterectomy) that affect self-image and sexual functioning
- For many, new possibilities and creativity in postreproductive years

Elderly
- Continuing interest in intimate and sexual relationships
- Physical and emotional changes accompanying aging, including the slowing of sexual responsiveness, lessened physical comfort, and embarrassment
- For many, the loss of intimate partner to death and a sense of loss in family, social, and societal roles
- Dealing with medical illness, medications, and surgery that affect sexual health, function, and self-image
- Sense of integrity and wholeness with respect to one's life, including one's sexuality

ise. The temporal pattern of a young woman's menstrual cycle may be inconsistent in adolescence, especially in connection with erratic nutrition and exercise patterns that in some cases are pathological (e.g., anorexia nervosa, bulimia). Within a few years, however, in the absence of severe physical and psychiatric pathology, menses normally tend to fall into a more regular rhythm with predictable ovulation.

The psychological work of adolescence is equally remarkable. A young woman's tasks include making changes in her self-image and body-image, exploring her gender identity and sexual orientation, learning about emotional and physical intimacy in peer relationships, becoming more autonomous and feeling competent in familial and other contexts, and forming a personal value system around relationships, school performance, sexual behavior, and other issues such as drug use and the problems that accompany sexual activity. Through such experiences, a young woman makes the transition from her family of origin to greater independence and prepares for the full responsibilities of adulthood.

During young and middle adulthood, a number of psychological and physical events of development may occur. At this time, women tend to become more comfortable with themselves and begin making committed attachments, marriages, and partnerships. They learn increasingly about their sexuality, sexual orientation, and personal health issues. Their menstrual cycles also become more settled and predictable. Menstruation may be viewed more positively than at other times as a link to desired fertility. Difficult menstrual patterns (e.g., premenstrual magnification, premenstrual exacerbation of other conditions, or premenstrual syndrome) may also become clearer as women gain greater insight into their cyclic symptoms. In addition, much of women's lives during young and middle adulthood may be affected by reproductive issues such as contraception, pregnancy and lactation, miscarriage and termination of pregnancies, infertility, and child-rearing, all of which may affect menstruation patterns and related cyclic mood and behavioral symptoms. A woman's view of her responsibilities in family and professional relationships may become consolidated during her 20s through 40s as she practices these skills as a wife or partner, a parent, a daughter, a sister, a neighbor, a citizen, and a worker. Taken together, such everyday experiences greatly influence a woman's tolerance and perception of physical symptoms, energy level, willingness to seek health care, self-esteem, libido and sexual desire, comfort, and self-understanding.

In later adulthood, women experience physiological, anatomic, and emotional changes throughout their postreproductive years. Menopause ordinarily occurs in women aged 45 to 55, preceded by approx-

imately 2 years of lengthened or missed menstrual cycles and occasional spotting. Premenstrual syndrome, per se, tends to worsen as menopause approaches and to remit after menopause. During this phase of life, women often experience medical illness, undergo surgical interventions, and receive medications that affect menstrual function and general physical well-being such as hormone replacement. During this period, women also face transitions in family relationships, including children moving away, divorce, or the death of a spouse or parent. Over the 20 or more years beyond menopause, many adaptations are required as women experience changes in intimate relationships, social and societal roles, and personal identity. If loneliness was present earlier in life, it may deepen in the postmenopausal years. Despite such difficulties, for many women, this period allows for creativity, generativity, and freedom not possible at a younger age. Ideally, late in life, women will feel a sense of integrity and completeness about all of their experiences in relation to their biological natures, their personal identities, and their familial and societal roles.

IV. PHENOMENOLOGY OF PREMENSTRUAL SYNDROME

A. PMS Symptoms and Their Timing

An immense number of symptoms have been attributed to PMS (Table II). The most common complaints include physical symptoms (breast swelling and tenderness, abdominal bloating, headaches, muscle aches and pains, weight gain, and edema), emotional symptoms (depression, mood swings, anger, irritability, and anxiety), and others (decreased interest in usual activities, fatigue, difficulty concentrating, increased appetite and food cravings, and hypersomnia or insomnia).

Four temporal patterns have been described for PMS. Symptoms can begin during the second week of the luteal phase (about Day 21). Alternatively, they can begin at ovulation and worsen over the entire luteal phase (about Day 14). In both of these patterns, symptoms remit within a few days after the onset of menses. Some women experience a brief episode of symptoms at ovulation, which is followed by symptom-free days and a recurrence of symptoms late in the luteal phase. Women who seem to be most severely affected experience symptoms that begin at ovulation, worsen across the luteal phase, and remit only after menses ceases.

Table II Examples of Premenstrual Symptoms

Abdominal cramps
Aches or pains
Anger
Anxiety
Bloating
Breast tenderness
Clumsiness
Concentration problems
Confusion
Cravings (e.g., carbohydrate, salt)
Depression
Excessive sleepiness
Fatigue
Forgetfulness
Headaches (migraine, tension)
Hot flashes
Insomnia
Impulsivity
Irritability
Moodiness
Rapid shifts in emotions
Swelling (hands, feet)
Weight gain

These women commonly have only 1 week a month that is symptom-free. It is unclear whether these four patterns represent distinct subtypes of PMS or whether they correspond to other conditions. These four patterns of symptoms must be differentiated from underlying illnesses that either are precipitated during the premenstrual phase or demonstrate a cyclic waxing and waning of intensity related to menstruation. They must also be differentiated from other problems associated with menses, including pelvic pain with menstruation (dysmenorrhea), infrequent menses (oligomenorrhea), absent menses (amenorrhea), frequent menses (metrorrhagia), and excessive bleeding with menses (menorrhagia).

The course and stability of PMS over time has not been systematically characterized. It has been observed that PMS can begin any time after menarche, but women most frequently seek treatment for their symptoms in their thirties. Symptoms are believed to remit with conditions, such as pregnancy, that interrupt ovulation. Women generally report that their symptoms worsen with age until menopause, when PMS usually ceases.

B. Prevalence

The true prevalence of PMS is unknown because a prospective, community-based epidemiological study of the syndrome has not yet been conducted. Nevertheless, it is estimated that 20 to 40% of women report some premenstrual symptoms and that 5% of women experience some degree of significant impairment of their work or lifestyle. These figures are consistent with retrospective epidemiological survey data that report the prevalence of PMS to be 6.8% and with two population-based studies that report the prevalence of PMS to be 4.6% and 9.8%, respectively.

The frequency of PMS in different cultures remains undetermined, although at least 24 countries have published studies of PMS. Retrospective surveys of premenstrual symptoms have led to the belief that PMS affects women equally, regardless of socioeconomic status or culture; this belief is a hypothesis that merits further investigation.

C. Etiology and Risk Factors

The etiology of PMS and the factors that place a woman at risk for developing PMS remain uncertain. Etiologic hypotheses that have been proposed include abnormalities in hormonal secretory patterns (ovarian steroids, melatonin, androgens, prolactin, mineralocorticoids, thyroxin, insulin), neurotransmitter levels (biogenic amines such as epinephrine and norepinephrine, endogenous opioids), circadian rhythms (temperature, sleep), prostaglandins, vitamin B6 levels, nutrition, allergic reactions, stress, and other psychological factors. Although investigators may advocate vehemently for one or more of these possibilities, no single, fully explanatory mechanism has been isolated as yet. Furthermore, there are physiological and behavioral correlates of menstrual cycle rhythms such as increases in appetite premenstrually and abdominal discomfort during menstruation that are present in women without PMS. These findings have led to the belief that the etiology of PMS resides in the interaction of many different factors that culminate in symptom expression.

Although not demonstrated conclusively, research suggests that genetic factors may place a woman at a relatively greater risk for the development of PMS or for greater severity of PMS symptoms. In one small study conducted by Dalton and colleagues, the pattern of identical twins both having PMS was found to be significantly higher (93%) than in nonidentical twins (44%) and in nontwin control women (31%). A questionnaire survey of 462 female volunteer twin pairs published by Van den Akker and colleagues further supports the possibility that a genetic predisposition for PMS exists. Similarly, evidence from developmental studies suggests a familial pattern as well. For instance, in a study of 5000 adolescent Finnish girls and their mothers, daughters of mothers with premenstrual "tension" were more likely to complain of PMS than were daughters of mothers who were symptom-free. In addition, 70% of daughters whose mothers had nervous symptoms in this study also had symptoms themselves, whereas only 37% of daughters of unaffected mothers experienced symptoms. These studies represent a crucial step toward clarifying the contributions of nature and nurture to the expression of PMS.

As with all medical illnesses, a number of psychological factors may contribute to PMS symptomatology in women. A young woman's symptoms and signs around menstruation may be interpreted as pathological or as normal according to her internalized sense of sexual health drawn from early family experiences, societal views of gender, and other influences. The ability to cope effectively with severe PMS symptoms may be hampered by the extraordinary stresses (e.g., balancing family and work responsibilities, single-parenting, dealing with financial pressures, or surviving the loss of a spouse) that have become commonplace in women's lives. Sadness and anxiety, vulnerability, and helplessness can become linked to a woman's experience of her menstrual cycle and may be attributed to PMS. Moreover, if a woman has disowned or devalued parts of herself, if she has endured interpersonal violence or other trauma, her suffering may be expressed symbolically through PMS symptoms. In summary, it is likely that the etiology of PMS resides in the interaction of multiple influences from a woman's biology, developmental events, and contemporary life circumstances which find expression in a unique cultural context.

V. RESTORING MENTAL AND PHYSICAL HEALTH RELATED TO THE MENSTRUAL CYCLE

Mild warning signs of the onset of menstruation, as Dalton describes (see Premenstrual Syndrome (PMS)), are a valuable gift of nature. The need to restore mental and physical health related to the menstrual cycle through formal clinical intervention occurs only when

Table III Objectives in Caring for Women's Health: PREVENTION

P   *Prevention*—Prevention of illness, high-risk behaviors, stresses associated with sexuality

R   *Resources*—Provision of resources for safety, learning, and social support

E   *Evaluation*—Evaluation of signs and symptoms, sexual history and practices

V   *Violence*—Exploration of issues surrounding violence and coercive sexuality

E   *Esteem*—Assessment of esteem and well-being associated with sexuality and intimacy

N   *Nonjudgmental*—Communication in a nonjudgmental, open manner

T   *Treatment*—Prompt and appropriate treatment of identified illnesses

I   *Intervention*—Intervention when necessary to ensure physical and emotional safety

O   *Options*—Provision of therapeutic options surrounding sexual health (e.g., contraception)

N   *Nonexploitative*—Establishment of a nonexploitative, ethical relationship with patient

these warning signs, or the experience of menstruation itself, become especially uncomfortable. In such cases, it is essential to take a clinical approach that remains mindful of the objectives in providing clinical care for women's sexual health (Table III) and involves three elements: prevention, accurate diagnosis, and appropriate treatment interventions.

A. Prevention

As evidenced by the virtual elimination of smallpox, polio, and measles in developed countries because of routine immunization practices, primary prevention may offer the greatest promise for many medical conditions that cause tremendous suffering. In the absence of greater clarity and specificity concerning the etiology of PMS, the creation of reliably effective primary, secondary, and tertiary preventive health strategies for this syndrome is difficult. Nevertheless, early work suggests that prevention of PMS hinges on two objectives: the pursuit of overall good health, including sexual health, and the process of unearthing and clarifying patient beliefs that may interfere with personal well-being. Education related to biological or psychological aspects of prenatal care, family patterns and roles, and social/cultural ideas may address these goals and may diminish the likelihood of the initial development of PMS (primary prevention) and increase the chances of recognizing, appropriately treating, and reducing the suffering associated with PMS (secondary and tertiary prevention).

A woman who experiences uncomfortable physical, psychological, and/or behavioral signs and symptoms in relation to her menstrual cycle should thus be understood with respect to her biological nature and the psychological aspects of her life experiences and her contemporary circumstances. In so doing, the clinician can pursue educational interventions that may decrease the incidence (number of new cases each year in a given population) of PMS, improve recognition of PMS, and reduce the morbidity associated with PMS. Three illustrations of preventive educational interventions follow.

I. Early Developmental Experiences and Health

Premenstrual syndrome differs from other endocrine-related mood disorders, such as depression induced by diabetes or hypothyroidism, in that blood hormone levels are essentially normal. These findings suggest that PMS may have special psychobiological features, and these should raise questions about the relationship of PMS to childhood health and nurturing. Early evidence indicates that tactile stimulation before weaning, for example, leads to antibody production, thought to be essential for proper functioning of the immune system in infancy and for immune and pituitary–adrenal activation in adulthood. Research should thus focus on the impact of early development on immunological and neuroendocrinological patterns that may permanently influence the person's susceptibility to or immunity from illness. As these complex issues become clarified, clinical attention should focus on the quality of the caregiver–infant relationship to ensure optimal maturation and enhanced neuroendocrine/immune function later in life. This example of early infant care is a valuable paradigm for exploring the interplay of biological, psychological, and social/cultural factors in preventive health.

2. Women's Development within the Context of the Family

Prevention related to the woman's personal developmental experiences focuses first on family. The family is the predominant institution in which growth and development of each individual member occurs and in which social and cultural values are translated into everyday terms. A girl's identity develops out of a sense of connectedness with others, first as a sense of being like and connected with her first caregiver, and later as a sense of being connected with others. By 18 months, a girl has learned the label, "I am a girl." The process of developing this label into an inner acceptance of herself as a woman—with the accompanying belief that it is *good* to be a woman—is complex. The outcome will depend in part on the convictions of the first caregiver with whom she identifies. It will also depend on the girl's observations of how women are treated in the family and in the world at large and how women's sexuality is understood. If women around her are socially stigmatized, despair and identity confusion may result. Where symptoms of PMS reflect such alienation, attention to these issues rooted in early family experiences may prevent the development of PMS.

Explicit discussion of different kinds of family roles may help women to examine their own family experiences and to reconsider their expectations of themselves. The behavior of each person may be defined by the roles he or she is assigned within a family system. Kinship roles define who is mother, father, daughter, son, sister, or brother. Stereotypical roles define who is nurturer, housekeeper, breadwinner, disciplinarian, and so on, and reflect society's shared beliefs that are passed from generation to generation, constantly reinforcing the structure of a given culture. Unrealistic and irrational role expectations may define the good mother/bad mother, good father/ bad father, good teenager/rebellious teenager, and others, and are generated by unconscious conflicts and shared myths among the family members. To the extent that people can discuss roles and reach an understanding about how roles emerge, the likelihood of role strain diminishes. With this, the likelihood of the expression of role strain through physical symptoms may also decline.

3. Women's Suffering in Relation to Contemporary Circumstances and the Effects of Culture

Prevention related to a woman's contemporary circumstances includes clarification of cultural stereotypes and of implicit social attitudes about women. To the extent that stereotypes and attitudes are applied to women indiscriminantly and without reflection, they can negatively affect the psychological health of women. For example, if early experiences foster the cultural ideal of caretaking as womanly and good, this ideal carries the potential for promoting stereotypes of caring as womanly and a good woman as selfless and self-sacrificing. Thus, self-giving may not be assessed in terms of the intentions of the woman and the consequences of her behavior, but on the basis of whether or not her behavior is viewed as inherently feminine. In other words, the worth of the woman's self-sacrifice may not be acknowledged and rewarded, but instead her behavior is viewed as nothing more than an indication of her fundamental feminine nature. As a result, a woman can believe that no effort she makes in her current situation is of significant value, leaving her feeling unappreciated and unhappy. Alternatively, if a woman insists on recognition for her contributions, is assertive, or expresses personal needs (e.g., through words, behaviors, and/or symptoms), her "request" may be disquieting for men, women, and institutions that equate femininity with self-sacrifice. Those who are threatened may retaliate against the woman rather than reward her. Such role conflicts may be especially likely to occur in cultures or subcultures that are rapidly changing and whose most vulnerable members (often women and children) may bear the brunt of such change.

Similarly, and more specifically, a society's beliefs about menstruation can influence both expectations about the menstrual cycle and the reporting of symptoms. Women with PMS may be greeted with skepticism and invalidation by others because of the cultural taboos that surround menstruation. Moreover, when a woman's complaints of PMS signal that she is not pregnant, her PMS symptoms can be interpreted from a cultural perspective as reproductive inadequacy or "deviance." For these reasons, women may need support as they grapple with how their needs are responded to by others in confusing and negative ways because of cultural stereotypes. Over time, women may learn how to gear their expectations and behaviors so that they can remain true to themselves but also respect others' views and seek appropriate affirmation.

B. Diagnosis

Each woman is unique in terms of her physical experience of menstrual cycle events, her cognitive inter-

Table IV Diagnostic Evaluation of Premenstrual Syndrome

General medical history
- Overall health
- Current medical and psychological issues
- Medications (prescribed and over-the-counter)
- Past medical and psychiatric history
- Habits (e.g., exercise, sleep, and eating patterns, smoking, alcohol, and drugs)
- Preventative health care (e.g., immunizations, cholesterol levels, pap smears, mammography)
- Developmental and social history
- Family illness history
- Sexual history (e.g., comfort with sexuality, current sexual functioning, past sexual experiences, high-risk behaviors)

Focused medical history
- Overall gynecological health
- Menstrual history (e.g., age at menarche, length of menstrual cycle, quantity and pattern of bleeding)
- Nature, timing, and severity of symptoms around menstruation
- Pattern of menstrual and premenstrual symptoms during adolescence and early adulthood
- Pattern of menstrual and premenstrual symptoms in relation to pregnancy, breast-feeding, and hormonal interventions (e.g., oral contraceptives)
- Unrecognized endocrine problems (e.g., thyroid dysfunction, androgen excess)
- Unrecognized psychiatric illness (e.g., depression, anxiety, posttraumatic stress disorder, somatoform disorder)

Physical examination
- Mental status examination
- Screening physical examination, including examination for signs of
  - endocrine dysfunction
  - gynecologic illness
  - overlooked health problems (e.g., anemia, infection)
- Screening laboratory tests (e.g., thyroid function tests)

Prospective symptom rating
  Patient records the timing and severity of physical and psychological symptoms for at least two menstrual cycles. The pattern is evaluated during a subsequent appointment.

pretation of sensations related to menstruation, her conscious and unconscious emotional responses to her internal rhythms and timing, and her adaptive behaviors toward menstrual cycle events. When a woman expresses concern about her menstrual cycle or offers complaints suggestive of PMS, the health care provider must attend to the whole person and understand, from a developmental perspective, the complex social context in which the woman lives (Table IV). Such an approach is essential for making an accurate diagnosis of PMS and pursuing appropriate treatment interventions.

As there is no absolute independent, verifiable biological marker (such as a blood test) or physio-behavioral measure (such as increased nocturnal temperature or other signs related to individual circadian rhythms) to identify PMS reliably, the diagnosis of PMS is believed to be a clinical judgment. It is thought to be present when three criteria are met: (1) no other condition is present that accounts for the patient's symptoms, (2) prospective daily symptom ratings demonstrate a marked change in severity of symptoms premenstrually for at least two menstrual cycles, and (3) there is a symptom-free week (usually Days 5 to 10) during the menstrual cycles. It is possible for a woman to have a psychiatric disorder or a physical disorder in addition to PMS as long as the symptoms of PMS are distinct from the other disorder and occur during the luteal phase and remit during menses.

Clinical investigation of PMS thus involves two kinds of information. First, it entails prospective documentation by the woman of symptoms and signs she experiences in clear association with phases of her menstrual cycle. Prospective daily ratings of symptoms with respect to quantity, quality, and severity for a minimum of 2 months are required to confirm a woman's retrospective report of premenstrual symptomatology (Table V). A retrospective history of PMS is not sufficient for a diagnosis because it introduces biases, leading to an overdiagnosis of PMS. Second, other medical conditions that may account for the patient's discomfort must be excluded. Clinicians must therefore perform a careful health history. A complete physical examination must also be conducted, including a mental status examination and a pelvic examination. Psychiatric conditions such as depression, anxiety, somatoform disorders, and others must be considered in the evaluation process. Gynecological conditions such as uterine fibroids, endometriosis, and fibrocystic breast disease, and other physical conditions such as anemia and endocrine dysfunction (e.g., diabetes mellitus, thyroid disease, Cushing's disease) must also be considered and appropriate diagnostic tests performed in the evaluation process. Coexistent medical and psychiatric disorders must be distinguished from disorders that might cause the patient's symptoms and signs.

C. Appropriate Treatment Interventions

Once a diagnosis has been established or refuted, results of the evaluation should be shared with the

Table V Daily Symptoms Calendar

Name: *Yolanda Johnson*

Choose the symptoms to be monitored and label the columns. Circle the appropriate number for each symptom every day of your cycle.

Symptom severity rating: 1 = Not at all, 2 = Minimal, 3 = Mild, 4 = Moderate, 5 = Severe, 6 = Extreme.

Menses: X = Normal flow, S = Light flow

Date	Menses	Symptom #1 Breast Tenderness	Symptom #2 Irritability	Symptom #3 Food Craving	Symptom #4 Bloating
		(1) 2 3 4 5 6	(1) 2 3 4 5 6	(1) 2 3 4 5 6	(1) 2 3 4 5 6
		(1) 2 3 4 5 6	(1) 2 3 4 5 6	(1) 2 3 4 5 6	(1) 2 3 4 5 6
		(1) 2 3 4 5 6	(1) 2 3 4 5 6	(1) 2 3 4 5 6	(1) 2 3 4 5 6
		(1) 2 3 4 5 6	(1) 2 3 4 5 6	(1) 2 3 4 5 6	(1) 2 3 4 5 6
		(1) 2 3 4 5 6	(1) 2 3 4 5 6	(1) 2 3 4 5 6	(1) 2 3 4 5 6
		(1) 2 3 4 5 6	(1) 2 3 4 5 6	(1) 2 3 4 5 6	(1) 2 3 4 5 6
		1 (2) 3 4 5 6	1 (2) 3 4 5 6	1 2 (3) 4 5 6	1 2 (3) 4 5 6
		1 2 (3) 4 5 6	1 2 (3) 4 5 6	1 2 (3) 4 5 6	1 2 (3) 4 5 6
		1 2 3 (4) 5 6	1 2 3 (4) 5 6	1 2 3 (4) 5 6	1 2 (3) 4 5 6
		1 2 3 4 (5) 6	1 2 3 4 (5) 6	1 2 3 4 (5) 6	1 2 (3) 4 5 6
		1 2 3 4 5 (6)	1 2 3 4 (5) 6	1 2 3 4 (5) 6	1 2 (3) 4 5 6
		1 2 3 4 5 (6)	1 2 3 4 (5) 6	1 2 3 4 5 (6)	1 2 (3) 4 5 6
		1 2 3 4 5 (6)	1 2 3 4 (5) 6	1 2 3 4 (5) 6	1 2 (3) 4 5 6
		1 2 3 4 5 (6)	1 2 3 4 (5) 6	1 2 3 4 (5) 6	1 2 (3) 4 5 6
	X	1 2 3 4 (5) 6	1 2 3 (4) 5 6	1 2 (3) 4 5 6	1 2 (3) 4 5 6
	X	1 2 (3) 4 5 6	1 (2) 3 4 5 6	(1) 2 3 4 5 6	1 2 (3) 4 5 6
	X	(1) 2 3 4 5 6	(1) 2 3 4 5 6	(1) 2 3 4 5 6	(1) 2 3 4 5 6
	X	(1) 2 3 4 5 6	(1) 2 3 4 5 6	(1) 2 3 4 5 6	(1) 2 3 4 5 6
	X	(1) 2 3 4 5 6	(1) 2 3 4 5 6	(1) 2 3 4 5 6	(1) 2 3 4 5 6
	S	(1) 2 3 4 5 6	(1) 2 3 4 5 6	(1) 2 3 4 5 6	(1) 2 3 4 5 6
		(1) 2 3 4 5 6	(1) 2 3 4 5 6	(1) 2 3 4 5 6	(1) 2 3 4 5 6
		(1) 2 3 4 5 6	(1) 2 3 4 5 6	(1) 2 3 4 5 6	(1) 2 3 4 5 6
		(1) 2 3 4 5 6	1 (2) 3 4 5 6	(1) 2 3 4 5 6	(1) 2 3 4 5 6
		(1) 2 3 4 5 6	1 2 (3) 4 5 6	(1) 2 3 4 5 6	(1) 2 3 4 5 6
		(1) 2 3 4 5 6	1 (2) 3 4 5 6	(1) 2 3 4 5 6	(1) 2 3 4 5 6
		(1) 2 3 4 5 6	(1) 2 3 4 5 6	(1) 2 3 4 5 6	(1) 2 3 4 5 6
		(1) 2 3 4 5 6	(1) 2 3 4 5 6	(1) 2 3 4 5 6	(1) 2 3 4 5 6
		(1) 2 3 4 5 6	(1) 2 3 4 5 6	1 (2) 3 4 5 6	(1) 2 3 4 5 6
		(1) 2 3 4 5 6	(1) 2 3 4 5 6	1 (2) 3 4 5 6	1 (2) 3 4 5 6
		(1) 2 3 4 5 6	(1) 2 3 4 5 6	(1) 2 3 4 5 6	(1) 2 3 4 5 6
		(1) 2 3 4 5 6	(1) 2 3 4 5 6	(1) 2 3 4 5 6	(1) 2 3 4 5 6
		(1) 2 3 4 5 6	(1) 2 3 4 5 6	(1) 2 3 4 5 6	(1) 2 3 4 5 6
		(1) 2 3 4 5 6	(1) 2 3 4 5 6	(1) 2 3 4 5 6	(1) 2 3 4 5 6
		(1) 2 3 4 5 6	(1) 2 3 4 5 6	(1) 2 3 4 5 6	(1) 2 3 4 5 6
		(1) 2 3 4 5 6	(1) 2 3 4 5 6	(1) 2 3 4 5 6	(1) 2 3 4 5 6

patient and various treatment strategies should be considered.

1. For Women Thought Not to Have PMS

Women with symptoms caused by another illness, but without demonstrable PMS, should receive reassurance and clarity about possible sources of their discomfort. Accurate information about sexual health, experiences normally associated with the menstrual cycle, and symptom patterns may be tremendously helpful. Treatment of a previously unrecognized or poorly controlled physical illness (e.g., hypothyroidism, diabetes mellitus) may eliminate the premenstrual complaints. New or more intensive treatment of a psychiatric disorder such as depression may lead to improvement in symptoms attributed to the premenstrual phase. Doses of psychotropic medication may need to be increased during the late luteal phase and early follicular phase to control symptoms. It should be made explicit that women who are thought not to have PMS will receive continued health care and will not be abandoned to cope with their symptoms alone.

Women whose evaluations do not yield clear evidence of PMS or of another physical or mental illness should be shown that their daily symptom ratings do not reflect a PMS pattern, that their physical examination and laboratory tests do not suggest another physical illness, and that their psychological evaluation has ruled out a mental disorder. Some time should be spent with women with these experiences to acknowledge the reality of their symptoms, even though the meaning of their symptoms is unclear. For example, these women could be in the incipient phases of developing PMS where their symptomatology is inconsistent or of too low a severity to qualify for the diagnosis of PMS. These women should be encouraged to continue charting their daily symptoms, to return in 3 to 6 months for reevaluation, and to ensure adequate sleep, proper diet, and healthy exercise. Alternatively, other sources of symptoms that are not disclosed early in the evaluative process, such as stressful life situations, can be explored and appropriate supports offered at this time.

2. For Women Diagnosed with PMS

Once PMS is documented, a wide variety of psychosocial and preventive health interventions should be considered. These treatments have not been demonstrated to be helpful to all women and their clinical

Table VI Premenstrual Symptom Interventions

Symptoms	Intervention
Psychological	
Anxiety	Biofeedback
	Benzodiazepines
	Relaxation training
	Serotonergic anxiolytic, i.e., buspirone
Depression	Cognitive–behavioral therapy
	Light therapy
	Serotonergic antidepressants (e.g., clomipramine, fenfluramine, fluoxetine, nefazadone, paroxetine, sertraline, and venlafaxine)
	Sleep deprivation
Physical	
Breast tenderness	Tocopherol (vitamin E)
	Bromocriptine
	Tamoxifen
Fatigue and/or insomnia	Sleep hygiene
	Serotonergic antidepressants
Food cravings	High tryptophan (carbohydrate) diet
	Cognitive–behavioral therapy
	Serotonergic antidepressants (e.g., fenfluramine)
Headaches	Aspirin (acetylsalicylic acid)
	Tylenol (acetaminophen)
	Ibuprofen
	Exercise
Multiple symptoms	Cognitive–behavioral therapy
	Group therapy
	Psychoeducation
	Serotonergic antidepressants
	Support group
	Wellness program (e.g., exercise, nutrition, stress reduction)
Weight gain	Diuretics (e.g., spironolactone)
	Salt restriction

scientific bases are not proven. Because the etiology of PMS is multifactorial and elusive, single pharmacologic interventions that "target" the causal mechanism of PMS have not been found. This fact should be reviewed carefully with each woman, and it should be understood that the goal of therapy is to find the unique approach that best addresses her specific needs and complaints (Table VI).

• Providing women with accurate information about their sexual health, the menstrual cycle, and PMS in general is crucial in dispelling myths and addressing the sense of helplessness a woman may feel in relation to her symptoms. Explanation of symptoms and the natural history of PMS, descriptions of various treatment strategies with anticipated benefits, risks, side effects, and alternatives may prove to be immensely reassuring.

- The temporal pattern of their symptoms should be reviewed with women who experience PMS. Visualizing the type, severity, and timing of her symptoms can bring to the woman a sense of control over her symptoms sufficient enough to relieve distress. Women should be encouraged to develop ways of "planning ahead" for their premenstrual symptoms and signs so that they can prepare their families, close associates, and themselves for their symptomatic times. Efforts to limit external stress as much as possible (e.g., not assuming extra obligations or tasks at certain times) may help some women to navigate their monthly cycles more effectively.
- Consuming large amounts of caffeine or its equivalent (theophylline and theobromine, or methylxanthines) has been associated with women's retrospective reports of more severe premenstrual symptoms. Because caffeine can cause irritability, insomnia, and gastrointestinal distress at any time of the month, it makes sense to limit the consumption of caffeine or related compounds throughout the month.
- Decreasing salt intake is commonly recommended as one way to minimize premenstrual bloating, although many women with this complaint do not actually gain weight premenstrually. As many women consume more salt than necessary and because some women do experience symptom relief from limiting their salt intake, it seems reasonable to recommend limiting salt intake at least prior to and during the usual symptomatic interval each month.
- Some researchers suggest that increased appetite and carbohydrate cravings have been linked to the need to increase sources of tryptophan for serotonin synthesis. A healthy diet of frequent meals including complex carbohydrates may relieve PMS symptoms and may be linked to the steady availability of tryptophan.
- Exercise has been shown to minimize some symptoms associated with fluid retention and to increase self-esteem. Except for women with obvious medical contraindications, women should be encouraged to participate all month in some kind of regular

Table VII Menstrual Cycle Interventions

Oral contraceptives
GnRH analogues
Oophorectomy
Danazol
Estradiol implants and patches

physical exercise. It is the frequency, not the intensity, of exercise that seems to make a difference.

If PMS symptoms persist after these measures have been tried, more rigorous pharmacologic and nonpharmacologic interventions may be necessary.

One approach to pharmacologic treatment of PMS is to control the overall menstrual cycle. This approach entails hormonal intervention. Four principal strategies have been used (Table VII):

- Oral contraceptives may minimize physical and psychological symptoms of PMS, as documented in both retrospective and prospective studies. Oral contraceptives may, however, also precipitate symptoms that resemble PMS, such as depression. In addition, risks and side effects of oral contraceptives include cardiovascular complications, migraine headaches, and increases in serum triglycerides. These considerations must be discussed and this strategy undertaken carefully.
- GnRH agonists and oophorectomy (i.e., surgical removal of ovaries) may effectively eliminate PMS symptoms, although this approach is associated with the unwanted effects of low estrogen production. Moreover, surgical risks must be balanced against the severity of PMS symptomatology to justify such an intervention. This strategy is best reserved for very debilitating PMS in older women, and only if less invasive methods have failed.
- Danazol is a synthetic androgen used to suppress the hypothalamic–pituitary–ovarian axis by inhibiting release of gonadotropin. It is superior to placebo when given daily, but many women cannot tolerate the side effects, which include weight gain and an imbalance of estrogen compounds and androgen (e.g., hirsutism, flushing, vaginitis).
- Estradiol implants have also been used successfully to treat PMS. The addition of synthetic progestin has been associated with a return of PMS symptoms but with significantly milder intensity than before hormonal treatment.

A second approach is to manage specific psychological symptoms. With respect to severe psychological symptoms, it is crucial first to verify that the woman, despite her discomfort, is sufficiently safe. A woman who is depressed to the point of being suicidal, or who is so angry that she might harm someone else, should be carefully protected. Four psychiatric medicines that address depression and anxiety have been used effectively in some patients with PMS: Xanax (benzodiazepine anxiolytic, GABA agonist), buspirone (anxiolytic, serotonin 1a agonist), nortryptiline (tricyclic antidepressant, noradrenergic and serotonergic agonist), and fluoxetine, sertraline, and others (antidepressants, selective serotonin reuptake inhibitors). These medications have both proven benefits and numerous side effects, and their use must be dictated by clinical judgment. For example, Xanax is a medication that addresses time-limited, target anxiety symptoms extremely well, but is sedating and highly addicting. Nortryptiline helps depressive symptoms effectively, but it may cause dry mouth, constipation, and sexual dysfunction. The serotonergic medications (e.g., Prozac, Zoloft) alleviate PMS symptoms (even in the absence of depression), but usually are taken daily and, while generally well-tolerated, may have unpleasant side effects (e.g., jitteriness, headaches, nausea). For these reasons, all medication choices must be approached carefully and monitored closely. [*See* Psychopharmacology.]

A third approach is to manage the predominantly physical symptoms of women with PMS. Here the interventions will depend on the medical issues and complaints. Diuretics can be helpful if patients have documented weight gain and evidence of fluid retention. Spironolactone has been a preferred diuretic medication because of its potassium-sparing properties. Other diuretics may be used so long as the possibility of hypokalemia is monitored. Vitamin E, bromocriptine (a dopamine agonist that can cause nausea), and tamoxifen (an oral nonsteroidal agent with antiestrogen properties that can cause headaches and fatigue) have all been shown to be beneficial for breast pain. Over-the-counter analgesics may be very valuable and safe in treating PMS-related headaches. In addition to good sleep routines for insomnia and healthy eating routines for food cravings, serotonergic antidepressants may be helpful for addressing fatigue and fostering stable eating patterns.

The choice of treatment should be grounded in the understanding of the woman's needs in terms of which symptoms are most troublesome for her, which treatment interventions are likely to be most effective for these symptoms, and which treatment strategies will be most acceptable to the patient according to her values and way of life.

BIBLIOGRAPHY

Barbieri, R. L. (1993). Physiology of the normal menstrual cycle. In I. Smith & S. Smith (Eds.), *Modern management of premenstrual syndrome* (Ch. 4). New York: Norton Medical Books.

Ferin, M., Jewelewicz, R., & Warren, M. (1993). *The menstrual cycle: Physiology, reproductive disorders, and infertility.* New York: Oxford University Press.

Frank, R. T. (1931). The hormonal basis of premenstrual tension. *Arch. Neurol. Psychiatry 26,* 1053–1057.

Gold, J. H., & Severino, S. K. (Eds.). (1994). *Premenstrual dysphorias: Myths and realities.* Washington, DC: American Psychiatric Press.

Golub, S. (1992). *Periods: From menarche to menopause.* Newbury Park, CA: Sage.

Jensvold, M. F. (1992). Psychiatric aspects of the menstrual cycle. In D. E. Steward & N. L. Stotland (Eds.), *Psychological aspects of women's health care: The interface between psychiatry and obstetrics and gynecology.* Washington, DC: American Psychiatric Press.

Severino, S. K., & Moline, M. L. (1989). *Premenstrual syndrome: A clinician's guide.* New York: Guilford.

Stewart, F., Guest, F., Stewart, G., & Hatcher, R. (1987). *Understanding your body: Every woman's guide to gynecology and health.* New York: Bantam.

Prenatal Stress and Life-Span Development

Pathik D. Wadhwa

University of Kentucky College of Medicine

Fetal Growth Restriction   Fetal or newborn weight below the 10th percentile for gestational age.
Low Birth Weight   Birth weight below 2500 g.
Neurodevelopmental Deficit   Age-specific structural and/or functional deficits of the central nervous system.
Prenatal   Before birth.
Preterm Birth   Birth before 37 completed weeks gestation.
Stress   A process where actual and/or perceived environmental demands exceed the adaptive capacity of an organism, resulting in psychological and/or biological changes.

The effects of **PRENATAL PSYCHOSOCIAL STRESS** on the fetus and related outcomes are examined along the entire developmental continuum. This overview is followed by further research questions in the area and a discussion of the implications of prenatal stress for processes related to health and development over the life span of the individual.

I. INTRODUCTION

Substantial empirical evidence supports a role for psychological and social processes in the maintenance of health and in the incidence and progression of chronic diseases of the nervous, cardiovascular, endocrine, immune, gastrointestinal, and musculoskeletal systems. More recently, concerns have been raised about possible effects of psychosocial factors such as stress during pregnancy, and a number of human and animal studies have been conducted to examine this question. The outcomes of pregnancy can be broadly classified into those affecting primarily the mother (e.g., maternal complications during pregnancy or following delivery, and labor and delivery parameters such as length of labor, mode of delivery, and maternal postpartum affect) and those affecting primarily the fetus (e.g., spontaneous abortion, fetal growth and maturation, gestational age at birth, neonatal complications, and indices of subsequent infant development). The primary focus here is on the effects of prenatal stress on the developing fetus and related outcomes; the effects of prenatal stress on maternal pregnancy outcomes will not be described here.

II. PSYCHOSOCIAL STRESS AND REPRODUCTIVE FUNCTION

Disruption of reproductive function in mammals is a well-known consequence of stress. Although not the focus here, it is important to note that the detrimental effects of stress may be apparent at the earliest juncture of the reproductive continuum—the ability to conceive and become pregnant. For example, in males, psychosocial stress has been associated with impaired spermatogenesis (decrease in the number and motility of normal sperm and increase in the number of immature sperm), psychogenic impotency, and premature ejaculation. In females, stress has been associated with suppression of ovulation (anovulatory amenorrhea) and failure of implantation. These effects of psychogenic stress have been estimated to account for a large proportion of the incidence of infertility in humans, and are believed to result from stress-associated increases in the level of sympathetic activity, increases in levels of stress hormones such as corticotropin-releasing hormone (CRH) and cortisol, and concomitant decreases in levels of sex hormones such as luteinizing hormone (LH), follicle-stimulating hormone (FSH), testosterone, estrogen, and progesterone. [*See* STRESS.]

III. PSYCHOSOCIAL STRESS IN PREGNANCY

Moving beyond fertilization and conception, psychosocial stress during human pregnancy has been associated with outcomes at various points along the developmental continuum, including early pregnancy loss (spontaneous abortion), fetal developmental outcomes (malformations, physiological activity, neurobehavioral maturation, growth *in utero*), the length of gestation, infant birth weight, neonatal neurological optimality, neonatal complications, infant neurodevelopmental indices related to cognition, affect and behavior, and childhood and adult psychopathology. The vast majority of these investigations have been conducted during the past two decades; a literature search of the databases of the National Library of Medicine and the American Psychological Association for the period between 1975 and 1996 identified approximately 100 studies of psychosocial factors in human pregnancy. An in-depth review of this litera-

ture is beyond the present scope. Instead, an overview that describes some of the major studies and findings is presented. On a related note, a number of studies have examined the role of social support in human pregnancy; a description of this literature is also beyond the present scope, and the interested reader is referred to an excellent review of social support and pregnancy by Christine Dunkel-Schetter and her colleagues.

A. Human Studies of Psychosocial Stress, Fetal Development, and Subsequent Outcomes

The belief that a mother's emotional state during pregnancy may influence the development of her fetus has existed since ancient times across all cultures. References to this notion can be found in an ancient Indian text—the *Mahabharata*—thought to have been written about 1050 BC, in the Old and New Testaments, in the writings of early Greek physicians such as Hippocrates, and in the works of a number of scholars through the Middle Ages into the present century. Research examining the effects of prenatal stress first appeared in the literature in the mid-1950s. Much of the earlier work in this area, however, was limited by conceptual and methodological problems, including inadequate conceptualization and operationalization of predictor as well as outcome variables, retrospective methodology, inadequate control of covariates of pregnancy outcome, and inappropriate statistical procedures. Over the last 15 years or so, larger, better-designed studies have begun to present a somewhat more consistent set of findings indicating that psychosocial stress may contribute, in part, to a wide array of adverse pregnancy outcomes.

I. Spontaneous Abortion

Spontaneous abortion is among the most frequent adverse pregnancy outcomes, occurring in approximately 40% of all pregnancies and in 15% of all clinically recognized pregnancies. One of the most commonly held beliefs about the role of psychosocial stress in pregnancy is that extreme or severe life stressors may trigger spontaneous abortion (SAB). However, few studies have systematically examined this hypothesis for several reasons. First, about 25% of very early abortions are not even recognized clinically. Second, in the case of clinically recognized spontaneous abortions, the vast majority occur in the first trimester of gestation, thereby posing practical problems for the conduct of prospective studies, and raising the issue of recall bias in retrospective studies. However, three noteworthy studies have been conducted. A prospective study of more than 3900 women in northern California examined psychological stress in the workplace and found that although stressful work was not associated with an overall increased risk of spontaneous abortion, stressful work was associated with a two- to threefold increased risk of SAB in three groups of women: over 32 years of age, cigarette smokers, and primigravid. Another prospective study of more than 5000 women in northern California by the same research team examined the relationships between life events, perceived stress, social support, and SAB. Results indicated no association between measures of perceived stress or social support and SAB. However, although the total number of negative life events in the 6 months prior to interview was not significantly associated with SAB, women with life events involving interpersonal difficulties, such as divorce or problems with relatives, had a 1.5-fold increased in the number of spontaneous abortions compared with women without such events. It is well established that approximately one-half of all spontaneous abortions are a direct consequence of genetic abnormalities. On the basis that the genetic composition of the fetus is determined at the time of conception and the logic that negative life events increase the risk of spontaneous abortion only in chromosomally normal fetuses, another group of researchers tested this hypothesis by interviewing 192 women visiting a medical center after a spontaneous abortion to assess negative events that occurred in the 4 to 5 months preceding the loss. At the time of the interview, neither the women nor the investigators knew whether there was a genetic abnormality in the aborted conceptus, because chromosomal karyotyping was conducted after the interviews had taken place. After adjusting for duration of recall, sociodemographic characteristics, and health practices, the results indicated that women who experienced negative life events after conception had a two- to fourfold increase in the risk of chromosomally normal spontaneous abortions, whereas no association was found between life stress and chromosomally abnormal losses.

2. Fetal Malformations

Although the incidence of major fetal malformations is relatively small, their consequences can often be quite severe. Prospective studies of fetal malformations require very large sample sizes, and retrospective studies are subject to reporting bias. The two studies described in this section reflect innovative approaches to investigate the possible role of maternal psychological stress in the incidence of fetal malformations. A study in Sweden used the national birth registry to compare the incidence of major fetal malformations in the children of more than 1200 women whose applications for legal abortion had been refused (proband series) with other children born in the same delivery wards (control series). Results indicated an overall increase in the frequency of fetal malformations in the proband series, with the increase achieving statistical significance in two subgroups—women over 25 years of age and women from a low social class. Moreover, one malformation—cleft palate—occurred at a significantly higher rate in the proband series than in the country as a whole. Another study of more than 22,000 births in Santiago, Chile, in the 9-month period following a large earthquake (8 to 9 on the Richter scale) found a significant overall increase in the incidence of fetal malformations (facial cleft palate) over previous years, with the largest increase in the cohort of babies born 6 months after the earthquake. To test the hypothesis that this effect may be related to maternal stress, the study investigators used a vibrator cage to expose two strains of 13-day-old mice embryos (the developmental equivalent of a 3-month-old human fetus) to the same intensity and duration of shock as in the original earthquake. Results indicated a significant increase in the incidence of cleft palate in the experimental group in one strain and a significant increase in the proportion of resorbed embryos in both strains, thereby providing support for the stress hypothesis in humans.

3. Fetal Heart Rate and Motor Activity

Can the developing fetus recognize and respond to the mother's emotional state? Going as far back as the 1960s, studies have reported associations between maternal emotions such as anxiety and fetal hyperactivity and tachycardia. A more recent correlational study reported a significant positive association between maternal state anxiety and fetal motor activity and behavioral state, and an experimental study demonstrated that the fetuses of women high in anxiety exhibited more pronounced heart rate responses to a taped stimulus than the fetuses of women low in anxiety. A similar pattern of fetal responses was noted after experimental applications of prenatal stress. Immediately after an earthquake in southern Italy, ultrasound examination of 28 panic-stricken women between 18 and 36 weeks gestation who happened to be attending an antenatal clinic at the time of the earthquake indicated that *all* fetuses showed intense hyperkinesia lasting between 2 and 8 hours, with numerous disordered and vigorous movements. In another study, exposure to a more mild form of psychological stress (listening to tape recordings of a baby cry and recalling an alarming situation) resulted in a sudden fall in fetal heart rate followed by overswing recovery. The opposite effects were noted in experimental studies of maternal relaxation. Playing their favorite music to mothers or providing reassuring feedback after an ultrasound examination were each found to result in a significant decrease in fetal activity.

A study of the effects of severe maternal trauma on the fetus examined the association between prenatal physical abuse and fetal and neonatal outcomes in a sample of more than 350 rural, low socioeconomic status women in the Appalachian region of the United States. Results indicated that 16% of the sample reported being abused since they became pregnant, and that physical abuse was significantly associated with a three- to fourfold increase in risk for fetal distress, fetal death, and neonatal complications.

4. Fetal Brain Development and Neurobehavioral Maturation

Few human studies have attempted to examine the possible relationship between prenatal stress and indices of fetal brain growth and maturation. From a sample of more than 3000 Danish women assessed during mid-gestation, birth and neonatal outcomes were compared across a group of 70 pregnant women reporting moderate to severe stressful life events and an inadequate social network (high stress group) and a group of 50 nonstressed pregnant women with an intact social network. Results controlling for smoking and birth weight indicated that neonates born to mothers in the high stress group had a significantly smaller head circumference and suboptimal neonatal neurological scores compared with neonates born to

nonstressed mothers, leading the authors to suggest a specific effect of prenatal psychosocial stress on fetal brain development.

An important limitation in the area of maternal–fetal medicine is the paucity of knowledge and methodology to quantify and assess precisely fetal neurological development and maturation in utero. A series of longitudinal studies by Janet DiPietro and colleagues examined the functional development of the fetal central nervous system over the course of gestation to identify risk factors for neurodevelopmental delays. The sequence and characteristics of fetal neurobehavioral development and maturation (i.e., fetal autonomic, motoric, state, and interactive functioning) were assessed serially at six time points between 20 and 38 weeks gestation. Findings indicated that fetal neurobehavioral maturation was characterized by slower heart rate, increased heart rate variability, reduced but more vigorous motor activity, coalescence of heart rate and movement patterns into distinct behavioral states, and increased cardiac responsivity to stimulation with advancing gestation. With reference to the effects of prenatal stress, results indicated that a measure of chronic maternal psychological distress was significantly and negatively related to the neurobehavioral maturation of the fetus; greater maternal stress was associated with reduced fetal heart rate variability and reduced coupling between fetal heart rate and movement.

5. Length of Gestation and Infant Birth Weight

Preterm birth (before 37 completed weeks gestation) and low birth weight (below 2500 g) are two major adverse outcomes of pregnancy; they frequently co-occur; their incidence in the United States varies between 7 and 15% of all births; their etiology is poorly understood; and they present severe short- and long-term developmental and health consequences for the newborn. For these reasons, the length of gestation and infant birth weight are among the most frequently studied outcomes of human pregnancy; approximately 65% of the human studies of maternal prenatal stress over the past 20 years have included measures of one or both of these birth outcomes. To date, almost all of these studies have been correlational in design, where various aspects of prenatal stress and related constructs have been assessed and their associations examined with one or both of these outcomes. A majority of these studies (approximately 75%) have incorporated one or more prospective assessments of prenatal stress, and the remaining studies have retrospectively compared prenatal characteristics of women with adverse birth outcomes to those of women with more favorable outcomes. Most studies have included broad, population-based samples; a few studies have focused on specific subgroups of women thought to be at higher risk for adverse outcomes, such as pregnant teenagers or African American women. Finally, fewer than one half of these studies have controlled for the effects of established sociodemographic, biomedical, or behavioral risk factors on outcome such as parity, socioeconomic status, race, maternal hypertension, and smoking, and a small number of these have examined the role of established risk factors as potential mediators of the stress–outcome relationship. Inconsistencies in study design and methodology have resulted in a set of mixed results that are difficult to interpret and to compare across studies. Nevertheless, the overall set of findings generally seems to support a role for prenatal stress in pregnancy outcomes related to length of gestation and birth weight.

Prenatal stress in human studies has been assessed most often with measures of frequency (and in a few instances, severity) of negative life events occurring either soon before or soon after the time of conception. This is followed by measures of maternal affect and appraisals of chronic stress. Most studies of prenatal life event stress have used standard or modified versions of life-event checklists; a few studies have examined the effects of specific stressors during pregnancy, such as death of a spouse, unemployment, war, and refugee status. Among studies of maternal affect, anxiety is the most commonly assessed affect, followed by depression. Most studies of maternal anxiety have measured state anxiety, a few have measured both state and trait anxiety, and only three studies have examined the effects of pregnancy-specific anxiety on outcome. Most studies of prenatal chronic stress have measured non-domain-specific appraisals of chronic stress; however, the effects of chronic stress in the workplace and in the context of family functioning were each examined in two studies, and the effects of chronic stress resulting from difficulties in the household role and a broken marriage were each examined in one study. [See ANXIETY; DEPRESSION.]

With outcomes related to the length of gestation, the human literature offers reasonably strong support for the hypothesis that higher levels of prenatal stress are associated with shorter gestation, earlier onset of spontaneous labor, and, in many instances, preterm delivery. In fact, according to a review of psychosocial factors and pregnancy outcome by K. Marieke Paarlberg and colleagues, the relationship between high prenatal stress and shorter gestation is among the more consistent and unambiguous findings in this area. The review of the relevant literature from 1975 to 1996 presented here finds a significant negative relationship between prenatal stress and gestational length in approximately 60% of the studies. The proportion of studies with this finding is higher among recent reports, which are more consistently characterized by prospective designs and appropriate adjustments for the effects of established sociodemographic and biomedical risk factors, either by study design or through statistical procedures. In most cases, prenatal stress was found to exert direct effects on the length of gestation, although in some instances the effects were indirect and were mediated by factors such as socioeconomic status, maternal weight gain, exertion, and medical problems during pregnancy. One of the most rigorous studies in the area was conducted recently by the Maternal–Fetal Medicine Network of the National Institute of Child Health and Human Development. In this study, various forms of psychosocial stress were assessed prospectively in a national representative sample of more than 2500 pregnant women recruited from 10 participating medical centers across the United States. Results indicated that after adjusting for maternal sociodemographic and behavioral characteristics, psychosocial *stress* was a significant predictor of spontaneous preterm birth. Each point increase on a four-point scale of stress was associated with a 16% increase in the risk for spontaneous preterm delivery. Another impressive prospective study conducted in Denmark on more than 5800 women reported a dose-response relationship between psychological distress in the 30th week of pregnancy and risk of preterm delivery after controlling for demographic, medical, and behavioral confounds; women in the moderate and severe distress groups had a 1.5- to 2.5-fold increase in the relative risk for preterm delivery compared with women in the low distress group. In the same study population, women who experienced one or more highly stressful life events (the severity of life events was assessed subjectively) primarily between the 16th and 30th week of gestation had a 1.75

times greater risk of preterm delivery than those without stressful events. Finally, yet another prospective study of more than 2400 women in Denmark found a similar significant effect of psychosocial stress on risk for preterm delivery.

The birth weight of a newborn is a direct consequence of two processes: the length of gestation and fetal growth. That is, infants may be born small because they were born too early or did not grow adequately *in utero* or both. Thus all the factors that negatively impact the length of gestation are also likely to impact birth weight, although the converse is not necessarily true. As in the studies of gestational length, most of the more recent studies of birth weight are prospective in nature and have controlled for the effects of established risk factors. A review of the relevant literature between 1975 and 1996 found that approximately one half of the studies reported significant negative effects of prenatal stress on infant birth weight. Among the studies that reported this finding, approximately 75% controlled for the effects of known sociodemographic, biomedical, or behavioral correlates of birth weight, whereas only 40% of the studies that reported no effect of prenatal stress on birth weight controlled for the effects of the above risk factors. In most instances, the effects of prenatal stress on birth weight were direct; however, some studies reported indirect effects mediated by factors such as parity, smoking, and maternal weight gain.

It is important to note that a relatively small number of studies in this area have controlled for the effects of gestational length on birth weight to examine the effects of prenatal stress on fetal growth per se. One noteworthy study assessed this association in a sample of more than 1500 predominantly African American women in Alabama. After controlling for length of gestation, smoking, race, infant sex, medical risk, and behavioral risks, high psychosocial stress was significantly associated with a 1.6- to 2.3-fold increase in the risk of fetal growth restriction (birth weight below the 10th percentile for gestational age). Further analyses in this sample indicated that this effect was seen only in women with a low body mass index (BMI less than 22); the finding did not hold for heavier women (BMI greater than 22). Another population-based study of a sample of more than 14,000 predominantly African American urban, indigent women in Detroit, Michigan, found that mothers from broken marriages (separated, divorced, or wid-

owed) had a 1.5-fold increased risk of fetal growth restriction compared with married women, and that this effect was primarily mediated through substance abuse. In a third study, perceived difficulty with the household role assessed at 20 weeks gestation predicted preterm birth and low birth weight in a sample of approximately 400 women in Glasgow, Scotland. After controlling for sociodemographic variables and smoking, women reporting a high level of difficulty had a threefold increase in the risk of preterm birth and a fourfold increase in the risk of low birth weight (length of gestation was not controlled); however, this association was not present using the same measure administered at 30 weeks gestation.

Some studies have attempted to differentiate the psychosocial determinants of preterm birth from those of fetal growth restriction. A retrospective, case-control study of 90 women found that severe life stress was one of three factors associated with preterm birth, whereas low social support was one of the three factors associated with small size for gestational age. This finding was replicated in a prospective study of more than 2400 women in Denmark. Prenatal life event stress was significantly associated with preterm delivery, whereas social network variables significantly predicted fetal growth restriction. Last, a study of more than 2500 Greek women examined various pathways that mediated the effects of *prenatal* risk factors on birth weight. Results suggested that perceived *stress* and the quality of interpersonal relationships (social support) during pregnancy each had significant and independent effects on birth weight, and that in both instances, about half of the effect was mediated through reduction of gestational length and the other half was mediated through fetal growth restriction.

The preceding studies involved the assessment of prenatal stress at the level of the individual. Some exceptions to this level of analysis can be found in studies of the effects of war on pregnancy outcome, which have adopted a broader and more sociological approach to the assessment of prenatal stress. A study of pre- and post-Gulf War changes in pregnancy outcomes in a Kuwati population found a significant increase in the number of spontaneous abortions, low birth weight babies, and babies with congenital anomalies during and in the year immediately following the war. Another study examined the effects of expatriation following war by comparing outcomes across three delivery populations just before and during the civil war in Croatia—7845 women from free Croatia, 712 women from occupied areas of Croatia (both nondisplaced populations), and 593 Croatian refugees from Bosnia and Herzegovina and Serbia (expatriated population). Results indicated a significant, twofold increase in the rate of preterm delivery and low birth weight rate in displaced women compared with nondisplaced women, supporting the notion that stress, fear, and exile may influence the length of gestation. This finding was, however, not replicated in a sample of more than 600 non-war refugees in Greece. Finally, in Israel, a study of developmental outcomes in a cohort of boys born during the year of the Six-Day War in 1967, reported a significant increase in developmental delays and regressive, nonaffiliative and dissocial behavior compared with a cohort born 2 years later.

6. Neonatal Neurobehavioral Development

A very small number of human studies have examined the possible effects of prenatal psychosocial stress on indices of neonatal neurodevelopment and temperament. A prospective study of various sociodemographic, biomedical, psychosocial, nutritional and behavioral predictors of neonatal neurodevelopment in a sample of 467 infants born to a predominantly low socioeconomic class of African American women reported significant associations between prenatal indices of maternal stress, social relations, and personality factors and indicators of neonatal neurobehavioral development and temperament (assessed with the Brazelton Neonatal Behavioral Assessment Scale), including orientation and habituation, motor performance, and regulation of state and autonomic response. Another prospective study of the prenatal correlates of neonatal temperament in a sample of 150 newborns reported a significant association between prenatal depressive symptoms and infant behavior (inconsolability and excessive crying) assessed 8 to 72 hours after birth. Yet another prospective study of more than 1000 women and their infants assessed maternal psychosocial distress during each of the three trimesters of gestation and infant temperament at 5 years of age. The study findings suggested a time- and sex-specific effect of prenatal stress on infant temperament; maternal emotional distress experienced during the first trimester, but not during the second and third trimesters, significantly predicted infant temperament

(negative emotionality) at 5 years of age. Moreover, this relationship was particularly strong in male offspring.

7. Infant, Childhood, and Adolescent Neurobehavioral Development

Again, a very small number of studies have examined the associations between reports of prenatal psychosocial stress and indices of subsequent neurobehavioral development in humans. A retrospective study of 265 children between 6 and 13 years of age found a significantly higher proportion of attention deficit disorder (ADD) among children of mothers reporting either emotional stress or smoking during pregnancy. Another retrospective case-control study of 58 severely emotionally disturbed children and adolescents between ages 4 and 19 in a partial-hospitalization program found that significantly more children in this group were born to unmarried mothers who had not planned to become pregnant, felt unhappy about being pregnant, and lived in family discord. A similar finding was reported in a retrospective study of 59 autistic children; mothers of these autistic children were found to have experienced significantly more family discord during pregnancy than mothers of children in a normal control group. Last, a prospective study in Sweden assessed psychosocial and other factors at the beginning of pregnancy in a sample of more than 500 women, followed by assessments of their children at 4 years of age with Griffith's developmental scales. Results suggested a sex-specific effect of prenatal stress on infant psychomotor and mental development, with boys, but not girls, from homes with high psychosocial stress having significantly lower developmental scores than boys from nonstressed homes. [See ATTENTION DEFICIT HYPERACTIVITY DISORDER (ADHD); AUTISM AND PERVASIVE DEVELOPMENTAL DISORDER.]

8. Adult Neurobehavioral Development

Only one study was found that examined the possible effects of prenatal psychosocial stress in human adults. This study was a retrospective epidemiological investigation conducted in Finland on persons born between 1925 and 1957 to assess the effects of a severe prenatal stressor on psychiatric and behavioral disorders. A group of 167 individuals were identified whose fathers had died during the prenatal period (index group), and the incidence of psychiatric morbidity was compared using a control group of 168 persons whose father died during the first year of life. The results indicated a significant increase in the numbers of diagnosed schizophrenics and documented criminals in the index group, thereby supporting a long-term effect of prenatal stress on neurobehavioral development.

B. Animal Studies of Psychosocial Stress, Fetal Development, and Subsequent Outcomes

The animal models that are used to study the effects of prenatal stress on the fetus offer some obvious advantages over studies of human pregnancy. Experimental manipulations performed in standardized and controlled settings allow causal inferences to be drawn; the use of inbred strains minimizes the effects of individual differences in the genotype; the use of invasive procedures during gestation and after birth facilitates cellular and molecular levels of analyses; and the time span of gestation and life of most animal species is relatively short. In animals, stressors such as immobilization, restraint, noise, crowding, injection, light, and shock are believed to be analogous to psychological stress in humans, and they have all been used in studies of prenatal stress. A literature search of the National Library of Medicine database for the period between 1975 and 1996 found more than 150 reports describing the effects of various forms of prenatal stress or stress hormones in animal models of pregnancy. Twenty percent of these studies were published in a foreign language, and an English translation of the study abstract was used when available. All studies used an experimental design. The majority were performed on various strains of rats; other animal species that were used include mice, nonhuman primates, sheep, guinea pigs, and, in one instance, cats. The results from these studies provide powerful evidence to support a causal role for prenatal stress in influencing critical developmental and health outcomes, such as brain morphology, receptor density and sensitivity, central nervous system function, sexual differentiation, baseline and challenge-induced activity of the autonomic nervous, neuroendocrine, immune, and reproductive systems, physical health (cardiac function, hypertension, ulceration), acceleration of aging (neuronal and cognitive loss), and longevity. These studies also offer valuable insight into putative physiological mechanisms that may be involved in mediating the effects of a stressful environment on the developing fetus. An overview of this literature, organized along the continuum of developmental outcomes, is provided here. Unless otherwise specified, all studies used rat models of prenatal stress.

1. Implantation, Early Pregnancy Loss, and Fetal Anomalies

Prenatal stress may inhibit reproductive processes related to implantation and early embryogenesis. Restraint stress in the early stages of pregnancy (days 1 through 6) in mice caused a dramatic reduction in the pregnancy rate from 90 to 52%; this effect was achieved by decreasing the number of normal corpora leutea (CL), increasing the number of abnormal CL, decreasing serum progesterone, decreasing the number of implantation sites, and producing abnormalities of embryo and implantation. Furthermore, prenatal stress in female offspring has been shown to reduce fertility and fecundity, producing estrous cycle disorders, spontaneous abortions, or vaginal hemorrhaging and high neonatal mortality. Prenatal restraint also produces a significant increase in the frequency of cleft palate in offspring.

2. Brain Monoamine and Adrenergic Systems

The neurotransmitters serotonin (5-HT) and norepinephrine (NE) are believed to play an important role in early neurogenic processes by acting as differentiation signals to regulate the time of neuronal genesis in cell populations. According to Lauder and colleagues, the ability of stress to interact with neurogenesis during the time in gestation when these monoamines are required as humoral signals suggests that maternal influences can interfere with ontogency of this circuitry during prenatal development. Low levels of maternal prenatal stress, such as crowding and injection stress, were found to produce persistent changes in serotonin (5-HT) binding in several brain regions of the offspring, including the cerebral cortex and hippocampus, at 60 days of age. Moreover, the discovery that the critical period for prenatal stress-induced changes in brain 5-HT neurons is between embryonic day 15 and birth suggests the mechanism involves an interaction with developmental events occurring within this time span, such as axonal growth and synaptogenesis. In another study, concentrations of brain catecholamines—dopamine (DA) and NE—in the cerebral cortex and locus coeruleus region were significantly reduced and concentrations of DA and NE metabolites were significantly elevated in prenatally stressed rats. Yet another study of the development of rat brain adrenergic receptors indicated that the offspring of prenatally stressed rats showed reduced receptor binding in the cerebral cortex, suggesting a role for stress in producing permanent neurochemical changes to cause delayed or impaired development of the postsynaptic elements of noradrenergic neurons. Moreover, *prenatal stress* induced long-term changes in the activity of tyrosine hydroxylase (TH), the key enzyme of catecholamine synthesis, the cortex and hypothalamus. It is therefore probable that stress-induced alterations in fetal brain monoamine synthesis and adrenergic activity may play a part in the mechanisms by which prenatal stress produces behavioral deficits in the offspring of stressed female rats.

3. Hypothalamic-Pituitary-Adrenal Axis

Several studies have demonstrated that the maternal and fetal autonomic and hypothalamic-pituitary-adrenal (HPA) axes respond rapidly to maternal stress; acute restraint stress in late gestation resulted in immediate, sex-specific changes in maternal and fetal hypothalamic and peripheral levels of catecholamines, corticotropin-releasing hormone (CRH), beta-endorphin, and corticosterone.

The effects of prenatal stress on the HPA system of the offspring include long-term alterations in the size of the hippocampus, the density and sensitivity of glucocorticoid receptors in the brain, and basal and stress-induced responses of pituitary–adrenal activity. Prenatal treatment of dexamethasone (DTX) in rhesus monkeys resulted in an irreversible deficiency of hippocampal neurons, as shown by a 30% reduction in size and segmental volume of the hippocampus assessed by magnetic resonance imaging, and an increase in basal and poststress levels of plasma cortisol. A similar effect of reduced hippocampal weight in both sexes was produced by prenatal stress in rats. Prenatal restraint stress also resulted in a significant decrease in type I and type II corticosteroid receptors in the hippocampus and altered corticosterone reactivity to stress at 90 days of age; the effect on brain glucocorticoid receptor density of the fetus was more marked in females than in males. The effects of hyperactivity of the maternal HPA axis during pregnancy on the development of the HPA axis and brain monoamine systems of the offspring were examined by ad-

ministering ACTH to the mother during the latter third of pregnancy. Results indicated that the adrenals of experimental animals weighed less and had aberrant morphology; this effect was more pronounced in female offspring. Moreover, basal plasma corticosterone levels were higher in experimental animals and lower after exposure to stress; in the brain, dopaminergic activity was decreased and serotonergic activity increased, indicating that prenatal stress affected brain development and as a consequence programmed the developing HPA axis to hyperfunction under basal conditions, leading to exhaustion and inability to mount an adequate response to stress. These effects of prenatal stress on the HPA axis of the offspring were shown to be mediated by maternal glucocorticoid secretion; maternal adrenalectomy blocked the prenatal stress-associated changes in corticosteroid receptors in the hippocampus and function, whereas substitutive corticosterone treatment reinstated the effects of prenatal stress.

4. Immune System

Prenatal maternal stress (foot-shock or the psychological stress of observing a nonpregnant partner being stressed) was shown to alter immune parameters and function in rat offspring. A study of cellular responses in 6-month-old rhesus monkeys of prenatally stressed mothers found that lymphocytes exhibited lower suppressor function and cytolytic activity against target cells, indicating that an acute stressor in the prenatal period could produce long-term effects on postnatal immunity. [See PSYCHONEUROIMMUNOLOGY.]

5. Sexual Differentiation and Reproductive Function

Sexual differentiation of the brain is regarded as a model for environment-dependent brain development mediated by systemic hormones and neurotransmitters. Abnormal concentrations of these substances, if occurring during a critical period of brain development, can lead to permanent developmental disabilities of fundamental processes of life. Several studies have demonstrated effects of prenatal stress on brain, hormone and behavioral processes related to sexual differentiation. For example, in males, prenatal stress produced a 50% decrease in the size of the sexually dimorphic nucleus of the preoptic area (SDN-POA) of the brain; the size of the SDN-POA was not altered in female offspring. This effect was mediated by stress-induced reduction of c-*fos* activity in the region of the POA; SDN-POA volume is predictive of sexual activity in male rats and is correlated with plasma testosterone levels. Basal testosterone levels in both plasma and testes were significantly lower, whereas basal plasma progesterone levels were significantly higher in adult offspring of prenatally stressed rats. Behaviorally, male offspring of prenatally stressed rats show demasculinization (i.e., significantly decreased male sexual behavior) and feminization (i.e., significantly increased female sexual behavior) in adulthood.

6. Cognition, Affect, and Behavior

A number of studies have demonstrated profound behavioral alterations in the offspring of prenatally stressed animals. These effects include impaired learning and cognitive function, impaired affect (increased emotionality, fearfulness, and depression), increased asocial behavior, and altered sexual behavior.

a. Cognition. Prenatal stress adversely affected learning ability in offspring; this effect was blocked by the simultaneous administration of an antianxiety drug (diazepam), suggesting that anxiolytics may overcome the adverse effects of prenatal stress through reduction of stress. Pregnant female rhesus monkeys or squirrel monkeys were exposed to a 2-week period of either repeated psychological disturbance in midgestation or ACTH. During the first month after birth, the infants were tested with a modified Brazelton Newborn Behavioral Assessment Scale. Infants of prenatally stressed monkeys from both groups showed early impairments in motor coordination and muscle tonicity and shorter attention spans, and were also more irritable and difficult to console.

b. Emotionality. Prenatal stress can influence emotional reactivity of offspring. In a series of studies, the effects of prenatal exposure to predictable or unpredictable stress were studied by exposing rats to different schedules of noise or light stress, and the development of their offspring was examined during the first 2 weeks of life. Results indicated that unpredictable stress caused significant delays of motor development and motivation-involved behavior, and also impaired development of hippocampal function, which lasted into adulthood and manifested as an increase in vulnerability and a decrease in habituation to stressful stimuli. Unpredictable noise and light stress during pregnancy also induced alterations in behavioral

asymmetries in the adult offspring. Dopamine and serotonin turnover rates were measured in three left and right brain areas of prenatally stressed rats; prenatal stress was shown to increase the degree of interhemispheric correlation of both neurotransmitters, suggesting that this facilitated communication may underlie the alterations in behavioral asymmetries (fearfulness to stressful situations) induced by prenatal stress.

c. Depression. Like humans, laboratory rats show sex differences in depression. Prenatal restraint stress produced reduced sex differences for depression but did not affect sex differences in open-field behavior. A follow-up study demonstrated an increase of behavioral depression and a decrease of dopaminergic neurotransmission in the nucleus accumbens (an established risk factor for depression) in the offspring of prenatally stressed rats, thereby supporting the hypothesis that prenatal stress may increase the risk of depression in the offspring.

7. Cardiac Function

Endogenous glucocorticosteroids provide natural differentiation signals for adrenergic neurons, and exposure to high exogenous steroid levels has been shown to disrupt the timing of neuronal maturation. Prenatal dexamethasone treatment produced a dose-dependent retardation of heart weight gain, accompanied by abnormalities of noradrenergic innervation, as assessed with measurements of norepinephrine levels and turnover, suggesting a prenatal stress effect on cardiac noradrenergic innervation and sympathetic activity. Moreover, this effect was still apparent in young adulthood. Another study found that the offspring of prenatally stressed rats had higher arterial blood pressure than controls.

8. Aging

Various lines of evidence suggest that glucocorticoids (GC), acting through GC receptors in the brain, can act as life-long organizing signals from early development to old age. With increasing age, the endangering actions of glucocorticoids on nerve cells prevail over neurotrophic ones, leading to reduced nerve cell survival.

IV. RESEARCH QUESTIONS

Evidence indicates that prenatal stress may influence the development of the fetus and subsequent related outcomes. However, several questions remain. These questions relate to outcome specificity, stressor specificity, the timing of stress during gestation, and the mechanism or mechanisms by which stress may act on the developing fetus.

A. Outcome Specificity

Is prenatal stress related to specific developmental outcomes? In humans, prenatal stress is associated with a range of adverse outcomes along the developmental continuum, most notably with a decreased length of gestation and fetal growth. Animal models of prenatal stress extend the findings of human studies and demonstrate a strong causal link with outcomes related to brain development and physiological function. Nevertheless, the existing human literature has neither proposed nor tested hypotheses related to outcome specificity. Several of the earlier studies combined distinct outcomes such as preterm birth, labor and delivery parameters, neonatal complications, and, in some instances, even antepartum risk conditions, into composite indices of "pregnancy complications." The next generation of studies looked at outcomes such as infant birth weight and gestational age at birth separately. More recent studies have examined stress effects on fetal growth by controlling for the effects of gestational length on birth weight. However, even preterm birth and fetal growth restriction are not homogenous outcomes. For example, preterm birth may be elective or spontaneous, and spontaneous preterm births may be precipitated by either preterm labor or preterm premature rupture of membranes. Fetal growth restriction has two distinct recognizable types: symmetrical growth restriction leading to stunted growth of all or most developing organs, and asymmetrical growth restriction with normal head and brain size but restricted abdominal viscera and subcutaneous fat. It is important to recognize this heterogeneity, because various categories within each of these outcomes may be differentially linked to stress. Finally, few prospective studies of prenatal stress and neurodevelopmental outcomes have been conducted. These studies are essential because the central nervous system (CNS) undergoes developmental changes all through gestation (as opposed to other organ systems that for the most part complete development by the end of the first trimester) and is therefore more susceptible to exogenous and endogenous insults for a longer period of time; the threshold of vulnerability of the CNS is probably lower than that of other systems; the effects of CNS insult may have longer and more permanent consequences than those on other systems; and the possible effects of stress on the brain may not be evident at birth but may be recognized only later in life at various time points along the neurodevelopmental continuum.

B. Stressor Specificity

There is no universally accepted definition of stress; however, it is clear that stress is not a unidimensional construct, but rather "a person–environment interaction," in which there is a perceived discrepancy between environmental demands and the individual's biological, psychological, or social resources. This transactional view of the stress construct calls for the identification of stressful stimuli, subjects' appraisal of these stimuli, and their response, especially emotional response. Most of the human studies of prenatal stress have used either stimulus-based or response-based definitions of stress, and have assessed prenatal stress with measures of life events (potentially stressful environmental conditions), state anxiety (nonspecific emotional response to stressful stimuli), and trait anxiety (predisposition to respond to stressful situations by experiencing anxiety). Several authors have directly compared the results of prenatal anxiety and life event studies, by implication suggesting that they measure the same construct. However, patterns of specific types of stress (chronic, episodic) may be differentially related to adverse pregnancy outcomes. In the present review, no studies to date have made predictions or tested hypotheses related to the specific nature or type of prenatal stress that may influence fetal developmental outcomes. On the basis of research in nonpregnant humans and animals, it seems reasonable to suggest that the effects of stress may depend, in part, on its salience along various dimensions, such as episodicity–chronicity, novelty–predictability, or controllability.

C. Timing of Stress

Fetal growth and development is a logarithmic process, with rapid mitosis at early stages and cellular hypertrophy and accumulation of fat, glycogen, and connective tissue later in gestation. As reviewed by Marc Bornstein, it is well established that there are several sensitive or critical periods in development, and there may be critical periods during pregnancy when the developing fetus is especially vulnerable to prenatal stress. These periods may be related to the times in gestation corresponding to specific developmental events, and/or to time-specific changes in maternal or fetal physiological responses to stress over the course of gestation. Although this premise of susceptible periods is well supported in the animal literature, few human studies of prenatal stress have incorporated multiple assessments of stress, and no studies have tested hypotheses about time-specific effects of prenatal stress. Some of the studies that incorporated multiple measures of prenatal stress at different time points in gestation lend inferential support to the premise that the timing of stress during gestation may be an important factor with regard to its influences on fetal outcome. For example, one study of birth weight assessed life event scores at each trimester of gestation. Life event scores during the first trimester were not associated with outcome, and an index of increases in life event scores from the second to the third trimester (but not high scores per se) was significantly associated with low birth weight. Another study reported an association between chronic stress measured at 30 weeks gestation and preterm birth, but not between chronic stress measured at 16 weeks gestation and outcome. Yet another study reported an association between life event stress during the first trimester and infant temperament at 5 years of age, but no associations between life event stress during the second and third trimesters and infant temperament.

D. Mechanisms of Stress Effects

The two major classes of mechanisms through which stress influences health in humans are, first, a direct physiological pathway mediated primarily by central and peripheral stress responses of the autonomic nervous, endocrine, and immune systems; and, second, an indirect behavioral pathway mediated by health-related behaviors such as smoking, alcohol and drug abuse, and reduced compliance with adherence to other aspects of health care. Each of these possible mechanisms is discussed here in the context of the effects of prenatal stress in humans.

1. Physiological Mechanisms

The participation of the autonomic nervous, neuroendocrine, and immune systems in response to psychological stress is well established and has been pro-

posed as a central mechanism linking psychosocial factors to health outcomes. Several researchers have suggested that stress-related responses of the neuroendocrine axis and the autonomic nervous system during pregnancy may contribute to adverse outcomes. For instance, elevated levels of hypothalamic, pituitary, and placental stress hormones have been implicated in the initiation of preterm labor. Vasoconstriction and hypoxia in response to sympathetic-adrenal-pituitary activation decrease uteroplacental perfusion, and may thereby contribute to fetal growth restriction. The immunosuppressive effects of stress and HPA activation may increase susceptibility to infection, which, in turn, is a risk factor for preterm birth. However, few systematic investigations have been conducted of these physiological processes as potential mediators of the prenatal stress and pregnancy outcome link in humans. Some studies have examined the association between catecholamines and anxiety at the onset of labor and between catecholamines and physical activity during pregnancy. A review of the relevant literature since 1975 revealed only two studies that examined the relation between psychosocial factors and neuroendocrine parameters during human pregnancy, and one study that examined maternal physiological reactivity to a behavioral stressor. In a sample of 40 pregnant adolescents assessed during the middle and latter part of gestation and postpartum, subjects with an increase in cortisol levels across a 40-minute period measured before 20 weeks gestation and at 2 to 3 weeks postpartum had fewer symptoms of anxiety and depression than subjects with no cortisol increase; there was, however, no relation between cortisol and symptoms of anxiety or depression at the 34 to 36 weeks gestation assessment. In a sample of 54 adult women with a singleton, intrauterine pregnancy, maternal plasma levels of adrenocorticotropin hormone (ACTH), β-endorphin (βE), and cortisol, measured at the beginning of the third trimester of pregnancy, were significantly correlated with maternal levels of prenatal stress, social support, and personality. After controlling for the effects of factors known to influence hormone levels during pregnancy, including gestational age, circadian variation, and obstetric risk, a combination of the maternal psychosocial and sociodemographic factors accounted for 36% of the variance in ACTH, 13% of the variance in cortisol, and 3% of the variance in βE. A study of 40 low-risk pregnant women examined the relationship between maternal blood pressure responses to a behavioral stressor (interactive arithmetic task) during pregnancy and infant birth outcomes. Results indicated that women with larger diastolic blood pressure responses to stress delivered infants with significantly lower birth weights and decreased gestational age. Recently, Pathik Wadhwa and colleagues have proposed a psychobiological model of prenatal stress in humans. According to this model, prenatal stress exerts significant, outcome-specific effects on fetal outcomes, in part, through its influence on maternal physiology. These effects are proposed to be modulated by the nature, timing, and duration of stress. The model specifically postulates that prenatal stress may perturb the maternal hypothalamic-pituitary-adrenal axis, which, in turn, may influence the production and release of placental CRH, a hormone that is thought to play a major role in fetal development and the timing of delivery.

2. Behavioral Mechanisms

The effects of maternal health-related behaviors during pregnancy on fetal development such as nutrition, smoking, alcohol, and drug abuse are well documented and include an increased risk of spontaneous abortion, fetal growth restriction, preterm delivery, and cognitive and motor deficits of the central nervous system. An emerging literature supports a significant role for psychosocial variables such as prenatal stress and depression in counter therapeutic health behaviors in pregnancy. For example, a review of the relevant literature between 1975 and 1996 found more than 30 studies that examined the associations between maternal psychosocial factors and smoking, alcohol, or drug abuse in human pregnancy. In overlapping reports, the correlates of smoking, alcohol, drug abuse, and unspecified combinations thereof were examined in 13, 9, 5, and 20 reports, respectively. For psychosocial factors, the role of social support, depression, stress, and maternal personality (self-esteem, locus of control, hostility, coping style, and attitudes toward pregnancy) was assessed in 16, 12, 11, and 9 reports, respectively. The study samples were representative of the general population and ranged from middle-class, married, Anglo women to low socioeconomic class, single, African American women and teenagers. Approximately 75% of the studies were prospective and assessed both psychosocial factors and health behaviors at one or more times during preg-

nancy; however, only a small number of studies (16%) included biologically validated measures of health behaviors such as carbon-monoxide or cotinine assays for smoking or toxicological assays for alcohol and illicit drugs. This literature provided strong support for the hypothesis that psychosocial factors are related to one of more of the preceding countertherapeutic health behaviors in human pregnancy. When analyzed separately, either by individual health behaviors or by psychosocial factors, approximately 80% of the studies reported significant finding—higher levels of prenatal stress or depression were associated with increased incidence of these behaviors; higher levels of social support were associated with decreased incidence of these behaviors; and among personality and individual difference variables, higher levels of self-esteem, locus of control, and positive attitudes toward pregnancy were associated with decreased incidence, and higher levels of hostility and defensive coping style were associated with increased incidence of these behaviors, respectively. [See SMOKING; SUBSTANCE ABUSE.]

V. IMPLICATIONS OF PRENATAL PSYCHOSOCIAL STRESS FOR LIFE-SPAN DEVELOPMENT

The implications of findings that prenatal stress may exert significant effects on fetal development and related outcomes can be considered (a) in terms of the significance of adverse developmental outcomes over the individual's life span, and (b) in terms of an epigenetic view of development in which bidirectional interactions between genes and environment shape the developmental trajectory over the course of the life span.

A. Significance of Adverse Pregnancy Outcomes

The term prematurity encompasses both preterm delivery and low birth weight. Prematurity is now recognized as the leading cause in the United States of infant mortality and morbidity in the nonanomalous fetus. The prevalence of prematurity is higher in the United States than in any other developed nation in the world, and has not decreased significantly over the last 40 years; the etiology is unknown in one-half to two-third of all cases; and prevention programs to reduce the incidence have largely been unsuccessful. Although the vast majority of premature newborns survive, studies of short-term outcomes find significantly higher rates of severe morbidity in the neonatal period, including asphyxia, meconium aspiration, hypoglycemia, polycythemia, and respiratory distress syndrome. Studies of long-term outcome find higher rates of sensorineural impairments and disabilities (e.g., cerebral palsy and visual, auditory, and intellectual impairments) and higher rates of complications of the respiratory, gastrointestinal, and renal systems. In the United States, more than 48 million people, or 15% of the population, suffer from some form of neurological disorder, exclusive of mental disease. A large proportion of such disorders are believed to originate during prenatal life, and elucidating their etiology presents a perplexing neurological problem. In addition to the health consequences, the economic impact of prematurity is enormous; recent estimates suggest that approximately 40% ($4 billion per annum) of the expenditure on infant health care was for costs related to prematurity. Last, the hardship and emotional toll of prematurity on individuals and families is incalculable. For these reasons, prematurity has been identified as the single most significant problem in maternal–child health in the United States.

As if the consequences of prematurity were not severe enough, new evidence now suggests that prematurity may confer an increased life-long risk for coronary heart disease (CHD)—the leading cause of morbidity and mortality among women and men in the United States. For example, a prospective study of CHD in more than 2500 men in South Wales over a 20-year period obtained birth weight data for approximately one half of the sample (n 1258). Results indicated a significant relationship between lower birth weight and higher risk of coronary heart disease after controlling for age, father's social class, social class, marital status, fibrinogen and cholesterol concentrations, blood pressure, and smoking history. This pattern of findings has been replicated in more than 16 studies of women, men, and children, including three population-based epidemiological studies in Britain with a combined sample of more than 16,000 individuals. The association between birth weight and CHD is large, highly statistically significant, and cannot be explained by associations with childhood or adult SES or other conventional risk factors for

CHD—it is found in each social group and is independent of health-related behaviors such as smoking. Consequently, a new model has been advanced for the origins of cardiovascular disease in which CHD results not primarily from external forces, but from the body's self-organization, homeostatic settings of enzyme activity, cell receptors, and hormonal feedback, all of which are established in utero and eventually lead to premature death. An animal model of in utero exposure to glucocorticoids and adult hypertension has also yielded highly supportive findings.

B. Role of Early Environment on Developmental Trajectory over the Life Span

It would be an understatement to assert that the developmental processes that transform a single-cell human embryo into a fully functioning organism, whose cerebral cortex alone contains some 10^9 neurons, within a mere span of 40 weeks are exceedingly complex and fascinating; indeed, one would be hard pressed to come up with any other example in the physical or biological world that even begins to approximate the elegance of intrauterine development. Sentimentality aside, the development of the embryo and fetus is characterized by proliferation and specialization of cells to form interconnected functional units. Whereas the structural and, for the most part, functional development of major organ systems is completed by the end of the first trimester of gestation, the central nervous system continues to grow and evolve all through gestation and for the first 10 to 12 years of life after birth. Stages of CNS development are characterized, in overlapping time periods, as those involved in the proliferation and migration of neurons and glial cells, differentiation and maturation of neurons (including axonal and dendritic development and synaptogenesis), myelination, and the development of neurotransmitter (noradrenergic, dopaminergic, serotonergic, cholinergic, GABA/EAA/peptide) systems. During peak growth, neurons generate at the rate of more than 250,000 per minute to form over 100 trillion connections in the brain by birth. Developmental biologists over the ages have asked the following question: Does the genetic material of the fertilized egg already contain a full set of building specifications for the human organism? Over the last few years, there has been a major paradigm shift in developmental neuroscience regarding fundamental concepts of how the nervous system and the rest of the organism develops and functions. The answer to this question is now believed to be an unequivocal no. Genes and environment are no longer believed to exert separate influences, and development is viewed not as a gradual elaboration of an architectural plan preconfigured in the genes but rather as a dynamic interdependency of genes and environment characterized by a continuous process of interactions in a place- and time-specific manner, and involving short- and long-term information storage, whereby genetic and epigenetic processes, at every step of development, become represented in the evolving structural and functional design of the organism. According to this epigenetic view of development, events at one point in time have consequences that are manifested later in the developmental process, and afferent activity has a profound influence on the developmental trajectory over the life span. Parenthetically, this paradigm shift renders moot many developmental questions regarding the relative influences of genetic versus environmental processes on outcomes, because environment can alter structure and function by acting through the genome.

In the context of this formulation, experience may play either a necessary or advantageous role for normal development or may play a noxious role to harm development. Clearly, if the nature of experience is perceived to be stressful, it may produce profound deleterious effects on development, as evidenced by the research literature presented here. Moreover, the central nervous system may be more vulnerable to environmental insult than any other system because it develops over a much longer period of time (11 to 12 years); it has limited repair capabilities (neurons do not multiply after the initial period); its units have highly specific functional roles; the blood–brain barrier is not fully developed *in utero*; and the sensitivity of neurotransmitter systems, which is set during critical developmental periods, affects the organism's response to all subsequent experience.

These new insights have prompted researchers such as David Barker and colleagues to propose a model of fetal programming of human disease based on the notion that "set points" for homeostatic feedback and control mechanisms are determined during intrauterine life and therefore alter the individual's response characteristics to her or his environment all through life. They also argue that relative to other animal species, humans may be more vulnerable to the noxious

effects of an adverse intrauterine environment because organisms are most susceptible to environmental insult during phases of rapid growth, and, in humans, cell division occurs *in utero* at a more rapid rate than in other animal species.

Not all experience is stressful; in fact, a rich or stimulating environment may promote and optimize developmental outcomes. In 1949, Donald O. Hebb posited a hypothesis of use-induced plasticity of the nervous system, the so-called "use it or lose it" theory. Many years and investigations later, empirical evidence in animals, and to a lesser extent, humans, support this postulate. Rats exposed to a stimulating environment after birth showed significant increases in the size and density of neurons and dendrites, the number of synapses per neuron, total brain volume, and brain vasculature. These changes have been correlated with significantly increased cognitive function and decreased stress responsiveness over the life span, reduced cognitive deficits in old age, and a longer life span.

Another important concept is that the postnatal environment can interact with the newborn to either attenuate or accentuate the effects of prenatal stress. For example, in rats, the decrement in male sexual behavior produced by prenatal stress was attenuated by raising the male with either a control female or male, and accentuated by raising the male in social isolation alone or in combination with stress. Similarly, retardation in motor development produced by prenatal stress was attenuated when the rat pups were raised by a nonstressed control mother, and accentuated when the pups were raised by a stressed dam. Handling has also been shown to reverse the effects of prenatal stress in animals. Neonatal handling (from postnatal days 1 to 21) of newborn rat pups reversed the effects of prenatal stress on emotionality and timidity of offspring and on endocrine and metabolic processes, suggesting that neonatal handling may influence postnatal organization of brain development in the opposite direction to that induced by prenatal stress. A similar reversal of the effects of prenatal stress was achieved by adoption at birth. Early adoption of the rat pup (during the first hour after birth), but not later adoption (on the 5th or 12th day after birth) prevented long-term impairments from prenatal stress in glucocorticoid feedback in the offspring. In humans, Tiffany Field and colleagues demonstrated that preterm neonates who were massaged daily for 45 minutes for 10 days gained almost 50% more weight than unmassaged controls, even though the groups did not differ in caloric intake; the massaged infants were awake and active a greater percentage of the observation period; and the massaged infants performed better on the Brazelton Scale on habituation, orientation, motor activity, and regulation of state behavior.

In conclusion, experience plays a critical role in development; the effects of early experience have longer lasting and more permanent consequences on development than those of later experience; adverse early experience in the form of prenatal psychosocial stress has the potential to impact negatively outcomes along the developmental continuum through physiological and behavioral mechanisms; and these suboptimal developmental outcomes in early life may have consequences over the life span of the individual and may affect processes related to mental and physical health, well-being, aging, and longevity. However, not all the news is bad. Sufficiently rich forms of pre- and early postnatal experience may not only be beneficial, but may in fact be necessary for the full growth and expression of brain characteristics and behavioral potential to promote and optimize developmental outcomes over the life span. Moreover, certain types of postnatal experience may even attenuate the detrimental effects of prenatal stress on the development of the individual.

BIBLIOGRAPHY

Barker, D. J. P., & Sultan, H. Y. (1995). Fetal programming of human disease. In M. A. Hanson, J. A. D. Spencer, & J. H. Rodeck (Eds.), *Growth*. Cambridge, UK: Cambridge University Press.

Bornstein, M. H. (1989). Sensitive periods in development: Structural characteristics and causal interpretations. *Psychological Bulletin 105*(2) 179–197.

Chrousos, G. P. & Gold, P. W. (1992). The concepts of stress and stress system disorders. Overview of physical and behavioral homeostasis. *Journal of the American Medical Association, 267*(9), 1244–1252.

Creasy, R. K. (1994). *Preterm labor and delivery*. In R. K. Creasy & R. Resnik (Eds.) *Maternal fetal medicine: Principles and practice*. Philadelphia: Saunders.

DiPietro, J. A., Hodgson, D. M., Costigan, K. A., Hilton, S. C., & Johnson, T. R. (1996). Fetal neurobehavioral development. *Child Development, 67*(5), 2553–2567.

Dunkel-Schetter, C., Sagrestano, L. M., Feldman, P., & Killingsworth, C. (1996). Social support and pregnancy: A comprehensive review focusing on ethnicity and culture. In G. R. Pierce, B. R. Sarason, & G. Sarason (Eds.), *Handbook of social support and the family*. New York: Plenum Press.

Field, T. (1995). Infant massage therapy. In T. Field (Ed.), *Touch in early development*. Mahwah, NJ: Lawrence Erlbaum.

Lauden, M., Wallace, J. A., & Krebs, H. (1981). Roles for serotonin in neuroembryogenesis. *Advances in Experimental Medicine and Biology, 133*, 477–506.

McEwen, B. S., & Stellar, E. (1993). Stress and the individual. Mechanisms leading to disease. *Archives of Internal Medicine, 153*(18), 2093–2101.

Paarlberg, K. M., Vingerhoets, A. J., Passchier, J, Dekker, G. A., & Van Geijn, H. P. (1995). Psychosocial factors and pregnancy outcome: A review with emphasis on methodological issues. *Journal of Psychosomatic Research, 39*(5), 563–95.

Sapolsky, R. (1994). *Why zebras don't get ulcers: A guide to stress, stress-related diseases, and coping*. New York: Freeman.

Smotherman, W. P., & Robinson, S. R. (1995). Tracing developmental trajectories into the prenatal period. In T. P. Lecanuet, W. P. Fifer, N. A. Krasnegor, & W. P. Smotherman (Eds.), *Fetal development: A psychobiological perspective*. Hillsdale, NJ: Laurence Erlbaum.

Wadhwa, P. D., Dunkel-Schetter, C., Chicz-DeMet, A., Porto, M., & Sandman, C. A. (1996). Prenatal psychosocial factors and the neuroendocrine axis in human pregnancy. *Psychosomatic Medicine, 58*(5), 432–446.

Procrastination

Joseph R. Ferrari

DePaul University

Arousal Procrastination Behavioral task delays motivated by a desire for a thrill-seeking experience. The person waits to begin or complete a task until there is little time remaining; then, with the deadline imminent, the person seeks to "beat-the-clock."

Avoidance Procrastination Behavioral task delays motivated by imagined or actual fears, such as fear of failure, fear of success, fear of social disapproval, and/or task aversiveness.

Decisional Procrastination A cognitive form of delay in which a person fails to make decisions in a timely manner; also known as "indecision."

Dispositional-Type of Procrastination Chronic or frequent rates of procrastination such that a person chooses to make chronic delays a global life-style pattern.

Procrastinatory Behavior Targets overt or covert behavior in which a person chooses to delay the start or completion of a task. This phrase also has been used to refer to ancillary acts a person performed other than the target act needing to be completed by a deadline.

Situational-Type of Procrastination High rates of task delays in selective, specific settings for certain target behaviors (e.g., academically related tasks).

PROCRASTINATION is the purposive delay in the beginning and/or completion of an overt or covert act, typically accompanied by subjective discomfort. Unlike prioritizing, procrastination involves the noncompletion of target tasks by deadline, or the "late start" of such tasks just prior to the deadline. This article provides an overview of current research concerning procrastinators and procrastinatory behavior.

I. HISTORICAL ROOTS AND CURRENT PREVALENCE

Procrastination is essentially a modern malady, since its occurrence seems only relevant in countries where technology is advanced and schedule adherence is important. The more industrialized a society, the more salient the construct of procrastination becomes. Many pre-industrialized societies do not have words comparable to our notion of procrastination. The ancient Egyptians, for example, possessed two verbs that have been translated as meaning *procrastinate*. One denoted the *useful* habit of avoiding unnecessary work and impulsive effort, while the other denoted the *harmful* habits of laziness in completing a task necessary for subsistence.

The term *procrastination* comes directly from the Latin verb *procrastinare*, meaning quite literally, to put off or postpone until another day ("pro," an adverb implying forward motion, and "crastinus," meaning belonging to tomorrow). The *Oxford English Dictionary* lists the earliest known English usage of the word *procrastination* as occurring in 1548, but without a pejorative connotation. The term reflected more of the concept of "informed delay" or "wisely chosen restraint" popular in Roman accounts than the modern malady it has become. By the early 1600s, the word *procrastination* was in relatively common usage, but the negative connotations of the term did not seem to emerge until the mid-eighteenth century, at approximately the time of the Industrial Revolution.

The term procrastination may have acquired its pejorative connotations by a gradual association with the term *sloth*, implying not only a personal avoidance of tasks but an active manipulation by an individual to get another to perform or complete the work necessary for one's own subsistence. In today's industrial society where the importance attached to punctuality is great, the manipulative aspect of the concept "sloth" becomes less important and words suggesting task avoidance, such as "procrastination," become more negatively imbued with meaning.

Within the United States, it has been estimated that nearly 70% of college students engage in academic procrastination. College students purposively delay the start and/or completion of studying for exams, writing term papers, reading assignments, and fulfilling academic procedures such as registering. Furthermore, it has recently been demonstrated that in America about 20% of the normal adult population engage in chronic procrastination. Adults report they frequently delay in tasks such as responding to the social or business requests of others, purchasing essential items such as food or gifts, and meeting important deadlines such as Christmas shopping and paying bills.

Although prevalence rates have not been determined in other countries, important research studies on procrastinators and procrastinatory behavior have occurred in Canada, Israel, Japan, and the Netherlands. In addition, it has been found that within the United States and other industrialized nations, self-reported rates of procrastinatory behavior is common among men and women; in short, there is no consistent gender difference in procrastinatory behavior or among dispositional procrastinators. Taken together, it appears that procrastination is common among both men and women residing in industrialized, Westernized nations.

II. TYPES OF PROCRASTINATION AND PROCRASTINATORS

The number of research articles on procrastination has been increasing since the late 1980s, although the total number of articles in major periodicals in psychology has been comparatively low. There seem to be two forms of procrastination repeatedly appearing in the literature: situational and dispositional. In *situational procrastination,* a person purposively delays overt (i.e., behavioral) acts within a specific setting. Most of the research and clinical literature in this area has focused on *academic procrastination.* Students (typically, college-age) report delaying on academic tasks such as studying for an exam, reading weekly assignments, or fulfilling academic requirements like course registration.

In *dispositional procrastination,* a person responds with a global use of chronic, habitual tendencies toward delay. Self-report instruments appear to measure *arousal procrastination,* a desire for thrill-seeking experiences by working "against the clock" as deadlines approach; *avoidance procrastination,* the use of delays to prevent demonstrations of poor, or quality, performance; and, *decisional procrastination* (or, indecision), a cognitive style of procrastination where making decisions is delayed typically as a method to cope with stressful events. Table I presents a sampling of variables positively and negatively correlated with arousal, avoidance, and decisional procrastination. Interested readers are asked to refer to Ferrari, Johnson, and McCown (1995) for further details.

III. ASSESSMENT OF PROCRASTINATION

Before theory construction and substantial research are performed on procrastinators and procrastinatory behavior, precise measurement of the constructs is needed. In this section, seven major self-report instruments are briefly discussed. Table II presents a short summary on these measures. For a summary of the measure's psychometric properties and actual items, see Ferrari et al. (1995). Keep in mind that these instruments provide self-report indices of procrasti-

Table I   Sample Correlates of Self-Reported
Procrastination

Arousal and avoidance procrastination

Positive correlates
  Academic procrastination
  Decisional procrastination
  Neurotic disorganization
  Dysfunctional impulsivity
  Depression
  Neuroticism
  Perfectionism
  Self-defeating behaviors
  Rebelliousness
  Revenge
  Cognitive failures and forgetfulness
  Self-handicapping
  Public and private self-consciousness
  Social anxiety
  Cross-situational variability
  Social comparison
  Defensive avoidance
  Protective and acquisitive self-presentation
  Diffuse-oriented identity
Negative correlates
  Organization
  Belief in a just world
  Self-esteem
  Self-control
  Self-reinforcement
  Information-oriented identity

Decisional procrastination (indecision)

Positive correlates
  Academic procrastination
  Arousal and avoidance procrastination
  Cognitive failure and forgetfulness
  Dysfunctional impulsivity
  Revenge
  Self-defeating behaviors
  Self-handicapping
  Public self-consciousness
  Social anxiety
  Social comparison
  Diffuse-oriented identity
  Interpersonal dependence
  State anger and anger-in
  Obsessive thoughts and compulsive behaviors
Negative correlates
  Self-esteem
  Decisional self-confidence
  Belief in a just world
  Hard-driving and competitive
  Information-oriented identity

Note. It may be worthy to note that dispositional procrastinators and nonprocrastinators do *not* differ significantly in intelligence or intellectual abilities.

Table II   Assessment Instruments of Self-Reported
Procrastination

Academic procrastination
  • "Procrastination Assessment Scale—Students" (PASS, 1984) 38 items; subscores—frequency, personal problem, reasons.
  • "Tuckman Procrastination Scale" (TPS, 1991) 16 items; no subscores.
  • "Procrastination Checklist Study Tasks" (PCS, 1995) 11 items; subscores—behavioral and intentional promptness.
  • "Academic Procrastination State Inventory" (APSI, 1995) 23 items; subscores—academic procrastinatory behavior, fear of failure, lack of study motivation.
Global procrastination tendencies
  • "Decisional Procrastination Scale" (DP, 1982) 5 items; no subscores.
  • "Tel-Aviv Procrastination Inventory" (TAP, 1983) 54 items; subscores—everyday, work-related, academic tasks.
  • "General Procrastination Scale" (GP, 1986) 20 items; no subscores.
  • "Adult Inventory of Procrastination" (AIP, 1989) 15 items; no subscores.

nation used for research purposes. At present, there seems to be no standardized, diagnostic measure of procrastination solely for clinical usage.

As noted from Table II, there exist four reliable and valid measures on academic procrastination. The most widely used instrument is the PASS, developed by E. Rothblum and L. Solomon at the University of Vermont. The instrument (using 5-point scales) asks students to indicate their prevalence of and personal problems with procrastination in six academic areas. Subsequently, students are asked to recall procrastinating on writing a term paper and are instructed to indicate (also with 5-point scales) the extent to which a series of reasons may have contributed to the procrastination.

B. Tuckman at Florida State University developed the TPS. This instrument contains 16 four-point scales embedded among 35 items. It provides a general index of academic procrastination resulting from a student's ability to self-regulate or control task schedules.

Recently, H. Schouwenburg of the University of Groningen, The Netherlands, developed two brief measures of academically related task delays. The PCS is a "yes-no" checklist that examines the promptness of executing and intending to execute academic tasks. A discrepancy score is computed from the difference between intention and action, as well as two promptness scores. The APSI examines changes or fluctuations in academic procrastinatory behavior along

5-point rating scales. This instrument assesses academic task delays as well as two motives for situational procrastination—fear of task failure and lack of motivation to study.

Within the area of global, everyday, more dispositional types of procrastination, there exist four reliable and valid measures. The first reported instrument was created by L. Mann at Flinder's University of Australia to examine indecision. The 5-item, 5-point DP scale is a unidimensional measure (embedded among other subscales) and examines decisional procrastination, the cognitive tendency to delay making decisions when confronted with threatening or stressful situations. In Israel, N. Milgram of Tel-Aviv University developed the TAP to assess dispositional procrastination of everyday tasks, work-related tasks, and (for students) academic tasks. Respondents complete the measure twice—once to determine when a person does a particular task (i.e., early or late within a timeframe), and again to determine the ease to schedule when to do a task.

However, most of the research literature that assesses behavioral tendencies toward dispositional types of procrastination have used two other instruments useful across a variety of settings. One measure is the GP scale by C. Lay from York University. This 20-item, unidimensional scale has been used in "true-false" format or 5-point scales, with half the items reverse scored. J. Johnson, Louisiana State University, and W. McCown, Northeast Louisiana University, developed the 15-item, 5-point AIP scale as a second measure. Both the GP and AIP scales are global measures that examine diligence across a variety of tasks.

IV. THEORIES OF AND MOTIVES FOR PROCRASTINATION

"Why do people procrastinate?" Different perspectives within psychology have proposed different theoretical models to address this question. Some psychodynamic theorists, for instance, point to faulty childrearing practices. Procrastinating adults are plagued by parents who "overcoerced" achievement, setting unrealistic goals for their child, and linking the attainment of these goals to parental love and approval. Others postulate that unconscious feelings of parental anger are expressed when children fail at parental imposed tasks. Children unconsciously respond to this anger by demonstrating a delay of future goal-oriented behavior. When these children become adults they respond to unconscious memories of parental conflict and subsequently find themselves unable to finish any task that is imposed with a deadline.

Burka and Yuen's (1983) self-help book offers a very popular layperson's guide to procrastination within a psychodynamic tradition. These authors claim common fears of success and failure, as well as anger toward authority, to be major contributors to procrastinatory behavior. They claim that the procrastinator views their self-worth as based on personal abilities, which are based on task completion. By delaying task completion, the procrastinator's true abilities are never tested; and, in turn, their self-worth is not tested or threatened.

Behavioral psychologists emphasize seeking rewards and avoiding punishers as motives for procrastination. Procrastinators engage in a variety of activities that they find more reinforcing or pleasing (e.g., "hanging out" with friends) than tasks that are difficult, challenging, effortful, or annoying (e.g., studying). Procrastinators, in fact, report that they lack self-control and engage in frequent self-reinforcement. Not surprisingly, "task aversion" has been a common motive by procrastinators for avoiding or escaping responsibilities.

Procrastination may be maintained by variable schedules of reinforcement. That is, by delaying a task perceived as aversive (e.g., washing dishes, doing laundry), the task may be completed by others (one's roommate or spouse). On other occasions, an aversive task (terminating a coworker's employment) may just "work out" if one waits long enough (the worker gets another job before being informed they were to be fired). Thus, people may procrastinate because the act of delaying is personally pleasurable (rewarding), and/or positive consequences from delaying *may* occur this time around (variable schedule).

Cognitive–behavioral theories of procrastination also have been proposed. A. Ellis and W. Knaus claimed that procrastinators seek to avoid rejection of irrational beliefs, such as "I must do well on a task; if not, then I'm no good," or "Life should be easy and I can't stand the fact that this might not be true." Academic procrastination has been attributed to fear of failure, and dispositional procrastinators report using irrational beliefs and self-defeating behaviors.

Decisional procrastination (indecision) has recently

been the focus of research psychologists. Indecisives compared to decisives do *not* differ in their ability to make decisions quickly, but choose to delay. Indecisives and decisives both seek the same amount of information on items that they desire. However, indecisives compared to decisives tend to avoid seeking information on items that are not of personal interest. The study of cognitive theories and forms of procrastination remains a fruitful line of study for psychologists.

Neuropsychological and biological theories of procrastination, at present, are lacking. Direct biological differences between procrastinators and nonprocrastinators is, at best, speculative. However, it is possible that biology may play a role in the subtypes of procrastination that a person displays. For instance, one type of procrastinator tends to be underaroused; hence missing appropriate cues for deadlines. This type was mentioned above as arousal procrastination, motivated by sensation seeking, a variable with a moderate genetic component. Avoidance procrastination tends to be overaroused, avoiding tasks because of anxiety and fears. Nevertheless, it seems that some forms of procrastination are motivated by genetic or genetic–environment interactions that have yet to be specified.

In sum, different psychological perspectives have offered models to explain "why" people procrastinate. Unfortunately, the empirical data on this topic has been limited and no tests between models have been conducted. Still, it appears that these models are plausible and probable explanations for low rates of diligence among some individuals.

V. DEVELOPMENT OF CHRONIC, DISPOSITIONAL PROCRASTINATORS

One issue that comes to mind concerning procrastinators is "Where does this tendency come from?" The answer to this question, as in determining motives, is complex. A couple of studies found that childhood traumas were related to adult tendencies for dispositional procrastination. In one study, adult children of alcoholics reported they were more likely to be chronic procrastinators than children of nonalcoholics. In another study, adult incest survivors scored high on dispositional measures of procrastination and reported difficulties regarding finishing tasks on time. [*See* Alcohol Problems; Child Sexual Abuse.]

Parenting appears to be an important aspect in the psychological development of procrastination. In one study young women were asked to complete dispositional procrastination measures (i.e., avoidant and decisional measures) and to identify their parents' authority styles. The parents also completed both measures of procrastination. Procrastination scores among these women were significantly related to their father's authoritarian parenting style. Furthermore, these women reported high rates of suppressed anger, and they had mothers who were indecisive. Another study found that procrastinators compared to nonprocrastinators experienced more personal conflicts with their father, than with their mother or their same or opposite sex best friends. Furthermore, it seemed that procrastinators were less likely to rely on their immediate family for support when stressed and faced with difficult life situations. [*See* Parenting.]

In short, these studies point to a person's home dynamics as an important role in the development of chronic procrastinators.

VI. DISPOSITIONAL PROCRASTINATORS AND SOCIAL RELATIONS

Research has also examined aspects of social relations among chronic procrastinators compared to nonprocrastinators. For example, procrastinators reported greater interpersonal dependence (e.g., allowing others to influence their behaviors and to make decisions for them) than nonprocrastinators. Within the workplace, men and women adult procrastinators in managerial positions tended to distance themselves from subordinates who were labeled procrastinators. That is, managers attributed responsibility and cause for delays in work settings to subordinates labeled procrastinators and recommended that the person be fired from their jobs—even though the managers themselves were procrastinators!

Another study found that dispositional procrastinators (high arousal and decisional types) and nonprocrastinators did not differ significantly in the size of their social support network. However, procrastinators were more likely than nonprocrastinators to report being unsatisfied with the support they received from their social network.

In terms of task performance, dispositional procrastinators compared to nonprocrastinators also self-handicapped their performance in order to facilitate the portrayal of a positive social image to others. In fact, procrastinators, but not nonprocrastinators, reported using perfectionism as a method to be liked by others (to "get along"), as opposed to attempting to do the best possible job (to "get ahead").

The role of social settings and self-presentation seems to be an important factor for chronic, dispositional procrastinators. Clearly, this variable should be considered in treatment programs, and remains an avenue for further research.

VII. PROCRASTINATION AND EXCUSE MAKING

It may come as no surprise that procrastinators are good excuse makers. In fact, this issue has been studied in several studies of situational and dispositional procrastination. One study examined academic procrastination and excuse making by college students from selective and nonselective (in terms of admission standards) institutions. It was found that across campuses procrastinators compared to nonprocrastinators reported using fraudulent excuses more often in the current semester and while in college. The primary goal for the excuse was to gain additional time for completing a task or exam. Although the types of phony excuses differed by setting and individual differences, it was interesting to note than in over 90% of the occasions instructors did *not* request "proof" for the excuse.

Adults who are chronic procrastinators also employ frequent excuses. In one study of Christmas holiday shoppers, procrastinators compared to nonprocrastinators were more likely to attribute their lack of diligence at shopping to self-personal factors (e.g., lack of energy, dislike of shopping, indecision), as opposed to situational factors (e.g., weather, current sale prices, business affairs). In another study of U.S. income tax filers, procrastinators compared to nonprocrastinators were likely to request extensions beyond the April 15th deadline to file, and they generated a greater number and more elaborate set of excuses.

Thus, as common knowledge suggests, individuals who engage in procrastination also may be excuse makers. The need to be "clever on your feet" when generating an excuse seems to be an important attribute of procrastination.

VIII. PROCRASTINATION AND CLINICAL PATHOLOGIES

Earlier in this article it was noted that dispositional procrastination may be associated with a large number of self-reported personality variables (see Table I). A quick scanning of those individual differences suggest that chronic, frequent procrastination is related to a maladjusted life-style. Experimental studies reveal that dispositional procrastinators engage in exaggerated self-handicapping of their task performances, avoid self-relevant diagnostic information, experience rejection-related emotions, and even recommend severe reprimands for poor performance observed in fellow procrastinators.

A few studies have tried to relate procrastination tendencies to clinical psychopathologies. One study found that dispositional procrastination was related to antisocial and narcissistic disorders. Another study found that dispositional procrastinators (avoidant and decisional forms) compared to nonprocrastinators reported higher states of passive-aggressive disorders. Across two samples of "normal" participants dispositional procrastination was not related to obsessive thoughts or compulsive acts. However, in a study using a sample of patients clinically diagnosed with obsessive-compulsive personality disorder (OCPD), decisional (but not avoidant) procrastination was related to obsessive thinking and compulsive behaviors. One study also found that obsessive-compulsive tendencies among one's family did not result in promoting dispositional procrastination in family members. [*See* OBSESSIVE-COMPULSIVE DISORDER.]

Thus, the relationship between procrastination and clinical pathologies seems to be a rich avenue for further study. Besides passive-aggressive and obsessive-compulsive tendencies, it is quite possible that other pathologies contain components of procrastination. Research into these areas would be useful for clinical interventions.

IX. TREATMENT MODALITIES

It seems that most treatment programs for procrastination make time management their major emphasis. Indeed, dispositional procrastinators compared to nonprocrastinators make poor judgments of time, often under- or overestimating the time needed to complete tasks. For the situational procrastinator, then, time-management strategies may be appropriate. Interventions should focus on what target situations are least likely to be completed. Then, it should be determined whether it is task aversiveness or personal fears (success and/or failure) that motivates the person not to complete the task. Subsequently, the situational procrastinator should be taught time management skills as well as how to cope and deal with stressful, aversive situations that promote diligence.

Still, after reading this article it appears that dispositional procrastination involves more than time management problems. To tell the chronic procrastinator to "just do it" would be like telling the clinically depressed person "cheer up!" It just does not work. Instead, dispositional procrastinators may benefit from brief counseling interventions to determine how and why the person delays often. It is unlikely that the procrastinator requires psychopharmacological treatment, but group (and, perhaps, family) treatments have been successful. Determining the person's stress levels and assessing the type of procrastination also is needed. It is suggested that interested readers review leading texts listed in the bibliography for details on effective intervention strategies.

X. CONCLUSION

In sum, it appears that the label of "procrastinator" or "procrastinatory behavior" would not be associated with a healthy personality. The term has existed only in modern times among industrialized nations. The notion that procrastination is simply a "time-management problem" does not seem complete when examining the number of negative personality variables associated with the term. In fact, there appears to be different forms of chronic procrastinators, and useful measurement tools have been developed to tap into the different types of procrastination. Theories and motives for why people procrastinate appear to be useful for research investigations.

In addition, it was noted that the development of procrastination tendencies may begin in the home. Procrastinators also seem to have difficult social relationships, but are excellent excuse makers. Further, it appears that some clinical pathologies may be related to dispositional procrastination. Fortunately, clinical interventions have been useful to treat both situational and dispositional procrastinators. Thus, in this article it has been demonstrated that procrastination is "not about time."

BIBLIOGRAPHY

Leading Texts

Burka, J. B., & Yuen, L. A. (1983). *Procrastination: Why you do it and what to do about it.* Reading, PA: Addison-Wesley.

Ellis, A., & Knaus, W. J. (1977). *Overcoming procrastination.* New York: Institute for Rational Living.

Ferrari, J. R., Johnson, J. A., & McCown, W. G. (1995). *Procrastination and task avoidance: Theory, research, and treatment.* New York: Plenum Publications.

Sample of Research Studies

Ferrari, J. R. (1993). Procrastination and impulsivity: Two sides of a coin? In W. McCown, M. B. Shure, & J. Johnson (Eds.), *The impulsive client* (pp. 265–271). Washington, DC: American Psychological Association.

Ferrari, J. R., & Olivette, M. J. (1994). Parental authority influences on the development of female dysfunctional procrastination. *Journal of Research in Personality, 28,* 87–100.

Lay, C. H. (1986). At last, my research on procrastination. *Journal of Research in Personality, 20,* 474–495.

Lay, C. H. (1990). Working to schedule on personal projects: An assessment of person-project characteristics and trait procrastination. *Journal of Social Behavior and Personality, 5,* 91–103.

McCown, W., Petzel, T., & Rupert, R. (1994). Personality correlates and behaviors of chronic procrastinators. *Personality and Individual Differences, 11,* 71–79.

Milgram, N. A., Gehrman, T., & Keinan, G. (1992). Procrastination and emotional upset: A typological model. *Personality and Individual Differences, 13,* 1307–1313.

Milgram, N. A., Sroloff, B., & Rosenbaum, M. (1988). The procrastination of everyday life. *Journal of Research in Personality, 22,* 197–212.

Protective Factors in Development of Psychopathology

Natalie Grizenko

McGill University

Protective Factors Elements that modify, ameliorate, or alter a person's response to some environmental hazards that predisposes a maladaptive outcome. Protective factors do not have any effect on the individual in the absence of stress.

Resilience The ability to recover readily from illness, depression, adversity, or the like. Resilience is the successful adaptation to stressful life events.

Risk Factors Elements that if present increase the likelihood of developing emotional or behavioral disorders.

Vulnerability Susceptibility to negative developmental outcomes under high-risk conditions. However, even under conditions of low risk or stress certain children could still be deemed vulnerable.

PROTECTIVE FACTORS IN DEVELOPMENT OF PSYCHOPATHOLOGY are elements that increase a person's chances of achieving competence in life. These factors may be biological, psychological, or social in nature. For example, a child's intelligence and temperament are innate factors. Psychological protective factors, such as high self-esteem, influence the mechanism by which a person deals with his or her environment. They influence the process by which an individual develops adequate coping strategies. Social protective factors include all of the protective elements of a familial and social support network.

I. INTRODUCTION

As clinicians working in the mental health field, we all have stories of families where the children may have grown up in severe poverty, been exposed to sexual and physical abuse, or had parents who were alcoholics. Many of these children end up similar to their parents, in difficulties with the law, in unstable relationships, and unable to maintain consistent employment. And yet, there is occasionally that one child who succeeds against all odds, who manages to achieve professional employment and a stable happy homelife, and who seems to have the warmth to make the people around him or her feel good. What is this quality of invulnerability or resilience and where does it come from? Studies to date suggest that there is no single source of resilience or invulnerability, instead there are many interacting factors. Factors that may have a genetic component, such as temperament and intelligence, are mediated through a number of environmental factors, such as the presence of consistent loving caregivers, which in turn may shape, through social learning, the development of appropriate self-esteem and positive future interactions and experiences.

This entry examines the multidimensional interactive components that shape resilience and how, once understood, this knowledge can be used to improve children's coping capacities and to develop programs that will improve the future of children at risk for developing psychopathology.

II. INTERACTIONAL MODEL

An invulnerable or resilient child has numerous protective factors that give him or her the ability to adapt to situations of high life stress. Invulnerability is a partial and dynamic state in constant interaction with a changing environment. Children who are vulnerable to a particular traumatic event at one stage of development may become invulnerable to the same event at another developmental stage. For example, for an infant, the loss of a mother followed by a severe lack of affectionate parental care may have much greater consequences than if he or she was an adult. Situations of high stress tend to affect the individual most during rapid phases of growth when he or she is most vulnerable.

It is also important to understand that life stress events are not synonymous with risk factors. Risk factors can be defined as factors that increase the vulnerability of a child, or that increase the likelihood that a child may develop difficulties in situations of any stress, even minor stress. The reverse is also true. Exposure to a certain limited degree of stress may actually increase the resilience of a person. Anxiety as a result of exposure to traumatic situations, according to Freud has two components. There is one form of anxiety that is paralyzing, overwhelming, and produces a "fright-neurosis"; on the other hand, there is an anxiety that protects against such powerful experiences by signaling and thus preparing the subject beforehand for the disturbing encounter. It is through this learning process that the person becomes better able to deal with future situations of stress. The ego, when confronted with challenges, does more than retreat or safeguard itself; it attempts to master the stimulus, to cope interactively with the environment, and to transform situations rather than permit itself to be transformed by them. [See ANXIETY; STRESS.]

Protective factors are not just the opposite of risk factors. Risk factors increase the probability that a person will develop psychopathology, whereas protective factors operate indirectly. The effect of protective factors is only apparent through their interaction with risk variables by lowering the potential for a maladaptive outcome.

From the 1976 longitudinal studies of Murphy and Moriarty, a profile has emerged of "good copers." These are children who are cognitively capable, affectively expressive, and effective. They have a certain degree of healthy narcissism, good insights into interpersonal situations, and realistic views. They are flexible, humorous, confident, warm, and creative. Furthermore, parents of "good copers" are often "good copers" themselves and provide models of resilience to their children.

The importance of certain risk and protective factors may vary in the development of various psychopathologies. For example, genetic factors are very important in the development of schizophrenia, whereas early parental loss or neglect may be associated with the development of depression in later years. Studies have shown that institutionalized children who do not become depressed later in life frequently have experienced more secure and stable attachment than the children who develop difficulties. It is a combination of biological or genetic factors, psychological factors, and environmental factors that make certain individuals more resilient to stress than others. [See DEPRESSION; SCHIZOPHRENIA.]

III. BIOLOGICAL PROTECTIVE FACTORS

A. Intelligence

Numerous studies have shown that intelligence (at times assessed as academic performance) is associated with better adaptation in situations of stress. For example, when exposed to increasing levels of stress, bright children do not show the decrease in social competence demonstrated by less intelligent children. In a study of 205 children between the ages of 8 and 13, Master and colleagues noted that children of lower intellectual ability, with lower socioeconomic status, and fewer positive family qualities appeared to be at greater risk of being less "competent" when under high levels of stress. Competence was assessed by teacher ratings, peer assessments, and school record data.

It is possible that so-called "resilient" children react to stressful situations in a primarily internalizing way rather than through externalizing uncontrolled behavioral disturbances. These internalizing presentations can often be missed by teachers. Parker and associates, in a study of urban elementary school children, were able to show that despite the superior behavioral competence of stress-resilient children, compared with stress-affected children, the resilient group did not show similar advantages in self-rated levels of depression or anxiety.

Other studies have shown that intelligence can sometimes be a vulnerability factor. For example, intelligence may be protective at lower stress levels, but when the levels become too high, intelligent children may lose their advantage. Explanations for such a finding are that intelligent children tend to have high levels of sensitivity to their environment which may heighten their susceptibility to stressors. [*See* INTELLIGENCE AND MENTAL HEALTH.]

B. Temperament

Children are born with very different temperaments. A common assumption people have is that congenital elements of temperament are fully expressed at birth and diminish in importance with interaction with the environment. Recent research indicates that genetically determined elements of temperament are poorly expressed at birth, being overshadowed by perinatal factors, and become more evident during the next few years of life. In one study of 316 newborn twins, monozygotic twins showed little concordance in temperament as neonates but found impressive concordance later in life. Environmental differences may obscure genetic influences in the neonatal period and genetic influences on temperament may increase with increasing age from infancy to early childhood. [*See* PERSONALITY.]

It is thus important to look at temperament not only as a biological phenomenon but also as a psychological one. The notion of "goodness of fit" between the mother and infant is of great importance. Poor fits occur when a mother is so temperamentally different from the baby that she cannot provide what the infant demands. For example, a very stimulating mother may lack the gentleness required by an infant of unusual sensitivity and an unforthcoming mother may find an overly energetic baby too much for her to manage. The situation of not being well fitted with the primary caregivers is not only stressful for the infant but may make the mother feel inferior and unsure about her parental competence. Therefore it is not only whether or not an infant has an easy temperament but also the quality of fit between the infant and parents that will determine whether the child's development will be smooth.

Finally, Maziade and associates, in a study of 980 children in Quebec, demonstrated that temperament alone is not a good predictor of outcome unless the mediating effects of family functioning are considered. By studying two groups of children, one with extremely easy temperaments and the other with extremely difficult temperaments, he was able to show that only in dysfunctional families was there an association between extreme temperament at age 7 and psychiatric status at ages 12 and 16.

IV. PSYCHOLOGICAL PROTECTIVE FACTORS

A. Positive Self-Esteem

Self-esteem has often been cited as a key variable in determining resilience. Self-esteem includes the thoughts that people have about their competence and work, about their abilities to effectuate change, to confront rather than retreat from challenges, to learn from both success and failure, and to treat themselves and others with respect. Our self-esteem influences our actions, which in turn affects how we see ourselves, so that a dynamic, reciprocal process is continuously in force.

The development of self-esteem occurs within the dynamic interaction of a child's inborn temperament and the environmental forces that respond to the child. Incongruences between the parent's (or teacher's or other adults') and the child's temperamental characteristics or expectations may be sources of anger and disappointment. Low self-esteem is a common outcome unless the adults are able to lessen the effect of the mismatch by being more empathic, by appreciating the child's unique style and needs, and by adapting their own expectations to the child's capacities. Although children with high self-esteem frequently display adaptive strategies that promote growth, those with low self-esteem frequently rely on maladaptive coping behaviors such as quitting, avoiding, cheating, and bullying. These behaviors may lead to further failure and an increased lowering of self-esteem.

Attribution theory, initially proposed by Weiner, offers a framework for understanding how low self-esteem influences behavior. This theory examines the causes to which people attribute their successes and failures. Children with high self-esteem see their success as being determined by their own efforts, resources, and abilities. They feel a sense of control over their lives and take realistic credit for their accomplishments. Children with low self-esteem tend to feel that their achievements are predicated on luck, chance, or fate. They do not feel they control their lives, thereby weakening their confidence in their ability to succeed in the future. Furthermore, children who experience low self-esteem do not see mistakes as something to learn from, but instead they attribute them to factors that cannot be changed, such as lack of ability or intelligence. Feelings of helplessness and hopelessness ensue. These children expect to fail, retreat from demands, and develop maladaptive coping strategies that exacerbate their situation. [See SELF-ESTEEM.]

B. Internal Locus of Control

An internal locus of control has also been shown to be a protective factor. For example, Werner and Smith in their longitudinal study of invulnerable children found that children who had a high faith in their control over their environment, thus showing an internal locus of control, did much better than those who believed that the external environment was random and immutable. It has also been demonstrated than an internal locus of control differentiates stress-affected elementary school children from those who are stress-resilient. The latter also had higher levels of empathy and more effective social problem-solving skills.

C. Secure Attachment

Secure early attachment is an important protective factor for populations at risk. Faber and Egel showed that there is a significant decline in competence of abused children during the first 5 years of life. The children who remain competent are more likely to have had a history of secure attachment.

Environmental factors such as the presence of a male partner in the home and the mother's emotional support of the child also play a major role. It has been demonstrated that resilient children have fewer prolonged separations from the primary caregiver in early childhood, leading to the development of close bonds and good emotional support, along with the development of positive self-esteem and positive self-concept.

A stable early attachment relationship basically means that the primary caregiver provides both a secure base for the infant's exploration and a safe haven to which the infant can return when frightened, tired, or hungry. The more secure the infant feels, the more willing the infant is to explore the world around him or her. Researchers have found that children who experience a secure attachment during infancy will later approach problem-solving tasks more positively and with greater persistence than will children who experience insecure attachment. Children with secure attachments tend also to be more empathic, unconflicted, and more competent in their relationships with adults and peers. The success or failure of an infant's early attachment frequently establishes a cluster of expectations that sets the stage for future social relations. In a study of children from low income families, it was shown that insecurely attached infants at late latency and early adolescence were more dependent, less sociable, had lower self-esteem, trusted others less, and were less resilient than those who were securely attached. [See ATTACHMENT.]

D. Positive Coping Strategies

Positive self-esteem and positive self-concept allow the individual to push the frontiers of the goals they set out to accomplish. A positive feedback loop is created, in that the more a person succeeds, the greater his or her self-esteem and the more he or she is prepared to take risks and learn new adaptive coping strategies, which in turn can lead to further success.

Coping strategies should not be confined with defense mechanisms. Coping strategies are largely flexible, oriented toward present reality, "secondary process thinking," and can often be taught and learned, which also means that parents can serve as appropriate models. Resilient children's capacity to tolerate frustration, handle anxiety, and ask for help when needed, differentiates them from more vulnerable children. Resilient children orient themselves rapidly to situations and communicate without inhibition. When faced with lots of material in their activities, they are able to accept substitutions; they allow others to get close to them and reciprocate in a warm manner. Their pattern of recovery from transient setbacks is also different from others in that they are able to retreat for awhile into safety, to take time out to recuperate, to play traumatic experiences out, and, if need be, transform unpleasant reality through the medium of fantasy. [See COPING WITH STRESS.]

V. SOCIAL PROTECTIVE FACTORS

A. Supportive Family Environment

The importance of family factors in resilience has been suggested by numerous studies. Resilient children are more likely to come from home environments that can be described as warm, affectionate, and emotionally supportive, and where structure and limits are fair and clear-cut. The parents provide a facilitating environment that allows for the child's growing individuality, fosters reliability and self-reliance, while at the same time giving support and safety. A good relationship with at least one parent can protect against the risks associated with family discord and child abuse.

B. Social Support Network

If family support is missing, children may find "protection" through grandparents, other extended family members, friends, and community groups and agencies. In a study of 100 children conducted by Grizenko and Pawliuk in 1994, it was shown that the presence of grandparents was a very significant protective factor for children under stress. In long term follow-up studies of young adults with attention deficit hyperactive disorder, when they were asked what they believed was most helpful to them as they were growing up, the most frequent reply was that there was someone—a parent, teacher, or other significant adult—who believed in them.

Children may also receive a great deal of support in school. This can enhance their self-esteem and feeling of competence. As Rutter describes, the long-term educational benefits from positive school experiences probably stems less from what children are specifically taught than from effects on children's attitude to learning, on their self-esteem, and on their task orientation and work strategies.

Resilient children appear to be quite able to find sources of support. Frequently, these children do not seek professional support but develop a network of informal relationships that includes friends, teachers, and members of community organizations. The way in which high-risk adolescents perceive the usefulness of these support systems varies with sex, grade, and ethnic background. It was shown in one study that, having informal social support was related to better peer self-concept but also with lower academic adjustment, indicating both the potential positive and negative influence of a peer group.

Social support may also not only act as a protective factor for adulthood, but may also benefit the next generation. The presence of social support has been shown to be important in differentiating parents who repeated an intergenerational cycle of child abuse from parents who did not. [See SOCIAL SUPPORT.]

C. Marital Support

A good marital relationship can also be a protective factor. In a study of girls reared in institutions, women who were reared in institutions and had warm supportive spouses were able to show a similar level of good parenting as a comparison group. Those who were reared in institutions but who did not have supportive spouses showed an absence of good parenting ability. It is important to go further to try to understand by what mechanism a good relationship with a spouse is a protective factor. It has been suggested that it may operate through an effect on self-esteem, through diffusion of task responsibilities by virtue of the husband sharing in parental roles, or through the possibility of having someone with which to discuss family problems and improve social problem-solving skills. Furthermore, there may have been a selection process that occurs, in that the psychologically more healthy women were able to select supportive spouses. As the study demonstrated, the most important explanatory variable was whether or not the women exercised "planning" in the choice of their spouse, meaning that they did not marry for negative reasons such as escaping an intolerable family situation or as a result of an unwanted pregnancy. [*See* MARITAL HEALTH.]

VI. DEVELOPMENT OF SPECIFIC INTERVENTION STRATEGIES TO IMPROVE RESILIENCE

As previously mentioned, stressors tend to affect the individual most during periods of change and rapid growth. It is during this time that the person is most vulnerable. However, resilience is not just a matter of constitutional strength or weakness; it is also a reflection of what the individual does about his or her plight. Adolf Meyer has long argued, through his psychobiological approach, for the developmental importance of the way in which people meet key life changes and transitions. He places emphasis on the importance of the person–environment interactions at these times. It is important to stress the role of the individual when in contact with difficult situations. It would be simplistic to assume that the protective factors discussed previously work in isolation. Specific protective factors should be viewed in terms of the development of a protective process, that is, to develop a specific interactional model for each individual and not just identify the pieces in the puzzle. What is most interesting is to examine how children and adults are able to use the pieces of the puzzle (or the various protective factors) to form a highly integrated functional whole.

Examples of mediating mechanisms in the protective process include (1) reduction of risk impact, (2) reduction of negative chain reactions, (3) establishment and maintenance of self-esteem and self-efficacy, and (4) opening up of opportunities. One way to reduce the impact of stressors is to have controlled exposure to the stressful situation and thus allow for coping mechanisms to develop. For example, it may be beneficial to visit with a child the hospital where he or she will have surgery before admission and to try to answer all of the child's questions. Another way to reduce risk factor impact is to distance oneself physically from the unalterable difficult situation. For example, children who live with a parent who is mentally ill may spend many hours in extracurricular activities outside the home.

Many of the protective factors identified actually act by reducing the negative chain reaction started by exposure to certain life stressors. For example, the ill effects of parental loss in early childhood have been demonstrated to stem from the lack of affectionate care or institutionalization that follows the loss, and not from the loss itself. The lack of affectionate care in early childhood can then lead to the development of poor self-esteem. Therefore, if one is able to support the remaining parent or provide stable and secure alternative care, the child may be able to develop and function well in the future, as secure early attachments often lead to feelings of high self-esteem and efficacy.

As has previously been discussed, positive self-esteem and self-efficacy are important protective factors that can be modified by addressing the environment. To foster self-esteem, one needs to create an environment at home and at school that increases the likelihood that the children will be successful and that they will experience this success as due to their own efforts and abilities. Hence, children should experience a greater sense of control, ownership, and responsibility for their lives. Also, children must learn that mistakes are a normal part of learning and are to be expected.

To develop self-esteem and self-efficacy, one needs to look at each child individually and identify his or her temperament, interests, strengths, weaknesses, cognitive skills, and coping strategies. Next, one needs to identify the "island of competence" in each child and try to reinforce it. Quite often a ripple effect is created: as the child feels success in one area of his or her life, he or she ventures to take greater risks and to face other challenges of life. In one observation of high-risk children, resilient children, even though they were not unusually talented, took much pleasure in hobbies (their "island of competence") that brought them solace and enabled them to develop even when things fell apart in their homes. [*See* SELF-EFFICACY.]

Guided by attribution theory, a number of simple strategies can be used in both the home and school setting to increase self-esteem and self-efficacy. First, children should be given the opportunity to take on responsibilities and to make a contribution to their home, school, or community environment. For example, a child whose "island of competence" consists of artistic ability may be encouraged to make the posters for the school fundraising activities. Second, children should be given the opportunity to make decisions and solve problems to increase a sense of control over their lives. Third, children should be offered encouragement and praise. All too often, parents and teachers are very attentive to children not listening or following instructions but forget to praise children for behaving well. What should be promoted is a policy of "catching children when they are good" and pointing it out to them. Also, adults need to help children develop self-discipline by creating clear guidelines and consequences. Children must not be humiliated or intimidated into following rules, but should be made to understand the purpose of the rules. If children are to develop high self-esteem, they must have a secure and comfortable sense of self-discipline. Finally, children should also be helped to accept mistakes and failures and see them as crucial ingredients in the learning process.

Grizenko and Pawliuk conducted a study in 1994 to examine risk and protective factors for disruptive behavior disorders in children. Significant protective factors were defined as those associated with a reduced risk of behavioral disorders under conditions of recent high stress. These factors included easy temperament as an infant, ability to cope well under stress, easy adaptation to change, positive self-image, and ability to express feelings easily. Social protective factors that discriminated between behavior problem and control children were having two or more hobbies, having a positive relationship with grandparents, and having friends. One can extrapolate from these findings certain intervention strategies that may cultivate protective factors in at-risk children. For example, after-school programs can be used to encourage outside activities, build friendships, and develop hobbies, all of which may serve as an escape from a stressful home situation and provide the child with successful experiences, thereby increasing self-image. Individual and family therapy can increase a child's ability to understand and express feelings before problems escalate. Teachers or guidance counselors can be encouraged to develop programs that help children under stress to identify, understand, and appropriately express feelings instead of acting them out through delinquent behavior. Finally, the protective role that grandparents can play with children should be supported and encouraged.

At present, there is a limited number of studies that examine the effectiveness, cost-effectiveness, and cost–benefit ratio of preventive programs that attempt to enhance protective factors. Cost-effectiveness is the ratio of treatment effect to treatment cost. The cost–benefit ratio is the ratio of the cost of treatment versus the cost of no treatment (potential long-term cost to society).

It has been demonstrated that children at risk who were exposed to parent-effectiveness training and social skills training programs were two times less likely to show serious academic and behavioral difficulties than an untreated group and were less likely to engage in delinquent activities as adolescents. In another examination of the cost–benefit analysis of a preschool education program on children growing up in poverty, children were followed up 25 years after discharge from the program. Comparing the cost of the program to such variables as cost to society of welfare, adult education, employment compensation, crime, and delinquency, a cost–benefit ratio in excess of 1:7 was demonstrated. The majority of the benefits from the preschool program—more than $88,000 per child—accrued to the general public, mainly in the reduction of crime. Another example of a preventive cost-beneficial program was the PALS program studied by Jones and collegues in 1989. PALS (for "participate and learn skills") was a nonschool, skill-development program offered to all children 5 to 15 years of age living in a publicly supported housing complex in Ottawa, Canada. Although only marginal effects in school performance or behavior in the home were observed, significant changes occurred on unobtrusive measures of antisocial behavior outside the home and school. A cost–benefit analysis indicated that potential savings, primarily in reduced vandalism and reduced police and fire costs, greatly exceeded the cost of the program.

VII. FUTURE RESEARCH

There are two basic approaches to studying protective factors. One is a general population survey. It is a costly technique that requires large numbers of subjects. But it does allow for a hierarchical analysis of the importance of various protective factors and an understanding of protective factors in situations not only of severe but also moderate to mild stress. The second approach examines protective factors in at-risk populations. This approach is less costly because it requires a smaller sample size, but the generalizability of the results is questionable, given that the protective factors found may be specific to the psychopathology and age group studied.

When either approach is used, it is important to keep in mind that the protective factors identified should not be looked at in isolation. Protective factors frequently have their own complex internal structure. For example, the protective factor of having a supportive grandparent may allow the child to have at least one person in his or her life who accepts him or her unconditionally, regardless of temperamental idiosyncracies, physical appearance, or intelligence. This in turns allows for the development of high self-esteem. The direction of future research in protective factors should lie in the understanding of the mechanisms of action of risk and protective factors and the direction of causality. Causality can only be determined by using a longitudinal study design. The difficulties with long-term follow-up is that there may be a high attention rate, it is costly, and operational definitions of particular disorders may change. Furthermore, long-term studies may be subject to cumulative testing effects, so that with repeated contact, subjects may be less likely to report psychopathology.

An example of an excellent longitudinal study was Werner's 32-year follow-up study of high-risk infants in Kauai who had experienced perinatal stress, low socioeconomic status, or life in a discordant or divorced family environment with parental alcoholism or mental illness. What was remarkable is that the author of the study was able to follow up 80% of the cohort. Starting from the perinatal period, the effects of risk factors, protective factors, and stressful life events on physical, intellectual, and psychosocial development were monitored. One third of the children were considered to be resilient because, as adults, they had more positive life experiences than the others. As children, these individuals had fewer eating and sleeping problems, were good-natured, and got along well with classmates. They were more advanced in communication, maturity, self-help skills, and reading. The family had four or less children, with spaces of 2 or more years between children. There had been few prolonged separations with the primary caregiver and the children had close bonds with grandparents, older siblings, or other significant adults. In high school, these children developed a positive self-concept and internal locus of control. The resilient group had all grown up in poverty, yet had finished at least high school, were almost all employed, and were coping successfully. An interesting finding was that more than half of the stressful life events that increased their chances of having a criminal record or broken marriage by age 30 took place in infancy or early childhood. The other im-

portant point raised in the study was that both vulnerability and resilience could change with time. Up to age 10, boys were more vulnerable than girls. Between ages 11 and 20, they became less so. The trend reversed again when they were in their 30s, when males again became the more vulnerable of the two.

Another difficulty for future studies of protective factors is the manner in which resilience is assessed. In earlier studies, a lack of psychopathology and behavioral disturbance under stress were seen as indicators of resilience. Recent studies have used social competence as an indicator. The problem with social competence is that it is composed of many factors. Children may present with a high degree of competence on behavioral indices but may still have underlying psychological problems such as depression or anxiety. Children who are resilient frequently demonstrate greater intellectual maturity. These children may respond to stress in a primarily internalizing manner other than presenting with socially inappropriate behavior.

It is also important to note that there are few psychometrically sound measures of stressful life events that enable an accurate assessment of levels of stress. A resilient child is one who is able to be socially competent even under stress. However, what may be seen as high stress for one child may not be for another. Furthermore, there is only one psychometrically valid scale that utilizes a biopsychosocial approach for the evaluation of risk and protective factors in children—the Risk Protective Scale by Grizenko, Looper, and Pawliuk.

In summary, further research is needed to understand, identify, and study the mechanism of action of protective factors. Longitudinal studies are necessary to examine what combinations of protective factors actually protect children and adults from developing psychopathology under stress and also to examine how different protective factors may have varying degrees of importance at various stages of development. There is also a need for more objective, psychometrically sound measures that allow for an evaluation of the full scope of biological, psychological, and social protective factors. Finally, studies are needed that test whether specific intervention strategies can be developed to improve the resilience of children. Research is needed to examine the effectiveness of various intervention strategies, such as social skills training programs and after-school programs aimed at improving the self-esteem and self-concept of children at risk.

VIII. SUMMARY AND CONCLUSIONS

Individuals' responses to stress and adversity can be very different; some succumb and others escape damage. What sets resilient individuals apart is that despite enormous odds their lives reveal a clear pattern of recovery and mastery. Protective factors that have been studied that enhance resilience are numerous but ill defined; they may vary with gender, age, and type of psychopathology. The focus should not be on specific protective factors but on the interactive mechanism of vulnerability and the protective process. Resilience should be examined not only in the context of what protective factors affect the individual at present, but also in the context of how people deal with life changes and what they do about stressful or adverse circumstances. Resilience is a result of a complex interplay of innate or biological factors, such as genetic loading for psychiatric disorders, intelligence, and temperament, combined with the psychological makeup of the individual that is modulated by factors such as self-esteem and expresses itself through various coping strategies. All of this is affected by social circumstances that may enhance or buffer the effects of stress. For example, a supportive social network of close family and friends may add to the ability of an individual to cope with many of life's adversities.

BIBLIOGRAPHY

Anthony, E. J., & Cohler, B. J. (Eds.). (1987). *The invulnerable child*. New York: Guilford Press.

Brooks, R. B. (1994). Children at risk: Fostering resilience and hope. *American Journal of Orthopsychiatry, 64*(4), 545–553.

Grizenko, N., & Fisher, C. (1992). Review of studies of risk and protective factors for psychopathology in children. *Canadian Journal of Psychiatry, 37*(10), 711–721.

Grizenko, N., & Pawliuk, N. (1994). Risk and protective factors for disruptive behavior disorders in children. *American Journal of Orthopsychiatry, 64*(4), 534–544.

Jones, M. B., Offord, D. R. (1989). Reduction of antisocial behavior in poor children by nonschool skill-development. *Journal of Child Psychology, Psychiatry and Allied Disciplines, 30*(5), 737–50.

Murphy, L. B., & Moriarty, A. E. (1976). *Vulnerability, coping and growth*. New Haven, CT: Yale University Press.

Rutter, M. (1990). Psychosocial resilience and protective mechanisms. In J. Rolf, A. S. Masten, D. Cicchetti, K. H. Nuechterlein, & S. Weintraub (Eds.), *Risk and protective factors in the developments of psychopathology*, pp. 181–214. New York: Cambridge University Press.

Werner, E. E., & Smith, R. S. (1982). *Vulnerable but invincible: A longitudinal study of resilient children and youth*. New York: McGraw-Hill.

Psychoanalysis

Mardi J. Horowitz

University of California, San Francisco

Abstinence The analyst avoids nonessential advice and reassurance, waiting to hear the patient's usually unspoken wishes and fears.

Dream Interpretation Explaining symbolic meanings behind dream images.

Dynamic Interpretation Explaining the wish-fear-and-defense configurations involved in forming maladaptive patterns of experience and behavior.

Genetic Interpretation Interpretation about situations, memories, and fantasies of infancy, childhood, and adolescence that lead to an understanding of the patient's present patterns.

Interpretation The main tool of the analyst.

Neutrality The analyst does not react as emotionally as he or she might in a personal social situation.

Reconstructive Interpretation Piecing together different topics and inferences to form a plausible story about how possibly significant early experiences account for current beliefs, attitudes, and behaviors.

Resistance Defensive operations that work against authentic emotional expressions and memory recovery thereby obstructing the progress of analysis.

Transference Interpretation Explaining the meaningful configurations of ideas and feelings about the relationship with the analyst.

Transference Neuroses A substitute pathology that reiterates fundamental developmental conflicts based on unconscious schematizations and motives concerning self and other roles in a relationship. In forming such transference-based reactions, the patient regresses to early stages of development, returning to the conceptual source of problems.

PSYCHOANALYSIS is a treatment that aims at a comprehensive exploration and understanding of unconscious conflicts, character, and personality development. Meetings are frequent and often go on for years. The aim of therapy is to alter the interaction of conscious and unconscious processes in the direction of better integration of identity leading to improved adaptation, maturity, and health. The central concepts of theory provide the basis for the treatment. These concepts focus on the interactions of wishes, fears, and defenses against threat, and the influence of enduring but often unconscious motives upon personality structure.

Personality is viewed as a knowledge and procedural structure that is the result of repeated behaviors and decisions for how to reduce or avoid dangerous manifestations of raw wishes, exposures to dreaded situations, and the experience of problems, symptoms, and uncontrolled moods. Thus, a psychoanalytic formulation of personality may include hypotheses about developmental antecedents in terms of how wishes, fears, and immediate defenses lead to more adaptive but still defensive compromises. Although relatively more adaptive compromises may be preferable to problem-filled or symptomatic compromises, they are not seen as substitutes for new, more optimal solutions that may be achieved through treatment.

I. THE BEGINNING OF PSYCHOANALYSIS: SIGMUND FREUD

Sigmund Freud established psychoanalysis as a combination of theory, mode of investigation, and technique of treatment. Dream work, multiple subpersonalities theory, recognition of unconscious determinants of behavioral patterns, hypnosis, and suggestive techniques were islands of fragmentary knowledge before Freud integrated them, added a developmental approach, described unconscious defensive mechanisms, and recognized transference and resistance.

In initial work, Josef Breuer and Freud emphasized the importance of psychic traumas. Repressed but dynamically active, memories of such traumas might affect conscious thoughts, feelings, and behaviors. Later, Freud added theories of repressed wishes and fears and their elaborations into unconscious but active fantasies.

In his early model, Freud viewed therapy as making the unconscious conscious. He developed one of the most important techniques in psychoanalysis, *free association,* as he gave up hypnosis and yet retained the attention-altering properties of trance and suggestion-induced reveries. No association is, of course, entirely free. The patient is encouraged not to suppress or edit what comes to mind and not to always focus only on one specific topic, instead saying in words all thoughts, images, feelings, and bodily sensations as they occur in the stream-of-conscious representations. Free association has been useful in counteracting unconscious defensiveness in general, in finding linkages between ideas in particular, and in understanding the power of certain symbols.

In order to associate freely, the patient must try to set aside restrictions on thought and reporting that occur because of feelings of embarrassment, shame, guilt, or fear that these emotions bring. A patient can experience such a process as confusing and anxiety provoking, which is why psychoanalysis is not always useful for persons who are vulnerable to conceptual disorganization.

Studying the flow of a patient's associations, therapists look not only at contents but at the sequences that indicate efforts to avoid or distort the communi-

cation of meanings. Together, the patient and therapist can observe the derailment of clear expression and elaboration of a topic. Thus, by developing free association as a rule in psychoanalysis, Freud was in a position to describe defense mechanisms.

Early theory dealt with repression as a defense against the repetition of emotionally distressing traumatic memories. Paradoxically, both intrusions into consciousness and omissions from consciousness were seen as the result of defense mechanisms. Omissions of traumatic memories were due to inhibitions; intrusions were due to sudden conscious representation in spite of efforts to inhibit the mental contents. Freud's early observations of both amnesia and excessive intrusion of traumatic memories have stood the test of time. Nonetheless, subsequent research has shown that the repressed memory theory of psychopathology was too limited.

After trauma psychology, Freud began to work on repressed wishes and then on how personality comes to be formed. He proposed that personality developed from the action of two basic drives or instincts, libido and aggression. From biological determinants these drives evolved into structures of learned knowledge during infancy, childhood, and adolescence. Social experiences in interactions with significant others affected the direction and linkages of such drives. Each individual was a complex result of nature and nurture. This was called id psychology.

Freud described the evolution of character in what was one of the first attempts to put psychology into a developmental sequence. He said the libidinal drives proceed in stepwise fashion to invest the oral, anal, and genital zones of evolving sensation, interpersonal communication, and erotism. This is the psychosexual theory of development within id psychology. Some observations of character traits that tended to occur together have been confirmed by subsequent investigations, but the general theory of id psychology has since been modified.

In altering his therapeutic technique from suggestion, hypnosis, and catharsis to free association, Freud simultaneously realized that a "different though not contradictory conception of the therapeutic process" was warranted. With the new emphasis on removal of amnesia and recovery of repressed memories, he observed that the same instinctive forces that brought about repression in order to obliterate pathogenic material from consciousness continued to exert a force—

resistance—against full disclosure through free association; moreover, unexpected feelings toward the analyst—*transference*—was noted.

Freud's view of transference was of ideas and feelings that arose from the past and recapitulated earlier ties with significant persons from childhood. In the case of Dora in 1905, he believed her hostile feelings resulted in her breaking off treatment, which he called "acting out." Just as Fraulein von R. had been the first pivotal failure with hypnosis leading to Freud's major technical shift away from its use, so the case of Dora was the turning point in psychoanalytic technique that highlighted for Freud the necessity to interpret feelings transferred onto the analyst.

II. POST-FREUD: EARLY TWENTIETH CENTURY TO PRESENT

The history and growth of the psychoanalytic movement from classical psychoanalysis to current practices has been marked by repeated revisions by Freud himself, as well as reappraisals and additions by others. From its beginnings, some analysts have argued against nearly all of Freud's basic conceptual premises, from the strictly sexual etiology of the neuroses to his views on feminine psychology. Reacting more directly to their clinical concerns that too few patients are amenable to the rigorous requirements associated with orthodox psychoanalysis, others have attempted to make the treatment more extensively applicable, affordable, and terminable.

Early efforts in the 1920s and 1930s by such analysts as Sandor Ferenczi, Otto Rank, and Wilhelm Stekel were aimed at increasing the applicability of psychoanalyses to a larger clinical spectrum by shortening treatment time (Rank was the first to propose an "endsetting" time limit) and emphasizing a more active, affective, and caretaking approach, particularly the use of the therapist as a substitute primary object in the treatment of young children. However, these therapists soon sparked a major controversy over whether their supportive therapy additions, a departure from a totally neutral-interpretive technique, would compromise treatment.

Karen Horney's rejection of Freud's libido theory of neurosis in favor of a more interpersonal approach in the analysis of neurotic patients also made less distinction between analysis and psychotherapy in that the analyst played a more active role, and dispensed with free association and the couch. Similarly, Harry Stack Sullivan's pioneering work with a population of schizophrenic patients drew attention to their distorted thinking and action patterns in adult interpersonal relationships, and influenced treatment techniques by defining the face-to-face psychiatric interview that examined the role of the analyst as a participant as well as an observer.

Within the framework of existential analysis (e.g., Medard Boss' *Daseinanalysis*), the role of the analyst was further altered by emphasizing the real, here-and-now encounter, as recently updated by Irving Yalom. Others who were engaged in the treatment of patients with character problems began to acknowledge the increasing need to enlarge the scope of treatment by introducing "parameters" (Kurt Eissler's term) that would help such patients in analysis. This technical direction was influenced by the growing effects of ego psychology on the understanding of ego defects and problems wrought by their presence.

Wilhelm Reich's analysis of character armor, as well as Otto Fenichel's investigations of problems of psychoanalytic technique, expanded the analysis of resistances in the form of pathological character traits. As analysts like Merton Gill, Leo Stone, Kurt Eissler, and Wilfred Bibring attempted to define and expand the horizons of psychoanalysis, Anna Freud's delineation of defense mechanisms also placed new emphasis on both their adaptive function and their characterological nature, and George Vaillant has brought this theory into the present.

At the same time, the European influence of the British object relations school, and the theories of Melanie Klein, Wilfred Bion, Donald Winnicott, and Michael Balint, led to modifications in technique to accommodate patients with impoverished or distorted early childhood learning patterns, as embodied in concepts of therapy as a "holding environment," the therapist as "container," and "healing the basic fault."

Elizabeth Zetzel, and later Ralph Greenson, followed Anna Freud's (and others') interests in the real relationship between analyst and patient by developing the now accepted notions of the therapeutic or working alliance that recognized the need to incorporate nontransferential elements into analysis; simultaneously advances were being made on a more theoretical front of interpersonal subjectivities and unconscious resonances as brought up to date by

Evelyne Schwaber, Robert Stolorow, Alan Skolnikoff, Owen Renick, and Morton and Estelle Shane.

Amplifications of ego functions' influence on adaptation were advanced by Heinz Hartmann, Ernst Kris, and Hans Lowenthal. Hartmann especially postulated the existence of a "conflict-free sphere" of the ego, and further defined the concepts of the self as a separate structure within the ego. Edith Jacobson's developmental model as a foundation of comprehensive psychoanalytic theory, which integrated drive theory with ego psychology and object relations theory, was supported by Renee Spitz's and Margaret Mahler's research that directly studied infants and their mothers during development. This work has been brought into current focus by Robert Emde, Fred Pine, and Daniel Stern.

Since the 1970s there has been an increased interest in narcissistic and borderline character disturbances. Heinz Kohut's psychology of the self in the understanding of narcissism and Otto Kernberg's application of psychoanalytic object relations theory to the development of psychoanalytic techniques in the treatment of borderline patients gained center stage. Their observations have profoundly influenced notions of the nature and kind of transference manifestations that appear in treatment.

John Bowlby added new theories having to do with how wishes and fears were incorporated into enduring, usually intrapsychic working models and schematizations of self and other. Like Edith Jacobson, Otto Kernberg, Heinz Kohut, and Mardi Horowitz, he attempted to integrate object relations theory and advances in developmental, cognitive, or ego psychologies. These object relations theorists described a variety of new ways people distort their views of self and others due to discomfort and trauma, including defenses of splitting, projection, and projective identification. Kohut then rejected many aspects of the original Freudian id-ego-superego theory in favor of what he called self-psychology.

Self-psychologists added views of others as extensions of self or self-objects, and of maladaptive patterns of idealization and devaluation to support fragile self-conceptualizations. Rather than real loved personas, with separate wishes and responses to the patient, self-objects are projections onto the other person of what the patient wishes them to be. Of course, these views often are quite at odds with reality and lead to relationship problems.

The control mastery theory of Joseph Weiss and Hal Sampson expanded on previous views of unconscious mental processes. They inferred that each person had unconscious plans at mastery of life. Unconscious calculations appraised the degree of safety or threat in trials of whether or not actions based on these plans could be successfully implemented. If unconscious assessments, based on past and perhaps outmoded developmental experiences nonetheless predicted danger, then processes of control inhibited the plans or led to distorted versions of them.

People like Arnold Cooper and Robert Wallerstein found ways to encompass the divergences in modern theory. Morton Reiser and Mardi Horowitz made efforts to develop a general psychodynamic theory that used modern cognitive neuroscience languages while integrating ego psychological and object relations theories into information processing terminologies. Horowitz developed formulation methods that identified states of mind, each with different schemas of self and models of relationship with other, and differing defensive control processes in each state. He suggested that shifts in control, memories, and person schemas, led to the state cycles of personality based patterns of repetitive but maladaptive interpersonal behaviors.

Table I contrasts the evolving differences between psychoanalysis and psychoanalytic psychotherapy, and Table II outlines the historical development of psychoanalytic psychotherapy.

III. MAJOR METAPSYCHOLOGICAL CONCEPTS

The *dynamic* perspective reflects the notion that all mental phenomena are the result of a continual interaction of forces that oppose one another. It implies that human behavior and motivation are active, goal and plan directed, and slowly changing at all times. It is the basis for such fundamental concepts as *conflict*.

The *topographical* perspective refers to the premise that mental phenomena reveal themselves at different levels of manifestation, from unconscious to the border of awareness or accessibility (preconscious) to conscious representation. This general orientation recognizes a human being's pervasive avoidance of painful feelings or experiences by keeping unpleasant thoughts, wishes, and affect from awareness. It also

Table I Psychoanalysis and Psychoanalytic Psychotherapy Contrasted

Feature	Psychoanalysis	Psychoanalytic psychotherapy	
		Expressive mode	Supportive mode
Frequency	Up to five times per week.	Regular one to three times per week.	Flexible.
Duration	Long term; usually 3 to 5 or more years.	Short or long term; several sessions to months or years.	Short or intermittent long term: single session or lifetime.
Modus operandi	Systematic analysis of all (positive and negative) transference and resistance: primary focus on analyst and intrasession events; transference neurosis facilitated; regression encouraged.	Focus on conflictual topics, interpersonal patterns and transference.	Focus on topics of current concern and increasing skills, reducing tendencies to transference by early interpretations of irrational beliefs.
Sample patient populations	Personality problems and psychosomatic disorders.	Symptom neuroses; personality problems; pathological responses to stressor life events.	Immaturity; severe personality disorders; latent or manifest psychoses; physical illness; ongoing stressor events.
Usual patient requisites	High motivation; psychological-mindedness; good previous relationships; good tolerance for ambiguity.	High to moderate motivation and psychological-mindedness; ability to form therapeutic alliance; frustration tolerance.	Modest degree of motivation and ability to contemplate.
Goals	Reschematization of knowledge structure; resolution of unconscious conflicts; insight into intrapsychic events; improved developmental level and new capacities.	Partial reorganization of personality and defenses; resolution of preconscious and conscious derivatives of conflicts; insight into current interpersonal events; improved relations; symptom relief.	Reintegration of ability to cope; stabilization or restoration of preexisting equilibrium; learning new skills; better adjustment or acceptance of pathology; symptom relief.
Major techniques	Reduced eye contact; free association; full interpretation (including confrontation, clarification, and working through) with emphasis on developmental reconstruction.	Limited free association; confrontation, clarification, working-through, and interpretation.	Expression of feelings and ideas, suggestion, clarification and logical views in the here-and-now, providing a safe relationship.
Treatment with medication	Usually avoided; if used, all negative and positive meanings and implications thoroughly analyzed.	May be used. If applied, negative implications explored and diffused.	May be used. If applied, negative implications explored and diffused.

acknowledges the persistence, resilience, and inaccessibility of underlying conflicts that remain alive and active, but may appear in diverse and disguised forms often unrecognizable by their recipient.

The *structural* perspective refers to the idea that the mental apparatus is organized into functional units of a tripartite nature—the it-like functions of id, the self-like functions of ego, and the over-self-like functions of superego. This basic personality organization forms the theoretical structure of intrapsychic conflict among instincts (*id*), a set of functions integrating identity with external reality demands (*ego*), and one's ideals, moral precepts or standards (*superego*).

The *economic* perspective relates to how psychic intentions are distributed, discharged, and transformed. It has implications for how ideas and affect are expressed (e.g., verbally or somatically), and for how the individual fends off psychic threat through a variety of defense mechanisms (e.g., *sublimation*, whereby unacceptable drives are diverted into socially acceptable forms; *reaction formation,* which turns an impulse into its opposite; or *displacement,* in which feelings belonging to one object are transferred to

Table II Historical Development of Psychoanalytic Psychotherapy

Theorist	Major contributions to psychoanalytic psychotherapy
1920s–1940s	
Rank, Ferenczi	Emphasized supportive as well as expressive technique with emphasis on affective experience: end-setting time limit.
Stekel	Psychoanalytically based brief psychotherapy.
Reich, Fenichel	Expanded analysis of character.
A. Freud, Spitz	Application of ego psychology to psychoanalytic treatment and child analysis, with emphasis on the adaptive function of defense mechanisms.
Alexander, French	Role of analyst to provide corrective emotional experience by being different from parents and offering alternative to early developmental experiences; short-term duration; emphasis on face-to-face interviews.
Horney, Fromm, Sullivan	Closed distinction between analysis and therapy; free association and couch not essential; active therapist role; short-term goals focused on patterns of interpersonal relationships.
1950s–1960s	
Eissler, Bibring, Stone, Gill	Expanded definition, indications, and scope (parameters) of psychoanalysis (Eissler, Bibring, Stone), including broadened analysis of transference (Gill).
Klein, Winnicott, Bion, Balint	Influence of British object relations school on psychoanalytic theory and technique (Klein): concepts of holding environment, good-enough mothering (Winnicott), therapist as container (Bion), healing the basic fault (Balint) addressed patients without adequate mothering in early months of life.
Zetzel, Greenson	Extension of therapeutic relationship to nontransferential aspects: concepts of therapeutic alliance (Zetzel) and working alliance (Greenson) advanced idea that analysis incorporate aspects of reality or real relationship into treatment, utilizing both observing and experiencing ego of patient.
Hartmann, Kris, Lowenstein	Advanced ego psychology in adaptation; postulated conflict-free sphere of ego and defined concept of self as separate structure: concept of regression in the service of the ego emphasized ego's participation in the analytic process.
Jacobson	Developmental model as basis of comprehensive psychoanalytic theory, integrating ego psychology, object relations, and drive theories in terms of multiple layered representations of self and others.
Mahler	Direct observation and research on infants and mothers; delineated separation-individuation subphases of child development, with impact on adult personality and pathology and implications for analytic treatment process.
Arlow, Brenner, Sandler, Stone, Rangell, Wallerstein	Clarified issues of unconscious fantasy and conflicted structures in relation to appraisals of reality. Studied expressive and supportive dimensions of therapy.
Edelson, Peterfreund, Klein, Rosenblatt, Thickstun, Schaeffer	Clarified need for a new theoretical language closer to observation.
1970s–1990s	
Kernberg, Ogden	Extension of object relations theory to psychoanalytic psychotherapy techniques in treatment of borderline disorders; delineation of expressive techniques for analyzing primitive transferences and defenses.
Kohut, Gedo, Goldberg, Basch, Ornstein	Development of self-theory in analytic treatment of narcissistic disorder; delineation of self-object (mirroring and idealizing) transferences; emphasis on empathic atmosphere to facilitate insight and transmuting internalization to crystallize self.
Weiss, Sampson	Developed, in control mastery theory, an enlarged view of unconscious processes as calculating whether life plans could be implemented to achieve mastery or needed to be held in check by processes of control because of dreaded consequences such as harming others.
Horowitz, Luborsky, Singer, Strupp	Integration of ego psychology and object relations theory with cognitive theory to develop coherent case formulations in terms of states of mind, schemas of persons, and habitual processes of control; added research methods.

another). Displacement has direct treatment implications for the phenomenon of *transference,* in which affect meant for early significant figures in the patient's life is placed onto the analyst or therapist.

The *genetic* perspective concerns the historical aspects of personality and its subsequent development. In this view, early experiences are repeated (*repetition compulsion*) until they can be neutralized through consciousness; that regression to infantile modes of behavior is both a manifestation of illness and a technical process facilitated to recreate within analysis the patient's original conflict (*transference neurosis*), whose resolution is the essence of classic analytic cure. It has broader implications for the idea of *psychic determinism,* which illuminates the crucial notion that present behavior is meaningfully related to one's past, and for developmental stages through which the individual evolves from infancy to adult maturity.

IV. FUNDAMENTAL TREATMENT CONCEPTS

A. Transference

Transference is broadly defined as the experience of feelings toward a person that do not befit the intended individual but belong to another person from the past. Intensive analysis of transference is the modus operandi that technically distinguishes psychoanalysis from all other forms of psychotherapy. Since Freud's original serendipitous discovery of the "strange phenomenon" of transference in the psychoanalytic treatment of every neurotic patient, its vicissitudes have been conceptualized in various related ways: (1) as a distinct type of therapeutic relationship, which has since been distinguished from nontransferential therapist–patient bonds (i.e., therapeutic alliance or real relationship); (2) as substitute pathology, expressed in the formation and resolution of a so-called transference neurosis; and (3) as a general phenomenon that transcends the boundaries of analysis into all human relationships.

B. Transference as a Therapeutic Relationship

The typical transference relationship is one in which the patient directs toward the analyst an unusual degree of attachment and affection that is not a realistic response to the relationship between them but can only be traced to wishful fantasies and idealizations that have remained unconscious. These fantasies are repeated in analysis as unresolved childhood attitudes and affects that are anachronistic and inappropriate, in part because repressed material necessarily contains infantile strivings and in part because the analyst may promote their appearance through special methods and analytic rules that intensify reactivation.

The peculiarity of the transference relationship to the analyst lies in its excess, in both character and degree, over what is rational and justifiable. Its major manifestation may include overendowment of the analyst as an idealized image, often including overestimation of the analyst's qualities, adoption of similar interests, and intense jealousy of other persons in the analyst's life. As the transference relationship is based on projection and fantasy on the part of the patient, and the analyst neither responds to the cravings of the patient nor reacts in a reciprocal or personal fashion, it is characterized (and often criticized) as being an artificial and asymmetrical bond. These qualities have been amended in later nontransferential concepts of the therapeutic relationship (e.g., working alliance, real relationship) that have been incorporated into theory and treatment.

Often, what distinguishes a transference from a nontransference reaction is not its content per se, but a group of qualities that tend to characterize transference responses and that may be used as signals to the analyst to denote their occurrence: inappropriateness (which refers to the largely irrational character of the transference response); intensity (which applies to the unusual strength of emotionality); ambivalence (which relates to the contradictions and shifts in affect that occurs toward the therapist); tenacity (which reflects the resilience with which such feelings tend to persist despite the analyst's actual behavior); and capriciousness (which describes the erratic, and sometimes trivial events that evoke the responses).

As transference distortions develop, their manifestations can be either positive or negative, paralleling the ambivalence that underlies all feelings that are in part unconscious. *Positive transference* refers to the expression of good feelings toward the analyst, of love and its many variations, manifested in (albeit excessive) interest, trust, admiration, respect, sympathy, and so on, that can predominate as the motive force behind the wish to change and receive the analyst's approval. In a state of positive transference, the patient overvalues and endows the analyst with some of the same magical powers attributed during infancy to the patient's parents. These feelings may be the basis for benign dependency, utilized by the analyst in gaining the patient's trust and establishing rapport insofar as the patient is well motivated and receptive to the analyst's influence. At the other end of the affective spectrum, *negative transference* refers to equally intense bad feelings toward the analyst—including hate, anger, hostility, mistrust, and rebelliousness—in which the patient undervalues the analyst in ways that also repeat comparable feelings toward parent or parent substitutes of the past. Both types are inevitable aspects of psychoanalysis and must be interpreted. Some analysts have considered positive transference to be libidinal, based on sexual drives, whereas negative transference is regarded predominantly as a function of unresolved aggressive strivings.

For the most part, however, it is negative transference that becomes most problematic and requires analysis if treatment is to proceed because it manifests itself in ways that interrupt treatment, whether through direct attacks on the analyst or by acting out negative feelings instead of exploring them. Nonetheless, very intense positive transference, often expressed in the patient's excessive passionate demands on the analyst, can be misleading in that it too may be manifestation of resistance as the patient defends against further probing into unresolved conflicts. Another obstacle to analytic progress may be the analyst's own strong reactions to the patient, *countertransference,* which can inappropriately enter the treatment if the analyst is not sufficiently aware of personal feelings.

As traditionally understood, transference refers primarily to unrealistic distortions from the past, whether positive or negative; it does not pertain to reactions resulting from reality factors, as when the patient may be legitimately angry. However, transference responses are increasingly recognized as having objective as well as subjective components, relating to significant figures of the past and to real responses of the analyst: "new editions" of old conflicts are exact replicas that are total projections, whereas "revised editions" attach themselves to actual characteristics of the therapist.

C. Transference Neurosis

The most vivid expression of transference is the formation of a *transference neurosis,* a substitute pathology that reiterates fundamental pathology, in which the patient psychologically regresses to early stages of development and returns to the source of personality problems in the past in order to transcend them. Manifestations of the transference neurosis do not arise immediately, but emerge in the so-called middle phase of analysis, when the patient is most subject to the regressive forces induced by the analytic situation and the emergence of infantile needs for gratification. Its appearance may be episodic, or it may never truly appear, although much of the work of the middle phase is spent removing resistances in order to allow the transference neurosis to surface. The transference neurosis was originally regarded as a serious obstacle to analytic work, but it also allows the analyst to observe directly the recapitulation of the patient's childhood responses.

D. Resistance

Resistance is defined as the forces or defensive operations of the mental apparatus that work against the recovery of memories and that obstruct the progress of analysis by opposing the analytic procedure, the analyst, and the patient's reasonable ego. Comparable to transference, analyzing or managing resistances is also central to analytic work, and functions in counterpoint to transference in two ways: (1) as resistance to the transference, which means that the patient fights against the development of a transference and thus prevents the analyst from being able to tap the source of intrapsychic conflict, and (2) as transference resistance, which means that the transference itself is used as a resistance by stubbornly adhering to irrational transference manifestations instead of utilizing the transference as a path to earlier experiences and memories.

Conscious resistance refers to the deliberate withholding of information from the analyst, or the like. Such resistance is transient and usually easily rectified by pointing it out to the patient. Unconscious resistance, however, refers to a much more significant and resilient phenomenon that arises as a defense against emotionality and memory.

The clinical signs and manifestations of resistance

are manifold. Any persistent, stereotyped, or inappropriate interruption of the treatment process may be a clue to resistance. Common examples include the silent patient, who impedes the progress by failure to verbalize, and, at the other end of the spectrum, the compulsive talker, who is ostensibly obeying the fundamental rule to say whatever comes to mind, but whose verbal productions are unconscious barriers to insight. Specific variations of resistant behavior may be undue focus on the past (fixation on a particular point in time) or incessant inclusion of trivia or external events in order to avoid painful or emotionally laden topics. Typical forms of resistance also include lateness, missed hours, and delaying (forgetting) to pay one's bill.

Managing resistances means that the defensive maneuvers of the patient are to be addressed before the material that is fended off can be approached. The analyst must discover how the patient resists, what is being resisted, and why. The immediate cause of resistance (e.g., anxiety, guilt, or shame) may be a superficial or surface indication of what is going on in the patient; repeated uncovering and confronting of resistances should reveal the underlying affects that are unconsciously behind such behaviors.

E. Countertransference

As previously mentioned, and as the name suggests, *countertransference* is transference in the reverse direction—from analyst to patient. It generally refers to unconscious emotional needs, wishes, or conflicts of the analyst evoked by the patient, which are brought into the analytic situation and thus influence the analyst's objective judgment and reason.

Countertransference manifests itself in many ways; it is commonly acute, temporary, superficial, and easily recognized and managed; but it can also be chronic, permanent, deeply rooted, largely unconscious, and out of the analyst's control. The former may occur in response to very specific content that arises or in identification with some concrete aspect of the patient's personality. The latter involves more generalized and ingrained patterns of behavior, often pathological, that pervade the analysis in a way that is untherapeutic and to which the analyst remains blind without external intervention.

The former type of countertransference, fortunately, is more typical and occurs in every analysis.

Comparable to the patient's acting out, the analyst brings into the analysis feelings, thoughts, or behavior that do not belong there. Classic countertransferences may manifest themselves in special consideration for an attractive patient, like eagerly making an unavailable hour available, or failing to remember the changed hour of an uninteresting patient. The following are considered common warnings of countertransference in analysis: experiencing uneasy feelings during or after sessions with certain patients; persistently feeling drowsy or actually falling asleep; altering sessions or showing carelessness regarding scheduling (e.g., extending hours or forgetting about them); making special financial arrangements (e.g., overly strict with some patients and underassiduous with others); wishing to help the patient outside the session; dreaming about one's patients or being preoccupied with them in one's leisure time; using the patient as an example to impress a colleague or having the urge to lecture or write about a particular patient; reacting strongly to what the patient thinks of the analyst (i.e., needing a particular patient's approval); not wanting the patient to terminate or wanting the patient to terminate; finding oneself unable to explore certain material or to understand what is going on with the patient; and evincing sudden or excessive feelings, such as anxiety, depression, or boredom.

Countertransference is presumed to relate primarily to unresolved and irrational responses; yet it may also refer to an analyst's relatively reasonable reactions to a patient's behavior, as when feeling aroused by a seductive patient, paternal to a deprived patient, frightened by an aggressive patient, burdened by a demanding patient, or jealous of a successful patient. As such, countertransference feelings are an inevitable part of any treatment. However, when these feelings are not simply situation-specific and evoke strong reactions that belong to former events or persons in the analyst's life, they can become problematic because the analyst is in danger of bringing these unconscious feelings into the analysis in the form of unnecessary, if not actually untherapeutic, behaviors.

Of more serious implication are those forms of countertransference reflecting chronic problems left unsettled in the analyst's own analysis. Some examples may be the analyst with an underlying masochism who accepts abuse from patients without adequately analyzing its reasons; the grandiose analyst who takes on the most difficult patients with promises of cure without recognizing the need for help if the treatment is not going well; the analyst who allows a seductive patient to act out, or reciprocates sexual advances instead of examining the patient's wish to arouse; or the lonely analyst who encourages the patient's dependency and will not terminate treatment for fear of abandonment. When the analysis becomes a source of narcissistic gratification for the analyst who encourages the love or idolatry of the patient without introducing a more realistic appraisal, or prematurely terminates patients who do not improve sufficiently, the analyst's own return to therapy may be indicated.

V. CHARACTEROLOGICAL FORMULATION

The theories of psychoanalysis are an aid to explaining characterological aspects of personality problems and to planning how they may be changed. Therapists combine theory with observation in order to develop a patient-specific set of hypotheses. Typically, in psychoanalytic case formulation, it is assumed that symptoms and problems in living are caused by the interaction of multiple processes at biological, social, and psychological levels. At the level of the individual's psychology, the symptoms and problems might be caused not only by deficits in normal capacity but by conflicts. Active conflicts may lead to the formation of compromises between or among wishes, and their feared consequences. In psychodynamics these compromises are often regarded as defensive mental strategies.

The formation of symptomatic traits is often understood as a compromise between expressive aims and the wish to avoid the threatening consequences of expression. Some traits are learned from identification with others. Because symptomatic character traits are seen as complexly rooted in such multiple causations, psychoanalysts use the term overdetermination or pluralistic determination in making formulations.

For example, an individual may want to both transgress a moral value and also express feelings of guilt over the transgression. He or she fears the distress that could occur and inhibits both the wish and the guilt. Because of the unresolved topic he or she may nonetheless experience anxiety that something dreadful is about to happen. For such a person, anxiety would be a presenting symptom. The topic of the type of transgression might be conflictual or emotionally evoca-

tive, but unclear. The warded-off wishes, guilt, and fear can be formulated as the unconscious reasons for forming anxious experiences. The symptoms of anxiety are viewed as the result of the conflict between the impulse to express the guilt and the defensive avoidance of such expressions. Social and biological factors might influence the manner in which the anxiety symptoms are experienced and communicated.

A patient may mysteriously have anxiety symptoms during encounters that are meant to be lovingly erotic. The patient may add descriptions that indicate fears of phenomena that are even worse than the anxiety symptoms, such as horror of becoming enraged upon sexual frustration, guilt about potentially acting on the hostility felt toward a spouse, and/or a warded-off despair on feeling rejected. Avoidance of erotic situations may reduce the frequency or intensity of anxiety symptoms at the expense of diminished opportunities for the satisfaction of sexual wishes. The person might report substitute behaviors such as becoming so interested in morality that he or she is investigating pornography because it is socially bad and ought to be banned.

A patient may present a set of signs and symptoms that are part of a problematic state of mind, but not necessarily the most dreaded. For example, the person may present with moods of tension in which there is preoccupation, diddling with peripheral details, and blockage of work on central aspects of a project. This may be a surface indicator of approach and avoidance conflicts about collaborating on a project or about competing to win a role in a project. The desired state might be one of working well, enjoying mutual effort and, when necessary, competing in a realistic way. A related dreaded state of mind with a work supervisor or rival peer might be guilt over doing so well that the other is harmed or defeated, or doing so poorly that the self is humiliated. Approach and avoidance conflicts can lead to a problematic compromise state, one presenting with symptoms of anxiety and work block. A relatively less symptomatic and so relatively more adaptive compromise state defends against dreaded consequences of working too well by taking a stance of aloofness in regard to work. By procrastinating and isolating the interests of the self from the project, the risks of being one-up or one-down are reduced, but the satisfactions cannot be obtained.

Similarly, on a sexual topic, the presenting state may be a problematic compromise state containing anxiety symptoms and a tense mood. The desire might be for states of sensuous pleasure and closeness. The patient may have even more dreaded states of mind such as a mood of despair over being used and then abandoned. A relatively more adaptive compromise state that the problematic state of anxious tension might be clowning around to ward off states of closeness and intimacy. Just as one does not take the surface symptoms as the whole picture, in making a psychodynamic formulation at the level of observing the states of mind that bring phenomena together into coherent patterns, one does not take the presenting or problematic states of mind as the whole picture.

Psychoanalytic formulations of why states of mind occur focus on unconscious aspects of identity of self and on internalized object relationships. Interpersonal experiences during development leave an enduring inner set of models, comprised of views of self and others, that can cause the styles, moods, and organizations of any particular state of mind. Moreover, these inner schemas about self and the surrounding world may have sequences that can lead to cycles of shifting from one state to another. These sequences can be a part of not only conscious but, very importantly to psychodynamic formulations, unconscious fantasies, plans, or scripts. Once again, the developmental antecedents of various schemas, plans, and scripts are important aspects of formulations, and dynamic formulations change with increased understanding—formed during explorations in treatment sessions—of how the past is influencing, perhaps very irrationally, the present and near future.

Personality is in part a repertoire of schemas of self and others, and of values and plans for how to handle wishes, fears, defenses, and coping. Self-organization is a set of schemas that leads to a conscious sense of identity, of an "I" or "me" that continues over time. Each person's experience of the self varies; this stems from the activity of multiple self-schemas that can lead to different self-images and styles in different states of mind.

Some self-schemas can be activated to ward off the effects of others. An inferior self-schema may organize a potential state of shame. If less inferior and more realistic self-schemas cannot be activated, then grandiose and unrealistic ones might be primed in order to avoid shame by bolstering pride.

Activation of ideal schemas of self, when matched to and discrepant from real or devalued schemas of self, can lead to emotional experiences of shame or guilt. Whether or not such self discrepancies lead to deflation of self-esteem or can be accepted while maintaining emotional equilibrium depends on an individual's level of personality maturity. One way to view maturity is in terms of degree of supraordinate integration of multiple schemas of self. People vary in the degree to which they have or have developed the capacity to develop schemas of schemas. Those who can manage this are said to have an integrated self-conceptualization because they can accept various types of self-discrepancies.

The technique of interpretation and working-through in treatment might differ for patients who do and do not have supraordinate self-schemas to integrate and control subordinate self-schemas. The existence of supraordinate schemas allows a patient to contain in a given state of mind the information relevant to the self-schemas that organized a different state of mind. Patients without this capacity are more vulnerable than others to explosive shifts in state and in how they can view the therapist. These aspects of a formulation can be understood using a tool of inference called *role-relationship models*. Such models contain views of self and other, and self with other, and how transactions may unfold. A role–relationship model, in its simplest diadic form, includes a set of characteristics of self, a set of attributes and roles of others vis à vis the self, and a script of automatically expected transactions between self and other. One example of such a script begins with a wish, goes on to a response of the other, and then to reactions of the self, which may include self-appraisals. This is the aspect that Lester Luborsky called a Core Conflictual Relationship Theme.

Any person may have multiple role–relationship models for internally interpreting any topic, for any relationship, and for any traumatic event. Theories about such unconscious beliefs separate psychoanalytic points of view from cognitive and behavioral approaches to therapy because they add these components to case formulations: (1) there are immature schemas that can influence behavior in some states of mind but not others; (2) there are more mature schemas that can inhibit activity of less mature schemas in some states but not others; and (3) there are defensive layerings so that some schemas may be activated in order to ward off dreaded states of mind that might be organized by other schemas. Psychoanalytic therapies explore this structure of knowledge about self and others, its lack of concordance with real interpersonal opportunities, and its developmental sources. Such insight seeks to achieve a process of working through in order to arrive at new behaviors that can be learned and practiced until new schemas function automatically in organizing behavior and states of mind.

Psychoanalytic formulations include control processes that act beyond full conscious awareness to reduce the expression of ideas and feelings. By uncovering and analyzing such processes the therapist and patient can act to change them if they are resulting in symptoms or obstructions to the patient's life. The idea is not only to increase work on warded-off topics but to modify in an adaptive direction the person's habitual and nonadaptive forms of defensiveness.

Inhibitions of conflicted and potentially emotional topics can lead to the defensive maneuvers known as suppression (conscious avoidance), repression (unconscious avoidance), denial (reducing the impact of the real implications of external stressors), and disavowal or negation (obscuring what has been revealed).

Inhibitions of schemas and facilitations of other schemas, as well as dislocations of roles and attributes, can lead to defensive maneuvers that distort views of self and others. These include such operations as projection (attributing something from self to other), displacement (putting something from one person onto a less dangerous person), and role reversal (exchanging positions to take the role of lesser danger to the self).

Another class of control processes, one that affect the form of expression, can be added to these controls of the topics of thought and communication and their schematic organizers. These are also important to understand because of their implications for technique. A patient may discourse on a conflictual topic in a flat, hyperlogical, or intellectualized, unengaged, or generalized manner. There may be communication only of ideas, without emotion, a defensive mechanism called isolation.

VI. THE GROUND RULES AND CONTEXT OF PSYCHOANALYTIC TREATMENTS

The goal of therapy is to improve the future for the patient. Each party to the treatment has tasks in relation to this goal. The patient is asked to speak truth-fully and completely about memories, fantasies, associations, images, dreams, bodily feelings, wishes, and fears that are usually not told to others. The therapist and the patient together observe what it feels like to do this, how it is done, what is communicated, and what the process does to their relationship. The therapist puts this understanding into words in the form of interpretations, which are intended to connect the patient's present feelings with his or her past, giving a broader picture about meanings, including those that have never before been verbalized.

In psychoanalysis, the two people explore private themes, personal dilemmas, conflictual memories, and unsettling feelings of one of them. Most people are not used to speaking openly on such matters. The analyst describes what can be done in the sessions to create this unusual environment of very frank discourse and interpretation. The therapy hour will begin on time and end on time. The patient's feelings about this are often one of the first topics relating to the therapy itself that comes up. Despite the fixed ending of each hour, the patient is not rushed to premature closures. An hour may end but a conflictual topic can be held over until the next session begins. As no one can be sure about interpretations, ambiguity as to meanings will have to be tolerated.

The analyst offers a relationship in which there is respect for the personal attitudes and feelings of the patient. The values of the therapist may be different from the patient and are not imposed on the patient. Clarification of the patient's values and how they may conflict with social norms is, however, an aspect of the dialogue. The therapist also displays more equidistance, abstinence, and neutrality, than one would expect of other relationships as with friends, teachers, parents, or religious counselors.

Equidistance means the therapist is "there" not just for the adult, poised, competent self-schema of the patient, and the states of mind organized by that set of concepts and images, but also "there" for the patient's ideals and values, and also "there" for the childlike self-schemas and immature passions of the patient. The patient may have a conflict among wishes to be taken care of, dangerous wishes to take over the lovers and careers of others, moral injunctions against ruthlessness or dependence, and adult concerns over how to appraise current dangers in the social, political, spiritual, and environmental worlds. The therapist does not side with any sector or any of a variety of self-schematizations of the patient, but remains available as a container for all facets of conflict.

For the therapist, the term abstinence means, at its best, avoiding unessential advice and reassurance while waiting to hear the unspoken and the hitherto unspeakable. The therapist is not there to gratify the patient's wishes but to foster adaptation to life so that the patient can seek constructive gratification in life outside the therapy. A related concept is neutrality, which means that the therapist does not react emotionally as he or she would in a social situation according to his or her own wishes, ideals, and moral standards. Neutrality is not coldness or indifference: warmth, compassion, concern, sympathy, empathy, and understanding are not deflections from neutrality but absolute requirements for the therapist if the treatment is to achieve its full goal.

The major general techniques of psychodynamic treatments are fostering expression, suggestion, clarification, interpretation, and repetition in order to facilitate working through. Working through means the process of revising knowledge structures so that warded-off topics can be confronted, traumatic memories integrated, and conflicts and contradictions resolved or accepted; working through is also the process by which deficiencies are reduced and unconscious fantasies are modified by conscious choices.

A. Fostering Expression

Fostering expression includes helping the patient to assume most of the responsibility for bringing up topics of importance. He or she is encouraged to broaden the topics of discussion beyond the scope of original complaints. The fundamental rule is to try to say everything that comes to mind or is felt in the body.

This fundamental rule of complete disclosure can be expanded to helping the patient to use free associative reveries and to report peripheral and fleeting thoughts and visual images. At times drawings, paintings, poems, letters, and discussions of bodily postures or impulses to move during the hour may be used to widen the modes of representation for initial expression of inchoate feeling states and ambiguous ideas. But while pictures in the mind's eye and bodily enactions are utilized as carriers of meaning, translation into words is emphasized as the clearest form of communication and the beginning of the possibilities for logical and psychological understanding of nonverbal

impulses and behavior and through that, the ability to change, if change is desirable.

B. Suggestion

The therapist may suggest that the patient attend to certain topics, follow certain principles of disclosure, or try out certain alternative modes of perceiving, thinking, feeling, or acting. The therapist may ask, for example, "What do you imagine you would feel if it were to happen that . . ." to suggest focusing in a specific direction. The choice about whether or not to follow such suggestions is left to the patient. Firm directions are seldom if ever given, and any type of manipulative or covert suggestion is avoided. This means giving up the use of certain positive effects of suggestion, as in the placebo effect, in favor of fostering a sense of joint exploration in the search for insight and understanding as vehicles to change.

C. Clarification

Clarification includes techniques of questioning or repeating what the patient has told the therapist. Even when the therapist repeats exactly a bit of dialogue spoken by the patient, it sounds different when the patient hears the remark. When the therapist reorganizes information reported by the patient it is usually to convey cause and effect sequences and to show the patient the meaningful relatedness of sequences that have seemed, to the patient, unrelated.

For example, the patient might tell a story like this:

"He really made me mad, implying I had not done my work. I'd like to quit that job. While I hadn't gotten the inventory together, I would have eventually."

The therapist might qualify:

"While you had intended to do it, you had not yet gotten the inventory together. He criticized you for that. Then you got mad and now want to quit."

This intervention is very minor, but it puts the sequence into a temporal order and gives the patient a chance to listen to that and then comment further.

It can be helpful to say how the discourse of the patient is being received. The therapist may say:

"I don't understand this story too well, maybe I haven't got the sequence of events in my mind yet."

Such remarks not only encourage the patient to elaborate on the sequence of events, they clarify the manner in which the patient is telling the story in question.

D. Interpretation

Interpretation is the central tool of the psychoanalyst and dynamic therapist. In an interpretation the therapist says what is important, why it is important, and/or how it comes about. Interpretations are so crucial to psychodynamic techniques that they can be categorized as follows.

Genetic interpretations link current patterns to their developmental antecedents, going back to adolescence, childhood, and infancy as necessary to understand the present. (The word "genetic" here is used to refer to the original or developmental source of current patterns, not to direct action of the genes.) A special form of genetic interpretations is the reconstruction. In a reconstruction the dynamic therapist pieces together different topics and offers a story about what significant early experiences might have been like in order to account for current, clear, important, and maladaptive beliefs, attitudes, wishes, or behavioral problems.

Transference interpretations explain to the patient the meaning of distortions in the relationship with the therapist. A transference interpretation may involve a contrast between the role–relationship models described as transference and the role–relationship model that might describe the current therapeutic alliance of the patient, or the potential for relationship in the treatment setting that takes into account the real opportunities of that setting.

Dynamic interpretations explain to the patient the forces involved in a conflictual constellation. Wishes, fears, and defenses on a given topic are described, and their interaction leading to experiences is also described. The advantage of working with levels of formulation that address phenomena, states of mind, person schemas, and processes of control is that the language of the formulation itself can be used directly in discourse with the patient about desires, threats, and defensiveness.

Dream interpretations explain to the patient the concerns and symbolic meanings that may lie behind the formation of dream images. Some schools of dynamic treatments rely partly on assumed general inclinations such as archetypes or mythic symbols, but most often dream interpretation is delivered in terms of what the therapist actually knows about this specific patient's schemas and role–relationship models. Accurate interpretation of a dream usually requires more knowledge than the description of the manifest content of the dream, and so the patient's free associations to elements in the dream are requested. They suggest the antecedent moods, schemas, and recent experiences that contribute to the dream elements.

Interpretations are tentative and may change over time as understanding deepens. That is why in technique the wording is often put in a tentative way, leading to some jokes about analysts who too invariably repeat "I wonder if perhaps you might be feeling. . . ." Interpretation is not enough to induce psychic change. The change process beyond interpretation is called working through.

E. Repetition and Working Through

The working-through process involves repeated examination of the same topic. If the treatment is progressing, each repetition is perhaps a bit different and contributes to the overall decrease in repression and increase in understanding. Some new aspect of conflict may be identified, and new linkages between topics are established. Realization of developmental antecedents of current conflicts helps the task of differentiating current reality from past fantasy.

Previously warded-off ideas and feelings may be allowed expression and modification during repetitions. Linkages to other domains of meaning may be established. In each repetition there may be a shift in the interaction of wishes, fears, defenses, and beliefs about reality. Should the whole topic again fall under repression, as it characteristically does after the treatment hour, it is in this revised form and can come up again, each time more easily, for further revision until it is completely analyzed.

F. Complications

It has been observed in exploratory psychoanalysis that some patients have an initial period of effective work and then have a deterioration in their condition. This has been called a negative therapeutic reaction. Sometimes character traits of self-punitiveness have been noted in such instances. It is important in such instances for the therapist to be self-observant for feelings of helplessness, guilt, and anger, and to aim instead for understanding with the patient why the condition has gotten worse.

Not to be confused with negative therapeutic reactions are negative transference phenomena. These are a common aspect of treatment. In developmentally immature patients, ones who have unintegrated self-schemas and who are vulnerable to feeling fragmented, empty, worthless, or bad, negative transference reactions can occur and seem to the patient "the whole picture." That is, they are not mitigated by simultaneous schemas of a therapeutic alliance. Early interpretation of the negative transferences and/or very early emphasis on signs of the therapist being helpful in a therapeutic alliance may be needed to prevent the patient from dropping out prematurely in the midst of a negative transference reaction.

VII. RESEARCH AND EVALUATION

Henry Bachrach, Robert Galatzer-Levy, Alan Skolnikoff, and Sherwood Waldron report the following in their review of psychoanalytic efficacy studies: Robert Knight reviewed analytic case outcome research before the late 1930s. The results indicate much improvement or better in 63% of neurotic cases, 57% of character disorder, 78% of psychosomatic conditions, and 25% of psychoses. In a study led by Weber of persons who applied for psychoanalysis and then received either analysis or time-unlimited analytic psychotherapy, the patients in different modalities had a 90% or greater report of being satisfied, and 75 to 90% were rated as improved. In a separate study Jerome Sashin, Stanley Eldred, and Suzanne van Amerowgen reported a 69% agreed-upon completion rather than breaking off of therapy, and a 75% level of achieving at least moderate improvement.

Brief forms of dynamic psychotherapy have been found to be effective in many empirical studies as summarized by Mary Lee Smith, Gene Glass, and Thomas Miller. At outcome the average patient is better than 72% (effect size .59) of subjects in waiting-list control groups. The current questions for research concern which therapy for which type of patient and with what type of emphasis on therapist action.

Different studies led by Robert Wallerstein and by Mardi Horowitz have indicated that therapist actions that are more probing for warded-off contents and more confrontational with respect to control processes may be more helpful for neurotic level cases and less helpful for narcissistically vulnerable, borderline, or psychotic levels of self-organization.

BIBLIOGRAPHY

Brenner, C. (1982). *The mind in conflict.* New York: International Universities Press.

Greenson, R. R. (1967). *The technique and practice of psychoanalysis.* New York: International Universities Press.

Horowitz, M. J. (1988). *Introduction to psychodynamics: A new synthesis.* Northvale, New Jersey: Aronson: masterworks series (first published by Basic Books).

Horowitz, M. J., Kernberg, O., & Weinshel, E. (Eds.) (1993). *Psychic structure and change in psychoanalysis.* New York: International Universities Press.

Pine, F. (1990). *Drive, ego, object, self.* New York: Basic Books.

Shapiro, T., & Emde, R. (1995). *Research in psychoanalysis.* New York: International Universities Press.

Wallerstein, R. F. (1995). *The talking cures: The psychoanalyses and the psychotherapies.* New Haven, CT: Yale University Press.

Psychoneuroimmunology

Robert Ader and Nicholas Cohen

University at Rochester School of Medicine and Dentistry

Autoimmunity   Immune reactions generated against an individual's own tissue or cellular antigens that can lead to diseases such as systemic lupus erythematosus and rheumatoid arthritis.

Cellular Immunity   Immunity mediated by antigen-stimulated, thymus-derived effector T lymphocytes (e.g., cytotoxic T cells) that does not involve antibody.

Conditioned Response   Response to a previously neutral (conditioned) stimulus after the neutral stimulus has been paired with a stimulus that unconditionally elicits the particular response being studied.

Humoral Immunity   Effector mechanism or immunity that is mediated by circulating antibodies produced by bone marrow-derived B lymphocytes. For many antigens, B cells produce antibody only after the occurrence of complex interactions among helper and suppressor T lymphocytes, certain accessory cells, and B lymphocytes.

PSYCHONEUROIMMUNOLOGY is, perhaps, the most recent convergence of disciplines (i.e., the behavioral sciences, the neurosciences, and immunology) that has evolved to achieve a more complete understanding of how the interactions among systems serve homeostatic ends and influence health and disease. The hypothesis that the immune system constitutes an underlying mechanism mediating the effects of psy-

chosocial factors on the susceptibility to and/or the progression of some disease processes is tenable, however, only if it can be shown that the brain is capable of exerting some regulation or modulation of immune responses. Several laboratories are now exploring such relationships at levels of organization ranging from the molecular to the organismic. Psychoneuroimmunology, then, refers to the study of the interaction among behavioral, neural, endocrine, and immune processes of adaptation. The present synopsis concentrates on the behavioral component of psychoneuroimmunological research.

I. INTRODUCTION

In practice, research in immunology has proceeded on the implicit assumption that the immune system is autonomous—an agency of defense that operates independently of other psychophysiological processes. Indeed, the self-regulating capacities of the immune system are remarkable and the interactions among subpopulations of lymphocytes occur and can be studied in vitro. The same can be said for other physiological processes. The endocrine system, too, was once thought to be autonomously regulated, and it is only in modern times that neural influences were identified. It may well be that immune responses can be made to occur in a test tube, devoid (presumably) of the (confounding or modulating) influences of the natural environment, but it is the immune system functioning in the natural environment that is of ultimate concern. Without denying the idiosyncratic properties of the immune system, it is becoming clear that behavioral factors and neuroendocrine factors play a critical role in the immunoregulatory processes that contribute to homeostasis.

It has been known for some time that manipulations of brain function can influence immune function. Lesions or electrical stimulation of the hypothalamus, for example, alters humoral and cell-mediated immune responses. Conversely, elicitation of an immune response (exposing an animal to an antigen) can influence hypothalamic activity. Following stimulation with different antigens, there is an increase in the firing rate of neurons within the ventromedial hypothalamus, and this increase corresponds to the time of the peak antibody response. Some of the most recent data documenting the potential for neural–endocrine–immune system interactions come from neuroanatomical studies of the innervation of lymphoid tissues (Fig. 1), which provides a foundation for functional relationships among these systems.

The observation that neurochemical and endocrine

signals influence immune responses is supported by the identification of receptors on lymphocytes for a variety of hormones and neurotransmitters. Also, recent data suggest that lymphocytes themselves are capable of producing neuropeptides and hormones. Again, not only do variations of hormonal state or neurotransmitter levels influence immune responses, but the immune response to antigenic stimulation induces neuroendocrine changes. At the neural and endocrine levels, then, there is abundant evidence of the potential for interactions between the brain and the immune system.

II. STRESS AND IMMUNE FUNCTION

A. Studies in Humans

Observations suggesting a link between behavior and immune function go back to the earliest observations of a relationship between psychosocial factors, including "stress," and susceptibility to those disease processes that we now recognize as involving immunological mechanisms. There are now abundant clinical data documenting an association between psychosocial factors and disease.

The death of a family member, for example, is rated highly on scales of stressful life events and has been associated with depression and an increased morbidity and mortality in the case of a variety of diseases, many of which are presumed to involve immune defense mechanisms. Bereavement and/or depression has also been associated with changes in some features of immunological reactivity such as a reduced lymphoproliferative response to mitogenic stimulation and impaired natural killer cell activity. Other studies have documented changes in immune reactivity associated with the affective responses to other "losses" such as marital separation and divorce. These are provocative and important observations. It should be emphasized, however, that the association between the response to "losses" and increased morbidity and the association between the response to "losses" and alterations in immune function do not, in themselves, establish a causal link between psychosocial factors, immune function, and health or disease. [*See* DEPRESSION.]

The death of a spouse is intuitively stressful, but changes in immune function are observed in humans exposed to less severe, but nonetheless effective, natu-

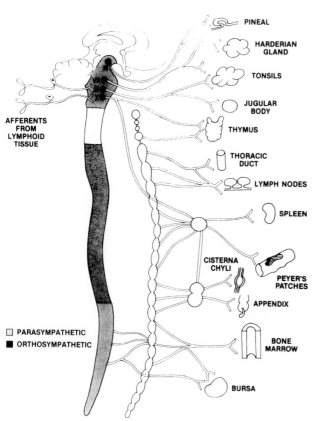

Figure 1 Recently collected data provide evidence for the innervation of lymphoid organs. [Reproduced, with permission, from J. B. Martin (1988). *Prog. Neuroendocrinimmunol.* **1,** 5–8.]

rally occurring "stressful" circumstances. The level of distress during student examination periods, for example, is invariably greater than that during control periods and, in a series of experiments conducted at Ohio State University, transient impairments in several parameters of immune function were observed in medical students at such times. Relative to a nonstressful baseline measurement, examination periods are associated with a decrease in mitogen responsiveness, natural killer cell activity, percentage of helper T lymphocytes, and interferon production by stimulated lymphocytes. In students who are seropositive for Epstein–Barr virus (EBV), exam periods are associated with elevated EBV titers, interpreted as a poorer cellular immune response control over the latent virus. The incidence of self-reported symptoms of infectious illness is also increased during examination periods. Personality tests have not revealed differences between the student volunteers and their classmates, and other life changes that could have influenced immune function during examination periods were minor and unrelated to changes in immunological reactivity.

An old (and continuing) experimental and clinical literature suggests that immune function can be altered by psychological means (e.g., hypnosis), and an increasing number of studies are attempting to relate different personality characteristics and affective states with alterations in immune function. These correlational studies must be considered preliminary at this time. They are difficult studies to implement, so it is hardly surprising that unequivocal evidence for causal relationships does not yet exist.

B. Studies in Animals

Most of the evidence for stress-induced alterations in immunity comes from basic research on animals. A variety of stressors (avoidance conditioning, restraint, noise) can, under appropriate experimental circumstances, influence the susceptibility of mice to a variety of infectious diseases (Coxsackie B, herpes simplex, polyoma, and vesicular stomatitis viruses). It thus appears that stressful circumstances can alter the host's defense mechanisms, allowing an otherwise inconsequential exposure to a pathogen to develop into clinical disease. Adult mice are generally resistant to Coxsackie virus and show no manifestations of disease when exposed to either virus or "stress" alone. Symptoms of disease are observed, however, when mice

are inoculated with virus and exposed to stressful environmental conditions. These results parallel clinical observations. For example, the presence of pollen alone may not be sufficient to elicit symptoms in a subject with hay fever, but the combination of pollen and a threatening life situation is.

Separation experiences (i.e., "losses") have also been studied in animals. Periodic interruptions of mother–litter interactions and/or early weaning decrease lymphocyte proliferation to mitogenic stimulation and reduce the plaque-forming response to subsequent challenge with sheep red blood cells (SRBC) in rodents. Monkey infants and their mothers respond to separation with a transient depression of in vitro mitogen responsiveness. Separation of squirrel monkeys from their mothers results in several changes in immunological reactivity, including a decline in complement protein levels (an effector mechanism in humoral immune responses), macrophage function, and immunoglobulin G antibody responses to immunization with a benign bacteriophage, the magnitude of one or another of the effects being a function of the psychosocial environment in which the animals were housed following separation.

In adult animals, a variety of behavioral manipulations are capable of influencing a variety of immune responses in a variety of species—and in a variety of ways. Heat, cold, and restraint (each of which is commonly referred to as a stressor and each of which is commonly thought to elicit a representative "stress" response) have different effects on the same immune response, and the same stressor (e.g., restraint) has different effects on different immune responses. The intensity and "chronicity" of the stressor are among the several parameters of stimulation that are likely to influence immune responses. The initial response to auditory stimulation, for example, is a depression of mitogenic responsivity. Repeated exposure to the loud noise (i.e., chronic stress), however, is associated with an enhancement of this same response. Moreover, the initial association of elevated adrenocortical steroid levels with decreased immunological reactivity is not necessarily observed under conditions of chronic stress. In another series of experiments, there was a graded suppression of mitogen responses with increasing intensities of electric shock stimulation, a relationship that persisted in adrenalectomized animals. As has been observed for other psychophysiological responses, the data suggest that it may be the organism's capacity to cope with stressful environmental circumstances that determines the extent to which immune processes are affected.

Neuroendocrine states provide the internal milieu within which immune responses occur. Stimulating animals during prenatal and early life, varying social interactions among adult animals, and exposing animals to environmental circumstances over which they have no control are among the psychological manipulations that induce neuroendocrine changes that are now implicated in the modulation of immune responses. Our knowledge of interactions between neuroendocrine and immune function under normal and stressful conditions, however, is incomplete. For example, glucocorticoids are, in general, immunosuppressive. It is therefore assumed that adrenocortical steroid elevations, the most common manifestation of the stress response, are responsible for the frequently observed suppression of immune function. There are numerous examples of stress-induced, adrenocortically mediated alterations of immune responses, particularly in vitro. However, there are numerous other observations of stress-induced alterations in immune function that are independent of adrenocortical activation. The subtleties that can characterize the involvement of hormones and neuropeptides in the mediation of stress-induced alterations of immunity are illustrated by the results of different regimens of electric shock stimulation. Intermittent and continuous schedules of inescapable electric footshocks result in an analgesia to subsequent footshock. Only the intermittent shock, however, was found to be an opioid-mediated analgesia and only the intermittent footshock resulted in a suppression of natural killer cell activity. These results apparently reflect the immunomodulating potential of endogenously released opioids. Thus, even a cursory review of the literature makes it evident that the in vivo immunological consequences of stress involve extremely complex neural, endocrine, and immune response interactions. Considering that immune responses are themselves capable of altering levels of circulating hormones and neurotransmitters, these interactions are likely to include complex feedback and feedforward mechanisms as well.

Stressful life experiences affect immunity, but the data yield an inconsistent picture of the direction, magnitude, and duration of the effects. At the very least, the effects of stress appear to be determined by:

(1) the quality and quantity of stressful stimulation; (2) the capacity of the organism to cope effectively with stressful circumstances; (3) the quality and quantity of immunogenic stimulation; (4) the temporal relationship between stressful stimulation and immunogenic stimulation; (5) the parameters of immune function and the times chosen for measurement; (6) the experiential history of the organism and the prevailing social and environmental conditions upon which stressful stimulation and immunogenic stimulation are superimposed; (7) a variety of host factors such as species, strain, age, sex, and nutritional state; and (8) interactions among these variables. Although we are far from a definitive analysis of the effects of stress and the means by which perceived events are translated into altered physiological states capable of modulating immune functions, the available data do provide a body of evidence that the immune system is sensitive to the modulating effects of psychobiological processes ultimately regulated by the brain.

III. EFFECTS OF CONDITIONING ON IMMUNE RESPONSES

A. Background

Behaviorally conditioned alterations in immune function provide one of the more dramatic lines of research implicating the brain in the modulation of immune responses. These studies derived from serendipitous observations of mortality among animals in which a saccharin-flavored drinking solution had been paired with an injection of cyclophosphamide (CY), a powerful immunosuppressive drug. Pairing a novel taste stimulus, a conditioned stimulus (CS), with an agent that induces temporary gastrointestinal upset, the unconditioned stimulus (UCS), will, after a single pairing, result in an aversion to that taste stimulus. Repeated reexposures to the CS in the absence of the UCS will result in extinction of the avoidance response. During the course of repeated extinction trials, conditioned animals began to die and, more critically, mortality rate, like the magnitude of the avoidance response, varied directly with the volume of saccharin consumed on the single conditioning trial. In an attempt to explain these results, it was hypothesized that, at the same time that a behavioral response was conditioned, an immunosuppressive response was condi-

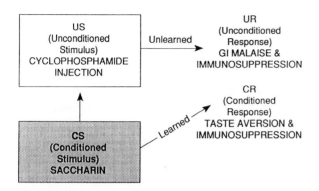

Figure 2 Schematic representation of the relationship between conditioned and unconditioned stimuli and conditioned and unconditioned responses. [Reproduced, with permission, from R. Ader (1987). *Immunopathol. Immunother. Lett.* **2**, 6–7.]

tioned and being elicited in response to reexposure to the CS (Fig. 2). If so, this might have increased the susceptibility of these animals to any latent pathogens in the laboratory environment.

B. Conditioned Changes in Immune Function

To test this hypothesis, the authors designed a study in which rats were conditioned by a single pairing of saccharin-flavored water and an injection of cyclophosphamide. When the animals were subsequently immunized with SRBC, one subgroup of conditioned animals remained untreated (to assess the effects of conditioning per se), another subgroup of conditioned animals was injected with CY (to establish the unconditioned immunosuppressive effects of the drug on the response to antigen), and an experimental subgroup was reexposed to the saccharin-flavored water (the CS). A nonconditioned group was also provided with saccharin-flavored water that had not previously been paired with their injection of CY. As hypothesized, conditioned animals reexposed to the CS at the time of antigenic stimulation showed an attenuated antibody response to SRBC in relation to nonconditioned animals and conditioned animals that were not reexposed to the CS. These results were taken as evidence of behaviorally conditioned immunosuppression and have now been independently verified and extended by several investigators.

The effects of conditioning have been quite consistent under a variety of experimental conditions. The magnitude and/or the kinetics of the unconditioned response vary as a function of the dose of CY, but one can still observe conditioned changes in immunological reactivity using different doses of CY. Also, there are several experiments in which the immunomodulating effects of "stress" have been conditioned. In addition to the effects of conditioning on antibody responses described here, conditioning is capable of influencing different parameters of cell-mediated immunity as well as a variety of nonspecific host defense responses. Not only has the release of histamine by sensitized animals been conditioned, but conditioned increases in a specific mediator of mucosal mast cell function have also been demonstrated.

The notion that conditioned immune responses are inextricably linked with conditioned avoidance responses or that there is some direct relationship between conditioned behavioral responses and conditioned immunological responses receives no support from the available literature. Taste aversions can be expressed without concomitant changes in immune function, and conditioned changes in immune function can be obtained without observable conditioned avoidance responses. Consistent with the relationship between conditioned behavioral and autonomic or endocrine responses, the available data suggest that different (multiple) conditioning processes and mechanisms are involved in the conditioning of behavioral responses and in the conditioning of different immune responses.

Both the acquisition and extinction of the conditioned enhancement of immunological reactivity have been observed using an antigen rather than pharmacological agents as the UCS. In one study, CBA mice were anesthetized, shaved, grafted with skin from C57BL/6J mice, and left bandaged for 9 days. In response to the grafting of allogeneic tissue, there was an increase in the number of precursors of cytotoxic T lymphocytes (CTLp) that could react against alloantigens of the foreign tissue. Since CTLp numbers did not return to baseline levels for 40 days, the conditioning manipulations were repeated three times at 40-day intervals. On the fourth trial, the procedures were repeated again, except that the experimental animals did not receive the tissue graft. Approximately half the animals, however, showed an increase in CTLp in response to the grafting procedures. When these "responders" were divided into groups that were exposed to additional conditioning trials or extinction trials (sham grafting), all of those that experienced additional conditioning trials showed a conditioned increase in CTLp, whereas none of the previous "responders" that were given unreinforced trials showed a conditioned response.

In another study, mice were repeatedly immunized with low doses of a common laboratory antigen following exposure to a gustatory conditioned stimulus. Three weeks after the last conditioning trial, half the animals in each of several experimental groups were reexposed to the CS alone, or they were reexposed to the CS in the context of a low-dose booster injection of the same antigen. Since it seemed unlikely that a CS could initiate antibody production by itself, this booster dose of antigen, insufficient to elicit more than a small antibody response, was administered to assure that a salient stimulus was available to activate the immune system. Reexposure to either the CS or the booster dose of antigen alone was not sufficient to elicit a robust antibody response. However, relative to several control groups, an enhancement of antibody titers was observed when conditioned mice were reexposed to the CS in the context of a minimally immunogenic dose of antigen.

The physiological mediation of conditioned alterations in immune function is not yet known. Some investigators have hypothesized that the conditioned suppression of immunological reactivity was the direct result of stress-induced responses since glucocorticoid elevations (taken as an index of "stress") frequently suppress some immune responses. The existing data, however, provide no support for stress-induced elevations in "stress hormones," notably adrenocortical steroids, as the mediator of conditioned alterations in immune function. In fact, most of the data stand in direct contradiction to such a hypothesis.

Although there are problems in interpreting extirpation experiments, it should be noted that, in one study, immunosuppression was not observed in adrenalectomized mice. On the other hand, no conditioned suppression of antibody production is observed when a drug, lithium chloride (LiCl), that elevates steroid levels but is immunologically neutral under defined experimental conditions is used as the UCS—or when steroid levels are elevated by injections of LiCl or corticosterone at the time of immunization. Conditioned suppression and/or enhancement of antibody- and/or cell-mediated responses occurs in the presumed ab-

sence of or with equivalent elevations in corticosterone and, presumably, other "stress hormones." In a two-bottle, preference testing procedure, fluid consumption is equal in experimental and control groups, and the thirsty animal is not faced with the conflict of choosing between drinking and the noxious effects that are associated with the CS solution. Under these experimental circumstances, conditioned immunosuppression is still observed in the antibody response to T-dependent and T-independent antigens, a graft-versus-host reaction, and in the white blood cell response to CY. Finally, in a discriminative conditioning paradigm, both the stimulus that signaled presentation of the UCS (the CS+) and a signal that was not associated with the UCS (the CS−) induce an elevation in adrenocortical steroid levels, but only the CS+ induces a conditioned release of histamine. It is reasonable to hypothesize that conditioned alterations of immunological reactivity may be mediated by conditioned neuroendocrine responses, but the data that have been collected thus far are inconsistent with the hypothesis that such effects are mediated simply by nonspecific, stress-induced changes in hormone levels.

Although the mechanisms underlying conditioned suppression and enhancement of immunological reactivity are not known, there is no shortage of potential mediators of such effects. Multiple processes are probably involved. Conditioned immunosuppressive responses, for example, occur when conditioned animals are reexposed to the CS before as well as after immunization. This observation could imply that the mechanisms do not involve antigen-induced immunological or neuroendocrine changes; they could also indicate that different mechanisms are involved when conditioning is superimposed on a resting or on an antigen-activated system. Also, different immunomodulating agents have different sites of action and the same immunomodulating drug may have different effects on activated or nonactivated lymphocytes. We now know that the immune system is innervated, that leukocytes and neurons share certain neuropeptide/neurotransmitter receptors, that lymphocytes can produce several neuroendocrine factors, and that cells of the immune system and the nervous system can produce and respond to the same cytokines. Thus, conditioned changes in neural and/or endocrine activity that can be recognized by activated lymphocytes or, conversely, the effects of conditioning on the release of immune products capable of being recognized by the nervous system constitute potential pathways for the conditioned modulation of immune functions. Indeed, in attempting to account for the conditioned enhancement of antibody production when antigen was used as the UCS, it was hypothesized that two signals were involved: one from the immune system in response to the booster injection of antigen, and one from the nervous and neuroendocrine systems in response to the conditioned stimulus.

Current research provides compelling evidence for the acquisition and extinction of conditioned suppression and enhancement of immunological reactivity. These studies dramatically illustrate the role of behavior in the modulation of immune responses, a modulation that is, presumably, ultimately regulated by the brain.

C. Clinical Implications of Conditioning Studies

There are strains of mice that spontaneously develop an autoimmune disease that is strikingly similar to systemic lupus erythematosus in humans. In this disorder, a suppression of immunological reactivity is in the biological interests of the organism. The (NZB× NZW)F1 female mouse, for example, develops a lethal glomerulonephritis that can be delayed by weekly injections of CY. Therefore, in an effort to determine the biological significance of conditioned alterations in immunological reactivity, the effects of conditioning were assessed in this animal model of autoimmune disease. If, as indicated earlier, the immunosuppressive effects of CY can be conditioned, could conditioned immunopharmacological effects be applied to a pharmacotherapeutic regimen, that is, could conditioned stimuli be substituted for some proportion of the active drug treatments received by these animals to delay the development of disease?

One group of mice (Group C100), treated under a traditional pharmacotherapeutic regimen, was given a saccharin-flavored solution to drink and, after each exposure to saccharin, the animals were injected with CY. As expected, this protocol delayed the development of proteinuria and mortality. An experimental (conditioned) group (Group C50) was injected with CY following saccharin on only half of the weekly occasions when the CS was presented. A nonconditioned control group (Group NC50) received the same number of saccharin and CY presentations as Group C50, but for this group the saccharin and CY were never paired.

Nonconditioned and placebo-treated animals did not differ. This indicated that half the total dose of CY administered to mice that were treated under the standard pharmacotherapeutic protocol was ineffective in modifying the course of autoimmune disease. Group C50 was also treated with half the cumulative dose of CY given to Group C100, but these animals developed proteinuria significantly more slowly than placebo-treated mice and significantly more slowly than nonconditioned mice treated with the same cumulative amount of drug.

The mortality data yielded the same results. There was no difference between nonconditioned animals and untreated controls, but conditioned animals treated with the same amount of CY as nonconditioned animals survived significantly longer than untreated controls and nonconditioned animals. The mortality rate of conditioned mice did not differ significantly from animals in Group C100, which received twice as much drug. These results indicate that, within the context of a pharmacotherapeutic regimen, conditioning effects were capable of influencing the onset of autoimmune disease using a cumulative dose of active drug that was not, by itself, sufficient to alter the course of disease.

After the period of pharmacotherapy, groups were divided into thirds that (1) continued to receive saccharin and CY on whatever schedule existed during therapy, (2) continued to receive saccharin and intraperitoneal injections of saline but no CY, or (3) received neither saccharin nor CY. Consistent with the interpretation that the effects on the development of lupus were conditioning effects, unreinforced presentations of the CS influenced the development of autoimmune disease in conditioned animals but not in nonconditioned animals. Among the animals conditioned under a traditional or continuous schedule of reinforcement (Group C100), mice that continued to receive CS exposures after the termination of active drug therapy survived significantly longer than similarly treated mice that were deprived of both the CS and the drug. In fact, animals that continued to be exposed to saccharin plus intraperitoneal injections of saline did not differ from animals that continued to be treated with active drug. These data, too, are consistent with the conditioned immunopharmacological effects described earlier. Consensual validity for these results is provided by studies in which repeated exposures to a CS previously associated with CY accelerated tumor growth and mortality in response to a transplanted syngeneic plasmacytoma and attenuated an experimentally induced arthritic inflammation. These findings document the biological impact of conditioned immunopharmacological responses. They also suggest that there may be some heuristic value in conceptualizing pharmacotherapeutic protocols as a conditioning (learning) process.

IV. IMMUNOLOGICAL EFFECTS ON BEHAVIOR

In the same way that there are reciprocal relationships between neural and immune functions and endocrine and immune functions, data are accumulating to suggest that there are immunological influences on behavior in addition to behavioral influences on immune function. Cytokines, a variety of chemical substances released by activated lymphocytes, facilitate intercellular communication within the immune system and, in addition, constitute a channel of communication from the immune system to the nervous system. Interleukin-1, in particular, is a cytokine released by activated macrophages that is capable of altering electrical activity in the brain, neurotransmitter functions, and a variety of behavioral and affective states. Several investigators have described the behavioral effects of (early) viral infections, the cognitive and emotional sequelae of autoimmune diseases, and behavioral differences between normal mice and those with a genetic susceptibility to autoimmune disease.

Furthermore, recent data suggest that behavioral changes associated with immunological dysfunctions may actually be adaptive with respect to the maintenance or restoration of homeostasis within the immune system. Lupus-prone (NZB×NZW)F1 mice do not acquire conditioned taste aversions in response to immunosuppressive doses of CY that are effective in inducing conditioned avoidance responses in healthy control (C57BL/6) mice. Also, when tested after the development of signs of autoimmune disease (lymph-

adenopathy and elevated autoantibody titers), Mrl-lpr/lpr mice, another strain of animals that spontaneously develop a lupus-like disorder, do not avoid flavored solutions paired with doses of CY that are effective in inducing taste aversions in congenic (Mrl+/+) control mice. These differences in behavior do not result from a learning deficit in the lupus-prone mice, since there are no substrain differences prior to the development of symptoms of disease nor when a nonimmunosuppressive drug is used as the UCS. Phenomenologically, it would appear that lupus-prone mice "recognize" the existence of their immunological deficit and/or the ameliorating effects of the immunosuppressive drug, despite its noxious gastrointestinal effects.

Mrl-lpr/lpr mice with symptoms of autoimmune disease also voluntarily consume more of a flavored drinking solution containing CY than do asymptomatic controls. Moreover, they drink sufficient amounts of the CY-laced solution to attenuate lymphadenopathy and autoantibody titers. Although not previously described with respect to the immune system, these data are consistent with a large literature indicating that behavioral responses are a primary means by which animals maintain and regulate some physiological states. Whether, in the case of a dysregulated immune system, the animal is responding to nonspecific, immunologically induced pathophysiological changes in one or another target organ or, consistent with the bidirectional pathways that link the central nervous system and immune system, whether the brain is capable of receiving and processing information emanating from the (dysregulated) immune system directly remains to be determined. To the extent that the brain is capable of acting on information provided by the immune system, it would appear that behavioral processes have the potential to serve an in vivo immunoregulatory function.

V. SUMMARY

The observations and research described in this article derive from a nontraditional view of the "immune system." It has become abundantly clear that there are probably no organ systems or homeostatic defense mechanisms that are not, in vivo, subject to the influence of interactions between behavioral and physiological events. The complex mechanisms underlying these interactions and their relationship to health and illness, however, are imperfectly understood. The most imperfectly understood, perhaps, are the interrelationships among brain, behavior, and immune processes.

Without attempting to be exhaustive, we have, using "stress" effects and conditioning phenomena as illustrations, pointed out that behavior is capable of influencing immune function. We have also noted that the immune system is capable of receiving and responding to neural and endocrine signals. Conversely, it would seem that behavioral, neural, and endocrine responses are influenced by an activated immune system. Thus, a traditional view of immune function that is confined to cellular interactions occurring within lymphoid tissues is insufficient to account for changes in immunity observed in subhuman animals and humans under conditions that prevail in the real world. The clinical significance of these interactions will not be fully appreciated until we understand more completely the extent of the interrelationships among brain, behavior, and immune functions. Behavioral research represents a new dimension in the study of immunity and immunopharmacology, but it has al-

ready yielded basic data that suggest new integrative approaches to an analysis of clinically relevant issues.

This article has been reprinted from the *Encyclopedia of Human Biology, Second Edition, Volume 7.*

BIBLIOGRAPHY

Ader, R., & Cohen, N. (1993). Psychoneuroimmunology: Conditioning and stress. *Annu. Rev. Psychol.* **44**, 53–85.

Ader, R., Cohen, N., & Felten, D. L. (Eds.) (1990). "Psychoneuroimmunology," 2nd ed. Academic Press, New York.

Felten, D. L., Felten, S. Y., Bellinger, D. L., Carlson, S., Ackerman, K. D., Madden, K. S., Olschowka, J. A., & Livnat, S. (1987). Noradrenergic sympathetic neural interactions with the immune system: Structure and function. *Immunol. Rev.* **100**, 225–260.

Fricchione, G. (Ed.) (1994). Stress mechanisms. *Adv. Neuroimmunol.* **4**, 1–56.

Glaser, R., & Kiecolt-Glaser, J. (Eds.) (1994). "Handbook of Human Stress and Immunity." Academic Press, New York.

Locke, S., Ader, R., Besedovsky, H., Hall, N., Solomon, G., & Strom, T. (Eds.) (1985). "Foundations of Psychoneuroimmunology." Aldine, New York.

Scharrer, B., Smith, E. M., & Stefano, G. B. (Eds.) (1994). "Neuropeptides and Immunoregulation." Springer-Verlag, Berlin.

Sheridan, J. F., Dobbs, C., Brown, D., & Zwilling, B. (1994). Psychoneuroimmunology: Stress effects on pathogenesis and immunity during infection. *Clin. Microbiol. Rev.* **7**, 200–212.

Psychopathology

Keith S. Dobson and Dennis Pusch

University of Calgary, Canada

Diagnosis The process of applying consistent labels to patterns of abnormal functioning.
Insanity A legal term, meaning that a person is not legally responsible for his or her actions.
Mental Health The absence of psychopathology, and the positive aspects of subjective well-being, development and use of abilities, social adaptation, and achievement of goals.
Mental Illness Largely synonymous with psychopathology, although implying an underlying disease or illness process.
Psychopathology An aberrant or dysfunctional way of functioning, defined in terms of behavioral, interpersonal, emotional, cognitive, and psychophysiological patterns.

The definition of **PSYCHOPATHOLOGY** has long been a matter of theoretical and practical importance to individuals involved in the mental health movement. It is primarily psychiatric and psychological professionals who have been involved in the conceptualization and definition of psychopathology. At the theoretical level, debates have centered around such issues as whether humans or their behavior is disordered or "ill," the different approaches that can be taken to define health and pathology, and the moral implications of defining some individuals as having a pathological condition. At the practical level, there have been exten-

sive discussions about how best to conceptualize and assess abnormal behavior, and how to minimize the potentially negative influences of labeling.

I. DEFINITIONAL ISSUES

A. Normalcy versus Abnormalcy

Within the overall frame of reference of psychopathology a number of related concepts must be defined and distinguished. As a term, *psychopathology* refers to an aberrant or dysfunctional (i.e., pathological) way of functioning, where functioning is defined in terms of behavioral, interpersonal, emotional, cognitive, and psychophysiological patterns. Whether a particular way of functioning is aberrant can be judged by a number of criteria. Included in such criteria is whether that functioning causes personal distress, causes others in the person's social sphere to become distressed, falls outside of accepted social norms or values for functioning, falls within certain criteria for abnormal functioning, or is a statistically rare functional pattern. Each of these approaches to establishing an aberrant pattern of functioning has advantages and disadvantages. It is due to the presence of these approaches that different approaches to conceptualizing psychopathology exist.

Mental illness is a term that is largely synonymous with psychopathology, although it carries the implication that the unusual or aberrant patterns of functioning seen in these conditions reflect some form of disease or illness. The medical model reflected in the illness term is rejected by some psychopathologists, as an inappropriate model for either all or some forms of psychopathology. Another term that is considered synonymous with psychopathology is *abnormal behavior*. This term is equally descriptive as psychopathology, as neither implies a belief in the cause of the unusual or aberrant patterns of functioning, but is more focused on the behavioral component of the dysfunction.

A term that is sometimes confused with psychopathology is *insanity*. Although such terms as insane, mad, and lunatic were once used in much the same way modern society uses the terms psychopathology and mental illness, insanity has taken on a much more narrow definition. Specifically, insanity is a legal term that addresses the question of whether a particular person can be held criminally responsible for his or her actions. Several different tests of insanity exist, but in every case the decision as to whether a person is legally insane is made by a judge or jury, and is made with respect to the crime they are alleged to have committed. It is the case that many different forms of abnormal or psychopathological behavior do not meet the criterion for insanity. Further, it is possible that a person can be legally insane (i.e., not legally responsible for their actions) when they have no discernable form of psychopathology, as defined by mental health practitioners.

A term that has relevance to psychopathology is *mental health*. While one can imagine mental health as the absence of psychopathology, it is also possible to conceptualize mental health in terms of its positive attributes. The World Health Organization has defined mental health as "inner experience linked to interpersonal group experience," and is associated with such characteristics as subjective well-being, optimal development and use of mental abilities, social adaptation, and achievement of goals.

In summary, psychopathology is a concept that is similar to mental illness and abnormal behavior, but is distinct from insanity. Mental health can be conceptualized as the absence of psychopathology, but also has other positive components not related to the concept of psychopathology.

B. Conceptual Approaches to Psychopathology

There are a large number of theoretical approaches to psychopathology, and these have steadily evolved over the centuries.

One dominant belief about the cause of abnormal behavior is that of possession; which is the idea that evil spirits or demons possess the mind and body of the person in question and cause them to behave in an aberrant fashion. There is fossil evidence that early humans believed in demonic possession as a cause of abnormal behavior, as there are skulls dating from prehistoric times which show purposeful cutting of the skull, or trephination. Trephination is often explained as an effort to release pressure in the skull, which may have been conceptualized by early humans as possession by an evil spirit. The idea of demonic possession as an explanation for abnormal behavior continues to persist (for example, the Roman Catholic Church still has procedures for exorcism as part of its accepted canon, and voodooism is still practised in some parts of the world today), but it has largely been supplanted by other explanations of abnormalcy.

One early alternative model to possession was the humoral theory promoted by Hippocrates. The humoral model proposed that four humors, or fluids, are in the body, and that each is associated with a particular attitude and time of life. Blood, for example, is associated with growth, optimism, and good health, while black bile, or melancholia, is associated with death, depression, and darkness. The humoral theory was a prominent one in medicine for centuries, but has been since shown to be false.

Contemporary conceptions of psychopathology can be broken down into the two major categories of categorical and dimensional types. Categorical conceptions of psychopathology view abnormal behavior as discontinuous with normal behavior; as something that has a qualitatively different sense to it. Such conceptions are apt to include ideas of illness or disease processes, as these processes are those that distinguish normal from abnormal functioning. Categorical approaches to psychopathology are consistent with the practise of diagnosing or labeling dysfunctional patterns of functioning. The categorical approach to psychopathology is very heavily subscribed to because diagnosis is often considered to be necessary prior to the provision of treatment in psychiatric settings.

Dimensional approaches to psychopathology view aberrant functioning as falling on a continuum, with some types or levels of functioning being more or less dysfunctional than others. Within a dimensional approach diagnosis and labeling are less accepted, except to the extent that labels are applied to individuals at agreed upon points along a continuum. For example, if a person bites his or her nails more than three times a week, we might label that as "abnormal"; less than three times a week might be considered "normal." Dimensional approaches are often used in combination with statistical conceptions of what is "average" or normal, and abnormalcy is defined as being atypical or highly different from the "average" person.

II. CATEGORICAL MODELS OF PSYCHOPATHOLOGY

A. Historical Precursors to the Diagnosis of Psychopathology

The labeling of abnormal behavior has taken place for centuries. In ancient Greek society, such disorders as melancholia (what we would today term depression), mania (agitated or excited behavior), and phrenitis (most other forms of psychopathology, including severe forms of thought and behavior dysfunction) were distinguished. Models for the onset (etiology) of these disorders were established, and these disorders had differentiated treatment programs.

After the Dark Ages, the Renaissance and Enlightenment periods of Western civilization saw a renewed and more sophisticated approach to the diagnosis of psychopathology emerge. With the creation of asylums, large institutions designed for the holding and treatment of persons with mental illness, came the ability to study, differentiate, and more carefully assess abnormal conditions. Different systems for diagnosing psychopathology began to emerge, with different labels being proposed, debated, and either accepted or rejected. By the end of the 19th century, the number of divergent systems for diagnosis was recognized as a serious problem for the credibility and acceptability of any diagnostic system.

The approach to diagnosis and labeling that has been generally accepted was formalized by a German physician, Emil Kraepelin, in 1883. Using an approach comparable to that used in the rest of medicine, his approach included the assessment of different symptoms that formed cohesive patterns called *syndromes*. These syndromes, once identified, could then be labeled. In the original Kraepelinian diagnostic system there were a relatively small number of syndromes and diagnoses, but each was conceptually distinct and had its own specific symptoms.

B. The International Classification of Diseases

The World Health Organization (WHO) adopted Kraepelin's system for diagnosing psychopathology, and has listed mental disorders as potential causes of death since 1939. The list of mental disorders included in the WHO directory has been revised a number of times, and the 1969 revision in particular received some acceptance. In 1979 the WHO published the ninth revision and the current version of the *International Classification of Diseases* (ICD). There are a total of 30 major categories of mental disorders in the *ICD-9* (see Table I). As many of these categories contain more specific forms of psychopathology, there are a total of 563 diagnostic categories in the *ICD-9*.

One of the principle features of the *ICD* is that it distinguishes organic from nonorganic forms and causes of abnormal behavior. For example, a major distinction is made between "organic psychotic conditions" and "other psychoses." This distinction has been severely examined in the diagnostic literature as potentially lacking validity. For example, it is sometimes the case that what appears to be the same type of abnormal behavior may have different etiological bases; it is often impossible, however, to know with certainty which of the different etiological possibilities is the correct one. A diagnostic system that requires the diagnostician to make etiological judgments may therefore force false decisions.

Another aspect of the *ICD* is that it distinguishes "psychotic" from "nonpsychotic" (also referred to as "neurotic") conditions. The psychotic–neurotic distinction within the *ICD* is also problematic. For example, depressive conditions are found listed both as psychotic (major depressive disorder) and neurotic (depressive disorder) conditions, but the distinction between these two hypothetically distinct types of depression is not clear.

Despite some problems with the *ICD* system for diagnosing mental disorder, it is a widely subscribed to international model for diagnosis. It is the dominant approach used in Europe, as well as countries that have been under European influence. The World Health Organization is currently at work on the *ICD-10*.

C. Diagnostic and Statistical Manual

Due to problems with earlier versions of the *ICD*, the American Psychiatric Association developed its own

Table I Major Mental Disorder Diagnostic Categories from the *International Classification of Diseases*

A. Organic psychotic conditions
  1. Senile and presenile organic psychotic conditions
  2. Alcoholic psychoses
  3. Drug psychoses
  4. Transient organic psychotic conditions
  5. Other organic psychotic conditions
B. Other psychoses
  1. Schizophrenic disorders
  2. Affective psychoses
  3. Paranoid states
  4. Other nonorganic psychoses
  5. Psychoses with origin specific to childhood
C. Neurotic disorders, personality disorders, and other nonpsychotic mental disorders
  1. Neurotic disorders
  2. Personality disorders
  3. Sexual deviations and disorders
  4. Alcohol dependence syndrome
  5. Drug dependence
  6. Nondependent abuse of drugs
  7. Physiological malfunction arising from mental factors
  8. Special symptoms or syndromes, not elsewhere classified
  9. Acute reaction to stress
  10. Adjustment reaction
  11. Specific nonpsychotic mental disorders due to organic brain damage
  12. Depressive disorder, not elsewhere classified
  13. Disturbance of conduct, not elsewhere classified
  14. Disturbance of emotions specific to childhood and adolescence
  15. Hyperkinetic syndrome of childhood
  16. Specific delays in development
  17. Psychic factors associated with diseases not elsewhere classified
D. Mental retardation
  1. Mild mental retardation
  2. Other specified mental retardation
  3. Unspecified mental retardation

system for diagnosis. Referred to as the *Diagnostic and Statistical Manual* (DSM), the system was first published in 1952, and has since been updated and republished three more times. The current *DSM* is the fourth version, which was published in 1994).

The first two editions of the *DSM* had many similarities to the *ICD*. Distinctions were made between psychotic and nonpsychotic disorders, for example, and the diagnostic system included many etiological terms in the diagnoses. In 1980, with the publication of *DSM-III*, the American Psychiatric Associa-

tion made a major departure from this approach and deleted, as much as possible, all references to putative causes of disorder. Instead, the *DSM* became a more descriptive system that attempted to label disorders solely on their objective features, with as little inference as possible about the cause of the disorders.

In addition to the more descriptive nature of the later editions of *DSM*, an additional feature was that it was multi-axial. The multi-axial nature of the *DSM-IV* meant that it examined different axes or dimensions of functioning within the person being diagnosed at a single time, in order to achieve a more rounded assessment of the person and their functioning.

DSM-IV has continued the basic descriptive approach of the *DSM-III*. The *DSM-IV*, as was true for the *DSM-III*, has five major axes. The first two axes are those most analogous to the *ICD* diagnostic system. Axis I comprises the major psychopathology diagnoses (see Table II), while Axis II is used to diagnose personality disorders and mental retardation. Axis III is used to diagnose physical disorders and conditions. Some of these disorders or conditions may be relevant to the other psychopathology diagnoses, whereas other medical disorders or conditions may simply help to round out a picture of the person's current problems. Axis IV of the *DSM-IV* is used to rate the severity of psychosocial stressors, whereas Axis V consists

Table II Major Mental Diagnostic Categories from Axis I of the *Diagnostic and Statistical Manual-IV*

Disorders usually first evident in infancy, childhood, or adolescence
Delirium, dementia, and amnestic and other cognitive disorders
Mental disorders due to a general medical condition
Substance-related disorders
Schizophrenia and other psychotic disorders
Mood disorders
Anxiety disorders
Somatoform disorders
Factitious disorders
Dissociative disorders
Sexual and gender identity disorders
Eating disorders
Sleep disorders
Impulse control disorders
Adjustment disorders
Other conditions that may be a focus of clinical attention

of a global assessment rating of the individual's functioning for the past year.

In order to diagnose a person using the *DSM-IV*, information should be provided on each of the five axes. Thus, whereas only Axes I and II are comparable to the *ICD*'s diagnostic labels, the *DSM* system is more comprehensive than the *ICD*, and provides more of a complete context in terms of the patient's medical and psychosocial issues. [*See* DSM-IV.]

D. Future Issues and Developments

A large number of conceptual, research, and ethical issues are relevant to the categorical approaches to psychopathology. At the conceptual level, issues of validity (i.e., accurate portrayal of reality) have been raised. These issues have taken a number of forms. For example, the fact that over time the total number of diagnostic categories has been increasing, and the fact that the *ICD* and the *DSM* systems have different numbers and types of diagnoses, leads to the question about which (if either) system best reflects the real range of psychopathology. Ideally, diagnostic systems should be both comprehensive (that is, include all potential diagnoses) and distinctive (that is, each diagnostic category should be distinct and minimally overlapping with other categories). It is not clear at present that either existing system meets these criteria. Nor is it easy to imagine how they could demonstrate that they are both comprehensive and distinctive.

Another validity issue that has been raised with regard to the two major diagnostic systems is the extent to which a categorical system best represents psychopathology. This issue has been particularly raised in the case of the personality disorders, where it has been argued that rather than being discrete disorders they represent the extreme ends of personality dimensions. According to this view, rather than diagnosing personality disorders such as dependent personality disorder, psychopathologists should speak about the relative strength or weakness of certain personality dimensions such as dependency. [*See* CLASSIFYING MENTAL DISORDERS: NONTRADITIONAL APPROACHES.]

Although the issue of whether disorders are dimensional or categorical in nature is most acute in the case of personality disorders, it is also clear that in other disorders judgments must be made about when a given behavioral pattern or other symptom falls outside the range of normal. Consider, for example, the diagnosis

Table III Diagnostic Criteria for Anorexia Nervosa

A. Refusal to maintain body weight at or above a minimally *normal* weight for age and height, e.g., weight loss leading to maintenance of body weight less than 85% of that *expected*; or failure to make *expected* weight gain during period of growth, leading to body weight less than 85% of that *expected*.

B. *Intense* fear of gaining weight or becoming fat, even though underweight.

C. *Disturbance* in the way in which one's body weight or shape is experienced, undue influence of body weight or shape on self-evaluation, or denial of the seriousness of the current low body weight.

D. In postmenarcheal females, amenorrhea, i.e., the absence of at least three consecutive menstrual cycles. (A woman is considered to have amenorrhea if her periods occur only following hormone, e.g., estrogen, administration.)

Source: Adapted from the *Diagnostic and Statistical Manual-IV*. Italics not in the original.

of anorexia nervosa (see Table III). Within that diagnosis are a number of judgments that a diagnostician would have to make, including what is an "expected body weight," when a fear of being overweight is "intense" and when thoughts about body size are "disturbed." While at the extremes of such judgments there would likely be high agreement across diagnosticians, less extreme fears and disturbances are more difficult to judge with certainty. Put otherwise, some of the symptoms are themselves not dichotomous, but reflect dimensions of disturbance, which are identified only if they cross some imaginal "line" of dysfunction. Decisions about how to recognize where that line has been crossed require some agreement among diagnosticians about what that line is, and how to recognize it is being breached. [*See* ANOREXIA NERVOSA AND BULIMIA NERVOSA.]

Similar arguments have been made with respect to most forms of childhood disorders, as these disorders are typically conceptualized in terms of extreme forms of behavior (for example, too much aggressive behavior) that might better be seen as extremes on a continuum rather than discrete forms of psychopathology.

A third issue about diagnoses has been that to some extent they do not reflect the real world of psychopathology, but rather society's beliefs about and experience of abnormal behavior. Critics of diagnosis have pointed out that the "emergence" of new disorders and deletion of others reflect changing societal values, rather than scientific advances that could validate such changes. For example, the diagnosis of homosexuality has had an interesting history within the *DSM* system. In the *DSM-II*, published in 1968, homosexuality was defined as a psychopathology diagnosis. By the time *DSM-III* was published in 1980 the system had changed, such that only ego-dystonic homosexuality (i.e., sexual preference for a same-sex person, but where the individual felt that this preference was inconsistent with their own wishes) was a recognized disorder; instances where the homosexual patterns were ego-syntonic (consistent with the persons's wishes) were not considered abnormal. Homosexuality has been totally deleted as a diagnostic label in the *DSM-IV* (*ICD* continues to include homosexuality). It has been pointed out that this evolution of approaches to homosexuality mirrors a growing recognition and acceptance of homosexuality in Western society. It has been argued, therefore, that the changing diagnoses related to homosexuality do not reflect changes in the scientific basis of that diagnosis, but rather reflect changes in the attitudes and biases that the developers of diagnostic systems share with society at large. It has been similarly argued that other disorders, such as anorexia nervosa, reflect societal beliefs and awareness about specific behaviors, rather than necessarily reflecting the "true" nature of psychopathology.

At the scientific level, the major issues that face categorical systems of psychopathology are those related to the internal consistency and reliability of diagnostic categories. If a perfect diagnostic system existed, then every person with psychopathology should be captured in the system, and every trained diagnostician should recognize an individual's unique diagnoses in a manner consistent with other diagnosticians. Research on these issues suggests that our current systems, although better than their precursors, do not closely approximate these goals. Clearly, further research and development are needed to clarify why consistency and reliability have been elusive.

Finally, there have been ethical arguments raised against the practice of diagnosis. It has been argued, for example, that diagnosis involves an artificial process of labeling people, and that once these labels are applied they become more than descriptions of the individual's current functioning, but become long-term crosses for the individual to bear. These abuses of the diagnostic process have been used as a basis for arguing that the utility of diagnosis is more than offset by its costs, and should be abandoned.

III. DIMENSIONAL MODELS OF PSYCHOPATHOLOGY

Dimensional models view psychopathology as deriving from underlying dimensional constructs that explain both normal and abnormal functioning. For example, it is possible to imagine a construct called interpersonal dependency. At one end of this construct is extreme dependency, as would be marked by such thoughts as being insufficient without others, having to have others around to feel comfortable, and marked by such behavior as constantly seeking out others to be with, talking to others, etc. At the other end of this construct is extreme interpersonal independency, which would be marked by such thoughts as never needing others, having to be alone to feel comfortable, and such behaviors as spending time alone, not starting conversations with others, etc. A person functioning at either of the extremes on this dimension would be considered dysfunctional or psychopathological; between these two extremes lies a wide range of normal dependency–independency options.

Research has shown that most constructs are more common at their middle range, and less common at their extremes. As such, if those constructs related to personality or behavior that are related to psychopathology could be identified, then it would be possible to identify those points along the continua where abnormal or extreme patterns could be identified. For example, using the dimension of interpersonal dependency–independency, it might be possible to identify a point along that continuum where the person is either so dependent or independent it causes distress and/or interpersonal problems for the person. It would be at those points we would talk about the person crossing an imaginary line from normal to psychopathological functioning (see Fig. 1).

A. Trait versus Symptom Approaches

Dimensional models of psychopathology can be viewed as typically being one of two major types. Some dimensional models focus on underlying theo-

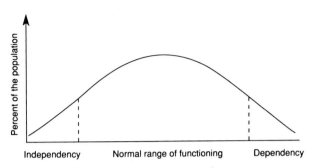

Figure 1 A dimensional approach to dependency.

retical dimensions or traits that might explain abnormal behavior, while other focus more on the range of symptoms or descriptive features of the dysfunctional behaviors themselves. Trait approaches are more theoretical than symptom approaches, and typically have an associated theory of normal personality as well as psychopathology, while symptom approaches focus more on the elements of psychopathology alone.

There are a number of trait approaches to psychopathology, and all cannot be described here. The work of Hans Eysenck is a good example of this approach, however, and will be used to provide an example. In Eysenck's earlier research, he identified two basic dimensions to normal and abnormal behavior. One of these was the dimension of introversion–extroversion, which had extremes of being highly introverted (shy, retiring, isolated) and highly extroverted (outgoing, sociable), while the other was neuroticism (which had two extremes of stable versus unstable patterns; where instability is marked by such attributes as anxiety, physical complaints, moodiness, etc.). According to Eysenck's research these two personality dimensions were unique from each other. An individual's placement on each dimension, according to Eysenck, reflects a basic disposition on the part of the individual which likely could be seen in different situations that the person finds him/herself in, and also lasts across time.

Within Eysenck's model of functioning, psychopathology is identified at the extremes of each dimension. Thus, a person who is "too" extroverted could be said to be dysfunctional; similarly, a person "too" high on neuroticism could be said to be dysfunctional. Eysenck developed questionnaires to measure these dimensions which allowed clinicians to identify how much of these dimensions were represented by an in-

dividual, and thereby identify if the person was in the normal range of functioning or not.

A later addition to Eysenck's theory was a third dimension, referred to as *psychoticism*. This dimension was theoretically distinct from the other two, and reflected an underlying tendency toward more extreme forms of abnormal behavior, including insensitivity toward and lack of caring about others, and opposition of accepted social customs.

A mental health professional using Eysenck's system to describe psychopathology would not talk about a given individual as "extroverted," "neurotic," or "psychotic," but would rather talk about an individual as being high on these dimensions. The mental health professional would know that certain forms of thought, emotion, and behavior are related to these dimensions, and would explain psychopathology in terms of these underlying trait dimensions.

As stated previously, Eysenck's is just one of a number of trait approaches to psychopathology. One of the major issues that has been addressed by theorists who use these models has been that of trying to develop a comprehensive and exhaustive system. In recent years, there has been considerable discussion about what are referred to as the "Big Five" personality traits that might explain most human behavior. These five factors include neuroticism, extraversion, openness, agreeableness, and conscientiousness. While we will not discuss the adequacy of this model here, it is important to note two elements: first, that many theorists are beginning to converge on the importance of these five factors in personality, and second, that one of these dimensions—neuroticism—is explicitly oriented toward identifying abnormal behavior of a neurotic type (anxiety, physical complaints, nervousness, edginess, etc.). [*See* PERSONALITY.]

As opposed to trait models of psychopathology, there are symptom dimensional approaches. One prominent example of this type of approach has been with regard to the personality disorders. Within the *DSM-IV*, there are 11 recognized personality disorder diagnoses. As is true for other diagnostic categories, *DSM-IV* lists the descriptive features of these disorders, and presents them as unique (although a given individual could have more than one diagnosis simultaneously). An alternative perspective to conceptualizing types of personality disorders is to conceptualize personality as having a number of dimensions, which at their extreme represent dysfunctional patterns of interpersonal relating. Such an alternative approach would view personality features in terms of their symptoms, as well as in terms of the severity of these symptoms. [*See* PERSONALITY DISORDERS.]

Symptom-based approaches, as seen in the area of personality disorders, can be imagined for most types of psychopathology. In the area of depression, for example, one can imagine that rather than diagnosing an individual as depressed or not based upon whether they meet certain diagnostic criteria, a psychopathologist could describe the severity or depth of depression. Such an approach would require a psychopathologist to determine the key symptoms of depression, to evaluate the severity of each of these symptoms, and then determine the overall depth or severity of depression for a given individual. The fact that the end result is an index of severity, though, means that an underlying dimensional, rather than categorical, approach has been used to conceptual and describe depression. [*See* DEPRESSION.]

Dimensional approaches to most forms of psychopathology exist. Typically, the assessment of psychopathology using such approaches relies on questionnaires, which are self-report means to determine the number and severity of different symptoms the person may be experiencing. A large number of trait and symptom questionnaires have been developed, predominantly by psychologists working in the fields of personality and psychopathology. A listing of all published questionnaires and psychological tests can be gained by examining the *Mental Measurements Yearbook,* which is an annual publication of the Buros Institute.

B. Models of Psychopathology

Psychopathologists are not content with conceptualizing and describing categorical and dimensional aspects of psychopathology. Another key activity of psychopathologists is to develop theoretical models that can potentially explain the cause, course, and required treatment of these disorders as well. A large number of theoretical models have been developed to attempt to explain psychopathology, many of which are very complex and well beyond the scope of this article. An excellent starting reference for interested readers is *Abnormal Psychology,* by Davison and Neale (1991).

Models of psychopathology fall into several major categories. One major dimension which can be used to think of these models is whether their focus is on factors that are external or internal to the person. Models that focus on external factors might place an emphasis on such issues as early childhood experiences, family dynamics, traumatic experiences, and even social and cultural issues that might lead to different forms of problematic behavior. These models are likely to focus on the need for changes external to the individual to correct psychopathology, including marital and family therapy. Some theorists who adopt this type of environmental or social perspective also focus on the need to change societal or cultural variables to lower the likelihood of some forms of psychopathology. For example, it has been argued that some eating disorders are encouraged by the value that society places on thinness, and that by changing societal values, we may actually be able to lower the future likelihood of some eating disorders.

Theorists who focus on factors internal to the individual typically adopt either a biological or a psychological perspective. Biologically oriented theorists might focus on genetic contributions to psychopathology, structural problems in the nervous system that cause abnormal behavior, or neurological processes that can be disordered and lead to psychopathology. These theorists are likely to focus on biological treatments to psychopathology, including psychoactive medications. A large number of medications for treating psychological disorders exist, many of which have documented benefit.

The third major theoretical approach to psychopathology is psychological in nature. Such approaches focus upon psychological models of both normal and abnormal personality, and try to explain psychopathology in terms of these processes. Within the psychological approaches are a number of discrete models, including psychoanalytic, behavioral, cognitive, humanistic, and other theoretical approaches. While all of these models share the assumption that there is something within the individual at the psychological level that explains abnormal behavior, the specifics of each model vary dramatically, as do the therapies they promote.

In summary, psychopathology researchers not only classify, diagnose, and assess abnormal behavior, but also are interested in the causes, course, and treatment of these conditions. Different models are used in the effort to explain psychopathology. While some models appear to be better suited for some forms of abnormal behavior, others may be more appropriate for other conditions. It is also possible that a given form of psychopathology, such as anxiety, may have multiple causes, which may vary from person to person having that disorder. Humans are extremely complex, and the large number of approaches helps to encompass that complexity in the way psychopathologists conceptualize their subject field.

IV. FUTURE ISSUES IN PSYCHOPATHOLOGY

As the above reveals, psychopathology is an intricate and often perplexing field of study. Although there are a large number of issues that face the field, major issues include the future of categorical and dimensional approaches, theoretical models, and treatment issues. Each is discussed in turn below.

A. Categorical and Dimensional Approaches

Both of the categorical and dimensional approaches to psychopathology face the issues of comprehensiveness and distinctiveness. How many diagnoses or dimensions, respectively, adequately account for the range of human dysfunction? Are these distinct diagnoses and dimensions, or is their overlap such that they call into question the theoretical basis for the approach to psychopathology?

Another question that both approaches face is how best to assess psychopathology. As has been stated, each of these approaches has its own methodology for assessment. Categorical approaches lend themselves to diagnoses, which are typically constructed as a result of interviews with individuals, and the decision as to whether the given individual qualifies for one or more diagnoses. Dimensional approaches are most often assessed using questionnaires that assess one or more dimensions of psychopathology, using traits or symptoms as the conceptual basis for assessment.

Interview and questionnaire assessment strategies are not necessarily contradictory, and many psychopathologists believe that using both leads to a more comprehensive understanding of the individual in question. It remains for the field to adequately address which strategy or strategies are best within each approach, and how best to integrate these two types of assessment.

B. Theories of Psychopathology

Theories of psychopathology, as is true for all scientific theories, are tested against their explanatory power. Within psychopathology, many research methods exist to test theoretical models, including the ability to discriminate groups with different types of psychopathology, or the correlation between certain theoretical constructs and the severity of psychopathology. The field of psychopathology is rich with research questions.

Psychopathology research is notoriously difficult to conduct for a number of reasons, including the large number of definitional, assessment and theoretical perspectives already discussed. Further, it is often difficult to easily obtain large numbers of research subjects that clearly have a distinct form of psychopathology, and for ethical reasons it is often not possible to conduct the experimental types of studies that might best test different theories of psychopathology. Finally, a good number of different forms of psychopathology need time to develop (indeed, sometimes it is the course of different disorders that itself is the object of scientific study), which requires long-term research funds and geographical stability of both researchers and research objects. Such control is not easy to obtain in the real world.

Despite the above problems, research in the field of psychopathology is increasingly driven by strong theoretical questions, and the answers to these questions are slowly being accumulated. The field has begun to contrast competing theories, and the overall adequacy of some theoretical models is beginning to become clear. It can be expected that over the next decades some "best models" for different forms of psychopathology will emerge.

C. Treatment Issues in Psychopathology

Many psychopathologists enter the field because of a desire not only to understand, but also to help people with behavioral problems. One hope is that with accurate assessment and diagnosis, treatment options may become clarified. Although there does not yet exist a clear correspondence between different forms of psychopathology and treatments, the field has advanced considerably in this direction. For a given disorder there likely are several viable treatments, some of which may have better success rates, but all of which have some potential for helping an individual in distress. With increasing sophistication of assessment, diagnosis, and conceptualization, it is likely that treatment of psychopathology will become an even more complex and successful enterprise in the future than now.

This article has been reprinted with updated references to *DSM-IV* from the *Encyclopedia of Human Behavior, Volume 3*.

BIBLIOGRAPHY

American Psychiatric Association (1994). "Diagnostic and Statistical Manual-IV." Washington, DC.

Buros Institute (1992). "Mental Measurements Yearbook." Gryphen, Highland Park, NJ.

Davison, G., and Neale (1991). "Abnormal Psychology," 5th ed. Wiley, New York.

World Health Organization (1979). "International Classification of Diseases," 9th ed. Geneva, Switzerland.

Psychopharmacology

Neil E. Grunberg, Laura Cousino Klein, and Kelly J. Brown

Uniformed Services University of the Health Sciences

Dose A specified amount of a drug.
Drug Any chemical compound that is used medically or recreationally.
Pharmacodynamics Actions of drugs on the body.
Pharmacokinetics Actions of the body on drugs.
Pharmacology The study of drugs.
Toxicity Adverse or untoward effects of a substance.

PSYCHOPHARMACOLOGY refers to the study of drugs as they relate to mind and behavior. This topic includes several different aspects of this relationship. It includes the study, development, and administration of drugs or medications to treat psychological and psychiatric disorders, such as anxiety disorders, mood disorders, and psychoses. It includes the study and development of drugs that affect behaviors in psychologically normal people, such as sleeping, feeding, and sexual functioning. It includes the study and development of drugs that affect cognitions and perceptions, such as attention, memory, learning, hunger, sensory perception, and pain. It includes the study of drugs that are addictive or abused and the study and development of drugs to treat drug addiction, to help alleviate withdrawal from addictive drugs, and to help maintain abstinence from addictive drugs. In addition, psychopharmacology includes the investigation of psychological, pharmacological, biological, neuroscientific, and molecular biologic mechanisms that underlie the actions of psychopharmacologic agents to help understand how these drugs work, underlying particular psychological disorders, and more general aspects of psychology and behavior.

Psychopharmacology can be traced back to the use of botanically derived medicinal agents, particularly alcohol and opium, in Greek culture and throughout the world by shamans or medicine men to achieve particular psychological states and to alter mood, anxiety, hunger, and pain. Psychopharmacology developed markedly in the twentieth century, especially after World War II. Sedative-hypnotics (e.g., barbiturates) and stimulants (e.g., amphetamines) were introduced at the beginning of this century, but it was the dramatic actions of antipsychotic medications (e.g., phenothiazines) that grabbed professional, public, and media attention. The pharmaceutical industry realized the potential market and profitability of psychopharmacologic agents beginning in the middle of this century and the development of psychopharmacologic medications became a major thrust. With cultural changes in the 1960s also came an explosion in popular, recreational use of a wide variety of mind-altering drugs, including marijuana, LSD, amphetamines, and opiates. This societal change also led to debates and discussions about addictive drugs, including drugs used for medicinal and nonmedicinal reasons. Technological and conceptual developments in behavioral sciences, neurosciences, and molecular biology from the 1960s to the present further added to interest in psychopharmacology. Today, it is taken as a given that drugs can alter mind and behavior, that drugs can be developed to treat psychological problems, that drugs not intended primarily as psychopharmacologic agents also can affect mind and behavior, and that psychopharmacology is a diverse and active discipline to study drugs and to help understand mind and behavior. The present article addresses major issues in psychopharmacology. This article discusses principles and paradigms of psychopharmacology; mechanisms of action of psychopharmacologic agents; clinical psychopharmacology; and issues related to special populations.

I. PRINCIPLES AND PARADIGMS OF PSYCHOPHARMACOLOGY

A. Psychopharmacology versus Behavioral Pharmacology

Within any field different camps develop for a variety of reasons, some historical, some conceptual, some methodologic, and some personal. The study of drugs and psychology is no exception to this truism. Whereas psychopharmacology has come to refer to a broad rubric of issues, methods, and topics, behavioral pharmacology has a narrower focus. This particular subfield is mentioned here because it is so important to the broader topic and it has made so many contributions to knowledge of drugs and behavior. It is singled out because scientists studying drugs and behavior either identify themselves as behavioral pharmacologists or psychopharmacologists. Behavioral pharmacology developed as behaviorists—that is, experimental psychologists who focused on behavior rather than on mind, perception, or motivations—began to study drugs. In addition, behavioral pharmacology refers to a series of techniques (especially operant techniques) that are used to examine drug effects on behavior and the actions of environmental or other variables on behavioral responses to drug actions. The behaviors of interest are operant (responses elicited by the environment) and conditioned behaviors, rather than unconditioned, naturally occurring behaviors. Traditional behavioral pharmacologists are primarily interested in the actions of drugs, the biological and behavioral mechanisms that underlie drug actions, and the identification and development of new drugs that alter behavior.

B. Conditional and Unconditional Behaviors

Conditional behaviors, also called conditioned behaviors, are behaviors that have come under the control of environmental stimuli or under the control of other external stimuli that in and of themselves do not elicit the given response. These conditional behaviors are either classically conditioned (Pavlovian conditioning) or instrumentally conditioned (operant or Skinnerian conditioning). Classical conditioning refers to the phenomenon in which a conditional stimulus (CS) (e.g., tone) is presented with an unconditional stimulus (UCS) (e.g., meat powder to a dog) that leads to an unconditional response (UCR) (e.g., salivation). After repeated pairings of the CS and UCS, the CS comes to elicit a similar response, which is known as the conditional response (CR). Operant conditioning refers to the phenomenon in which the behaviors emitted are shaped by the consequence (e.g., reward or punishment) of the behavior. This approach is typically studied in operant chambers (Skinner boxes). Psychopharmacologists, especially behavioral pharmacologists, use variations of these learning principles and paradigms to study drug actions on behaviors.

Unconditional behaviors refer to innate, or naturally occurring, behaviors. These behaviors include: feeding, drinking, sleeping, moving, exploring, jumping, startling, touching, grabbing, grooming, playing, fighting, nesting, and copulating. Psychopharmacologists examine effects of drugs on these and other unconditional behaviors in order to learn about drug actions, to compare different drugs, and to understand various behaviors.

Together, the study of drugs on unconditional and conditional behaviors offers a more complete picture of behavioral effects of drugs. The conditional behaviors offer the advantage of exquisite control and sensitive measure of drug effects. The unconditional behaviors offer the advantage of information that is of direct clinical relevance as well as information about basic, everyday behaviors.

C. Human and Animal Subjects

Psychopharmacology uses human and animal subjects. Human subjects include patients with particular disorders, conditions, or injuries, and healthy, normal volunteers. It is relevant and important to stipulate and consider the age, gender, race, ethnicity, genotype, and other major demographics of the patients or subjects. Animal subjects are taken from a wide variety of species, including monkeys, rabbits, rats, mice, gerbils, hamsters, and pigeons. Age, sex, and genotype are important variables to consider when examining effects of drugs on animal subjects.

D. Pharmacokinetics and Pharmacodynamics

Pharmacokinetics refers to the actions of the body on drugs (e.g., distribution, metabolism, reabsorption, elimination of a drug). Pharmacodynamics refers to the actions of drugs on the body (e.g., binding to a particular receptor, stimulation of a chemical or electrical response, stimulation of a physiologic or organ response, stimulation of a behavioral or psychological response). Both of these principles are important when studying psychopharmacologic agents. They are relevant to the characterization of the relationship between drugs and the body. In addition, particular situations or stimuli (e.g., stressors, other drugs, history of exposure to the drug of interest, individual difference variables) can alter pharmacokinetics or pharmacodynamics or both types of processes. Identification of the contribution of these mechanisms of action are relevant to the prescription of appropriate drugs and dosages and to elucidate the mechanisms underlying a given drug or condition.

E. Toxicity and Adverse Side Effects

As with all drugs, psychopharmacologic agents have an effective dose range. Outside this range, the drugs either are ineffective or have toxic and adverse side effects. For example, stimulants used to treat attentional problems, to regulate hunger, or to control asthmatic attacks, can cause anxiety, shakiness, dizziness, and panic. Antibiotics used to kill or to control infectious diseases can lead to psychotic-like episodes and hallucinations. Analgesics can result in respiratory distress. The combination of various drugs, especially when used with alcohol, can potentiate these toxic and adverse side effects. It is relevant to consider this issue in the present context because drugs that are not normally considered to be psychopharmacologic agents can cause psychological effects in high dosages or in combination with other drugs. In addition, drugs can have a range of behavioral effects (e.g., discomfort, headache, dizziness, nausea, sedation, altered appetite, sexual impotence) that decrease the likelihood of adherence to prescribed medication regimens. The study of these effects also contributes to psychopharmacologic knowledge.

II. MECHANISMS OF ACTION OF PSYCHOPHARMACOLOGIC AGENTS

A. Neuroanatomy

The brain, central nervous system, and peripheral nervous system all are relevant to the actions of psychopharmacologic agents. The vast array of effects of these drugs is reflected in the range of relevant neuroanatomical sites affected by these drugs. The specific loci of action reveal information about the underlying mechanisms of drug action and also reveal information about the anatomical substrates of specific psychological and behavioral responses. Brain regions that are relevant to the present discussion include the reticular activating system (for arousal and consciousness), pons and medulla (for autonomic control), cerebellum (for motor function and locomotion), pituitary (for hormonal regulation), hypothalamus (for body weight and hunger regulation), amygdala (for aggression), limbic system (for emotions and mood), hippocampus (for memory and learning), ventral tegmental area and nucleus accumbens (for reward), occipital lobe (for vision), parietal lobe (for somatosensory perception), temporal lobe (for audition), and the cortex (for higher cognitive and sensory-motor processing). Increasingly, psychopharmacologists are investigating neuroanatomical structures and loci via electrophysiological (e.g., single cell recording), surgical (e.g., ablation), and pharmacological (e.g., specific agonists and antagonists, radioactively labeled drugs) techniques in conjunction with functional assessment of drug effects. This work can be done on a molecular and cytoarchitectural level in animal subjects. Developments in receptor biology, structure and function, allow for detailed analyses of the cellular bases for psychopharmacologic drug actions. In addition, brain imaging techniques (including positron emission tomography [PET], magnetic resonance imaging [MRI], computed tomography [CT], single photon emission computed tomography [SPECT], and magnetoencephalography [MEG]) allow for the examination of structural and functional information relevant to psychopharmacologic agents in humans.

B. Neurophysiology and Electrophysiology

The function and actions of neurons, nerves, neural tracts, and neural tissue can be evaluated by invasive and noninvasive techniques and are included in psychopharmacologic investigations. In animal subjects, current technology allows for single cell recording of electrical activity relevant to neurophysiologic function. Action potentials, excitatory postsynaptic potentials (EPSPs), inhibitory postsynaptic potentials (IPSPs), long-term potentiation (LTP), and kindling all are studied in response to psychopharmacologic agents. Sensory and motor nerve recording, in animal subjects and in human patients, also provide useful information in this context. Electromyography (EMG) can be used in human patients to evaluate muscular responses, for example, to muscle relaxants and in cases of anxiety and pain. Electrocardiography (ECG or EKG) is used to assess heart function and is relevant in the present context to evaluate side effects of psychopharmacologic agents, as an index of stress responses, and to evaluate effects of psychopharmacologic drugs that may be revealed in cardiovascular arousal (e.g., anxiety, general arousal). Electroencephalography (EEG) is a noninvasive technique used to evaluate electrophysiologic activity of the brain. Detailed analyses of this information (e.g., contingent negative variation [CNV], auditory evoked potentials [AEP], visual evoked potentials [VEP], somatosensory evoked potentials [SEP], and positive or negative deflections in these responses) reveal the relay of information through specific brain regions and, thereby, can be used to evaluate the actions and to suggest mechanisms of psychopharmacologic agents.

C. Neurochemistry

The chemical bases of communication among neurons and the chemical regulation or modulation of this communication are affected by psychopharmacologic agents. These drugs can alter all of the known chemical neurotransmitters, including: amino acid transmitters (e.g., γ-amino-butyric acid [GABA], glycine, taurine, beta-alanine, glutamate, aspartate, cysteic acid), acetylcholine, catecholamines (e.g., norepinephrine, epinephrine, dopamine), indoleamines (e.g., serotonin), histamine, and neuroactive peptides (e.g., pro-opiomelanocortin [POMC], β-endorphin, leu-cine-enkephalin, methionine-enkephalin, dynorphin, neuropeptide-Y). Psychopharmacologic agents also can alter neuromodulators and chemicals that affect body functions, including: adrenocorticotrophin hormone (ACTH), corticotropin releasing factor (CRF), corticosteroids, and many peptides (e.g., Substance P, galanin, cholecystokinin [CCK], neurotensin, vasopressin, antidiuretic hormone [ADH], thyrotropin releasing hormone [TRH]). In addition to these relatively large molecules, psychopharmacologic agents can affect chemical ions (charged particles, such as Na^+, Ca^{++}, K^+, Mg^{++}, Cl^-) that alter neuronal transmission. Further, psychopharmacologic agents can affect second messengers (e.g., cyclic adenosine monophosphate [cAMP], guanine diphosphate [GDP], nerve growth factor [NGF]) and G-proteins that act to modulate neuronal communication. Genes with altered expression after drug exposure also are under investigation. Evaluations of these actions are active topics of research.

III. CLINICAL PSYCHOPHARMACOLOGY

Psychopharmacologically active agents (e.g., alcohol, opium) have been used for millennia to alter psychological state. Over the past 200 years, specific gases and chemicals have been identified (e.g., nitrous oxide, barbituric acid) that also alter consciousness and psychological state. It was not until the 1950s, however, that use of drugs to treat mental disorders and conditions became formalized and a focus of research and clinical attention. The dramatic reports in the early 1950s of chlorpromazine (Thorazine) to treat psychoses was a breakthrough that allowed previously uncontrollable patients to be cared for in a humane manner. This important development proved to be the genesis of clinical psychopharmacology as a central element in modern psychiatry and as a valuable adjunct to psychotherapy. No single pharmacological class is the panacea for the treatment of mental disorders. In fact, the identification and distinction among mental health disorders continues to be accompanied by the development of many different psychopharmacological agents that either treat the mental health condition or the symptoms associated with the condition. This section addresses the available psychopharmacologic treatments of the major categorizations of mental health disorders presented by the *Diagnostic and Statistical Manual of Mental Disorders* (Fourth Edition; *DSM-IV*) of the American Psychiatric Association and of other important psychological conditions. [*See* DSM-IV.]

A. Anxiety Disorders

Psychopharmacologic treatment of anxiety disorders began with the use of sedative-hypnotics (e.g., bromide salts, alcohol, chlorol hydrate) at the turn of the twentieth century. Barbiturates (e.g., phenobarbital, pentobarbital) were introduced early in the twentieth century but their adverse side effects, including addiction liability and toxic overdose, limited the use of these agents. The development of the benzodiazepines (e.g., chlordiazepoxide, diazepam) in the 1960s as general anxiolytics (separate from the muscle relaxant properties) was a major breakthrough because of the wide effective dose range and the limited adverse side effects. Subsequently, beta-adrenergic receptor antagonists (e.g., propranolol), antihistamines (e.g., hydroxyzine), and anticholinergic agents were used to treat specific cases of anxiety disorders (e.g., speech anxiety, posttraumatic stress disorder [PTSD]). More recently, azapirones (e.g., buspirone) that act via serotonergic antagonism and some dopaminergic antagonism have proven useful for mild forms of generalized anxiety. In the late 1980s, selective serotonin reuptake inhibitors (SSRIs) (e.g., fluoxetine [Prozac], sertraline [Zoloft], paraxetine [Paxil]) were introduced and, in the 1990s, were approved for treatment of specific anxiety disorders (e.g., panic, agoraphobia, PTSD). In addition, tricyclic drugs (e.g., clomipramine, imipramine, amitriptyline) and monoamine oxidase inhibitors (MAOIs) (e.g., phenelzine, tranylcypromine) are used in the treatment of some anxiety disorders (e.g., panic, agoraphobia, PTSD). [*See* Anxiety.]

B. Eating Disorders

Eating disorders usually are characterized by a morbid fear of becoming fat and a preoccupation with body weight, food, and body image. Eating disorders include anorexia nervosa (restricting type and eating/purging type) and bulimia nervosa (purging and nonpurging type) and occur more commonly among females than among males. Anorexia nervosa is associated with a 5 to 18% premature mortality rate. In addition, these individuals are at risk for comorbid depression, mood disorders, and an increased risk of physical health problems as a result of poor nutrition. Given the serious implications of this illness, hospitalization can become necessary in an effort to restore the patient's nutritional status, electrolyte balance, and hydration. Unfortunately, no psychopharmacologic agent or class of agents cures the primary symptoms of anorexia nervosa. Various drugs are used to treat secondary symptoms associated with these eating disorders. For example, amitriptyline (i.e., the tricyclic antidepressant Elavil) has been used effectively in some patients with this disorder, and cyproheptadine, a drug with antiserotonergic and antihistaminic effects, is effective with some restrictive-type anorexia patients. Some studies suggest that fluoxetine (i.e., an SSRI) administration may result in weight gain, but most studies indicate that antidepressants provide little benefit to these patients. There are risks (e.g., hypotension, cardiac arrhythmias, dehydration) associated with the use of tricyclic antidepressants in these patients and, therefore, it is not recommended that they be used. There are no data on the use of other SSRIs in patients with anorexia nervosa. MAOIs (phenelzine or tranylcypromine) may be useful, but few data are available to establish their value unequivocally. Antidepressant medications seem to be particularly useful with bulimic patients. Imipramine, desipramine, trazodone, fluoxetine, and MAOIs have been successful in treating binge–purge cycles. Antidepressants are effective when used in dosages suggested for the treatment of depressive disorders. However, higher dosages of fluoxetine usually are needed to alleviate binge episodes than those dosages suggested for treating depression. Carbamazepine and lithium are useful in bulimic patients with comorbid mood disorders but are not useful in treating binge episodes alone. Bupropion is contraindicated in patients with a history of anorexia nervosa and bulimia nervosa because it may result in seizures. [*See* Anorexia Nervosa and Bulimia Nervosa.]

Although not usually defined as classical eating disorders, there certainly are many cases of overeating that lead to obesity and excessive body weight. Some people overeat in response to psychological or environmental conditions; others are night-eaters (i.e., they get up and eat excessively after they have gone to bed); and others eat to the point of obesity and excessive body weight as a result of biological variables. Appetite suppressant medications (e.g., dexfenfluramine, diethylpropion, fenfluramine, mazindol, phendimetrazine, phentermine) are useful for some people but the effects are modest. Other appetite suppressant medications (e.g., amphetamines) are not recommended for use because they are addictive. Various antidepressants are used in some cases of overeating. [See OBESITY.]

C. Learning, Memory, Attention, and Related Cognitive Disorders

There is a wide variety of cognitive conditions that deleteriously affect learning, memory, and attention but that do not involve other psychopathology. For example, Attentional Deficit Disorder with and without hyperactivity (ADHD and ADD), senile dementia, and Alzheimer's disease are familiar to the public. Each of these conditions can have profound negative effects on daily living and quality of life. Psychopharmacologic treatment for these conditions is an active, current topic of interest with modest success to date. For example, ADHD is treated with stimulants (including dextroamphetamine, methylphenidate [Ritalin], and pemoline), antidepressants (including imipramine, desipramine, and nortriptyline), and clonidine. Memory deficit-related conditions are an area of great interest and experimental investigations are examining various medications, including drugs that act as: dopaminergic agonists, α-2 adrenergic agonists, cholinergic agonists, general cerebral metabolic enhancers, calcium channel blockers, and serotonergic agents. [See ALZHEIMER'S DISEASE; ATTENTION DEFICIT HYPERACTIVITY DISORDER (ADHD); DEMENTIA.]

D. Mood Disorders

Mood disorders are manifested as either depressive or manic episodes. Among the most serious of the mood disorders are major depressive disorder or unipolar depression, in which a patient only experiences depressive episodes, and bipolar disorder, in which a patient experiences both manic and depressive episodes or only manic episodes. The history and current use of pharmacological agents to treat these separate mood disorders differ. With regard to unipolar depression, amphetamines were first used in the late 1930s. In the 1950s, the tricyclic and tetracyclic antidepressants (TCAs) (e.g., imipramine, amoxapine) and MAOIs

(e.g., phenelzine) were serendipitously discovered to elevate depressive moods. These prototypal compounds, however, affect many systems indiscriminately, have a slow action of onset, and produce numerous unwanted side effects that deter patient compliance. The largest new drug class of antidepressants includes SSRIs (e.g., fluoxetine). In general, the SSRIs are no more effective than TCAs but cause limited and more tolerated side effects and have a reduced risk of overdose. Two new antidepressants, with pharmacologic actions and side effects profiles that differ from those of SSRIs, are nefazodone and venlafaxine which inhibit serotonin reuptake and also either exhibit $5\text{-HT}_{2A}/5\text{-HT}_{2C}$ antagonism or inhibit the reuptake of norepinephrine, respectively. Other nonuptake-inhibiting serotonergic drugs that increase serotonin release and function through partial agonism of the 5-HT_{1A} (e.g., buspirone) and 5-HT_{2C} (e.g., *m*-chlorophenylpiperazine) receptors are being investigated. Manipulation of the serotonergic system is the most common, current approach in antidepressant drug therapy, but new selective and reversible MAO-A inhibitors (e.g., moclobemide) are being tested and have been reported as effective to treat unipolar and bipolar patients with no anticholinergic or cardiovascular side effects and minimal dietary restrictions. With regard to bipolar disorder, lithium remains the major pharmacological treatment since its discovery as a calming agent in 1949. Only 60 to 80% of bipolar patients, however, respond to lithium treatment alone. Patients who do not respond to lithium are often given antidepressants in combination with antipsychotics despite the higher risk of developing tardive dyskinesia. Over the past few years, a variety of other drugs, including anticonvulsants (e.g., carbamazepine) and calcium channel blockers (e.g., verapamil), have been used to treat bipolar disorder. Mania also can be treated with benzodiazepines, anticonvulsants, antipsychotics, or calcium channel blockers. In most cases of bipolar disorders, patients receive a combined pharmacotherapeutic treatment during the course of their illness. [See DEPRESSION; MOOD DISORDERS.]

E. Pain

Pain is the unpleasant psychological experience associated with actual or potential tissue damage. Pain may be acute, periodic, or continuous; sharp, dull/aching, or burning; annoying, uncomfortable, or unbearable. Pain occurs in response to readily identifiable accidents, injury, or medical treatments (e.g., surgery); to ambiguous or mixed causes (e.g., weather conditions, disturbed sleep, work environment); and to unknown immediate causes (e.g., undiagnosed pathology, forgotten injury). Pain is treated by a variety of pharmacologic agents including: opiates (e.g., morphine, meperidine, fentanyl, codeine), nonsteroidal anti-inflammatory agents (e.g., salicylic acid derivatives such as aspirin; para-aminophenol derivatives such as acetaminophen; indole and indene acetic acids such as indomethacin) and drugs that are selectively used to treat specific pain-related disorders (e.g., the 5-HT_{1D} agonist, sumatriptan, to treat migraine headaches). With regard to pain of known cause, pharmacologic treatments are relatively effective for the vast majority of people. With regard to pain of ambiguous or unknown origin and with regard to continuous pain, pharmacologic treatments have mixed results. For example, opiate medications alter how chronic pain patients perceive and cope with pain but do not completely alleviate the pain.

Unfortunately, currently available analgesics have many undesirable side effects including sedation, respiratory depression, gastrointestinal upset or constipation, pruritus, and addiction. Ongoing investigations are attempting to develop analgesic medications with greater efficacy and few side effects. [See PAIN.]

F. Psychoses

Psychotic disorders are characterized by delusions, hallucinations, disorganized speech, or disorganized or catatonic behavior. The major psychotic disorders include schizophrenia, schizophreniform disorder, schizoaffective disorder, or delusional disorder. The most widely prescribed antipsychotic drugs are referred to as neuroleptics. The major antipsychotics are: tricyclic phenothiazines, thioxanthenes, dibenzepines, butyrophenones, benzamides, clozapines, and risperidone. Most drugs of these types block D2 dopaminergic receptors and inactivate dopamine neurotransmitters in the forebrain. Some of these medications also affect D1 dopaminergic, 5-HT_2 serotonergic, and α-adrenergic receptors. Unfortunately, none of these medications cures psychoses, each one helps only some patients, and there are deleterious side effects, including: akathisia, rigidity, tremors, and other neuromuscular effects. In addition to these major drugs, lithium, anticonvulsants, and benzodiazepines are prescribed. [See SCHIZOPHRENIA.]

G. Sexual Dysfunction

DSM-IV distinguishes among sexual dysfunctions as: Sexual Desire Disorder, Sexual Arousal Disorder, Orgasmic Disorder, Sexual Pain Disorders, Sexual Dysfunction Due to a General Medical Condition, Substance-Induced Sexual Dysfunction, and Sexual Dysfunction Not Otherwise Specified. These conditions are different from Paraphilias (e.g., intense sexual urges to unusual objects, Exhibitionism, Voyeurism). Psychopharmacology has played a relatively small role in the treatment of these conditions but that role is increasing. Antianxiety agents and antidepressants are helpful in some patients. Other medications (e.g., methohexital sodium) have been used in conjunction with desensitization therapy. Sex hormones (e.g., estrogen, testosterone) have been used in specific cases. With changes in societal attitudes to the discussion of these types of problems also may come increased attention to the development and study of treatment for these conditions. [See SEXUAL DYSFUNCTION THERAPY.]

H. Sleep Disorders

Humans spend one-quarter to one-third of their lives sleeping and roughly one-third of all adults experience some type of sleep disorder during their lives. Sleep disorders are categorized by the DSM-IV as: Primary Sleep Disorders (including Dyssomnias and Parasomnias), Sleep Disorder Related to Another Mental Disorder, Sleep Disorder Due to a General Medical Condition, and Substance-Induced Sleep Disorder. The most common Sleep Disorder is Insomnia, but other Dyssomnias include: Hypersomnia, Narcolepsy, Breathing-Related Sleep Disorder, and Circadian Rhythm Sleep Disorder. Parasomnias include: Nightmare Disorder, Sleep Terror Disorder, and Sleepwalking Disorder. Primary Insomnia is treated with benzodiazepines or sedative-hypnotics. Primary Hypersomnia is treated with stimulants, such as amphetamines, or SSRIs. Narcolepsy is treated with stimulants, antidepressants, and sometimes with α_1 agonists. Benzodiazepines and other antianxiety medications are used selectively to treat other sleep disorders. [See SLEEP.]

I. Substance-Related Disorders

In the *DSM-IV*, Substance-Related Disorders include taking drugs of abuse, side effects of medication, and toxic exposure. Substance-Related Disorders are categorized as Substance Use Disorders (Substance Dependence and Substance Abuse) or as Substance-Induced Disorders (Substance Intoxication, Substance Withdrawal, any Substance-Induced adverse psychological or behavioral effect). A wide variety of psychopharmacologic agents are used in conjunction with psychological approaches to treat the varied aspects of Substance-Related Disorders. This section provides a brief synopsis of this expansive aspect of psychopharmacology. [*See* SUBSTANCE ABUSE.]

Alcohol and nicotine (e.g., in cigarettes, cigars, and other tobacco products) are the most commonly used and abused substances in our culture. Other drugs also are used recreationally and have deleterious effects. Psychopharmacologic treatments can be used to discourage drug use, to decrease withdrawal symptoms, or to treat comorbid psychological conditions. The major Substance-Related Disorders and their Treatments are:

1. Alcohol-Related Disorders

Psychopharmacologic agents used for the treatment of alcohol abuse include disulfiram (i.e., Antabuse). When ingested, disulfiram inhibits the enzyme aldehyde dehydrogenase so that consumption of alcohol results in a toxic reaction to the accumulation of acetaldehyde in the blood. Consumption of alcohol while taking disulfiram leads to flushing, feelings of heat and numbness in the limbs and upper chest, nausea, dizziness, malaise, blurred vision, air hunger, and palpitations. Psychotropic medications that are used to treat anxiety and depressive symptoms in these patients are useful. Recently, these drugs and SSRIs have been used to control craving for alcohol. Specifically, trazodone, serotonin type 3 (5HT$_3$) antagonists, and dopaminergic agonists (e.g., apomorphine, bromocriptine) may be effective in decreasing cravings. Naltrexone, an opioid antagonist, also has shown promise as a possible treatment for alcohol dependence. Benzodiazepines are the primary medications for controlling alcohol withdrawal symptoms (seizures, delirium, anxiety, tachycardia, hypertension). Carbamazepine, β-adrenergic receptor antago-

nists, and clonidine also have been used to treat sympathetic activity associated with alcohol withdrawal. However, these drugs are not effective in the treatment of seizures or delirium. [*See* ALCOHOL PROBLEMS.]

2. Amphetamine-Related Disorders

The pharmacologic treatment for amphetamine-induced psychotic disorder and amphetamine-induced anxiety disorder is usually antipsychotics (phenothiazine, haloperidol) and anxiolytics (diazepam), respectively, on a short-term basis. Chronic lithium treatment to attenuate the euphoria associated with amphetamine use, thereby decreasing the likelihood of continued use, is not recommended.

3. Caffeine-Related Disorders

Analgesics such as aspirin, ibuprofen, and acetaminophen usually are sufficient for treating headaches and muscle aches associated with caffeine withdrawal. Benzodiazepines rarely are needed and should only be prescribed for a short period of time (less than 7 days).

4. Cannabis-Related Disorders

Psychopharmacologic treatment for these disorders is less clear, but some patients may respond to anxiolytics for the treatment of withdrawal symptoms. In addition, antidepressants may be useful in treating any underlying depressive disorder associated with cannabis abuse.

5. Cocaine-Related Disorders

Several pharmacologic agents have been used to decrease cocaine craving in cocaine abusers. Dopaminergic agonists, amantadine and bromocriptine, and TCAs such as desipramine and imipramine seem to decrease drug cravings, increase energy, and improve sleep. Carbamazepine also decreases cravings, but not in patients with antisocial personality disorder.

6. Hallucinogen-Related Disorders

Pharmacologic agents such as dopaminergic antagonists are often used to treat psychotic symptoms associated with withdrawal and benzodiazepines can be used to treat anxiety symptoms on a short-term basis.

7. Inhalant-Related Disorders

There are no prescribed methods of psychopharmacologic treatments for these disorders.

8. Nicotine-Related Disorders

Administration of nicotine through a transdermal patch is a useful approach to help individuals quit smoking because it curbs withdrawal symptoms associated with nicotine cessation (e.g., hunger, irritability, inattention). Nicotine also can be administered via chewing gum or in a nasal spray. Clonidine and antidepressants (fluoxetine and buspirone in particular) have been used to help some people who abstain from tobacco use. [*See* SMOKING.]

9. Opioid-Related Disorders

Methadone, a synthetic opioid agonist that is administered orally, is used as a substitute for heroin to help the patient move away from injectable opiates, maintain a steady job, and reintegrate into a daily lifestyle that is not associated with drug-taking. Levo-α-acetylmethadol (LAMM) is a longer acting opioid agonist that is similar to methadone and only needs to be administered about three times a week. Buprenorphine is a mixed opioid agonist-antagonist that has shown promise as an opioid substitute in the treatment of opioid addiction. Naltrexone can be used to block the pharmacologic actions of opioids, including the subjective high, and, possibly the subsequent drug craving and physical dependence. Clonidine is administered during the initial stages of opiate withdrawal and naltrexone is administered to treat opioid overdose.

10. Phencyclidine (or Phencyclidine-like)-Related Disorders

Benzodiazepines and dopamine receptor antagonists (haloperidol) are used for controlling behavioral disorders associated with phencyclidine intoxication.

11. Sedative-, Hypnotic-, or Anxiolytic-Related Disorders

Carbamazepine may be useful in the treatment of benzodiazepine withdrawal. The treatment for barbiturate abuse is far more complicated than benzodiazepine withdrawal because sudden death can occur during withdrawal. It is recommended that phenobarbital be substituted in the withdrawal procedure and the dosages gradually decreased over a long period of time. Once complete withdrawal has occurred, non-barbiturate sedative-hypnotics should be used as a substitute for the barbiturate. However, this substitution typically translates the drug dependence to a new substance and does not cure the addiction.

IV. SPECIAL POPULATIONS

A. Pediatric

Age influences pharmacokinetic and pharmacodynamic responses. With regard to psychopharmacology, it is generally assumed that children are small adults and, therefore, adjustments in psychopharmacologic treatments simply need to be made based on body weight. This assumption, however, may be wrong. There are rapid, age-related biological and psychological changes that begin in the newborn and continue throughout childhood and adolescence. These changes demand a psychopharmacologic treatment approach that differs from adults and is sensitive to developmental stages, both physical and psychological. As of now, our understanding of pediatric psychopharmacology is limited and many important investigations of drug actions across developmental periods have yet to be conducted.

B. Geriatric

Aging is a highly individualized process that results in various changes over time that can alter significantly the actions of psychotropic medications in the body and how the body affects the drugs. In elderly patients there are changes in: organ system function, drug distribution, drug action, drug metabolism, and drug elimination. In addition, cumulative drug actions are common among elderly persons who take many prescription medications, over-the-counter medications, and other substances (e.g., alcohol, nicotine, caffeine). Psychopharmacologic treatments in the elderly require coordinated, integrated medical care that captures a complete picture of functioning within each individual. Quality of life in elderly patients can be greatly improved and prolonged by thoughtful use of medications and medical interventions. However, there are several obstacles to compliance that the prescriber should consider, including the expense of medications and treatment, the forgetfulness of some patients, and the deliberate choice by a patient not to take a particular treatment. The same sets of medical advances that offer improved quality of life for some, may represent threats to autonomy if thoughtfulness is not included in the clinical decision-making for each patient. [*See* AGING AND MENTAL HEALTH.]

C. Individual Differences

Besides age, many factors can influence interindividual variability in drug responsivity, susceptibility to negative side effects, and potential drug abuse liability. These factors include biological (e.g, genetics, gender, ethnicity, disease state), environmental (e.g., stress, culture), and behavioral (e.g., diet, drug use, drug history) influences as well as the interactions of any two or more of these variables. The mechanisms by which these variables influence the actions of drugs can be molecular, biological, pharmacokinetic, pharmacodynamic, psychological, or social in nature. The identification of individual difference variables and their contribution to drug action are relevant to the clinical administration of medications as well as to our understanding of the mechanisms underlying drug addiction. [*See* INDIVIDUAL DIFFERENCES IN MENTAL HEALTH.]

BIBLIOGRAPHY

American Psychiatric Association. (1994). *Diagnostic and Statistical Manual of Mental Disorders* (4th ed.). Washington, DC: Author.

Bloom, F.E., & Kupfer, D.J. (Eds.). (1995). *Psychopharmacology: The fourth generation of progress.* New York: Raven Press.

Cooper, J.R., Bloom, F.E., & Roth, R.H. (1996). *The biochemical basis of neuropharmacology* (7th ed.). New York: Oxford University Press.

Hardman, J.G., Limbird, L.E., Molinoff, P.B., Ruddon, R.W., & Gilman, A.G. (Eds.). (1996). *Goodman & Gilman's The pharmacological basis of therapeutics* (9th ed.). New York: McGraw-Hill, Inc.

Julien, R.M. (1988). *A Primer of Drug Action* (5th ed.). New York: W.H. Freeman and Company.

Kaplan, H.I., Sadock, B.J., & Grebb, J.A. (1994). *Kaplan and Sadock's synopsis of psychiatry: Behavioral sciences, clinical psychiatry* (7th ed.). Baltimore, MD: Williams & Wilkins.

Katzung, B.K. (Ed.). (1992). *Basic & clinical pharmacology* (5th ed.). Norwalk, CT: Appleton & Lange.

Melmon, K.L., Morrelli, H.F., Hoffman, B.B., & Nierenberg, D.W. (Eds.). (1992). *Melmon and Morrelli's clinical pharmacology: Basic principles in therapeutics* (3rd ed.). New York: McGraw-Hill, Inc.

Pirodsky, D.M., & Cohn, J.S. (1992). *Clinical primer of psychopharmacology: A practical guide* (2nd ed.). New York: McGraw-Hill, Inc.

R

Racism and Mental Health

Carolyn B. Murray

University of California, Riverside

Cultural Awareness An understanding of the worldview of a culturally different client.

Cultural Sensitivity A respect and appreciation for the worldview of a culturally different client.

Culturally Skilled Professional A mental health practitioner who is self-aware, culturally aware, and culturally sensitive.

Culture Everything man has made.

Definitional Power The ability to act or produce the effect of describing, explaining or determining the meaning of a phenomenon.

Etiology The causes of abnormal behavior.

Nondominant Ethnic Groups Minority groups who lack power.

Racism Results from the transformation of race prejudice and/or ethnocentrism through the exercise of power against a racial group defined as inferior, by individuals and institutions with the intentional or unintentional support of the entire culture.

Self-Awareness A person who is knowledgeable about his or her own behavior, values, biases, preconceived notions, personal limitations, and so on.

Worldview The particular set of assumptions that we rely upon to give structure to our reality.

RACISM should be distinguished from the related concepts of prejudice and discrimination. *Prejudice* is a type of attitude; generally negative toward the mem-

bers of some social group; *discrimination* refers to unfair or unjust actions toward those individuals. Racism refers to more than attitudes and behaviors of individuals; it is the institutionalization form of that attitude. This article discusses the impact of racism on mental health. It begins with a general discussion of the debilitating psychological effects that centuries of American racism has had on people of color, narrows to how racism within the mental health profession has often led to the revictimization of people of color within the therapeutic environment, and ends with a discussion of strategies for reducing racism in mental health practice.

I. INTRODUCTION

A comprehensive meaning of racism encompasses both individual attitudes and behaviors, and includes concepts of power, stratification, and oppression. Specifically, racism is an energizing cultural force that bestows identity to societal members by organizing expectations on the basis of the assumed biological principle of race. The organization of such expectations gives rise to a social system that distributes rewards unequally to the various races and that protects the idea of White supremacy through the use of propaganda, force, and intimidation. Racism is consciously and unconsciously enforced and maintained by legal, cultural, religious, educational, economic, political, environmental, and military institutions. Manifestations of racism are both overt (e.g., physical attacks, segregation) and covert (e.g., tokenism, school curricula). While racism is obviously injurious to the mental health of its victims, it is also debilitating to the victimizers.

Racism in the United States has been and is both systematic and cumulative. Particular instances of racial or ethnic discrimination may seem minor to an observer, but the effects of subtle and covert slights such as sabotage (e.g., allowing an African American student to do inadequate schoolwork without the proper feedback or evaluation) are magnified when they occur in contexts that include more blatant actions such as verbal harassment or physical attack. The cumulative impact of discrimination over months, years, and lifetimes is usually far more than the sum of individual instances.

A. Racism and Its Mental Health Consequences: A Historical Overview

The link between racism and mental health has a long history; the foundation for patterns of racial conflict and racism were in fact established with the arrival of Europeans on the American continent. Native Americans, African Americans, Asian Americans and Mexican Americans have all experienced racism in their encounters with Europeans. Other groups (e.g., Italians, Jews, Poles, Irish and others) have been discriminated against and economically exploited, but members of these groups were assimilated due to their similar physical characteristics. Members of these groups have also internalized racist ideologies and practices toward people of color.

1. Native Americans
As the celebration of the 500th anniversary of Columbus' 1492 voyage to the Americas began Native American groups across the nation held protests. These protests were termed "a commemoration of centuries of racism in the Americas." Native Americans pointed out that Columbus' voyage had meant "500 years of genocide" for their people, despite the fact that the Europeans had been initially welcomed and were even aided by the native population. The early Europeans found it necessary, in order to exploit the Native American, to characterize the Indian as a "savage" in need of "civilization." Concomitant with such characterization was a series of dehumanizing actions and deceptive treaties that enabled the settlers to steal Native American land and thus destroy their means of livelihood.

Although somewhat more subtle, racism against Native Americans is still the rule rather than the exception. White racism today exists in the form of a backlash against land and fishing claims. Less subtle racism exists in the form of a documented increase in harassment and violence, and other practices that aid in the destruction of their culture under the guise of assimilating them.

The mental health consequences of this racist treatment are overwhelming. The most obvious is an exorbitant substance abuse problem. In some surveys, up to 70% of Indian adolescents use alcohol and drugs. Mental health literature indicates that social drinking may be a mechanism to release frustration and boredom, allowing Native Americans to express emotions that are normally under control. In addition, drinking may serve as a social event, which is why it is actually encouraged in many tribal groups. It is important to note that such substance abuse is not an indigenous trait; alcoholism was unknown in Native American society until the arrival of the European.

2. African Americans
From the very beginning of European conquest, Africans were part of the American experience. Some came as explorers with Columbus, but most were brought to America as slaves, unlike other immigrants who came voluntarily. The oppression faced by the enslaved African Americans, thus, differed dramatically from the discrimination found by White immigrants (e.g., Italians) who came later. Enslaved Africans experienced an almost total loss of their languages, cultures, kinship bonds, religion, and family functions. Literally, tens of millions were murdered during the 300 years of the slave trade. Moreover, inhuman treatment of African Americans was rationalized by distorting religious doctrine (e.g., the use of Cain's mark to conclude that the Black race was cursed by God), political ideology (e.g., "White man's burden"), and "pseudo" ideological treatises (e.g., "Social Darwinism"). Even after their emancipation from slavery African Americans were exploited under the systems of sharecropping, education, and commerce. In addition, while the Supreme Court institutionalized "separate but equal" thousands were lynched and often castrated. Even though they were citizens, African Americans were disenfranchised and considered to possess *no* rights that White men had to respect.

During the 1960s and 1970s African Americans made some measurable economic and social progress, but many of these gains were eroded with a later upsurge of racism in the 1980s and 1990s. The situation is even more disturbing in light of the recent dismantling of civil rights legislation by the U.S. Supreme Court and state voter referendums (e.g., California's Proposition 209). Negative portraits of African Americans in the mass media (e.g., coverage of the O. J. Simpson trial) continues to add to an exploitive situation. Moreover, conservative think tanks, aided by the mass media (e.g., Herrnstein & Murray's *The Bell Curve*) have carried out extensive campaigns to eliminate policies (e.g., affirmative action laws) and programs that facilitate upward mobility (e.g., Headstart).

While racism is not the only cause of problems experienced by African American people, it does put an added burden on the psychological adaptation by presenting direct assaults (e.g., police brutality) and indirect assaults (e.g., unemployment). However, the literature investigating the incidence of mental disorders among African Americans is contradictory. Some studies have found that African Americans have more mental disorders than Whites; others report the opposite finding. In either case, a pejorative inference is drawn. In the former instance African Americans are seen as having inferior ego strength; in the latter, African Americans are seen as being too intellectually deficient to appreciate and be affected by the stresses of life in a technological society. A number of studies have suggested that along with anger and rage, a widespread feeling of sadness (i.e., a kind of cultural depression) is a part of the African American's response to historical and current conditions in America. Also, the rising tide of drug addiction, hypertension, homicide, and alcoholism are mental health issues that often mask depression and hopelessness.

3. Mexican Americans

The Latino population in America is a heterogeneous group that differs in its histories and in cultural forms (e.g., in food, religious shrines, and music). Given this diversity, the focus of this review will be on Mexican Americans who constitute two-thirds of the U.S. Latino population.

In the early 1500s, Spanish invaders conquered, colonized, and sought to Catholicize the native population in what is now Mexico and the southwestern United States. Since few women migrated to the Americas, sexual liaisons (often forced) between Spanish men and indigenous women were common, resulting in today's *mestizos* (mixed peoples). After centuries of colonial domination, Mexico finally won its independence from Spain in 1821. Due to the resentment of White slave holders toward Mexican antislavery laws, and the growing number of illegal U.S. immigrants coming from the north, the United States and Mexico went to war. As a result, the Mexican government was forced to cede the Southwest in 1848. Mexican residents had the choice of remaining or moving South; most stayed, assured on paper of protection of their legal rights, and their language and cultural heritage by Article IX of the Treaty of Guadalupe Hidalgo.

With the discovery of gold in California, Whites poured into the region using any means necessary (e.g., lynching, armed theft, and/or legal action) to wrest control over the lands and politics of the region. In spite of treaty promises, grants were ignored and the land was treated as U.S. government property and given or sold cheaply to Whites. Since that time, Mexican Americans and Mexican immigrants have been exploited for their labor. They have suffered racial stereotyping (e.g., unintelligent, violent, etc.) similar to that of other people of color, and are still discriminated against in economics, education, and politics.

Epidemiological studies conducted before 1980 found a lower prevalence of psychiatric disorder among Mexican Americans as compared with the general population. More recent surveys, however, suggest that the prevalence of psychological distress among Mexican Americans is at least as high as the overall population and, in some instances, higher. However, it is doubtful that Mexican Americans seek mental health services at a rate commensurate with their actual prevalence of psychological disturbance.

Many of the existing studies are confined to small ethnic enclaves. Some report that Mexican American farm workers have symptom levels resembling those of other low-income social economic groups, such as southern African Americans. It is generally acknowledged that Mexican American farm workers experience psychiatric symptom levels that place them at extraordinary risk because of limited social mobility, poverty, and racial discrimination. In addition, alcoholism, drug use, and juvenile delinquency have been on the increase.

4. Asian Americans

In contrast to the other three groups, the contemporary image of Asian Americans is that of a highly successful *nondominant* ethnic group ("the model minority"). A closer analysis of the status of Asian Americans, however, does not completely support this success story.

The differences among the Asian American population should be noted. Asians consist of at least 29 distinct subgroups that differ in language, religion, and values. Compounding the difficulty in making any generalizations about the Asian American population are within group differences. Individual Asian Americans differ with respect to variables such as country of origin, English language proficiency, education, family structure, and religiosity. Despite these differences Asian Americans have, historically, experienced the same type of discrimination suffered by African Americans and Latinos: they have been exploited by U.S. employers, denied property and citizenship rights, assaulted, murdered, and (during World War II) placed in "internment" camps. In addition, the immigration Act of 1924 was used to exclude Asian immigrants, who were seen by the Congress as racially inferior and a threat to the society. In sum, Asians in America have at one time or another been subjected to the most appalling forms of racism.

Today the image and the status of Asian Americans has drastically improved. Specifically, Chinese and Japanese exceed the national median income, and even Filipinos who, in 1968, were far below the nation's median income level, have now attained parity with Whites. However, increasing unemployment in the wake of the recessions of the 1980s and 90s has fueled a tendency among Whites to blame the Japanese for U.S. economic troubles. One consequence of this perception has been the introduction of anti-Japanese legislation (e.g., protectionist bills). Japanese executives and investors who recently arrived in the United States sometimes face racial discrimination. Moreover, a closer examination of the higher median income reveals it is partially due to a larger number of earners in Asian families. In addition, there considerable poverty despite the higher median income.

In spite of the historical and present racism experienced by Asian Americans, mental health statistics reinforce the belief that Asians in America are relatively well adjusted, function effectively in society, and experience few difficulties. Studies consistently report that Asian Americans have low official rates of juvenile delinquency, low rates of psychiatric contact and hospitalization and low rates of divorce. Indeed, there seems to be a prevalent belief that Asian Americans are somehow immune to the forces of prejudice and discrimination.

However, as pointed out by Sue and Sue in a 1991 book entitled *Counseling the Culturally Different*, apart from being tourist attractions, Asian communities in San Francisco and New York represent ghetto areas with high levels of unemployment, poverty, health problems, and juvenile delinquency. The Chinese community, for instance, has an extremely high tuberculosis rate and a suicide rate three times that of the national average. Over the years, numerous mass murders have occurred that are linked to Chinese juvenile gangs, and recent news report an increasing trend in criminal activities. Recent studies conducted on Asian immigrants in middle-size cities found evidence of unusual high levels of psychological anxiety even among professionals. Their seemingly "trouble free" status can be explained by the fact that there are few statistics on Asian Americans in the psychiatric epidemiological literature, which may be due to the fact that Asian Americans underutilize mental health services.

B. Racism's Impact on Whites

Racism's impact on mental health has been discussed predominantly in terms of its effects on people of color. Such an approach redirects efforts to eliminate racism to helping oppressed people tolerate it. Any comprehensive strategies for significantly reducing racist attitudes and behaviors in America must take into account the causes of racism among Whites, the benefits and costs to Whites, and the societal structures that facilitate and maintain it. By examining racism's impact on Whites we have a chance to alter the circumstances that lead to oppression.

Research has concluded that approximately a fifth of White Americans have strong personal and psychological motivation for their racist beliefs. The remaining 80% are believed to be prejudiced due to environmental, social, and cultural influences (such as those produced by mass media, educational, and family systems).

One of the oldest and most popular theories to explain racism is economic competition. This theory argues that it is reasonable to expect racism to *decrease* whenever labor is in short supply and to *in*crease under the competitive pressures of a labor surplus. Thus, the more prosperous the economy, the greater will be prosperity for the overwhelming majority of the people. Recent evidence indicates that racism *does not* benefit the masses of Whites economically as once believed. For example, labor market analyses report that increases in racial equality are correlated with higher earnings for low- and middle-income Whites (as well as for Blacks). In addition, an increase in racial equality is correlated with increased unionization. On the other hand, increases in racial equality is correlated with falling industrial profit rates. In sum, *de*creases in racial equality resulted in losses for low- and middle-class Whites, while the upper 1% of White incomes significantly increased.

These findings indicate that there are good reasons for Whites to eliminate racism, at least in the workplace. On the other hand, upper-class industrialists and management have historically and even today acted to maintain high profits and incomes by manipulating racial fears (e.g., status loss, job loss, housing value loss) of lower and middle-income Whites. In response, lower and middle-income Whites have rarely acted in their own best economic interest. Throughout history, politicians have used Blacks as scapegoats for failed economic or political policies. Before the Civil War, rich slave owners persuaded the White working class to stand with them against the danger of slave revolts—even though the existence of slavery relegated White workers to a life of economic privation.

By the 1890s, Black farmers and poor Whites, both exploited by Southern upper class Whites were forging a coalition—the Populist party—to deal with economic issues. White opponents to this new coalition resorted to their first line of defense—racism—using racial fears of poor Whites (e.g., intermarriage, Black domination, etc.) to destroy the movement. Today, millions of Americans—Whites as well as Blacks—face steadily worsening conditions: unemployment, mediocre education, inaccessible health care, and so on. The top fifth of Americans now earns more than the bottom four-fifths combined. But instead of White Americans voting to expand opportunity, they are willing to accept their often diminished status as long as they have priority over Blacks and other people of color for access to the few opportunities available. Such Whites vent their frustrations by opposing any serious programs that advance people of color. This explains their support for proposition 209 eliminating Affirmative Action. Thus, racism provides short-term differential status and material benefit to some White people, but the hierarchical social reward structure it has helped sustain has worked against the vast majority of working- and middle-class Whites.

There is very little information available concerning the impact of racism on the mental health of Whites. Almost all of what is available is speculative. Even so, the conclusions are that racism adversely affects the psychological well-being of Whites by (1) creating a false sense of supremacy; (2) creating feelings of racial insecurity; (3) distorting reality; (4) feeding or aggravating psychiatric disturbances; (5) promoting ignorance and disdain of other races and cultures; (6) creating ingroup behavioral habits that oppress outgroups; and (7) letting false fears control and limit their lives. Today, many Whites believe their way of life is being eroded due to the demands of people of color. These perceptions are increasingly stressful, thus, creating psychological discomfort in the form of anxiety and dread.

II. RACISM IN THERAPEUTIC INTERVENTION

It is estimated that there are more than a million mental health workers in the United States. Mental health professionals have been no less immune to possessing and expressing racism than other members of society. Estimates of the extent to which racism is an issue within the mental health profession has varied greatly from a fringe element to the core of the entire field. The evidence appears to support the latter.

To investigate the extent to which racism plays an important role in mental health, a 1995 review piece by Castellano B. Turner and Bernard M. Kramer, entitled "Connections Between Racism and Mental Health," pointed out that the following seven aspects of the profession must be considered: (1) the *definition* of mental health and illness; (2) the theories of the *etiology* of mental illness; (3) the *evaluation* process (assessment and diagnosis); (4) the provision of *direct services*; (5) the organizing and structuring of mental health *institutions and programs*; (6) the *research* carried out to understand the mental health problems of racial groups; and (7) the *training* of mental health professionals to provide direct service and organize intervention programs. Each of these aspects of the mental health profession will be discussed below in terms of the role that racism plays.

A. The Role of Racism in the Definitions of Mental Health

There are at least two major forms of power—physical power and definitional power. Definitional power is the ultimate form of power, because with definitional power physical power is not necessary. This is relevant to the present thesis in that dominant racial groups may construct definitions of mental illnesses that justify their "superiority" or the subjugation of "inferior" groups. For example, behavior that is common in the subjugated group may be defined as abnormal, and thus the members of the subjugated group will be considered abnormal. In comparison to the dominant group, both overdiagnosis and underdiagnosis of a mental disorder within the subjugated group is assumed to be a mental deficiency. The best well-known example in the United States is the theory that African slaves were *not* subject to depressive disorders. While genetics was the established explanation for this lower incidence of depression in African Americans, it was also argued that the living conditions of slaves—not having the pressures of making decisions—was a major contributor. This, of course, legitimized a dehumanizing, exploitive, oppressive system—slavery.

B. The Role of Racism in the Etiology of Mental Illness

Theories regarding the origins of mental illness range from those that are biological (e.g., genetic predisposition, biochemical imbalances, etc.) to those that are environmental factors (e.g., deplorable child rearing practices, stress, etc.). Racism plays a role in the etiology of mental illness to the extent to which epidemiological differences between racial groups are explained in terms of the genetic or cultural inferiority of the subjugated group. While it is not always the case that a genetic or cultural interpretation is racist, it is true that even the most severe forms of mental illness (e.g., schizophrenia and severe depression) occur in all racial groups. The variations that do exist are readily interpretable as emerging from environ-

mental stressors (e.g., poverty) and to a certain degree variations in the willingness of health professionals to label certain groups as suffering from a severe form of mental illness (e.g., schizophrenia). Generally, therapists are more reluctant to apply the label "schizophrenia" to higher income patients because it may have a damaging effect on their clients' future endeavors. [*See* SCHIZOPHRENIA.]

Not only does racism play a major role in explaining the origins of racial group mental health differences, it also has an enormous impact on explaining how mental illness is maintained. While the link between stress and mental illness is well accepted, mental health professionals and researchers have not been sufficiently concerned with the stress that racism produces in people of color. The lack of concern about the role of racism and mental health exists in theory, research, clinical practice, and in graduate education. Persons of color who are the victims of mental illness are blamed (e.g., genetic inferiority, culturally deficit), just as victims of racism are blamed (e.g., genetic inferiority, culturally deficit). Because much of the development of mental health problems is linked to stress, racism must be regarded as a major source of illness for African Americans, Asian Americans, Mexican Americans, and Native Americans. [*See* STRESS.]

C. The Role of Racism in the Evaluation of Mental Illness

Racism also plays an important role in the assessment and evaluation of mental disorders as our earlier discussion of definitional power implied. While assessment and evaluation are both necessary and invaluable for developing effective treatment strategies, such assessment instruments are hardly "value free" or more valid than subjective evaluation methods (e.g., clinical diagnosis). For people of color, psychological assessment instruments may be *no* more valid than the testers themselves. Indeed such measures may be more injurious because they are covered in the cloak of "objectivity." The impact of racism on psychological assessment and diagnosis has been a particular concern in African American and Latino communities.

One major issue is that standardized psychological assessment instruments were constructed on the basis of acceptance and use of a psychometric paradigm developed and applied in the United States and Western

Europe—primarily to and by White males. The tests are therefore *culture*-specific and appropriate primarily for those holding an Eurocentric worldview. This worldview embraces shared group and individual identity components originating in childhood socialization. The use of diagnostic criteria based on such limited experiences often fails to take into account major cultural and social class differences between Whites and people of color. And it is this that leads to invalid conclusions concerning the type and degree of mental health problems.

Although the inadequacies and errors of measuring instruments are many and well documented, the most important problem involves the testers themselves. Even an inadequate instrument sometimes can be useful in the hands of an examiner who acknowledges its limitations and make appropriate adjustments. Unwitting distortion of information contained in test protocols may occur on the basis of an often unacknowledged assessor belief that all "healthy" persons should be assimilated as Americans. The guiding value is that historic differences in ethnicity should be eliminated in the "melting pot" of the United States.

Institutional racism may also cause misdiagnosis. Until recently, due to a "Eurocentric bias" inherent in the *Diagnostic and Statistical Manual of Mental Disorders*, nondominant ethnic members were often diagnosed as being more disturbed than they really were. For example, schizophrenic delusions or hallucinations may be confounded with religious and cultural beliefs of some Native and African Americans (e.g., speaking in tongues, hearing the voice of God, spiritual visions, etc.). On the other hand, if a symptom is extreme within a particular culture, but not extreme within the dominant culture, it may not be recognized as pathology. For example, Asian American children are often under diagnosed with hyperactivity because they are measured against the White American cultural norm instead of against their own cultural norm. In the 1994 *Diagnostic and Statistical Manual of Mental Disorders* (4th edition), new features were introduced to increase sensitivity to variations in "how mental disorders may be expressed in different cultures and to reduce the possible effect of intended bias stemming from the clinician's own cultural background" (p. xxv). In sum, what diagnosticians typically regard as abnormal behavior cannot be separated entirely from their own cultural background.

This becomes extremely problematic when the cultural background is inherently racist. [*See* DSM-IV.]

D. The Role of Racism in Service Delivery

Racism affects service delivery in terms of (1) types of services delivered; (2) length of treatment received; (3) type of diagnosis; (4) degree of sensitivity to client's culture; and (5) relevance of services to the needs of the client. With regard to services delivered, nondominant ethnic members do not receive their fair share of the resources. On every index, minorities receive fewer services and a poorer quality. Specifically, African Americans and Latinos, in contrast to Whites, were less often given individualized psychotherapy, more frequently jailed instead of hospitalized, and more often treated with pharmacotherapy. Many studies have demonstrated that clinicians, given identical test protocols, tend to make more negative prognostic statements and judgments of greater maladjustment when the individual was said to come from a lower rather than a middle-class background. Significantly, African Americans, Latinos and Native Americans are assumed to be lower class.

Several studies investigating racial differences in treatment modalities reported that people of color, particularly African American men, are denied access to more prestigious treatment because they are perceived as not fitting the service treatment model. What are the criteria for fitting the service model? The most important are being verbal and insightful, or in other words, "intelligent." Moreover, nondominant men, especially African Americans, are perceived as physically dangerous and sexually threatening, even when their symptomology does not exemplify these tendencies.

The length of treatment also favors Whites. A 1990 National Institute of Mental Health study revealed that African Americans and Latinos have significantly briefer stays in psychiatric inpatient facilities, but a significantly higher recidivism rate. One explanation is that they are discharged prematurely, only to be returned more frequently. Another explanation, for which there is some research evidence, is that mental health professionals are less than enthusiastic about treating ethnic nondominant clients. And, thirdly, it is highly probable that more recidivism exemplified by ethnic minorities is due to greater stress (which, again, is primarily a function of racism).

The third way in which racism affects service delivery is in terms of type of diagnosis. Nondominant ethnic minorities are more likely to receive diagnoses of serious and long-standing psychopathology. As stated previously, some psychotherapists may be reluctant to label certain groups (i.e., middle- and upper-class Whites) as suffering from a severe form of mental illness (e.g., schizophrenia). This is not the case for African Americans and Latinos. Moreover, there is no valid evidence that the frequency of mental illness differs between Whites and African Americans when social economic status is held constant. However, the literature does suggest that racist attitudes in American society, internalized by mental health professionals, can hamper the efforts of people of color to make themselves understood. [*See* ETHNICITY AND MENTAL HEALTH; SOCIOECONOMIC STATUS.]

The degree of sensitivity to the client's culture, and relevance of services to his or her needs are intimately tied together. Cultural background plays a definitive part in the way one copes or responds to stress. Additionally, social forces play a part, as do attitudes and expectations held by societal authorities (e.g., police; welfare agencies, and so on).

Given the complexity of human behavior it is futile to attempt an understanding of ethnic minorities without an adequate exploration of their historical background, subcultural values, and unique conflicts. Unfortunately, however, the lack of knowledge of ethnic culture and the insensitivity of mental health professionals to the plight of minorities has done more harm than good.

E. The Role of Racism in the Structuring of Mental Health Institutions

Systemic racism also affects the provision of mental health services. For example, the Community Mental Health Center Act of 1963 specified that clients in a given catchment area were to be cared for in a common place for that particular area. The stated purpose was to ensure community connectedness rather than isolation, and to ensure continuity rather than fragmentation of care among the state psychiatric facilities and community mental health services. However, what resulted for ethnic minorities were "ghetto facilities" and "ghetto wards" (e.g., clients are predominantly, if not entirely one ethnic group) within predominantly White facilities. Staffing patterns reflected the occupational structure of the society, with nondominant ethnic orderlies and White mental health professionals. More striking is the nature of the relationship of these wards or facilities to the rest of the hospital or system. Predominantly African American, Latino, or Native American facilities and wards experience more difficulty getting routine services—pickups and deliveries, repairs, and laboratory services. In addition, there is a perception by some that these places are plagued with violence and sexual activity. Thus, out of fear delivery personnel are reluctant to deliver services or work to these areas. In essence, mental health settings represent specific contexts for racist practices.

F. The Role of Racism in Mental Health Research

Prior to 1970 there was a dearth of research on the impact of racism on its victims and its necessary treatment strategies. While in most recent years more attention has been paid to the effects of racism on its victims, mental health researchers have not dealt with the possibility that racism may be a manifestation of individual mental illness or, collectively, of a "sick society."

Given the pervasiveness of racism in American society, it is highly probable that research is often influenced by racist perspectives and values. Researchers bring biased attitudes to the scientific enterprise. Throughout the recent history of the sciences in general, and the social sciences in particular, the objective to establish the superiority of Whites, and the inferiority of nondominant ethnics (e.g., African Americans, Latinos, and others) has been consistently pursued. Manifestations of the higher economic and educational status of Whites, in comparison to nondominant ethnics, have been explained in terms of genetic or cultural deficits inherent in the latter. Evidence for such racist interpretations have been gleaned from faulty research designs (e.g., comparing middle-class Whites to lower class African Americans) and culturally biased instruments (e.g., as discussed earlier, using instruments normed on White males as the standard for all others). Moreover, ethnocentric theories and research findings have been used to establish intervention policies and programs.

G. The Role of Racism in Training Mental Health Professionals

Although the number of nondominant ethnics (African Americans, Asian Americans, Latinos, and Native Americans) is increasing in the United States, only superficial interest has been paid to training mental health professionals to deliver culturally sensitive services. Furthermore, most graduate mental health training programs foster *cultural encapsulation,* a term first coined in 1962 by G. C. Wrenn. The phrase refers to the practice of substituting a model stereotype (i.e., the most frequent behaviors of middle class White males) for the real world, while disregarding cultural variations in a dogmatic adherence to some universal notion of truth, culminating in a technique-oriented definition of the therapeutic process. The results are that mental health professional roles are rigidly defined and impregnated with an implicit belief in a universal concept of "healthy" and/or "normal." For example, the psychoanalytic emphasis on "insight" as a determinant of mental health is a value inherent in Euro-American or Western culture, but not particularly valued in certain socioeconomic groups and ethnic groups. Moreover, many nondominant ethnics are reluctant to initially self-disclose because it can place them in a situation where they are judged to be mentally unhealthy. A prime example is the tendency to interpret the findings on a personality test as supporting paranoid delusion when African Americans score higher on suspiciousness than their White counterparts. In fact, for African Americans to be suspicious often represents a more healthy and accurate assessment of their reality—given their history of slavery, oppression, and present-day discrimination.

The collection and dissemination of information on cross-cultural therapy and the training of culturally skilled professionals have been hindered by several problems—in addition to the obvious pervasive bias and racism inherent in such programs. While there has been much discussion about what is wrong with present programs, very little has been done in the way of change. This is due primarily to the fact that the people interested in changes to the status quo are usually members of ethnic groups who are underrepresented in mental health facilities. Also, there exists a gap between problem awareness and knowledge of cultural based solutions. Finally, and perhaps most importantly, there is a general failure to appreciate the role of therapist *self-knowledge* in the implementation of necessary changes. While cognitive understanding and therapeutic skill training are important, without self-exploration of one's own racism, any acquired information will be tainted by the existing value system. The importance and necessity of "self-knowledge" in the pursuit of antiracist and culturally sensitive mental health practices will be discussed in the next section.

III. A VIABLE SOLUTION TO RACIST PRACTICE IN MENTAL HEALTH

The major emphasis of cross cultural psychotherapy has been on training therapists to become aware of ethnic-group experiences, and class factors, as well as techniques that correspond to each individual culture. However, while it is important and necessary to be aware of a client's culture, such awareness is not sufficient. A more important aspect of cross-cultural psychotherapy—therapist self-awareness has received very little attention.

A valid understanding of ethnic group experiences can only be acquired by a self-enlightened, nondefensive, open and skilled professional. Because most therapists, including ethnic persons of color, have internalized the values of mainstream America—including those values associated with negative images of ethnic group members—such professionals are exceedingly rare.

A. Knowledge of Ethnic Culture

The inability of therapists to provide culturally responsive forms of treatment is the single most important reason given for ethnic minorities being underserved, inappropriately served, as well as having a significantly higher drop-out rate. In response to this inability some therapeutic training programs, and conferences have incorporated culturally sensitive curricula. The following knowledge of ethnic cultures and communities is the cornerstone of this curriculum:

1. Native American cultural orientation emphasizes cooperative or group accomplishments (not competitive individualism), a present-time orientation, creative and nonverbal expressiveness, a focus on sat-

isfaction of present needs, the use of supernatural explanations, an extended family constellation, and harmony with nature.

2. African American cultural orientation emphasizes a sense of "peoplehood" or race consciousness, an action orientation, a paranoia due to oppression, a flexible concept of time, nonverbal behavior, spirituality, and an extended family system.

3. Latino cultural orientation emphasizes group centeredness, respect, cooperation, a flexible time orientation, a family orientation, and a religious distinction between mind/body.

4. Asian cultural orientation emphasizes a family centeredness, restraint of feelings, one-way communication from authority figure to person, respectful silence, advice seeking, well-defined patterns of interaction (concrete structured), a public suppression of emotion, and an extended family system.

Unfortunately, knowledge of ethnic culture is frequently applied in inappropriate ways. This is because its application and relevance cannot always be assumed due to individual differences among members of a particular ethnic group. Therapists with some knowledge of these groups often act upon insufficient knowledge or overgeneralize about what they have learned about culturally dissimilar groups. Moreover, given the Eurocentric educational system, it is virtually impossible to gain sufficient knowledge of the different ethnic groups through attendance in one course, one conference, or one seminar. This is easily understood once it is appreciated that there exist approximately 530 distinct Native American tribes, varying in customs, language, and family structure. Moreover, when tribal variations are multiplied by whether the Native American clients are urban or reservation, and the degree of acculturation, the prospect of acquiring enough knowledge about each group becomes overwhelming indeed.

In addition to the overwhelming task of knowing the cultural background of the client, some therapists have advocated the development of specific intervention strategies to use with ethnic clients. For instance, Asian clients are presumably more culturally familiar with structured relationships, and thus, prefer therapists who provide structure, guidance, and direction rather than nondirectness in interactions. The major problem with approaches emphasizing either cultural knowledge or culture-specific techniques is that neither has been demonstrated to result in effective psychotherapy.

B. The Role of Human Cognition

The underlying assumption is that knowledge of another's culture makes one more culturally sensitive. Recent literature has argued that recommendations and training that encourage mental health therapists to be culturally sensitive have not been very successful. The emphasis has shifted from knowing the client's culture to self-knowledge. The mental health professional's pursuit of self-knowledge is said to better equip him or her to understand and appreciate others. Moreover, the research from the social cognition literature, though indirectly related to cross cultural therapy, does not support the assumption that beneficial gains (i.e., cultural sensitivity) result from the knowledge of ethnic cultures. The process of learning about other cultures or even bringing people together for the purpose of developing more sensitivity, less prejudice, and so on, can backfire and reinforce and even increase prejudices, social distance, and conflict.

In addition, receiving information about a group's culture has been found to actually lead to stereotyping or reconfirm existing stereotypes. Whenever statements are made that "Blacks are . . . ," "Native Americans do not . . . ," or "Japanese prefer . . . ," the content is stereotypical because there is no attention given to the differences among individual Blacks, Native Americans, and Japanese. Thus, the previously mentioned cultural traits, rather than resulting in cultural sensitivity, may result in stereotyping or reinforcing existing stereotypes.

Stereotyping often results in people not examining important concepts beyond those with which they are already familiar. For instance, if a counselor discovers that a certain type of intervention or a certain approach works well with a particular Japanese client, then he or she may generalize this to his or her entire Japanese clientele.

To reiterate, an unbiased understanding of ethnic-group experiences and issues can only be appropriately implemented by a self-enlightened, nondefensive, open, and skilled professional. Exposure to cultural materials about ethnically diverse groups can reinforce stereotypes for some students, creates resentment in others, and causes confusion and anxiety for still others. For instance, a simple statement like "African Americans are relatively more likely to be a part of an extended family system, in which the members help each other emotionally and economically," has been responded to by such statements as: (1) "I resent the connotation that somehow their family system is better than that of Whites"; (2) "I feel less than adequate having come from a nuclear family system"; and (3) "I wish I had come from an extended family system."

A significant part of cross cultural awareness acknowledges disadvantaged people's experience with oppression, discrimination, and racism. This type of information is often met with defensiveness and hostility. The general consensus among many people is that discrimination was in the past, and that the previously oppressed groups need to stop blaming Whites for their troubles. In spite of demonstrable facts (e.g., while White males represent only 37% of the population, they account for 92% of state governors, 82.5% of Forbes 400, 70% of tenured college professors, etc.), White males believe they are the ones that were being discriminated against and that people of color have made progress in the society at their expense. They also believe that ethnically diverse people do not deserve the progress they have made.

A shortcoming of the social cognition literature, however, is that its proponents would have us to believe that human cognition occurs in a vacuum. On the contrary, prejudices and stereotypes are gleaned from the social context in which it occurs and shaped by a hierarchy of values. For example, many persons of color may eventually come to believe the stereotypes held in the larger society about themselves, and about other ethnic groups. Thus, when presented with ethnic cases, some people of color, in contrast to Whites, are more stereotypic in their diagnosis and suggestions for intervention, and less critical of Whites clients.

In sum, to effectively deliver services to members of a negatively stereotyped group, both the dominant and the nondominant mental health professional must first become aware of their own assumptions about human behavior, values, biases, preconceived notions, and personal limitations. Secondly, they must actively attempt to understand the worldview of culturally different clients. Part of the self-awareness process, in addition to understanding how human cognition acts to

perpetuate stereotypes and prejudices, should also include an understanding of the influence of culture.

C. Culture: When Knowledge Isn't Necessarily Reality

Recent focus of training culturally sensitive health professionals has been on the role of culture. Culture consists of those aspects of the environment that people make. Culture is transmitted generation to generation by parents, teachers, religious leaders, other respected elders in a community, and the media. Thus, culture also consists of ideals, values, and assumptions about life that guide specific behaviors. Successful social adjustment is in effect the process of learning the habits, norms, and ways of thinking essential for fitting into the society of one's culture. Since culture is widely shared and accepted, there is little reason to discuss it, and therefore, we are not even aware of its influence.

During the late 1980s Linda James Myers and her colleagues proposed a new approach to training therapists that advocated the adoption of an "Optimal theory," which represented a shift from an Eurocentric to an Afrocentric worldview. Proponents of the Optimal theory argue that the difficulties previously mentioned in the training of mental health professionals and mental health service delivery arise directly from interpreting multiculturalism through Eurocentric conceptual systems. Western culture assumes that the universe is comprised of opposing separate good and evil forces. It further assumes that all beings can be ranked based upon the relative proportions of good and evil, or superiority versus inferiority. Because—within a Eurocentric cultural framework—worth is not intrinsic, individuals are left to rely on external realities for feelings of self-worth. Hence one's skin color, class, sex, age, income, education, occupation, and ethnicity all become critical factors in defining individuals.

Optimal theory, on the other hand, assumes the unity of spirit and matter, with spirit being preeminent. According to optimal theory the individual is a unique manifestation of spirit; therefore self-worth is intrinsic and independent of external criteria. Proponents of Optimal theory argue that to truly value and appreciate the diversity of human expression and experience, one must adopt an optimal worldview and see the interrelatedness and interconnectedness of all life. The shift in worldview requires considerable introspection; thus, Optimal theory emphasizes self-knowledge. While empirical evidence in support of the effectiveness of Optimal theory is lacking, the importance of self-knowledge in the delivery of culturally sensitive mental health services has been validated.

IV. RECOMMENDATIONS AND CONCLUSIONS

A. The Role of Self-Awareness

Recent literature indicates that keys to developing a positive cross-ethnic therapist/client relationship and effective intervention are (1) understanding the importance of knowing one's own culture, (2) the extent to which one has internalized "Western culture," and (3) knowing the impact of culture on interpersonal perceptions and behaviors. This is true for both the mainstream therapist and the ethnic therapist. Training programs stress the importance of not allowing our own biases, values, or "hang-ups" to interfere with the ability to work with clients. In most cases, however, this aspect of counseling is explored at an intellectual level with very little training directed at having trainees get in touch with their own values and biases about human behavior. Moreover, training which facilitates an exploration of the worldview that a person has internalized are few and far between.

One vehicle for a person to explore his or her worldview is personal psychotherapy. Although required by some training programs and encouraged by others, personal psychotherapy traditionally does not explore cultural and/or racial issues. The reasons for this void in personal psychotherapy are many. The most apparent reason is that culture is like the air we breathe; thus, we take it for granted, and we do not think about it unless we are so challenged to think about it. In addition, we tend to gravitate toward therapists who are similar to ourselves, and who do not challenge our worldview. Thus, personal therapy focuses mainly on personal issues that cause us discomfort, such as difficulties we had with our mothers that may result in countertransference (i.e., displacement of the analyst feelings on to the client). To be effective, a cross-cultural counselor must have dealt adequately with and worked through racial biases, feelings, fears, and guilt.

B. The Culturally Skilled Professional

A 1990 book written by Sue and Sue, entitled *Counseling the Culturally Different,* describes a culturally skilled mental health professional, and offers comprehensive training tips. The culturally skilled professional is said to be a person who has moved from being culturally unaware to being aware and sensitive to his or her own cultural heritage, while valuing and respecting differences. To do so one must conduct a values exploration, which concentrates on becoming aware of the stereotypes held and how they affect nondominant clients. The culturally skilled professional actively looks for exceptions, conscientiously suspends making value judgments, and challenges ethnocentric beliefs. She monitors her progress via consultation and supervision.

In addition, culturally skilled professionals are comfortable with differences that may exist between themselves and their clients in terms of race and beliefs. Awareness is facilitated by acknowledging one's own racist attitudes, beliefs, and feelings, and dealing with it in a nondefensive, guilt-free manner. Moreover, the culturally skilled professional is aware of his or her own limitations and, is thus sensitive to circumstances that may dictate referral of an ethnic client to a member of his or her own race/culture or to another counselor.

These modifications of one's awareness and perception do not mean that the culturally skilled professional cannot hold their own worldview, but rather that they can see and accept the client's worldview in a nonjudgmental manner. Cross-cultural sensitivity has been accomplished when the therapist has: (1) achieved self-awareness and understanding of his or her own culture—self-awareness is the basis of all knowledge; (2) has an understanding of the client's culture; (3) has an understanding of the client's relationship to the sociopolitical system; (4) has an understanding of the ways in which generic counseling and therapy may limit the potential of the client; (5) has an array of therapeutic techniques at his or her disposal; and (6) is willing to exercise institutional intervention on behalf of the client when appropriate.

In conclusion, cultural barriers *can be* overcome in the delivery of mental health services. We must begin with individual therapists, focusing on the training level. As the number of culturally skilled therapists grow, we can bring pressure on societal institutions to suspend the negative stereotyping and racist treatment of people of color. An important and necessary component for a mentally healthy society is one in which the true histories and contribution of all peoples are included and valued in the lessons taught to the young, thus creating a new worldview of mutual respect for our differences.

BIBLIOGRAPHY

American Psychiatric Association. (1994). *Diagnostic and statistical manual of mental disorders* (4th ed.). Washington, DC: Author.

Aponte, J. F., Rivers, R. Y., & Wohl, J. (Eds.). (1995). *Psychological interventions and cultural diversity*. Boston: Allyn and Bacon.

Bowser, B. P., & Hunt, R. G. (1981). Afterthoughts and reflection. In B. P. Bowser & R. G. Hunt (Eds.), *Impact of racism on White Americans*. Newbury Park, CA: Sage.

Jackson, J. S., & Inglehart, M. R. (1995). Reverberation theory: Stress and racism in hierarchically structured communities. In S. E. Hobfoll & M. W. deVries, (Eds.), *Extreme stress and communities: Impact and intervention*. Boston: Kluwer Academic Publishers.

Pedersen, P. (Ed.). (1985). *Handbook of cross-cultural counseling and therapy*. Westport, CT: Greenwood Press.

Turner, C. B. & Kramer, B. M. (1995). Connections between racism and mental health. In C. V. Willie, P. P. Rieker, B. M. Kramer, & B. S. Brown (Eds.), *Mental health, racism and sexism*. Pittsburgh, PA: University of Pittsburgh Press.

Speight, S. L., Myers, L. J., Cox, C. I., & Highlen, P. S. (September/October 1991). A redefinition of multicultural counseling. *Journal of Counseling and Development, 70*, 29–35.

Sue, D. W., & Sue, David. (1990). *Counseling the culturally different*, (2nd ed.). New York: John Wiley & Sons.

Willie, C. V., Kramer, B. M., & Brown, B. S. (1973). *Racism and mental health*. Pittsburgh, PA: University of Pittsburgh Press.

Rape

Mary Koss and Laura Boeschen

University of Arizona

Acquaintance Rape Rape involving a perpetrator who is known to the victim.

Date Rape Rape involving a perpetrator who has some level of romantic relationship with the victim ranging from having just met to being established partners.

Marital Rape Rape involving the legal or common-law spouse or ex-spouse of the victim.

Non-normative Rape Illicit, uncondoned sexual abuse that is both against the will of the recipient and in violation of social norms for expected behavior.

Normative Rape Sexual penetration that is unwanted, but the victim's participation is coerced by social processes and norms that support the practice and deny justice.

Sexual Assault Forced or coerced sexual acts not involving penetration.

Unacknowledged Rape Victim A person who has experienced unwanted sexual penetration through force or threat, but who does not use the label "rape" to conceptualize the incident.

Victim/Survivor The person to whom an intentional harm or wrong is done. Trauma service providers often use survivor instead of victim to signify that the victim has overcome possible death or serious injury. However, the survivor still faces many months of recovery to overcome the effects of rape on physical, psychological, and social health.

The definition of **RAPE** varies by state and changes over time in response to legislative advocacy. However, most North American statutes currently define rape as the nonconsensual oral, anal, or vaginal penetration of the victim by the penis, fingers, or other parts of the body, or by objects, using force, threats of bodily harm, or by taking advantage of a victim incapable of giving consent. Penetration, however slight, completes rape; emission of semen is not required. Laws defining rape have been revised in all states of the United States in recent years. In contrast to older definitions, the crime of rape is no longer limited to female victims, to vaginal penetration alone, or to forcible situations only, and the exclusion of spouses as possible perpetrators of rape has been dropped. Thus, rape laws criminalize assaults by intimates, as well as assaults by strangers, and they are gender neutral, suggesting that both men and women can be raped. However, the rape of women is 10 times more common than rape of men, and perpetrators are almost always men regardless of the sex of the victim. Perpetration by women is very uncommon. Finally, rape is universal in that it occurs cross-culturally, although the prevalence rates differ among cultures.

I. PREVALENCE

Rape is one of the most underreported crimes in the United States. Therefore, determining the prevalence rates of rape is difficult, as the information must come from the victims themselves. Complicating matters, most victims live in societies that have a history of either blaming rape victims or denigrating them as damaged goods. As a result, many of them are not willing to reveal their experiences to outside authorities or interviewers. The United States has two federal sources of rape incidence data. The Uniform Crime Reports (UCR) is a compilation of crimes reported to local authorities. The UCR reported that 104,806 crimes qualified as rapes in 1993, a figure that includes both completed and attempted rape. Only about 8% of these reports were rejected as "unfounded" by police nationwide. Unfounded is not synonymous with a false complaint. The term also applies to circumstances where police believe that rape may have occurred but it will be impossible to prove. Larceny crimes such as auto theft, where the possibility of insurance claims lurk, are the crimes most often falsely reported. Depending on source, estimates of the percentage of rapes that are reported to police range from 8 to 54%. The second federal data source is the National Crime Victimization Survey (NCVS), a nationwide, household-based crime victimization survey intended to determine the true amount of crime, including both reported and unreported cases. The NCVS reported that 316,000 rapes (including attempts) occurred in 1993 and 1994, 66% of which were unreported. This number reflects a 400% increase in the number of completed rapes reported between the year prior to revision in the rape questions and the current year (316,000, up from 83,080). However, there are still reasons to believe that many rapes remain undetected because of survey features that favor recall of violent crime over intimate crime, impede rapport, and lack confidentiality for responses. An independent estimate of the number of rapes among adult women for 1992 conducted by the National Victims Center and using a national telephone sample was 683,000, whereas the NCVS reported 313,600 rapes during the same period.

Many quotes of rape risk are given in percentages and range between 13 and 25% in the majority of sources, including in several large community samples and a national sample. These numbers suggest much higher chances of rape than federal estimates. One reason for the difference in findings is that the percentage figures represent rape *prevalence* and count women as victims if they have been raped at any point in their lifetime, as opposed to the crime *incidence* figures that count only individuals who were victimized during the preceding 12 months. Because the recovery period for rape is extensive, and because some key changes such as increased fear of crime may be permanent, rape experts argue that prevalence rates more accurately portray the true toll of rape on women. Incidence figures, on the other hand, are useful for tracking crime trends and for estimating the level of need for intervention services.

The differences in prevalence rates found among sources is explained by differences in sampling and methodology. Specifically, differences in the composition of samples, the questions asked, and the context in which the questions are placed can lead to sizable variation in the rates of rape recorded. First, the method of data collection is important. If the participants are hard to reach, have language barriers, and/or do not trust the interviewer, the researcher will underdetect a sensitive issue such as rape. How the questions are asked will also affect the amount of disclosure. If the screening questions use different conceptual labels than respondents use to remember their experience, the respondent's memory may not be jogged for a relevant experience. Many victims do not answer affirmatively to questions that use the words "rape" or "sexual assault," either because they are not aware of the full definition, or because they do not want to be stigmatized as a rape victim.

Equally important to uncovering rape experiences is the type of questions asked. Although some researchers ask a single "gate" question to save time in their attempt to stimulate recall of a range of sexually unwanted experiences, data suggest that this approach results in lowered efficiency in identifying rape cases. A single item cannot cue the respondent to recall the variety of guises under which rape can occur. Behaviorally specific screening questions pose a more effective strategy for detecting rape. These questions allow the interviewer to bypass the individual labels the respondent may use by confining questions to specific acts and behaviors that exemplify how the investigators are defining rape. It is a common finding that women will endorse affirmatively that they have had intercourse against their will because a man used force, but will say no when asked if they have been raped. Finally, the context of the questioning, the timing and placement of the questions, as well as the gender and ethnicity of the person asking the questions are other important factors when interviewing rape victims. Less than optimal conditions for any of these factors can lead to underdetection of rape.

Regardless of the source of data, there are several findings about rape that are undisputed. The typical victim is young, with the peak ages for rape being 12 to 24 years. More than 80% of rapes are committed by people the victims know, and these incidents are less likely to be reported to the police. In one national survey, an estimated one third of stranger rapes were reported to police compared with only 13% of acquaintance rapes. Contrary to stereotypes, the level of violence is often equal or greater in rapes involving acquaintances, especially among partners in a steady relationship or formally married, compared with rapes involving complete strangers. Likewise, the fear of being seriously injured or killed is similar, regardless of the victim–offender relationship.

Recent awareness that rape prevalence may vary, and that rape may play a different role or induce different responses depending on a victim's cultural background, has led to attempts to calculate prevalence statistics across ethnicities within the United States and cross-nationally. Most of these studies suggest that rape is a significant concern for women universally. Data for the United States suggest that prevalence rates are similar for African-American women and white women. However, some studies show that the prevalence of sexual assault is lower among recently immigrated Hispanic women than Hispanic U.S. citizens and among non-Hispanic white women. An alternative explanation for this finding is that it is not the level of rape that differs but the attitudes and level of comfort over discussion of intimate matters with a complete stranger. More extensive research is needed in this area before firm conclusions are drawn. Some cross-national figures, drawn from studies administered to college students in several countries, show lifetime prevalence of completed and attempted rape combined is universally above 20%.

It is obviously perilous to draw conclusions about international prevalence from crime statistics, as few women choose to report these acts where laws are unsupportive. Unfortunately, individual researchers also face obstacles in obtaining numbers. They encounter difficulty in overcoming the cultural norms for secrecy over sexual matters, the distrust of authorities and even of fellow citizens under conditions of social stress, and the issues of privacy in such tight quarters

and close-knit societies. Methodologically, it becomes difficult to compare studies cross-culturally because of the varying definitions of rape used by researchers and the cultural and geographic representativeness of samples of societies examined.

The stereotypical rape, a surprise attack on a virtuous woman by a complete stranger, violates the norms of most human societies. Thus, it is called nonnormative rape. However, attitudes and laws differ among societies in their stance toward unwanted forcible sex that involves nonvirgin older girls and women, women forced to have sex by their legal husbands, and unwanted sex that is part of puberty rights and marriage rituals, for example. Virtually every society has social processes that deny labeling various forms of unwanted sexual behavior as rape, condone rape as a punishment for women, pressure women into accepting unwanted sex, and create insurmountable obstacles toward sanctioning the perpetrator. Rape and sexual assault that is tacitly supported by society is called normative rape. Several investigators have combed ethnographic databanks to determine the rates of rape in nonindustrial and preliterate societies. Non-normative rape was universally found to be rare. Normative rape, in contrast, occurred in 42 to 90% of societies.

Unfortunately, in some societies, laws declare that the wrongness of rape is determined by the moral status of the woman, suggesting that only certain types of women deserve protection from rape. Countries such as Costa Rica, Ecuador, Guatemala, Pakistan, and Sri Lanka have laws that recognize rape only when the victim is determined to be honest and chaste. Outside the English-speaking world, laws prohibiting husbands from forcing sex with their wives are rare. International human rights organizations have documented the use of rape as a method to control women, particularly those who work toward the betterment of life for women and children, in countries including Peru, India, Pakistan, and several throughout Latin America. Finally, as recent world news has revealed, rape can be widespread under conditions of war and social disorganization, such as occurred in Bosnia-Herzegovina and Somalia. Fortunately, some progress has been made to free women from gender-based sexual abuse. In 1992, the United Nations passed a general resolution recognizing women's rights as human rights and called on the world's nations to reduce and ultimately eliminate all forms of gender-based abuse. Rape in wartime has been forbidden by the Geneva Conventions since 1949.

II. CAUSES OF RAPE

Many theories have highlighted a primary cause of rape. Some of these theories focus on the individual characteristics of men who commit rape, and others emphasize institutional or social causation. Research suggests, however, that no single theory can explain all types of rape all of the time. Therefore, current emphasis is on the development of more complex multifactor models of causation that combine findings from earlier work. One of the more popular theories of individual determinants is based on evolution, where the goal of sexual behavior is to maximize the likelihood of passing on one's genes. In ancestral environments, men were best served by mating with as many fertile females as possible. A number of recent studies have shown that young men are more interested in partner variety, less interested in committed long-term relationships, and more willing to engage in impersonal sex than young women. However, this explanation is criticized as limited in the explanation of rape among modern human beings. For example, it cannot explain the proportion of rapes lacking reproductive consequences because they involve oral or anal penetration, or victims who are prepubescent or male. More recent evolutionists modify their approach by combining it with other factors such as psychopathology and an erotic interest in coercive sexual behavior. [See EVOLUTION AND MENTAL HEALTH.]

Other recent theories of individual determinants are based on physiology and neurophysiology. Most of this research involves animal studies or human correlations that do not imply causation. These studies concentrate on steroid hormones, neurotransmitters, neuroanatomical abnormalities, and brain dysfunctions, showing a correlation between biological factors and aggression. Although there is an increasing interest in the role played by biological factors in aggression, current researchers realize that an interaction of biological, developmental, and environmental factors contribute to rape. [See AGGRESSION.]

Certain psychopathology and personality traits have also been diagnosed among sexual offenders. Sexual offenders are most frequently diagnosed with some type of antisocial personality disorder and distinctive personality profiles have been reported for rapists. However, the only perpetrators tested are those who are caught, and this group is a limited sample distinguished by greater poverty and lower education than rapists who remain free in the community. Even within incarcerated groups, it is frequently impossible to differentiate sex offenders from offenders who were not convicted of a sexual offense. Efforts to create typologies of rapists have led to the conclusion that there is a great deal of heterogeneity, even among the narrow range of men confined in centers for treatment of sexually dangerous persons.

Social and institutional theories argue that although rape affects individuals and is perpetrated by individuals, it is ultimately a problem of the society that spawns and perpetuates it. Adherents of social explanations note that rape is so pervasive it cannot be explained as the product of individual psychopathology or biology. From this perspective, rape occurs in a sociocultural context and is viewed as one manifestation of gender inequality. Gender has always been an integral organizing feature of human social structures and institutions. These social structures and institutions, such as family, peer groups, school, military, sports, and religion, directly impinge on the daily lives of men and women and define the gendered sociocultural context we live in. For example, a woman's conflict between work and home is viewed as an individual problem rather than as a problem of the design of home and work environments that make it difficult to combine the activities of these two worlds. Because gender pervades our social structures, its relationship to rape must be conceptualized and addressed not only at individual levels, but at institutional levels as well.

Understanding rape also requires examination of the legal, economic, and physical power inequalities between men and women. Rape is one mechanism for maintaining these inequalities and reinforcing the male dominance and female subordination in society. From this perspective, it is not rape itself but the fear of rape that controls women. Fear may drive women to seek protection from men. Some research supports this hypothesis that rape has a basis in societal inequalities. For example, some researchers have discovered that more male-dominant societies support the highest levels of rape and also that significantly greater frequencies of rape are found in preliterate societies characterized by patrilocality and an ideology of male toughness. Furthermore, it has been found in the United States that rape rates in individual states are correlated with societal-level indicators of social disorganization and inequality.

Cultural norms and expectations pervade everyday life. Myths such as "women provoke rape by the way they dress" and "women say no when they mean yes" appear to prevail throughout our society. Groups in the United States who have been identified by researchers as endorsing rape myths include average citizens, police officers, and judges. The prevalence of these myths helps explain why intervention efforts have often been victim-focused and have often been victim-blaming, and why the responses of health professionals, the justice system, and the family frequently increases, rather than ameliorates, the impact on victims. Furthermore, these myths trivialize the consequences of rape, minimize the responsibility of men, and therefore prevent the development of effective policies and programs to support victims and prevent rape.

Gender inequality can also be found in the sexual scripts that widely characterize and govern the behavior of boys and girls, men and women. These scripts assign different roles and behaviors to men and women and guide their interactions. Women are expected to have relationships with men who are bigger, smarter, older, more educated, higher in status, more experienced, more confident, and more highly paid than themselves. Men are cast in the role of sexual initiators, women as gatekeepers. Sexual experience is valued in men, but even in a sexually liberated age, too much sexual experience detracts from a woman's reputation. From the vantage point of these scripts, rape represents a man performing vigorously in his expected role while the woman fails to perform hers. This traditional script explains why many men who have been sexually aggressive do not realize they have raped, and why many rape victims blame themselves for what happened. Heterosexual scripts are learned early. Adults and children alike are bombarded with images that equate physical and psychological domination and abuse of women with sexual pleasure through television, film, magazines, and music. Furthermore, parents tend to socialize their daughters to resist sexual advances and socialize their sons to initiate sexual activity. One study found that 50% of the girls and 65% of the middle school boys sampled believed that it is acceptable for a man to force a woman

to have sex if they have been dating for more than 6 months. Approximately 25% of the boys said that it was acceptable for a man to force sex on a woman if he had spent money on her. Research also shows that men who use traditional dating scripts, where they initiate the date, pay all of the expenses, and drive the car, are more likely to be sexually aggressive than other men.

Cultural expectations and norms associated with alcohol use also serve to perpetuate rape. Alcohol appears to not only serve as a disinhibitor for the man, but as an excuse for his behavior after the fact. It also serves as a blaming mechanism for the victim if she has been drinking and may be used by women to "medicate" the tension they experience over expressing sexuality in a double-standard environment and pursuing the conflicting goals of affiliation and safety. Research also suggests that alcohol may interfere with social cognitions. Recent studies demonstrate that men under the influence of alcohol are more likely to perceive ambiguous or neutral cues as suggestive of sexual interest and to ignore or misinterpret cues that a woman is unwilling. Obviously, many sexual assaults occur in the absence of alcohol. However, alcohol use plays an important role in sexual assault—it has been reported in 75% of all acquaintance rapes by men and 50% by women. [See ALCOHOL PROBLEMS.]

Regardless of the theoretical leanings of a particular researcher, it is now accepted that multiple classes of influences, from the individual to the societal level, determine the expression of sexually aggressive behavior in men. The heterogeneity of sexually aggressive men precludes an all encompassing explanatory theory. Rather than focusing on a single set of causes, researchers have turned to multivariate models of sexual assault. These models understand rape as *gendered* violence, addressing *multiple levels of influence* from macrosocial to intrapsychic and neurophysiological. They hypothesize processes through which culture at the societal level is transmitted and becomes represented within the minds of individuals. They use a *life-span perspective* that focuses on the development of a man's violent career, including how his early life experiences become transformed into perpetration and the trajectory of escalation within a career of violence. Finally, they are *probabilistic* in that it is recognized that not all variables may operate in every case. Thus, people bring their past into the present in their attitudes, respond to biological drives, and reflect the influences of their families and formative institutions in the sexual scripts they follow, and these features influence selection of the environments and strategies they use in pursuing intimate connection. Sexual violence is also responsive to its consequences. In a society where few men are arrested, prosecuted, or convicted of raping a female acquaintance, little constructive feedback counters the immediate reinforcement of achieving sexual aims through whatever means necessary.

III. PSYCHOLOGICAL IMPACT

Immediate responses to rape may include shock, intense fear, numbness, confusion, extreme helplessness, and disbelief. Many victims also experience feelings of guilt, shame, and self-blame that may be a result of cultural myths about rape and unsupportive responses of their social support network. These negative feelings may be worse in victims who were raped by known partners. Although self-blame has been found to be an adaptive means of retaining "just" world beliefs in certain trauma victims, it is not the case with rape victims, who are often already blamed by their societies. Self-blame has repeatedly been found to predict poorer adjustment and greater distress in rape victims. A rape victim's cognitive beliefs and schemas about safety, power, trust, esteem, and intimacy are also often affected by this type of experience. Many victims experience feelings of vulnerability and loss of control that often stem from no longer believing that they are secure in the world, that the world has order and meaning, and that they are worthy persons. Although some victims may actually gain a more flexible belief system through a destabilizing experience such as rape, others may suffer from pervasive negative beliefs that she is bad, evil, responsible, and untrustworthy. Some rape victims experience a general distrust or fear of men.

There is no "correct" or "healthy" time span for victims in coping with their assaults. For some, symptom elevation subsides by the third month, but approximately one quarter of rape victims go on to experience long-term and sometimes severe symptoms. Although many victims may not feel "recovered" within a few months or even years after an assault, and many never view the world in the same way again, the majority of survivors continue to function

in everyday life and within 4 to 6 years feel that they have healed.

The most common long-term symptoms experienced by rape victims are those of fear and anxiety. Fear is often triggered by stimuli associated with the attack itself or by situations that are perceived by the victim as reminders of rape. Generalized anxiety may lead to jumpiness, sleep disruptions, and a lack of concentration. Some rape victims will also experience symptoms of depression. These symptoms include sleep and appetite disturbance, a loss of interest in normal activities, a decrease in the ability to concentrate, and feelings of alienation and loneliness. Although some rape victims actually develop major depressive disorders after the rape, others will only experience some of the symptoms, and not for extended periods of time. One study found that almost one in five raped women in the community had attempted suicide. Rape victims are also more likely than nonvictims to receive several psychiatric diagnoses, including alcohol abuse/dependence and drug abuse/dependence even several years after the assault. Some victims report deterioration in their sexual functioning after an assault. These women experience a fear of sex, arousal dysfunction, and/or decreased sexual interest which may be the result of a lowered sexual self-esteem, negative feelings about men, and/or increased insecurities concerning sexual attractiveness because of the rape. [*See* ANXIETY; DEPRESSION.]

Posttraumatic Stress Disorder (PTSD) is the predominant psychiatric diagnosis applied to victims of rape, as well as to survivors of other traumas who are exposed to the threat of injury and death. Characteristic symptoms of PTSD include repeated daytime intrusive memories and/or nightmares that are so discomforting as to motivate patients to go to great lengths to avoid reminders of the trauma. It has been diagnosed in as many as 94% of rape victims assessed immediately after an assault. Lifetime prevalence of PTSD is about 15% among victims of rape, a figure similar to that among male combat veterans. Because of the high prevalence of rape, combined with a high likelihood of inducing symptoms, rape victims make up the largest single group of PTSD sufferers. The primary limitation in applying PTSD to rape victims is that the diagnosis focuses on a narrow range of symptoms, while actual reactions to rape are broader. Not included in the PTSD diagnosis are cognitive impacts of rape and sexual dysfunctions. Some mental health care providers, especially in Latin America, are critical of the PTSD diagnosis because they feel it medicalizes a social problem and focuses the victim on her individual psychology, rather than directing her energy toward affiliating with other targets of violence and using their cumulative energy to attack the root causes of violence within the society. [*See* POSTTRAUMATIC STRESS.]

Although all women are affected in some way by the experience of rape, it is difficult to predict the magnitude of impact and the type of response specific individuals will have to sexual assault. Research suggests trends for certain demographic variables of the victim as well as for certain aspects of a victim's history. For example, research has found that income and education do not appear to be related to type or severity of symptoms, but being married and being elderly have been associated with greater postassault distress. In addition, women with preexisting psychological distress also tend to have higher levels of postassault psychological symptoms. Previous victimization, however, creates a more complex picture. Although first-time victims show more distress immediately after a rape, prior victims experience increased stress over time, show more depression, and have a longer recovery overall. Women who are raped more than once are also more likely to abuse substances and have a lifetime diagnosis of depression. Finally, having experienced other negative life stressors is also associated with greater postassault stress. [*See* STRESS.]

The nature of the attack has also been linked to the degree to which victims experience symptoms. First, women who have been sexually assaulted by acquaintances or family members suffer as serious psychological aftereffects as women who are assaulted by strangers. However, women raped by men they know are less likely than stranger rape victims to realize that the unwanted sexual experience meets the requirements for rape, and consequently are less likely to report their victimization to police. These women have been called unacknowledged rape victims. Second, it appears that the actual violence may be less crucial in predicting response than the perceived threat, even though number of assailants, physical threat, injury requiring medical care, and medical complications are all predictive of symptoms. Finally, research suggests that victims who were fondled and caressed tend to experience more symptoms, which may be associated with later confusion about subsequent displays of af-

fection that remind them of the attack, causing anxiety and other symptoms. Social support may moderate the impact of rape, but it appears that unsupportive behavior by significant others in particular predicts poorer social adjustment. [*See* SOCIAL SUPPORT.]

Ethnicity is also an area that deserves more study. Research suggests that Asian and Mexican American women have more difficult recoveries than do other women, possibly because of cultures that link intense, irremediable shame to rape or that hold women responsible for assaults. No ethnic differences in rates of mental disorders have been found among Hispanic, African American, and white women. Even though there may be general similarity in levels of symptoms, the meaning of the experience, the meaning of the symptoms, and preferred avenues of healing may differ.

IV. PHYSICAL IMPACT

If a victim seeks any professional help at all after a rape, she is most likely to visit a physician. Many victims who go to a health provider, however, are not asked and do not disclose that they have been raped. Furthermore, many physicians do not have the training to identify the warning signs of sexual assault, so victims are treated for physical surface wounds only. Fortunately, forensic exams and acute care are now offered by specially trained nurse examiners in many communities. However, the role of the medical system transcends the traditional focus on emergency and forensic intervention. Current research demonstrates that rape has long-lasting effects on health. Adult victims of sexual assault seek help from physicians twice as frequently as other women, most often in the second year after victimization. Victimization was a more powerful predictor of medical care utilization among women HMO patients than other variables with well-known links to disease, including smoking, drinking, life stress, age, and education.

Like psychological symptoms, victims of rape may experience to varying degrees a wide range of physical symptoms. In the immediate aftermath of rape, there are nongenital injuries, including abrasions and bruising, as well as genital injuries, including vaginal tears that can range from catastrophic to microscopic. Colposcopy, which involves bright illumination and magnification of the vagina allows sexual assault examiners to better document genital injuries. Rapes also result in nongenital injuries from the force used to accomplish penetration, or from gratuitous force beyond that necessary to accomplish the crime. Some reports indicate that 40% of rape victims experience nongenital injuries, 54% of whom seek medical treatment. However, in terms of costs both to the medical care system and in individual distress, the chronic somatic consequences of rape are more alarming. Several medical diagnoses are made disproportionately among women who have a history of sexual assault, including gastrointestinal syndromes, chronic pain syndromes including pelvic pain, and tension headaches.

V. INTERVENTIONS

If effective treatments for sex offenders were developed, interventions for victims would not be as necessary. Currently, cognitive behavioral interventions are used in treatment centers to try to teach offenders to identify situational and emotional states in which they are likely to reoffend and teach them how to avoid or cope effectively with triggers. These interventions occur in group and individual settings, where offenders are taught empathy, coping skills, and anger management, for example. One study of this type of cognitive behavioral treatment, which used a random assignment design with control groups, found that the recidivism rates were lower for the group who received treatment than for the control group, suggesting that treatment may have some positive effect. However, of those offenders who were removed from the treatment group for disruptive behavior, 100% reoffended within 5 years, suggesting that those who are most likely to reoffend are too disruptive to receive treatment.

Recent meta-analyses of sex offender treatment studies have concluded that their success rates are not promising. The research on treating sex offenders appears to suffer from intractable methodological problems, precluding any definitive conclusions. For example, definitive conclusions about treatment effectiveness demand random assignment to treatment and no-treatment comparison groups. However, many investigators feel that it is both unethical and immoral to withhold treatment from known sex offenders in an attempt to compare the recidivism rates. In addition, it is very difficult to compute recidivism rates adequately, as not all reoffenders are caught. Finally, the treatments that have been studied are created for offenders who are already incarcerated. Given the low rate of conviction for men who sexually assault, this intervention is therefore structured for the minority of rapists. The only intervention geared toward the majority of offenders, who are residing undetected in the community, is prevention.

Most rape victims do not contact mental health professionals. Many African-American women, for example, prefer parents and friends for assistance to the formal system. Victims tend to resist a patient identity. After all, the rape was done to them, outside of their control; survivors dislike being viewed as having emotional problems because of it. Furthermore, rape victims are less likely than other crime victims to disclose their victimization to anyone, thereby reducing their recovery resources. Resolution of rape on one's own is difficult, especially because victims face a culture that challenges their credibility and holds them at least partially culpable for the sexual assault against them. Many women try to block the rape from their minds, believing that if they do not think about it, they can put it behind them. There are some indications that this strategy may work for some trauma survivors. For others, recovery from rape-related symptoms is more elusive and they eventually request assistance for psychological or physical distress.

As discussed previously, physicians are the health professionals most often approached by rape victims. Because they are the ones on the front lines, it is most important that physicians be trained to screen for victimization by violence, acknowledge disclosure, and direct women to other resources if they so desire. Currently, the bulk of victim care is provided by grassroots agencies. These agencies have accomplished more for rape victims than any other component of the response system. Before 1970, there were no agencies nor advocacy groups to fight for victims rights or to provide victim services. However, rape crisis centers began opening across the United States throughout the 1970s. By 1979, there was one rape center in at least one community in every state, Puerto Rico, and the District of Columbia. Crisis centers are settings for community action, legal advocacy, provision of victim services, and community education. Most of the community response to rape today can be traced to their advocacy efforts. In addition to advocating for improved community response to rape, centers support groups for survivors and offer hospital and police accompaniment services to victims, court accompaniment programs, volunteer hot lines, self-defense training, and advocacy. They also often offer training for police, court, medical, and mental health professionals. They educate the community and professionals about victims and the normal responses to a rape experience to prevent incorrect diagnoses of psychopathology. Finally, the centers emphasize prevention by presenting programs in the schools and colleges to educate young people about rape, particularly within intimate relationships.

Unfortunately, these agencies rely on funding from local and state money, which has become more and more difficult to obtain. The result is that most centers cannot offer all of their community programs. Many have to focus solely on their crisis intervention services, others have merged with other agencies, and some have closed altogether. Reinvesting in these community centers is crucial not only for providing continued help for victims in crisis, but also for changing the attitudes of society and its community leaders and professionals as a means of prevention. Adequate funding is necessary to maintain current programs, to retain qualified staff, and to extend service out to jails, detention centers, prisons, substance-abuse programs, and other settings where a large proportion of women are sexual assault survivors. These agencies and their communities also need to develop strategies to link rape centers with medical, mental health, and justice systems.

In spite of the current funding drain, the legal advocacy efforts of these agencies have continued the fight for change in the justice system. Their aim has been to increase reporting, arrest, prosecution, and conviction of rape by changing prevailing laws, law enforcement practices, and the treatment of victims in the courtroom. Several reforms dealing with these issues have been fought for and won at the state level. For example, the legal definitions of sexual assault were expanded to replace the single crime of rape with a series of gender-neutral graded offenses and to create an accompanying set of graded penalties. In addition, the need for corroborating evidence and proof of resistance were eliminated in courts throughout the country, and rape shield laws were implemented, prohibiting the use of certain evidence of the victim's history in trial. Finally, marital exceptions have been eliminated in many states. Recent literature, however,

questions whether these laws have been implemented as they were intended and whether they actually have an impact in the community on police, prosecutors, and juries, for example.

Several federal programs have been created to help fight violence against women. The Victims of Crime Act (VOCA) was developed in 1984 to authorize yearly grants to states to assist and compensate victims. The Office for Victims of Crime was established in 1993 by the Justice Department to support training programs for professionals who come into contact with victims of violence. It sponsored a sexual assault medical examination protocol that standardized procedures for hospital personnel which has been replicated in 14 states. The National Institute of Mental Health (NIMH) provides funding for research on the sexual assault of women. The National Institute on Alcohol Abuse and Alcoholism (NIAAA) has also supported research on the interaction of sexual assault and alcohol. Finally, the Centers for Disease Control and Prevention (CDC) appropriates money to support the fight against sexual assault. The Violence Against Women Act, passed as part of the crime bill of 1995, contained increased funds for rape crisis centers and for prevention approaches to sexual assaults.

Although relatively few rape victims seek specialty mental health treatment immediately after a rape, more eventually seek help for rape-related issues, such as a breakup, persistent symptoms, an impending trial, or withdraw of support from family and friends. If victims choose to seek mental health treatment, they have many options ranging from different formats such as individual and group therapy to differing techniques within each format. Research on individual psychotherapy has focused on behavioral and cognitive-behavioral techniques for rape victims. Behavioral exposure techniques such as in vivo flooding, systematic desensitization, and prolonged exposure treatment confront the victim with the feared situation through varying degrees of exposure or imagination. These techniques show mixed empirical results. The prolonged exposure treatment appears to be the most helpful, but all of these techniques are somewhat aversive for the victim and may result in high dropout rates or reactivation of chemical abuse and suicide attempts unless practiced by a qualified specialist.

Anxiety management techniques, such as stress inoculation training, focus more on the victims' cognitions by teaching them to feel in control of the fear, rather than activating and habituating the fear. New hybrid approaches such as cognitive-processing therapy and eye movement desensitization and reprocessing therapy (EMDR) combine elements of exposure and anxiety management. A recent study suggests the efficacy of brief prevention programs that combine education about common reactions to rape with cognitive-behavioral procedures in diminishing the symptoms of PTSD. Victims receiving the brief prevention program showed less severe reexperiencing and arousal after 2 months than victims who only received repeated assessments of their psychopathology.

Current individual psychotherapeutic treatments may not be appropriate for many of those in need. Of those victims who do seek out this type of treatment, 20 to 30% drop out of treatment before completion. Little study of culturally appropriate methods has been done. Individual therapy for rape victims has been criticized as an inappropriate approach because it reduces rape from a social or political issue to an individual issue. These individualistic treatments, it is argued, encourage women to adjust to living in a rape-supportive society by focusing energy on their own recovery rather than also on political action that could ultimately prevent rape.

Group psychotherapeutic treatment for rape victims has become the intervention of choice of clinicians, as it both builds a community feeling of activism and empowerment and also provides individual support by peers who are able to validate feelings, share grief, and counteract self-blame. Group therapy is widely used both in community-based programs and within the formal mental health system. The effort directed at evaluation of group interventions is very disproportionate to the number of survivors treated by it. Whereas most evaluation studies have focused on individual treatment, most survivors receive group interventions. However, the few studies that exist have suggested promising results.

No one therapy has proven to be effective for every client, and no one treatment has proven to be superior for rape-related symptoms. All efficacious treatments share common features. Such features include the avoidance of victim blame, a supportive, nonstigmatizing view of rape as a criminal victimization, an environment in which to overcome cognitive and behavioral avoidance, provision of information about traumatic reaction, and the expectation that symptoms will improve. If specialty mental health care is going to be used more by rape victims, the victims need to know that their specific concerns will be addressed. Very little data currently exist on treatments for adolescents, for example, which is the largest population of rape victims. In addition, more study is needed on the specific concerns of different ethnic groups. Even the area of crisis intervention, which is used the most out of all specialized treatment, is lacking in empirical evaluation. The current treatment evaluations are brief and the current treatment studies deal only with uncomplicated cases and have only a small number of participants, treated by an unrealistically small number of therapists. Finally, research is needed to document that treatments incorporating a focus on the rape event itself are more effective than more traditional approaches that focus on symptoms of depression, anxiety, and sexual dysfunction. This includes the need to investigate the effectiveness of treatments in fostering adaptive accommodation, altering maladaptive schema changes, and applying cognitive strengths to the reconstruction of trauma memories.

VI. CONCLUSIONS

Over the years, the public has believed that rape was rare. We now know better. Stereotypes have also misled the public to think that most rapes involved strangers. Actually, the majority of perpetrators are known by their victims. Understanding the roots of rape requires moving beyond individual biology or pathology. The social context that supports rape must be acknowledged and the systemic response to rape scrutinized. Rape in the United States must be viewed from the perspective of the entitlements that have been granted, the attitudes that are modeled, and the feeble justice response mounted against it. Rape is reinforcing to those who use it, and cannot be eliminated without changing its payoff. Although rape affects individuals, it must be fought at a societal level. Treatment programs for sexual offenders have not lived up to expectations, and treatment for victims is provided through grassroots agencies perennially strapped for money. On the basis of these observations, the directions most likely to bring about significant change are in prevention and advocacy.

BIBLIOGRAPHY

Abbey, A., Ross, L. T., & McDuffie, D. (1995). Alcohol's role in sexual assault. In R. R. Watson (Ed.), *Drug and alcohol abuse reviews: Vol. 5. Addictive behaviors in women.* Totowa, NJ: Humana Press.

Bart, P. B., & Moran, E. G. (Eds.). (1993). *Violence against women: The bloody footprints.* Newbury Park, CA: Sage.

Crowell, N. A., & Burgess, A. W. (Eds.). (1996). *Understanding violence against women.* Panel on Research on Violence Against Women, Committee on Law and Justice, Commission on Behavioral and Social Sciences and Education, National Research Council. Washington, DC: National Academy Press.

Furby, L., Weinrott, M. R., & Blackshaw, L. (1989). Sex offender recidivism: A review. *Psychological Bulletin, 105,* 3–30.

Heise, L., Pitanguy, J., & Germain, A. (1993). *Violence against women: The hidden health burden.* Washington, DC: The World Bank.

Koss, M. P., Goodman, L. A., Browne, A., Fitzgerald, L. F., Keita, G. P., & Russo, N. F. (1994). *No safe haven: Male violence against women at home, at work, and in the community.* Washington, DC: American Psychological Association.

Koss, M. P., & Harvey, M. R. (1991). *The rape victim: Clinical and community interventions.* Newbury Park, CA: Sage.

Miczek, K. A., Mirsky, A. F., Carey, G., DeBold, J., & Raine, A. (1994). An overview of biological influences on violent behavior. In A. J. Reiss, K. A. Miczel, & J. A. Roth (Eds.), *Understanding and preventing violence: Vol. 2. Biobehavioral influences* (pp. 1–20). Panel on the Understanding and Control of Violent Behavior, Committee on Law and Justice, National Research Council. Washington, DC: National Academy Press.

Parrott, A., & Bechhofer, L. (Eds.). (1991). *Acquaintance rape: The hidden crime.* New York: John Wiley.

Resick, P. A., & Schnicke, M. K. (1993). *Cognitive processing therapy for rape victims: A treatment manual.* Newbury Park, CA: Sage.

Reactivity

Jim Blascovich

University of California, Santa Barbara

Kristen Salomon

University of Pittsburgh

Cardiac   Of or pertaining to the heart, a muscular organ responsible for pumping and distributing blood throughout the body.

Cardiovascular System   Provides a continuous supply of nutrients and minerals to meet the metabolic demands of bodily tissues and consists of the heart (pump), vasculature (vessels), and blood (fluid).

Cognitive Appraisal   Mental process by which individuals assess or construe situations resulting in various emotional and motivational states.

Psychophysiological   Of or pertaining to the study of neurally, hormonally, and immunologically driven physiological processes and mechanisms as they relate to psychological factors.

Vascular   Of or pertaining to the blood vessels, including arteries and veins.

REACTIVITY typically refers to physiological changes in response to psychological stimulation. Although reactivity as a generic term can and has referred to nonphysiological changes (e.g., changes in self-reported emotion), reactivity refers more typically to physiological changes, particularly changes involving the cardiovascular system. Health psychologists, psychophysiologists, and others have investigated both the antecedents and consequences of cardiovascular reactivity.

I. BACKGROUND

A. The Emergence of Reactivity as a Field of Study

Anecdotal information amassed over the centuries supports a positive relationship between stress-related personality dispositions and cardiovascular problems such as hypertension and coronary heart disease, leading many laypersons to accept implicitly the connection between the two. This intuitive association adds to the evidence provided by epidemiological investigations identifying a set of traditional risk factors (including family history, smoking, level of exercise, obesity, etc.) that in the aggregate predict only about half of the incidence of cardiovascular pathology. This evidence has led behavioral scientists, particularly psychologists, to examine the relationships between psychological factors and cardiovascular disease more explicitly.

In the last quarter of the twentieth century, investigators moved beyond the mere association of psychological factors, such as dispositions and stress, and disease to a consideration of possible mechanisms causally mediating the relationship. As often is the case in science, what appeared early on as a relatively simple and straightforward causal account now appears much more complicated.

B. Developments Contributing to the Understanding of Reactivity

As conceptual, technological, and analytic sophistication in psychophysiology has grown, behavioral scientists have made substantial advances in understanding probable mechanisms mediating relationships between psychological antecedents and disease. Investigators now understand the limits and empirical shortcomings of unitary arousal constructs for explaining the relationship between psychological factors and disease. Researchers now can assess a wide range of meaningful cardiovascular physiological responses noninvasively and continuously. Finally, analysts have more powerful statistical models and techniques to apply to reactivity data.

1. Increases in the Sophistication of Arousal Constructs

Cannon's claim of concurrent activation of most or all sympathetically controlled physiological systems in response to psychological stimuli provided a physiological basis for Hull's drive-reduction motivational model. Hull's model, in turn, provided the motivational underpinnings of various arousal-based theories such as Selye's general adaptation syndrome model of stress, Festinger's theory of cognitive dissonance, and Schachter and Singer's cognitive labeling theory of emotion. In theories of this type, arousal represents a departure from resting levels, albeit a sisyphean one, destined to return back to resting levels via psychological and behavioral adjustments of the organism. Cannon's notion of general sympathetic activation also provided justification for the measurement and indexing of arousal constructs via unitary and apparently interchangeable measures such as heart rate and skin resistance because, according to his fight-or-flight model, all such measures of sympathetic activation covaried positively.

Not surprisingly, the notion of general arousal set the stage for the premise that stress-related psychological factors lead to increased cardiovascular responses such as heart rate and blood pressure. Given that these responses occur in the absence of bodily (i.e., metabolic) demands for them, their occurrence unnecessarily strains and ultimately injures the organism. Hence, individuals at risk for relatively high or hyper-reactive responses (e.g., excessive elevations in blood pressure) by virtue of dispositional or other psychological factors could expect a higher likelihood of pathology (e.g., hypertension), and one could identify such individuals via simple heart rate and blood pressure measurements during relevant experiences (i.e., presumably stressful). [See HYPERTENSION; HEART DISEASE: PSYCHOLOGICAL PREDICTORS; STRESS.]

A variety of factors contributed to the fact that the premise of psychologically driven arousal underlying pioneering reactivity studies differed little from Cannon's notion of the early 1900s. For example, many reactivity researchers lacked formal psychophysiological training. However, as more psychophysiologically sophisticated investigators demonstrated the naivete of general arousal constructs, more sophisticated arousal notions emerged, enabling reactivity researchers to improve their theoretical models and measures accordingly. In 1981 Obrist distinguished between psychologically passive situations such as viewing horror films and psychologically active situations such as giving a speech arguing that only the active situations induced cardiovascular responses (presumably malignant) uncoupled with metabolic demands. In 1989 Dienstbier distinguished between benign and malignant cardiovascular responses within psychologically active situations, leading Blascovich and Tomaka in 1996 to identify distinctly different patterns of cardiovascular responses (see below) in psychologically active situations phenomenologically experienced as challenging (benign) or threatening (malignant). That benign cardiovascular responses to psychological stimuli exist explains the evidence that certain "hardy" or "physiologically tough" individuals appear immune to the development of cardiovascular diseases despite repeated exposure to potentially stressful or threatening psychological stimuli. [See HARDINESS IN HEALTH AND EFFECTIVENESS.]

2. Advances in Noninvasive Cardiovascular Recording

The simple heart rate and blood pressure measurement devices that previously constituted the reactivity researcher's tool box have been supplemented in the nineties by more sophisticated recording devices that, when coupled with high-performance laboratory computers, enable reactivity researchers to assess an abundance of theoretically important cardiovascular responses, including chronotropic, inotropic, hemodynamic, and vascular measures. Generally, these devices also provide continuous recordings allowing greater sensitivity both to acute and transient cardiovascular responses and to dysfunctional pathophysiological responses as well as providing time-based topological information (e.g., patterns of response recovery from peak reactivity to rest). Further, lightweight portable versions of these devices have begun appearing, allowing for ambulatory or field-based investigations in addition to the more traditional laboratory-based ones.

Chronotropic or time-based measures include not only the familiar heart rate (HR) but also systolic time intervals including left-ventricular ejection time (LVET) or the elapsed time between the opening and closing of the aortic valve that together with pre-ejection period comprises electromechanical systole (or EMS). Force-based or inotropic measures include most importantly pre-ejection period (PEP), which is the elapsed time between the onset of ventricular contraction and the opening of the aortic valve and constitutes an inverse index of the strength of ventricular contraction (i.e., the shorter the pre-ejection period, the greater the ventricular contractile force). Blood-based or hemodynamic measures include stroke volume (SV) or the amount of blood ejected from the left ventricle during a given cardiac cycle, cardiac output (CO) or the amount of blood ejected from the left ventricle per minute (equal to SV · HR), and blood pressure measures. The latter include systolic blood pressure (SBP) or peak blood pressure occurring when the aortic valve opens and the heart begins expelling blood, diastolic blood pressure (DBP) or the lowest level of the blood pressure occurring when the aortic valve closes and the heart relaxes, and mean arterial pressure (MAP) or average blood pressure across the cardiac cycle. Finally, vascular measures include importantly total peripheral resistance (TPR) a measure of vascular constriction (as indicated by increases in TPR) or dilation (as indicated by decreases in TPR).

Impedance cardiography represents perhaps the most important recent advance in cardiovascular measurement techniques. This technique rests on principles of electrical conduction defined in Ohm's Law (specifically stated as resistance or impedance equals voltage divided by current). Impedance cardiographs operate by passing a safe high-frequency alternating current through the thoracic cavity (see Fig. 1) and continuously assessing changes in impedance. The latter vary as a function of conductance changes in the thoracic cavity itself, which vary in large part as a function of pulsatile changes in blood flow into and out of the heart. Key inflections in continuous analog waveforms depicting changes in thoracic impedance have been associated with critical cardiac events, particularly the opening and closing of the aortic valve (see Fig. 2). Because key inflections on an electrocardiogram are associated with other cardiac events, particularly the onset of ventricular contraction (as seen

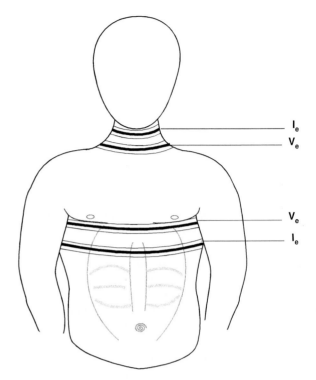

Figure 1 Impedance cardiographic band electrode configuration.

in Fig. 2), simultaneous recording of impedance cardiographic and electrocardiographic waveforms provide the researcher with the opportunity to measure chronotropic responses such as HR, LVET, and EMS, and inotropic responses such as PEP. Further, ampli-

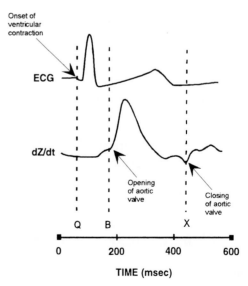

Figure 2 Derivation of cardiac measures using impedance and ECG signals.

tude measurements at critical points in the impedance waveforms provide the basis for computing hemodynamic measures such as SV. The latter when combined with HR allows the computation of CO (see Fig. 2).

Sophisticated automatic blood pressure recording devices have also appeared relatively recently. Some of these devices allow indefinite or continuous heartbeat-to-heartbeat SBP, DBP, and MAP assessment. The latter blood pressure devices do not repeatedly occlude arteries and thereby avoid repeatedly startling research participants with pain. Because CO and MAP fully determine TPR, blood pressure recording together with impedance cardiography and electrocardiography allows the computation of TPR (i.e., TPR = CO/MAP).

In addition to an improved set of cardiovascular response measurement tools, reactivity researchers now have more sophisticated devices at their disposal enabling them to assess more specific pathophysiological outcomes. For example, improved cineangiographic techniques allow more precise measurement of structural problems such as coronary artery disease. Radionuclide ventriculography allows more precise measurement of functional problems such as ventricular wall dysfunctions.

3. Advances in Analytic Techniques

Although most of the cardiac and vascular measures described above provide independent information about the cardiovascular system, the fact that the heart and the vasculature operate as a well-integrated system leads to positive correlations among these cardiovascular responses. Analysts must ordinarily remove such covariation effects statistically because the independent contributions of these variables constitute the information of interest. Furthermore, continuous measurement allows more powerful and sensitive examination of reactivity data via multivariate statistical techniques, including multivariate analyses of variance, multiple regression, multidimensional topographical representations, and structural equation modeling.

II. PATTERNS OF CARDIOVASCULAR REACTIVITY

As the conceptual, technological, and analytic advances described above unfolded, researchers assessed the convergence of various cardiovascular responses during potentially stressful episodes. It soon became apparent that not only did type of task or situation influence patterns of cardiovascular responses, as Obrist had demonstrated in his work on active and passive tasks, but also that at least two patterns of cardiovascular responses could be distinguished within active task situations themselves. Regarding the latter, investigators initially distinguished cardiac from vascular reactivity noting differences such that some research participants evidenced reactivity primarily in terms of cardiac or heart-based responses such as increases in HR and SV volume whereas others evidenced reactivity primarily in terms of vascular-based responses such as increases in TPR.

Blascovich and Tomaka took another approach arguing that the two types or categories of cardiovascular reactivity mapped better onto different phenomenological experiences (positive vs. negative) within active coping situations than to different types of individuals across active coping situations. Specifically, they suggested and demonstrated that benign (challenging, nonthreatening, nonstressful) perceptions of active coping tasks resulted in a pattern of increased cardiac and decreases vascular response (a pattern reminiscent of aerobic exercise), and that less benign (threatening, stressful) perceptions resulted in a pattern of both increased cardiac and increased vascular response (see Fig. 3).

Physiologically these patterns appear to follow Dienstbier's model of physiological toughness. Dienstbier noted that increased cardiovascular performance during potentially stressful situations can indicate positive or nonmalignant phenomenological states. Dienstbier associated increased sympathetic-adrenomedullary (SAM) activity with benign states

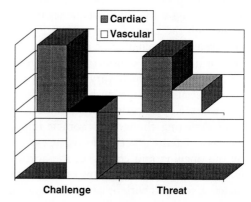

Figure 3   Cardiovascular indices of challenge and threat.

and improved performance and increased pituitary-adrenocortical (PAC) activity with malignant states when such activation occurs alone or concomitant with SAM activation.

Based largely on the work of Dienstbier, Blascovich and Tomaka posited that the benign pattern of physiological activation marked by SAM activation caused: (1) sympathetic neural stimulation of the myocardium increasing cardiac performance and (2) adrenal medullary release of epinephrine causing vasodilation in the large muscle beds and lungs and an overall decrease in systemic vascular resistance, as well as some additional enhancement of cardiac performance. These investigators posited that the malignant pattern marked by dual activation of the PAC and SAM axes caused: (1) elevations of cardiac performance over resting levels (SAM activity) and (2) decreased release of epinephrine and norepinephrine from the adrenal medulla (PAC activity) causing moderate increases in cardiac output without accompanying decreases in systemic vascular resistance. All other things equal, the malignant pattern should be accompanied by larger increases in blood pressure responses than the benign pattern.

The description and demonstration of qualitatively different patterns of cardiovascular reactivity allows for the integration of largely separate literatures that heretofore had little overlap: one in which increases in cardiovascular responses are associated with positive outcomes, including performance, and one in which increases are associated with negative outcomes not only in terms of performance but also in terms of cardiovascular health. Further, this distinction between patterns of reactivity helps better account for the apparently stronger epidemiological relationship between vascular reactivity and cardiovascular disease than exists between cardiac reactivity and disease.

In sum, measures of both cardiac and vascular responsivity appear necessary if one wants to draw strong inferences regarding psychologically generated cardiovascular reactivity. Furthermore, within the cardiac set of responses inotropic measures such as PEP and SV appear more informative than chronotropic ones such as heart rate.

III. THEORETICAL MODELS

Historically, two general types of theoretical frameworks, dispositional and transactional, have guided reactivity researchers. The former assumes that traits or dispositions drive reactivity, and the latter that the interactions or transactions of individuals with specific environments do. Gradually, as research has accumulated, the transactional type of reactivity model has supplanted the older, more simplistic dispositional type.

A. Dispositional Models

Dispositional or trait models of reactivity received their impetus from the attempts of researchers to relate global personality characteristics to cardiovascular disease. In this regard, the epidemiologically established relationship of the popular construct "Type A personality," or coronary-prone behavioral style, to cardiovascular disease provided a driving force.

Researchers within the dispositional framework generally based their investigations on simple causal models of the type illustrated in Fig. 4 (see panel A), which depicts cardiovascular reactivity as a mediator of the relationship between dispositions and disease. Interestingly, however, some investigators have used empirical assessments of cardiovascular reactivity in theoretical discussions as evidence of either the dispositional antecedent or the consequent pathology (see Fig. 4, panels B and C) rather than as indexes of the mediating physiological process.

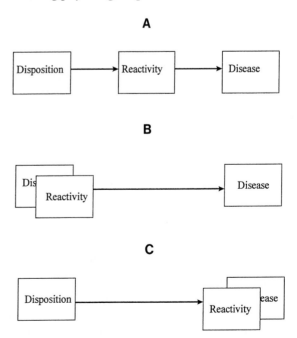

Figure 4 Generic dispositional reactivity model.

Although some reasonable arguments, particularly the assumption that vascular reactivity comprises part of the actual pathophysiological process, support the use of cardiovascular reactivity as a proxy for disease, little support exists for the use of cardiovascular reactivity as a proxy for a dispositional process. Nevertheless, some investigators have gone so far as to suggest that reactivity is a dispositional or trait construct itself and use labels such as "hot reactors" and "cold reactors" to anchor the assumed underlying dispositional reactivity dimension. In the view of many, claiming reactivity as the disposition itself represents a case of definitional operationism in the extreme on perhaps the same order as claiming that intelligence is what intelligence tests measure.

Furthermore, little evidence exists that would support such a view. First, although proponents demonstrate positive relationships within individuals' reactivity assessments across time and tasks, the limited types of situations within which these assessments occur share considerable overlap in situational influences (e.g., attachment of sensors to participants' bodies, presence of "polygraphs" and other physiological recording equipment, sequence of experimental procedures and events) leading to common demand characteristics and levels of evaluation apprehension. Thus, one could argue that the data purported to support the notion of within-person reliability in terms of cardiovascular responding across tasks and times also supports person-by-situation reliability across tasks and times. Second, within-person differences in cardiovascular reactivity have been demonstrated across tasks as a function of task appraisal (see below) providing serious logical problems for the reactivity as trait notion.

In sum, purely dispositional models of cardiovascular reactivity appear inadequate and oversimplified. Nonetheless, the deficiencies of the model do not detract from the wealth of evidence supporting the notion of dispositional influences on cardiovascular reactivity. These models simply do not explain all the variance in cardiovascular reactivity.

B. Transactional Models

Transactional models take the general form depicted in Fig. 5. Typically, the process linking situations and reactivity is mediated by some sort of cognitive appraisal or construal process. Thus, investigators in

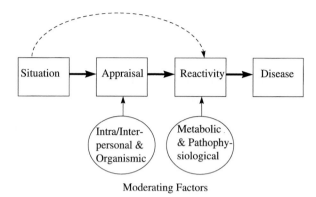

Figure 5 Generic transactional reactivity model.

this tradition assume that situations engender reactivity only as a function of the meaning (e.g., stressful vs. nonstressful, threatening vs. challenging) assigned to them by the actor. Holding the type of situation constant, generally or specifically, does not guarantee any particular pattern or intensity of cardiovascular response; whereas, controlling the meaning of the situation does.

According to transactional models, several types or categories of factors influence or moderate situational appraisals or construals. These categories include intrapersonal factors such as dispositions, cognitions, and affect; interpersonal factors such as liking and evaluation; and socially relevant organismic factors such as sex, race, and body type. Still other factors moderate appraisal induced cardiovascular reactivity. These include physiological ones such as metabolic factors and pathophysiological ones such as disease.

Finally, transactional models often include (as depicted in Fig. 5 by the broken line) a secondary pathway directly linking mere perception of the situation to reactivity independent of intervening processes and moderating factors. This pathway illustrates the possibility that the transactional process up to this point may be so well learned that reactivity occurs nearly instantaneously as a result of strong associations between specific types of situations, relevant appraisals, and cardiovascular responses.

Compared to dispositional approaches, transactional approaches better accommodate the many biological, psychological, and social factors, and processes thought to influence reactivity and its relationship to disease. In essence, such biopsychosocial approaches better encompass the complicated nature of reactivity.

IV. RESEARCH FINDINGS

Literally thousands of empirical studies have investigated various issues related to cardiovascular reactivity. This evidence of interest in reactivity stems from well-placed concerns of clinicians, investigators, and funding agencies regarding the multiplicity of causal mechanisms underlying cardiovascular diseases including psychological ones. Such a profusion of research findings also suggests the relevance of many subdisciplines of psychology including not only psychophysiology and health psychology but also clinical, personality, and social psychology. The transactional approach also facilitates summary and integration of the multidisciplinary nature of research findings involving cardiovascular reactivity.

A. Situational Influences

Clearly the nature of situations influences overall patterns of cardiovascular reactivity. One can draw the highest order distinction in this regard between goal-relevant and non-goal relevant situations. A potentially evocative or reactivity-related situation must engage the individual's motivation. If the situation remains unnoticed or irrelevant to the individual, meaningful reactivity will not occur. For example, taking the college board examination merely because one's school or parents require it may not engage the student who has little or no intention of attending college. Viewing a disturbing film may not engage the projectionist, at least in the same way that it does viewers.

A second order distinction lies between metabolically demanding and non-metabolically demanding goal relevant situations. The former; for example, athletic endeavors, clearly evoke substantial cardiovascular reactivity. However, most clinicians and researchers agree that such patterns generally do not predispose individuals to cardiovascular disease. However, evidence exists that engagement in metabolically demanding activities such as moderate aerobic exercise does not necessarily mask or prevent the more malignant patterns of reactivity associated with non-metabolically demanding goal-relevant tasks when they occur jointly (e.g., mental problem solving while jogging).

As discussed above, the nature of task demands within non-metabolically demanding, goal-relevant situations provides an important third level distinction. Specifically, whether task performance requires passive endurance (e.g., viewing a disturbing film) or active instrumental responding (e.g., giving a speech) affects resultant patterns of cardiovascular reactivity. With regard to reactivity, we know most about this type of situation; that is, active, non-metabolically demanding, goal-relevant ones. These situations pervade modern life, and thus this somewhat limited focus does not preclude important and clinically relevant theoretical and empirical advances.

B. Appraisal and Its Moderators

Clearly, cognitive appraisal of goal-relevant situations constitutes the key mediating process within transactional models of reactivity. How the individual appraises the situation affects the nature and pattern of resulting cardiovascular reactivity. As described above, Blascovich and Tomaka, as well as others, distinguish between benign challenge and malignant threat appraisals that result in distinguishable patterns of reactivity (see Fig. 3).

The evidence linking challenge and threat appraisals with these arguably benign and malignant cardiovascular reactivity patterns derives from laboratory studies in which participants freely appraised upcoming active performance tasks, studies in which investigators manipulated appraisals via instructional set, and studies in which investigators manipulated cardiovascular patterns resembling benign and malignant ones prior to situational appraisal. The former two groups of studies evidenced the patterns associated with specific overall appraisals (i.e., challenge and threat) while the latter set did not produce differences in appraisals lending support to the contention that cognitive appraisal mediates cardiovascular reactivity rather than the reverse. In addition, research has shown that variation in cardiovascular response pattern (i.e., malignant vs. benign) accompanies within-person changes in appraisal (i.e., challenge vs. threat).

1. Intrapersonal Moderators

As Fig. 5 depicts, intrapersonal factors comprise one category of situation-appraisal moderators. This category includes dispositional or personality, cognitive, and affective influences.

By far, most research on intrapersonal factors has focused on dispositions. Initially, investigators focused on Type A or coronary-prone personality style, establishing the relationship between this disposition and cardiovascular reactivity (though not necessarily distinguishing between the benign and malignant pattern suggested above). Later, researchers focused on specific components of the Type A construct resulting in general consensus that hostility provided the most influence or moderation. Other dispositions that investigators have shown to influence reactivity and by extension of the transactional view to appraisal include trait anger, anxiety, belief in a just world, and locus of control [See ANGER; ANXIETY.]

Clearly, cognitive factors also moderate appraisals of goal-relevant, motivated performance situation although researchers have devoted not nearly so much effort to this intrapersonal factor as on dispositional ones. To the extent that individuals bring specific knowledge and mental skills to bear on goal-relevant tasks, cognitive factors such as learning and memory remain important. Researchers have investigated attitudes as a cognitive moderator of the appraisal process and resulting reactivity. These experiments demonstrate that individuals possessing preexisting task-relevant attitudes exhibit benign patterns of reactivity during task performs compared to individuals who do not possess such attitudes.

Finally, affective states also likely moderate cognitive appraisal and eventual patterns of reactivity, although the amount of research in this area remains relatively sparse. One might expect that positive mood or affective states would predispose individuals to positive or challenge appraisals and that negative mood or affective states would predispose individuals to negative or threat appraisals. Indeed, work on dispositional affective traits such as anger, anxiety, depression, temperament, and hostility supports such a view. However, more research appears necessary if we want to understand the intricacies of non-dispositional mood states on appraisal and patterns of cardiovascular reactivity.

2. Interpersonal Moderators

According to the transactional view, a second category of cognitive appraisal moderators involves the presence of others in the goal-relevant, active performance situations (see Fig. 5). Much of the relevant work on this issue falls within the category of social support research. Social support investigators reason that the presence of supportive others should dampen

malignant reactivity patterns. According to the transactional view, the presence or availability of supportive others provides an important resource (i.e., an emotional one) in the demands/resources equation.

Interestingly, experimental research has demonstrated a quite interesting picture. Friendship, interpersonal closeness, and even marriage do not appear necessarily to cause the hypothesized benign effects of the presence of others during active performance situations on appraisal and reactivity. Rather, the extent to which performers regard any others present as evaluative. Furthermore, without special precautions to assure that they remain nonevaluative, even close friends and spouses can contribute to the evaluation apprehension of performers, thereby increasing the likelihood of threat. The fact that the presence of pets appears to lessen threat patterns of reactivity suggests performers consider them as nonevaluative supportive others. [See SOCIAL SUPPORT.]

3. Organismic Moderators

Biologically based individual characteristics such as sex, race, body size, and so on, appear relevant to the appraisal process. To the extent that such characteristics increase the perceived demands of the situation and/or decrease the perceived resources of the individual, they should moderate appraisal and thereby influence reactivity. For example, actors may feel greater evaluation apprehension to the extent they feel observers hold stereotypical beliefs regarding their race, sex, and so on. In addition, actors may hold self-stereotypes consonant with cultural stereotypes believing that as members of a stereotyped or stigmatized group they do not possess the skills or abilities to perform well (e.g., women on math tasks, African Americans on academic tests).

C. Reactivity and Its Moderators

According to the transactional view, the type and severity of cardiovascular reactivity patterns depends primarily on appraisal outcome. However, certain biological factors may moderate at minimum the severity of these patterns, including metabolic and pathophysiological ones.

I. Metabolic Moderators

Physiological processes, including metabolic demand and processes, likely moderate the strength of reactivity responses. Although, as mentioned above, moderate exercise does not appear to diminish the effects, higher levels of exercise may well provide sufficient metabolic demands to alter or mask psychologically generated reactivity patterns. Furthermore, the quality of the metabolism of cardiovascularly important chemicals and nutrients (e.g., sodium, lipids) can potentiate or diminish cardiovascular responses, thereby altering patterns of reactivity.

2. Pathophysiological Moderators

Because investigators regard the pernicious patterns of cardiovascular reactivity as antecedents of disease, once clinically significant levels of disease appear, these patterns may change. Cardiovascular diseases themselves may alter the pattern and severity of cardiovascular reactivity. Certainly, chronic diseases such as cardiomyopathy and arteriosclerosis affect at least the variability and sometimes the direction of cardiovascular responses during goal-relevant performance situations. In addition, the permanent effects of more acute pathophysiological events such as necrosis of cardiac muscle following myocardial infarction can have similar moderating influences.

D. Disease

Importantly, researchers have established that malignant patterns of reactivity appear related to chronic cardiovascular diseases, especially coronary heart disease and hypertension (which itself represents a cause of coronary heart disease). This link has been shown both experimentally in much significant animal research and in correlational studies involving the diagnostic utility of reactivity measures for both chronic disease states and functional cardiovascular problems (e.g., ventricular wall performance abnormalities).

Investigations to date suggest multiple pathophysiological vectors connecting psychologically generated cardiovascular reactivity to each of a large set of acute and chronic disease outcomes. Researchers have suggested many plausible pathways linking reactivity to disease, including maladaptation resulting from repeated sympathoadrenal medullary and pituitary adrenal cortical activation, endothelial injuries of the coronary arteries, and cardiac functional abnormalities. However, definitive specification of the exact pathophysiological mechanisms remains for future researchers.

V. CLINICAL AND HEALTH IMPLICATIONS

Psychologically driven patterns of cardiovascular reactivity likely serve as markers of mental as well as heart health. On an individual level, whether or not repeated malignant reactivity episodes eventuate in serious acute or chronic cardiovascular diseases, such patterns evidence the experience of threat, a likely harbinger of mental health problems and psychopathology.

Depending upon the actual or imagined situational context, threat reactivity may indicate the existence of various acute and chronic mental health problems such as burnout, posttraumatic stress disorders, anxiety, depression, and relationship problems. Although few if any clinicians currently assess cardiovascular reactivity patterns using sophisticated, state-of-the-art techniques, such assessments are possible. If clinicians can craft active performance tasks (e.g., role playing, speech anticipation and giving) phenomenologically capturing appropriate contexts related to potential problem areas in a client's life (e.g., romantic relationships, work, children), they may better identify important client problems and issues and better evaluate both therapy-based and pharmacological interventions and treatment outcomes over time.

That resource appraisals together with demand appraisals determine the benign or malignant nature of cardiovascular reactivity suggests a basis for therapeutic strategies to ameliorate threat experiences. Specifically, interventions designed to decrease the individual's perceptions of demands, dangers, and uncertainties in goal-relevant, active performance tasks together with interventions designed to increase the individual's perceptions of his or her own abilities, skills, and resources should help reduce meaningful threat and its mental and heart health sequelae.

BIBLIOGRAPHY

Anderson, N. B., McNeilly, M., & Myers, H. (1993). A biopsychosocial model of race differences in vascular reactivity. In J. Blascovish and E. S. Katkin (Eds.), *Cardiovascular reactivity to psychological stress and disease: An examination of the evidence* (pp. 83–108). Washington, DC: American Psychological Association.

Blascovich J., & Katkin, E. S. (Eds.) (1993). *Cardiovascular reactivity to psychological stress and disease.* Washington, DC: American Psychological Association.

Blascovich, J., & Tomaka, J. (1996). The biopsychosocial model of arousal regulation. In M. Zanna (Ed.), *Advances in Experimental Social Psychology, Vol. 28,* (pp. 1–51). New York: Academic Press

Dienstbier, R. A. (1989). Arousal and physiological toughness: Implications for mental and physical health. *Psychological Review, 96,* 84–100.

Lazarus, R. S., & Folkman, S. (1984). *Stress, appraisal, and coping.* New York: Springer.

Matthews, K. A., Weiss, S. M., Detre, T., Dembroski, T. N., Falkner, B., Manuck, S. B., & Williams, R. B. (1986). *Handbook of stress, reactivity, and cardiovascular disease.* New York: Wiley & Sons.

Obrist, P. A. (1981). *Cardiovascular psychophysiology: A perspective.* New York: Plenum.

Turner, J. R., Sherwood, A., & Light, K. C. (1993). *Individual differences in cardiovascular response to stress.* New York: Plenum.

Religion and Mental Health

Harold G. Koenig and David B. Larson

Duke University Medical Center

Health Professionals   Persons specially trained to deliver health care to others, including physicians, nurses, counselors, psychologists, social workers, and others.

Mental Health   The capacity to love and to receive love.

Neurotic   This refers to someone with internal conflicts; person may appear nervous, inhibited, excessively controlled or controlling, and/or emotionally unstable.

Religion   Beliefs, practices, and rituals related to a specific established religious tradition.

Spirituality   A sense of relatedness to a transcendent dimension or to something greater than the local self. While religion is included within spirituality, spirituality extends beyond religion and can include almost any human experience.

Religious beliefs and activities are widely prevalent and play an important role in the lives of many Americans. When asked about these practices, many persons report that they receive comfort and support from religious beliefs and activities. When studies have examined the relationship between **RELIGIOUSNESS AND MENTAL HEALTH**, they have found lower rates of depression, anxiety, and substance abuse among those who are more religiously committed. Treatment studies which have integrated religious beliefs and practices into traditional cognitive-behavioral therapy have reported quicker resolution of depression and anxiety disorders among religious patients than have traditional therapies. Because of high rates of emotional disorders and substance abuse among younger adults and the growing inability of our government to provide for such services (especially for the increasing number of older adults), a closer cooperation between religious bodies, community service agencies, and health care providers is necessary.

I. INTRODUCTION

Why have an article about faith and religion in an encyclopedia that focuses on the promotion and restoration of mental health? Sigmund Freud and some modern-day mental health professionals have emphasized the neurotic aspects of religious belief and practice. As a result, religiousness has been linked with emotional instability, rigidity, inflexibility, repression, and even delusional thinking. How then might religion be related to the promotion of mental health, improved coping, or the restoration of those who are mentally ill? While this topic at first may seem misplaced, there are a number of important reasons why an article on religion should be included.

These reasons include (1) the frequency of religious belief and practice in America; (2) the relationship between religiousness and mental health (as determined by systematic research); (3) the changing demographics, frequency, and pattern of mental illness in the community over the next 40 years; and (4) the increasing cost of health care and the increasing inability of government-sponsored programs to provide for mental health needs. Consequently, there has arisen a search for community resources that might help fill the widening cracks in mental health care left by dwindling government supports.

Religious bodies represent one such community resource. They are present in every community; a large proportion of each community is engaged and actively participating; religious bodies have traditionally cared for and helped the vulnerable, disadvantaged, and poor in society; and they proscribe a philosophy conducive to mental health. Most mental health professionals will have little problem with all but the last of these claims. Is religion really conducive to better mental health, or does it breed neurosis and mental instability as Freud and Ellis have argued and many in the mental health community still assume? We will address this question later on. For now, however, let us examine the types and frequency of religious beliefs and activities among Americans today.

II. RELIGIOUS BELIEF AND ACTIVITY

A. Religious Affiliation

A rich variety of different religious traditions flourishes in the United States. The founders of this country were drawn here at least partly in search of religious freedom, and this principle continues to draw persons from all over the world. All of the major world religions are represented here: Christianity, Judaism, Islam, Hinduism, and Buddhism (including Confucianism, Taoism, and Shintoism). However, it is important to consider what religious traditions Americans are most frequently affiliated with when we select a tradition to report details about religious belief and practice. For more than the past 50 years, the Gallup Polls have provided important information on religious preferences of Americans. According to the latest of these polls, conducted in 1994, 85% are traditional Christian (61% Protestant and 24% Catholic), 2% Mormon, 2% Jewish, 1% Greek or Russian Orthodox, 3% other than Christian or Jewish, and 6% none; less than 1% of Americans are Hindu, Muslim, or Buddhist. These distributions have changed little over the past 50 years.

Thus, more than 90% of Americans who claim a religious preference are affiliated with a Judeo-Christian religious tradition. For this reason, we have chosen to report in this article primarily on the practices of Christians and Jews, although the religious practices of persons from other world religions will also be briefly addressed. Furthermore, the reader should be aware that the statistics on religious practices for Christians and Jews are seldom reported separately; instead information on organizational practices is typically in the form of frequency of "church or synagogue" attendance while private religious practices are enumerated in terms of frequency of private prayer or scripture reading.

B. Judeo-Christian Beliefs and Practices

The religious faith of Protestant Christians, who make up almost two-thirds (61%) of all persons in the United States, can be expressed in terms of personal beliefs, organized religious activities (church attendance, home-centered Bible study or prayer groups, other social group activities), nonorganized religious activities (private prayer, scripture reading, listening to religious radio programs or watching religious television shows), and the subjective importance of religion in their lives. Catholic Christians express their faith in a manner similar to Protestants, although there is more emphasis on church tradition and ritual, Jesus' mother Mary, the saints, and the practice of praying the rosary.

A December 1994 Gallup poll reported that 96% of Americans believe in God or a Universal Spirit. There was little difference for age groups, with 94% of younger adults and 97% of older adults claiming to believe. These figures contrast markedly with belief in God by mental health professionals. A survey of more than 3000 mental health professionals revealed that almost one-third were agnostics or atheists (40% of those who were psychoanalytically trained). In a 1990 survey of religious beliefs and practices of psychologists, only 18% participated in organized religion and about one-half indicated that their personal religious beliefs encompassed "an alternative spiritual path."

Not only is belief common among the American public, but many claim that religion has an important influence in their lives as well. Surveys by the Princeton Religion Research Center (Gallup Poll) reveal that almost 70% of Americans indicate "completely true" or "mostly true" to the statement "Religion is the most important influence in my life." Conservative Christian beliefs are likewise common, with 85% indicating completely or mostly true to the statement "I believe in the divinity of Jesus Christ."

According to recent Gallup polls, both communal and private religious activities are likewise prevalent in the United States. Approximately 40% of the general population attends church weekly or more often (more than 50% for persons age 65 or older), 40% read the Bible weekly or more often (52% of those age 50 or older), 90% pray (95% of persons age 50 or over), and 49% watch religious television (64% of those age 65 or over). Thus, religious beliefs and activities are important for the majority of persons in the United States.

Christian religious beliefs and practices play an even greater role in the lives of Americans who belong to minority population groups. This is particularly true for Hispanic and African Americans. Hispanic Americans, the majority of whom are Catholic, report that religious beliefs and church activities provide them with personal as well as social support when dealing with stress, especially the stress of caring for sick or elderly family members. Most importantly, one of the most religious race-gender populations in American society is elderly African American women. Despite being at risk for suicide because of poor health and low socioeconomic status, elderly African American women surprisingly have by far the lowest suicide rate of any population subgroup. While elderly White divorced males have a suicide rate greater than 100 per 100,000 per year, the rate in elderly African American women is less than 3 per 100,000 per year. The church is known to be a vital informal source of support for many African Americans, particularly those who are older and who actively practice their faith.

Jewish Americans, on the other hand, express their religious faith by belief in God, synagogue attendance, special dietary practices (eating "kosher" foods) and fasting, and observance of Jewish holidays (Passover, Yom Kippur, etc.). A 1979 survey of the population of Israel by researchers Ben-Meir and Kedem revealed that 64% of Jews believe in God, 56% believe that God gave the Torah on Mt. Sinai, and 29% believe that the soul continues to exist after death; Jewish practices included praying on the Sabbath (23%), refraining from travel on the Sabbath (22%), fasting on

Yom Kippur (74%), buying only Kosher meat (79%), lighting Chanukah candles (88%), affixing a Mezuzah to home's entrance (89%), and participating in a Passover Seder (99%). To our knowledge, there has been no systematic survey of the beliefs and practices of Jews in the United States.

C. Other World Religions

Islam, Buddhism, and Hinduism are the other three great world religions that have a small but significant representation among Americans. Muslims believe in one God and in his Holy Prophet Mohammed. Religious teachings come from the Holy Koran, and conservative Muslims pray four times each day. Islam discourages ascetic life-styles and emphasizes the family. While Christianity, Judaism, and Islam are monotheistic religions, Buddhism and Hinduism may be described as pantheistic; rather than seeing God as a discrete personality outside of and apart from creation, pantheists see God as being all the laws, forces, and manifestations (including all living creatures) of the self-existing universe.

Buddhism is a more introspective, monastic form of religion that emphasizes the renunciation of this life. It draws attention to the suffering that occurs in life in order to motivate persons to detach from this world, to achieve a calming of the self, and to come to a fuller sense of the "ageless presence." Hinduism, on the other hand, tries to balance the priorities of family life and monasticism. Hindu faith is manifested in diverse traditions and rituals. It views the life cycle as being constantly renewed as the person moves upward in the Indian caste system. Islam, Buddhism, and Hinduism all play important roles in the lives of their adherents; systematic research is needed to better understand how these religious belief systems impact on mental health.

III. RELIGION AND MENTAL HEALTH INTERFACE

A. Attitudes toward Religion and Mental Health

Freud, Feuerbach, and Pruyser hypothesized that as persons grew older, their infantile notions of religion and God (as manifested by traditional Judeo-Christian beliefs) would gradually mature and lessen in importance; in effect, persons would "grow out" of their primitive need for such beliefs. Sigmund Freud, later affirmed by Albert Ellis, went so far as to say that religious influences were unhealthy and would eventually be replaced by the "rational operation of the intellect" as not only the person, but society as well, matured and advanced. Most recently, McMaster's professor of psychiatry Wendell Watters has written about the negative effects of religion on mental and physical health, claiming that Christianity in particular can be the cause of neuroses, depression, and even schizophrenia. In spite of predictions of religion's eventual demise and the passionate arguments for and against religion's negative effects on health, empirical research is beginning to move this topic out of the arena of personal opinion and public debate.

Large public surveys by the Gallup organization have recently eliminated substantial doubt about the continued importance and high frequency of traditional religious beliefs and practices among Americans, particularly the aged and those suffering with illness (see earlier section). In fact, from a societal perspective, weekly church attendance in the United States has changed little in the 60 years since Freud's death, and there is evidence that the secularization trends of the 1960s and 1970s are now beginning to reverse. Less clear until recently, however, has been religion's impact on mental health.

B. Research on Religion and Mental Health

Over the past 20 years, research on religion and health has increased substantially. During this period, literally hundreds of papers have been published on religious belief or practice and some aspect of health. Research reports have appeared in many different professional journals in the fields of psychology, psychiatry, pastoral counseling, medicine, nursing, social work, and gerontology. Because this research is so widely scattered (and still somewhat limited), professionals in one field often have little idea about advances in other professional fields. For this reason, there is little consensus about the impact of religion on health. A comprehensive review of almost 300 recent publications in the field of aging alone, however, has uncovered a set of consistent findings.

The majority of these studies, particularly those conducted within the past decade, have demonstrated

a positive relationship between Judeo-Christian beliefs and practices (the most frequently studied in the United States) and mental health. This research can be divided into: (1) self-reports by research subjects about the effects of religious commitment on their ability to cope and adapt to life stressors; (2) objective examinations of the relationship between religiousness and emotional health in epidemiological surveys; and (3) treatment studies that have integrated religious beliefs and behaviors into traditional therapies for depression and anxiety disorders.

C. Self-Reported Benefits of Religion

Participants in community and clinical research studies commonly report that their religion aids them in understanding, coping with, and adapting to negative life events and health problems. In studies that have asked subjects open-ended questions such as "What is it that enables you to cope with stress?" between one-quarter and one-third consistently provide religious responses (this is especially true for older respondents). When asked a direct question on whether religious beliefs or practices provide comfort and support, between 69% and 89% of persons give affirmative responses. [See COPING WITH STRESS.]

This well-documented tendency for people to *turn to religion* for comfort during times of physical illness or emotional turmoil, however, can complicate, or confound research results when we examine the cross-sectional relationship between religious behaviors and well-being or emotional health. This "dynamic factor" (persons turning to religion when upset or distressed) will at least partially cancel out an inverse relationship between religiousness and emotional distress that might indicate a protective effect for religion. An appropriate clinical comparison would arise if psychiatric patients were asked about the number of times they saw a psychiatrist in the past year and this number was then correlated with test scores indicating level of emotional distress. Despite the fact that psychiatrists actually treat patients' symptoms, it is likely that the researcher would find a positive relationship between emotional symptoms and the number of visits to mental health professionals. One could hardly conclude (although some decision makers have tried) that seeking help from such providers worsened the patients' psychiatric symptoms. The same line of thinking holds true for religious beliefs and practices. Mental health professionals have drawn this faulty conclusion about religion for more than half a century now.

D. Epidemiological Studies

Despite the difficulty of demonstrating an inverse relationship between religion and mental distress, there have been at least 50 published reports (mostly cross-sectional) in the past 15 years showing that religious persons experience not only greater well-being and higher life satisfaction, but less anxiety and depression, lower rates of suicide, less alcoholism, less loneliness, and better adaptation to stress than do persons without spiritual resources. This is particularly true for Black Americans and other minority and low income groups. In a 1995 study of a representative national sample of 1848 African Americans of all ages, Levin and colleagues, using state-of-the-art statistical modeling, found that religious activities were associated with better health and higher life satisfaction; in fact, religious activities were as strong a predictor of life satisfaction as overall health status. Their model fitted equally well in both younger and older African Americans.

Instead of religious coping behaviors disintegrating during periods of high stress (as predicted by mental health traditionalists, consistent with Freud), they appear to function even better during these periods than do less religious persons. In 1989, Manton directly examined the relationship between "spiritual support" and indicators of well-being in two study samples, dividing each sample into persons experiencing high psychosocial stress and those experiencing low stress. For both high stress subsamples, spiritual support was significantly related to personal adjustment (assessing in this case low depression and high self-esteem), whereas no relationship was found in the low-stress subsamples. Likewise, in a study of 850 medically ill patients admitted to an acute care hospital, Koenig and colleagues found an inverse relationship between religious coping and depression. Once again, this relationship was stronger among patients with severe disability than among those who were more functional and independent. In the latter study, religious coping was the only one of 15 psychosocial and health factors that predicted lower rates of depression when patients were readmitted to the hospital months later. [See DEPRESSION.]

Ellen Idler's work from the Yale Health and Aging Project has also demonstrated that for the chronically ill, religiousness can affect not only the relationship between disability and depression, but also an individual's perception of their disability. At any level of chronic illness, Idler found that the more religious the person was, the less disability they tended to report. Likewise, the relationship between disability and depression weakened as religiousness increased. These findings have important public health implications for an expanding population of elderly persons in the United States with high rates of chronic illness and disability, especially at a time when funds for mental health services may be increasingly limited.

E. Treatment Studies

In 1992, Propst and colleagues compared the efficacy of two versions of Cognitive-Behavioral Therapy (CBT) in treating depressed patients (average age 40 years). One version was a standard CBT protocol; the other version included specific religious content based on counseling practices used by Protestant and Catholic clergy when treating depressed congregants (religious CBT). Religious CBT gave Christian religious rationales for the therapeutic interventions, used religious arguments to counter irrational thoughts, and used religious imagery as part of the behavioral component. Forty religious patients were randomly allocated to either standard CBT, religious CBT, a pastoral counseling group, or a wait-list control group (10 in each of the four groups). Each of the intervention groups received 18 fifty-minute sessions, and was assessed with multiple measures of depression and overall illness severity pretreatment, at study termination, and at 3 and 24 months thereafter. The measures used were based on a previous National Institute of Mental Health multisite depression intervention study. Results showed that religious CBT and pastoral counseling groups achieved significantly lower posttreatment depression and adjustment scores than did either the standard protocol or wait-list control groups. Improvement for the three treatment conditions, however, was equal at 3 months and at 2 years followup.

A second study by Azhart and colleagues in 1994 assessed the effectiveness of religious psychotherapy in the treatment of Muslim patients with anxiety disorder. Sixty-two patients (again, average age 40 years) were randomly assigned to either study or control groups. Both groups received from 12 to 16 weekly sessions of supportive psychotherapy for anxiety and

8 weeks of benzodiazepines. In addition, however, the study group was given religious psychotherapy that involved having patients read verses from the Holy Koran and encouraging prayer. At 3 months, the study group scored significantly lower on the Hamilton Anxiety scale (rated by a psychiatrist blinded to treatment group); by 6 months, however, again there was no significant difference between study and usual treatment groups. These two studies document the beneficial effects of a religious intervention, if only short-term, for emotional disorders in religious persons. It is important that future research not only looks at clinical outcomes but religious outcomes as well. [*See* ANXIETY.]

F. Possible Mechanisms of Effect

Questions that remain unanswered include *how* religious beliefs and activities might buffer against emotional distress or facilitate its resolution, and to what extent all world religions—regardless of belief or activity—have similar effects. Unfortunately, the second part of this question is not answerable at this time. There have been no detailed systematic studies comparing the effects of Christian, Jewish, Muslim, Bud-

dhist, or Hindu belief systems and practices on mental health. Most studies published to date on religion and mental health have been done in subjects affiliated with a Judeo-Christian faith tradition. The 1994 Azhart study on Muslims is a rare exception. For this reason, the results from these studies cannot be generalized to other world religions nor to other even newer forms of spirituality. Indeed, there may be specific aspects of the Judeo-Christian belief system that can be particularly conducive (or harmful) to mental health. Little is known, however, about what those characteristics might be.

G. Prevention of Mental Health Problems

The research that has been conducted on the relationship between Judeo-Christian belief systems and mental health offers interesting insights into the possible mechanisms by which religious beliefs and behaviors might prevent the development of emotional problems (Fig. 1) or facilitate their resolution (Fig. 2). These influences can be divided into cognitive or intrapsychic effects and social or interpersonal effects. It is likely that such factors could have an impact over the lifetime of the individual. First, the religious back-

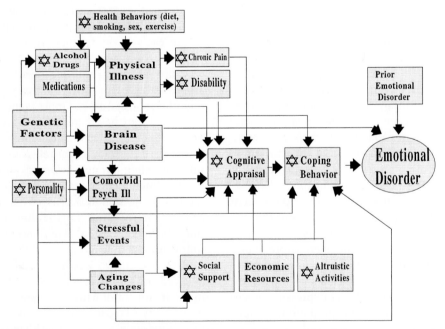

Figure 1 Hypothesized model of the way religious beliefs and activities help prevent emotional disorder in later life. From Koenig, H. G. (1995). *Research on Religion and Aging.* Westport, CT: Greenwood Press. Used with permission.

ground and beliefs of parents may affect early childhood development. Religious beliefs influence how parents discipline children, what types of values and morals are instilled, how much tenderness and love they express toward them, and how they view children in general (as a "blessing" or a hindrance). Furthermore, if religion is an effective coping strategy, then it could affect the emotional adjustment of parents and help determine their emotional availability to children. Each of these factors can have a profound influence on personality development.

Second, religious prohibitions against substance abuse can affect the development of alcoholism or drug abuse and the consequent physical and mental health problems associated with the more severe disorders. These prohibitions can also influence whether a person turns to alcohol or drugs in response to stress, or chooses healthier coping responses. Promiscuous sexual practices, unhealthy dietary habits, and smoking can also adversely affect health over a lifetime and increase an individual's vulnerability to physical health problems in later life, as well as to depression, anxiety, or substance abuse that can follow such health problems. Thus, religious beliefs may limit risk-taking behaviors and foster healthier life-styles.

Third, as discussed earlier, religious beliefs can shape a person's psychological perception of pain or disability at any given level of objective physical illness severity. Most importantly, religious cognitions may play an important role in maintaining hope and stimulating motivation toward recovery. In the same way, religious beliefs can affect the person's *cognitive appraisal* of stressful events unrelated to health. In all these cases, it is not the event itself that causes distress, but the person's interpretation of that event and its meaning for him or her. Religious beliefs and attitudes can help persons to view negative situations in a more positive light by thinking about and focusing on, for example, the hopes stated in their holy scriptures or on their religious role models. Belief in a caring, compassionate, interested, and all-powerful God who is in control and who can be coaxed into action on their behalf through personal prayer can provide a person with hope and a sense of control that he or she otherwise would not have.

Fourth, religion may affect the types of coping responses a person chooses as they attempt to deal with different losses in life (job, health, loved ones, social position). Because of its effectiveness in reducing distress in the setting of physical illness, religious cop-

ing may help prevent frank denial of the problem and thus facilitate early recognition and more appropriate health-seeking behavior (as in cancer or heart disease). Likewise, as noted before, religious beliefs may help discourage excessive use of alcohol or addicting sedatives in response to life stressors, behaviors that could lead to even greater health problems down the road. Respect and honor for one's life and physical body is a basic Judeo-Christian tenet that may enhance timely health care and improve compliance with treatment. The latter is an important arena for future clinical research.

Fifth, besides reducing emotional distress through healthy cognitions and coping behaviors, religion might also forestall the development of depression or anxiety disorders by its promotion of communal or social interaction. Houses of religious worship are a readily available, acceptable, and inexpensive source of support for many persons, particularly the elderly and those with medical care needs. Studies of patients seeking medical care for health problems have reported that more than 50% of patients report that all or most of their closest friends come from their church congregation. The socialization provided by religious organizations can help prevent loneliness and isolation, and it can provide healthy leisure activities among age-matched peers. In religious settings, support groups naturally form for those who have lost a spouse, for those struggling with disability or specific illnesses (cancer), or for family members burdened with the responsibility of caring for an elderly parent or spouse. In addition, Judeo-Christian tenets encourage a sense of community, caring for others, and love of one's neighbor that may help stimulate volunteer activities that take the person's attention away from their own problems and refocus energy on providing for the needs of others. The latter fulfills the dual function of providing for the instrumental needs of less-fortunate members of the congregation, and giving the helper a sense of purpose and meaning in life by "serving God." Neal Krause at the University of Michigan has now published objective evidence that volunteer activities focused on helping others is associated with greater well-being. [*See* SOCIAL NETWORKS; SOCIAL SUPPORT]

H. Resolution of Mental Health Problems

Should depression or anxiety disorders develop, religious beliefs and practices may also help accelerate re-

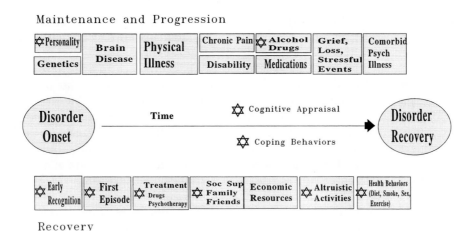

Figure 2 Hypothesized model of the way religious beliefs and activities help facilitate recovery from emotional disorder in later life. From Koenig, H. G. (1995). *Research on Religion and Aging*. Westport, CT: Greenwood Press. Used with permission.

covery (Fig. 2). Religious cognitions and social activities help to speed recovery in much the same way that they act to prevent the development of emotional disorders. Adjustment problems are usually time-limited and most persons move naturally toward adaptation and recovery. Religion may facilitate this movement by discouraging unhealthy coping behaviors that could exacerbate the problem (drugs or alcohol), by promoting early recognition and treatment within the church setting, by enhancing compliance with psychotherapy or psychotropic medications, by encouraging continued social participation and involvement, and by providing a social group to whom one can turn for comfort and support. High social support has been found to predict both a lower rate of onset of major depression and a more rapid recovery in middle-aged and older adults. Finally, religion may reduce the risk of suicide by providing the person with hope and a belief system that discourages self-destructive acts.

I. Negative Effects of Religion

This review would be incomplete if only the positive features of religion were considered. Religion, like all other potentially good things in life, can also have its negative sides. The negative or clinically harmful aspects of religion, in the opinion of these authors, are primarily due to its rigid use, misuse, and manipulation by persons who were neurotic or otherwise mentally disturbed before they became religious or by those whose life practices seem to have little in common with what they believe. Several examples follow. A narcissistic person might use religious doctrines to build, if not inflate, their sense of pride; justify their sense of "correctness"; or excuse their insensitivity to others whom they view as different (thus having less worth) than them. Similarly, an obsessive-compulsive person might focus on church work to the exclusion of other family or job responsibilities, adversely affecting family life or outside relationships. A perfectionistic, controlling person may hold onto religious doctrines so rigidly and inflexibly that he or she is unable to tolerate either his or her own faults (without exaggerated guilt) or the imperfections in others (without being critical and rejecting). Finally, the untrusting, paranoid person may project their hostility onto nonreligious peers, labeling them as "religious" persecutors, or may keep others at a distance by angrily condemning the "errancy" of their beliefs, even though these beliefs may vary only slightly from their own.

For more severely disordered persons, religion may be the direct manifestation of psychosis. The grandiose manic may feel that he or she has a special relationship with God, a message from God, or, in fact, is God. The depressed elder may experience delusions of pathological guilt for having committed an imagined sin for which they believe there is no forgiveness. Despite these pathological uses and manifestations of religion, traditional beliefs and practices are in general positively related to better mental health outcomes. In what way might this observation be relevant to mental health professionals and health care planners?

IV. CHANGES IN DEMOGRAPHICS AND PATTERNS OF MENTAL ILLNESS

A. Demographic Changes

A decreasing birth rate and improvements in health care that are reducing infant and childhood mortality and allowing older persons to live longer has brought on the "aging of America." While there were only about 28 million persons age 65 or over in the United States in 1985 (i.e., 12% of the population), in the year 2000 there will be 35 million, in the year 2020, 55 million, and in 2040, an estimated 70 million persons in this age group (25% of the population). Aging of the 76-million-member baby-boom cohort is primarily responsible. Indeed, persons age 85 or older are the most rapidly growing age group in America today.

B. Distribution of Mental Illness

National surveys indicate a distinct age distribution of psychiatric disorders in the community. Low rates of depression, anxiety disorder, and substance abuse have been found among the current cohort of older adults (who also are less likely to utilize mental health services). High rates of psychiatric disorder, on the other hand, have been documented in younger and middle-aged cohorts (who are much more likely than older adults to utilize mental health resources). At a time when rates of psychiatric disorder and use of mental health services are at their lowest in the elderly (only 2 to 3% of the Medicare budget is spent for mental health services), there is already a growing problem with access to care for geriatric patients on Medicare. What will happen when these younger cohorts with higher rates of psychiatric illness and higher demand for mental health services reach old age? Furthermore, with increasing numbers of severely disabled elderly and 14 million (or more) persons with Alzheimer's disease projected for the mid-twenty-first century, rates of associated depression and adjustment disorders among patients and family caregivers are expected to increase even further, possibly overwhelming health service networks.

C. Increasing Costs of Health Care

According to the American Hospital Association, Medicare expenditures increased from $38 billion in 1980 to $170 billion in 1995. To stem the continuing rapid growth in this program, attempts are being made to cut back on Medicare spending. The intention is to help reduce overall federal spending (which is now 4% higher than income from taxes), prevent the deepening of a $6 trillion national debt, and free up funds to pay for much needed health care reform. Yet these cutbacks in Medicare will be coming at a time of increased need for geriatric services, particularly mental health care. It appears possible, then, that government programs over the next half-century will not be able to meet the rising demand for mental health services (both geriatric and nongeriatric). Consequently, there is a need to identify resources within the community that might help supplement existing programs.

D. The Church and Synagogue as Community Resources

As we discussed earlier, 70 to 80% of Americans are members of a church or synagogue and 40% attend services at least weekly. Numbers like these make organized religion the most common form of voluntary social activity (outside of the family) in the United States; in fact, involvement in religious organizations is probably greater than all other forms, of voluntary community activity combined. Religious institutions are present in every community, are privately funded, and hold a philosophy of caring for others and meeting the needs of the less fortunate. Before government-funded welfare programs were in place for the poor and the sick, who took on the responsibilities for their needs and care? Either their families did, or the church did.

V. RESPECT FOR RELIGION IN CARE AND TREATMENT

A. Cooperation between Church and State

What is the clinical significance of these new research findings and their implications for the delivery of mental health services to persons living in the United States? Given the increasing demand for mental health services, the increasing inadequacy of public resources to meet these needs, the traditional role of the religious sector in meeting such human needs, and the positive effects of Judeo-Christian beliefs and behaviors on mental health (particularly among high-risk groups such as the poor, the chronically ill, and the disabled), it would appear prudent that a working alliance be developed between church, community social service agencies, and family caregivers to help meet mental health needs.

Such a collaboration is especially important from a public health standpoint. There is an increasing need in this country to foster groups as well as personal practices that promote mental health and prevent emotional distress. This is true for the healthy persons living in the community, for frail homebound or institutionalized persons, and for their family caretakers. While it is necessary to bear in mind the need to preserve religious freedom and respect individual beliefs of all kinds, the encouragement and recognition of healthy religious beliefs and behaviors should be a priority for both public service programs and individual health care providers.

Educational seminars sponsored by social service agencies could educate clergy and their staff about the mental health needs of their congregants. Mental health professionals might be brought in to teach basic counseling skills, as well as to provide information about how to recognize common psychiatric diagnoses, and to determine what disorders can be handled within the church and which require timely referral to mental health specialists. In this way, churches could act as a front line for mental health screening, facilitating early detection and treatment before emotional conditions advance to the point that they require more costly outpatient or even inpatient professional care. When persons do develop mental illness that requires professional help, then a treatment plan could be developed that includes local followup within the church by lay counselors (or parish nurses) acting as case managers.

B. Religious Interventions by Mental Health Professionals

How can health professionals utilize the spiritual resources of patients to facilitate adaptation and speed recovery, while at the same time showing respect for the patients' religious beliefs and practice, which may vary from their own? Do patients want health professionals to address religious issues? Are health pro-

fessionals willing and able to address such issues? How many health professionals address religious issues with patients? These are difficult questions, and there is clearly a need for further research to provide adequate answers. Some information, however, may be learned from research already done in older adults seeking care in the medical setting.

In 1988, Koenig and colleagues surveyed a random sample of 160 Illinois physicians about their attitudes toward and experiences with religious issues among their older patients. Almost half of physicians (49%) indicated that patients at least sometimes mentioned religious issues during a clinical visit. When asked if religious issues should be left entirely up to the clergy to deal with, 69% of physicians disagreed, indicating that doctors should be able to address these issues at least some of the time. When asked what types of religious interventions were appropriate for physicians during a clinic encounter, 77% of physicians indicated that encouraging a patient's own beliefs was appropriate, 66% indicated that joining in prayer with the patient was appropriate, and 63% indicated that sharing their own beliefs with a patient was appropriate. When asked whether these clinicians had ever prayed with patients, 37% indicated that they had; interestingly, this was roughly the same percentage of physicians who thought that patients would want their physician to pray with them (63% felt that patients would not want this).

As a followup to this study, 72 persons were asked the following question: "If you were experiencing great emotional distress, were very sick, or were near death, would you like your personal physician to pray with you?" The four possible responses were "No, definitely not," "No, probably not," "Yes, somewhat," and "Yes, very much." Seventy-eight percent of respondents indicated an affirmative response (51% very much, 27% somewhat). While these data cannot be applied to mental health professionals and their patients, they give the reader a sense that both medical physicians and patients are quite open and willing to deal with religious issues in the clinical setting.

In one of the few published discussions in a contemporary mental health journal that examines how knowledge about a patient's religious beliefs can help facilitate diagnosis and treatment, Waldfogel and Wolpe use six dimensions of religious experience to discuss approaches to incorporating religious factors in the psychiatric evaluation and treatment of medically ill hospitalized patients. They conclude that the role of the psychiatrist is to seek to understand the patient's beliefs and then use them to help the patient to better cope with his or her illness. Consultation with clergy is also stressed both to help overcome resistances by a patient who views psychiatrists as anti-religious and to help the patient accept the psychiatric evaluation and treatment plan. If the patient asks the psychiatrist about his or her own religious beliefs, the authors suggest that the psychiatrist may or may not choose to respond. Those who feel uncomfortable about revealing their personal beliefs are encouraged to acknowledge the importance of the search for meaning and to state that not everything in the world can be scientifically explained. This response may help open a dialogue with patients who are fearful that their beliefs will not be respected. Finally, Waldfogel and Wolpe suggest that psychiatrists examine their own religious beliefs and spiritual needs so that these do not interfere with the evaluation and treatment of their patients. Formal training in residency programs and collaborative work with clergy are suggested.

The above suggestions are useful for mental health professionals when dealing with religious issues of their patients. In these instances, the clinician should obtain a religious history from the patient. This can be done in a routine, matter-of-fact fashion and it can be included in the developmental history section of the initial evaluation. At a minimum, this should include the religious background of the parents, the patients' current religious denomination, whether they are currently active members of a church, whether they find religious beliefs or activities helpful in enabling them to cope, examples of how religion has helped or harmed them, and to what extent they feel religious issues are involved in their current situation. Simply taking a history is often therapeutic; it is also helpful for clarification and for a deeper understanding for the therapist of the patient's issues.

If the clinician feels the religious beliefs and behaviors of the patient are healthy and are facilitating adjustment, then he or she should learn how this can be supported or encouraged. If, on the other hand, the clinician feels that the patient's religious beliefs are contributing in some way to psychopathology, then consultation with the patient's clergy (after approval from the patient) might be advisable. While most patients are quite open about discussing religious issues, there are some patients who wish to keep religion and

psychotherapy separate. While this feeling should always be honored by the therapist, he or she might gently explore why the patient feels this way.

Existential and spiritual issues frequently overlap with psychological concerns of patients. Such issues involve finding meaning and purpose in life, coming to terms with one's mortality, dealing with the loss of loved ones, resolving old wounds and conflicts, and putting together one's life history and making sense of it all. Religion can provide answers to questions that the social and psychological sciences have understandable difficulty in addressing. As clinicians and members of community service agencies come to better understand the role that religious beliefs play in helping persons to adapt to stress, they will begin to develop respect and appreciation for them as the immense resource that they can be.

VI. CONCLUSION

Religious beliefs and activities are widely prevalent and play an important role in the lives of many Americans. When asked about these practices, many persons report that they receive comfort and support from religious beliefs and activities. When studies have examined the relationship between religiousness and mental health, they have found lower rates of depression, anxiety, and substance abuse among those who are more religiously committed. Treatment studies that have integrated religious beliefs and practices into traditional cognitive-behavioral therapy have reported quicker resolution of depression and anxiety disorders among religious patients than have traditional therapies. Because of high rates of emotional disorders and substance abuse among younger adults and the growing inability of our government to provide for such services (especially for the increasing number of older adults), a closer cooperation between religious bodies, community service agencies, and health care providers would appear prudent as we seek to better meet and effectively deal with the mental health needs of Americans in the twenty-first century.

ACKNOWLEDGMENTS

Funding provided in part by a grant from the John Templeton Foundation and King Pharmaceuticals, Bristol, TN (Dr. Larson); by an

NIMH Clinical Mental Health Academic Award MH01138 (Dr. Koenig); and by the Center for the Study of Religion/Spirituality and Health at Duke University Medical Center.

BIBLIOGRAPHY

Ben-Meir, Y., Kedem, P. (1979). Index of religiosity of the Jewish population of Israel. *Megamot 24*; 353–362.

Koenig, H. G., Smiley, M., & Gonzales, J. P. (1988). *Religion, health, and aging* (pp. 136–139). Westport, CT: Greenwood Press.

Koenig, H. G., Cohen, H. J., Blazer, D. G., Pieper, C., Meador, K. G., Shelp, F., Goli, V., & DiPasquale, R. (1992). Religious coping and depression in elderly hospitalized medically ill men. *American Journal of Psychiatry 149*, 1693–1700.

Koenig, H. G. (1994). *Aging and God*. New York: Haworth Press.

Koenig, H. G. (1995). *Research on religion and aging*. Westport, CT: Greenwood Press.

Koenig, H. G. (1996). Religion and psychotherapy with older adults. *Journal of Geriatric Psychiatry 29*, 155–184.

Koenig, H. G. (1997). *Is Religion good for your health?* New York, NY: Haworth Press.

Larson, D. B., Lu, F. G., & Swyers, J. P. (1996). *Model curriculum for psychiatry residency training programs: Religion and spirituality in clinical practice*. Rockville, MD: National Institute for Healthcare Research.

Levin, J. S., Chatters, L. M., & Taylor, R. J. (1995). Religious effects on health status and life satisfaction among Black Americans. *Journal of Gerontology (social sciences) 50B*, S154–S163.

Manton, K. I. (1989). The stress-buffering role of spiritual support: Cross-sectional and prospective investigations. *Journal for the Scientific Study of Religion 28*, 310–323.

Matthews, D. A., Larson, D. B., & Barry, C. P. (1993–1995). *The faith factor: An annotated bibliography of clinical research on spiritual subjects* (Vols. I–IV). Rockville, MD: National Institute of Healthcare Research.

Waldfogel, S., & Wolpe, P. R. (1993). Using awareness of religious factors to enhance interventions in consultation-liaison psychiatry. *Hospital and Community Psychiatry 44*, 473–477.

Retirement

Phyllis Moen and Heather E. Quick

Cornell University

Cumulation of Advantage or Disadvantage The situation in which personal characteristics (e.g., gender, race) or early events (e.g., educational achievement, occupational choice) have either a positive or negative influence throughout life, with a widening gap developing over time between the advantaged and the disadvantaged.

Ecological Context A general term referring to the physical or social environment unique to a group or individual.

Life Course Paradigm (Perspective) A theoretical perspective that emphasizes the importance of understanding individual change and development as the product of experiences throughout life, the timing of those experiences, and the context of social and historical time.

Role Enhancement Perspective A theoretical perspective that suggests that occupying multiple roles has certain benefits for well-being.

Role/Social Role A position (e.g., worker, volunteer, mother) that an individual holds in any group organization (e.g., company, community, family).

Role Strain Perspective A theoretical perspective that suggests that holding many roles is stressful for the individual and therefore has a negative impact on well-being.

Social Integration When an individual occupies social roles (the opposite of social integration is social isolation).

Trajectory A pathway or series of role involvements throughout the life course involving the movement in and out of social roles, the timing of these changes, and the time spent in each role (e.g., the employment trajectory is made up of the years spent in particular jobs as well as the job changes that occur between the first and final jobs).

Transition A major shift in roles or relationships, as when an individual leaves a role, takes on a new role, or changes roles.

RETIREMENT has traditionally meant the movement from full-time employment to full-time leisure at the end of a lifetime of work (usually at age 65). However, retirement has become more complicated. Some individuals "retire" from their career job but take on a second or third career. Thus retirement and work are no longer mutually exclusive. Also, norms regarding the appropriate age to retire are changing, and growing numbers of workers are retiring earlier (in their 50s and early 60s), while a few retire much later or never retire.

Encyclopedia of Mental Health
Volume 3

I. OVERVIEW OF THE RETIREMENT TRANSITION

Retirement is an important transition in later life and a focal point for understanding the path to successful aging. However, to date, there is little consensus as to what contributes to mental health after retirement. The relationship between the transition to retirement and psychological well-being is not a simple one; retirement may mean an increase in mental health, a decrease in mental health, or no change whatsoever. Studies comparing older workers and retirees often find both to be satisfied with their lives.

The effect of the retirement transition on mental health must be understood within the context of the life experiences prior to retirement (including the preretirement job), the nature of the retirement transition, and life after retirement. It is this more complex, ecological and life-course focus that is the most fruitful for an understanding of what promotes mental health in retirement. In this entry, we draw on this perspective (1) to examine aspects of the retirement transition that are important for mental health, (2) to discuss some of the empirical findings regarding the relationship between mental health and retirement, and (3) to propose a life-course model of the retirement transition.

A. Retirement: From Employment to Old Age?

One could view the retirement transition as little more than a passage to old age, an abrupt relinquishing of productive engagement in the form of paid work. But two trends—an increase in longevity and progressively earlier retirement—mean that men and women face an extended postretirement phase of activity and vitality. Societal views and expectations about retirement are in transition, and the mental health implications of retirement are far from self-evident.

Despite widely held beliefs regarding boredom and inactivity in retirement, research indicates that retired men and women often remain active in their communities through participation in volunteering, clubs, and religious organizations. Many take on postretirement employment. Thus, although men and women may be retiring earlier, they are not necessarily leaving the labor force or stopping being productive.

B. Retirement as Relief or Loss?

The presumed negative impact of retirement on mental health stems from the long tradition of linking employment with mental health. Studies have shown that work has emotional health benefits. Holding a job not only provides earnings, but also promotes feelings of efficacy, prestige, a sense of purpose, and positive identity. From this *role enhancement* perspective, men and women who retire from their career jobs are vulnerable to feelings of role loss, which can lead to psychological distress, compared with those who remain actively engaged in employment.

An alternative argument, the *role strain* perspective, emphasizes the costs rather than the benefits of paid work. From this point of view, retirement from the strains of a demanding or unsatisfactory job should reduce psychological distress and promote well-being. But most studies of the relationship between employment and well-being do not look specifically at the retirement transition.

II. AN ECOLOGICAL LIFE-COURSE APPROACH

Combining Urie Bronfenbrenner's notion of the ecology of human development with Glen Elder's life course paradigm offers a useful way to view the links between the retirement transition and mental health. This perspective highlights the importance of social context as well as the processes of development and change that occur in retirement.

A life-course perspective underscores the importance of considering not only whether people are employed or retired, but also their role trajectories, including the duration of their work careers and the timing of their retirement. The impact of retirement cannot be understood without reference to issues of timing, trajectory, and transitions in one's work career, but also one's family and health "careers" must be considered.

An individual's mental health is the product of a life history of events, relationships, and behaviors. Four interrelated themes characterize an ecological life-course approach to mental health and retirement: (1) an emphasis on context, (2) recognition of the importance of transitions and trajectories, (3) attention to the subjective sense of identity, and (4) acknowledgment of the interplay between social change and individual lives.

III. ECOLOGICAL CONTEXT

Bronfenbrenner proposes that location in different ecologies may render the same experience—such a retirement—individually distinctive and may produce quite different effects. Key contextual factors that figure prominently in shaping psychological well-being and quality of life are health, social class, and gender. These factors affect both the opportunities available to retirees as well as their motivation, generally, to seek out new roles (e.g., as a club member or volunteer).

A. Current or Past Health

Good physical health has been shown to be positively related to mental health and life quality for both retired men and women. In fact, research points to good health as the single most important factor related to retirement quality among women. Retirees in good health are more likely to engage in social activities that might enhance well-being. At the same time, healthier individuals are more apt to delay retirement or to seek work after retirement.

There are some who speculate that retirement actually diminishes health. Although physical health tends to deteriorate with age, longitudinal studies find no connection between retirement and a decline in health. Furthermore, some research suggests that retired men and women have better health habits (e.g., exercising more regularly and consuming less alcohol) than those who have not yet retired.

Research and theory suggest a certain "cumulativeness" to well-being, with those men and women reporting high levels of mastery, self-esteem, or general life satisfaction in earlier adulthood being the most likely to report these same positive views in their later years. Elder and Caspi underscore the potential for the accentuation of traits over time, as well as the cumulation of advantage or disadvantage. Thus for some, the impact of earlier stressors is magnified with time, and for others, early psychological health fos-

ters a sense of well-being throughout life, including retirement.

B. Social Class

Position in the social structure also seems to be important in the transition to retirement. On the one hand, blue-collar workers are more apt to retire from physically stressful and less rewarding jobs. For workers whose jobs are psychologically demanding or boring, retirement may be a way out of unpleasant work. Jobs that are demanding and that provide little sense of control have been shown to be negatively related to health and well-being—both throughout the work career and after retirement. Those who see their jobs as stressful or unrewarding are likely to view retirement as a relief. Studies have found that blue-collar workers are especially pleased to retire early, whereas those in higher status jobs are more apt to keep their employment and retire later. In this sense, retirement may be associated with good mental health among those in lower socioeconomic strata.

However, overall, social class differences in mental health favor those in higher level occupations; thus a person leaving an unsatisfactory job does not necessarily experience an improvement in mental health. One reason is that social class is associated with economic situation, with blue-collar retirees having lower pensions and fewer financial resources than those higher on the occupational ladder. Postretirement income, in turn, is a strong predictor of well-being. Studies also show that men in clerical and service occupations are also more likely than those in other jobs to leave workforce as a result of a disability, a factor associated with a more difficult adjustment to retirement.

Men and women retiring from professional occupations may have social-psychological advantages as well. Research indicates that professionals are more likely to maintain contact with co-workers and colleagues throughout their retirement years; these ties continue to provide social support as well as a link to their professional identity. Moreover, research on motivational orientations indicates that men and women with lower levels of education and low preretirement occupational status tend to focus more of their energy on disengaging from social commitments rather than on increasing social participation, which might enhance mental health. [See SOCIOECONOMIC STATUS.]

C. Gender

The differences in mental health between men and women are evident at all stages of the life course, including the retirement years. Historically, gender relations have had a profound influence on the role options of men and women, traditionally limiting women's participation in, and hence retirement from, paid work. However, a number of social changes in both attitudes and behavior have substantially increased the labor force participation of American women. Thus more women are retiring from paid work than has ever been the case in history. At the same time, men are retiring at increasingly earlier ages.

Given the occupational segregation of jobs by gender, women tend to be concentrated in service and clerical occupations, jobs that typically offer low wages and pension benefits. Thus older women often need to continue working longer to accrue enough pension credits to retire comfortably. Research findings link retiring late to a decline in well-being, which, along with other findings, suggests that retired women may fare less well in terms of mental health than retired men. For example, recent studies find that more retired women than men report lower satisfaction and increased stress at retirement. The differential experiences of men and women in retirement are only beginning to be documented.

IV. TRANSITIONS AND TRAJECTORIES

A. Pathways to and through Retirement

An understanding of how past experiences affect retirement, as well as how experiences in retirement shape subsequent mental health, is critical to a life-course approach to retirement. Few studies of people in retirement focus on how their roles and relationships throughout adulthood shape the quality of their retirement experience. Recent theoretical advances focusing on the developmental course of adulthood recognize that individuals are products of a life history of events, relationships, and behavior.

There is some evidence that (1) married men and women tend to be more satisfied with the retirement years than those who are single, (2) retirees who maintain social contacts—who spend time visiting with friends and neighbors—are less apt to feel useless, and (3) postretirement employment, club membership, and volunteering are all associated with psychological well-being.

Recent findings suggest that subjective cognitions—*perceiving* oneself as being socially active—are a key to well-being in retirement. Feelings of loneliness, boredom, and unproductivity are consistently associated with low levels of well-being. Thus perceptions of involvement may be the mechanism through which social participation improves psychological health.

B. Timing

A life-course focus on retirement highlights the "social clock" aspects of this transition, with individuals being either on time or off time (with off time meaning retiring earlier or later than the norm). Some research suggests that early retirement may have negative consequences for men's lives, producing more adverse effects than later retirement. On the other hand, if individuals retire early because of health problems, they may feel better off when they do not have to face the physical and psychological demands of their job.

The timing of retirement in men's and women's lives cannot be separated from choice and control over the decision of when—or even whether—to retire. Michael Rutter points out that individuals often shape their own behavior patterns, either through selecting or creating their environments. Those who control the timing of their retirement and the nature of their postretirement life are better able to shape the quality of the retirement transition and its meaning in their lives.

Also critical to an understanding of the mental aspects of retirement is its *degree of predictability*. Retirement can be long anticipated and planned for, or unexpected, abrupt, and disconcerting. Planned or expected changes in roles and resources are more easily adapted to than unanticipated crisis events, such as a sudden change in health. Most research on retirement finds that those who stopped work and who felt that they had little or no choice reported lower levels of mental health compared with both the voluntarily retired and those working their preferred amount. Planning may serve as a protective mechanism, reducing the stressfulness of the retirement transition.

C. Retirement as a Process

Retirement is both a transition (the act of leaving one's career job) and a life stage (the years that follow the transition). As a life stage, the experience of retirement may change not only from individual to individual, but also from year to year. Key to a life-course formulation of mental health and well-being is the importance of considering the duration of time spent in retirement.

In their study of retirement adjustment over time, Richardson and Kilty found that men and women experienced marked changes within the first year of retirement. Compared with right after retirement, at 6 months after leaving their preretirement jobs, men and women felt less satisfied with their social relationships and reported decreased levels of well-being overall. At the end of 1 year, however, their reports of well-being began to improve, indicating that there may be an initial adjustment period during which individuals begin to develop coping strategies or find social activities to compensate for their role loss.

V. SUBJECTIVE DEFINITIONS

Changes in roles and resources are presumed to lead to changes in identity. Bronfenbrenner suggests that the cognitive responses of individuals are related to both the characteristics of the person and the characteristics of his or her environment, along with the processes that shape and bind them over time. The retirement transition is a significant life event that alters both the physical and social world of workers. The changes in routines, roles, and relationships that retirement entails affect how individuals perceive themselves, their abilities, and their experience of stress or well-being.

Robert Kahn discusses the goodness of fit between the demands of a job and the abilities and aspirations of the person who holds it. A similar goodness of fit can be applied to retirement, and the nature of this fit should affect the stressfulness of the retirement transition. It follows that the effects of retirement on psychological functioning are contingent on an individual's thoughts and feelings about retirement.

Stress researchers have underscored the variety of ways in which people respond to the loss of roles and relationships. Comparing the perceived impact of re-

tirement relative to other life events, Martin Matthews and Brown found that in a sample of recent retirees, the transition to retirement was less stressful than expected. From a list of 34 life events, retirees ranked the transition to retirement 28th in perceived importance. Some research suggests that the transition to retirement might even reduce stress levels. Contrary to many younger people's expectations, retirement does not seem to be a stressful transition. This may be especially true for those who look forward to this life phase and who feel they planned sufficiently for retirement. Similarly, those who, over the years of employment, develop a sense of mastery and self-esteem should be able to use these psychological resources to their advantage in their retirement years as well. [*See* STRESS.]

VI. SOCIAL CHANGE AND INDIVIDUAL LIVES

Individual lives are embedded in a changing social, cultural, and economic environment. This means that different cohorts of individuals born at different historical times will have unique experiences, including the experience of retirement. Retirement will be vastly different for the baby-boomers compared with persons born before the turn of this century who faced retirement during the Great Depression years. Individuals in different age cohorts come to retirement with different motivations, impediments, and opportunities. For example, the women's movement of the 1970s transformed women's employment and educational experiences, meaning that more women are retiring after an extended period in the labor force. And white-collar managers in their 50s and 60s in the 1980s and 1990s were more apt to be "encouraged" to retire with early-retirement incentive packages associated with downsizing. Future retirees will be younger, healthier, and better educated, meaning that retirement for them will be a different experience from what it was for their parents or grandparents.

VII. SUMMARY: RETIREMENT AND RESILIENCE

Is the retirement transition a passage to the "golden" years or a key life stressor that triggers depression?

Does retirement increase the risk of emotional distress? Retirement, by definition, involves role loss, but research suggests that it may not necessarily involve disappointment, regret, isolation, or increased risk of depression. In fact, retiring from a stressful job may reduce the ongoing difficulties of life, thereby reducing vulnerability to emotional distress. In general, research findings do not support the notion that the transition to retirement has a strong negative impact on mental health. [*See* DEPRESSION.]

An ecological life-course approach highlights the importance of examining the retirement transition from the perspective of (1) continuity and change in roles and psychosocial development, (2) the ways previous life experiences shape current circumstances and mental health aspects of retirement, (3) individuals' definitions of options, expectations, and personal identities, and (4) the social and historical context.

Current role involvements are important for well-being in retirement, but recent studies suggest that whether or not retirees *feel* involved may be more critical. Furthermore, research findings by Moen and others suggest that it is not only current roles and resources that are related to psychological well-being in later life, but that life experiences throughout adulthood are also important. The more personal and social resources available to individuals undergoing the retirement transition, the more likely those in this life phase will experience high levels of well-being. A life-course formulation points to a certain "cumulativeness" to well-being, with individuals high in self-esteem or general life satisfaction in earlier adulthood being the most likely to report the same positive views in their retirement years.

ACKNOWLEDGMENT

Support for the preparation of this entry was provided in part by National Institute on Aging Grant IT50 AG11711-01 (Karl Pillemer and Phyllis Moen, coprincipal investigators).

BIBLIOGRAPHY

Bronfenbrenner, U. (1995). Developmental ecology through space and time: A future perspective. In P. Moen, G. H. Elder, Jr., and K. Lüscher (Eds.), *Examining lives in context.* Washington, DC: American Psychological Association.

Elder, G. H., Jr. (1995). The life course paradigm: Social change and individual development. In P. Moen, G. H. Elder, Jr., and K. Lüscher (Eds.), *Examining lives in context.* Washington, DC: American Psychological Association.

Elder, G. H., Jr., & Caspi, A. (1990). Studying lives in a changing society: Sociological and personological explorations. In A. I. Rabin, R. A. Zucker, R. A. Emmons, & S. Frank (Eds.), *Studying persons and lives.* New York: Springer.

Kahn, R. L. (1994). Opportunities, aspirations, and goodness of fit. In M. W. Riley, R. L. Kahn, A. Foner, & K. A. Mack (Eds.), *Age and structural lag: Society's failure to provide meaningful opportunities in work, family, and leisure.* New York: Wiley.

Martin Matthews, A., & Brown, K. H. (1988). Retirement as a critical life event: The differential experiences of women and men. *Research on Aging, 9*(4), 548–571.

Moen, P. (1996). A life course perspective on retirement, gender, and well-being. *Journal of Occupational Health Psychology, 1,*(2), 131–144.

Moen, P. (1997). Women's roles and resilience: Trajectories of advantage or turning points? In B. Wheaton & I. Gotlib (Eds.), *Stress and adversity over the life course.* New York: Cambridge University Press.

Richardson, V., & Kilty, K. (1991). Adjustment to retirement: Continuity versus discontinuity. *International Journal of Aging and Human Development, 32*(2), 151–169.

Rutter, M. (1987). Psychosocial resilience and protective mechanisms. *American Journal of Orthopsychiatry, 57,* 316–331.

S

Schizophrenia

Jason Schiffman and Elaine Walker

Emory University

Antipsychotics Medications that have been demonstrated to reduce the symptoms of schizophrenia.
Behavioral Genetics The study of the extent to which individual differences in behavior are attributable to genetic factors as opposed to environmental influences.
Dopamine A catecholamine neurotransmitter located throughout the brain, particularly the substantia nigra and basal ganglia.
Frontal Lobes The portion of each cerebral hemisphere that is anterior to the central sulcus and above the lateral fissure, and is active in reasoning, planning, and other higher mental processes.
Neuropsychology The study of the relation between brain function and behavior.
Ventricles Cavities in the brain that are continuous with the central canal of the spinal cord and are filled with cerebrospinal fluid.

SCHIZOPHRENIA is a psychotic disorder characterized by disturbances in thought, emotion, and behavior. This article discusses the symptoms, etiology, treatment, and other pertinent issues concerning this mental illness.

I. DESCRIPTION AND CLASSIFICATION

Schizophrenia is a serious mental illness that afflicts about 1% of the population at some point in their lifetime. In the current *Diagnostic and Statistical Manual of Mental Disorders (DSM-IV)*, it is described as an illness that is characterized by psychotic symptoms and significant interpersonal or occupational dysfunction that persist for a period of at least 6 months. The term psychotic refers to symptoms that indicate an impairment in the patient's ability to comprehend reality. This includes beliefs that have no basis in reality and that are not susceptible to corrective feedback (delusions), and sensory perceptions that have no identifiable external source (hallucinations). In addition to hallucinations and delusions, the *DSM* lists three other key symptoms of schizophrenia: disorganized speech, disorganized or catatonic behavior, and negative symptoms. [*See* DSM-IV.]

A. Symptoms

1. Delusions
Delusions are the primary example of abnormal thought content in schizophrenia. Delusional beliefs conflict with reality and are tenaciously held, despite evidence to the contrary. There are several types of delusions. *Delusions of control* is the belief that one is being manipulated by an external force, often a powerful individual or organization (e.g., the FBI) that has malevolent intent. *Delusions of grandeur* refers to patients' beliefs that they are especially important and have unique qualities or powers (e.g., the capacity to influence weather conditions). In contrast, some pa-

tients express the conviction that they are victims of persecution or an organized plot, and these beliefs are referred to as *delusions of persecution.* Examples of more specific delusions include *thought broadcasting,* the patient's belief that his or her thoughts are transmitted so that others know them, and *thought withdrawal,* the belief that an external force has stolen one's thoughts.

2. Hallucinations

Hallucinations are among the most subjectively distressing symptoms experienced by schizophrenia patients. These perceptual distortions vary among patients and can be auditory, visual, olfactory, gustatory, or tactile. The majority of hallucinations are auditory in nature and typically involve voices. Examples include the patient hearing someone threatening or chastising him or her, a voice repeating the patient's own thoughts, two or more voices arguing, and voices commenting. The second most common form of hallucination is visual. Visual hallucinations often entail the perception of distortions in the physical environment, especially in the faces and bodies of other people.

Other perceptual distortions that are commonly reported by schizophrenia patients include feeling as if parts of the body are distorted in size or shape, feeling as if an object is closer or farther away than it actually is, feeling numbness, tingling, or burning, being hypersensitive to sensory stimuli, and perceiving objects as flat and colorless. In addition to these distinctive perceptual abnormalities, persons suffering from schizophrenia often report difficulties in focusing their attention or sustaining concentration on a task.

It is important to note that in order for an unsubstantiated belief or sensory experience to quality as a delusion or hallucination, the individual must experience it within a clear sensorium (e.g., unsubstantiated sensory experiences that occur only upon awaking from sleep or when falling asleep would not qualify as delusions). Thus, for example, if a patient reports hearing something that sounds like voices when alone, but adds that he or she is certain that this is a *misinterpretation* of a sound, such as the wind blowing leaves, this would not constitute an auditory hallucination.

3. Disorganized Speech

The *DSM* uses the term *disorganized speech* to refer to abnormalities in the form or content of the individual's verbalizations. It is assumed that these abnormalities reflect underlying distortions in the patient's thought processes. Thus the term thought disorder is frequently used by researchers and practitioners to refer to the disorganized speech that often occurs in schizophrenia.

Problems in the form of speech are reflected in abnormalities in the organization and coherent expression of ideas to others. One common abnormality of form, *incoherent speech,* is characterized by seemingly unrelated images or fragments of thoughts that are incomprehensible to the listener. The term *loose association* refers to the tendency to abruptly shift to a topic that has no apparent association with the previous topic. In general, the overall content of loosely associated speech may be easier to comprehend than incoherent speech. In *perseverative speech,* words, ideas, or both are continuously repeated, as if the patient is unable to shift to another idea. *Clang association* is the utterance of rhyming words that follow each other (e.g., "a right, bright kite"). Patients choose words for their similarity in sound rather than their syntax, often producing a string of rhyming words.

4. Disorganized or Catatonic Behavior

The overt behavioral symptoms of schizophrenia fall in two general areas: motor functions and interpersonal behavior. Motor abnormalities, including mannerisms, stereotyped movements, and unusual posture, are common among schizophrenia patients. Other common signs include bizarre facial expressions, such as repeated grimacing or staring, and repeated peculiar gestures that often involve complex behavioral sequences. As with other symptoms of the psychosis, the manifestation of motor abnormalities varies among individuals. Schizophrenia patients sometimes mimic the behavior of others, known as echopraxia, or repeat their own movements, known as stereotyped behaviors. Although a subgroup of patients demonstrate heightened levels of activity, including motoric excitement (e.g., agitation or flailing of the limbs), others suffer from a reduction of movement. At the latter extreme, some exhibit *catatonic immobility* and assume unusual postures that are maintained for extended periods of time. Some may also demonstrate *waxy flexibility,* a condition in which patients do not resist being placed into strange positions that they then maintain. Catatonia has decreased dramatically in recent decades, so that it is now rare. Several researchers have attributed this decline to the introduction of antipsychotic medication (described later).

In the domain of interpersonal interactions, schizophrenia patients frequently demonstrate behaviors that are perceived as bizarre or inappropriate by others. For example, it is not uncommon for patients to use socially unacceptable language and unusual tones of voice, or to show overly dependent or intrusive behavior. Another common symptom, *inappropriate affect,* involves unusual emotional reactions to events and experiences. For example, patients may laugh at a sad or somber occasion, or be enraged by insignificant events. Finally, many patients manifest increasingly poor hygiene as their illness progresses. Their appearance may also be marked by disheveled clothing or inappropriate clothing, such as gloves and coats in the summer.

5. Negative Symptoms

The symptoms of schizophrenia can be classified into the general categories of positive and negative. Positive symptoms involve behavioral excesses and most of the symptoms described earlier fall in to this category (e.g., delusions, hallucinations, and bizarre behaviors). In contrast, negative symptoms involve behavioral deficits. Examples include *flat affect* (blunted expressions of emotion), *apathy,* and *social withdrawal.* In the domain of verbal expression, schizophrenia patients who manifest a very low rate of verbal output are described as showing *poverty of speech.* Patients whose speech is normal in quantity, but lacks meaning, suffer from *poverty of content.* Recently, some researchers have suggested that positive and negative symptoms may be caused by different neural mechanisms.

It is important to mention that a reduction in overt displays of emotion does not necessarily imply that patients have less intense subjective emotional experiences than the average person. In fact, recent findings indicate that blunted emotional expressions can coexist with intense subjective feelings of emotion.

B. Variability of Symptoms among Patients

According to *DSM-IV,* patients must show two or more of the preceding five symptoms to meet the diagnostic criteria for schizophrenia. Thus, no one of these symptoms is required for the diagnosis. Furthermore, the following four criteria must also be met: (1) the patient shows marked deterioration in occupational, interpersonal, or domestic functioning; (2) the patient manifests continuous signs of symptoms or dysfunction for at least 6 months; (3) the patient does not manifest predominant signs of mood disturbance (e.g., depression or mania); and (4) the symptoms are not caused by substance abuse or a primary medical condition.

Because the diagnostic criteria for schizophrenia are relatively broad, with no one essential symptom, there is a great deal of variability among patients in their symptom profiles. It has therefore been proposed that schizophrenia is a heterogeneous disorder with multiple causes. It is also the case, however, that patients must show a marked and persistent impairment to meet the diagnostic criteria for schizophrenia. Thus, those who meet criteria for the diagnosis are significantly impaired in everyday functioning. For many individuals who are diagnosed with schizophrenia, independent functioning is never achieved.

C. Subtypes of Schizophrenia

The *DSM* lists five subtypes of schizophrenia. In schizophrenia of the *paranoid type,* delusional concerns about persecution and/or preoccupation with threat dominate the clinical presentation, although delusions of grandeur are also often present. *Disorganized* schizophrenia is distinguished by extremely incoherent speech and behavior, as well as blunted or inappropriate affect. In *catatonic* schizophrenia, the clinical picture is dominated by abnormalities in movement and posture, such as those described earlier. Patients classified as having *undifferentiated* schizophrenia do not meet criteria for any of the previous subtypes. Finally, the diagnosis of *residual* schizophrenia is applied to patients who have had at least one episode of schizophrenia and who continue to show functional impairment, but who do not currently manifest any positive symptoms.

II. HISTORY

During the late 1800s and early 1900s, Emil Kraepelin and Eugen Bleuler provided the first conceptualizations of schizophrenia. Kraepelin defined "dementia praecox," the original term for schizophrenia, as an endogenous psychosis characterized by intellectual deterioration (dementia) and early onset (praecox). Kraepelin included negativism, hallucinations, delusions, stereotyped behaviors, attentional difficulties, and emotional dysfunction as major symptoms of the disorder. Kraepelin's work focused on description and phenomenology, leaving subsequent researchers to investigate the cause or causes of the disorder.

In contrast to Kraepelin, Eugen Bleuler, a Swiss psychiatrist, proposed a broader view of dementia praecox, with a more theoretical emphasis. Bleuler contested two of Kraepelin's defining assumptions: specifically, that the psychosis was typically characterized by early onset and intellectual deterioration. Bleuler attempted to identify an underlying commonality among the diverse variations of what Kraepelin referred to as dementia praecox and concluded that all of the patients suffered from a "breaking of associative threads," causing a disharmony among communicative and thought processes. He believed this abnormality accounted for the problems of thought, emotional expression, decision making, and social interaction associated with schizophrenia. Guided by the defining principle of disharmonious mental structures, Bleuler renamed the disorder "schizophrenia," meaning "split mind."

In the early to mid-1900s, American psychiatrists continued to use a broad definition of schizophrenia. The distinction between process and reactive schizophrenia was considered important, however, because it was assumed to distinguish between cases characterized by gradual deterioration (process) and cases that were precipitated by acute stress (reactive).

During this time, some clinicians and researchers viewed the specific diagnostic criteria for the major mental illnesses (schizophrenia, bipolar disorder, major depression) as artificial and discretionary, and used instead flexible and inconsistent standards for diagnoses. Studies that compared the rates of disorder across nations revealed that schizophrenia was diagnosed at a much higher rate in the United States than in Great Britain and some other countries. This national difference resulted from the use of broader criteria for diagnosing schizophrenia in the United States. Many patients who were diagnosed as having depression or bipolar disorder in Britain were diagnosed with schizophrenia in the United States. Because subsequent revisions in the *DSM* have included more restrictive criteria for schizophrenia, U.S. diagnostic rates are now comparable with other countries.

In addition to a more restrictive definition of schizophrenia, subsequent editions of the DSM have included additional diagnostic categories that contain similar symptoms. Thus the range of "schizophrenia-spectrum disorders" continue to broaden with the description of variants of schizophrenia, such as schizoaffective disorder, which is characterized by a mix of affective and psychotic symptoms. The diagnostic category of schizophreniform disorder was also added. This diagnosis is given when the patient shows the typical symptoms of schizophrenia, but does not meet the criterion of 6 months of continuous illness.

III. DEMOGRAPHIC CHARACTERISTICS OF SCHIZOPHRENIA

Estimates of the prevalence of schizophrenia converge at around 1% of the population. Although there is evidence of cross-national differences in the rate of schizophrenia, the differences are not large (i.e., 1 to 2% difference). It is, in fact, striking that the rate of occurrence is so consistent across cultures.

The modal age at onset of schizophrenia is in early adulthood, usually before 25 years of age. Thus most patients have not had the opportunity to marry or establish a stable work history before the onset of the illness. As a result of this, and the often chronic nature of the illness, many patients never attain financial independence. It is relatively rare for preadolescent children to receive a diagnosis of schizophrenia. Similarly, it is rare for individuals beyond the age of 40 to experience a first episode of the illness.

A. Sex Differences

Although it has traditionally been assumed that there is no sex difference in the rates of schizophrenia, some recent research findings indicate that a somewhat larger proportion of males than females meet the *DSM-IV* criteria for the disorder. Nonetheless, the overall rates do not differ dramatically for men and women. It is well established, however, that women are more likely to have a later onset of illness, as well as a better prognosis. Women also show a higher level of interpersonal and occupational functioning during the period prior to illness onset. The reasons for this sex difference are not known, but it has been proposed by several theorists that the female sex hormone, estrogen, may function in attenuating the severity of the illness. [*See* Gender Differences in Mental Health.]

B. Social Class Differences

Compared with the general population averages, schizophrenia patients tend to have significantly lower incomes and educational levels. Poor urban inner city districts, inhabited by the lowest socioeconomic class, contain the largest proportion of schizophrenia patients. There is a sharp contrast between the rates of schizophrenia in the lowest socioeconomic class and all other levels, including the next higher level. Findings from various cultures suggest that rates of schizophrenia are almost two times higher in the lowest social class group compared with the next lowest.

These social class differences appear to be a partial consequence of the debilitating nature of the illness. The *social-drift theory* suggests that during the development of schizophrenia, people drift into poverty. When the incomes and educational levels of the parents of patients are compared with those of the general population, the differences are not as striking.

There is, nonetheless, evidence that patients do come from families where the incomes and educational backgrounds of the parents are slightly below the average. These findings have led researchers to conclude that there may be a causal link between social class and risk for the illness. The *sociogenic hypothesis* posits that situational factors associated with low social class, such as degrading treatment from society, low levels of education, and few opportunities for achievement and reward, produce stress that contributes to the risk for schizophrenia. [*See* Poverty and Mental Health; Socioeconomic Status.]

IV. LIFE FUNCTIONING AND PROGNOSIS

Before the introduction of antipsychotic medications in 1950, the majority of patients spent most of their lives in institutional settings. There was little in the way of programs for rehabilitation. But contemporary, multifaceted treatment approaches have made it possible for most patients to live in community settings.

Of course, during active episodes of the illness, schizophrenia patients are usually seriously function-ally impaired. They are typically unable to work or maintain a social network, and often require hospitalization. Even when in remission, some patients find it challenging to hold a job or to be self-sufficient. This is partially due to residual symptoms, as well as to the interruptions in educational attainment and occupational progress that result from the illness. However, there are many patients who are able to lead productive lives, hold stable jobs, and raise families. With the development of greater community awareness of mental illness, some of the stigma that kept patients from pursuing work or an education has diminished.

A. Long-Term Course

For about one third of patients, the illness is chronic and is characterized by episodes of severe symptoms with intermittent periods when the symptoms subside but do not disappear. For others, there are multiple episodes with periods of substantial symptom remission. About one third of those who receive the diagnosis eventually show a partial or complete recovery after one or two episodes.

Several factors have been linked with a more favorable prognosis for schizophrenia. Early treatment seems to be important in that the shorter the period between the onset of the patient's symptoms and the first prescribed medication, the better the clinical outcome. Another indicator of better prognosis is a high level of occupational and interpersonal functioning in the premorbid period. Also, as noted earlier, women and patients who have a later onset of symptoms have a better long-term outcome.

B. Premorbid Characteristics of Schizophrenia

Some of the difficulties experienced by individuals with schizophrenia can be observed before the onset of the clinical symptoms. Deficits in social skills, concentration, emotional expression, motivation, and occupational or academic performance often precede the first clinical symptoms. This period of gradual decline in functioning before the first illness episode is referred to as the prodromal phase.

However, there are often more subtle signs of dysfunction long before the onset of the prodromal period. Controlled studies using archival data sources, such as medical and school records or childhood home-movies, indicate that subtle differences are discernible as early as infancy in some patients. Individuals who succumb to schizophrenia in adulthood sometimes have abnormal motor development and show deficits in emotional expression and interpersonal relationships in early childhood. Cognitive impairment and difficult temperament have also been observed. During middle childhood and adolescence, researchers have found evidence of neurological abnormality, poor emotional control, social immaturity, and academic performance deficits. Premorbid behavioral problems often become marked through the adolescent years, and many exhibit behavioral disturbances and cognitive abnormalities that resemble the clinical symptoms of schizophrenia.

V. ETIOLOGY: THEORIES AND RESEARCH FINDINGS

The causes of schizophrenia are unknown, but it is now widely accepted by both researchers and clinicians that schizophrenia is biologically determined. This is in striking contrast to the early and mid-1900s, when many subscribed to the theory that faulty parenting, especially cold and rejecting mothers, caused schizophrenia in offspring.

A. Brain Abnormalities in Schizophrenia

There are several sources of evidence for the assumption that schizophrenia involves an abnormality in brain function. First, studies of schizophrenia patients have revealed a variety of behavioral signs of central nervous system impairment, including motor and cognitive dysfunctions. Second, when the brains of patients are examined with *in vivo* imaging techniques, such as magnetic resonance imaging (MRI), many show abnormalities in brain structure. Similarly, postmortem studies of brain tissue have revealed irregularities in nerve cell formation and interconnections.

Laboratory studies of schizophrenia patients have revealed a variety of abnormalities, including irregularities in smooth pursuit eye movements, psychophysiological responses to sensory stimuli, and concentration. Research on the neuropsychological performance of schizophrenia patients was first conducted in the 1950s and continues to the present time. Individual neuropsychological tests are designed to measure functions subserved by specific regions or

systems of the brain. An early finding in this area was that schizophrenia patients were the one psychiatric group whose performance on neuropsychological tests was indistinguishable from people with known brain damage. The findings suggested a generalized cerebral dysfunction in schizophrenia. However, patients show the most consistent deficits on tests of attention and memory, indicating dysfunction of the frontal and temporal lobes and the hippocampus. Further evidence of dysfunction in these brain regions is derived from poor performance on tests of executive functions: the ability to formulate, maintain, and adapt appropriate responses to the environment.

Brain-imaging studies of schizophrenia have yielded results that mirror those obtained from neuropsychological research. Some relatively consistent findings are that the brains of schizophrenia patients have abnormal frontal lobes and enlarged ventricles. Enlarged ventricles suggest decreased brain mass, particularly in the limbic regions, which are intimately involved in emotional processing. Furthermore, ventricular size correlates with negative symptoms, performance deficits on neuropsychological tests, poor response to medication, and poor premorbid adjustment. These associations between ventricular enlargement and both premorbid and postmorbid characteristics suggest that the brain abnormalities are long-standing, perhaps congenital.

In addition to brain structure, investigators have examined biological indices of brain function in schizophrenia. Functional brain-imaging studies, with procedures such as positron emission tomography (PET) and measurement of regional cerebral blood flow, reveal that schizophrenia patients have decreased levels of blood flow to the frontal lobes, especially while performing cognitive tasks.

Researchers are now pursuing the question of what causes the brain abnormalities observed in schizophrenia. Although as yet there are no definitive answers, investigators have made continuous progress in identifying factors that are associated with risk for the disorder.

B. Biochemical Factors

The structural brain abnormalities that have been observed in schizophrenia support the assumption that it is a disorder of the central nervous system. But it has also been shown that similar structural abnormalities (i.e., ventricular enlargement and volume reductions) are present in other disorders, both neurological and psychiatric. It is therefore assumed that specific abnormalities in brain biochemistry may play a role in schizophrenia.

The functioning of the central nervous system is dependent on a host of chemicals that serve as the "messenger substances" among neurons. These chemicals or neurotransmitters have been the subject of intense investigation. Among the various neurotransmitters that have been implicated in the neuropathophysiology of schizophrenia is dopamine. Dopamine is viewed as a likely candidate for two main reasons: (1) drugs that act to enhance the release or activity of dopamine can produce psychotic symptoms, and (2) drugs that have been established to have antipsychotic properties (i.e., reduce psychotic symptoms) reduce the activity of dopamine in the brain. Current theories of the role of dopamine in schizophrenia have focused on dopamine receptors. There is evidence that there may be an abnormality in the number or sensitivity of certain dopamine receptors in the brains of schizophrenia patients. To date, however, this evidence remains inconclusive.

Several other neurotransmitters have also been hypothesized to play a role in schizophrenia. Current theories under investigation include a malfunction of the receptors for a neurotransmitter called glutamate and an abnormality in the balance between dopamine and serotonin (another neurotransmitter which, like dopamine, has been implicated in the pathogenesis of schizophrenia). As research findings on the biochemical aspects of schizophrenia accumulate, it increasingly appears that the illness may involve multiple neurotransmitters, with different biochemical profiles for different patients. [*See* CATECHOLAMINES AND BEHAVIOR.]

C. Genetics

A convincing body of research supports the notion of a genetic predisposition to schizophrenia. Behavioral genetic studies of families, twins, and adopted offspring of schizophrenia patients indicate that an inherited vulnerability is involved in at least some cases of the disorder.

There is an elevated risk of schizophrenia for individuals with a biological relative who suffers from the disorder, and the risk rates increase as a function of the genetic closeness of the relationship. For example, it has been estimated that children of schizophrenia

patients have a 9 to 15% likelihood of developing the illness, siblings of patients have an 8 to 14% likelihood, and cousins have a 2 to 6% likelihood of being diagnosed with schizophrenia. Given the general population rate of approximately 1%, relatives of patients are at statistically increased risk. It must be noted, however, that relatives share common experiences as well as common genes. Therefore, examinations of the prevalence of schizophrenia in the relatives of patients cannot elucidate the relative contributions of environmental and genetic factors.

Some investigators have studied the development of adopted children whose biological mothers had schizophrenia. This approach has the potential to provide more conclusive information than family studies. The results of these investigations show that when biological offspring of schizophrenic mothers are reared from infancy in adoptive homes they are more likely to develop schizophrenia than are adopted children from healthy mothers. Furthermore, these children also exhibit a higher rate of other adjustment problems when compared with controls. Studies of this type have clearly illustrated that vulnerability to schizophrenia can be inherited.

Research on twins examines differences in concordance rates between identical (monozygotic or MZ) and fraternal (dizygotic or DZ) twins. Twin studies rely on the fact that MZ twins essentially share 100% of their genes. Thus, environmental influences account for any behavioral differences between MZ twins. In contrast, DZ twins are no more genetically similar than regular siblings; DZ twins do, however, share more similar environmental factors than do nontwin siblings. To date, the results of twin studies have consistently shown that MZ twins are significantly more likely to be concordant for schizophrenia than are DZ twins.

At the same time, it is important to note that in at least 50% of the cases in which one member of an MZ twin pair has schizophrenia, the other does not. Such "discordant" pairs have been the subject of a recent, comprehensive investigation in the United States. Among the most important findings from this research project are those from the MRI scans conducted on the twins. The ill twins in the pairs showed significantly more brain abnormalities than the healthy twins. Most notable were reductions in the volume of certain brain regions, especially the hippocampus, and increases in the size of the ventricles. These results clearly indicate the importance of environmental factors in the etiology of schizophrenia. [*See* GENETIC CONTRIBUTORS TO MENTAL HEALTH.]

D. Obstetrical Complications

As is the case with many other disorders that involve brain dysfunction, there is evidence that schizophrenia is associated with exposure to prenatal and delivery complications. Obstetrical complications (OCs) are defined as physical deviations from the normal course of events during pregnancy, labor, or the neonatal period. Estimates of OCs in schizophrenics have been as high as 67%, significantly higher than the rate of OCs found in normal controls.

Among the prenatal factors that have been found to be associated with increased risk for schizophrenia are prenatal maternal nutritional deficiency, viral infection, bleeding, and toxemia. Complications of delivery that can result in hypoxia have also been linked with heightened risk for the disorder. Hypoxia, a deficiency in the amount of oxygen available to the fetus, can affect the development of various parts of the brain. Some researchers argue that hypoxia results in hippocampal damage, thus contributing to vulnerability for schizophrenia. Low birth weight, a neonatal complication, is another potential early factor contributing to schizophrenia. There is evidence that low birth weight is related to increased ventricular size, which is a common characteristic of schizophrenia patients.

The findings on prenatal complications support the notion that fetal brain development may be disrupted in individuals who later manifest schizophrenia. A central question raised by these findings concerns the nature of the etiologic role of OCs. Some hypothesize that OCs produce the neural predisposition to schizophrenia, whereas others posit that OCs exacerbate or interact with an existing genetic predisposition. [*See* PRENATAL STRESS AND LIFE SPAN DEVELOPMENT.]

Findings from prospective, high-risk research projects lend support to the hypothesis that OCs interact with genetic vulnerabilities in the etiology of schizophrenia. High-risk studies involve the repeated assessment of children of schizophrenia patients, based on the expectation that a larger percentage of these children will eventually develop the illness than individuals in the general population. The high-risk method offers some advantages when compared with retrospective studies of the precursors of schizophrenia.

One advantage is that it allows for the direct assessment of subjects in the premorbid period, as well as the selection and study of variables that are thought to have prognostic relevance. Furthermore, because a significant portion of the data collection takes place during the premorbid period, this reduces confounds that often occur in the study of diagnosed patients (e.g., medication and institutionalization).

Studies using the high-risk method have shown an interactive effect of genetic risk and exposure to OCs in predicting adult psychiatric outcome. In other words, the correlation between OCs and adult psychiatric symptoms was greater for offspring of schizophrenia parents than for children of healthy parents. The same pattern was apparent for the relation between OCs and adult brain morphology, suggesting that pre- and perinatal factors contribute to brain abnormalities.

E. Viral Infection

As noted earlier, prenatal exposure to maternal viral infection has also been linked with schizophrenia. Specifically, the rate of schizophrenia is increased for cohorts who were in the second trimester during flu epidemics. Another source of evidence for the viral hypothesis is the finding that the births of schizophrenia patients do not seem to be randomly distributed throughout the course of the year. Instead, the births of schizophrenia patients occur more frequently in winter months.

Some researchers have suggested that postnatal viral infection may also be relevant to schizophrenia, and that the illness may be caused by a long-acting virus. This hypothesis claims that "slow viruses," which are active over a long period of time, interact with a genetic predisposition to produce schizophrenia. Various findings are cited in support of this hypothesis. Some researchers have identified a viral infection in fatal catatonia, a disorder characterized by schizophrenia-like symptoms, suggesting that a similar viral infection may be found for schizophrenia. Other researchers have found signs of viral activity in the cerebrospinal fluid of patients with schizophrenia.

F. Diathesis-Stress Model

The diathesis-stress model has dominated theories about the etiology of schizophrenia for several decades. This model assumes that certain individuals inherit or acquire a vulnerability to schizophrenia (the diathesis), and that the behavioral expression of this vulnerability is determined or triggered by environmental stressors. Although "stress" was originally conceptualized as psychosocial in origin, contemporary versions of this model broaden the definition of stress to include prenatal and postnatal insults to the central nervous system. Thus the diathesis, combined with exposure to environmental stressors, can produce schizophrenia.

Exposure to stress within the context of the family has been the focus of researchers in the field. Families in which there is a schizophrenia patient show more conflict and abnormalities in communication than do other families. However, it has also been shown that there is greater conflict and more abnormalities of communication in families in which any member has a severe debilitating illness. Thus, family communication styles are unlikely to play a unique causal role in schizophrenia. [*See* STRESS.]

There is good evidence, however, that exposure to high levels of criticism from family members can increase the likelihood of relapse in schizophrenia patients. The number of critical comments, expressions of hostility, and emotional overinvolvement comprise a construct referred to as expressed emotion (EE). Recovering schizophrenia patients in families high in EE are much more likely to have a relapse compared with patients in families low in EE. There is also evidence from studies of the adopted offspring of schizophrenia patients suggesting that familial stress can hasten the onset of symptoms.

VI. TREATMENT AND THERAPY

Before 1900, knowledge of the nature and causes of mental disorders was limited. Individuals with psychiatric symptoms, particularly psychotic symptoms, were typically viewed by others with disdain or amusement. However, social trends and advances in medical knowledge converged to produce greater sympathy for those with mental illness. This led, especially during the early part of the century, to the construction of public and private hospitals devoted to the care of the mentally ill.

Today, most schizophrenia patients experience at least one period of inpatient treatment. This is typically precipitated by the first psychotic episode. During this initial hospitalization, an extensive assessment is usually conducted to determine the most appropriate diagnosis. Treatment is then initiated to reduce symptoms and stabilize patients so that they can return to the community as soon as possible.

In the past, periods of hospitalization were longer in duration than they are today. This is due, in part, to the availability today of better medical treatments. Another factor that has contributed to shorter hospital stays is the deinstitutionalization movement. Initially spurred by concerns that too many of the mentally ill were becoming "institutionalized" and were losing their ability to function in the community, financial support for state psychiatric hospitals was gradually cut. But community support services and transitional living arrangements were not readily available to many patients. As a result, former psychiatric inpatients now constitute a substantial proportion of the homeless found in U.S. cities. [*See* MENTAL HOSPITALS AND DEINSTITUTIONALIZATION.]

A. Antipsychotic Medication

Introduced in the 1950s, antipsychotic medication has since become the most effective and widely used treatment for schizophrenia. Research indicated that the "typical" antipsychotics, such as haloperidol, decreased the symptoms of schizophrenia, especially positive symptoms, and reduced the risk of relapse. However, they were not as effective in reducing the negative symptoms. Furthermore, some patients showed no response to antipsychotic drugs.

Chlorpromazine (Thorazine) was among the first antipsychotic commonly used to treat schizophrenia. Since the 1950s, many other antipsychotic drugs have been introduced. Like chlorpromazine, these drugs reduce hallucinations, delusions, and thought disorder, and engender more calm, manageable, and socially appropriate behavior. As mentioned, all currently used antipsychotic drugs block dopamine neurotransmission. Thus it has been assumed that their efficacy is due to their capacity to reduce the overactivation of dopamine pathways in the brain.

Unfortunately, the benefits of standard or typical antipsychotic drugs are often mitigated by side effects. Minor side effects include sensitivity to light, dryness of mouth, and drowsiness. The more severe effects are psychomotor dysfunction, skin discoloration, visual impairment, and tardive dyskinesia (an involuntary movement disorder that can appear after prolonged use of antipsychotics). It is especially unfortunate that tardive dyskinesia is sometimes irreversible when patients are withdrawn from neuroleptics. Many of these physical signs are known to be caused by chronic blockade of dopamine pathways. Although additional medications can counter some of the negative effects of the typical antipsychotics, schizophrenia patients often resist taking them because of an aversion to the side effects.

Within the past decade, some new, "atypical" antipsychotic drugs have been introduced. It was hoped that these drugs would be effective in treating patients who had not responded to standard antipsychotics. Also, researchers hoped to identify medications that had fewer side effects. One example is Clozapine, released in 1990, which seems to reduce negative symptoms more effectively than typical antipsychotic drugs. Clozapine not only offers hope for patients who are nonresponsive to other medications, but it also has fewer side effects than typical antipsychotics. However, clozapine can produce one rare, but potentially fatal, side effect, agranulocytosis, a blood disorder. Consequently, patients who are on this medication must be monitored on a regular basis. It is fortunate that several other new antipsychotic medications have recently become available, and some of these appear to have no serious side effects.

It appears that it is important to begin pharmacological treatment of schizophrenia as soon as possible after the symptoms are recognized. The longer patients go without treatment of illness episodes, the worse the long-term prognosis. Medication also has the benefit of lowering the rate of mortality, particularly suicide, among schizophrenia patients. Patients who are treated with antipsychotic medication generally require maintenance of the medication to obtain continued relief from symptoms. Medication withdrawal often results in relapse. At the same time, the associated long- and short-term side effects of antipsychotics, especially the typical antipsychotics, are of continuing concern to patients, their families, and physicians. It is possible that future research on the neural mechanisms involved in schizophrenia will lead to the development of novel treatments that eliminate the need for maintenance medication.

Many schizophrenia patients also suffer from depression and, as noted, are at elevated risk for suicide.

The reason or reasons for the high rate of co-occurance of depression with schizophrenia is not known. Given the debilitating and potentially chronic nature of schizophrenia, however, it is likely that some patients experience depressive symptoms in response to their condition. For others, depressive symptoms may be medication side effects or a manifestation of a biologically based vulnerability to depression. [See PSYCHOPHARMACOLOGY.]

B. Psychological Treatment

Clinicians have used various forms of psychological therapy in an effort to treat schizophrenia patients. Early attempts to provide therapy for schizophrenia patients relied on insight-oriented or psychodynamic techniques. The chief goal was to foster introspection and self-understanding in patients. Research findings provided no support for the efficacy of these therapies in the treatment of schizophrenia.

It has been shown, however, that supportive therapy can be a useful adjunct to medication in the treatment of patients. Similarly, psychoeducational approaches that emphasize providing information about symptom management have proven effective in reducing relapse. Among the most beneficial forms of psychological treatment is behavioral therapy. Some psychiatric hospitals have established programs in which patients earn credits or "tokens" for appropriate behavior and then redeem these items for privileges or tangible rewards. These programs can increase punctuality, hygiene, and other socially acceptable behaviors in patients.

In recent years, family therapy has become a standard component of the treatment of schizophrenia. These family therapy sessions are psychoeducational in nature and are intended to provide the family with support, information about schizophrenia, and constructive guidance in dealing with the illness in a family member. In this way, family members become a part of the treatment process and learn new ways to help their loved one cope with schizophrenia. [See FAMILY THERAPY.]

Another critical component of effective treatment is the provision of rehabilitative services. These services take the form of structured residential settings, independent life-skills training, and vocational programs. Such programs often play a major role in helping patients recover from their illness.

VII. SUMMARY

It is now firmly established that schizophrenia is caused by an abnormality of brain function that in most cases has its origin in early brain insults, inherited vulnerabilities, or both. But the identification of the causal agents and the specific neural substrates responsible for schizophrenia must await the findings of future research. There is reason to be optimistic about future research progress. New technologies are available for examining brain structure and function. In addition, dramatic advances in neuroscience have expanded our understanding of the brain and the impact of brain abnormalities on behavior. We are likely to witness great strides in our understanding of the causes of all mental illnesses within the coming decades.

It is hoped that advances will also be made in the treatment of schizophrenia. New drugs are being developed at a rapid pace, and more effective medications are likely to result. At the same time, advocacy efforts on the part of patients and their families have resulted in improvements in services. But a further expansion of services is greatly needed to provide patients with the structured living situations and work environments they need to make the transition into independent community living.

BIBLIOGRAPHY

Breier, A. (Ed.). (1996). *The new pharmacotherapy of schizophrenia.* Washington DC: American Psychiatric Press.

Keefe, R. S., & Harvey, P. (1994). *Understanding schizophrenia: A guide to the new research on causes and treatment.* New York: Free Press.

Miller, G. A. (Ed.). (1995). *The behavioral high-risk paradigm in psychopathology.* New York: Springer.

Shriqui, C. L., & Nasrallah, H. A. (Eds.). (1995). *Contemporary issues in the treatment of schizophrenia.* Washington DC: American Psychiatric Press.

Torrey, E. F. (1994). *Schizophrenia and manic-depressive disorder: The biological roots of mental illness as revealed by the landmark study of identical twins.* New York: Basic Books.

Walker, E. F. (1991). *Schizophrenia: A life-course developmental perspective.* New York: Academic Press.

Self-Disclosure

Crystal L. Park and William B. Stiles

Miami University

Alexithymia Individual characteristic involving an inability to identify feelings or to put them into words.
Assimilation Integration of new information or experience into an already-existing framework or way of understanding.
Catharsis Gaining of relief by expression of feelings.
Expressive Disclosure Disclosure meant to gain intrapersonal goals, such as cathartic relief or self-understanding.
Fever Model A theory that proposes that disclosure of psychological distress is analogous to a fever: both a signal of disturbance and a part of a restorative process.
Inhibition A state in which an individual consciously restrains, holds back, or in some way exerts effort not to think, feel, or behave.
Repression Motivated forgetting; inability to recall feelings or events because thinking about them would be psychologically painful.
Strategic Disclosure Disclosure that is meant to achieve social or interpersonal goals.

SELF-DISCLOSURE refers to the act of verbally revealing personal information about oneself (particularly thoughts, feelings and secrets) to another. The effects of self-disclosure on mental health are com-

plex: Self-disclosure produces certain types of effects within the discloser, and also profoundly influences the development and maintenance of the discloser's personal relationships with others. This article discusses functions of self-disclosure, the contexts in which self-disclosure occurs, the consequences of self-disclosure, the proposed mechanisms through which self-disclosure exerts effects on mental health and well-being, individual and situational differences in self-disclosure, and applications of self-disclosure.

Research on self-disclosure has tended to focus on three rather different aspects: (1) the effects of individual differences on self-disclosure and self-disclosure as a personality style; (2) the role of self-disclosure in developing and maintaining personal relationships (including relationships with romantic partners, friends, and strangers); and (3) the role of self-disclosure in the etiology and treatment of psychological distress. We discuss findings from all of these areas as they inform the relationship of self-disclosure to mental health and well-being.

I. FUNCTIONS

People's decisions about when, how, and what to disclose have consequences not only for the individuals but also for the relationships in which disclosure does or does not take place. Self-disclosure serves many purposes; these purposes can be classified broadly as either "strategic" or "expressive" functions. Strategic functions are extrinsic or instrumental; the purposes or benefits of disclosure are derived from the external consequences, principally effects on the intimacy, status, or other aspects of relationships among people. Expressive functions, on the other hand, are those in which the purposes or benefits of disclosing are derived from the act itself, such as gaining self-understanding or experiencing relief through catharsis. All disclosures probably serve some mixture of strategic and expressive functions, but in many cases one or the other function predominates.

A. Strategic Self-Disclosure

In their daily lives, people engage in many types of self-disclosure for strategic purposes. For example, individuals maintain their relationships with others through their decisions about what to disclose and what to withhold. Through their disclosures, individuals decide how intimate they want to be with others. Through their disclosures, people also elicit feedback from others about their own thoughts and feelings. For example, individuals may receive help or social support in response to disclosures indicating need.

1. Management of Relationships

Self-disclosure is an important component in developing and maintaining relationships. Disclosure provides opportunities to establish trust and convey interest in others. Research in this area is complex, but results generally indicate that people who disclose intimate information tend to be liked more than people who disclose less, and that people reciprocate disclosure to the extent that they like the discloser. Self-disclosure can promote and inform the development of close relationships (e.g., one person's disclosure may be used by the other person to draw inferences about compatibility). Through increasingly personal and reciprocal self-disclosures, people may become close and intimate.

Self-disclosure also occurs as a part of ongoing social interactions between relationship partners. In such ongoing close relationships, partners negotiate what they will and what they will not talk about. Disclosure over time is one way that people in relationships maintain a vital connection and closeness with one another.

2. Self-Presentation

People have a virtually unlimited amount of private, personal information and inner experience that is available only to themselves. Their choices about what information to disclose, how to disclose it, and to whom to disclose are important determinants of how

others will respond to them, and, over time, such decisions strongly influence individuals' social relationships. Research suggests that these choices may not be made deliberately or consciously, and that individuals differ in the extent to which they are skilled at impression management (sometimes called "self-monitoring"). High self-monitors are more sensitive than low self-monitors to feedback from others, such as nonverbal communication, and they tend to adjust and modify their behaviors to make them more socially acceptable. Evidence suggests that when those high in self-monitoring disclose personal information to others, they tend to do so in a more thoughtful, sensitive way than those low in self-monitoring.

3. Receiving Feedback/Social Validation

By disclosing information to others, individuals avail themselves of information that others provide for them in the form of feedback. The responses of others to whom one discloses can be very helpful in appraising or understanding the disclosed information. These responses include both specific responses (e.g., That's not such a big problem; I've known lots of people . . .) as well as their general reactions (e.g., approval, interest, compassion, shock, disgust, boredom).

4. Requesting Information and Help from Others

An important strategic function of self-disclosure is asking for advice or help from others. When people disclose their problems or make known their needs for information or tangible help, they make it more likely that others will respond favorably with the needed support.

B. Expressive Functions

The expressive, stress-relieving function of self-disclosure becomes important when people are psychologically distressed. Experiencing upsetting or stressful events often generates a feeling of internal pressure, incorporating emotions such as anger or sadness or some other negative feeling, along with a need to relieve or release the pressure. Under such duress or pressure, people tend to disclose more. Although the pressure is greatest immediately or shortly after a stressful or traumatic experience, psychologically powerful or important events can leave people with a need to talk that lasts for months or years afterward (e.g., bereavement, traumatic war experiences).

There seems to be a connection between personal disclosure and distress. Studies have found that people who are psychologically disordered tend to disclose more when they are distressed than when they are not. The most important differences between normal and abnormal or psychologically disordered groups are probably in the type rather than amount of self-disclosure made, and in the appropriateness of specific disclosures. [*See* COPING WITH STRESS; STRESS.]

II. CONTEXTS AND CONDITIONS

A. Kinships, Friendships, and Other Personal Relationships

Self-disclosure occurs most frequently within interpersonal relationships. Disclosure of many kinds of information is such a natural part of the human experience that such an observation seems unnecessary. However, it is important to note the types and extent of such disclosure in order to understand why disclosure in these types of relationships is sometimes inadequate to meet a person's needs. Under normal circumstances, people tend to talk about their emotionally significant experiences with their relatives, friends, and associates soon after the experience occurs. Often this forum for disclosure is adequate and helps the discloser feel better.

On the other hand, these listeners often have a limited tolerance for such expressive disclosure. In the case of extended and repeated disclosures, an individual's normal social support network may "burn out" and become unreceptive or even hostile. Sometimes individuals do not have adequate personal relationships, or they sustain a loss that involves the very social relationship they would normally have relied on for disclosure and comfort. Psychotherapists, clergy, and other professional listeners can be regarded as sources of social support for such extenuating circumstances. [*See* BURNOUT.]

B. Therapy

Many theoretical perspectives view a high level of client disclosure as critical in counseling and psychotherapy, and the techniques of many schools of psychotherapy attempt to facilitate clients' disclosure. Disclosure is typically considered to be "good process" in therapy, whereas its absence tends to be associated with defensiveness or resistance. Through making personal disclosures to their therapist, clients can become aware of and acceptant of their own experiences, learn about their unconscious impulses and conflicts, or develop a genuine relationship with the therapist. In addition to being trustworthy and receptive listeners, psychotherapists, through their responses to the disclosure, may help clients to identify and express their emotional experiences. For example, client-centered therapists use reflections to help their clients put their internal experience into words; gestalt therapists use "process directives" to encourage clients to express their feelings toward others in empty chair procedures; and therapists of many orientations ask questions about their clients' feelings. Although their preferred techniques vary, and although they may guide their clients' disclosures in theory-specific directions, different schools of therapy appear to share a common goal of facilitating client disclosure.

C. Situational Factors; Privacy and Anonymity

The particular situations with which individuals find themselves dealing also influence their willingness and ability to disclose. The need to "find a quiet place to talk" speaks to the importance of setting and atmosphere. Professionals such as clergy and psychotherapists, whose jobs involve facilitating self-disclosure, consistently favor quiet, comfortable, private surroundings, in which there are few distractions.

The content of the information to be disclosed has obvious and powerful effects on the ease and likelihood of disclosure. Particularly difficult are disclosures of information of which the hearers may disapprove. Research has shown that individuals find it harder to disclose socially stigmatized information, such as that regarding incest or rape, than other types of negative experiences, such as bereavement. For some people, the assurance of confidentiality offered by clergy and psychotherapists is essential if they are to disclose information or feelings that may be embarrassing, illegal, or otherwise objectionable to others.

D. Is a Listener Necessary for Self-Disclosure?

One unresolved issue in self-disclosure research is that of the importance of the relationship between the discloser and the listener, or even of the necessity of having a listener at all. For example, is it necessary to have someone hear or receive the disclosure in order for it to have effects? Or does writing one's deepest feelings in a diary or journal function as disclosure? How do the effects of disclosing to a friend differ from those of disclosing to a stranger? Does the feedback provided by the listener influence the internal effects of the disclosure on the person who disclosed? Some research indicates that disclosure through anonymous writing has effects similar to those of talking to a friend or therapist, although other research indicates that speaking to a therapist produces more potent effects.

III. CONSEQUENCES OF DISCLOSURE

What benefits do people obtain from disclosing? Although researchers have begun to explore this area using an array of methods, there are some inherent difficulties in the field. For example, self-disclosing behaviors and tendencies do not exist randomly in the population, nor are they easily manipulated by researchers. Instead, self-disclosure is internally regulated by individuals who differ in their self-disclosure behaviors, life experience, and many other characteristics. Further, the study of the effects of disclosure in various contexts is complex. Disclosure serves certain personal and interpersonal functions and also occurs within a cultural context that has normative expectations about disclosure. Therefore, the effects of disclosure must be studied in terms of the amount and the content of disclosures, in the functions served by the disclosures, and in the extent that the listener adheres to social norms. Much remains to be learned regarding the complex effects of disclosure.

In spite of these difficulties in studying self-disclosure and mental health and well-being, there is a fair amount of evidence suggesting that self-disclosure has strong effects on various aspects of psychological and physical functioning. Research into the consequences of disclosure have focused on three areas: (1) the effects of self-disclosure in intimate relationships; (2) the effects of self-disclosure on psychotherapy outcomes; and (3) the effects of disclosure of stressful or traumatic experiences on psychological and physical health.

A. Relationship Outcomes

Self-disclosure tends to both reflect and affect other interpersonal processes. For example, physically at-

tractive people tend to give and receive more disclosure than physically unattractive people. It may be that others find attractive people's thoughts, feelings, perceptions, and intentions more interesting than those of unattractive people and encourage such expression by attractive people more than by unattractive people. At the same time, others are more likely to disclose their own thoughts and feelings to attractive than to unattractive people, as a strategy to engage the former in closer relationships.

Between people of equal social status, disclosure often promotes intimacy, both by the revelation of private knowledge and feelings to another and by encouraging reciprocity of disclosure from the other. Widening and deepening of mutual disclosure is characteristic of the growth of intimate relationships, and a feeling of knowing and being known to another is a central feature of intimacy. People low on self-disclosure tend to have more relationship problems, including loneliness, alienation, lower marital satisfaction, and fewer sources of social support.

B. Mental Health

Victims of stressful experiences, such as trauma or bereavement, are less likely to become depressed or develop psychological symptoms if they confide their feelings in others with whom they feel close. Although an inability to disclose appropriately need not imply other psychological disorders, it is likely to lead to difficulties in dealing with life's stresses. Those who report they can and do discuss their problems and distressing feelings with friends and family are less likely to show symptoms of serious depression. There is also evidence that interventions aimed at encouraging victims to disclose their distressing thoughts and feelings help to ease their emotional pain.

Another, perhaps more lasting intrinsic benefit of disclosure is the growth of self-awareness, self-acceptance, and self-understanding or insight. This process has been extensively discussed by psychotherapy theorists, and appears to lie at the core of many psychotherapies. Such increases in self-awareness are related to self-disclosure of affectively laden experiences.

On the other hand, self-disclosure is not always associated with better mental health. Some people may disclose excessively, inappropriately, or counterproductively (as in self-focused depressive rumination).

C. Therapy Outcomes and the Fever Model

In view of the apparent benefits of disclosure for people who are troubled, one would expect that the amount of disclosure made by a client in therapy would predict that client's success in therapy outcome. When clients disclose at high levels, they are judged by experts as making good use of the setting. Paradoxically, however, clients who disclose a great deal in therapy have outcomes that are no better, on the average, than those who disclose less.

One attempt to resolve this paradox has been called the fever model of disclosure. The fever model suggests that clients normally disclose at optimum levels. Those who are more distressed tend to disclose more and those who are less distressed disclose less. At the same time, disclosure helps relieve distress and hence reduce the need to disclose. Thus, disclosure serves as part of a psychological homeostatic system, helping to maintain a psychological equilibrium. The relation of disclosure to psychological distress is analogous to the relation of fever to physical infection: both serve as a signal of some underlying disturbance and operate as part of the restorative process.

The fever model shows how self-disclosure can be associated both with sickness and with restoration of health. Because disclosure signals current distress but also tends to reduce future distress, disclosure is associated with distress at given points in people's lives, but with psychological well-being in the long run.

Statistically, a high level of distress is associated with disclosure in psychotherapy; however, more distressed clients do not necessarily have better outcomes. Indeed, one might expect clients who are initially more dysfunctional to have worse outcomes. Consequently, high disclosure may not predict positive outcomes. Analogously, a high fever is not a particularly good predictor of full or rapid recovery from physical infection, and inducing a fever is rarely an effective treatment. Moreover, as clients improve, they presumably feel less distressed, and their rate of disclosure should decrease, so their average level across sessions may be lower than the level for clients who fail to improve. For these reasons, assessing the true nature of the relationship between the process and the outcome of therapy is difficult.

Psychological disorders may arise because of failures in disclosure regulation. This automatic mechanism may not work perfectly for all individuals. For example, some people may have no relationships that are suitable for free disclosure. For others, psychological defensiveness or lack of social skills may inhibit disclosure.

The fact that some people inhibit disclosure, whereas others disclose excessively, suggests that disclosure level may bear a curvilinear relation to adjustment—that both very high and very low rates of disclosure may reflect disorder. However, the fever model distinguishes high disclosure attributable to distress (a normal restorative response) from high disclosure attributable to specific disclosure-related personality problems. In the same way, the fever model distinguishes low disclosure attributable to low distress (healthy concern for other people and events) from low disclosure attributable to social impediments (e.g., roles that inhibit disclosure) or psychological blocks (e.g., defensiveness).

D. Physical Health

Individuals restriction or inhibition of emotional expression, because of either their personality style or a fear of negative social consequences, seems to result in compromised immunological function and increased risk of health problems. There is strong evidence that factors that reduce individuals' ability to confide or discuss stressful events may aggravate immunological dysfunction and increase the likelihood of illness. Previous studies have found that both acute and chronic stressors can compromise immune function and increase the susceptibility to infectious illness. It also seems that individuals in situations that prevent disclosure of stressful situations are at increased risk of negative health consequences. For example, a number of investigators have found lower levels of social support to be associated with poorer immunological functioning. Some evidence indicates that the use of a repressive coping style is associated with the onset or progression of cancer.

A series of studies using a paradigm pioneered by James Pennebaker has highlighted the effects of self-disclosure on health. The research paradigm involves asking participants to write for four consecutive days about their thoughts and feelings regarding a trauma they have experienced. A control group of participants writes about innocuous topics, and then the physical and mental health of the groups are compared. These studies have documented that during the months following the writing, those participants who disclosed trauma-related thoughts and feelings make fewer doctor visits, and show increases in various aspects of immune functioning, as compared with the control group.

Self-disclosure might also exert secondary effects on physical health through its effects on mental health. For example, high levels of depression may lead an individual to perform fewer health behaviors, to exhibit lower compliance with medical regimens, or to stop exercising. To the extent that self-disclosure is related to less depression, it would be expected to improve health by promoting better health habits.

E. Caveat: When Disclosure Is Not Helpful

Although the overall effects of self-disclosure appear to be beneficial, disclosure is not always helpful. Self-disclosure of negative information may intensify unpleasant feelings by increasing self-awareness: if someone discloses intimate information that is negative, it may focus the discloser's attention on her or his real or imagined weaknesses and faults, leading that individual to feel worse about herself or himself. The self-awareness associated with high self-disclosure may thus aggravate a person's negative mood state by focusing on the discrepancy between the real self and an ideal self. Some evidence exists that self-disclosure that focuses on personal problems may heighten negative affect immediately after disclosure, but that it is likely to have positive, long-term effects.

Further, by sharing upsetting personal experiences with others, the discloser risks causing the listener to at least temporarily feel upset and embarrassed. Another risk is that if negative feelings are aroused in the listener, the discloser may experience rejection. Thus, others' nonsupportive reactions to the self-disclosure of upsetting events and experiences can worsen the discloser's negative feelings.

The timing of self-disclosure may influence whether benefits occur or not by influencing people's coping reactions. If people anticipate going through a stressful event, disclosure of feelings before the stressful event may heighten negative emotions and lead to higher appraisals of threat and less adaptive coping. On the other hand, people who talk about their feelings after a stressful event may experience better adaptation through venting negative feelings or gaining insight about what happened.

IV. PROPOSED MECHANISMS

Disclosure can be generally understood as a means for maintaining psychological homeostasis. The propositions that distress leads to disclosure and that disclosure leads to relief imply that disclosure automatically leads to psychological adjustment. The fever model holds that disclosure is an element in a naturally, internally regulated process of maintaining psychological well-being. It suggests that an individual's level of disclosure normally rises and falls to express, and that the individual can thus come to terms with the emotional meaning of day-to-day life experiences. It follows that under normal circumstances, the level of an individual's disclosing will approximate an optimum level. This internally regulated process likely operates through a number of different mechanisms to influence adjustment. Mechanisms that have been proposed to account for the effects of self-disclosure include the provision of social support, the lessening of shame and guilt through the perception of universality, decreased inhibition, assimilation and the making of meaning from stressful experiences, the promotion of insight and self-understanding, and the experiencing of catharsis.

A. Social Support

The socially mediated benefits of disclosing to a confidante are many; these include obtaining esteem support, informational support, instrumental support, and motivational support. Self-disclosure may be the mechanism for the reported buffering effect of social support on stress. People with strong interpersonal relationships, in which they can disclose freely, use these relationships when stress arises. In addition to acquiring needed tangible and intangible social support, individuals who self-disclose may get important feedback from those in their social networks.

Although there is no certainty that revealing problems and negative feelings to others will prompt them to provide the help that is needed or wanted, nondisclosure virtually guarantees that sufficient comfort or aid will not be provided. Failure to disclose distress is likely to minimize the instrumental aid others offer. Keeping problems to oneself, then, can undermine the impact of any expressions of caring or intimacy that others provide, and can reduce both the extent and effectiveness of advice and instrumental assistance from the individual's social environment.

The relation between social support and self-disclosure is complicated, however. If others find distress disclosure unpleasant, individuals engaging in such disclosure may lose some of their social support. Because social support is an important ingredient in the process of successfully coping with stressful experiences, the loss of such support could ultimately have detrimental effects on their adjustment and well-being. The disclosure of enough of one's misery to gain the benefits of such revelations, without disclosing in such a way or to such an extent that it will drive others away, is an important social competency, one in which individuals vary (this individual difference issue in disclosure is addressed in Section V.) [*See* SOCIAL SUPPORT.]

B. Acceptance of Feelings/ Universality of Experience

Nondisclosure can lead to feelings of shame and guilt. The act of self-disclosure may relieve feelings of shame and guilt over difficulties that were previously kept hidden. The act of disclosure may help people see themselves more positively because of the very fact that they have divulged the information. On the other hand, people who have not disclosed difficult or distressing events may feel worse and more ashamed about themselves because they infer that concealing the information implies that it is somehow negative. For example, when people experience serious emotional distress, they are often inclined to doubt that such feelings are normal, which can lead to shame and guilt for not coping as well as others seem to. If people talk over their negative feelings with others, many of these secondary doubts and fears can be alleviated through normalizing information from the social environment. When people try to conceal their troubles, such doubts and anxieties will likely further exacerbate the original distress.

C. Decreased Inhibition

Inhibition, or lack of disclosure, increases physiological stress. Actively inhibiting one's thoughts, feelings, or behaviors requires physiological work and is stressful. In the short run, inhibition is reflected by increases in the activity of the autonomic nervous system. Over time, the stressfulness of the physiological work of inhibition takes its toll on the body, which might lead to increases in the probability of illness and other stress-related physical and psychological problems.

Research has shown that disclosing or confronting a trauma immediately reduces the physiological work of inhibition. During self-disclosure, reduction in autonomic nervous system activity, such as skin conductance level, is evident. Over time, the overall physiological work is reduced, lowering the overall stress on the body.

D. Promotion of Insight and Self-Understanding

Some theories of psychotherapy, including traditional Freudian psychoanalysis, suggest that overcoming psychological problems requires insight—emotional and cognitive understanding of the roots of the problem. From this perspective, disclosure is a necessary first step toward insight, providing the raw material from which an understanding can be built. In psychoanalysis, a client is given the task of revealing everything that enters his or her mind, including feelings, memories, and passing thoughts. As this information is revealed, the client and therapist, working together, can piece together an understanding of what led to the problem and what psychological forces are maintaining it.

E. Assimilation/Meaning Making

Translating an event or experience into language affects the way the experience is organized and encoded in the mind. The mere act of putting it into words changes the person's memory of it, causing it to evolve from an unwieldy, chaotic emotional experience into a coherent narrative or story. By talking or writing about previously inhibited experiences, individuals translate the event into language. Once encoded linguistically, they can more readily understand or find meaning in, or attain closure of, the experience. Once the experience is organized, it can more readily be assimilated and set aside.

On the other hand, nondisclosure increases obsessional thinking. The more one tries to avoid talking about a traumatic life event, the more difficult it might be to get rid of the unwanted thoughts. Research demonstrates that people who try to suppress certain thoughts may become preoccupied later with the thoughts they seek to avoid. Self-disclosure may thus provide a release from thinking about upsetting events, allowing the person to organize and make sense of what happened.

The failure to talk about, and to account for, stressful events or experiences impedes the cognitive and emotional assimilation process. Stressful events and experiences that are not assimilated are more likely to remain in consciousness as unwanted and ruminative thoughts, and the suppression of these thoughts is associated with increased physiological arousal.

Active inhibition is also associated with potentially deleterious changes in information processing. By holding back significant thoughts and feelings associated with stressful events and experiences, individuals typically do not fully process their experiences. By not talking about an inhibited event, for example, individuals usually do not translate the event into language that aids in the understanding and assimilation of the event.

Research indicates, however, that it is not just reviewing and reorganizing factual material that is involved in the effects of self-disclosure on adjustment. Instead, it seems that individuals must also process the emotional concomitants of the experience. The association between emotional experiencing and beneficial effects of disclosure is supported by research comparing the disclosures of those who, following disclosure, demonstrate subsequent health improvement to those who do not. Improved health is related to the use of more negative than positive emotion words, suggesting that improvement may not occur unless the discloser discusses emotions as well as facts.

F. Catharsis

Catharsis involves the sense of relief that individuals feel after having successfully explained a personal difficulty to another person. This cathartic effect, sometimes described as "getting it off my chest," seems to be facilitated by some indication of understanding from the other. The primary source of benefit, however, seems to be more strongly related to the depth of the disclosure itself and to the intensity of the accompanying emotion than to any specific quality of the listener's response.

V. INDIVIDUAL DIFFERENCES

There are clear differences in the disclosure-related behaviors of different people in different circumstances. These differences can be viewed as personality differ-

ences (e.g., tendency to inhibit disclosure), as differences in resources (such as coping skills or social support), or as differences in cultural norms. These differences affect the interpretation of relationships between self-disclosure and well-being. [See INDIVIDUAL DIFFERENCES IN MENTAL HEALTH.]

A. Personality Differences

Individuals vary widely in the degree to which they can be classified as inhibitors or disclosers, and a number of personality characteristics have been advanced to account for these differences. For example, researchers have proposed that people vary on traits known as alexithymia and repression. Those high in alexithymia have an inability to identify or describe their emotions. Alexithymics, then, are generally not likely to be high on self-disclosure. A related characteristic, repression, refers to the tendency to report experiencing little anxiety combined with a tendency to present oneself in a very positive social light. This personality characteristic is also related to less self-disclosure.

Some differences in self-disclosure behaviors may be due to innate differences in temperament. The socialization processes through which individuals mature will also affect their self-disclosure behaviors. For example, some people are socialized to be or to value being stoic or nondisclosing, while others learn to express their emotions freely.

People also vary in their social competencies regarding disclosure. Some may reveal their personal information and problems in a more restrained, tactful, or sensitive way that enables them to bring up and discuss difficulties without alienating the people around them while still maintaining their social support. Others are less skilled at making disclosures, and either inappropriately continue to disclose their distress, driving away their social support, or try to maintain their relationships by keeping their problems to themselves. [See PERSONALITY.]

B. Differences in Resources

Individuals differ in their coping abilities, including the degree to which they actively confront or disclose a trauma. The coping style of emotional inhibition is related to personality characteristics such as alexithymia and repression. Inhibition involves a paucity of thought about emotions, dissociation between subjective and bodily emotional reactions, a lack of communication about emotions, and extreme conflicts between wanting to confide and repression of this desire.

As noted above, much self-disclosure occurs in social contexts. Some of the differences seen in self-disclosure may be due to the actual lack of a social support network in which this disclosure might take place. Such a lack could be due to poor social competencies (see Section V. A.), or to temporary circumstances (e.g., in the case of someone who just moved to a foreign country to begin a program of study).

C. Differences in Cultural Norms

A rather unexplored area in self-disclosure research involves the role that cultural norms play in determining when, what, and how individuals will disclose personal information. There is research that suggests that Western cultures, particularly that of the United States, encourage more and broader personal disclosures, and that individuals from Eastern cultures, such as China, tend to disclose less. There are likely many cultural and subcultural norms and dictates that influence individuals self-disclosure behaviors. Cultures also vary in who is seen as an appropriate recipient for disclosures. In some groups, disclosure within the family is accepted, but disclosure of negative feelings or events to people outside the family may be seen as inappropriate or disloyal. Psychotherapists and others who deal with such groups should be aware that what appears to be a client's emotional inhibition may be a manifestation of family loyalty or a different cultural norm.

D. Role of These Individual Variables in Determining Disclosure–Benefit Relationships

Making generalizations about the effects of self-disclosure is difficult. Individuals experiencing the same event may vary widely in their disclosure of the event, and the same individual may disclose about two different events very differently.

Interpretations of research on self-disclosure may differ depending on whether the tendency to disclose is conceptualized as an individual difference variable or as a situational response. For example, studies us-

ing the writing-about-trauma research paradigm developed by Pennebaker will yield different interpretations if researchers consider self-disclosure as a personality variable than if researchers assume all people disclose similarly. If people are assumed to differ, then those who are high in self-disclosure would be likely to have already disclosed a great deal, and may have less to disclose in the experimental condition. Experimentally inducing disclosure in high disclosers is unlikely to effect improvements, whereas inducing disclosure in individuals who are initially inhibited may yield dramatic benefits. Some research evidence supports such an interpretation.

The potential benefits of emotional disclosure for mental and physical health presume that people are both motivated and able to disclose. If repression involves an active inhibitory mechanism, and if the motivation for this mechanism is self-protection, then the effectiveness of emotional disclosure in repressing or inhibiting individuals may be limited. People with limited emotional awareness or expressive abilities regarding feelings and emotional experiences not only have a limited capacity for disclosure, but potentially beneficial effects of disclosure may be limited as well. Systematic research on individual differences in openness to emotional experience and on emotional expressiveness as moderators of the effects of self-disclosure is clearly needed.

VI. IMPLICATIONS

Is more disclosure better? The fever model suggested that disclosure is a common active ingredient in many different therapies. However, this does not imply that more disclosure is necessarily better or that everyone would benefit from high levels of disclosure. Manipulating or forcing distressed people to disclose more than they do may not be helpful. The fever model implies that expressive disclosure is a homeostatic restorative mechanism. Normally, it should be most beneficial to allow it free reign rather than to artificially increase or decrease it. Of course, some distressed people who show up in therapy may be blocked in their ability to disclose, either because of defensiveness, early training for stoicism, or constricting social norms. For such people, training in intensive disclosure could enhance their ability to make use of their friends or psychotherapy.

BIBLIOGRAPHY

Collins, N. L., & Miller, L. C. (1994). Self-disclosure and liking: A meta-analytic review. *Psychological Bulletin, 116,* 457–475.

Derlega, V. J., & Berg, J. H. (Eds.). (1987). *Self-disclosure: Theory, research, and therapy.* New York: Plenum Press.

Derlega, V. J., Metts, S., Petronio, S., & Margulis, S. T. (1993). *Self-disclosure.* Newbury Park, CA: Sage.

Pennebaker, J. W. (1993). Putting stress into words: Health, linguistic, and therapeutic implications. *Behaviour Research and Therapy, 31,* 539–548.

Pennebaker, J. W. (Ed.). (1995). *Emotion, disclosure, and health.* Washington, DC: American Psychological Association.

Self-Efficacy

Albert Bandura

Stanford University

Affective Processes   Processes regulating emotional states and elicitation of emotional reactions.
Cognitive Processes   Thinking processes involved in the acquisition, organization, and use of information.
Motivation   Activation to action. Level of motivation is reflected in choice of courses of action, and in the intensity and persistence of effort.
Perceived Self-Efficacy   People's beliefs about their capabilities to produce effects.
Self-Regulation   Exercise of influence over one's own motivation, thought processes, emotional states, and patterns of behavior.

Perceived **SELF-EFFICACY** is defined as people's beliefs about their capabilities to produce designated levels of performance that exercise influence over events that affect their lives. Self-efficacy beliefs determine how people feel, think, motivate themselves, and behave. Such beliefs produce these diverse effects through four major processes. They include cognitive, motivational, affective, and selection processes.

A strong sense of efficacy enhances human accomplishment and personal well-being in many ways. People with high assurance in their capabilities approach difficult tasks as challenges to be mastered rather than as threats to be avoided. Such an efficacious outlook fosters intrinsic interest and deep engrossment in activities. They set themselves challenging goals and maintain strong commitment to them. They heighten and sustain their efforts in the face of failure. They quickly recover their sense of efficacy after failures or setbacks. They attribute failure to insufficient effort or deficient knowledge and skills which are acquirable. They approach threatening situations with assurance that they can exercise control over them. Such an efficacious outlook produces personal accomplishments, reduces stress, and lowers vulnerability to depression.

In contrast, people who doubt their capabilities shy away from difficult tasks which they view as personal threats. They have low aspirations and weak commitment to the goals they choose to pursue. When faced with difficult tasks, they dwell on their personal deficiencies, on the obstacles they will encounter, and all kinds of adverse outcomes rather than concentrate on how to perform successfully. They slacken their efforts and give up quickly in the face of difficulties. They are slow to recover their sense of efficacy following failure or setbacks. Because they view insufficient performance as deficient aptitude it does not require much failure for them to lose faith in their capabilities. They fall easy victim to stress and depression.

I. SOURCES OF SELF-EFFICACY BELIEFS

People's beliefs about their efficacy can be developed by four main sources of influence. The most effective way of creating a strong sense of efficacy is through *mastery experiences*. Successes build a robust belief in one's personal efficacy. Failures undermine it, especially if failures occur before a sense of efficacy is firmly established.

If people experience only easy successes they come to expect quick results and are easily discouraged by failure. A resilient sense of efficacy requires experience in overcoming obstacles through perseverant effort. Some setbacks and difficulties in human pursuits serve a useful purpose in teaching that success usually requires sustained effort. After people become convinced they have what it takes to succeed, they persevere in the face of adversity and quickly rebound from setbacks. By sticking it out through tough times, they emerge stronger from adversity.

The second way of creating and strengthening self-beliefs of efficacy is through the *vicarious experiences* provided by social models. Seeing people similar to oneself succeed by sustained effort raises observers' beliefs that they too possess the capabilities to master comparable activities to succeed. By the same token, observing others fail despite high effort lowers observers' judgments of their own efficacy and undermines their efforts. The impact of modeling on perceived self-efficacy is strongly influenced by perceived similarity to the models. The greater the assumed similarity the more persuasive are the model's successes and failures. If people see the models as very different from themselves their perceived self-efficacy is not much influenced by the models' behavior and the results they produce.

Modeling influences do more than provide a social standard against which to judge one's own capabilities. People seek proficient models who possess the competencies to which they aspire. Through their behavior and expressed ways of thinking, competent models transmit knowledge and teach observers effective skills and strategies for managing environmental demands. Acquisition of better means raises perceived self-efficacy.

Social persuasion is a third way of strengthening people's beliefs that they have what it takes to succeed. People who are persuaded verbally that they possess the capabilities to master given activities are likely to mobilize greater effort and sustain it than if they harbor self-doubts and dwell on personal deficiencies when problems arise. To the extent that persuasive boosts in perceived self-efficacy lead people to try hard enough to succeed, they promote development of skills and a sense of personal efficacy.

It is more difficult to instill high beliefs of personal efficacy by social persuasion alone than to undermine it. Unrealistic boosts in efficacy are quickly disconfirmed by disappointing results of one's efforts. But people who have been persuaded that they lack capabilities tend to avoid challenging activities that cultivate potentialities and give up quickly in the face of difficulties. By constricting activities and undermining motivation, disbelief in one's capabilities creates its own behavioral validation.

Successful efficacy builders do more than convey positive appraisals. In addition to raising people's beliefs in their capabilities, they structure situations for them in ways that bring success and avoid placing people in situations prematurely where they are likely to fail often. They measure success in terms of self-improvement rather than by triumphs over others.

People also rely partly on their *somatic and emotional states* in judging their capabilities. They interpret their stress reactions and tension as signs of vulnerability to poor performance. In activities involving strength and stamina, people judge their fatigue, aches, and pains as signs of physical debility. Mood also affects people's judgments of their personal efficacy. Positive mood enhances perceived self-efficacy, and despondent mood diminishes it. The fourth way of modifying self-beliefs of efficacy is to reduce people's stress reactions and alter their negative emotional proclivities and misinterpretations of their physical states.

It is not the sheer intensity of emotional and physical reactions that is important but rather how they are perceived and interpreted. People who have a high sense of efficacy are likely to view their state of affective arousal as an energizing facilitator of performance, whereas those who are beset by self-doubts regard their arousal as a debilitator. Physiological indicators of efficacy play an especially influential role in health functioning and in athletic and other physical activities.

II. EFFICACY-ACTIVATED PROCESSES

Much research has been conducted on the four major psychological processes through which self-beliefs of efficacy affect human functioning.

A. Cognitive Processes

The effects of self-efficacy beliefs on cognitive processes take a variety of forms. Much human behavior, being purposive, is regulated by forethought embodying valued goals. Personal goal setting is influenced by self-appraisal of capabilities. The stronger the perceived self-efficacy, the higher the goal challenges people set for themselves and the firmer is their commitment to them.

Most courses of action are initially organized in thought. People's beliefs in their efficacy shape the types of anticipatory scenarios they construct and rehearse. Those who have a high sense of efficacy, visualize success scenarios that provide positive guides and supports for performance. Those who doubt their efficacy, visualize failure scenarios and dwell on the many things that can go wrong. It is difficult to achieve much while fighting self-doubt.

A major function of thought is to enable people to predict events and to develop ways to control those that affect their lives. Such skills require effective cognitive processing of information that contains many ambiguities and uncertainties. In learning predictive and regulative rules people must draw on their knowledge to construct options, to weight and integrate predictive factors, to test and revise their judgments against the immediate and distal results of their actions, and to remember which factors they had tested and how well they had worked.

It requires a strong sense of efficacy to remain task oriented in the face of pressing situational demands, failures, and setbacks that have significant repercussions. Indeed, when people are faced with the tasks of managing difficult environmental demands under taxing circumstances, those who are beset by self-doubts about their efficacy become more and more erratic in their analytic thinking, they lower their aspirations, and the quality of their performance deteriorates. In contrast, those who maintain a resilient sense of efficacy set themselves challenging goals and use good analytic thinking which pays off in performance accomplishments.

B. Motivational Processes

Self-beliefs of efficacy play a key role in the self-regulation of motivation. Most human motivation is cognitively generated. People motivate themselves and guide their actions anticipatorily by the exercise of forethought. They form beliefs about what they can do. They anticipate likely outcomes of prospective actions. They set goals for themselves and plan courses of action designed to realize valued futures.

There are three different forms of cognitive motivators around which different theories have been built. They include *causal attributions, outcome expectancies,* and *cognized goals.* The corresponding theories are attribution theory, expectancy-value theory, and goal theory, respectively. Self-efficacy beliefs operate in each of these types of cognitive motivation. Self-efficacy beliefs influence causal attributions. People who regard themselves as highly efficacious attribute their failures to insufficient effort, those who regard themselves as inefficacious attribute their failures to low ability. Causal attributions affect motivation, performance, and affective reactions mainly through beliefs of self-efficacy.

In expectancy-value theory, motivation is regulated by the expectation that a given course of behavior will produce certain outcomes and the value of those outcomes. But people act on their beliefs about what they can do, as well as on their beliefs about the likely outcomes of performance. The motivating influence of outcome expectancies is thus partly governed by self-beliefs of efficacy. There are countless attractive options people do not pursue because they judge they lack the capabilities for them. The predictiveness of expectancy-value theory is enhanced by including the influence of perceived self-efficacy.

The capacity to exercise self-influence by goal challenges and evaluative reaction to one's own attainments provides a major cognitive mechanism of motivation. A large body of evidence shows that explicit, challenging goals enhance and sustain motivation. Goals operate largely through self-influence processes rather than regulate motivation and action directly. Motivation based on goal setting involves a cognitive comparison process. By making self-satisfaction conditional on matching adopted goals, people give direction to their behavior and create incentives to persist in their efforts until they fulfill their goals. They seek self-satisfaction from fulfilling valued goals and are prompted to intensify their efforts by discontent with substandard performances.

Motivation based on goals or personal standards is governed by three types of self-influences. They include self-satisfying and self-dissatisfying reactions to one's performance, perceived self-efficacy for goal attainment, and readjustment of personal goals based on one's progress. Self-efficacy beliefs contribute to motivation in several ways: They determine the goals people set for themselves; how much effort they expend; how long they persevere in the face of difficulties; and their resilience to failures. When faced with obstacles and failures people who harbor self-doubts about their capabilities slacken their efforts or give up quickly. Those who have a strong belief in their capabilities exert greater effort when they fail to master the challenge. Strong perseverance contributes to performance accomplishments.[See OPTIMISM, MOTIVATION, AND MENTAL HEALTH.]

C. Affective Processes

People's beliefs in their coping capabilities affect how much stress and depression they experience in threatening or difficult situations, as well as their level of motivation. Perceived self-efficacy to exercise control over stressors plays a central role in anxiety arousal. People who believe they can exercise control over threats do not conjure up disturbing thought patterns. But those who believe they cannot manage threats experience high anxiety arousal. They dwell on their coping deficiencies. They view many aspects of their environment as fraught with danger. They magnify the severity of possible threats and worry about things that rarely happen. Through such inefficacious thinking they distress themselves and impair their level of functioning. Perceived coping self-efficacy regulates avoidance behavior as well as anxiety arousal. The stronger the sense of self-efficacy the bolder people are in taking on taxing and threatening activities.

Anxiety arousal is affected not only by perceived coping efficacy but also by perceived efficacy to control disturbing thoughts. The exercise of control over one's own consciousness is summed up well in the proverb: "You cannot prevent the birds of worry and care from flying over your head. But you can stop them from building a nest in your head." Perceived self-efficacy to control thought processes is a key factor in regulating thought produced stress and depression. It is not the sheer frequency of disturbing thoughts but the perceived inability to turn them off that is the major source of distress. Both perceived coping self-efficacy and thought control efficacy operate jointly to reduce anxiety and avoidant behavior. [See ANXIETY; STRESS.]

Social cognitive theory prescribes mastery experiences as the principal means of personality change. Guided mastery is a powerful vehicle for instilling a robust sense of coping efficacy in people whose functioning is seriously impaired by intense apprehension and phobic self-protective reactions. Mastery experiences are structured in ways to build coping skills and instill beliefs that one can exercise control over potential threats. Intractable phobics, of course, are not about to do what they dread. One must, therefore, create an environment so that incapacitated phobics can perform successfully despite themselves. This is achieved by enlisting a variety of performance mastery aids.

Feared activities are first modeled to show people how to cope with threats and to disconfirm their worst fears. Coping tasks are broken down into subtasks of easily mastered steps. Performing feared activities together with the therapist further enables phobics to do things they would resist doing by themselves. Another way of overcoming resistance is to use graduated time. Phobics will refuse threatening tasks if they will have to endure stress for a long time. But they will risk them for a short period. As their coping efficacy increases the time they perform the activity is extended. Protective aids and dosing the severity of threats also help to restore and develop a sense of coping efficacy.

After functioning is fully restored, the mastery aids are withdrawn to verify that coping successes stem from personal efficacy rather than from mastery aids. Self-directed mastery experiences, designed to provide confirmatory tests of coping capabilities, are then arranged to strengthen and generalize the sense of coping efficacy. Once people develop a resilient sense of efficacy they can withstand difficulties and adversities without adverse effects.

Guided mastery treatment achieves widespread psychological changes in a relatively short time. It eliminates phobic behavior and anxiety and biological stress reactions, creates positive attitudes, and eradicates phobic ruminations and nightmares. Evidence that achievement of coping efficacy profoundly affects dream activity is a particularly striking generalized impact.

A low sense of efficacy to exercise control produces depression as well as anxiety. It does so in several different ways. One route to depression is through unfulfilled aspiration. People who impose on themselves standards of self-worth that they judge they cannot attain drive themselves to bouts of depression. A second efficacy route to depression is through a low sense of social efficacy. People who judge themselves to be socially efficacious seek out and cultivate social relationships that provide models on how to manage difficult situations, cushion the adverse effects of chronic stressors, and bring satisfaction to people's lives. Perceived social inefficacy to develop satisfying and supportive relationships increases vulnerability to depression through social isolation. Much human depression is cognitively generated by dejecting ruminative thought. A low sense of efficacy to exercise control over ruminative thought also contributes to the occurrence, duration, and recurrence of depressive episodes. [See DEPRESSION.]

Other efficacy-activated processes in the affective domain concern the impact of perceived coping self-efficacy on biological systems that affect health functioning. Stress has been implicated as an important contributing factor to many physical dysfunctions. Controllability appears to be a key organizing principle regarding the nature of these stress effects. It is not stressful life conditions *per se,* but the perceived inability to manage them that is debilitating. Thus, exposure to stressors with ability to control them has no adverse biological effects. But exposure to the same stressors without the ability to control them impairs the immune system. The impairment of immune function increases susceptibility to infection, contributes to the development of physical disorders, and accelerates the progression of disease. [See PSYCHONEUROIMMUNOLOGY.]

Biological systems are highly interdependent. A weak sense of efficacy to exercise control over stressors activates autonomic reactions, catecholamine secretion, and release of endogenous opioids. These biological systems are involved in the regulation of the immune system. Stress activated in the process of acquiring coping capabilities may have different effects than stress experienced in aversive situations with no prospect in sight of ever gaining any self-protective efficacy. There are substantial evolutionary benefits to experiencing enhanced immune function during development of coping capabilities vital for effective adaptation. It would not be evolutionarily advantageous if acute stressors invariably impaired immune function, because of their prevalence in everyday life. If this were the case, people would experience high vulnerability to infective agents that would quickly do them in. There is some evidence that providing people with effective means for managing stressors may have a positive effect on immune function. Moreover, stress aroused while gaining coping mastery over stressors can enhance different components of the immune system.

There are other ways in which perceived self-efficacy serves to promote health. Lifestyle habits can enhance or impair health. This enables people to exert behavioral influence over their vitality and quality of health. Perceived self-efficacy affects every phase of personal change—whether people even consider changing their health habits; whether they enlist the motivation and perseverance needed to succeed should they choose to do so; and how well they maintain the habit changes they have achieved. The stronger the perceived self-regulatory efficacy the more successful people are in reducing health-impairing habits and adopting and integrating health-promoting habits into their regular lifestyle. Comprehensive community programs designed to prevent cardiovascular disease by altering risk-related habits reduce the rate of morbidity and mortality.

D. Selection Processes

The discussion so far has centered on efficacy-activated processes that enable people to create beneficial environments and to exercise some control over those they encounter day in and day out. People are partly the product of their environment. Therefore, beliefs of personal efficacy can shape the course lives take by influencing the types of activities and environments people choose. People avoid activities and situations they believe exceed their coping capabilities. But they readily undertake challenging activities and select situations they judge themselves capable of handling. By the choices they make, people cultivate different competencies, interests, and social networks that determine life courses. Any factor that influences choice behavior can profoundly affect the direction of personal development. This is because the social influences operating in selected environments continue to promote certain competencies, values, and interests long after the efficacy decisional determinant has rendered its inaugurating effect.

Career choice and development are but one example of the power of self-efficacy beliefs to affect the course of life paths through choice-related processes. The higher the level of people's perceived self-efficacy the wider the range of career options they seriously consider, the greater their interest in them, the better they prepare themselves educationally for the occupational pursuits they choose, and the greater is their success. Occupations structure a good part of people's lives and provide them with a major source of personal identity.

III. ADAPTIVE BENEFITS OF OPTIMISTIC SELF-BELIEFS OF EFFICACY

There is a growing body of evidence that human accomplishments and positive well-being require an optimistic sense of personal efficacy. This is because ordinary social realities are strewn with difficulties. They are full of impediments, adversities, setbacks, frustrations, and inequities. People must have a robust sense of personal efficacy to sustain the perseverant effort needed to succeed. In pursuits strewn with obstacles, realists either forsake them, abort their efforts prematurely when difficulties arise, or become cynical about the prospects of effecting significant changes.

It is widely believed that misjudgment breeds personal problems. Certainly, gross miscalculation can get one into trouble. However, the functional value of accurate self-appraisal depends on the nature of the activity. Activities in which mistakes can produce costly or injurious consequences call for accurate self-appraisal of capabilities. It is a different matter where difficult accomplishments can produce substantial personal and social benefits and the costs involve one's time, effort, and expendable resources. People with a high sense of efficacy have the staying power to endure the obstacles and setbacks that characterize difficult undertakings.

When people err in their self-appraisal they tend to overestimate their capabilities. This is a benefit rather than a cognitive failing to be eradicated. If efficacy beliefs always reflected only what people can do routinely they would rarely fail but they would not set aspirations beyond their immediate reach or mount the extra effort needed to surpass their ordinary performances.

People who experience much distress have been compared in their skills and beliefs in their capabilities with those who do not suffer from such problems. The findings show that it is often the normal people who are distorters of reality. But they display self-enhancing biases and distort in the positive direction. People who are socially anxious or prone to depression are often just as socially skilled as those who do not suffer from such problems. But the normal ones believe they are much more adept than they really are. The nondepressed people also have a stronger belief that they exercise some control over situations.

Social reformers strongly believe that they can mobilize the collective effort needed to bring social change. Although their beliefs are rarely fully realized they sustain reform efforts that achieve important gains. Were social reformers to be entirely realistic about the prospects of transforming social systems they would either forego the endeavor or fall easy victim to discouragement. Realists may adapt well to existing realities. But those with a tenacious self-efficacy are likely to change those realities.

Innovative achievements also require a resilient sense of efficacy. Innovations demand heavy investment of effort over a long period with uncertain results. Moreover, innovations that clash with existing preferences and practices meet with negative social reactions. It is, therefore, not surprising that one rarely finds realists in the ranks of innovators and great achievers.

In his delightful book titled *Rejection*, John White provides vivid testimony that the striking characteristics of people who have achieved eminence in their fields is an inextinguishable sense of personal efficacy and a firm belief in the worth of what they are doing. This resilient self-belief system enabled them to override repeated early rejections of their work.

Many of our literary classics brought their authors countless rejections. James Joyce's *Dubliners* was rejected by 22 publishers. Gertrude Stein continued to submit poems to editors for 20 years before one was finally accepted. Over a dozen publishers rejected a manuscript by e. e. cummings. When he finally got it published, by his mother, the dedication read, in uppercase: "With no thanks to . . ." followed by the list of 16 publishers who had rejected his manuscript.

Early rejection is the rule, rather than the exception, in other creative endeavors. The Impressionists had to arrange their own exhibitions because their works were routinely rejected by the Paris Salon. Van Gogh sold only one painting during his lifetime. Rodin was rejected three times for admission to the Ecole des Beaux-Arts.

The musical works of most renowned composers were initially greeted with derision. Stravinsky was run out of town by enraged Parisiens and critics when he first served them the *Rite of Spring*. Entertainers in the contemporary pop culture have not fared any better. Decca records rejected a recording contract with the Beatles with the nonprophetic evaluation, "We don't like their sound. Groups of guitars are on the way out." Columbia records was next to turn them down.

Theories and technologies that are ahead of their time usually suffer repeated rejections. The rocket pioneer Robert Goddard was bitterly rejected by his scientific peers on the grounds that rocket propulsion would not work in the rarefied atmosphere of outer space. Because of the cold reception given to innovations, the time between conception and technical realization is discouragingly long.

The moral of the *Book of Rejections* is that rejections should not be accepted too readily as indicants of personal failings. To do so is self-limiting.

In sum, the successful, the venturesome, the sociable, the nonanxious, the nondepressed, the social reformers, and the innovators take an optimistic view of their personal capabilities to exercise influence over events that affect their lives. If not unrealistically exaggerated, such self-beliefs foster positive well-being and human accomplishments.

Many of the challenges of life are group problems requiring collective effort to produce significant change. The strength of groups, organizations, and even nations lies partly in people's sense of collective efficacy that they can solve the problems they face and improve their lives through unified effort. People's beliefs in their collective efficacy influence what they choose to do as a group, how much effort they put into it, their endurance when collective efforts fail to produce quick results, and their likelihood of success.

IV. DEVELOPMENT AND EXERCISE OF SELF-EFFICACY OVER THE LIFE SPAN

Different periods of life present certain types of competency demands for successful functioning. These normative changes in required competencies with age do not represent lock-step stages through which everyone must inevitably pass. There are many pathways through life and, at any given period, people vary substantially in how efficaciously they manage their lives. The sections that follow provide a brief analysis of the characteristic developmental changes in the nature and scope of perceived self-efficacy over the course of the lifespan.

A. Origins of a Sense of Personal Agency

The newborn comes without any sense of self. Infants' exploratory experiences in which they see themselves produce effects by their actions provide the initial basis for developing a sense of efficacy. Shaking a rattle produces predictable sounds, energetic kicks shake their

cribs, and screams bring adults. By repeatedly observing that environmental events occur with action, but not in its absence, infants learn that actions produce effects. Infants who experience success in controlling environmental events become more attentive to their own behavior and more competent in learning new efficacious responses than do infants for whom the same environmental events occur regardless of how they behave.

Development of a sense of personal efficacy requires more than simply producing effects by actions. Those actions must be perceived as part of oneself. The self becomes differentiated from others through dissimilar experience. If feeding oneself brings comfort, whereas seeing others feed themselves has no similar effect, one's own activity becomes distinct from all other persons. As infants begin to mature, those around them refer to them and treat them as distinct persons. Based on growing personal and social experiences they eventually form a symbolic representation of themselves as a distinct self.

B. Familial Sources of Self-Efficacy

Young children must gain self-knowledge of their capabilities in broadening areas of functioning. They have to develop, appraise, and test their physical capabilities, their social competencies, their linguistic skills, and their cognitive skills for comprehending and managing the many situations they encounter daily. Development of sensorimotor capabilities greatly expands the infants' exploratory environment and the means for acting upon it. These early exploratory and play activities, which occupy much of children's waking hours, provide opportunities for enlarging their repertoire of basic skills and sense of efficacy.

Successful experiences in the exercise of personal control are central to the early development of social and cognitive competence. Parents who are responsive to their infants' behavior, and who create opportunities for efficacious actions by providing an enriched physical environment and permitting freedom of movement for exploration, have infants who are accelerated in their social and cognitive development. Parental responsiveness increases cognitive competence, and infants' expanded capabilities elicit greater parental responsiveness in a two-way influence. Development of language provides children with the symbolic means to reflect on their experiences and what others tell them about their capabilities and, thus, to expand their self-knowledge of what they can and cannot do.

The initial efficacy experiences are centered in the family. But as the growing child's social world rapidly expands, peers become increasingly important in children's developing self-knowledge of their capabilities. It is in the context of peer relations that social comparison comes strongly into play. At first, the closest comparative age-mates are siblings. Families differ in number of siblings, how far apart in age they are, and in their sex distribution. Different family structures, as reflected in family size, birth order, and sibling constellation patterns, create different social comparisons for judging one's personal efficacy. Younger siblings find themselves in the unfavorable position of judging their capabilities in relation to older siblings who may be several years advanced in their development.

C. Broadening of Self-Efficacy through Peer Influences

Children's efficacy-testing experiences change substantially as they move increasingly into the larger community. It is in peer relationships that they broaden self-knowledge of their capabilities. Peers serve several important efficacy functions. Those who are most experienced and competent provide models of efficacious styles of thinking and behavior. A vast amount of social learning occurs among peers. In addition, age-mates provide highly informative comparisons for judging and verifying one's self-efficacy. Children are, therefore, especially sensitive to their relative standing among the peers in activities that determine prestige and popularity.

Peers are neither homogeneous nor selected indiscriminately. Children tend to choose peers who share similar interests and values. Selective peer association will promote self-efficacy in directions of mutual interest, leaving other potentialities underdeveloped. Because peers serve as a major influence in the development and validation of self-efficacy, disrupted or impoverished peer relationships can adversely affect the growth of personal efficacy. A low sense of social efficacy can, in turn, create internal obstacles to favorable peer relationships. Thus, children who regard themselves as socially inefficacious withdraw socially, perceive low acceptance by their peers, and have a low sense of self-worth. There are some forms of behavior

where a high sense of efficacy may be socially alienating rather than socially affiliating. For example, children who readily resort to aggression perceive themselves as highly efficacious in getting things they want by aggressive means.

D. School as an Agency for Cultivating Cognitive Self-Efficacy

During the crucial formative period of children's lives, the school functions as the primary setting for the cultivation and social validation of cognitive competencies. School is the place where children develop the cognitive competencies and acquire the knowledge and problem-solving skills essential for participating effectively in the larger society. Here their knowledge and thinking skills are continually tested, evaluated, and socially compared. [See COGNITIVE DEVELOPMENT.]

As children master cognitive skills, they develop a growing sense of their intellectual efficacy. Many social factors, apart from the formal instruction, such as peer modeling of cognitive skills, social comparison with the performances of other students, motivational enhancement through goals and positive incentives, and teachers' interpretations of children's successes and failures in ways that reflect favorably or unfavorably on their ability also affect children's judgments of their intellectual efficacy.

The task of creating learning environments conducive to development of cognitive skills rests heavily on the talents and self-efficacy of teachers. Those who have a high sense of efficacy about their teaching capabilities can motivate their students and enhance their cognitive development. Teachers who have a low sense of instructional efficacy favor a custodial orientation that relies heavily on negative sanctions to get students to study.

Teachers operate collectively within an interactive social system rather than as isolates. The belief systems of staffs create school cultures that can have vitalizing or demoralizing effects on how well schools function as a social system. Schools in which the staff collectively judge themselves as powerless to get students to achieve academic success convey a group sense of academic futility that can pervade the entire life of the school. Schools in which staff members collectively judge themselves capable of promoting academic success imbue their schools with a positive atmosphere for development that promotes academic attainments regardless of whether they serve predominantly advantaged or disadvantaged students.

Students' belief in their capabilities to master academic activities affects their aspirations, their level of interest in academic activities, and their academic accomplishments. There are a number of school practices that, for the less talented or ill prepared, tend to convert instructional experiences into education in inefficacy. These include lock-step sequences of instruction, which lose many children along the way; ability groupings which further diminish the perceived self-efficacy of those cast in the lower ranks; and competitive practices where many are doomed to failure for the success of a relative few.

Classroom structures affect the development of intellectual self-efficacy, in large part, by the relative emphasis they place on social comparison versus self-comparison appraisal. Self-appraisals of less able students suffer most when the whole group studies the same material and teachers make frequent comparative evaluations. Under such a monolithic structure students rank themselves according to capability with high consensus. Once established, reputations are not easily changed. In a personalized classroom structure, individualized instruction tailored to students' knowledge and skills enables all of them to expand their competencies and provides less basis for demoralizing social comparison. As a result, students are more likely to compare their rate of progress to their personal standards than to the performance of others. Self-comparison of improvement in a personalized classroom structure raises perceived capability. Cooperative learning structures, in which students work together and help one another also tend to promote more positive self-evaluations of capability and higher academic attainments than do individualistic or competitive ones.

E. Growth of Self-Efficacy through Transitional Experiences of Adolescence

Each period of development brings with it new challenges for coping efficacy. As adolescents approach the demands of adulthood, they must learn to assume full responsibility for themselves in almost every dimension of life. This requires mastering many new skills and the ways of adult society. Learning how to

deal with pubertal changes, emotionally invested partnerships, and sexuality becomes a matter of considerable importance. The task of choosing what lifework to pursue also looms large during this period. These are but a few of the areas in which new competencies and self-beliefs of efficacy have to be developed.

With growing independence during adolescence some experimentation with risky behavior is not all that uncommon. Adolescents expand and strengthen their sense of efficacy by learning how to deal successfully with potentially troublesome matters in which they are unpracticed as well as with advantageous life events. Insulation from problematic situations leaves one ill-prepared to cope with potential difficulties. Whether adolescents forsake risky activities or become chronically enmeshed in them is determined by the interplay of personal competencies, self-management efficacy, and the prevailing influences in their lives. Impoverished hazardous environments present especially harsh realities with minimal resources and social supports for culturally valued pursuits, but extensive modeling, incentives, and social supports for transgressive styles of behavior. Such environments severely tax the coping efficacy of youth enmeshed in them to make it through adolescence in ways that do not irreversibly foreclose many beneficial life paths.

Adolescence has often been characterized as a period of psychosocial turmoil. While no period of life is ever free of problems, contrary to the stereotype of "storm and stress," most adolescents negotiate the important transitions of this period without undue disturbance or discord. However, youngsters who enter adolescence beset by a disabling sense of inefficacy transport their vulnerability to distress and debility to the new environmental demands. The ease with which the transition from childhood to the demands of adulthood is made similarly depends on the strength of personal efficacy built up through prior mastery experiences. [*See* ADOLESCENCE.]

F. Self-Efficacy Concerns of Adulthood

Young adulthood is a period when people have to learn to cope with many new demands arising from lasting partnerships, marital relationships, parenthood, and occupational careers. As in earlier mastery tasks, a firm sense of self-efficacy is an important contributor to the attainment of further competencies and success. Those who enter adulthood poorly equipped with skills and plagued by self-doubts find many aspects of their adult life stressful and depressing.

Beginning a productive vocational career poses a major transitional challenge in early adulthood. There are a number of ways in which self-efficacy beliefs contribute to career development and success in vocational pursuits. In preparatory phases, people's perceived self-efficacy partly determines how well they develop the basic cognitive, self-management, and interpersonal skills on which occupational careers are founded. As noted earlier, beliefs concerning one's capabilities are influential determinants of the vocational life paths that are chosen.

It is one thing to get started in an occupational pursuit, it is another thing to do well and advance in it. Psychosocial skills contribute more heavily to career success than do occupational technical skills. Development of coping capabilities and skills in managing one's motivation, emotional states, and thought processes increases perceived self-regulatory efficacy. The higher the sense of self-regulatory efficacy the better the occupational functioning. Rapid technological changes in the modern workplace are placing an increasing premium on higher problem-solving skills and resilient self-efficacy to cope effectively with job displacements and restructuring of vocational activities. [See COPING WITH STRESS.]

The transition to parenthood suddenly thrusts young adults into the expanded role of both parent and spouse. They now not only have to deal with the ever-changing challenges of raising children but to manage interdependent relationships within a family system and social links to many extrafamilial social systems including educational, recreational, medical, and caregiving facilities. Parents who are secure in their parenting efficacy shepherd their children adequately through the various phases of development without serious problems or severe strain on the marital relationship. But it can be a trying period for those who lack a sense of efficacy to manage the expanded familial demands. They are highly vulnerable to stress and depression. [See PARENTING.]

Increasing numbers of mothers are joining the work force either by economic necessity or by personal preference. Combining family and career has now become the normative pattern. This requires management of the demands of both familial and occupational roles. Because of the cultural lag between societal practices

and the changing status of women, they continue to bear the major share of the homemaking responsibility. Women who have a strong sense of efficacy to manage the multiple demands of family and work and to enlist their husbands' aid with childcare experience a positive sense of well-being. But those who are beset by self-doubts in their ability to combine the dual roles suffer physical and emotional strain.

By the middle years, people settle into established routines that stabilize their sense of personal efficacy in the major areas of functioning. However, the stability is a shaky one because life does not remain static. Rapid technological and social changes constantly require adaptations calling for self-reappraisals of capabilities. In their occupations, the middle-aged find themselves pressured by younger challengers. Situations in which people must compete for promotions, status, and even work itself, force constant self-appraisals of capabilities by means of social comparison with younger competitors.

G. Reappraisals of Self-Efficacy with Advancing Age

The self-efficacy issues of the elderly center on reappraisals and misappraisals of their capabilities. Biological conceptions of aging focus extensively on declining abilities. Many physical capacities do decrease as people grow older, thus requiring reappraisals of self-efficacy for activities in which the biological functions have been significantly affected. However, gains in knowledge, skills, and expertise compensate some loss in physical reserve capacity. When the elderly are taught to use their intellectual capabilities, their improvement in cognitive functioning more than offsets the average decrement in performance over two decades. Because people rarely exploit their full potential, elderly persons who invest the necessary effort can function at the higher levels of younger adults. By affecting level of involvement in activities, perceived self-efficacy can contribute to the maintenance of social, physical, and intellectual functioning over the adult lifespan.

Older people tend to judge changes in their intellectual capabilities largely in terms of their memory performance. Lapses and difficulties in memory that young adults dismiss are inclined to be interpreted by older adults as indicators of declining cognitive capabilities. Those who regard memory as a biologically shrinking capacity with aging have low faith in their memory capabilities and enlist little effort to remember things. Older adults who have a stronger sense of memory efficacy exert greater cognitive effort to aid their recall and, as a result, achieve better memory.

Much variability exists across behavioral domains and educational and socioeconomic levels, and there is no uniform decline in beliefs in personal efficacy in old age. The persons against whom the elderly compare themselves contribute much to the variability in perceived self-efficacy. Those who measure their capabilities against people their age are less likely to view themselves as declining in capabilities than if younger cohorts are used in comparative self-appraisal. Perceived cognitive inefficacy is accompanied by lowered intellectual performances. A declining sense of self-efficacy, which often may stem more from disuse and negative cultural expectations than from biological aging, can thus set in motion self-perpetuating processes that result in declining cognitive and behavioral functioning. People who are beset with uncertainties about their personal efficacy not only curtail the range of their activities but undermine their efforts in those they undertake. The result is a progressive loss of interest and skill.

Major life changes in later years are brought about by retirement, relocation, and loss of friends or spouses. Such changes place demands on interpersonal skills to cultivate new social relationships that can contribute to positive functioning and personal well-being. Perceived social inefficacy increases an older person's vulnerability to stress and depression both directly and indirectly by impeding development of social supports which serve as a buffer against life stressors.

The roles into which older adults are cast impose sociocultural constraints on the cultivation and maintenance of perceived self-efficacy. As people move to older-age phases most suffer losses of resources, productive roles, access to opportunities, and challenging activities. Monotonous environments that require little thought or independent judgment diminish the quality of functioning, whereas intellectually challenging ones enhance it. Some of the declines in functioning with age result from sociocultural dispossession of the environmental support for it. It requires a strong sense of personal efficacy to reshape and maintain a productive life in cultures that cast their elderly in powerless roles devoid of purpose. In societies that emphasize the potential for self-development throughout the lifespan, rather than psychophysical decline with aging, the elderly tend to lead productive and purposeful lives.

V. SUMMARY

Perceived self-efficacy is concerned with people's beliefs in their capabilities to exercise control over their own functioning and over events that affect their lives. Beliefs in personal efficacy affect life choices, level of motivation, quality of functioning, resilience to adversity, and vulnerability to stress and depression. People's beliefs in their efficacy are developed by four main sources of influence. They include mastery experiences, seeing people similar to oneself manage task demands successfully, social persuasion that one has the capabilities to succeed in given activities, and inferences from somatic and emotional states indicative of personal strengths and vulnerabilities. Ordinary realities are strewn with impediments, adversities, setbacks, frustrations, and inequities. People must, therefore, have a robust sense of efficacy to sustain the perseverant effort needed to succeed. Succeeding periods of life present new types of competency demands requiring further development of personal efficacy for successful functioning. The nature and scope of perceived self-efficacy undergo changes throughout the course of the lifespan.

This article has been reprinted from the *Encyclopedia of Human Behavior, Volume 4.*

BIBLIOGRAPHY

Bandura, A. (1986). "Social Foundations of Thought and Action: A Social Cognitive Theory. " Prentice-Hall, Englewood Cliffs, NJ.

Bandura, A. (1991). Self-efficacy mechanism in physiological activation and health-promoting behavior. In "Neurobiology of Learning, Emotion and Affect" (J. Madden, IV, Ed.), pp. 229–270. Raven Press, New York.

Bandura, A. (1991). Self-regulation of motivation through anticipatory and self-regulatory mechanisms. In "Perspectives on Motivation: Nebraska Symposium on Motivation" (R. A. Dienstbier, Ed.), Vol. 38, pp. 69–164. University of Nebraska Press, Lincoln.

Bandura, A. (Ed.) (1995). "Self-efficacy in Changing Societies." Cambridge University Press, New York.

Bandura, A. (1997). "Self-efficacy: The Exercise of Control." W. H. Freeman, New York.

Lent, R. W., & Hackett, G. (1987). Career self-efficacy: Empirical status and future directions. *J. Vocational Behav.* **30,** 347–382.

Maddux, J. E., & Stanley, M. A. (Eds.) (1986). Special issue on self-efficacy theory. *J. Soc. Clin. Psychol.* **4**(3).

Schunk, D. H. (1989). Self-efficacy and cognitive skill learning. In "Research on Motivation in Education." (C. Ames and R. Ames, Eds.), Vol. 3, pp. 13–44. Academic Press, San Diego.

Schwarzer, R. (Ed.) (1992). "Self-Efficacy: Thought Control of Action." Hemisphere, Washington, DC.

White, J. (1982). "Rejection." Addison-Wesley, Reading, MA.

Wood, R. E., & Bandura, A. (1989). Social cognitive theory of organizational management. *Acad. Management Rev.* **14,** 361–384.

Self-Esteem

Robert A. Wicklund

University of Bielefeld

Compensation   Projecting one's would-be strengths in proportion to actual weakness.
Performance Potential   The ability, power, or disposition to undertake certain actions.
Self-Awareness   Attention directed toward one's own person.
Self-Esteem   Subjective self-appraisal of one's own performance potential.
Validity   The relation of a self-appraisal to a behavioral criterion.

SELF-ESTEEM, characteristically treated as individuals' subjective appraisals of their cumulative successes and failures, is the central topic of this article. Following a short encapsulation of the traditional literature, a number of issues are taken up that bear on the usefulness of the concept of self-esteem, as it is generally researched and applied.

I. INTRODUCTION TO THE LITERATURE

The considerable literature on the topic of self-esteem, or self-worth, reflects a denominator that is common to practically all theory and research in this field, as reflected in an overview by Oosterwegel and Oppenheimer. This denominator is a performance-related one. Self-esteem, as exemplified through the measuring instruments and case histories, has to do with indi-

viduals' subjective appraisals of their own performance potentials. Performance potential, in this context, means not only behavioral repertoires such as athletic or intellectual abilities, but also fixed physical characteristics—such as height or good looks—that have implications for success/failure. Self-esteem is almost invariably treated as the sum of several such performance potentials, and not just as a self-appraisal of some single, preferred aspect. Self-esteem is thus multidimensional.

Although the actual measurement of self-esteem is prone to abide by such a self-appraised performance potential approach, much of what is written conceptually about self-esteem suggests that self-esteem is not simply the sum of high self-evaluations. As Rosenberg made explicit in 1979, a person with high self-esteem is also "accepting" of weak points, self-critical, and not merely aggrandizing of one's own person. But the translation of the *concept* of self-esteem into the measurement of self-esteem belies this direction of thinking, and to be sure, the focus of psychology is well indicated by self-report measures that are indeed reducible to "I am good"/"I am bad" across a number of dimensions.

What do these performance dimensions look like more concretely? A sample of the questionnaire items from the Piers-Harris self-concept scale, as summarized in Robinson and Shaver, is informative here.

I am well behaved in school (Factor 1, Behavior).
I have good ideas (Factor 2, Intellectual).
I am good looking (Factor 3, Physical).
I am often afraid (Factor 4, Anxiety).
I have many friends (Factor 5, Popularity).
I am a happy person (Factor 6, Happiness).

Encyclopedia of Mental Health
Volume 3

Intellectual performance, physical good looks, and numerous other attained or given strengths thus make up the self-appraisal. The case is similar with the Janis-Field Scale:

> How often do you feel that you have handled yourself well at a social gathering?
> How confident are you that your success in your future job or career is assured?
> How often do you feel that you are a successful person?

Many self-esteem scales take a highly global approach in their formulations, as does Rosenberg's New York State Self-Esteem Scale:

> Item 1: On the whole, I am satisfied with myself. (strongly agree/agree/disagree/strongly disagree)
> Item 10: I take a positive attitude toward myself. (strongly agree, etc.)

As Robinson and Shaver point out, a person's self-assessed "goodness" can be framed in either of two ways, within the parameters of questionnaires such as those just cited. (1) The raw favorability of the self-appraisals can be summed up, or else (2) the respondent also indicates an *ideal* level, that is, an aspiration on each performance dimension, and the discrepancies between *ideal* and so-called *real* are then computed. The greater the discrepancies, the lower the self-esteem. In effect, the two methods generally produce about the same result.

Although some scale authors allow the respondent a certain freedom with respect to which dimensions will be evaluated, the literature reflects an overriding tendency to offer respondents the performance dimensions in a fixed manner. This procedure of course simplifies the calculation of self-esteem, and allows more readily comparisons between subjects and between samples.

II. THE ISSUES

A. The "Use" or Validity of Self-Esteem

Is self-esteem, as something to be measured verbally, simply a verbal report? Do we know anything about the masses of responses to numerous self-esteem questionnaires, other than that verbal behavior has been measured? The issue here is one of "to what use?" and this leads us to ask whether a high or low self-esteem

person, as defined via the usual questionnaire devices, is simultaneously high or low in psychologically interesting, independently assessed respects.

Many of the "uses" or validities of individual self-esteem questionnaires consist of showing that a person who is, for instance, "high-medium" self-esteem on Measure X also tends to show "high-medium" self-esteem on some older, more established Measure Z. In this manner the introduction of a new measure can be justified to the research community; this procedure, which often consists just of correlating responses to the two measures, is called "convergent validity" by Robinson and Shaver.

Even though researchers among themselves may be convinced that an interesting and useful construct (i.e., self-esteem) is being tapped into via the agreement among these various measures, the wider readership likely wants something more definite and concrete when looking for the usefulness of self-esteem instruments. It is here that we step into what is commonly called "predictive" validity, and to be sure, lots of studies point to the relation between high/low self-esteem scores and "hard" criteria.

Among others, it can sometimes be demonstrated that significant success or failure experiences affect self-esteem scores. These kinds of studies are especially useful, in that they show that objective changes in one's performance potential, such as success or failure in running for political office, are reflected in self-appraisals of performance potential. In other words, objective success/failure can result in corresponding changes in self-esteem scores. Certain research also demonstrates that people who are members of deviant or less-than-idealized social categories show lower self-esteem scores, as in Rosenberg and Kaplan. A particularly telling study, reported by Rosenberg and Kaplan, demonstrates a telling point: First respondents were divided up according to their aspirations—in this case, according to the importance that they attached to being a member of a prestige social class. Second, they divided the sample further into levels of occupational attainment, ranging from "unskilled and semiskilled" to "professional." Interestingly, respondents' self-esteem levels were then predictable based on the fit of their current status to their aspiration level. For instance, people in the unskilled/semiskilled group who aspired strongly to membership in the prestige class evidenced a markedly low self-esteem level. Their counterparts, who had no special aspirations, had a higher level of self-esteem. On the other hand, for those who were already professionals, level of aspiration had no marked impact on their self-esteem levels. In other words, the frustrations of the high-aspiring unskilled/semiskilled respondents were reflected in low self-esteem.

The results of this study thus fit the discrepancy model of self-esteem beautifully, in that falling well short of one's aspirations appears to result in unfavorable self-appraisals. And, generally, it is not difficult to find support for the thesis that people who have gained actual membership in socially valued categories also evidence relatively high reported self-appraisals. For example, it can be shown that those in higher intellectual categories, people not classified as mentally ill, and noncriminals have higher self-esteem. But on the other hand, we should not expect it all to be so straightforward.

Common sense would imply that ethnic group membership would contribute a good deal to lowering individuals' self-esteem. After all, ethnic groups that have long been subject to discrimination are, on the average, less "successful" members of the society at large than are the more accepted subgroups. The common-sense thesis would then suggest that the discriminated-against groups will evidence lower self-esteem. But an example to the contrary can be found in Rosenberg. In examining the self-esteem scores of various religious and ethnic groups in the United States, Rosenberg divided the respondents into high, medium, and low self-esteem subgroups. For his English/Welsh Protestant sample, 39% of the people fell into the high self-esteem category by way of their self-reports on the self-esteem measure. But for the Black Protestant sample, there were also 39% in the high self-esteem category.

Rosenberg goes on to cite studies indicating findings of equal or higher self-esteem among black respondents than for white samples; similar patterns are found in comparing Latin-Americans with Anglo-Americans. That is, Latin-Americans frequently show self-esteem levels as high as, or higher than, the Anglo-American levels. How can this be? On the average, groups who have long been discriminated against cannot very well belong to the favored performance categories as often as the "mainstream" groups. [See ETHNICITY AND MENTAL HEALTH.]

Among other possibilities, it may well be that a minority group has its own reference points for success/failure, as well as self-esteem dimensions that are relatively group-specific. This implies that the in-dividual self-esteem dimensions would then have to be weighted, depending on their relative importance within any given group. Further, the breadth of each individual's reference standards would have to be taken into consideration. Does a person compare just within the familiar group, or also across social groups and classes? There are numerous conceptions that come to terms with the individual's deriving a self-esteem level, but these issues will not be pursued here; it is time to return to the issue of validity, or use, of the self-esteem concept.

B. Compensation and "Negative" Validity

If we take Adler's compensation thesis of 1912 seriously—the notion that weakness underlies the person's trying to manifest strength—we then need to draw into question the naive assumption that objective performance potential (a person's athletic, social, or intellectual prowess) will be reflected automatically in some linear fashion in the person's self-esteem scores. But in order to follow this thesis, it is first necessary to shunt aside the multidimensional self-esteem score concepts, and to consider just one central performance area. This should be one that is vital in the motivations and habits of the respondent in question. Once such a central performance area is isolated, it is then interesting to see what occurs when the person's capabilities in that area are poorly developed, and/or rendered momentarily insecure. To be sure, the person can then be shown to talk and behave as if the performance potential were indeed present and thriving.

A number of controlled studies by Wicklund and Gollwitzer illustrate what is meant here. One can begin, for instance, with business administration majors, potentially headed toward careers as managers or the like. Then, and this is a crucial step, those highly committed to business/management can be separated out from those not so committed. It can be said that those highly committed have an ongoing motive, a current concern or project, to excel in the business world.

A variable of insecurity then needs to be defined. For example, if certain respondents come to realize that their personalities are not suitable for the business world, insecurity with respect to their future careers should be present. Or, if certain respondents have poor grades, no relevant applied experience, no chances for job interviews, their security will similarly be undermined.

Now comes the self-esteem element, although in more specified form. If the business students are asked such questions as "How capable are you, relative to your fellow students, in your chosen field?" or "How many people would you like to have serving under you in your first professional position?" a systematic phenomenon occurs. Those who are definitely committed, but who are lacking in the objective or socially recognized underpinnings for performance, will overclaim competence and will also want to command more people. In short, they are more oriented toward power, especially within the central performance area, and are particularly self-aggrandizing.

What does this mean for the validity of a self-esteem measuring instrument? If a weak background, inadequate grades, and the like lead to compensatory, self-aggrandizing self-appraisals, then the focused, business-relevant self-esteem measure acquires a negative validity. The less well-equipped the person is to carry out the performance, the *higher* is the self-esteem. One cannot say that the measuring instrument is *in*valid; after all, it predicts something concrete, but it predicts in what would be regarded as a perverse manner. Correspondingly, of course, the person who is objectively well equipped, experienced, and the like tends toward relative modesty.

But a different picture, a "normal" picture, emerges among less committed respondents. Across several studies there is a tendency toward a positive relation between the person's objective basis for good performance and the same person's self-appraisals for those performance areas. In other words, among those who are not very motivated in the given performance realm, the self-esteem measure (i.e., the self-estimate measure pertinent to that performance area) is related in a positive, seemingly linear manner to actual, or objective potential in that area.

Given that more specific forms of self-esteem measures are in use frequently, such as social self-esteem or athletic self-esteem, the validity issue becomes highly interesting. As long as respondents are actively involved in the area chosen for study—be it music, business administration, or tennis—the focused self-esteem measure is quite likely to produce a negative validity, through the ill-equipped persons' compensating.

As it happens, this issue is systematically overlooked in research carrying the flag "self-esteem." Research efforts allow for a certain amount of "noise" in the measuring instruments, but it is virtually always assumed, whether implicitly or explicitly, that self-reports of one's performance potential are veridical with something valued. This assumption is tantamount to a regular failure among efforts to show that high self-esteem, in itself, is valuable, healthy, or otherwise socially valued. High self-esteem, as measured, can easily be nothing but the verbal reflection of a motivated compensation effort. High self-esteem as conceptualized, which sometimes includes a self-critical posture as integral to high self-esteem, has little to do with these dominant measures that receive psychology's attention.

The same difficulty is present when the multidimensional self-esteem scales (the usual scales) are administered. The difference is that the negative validities may submerge, in that crucial performance dimensions, to which respondents are committed, are then only a minor segment of the whole scale. That is, the negative validity problem still exists, but it will not be so readily recognizable.

C. Multidimensionality

Self-esteem is treated per definition as a molar "trait," a cumulation of multiple kinds of performance potentials. A person's total score across these multiple dimensions is regarded as the individual's sense of success, attainment, social recognition, and the like. As such, the ideal high self-esteem person is a positive prototype for the society that develops self-esteem concepts and especially for that society's self-esteem measures. The prototype is a seemingly well-rounded person, a member of the groups that perform well across the board.

One of the bases for placing so many diverse behavioral potentials together is the assumption that a person who scores high on one dimension will tend to score high on other dimensions. And this assumption likely holds, statistically, across various self-esteem measures. However, do these congruencies within respondents simply signal propensities to be consistent *verbally* across items, or do the consistencies signal an underlying "hanging together" of high (or alternatively, low) performance potentials? Within the context of any given set of measurements, this question is impossible to answer.

The establishing of validities for individual performance areas is difficult enough, as one requires an external performance criterion, such as information about the respondents' actual (objective) strength/

weakness in that area. To undertake such a research project for *all* of the 10, 20, or 30 self-esteem dimensions within one questionnaire is a task that no one has heretofore accomplished. In fact, the analysis of predictive validity for any given self-esteem item or group of items is a rarity.

Accordingly, the summing up of self-appraisals in numerous different performance areas becomes a highly questionable procedure, given that the individual validities for the numerous different dimensions can vary widely, from positive to negative, in ways completely unknown to the investigator or practician. Ultimately, then, the self-esteem administrator must have blind faith in subjects' reports being "accurate" across all the dimensions. But there is still another issue, this one having to do with a psychological process that appears to mediate truthful or veridical answering.

D. Self-Awareness with Respect to Salient Dimensions

A considerable amount of research on self-appraisals has been conducted to look at the validity of such appraisals as influenced by respondents' self-awareness, as summarized by Wicklund in 1982 and Gibbons in 1990. As such, this research also counts as self-esteem research, although it usually does not carry the self-esteem label. The paradigms are no different from any other predictive validation study, in that a hard behavioral criterion is chosen, and respondents' self-reports about an ability, trait, or attitude pertinent to that behavior are measured.

When the verbal measurement takes place under relatively normal conditions, without prodding respondents into a self-reflective state, the answers tend often toward zero validity. This result can be shown for dimensions such as hostility, sociability, and even for reporting one's own college entrance examination scores. If the validities are not zero, then they tend to be modest—correlations in the range of .10 and certainly not anything that a scalemaker would be pleased to report within the context of claiming that the scale is useful or otherwise valid.

But when conditions are arranged so that respondents are brought to focus inward on themselves, such as via a simple mirror, then a sizable and *positive* validity develops—a phenomenon discussed by Gibbons as well as Wicklund. As it happens, all of the research

using this self-awareness variable to bolster validity has limited itself to one kind of performance potential or trait, such as sociability or intellectual potential. The reason, of course, is that the instituting of more than one hard criterion for validity in the context of a single study is cumbersome, at best. Whether the self-focusing technique would function to enhance validity during the filling out of entire self-esteem scales is an entirely open question.

Thus again, we are confronted with an argument that implies a problem when numerous, heterogeneous performance dimensions are thrown together into one questionnaire and the verbal self-appraisals simply added up. There is no way of knowing whether respondents are going to be self-reflective to an adequate degree for the veridical answering of each and every item. For this reason there is basis for seriously questioning whether 20, 30, or more separate answerings are going to result in corresponding valid self-appraisals, and this places the researcher in the odd position of having to take a rather conservative posture with respect to self-esteem scores, in the following sense: Self-esteem as currently operationalized can easily be little more than the verbal answers themselves, ambiguous with regard to a connection to psychological aspects of the respondents.

III. STRIVING TOWARD HIGH SELF-ESTEEM: A VALUED ENDEAVOR, OR NEUROSIS?

An often encountered, somewhat primitive assumption in the self-esteem literature has to do with "building" or "improving" the self. People who manage to raise their self-esteem scores are regarded as working toward a valued end. To "feel good" about oneself is an end in itself; to have "self-confidence" (practically a synonym of self-esteem—see Robinson and Shaver), so it goes without saying, is a marvelous goal for all people. The same is said of not being shy (which approximates "high sociability") and assertiveness, argumentativeness, and expressed readiness to take risks. Popular psychology and much of research psychology esteem people's striving toward high self-esteem, which, perhaps regrettably, is measured regularly by self-appraisal on performance dimensions.

But what happens when we alter the formulation just slightly, and rather than speaking of self-esteem as a desirable goal, refer to it as a need, as something toward which people are driven? At this point we enter a world of rather different considerations.

Horney as well as Adler has referred to the *neurotic* desire to show oneself to be better, to take claim for achievements, to come across favorably in social comparisons. The root problem, according to the compensation model forwarded by Adler and Horney, is that the person in charge of these inflated self-appraisals and claims does not have the patience to *develop* positive traits in a natural or socially useful way, but rather, the *apparent* high self-esteem comes about via the static process of simply projecting an idealized, fabricated image into the verbal self-appraisal. This is, of course, the root of the negative validity in self-esteem questionnaires.

It works similarly in the example of the authoritarian personality. Burdened with status anxiety, thus a socially based inferiority complex, the authoritarian personality of Adorno and colleagues denies weaknesses, shuts out failures, lays claim to strengths, and these self-aggrandizing tendencies even extend to the authoritarian's own family, which is placed in a golden light. Such claims may well result in a picture that resembles high self-esteem, but the underlying issue remains "What drives or forces these favorable self-reports?"

Solomon, Greenberg, and Pyszczynski have established that anxiety in the face of death perpetuates and energizes the need for high self-esteem. They show how self-esteem can be propped up by the person's abiding by cultural prescriptions. The more the individual is a "good boy or girl" in cultural contexts, the higher will be the death-threatened individual's self-esteem. Again, one can hardly say that this kind of self-esteem is the mere reflection of *actual* performance potential. Rather, one's pursuit of such self-appraisals goes into gear because of insecurities, in this case, due to the threat of death.

Thus, psychologically, it makes sense to turn the perspective around, and rather than being concerned about whether positive self-appraisals are a healthy end in themselves, we might concern ourselves with the long-recognized possibility that favorable self-esteem owes to insufficiencies or threats. Whether the self-aggrandizing "self-esteem" stemming from such threats is neurotic is a question of value judgment, but at the very least, such self-esteem strivings are largely anti-social in two respects:

1. The larger community that accepts the veracity of self-esteem reports is then misled, often seriously, to the extent that the self-esteem scores, or components of them, are invalid or negatively valid.
2. The individuals with ongoing self-esteem-shoring-up projects are disinclined to appreciate or acknowledge others' perspectives and such a self-concerned, non-perspective-taking orientation is perhaps well characterized as neurotic, particularly if we consult Horney's analysis.

A corresponding recommendation for self-esteem theory and research can be made in a twofold manner. First of all, the field is in urgent need of recognizing that self-appraisals are frequently psychologically driven. They are not simple self-observations, self-perceptions, building blocks of self-knowledge, or the like. Second, the self-esteem area of research should return to the theoretical drawing board. What are we actually after? A portrait of the all-around high-level performer, or a sketch of the prototypically "well-functioning" human? Does one require a self-report measure of the socially integrated, self-accepting, self-critical person? If a certain culturally esteemed portrait is desired as a practical end, then the current self-description methods will never do, as they are subject to the various psychological forces detailed already. The person in search of the portrait may have to go directly to the "hard" validity criteria, and simply define socially esteemed individuals by means of their possessing objective indicators of performance potential. Such an enterprise is simple, but it would then render *self*-esteem unnecessary; the "self" part of it all is then simply replaced by *culturally* esteemed.

BIBLIOGRAPHY

Adler, A. (1912). *Über den nervösen Charakter: Grundzüge einer vergleichenden Individual-Psychologie und Psychotherapie.* Wiesbaden, Germany: Bergmann.

Gibbons, F. X. (1990). Self-attention and behavior: A review and theoretical update. In M. P. Zanna (Ed.), *Advances in experimental social psychology* (Vol. 23, pp. 249–303). New York: Academic Press.

Horney, K. (1945). *Our inner conflicts: A constructive theory of neurosis.* New York: W. W. Norton.

Oosterwegel, A., & Oppenheimer, L. (1993). *The self-system: Developmental changes between and within self-concepts.* Hillsdale, NJ: Erlbaum.

Robinson, J. P., & Shaver, P. R. (1973; original 1969). *Measures of social psychological attitudes.* Ann Arbor, MI.: Institute for Social Research, University of Michigan.

Rosenberg, M. (1979). *Conceiving the self.* New York: Basic.

Rosenberg, M., & Kaplan, H. B. (Eds.) (1982). *Social psychology of the self-concept.* Arlington Heights, IL: Harlan Davidson.

Solomon, S., Greenberg, J., & Pyszczynski, T. (1991). A terror management theory of social behavior: The psychological function of self-esteem and cultural worldviews. In M. P. Zanna (Ed.), *Advances in experimental social psychology* (pp. 91–159). San Diego: Academic Press.

Wicklund, R. A. (1982). Self-focused attention and the validity of self-reports. In M. P. Zanna, E. T. Higgins, & C. P. Herman (Eds.), *Consistency in social behavior: The Ontario Symposium* (Vol. 2, pp. 149–172). Hillsdale, NJ: Erlbaum.

Wicklund, R. A., & Gollwitzer, P. M. (1982). *Symbolic self-completion.* Hillsdale, NJ: Erlbaum.

Self-Fulfilling Prophecies

Mark Snyder

University of Minnesota

Arthur Stukas

University of Pittsburgh

Behavioral Confirmation When, in the course of social interaction, one person (the "perceiver") acts on his or her beliefs about another person (the "target") in ways that cause the target to behave in ways that confirm the perceiver's expectation, behavioral confirmation is said to occur (see also, self-fulfilling prophecy).

Behavioral Disconfirmation An outcome of social interaction in which the initial beliefs of one person about another person are not supported by, and may even be directly contradicted by, the other's actual behavior in the interaction.

Expectation A belief or preconception about the ways in which another person will behave in social interaction.

Perceiver Any person who holds beliefs about another person in social interaction.

Perceptual Confirmation A phenomenon of social interaction in which a person holding initial beliefs about another person comes to feel that those beliefs have been confirmed during their interaction with that other person.

Self-Fulfilling Prophecy A consequence of social interaction that occurs when a person's initial beliefs about another person lead him or her to behave in a way that elicits behavior from that other that confirms the initial beliefs.

Target Any person about whom beliefs are held by another person in social interaction.

When people interact with other people, they often use their preconceived beliefs and expectations as guides to action. Their actions, in turn, may prompt their interaction partners to behave in ways that confirm these initial beliefs. This phenomenon, in which belief creates reality, is known by several names—the SELF-FULFILLING PROPHECY, expectancy confirmation, and behavioral confirmation.

I. THE PHENOMENON

In social interactions, individuals often hold expectations about those with whom they are interacting based on past experience, information gained from third parties, or beliefs about the characteristics associated with the group membership of their interaction partners. When individuals use these expectations to guide their behavior in social interaction, they may indicate to the targets of their expectations that only expectation-congruent behavior is appropriate. Or their behavior may only allow expectation-congruent responses from their partners. For example, men who believe that women typically act submissively in social interaction may act more dominantly with women. This dominant behavior may encourage submissive behavior or prevent nonsubmissive behavior by female interaction partners in response. Even women who typically act in a dominant fashion may act submissively under such conditions. This is the essence of the self-fulfilling prophecy.

The self-fulfilling prophecy has been demonstrated to occur in a wide variety of domains and for a wide variety of beliefs and expectations. Recently, after documenting the existence of the phenomenon, researchers have moved to examine both the limits of the self-fulfilling prophecy and the social and psychological factors associated with its occurrence, as well as theoretical and practical implications of the self-fulfilling consequences of beliefs and expectations.

A. Self-Fulfilling Consequences of Expectations

The self-fulfilling prophecy in social interaction has been demonstrated in a series of empirical investigations in which one person (the perceiver), having adopted beliefs about another person (the target), acts in ways that cause the behavior of the target to confirm these beliefs. As a result, the perceiver finishes the interaction with his or her initial expectations intact, believing that these expectations have been confirmed by the target's behavior. Additionally, in the course of the interaction, the target actually comes to behave in ways that appear to confirm the perceiver's expectations. The consequences of perceiver's expectations thus can be separated into two kinds: (1) perceptual and/or cognitive confirmation of expectations in the mind of the perceiver; and (2) behavioral confirmation of expectations by the actions of the target during the interaction. The defining features of perceptual and behavioral confirmation have been examined in the social psychological laboratory using experimental methods.

Typically, in research on the self-fulfilling effects of beliefs and expectations, perceivers are led to expect certain traits and/or behaviors from the persons with whom they will interact—for example, a commonly used expectation in such research is that the target is either extraverted or introverted. To the extent that the perceiver believes that the target is indeed extra-

verted or introverted after their interaction is over, *perceptual confirmation* can be said to have occurred. If objective third parties, upon listening to recordings of the interaction (usually to targets' contributions only), also deem those targets who were expected to be extraverts by perceivers as more extraverted and those who were expected to be introverts as more introverted, then *behavioral confirmation* can be said to have occurred.

B. A Prototypic Demonstration and Research Paradigm

As a prototypic demonstration of the self-fulfilling prophecy, consider the 1977 experiment by Snyder, Tanke, and Berscheid that examined the effects on interactions between college-aged men and women of the stereotyped assumption that physically attractive people have socially appealing personalities. Before a telephone conversation with a female partner, each man was randomly assigned a snapshot (ostensibly of his partner) of a physically attractive or physically unattractive woman. Men who were led to believe their partners were attractive treated them with more warmth and friendliness then men who believed their partners were unattractive. Women thought to be attractive (regardless of their actual looks) reciprocated these overtures and behaved in a friendly and sociable manner; in contrast, women assumed by their partners to be unattractive were cool and aloof during the conversations. As a result, the perceivers ended the conversations with support for their initial stereotypic assumptions.

This study contains all of the elements that are typical of investigations of the self-fulfilling consequences of beliefs and expectations. Participants arrived at the laboratory separately and were placed in separate rooms, connected by a "telephone." The perceiver was randomly assigned to receive one of two opposing expectations about his partner. In this case, the expectation was transmitted by providing a picture, ostensibly of the target. In other studies, the expectation has been conveyed differently, frequently by demographic information about the target or by profiles of the personality of the target. The perceiver is typically told that he or she has been randomly assigned to get the information provided as it may aid him or her in planning the ensuing interaction with the target. As in most investigations of the self-fulfilling prophecy, the target in the study was unaware of the expectation given of her and was also not prompted with any expectations about her partner.

The two participants conversed for a short while and then completed questionnaires asking for their perceptions of their partners and of themselves. These questionnaires provided evidence of *perceptual confirmation*. Also, because the interactions were audio-recorded, objective raters were able to evaluate the targets' behaviors and to determine the extent to which *behavioral confirmation* occurred. Thus, Snyder and his colleagues were able to show that perceivers' expectations about the physical attractiveness of their partners elicited behavior for these partners in accordance with stereotypic assumptions about beauty and sociability (regardless of the partners' actual physical attractiveness)—the self-fulfilling prophecy.

C. The Variety of Domains and Expectations for Which Self-Fulfilling Effects Have Been Documented

In addition to investigating self-fulfilling prophecies in casual social interaction, researchers have documented perceptual and behavioral confirmation effects in many other domains. For example, in an educational context, Rosenthal and his colleagues demonstrated that teachers who were led to expect particular patterns of performance from their students acted in ways that influenced those performances to confirm initial expectations. Thus, students expected by teachers to perform poorly in school may be aided in this poor performance by the teachers themselves. Investigations in this domain are notable exceptions to the prototypic laboratory demonstration described above in that researchers have observed teachers and students in their natural environments, interacting face to face over a longer course of time.

Similarly, even scientific researchers are susceptible to the self-fulfilling consequences of their expectations. Research, again by Rosenthal and his colleagues, has demonstrated that experimenters induced to have expectations about the behavior of subjects in an experiment acted in ways that brought about these expected behaviors. Thus, experimental hypotheses, that were by nature explicitly specious, were confirmed. This research effectively sensitized researchers to the need for methodological safeguards to avoid any self-fulfilling biases in scientific inquiry.

Additional studies have demonstrated that self-fulfilling prophecies can occur in organizational settings and in counseling and therapeutic settings. Employers and therapists may act in ways that lead employees and clients, respectively, to confirm preexisting expectations that may not be based on the actual behavior of the targets. Thus, it appears that self-fulfilling effects are not limited to casual social interactions but may occur in settings where consequences of these effects may be more important. Indeed, perceivers' expectations could have a strong impact on targets' educational attainment, employment success, or mental health.

In addition to the numerous domains in which self-fulfilling effects have been documented, a wide array of expectations have been shown to have self-fulfilling properties. Thus, there have been demonstrations of the behavioral confirmation and perceptual confirmation of stereotypes about the typical personalities of women and men, assumptions about racial differences, beliefs about age differences, self-images, anticipations of the likely personalities of other people, expectations of being liked or disliked, hypotheses about the personalities of other people, imputations of stigmatizing conditions to other people, mothers' stereotyped expectations about infants, and arbitrary designations of differences in ability and performance competence. The wide variety of these expectations attests to the generality of the self-fulfilling prophecy. Self-fulfilling effects seem possible whenever a perceiver holds an expectation about a target, whether it be positive or negative, important or less important.

II. THE MECHANISMS OF SELF-FULFILLING PROPHECIES IN SOCIAL INTERACTION

After documenting the existence of the self-fulfilling prophecy and charting the various areas and expectations for which it may occur, researchers have turned to the mechanisms of these phenomena. Four steps in the self-fulfilling prophecy sequence have been outlined: (1) perceivers adopt beliefs about targets; (2) perceivers act as if these beliefs were true and treat targets accordingly; (3) targets assimilate their behavior to perceivers' overtures; and (4) perceivers interpret targets' behavior as confirming their beliefs.

Much research has focused on the second step of this sequence, specifically on how perceivers elicit confirmation of their beliefs. Snyder and Swann suggested that self-fulfilling effects may result from confirmatory hypothesis-testing strategies that perceivers may use. Perceivers motivated to determine whether their partner fits their expectation typically act as though the expectation is true, asking questions that seek only confirmatory evidence and not questions that might bring out disconfirmation. This hypothesis-testing strategy may allow targets only enough latitude to provide answers or behaviors that are consistent with perceivers' expectations.

Perceivers may also design their own behaviors based on the assumption that their expectation is true. For example, perceivers expecting a cold target may act in a cold manner themselves, or perceivers expecting a competitive or hostile target may act more competitively or hostile themselves. Thus, when perceivers base their behaviors on the anticipated responses of targets, they may actually promote these behaviors for targets. When targets respond in fashion, the expectation is confirmed.

Research by Rosenthal, in which teachers elicit expectation-confirming behavior from their students, has examined particular behaviors that may also play a part in mediating self-fulfilling consequences. Investigators identified four classes of behaviors in which teachers (the perceivers) may engage to create the effects produced. Specifically, teachers may construct a distinct socioemotional climate (i.e., warm or cold), utilize or fail to utilize positive feedback, provide greater or lesser opportunity in terms of the amount and difficulty of the material presented, and provide greater or fewer chances for student response and interaction. All of these types of behaviors vary according to the expectations the teacher has about each student's potential and can lead to corresponding performance by the student. Rosenthal has pointed out that the climate created and the amount of material presented by teachers may have the strongest effects on students' behavior.

III. MOTIVATIONAL ASPECTS OF SELF-FULFILLING PROPHECIES IN SOCIAL INTERACTION

In recent years, researchers have also begun to probe the social and psychological processes that underlie and motivate behavioral confirmation and disconfir-

mation in interactions between the holders of expectations and the targets of expectations. That is, they have been seeking to understand why perceivers act on their beliefs in ways that initiate confirmation and disconfirmation scenarios, and why targets come to behave in ways that confirm or disconfirm expectations. To do so, students of social interaction have turned increasingly to theoretical and empirical research on the motivational foundations of these self-fulfilling prophecies.

One line of research by Darley and his colleagues has examined the distinct "interaction goals" that arise for both targets and perceivers in the context of a particular interaction. These goals are seen as desired end states that can be produced as a result of the interaction. For example, the job seeker wishes to be perceived as qualified and competent whereas the interviewer wishes to obtain an accurate assessment of the seeker's abilities. These different goals are theorized to arise from the situational context and to initiate or to inhibit self-fulfilling prophecies in conjunction with the nature of the expectation held by the perceiver.

Different types of expectations suggest different "tactics" that may be used by participants to meet their current (or long-standing) interactions goals. For example, negative expectations may influence perceivers to seek information that allows them to justify avoiding targets, while targets, if aware of these expectations, may seek to actively disconfirm them. It is crucial to note that these predicted behaviors are based on knowledge about both the situational context and the nature of the expectancy. In an interview context, the above behaviors may be elicited, but in a casual conversation different interaction goals may predominate. For instance, in casual settings, it may not be as important for targets to disconfirm a negative expectation and the self-fulfilling prophecy may be more likely to occur. Thus, knowledge of the perceiver's specific impression formation goals, derived from the context of the interaction and the content of the expectation, allows predictions about the type of behaviors that he or she will initiate. In conjunction with the interaction goals of the target, these behaviors may elicit perceptual and behavioral confirmation.

Another line of research, by Snyder and his coworkers, has examined the behavioral confirmation sequence from a "functional" perspective, that is, one that involves an explicit examination of the reasons and purposes, needs and goals, and plans and motives that underlie and generate the sequence. Researchers using this motivational framework seek to identify the psychological functions being served by those activities of perceivers and targets that generate behavioral confirmation. Thus, specific motivations can be identified that tend to produce those behaviors that create the self-fulfilling prophecy and its consequences. These motivations may operate in a variety of situations and the presence of particular pairings of perceiver and target motives, in any context, should result in behavioral confirmation. [See INTRINSIC MOTIVATION AND GOALS.]

Empirical investigations have thus far indicated that behavioral confirmation occurs most readily when the activities of the perceiver serve the function of acquiring knowledge and the activities of the target serve the function of facilitating interaction. In other words, perceivers who, by virtue of their role or personal characteristics, seek to gain a stable and predictable understanding of the target may be likely to enact the behaviors that initiate the self-fulfilling prophecy. They may use the available expectation as a hypothesis that they then seek to confirm by giving the target opportunities to act in accordance. It is important, however, to distinguish the goal of a stable and predictable understanding from the goal of an accurate understanding. Perceivers who are explicitly instructed to gain an accurate impression of targets may be unlikely to use confirmatory hypothesis-testing strategies. As Neuberg has shown, these perceivers are less likely to elicit behavioral confirmation than those who seek a stable or predictable understanding. Targets who seek to ensure that the interaction is a smooth or pleasant one often respond with behavior that confirms the perceivers' initial expectations, usually unknowingly. Choosing behaviors that mesh with perceivers' overtures (based on their expectations) may allow targets to facilitate a positive interaction for all involved. However, this positive interaction may also have the possibly unpleasant side effect of creating a self-fulfilling prophecy. Therefore, given the strong empirical support for the effects of these perceiver and target motivations on confirmation sequences, this line of research implicitly suggests that interactions in which perceivers are not motivated to acquire a stable understanding of targets and targets are not motivated to facilitate a smooth interaction will not lead to behavioral confirmation.

IV. STRUCTURAL ASPECTS OF SELF-FULFILLING PROPHECIES IN SOCIAL INTERACTION

Throughout the various conceptualizations of the self-fulfilling prophecy sequence, the role of the perceiver has been defined in terms of the guiding influence of his or her beliefs about the target. After all, it is the perceiver and not the target who holds preconceived beliefs and expectations. It is also the perceiver who often has more explicit opportunities than the target to use their interaction as an opportunity to evaluate those beliefs. For example, in interview formats for studying behavioral confirmation, the perceiver asks the questions and the target answers them. Similarly, in the getting-acquainted situations used in many behavioral confirmation experiments, it is typically the perceiver who initiates conversation by speaking first and taking a guiding and directing influence in the ensuing interaction. By contrast, the role of the target is defined in relation to behavioral reactions to the perceiver's overtures. Indeed, these overtures may provide ready guidelines for targets who find themselves pressed to interact with unfamiliar partners in unfamiliar situations. Thus, in the absence of competing considerations, the role of the target seems to be defined to promote taking cues from and fitting oneself into the outlines laid down by one's interaction partner.

In effect, these considerations point to *power differences* inherent in the roles of perceiver and target. Structural differences in information available to them combined with differing potential to direct interaction make the perceiver's role one of greater power and the target's role one of lesser power. In addition, perceivers and targets often interact in circumstances that themselves dictate an imbalance in power. Many demonstrations of the self-fulfilling prophecy have occurred in real or simulated interactions between teachers and students, between employers and employees, and between therapists and clients. In these cases, therapists, employers, and teachers, by virtue of their roles, can be thought of as often functioning in the role of perceivers. Individuals in these roles also have the power to influence those who depend on them for their jobs, education, or for solutions to problems, and who may serve as the targets of expectations about likely job performance, educational attainments, and therapeutic prognosis. These differences in power between perceivers and the dependent targets of their expectations may set the stage for self-fulfilling prophecies.

An empirical examination of the effect of differential levels of power on the behavioral confirmation sequence has been conducted by Copeland. The presence of an expectation about the partner and the ability to control the partner's outcomes were experimentally manipulated. Each participant was told that three students had been invited to the study, only two of whom would advance to a second phase in which they would play a game and perhaps win a prize of $25. The experimenter also announced that one of the students was already guaranteed (by random assignment) to go on to the game and therefore that person would interact with each of the other two and choose which one to invite to the game. In reality, though, only two students came to the lab and only one interaction occurred. In addition, one of the students was randomly assigned to have information about the other, information that suggested that his or her partner was either an extravert or an introvert. A getting-acquainted interaction ensued and a self-fulfilling prophecy was demonstrated only for those conditions in which the perceiver (the individual with the expectation) had the power in the interaction. When targets had the power to influence the perceivers' outcomes, behavioral confirmation did not occur—whether perceivers believed their partners to be extraverts or introverts had no detectable impact on the behavior of the targets of these expectations under these conditions.

Relating these structural effects to past research on the motivations involved in behavioral confirmation, Copeland reported that the motivations of perceivers and targets changed with the power they were granted in the interaction. When perceivers had power over targets' outcomes, they were motivated to seek knowledge about targets (which helped to elicit the self-fulfilling prophecy) but when they did not have power, perceivers were motivated to facilitate favorable interaction outcomes. Similarly, targets with power were knowledge-motivated, but those without such power over perceivers' outcomes, were motivated to facilitate pleasant interactions (which has been shown to be a target function that contributes to the self-fulfilling prophecy). Thus, the structural effect of power, often inherent in the roles of perceiver and target, may serve

to create the very motivations that underlie the behavioral confirmation sequence.

V. SELF-FULFILLING PROPHECIES IN APPLIED SETTINGS

Although research on the factors that combine to elicit self-fulfilling prophecies has mainly been conducted in the social psychological laboratory (with research on the linkages between teachers' expectations and students' performance in the classroom as the notable exception), it is clear that research on self-fulfilling effects of beliefs and expectations is readily applicable to a wide array of naturally occurring situations. For example, as we have just noted, role relationships that exist between people in various contexts can serve to designate one individual as the perceiver and one as the target, in addition to conveying differential levels of power to each. The therapeutic setting provides the therapist both with greater information about the client and with the explicit power to influence the course of interaction. Similarly, other relationships that contain explicit status differences (such as employer–employee and interviewer–interviewee) also allow differential access to information about the other, thus placing the individual with greater power in the role of the perceiver and the individual with lesser power in the role of the target. If these differences also promote knowledge-gathering motivations in perceivers and interaction-facilitating motivations in targets, then a self-fulfilling prophecy sequence is likely to be enacted.

Although these institutionalized role relationships provide clear examples of naturally occurring conditions that, through their inherent structural and informational power differences, may elicit behavioral confirmation, it is likely not the case that the self-fulfilling prophecy only occurs when perceiver-target differences are so explicit. Many social interactions take place between individuals with differential levels of power and information that are the result of more subtle factors, an issue to which we turn next.

Research and casual observation have long demonstrated that individuals in society may, by virtue of overt differences (differences in race, sex, sexual orientation, religion, ethnicity, nationality, life-style, or ideology), find themselves the targets of prejudice and discrimination. It is perhaps not surprising that the characteristics of these individuals that elicit prejudice are often the very characteristics that distinguish them from individuals who currently hold positions of social and institutional power in society. Many of these victims of prejudice are also the targets of stereotypes—simple, overgeneralized assertions about what "they" are like, "they" being the members of social categories who are robbed of their individuality by having applied to them a set of beliefs that ascribe to them, one and all, a set of shared attributes of character and propensities of behavior. Even though they may be held with little or no foundation in fact, many stereotypes also have a pernicious way of persisting over time. To some extent, people may cling to social stereotypes that have minimal validity because they elicit behavioral confirmation from the targets of their stereotypes. If, using stereotypes, people treat others in ways that bring out behaviors that appear to confirm stereotyped expectations, they may get little opportunity to discover ways in which their stereotypes are wrong.

As the targets of stereotyping, prejudice, and discrimination are often members of relatively powerless, or disadvantaged, groups, their interactions with members of powerful groups should be examined in the context of research on power differences and the self-fulfilling prophecy. Powerless targets have been demonstrated to more frequently confirm the expectations of powerful perceivers than when the power difference is reversed. In the case of prejudice, it may be that the power differences conveyed by societal status and the stereotypic expectations often held by the more powerful contribute to a self-fulfilling prophecy that perpetuates both the expectations themselves and the power differences that already exist. Powerless targets may be motivated to have interactions with powerful perceivers that do not serve to increase personal misfortune but instead end with targets gaining some desired outcomes from those with control over them. In this circumstance, these targets may help to initiate the self-fulfilling prophecy sequence by seeking to facilitate a positive interaction. Of course, targets might not choose to explicitly act in stereotypic ways for the perceivers' benefit but, in an effort to avoid confrontation with perceivers over stereotypical beliefs, they may choose to act in ways that are ambiguous enough to allow perceivers to see confirmation. Perceivers who come to see their stereotypic expectations as confirmed by targets' behaviors may use that "evidence" to further justify targets' lower status in society, thus perpetuating the status quo.

The same analysis may be applied to mental health issues. Much research has demonstrated the persistent nature of labels when applied to individuals, especially labels that refer explicitly to mental health status. For example, individuals once labeled schizophrenic may find that that information travels with them from situation to situation, from job to job, and so on. The behavior of those who interact with such labeled individuals may be markedly different when they are aware of the label. Due to the stigma attached to mental illness in our society, individuals who are tagged with a mentally ill label are simultaneously stereotyped and robbed of power. Thus, the conditions are again ripe for the self-fulfilling prophecy.

Indeed, research has demonstrated that the label of "mentally ill" can lead perceivers to interpret both the target's present and past behaviors as consistent with the diagnosis, even when the label is actually a fiction. The effect of labels does not seem to be alleviated by training as a mental health professional. One demonstration by Rosenhan of the power of labels to elicit perceptual confirmation led to the involuntary commitment of a number of research assistants, with a variety of different past experiences but each complaining of a single instance of having heard voices. Despite displaying a total lack of symptoms after being institutionalized, the researchers were kept for 7 to 52 days and then released with the diagnosis intact but "in remission." Thus, any of us may provide biographical information or behavior that, when seen in the light of a label, may show us to be deviant or deserving of differential treatment by others.

Within the context of interactions between therapists and clients, other research, reviewed by Snyder and Thomsen, also suggests that diagnostic labeling is performed rather quickly, thus providing therapists with a hypothesis about their client that they may then test, often using a confirmatory strategy. If these early diagnoses are derived from sources lacking in validity (such as the clients themselves), then confirmation of such diagnoses may prove detrimental to the therapeutic process. It seems likely that therapists may engage in the same biased search processes as perceivers in other contexts, soliciting information from clients that selectively confirms their beliefs about the symptomatology and precipitating events related to the clinical expectation. Clients may also provide behavioral confirmation of therapists' expectations by taking their cues from the apparently educated views of therapists and the categorical behavior they produce. In a positive light, however, therapists' expectations about what types of treatment will benefit their clients may also have self-fulfilling effects, encouraging clients to conform to the behaviors suggested by the treatment as expected.

The same process may occur in the organizations for which individuals work. Much research has demonstrated that employment interviewers may elicit expectation-confirmatory information and behaviors from interviewees based on their expectations about race, gender, job-related personality characteristics and potential performance on the job (see the 1974 study by Word, Zanna, and Cooper for a prime example). Thus, perceivers' expectations may prevent certain individuals from even getting hired. Once on the job, expectations may continue to affect workers' performances. Research by King and others demonstrated that positive expectations for specific employees by supervisors reduced absenteeism, increased motivation to learn the job, increased actual performance at required tasks, and subsequently, increased co-worker esteem.

Doubts about the ability of some individuals to perform adequately in work roles may be especially prevalent in occupational settings where certain groups of individuals are underrepresented. Research by Borgida and his colleagues, for example, has demonstrated that stereotyping may be heightened when members of an underrepresented group begin to enter new work arenas. For example, women steelworkers or executives may elicit greater stereotyping, prejudice, and discrimination in the workplace than would women in more stereotypically congruent positions such as secretary and teacher. Again, because the targets of these stereotypic expectations are often relatively powerless in these situations, and may have little choice but to rely on those in power to successfully accomplish their organizational duties, they are placed in a prime position to become targets (and victims) of self-fulfilling prophecies. Such prophecies, elicited by and confirmed for powerful perceivers, may result in poor performance reviews, fewer promotions or raises, and perhaps ultimately, termination of targets.

In the event that targets seek to provide evidence that disconfirms stereotypical expectations held of them, they are often subject to negative repercussions. These negative outcomes may occur despite behavior by targets that conforms more generally to perceivers' expectations for satisfactory performance but *not* to perceivers' expectations of stereotype-consistent behavior. Thus, those individuals who have not entered certain occupations, usually occupations associated with greater status, power, and economic benefit, may be blocked, explicitly or implicitly, by individuals higher in the organizational hierarchy. These bosses and supervisors may feel that the behavior of the newcomers is not satisfactory regardless of whether it represents the confirmation or the disconfirmation of their stereotypical beliefs.

VI. THE MATTER OF DISCONFIRMATION

Still, as widespread as self-fulfilling effects seem to be, they are not inevitable. Some situations may produce outcomes that neither validate nor dismiss initial expectations, while others may provide greater opportunities for targets to disconfirm rather than confirm expectations. On yet other occasions, as Jussim has pointed out, expectations that may have appeared to have self-fulfilling effects can be considered to have been, in retrospect, accurate expectations rather than expectations that have in some way influenced behavior. This is most likely the case when expectations are based on more valid and detailed information rather than on questionable stereotypes or other less valid assumptions.

Still it is clear that not every interaction in which one person holds an expectation about another person ends with the confirmation of that expectation, whether the expectation is accurate or not. In fact, the empirical literature contains several demonstrations of behavioral disconfirmation outcomes, in which targets did not act in ways consistent with the perceivers' initial beliefs and at times behaved directly counter to the perceivers' expectations. It should be noted that, in some of these studies, perceivers did cling to their initial expectations, despite the lack of "objective" behavioral evidence from targets in support of them. Although perceptual and behavioral confirmation commonly occur together, there are examples in the research literature of each occurring separately, with perceptual confirmation more frequently occurring in the absence of behavioral confirmation than vice versa.

What factors lead to disconfirmation rather than confirmation of expectations? As Copeland has demonstrated, when the power dynamics between the perceiver and target are altered such that their interactional motivations are reversed (targets seek to gather knowledge and perceivers seek to facilitate interaction) then behavioral confirmation can be attenuated and perhaps behavioral disconfirmation will occur. Similarly, Neuberg and his colleagues have shown that when perceivers are motivated to get targets to like them, even when perceivers have explicit power over targets' outcomes, these perceivers do not elicit self-fulfilling outcomes. Perhaps, the motivation to gain liking from another is of a kind with motivations designed to facilitate positive interactions. If perceivers interact with either of these goals in mind, then the outcome may be disconfirmation, or, at least, the absence of confirmation, of initial expectancies.

In the typical behavioral confirmation sequence, it seems that both perceivers and targets do not necessarily seek to express their own personality characteristics. Instead, perceivers seem to act on their beliefs and expectations and targets seem to respond to cues provided by perceivers. For example, a dispositionally friendly perceiver may act in a reserved fashion toward a target whom he or she expects to be unfriendly. As a result, a typically sociable target may reciprocate this aloof treatment by the perceiver. Research suggests, however, that when perceivers and targets do become motivated to express their personal attributes in social interaction, they may inhibit behavioral confirmation and possibly produce behavioral disconfirmation. As Swann has shown, targets possessed of especially certain and valued self-concepts in the area of the expectation may defy perceivers' behaviors that ordinarily elicit confirmation by instead seeking to express their identities. Perceivers seeking to express their identities or to express important values (like fairness or open-mindedness) may also short-circuit the self-fulfilling prophecy sequence by initiating behaviors that are more related to their own self-concepts than to their expectations of targets, thereby providing cues that do not elicit confirmation of these expectations and perhaps elicit disconfirmation.

Similarly, when people experience others' views of them as threatening to their identities, they can and do take actions that, in their roles as perceivers and targets, generate behavioral disconfirmation outcomes. These disconfirmatory outcomes can be interpreted as serving an identity-defensive function of protecting perceivers and targets from accepting potentially unpleasant, unflattering, threatening, or otherwise unwelcome beliefs about the self. Research by Hilton and Darley has demonstrated that targets, made aware of perceivers' negative expectations about them, may actively seek to disconfirm these expectations. Perceivers may also seek to disconfirm beliefs about targets that have a direct bearing on the perceivers' own identities. For example, perceivers who believed that targets thought them submissive worked to elicit submissive behavior from these targets (rather than expectation-congruent dominant behavior).

Other more structural characteristics of interactions may lead to disconfirmation outcomes as well. The likelihood of future interactions between target and perceiver may act as a moderator of the self-fulfilling prophecy. Recent research, presented by Haugen and Snyder, has demonstrated that perceivers who expect that future interactions are guaranteed do elicit self-fulfilling prophecies whereas perceivers who believe that future interactions are impossible do not. A possible reason for this moderation effect is again motivational in nature. It may be that perceivers who expect to interact subsequently with targets are more motivated to attain a stable and predictable sense of who these targets are than are perceivers who do not expect to ever meet their targets again. In the event of no possible future meetings, behavioral disconfirmation may be a more likely outcome.

VII. LONG-TERM EFFECTS OF SELF-FULFILLING PROPHECIES

As the bulk of the research on self-fulfilling prophecies has studied very short interactions between strangers in the laboratory (again, with the notable exception of research by Rosenthal on teacher–student interactions), relatively little is known about the longer term consequences of self-fulfilling prophecies. There are several possible continuing consequences of the confirmation of perceivers' expectations by targets' behaviors. First, research by Bem suggests that one's self-concept may be developed in part by reflecting upon the behaviors one has engaged in. If this theory is true, then targets from whom confirmatory behaviors are elicited may come to see themselves as the type of people who normally engage in such behaviors. In other words, targets' self-concepts may change as a result of perceivers' expectations. This may lead targets to act on these new self-conceptions in contexts beyond those that include the perceivers who initiated the behavioral confirmation process. Of course, this self-perception theory also maintains that behaviors attributed to situational causes will not affect one's self-concept. Much research has demonstrated, however, that targets are usually unaware of the effect of perceivers' expectations on them when they actually confirm them, and thus, may be unlikely to attribute their behavior to situational causes.

Second, if targets have provided behavioral confirmation of perceivers' expectations, this "evidence" may be taken by perceivers to justify further actions toward targets, or to dictate treatment, status, or privileges to which targets are entitled, either in the presence of perceivers or not. Therefore, perceptual confirmation, which has been shown to occur both with and without behavioral confirmation, can have its own consequences. These consequences can range from not receiving a job or a promotion, to actually being institutionalized; clearly, these are very real life-affecting consequences.

VIII. CONCLUSIONS

For social scientists, then, the self-fulfilling prophecy continues to be of very special significance. It represents a particularly complex intertwining of cognitive activities and behavioral processes in the context of ongoing social interaction and interpersonal relationships. As such, it has intriguing implications for the reciprocal influences of "subjective" reality (the perceiver's beliefs) and "objective" reality (the target's behavior) in a wide range of interaction contexts of considerable theoretical and practical significance.

Research on self-fulfilling prophecies has moved from initially documenting the existence of the phenomenon and its many consequences to investigating mediators and moderators of the effects. Current research has focused explicitly on the motivational and structural elements of social interactions that involve self-fulfilling prophecies so as to better understand when and why they occur. Future research will need to more thoroughly examine the role of the self-fulfilling

prophecy in applied settings and begin to design and test interventions that can inhibit or attenuate any negative consequences of this phenomenon.

ACKNOWLEDGMENTS

The authors would like to thank Marc Kiviniemi, Steven Martino, Galen Switzer, Matthew Winslow, and two anonymous reviewers for their helpful comments.

BIBLIOGRAPHY

Bem, D. J. (1972). Self-perception theory. In L. Berkowitz (Ed.), *Advances in experimental social psychology* (Vol. 6). New York: Academic Press.

Burgess, D., & Borgida, E. (1997). Sexual harassment: An experimental test of sex-role spillover theory. *Personality and Social Psychology Bulletin, 23,* 63–75.

Copeland, J. T. (1994). Prophecies of power: Motivational implications of social power for behavioral confirmation. *Journal of Personality and Social Psychology, 67,* 264–277.

Haugen, J. A., & Snyder, M. (1995, June). *Effects of perceivers' beliefs about future interactions on the behavioral confirmation process.* Paper presented at the annual meetings of the American Psychological Society, New York, NY.

Hilton, J. L., & Darley, J. M. (1991). The effects of interaction goals on person perception. In M. P. Zanna (Ed.), *Advances in experimental social psychology* (Vol. 24, pp. 236–267). Orlando, FL: Academic Press.

Jussim, L. (1986). Self-fulfilling prophecies: A theoretical and integrative review. *Psychological Review, 93,* 429–445.

King, A. S. (1971). Self-fulfilling prophecies in training the hardcore: Supervisors' expectations and the underprivileged workers' performance. *Social Science Quarterly, 52,* 369–378.

Neuberg, S. (1989). The goal of forming accurate impressions during social interactions: Attenuating the impact of negative expectations. *Journal of Personality and Social Psychology, 56,* 374–386.

Neuberg, S., Judice, T. N., Virdin, L. M., & Carrillo, M. A. (1993). Perceiver self-presentation goals as moderators of expectancy influences: Ingratiation and the disconfirmation of negative expectancies. *Journal of Personality and Social Psychology, 64,* 409–420.

Rosenhan, D. L. (1973). On being sane in insane places. *Science, 179,* 250–258.

Rosenthal, R. (1974). *On the social psychology of the self-fulfilling prophecy: Further evidence for Pygmalion effects and their mediating mechanisms.* New York: M. S. S. Inf. Corp. Modular Publications.

Rosenthal, R., & Fode, K. L. (1963). Three experiments in experimenter bias. *Psychological Reports, 12,* 491–511.

Snyder, M. (1984). When belief creates reality. In L. Berkowitz (Ed.), *Advances in experimental social psychology* (Vol. 18, pp. 248–305). Orlando, FL: Academic Press.

Snyder, M. (1992). Motivational foundations of behavioral confirmation. In M. P. Zanna (Ed.), *Advances in experimental social psychology* (Vol. 25, pp. 67–114). Orlando, FL: Academic Press.

Snyder, M., & Swann, W. B., Jr. (1978). Hypothesis-testing processes in social interaction. *Journal of Personality and Social Psychology, 36,* 1202–1212.

Snyder, M., Tanke, E. D., & Berscheid, E. (1977). Social perception and interpersonal behavior: On the self-fulfilling nature of social stereotypes. *Journal of Personality and Social Psychology, 35,* 656–666.

Snyder, M., & Thomsen, C. J. (1988). Interactions between therapists and clients: Hypothesis-testing and behavioral confirmation. In D. C. Turk & P. Salovey (Eds.), *Reasoning, inference, and judgment in clinical psychology: Theory, assessment, and treatment.* New York: Free Press.

Swann, W. B., Jr., & Hill, C. A. (1982). When our identities are mistaken: Reaffirming self-conceptions through social interaction. *Journal of Personality and Social Psychology, 43,* 59–66.

Word, C. O., Zanna, M. P., & Cooper, J. (1974). The nonverbal mediation of self-fulfilling prophecies in interracial interaction. *Journal of Experimental Social Psychology, 10,* 109–120.

Self-Healing Personalities

Howard S. Friedman

University of California, Riverside

Disease-Prone Personality A personality at higher risk of disease or premature mortality due to chronic internal psychophysiological disturbances and external risky behaviors.

Hostility A complex emotional and motivational reaction pattern often characterized by cynical beliefs, aggressive behavior, and the frequent experience of anger.

Personality The traits, motives, and emotional and behavioral patterns unique to each individual; a person's usual ways (persistent patterns) of responding to life events, a synthesis of biological tendencies, family upbringing, and the culture.

Self-Healing The process through which the body combats and repairs disease and disruption, without (or in addition to) external medical treatment.

SELF-HEALING PERSONALITY is a healing emotional style involving a match between the individual and the environment, which maintains a physiological and psychosocial homeostasis, and through which good mental health promotes good physical health. The term was proposed by psychologist Howard S. Friedman in his 1991 book of the same name. Self-healing, emotionally balanced people are alert, responsive, and energetic, but may also be calm and conscientious. They are not ecstatic nor manic, but are generally curious, secure, and constructive. Research suggests that they are also people others like to be around. Many people with mental health problems are at higher risk of disease and premature death, but people with self-healing personalities have better odds of a longer, healthier life.

I. BACKGROUND

The ancient Greeks, keen observers but poor scientists, described striking associations between mental and physical states. They proposed four bodily humors—blood, black bile (or melancholy), yellow bile (or choler), and phlegm—which were said to lead to a sanguine and ruddy person; or to proneness to depression (melancholy) and degenerative disease; or an angry (choleric), bitter personality; or to a phlegmatic, cold apathy. This scheme of four emotional aspects of personality heavily influenced medical practice for almost 2000 years, and it turns out that cheerfulness, depression, hostility, and apathy are indeed useful patterns for understanding the relations of mental and physical health. In terms of causal explanations, "humors" have been discarded, to be replaced by neurohormonal mechanisms and health-relevant behavior patterns.

Throughout the twentieth century, various ideas about the relations between chronic negative emotional patterns and physical health have been proposed and discussed, but not widely adopted. One of the roots of this tradition began in cardiology with the notion of the "Type A behavior pattern," which supposedly puts one at risk of coronary heart disease.

"Type B" was the healthy personality. On the surface, however, the relations of psychology, emotions, and health seem riddled with contradictions. For example, many individuals who work hard and hurry around like Type A people (who are supposedly prone to heart disease) are not coronary prone; on the contrary, they are especially healthy. It turns out that they are also extremely active and expressive. In brief, research in the Type A tradition has led toward a more sophisticated understanding of the psychoemotional disruptions of hostility that can lead to disease, rather than reliance on the idea that Type A is simply a medical syndrome (or collection of symptoms).

Analogously, many so-called "Type B" people (supposedly stress free) who become ill are not really calm and healthy, even though they look superficially like true Type Bs. Rather, their emotional conflicts are repressed. Repression of emotional conflict has been noted as a cause of disease since the days of Sigmund Freud, but the causal pathways have proved difficult to define and assess in a scientific manner. In recent years, careful attention to concepts and measurements has revealed why people with such long-noted emotional disturbances are often at higher risk for disease. [See TYPE A–TYPE B PERSONALITIES.]

II. DISEASE-PRONENESS

Although if often seems as if disease involves a simple causal sequence—for example, exposure to the flu virus and "catching" the flu—the actual process is much more complicated. For example, why do some people exposed to the infectious agent not contract disease? Why do some people recover more quickly than others? Why are some people more likely to be exposed to the infectious agent in the first place? Furthermore, most serious threats to health and life are now the complex chronic diseases—cardiovascular disease, cancer, diabetes, lung disease, and so on. Here, the causes are much more complicated than simple infections.

The most current research suggests that certain people are psychologically predisposed to be vulnerable or resilient due to a combination of temperament and early socialization. When vulnerable people encounter psychosocial environments that are a poor match for their needs, chronic negative emotional patterns often result. These reactions are accompanied by

physiological disturbance, and unhealthy behaviors such as substance abuse may also occur. Finally, these disturbances interact with disease-proneness caused by heredity (e.g., genetic proneness to cancer, hypercholesterolemia) and environment (e.g., toxins, high-fat diets).

A major link between personality and health involves those physiological changes occurring inside our bodies during stress. Although the psychophysiological mechanisms are complex, there is no doubt that they exist and are important. Well-documented physiological disturbances associated with stress include high levels of sympathetic activation, release of stress hormones such as cortisol, and decreased levels of certain sex hormones. There are both acute and chronic changes in arousal level, and associated changes in breathing patterns, metabolism, sleep habits, sexual activity, immune function, and attempts to self-medicate. [See PSYCHONEUROIMMUNOLOGY; STRESS.]

Some of the most potent stress relates to emotionally charged experiences. Such psychological stress is uniquely individual. As an illustration, let us consider why some people (but not others) drop dead of cardiac arrest when they encounter a severe emotional shock. (During major traumas such as earthquakes, a certain number of people seem to be literally scared to death.) Work by Bernard Lown and many others suggests a three-part model to account for the variability in sudden cardiac death after encountering stress. First, some electrical instability must already be present in the heart muscle; this is often but not always due to partially blocked arteries. Second, the person must be feeling a pervasive negative emotional state such as depression. Third, there must be an acute triggering event, which is exceptionally meaningful (or terrifying) to the individual. The self-healing personality is most relevant to the second of these factors—the harmful effects of a pervasive emotional disturbance and the protective effects of emotional balance.

The other major link between personality and health involves behavior. This connection is not so simple as it first sounds. Anyone could be hit by lightning or lose their family or be involved in an auto accident. Because such events are seemingly random, we often assume that there is little we can do to protect ourselves. But consider: Who is more likely to wander aimlessly across a busy street: a happy, fulfilled person or a lonely, depressed, preoccupied person? Who is more likely to go out for a late-night drive alone and without wearing a seat belt? Who is more likely to inject illegal drugs into their veins? It is obvious that people who are depressed, lonely, angry, or otherwise psychologically disturbed are more likely to put themselves into unhealthy situations. In other words, the other key way that personality relates to health is through behaviors that lead to more or less healthy habits and environments. The unhealthy behaviors associated with stress vary widely, as a function of individual personality, the social situation, and the society and culture. In modern Western society, they often include drinking alcohol, smoking cigarettes, taking psychotropic drugs (such as tranquilizers, both legal and illegal), overeating, and engaging in a variety of risky activities.

Some people are predisposed to addiction. It is hard to know the extent to which this is determined by biological temperament or by upbringing (both are involved), but there is evidence that there is an addictive personality. Some people are more likely than others to overeat, drink too much, become addicted to cigarettes, seek out dangerous thrills, and so on. In the wrong environment, these addictive personalities are likely to ruin their health unless their personality problems are addressed. In fact, the most important external route through which personality affects health involves our daily habits. Personality problems often lead to unhealthy habits, which in turn help maintain the personality problems while ruining health. Although the resulting increased risk of illness is not overwhelming, it is comparable in size to that of many other commonly noted health risks.

III. DISEASE-PRONE PERSONALITIES

Because we cannot randomly assign people to various personalities and stresses and then follow their health for many years, the results of any single study in this area are bound to be equivocal. Valid inference depends on piecing together various sorts of evidence. These pieces include reviews of many different studies of the associations between personality and disease; biological studies of behavioral patterns associated with disease and the corresponding disease mechanisms; and social and epidemiological studies of psychosocial reaction patterns and illness. Developments

in epidemiology, clinical studies of stress, assessment of emotional coping, and laboratory animal research together are painting a coherent picture of disease-prone and self-healing personalities.

The overall pattern of associations between chronic negative emotions and disease has been clearly shown using the statistical technique called metaanalysis, which is a sophisticated kind of statistical average, across different studies. Metaanalyses have looked at the relations of chronic emotional states to a wide range of chronic illness including arthritis, asthma, headaches, ulcers, and especially coronary heart disease. In these systematic analyses, involving many thousands of people, the degrees of consistency in the relations between disease and emotional aspects of personality turns out to be remarkably high.

The clearest evidence concerns chronic hostility. "Cholerics" tend to have emphatic gestures and loud voices, are dominant and forceful, with tense lips and stiff postures. Some are overtly aggressive and show the physiological correlates of chronic anger. They are excitable, easily frustrated, and may move around a lot and respond aggressively when challenged. Others are more cynical and alienated. Such hostile people seem especially likely to have interpersonal disputes, due to their suspicious, competitive style. There is also some evidence that they are more likely to smoke, drink, and use drugs. Although most studies focus on hostility's effects on cardiovascular disease, there is evidence that it also affects other diseases and all-cause morality. [See AGGRESSION; ANGER.]

Studies of nonhuman primates demonstrate that social stress promotes atherosclerosis among monkeys straining to maintain a position of social dominance. Further, those animals with the greatest heart-rate reactivity show the most coronary artery damage and act more aggressively, confirming clinical studies of humans. Since the artery damage can be prevented by a beta-blocker (propanolol), the evidence points to harmful effects of excessive activation of the sympathetic nervous system by social struggle. Everything else being equal, the modulation of sympathetic arousal is likely to promote physical as well as mental health. [See REACTIVITY.]

Research linking depression to illness is simultaneously the most intriguing and most controversial, because depression can obviously be a result as well as a cause of illness and because both depression and illness may be caused by an underlying third factor.

"Melancholics" generally speak softly, look tired, and sigh often, with slumped body posture or bowed heads. Most attention has been directed toward linking depression and cancer, since depression may suppress immune function. However, as metaanalytic reviews and subsequent clinical studies reveal, there is also good reason to believe that depression plays a role in cardiovascular and other diseases. Although there is solid evidence that depression is linked to high cortisol levels, the causal pathways are murky. No study has yet followed the whole long-term process from stress and depression to impaired physiological functioning and consequent disease. Depression often is associated additionally with a whole host of behavioral risk factors for disease including disturbances in eating and sleeping, impaired social relations, and substance abuse. Chronic depression is, of course, easy for health professionals to recognize but is often overlooked by the general public. Thus, although the various casual pathways are not yet disentangled, efforts to prevent and treat depression will likely have a salutary effect on physical health (in addition to suicide prevention), an effect often ignored in discussions of depression. [See DEPRESSION.]

The least understood among those with disease-prone patterns are the repressed. To a casual observer, this cool and sluggish style may not seem so bad. These "phlegmatic" people may have pleasant associations with their neighbors, and they may appear compliant, unassertive, appeasing, and cooperative, but would not be good candidates for close friends. Phlegmatics do not report being very anxious. They are out of touch with the emotional disturbances in their own bodies. Their hidden feelings can often be observed in their closed body positions, their protectively crossed arms or legs, and their tense, submissive movements. Their voices have hesitations, higher pitch, and often an anxious quality. For example, one young repressed woman asserted a strong desire to get on and accomplish things in her life; but testing revealed her feelings of powerlessness, alienation, and external control. Although she showed absolutely no signs of outward hostility either in person or on psychological tests, she harbored high levels of inner anger. Her "traditional" father did not want her to attend college, saying she would only "play around."

There is accumulating evidence that the holding back of thoughts or feelings is a form of stress that may produce psychophysiological arousal similar to that of the other disease-prone states. Some, such as psychologist James Pennebaker, have argued that psychotherapy or other, simpler forms of self-disclosure can relieve this inner conflict and thus promote health. Studies such as the Stanford study of social support and increased longevity in women with terminal breast cancer (in which women who talked to other victims about their feelings lived longer) are inconclusive by themselves but are part of a rapidly forming picture. This topic is now receiving intense analysis, but it is likely that the answers will lie in a more complex understanding of emotional self-regulation rather than in a simple hydraulic model of "bottling-up" versus emotional "discharge." Indeed, the issue of whether to repress or express negative emotion may be a red herring; the problem is having the chronic imbalance in the first place. Further, repression does not cause cancer, but, as noted above, emotional balance is one key factor in many disease processes and risks. [See SOCIAL SUPPORT.]

IV. THE SELF-HEALING PERSONALITY

Too often, scientists describe what is unhealthy but ignore what is healthy. In part, this is because we generally assume that the normal or default state is to be healthy and that it is unusual to be ill. It is also the case that there is a well-established professional structure (of physicians) for attempting to cure disease but much less organization focused on prevention. We thus tend to overlook the psychological and behavioral factors that promote a state of health. Fortunately, however, scientific attention is turning significantly toward the proactive elements of mental health that promote physical health.

Briefly stated, a nontechnical way to characterize a self-healing personality is in terms of enthusiasm. The word *enthusiasm* literally means "having a godly spirit within." Self-healing people smile naturally—the eyes, eyebrows, and mouth are synchronized and unforced. Such enthusiastic, sanguine people have smooth gestures that tend to move away from the body. They are unlikely to fidget, and they are less apt to make aggressive gestures. Emotionally balanced individuals not only walk smoothly, but they talk smoothly, showing fewer speech disturbances and more modulated tones. Their voices are also less likely to change their tone under stress. Obviously, there are exceptions to these rules: A single nonverbal gesture does not tell us much. Still, substantial valid information can be gathered about a person's healthy emotional style from just a few episodes of social interaction. This is why a careful in-take interview can be so valuable to a health care professional.

Although the most stressful situation is unexpected calamity in an area we value, most threats develop more slowly. To take a corporate example, as threats to a company's economic survival appear, everyone on the management board sees the challenges and feels the escalating stress, and the likelihood of illness rises. Who can best maintain emotional balance? Interestingly, often it is the CEO—the leader and chief executive. Although the CEO has the greatest amount of work and responsibility, this position paradoxically is *not* necessarily the most stressful. If the CEO has the best information, can exercise the most control, and has the right personality for the job, then health even may be enhanced rather than impaired. In other words, the stress is neither wholly external nor wholly internal; taking charge of and responding to one's environment in a way that fits with one's inclinations and temperament can be health promoting, despite a heavy workload or rapid change.

In fact, a healthy work environment is one that provides a challenging, socially valued job and the resources and support with which to do the job. However, a wild sense of optimism and great power is not necessary for a self-healing personality. Instead, a sense that one can control one's own behavior is most important. A sense of continual growth and resilience is also relevant. [*See* HEALTHY ENVIRONMENTS.]

Self-healing personalities have sometimes been described by humanistic psychologists, although the artificial mind–body dichotomy usually led them to focus on describing mental health, not physical health. For example, Abraham Maslow pointed out that healthy people first need to achieve balance in their basic biological needs, then affection and self-respect, and then self-actualization—the realization of personal growth and fulfillment. People with this growth orientation are spontaneous and creative, are good problem solvers, have close relationships to others, and have a playful sense of humor. They become more concerned with issues of beauty, justice, ethics, and understanding. They develop a sense of humor that is philosophical rather than hostile. These characteristics of the self-healing personality are not merely the opposite of such disease-prone characteristics as suspiciousness, bitter cynicism, despair and depression, or repressed conflicts. Rather, they are positive, meaningful motives, behaviors, and goals in their own right.

It is a misconception that self-healing involves the avoidance of stress. Many well-adjusted adults choose to tackle maddening puzzles, or engage in highly competitive sports, or volunteer their time to help the needy and distressed, or travel to exotic, stimulating locales. All these activities are stressful in the sense of being challenging, but the challenge is often not harmful. On the contrary, it can be healthy stimulation. In fact curiosity, stimulation, and exploration are important elements of a healthy individual. It is not stress per se but rather chronic negative emotion that is a problem.

Consider Mohandas K. Gandhi (called Mahatma or "Great Soul"), who was one of the greatest workaholics of all time and faced terrible conflicts but was not sickly although he spent over 2300 days in prison and endured numerous self-imposed fasts. What defined Gandhi's life was a commitment to principle. As he aged, he grew more and more content with his life, but remained humble. He certainly was not blindly optimistic, carefree, or lackadaisical. This case illustrates the well-documented finding that alienation is unhealthy. Obligation and dedication are healthy. Some people find this commitment in religion, others in philosophy. Other people seek political reform. Some people simply have a hobby such as preserving old cars or old trees or old books. What they have in common is a sense of purpose.

Indeed, the experience of moderate challenge can help condition healthy emotional responses. Walter Cannon, who developed the idea of homeostasis, emphasized that the body has developed a margin of safety. By this Cannon that the body is not built with "niggardly economy," but rather has allowance for contingencies that we may count on in times of stress. The lungs, the blood, and the muscles have much greater capacity than is ordinarily needed. In other words, the body naturally prepares itself for the rare "extra" challenge, and so it is natural and prudent to do what we can to increase these margins of safety in the emotional realm. In his classic 1890 work *Principles of Psychology,* the turn-of-the-century philosopher and psychologist William James, who anticipated much of our modern scientific understanding of emotional responses, summed up this idea succinctly when he advised, "Keep the faculty of effort alive in you by a little gratuitous exercise every day. That is, be systematically ascetic or heroic in little unnecessary points, do every day or two something for no other reason than that you would rather not do it, so that when the hour of dire need draws nigh, it may find you not unnerved and untrained to stand the test" (p. 97).

Self-healing personalities seek a match between their abilities and interests, on the one hand, and the exigencies of the environment on the other. That is, they seek out friends, careers, and hobbies that fit their individual temperaments, abilities, education, and predispositions. Self-healing personalities often rate highly on "hardiness," but whereas hardy people always have an inner sense of control and are involved and challenge-seeking, self-healing people find the match between their dispositions and their environments. Hence, a person of limited abilities in many domains and corresponding limited goals could be "self-healing" but not "hardy." [*See* HARDINESS IN HEALTH AND EFFECTIVENESS.]

V. THERAPEUTIC IMPLICATIONS

Simple cognitive and educational exhortations to "Stop those negative thoughts," "Don't worry so much," "Be more reasonable," are often ineffective in redressing emotional imbalance. If one could readily take such advice, the problem probably would not exist in the first place. For most people in most situations, we cannot simply "will our way" to health. Self-healing thus is not usually achieved through advice to relax and think positively.

A serious and common problem in designing therapeutic intervention is that people (or their therapists) often fail to evaluate sufficiently which changes are best for them as individuals. The same advice to "buy a music player and go jogging" would not be suitable for both an anxious, competitive 25-year-old businessman with migraines and a depressed, isolated 60-year-old woman with breast cancer. Solutions must be tailored for the needs of the individual. This is obvious when stated, but too often ignored. Anecdotally, forced vacations (such as dragging a spouse away from the "stress" of work) often seem to create more problems than they solve. Instead, for example, a high-energy person should be helped to funnel the high energy into more positive directions (rather than "slow down").

Changing toxic psychoemotional responses into a stable, healing system usually involves doing two things: (1) slowly changing habits and (2) selectively altering social environments. When one starts doing things in different ways and in different environments, then the personality gradually changes in a corresponding salutary manner. These changes are relatively stable; there is little relapse. At age 70, Dr. Jonas Salk, inventor of the polio vaccine, described his secret to staying young: "I keep working at what I like to do *and* I remain part of the community." In other words, a self-healing personality not only knows how to seek out situations that lead one to think positively and productively about life, but also recognizes the importance of other people—the importance of community social support.

Some people turn to telling a bedtime story to their children or grandchildren each night, or going to a community discussion group each week, or attending church regularly. They have routine habits of positive social interactions. Some workers read a book for 20 minutes every day during their lunch hour, or listen to classical music during their commute to work, or make concise lists of their weekly goals and accomplishments. They have developed regular habits of coping with intrusive, stressful thoughts in ways that are appropriate for them. Many discover that reaching out to help afflicted others is one of the best ways to help oneself. Unfortunately, these styles are often developed later in life, after serious illness strikes. It would be much better, of course, if these patterns had been learned before cancer or heart disease or other illness demanded one's attention to self-healing.

When a person develops a more healing emotional style, the nonverbal expressions become more healthy-looking. For example, a melancholic's voice becomes louder, his gaze becomes more direct, and his gestures become more animated. A choleric's body tension relaxes, his posture opens up, and his facial expressions become less threatening. A phlegmatic's expressions become more emotionally revealing, her gestures become more dominant, and her speech becomes more emphatic. We might not immediately recognize why, but we thus find self-healing people to be more likable. These nonverbal expressions may be employed as a gauge as to whether progress is being made.

With this framework, it is also easier to see where some therapies go wrong. For example, some people are advised to strive for the days when they can retire (or take more vacations) to get away from the stress of the workplace. In reality, retiring may be stressful and unhealthy or it may be helpful and healing. It depends on the particular individual and the particular situation—whether the workplace provides positive challenge, friendships, and financial and informational resources that are healthy, or arouses the chronic disturbance that is unhealthy. Relatedly, it is not unhealthy to be a "workaholic" if all other elements of self-healing are in place. In one case, a psychiatrist was especially successful with a distressed client when he gave up on relaxation therapy and helped rechannel the client's high energy level away from aggressive competitiveness and toward aggressive philanthropy.

It is often asserted that it is healthy to be optimistic. Although it does seem to be the case that a sense of willpower and positive hopes for the future can help one through difficulty (such as an acute illness), it is also the case that optimism can lead one to be shocked by reality or to avoid taking necessary prophylactic measures. The optimist who believes "I'm the lucky one who can smoke cigarettes with impunity" is not the true healthy sanguine, and constant advice to "cheer up" is not only pedestrian, but invalid.

The bottom line is that there is substantial evidence that chronic hostility, depression, and repression (and their concomitants) affect physical health and recovery from illness. Some of the mechanisms are psychophysiological: chronic stress disrupts the neurohormonal system that regulates metabolic and immune functions. Many of the other mechanisms are behavioral: emotional disruption is associated with homicides, suicides, smoking, alcoholism, drunken driving, and various failures to take prophylactic measures

(ranging from condom use to seat belts). Still other problems of disease-prone personalities are somewhere in between—sleep disturbances, eating disturbances, and exercise disturbances. Thus, the self-healing personality is directly relevant to preventing most of the causes of premature death in developed countries. As attention shifts from the pathology of mental illness to greater emphasis on the prevention of mental illness and the promotion of mental health, the many ways in which good mental health is a part of good physical health will become increasingly apparent. Indeed the mind–body distinction will fade, and the self-healing personality will be seen simply as essential to health.

BIBLIOGRAPHY

Antonovsky, A. (1979). *Health, stress and coping.* San Francisco: Jossey Bass.

Eysenck, H. J. (1991). *Smoking, personality, and stress: Psychosocial factors in the prevention of cancer and coronary heart disease.* New York: Springer-Verlag.

Friedman, H. S. (ed.) (1990). *Personality and disease.* New York: Wiley & Sons.

Friedman, H. S. (1991). *Self-healing personality: Why some people achieve health and others succumb to illness.* New York: Henry Holt.

Friedman, H. S., & Booth-Kewley, S. (1987). The "disease-prone personality": A meta-analytic view of the construct. *American Psychologist, 42,* 539–555.

Friedman, H. S., Tucker, J. S., Schwartz, J. E., Tomlinson-Keasey, C., Martin, L. R., Wingard, D. L., Criqui, M. H. (1995). Psychosocial and behavioral predictors of longevity: The aging and death of the "Termites." *American Psychologist, 50,* 69–78.

Lown, B. (1996). *The lost art of healing.* Houghton Mifflin.

Miller, T. Q.; Smith, T. W.; Turner, C. W.; Guijarro, M. L. (1996). Meta-analytic review of research on hostility and physical health. *Psychological Bulletin, 119,* 322–348.

Pennebaker, J. (Ed.) (1995). *Emotion, disclosure, and healing.* Washington, DC: American Psychological Association.

Sexual Behavior

John D. Baldwin and Janice I. Baldwin

University of California, Santa Barbara

I. A Multifactor Model of Sexuality
II. Sexual Orientation
III. Developmental Patterns of Sexual Behavior

Erotophiles People who like and have positive attitudes about sex.
Erotophobes People who have a fear or phobia about sexuality and sexual cues.
Kinsey Scale A continuum of different levels of heterosexual to homosexual orientation, with 0 being pure heterosexual and 6 being pure homosexual.
Psychogenic Excitation that has its origins in mental activity.
Scripts Patterns of talk and action that people learn from other people, books, movies, and other media. There are sexual scripts for dealing with every stage of relationships, from meeting a potential partner to making love.
Sexual Orientation The degree to which a person is sexually attracted to the other sex, the same sex, both sexes, or neither sex.

Human **SEXUAL BEHAVIOR** is influenced by countless biological, psychological, and social factors. From an evolutionary perspective, sexual behavior functions primarily to assure reproduction; and throughout most of human evolution, sexual activity was closely related to pregnancy and childbearing. Sexual behavior is usually pleasurable and may at times seem like an end in itself, but before the development of reliable birth control techniques, the link between sex and reproduction was much closer. The pleasures of sex also help create social bonds between two people,

but these bonds are often not strong enough by themselves to guarantee monogamy. Most cultures have surrounded sexuality with symbolic qualities, ritual meaning, or moralistic implications that often function to increase monogamy and family orientation. This social overlay makes human sexuality far more complex than the relatively basic reproductive activities seen in other primates. Some societies have discovered special ways in which sexual pleasures can be heightened and enjoyed for themselves, without always being linked with pregnancy. The development of increasingly effective birth control and abortion techniques in the past three decades has allowed considerable separation of sexual activity from reproduction and the subsequent sexual revolution.

I. A MULTIFACTOR MODEL OF SEXUALITY

As late as the early 1900s, it was common to "explain" human sexual behavior in terms of instincts. For example Freud postulated a sexual instinct and "explained" people's sex drive in terms of an instinctual energy he called libido. Gradually instinct theories have been recognized as weak hypothetical constructs and replaced by more detailed models of the biological, psychological, and social causes of motivation and behavior. Current theories of sexuality recognize that sexual behavior involves multiple components that interact complexly. The most basic elements of this multifactor model of sexual behavior are the reflex mechanisms that cause vaginal lubrication, penile erection, other genital responses, and orgasm. These reflexes influence and are influenced by both instrumental learning and classical conditioning, which in turn are affected by the type of home, community, and culture in which a person lives. Finally, as children develop more cognitive capacities, they can increasingly plan unique and creative ways of directing their sexual experiences.

A. Reflexes

The sexual responses of the genitals are mediated by several reflex centers located in the lower spinal cord. The most basic way to activate the sexual reflexes is by touch to the genitals. Nerves connecting the genitals to the spinal reflex centers respond to touch as the *unconditioned stimulus* that activates them—without the need for any prior conditioning. The reflex mechanisms then activate all the genital changes associated with sexual arousal, such as vaginal lubrication, penile erection, and—after enough stimulation—orgasm. They also send signals to and respond to signals from the brain. The connections with the brain allow sexual responses to influence and be influenced by learning, memory, and thought.

The sex reflexes operate from birth, but the hormonal changes of puberty lead to increasing sexual sensitivity and spontaneous responses in the genitals. The reflexive and inborn facets of sexual behavior are not, by themselves, adequate for assuring intercourse or successful reproduction. Considerable learning is needed for an individual to become sexually active. Since learning is influenced significantly by individual, social, and cultural variables—and each person has a unique history of learning experiences—there is considerable variability in human sexual activities both within and between societies.

B. Perception and Instrumental Learning

The neural pathways that connect the reflex centers in the lower spine to the brain connect with the sensory centers in the cerebral cortex, allowing people to perceive many types of sensations from the genitals. Some of these perceptions enter into long-term memory and influence later thoughts and actions.

In addition, some of the neural inputs from the genitals innervate the pleasure and pain centers in the brain, such that certain types of genital stimulation are experienced as pleasant, while other types are painful. Through instrumental learning (also known as oper-

ant conditioning), people usually learn to repeat those activities that are followed by pleasurable, rewarding experiences and avoid those followed by aversive sensations. We learn to do things that are instrumental in attaining pleasure (such as those things leading to orgasm) and avoiding pain (or reinforcement) and punishment help assure that most people learn sexual practices that are instrumental in attaining sexual pleasure—which, before the advent of birth control, often served the biological function of promoting pregnancy and the reproduction of the species.

The more rewarding—and less aversive—a person's experiences with sex, the more positive associations and memories the person tends to have about sex; and this usually translates to greater sexual motivation—or "sex drive"—if there are no biological problems that detrimentally affect the sexual response systems.

C. Classical Conditioning

The sexual reflex is among the reflexes that are capable of being conditioned via classical conditioning (also known as Pavlovian conditioning). Namely, when a neutral stimulus is paired repeatedly with the unconditioned stimulus of appropriate touch to the genitals, that neutral stimulus gradually becomes a *conditioned stimulus* capable of eliciting the sexual reflex. In common parlance, these conditioned stimuli are called "erotic stimuli" or "sexual turn-ons." Usually, the more frequently that an erotic stimulus or turn-on has been paired with the unconditioned stimulus to touch to the genitals, the more capable that conditioned stimulus is of eliciting sexual responses—unless a person has so many negative associations with or biological problems affecting sex that they suppress the sexual response.

Through classical conditioning, almost any stimulus that is frequently paired with and is predictive of the sexual arousal can become an erotic stimulus or sexual turn-on. The specific stimuli that people respond to as sexually exciting differ from person to person, depending on each individual's prior sexual experiences. Many people learn to respond to pictures or fantasies of nude bodies as erotic stimuli, if these have been paired with masturbation or sexual interactions in the past. Some come to find "talking dirty" to be sexually arousing, if such talk has been a common part of their exciting sexual experiences. Although many people would be offended by vulgar language and do not understand how anyone could find it sexually exciting, the principles of classical conditioning allow us to understand that almost *any* stimulus can become an erotic stimulus or sexual turn-on, for those individuals who have experienced it in conjunction with sexual excitement.

When people learn to imagine their erotic stimuli (in the absence of any external stimuli), they gain the ability to fantasize about their turn-ons. Since having sexual fantasies is often pleasurable, many people learn this cognitive activity—unless guilt or other bad feelings punish such fantasies. Some people cultivate elaborate sexual fantasies because of the pleasure and sexual arousal that they bring.

Nerves that connect the cortex to the sexual reflex mechanisms in the lower spinal cord allow cortical activity—such as seeing or fantasizing about sexual turn-ons—to activate the sexual reflexes. This is called *psychogenic* stimulation of the sexual reflexes, since the excitation is psychological in origin. For some people, psychogenic stimulation only produces a mild sexual response, such as slight vaginal lubrication or partial penile erection; but in other people, the response can be quite strong, sometimes leading to orgasm. There is a great deal of variation among people in the strength of these psychogenic responses, these differences being due to the number and intensity of positive and negative learning experiences that any given individual has had with sexuality.

During sexual intercourse, fantasies and psychogenic sexual stimulation can add to the total excitement that enhances the sexual response. Fantasies also serve to distract people from some of the stimuli that can inhibit the sexual response—e.g., guilt about sexual activities, fears of not being attractive enough to one's partner, or fears about the adequacy of one's sexual performance.

The sexual reflexes can be inhibited by aversive conditioning. Any of a variety of sex-related stimuli can become associated with fear, worry, or anxiety—depending on each individual's unique history of classical conditioning. For one person, fears of becoming pregnant can interfere with the sexual response, whereas another person may have no fears of pregnancy. Fear of not pleasing one's partner, not being able to have orgasms, or anything else can inhibit the sex reflex. Given the pervasive social attention to physical attractiveness—especially for females—

some people feel anxious that their partner will not think that their body is attractive enough.

D. Nonsocial and Social Learning

Some learning is clearly social, as when we watch other people's actions—perhaps via movies or videos—and learn from them. However, sexual learning may occur alone, as when a child explores touching his or her body, discovers masturbation, and pairs certain fantasies with sexual activities. But even these relatively nonsocial activities, done in private, are usually not devoid of social influence. For example, the child's frequency of masturbation is influenced by the degree to which the parents accept or punish masturbation. Each individual's choice of fantasy images used during masturbation is often affected by prior social experiences.

Social learning theory emphasizes that we learn a great deal from observing the actions and listening to the words of others, who are called *models*. Although sexual intercourse is usually not done publicly in our society, people learn about sex in private from observing and listening to their sexual partners. People also learn the sexual activities of *symbolic models* presented in magazines, books, movies, TV, and videos. In addition, there are many sex-related activities—such as meeting, becoming intimate, and suggesting sexual activities—that are modeled more often in public than in sexual behavior per se. Once information is acquired by observing others, people may later attempt similar actions. The degree to which they fully adopt the behavior depends on how instrumental it is in bringing them rewarding effects. Did a sexual position modeled in a video bring pleasure or complaints from one's partner?

Not only do people learn the physical activities of sex by observing and listening to others, they learn how others talk about sex and play out sexual roles. Patterns of talk and action are often called "scripts," and sexual scripts are involved at every stage from meeting a potential partner to making love. For example, there are countless opening lines a person can use to meet another, and research indicates that women are more discerning among them than are men. Men like almost all types of opening lines that women use to strike up a conversation; but women tend to like direct and innocuous lines and be turned off by cute-flippant lines from men. There are the countless scripts for dealing with sex, and they vary from society to society—from subculture to subculture. This can create confusion when people move from one social sphere to another or try to become intimate with someone from a different subculture.

E. Cognitive and Social Psychology

Cognitive psychology adds another level of complexity to the multifactor model of sexuality. Our perceptual experience enters inputs from all sense modalities into thought and memory. Our thoughts are composed mostly of visual imagery, sounds, and the inner words we "hear" in our minds as we think to ourselves. Whereas sexy pictures can influence our visual sexual fantasies, the sexual scripts we learn tend to influence the inner words we use to think about sex. When teens see TV shows or movies in which certain lines or scripts lead to sexually exciting outcomes, they may find themselves rehearing those words in their minds and then using parts of combinations of those scripts with others.

Social psychology stresses how much each individual is influenced by his or her position in society. Two people living in the same country—but exposed to different subsets of the multiple cultures possible within a society have access to different models, media, books, videos—which provide them with different ideas about sexual conduct. Some obtain vast amounts of information about sex, birth control, and relationships, while others obtain little. From each person's unique perspective on life, each develops personal views and opinions. As a result, two people can interpret the same event very differently: Two people can see the same erotic movie, and one calls it interesting while the other calls it repulsive pornography.

Cognitive and social psychology emphasize the importance of people's cognitive processes in interpreting their situations, creating unique and personal plans of action and making novel contributions to their social interactions. People are not passive receptacles, only being shaped by society. They are active, creative makers of their own social lives. They modify and creatively reconstruct the scripts and action patterns learned from society, producing their own unique contributions and social constructions. Creativity stems from many sources, two of which, for example, are fantasy and problem solving. People often invent creative fantasies, involving images and scripts, that can lead to plans for doing sexual activities they have never done before. People may consciously attempt to create a special sexual experience that is uniquely their own. Through the creative recombination of different scripts, fantasies, and novel ideas, people can construct sexual plans and actions that differ from anything they have ever seen used by others. Though perhaps not radically different from their culture, their actions are creative variations. Problems often cause people to search for creative solutions. When people face a problem, such as increasing boredom with sex after 10 years of marriage, the problem may stimulate creative efforts to devise novel and interesting sexual experiences.

As millions of creative people invent novel ideas and share them with others, the total contributions have their impact in changing the sexual practices of the larger society. Many new ideas are lost after being tried a few times, but others (usually the most rewarding ones) spread and become widely popular. Magazines and books may help popularize a sexual position or fantasy. People also change their society by voting, for example using the ballot to express their values about abortion, nude beaches, pornography, and other sex-related topics. By showing how people's values and creative thoughts affect their society, cognitive and social psychology empower people to take a stronger role in changing social conditions related to sexuality, gender, and reproductive rights.

F. Sex Drive

Psychology used to conceive of behavior as a function of drives and people today still talk about sex drive and libido. But with the development of multifactor models of behavior, the concept of drive is now seen as simplistic. People's desires and motivations for sex result from multiple causes, some biological and other social-psychological in origin.

Testosterone heightens sexual motivation in males—and probably in females. (Normally women have small amounts of testosterone in their bodies that are adequate for promoting sexual interest.) Good health tends to facilitate sexual desire and pleasure; whereas illness, depression, drug abuse, and other biomedical factors tend to reduce sexual motivation. Also, the more prior rewards and less prior punishment a person has experienced with sex, the stronger the person's sexual interest and motivation tends to be. Punishment related to sex leads to inhibition that can reduce a person's sexual motivation. The more sexual turn-ons and fantasies a person developed (via classical conditioning), the more likely his or her sexual interest will be piqued by numerous events of everyday life that might not be perceived as sexual by another [who has not eroticized those stimuli]. Also, the more sexual scripts a person has learned, the more the person tends to think and act in sexual ways.

There is no single "normal" level of sexual desire. Two people with high sexual desire may be very happy with their sexual life having sexual interactions every day; and two people with low sexual desire may have an equally satisfactory sex life, engaging in intercourse twice a month. Sexual desire is most likely to be a problem in a couple's relationship when the two have discrepant sexual desire—one wanting sex much more than the other.

II. SEXUAL ORIENTATION

Although many people think that there are only two types of sexual orientation—heterosexual and homosexual—the issue is much more complex. There is a continuum of positions between these two extremes with bisexuality lying in the middle. The definitions of these three terms set the stage for understanding the whole continuum. "Heterosexuals" are people whose primary erotic, psychological, emotional, and social interest is in members of the other sex—even though that interest may not be overtly expressed. "Homosexuals" are people whose primary erotic, psychological, emotional, and social interest is in members of the same sex—even though that interest may not be overtly expressed. "Bisexuals" have both of these capacities. [*See* HOMOSEXUALITY.]

Alfred Kinsey was the first sex researcher to provide a method of describing sexual orientation on a continuum, with 0 being pure heterosexual, 3 being bisexual, and 6 being pure homosexual. People who are at position one are mostly heterosexual, but have some homosexual orientation. Each higher number represents greater homosexual orientation. Kinsey and his coresearchers actually devised two separate scales. One measured *overt sexual experience,* and the other *psychosexual reactions,* such as erotic feelings, emotions, and fantasies. In most cases a person's position on one scale is the same as on the other scale. However, there are cases in which people's overt sexual behavior does not completely parallel his or her psychosexual reactions. For example, some homosexuals can respond sexually to the other sex, even though they find that their emotional and psychological attachment is to the same sex. Also, a person can be a homosexual and never engage in sexual relations with a member of the same sex.

III. DEVELOPMENTAL PATTERNS OF SEXUAL BEHAVIOR

Developmental models of human conduct are useful in showing how the numerous elements of a multifactor model interact across the lifespan. They help avoid debates about nature and nurture by clarifying how both biological and environmental factors influence behavior at each phase of life.

A. Childhood

The sexual reflexes function from the first days of life: Soon after birth, many boys have penile erections; and some girls, vaginal lubrication and clitoral tumescence. Even before birth, ultrasound studies suggest that erections may occur in male fetuses.

In the first year of life, many babies show the simplest forms of masturbation. Early in infancy, babies explore their environments and their own bodies, touching and looking at many parts of the anatomy with as much interest as they show for the world around them. Out of simple curiosity, they touch their arms, legs, and other parts, and discover their genitals in this process. Touch to the genitals elicits the sexual response, along with pleasurable feelings that reward genital self-stimulation. There are documented cases of babies learning to masturbate to orgasm before 1 year of age (though boys do not ejaculate any fluid before puberty). There is, however, considerable variation among children in early sexual self-stimulation, depending largely on their parents' response to the activity. Some parents punish and suppress early sexual behavior; whereas others are more accepting. Children who are punished for genital exploration may not learn to touch their genitals. Punishment may in fact condition inhibitions and fears about self-touching.

Sometimes children are inquisitive to learn what other children's bodies look like. Since children's play is not always monitored closely by adults, sexual exploration can lead in many possible directions. Often it leads to nothing more than one child's simply looking at and briefly touching the other child's body, but other outcomes are possible. A 9-year-old brother and his younger sister may innocently engage in mutual sexual exploration and discover that sexual play is pleasurable. In rare cases, after weeks of repeated sex play, they may discover intercourse, without knowing that adults would disapprove. Only later may the children discover that these activities are called "incest" and deemed unacceptable in the larger society.

In cultures where people sleep together in a common room or hut, children may see their parents making love and later imitate coital activities during play with other children. There is a great deal of variability among cultures in childhood sexuality; and in societies where parents do not inhibit their children, sexual exploration and play continue throughout childhood: There is no biologically determined "latency period" for sexuality.

In homes where early childhood sexual exploration is punished and little sexual information is given to the child, children can grow up with little knowledge and considerable guilt about touching their sexual organs or masturbating. Small degrees of such inhibition may not have long-lasting effects on the person's sexuality; but high levels of guilt and sexual ignorance can make it difficult for a person to develop a happy, uninhibited sexual life in subsequent years. Children who have negative socialization about sex often develop erotophobia, which is a fear or phobia of sexuality and sexual cues, leading to negative attitudes about sex. In contrast, a positive sexual socialization tends to lead to erotophilia, positive attitudes about sexuality and sexual cues.

In most societies, including ours, there is a double standard that imposes more sexual inhibitions, guilt, and erotophobia on girls than on boys. Parents are more likely to disapprove of masturbation for girls than boys. Girls are given fewer names for their genitals and are less likely to know the correct names than are boys, and few girls are told they have a clitoris. As a result, girls are less likely to masturbate or talk about their genitals than are boys.

B. Early Adolescence

Puberty usually begins between ages 9 and 13 in girls and 10 and 14 in boys. Most girls begin to menstruate between 11 and 14. Boys usually begin to be able to ejaculate at 11 or 12. The hormonal changes of puberty make the genitals more sensitive and more responsive. Adolescents—especially males—begin to experience spontaneous sexual arousal during the daytime and at night—in the form of nocturnal sexual arousal, erections, and orgasms. As a result teenagers typically become increasingly interested in sexuality—unless they have been made to feel very guilty or inhibited about sex. [See ADOLESCENCE.]

Boys typically develop sexual interests earlier and more intensely than girls. This is due to both biological and social factors. For biological reasons, boys usually begin to notice sexual arousal—such as spontaneous penile erections—2 or 3 years earlier than girls notice their first sexual arousal. Boys have more penile erections and orgasms—both while awake and sleeping—than girls have noticeable sexual arousal and orgasms. Boys are more likely than girls to be aware of their spontaneous sexual arousal and find it intense. Nocturnal erections occur during dream sleep and boys often wake in the morning with erections, which can help them discover the heightened level of pleasure that comes from masturbation after the onset of puberty. Also, boys have more nocturnal orgasms—or wet dreams—than do girls, and these are often coupled with sexual imagery that promote the development of sexual fantasies. As a result, the sexologist John Money calls wet dreams "nature's own pornography show"—just one more reason why boys tend to develop more erotic turn-ons and sexual fantasies than girls do.

There are exceptions to these generalizations. Erotophobic boys may deny their emerging sexuality, and erotophilic girls may actively explore their sexuality, even though they experience fewer biological impulses to aid them than boys do. However, most boys feel sexual arousal and interest much more often each day than most girls do.

Boys are much more likely than girls to learn to masturbate to orgasm during the adolescent years. This is due, in part, to the more frequent occurrences of spontaneous sexual arousal and orgasm in boys and the double standard that imposes less punishment and social inhibition on boys than girls. In our culture, many boys also experience peer pressure to experiment with sexuality, gain sexual knowledge, and become "sexperts." Talk in the male peer group often turns to sex, and many boys feel pressure from their peers to lose their virginity and prove their manhood. Success is greeted with social approval, which rewards even more interest in sex.

Girls, in contrast, tend to experience a more cautious socialization about sex. Yes, there is talk about sex in their peer groups, what it feels like and who is doing it. There is a great deal of variation among girls' peer groups, but these groups are more likely to pass on messages of caution about sex than are boys' peer groups. Girls learn that their more sexually active peers are called "sluts," or worse, and fear of social disparagement can make many girls reluctant to earn that label. Girls' peers may share frightening stories about girls who were taken advantage of by boys, stories of unwanted pregnancies and the subsequent problems, studies showing that STDs create many more complications for females than for males. In addition, girls may continue to hear words of caution from their parents.

Boys tend to want sex more than girls and to push more for it, while girls are more likely to play the gatekeeper role, wanting to know if he really cares about her before proceeding all the way to sexual intercourse. Hence, many girls and boys go through a period of petting or "fooling around" before engaging in sexual relations. Because physical touch to the skin, lips, and other body parts are all pleasurable, it is not surprising that couples enjoy the sensations of touching, fondling, kissing, and hugging. In such close interactions, pressure and touch to the genital areas are quite likely, which can heighten sexual arousal.

Erotic petting may be inhibited in societies that make young people feel guilty about premarital sex; or it can be facilitated in societies that inundate their youth with movies, videos, and stories of people doing sexual activities. Societal messages also influence the next step of sexual exploration: Societies with clear messages that premarital sex will be strongly punished may suppress further sexual exploration until marriage (or at least engagement); but such prohibitions are not very strong in most Western societies.

C. Premarital Sex

Many cultures have strict rules against premarital sex. Since most people throughout history have not had effective means of birth control, premarital sexual activity often led to pregnancy; and young unmarried mothers usually could not find marriage partners.

Males often did not want to marry a pregnant woman or a woman with a child—unless it was theirs—because they did not want to devote their child-rearing efforts to raising someone else's children. In such cultures, virginity is very important; and a man may give a woman back to her family if she is found (or suspected) not to be a virgin at marriage. Naturally, there is much variation among cultures, and some societies allow a certain amount of premarital sex, perhaps with a fiance just before marriage.

Since the advent of the sexual revolution, many modern Western nations have experienced significant increases in premarital sexuality, this being due to the development of increasingly effective forms of birth control, the decreasing influence of rigid religious codes, and increased secular culture showing sexy images in videos, TV, and movies. In the United States, increasing premarital sex has led to an increasing amount of teenage pregnancy and teenage abortion, in part because many parents and teachers have been reluctant to provide good birth control information to teenagers. Even though a majority of American parents want sex education in the schools, a vociferous minority tends to block it in many schools. In Western Europe and Canada, where rates of teenage premarital sexual activity are similar to those in the United States, the teen pregnancy and abortion rates are considerably lower. For example, the pregnancy rate among 15 to 19 year olds is 96 per 1000 in the United States, compared to 35 per 1000 in Sweden and 14 per 1000 in the Netherlands. In modern Western European countries, teenagers are given better sexual education and better access to birth control services than in the United States. Also traditional religious influence is less powerful/influential in Europe.

While the prevalence of premarital sexual intercourse has gradually increased, the age of onset has gradually declined. For example, Alfred Kinsey, a pioneer sex researcher, found that half of the women he interviewed some 40 years ago had intercourse before marriage; but Morton Hunt found that 81% of 18- to 24-year-old married women had done so in the early 1970s. In 1971, only 46% of unmarried 19-year-old women had engaged in intercourse; but this percentage increased to 55% in 1976 and 69% in 1979. This trend for increasing early sexuality is believed to have leveled off in the 1980s. In 1990, 54% of high school students grades 9 to 12 have had sexual intercourse.

Most parents do not tell their children or adolescents many details about the scripts for sexual intercourse, and many signal a reluctance or unwillingness to talk about premarital sex. As a result, many teens turn to their peers and the media for this information. These multiple and different sources often provide confusing or inaccurate information, with jumbled and often contradictory messages about the events surrounding first sex. Because it can be difficult to tell which of the countless different scripts presented by the media and peers is the best, adolescents often experiment with numerous lines and scripts, combining elements from various ones, not knowing which ones will work best for them until they have tried many. The less accurate information they have, the more likely they are to make mistakes. Because many of the scripts used on TV and in movies do not work well in everyday life, adolescence can involve much frustrating experimentation and embarrassment. (The more accurate information that teens receive from parents, sex educators, and books, the more likely they are to be well prepared for adolescent sexual exploration and first intercourse.)

In a study of girls' experiences around the time they have their first sex, Sharon Thompson found that many girls worried about a boy's putting a "big thing in small hole." Many did not know the ways that boys are likely to approach them for first sex and are surprised by the rapidity with which first sex occurred. Some were taken advantage of because they did not have realistic expectations and scripts for dealing with the boys. Those girls who were least likely to be abused or taken advantage of during their early sexual activities had mothers who talked honestly with them about the sexual scripts needed for good experiences with sex. First intercourse is usually less problematic for boys than girls. Typically, boys have orgasm and like losing their virginity. Girls are less likely to orgasm and less happy about their loss of virginity. However, after a year or two of sexual experience, many females and males begin to learn which scripts work best, how to have better sex, and how to avoid some of the problems related to sex—such as pregnancy, sexually transmitted diseases (STDs), and abusive partners.

Although some parents may believe that a guilt-inducing sex socialization will keep their child from experimenting with premarital sex, the erotophobia they condition in their children can create serious problems. Erotophobic teens often feel so guilty about sex that they avoid sex education information and do not learn effective means of birth control. This can leave them vulnerable to sexual accidents if their erotophobia is overcome by curiosity about sex or pressure from another person to experiment with sex. Although students with high sex guilt may begin sex as early as students with low sex guilt, they wait about a year longer than those with low sex guilt before using contraception. Erotophobic people can become pregnant and contract sexually transmitted diseases as easily as other people; and their lack of knowledge about sex puts them at a greater risk of such mishaps, since they have not planned ahead for sex and have limited knowledge about ways to avoid the problems.

Since AIDS has become a serious health problem, considerable effort has been directed at teaching adolescents safer sexual practices—such as the use of condoms and avoiding anal sex. Although some teens are following this advice, many teens are not using condoms for safer sex. In 1991, 46% of high school students reported using condoms during their last sexual intercourse. Since one-fifth of all people with AIDS contracted the virus as teens, there is room for improvement in education and honest communication with teens about sex. [*See* HIV/AIDS.]

D. Cohabitation

Although cohabitation is less common in the United States than in France or Sweden, increasing numbers of people are living with a partner without being married. In the United States, approximately 4% of unmarried adults are cohabiting, in contrast to 1% in 1960.

In the early 1950s, the typical age of marriage was about 20 years in women and 22.5 in men. Today it is about 24 in women and 26 in men. Since teens are also beginning sex at earlier ages than in the 1950s, it is clear that many young people are spending more years of their lives as sexually active but unmarried than was true before the sexual revolution. Some individuals have 2 to 5 years before they enter a relationship that will lead to marriage; for others it may be 10 years or more. Those who postpone marriage are more likely to cohabit than those who do not.

People who cohabit tend to be more liberal, and less religious, and more critical of marriage as an institution than people who do not cohabit. Although cohabitation is becoming increasingly routine before marriage, there is no evidence that it helps people make better choices of marital partners. Most cohabiting unions do not lead to marriage, dissolving relatively quickly. Also, cohabitors are more likely to divorce than people who do not cohabit, perhaps because they are more critical of marriage both before and after the wedding.

E. Marriage

In their 20s and 30s, married couples typically engage in coitus two or three times a week. Erotophiles often seek out ways to expand their sexual lives, add new activities and keep their erotic love strong. Many erotophobes expected that sex would be good once it was legitimated by marriage; but even after marriage, many erotophobes continue to feel that sex is "dirty," "sinful," or "base"; and these feelings can interfere with the enjoyment of intimate sexual relations for years or all through life.

The frequency of intercourse usually declines as people age. Many married people report that sexual relations are most fulfilling in the first year after marriage and that the quality of their sexual experience declines thereafter. People also report a decline in communication, listening, respect, and romantic love after marriage. These changes are not biologically determined or inevitable; but they do indicate that many people do not devote much attention to making their marriages successful. They also suggest that many people do not have the time, effort, or skill to solve their marital and sexual problems and/or that the multiple other demands of adult life—jobs, careers, children, socializing—are so demanding or rewarding that their marriages become neglected. [*See* MARITAL HEALTH.]

Heterosexual couples commonly engage in noncoital sex play before penile-vaginal intercourse. Foreplay typically lasts some 5 to 15 minutes, though the time varies from couple to couple and from time to time for any given couple. Various stimulative techniques are used in foreplay, including touching, caressing, and kissing of the genitals, breasts, lips, and other body parts. Couples use a variety of positions for engaging in intercourse, which usually lasts approximately 10 minutes. While the male-on-top, face-

to-face position is very common, couples are increasingly using the female-on-top position. Side-by-side positions and combinations of female superior and side-by-side positions are also used. Rear-entry positions are less commonly explored.

Many couples engage in oral-genital stimulation. Hunt's research found that 90% of people married less than 25 years had engaged in oral sex during the preceding year. Anal intercourse is not a common practice for most couples. Hunt's data indicate that for married people between 18 and 35, approximately 50% of men and 25% of women had engaged in anal intercourse on at least one occasion. A 1991 study of men ages 20–39 found that 20% had engaged in anal intercourse, 75% had performed oral sex, and 79% had received it.

Gay and lesbian couples use manual and oral stimulation of the genitals, breasts, and anus, along with caressing, kissing, and body rubbing for sexual arousal. Since the advent of AIDS, many gay males have reduced their use of anal sex, since it is one of the activities most likely to transmit HIV (the virus that causes AIDS).

Although females tend to be less interested in sex than males in the teens and 20s, female sexual interest tends to increase in the 20s, 30s, and 40s. Many of the inhibitions that girls learned while young are gradually overcome. As women learn how to avoid irresponsible partners, unwanted pregnancies, and STDS, they learn how to avoid some of the problems that had caused them to worry about sex earlier. Also, many learn how to have orgasms more easily, making sex more exciting and fulfilling. Many overcome guilt and other inhibitions as supportive sexual partners, the legitimacy of marriage, and access to more reliable information about sex counteract earlier fears and myths (ignorance). These factors have led many to the generalization that male sex drive peaks at 20 while females peak in their 30s or 40s. This generalization is somewhat misleading, since (1) many males have very strong sexual interests all through young and middle adulthood, and some even longer, and (2) increasing numbers of young women have fewer sexual inhibitions or are overcoming their sexual inhibitions at an earlier age than their mothers did. Modern books, courses, and workshops on sexuality help them do this.

People in their teens and 20s often explore novel

sexual positions and activities, but married couples often settle into a few favorite positions after they have explored a range of possibilities and discovered the ones they like the best. This can eventually lead to boredom with sex. If married couples report that they are losing interest in sex because it has become too routine, sexual therapists and marriage counselors sometimes give couples books that show multiple sexual positions and encourage them to try novel ones. There are several good books—such as *Sexual Awareness* by Barry McCarthy and Emily McCarthy, *How to Make Love to the Same Person for the Rest of Your Life,* and *Still Love It* by Dagmar O'Connor, and *The New Joy of Sex* by Alex Comfort—that contain pictures of multiple sexual positions, describing the pros and cons of each for males and females.

F. Extramarital Sex

Although marriage vows require faithfulness, studies reveal that a considerable number of people break the traditional marital contract. Hunt's survey in the 1970s found that 50% of married men and 20% of married women had at least one extramarital relationship by the age of 45. However, the rates for younger women were similar to those of men. Other more recent surveys of magazine readers indicate higher rates of extramarital sex. For example, a *Cosmopolitan* survey found that 60% of the women and 75% of men had extramarital sexual experience. There is historical and cross-cultural evidence that extramarital sex has been common at other times and in other societies. Although most individuals attempt to keep their extramarital affairs secret, they do not always succeed; and the discovery that there has been extramarital sex can be very damaging to the quality of a marriage, undermining trust and sometimes leading to divorce.

Some people, most notably Nena and George O'Neil in the book *Open Marriage,* recognize that secret affairs are common yet potentially deleterious to marriage and advocate "open marriage" as an alternative. Built on the assumption that most people want both a committed relationship and freedom, open marriage is designed to allow a couple to see other people and decide if this should include sexual relations or not. There are too few studies on open

marriage to know how common it is. One study found that in 15% of marriages, both partners had agreed that extramarital sex was acceptable under certain circumstances.

G. Divorce

About 50% of marriages end in divorce in the United States, though there has been a gradual decline in divorce since its peak in 1981. For many couples, marital happiness is the highest in the first year of marriage. As incompatibilities and fights begin to detract from the feelings of love, many couples cease to feel the passion and commitment needed to keep a relationship together. The peak in divorce occurs at 1.5 years after marriage. Many married people stop trying as hard at making their relationship work, and many experience a decline in marital happiness, sexual pleasures, and love. This need not occur if people continue to value their relationship and put time and effort into it. Unfortunately, the numerous obligations of adulthood—job, parenthood, maintaining a home—can take so many hours a week that many adults simply do not have the time to devote to their relationship. Thus, one study found that "difficulty in communication" was the most common reason given for divorce. Other reasons were unhappiness and incompatibility. Also, the birth of the first child is one of the greatest stresses on a relationship, and the sooner the child comes after marriage, the greater the chances of divorce. Waiting a couple of years before beginning a family allows a couple to solve many of their interpersonal problems and establish a stable relationship before adding the complexities of childrearing. Counselors, marriage workshops, and books can help, too. [*See* DIVORCE.]

This article has been reprinted from the *Encyclopedia of Human Behavior, Volume 4.*

BIBLIOGRAPHY

Crooks, R., & Baur, K. (1993). "Our Sexuality," 5th ed. Benjamin/Cummings, Redwood City, CA.
Heiman, J., & LoPiccolo, J. (1988). "Becoming Orgasmic: A Sexual Growth Program for Women." Prentice-Hall, New York.

Kaplan, H. S. (1987). "The Illustrated Manual of Sex Therapy," 2nd ed. Brunner-Mazel, New York.

Masters, W. H., Johnson, V. E., & Kolodny, R. (1992). "Human Sexuality," 4th ed. Harper Collins, New York.

Reinisch, J. M. (1990). "The Kinsey Institute New Report on Sex." St. Martin's Press, New York.

Silverstein, J. (1986). "Sexual Enhancement for Men." Vantage Press, New York.

Thompson, S. (1990). Putting a big thing into a little hole: Teenage girls' accounts of sexual initiation. *J. Sex. Res.* **27**, 341–361.

Zilbergeld, B. (1992). "The New Male Sexuality." Bantam Books, New York.

Sexual Disorders

Ronald M. Doctor and Bryan Neff

California State University, Northridge

Biological Sex Refers to one's status as male or female in terms of basic physiological characteristics, e.g., chromosomes, hormones, genitalia, etc.

Exhibitionism A paraphilic condition in which sexual gratification is obtained by inducing surprise, fear, or disgust in an unsuspecting person by the "flashing" of one's genitalia.

Fetishism A paraphilia that involves sexual gratification through rubbing, fondling, or usage of body parts or nonhuman objects such as underwear, garters, shoes, silk, etc.

Gender Identity Refers to a person's psychological identification with culturally defined traits and behaviors that constitute being a man (masculine) or woman (feminine).

Gender Identity Disorders Sexual disorders in which a person experiences a psychological confusion or mismatch between their biological sexual characteristics and their culturally assigned gender identity.

Paraphilias Sexual disorders that are characterized by an intense focus upon (1) nonhuman objects, (2) the suffering or humiliation of oneself or a partner, or (3) children or other nonconsenting persons; and result in great personal distress or disturbance.

Sexual Orientation One's emotional and physical attraction toward the same sex (homosexual), opposite sex (heterosexual), or both (bisexual).

Transsexualism An extreme form of gender identity disorder in which a person exhibits a life-long sense of gender incongruence (e.g., feeling trapped in the body of the opposite sex) and an overriding desire to undergo reassignment surgery.

Transvestism A paraphilia that is marked by a compulsion to cross-dress in clothing of the opposite sex. The amount of cross-dressing can be partial or regular. Most transvestites are heterosexual.

Voyeurism A paraphilic condition characterized by a recurrent, intense, and sexually oriented act that involves the observation of unsuspecting people who are naked, disrobing, or engaged in sexual activity.

SEXUAL DISORDERS encompass the full range of human sexual thoughts, feelings, and actions that are generally regarded as abnormal, dysfunctional, or disordered. With three exceptions (homosexuality, sexual addictions, and rape), the disorders discussed here are listed in the *Diagnostic and Statistical Manual Version IV* (*DSM-IV*) used in psychiatry and psychology as a means of listing the various diagnostic categories treated with psychotherapy or medications. Since the *DSM-IV* represents our current cultural values regarding human sexuality, it will serve as the basis for identifying various "disorders" that we feel are unacceptable in mainstream society. The disorders discussed are listed under "sexual and gender identity disorders" in the *DSM-IV*. The gender identity disorders, while they begin in childhood, have a profound effect on adult behavior and the ways in which adults cope with this disorder. Homosexuality has been excluded from the *DSM-IV* but remains a topic in the sexual disorders literature and cannot be excluded as a form of sexual variation that has significant socio-cultural history. The sexual addictions are included in this discussion for information purposes since the terminology has been used extensively in the public literature and media. Finally, rape, which is not represented in the *DSM-IV*, is discussed in this article, although we emphasize its aggressive and violent nature rather than sexual nature. Rape, as with such crimes as murder, are usually considered symptoms of other underlying problems, not a disturbance in itself.

I. INTRODUCTION

Few topics regarding human behavior hold as much interest and as much pathos as that of deviations and dysfunctions in human sexuality. What constitutes deviations and dysfunctions, however, are heavily dependent on contemporary cultural attitudes and values and these are often blind to the past history of sexuality in the culture.

We know, for example, that sexuality was represented in the rock art of the earliest human cultures. Paleolithic (30,000 to 10,000 B.C.) rock art, for example, is replete with both human and animal fertility symbols that were thought to endow the represented forms with abundant offspring. The Egyptians (3000 B.C.) are thought to have added power to the concept of fertility as represented in their symbols. In Western culture, our sexual values came mostly from the Judeo-Christian traditions. The Judaic tradition emphasized reproductive sexual behavior without guilt. The core concern was to protect the integrity of marriage with all other considerations of secondary value. Strict laws of adultery were applied to women but the husband was instructed only to "not covet your neighbor's wife . . . ," otherwise sex outside the marriage was tolerated. While the Jews were nomadic and their values emphasized family and procreation, sexual values for the Greeks emanated from their more settled agricultural lifestyle. Here family was still central but the Greeks allowed far more freedom of sexual expression in varied forms. For example, bisexuality was common among Greek males. Since beauty was the primary value or attraction, sexual behavior and arousal could arise in response to both boys and young or mature women of beauty. With the rise of Christianity more ascetic beliefs began to emerge. In general, sex had a procreative function, not the pleasure role noted with the Greeks and Hebrews. By the 18th century, religious views of life shifted from emphasis on eternal life in heaven to attaining happiness on earth and romantic love was valued. Sexual "deviations" started to become cultural issues with particular emphasis on homosexuality and masturbation. As venereal diseases became widespread, cultural values shifted to the physician as the arbiter of sexual morality, and to the repression of sexual behavior, particularly that of males. In the 20th century sexual notions are clearly shifting towards a continuum of behaviors. Modern sexologists not only have described the physiological, emotional, and psychological aspects of sexual behavior but have also highlighted the various forms of sexual behavior that exist whether in overt or covert forms.

This article deals with the full range of human sexual thoughts, feelings, and actions that are generally regarded as abnormal, deviant, or disordered. Our focus will be on these extremes but it should be noted that "deviant" and "disordered" are concepts that rest upon the assumption of a medical, disease, or psychiatric model of behavior that dichotomizes human actions into two qualitatively separate categories of "normal" and "abnormal." Some sexologists, on the other hand, view these sexual behavior variations not as diseases to be cured but as atypical expressions representing quantitative rather than qualitative differences. To them, sexual behavior falls on a broad continuum with the extremes being vulnerable to labels like "disordered" and "abnormal." Here we are dealing with differences in intensity and narrowness of behavior rather than qualitatively different behaviors. We can see this, for example, in the husband who might be aroused by his wife wearing lingerie versus the fetish individual who can only become sexually aroused by lingerie. Furthermore, the demarcation between abnormal and normal categories is not fixed or absolute. Rather, it consists of an ever changeable subjective value judgment derived from psychiatric, cultural, and political forces. For example, masturbation, once considered a sin then a disease, is now acceptable and understood. Likewise, homosexuality was actually removed from the psychiatric nomenclature due to political pressures and changes in culture norms. These are examples of the changeable nature of categorization and labeling and the subjective social value judgments they represent. [*See* SEXUAL BEHAVIOR.]

Our discussion will follow closely the psychiatric nomenclature and diagnostic categories since these represent our current values regarding human sexuality and the types of behaviors that are considered unacceptable in mainstream society. We will use the terms or labels often used in psychiatry and law to denote these patterns. Although it is not a psychiatric disorder, we will discuss homosexuality since it is a form of sexual behavior that has socio-cultural historical relevance and is still a controversial topic among some peoples. We will also discuss rape, gender identity disorders, and sexual addictions which are listed in the psychiatric diagnostic system but not under sexual disorders.

The behavioral area of sexual dysfunctions is not discussed since it usually represents inhibitions in sexual drive or performance and is not as comprehensive a manifestation of one's being as are the problems and stresses characteristic of sexual disorders. Finally, we will briefly discuss the topic of rape, emphasizing its aggressive and violent nature rather than sexual nature.

Our starting place in discussing sexual disorders is to focus on the notion of "sexual identity." A person's sexual identity can be seen as an interrelationship among the three basic elements of human sexual behavior, namely, biological sexual characteristics, gender identity, and sexual orientation. In the diagram below you can see that sexual identity is formed from the interaction between biological sex characteristics (such as male and female sex organs, hormones, etc.), gender identity (or one's identification with or feeling of femininity or masculinity), and sexual orientation (homo-, bi-, heterosexual, or other objects of stimulation as found, for example, in the paraphilias). In examining the gender identity disorders we will be discussing biological sex and gender identity. On the other hand, when we discuss the paraphilias, we will be focusing in part upon sexual orientation.

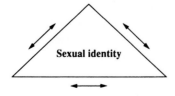

Sexual orientation
(homo-, bi-, hetero-, or other sexual objects)

Sexual identity

Gender identity
(feminine vs masculine)

Biological sexual characteristics
(male vs female)

II. GENDER IDENTITY DISORDERS

A person with gender identity disorder (GID) experiences a confusion or mismatch between biological sexual characteristics and their culturally assigned gender identity. The identity problem is psychological in nature rather than a biological ambiguity. Biologically, they are dimorphic (male vs female) in terms of chromosomal, gonadal, genital development, and hormonal levels. The ambiguity exists in terms of the individual's identification with culturally defined traits that constitute being a woman or man, i.e., the degree of femininity or masculinity the person exhibits through thoughts, feelings, and their actions. Not all people are comfortable with what they feel is their true sense of being a woman or man and their biological sex. The amount of disturbance can range from a mild sense of inappropriateness, to feeling like a woman trapped in a male's body, and vice versa.

GID should not be confused with transvestism, homosexuality, and hermaphroditism. Transvestites, as we will see later in more detail, cross-dress for fetishistic pleasure, and, with few exceptions, rarely find an incongruity between their sex and gender. A person who is emotionally and sexually attracted to a member of their same sex is, likewise, not inherently disturbed in regards to their gender identity. Finally, the hermaphrodite has to some degree the sexual organs for both sexes. Since this confusion stems from being biologically intersexed, the hermaphrodite's dilemma is not considered a psychological disorder. Once again, those with GID are unambiguously biologically formed in one sex, and their confusion is at the emotional and psychological levels.

GIDs are conceptually divided into three categories: GID of childhood, GID of adolescence and adulthood (not transsexual), and transsexualism. Let us look at each of these three categories. [*See* GENDER IDENTITY.]

A. Gender Identity Disorder of Childhood

GID of childhood is reserved for prepubescent children and is relatively uncommon. The sex ratio for the population in general is unknown, yet through clinical work it appears that there are many more boys than girls diagnosed with this condition. Generally, the age of onset for both sexes is age 4; however, in some cases it may appear as early as age 2. The majority of children will return to their expected gender roles by puberty, while the remaining minority will continue experiencing what is called "gender dysphoria" or role confusion. Reliable predictions of adult pathology, based upon nontypical childhood behavior have proved elusive. The primary symptoms needed to make a diagnosis are: (1) a persistent and severe discomfort regarding her or his own biological sex, and (2) a belief that they are, or desire to be, of the opposite sex. Such feelings and behaviors are chronic and problematic, thereby transcending any normal variation of stereotypical gender roles, such as being a "tomboy" or a "sissy."

A female with this disorder exhibits intense feelings of frustration at being a girl with a corresponding desire to become a boy, or, in some cases, they may even believe that they are of the opposite gender already. They often seek male peers and are repulsed by traditional feminine toys, games, etc., preferring instead the masculine equivalents. Lastly, there is an intense disgust toward and rejection of their anatomy, often illustrated by beliefs that they will grow a penis or not go through normal female pubescent body changes. The overall pattern with males is identical to the female description except that the specifics are reverse. For example, GID boys typically show severe distress at being a boy, they engage in cross-dressing, and prefer female toys, peers, and so on. They are repulsed by their genitalia, often wishing that it would disappear or that they would grow up and become a woman.

A major difference between the two sexes is found in the fact that many more boys than girls are treated for this condition. It is thought that differential socialization patterns may account for the discrepancy in prevalence rates. For example, boys are more often subjected to rigid parental expectations and therefore any nontypical gender behavior is often more apparent. Boys also tend to display more signs of secondary pathology, e.g., depression, anxiety, and withdrawal, perhaps due to harsher social consequences from peers for their feminine-like behavior. On the other hand, females who cross the gender line ("tomboys") tend to be more readily accepted than "sissies," or boys who violate gender expectations.

B. Gender Identity Disorder of Adolescence or Adulthood (Nontranssexual)

A person with this condition must have reached puberty, exhibit reoccurring discomfort with their biological sex, and habitually cross-dress. Motivation for wearing the apparel of the opposite sex is for emulation purposes, not for fetishistic pleasure. They are psychologically identified with the opposite sex and exhibit intermittent to constant cross-dressing. Despite the person's sense of discomfort, they usually have no preoccupations with changing their sex to match their gender identity.

Some researchers theorize that GIDs should be conceptualized on a continuum rather than as separate diagnostic categories. Accordingly, they might prefer the term *transgenderism,* which can be seen as an intermediate stage between the two extremes of GID of childhood and secondary transsexualism, i.e., someone who after a period of time decides to make a sex change. The transgenderist is someone who is living permanently in the role of the opposite sex *but* does not have the desire for a complete sex change. Essentially, their change is in gender, not in sexual biological characteristics.

C. Transsexualism

The transsexual condition can be distinguished from other GIDs essentially because of a life-long sense of gender incongruence or inappropriateness and a persistent preoccupation or obsessive quest for sex realignment or "reassignment" surgery. This preoccupation for sex change surgery must be present for at least 2 years to be diagnosed transsexualism. As you can see, we are now at the more extreme end of the GID continuum.

Some theorists have attempted to distinguish between primary and secondary transsexualism, with the former evidencing a history of gender dysphoria since childhood while the latter may be long-term cross-dressers or transgenderists but they seek reassignment surgery later in life usually after experiencing a traumatic stressor.

Secondary pathology for transsexuals is common and most often includes anxiety and depression. For those who are driven to change their sex, the difficulty in getting the funds to pay for surgery can result in self-mutilation and even suicide. In a culture that defines their dilemma as pathological and abnormal, transsexuals have many stories to relate about the pain and suffering they experience. This brief glimpse into the recollection of a girl "trapped" in a male body should partially convey their struggle for recognition as legitimate human beings:

> . . . I wanted above all to walk down the hall at school and be looked at and respected as were the normal girls. Yes, nor-

mal girls; for I was a girl with all my heart, but I was not a normal girl. I was a freak of a girl, one who had to look like a boy. . . . (Benjamin, 1966, p. 199)

It is generally believed that transsexualism is present in about 1 out of 30,000 males and 1 out of every 100,000 females. More males seek out treatment than females, with ratios as high as 8 to 1. In the United States alone, it is estimated that there are between six and ten thousand postoperative transsexuals, i.e., people who have had sex change operations.

D. Etiology of Gender Identity Disorders

As the current body of knowledge now stands, the causal roots of GID remain undiscovered. The various approaches that attempt to explain this particular disorder can be broken down into the biological/medical, psychodynamic, and developmental/learning models. The first approach purposes genetic, hormonal, neurological, and chromosomal abnormalities as a causal factor. Despite a few leads, such as the effects of prenatal hormones on gender behavior, there is a meager amount of data to support the notion of biology as a sole or even major influence. The psychodynamic model emphasizes early childhood and personality development. Causal roles are attributed to difficulty with mother-child relations and the failure to psychologically identify with the parent of the opposite sex. Again, this is not a universal or even major phenomenon. Furthermore, it is very difficult to tease out what is the chicken and what is the egg. In other words, do parents shape children's behavior or does the child's behavior shape the parents' difficulty with the relationship? Finally, the importance of socialization processes and the acquisition of atypical childhood behaviors via modeling or conditioning represents the learning and developmental point of view. Unfortunately, contrary to both the psychodynamic and learning models, there is very little indication that the family environment has any serious effect in the development of gender identity disorders for substantial numbers of cases. For example, in a study by R. Green (*American Journal of Psychiatry,* 1978), of 16 children who were raised by transsexuals all were found to have heterosexual orientation with no disturbance in their gender identity.

E. Treatment Approaches to Gender Identity Disorders

The general consensus is that many or all behavioral and psychodynamic treatments for GID are ineffective.

Behavioral therapies have produced a few "successes" in strongly motivated clients, but even then some of the behavioral modification techniques used have raised disturbing moral questions. For example, reports of behavior therapies describe asking children to overemphasize the gender identity differences so as to produce aversive social reactions which, presumably, would diminish these opposite-sex behaviors and attitudes. In contrast, psychodynamic treatments aim at resolving childhood conflicts in the hope of producing acceptance of one's sex and the corresponding gender identity. After many case histories and grueling therapeutic hours, personality reorganization approaches have almost always ended in total failure. Both approaches subject children to personal pain in addition to the feelings of failure they must experience in therapies are ineffective. [*See* BEHAVIOR THERAPY.]

For transsexuals, sex reassignment treatment (sex change surgery) has proven in a majority of cases to be successful in bringing happiness and relief. After a careful screening process, a qualified individual must undergo intensive counseling and instruction on matters of grooming, vocation, legal rights, voice training, and the proper use of stereotypical gender role mannerisms. Then they may begin hormonal therapy in order to produce the desired secondary sex characteristics, e.g., breasts in males, facial/body hair modification, changes in body fat distribution, and some voice alteration. After living and working in one's new gender role for 1 to 2 years, only then can the candidate undergo genital reconstruction. The artificially constructed vagina is much more realistic in appearance and function than its male counterpart. While female genitalia is capable of lubrication and orgasm, the penis is less sensitive and lacks natural erectile capacities. Though limited in number and with sometimes inconclusive findings, some follow-up studies have indicated an 80 to 85% satisfaction rate for transsexual operations, with male-to-female transsexuals usually faring better than their counterparts. Dissatisfaction is usually the result of poor surgical techniques and personal and social instability that preceded surgery.

III. THE PARAPHILIAS

The term *paraphilia* is derived from the notion of a deviation or separation (para-) from what most people are attracted to (-philia). Originally, these were called "perversions," but modern terminology generally describes them as "deviations" or, more recently, as "variations." The *DSM-IV* describes these deviations as ". . . recurrent sexually arousing fantasies, sexual urges, or behaviors generally involving either (1) non-human objects, (2) the suffering or humiliation of oneself or one's partner, or (3) children or other nonconsenting persons." The diagnosis, however, is made only if the person has acted on their urges or is greatly disturbed or distressed about them. Paraphilic fantasy (such as sex with animals, arousal from undergarments, sado-masochistic thoughts, cross-dressing, or sex with children, etc.) as such is not sufficient to warrant clinical diagnosis. These preoccupations must be intense and recurrent, or undesired and disturbing to the individual, the preferred or exclusive forms of sexual gratification, or acted out overtly to be considered pathological. The paraphilias are usually multiple in nature rather than singular. They are almost exclusively confined to men with the exception of masochism, in which we see a significant number of females.

Current views of paraphilias have been heavily influenced by Freudian theory and analysis of sexual behavior. Within the psychodynamic model, a healthy or natural sexual relationship consists of opposite sexed partners whose object is coitus (sexual gratification through intercourse). These deviations in sexual orientation involve the use of an object other than the opposite sex partner, such as one of the same sex (homosexual), children (pedophilia), close relative (incest), animals (zoophilia), inanimate objects (fetish), or even dead people (necrophilia), as sexual objects. Likewise, instead of seeking coitus, departures include watching others (voyeurism), exposing genitals (exhibitionism), infliction of pain (sadism), or suffering pain (masochism) as deviant aims. In the paraphilias, the erotic object has a role or characteristic that is more important than their personality and personal characteristics of the object and the aim is to enact the paraphilic fantasy.

Mainstream diagnostic systems have been strongly influenced by these two major departures from object and aim. Alternatively, others have argued that perhaps the impact on others should be used as the diagnostic criterion. Here, fetishes and transvestism, and perhaps gender identity disorders, would be excluded in that they usually have little or no direct negative impact on others. All this is brought to your attention to highlight the subjective and consequently changing nature of diagnosis and categorization. Basically, as with most other mental illness categories, we are dealing with social value judgments rather than specific "diseases" and as such cultural and political values and attitudes influence the diagnostic process.

A. Pedophilias

The pedophile (derived from the Greek for "child lover") sexually prefers children of either sex for erotic gratification. It is usually thought that perpetrators must be at least 10 years older than their victims, but this age difference may differ considerably depending on circumstances. Pedophilia is also called "child sexual abuse" and "child molestation." Child molestation is most often perpetrated by males and usually involves such actions as manipulation of the child's genitalia, stroking of the body, forcing the child to manipulate the adult's genitalia, and, to a lesser degree, intromission. Pedophilia is the most common form of paraphilias and involves the most vulnerable victims—children.

Heterosexual men are responsible for most sex abuse against girls. Two out of three sexually abused children, however, are girls. *Conservative* estimates are that 10% of females and 2% of males were sexually abused as children. There is no well-delineated personality for the pedophilic. However, the concept of the "dirty old man" as perpetrator is misguided in that most pedophiles are in their late 30s with only about 5% being aged men. If we had to generalize, we could say that pedophiles are generally immature developmentally even though they may have married and have children of their own. Second, we often see the behavior under stress, i.e., during stressful life periods often accompanied by marital and sexual problems. Alcohol is consistently involved in pedophilic encounters. The majority of victims are relatives, neighbors, or acquaintances; and encounters, while usually brief, occur in series of extended contacts. Generally the younger the child, the more immature the perpetrator. Actual penetration and coitus occur in only 4% of cases. Interestingly, the vast majority (80%) of perpetuators have themselves been abused as children.

B. Incest

Incest is treated here as a subcategory of pedophilia. However, since pedophiles differ in age from their victims, incest may not necessarily meet the criteria. For example, the majority of incest cases seem to involve cousins and siblings who might be similar in age. Incest (from the Latin "impure") is a form of pedophilia involving close relatives, most commonly between cousins but parent–child or sibling–sibling incest is the most repugnant and most often the focus of treatment or criminal proceedings. Taboos against incest are present in all cultures, particularly against mother–son incest. Surveys among adults indicate that 14% of males reported having had sexual contact with a relative before adulthood (95% of which were heterosexual in nature) and 9% of females have had such contact. Most of these experiences were with cousins and essentially involved some form of "petting." Among a university sample, however, 10% of females reported incestuous relationships with their fathers (including stepfathers). Almost 90% of cases brought to court for incest involve father–daughter while only 5% are father–son incidents. Transgenerational incest seems to occur in about 10% of incest cases but probably has different dynamics than immediate parents and children or children and children.

The studies of incest have concluded that these events occur within seriously disturbed or dysfunctional families and that a code of silence develops in which these events are not spoken about and often repressed by the victims. Furthermore, the parents in this unhappy marriage typically consist of a domineering, authoritative, and impulsive husband and a dependent and emotionally distant wife. The husbands often also abuse the wives as well as the children.

Incest is a criminal as well as psychological disorder. The experience of incest is traumatic and psychologically damaging to the children involved (and even to those who know about it). Criminal prosecution does not erase the trauma of incest. These deep psychological scars must eventually be addressed in order for the victim to heal and live a fully mature life.

C. Voyeurism

Voyeurs are also called "peepers" or "Peeping Toms." The psychiatric diagnostic system describes this condition as a recurrent, intense, and sexually oriented "act of observing unsuspecting people, usually strangers, who are either naked, in the process of disrobing, or engaging in sexual activity. . . ." Looking (or "peeping") provides sexual arousal but no actual sexual contact with the observed person is sought. Orgasm, usually produced by masturbation, may occur during the voyeuristic activity, or later in response to the memory

of what the person has witnessed. Often these people enjoy the fantasy of having a sexual experience with the observed person, but in reality this does not occur. In its severe form, peeping constitutes the exclusive form of sexual activity.

Lady Godiva's ride through the streets of Coventry to remit an oppressive tax was watched by no one from the town—out of respect and gratitude for her actions—with the exception of Tom the tailor, who peeped through the curtains and for this act went blind. The "Peeping Tom" of today does not go blind literally but they are almost always men. To be considered a paraphilia, there must be a recurrent and intense preoccupation with looking from hiding or secret places. Just looking at live nudes or pictures of nudes is not a paraphilia.

Voyeurs tend to be younger men (convicted age is 23.8 years), unmarried and with little or no alcohol, drug, or other mental illness problems. While they tend to be heterogeneous as a group, they do commonly have deficiencies in heterosexual relationships. As a matter of fact, it has been conjectured that the voyeuristic practices are a safe and protected way of avoiding a possible relationship with a woman.

D. Exhibitionism

The legal term for exhibitionism is "indecent exposure" because of the shock or offensive value of the act to others. Again, this is mainly a male disorder. Like other paraphilias, it involves repetition, intensity, and sexual urges or arousing fantasies of at least 6 months duration. For the exhibitionist or "flasher" gratification seems to come from the disgust, shock, fear, and surprise of the unsuspecting usually female victims. There is usually a compulsive, driven quality to this behavior (as with most paraphilias) but they are also prone to be caught as they return to the same situation or place repeatedly. There is some evidence that at some level they may wish to be caught and that this consequence is deliberate and desired. The exhibitionists' behavior has a distinctive hostile air to it and this, coupled with the fact that they often have serious sexual problems might suggest intense, perhaps unconscious, hostility exists toward women. As a group they tend to be younger (30s) with about 30% married, 30% divorced or separated, and 40% never married. They are often above average in intelligence and do not have more serious forms of mental illness.

Anxiety, which forms a part in all the paraphilias, is also apparent in exhibitionists both in terms of the excitement or anxiety associated with the act itself and with the desire for anxiety relief that results from the act. There is also evidence that exhibitionists are sexually aroused by stimuli that usually have little or no arousal potential for most people (such as seeing fully clothed women in normal activities) and thus may misread the motives and intentions of others (perhaps seeing them as sex crazed as they are). A fairly large percentage of women (between 45 and 50%) report having seen or had direct contact with a "flasher."

E. Fetishism

Fetishism involves sexual arousal from some inanimate or nonliving object. Exposure to the object or preference for the object is usually necessary to maintain erectile states. Common objects include shoes, sheer stockings, gloves, toilet articles, undergarments particularly underpants, and many tactilely stimulating substances (soft fetishes) such as fur, velvet, and silk garments, and smooth solid objects (hard fetishes) that can be rubbed and fondled such as shoes, leather objects, and so on.

In ancient cultures, fetishes were objects that had magical powers. For the fetishist the object itself is endowed with sexual power and the owner is of little or no interest. Panties, stockings, and garters may be alluring and channel excitement to the wearer but to the fetishist, the object itself is the allure and goal, not the user.

Almost any object can acquire fetish properties. One mechanism for acquisition is classical conditioning in which a neutral object comes to acquire arousal properties by association with sexual arousal and stimulation (i.e., masturbating with the object present). By this process, any stimulus, even body parts, can become a fetish object.

Orgasm may occur with the fetish alone or the fetish object may need to be present during intercourse in order to maintain stimulation toward orgasm. Again, poorly developed heterosexual relationships are found in fetishes as in other paraphilias. Here, however, there is usually a strong mother–son bond with the fetish individual. Fetishes usually develop during adolescence. Fetishists are seldom distraught enough by the behav-

ior to seek out psychotherapy and they are usually not overt or foolish enough to be arrested or detected.

F. Transvestism

The Latin *trans* meaning "across" and *vestia* meaning "dress" for the term for "cross-dressing" or "transvestism." As pointed out earlier, transsexuals often manifest cross-dressing as a first expression of opposite sex feelings. This behavior, along with men who dress in "drag" to attract other men for sexual purposes, is not usually considered manifestations of transvestism. Likewise, female impersonators and actors who play female parts are not included under this diagnosis. To qualify as transvestism, there must be a compulsive desire to cross-dress and an intense frustration when the practice is interfered with. The transvestite is usually heterosexual in orientation, married, and otherwise masculine in appearance, demeanor, and sexual preference. The cross-dressing, while compulsive, is done in secret and does not lead to homosexuality or gender identity problems—although transvestites report feeling like a woman during the cross-dress episodes. Often wives will be overt or covert conspirators in the cross-dressing activities. Cross-dressers will often seek each other out for social occasions while made up as women.

The compulsion to cross-dress begins by adolescence, although most children who cross-dress will "grow out of it" by adulthood. Some male transvestites recall their parents forcing them to wear girls clothing as a form of humiliation and punishment. As an adult, however, the wearing of women's clothing usually has more significance than just sexual arousal or punishment. It affords the transvestite male an opportunity to escape from pressures and responsibilities. Some males only *partially* cross-dress, usually by covertly wearing female undergarments under their male clothing. Others are *complete* cross-dressers, who overtly carry out this practice either occasionally or, for some, all the time.

G. Sadomasochism (S-M)

The term *sadomasochism* is derived from the family names of two historical characters. The first is the French nobleman Marquis de Sade (Donatien Alphonse Francois was his "first" name, 1740–1814), whose writing consisted of vivid accounts of pain inflicted on one partner in sexual encounters of various kinds. *Sexual sadism* is defined as the infliction of physical pain and/or personal humiliation and degradation on a sexual partner. While de Sade portrayed infliction of excruciating pain on individuals, most sadism involves mild to moderate pain. It is estimated that about 5% of men and 2% of women have obtained sexual pleasure by inflicting pain on a regular basis.

While sadists inflict pain on willing or nonconsenting partners, sexual masochists (from Leopold von Sacher-Masoch, a German novelist who described this behavior in the late 19th century) enjoy suffering for erotic excitement as a preferred form of sexual activity. While sadists overwhelmingly tend to be men, masochists are more often females. The study of sadomasochism has only just begun. What little is known about these practices comes mainly from case studies, i.e., examination of S-M activities at centers for such activities or through paid dominance and submission sexual surrogates hired for these purposes.

Sadomasochistic activities center on use of dominance-aggression and submission in sexual activities. Terms that denote these activities abound such as bondage and domination (B-D), master–mistress, dominatrix, humiliation, restraints, whipping, leather/rubber, slave, bottom or submissive, and so on. Activities often involve elaborate interactions, sometimes with predetermined code words that will lead to the immediate release of a victim if desired and often use fetishistic trappings such as leather/rubber garments, chains, whips, shackles, harnesses, and other props. Rarely do sadomasochistic practices lead to physical injury, mutilation, or death. Victims, however, may be nonconsenting or willing and, not infrequently, paid sexual partners. The most frequent S-M activities are spanking, master–slave bondage, humiliation situations, oral–anal S-M contexts, whipping, and to a lesser degree, verbal abuse, enemas, torture, "golden showers" (urinating on someone), and use of toilet articles.

There is a well-defined S-M subculture that includes paraphernalia sex shops, stages for bondage scenes, magazines, prostitutes trained in S-M skills, and videos. Participants are predominantly heterosexual males with a greater concentration of bisexual female participants. Sadomasochistic activities are defined as paraphilias if they are recurrent and intense. To just tie up a sexual partner occasionally is not S-M activity.

H. Miscellaneous Paraphilias

Sexual arousal can become conditioned to a wide variety of eliciting stimuli. In this section, we will describe some relatively uncommon paraphilias that involve unusual and sometimes noxious objects of sexual arousal. The miscellaneous paraphilias described below not only occur rarely but are often not detected due to their secretive nature and the fact that persons who engage in these acts are rarely motivated to seek treatment for their behavior.

A number of paraphilias are difficult to clarify. Some seem closely linked to fetishism but instead of body parts, body discharges take on erotic significance. Coprophilia, for example, involves erotic fascination with feces; klismaphilia with enemas; urophilia with urine; and mysophilia with filth. These stimuli may excite or be used for orgasm. Soiling others—by urinating or defecating on them—can also serve sadomasochistic purposes and is sometimes seen in assaults and rape situations.

Some paraphilias may have a sexual goal that is not immediately obvious. For example, pyromania (fire setting) and kleptomania (stealing for excitement) are thought to sometimes represent sexualized activities and thereby qualify as paraphilias.

Frotteurism (or toucherism) is a paraphilia that involves sexual gratification or arousal by rubbing against or fondling an unsuspecting, nonconsenting person. The frotteur acts on urges to touch, rub, or fondle usually in crowed places, often accompanied by fantasies of having sex with the singled-out person. Contact is brief to avoid detection.

Finally, the 20th century has brought a host of telephone scatologia, or efforts to seek sexual gratification by making obscene telephone calls. Anonymity and escape from detection are enhanced in use of this media for contact.

IV. CAUSAL MODELS AND TREATMENTS

Several key observations and assumptions should be noted before addressing the etiology and treatment of sexual disorders. First, contemporary sexologists have had little success in identifying specific causal factors and in designing and implementing successful treatment modalities. Such a state is due, in part, to limited theoretical models and problematic methodology. Criticism of existing causal models has been in terms of their myopic and/or reductionistic focus. In other words, most theories have focused solely on cognitive/emotional, behavioral, or environmental elements rather than on how all three elements interact and affect an individual's sexual identity. Another factor may be methodological problems, e.g., the difficulty in forming operational definitions for, and measuring such abstract concepts as, gender identity or sexual orientation. A more important and subtle point however, is the view that by separating the range of sexual behaviors into specific categories and calling these "abnormal," we are, by this process alone, not asking the critical questions about *how* sexual identity and orientation develop as a phenomenon. Instead, we are caught up in treating our categorizations as if they are real and true medical diseases or abnormalities. In fact, it appears that sexual expression can vary greatly and lies on a continuum. Even though experience and socialization can affect the location of one's position on the continuum, we know very little about how individuals get to a particular place on the continuum in the first place.

Biological theories have predominated as causes of sexual disorders. The specific biological determinant or process would have to be in the male and not female structures. No absolute causative biological mechanisms have been identified. Most behavioral scientists see very little value in the psychoanalytic or psychodynamic theories. Both deficient psychosexual development and Oedipal fixations have been used to account for sexual disorders. Repressed hostility is thought to be at the roots of most paraphilias and the disorder allows a symbolic acting out of these repressed urges.

Learning theory models emphasize classical conditioning or associative learning linking sexual arousal with previously neutral objects or situations, masturbation becoming a key activity for this linking to occur. Learning theory seems to account for some paraphilias and for some portion of the sexual disorders but it lacks sufficient empirical power and predictability.

As mentioned previously, treatments for the paraphilias and other sexual disorders are very ineffective and positive effects seem to be confined to highly motivated clients with milder forms of the disorders. Biological treatments essentially attempt to dull or reduce sexual drive. The behavior therapies utilize counter-conditioning and desensitization methods. Various forms of group therapies (structured in a self-help manner) seem to be effective with the motivated client.

V. SEXUAL ADDICTION

How far do normal sexual activity levels extend? Where do we draw the line for pathological levels of sexual activity? Again, changes in social values have defined different patterns and points on the sexual activity continuum as pathological at different times. As a matter of fact, lack of precision in defining this category and the subjective nature of judgments resulted in the elimination of sexual addiction from the paraphilias in the *DSM-III-R* edition.

The terms "sexual addiction" and "sexual compulsion" began to appear in the scientific and clinical literature in the 1970s. They soon became popular terms to describe individuals who seemed obsessed with sexual behavior, i.e., nymphomaniacs, etc. Usually, sexual activity had to reach a level where it interfered with their job, relationships, career, or even their health. The behavior was often described as uncontrolled sexual behavior but functional analysis showed that it tended to lower anxiety states and probably helped enhance self-esteem and the sense of power and control.

Critics of the use of these concepts or diagnostic categories argued that they lacked precision and behavioral clarity, that they were often unreliable, and full of subjective judgments. Critics pointed out that the concepts did not fit our knowledge of the addictions nor of the compulsive processes. Furthermore, they were often applied to gay men with many partners and thus seemed discriminatory.

Supporters of this category argued that frequency was not the issue, rather one had to look at the purpose and meaning to the individual as critical components. Here, seeking out transient relationships in an indiscriminate manner certainly had the ring of self-defeating and self-destructive patterns of behavior that qualified as paraphilias. At this point, however, sexual addiction is an historical term.

VI. RAPE

Rape (Latin, "to seize") or the actual act of seizing a person by physical force or threat is an extreme form of sexual aggression and coercion. Rape is technically a legal term but it can be viewed from a psychological perspective. Current definitions of rape have extended the violation to deliberate intrusion into the emotional, physical, or rational integrity of the individual and even debasement through voyeurism ("visual rape"). Legally, rape is divided into statutory (seduction of minor) and forcible seizure of an unwilling partner over age 18. Recent attention has been focused on "date rape" or the use of coercion by dates, acquaintances or even boyfriends. The victims are almost always women. No woman is entirely safe from rape. Almost 100,000 rapes are reported each year but estimates are the majority of rapes go unreported. Most occur outside or in the victim's home. National studies have found that the incidence of rape has increased more rapidly than any other type of violent crime.

There are many factors and levels of causation to rape. Certainly, cultural and subcultural attitudes toward women and about men contribute to the setting for rape. Psychological studies of rapists have identified some broad typologies of rapists. These types were derived from a psychological examination of rape cases. In none of these cases was it found that rape was motivated by sexual satisfaction. All the cases were characterized by a predominance of power motive or anger. This led to the classification of rapists as (1) power assertive types (intimidation and control), (2) power reassurance types (to compensate for an underlying sense of weakness and inadequacy), (3) anger–retaliation type (rage, hatred, and violence predominate), and anger–excitation rape (the pathological sadist).

Prediction of rape from psychological profiles is not possible even though a proportion of rapists are obviously disturbed. The literature in this area is replete with instances of rape, in which, prior to the attack, the rapist had given no hint whatsoever of being a dangerous person. Conviction rates for rape are low and treatment or therapeutic interventions have generally been ineffective and disappointing. In addition to the need to develop adequate predictive and therapeutic measures for rapists, there is a tremendous need to improve treatments for the traumatized victims of these violent crimes. [*See* RAPE.]

VII. HOMOSEXUALITY

Sexual orientation, as it relates to homosexuality, is one's erotic attraction toward the same sex. Sexual orientation is a part of one's sexual identity, which, in turn, is primarily related to physical and emotional disposition, and is simultaneously interconnected yet distinct from biological and gender identity.

In Western culture, the most prominent means of conceptualizing sexual orientation is in terms of hetero- versus homosexuality. Traditionally, such distinctions are oversimplified and create oppositional positions. For these reasons, some theorists would rather conceive of orientation as being on a continuum, with heterosexuality and homosexuality at either end and in between a vast gradation of overlap reflecting bisexuality. Dichotomous thinking, coupled with rigid cultural values biased in favor of the heterosexual majority have led to a lengthy history of intolerance towards and oppression of homosexual and bisexual individuals.

Two forces helped shape negative and oppressive attitudes toward homosexuality. The first was Judeo-Christian values and beliefs that held that nonprocreative sexual acts were regarded as "sins against nature" and consequently frowned on in the culture. The second force was the rise of medicine and psychology as powerful authorities and arbiters of social morality by defining and controlling "deviant" and "diseased" behaviors. This control led to the condemnation of many fringe or nontraditional sexual practices with homosexuality in the forefront. Psychiatry, for example, included homosexuality in their diagnostic manual thus sanctioning intervention and treatment. Sin was now replaced by pathology. Being identified as mentally ill meant that homosexuals could be stripped of their civil and human rights while the heterosexual population looked on.

Under fire from within and outside their ranks, on December 15, 1973, the American Psychiatric Association board of trustees voted to remove homosexuality from the categories of mental illness. After much struggle and debate, homosexuality was replaced with a new category, ego-dystonic homosexuality, denoting those homosexual individuals who were distressed by their orientation and wanted to become heterosexual. This compromise category did not last for long, as many professionals and lay persons could see that it was just another more subtle means of perpetuating prejudice and oppression. Finally, all reference to homosexuality was removed from the official nomenclature.

A. Prevalence

The problem in measuring the prevalence of homosexuality is that it must be operationally defined. Renowned sex researcher Alfred Kinsey chose to operationally define sexual orientation on a continuum in terms of behavior frequency of homo-, hetero-, and degree of combined sexual behaviors. The following scale was developed:

0. Exclusive heterosexual with no homosexual
1. Predominately heterosexual, only incidental homosexual
2. Predominately heterosexual, but more than incidental homosexual
3. Equally heterosexual and homosexual
4. Predominately homosexual, but more than incidental heterosexual
5. Predominately homosexual, but incidental heterosexual
6. Exclusively homosexual

What resulted from his pioneering assessment of the sexual practices of the American public was surprising. Kinsey found that 37% of males surveyed had had physical contact to the point of orgasm, at least once, with another man. In addition, another 4–6% were either primarily or exclusively homosexual. It was found that of the females questioned, 13% had at least one such encounter with another female.

To conceive of homosexuality in strict behavioral terms challenged the more prevalent practice of using the terms to represent a personality deficit. The latter approach, of course, leads to social stigmatization. Kinsey also avoided applying sexual orientation labels in an either/or manner, by conceiving of sexuality as a range of behaviors on a continuum. Despite his popularity, his results were criticized on methodological and theoretical grounds. Specifically, grave doubts were raised about the generalizability of his data from the limited sampling he used. Other researchers conducting surveys with better sampling methods found similar to much lesser rates of incidence; usually between 4 and 16% homosexual behavior of some kinds. Theoretically, Kinsey was criticized for being too reductionistic by trying to conceptualize the homosexual expe-

rience in terms of the frequency of same sex behaviors. Regardless of the precise percentages and how one exactly conceives of it, homosexuality is and has been a pervasive part of our culture and population.

Since the early 1970s, there appears to have been a radical rethinking of how we treat those of homo- or bisexual orientations. Still, some lay persons and professionals find these orientations pathological and must seek causes and roots for these disorders. Katchadourian responds to these efforts in the following manner:

> Those who accept homosexuality as an illness seek its causes. Those who do not, object to this approach. "Causes" implies that there is something wrong; why not seek the "causes" of heterosexuality? The search for the origins of sexual orientation—homosexual or heterosexual—is a more legitimate quest.

The causal agents responsible for producing any sexual orientation are basically unknown. If we hope to gain insight by relying on a single explanation, then we will surely miss the dynamic and interactive nature of sexual identity. Whether the theoretical model is based upon genetic inheritance, developmental influences, or psychodynamic conflict, the nature of sexual orientation, regardless of sexual preference, seems better understood as having multiple roots. [See HOMOSEXUALITY.]

B. Treatments

Contemporary thought rejects the outdated notion of homosexuality and bisexuality as diseases to be treated and cured. Attempts by professional to change or convert homosexuals into heterosexuals have almost always been exercises in futility. Despite long and intensive therapeutic hours, psychoanalysis has had no success. With their aversive counter-conditioning techniques, the behavioral therapies have only faired marginally better. Irrespective of the theoretical model, when a person (homosexual or not) is forced into the therapy room, not only is change highly unlikely but the chances for negative psychological consequences are greatly increased.

An apparent exception to this lack of success was the Masters and Johnson sex therapy study, which reported to have "helped" two-thirds of those who volunteered for a 2-week treatment program. Criticisms of their work include the fact that the male and female participants were carefully screened to ensure that they exhibited high levels of desire to change and were the beneficiaries of very supportive partners. In addition to such biases in sampling, further analysis of the follow-up data revealed that the claimed failure rate of only 28% was probably too low. Perhaps a rate of about 45% would be more accurate.

C. Differences in Health and Personality

As pointed out earlier, psychiatrists have conceptualized the homosexual as inherently pathological and heterosexual as "normal." Numerous scientific studies have compared homosexuals who sought treatment against normal heterosexuals who were *not* in treatment. Differences were found between these groups on health and personality variables. More recent studies, with improved methodology, have shown that very few differences in pathology actually exist between equivalent heterosexual and homosexual samples. Differences in depression and suicide rates previously attributed to pathology or flaws in the individuals are now seen from a broader socio-psychological level of causation, i.e., environmental pressures to live up to one's societal status as deviant.

Another area in which scientific bias has played a mystifying role is in the realm of personality differences between homo- and heterosexuals. Specifically, there have been studies showing gay men were more feminine than straight men and that lesbians were more masculine than their heterosexual counterparts. Once again, such findings have been shown to be based on methodologically flawed clinical/nonclinical designs. Once corrected for biased sampling, such studies show that the differences in gender identity are minimal. Yes, "butch" lesbians and effeminate gays exist, but as a stereotype they are not representative of the homosexual and bisexual population as a whole.

This article has been reprinted with updated references to *DSM-IV* from the *Encyclopedia of Human Behavior, Volume 4.*

BIBLIOGRAPHY

American Psychiatric Association. (1994). "Diagnostic and Statistical Manual," 4th ed. Washington, DC.

Bancroft, J. (1983). "Human Sexuality and Its Problems." Churchill Livingston, London.

Bayer, R. (1987). "Homosexuality and American Psychiatry: The Politics of Diagnosis." Princeton University Press, NJ.

Benjamin, H. (1966). "The Transsexual Phenomenon." Julian Press, New York.

Bullough, V. L., & Brundage, J. (1982). "Sexual Practices in the Medieval Church." Prometheus, Buffalo, NY.

Carnes, P. J. (1983). "The Sexual Addiction." CompCase, Minneapolis.

Doctor, R. F. (1988). "Transvestites and Transsexuals: Toward a Theory of Cross-Gender Behavior." Plenum, New York.

Freeman, E. B. (1988). "Intimate Matters: A History of Sexuality in America." Harper and Row, New York.

Finkelhor, D. (1984). "Child Sexual Abuse." Free Press, New York.

Gonsiorek, J. C., & Weinrich, J. D. (Eds.) (1991). "Homosexuality: Research Implications for Public Policy." Sage, Newbury Park.

Katchadourian, H. A. (1989). "Fundamentals of Human Sexuality," 5th ed. Holt-Rinehart and Winston, San Francisco.

Sexual Dysfunction Therapy

Dinesh Bhugra and Padmal de Silva

University of London

Desire Disorders   Problems related to the degree of sexual desire.
Erectile Disorders   Problems in obtaining or sustaining a sufficiently strong erection for sex.
Orgasmic Disorders   Problems in achieving a climax in sex.
Premature Ejaculation   In the male, reaching a climax too soon, thus preventing enjoyable coital activity.
Sexual Dysfunction   Difficulties in sexual functioning.

SEXUAL DYSFUNCTION has been classified according to the four phases of sexual activity in both males and females. At each stage the individuals can suffer from high or low levels of activity and additional physical problems and pain at various stages during these phases.

I. INTRODUCTION

Sexual dysfunction and its treatment have been well described in historical, medical and psychiatric texts.

The presentation of patients with sexual dysfunction to clinicians is determined by social norms, mores, and expectations. In societies and cultures where sex is seen as a purely procreative process, people are less likely to present with sexual dysfunction—especially if the dysfunction is not interfering with procreation. On the other hand, in societies where sexual satisfaction is seen as a personal pleasure and fulfillment, more people are likely to seek help with the slightest dysfunction. The more severe the problem, the more likely it will be that the individuals seek therapeutic intervention. If there is stigma attached to sexual inadequacy in a society and the individuals believe that they are going to see a mental health professional, it is more likely that their attitudes may well produce a scenario where the pressure is on them and the therapist to do something about the problem furtively and quickly. The decision to seek professional help is very difficult for most people. Under the circumstances, the first impressions of the therapist and his/her response to the problem will be of paramount importance. An additional problem that the individuals may bring with them is an underlying relationship difficulty. A further complication is that the individual's demand may be for physical treatments and not for psychological therapies.

II. CLASSIFICATION OF SEXUAL DYSFUNCTION

The problems of classification in psychiatry are many, and these are reflected in the classification of dysfunction (see Table I). Such a simple division has its advan-

Table I General Classification of Sexual Dysfunction

Phase	Male	Female
Desire/drive/interest	Low interest	Low interest
	Excess interest	Excess interest
Arousal/excitement	Erectile dysfunction	Impaired arousal
Orgasm	Premature ejaculation	Orgasmic dysfunction
	Retarded ejaculation	
Sexual pain/other	Dyspareunia	Vaginismus
		Dyspareunia
	Sexual phobias	Sexual phobias

tages, but it does not take into account any underlying causative factors that would need to be taken into consideration while planning any therapeutic interventions. Precise labeling of the problem often ignores the relationship, cultural, and physical contexts. In addition, the physical causation of sexual dysfunction may be either central—in the brain, or peripheral—in the genito-urinary system. There may be an underlying biological substrate and there may be biological abnormalities, but on their own these may be insufficient for a full understanding of the disorder in question. The International Classification of Diseases (ICD-10) and the *Diagnostic and Statistical Manual (DSM-IV),* the two principal classificatory systems around the world, use a categorical classification and, apart from minor differences, are broadly similar in their approaches to diagnosis, including a multi-axial approach.

Female sexual dysfunction includes sexual desire disorders along with impaired arousal, orgasmic disorder, and vaginismus. Females may perceive their sexuality differently, and their sexual activity is, in part, culturally defined. This definition impacts upon the way in which women understand their own sexuality and whether they can adjust their expectations of their sexual functioning. Female sexual dysfunction may be due to early childhood experiences, or to later trauma, including sexual abuse, childbirth, and infertility, among others. Myths about sexual activity and sexual functioning may well affect both males and females.

In males, while orgasm and emission are normally linked, they can be separated, because in the latter phase organic muscle contraction and emission are responsible for ejaculation. Male sexual dysfunction includes premature ejaculation, retarded ejaculation,

painful ejaculation, and erectile difficulties. The latter could be linked with Peyronie's disease.

Various psychological factors that contribute to sexual dysfunction in both males and females include anxiety, anger, and "spectatoring," and these may result from misunderstandings and ignorance, unsuitable circumstances, bad feelings about oneself, one's partner, or the relationship, as well as poor communication within the relationship. A psychosomatic circle of sex that links cognitions with awareness of response leading on to peripheral arousal and genital response on the one side and activating the limbic system and spinal centers to orgasmic conclusion on the other is often used to describe various etiological points that may contribute to precipitation and perpetuation of sexual anxiety and sexual dysfunction. Thus, a complex set of factors is usually involved.

III. PRINCIPLES OF SEXUAL DYSFUNCTION THERAPY

After assessment of the exact nature of the dysfunction and possible etiological factors, two basic steps mark the early stages of therapy: managing anxiety and education. Quite often, the partners find it difficult to discuss sexual problems with each other or with the therapist, and the underlying lack of sexual education may well contribute to this and to sexual anxiety. Simple reading materials often allow the therapist to discuss problems, offer solutions, and peg the treatment planning. This basic education is often crucial in sex therapy.

Anxiety management is usually carried out in a number of ways—from physical muscle relaxation to yoga training or using tai chi or the Alexander technique. A valuable part of this anxiety management is the process of "despectatoring," which encourages individuals to get away from focusing on the sexual act and instead allowing relaxation in their physical and intimate contact. If the therapist discovers that there are underlying angry or depressive feelings, these may need to be treated medically or with psychological interventions. Bad feelings about sex, oneself, or one's partner need to be aired and discussed at length. If there is any underlying relationship discord, it would need to be assessed and managed. Sometimes this work may need to precede sexual dysfunction therapy. [*See* ANXIETY.]

The principles of managing sexual dysfunction

from a psychological perspective are described in detail below. In the first instance, it is necessary to deal with physical management of sexual dysfunction.

IV. PHYSICAL THERAPIES

There are at least four physical methods—oral medication, intrapenile injections, artificial devices, and surgical procedures. Physical methods are mostly used for treating male patients.

A. Oral Medication

Yohimbine has been shown to be an effective drug in managing erectile difficulties. It works better than placebo and is an α-2 adrenergic receptor blocker. Idazoxan is another selective and specific α-2 adrenoceptor antagonist and works in some cases, although it tends to have more side effects. The heterogeneity in etiology makes the existing clinical trials difficult to interpret.

B. Intracavernosal Injections

Phenoxybenzamine hydrochloride, papaverine hydrochloride, phentolamine mesylate, and prostaglandin-E have been used as intracavernosal injections for erectile difficulties. Phenoxybenzamine usage had led to priapism or painful erections lasting for up to 3 days and has largely fallen into disuse. Papaverine hydrochloride is a smooth muscle relaxant that, when injected intracorporeally, will result in active arterial dilation, corporeal smooth muscle relaxation, and venous outflow restriction—thus producing an erection. It is also less painful to inject, and these injections produce erections that are less painful and last for a few hours generally, at the maximum. A mixture of papaverine and phentolamine has been shown to be superior to papaverine alone.

Such vasoactive substances are also used to diagnose erectile problems, and evaluate indications for surgery of Peyronie's disease. In treatment, they are used for occasional self-injection and for regular self-injection in cases of persistent erectile failure. It has been shown that patients, having obtained erections with injections initially, often go on to have spontaneous erections.

The cases most likely to respond to this form of treatment are: mild cases of arteriogenic etiology, all cases of neurogenic etiology, mild cases of abnormal leakage, and those who have had unsuccessful surgical procedures. Some cases of psychogenic etiology also respond well to it.

The dosage of the drug papaverine should be increased gradually. In the first instance, from 8 to 15mgs should be used and usually this amount is sufficient to produce a slight enlargement of the penis lasting for 15 minutes or so. At subsequent consultations, higher doses may be used until the optimum dose is reached (leading to an erection of good quality (9 out of 10 or better) lasting for perhaps 30 minutes). There is still a lot of variation in individual responses so it is essential that individual doses are determined slowly and carefully. If a mixture of phentolamine and papaverine is used, the first trial dose of papaverine is limited to 15mg. If the response is poor, then a further injection of 0.5 mg phentolamine is given. In subsequent visits, a mixture of 0.5mg phentolamine and 30 mg papaverine is used, going up to a maximum recommended 2 mg phentolamine and 60 mg papaverine. These injections are usually given at the base of the penis at 3 o'clock or 9 o'clock positions (posterolaterally)—away from neurovascular bundle and urethra—using an insulin syringe and a gauge 26 or 27 needle. After cleaning the skin, holding the syringe perpendicular to the penis, the physician on the first occasion, and the patient himself subsequently (or his partner), inserts the needle through the tough tunica albuginea into the left or right corpus cavernosum. As the resistance is overcome and the needle enters the tunica a sensation is experienced at which point the medication is injected. If phentolamine is used first, the injection should be given with the patient lying flat as postural hypotension may occur if there is a leak into the venous system. The patient may then stand and an erection will appear in 10 to 20 minutes. The couple may be taught the technique together, and some patients prefer their partner to do the injecting as part of their foreplay. The patient should be advised not to use injections more than twice a week with a 2-day interval at least. Erectile capability may well return after some months of self-injection treatment. If the injection of papaverine and a combination with phentolamine fails to produce an erection, the possibility of a venous leak must be investigated.

In the United Kingdom in recent years, prostaglandin E has been used in the same way as papaverine and phentolamine but the patient needs to learn to dissolve the powdered compound for injection. The starting dose is 5 to 10 micrograms, with a maximum of from 20 to 40 micrograms. There is some clinical evidence to suggest that this preparation is more effective than papaverine alone and has a lower incidence of priapism or prolonged erections. In some cases, however, the patient may experience pain in the shaft or the glans following the injection.

Cardiovascular problems need to be investigated thoroughly prior to commencing treatment. Severe liver dysfunction, severe substance misuse, allergic reactions, and a history of sexual offending are some of the other contraindications. The most serious side effect is priapism. Other side effects described include painful nodules in the penis, fibrotic nodules, liver damage, pain, infection at the injection site, and bruising. Between 2 and 15% of patients will develop priapism. When this happens, the patient is advised to go to the nearest emergency room to have blood withdrawn from the corpora, and metaraminol (2mgs) or adrenaline (20 micrograms in 0.1 ml) injected at the base of the penis to be repeated half an hour later if indicated. In rare cases, surgical intervention may be indicated.

Using written information sheets and audiovisual aids to inform the patients and their partners, including advice on what to do if priapism occurs, should be encouraged. Written consents are recommended. Ethically, there remain several issues in offering physical treatments where underlying causes may well be psychogenic and the focus of the relationship appears to be on the erection rather than on more general factors. There is no doubt that, in some cases, the quality of the relationship following an improvement in sexual satisfaction due to frequency of intercourse increases intimacy and sexual arousal.

C. Artificial Devices

In 1917 Otto Lederer first patented a vacuum pump that induced erection by creating a vacuum around the penis, and maintained erection by the use of a constriction ring around the base of the penis. The different devices tend to vary according to the use of a pressure-limiting device, the shape of the cylinder, the design of the tension rings, and external versus attached pumps.

The basic mechanism of action is the filling of the corpora cavernosa due to suction and venous stasis, secondary to constriction, which are both passive mechanisms. As the additional volume can only be maintained by the use of the constriction device at the base of the penis, the patient and his partner often find it very difficult to deal with, when compared to papaverine injections. Furthermore, in this method, skin temperature of the penis falls and the erection is often not very strong. The commonest device in use is a rigid tube made of plastic, which is connected to a hand pump at one end and an opening at the other through which the flaccid penis is inserted. Prior to this, the penis and the tube are well lubricated and a rubber constriction band is placed around the open end of the tube. When the pump is used, air is pumped out and the resulting negative pressure draws blood into the corpora, producing an erection. Following this, the constricting rubber band can be slipped off to place it at the base of the penis to limit venous outflow. This band can be left in situ for half an hour. Another appliance—Correctaid—works on the same principle but the condom-shaped device is made of transparent silicon rubber. A tube is passed through at its base to open the inside of the tip of the sheath. The device is worn over the penis. Yet another appliance is the Blakoc suspensory energizer ring, which is rectangular and is made of ebonite, which can be fitted around the base of the penis and under the scrotum. With its small metal plates it can have some stimulatory effect on the erectile mechanism. The success rates using vacuum devices are variable. The side effects include hematoma, pain, ecchymosis, numbness, painful or blocked ejaculation. As in injection therapies, spontaneous erectile activity may return with the use of vacuum devices as increased self-confidence reduces performance anxiety.

D. Surgical Procedures

Surgical revascularization and surgical implants have been tried. Pre-operative counseling, education, and adequate preparation for the surgical procedures and informed consent with some risk/benefit analysis are essential. Originally, arterial bypass was attempted to join the epigastric artery into the side of the corpora cavernosa. Other attempts have included utilizing saphenous vein bypasses from the femoral artery to the corpora, and saphenous vein bypass from the inferior epigastric artery to the corpora cavernosa. The best results are said to be in younger males, although most authorities will agree that the theoretical disadvantages associated with these surgical procedures are genuine. The epigastric artery-dorsal artery revascularization is said to be more advantageous.

The selection of patients for sexual surgery is problematic because of significant areas of disagreement on the indications and the success criteria of various procedures. In spite of surgical intervention, underlying psychological factors often need to be taken into account. Some of these have been identified as poor sexual communication, lack of foreplay, and loss of interest. Preoperative counseling as part of the assessment should help in ruling out some of these problems.

E. Prosthesis

The use of plastic splints for the penis was first described in 1952. Semi-rigid silastic rods result in an almost permanently erect penis which can be bent to different angles. Acceptability of these processes has been improved by using modified appliances. An inflatable penile implant has been used to provide improvements in both girth and rigidity. Such a device works on a fluid-filled system that allows the flaccid and erect penis to appear normal. The choice between semirigid or inflatable devices depends very much on the patient's and his partner's preferences.

The semirigid prosthesis is made of medical grade silicone rubber with a sponge core. The device may be implanted by using perineal approach to insert it in the corporeal bodies. The device is available in lengths of 12 to 22cm, and diameters of 0.9, 1.12, and 1.3 mm. A flexirod prosthesis differs from the above by having a hinged area that enables the phallus to be placed in a dependent position when not being used for intercourse. The diameters here range from 0.9 to 1.2 cm and the length from 7 to 13 cm, and it can be shortened if necessary. Another type of prosthesis (called the "Jonas prosthesis") is used commonly and can be inserted through subcoronal, midshaft, penoscrotal, and suprapubic approaches, as well as through the perineal approach. In addition, it has 3 diameters of 9.5, 11.0, and 13.0 mm, and lengths of 16 to 24 cm. It is malleable and thus the penis can maintain a dependent position as well as an upright one. Variable versions of this prosthesis are now available. A newer prosthesis on the market is made of fabric-wrapped stainless steel that has flexibility of size and positioning.

F. Inflatable Prosthesis

As mentioned above, the inflatable prosthesis in its initial model consisted of an inflate pump, a deflate pump, a reservoir, and paired inflatable penile cylinders. However, the inflate and deflate pumps have been combined into one mechanism, and the original six segments of silicone rubber tubing have been reduced to three. The inflatable prosthesis has the advantage of being cosmetically appealing, it conforms to the patient's own corporal anatomy, and the erosion of the prosthesis through the glans is unlikely. Its side effects include aneurysm formation, high mechanical failure rate, kinking of the tubes, infection, puminosis, and scrotal hematoma. The age of the patient, coexisting medical problems, patient preference, and the risk of complications are some of the factors that need to be taken into account when a decision is being considered.

V. PSYCHOLOGICAL THERAPIES

There is a great deal of literature on the psychological approaches to the treatment of sexual dysfunction. Many authorities consider psychological therapy as the treatment of choice when help is sought for sexual dysfunction, although obviously there are instances where a physical approach might be more appropriate.

Psychological therapies take different forms. Psychodynamic therapy aims to understand the presenting problem as a manifestation of an underlying, unconscious conflict or memory, and it is often assumed that this has its origins in childhood. The therapy takes the form of a verbal, interactive endeavor, which also uses the transference (emotional responses of the patient to the therapist) as a means of resolving problems. Psychodynamic therapy for sexual dysfunction has not been adequately evaluated. There is a practical problem, too, in that such therapy is quite time consuming. However, there are circumstances when such an approach may be appropriate. [See PSYCHO-ANALYSIS.]

The more widely used psychological therapies for sexual dysfunction are best described as behavioral, although in recent years cognitive approaches have also been added.

In the behavioral approach, the treatment is directed toward the sexual problem itself. An important element of this is the reduction of anxiety, as in most cases anxiety acts as a factor that perpetuates the dysfunction. The more one fails in sex, the more anxious one gets. One tends to become a "spectator" of one's own performance, thus inhibiting spontaneous sexual responses and sexual enjoyment. Hence, in therapy the reduction of anxiety becomes a major priority. Early behavior therapists like Joseph Wolpe used this approach in the treatment of sexual problems. He used a method that he called "systematic desensitization," in which the sexual problem was dealt with in graded, nonthreatening stages. As a first step, the couple were asked to refrain from intercourse, but to engage in other intimate behaviors, mainly touching and caressing, in a gentle, step-by-step way. In this fashion, anxiety could be overcome gradually, and full sexual functioning restored. This basic behavioral approach was followed by a more formal, essentially behavioral, treatment package developed by William Masters and Virginia Johnson—universally known as the "Masters and Johnson approach." In this, after the assessment, the couple are asked to agree to a ban on intercourse, and they are then given detailed instructions in graded sexual exercises. The first stage is touching and caressing, excluding the genital area and the woman's breasts; this is called "nongenital sensate focus." After some practice sessions of this, which the couple carry out at home, they move on to the "genital sensate focus" stage, where the genitals and the breasts are not excluded. In these stages, the couple are also encouraged to engage in enhanced communication, both verbal and nonverbal. After the second stage, specific additional behavioral strategies are used, to deal with whichever specific problems the couple have presented with. Examples are the "squeeze" technique for premature ejaculation, "overstimulation" for retarded ejaculation, and the use of graded dilators in the treatment vaginismus. In erectile difficulties, a "teasing" approach may be used, enabling the male to learn to defocus on the erection and to relinquish control. [*See* BEHAVIOR THERAPY.]

The principles of the Masters and Johnson approach can also be used with patients who do not have partners, with certain modifications. In the early stages, they are usually asked to engage in "self-focusing."

Relaxation strategies are often taught to the patients in both couple and individual therapy as an additional technique for reducing anxiety and tension. This is usually done at an early stage.

This basic behavioral approach is often augmented by cognitive interventions. This involves identifying those cognitions that the patient may have that are faulty or dysfunctional. Such dysfunctional cognitions (thoughts, beliefs, attitudes) are often major factors in the etiology and more commonly of the perpetuation of sexual dysfunctions. They include cognition like "I am sure to fail again," "If I do not get an erection, my partner will ridicule me," and "It is going to be painful again." The therapist elicits such cognitions from the patient as part of the assessment, and then works on modifying these, using techniques of cognitive therapy (such as creating situations where they are shown to be false, and pointing out their self-fulfilling nature). [*See* COGNITIVE THERAPY.]

In the practice of psychological therapy, behavioral and cognitive elements are often used in conjunction; hence the term "cognitive-behavior therapy," which many therapists these days use to describe what they do. Cognitive techniques are particularly applicable for those without partners, who tend to avoid developing relationships because of fear of repeated failure.

In recent years, this basic psychological approach has been extended to include a systemic dimension. The sexual dysfunction is viewed in the context of the overall relationship of the couple. Relationship factors such as jealousy, resentment, and dominance often contribute to sexual problems, and the therapist takes these into account and intervenes appropriately. These systemic interventions can be, and often are, undertaken within the context of an overall behavioral framework. There is evidence that this expanded approach is rapidly gaining popularity among therapists who specialize in the psychological treatment of sexual dysfunction.

Group approaches are also used in this field. Therapists sometimes run groups for patients without partners, or even see couples in groups. In these, much cognitive work is done in the group setting, and in addition behavioral exercises are discussed and outlined, which the patients would implement as homework. Sometimes, those in group therapy are given brief individual or couple sessions with the therapist as an additional measure.

The original Masters and Johnson approach always used a team of two therapists, one male and one female, with every couple. In the practice of sexual dysfunction therapy today, this is the exception rather than the rule. In most instances, one therapist sees the couple, or the individual who has no partner, for regular sessions.

It was noted above that a psychodynamic approach is useful in certain circumstances. There are instances where the behaviorally based treatment may lead to some improvement, but progress reaches a plateau. It is considered useful, in these circumstances, to explore intrapsychic factors that may be relevant to the problem. Such exploration is usually undertaken within a psychodynamic framework. Early memories, conflicts, and so on, that may have contributed to the problem, and/or unacknowledged current psychological factors, are explored and, where possible, resolved.

VI. ETHICAL ISSUES

If the couple perceives the male erectile dysfunction as the only problem and the focus is on obtaining erections without looking at underlying problems, ethical dilemmas are raised for the therapist. Equally, if a child molester presents for therapy for sexual dysfunction, there is a clear and serious dilemma for the therapist. It is possible that under these circumstances the patient may not divulge his complete history. The forensic aspects of the underlying problems will need to be taken into account as part of the assessment. When couples are about to break up and the underlying sexual dysfunction tends to take on a greater importance, the couple's energies may be focused on the sexual problem rather than on the relationship itself. Often the patients, their partners, and some therapists may see psychological treatments as time consuming and prolonged, painful experiences, whereas physical treatments may be more appealing. Physical treatments should be offered only after a thorough investigation of the dysfunction, and treatment should not be employed simply to fulfill the patient's or their partner's unrealistic dreams of the "ever-ready potent man."

VII. PROGNOSIS

Prognosis of sexual dysfunction varies according to the type of dysfunction. The literature on sex therapy indicates that prognosis in general depends on a number of factors. One is the motivation of the patient/couple. A good overall relationship is also associated with a good outcome. Concurrent psychiatric disorder is a hindrance to good progress. While the different disorders have varying degrees of success, the prognosis for vaginismus is probably the most positive. In female orgasmic dysfunction, it appears that younger patients do better in treatment.

VIII. SPECIAL GROUPS

A. Gay, Lesbian, and Bisexual Adults

These three groups present with the same varieties of sexual dysfunction discussed above, and the treatment plans, whether physical or psychological, are about the same. However, there are some additional factors that need to be taken into account. The first of these is the fact that, even though a gay or lesbian individual is seeking help, this does not necessarily mean that they are publicly "out" and that everyone knows of their sexual orientation. A second factor is the common use of high-tech sex toys, pornography, and in men, "fist-fucking," sadomasochistic practices, and water sports (urination). Lesbians, on the other hand, may well have feminist views and may have political views on sexual intercourse that may appear to be at odds with those of the therapist. Furthermore, views on pornography, sexual exploitation, and the existence of a patriarchal society may well contribute to models of behavior and expectations of treatment at variance with those of heterosexual women.

Some additional issues in working with these three groups include problems of society's widely held homophobic views and practices, the individual's internalized homophobia, and difficulties inherent in same-sex relationships. On the other hand, same-sex couples have the advantage of not being bound by opposite sexual role expectations, for example, the male must always initiate, and the female must be submissive. Gay men and lesbians tend to have a more varied sexual repertoire, and penetration is not the main focus of the sexual activity. The relationships may be open and nonmonogamous. The therapist's views on nonmonogamy and knowledge of the gay subculture may prove to be of great relevance for the success of therapy. The therapist must inquire closely about the development of sexual identity, detecting discrepancies in sexual orientation in the two partners, identifying the problem areas in the relationship and then setting up appropriate intervention procedures. [See HOMOSEXUALITY.]

Bisexual individuals may feel unable to bring either

partner, and their problems may be with one gender or the other. The nonheterosexual orientation must be seen as equal but different, and the clinician must be familiar with group subcultures. Sexuality carries different meanings for gay men and lesbians and bisexual individuals, and these need to be ascertained and the emphasis on nonpenetrative pleasure encouraged.

B. Older Adults

Both therapists and patients need to question their assumptions about aging adults. There is some truth in the observation that desire for sexual intercourse falls off with age. However, ageist views on the clinician's part do not help the process of therapy. Older adults may change their practices and become more interested in nonpenetrative sexual activity. In addition, the loss of a partner may be more likely and newer relationships may have the additional burden of opprobrium by the extended families. Female and male sexual responses change with aging, usually due to hormonal changes. Whereas a young male may achieve a full erection in a matter of seconds, an older man may require several minutes to achieve the same response. He may also require a lot of physical stimulation to achieve an erection. Seminal fluid may be decreased. In addition, physical debility may contribute to lowered sexual interest and physical functioning. Drugs prescribed for physical conditions may also lead to impaired sexual functioning. Various psychological factors affecting sexuality in the elderly include lack of partners, lack of interest, and social stigma regarding older individuals "indulging" in sex. The therapist needs to be aware of the three fundamental areas of biological changes, attitudinal factors, and the role of life events. Pain, dryness, hot flushes, and physical mobility problems, especially those due to medical conditions like arthritis, are common and the therapist needs to deal with these. In this age group greater care must be taken to exclude physical causes of dysfunction. Psychological and physical therapies can be used in the same way as in younger adults, bearing in mind the essential factors specific to the older adult as highlighted above.

C. Ethnic Minorities

Various ethnic minorities have different cultural values placed on sex and sexual intercourse. As men-

tioned earlier, if the culture sees sexual intercourse as procreative and not for pleasure, the presenting complaint may be an inability to conceive rather than lack of pleasure. In cultures where semen is considered highly important and valuable, the individual may well have difficulties with suggestions of masturbation, sensate focus activity, and so on, as recommended by the therapist. In some cultures, various sexual taboos may well contribute to the anxiety that the couples experience. Under these circumstances, it would be useful to include this as part of the assessment and to ensure that appropriate therapeutic measures are taken. In some communities, the underlying causation of sexual dysfunction is generally seen as physical rather than psychological, and the patients and their partners may refuse to consider psychological intervention and demand physical treatments only. Under such circumstances, the therapist needs to be innovative in planning and delivering a combination of treatments. Using yohimbine or other physical agents in combination with a psychological approach can be fruitful. The therapist needs to be aware of the cultural nuances and social mores as well as cultural expectations in order to deal with sexual dysfunction problems satisfactorily. [See ETHNICITY AND MENTAL HEALTH.]

D. Those with Disability/Chronic Physical Illness

Not only do certain chronic physical illnesses such as autonomic neuropathy, damage to nerves, and neurotoxic chemotherapies produce problems with sexual functioning, many drugs that are used for these conditions also contribute to sexual dysfunction. Cardiovascular disease, cancer, arthritis, and so on, increase with aging, and chronic pain may further contribute to low sexual interest and orgasmic dysfunction. A thorough physical assessment must be an integral part of the assessment of sexual functioning. A number of patients may simply be seeking reassurance, education, or permission to carry on with their sexual activity, and a significant proportion may benefit from very simple and focused counseling or intervention. However, in some cases more prolonged therapy may be needed. In a majority of cases, education to change attitudes is a crucial part of therapy. Such an attitude change can be fostered by using a mixture of written and/or audiovisual materials and cognitive methods to combat false beliefs and to deal with inappropriate and handicapping worries. Overcoming physical handicaps along with working on relationship problems may mean that the goals of sex therapy need to be changed and appropriate interventions put in place. Physical treatments need to be combined with sex therapy. The goals of treatment may be limited by the physiological impact of the disease or disability. However, enhancing sexual functioning and enjoyment is generally achievable.

E. HIV/AIDS

The AIDS epidemic has contributed to a change in patterns of sexual activity not only in gay and bisexual communities, but to some degree in the heterosexual community as well. AIDS has also affected how people view their sexuality. In clinics, HIV-positive patients not infrequently present with sexual dysfunction. When dealing with such patients the therapist needs to establish their views on the illness, their knowledge about the illness as well as sexual dysfunction, and their attitudes toward therapy. There is no doubt that HIV-positive individuals can be helped using similar models of therapeutic intervention as those used with others, even though some therapists may find recommending physical interventions like penile prosthesis difficult. A thorough clinical assessment will allow the therapist to deal with some of these difficulties. [*See* HIV/AIDS.]

F. Paraphiliacs

Those with paraphilias, or variant sexual desires and practices, sometimes present with sexual dysfunction. Paraphiliacs seeking treatment in this way are almost always male, reflecting the vast preponderance of males over females among paraphiliacs. In their presentation, they often complain of difficulties in nonparaphiliac sexual relationships. For example, a man with a strong shoe fetish might seek help for an inability to obtain or maintain an erection in sex without contact with a woman's shoe. These patients need to be assessed carefully, and individually tailored treatment needs to be considered. The aim should be, as far as possible, to incorporate the paraphilia in a limited, controlled way into the person's sexual repertoire. Needless to say, criminal paraphilias such a pedophilia or zoophilia, or any paraphilia that the patient's

partner finds intolerable, can not be considered for such incorporation. In such cases, help should be directed toward the control of the person's paraphiliac urges. Various psychological techniques are available for the control of paraphiliac desires and behaviors—for example, orgasmic reconditioning and covert sensitization. At the same time, help should also be given to reduce any anxiety about nonparaphiliac sex, and to build up skills and competencies needed for such activity. In other words, a multifaceted treatment program is often required.

It is also important to note that little can be achieved in the treatment of paraphiliacs unless the patient has motivation and is cooperative.

IX. CONCLUSIONS

Sexual dysfunction therapy is widely practiced today, and many mental health professionals offer this service. Recent years have witnessed several major developments: new physical treatments for males, the use of cognitive therapy principles where needed, the combination of cognitive-behavioral treatment with a systemic approach, and the recognition of cultural differences. The demand for sexual dysfunction therapy is high, and more training is needed in this area within the mental health professions. Where competently used, on the basis of careful assessment, the therapy helps many patients and couples make significant improvements. Needless to say, further research is needed into the treatment techniques as well as into the dysfunctions themselves. One can expect further major progress in several areas in the next few decades.

BIBLIOGRAPHY

Bancroft, J. (1989). *Human sexuality and its problems* (2d ed.). Edinburgh: Churchill Livingstone.

Hawton, K. (1992). Sex therapy: For whom is it likely to be effective? In: K. Hawton & P. Cowen (Eds.), *Practical problems in clinical psychiatry*. Oxford: Oxford University Press.

Kaplan, H. S. (1995). *The sexual desire disorders: Dysfunctional regulation of sexual motivation*. New York: Brunner/Mazel.

Rosen, R. C., & Leiblum, S. R. (1992). *Erectile disorders: Assessment and treatment*. New York: Guilford Press.

Wince, J. P., & Carey, M. P. (1991). *Sexual dysfunction: A guide for assessment and treatment*. New York: Guilford Press.

Shyness

Lynne Henderson

The Shyness Institute

Philip Zimbardo

Stanford University

Attribution Style How people assign causality for behavior and events.

Avoidant Personality Disorder Chronic and long-standing fear of negative evaluation and the tendency to avoid interpersonal situations without a guarantee of acceptance and support, accompanied by significant fears of embarrassment and shame in social interaction.

Extroversion A personal preference for socially engaging activities and settings.

Introversion A personal preference for solitary, nonsocial activities and settings.

Self-Complexity Holding many different views of the self rather than a narrow conception.

Shy Extrovert A person who performs well socially, but experiences painful thoughts and feelings.

Social Fitness Desired general state of wellness in which the degree of social participation is determined by personal preference rather than by discomfort and fears of negative evaluation. Social fitness assumes a proactive orientation, adaptive functioning, so-cial empathy, and responsivity to people and social stimuli.

Social Fitness Model Education and training in adaptive social behavior, thinking patterns, and emotional states.

Social Phobia A DSM-IV diagnostic category defined as persistent avoidance and/or discomfort in social situations that significantly interferes with functioning.

SHYNESS may be defined experientially as discomfort or inhibition in interpersonal situations that interferes with pursuing one's interpersonal or professional goals. It is a form of excessive self-focus, a preoccupation with one's thoughts, feelings and physical reactions. It may vary from mild social awkwardness to totally inhibiting social phobia. Shyness may be chronic and dispositional, serving as a personality trait that is central in one's self-definition. Situational shyness is to experience the symptoms of shyness in specific social performance situations but not to incorporate it into one's self-concept. Shyness reactions can occur at any or all of the following levels: cognitive, affective, physiological, and behavioral (see Table I). It can be triggered by a wide variety of arousal cues. Among the most typical of these are authority figures, one-on-one opposite sex interactions, intimacy, strangers, having to take individuating action in a group setting, and initiating social actions in unstructured, spontaneous behavioral settings. Metaphorically, shyness is a shrinking back from life that weakens the bonds of human connection.

Table I Symptoms of Shyness

Behavioral	Physiological	Cognitive	Affective
Inhibition and passivity	Accelerated heart rate	Negative thoughts about the self, the situation, and others	Embarrassment and painful self-consciousness
Gaze aversion	Dry mouth	Fear of negative evaluation and looking foolish to others	Shame
Avoidance of feared situations	Trembling or shaking	Worry and rumination, perfectionism	Low self-esteem
Low speaking voice	Sweating	Self-blaming attributions, particularly *after* social interactions	Dejection and sadness
Little body movement or expression or excessive nodding or smiling	Feeling faint or dizzy, butterflies in stomach or nausea	Negative beliefs about the self (weak) and others (powerful), often out of awareness	Loneliness
Speech dysfluencies	Experiencing the situation or oneself as unreal or removed	Negative biases in the self-concept, e.g., "I am socially inadequate, unlovable, unattractive."	Depression
Nervous behaviors, such as touching one's hair or face	Fear of losing control, going crazy, or having a heart attack	A belief that there is a "correct" protocol that the shy person must guess, rather than mutual definitions of social situations	Anxiety

I. PREVALENCE AND DIAGNOSIS

The percentage of adults in the United States reporting that they are chronically shy, such that it presents a problem in their lives, had been reported at 40%, plus or minus 3%, since the early 1970s. Recent research indicates that the percentage of self-reported shyness has escalated gradually in the last decade to nearly 50% (48.7 ± 2%). The National Co-Morbidity Survey in 1994 revealed a lifetime prevalence of social phobia of 13.3%, making it the third most prevalent psychiatric disorder. The two disparate results suggest that the proportion of the population suffering from chronic, even debilitating shyness is not reflected in the numbers of people who visit anxiety disorder clinics. Most referrals to shyness clinics meet criteria for generalized social phobia, and many meet criteria for avoidant personality disorder. Although it has been suggested that there is a greater heterogeneity of presentation among shy people than among those diagnosable with generalized social phobia, both shys and those with generalized social phobias demonstrate similar difficulties with meeting people, initiating and maintaining conversations, deepening in-

timacy, interacting in small groups and in authority situations, and with self-assertion. Other frequent co-morbid diagnoses are dysthymia, alcohol or substance abuse, generalized anxiety disorder, specific phobias, dependent personality disorder, and schizoid personality disorder. Obsessive–compulsive personality and paranoid personality are also seen. Chronically shy individuals frequently have obsessive and/or paranoid tendencies.

Research has distinguished shyness from introversion, although they are typically related. Introverts simply prefer solitary to social activities, but they do not fear social encounters as do the shy, whereas extroverts prefer social to solitary activities. Although the majority of shy persons are introverted, shy extroverts are found in many behavioral settings. They are privately shy and publicly outgoing. They have the requisite social skills and can carry them out flawlessly in highly structured, scripted situations where everyone is playing prescribed roles and there is little room for spontaneity. However, their basic anxieties about being found personally unacceptable if anyone discovered their "real self" emerge in intimate encounters or in other situations where control must be shared or is irrelevant, or wherever the situation is ambiguous in terms of social demands and expectations. [See PERSONALITY.]

II. RESEARCH SUMMARY: EXPERIMENTAL AND NATURALISTIC

Before 1970, virtually all research on shyness was focused exclusively on children, especially adolescents, studied by developmental psychologists usually relying on reports of teachers and parents. However, that changed in the early 1970s with research instituted by the Stanford Shyness Research Program, headed by Philip Zimbardo. Zimbardo's interest in shyness in adults stemmed from observations made in a mock prison study he and his colleagues conducted in 1971. Preselected normal, healthy college student participants played the randomly assigned roles of prisoners and guards within a simulated prison environment. The scheduled 2-week study had to be terminated after only 6 days because of the pathology that became evident in the "breakdowns" of those playing the prisoner role in response to the sadistic use of power by the student- guards. Many of the prisoners adapted to a shocking degree to the coercive and arbitrary tactics of behavior control imposed arbitrarily by the guards. They seemed to need desperately the approval and acceptance of their guards, from whom approval was rarely given, and ended up trading autonomy for the role of "good prisoner," internalizing negative images of themselves in the process. The guard mentality is designed around ways to limit prisoners' freedom of action, thought, and association in order to manage more easily prisoner behavior, individually and collectively. The prisoners, in this dynamic dyadic interaction, are cast in a reactive mold either to rebel and get punished for their heroism or to conform to the coercive rules and—although "good prisoners"—come to despise themselves for surrendering their freedom and to be despised by their guards as weak and ineffectual. Similarities became evident between the mentality of the guard/prisoner roles and the thinking of shy people who incorporate both of these roles. The guard-self imposes the coercive control rules that the prisoner-self ultimately accepts; together, they thereby limit the shy person's freedoms. Expecting others to act like powerful and harsh critics who ultimately reject any contribution or action of theirs leads shy

people to develop coping strategies of minimal involvement in social life and avoidance of situations that carry potential risk of rejection. This prisoner–guard metaphor led to conceptualizing shyness as a self-imposed prison of silence and solitary confinement.

When a literature search of shyness in adults failed to find any substantial research, Zimbardo and his students conducted a large-scale survey, first with open-ended questions and then with a self-report checklist that was administered to more than a thousand people in the United States and in many other countries. In addition to survey research, the Zimbardo research team conducted hundreds of in-depth interviews, numerous case studies, experimental–behavioral research, and cross-cultural research on shyness for more than 20 years, culminating in the creation of a treatment program for shy adults.

In addition to the 40% of respondents who reported being chronically shy, another 40% indicated that they used to consider themselves as shy but do so no longer, 15% reported being shy in some situations, and only about 5% believed they were never shy. The reported 40% statistic has increased by about 10% in a recent partial replication of Zimbardo's work by Bernard Carducci at Indiana University Southeast, where 1642 students were surveyed between 1979 and 1991. Strangers, authorities, and persons of the opposite sex in both group and one-to-one interactions continue to comprise the most difficult situations.

Since Zimbardo's pioneering efforts, shyness has been studied primarily in university student populations by personality theorists and social psychologists interested in the subjective experiences of shy people, links between shyness and self processes, behavioral responses to shyness-arousing stimuli, and the consequences of shyness.

A. The Consequences of Shyness

The consequences of shyness are deeply troubling. People for whom shyness is an ongoing problem do not take advantage of social situations, date less, are less expressive verbally and nonverbally, and show less interest in other people than non-shys. Shy students, particularly if they are interacting with a socially confident person, anxiously focus on themselves rather than on the other person or on the conversation. Shy individuals are frequently painfully self-conscious and report more negative thoughts about themselves and others in social interactions, seeing themselves as inhibited, awkward, unfriendly, and incompetent, particularly with people to whom they are sexually attracted. They also see themselves as less physically attractive, although research indicates that shyness is uncorrelated with observers' ratings of attractiveness. Ten to 20% of shy individuals may also lack basic social skills. This may mean not knowing what to say or do (content), how to do (style), and when best to respond (timing). Objective ratings have shown that some shy individuals talk less, initiate fewer topics of conversation, avert their gazes more often, touch themselves nervously, and show fewer facial expressions. They agree more often than not, however, with non-shys about what constitutes appropriate social behavior. Their lowered likelihood of enacting social behaviors appears to be related to their lowered confidence in their ability to carry out the required behaviors and to their lack of self-efficacy beliefs.

Research has been limited by the dearth of naturalistic studies, and recent studies of both adults and children have shown greater variability and specificity in behaviors related to shyness. For example, in initial, unstructured heterosexual interactions, shy men exerted avoidant control over mutual gazes by denying female partners opportunities to initiate and terminate them. That is, they looked away when women met their gazes and terminated their own gazes quickly, which promoted negative reactions in interaction partners. Women's shyness also limited the frequency of gazing behavior, but, in contrast to men, their shyness did not seem to induce negative reactions in interaction partners or to inhibit their verbal interaction. This suggests that the cultural burden of shyness may rest more on men, who are expected to take the initiative in heterosexual encounters. Studies where shy women have had a negative impact on an interaction partner involved same-sex dyads, and for many women, shyness may be more of an issue with same-sex peers.

Although shy individuals are perceived as less friendly and assertive than others, they are not usually viewed as negatively as they fear. Shy people remember negative feedback more than do less socially anxious people, and they remember negative self-descriptions better than positive self-descriptions. They overestimate the likelihood of unpleasantness in social interaction and are exquisitely sensitive to potential nega-

tive reactions in others, dealing with perceived threat by rumination and worry. In fact, cognitive distraction has been shown to interfere more than anxiety with social interaction, particularly in sexual encounters, in the form of lowered pleasurable arousal, with social phobics reporting more sexual dysfunction than controls in the form of erectile difficulty and orgasmic inhibition. Shy individuals underestimate their own ability to cope with social situations and are pessimistic about social situations in general, failing to expect favorable responses even when they believe that they are able to perform appropriately and efficaciously. Shyness thus becomes a self-handicapping strategy—a reason or excuse for anticipated social failure that over time becomes a crutch, "I can't do it because I am shy." Shy men have been found to marry and have children later than their peers, to have less stable marriages when they do marry, to delay establishing careers, and to achieve less, although shyness and grade-point average is uncorrelated in both men and women. Shy college students are less likely to use resources for information and guidance in career planning and more likely to experience loneliness. They are more likely to forget information presented to them when they believe that they are being evaluated, but not when they think they are evaluating the speaker. Shy students do not expect to engage in assertive behaviors in job interviews, and shy male students do not think assertive behaviors will receive a favorable response by potential employers. Shy extroverts perform well socially, but experience painful thoughts and feelings. Shy people have been found to use alcohol in an effort to relax socially, which may lead to abuse and to impaired social performance, although there is some evidence that suggests that socially phobic individuals drink more frequently, but consume less than others. In any case, suppression of the fear response by alcohol reinforces the avoidance of emotional experience and prevents desensitization.

Two of the more profound, although less obvious, negative consequences of shyness include (a) greater health problems from lack of a social support network, so essential for health maintenance, and failure to disclose personal or sensitive problems fully to medical and psychological caregivers; and (b) making less money in less suitable jobs because of less frequent requests for raises, lower visibility on the job, interview-setting difficulties, and limits on job advancement that require greater verbal fluency and leadership skills. If shyness becomes chronic and continues into the later years of life, chronic social isolation leads to increasingly severe loneliness and related psychopathology, and even to chronic illness and a shorter life span. [*See* LONELINESS; SOCIAL SUPPORT.]

Comparisons between laboratory and naturalistic research lead to caution about overgeneralizing the findings regarding the patterns of behavior of shy people from the laboratory to natural field settings. A recent naturalistic study with children who were continuously monitored in everyday situations, and who were free to move about, revealed that shyness was unrelated to heart rate reactivity in unfamiliar situations, which was in contrast to findings from laboratory situations. Yet another study demonstrated that lower social self-esteem was not characteristic of chronically high shyness with strangers during preschool or early elementary school, also in contrast to findings by researchers studying adolescent and adult shyness. A major review of the literature regarding peer relations and later adjustment, published in 1987, reflected inadequate findings that demonstrated that shyness was predictive of later maladjustment. The authors further cautioned against generalization from abstract conceptualizations of adult shyness to children, maintaining that conclusions drawn from these sources were premature. The best summary of conceptualizations, research, and treatment perspectives on shyness can be found in a 1986 edited volume of 26 chapters by Jones, Cheek, and Briggs. [*See* REACTIVITY; SELF-ESTEEM.]

III. SHYNESS AND CHILDREN: INTERACTION OF GENETICS AND ENVIRONMENT

The research literature supports an interactionist interpretation of the origins of shyness: strong genetic predispositions in some newborns and strong experiential factors operating in some adolescents and adults to create shyness. Being born timid, easily aroused, and not responsive to social engagement overtures leads to less frequent social interactions with parents, siblings, family, and friends, thus promoting a shy response style. Although many children who are shy overcome it in time, many others remain shy all of their lives. However, research also shows that some people have become shy in adulthood who were not so previously, usually from experiences of rejection, conditions that lower self-esteem, and fears of failure in social domains.

Research with infants conducted by Jerome Kagan, Nancy Snidman, and their colleagues at Harvard University has shown that physiological differences between sociable and shy babies show up as early as 2 months. Approximately 15 to 20% of newborns may be quiet, vigilant, and restrained in new situations. Stimuli such as moving mobiles and tape recordings of human voices trigger an easily arousable sympathetic nervous system which manifests itself in an increased heart rate, jerky and vigorous movements of arms and legs, excessive crying, and urgent signals of distress. High heart rates have been detected in utero in neonates later defined operationally as timid or shy. At 4 years, another sign of sympathetic arousal is shown, a cooler temperature in the right ring finger than in the left in response to emotionally evocative stimuli. Timid children also show more brain wave activity in the right frontal lobe in contrast to normally reactive children who display more left-side activity. Other research has shown that the right side of the brain is involved in anxiety.

At the opposite end of the continuum are another 15 to 20%, bold newborn children who are sociable and spontaneous regardless of the novelty of the situation. The rest of newborns fall between these extremes of timidity and boldness. Longitudinal studies into the eighth year suggest that 75% of shy children and the same percentage of sociable children may maintain their behavioral styles. Furthermore, many shy adolescents up to the age of 14 were previously identified as "inhibited" when they were toddlers. Evidence that these biological components of shyness are a manifestation of a genetic predisposition is found in parents and grandparents of inhibited infants who report childhood shyness more often than relatives of uninhibited children. Furthermore, inhibited infants are more often born in September or October, a time in which the body is producing more melatonin, a neurally active hormone which may be transmitted to the fetus. Other biological correlates are blue eye color with blond hair and pale skin, and allergies, especially hay fever, which have been reported more frequently in families of inhibited children and in the most introverted and fearful of a sample of college undergraduates.

When continuities in shy children were traced into adulthood using archival data, adult males were described as lacking poise, aloof, withdrawing when frustrated, disliking demands, and reluctant to take action, but adult females in midlife evidenced no particular problems, following more conventional patterns of marriage and homemaking than their nonshy counterparts. These results were discussed in terms of cultural fit, that is, shy women were seen as more dispositionally suited to traditional roles than shy men.

Parallel evidence for a substantial genetic contribution to behavioral inhibition in animals has been found in puppies, rhesus monkeys, cats, and rats. In addition, behaviorally inhibited animals are more likely to be submissive, acquiescent, and more timid in their heterosexual interactions, patterns that are common in shyness and in social phobia in humans. Based on conditioning and ethological models of social phobia, the hypothesis has been advanced that a second-order general factor taps a common predispositional core that is a risk factor for the development of all of the anxiety disorders, although other explanations are plausible. Evidence is cited in studies that demonstrate that introverts learn to inhibit responses to avoid punishment more quickly than extroverts. Introversion, negative affectivity, and constraint have all been hypothesized to relate to behavioral inhibition and to an ease of acquisition of aversive associations and avoidance responses. Therefore, traumatic experiences or vicarious conditioning may lead to higher levels of fear and avoidance in inhibited children and adults.

It is notable, however, that the physiological or genetic predisposition to inhibition does not develop into shyness 25% of the time. A reactive temperament may need to be aggravated by environmental triggers, such as inconsistent or unreliable parenting, insecurity of attachment in the form of difficult relationships with parents, family conflict or chaos, frequent criticism, a dominating older sibling, or a stressful school environment. Empirical evidence of familial factors has been found in retrospective studies of the childhoods of social phobics relative to those of normal controls; these include criticism for not overcoming fears or embarrassing the family, fewer parental friendships, fewer family social activities, and teaching social skills by correction rather than by modeling. In addition, shyness was negatively correlated with perceived maternal acceptance, but positively correlated with maternal psychological control in shy female college students. Furthermore, many children overcome shyness themselves, some through altruism, others through an association with younger children that promotes leadership behaviors, and still others through contact with sociable peers. Nothing succeeds in overcoming shyness like experiencing social successes, if the child or adult takes the initial risk of engaging in some social activity. Shyness correlates with empathic concern on measures of empathy, and youngsters' emotional responsiveness may promote compassion for others. Parents who are supportive of a child's temperament, but not overprotective, appear to facilitate overcoming an initial inhibition in new and developmentally challenging situations. Overprotected children, however, are more at risk for anxious self-preoccupation, which interferes with taking others' perspectives, another aspect of empathy that becomes increasingly important as children become adults.

IV. BIOLOGY OF SHYNESS

The biological foundation of the social fear/anxiety component of shyness is found in the action of the amygdala and hippocampus. The amygdala appears to be implicated in the association of specific stimuli with fear. The more general, pervasive conditioning of background factors related to the conditioning stimuli is known as contextual conditioning. This diffuse contextual conditioning occurs more slowly and lasts longer than most traditional classical conditioning (pairing a conditioned stimulus to an unconditioned stimulus). It is experienced as anxiety and general apprehension in situations that become associated with fear cues, such as classrooms and parties, for shy people. Contextual conditioning involves the hippocampus, crucial in spatial learning and memory, as well as the amygdala. The bed nucleus of the striate terminalis (BNST) also functions in emotional–behavioral arousal and extends to the hypothalamus and the brain stem. Both the hypothalamus and the brain stem relay anxiety to the rest of the body. The hypothalamus triggers the sympathetic nervous system and the physiological symptoms of shyness, among them, trembling, increased heart rate, and muscle tension.

V. ATTRIBUTION STYLE, AFFECT, AND SHAME-BASED SELF-CONCEPT

Our research with community college students, as well as our clinic population, has shown that fearful and privately self-aware people blame themselves and experience shame in social situations that have perceived negative outcomes. This tendency appears to be exacerbated by private self-awareness. Shy individuals are higher than controls in state shame in social situations with negative outcomes and in trait shame. Shame may be experienced internally or expressed verbally. The results are consistent with previous research suggesting that shy people reverse what is known in social psychology as the "self-enhancement bias." Ordinarily, people tend to take credit for success and to externalize failure, or at least attribute it to unstable, specific, and controllable factors. This attribution style protects self-esteem and promotes continuing efforts toward interpersonal and professional goals. In contrast, self-reported shy individuals reverse this bias in social situations by blaming themselves for failure while also externalizing success. Furthermore, when they fail they often see the failure in stable, global, or uncontrollable terms. This attribution style engenders state shame, a painful affective state that interferes with both cognition and behavior. Many shy individuals report self-abusive cognitions and "freezing" in social encounters, which lowers self-esteem and interferes with motivation and proactivity, frequently leading to an avoidant and passive interaction style. Those who engage in self-blaming attributions are also higher in trait shame. Although self-blame among the shy is often confined to specific types of social situations, over a lifetime of shyness, this self-blame can become an insidious part of the mechanism that leads to loneliness, isolation, and depression. In chronic depression this reversal of the self-enhancement bias becomes much more pervasive, generalizing to virtually all areas of life.

In a recent sample of unselected high school students, half acknowledged self-blaming tendencies, and those who did so were significantly higher in social anxiety, fear of negative evaluation, and social avoidance and distress. Private self-awareness was associated with these self-blaming tendencies. The sample was notable in that it consisted of students who were well above average in mental ability and had striking advantages in terms of academic and social opportunity. In another similar sample of shy adolescents, shyness, self-blame, and private self-consciousness were significant predictors of social anxiety. Self-blame and private self-consciousness were significant predictors of fear of negative evaluation, whereas shyness and self-blame were significant predictors of social avoidance and distress. Self-blame was the common con-

tributor to all three indicators of distress. Furthermore, correlations of self-blame with social anxiety, fear of negative evaluation, and social avoidance and distress were .47, .56, and .40, respectively. In all three cases, however, the willingness to make a second effort was a significant negative predictor, and a belief in control of the impression one was making on another was a significant negative predictor of social anxiety. Furthermore, a nonblaming attribution style was negatively correlated ($-.38$) with shyness. The belief in the control of one's behavior also showed a negative correlation with shyness ($r = -.39$). A body of reliable research reveals that attributing both successful and failed heterosocial interaction to controllable causes is associated with reduced anxiety and a more adaptive balance of positive and negative thoughts during the conversation.

Frequent self-blaming appears to lead to negative biases about the self as a result of organizing all self-relevant information around highly elaborated negative beliefs about the self. Furthermore, people high in private self-awareness evidence greater reliability of self-reports across time than those lower in private self-consciousness, which suggests that private self-awareness contributes to the consistency of these beliefs. Information that is inconsistent with these well-articulated beliefs is less likely to be assimilated and is frequently discounted altogether. This means that positive information about the self, which is necessary for the development and maintenance of self-esteem and motivation, may not actually be processed. In fact, research has demonstrated that socially anxious subjects perceive unfavorable feedback as being more accurate than do non-socially anxious subjects; they discount positive feedback and exhibit marked discomfort in the face of positive feedback. Therefore, fearful and/or shy adolescents may be at significant risk for the development of shame-based self-concepts, and thus for the belief in personal inadequacy.

Accumulating evidence suggests a positive role for high self-complexity in coping with failure and stress. Self-complexity means holding many different views of the self rather than a simpler, narrow conception of oneself. Higher levels of self-complexity serve as a buffer against failure and the effects of stress, and research shows that performance after failure improves in subjects with high self-complexity. But if that complexity is organized around negative components, then the opposite outcome can be expected. Self-awareness is aversive when people compare themselves against unrealistically high, vague, or shifting standards. The desire to escape from the resulting painful self-awareness is common to many self-defeating behavior patterns, such as withdrawal and the cessation of problem solving. When shy or fearful individuals are self-blaming and shame prone, private self-awareness may contribute to a highly articulated negative view of the self that contains predominantly negative beliefs about the self, particularly in the face of perceived social failure. This composite is likely to contribute to self-defeating behavior. A major implication of these findings is the need to attend to the importance of the development of self-complexity in shy adolescents and its positive–negative valence.

Cognitive biases about social interaction and the self combine to inhibit social performance even when appropriate social skills are available. In fact, shy clients who show the most cognitive change are more likely to maintain treatment gains. In some cases, however, behavioral change may precede cognitive and affective change. Shy males who participated in positively biased social interactions with friendly, facilitative confederates showed increased dating frequency and long-term reduction in heterosexual anxiety, without any other intervention, in a follow-up after 6 months. Because self-consciousness and negative self-evaluation interfere with shy people's ability to pay attention to social cues and the needs of others, they must also learn to observe other people actively and to attend to others' wants and needs. This facilitates social interaction and reduces anxiety. In general, we would conclude that all shyness treatments, both professional and laity-based, should include two basic features: (a) facilitate success experiences in social situations tailored to the individual that proceed over trials in a hierarchy from safe to more risky; and (b) encourage shy individuals to focus on what they actively can do to help others, which is essential for shy people to break out of their passive egocentric preoccupation.

VI. SHYNESS AND CULTURE

Research in the United States typically indicates that shyness is highest among Asian Americans and lowest among Jewish Americans. This difference prompted efforts to assess shyness across diverse cultures. Using culturally sensitive adaptations of the Stanford Shyness Inventory, colleagues in eight countries administered the inventory to groups of 18- to 21-year-olds, usually in college or work settings. The overall pattern of results indicates a universality of shyness as a large proportion of participants in all cultures reported experiencing shyness to a considerable degree—from a low of 31% in Israel to a high of 57% in Japan and 55% in Taiwan. In Mexico, Germany, India, and Newfoundland, shyness was similar to the 40% U.S. statistic. Other data from this cross-cultural research show that the majority in each country perceive many more negative than positive consequences of being shy, and 60% or more consider shyness a problem (except for Israel, where the figure is 42%). There is no gender difference in reported shyness, but men have typically learned tactics for concealing their shyness because it is believed to be a feminine trait in most countries. In Mexico, males are less likely than females to report shyness.

One explanation for the cultural difference between Japanese and Israelis lies in the ways each culture deals with attributing credit for success and blame for failure. In Japan, an individual's performance success is credited externally to parents, grandparents, teachers, coaches, and others; whereas failure is entirely blamed on the individual. The consequence is an inhibition to initiate public actions and a reticence to take risks as an individual, relying instead on group-shared decisions. In Israel, the situation is entirely reversed. Failure is externally attributed to parents, teachers, coaches, friends, anti-Semitism, and other sources; whereas all performance success is credited to the individual's enterprise. The consequence is an action orientation toward always taking risks, as there is nothing to lose by trying and everything to gain. The concept of "chutzpa" emerges from such a positive risk-taking orientation as bold assertiveness regardless of personal skills or even requisite expertise. Much additional research is needed to appreciate fully the role of culture and societal norms in fostering shyness as a lifestyle or as an unacceptable response pattern, along with an analysis of the ways in which social agents transmit these values across generations. It is also important to distinguish between cultural values that promote shyness as a social control mechanism or a desired form of modesty and respect for authority, on the one hand, and personal values on the other hand that make shyness an undesirable constraint on autonomy and self-development.

VII. SHYNESS AND TECHNOLOGY

The steadily increasing percentage of young adults who report being shy (from the earlier 40% to the current nearly 50% level) may be analyzed as negative acculturation to a confluence of social forces operating in the United States. We maintain that this rise in shyness is accompanied by spreading social isolation within a cultural context of indifference to others and a lowered priority given to being sociable or in learning the complex network of skills necessary to be socially competent. A number of interacting social, technological, and economic processes operate to reduce daily ordinary, "real time" face-to-face interactions with other people. This lessened frequency of shared social experiences means that young people may not be learning the complex verbal and nonverbal language of social interaction. Without observing models engaging in pleasurable interactions, and without regularly practicing in this social exchange medium, there is a failure to develop adequate social skills, an awkwardness when having to interact with others, and thus a lowered priority for doing so. In addition to the failure to develop social skills, there seems to be an emerging reduction in emotional exchanges that promote intimacy, and in social sharing that promotes reciprocity.

The new cyberspace generation of the 1990s may be seen as an accretion on the TV generation that fostered passive, often isolated viewing of television for many hours a day. The use of video games, CD-rom games and stories, web surfing, email, and other technological marvels all obviate the need to take time to seek out direct contact with other people for fun, friendship, or work exchanges. Indeed, social time is being replaced with nanosecond-based efficient exchange of information within a highly structured, externally imposed format. Although some shy people benefit from using the anonymity and structural control features of email, the danger is that for many others, virtual on-line reality may become a substitute for the reality of human connectedness. We have been told by concerned parents that their young children prefer "chat time" on their computers to actually talking face to face with their classmates. Computer interaction enables the user to maintain a higher degree of control over the interaction than in direct, informal social communication.

Other societal forces are also contributing to less personalized exchanges between people, thereby possibly also promoting shyness in the current generation. Among these factors: automation of many services, fear of crime in the streets, smaller, more mobile, less intact nuclear and extended families, and a changing economic structure that is creating deep levels of existential anxiety among many workers through the enactment of obvious corporate values of enhanced profits taking priority over any sense of job security.

Automation is replacing people serving people with machines. In many areas of everyday life, from bank automated tellers to gas stations and telephone services, it is possible to complete needed interactions without ever dealing with a human being. Fear of crime has meant that one rarely sees children playing in groups in the streets, learning essential social skills on their own, without close adult supervision. Today's children are growing up in families with relatively few members, rarely with relatives living together or nearby, with a single parent, or with both parents working full-time, with little socializing to be observed in their home, or of neighbors and friends enjoying being with them and their parents. In recent years, as many U.S. businesses are feeling the need to be ever more competitive in the international global market place, the nature of the American workplace has been changing dramatically. Fewer workers are expected to produce more in less time, thereby enhancing productivity and raising profits through the extensive use of "downsizing." This destructive force is changing workers' sense of loyalty and their self-image, which is often based on their job definition. As job anxiety and related work stress get carried over to one's private life, there is a growing sense of being busier, working harder, and having less time and energy available for friends, family, hobbies, and recreational activities. Recent national surveys reveal that those negative social consequences are becoming normative for the majority of the population.

We would like to propose that the recent increases in statistics of shyness prevalence may be diagnostic not only of the extent of personal social anxiety, as viewed within the framework of a traditional medical model, but also of societal pathology within a public health model. As such, we may want to take note of increasing levels of shyness as a warning signal of a public health danger that appears to be heading toward epidemic proportions.

VIII. ASSESSMENT AND TREATMENT

This final section outlines methods of evaluating prospective clients for shyness treatment and the treatment protocols we have developed over a number of years of successfully treating shyness in adults at our Shyness Clinic in both individual and group therapy.

A. Initial Evaluation

An initial evaluation is generally a structured clinical interview, using either the SCID or the ADIS IV and an Avoidant Personality Disorder questionnaire. In addition to the structured interview, frequently used self-report questionnaires are the Stanford Shyness Inventory, a social anxiety or reticence questionnaire; the Beck Depression Inventory, a self-esteem inventory; the Fear of Negative Evaluation Scale; the Social Avoidance and Distress scale, a shame scale; and Spielberger's State/Trait Anxiety and Anger scales.

The Minnesota Multiphasic Personality Inventory (MMPI) is used to assess current symptomatology, and the Millon is used to assess the presence of personality disorders, long-standing traits, or patterns of behavior that have been maladaptive in work or in interpersonal relationships. The Multimodal Life History Questionnaire may be taken home and allows clients to record any stressful or traumatic events that may not have been discussed in the screening sessions, either due to the discomfort of discussing painful memories with a stranger or because the significance of an event had previously gone unrecognized.

Current behavior in a feared situation is usually assessed with a behavior performance/assessment test (BAT), which consists of a brief role-play or impromptu speech, usually videotaped, and includes a small audience. Subjective anxiety, SUDS, levels are usually assessed at intervals prior to the BAT for baseline and anticipatory levels, during, and immediately afterward. A hierarchy of 10 feared situations is constructed, with the client to role-play in simulated exposures in the group sessions and to practice in vivo during self-assigned behavioral homework between sessions. Our clients are given copies of these hierarchies to guide their practice and to be revised as goals are met or changed. Clients are also given social interaction diaries to record social anxiety, negative thoughts, and emotions in situations in which shyness occurs. The initial evaluation lasts anywhere from three to six sessions depending on the client's degree of difficulty across situations and across diagnostic categories. Individual goals in shyness groups include improved social skills, better interpersonal communication, reduced physiological arousal, increased emotional well-being, more adaptive thinking about the self and others in social situations, a more adaptive attribution style, and a more realistic view of the self.

Self-report tests and the BAT are repeated immediately after treatment. Some of our clients are willing to give a standardized letter to two or more friends that is returned to the clinic with instructions to share it with the client or keep it confidential. Letters with permission to share with clients are photocopied and sent to them. These include questions about changes in behavior, changes in observed comfort level, and an open-ended question about anything the friend notices that is different. In some studies with social phobia treatment, follow-up has continued up to the fifth year.

B. Treatment

Effective treatments for shyness exist. Existing treatments generally include exposure to feared situations usually simulated in treatment sessions or in vivo, and sometimes exposure to visualized feared situations in imaginal desensitization. These include some kind of anxiety management and/or coping skills training, such as coping self-statements. Research has shown, however, that the use of positive coping statements, although they reduce social anxiety, may also interfere with attending to the social task at hand, suggesting that challenging and reducing negative thoughts may be more effective. Flooding treatment, that is, exposure to the feared stimulus (imaginal and/or in vivo) until extinction (lowered anxiety or SUDS levels) occurs—has also proven effective with significant reductions in SUDS and pulse rate reported over the course of treatment. According to some studies of flooding techniques, between session extinction as well as within session extinction is necessary, but other researchers report that within-session extinction is sufficient. [See COPING WITH STRESS.]

Our comprehensive treatment includes exposure and behavioral practice in feared situations, social skills training, cognitive restructuring for negative thoughts about self and others, communication exercises both for getting acquainted and deepening relationships, and assertiveness training for situations where shy individuals make requests of others or say no to unreasonable requests. Additional techniques reported to be effective are the following: paradoxical intention, where clients deliberately intensify feared internal or external responses, like blushing, and discover more control than they imagined; the use of affirmations, short positive statements about the self that are written up to 20 to 30 times daily; and relaxation training, including progressive relaxation by each major muscle group and/or controlled breathing.

Treatments for shyness and social phobia are similar, but more systematic treatment outcome research has been conducted and published in the area of social phobia. Analyses of cognitive–behavioral and pharmacological treatments of social phobia have reported effective treatments for social phobia that are superior to placebo-controlled conditions, with exposure-based techniques that combine anxiety management strategies showing the highest effect sizes. MAOIs demonstrate the largest effect sizes in studies of pharmacological treatments, but SSRIs such as Prozac, Zoloft, and Paxil are being used with some success. There is controversy over the use of stimulants such as Ritalin in the treatment of social phobia, with early clinical reports suggesting that they are efficacious in some cases. Controlled studies are needed to assess the effects of these agents. There are no significant short-term differences between pharmacological and cognitive behavioral treatment (CBT) approaches; attrition rates are similar (between 14 and 18%), but investigators in a study that combined approaches found that subjects who received CBT plus Buspirone did worse than those who received either treatment alone. Studies with phenelzine and cognitive–behavioral group therapy (CBGT) showed that phenalzine had a faster onset (6 weeks compared with 9 weeks), but one half of the phenelzine responders relapsed during the follow-up period, whereas responders to cognitive behavioral group therapy maintained gains or continued to improve. A substantial number of generalized social phobics fail to respond to either, and combined treatments are being investigated. A methodological difficulty is that studies vary widely in diagnostic criteria for inclusion, particularly in terms of the inclusion of subjects who meet criteria for avoidant personality disorder. Another caution is recognizing the degree to which shyness or social phobia is a consequence of inadequate social skills, which are not improved by merely taking medication such as Prozac, which has been given media prominence as a shyness cure-all. [See PHOBIAS; PSYCHOPHARMACOLOGY.]

C. Stanford/Palo Alto Shyness Clinic Treatment: Social Fitness Training

Treatment for shyness at the Stanford/Palo Alto Shyness Clinic continues to focus on a health or wellness model, with techniques described as enhancing social interaction and increasing pleasure and emotional well-being in interpersonal relationships. Because controllability appears to be an important negative predictor of shyness, a model of cure that implies a passive recipient is unlikely to be useful or efficacious. The most recent innovation at the Shyness Clinic has been the development of the Social Fitness Model, which is analogous to a physical fitness model. People are provided with a tool kit (like tennis drills or calisthenics) that includes education about and training in positive social behavior, exercises to convert maladaptive thoughts, attributions, and self-concept distortions to more adaptive cognitive patterns, and training in effective communication skills, including healthy assertiveness and negotiation. People move from social dysfunction, withdrawal, passivity, and negative self-preoccupation to adaptive functioning, increased social participation, a proactive orientation, and empathy and responsiveness to others, that taken together is referred to as "social fitness." The intent of shyness treatment is not to create perfect social performers. Few people are world-class physical athletes, but most can enjoy physical exercise from sports that use high degrees of precision and finesse such as tennis, windsurfing, and dancing, to those that simply require moving in enjoyable, healthy ways, like hiking and walking. There are many choices about activity and degree of skill. What is important is a sense of health and well-being. Analogous to the physical fitness model, few people are world-class social athletes, but all can connect with other people in ways that are emotionally satisfying and productive. The best strategies for satisfying social interaction frequently develop in the group itself. What is provided is a safe situation, tools, and an educative framework.

Treatment at the Shyness Clinic consists of 26 weeks of cognitive-behavioral group psychotherapy beginning with 12 weeks of in-group simulated exposures (i.e., role-plays of feared situations with other group members and/or "confederates" who come into the groups specifically for a given interaction) and between-session in vivo exposures called behavioral homework. Between group sessions, clients enter feared situations and stay in them long enough to meet specific behavioral goals, such as starting and maintaining a conversation for several minutes, making eye contact and saying hello to a specified number of people at a social gathering, making a comment about the weather at a checkout stand in a supermarket, or asking someone to go out for coffee or to a movie.

The initial phase of treatment is followed by 10 to 11 weeks of verbal and nonverbal communication training, including on skills such as active listening, self-disclosure, trust building, handling criticism, and managing and expressing anger constructively. The last 3 to 4 weeks are spent writing and practicing scripts for situations in which clients need to assert themselves. Videotaped feedback is provided for those clients who are willing to use it (see Table II).

Outcome data for 6-month treatment groups at the Shyness Clinic demonstrate statistically significant reductions in fear of negative evaluation, social avoidance and distress, social anxiety, depression, and guilt. There has been a trend in shame reduction, which became significant with our recently increased focus on self-blame and self-concept distortions in the cognitive restructuring techniques used in our Social Fitness Model. Many clients get clinically significant reductions on these variables, meaning that they move into the normal range on standardized questionnaires. Some do not, but if they continue behavioral homework, most continue to improve; some relapse without continued group support. Clinical observation suggests that this effect is related to a loss of motivation that is related to persistent self-blaming tendencies and self-concept distortions.

Because most of the Shyness Clinic clients meet criteria for generalized social phobia and generalized anxiety disorder, many meet criteria for avoidant personality disorder, schizoid personality disorder, and dependent personality disorder, and some meet criteria for passive–aggressive disorder and paranoid personality disorder, these results hold out a good deal of hope for highly distressed clients as well as those with

Table II Multimodal Treatments for Shyness in Individual and Group Therapy

Description	Individual	Group
Social skills training	Modeling, behavioral rehearsal, video feedback	Modeling, role-plays with coaching and feedback
Simulated exposures to feared stimuli	Therapist and staff assisted	Therapist, group members, confederates
Flooding	Therapist and staff assisted, behavioral homework	
In vivo exposures	Therapist assisted, behavioral homework	Group members, behavioral homework
Communication training	Modeling; behavioral rehearsal, therapist and staff assisted, bibliotherapy, behavioral homework	Modeling, behavioral rehearsal, therapist and group assisted, bibliotherapy, behavioral homework
Assertiveness training	Modeling, behavioral rehearsal, script writing, behavioral homework	Modeling, behavioral rehearsal, script writing, behavioral homework, video feedback
Thoughts/attributions/ self-concept restructuring	Training, identification, and practice during simulated exposures, therapist and staff assisted	Training, group identification and practice during simulated exposures and communication exercises

more circumscribed difficulties. Our research at the Stanford Student Health Center with 8-week groups for students using the Social Fitness Model demonstrates similar findings, including significant reductions in shame and general fearfulness.

D. Long-Term Groups

Although there is little outcome data published for unstructured, interpersonal, long-term psychotherapy treatment groups, clinical observation strongly suggests that they are effective for shyness in that they provide a place to practice communication skills, to develop spontaneous expression of thoughts and feelings, to participate more fully in a group setting, and to assume leadership roles. Some data suggest that drop-in groups may be more useful for some kinds of shyness than groups that carry a commitment to weekly meetings. Clients at the Shyness Clinic enter a long-term group after an initial 6-month group if they need continued practice in performing new behaviors, changing negative thinking patterns with concomitant negative emotional states, and in developing trust and intimacy. Members work to build a culture free of the destructive evaluation of self and others. Shame arises in manageable doses, occurring when clients are dissatisfied with specific behaviors and have immediate opportunities to try new skills. The group becomes an environment for the emergence of stifled talents and self-expression, a phase that is highly gratifying for group therapists.

It has been our mission to persuade therapists and mental health professionals to recognize the serious need for treatment of shy adults and children, and to develop treatment approaches to liberate the millions of people who are trapped in their silent prisons of shyness.

BIBLIOGRAPHY

Carducci, B. J., & Zimbardo, P. G. (1995). Are you shy? *Psychology Today, 28,* 34–40, ff.

Crozier, W. R. (Ed.). (1990). *Shyness and embarrassment: Perspectives from social psychology.* New York: Cambridge University Press.

Jones, W. H., Cheek, J. M., & Briggs, S. R. (Eds.). (1986). *Shyness: Perspectives on research and treatment.* New York: Plenum.

Kagan, J. (1994). *Galen's prophesy: Temperament in human nature.* New York: Basic Books.

Leitenberg, H. (Ed.). (1990). *Handbook of social and evaluation anxiety.* New York: Plenum.

McKay, M., & Paleg, K. (1992). *Focal group psychotherapy.* Oakland, CA: New Harbinger.

Zimbardo, P. G. (1990). *Shyness: What it is, what to do about it.* Reading, MA: Addison-Wesley. (Original work published in 1977)

Sleep

Roseanne Armitage

University of Texas Southwestern Medical Center, Dallas

Biological Rhythm   Predictably recurrent change in physiology or behavior with a fixed period length.
Desynchronous EEG   Low-voltage, fast-frequency brain activity.
Sleep Architecture   Pattern of changes in sleep stages during sleep.
Synchronous EEG   High-voltage, slow-wave brain activity.

SLEEP is a distinct behavioral state that is defined on the basis of postural changes, reduction in response to external stimuli, and the presence of characteristic changes in brain wave activity, changes in temperature, and a variety of hormonal and neuroendocrine changes. Interest in sleep goes well beyond scientific inquiry. Poets, philosophers, and artists have contemplated the mysteries of sleep for centuries. Further, sleep is one of the few areas of scientific discovery to which all people can relate. Most everyone has experienced first-hand, the effects of both good and poor sleep. The following article will review our current knowledge of sleep physiology, biological rhythms, and the impact of sleep on daytime performance.

I. SLEEP EEG MEASUREMENT

Research on sleep electroencephalography (EEG) dates back to the mid-1930s, although the majority of scientific discoveries have taken place since 1951, when Aserinksy and Kleitman first identified rapid eye movement (REM) sleep in infants. Sleep EEG is recorded from electrodes affixed to the scalp that detect underlying bioelectrical potentials from the brain. Electrodes placed at the outer ridges of the eyes and under the chin monitor changes in eye movement (electroculograms or EOG) and muscle activity (electromyograms or EMG), respectively. These signals are then amplified by a factor of 10,000–50,000 and the resulting voltage values are displayed on paper. Recent advances in microcomputer technology have permitted the development of "paperless" polygraph systems where EEG data are displayed on a computer monitor and stored on large-volume disks or tape.

II. REM AND NREM SLEEP ARCHITECTURE

Five distinct stages of sleep have been identified based on the appearance of certain EEG characteristics that recur throughout the night. REM sleep, the stage most often associated with good dream recall, is characterized by a pattern of low-voltage, mixed-frequency, desynchronous EEG activity. Binocularly symmetrical rapid eye movements (REMs) and inhibition of motor activity (atonia or paralysis of antigravity muscles) are also associated with REM sleep. Only the diaphragm and extraocular muscles are active in this sleep stage. REM has been called paradoxical or active sleep because the pattern of EEG activity closely resembles that of wakefulness. It is somewhat akin to being awake in a body that is asleep.

Four stages of nonrapid eye movement (NREM) sleep have also been identified in humans. Stage 1 sleep is characterized by relatively low-voltage, fast-frequency EEG in the absence of REMs. Stage 1 sleep occurs at the beginning of the night and during the transition between other sleep stages. Stage 2 sleep is associated with sinusoidal spindle activity (12–14 cps) and biphasic, single delta waves (0.5–2 cps), called K-complexes. Background EEG activity in Stage 2 is generally higher voltage and slower frequency than Stage 1 or REM sleep. Stages 3 and 4 sleep are considered slow-wave or deep sleep, based on the predominance of delta waves. A sleep record with 20–50% delta is classified as Stage 3 and more than 50% delta identifies Stage 4 sleep.

In a healthy adult, the first episodes of Stage 1 identify sleep onset followed by the emergence of Stage 2, approximately 10 min later. Delta activity gradually appears, with a descent to slow-wave usually within the first hour of sleep. The first episode of REM occurs during the second hour of sleep and subsequent REM periods occur approximately 90 min after the previous one. Each REM period lengthens progressively, with three or four REM periods in a given night. An illustration of typical sleep architecture is shown in Figure 1.

NREM sleep comprises 70% of total sleep time, and approximately 50% of the night is spent in stage 2 sleep. REM constitutes 20–25% of total sleep time whereas 10–15% of the night is devoted to slow-wave sleep. Stage 1 and intermittent wakefulness generally make up less than 10% of the night.

III. AGE EFFECTS ON SLEEP

Human infants spend about 16 hr a day sleeping with 50% of total time in REM sleep, whereas premature infants have over 75% REM-sleep time. By age 2, REM sleep drops to less than 35% of total sleep. The percentage of REM further decreases to adult levels (20%) by age 5 or 6. The REM/NREM sleep cycle is approximately 50 min in length in neonates, lengthening to 90–100 min by early adolescence, and remains relatively constant throughout adulthood.

In general, the latency to the first REM period shortens to less than 70 min in the elderly, coupled with a decline in the amount of slow-wave sleep. There is some evidence to suggest that body temperature, usually at its lowest point in slow-wave sleep, is altered in the elderly, perhaps accounting for the decline in Stages 3 and 4 sleep. Overall, total sleep time is reduced in older adults, often accompanied by early morning awakenings. The ontogenetic changes in sleep architecture have been used as evidence for the functional significance of REM sleep.

IV. CONTROL MECHANISMS AND FUNCTIONS OF SLEEP

The mechanisms controlling sleep and wakefulness have been identified through animal research using electrode implants. As such, our knowledge is limited to the sleep stages that are similar in humans and animals, namely REM and slow-wave sleep. Little is known, for example, about the control mechanisms or functions of other NREM sleep stages, as they are identifiable in humans, but not usually in animals. Notable exception is recent work exploring computer-quantified EEG frequencies in low-amplitude NREM sleep in rats. As the precise frequency characteristics that underlie each sleep stage become known, exploration of animal models of EEG regulation may identify the mechanisms involved in initiating and maintaining low-voltage NREM sleep.

Slow-wave sleep is presumed to be controlled by limbic forebrain structures including the basal fore-

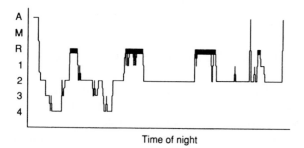

Figure 1 Typical sleep architecture in a normal healthy adult. A-awake, M-movement, R-REM sleep, 1-Stage 1 Sleep, 2-Stage 2 sleep, 3-Stage 3 sleep, 4-Stage 4 sleep.

brain, anterior hypothalamus, preoptic area, and thalamus. Electrical stimulation of these areas will result in drowsiness followed by sleep. The thalamus has been implicated in the generation of spindle activity, but is not necessary for the generation of cortical slow waves, which persist even after ablation of this region. There are also regions of the medulla, that when stimulated, produce cortical synchronization in an awake animal. Stimulation of this region during sleep will, however, produce wakefulness. Thus, a complex interaction of various areas in the brain regulates sleep and wakefulness. Catecholamine and adrenergic neurotransmitters have been implicated in the control of this sleep stage. The depletion of monoamines and dopamine, for example, results in the initiation of sleep. [See LIMBIC SYSTEM.]

Slow-wave sleep is associated with a reduction in cerebral metabolic rate, decreased temperature, and increased energy conservation. This sleep phase has been implicated in body and cell repair, leading to the view that slow-wave sleep serves a restorative-metabolic function and is required for homeostasis.

REM sleep is associated with acetylcholine, a neurotransmitter that is antagonistic toward catecholamines. Levels of acetylcholine are presumed to be highest in REM sleep, intermediate in wakefulness, and lowest in slow-wave sleep. These two major classes of neurotransmitters are presumed to have reciprocal interactive effects on the regulation of sleep stages. In dwelling electrode studies in animals have shown an increase in synchronous theta (4–8 cps) activity in the hippocampus during REM. REM sleep is largely controlled by the brainstem, not the cortex. The pons also generates distinct ponto-geniculo-occipital (PGO) waves during REM, that are not observable in scalp-recorded EEG. Phasic REMs, and middle-ear muscle potentials, presumed to be controlled by similar mechanisms, have been taken as evidence for PGO activity in humans.

Increased cerebral metabolism and activation of the visual cortex are found in REM sleep. This sleep stage is considered vital in facilitating structural differentiation and maturation of the central nervous system in neonates. REM deprivation in animals results in poor neural growth and development, interferes with the acquisition of new skills, and eventually leads to death. The prevalence of REM sleep in infant mammals argues strongly in favor of its role in neural development.

There is no one sleep center, but several areas in the forebrain and brainstem connected through ascending and descending projections to the cortex seem to initiate sleep.

V. BIOLOGICAL RHYTHMS

During approximately the same time period as the discovery of REM sleep, a vigorous growth of biological-rhythm research occurred. Of primary interest were rhythms in physiology and behavior with a period of approximately 24 hr, termed circadian (from the latin *circa dies*: about a day). Circadian rhythm research has formed the basis for theories on jet-lag effects, shift work, and biological clocks that control rhythms. The term ultradian (*ultra dies*), used to identify shorter duration rhythms such as the 80- to 120-min REM/NREM sleep cycle, was introduced a few decades later. Infradian rhythms, with a periodicity longer than 24 hr, have also been identified, of which lunar and menstrual cycles are examples.

Biological rhythms are presumed to be controlled by an internal clock or pacemaker that responds to a variety of exogenous (external) and endogenous (internal) influences. Light and temperature can be strong exogenous entrainers of biological rhythms, altering the periodicity and the strength or amplitude of rhythms, depending on time of exposure. Internal entrainment mechanisms can include neuroendocrine function, hormones, and neurotransmitter release, among others. Further, the need for energy conservation and homeostasis may be the driving force behind rest and activity cycles.

Circadian rhythms are presumed to be controlled by the suprachiasmatic nucleus (SCN) located in the anterior hypothalamus, also implicated in the regulation of temperature and slow-wave sleep. Ablation of the SCN will result in arrhythmic activity cycles that can be restored to a 24-hr period by transplantation of SCN cells from another animal. Light is the primary stimulator for the SCN, relayed through specialized photoreceptors. Very recent work has shown that the timing of exposure to light can be manipulated to disrupt sleep schedules, or alternatively, to improve sleep in shift workers. Bright light exposure has also been used to diminish the effects of jet-lag and as a treatment for seasonal depression.

Given that most functions within the brain are subsumed by several regions, is unlikely that a single pacemaker system controls all circadian and ultradian rhythms. It seems more plausible to assume that multiple pacemakers control the timing of physiology and behavior. Considerable debate remains over whether circadian and ultradian rhythms are, in fact, independent processes, or whether they are likely to be controlled by the same oscillatory mechanisms. Further research is necessary to resolve these issues.

Humans may be somewhat unique in that they are able to override sleepiness and to ignore cues of light and darkness. Occupational accidents are, however, examples of the impact of pushing the biological clock too far. Nuclear power-plant accidents such as Three-Mile Island and Chernoble, the Exxon Valdez oil spill, and increased air and auto accidents at night have all been attributed to trying to maintain alertness when the body is biologically prepared for sleep. Stated differently, these accidents result from unsuccessful attempts to override the biological clock that controls sleep and wakefulness. Trying to stay awake between 3 and 5 A.M. is the most difficult, as any shift-worker, diligent student, or sleep researcher can attest.

VI. THE BRAC HYPOTHESIS

In the mid-1960s, Kleitman theorized that variations in task performance, attention spans, and fatigue in wakefulness were related to the sleep cycle. This ground-breaking theory, the so-called basic rest—activity cycle (BRAC), suggested that similar mechanisms controlled rhythms in physiology and behavior throughout the 24-hr period. He further proposed that the 80- to 120-min REM/NREM sleep cycle had a waking analog. A variety of circadian and ultradian rhythms related to the sleep cycle have since been identified.

VII. RHYTHMS IN SLEEP PHYSIOLOGY

Growth hormone, body temperature, testosterone, melatonin, a variety of pituitary hormones, metabolic function, and blood constituents all show circadian rhythms related to the sleep/wake cycle. Melatonin, luteinizing hormone, prolactin, and growth hormone, for example, show peak concentrations during the night, particularly in slow-wave sleep. Urine flow and electrolytic concentrations show ultradian rhythms during sleep and are coupled with phases of the REM/NREM cycle.

VIII. RHYTHMS IN COGNITIVE ACTIVITY

A. Dreaming

In addition to the physiological changes associated with the sleep cycle, Kleitman and colleagues suggested that REM sleep was associated with dreaming. Early work indicated that detailed dream recall could only be obtained following REM awakenings, and led to the assumption that the appearance of REMs signified dreaming. More recent work has shown that dream recall rates are generally higher following awakenings from REM sleep (70–100%), lowest following slow-wave sleep (0–25%), and intermediate from Stage 2 awakenings (25–60%). It is clear from this research that REM sleep cannot be equated with dreaming. However, dream *recall* is facilitated in REM sleep, largely due to the presumed activation of memory and linguistic capabilities in this sleep stage. [*See* DREAMING.]

Individual differences also contribute to dream recall. In surveys of university students, about 10% remember dreams every morning upon awakening. Approximately 10% of students rarely recall a dream, whereas the majority of students recall dreams one to four times a week. In addition, cognitive style seems to play a role in recall. Individuals with more flexible and fluid cognitive styles tend to remember more dreams, in support of the proposed relationship between creative thinking and dreaming.

At the height of interest in hemispheric asymmetries and laterality, several theorists proposed that dreaming was correlated with greater activation of the right hemisphere. Although EEG and dream studies conducted since 1980 clearly indicate that neither good dream recall or manifest content is correlated with EEG asymmetries, the purported link between the right hemisphere and REM sleep remains a strong influence on current views.

B. Hemispheric Asymmetries in Sleep EEG

Early work suggested that EEG amplitude was lower in the left hemisphere during NREM stages and lower in the right hemisphere during REM sleep. Decreased EEG amplitude is generally interpreted to reflect a higher degree of cortical activation, suggesting that REM was associated with greater activation of the right hemisphere and that the left hemisphere was involved with NREM sleep. Several studies attempted to replicate this finding without success. More recent research tends to support the view that REM sleep is associated with small interhemispheric differences, not greater activation of the right hemisphere. Nevertheless, the notion that the two sides of the brain are differentially activated during REM and NREM sleep initiated a number of task-performance studies following awakenings from sleep.

C. Cognitive Task Performance and Hemispheric Asymmetries during Sleep

Most cognitive tasks are presumed to be lateralized; mathematical and logical tasks are associated with the left hemisphere of the brain, whereas visuo-spatial tasks are presumed to be mediated by the right hemisphere, in most right-handed individuals. The mode of presentation and the complexity of tasks is, however, critical. It is important to note that only stimuli presented to the right visual hemifield project directly to the left hemisphere. Similarly, stimuli presented to the left hemifield have a direct pathway to the right hemisphere. The presentation of stimuli outside the hemifields will project to both hemispheres and cannot be used to assess functional lateralization. These technical issues are important to bear in mind when interpreting task-performance data and their relationship to sleep stages.

D. Perceptual After-Effects

Lavie and colleagues have conducted a number of studies on perceptual after-effects following REM and NREM awakenings. The idea behind their work has been that if REM sleep was associated with increased cortical arousal of the right hemisphere, the duration of perceptual after-effects should be greater following awakenings from REM compared to Stage 4 sleep. In several studies they obtained longer-duration after-effects following REM awakenings, although these differences were not always significant. Their results support the view that cognitive processing is enhanced in REM sleep.

E. Mathematical and Spatial Tasks

Lavie and colleagues have also investigated performance on digit-span and word-fluency tasks, presumed to involve left hemisphere processing, and dot localization, pattern recognition, and spatial tasks, mediated by the right hemisphere. Better performance on left-hemisphere tasks was obtained following NREM awakenings. Performance on dot-localization tasks was most accurate following REM awakenings and significantly worse following NREM sleep. Other tasks did not, however, show significant differences between REM and NREM awakenings. Further research has also suggested that tactile tasks show a left-hand superiority following awakenings from REM sleep.

Taken together, these data suggest that a shift in cognitive-task performance is likely to occur in REM sleep. It is debatable, however, whether this shift is associated with unique characteristics and functions of the right hemisphere. As EEG studies suggest small asymmetries in REM sleep, it seems more reasonable to postulate that information processing in general is facilitated in REM. The cognitive and electrophysiological profile may be less disrupted in the transition from REM to wakefulness than from NREM to wakefulness. Performance data alone, however, suggest at least some lateralized tasks are enhanced following REM awakening.

IX. ULTRADIAN RHYTHMS IN WAKEFULNESS

One strategy for testing the BRAC hypothesis is to monitor ultradian rhythms in task performance in wakefulness. In addition to their work in sleep, Lavie and colleagues have investigated rhythms in perceptual phenomena in wakefulness and have shown 80- to 120-min rhythms in the duration of after-effects. Performance on spatial and mathematical tasks may also show an ultradian rhythm, but not always at 80–120 min. Further, manipulation of the demand characteristics of studies will alter the periodicity of performance. Offering monetary incentives for peak performance will suppress rhythmicity, further evidence of our ability to override the biological clock that controls sleep and wakefulness.

These data are suggestive of a BRAC but are not

conclusive. Because two rhythms have the same periodicity does not indicate they are controlled by the same mechanism(s). A more accurate test of the BRAC hypothesis requires 24-hour monitoring of performance and associated physiological variables such as EEG. If rhythms in EEG activity are continuous throughout sleep and wakefulness, no phase shift will occur in the transition from sleep to wakefulness or vice versa. Such an endeavor is, however, very labor intensive and, to date, has not been published.

A. Gender Differences

Several studies have shown that 80- to 120-minute rhythms in task performance are more pronounced among females. Hemispheric asymmetries in EEG activity, collected during the task performance episode, may also differentiate males from females. Males show larger interhemispheric differences during both mathematical and spatial tasks. Females, on the other hand, show small EEG differences associated with accurate performance on both types of tasks. While females may show stronger rhythms in wakefulness, the opposite effect has been observed during sleep. Ultradian rhythms in sleep EEG may be considerably stronger among males and generally of a shorter periodicity. This finding suggests that the mechanism or clock that controls rhythms in females may be stronger during the daytime. Perhaps females are more influenced by time and environmental cues that entrain or drive the biological clock. Most biological rhythm and sleep research, however, is conducted on male subjects. In studies where both male and female subjects were included, less than 30% analyzed potential gender effects. Even fewer take phase of the menstrual cycle into account, despite the known thermogenic influences of progesterone and other gonadal hormones that are likely to alter sleep architecture. Thus, there is insufficient work identifying gender differences and what factors may contribute to differential biological-rhythm control in males and females. What work has been completed suggests the timing of biological rhythms in sleep and wakefulness do show gender effects.

X. SLEEP DEPRIVATION EFFECTS ON PERFORMANCE

There is ample anecdotal information on the effect of sleepiness on performance in wakefulness, indepen-

dent of the BRAC hypothesis. There are natural fluctuations in alertness during the waking hours such as a dip in performance in the afternoon, usually following lunch. Some researchers have taken this as evidence for pressure to nap, like the afternoon siesta observed in some Latin and European cultures. Others have suggested this "postlunch dip" is the result of insufficient nocturnal sleep. Kleitman, among others, has suggested that performance fluctuations reflect the endogenous, circadian pacemaker at work, though the nature of the tasks themselves may influence performance. There is strong evidence to suggest that daytime alertness is under the control of both the sleep cycle and an endogenous circadian rhythm, independent of sleep. These two processes are likely to function interactively to control sleep and performance.

The impact of sleep on performance has been evaluated in numerous studies on sleep deprivation and shift work. Shift work is associated with increased daytime sleepiness, decreased performance on rote tasks, and increased accidents, as reported above. Shift work also has an impact on the quality of sleep obtained during the daytime, reducing total sleep time and increasing the amount of wakefulness after sleep onset.

Performance also shows a monotonic decline as a function of sleep deprivation. Reaction time is slower following total sleep deprivation and accuracy on memory tasks is generally reduced. Sleep deprivation also results in decreased concentration and an increase in distractive thoughts during task performance.

The precise effects of REM sleep deprivation on performance have been harder to identify. Some early work suggested that reaction time may actually improve with REM deprivation, and only a few studies have identified associated performance decrements. More recent work in animals suggests that REM deprivation interferes with learning an avoidance task. Appetitive tasks performance does not appear to be influenced by REM deprivation. Humans show decreased performance on logic tasks for several days following REM deprivation. College students are still able to recite the rules of tasks, but are unable to apply them.

Additionally, REM deprivation has an impact on sleep physiology during recovery periods. A REM-rebound phenomenon has been observed where the amount of REM on subsequent recovery nights is increased, and the latency to the first REM period is shortened. Further, as the length of REM deprivation increases, attempts to enter REM sleep become more frequent. In essence, it becomes harder to stop the emergence of REM sleep as the deprivation period increases. However, follow-up studies indicated strong individual differences in the amount of REM rebound.

Both REM and total sleep deprivation have an impact on mood, resulting in irritability and increased negative affect that may also contribute to poor performance. Research in the mid-1960s suggested that five nights of REM deprivation resulted in profound psychological disturbances. Subsequent studies, however, did not find dramatic personality changes following a week of REM deprivation. A few studies suggest that sleep deprivation and, in particular, REM deprivation, may alleviate depression. The mood alleviation effects are, however, short-lived.

Slow-wave sleep deprivation also results in a rebound on recovery nights. In general, it is harder to stop individuals from entering slow-wave than it is to deprive them of REM sleep, suggesting that the "pressure" for slow-wave sleep may be greater and may reflect an increased biological need for deep sleep. On the other hand, slow-wave sleep deprivation does not produce a larger performance decrement than REM deprivation nor is slow-wave rebound and recovery stronger. Total sleep deprivation is likely to have more deleterious effects on mood and performance than does selective deprivation of REM or slow-wave sleep. It should be noted, however, individual differences may have a strong impact on sleep deprivation effects. A case study of a young man who was sleep deprived for 264 hr revealed few mood or performance difficulties. Further, recovery sleep lasted a mere 14 hr and subsequent sleep was its usual 8-hr duration.

This resilience to the effects of sleep deprivation reflects our ability to override the biological clock that regulates sleep and wakefulness and to compensate for sleepiness. It is only when the pressure for sleep becomes overwhelming that serious performance and alertness decrements occur. Further, the effects of sleep deprivation may be cumulative, building up over many days before performance deterioration is noticeable. As the more recent REM-deprivation studies have shown, although performance decrements may be subtle, they may have serious consequences. Occupational accidents may result from subtle alterations in decisional processes that may result from too many nights of sleep restriction or total deprivation.

The impact of sleep disruption can also be seen in psychiatric disorders such as depression, obsessive-compulsive disorders, and anxiety disorders, where difficulty in sleeping is used as one of the diagnostic criteria. Most notably, REM sleep abnormalities such as shortened REM latency and increased total REM time have been offered as biological markers of depression. Further, depression has been linked to abnormalities of the hypothalamic-pituitary-adrenal axis, implicated in the control of sleep/wake cycles, and several sleep-related biological rhythm disturbances have been reported in this group. Thus, the effects of sleep loss and disturbance in biological rhythms have an impact that extends across several scientific disciplines.

Our understanding of the regulation of sleep and wakefulness has improved tremendously over the past three decades. New fields of research and medicine have emerged as a result of the discovery of REM sleep and interest in sleep/wake cycles. Sleep-disorders medicine, the study and diagnosis of insomnia, narcolepsy, sleep apnea, and REM behavioral disorders, among others, has emerged as separate discipline within sleep research. Chronobiology, the study of biological rhythms, owes its origins in part to sleep research. Courses in sleep and dreams now appear in college curricula and several graduate programs now offer specialization in sleep research.

This article has been reprinted from the *Encyclopedia of Human Behavior, Volume 4,* "Sleep: Biological Rhythms and Human Performance."

BIBLIOGRAPHY

Antrobus, J., & Bertini, M. (Eds.) (1992). "The Neuropsychology of Dreaming Sleep." Erlbaum, NJ.

Kryger, M., Roth, T., & Dement, W. (Eds.) (1989). "Principles and Practice of Sleep Medicine." Saunders, Philadelphia.

Moffitt, A., Kramer, M., & Hoffmann, R. (Eds.) (1993). "The Functions of Dreaming." State University of New York Press, Albany.

Neidermeyer, E., & Lope da Silva, F. (Eds.) (1982). "Electroencephalography." Urban and Schwarzenberg, Baltimore.

Spring, S., & Deutsch, G. (Eds.) (1981). "Right Brain-Left Brain." Freeman, San Francisco.

Touitou, Y., & Haus, E. (Eds.) (1992). "Biologic Rhythms in Clinical and Laboratory Medicine." Springer-Verlag, Berlin.

Wauquier, A., Dugovic, C., & Radulovacki, M. (Eds.) (1989) "Slow Wave Sleep: Physiological, Pathophysiological, and Functional Aspects." Raven Press, New York.

Webb, W. (Ed.) (1982). "Biological Rhythms, Sleep and Performance." Wiley, Chichester.

Smoking

Richard M. Millis

Howard University College of Medicine

Atherosclerosis Deposition of cholesterol and other lipids with proliferation of fibrous connective tissue in and narrowing of the inner walls of the arteries. Atherosclerosis progresses to arteriosclerosis as the arterial walls become more rigid from lipid invading the middle layer of the arterial wall.

Bronchiolitis Inflammation of the lung's small airways that commonly results from continuing irritation by cigarette smoking. Bronchiolitis is associated with excessive mucus production, plugging, loss of elasticity, and increased collapsibility of small airways, thereby providing a limitation to airflow during forced expiration that can be detected during routine pulmonary function tests. The early detection of small airways disease is made difficult because it is clinically silent, that is, people with small airways disease are usually symptom-free.

Chronic Obstructive Pulmonary Disease (COPD) Group of lung disorders including chronic bronchitis, bronchial asthma, bronchiectasis, and emphysema. Cigarette smoking commonly produces chronic bronchitis with inflammation of small airways (bronchiolitis).

Coronary Artery (Heart) Disease (CAD, CIHD) Condition that blocks the coronary arteries and decreases the blood supply to the heart muscle, usually associated with atherosclerosis. The risk of CAD is increased by elevation of the blood lipids, specifically an unfavorable balance between the low-density lipoproteins that transport cholesterol in the blood and the high-density lipoproteins that transport cholesterol and other fats to the liver and clear them from the blood.

Emphysema Enlargement of the air sacs (alveoli) of the lungs associated with loss of elasticity and increased collapsibility of the lung's small airways (bronchioles). Familial emphysema is a genetic disease from deficiency of an enzyme (α-1-antitrypsin) that protects the lung against destruction of its structural proteins collagen and elastin, which are responsible for its natural mechanical property (elasticity) to recoil (deflate) during expiration. By far the most common form of emphysema is that associated with chronic bronchitis, bronchiolitis, and COPD in smokers.

Mucociliary Escalator Lung's system for removal of potentially damaging airborne foreign particles such as bacteria, viruses, and debris. It consists of cilia that are specialized projections from the surface of the epithelial cells that line the airways and that beat in a coordinated rhythmic manner. The ciliary movement occurs in a milieu of an underlying thick blanket of mucus and an overlying more watery fluid that helps trap particles and move them upward, like the movement of an escalator, toward the mouth for removal by a cough (expectoration).

Stroke Acute decrease in the blood supply to the brain with loss of brain function. Stroke is commonly associated with arteriosclerosis.

Sudden Infant Death Syndrome (SIDS, crib death) Sudden death of a sleeping infant without an apparent cause. There is evidence of an abnormal distribution of nicotinic receptors in the brain stems of SIDS infants. The risk of SIDS is increased in premature infants, low-birth-weight infants, infants of mothers who smoke, and infants from mothers who take other addictive drugs such as alcohol and cocaine.

CIGARETTE SMOKE is a complex mixture of organic and inorganic chemical compounds generated by combustion of tobacco and additives. Cigarette smoke drawn through the mouthpiece of the cigarette is known as mainstream smoke. Sidestream smoke is the smoke given off by smoldering tobacco between puffs as well as the smoke diffusing through the cigarette paper and escaping from the burning cone during puffing. Passive smoking refers to a nonsmoker's inhalation of tobacco smoke. The term "environmental tobacco smoke" is used to refer to the mixture of sidestream smoke, primarily, but it also includes the exhaled mainstream smoke that is inhaled by a (passive) smoker who is inhaling tobacco smoke from the surrounding air. In a household where the parents smoke, the passive smoking that a child experiences can increase the number of the child's respiratory tract infections and illnesses as well as the child's rate of lung growth. The symptoms of childhood asthma also appear to be more severe when the parents smoke, and an infant born to parents who smoke appears to have a substantially increased risk of dying from sudden infant death syndrome (SIDS, crib death).

I. SMOKING-RELATED HEALTH PROBLEMS

Thousands of individual compounds have been found in cigarette smoke, including the addicting drug known as nicotine. Other toxic chemicals such as carbon monoxide, hydrogen cyanide, and acrolein can decrease the ability of the red blood cells (erythrocytes) to deliver oxygen and of virtually all tissues of the body to use oxygen. Various mutagens and carcinogens

in tobacco smoke, collectively known as polycyclic aromatic hydrocarbons, can transform normal cells (metaplasia) into cells that grow abnormally as tumors (neoplasms). Cancers are (malignant) tumors whose uncontrolled growth spreads (metastasis) through the body by the blood and lymphatic circulations and results in death of the person. In addition, the repeated (e.g., daily) inhalation of cigarette smoke acts as a continuing irritant to the lung's airways that produces inflammation.

Cigarette smoking is an addictive behavior. It is often the first addictive behavior that leads to usage of alcohol and illicit drugs such as marijuana, cocaine, and heroin. Currently, few people begin to use tobacco as adults. Thus, cigarette smoking is the addictive behavior most likely to become established during adolescence, usually by the age of 16. The tobacco industry makes a substantial investment ($4 billion annually) in advertising and promotional strategies that are thought to contribute significantly to influencing people to smoke at an early age. Those that smoke at an early age are more likely to develop severe levels of nicotine addiction than those that start at a later age. Cigarette smoking produces excessive cough and lung mucus (phlegm) production, an increased number and severity of respiratory illnesses, decreased physical fitness, blood lipid (fat) levels that can make people more susceptible to cardiovascular diseases (e.g., coronary artery disease, arteriosclerosis, and stroke), and retardation in the rate of lung growth and the level of maximum lung function. The usage of chewing (smokeless) tobacco is associated primarily with early indicators of (periodontal) degeneration of the gums and with damage to other soft tissues in the mouth. There is also some evidence that muscle fatigue during exercise might occur earlier in users of smokeless tobacco than in nonusers of tobacco products.

II. EFFECTS OF SMOKING ON MATERNAL AND CHILD HEALTH

Smoking by a mother during pregnancy retards fetal growth and is thought to contribute to unexplained death (mortality) of fetuses late in pregnancies. Smoking is also associated with a variety of abnormalities in the placental membranes that result in the premature delivery of babies. Consequently, smoking seems to contribute to the delivery of babies having low birth weight and to spontaneous abortions. Lower levels of intellectual achievement have been found in school-aged children whose mothers smoke compared to those whose mothers are nonsmokers. As mentioned earlier, maternal smoking is also associated with increased risk of SIDS.

III. RESPIRATORY EFFECTS OF SMOKING

Studies have shown a higher frequency of disorders of lung function in smokers than in nonsmokers. Effects of smoking on lung structure, particularly the small airways (those less than 2 mm in diameter), have been found in smokers as early as their mid-twenties. Respiratory bronchiolitis consists of an inflammatory process in the small airways with numerous clusters of macrophages (cells that ingest and deactivate potentially harmful foreign particles such as bacteria) with swelling (edema) and proliferation (hyperplasia) of the inner lining (epithelium) of the airways. Respiratory bronchiolitis is rarely found in nonsmokers in their twenties, but is a common finding in smokers in that age group. Because the effects of smoking begin in the small airways, they are usually clinically silent (without symptoms) until they progress to a stage that also affects the large airways (emphysema).

Normal breathing is virtually effortless because airflow through the respiratory tract occurs with little resistance. The airflow resistance in small airways is responsible for less than 20% of the lung's total airflow resistance. Thus, the large airways (bronchi trachea and nasal passages) contribute 80% of the lung's resistance to airflow, and numerous small airways can become totally obstructed without seriously affecting the total airflow resistance. This phenomenon can be appreciated by using a simpler example of the hindrance or congestion (resistance) of automobile traffic flow that would occur if one hundred small neighborhood residential streets were feeding automobile traffic into just a few large main streets. Assume the traffic flow is constant in one direction toward the largest street common to all of the pathways and that blockage of streets occurs only in the small streets. Under these conditions, a serious hindrance to traffic flow in the largest street (corresponding to airflow out of the lungs in the trachea) would not be noticed until a substantial number of small streets (small airways) had become blocked.

The progression from the early symptom-free condition of small airways disease to chronic obstructive pulmonary disease (COPD) can take two to three decades. During this time period, the smoker usually feels healthy and denies symptoms associated with poor lung function or injury. In high school and college students who smoke, tests of lung function (spirometry) have consistently shown reduced airflow rates indicative of injury to the small airways. When COPD is finally detected, years of inflammation, infection, excess mucus production, mucus plugging, and narrowing of the small airways have made a substantial number of them resistant to airflow and a condition known as emphysema is also found. Toxic components of tobacco smoke inhibit biochemical reactions that protect against destruction (oxidation) of important lung tissue proteins such as collagen and elastin. These structural proteins are largely responsible for the lung's mechanical properties that make it recoil without effort during the expiratory phase of breathing. Cigarette smoking, therefore, changes the lung's ability to recoil without effort during normal expiration and results in insufficient deflation of the lungs during normal expiration. This can be observed on a standard chest X ray as lung overinflation. Overinflation is associated with enlargement of the lung's air sacs (alveoli), where gas exchange occurs, thereby decreasing the size of the lung's surface area available for oxygenating the blood (lung gas exchange) and leading to decreased oxygenation of the blood (hypoxemia).

Toxic components of cigarette smoke also paralyze the specialized projections from the surface of airway epithelial (lining) cells (cilia) that remove airway debris and protect the lungs against particles of air pollutants, bacteria, and viruses. The cilia are like tiny motors on the surface of the epithelial cells that beat rhythmically to move potentially damaging particles that are trapped in the airway mucus upward toward the mouth (via the mucociliary escalator) for removal by a cough. This effect on cilia (ciliostasis) is thought to contribute substantially to the higher frequency of respiratory tract infections in smokers than in nonsmokers.

The signs and symptoms of respiratory tract injury and the early stages of COPD are cough, excessive respiratory tract mucus (phlegm, sputum) production, abnormal whistling sounds that are made when air flows out, usually, of the lungs during expiration (wheezing), and shortness of breath (dyspnea). The frequency of the symptoms is known to rise with the number of cigarettes smoked per day. Testing of lung function by spirometry has consistently shown that cigarette smokers have a lower level of lung function than persons who have never smoked. Spirometry is the measurement of the amount of air breathed in and out of the lungs. The forced expiratory volume in one second (FEV_1) is the amount of air breathed out during a maximal expiration that follows a maximal inspiration. In persons who have never smoked, FEV_1 begins to decline in the third or fourth decade of life. However, in smokers, the age-related decline begins at a younger age and occurs at a faster rate than in nonsmokers. When people stop smoking, their average decline in FEV_1 gradually returns to the rate observed in nonsmokers.

IV. CARDIOVASCULAR EFFECTS OF SMOKING

Cigarette smoking is a cause of coronary artery (heart) disease (CAD, CHD), atherosclerotic vascular disease, and stroke. These diseases rarely occur in adolescents, but autopsy studies of young adult male victims of combat in the Korean and Vietnam wars have shown that atherosclerosis begins in childhood and may become clinically significant as early as young adulthood. Similar autopsy studies on young people have also shown that the development of atherosclerosis in the coronary arteries and the aortas was consistently greater with higher levels of smoking.

Compared to nonsmokers, the blood of smokers seems to have higher levels of the low-density lipoproteins that are associated with transporting excess cholesterol and other fats and depositing them in the walls of blood vessels (atherosclerosis) and lower levels of the high-density lipoproteins that are responsible for carrying excess cholesterol to the liver for clearance from the blood. This blood lipid profile, together with the increased ability of smokers' blood platelets (thrombocytes) to clump together (aggregate), is thought to make people more susceptible to atherosclerosis, coronary artery disease, and stroke. In addition, nicotine's ability to increase the blood levels of the hormones epinephrine and norepinephrine (catecholamines), which are responsible for the body's fight-or-flight response, also narrows blood vessels in certain regions such as the skin, thereby increasing the

peripheral resistance to blood flow and decreasing the skin's temperature. This effect of nicotine on the blood supply to the skin and other peripheral tissues could contribute to the increased blood pressure associated with hypertension and to the ability of a person to control the buildup of heat in the body (thermoregulation) during exposure to hot environments and during exercise. Increases in circulating catecholamine levels associated with smoking can also produce abnormal heart rhythms (arrhythmias) that can contribute to poor physical performance as well as to sudden death.

Smoking also raises the free fatty acid levels of the blood by inhibiting storage of fats in subcutaneous adipose tissue. This effect appears to be partially responsible for the increased basal metabolic rate and leaner body mass found in smokers compared to nonsmokers as well as for the 5- to 9-pound gain in body weight that usually occurs when a person stops smoking. This weight gain has also been partially explained by nicotine's ability to inhibit the appetite regulation (feeding) center in the hypothalamus of the brain.

Smoking appears to compromise physical fitness, performance, and endurance. The mechanisms for this performance decrement are not entirely clear. However, reduction in the blood's oxygen-carrying capacity and increases in both the resting heart rate and the body's basal metabolic rate could produce the physical performance disadvantage that has been found in several studies of adolescents and young adult smokers competing against nonsmokers of the same age in various running races.

V. SMOKING-ASSOCIATED CANCERS

Cigarette smoking is presumed to be either a cause or promoter of cancers of the lung, lip, tongue, mouth, pharynx, larynx, esophagus, urinary bladder, pancreas, and liver. Exposure to other environmental carcinogens that can be found in the workplace or home, such as asbestos and radon gas (ionizing radiation), can act as promoters of lung cancer. Passive smoking is also associated with an increased risk of developing lung cancer.

Carcinogenesis is a multistage process. It is presumed that lung tumors occur many years before they are diagnosed as lung cancer. The polycyclic hydrocarbons, such as benzopyrenes and benzanthracenes, and the nitrosamines are thought to be the primary carcinogens in cigarette smoke. These carcinogens probably act as initiators of cancers by binding to deoxyribonucleic acid (DNA), thereby producing genetic mutations by causing errors in the transcription and replication of DNA. When these permanent alterations of DNA occur in the genes controlling cellular growth (oncogenes), they can produce an increased growth rate (proliferation, hyperplasia) and abnormal growth (metaplasia) of the lung's tissues. These changes in cell growth are indicative of a precancerous condition and the subsequent development of tumors (neoplasms).

The ability of a tumor's growth to become malignant and metastasize to other organs (e.g., liver and brain) is dependent on the genetic makeup of the individual and family history of cancer and on levels of other cancer-promoting chemical cofactors (risk factors), some normally produced in the body and others that are related to a person's life-style, such as hormones, growth factors, and drugs like alcohol. Many components of cigarette smoke also initiate an inflammatory response in which growth-promoting proteins are synthesized and released by cells (cytokines) that function as mediators of immunity. Continuing inflammation of the lung's airways from repeated (usually daily) irritation by cigarette smoke seems to be an important part of the multistage process of developing lung cancer. Thus, the risk of lung cancer gradually declines to that of nonsmokers when a person stops smoking.

VI. NICOTINE ADDICTION

The addictive properties of nicotine are produced by its actions in the central nervous system (brain and spinal cord). Most of the biologic effects of nicotine are produced by its actions on the brain's nicotinic receptors for the neurotransmitter acetylcholine. In the brain's emotional centers (limbic system), activity of acetylcholine at nicotinic receptors appears to be involved in the regulation of a person's mood. In the nucleus accumbens, stimulation of nicotinic receptors by acetylcholine releases the neurotransmitter dopamine, which produces reinforcement–reward responses thought to be important in the craving of food, sex, and drugs such as amphetamines, cocaine, and

alcohol (drug dependence). Similar to other addictive behaviors, nicotinic stimulation of the nucleus accumbens is thought to produce feelings of relaxation and well-being (euphoria). Personality differences seem to play a role in the establishment of addictive smoking behaviors. The incidence of smoking appears to be greater among individuals classified as extroverts than those classified as introverts. [*See* SUBSTANCE ABUSE.]

VII. TOLERANCE

Nicotine often produces a biphasic action on nerves that is dependent on the administered dosage. For example, at high doses, nicotine increases heart rate and, at low doses, it decreases it. Tolerance to nicotine develops quickly. Nonsmokers who smoke an occasional cigarette often experience greater increases in heart rate and blood pressure, trembling of the muscles of the hand (decreased hand steadiness, tremors), and susceptibility to experiencing the adverse effects of nicotine such as dizziness, nausea, mood disturbances, and headaches following smoking than do smokers. During the course of a daily smoking cycle, tolerance can be observed as smaller increases in heart rate and blood pressure and fewer adverse effects of nicotine. After a substantial period of abstinence, for example, one week, the smoker loses his or her tolerance for nicotine, but it is rapidly reestablished over subsequent cycles of smoking.

VIII. SMOKING-INDUCED ENHANCEMENT OF PERFORMANCE

There are many studies showing that nicotine increases a person's attention span, especially on monotonous tasks when it is necessary to sustain attention over a substantial time period (e.g., driving an automobile), and that nicotine administration might be beneficial in people with attention-deficit-hyperactivity disorder (ADHD). There appears to be a substantial amount of inter-individual and situational specific variability in the experiencing of these nicotine-induced performance enhancements. For example, nicotine administered to individuals who experience performance enhancement under conditions of excitement and stress often produces the opposite effect of decremental performance when given under nonstressful, low-excitement conditions.

IX. NICOTINE DEPENDENCE AND WITHDRAWAL

The rate of nicotine's breakdown (metabolism) varies with the nicotine intake. Smokers seem to metabolize nicotine faster than do nonsmokers. In smokers, within 3 hr after smoking, the blood nicotine level is virtually zero, and the signs and symptoms of nicotine withdrawal can be observed. It is thought that, like the dependence to other drugs, a smoker continues to smoke in order to alleviate the adverse effects of nicotine withdrawal (self-medication or self-stimulation). The most common effects of nicotine withdrawal include irritability, anxiety, decreased attentiveness, restlessness, impatience, sleeplessness (insomnia), and craving for tobacco.

X. TREATMENT OF NICOTINE ADDICTION

Mecamylamine is a drug that blocks the actions of acetylcholine at nicotinic receptors, and it has been shown to be highly effective in blocking the emotional relaxation and euphoric feelings associated with cigarette smoking. Smoking behavior can be influenced by sensations produced in the back of the mouth and in the tracheobronchial tree by nicotine-free products. For example, black pepper extract has been shown to produce mouth, throat, and respiratory tract sensations similar to those of cigarette smoke and to temporarily reduce a smoker's craving for cigarettes. Low-nicotine products, such as nicotine gum, which replicates the taste and flavor of smoking, or the transdermal nicotine patch, which produces a more gradual amount of nicotinic receptor stimulation than smoking, can also reduce the craving for cigarettes as well as certain nicotine withdrawal symptoms. Psychological counseling and smoking cessation support groups can also be effective in treating nicotine addiction.

XI. SUMMARY

Nicotine is the addictive agent in tobacco products such as cigarettes and chewing tobacco. Cigarette smoking-related health problems are a function of the number of years of smoking and the number of cigarettes smoked per day. Smoking has been causally linked to cancers of the lung primarily, and secondarily to cancers of the lip, tongue, mouth, pharynx, larynx, esophagus, urinary bladder, pancreas, and liver. Smoking is associated with an increased incidence of respiratory tract infections and COPD, which often is a smoking-induced disease of the lungs associated with loss of the lung's elasticity, emphysema, hypoxemia, and difficulty breathing. CAD and stroke are cardiovascular diseases in which cigarette smoking appears to be a risk factor for substantial illness and death (morbidity and mortality). Parental smoking is a risk factor for spontaneous abortions, low birth weight, retarded fetal growth, poor intellectual development, childhood asthma, and SIDS.

This article has been reprinted from the *Encyclopedia of Human Biology, Second Edition, Volume 8*, "Tobacco, Smoking, and Nicotine: Impact on Health."

BIBLIOGRAPHY

Balfour, D. J. K. (1991). The influence of stress on psychopharmacological responses to nicotine. *Br. J. Addict.* 86, 489–493.

Benowitz, N. L. (1992). Cigarette smoking and nicotine addiction. *Med. Clin. N. Am.* 76, 415–437.

Craig, W. Y., Palomaki, G. E., Johnson, A. M., and Haddow, J. E. (1990). Cigarette smoking-associated changes in blood lipid and lipoprotein levels in the 8- to 19-year-old age group: A meta-analysis. *Pediatrics* 85, 155–158.

Glantz, S. A., and Parmley, W. W. (1991). Passive smoking and heart disease: Epidemiology, physiology, and biochemistry. *Circulation* 83, 1–12.

Heishman, S. J., Taylor, R. C., and Henningfield, J. E. (1994). Nicotine and smoking: A review of effects on human performance. *Exp. Psychother.* 4, 345–395.

Rose, J. E., and Behm, F. M. (1994). Inhalation of vapor from black pepper extract reduces smoking withdrawal symptoms. *Drug Alcohol Dependence* 34, 225–229.

U.S. Department of Health and Human Services (1994). "Preventing Tobacco Use among Young People: A Report of the Surgeon General." U.S. Government Printing Office, Washington, D.C.

Social Networks

Barry Wellman

University of Toronto

I. Development and Principles
II. Personal Community Networks
III. Dense, Bounded, Stable Groups and Sparse,
     Loose, Changing Networks
IV. Network Size
V. Spatially Dispersed, Socially Ramified Networks
VI. From Public Sociability to Private Intimacy
VII. Social Support
VIII. A Comparative Perspective

Network Density The ratio of the number of ties actually present in a social network to the maximum number of ties that would exist if all network members were directly connected.

Personal (or Ego-Centered) Network A social network whose composition, structure, and contents are defined from a standpoint of the focal person at its center.

Social Network A set of nodes or network members (which may be persons, groups, organizations, nations, etc.) who are connected by a set of ties. The ties are flows of resources that reflect relations of control, dependency, and cooperation.

Social Support The interpersonal resources network members convey to each other, such as emotional aid, goods and services, financial aid, companionship, information, and a sense of belonging.

Whole Network A social network linking all of the members of a population by one or a few specified kinds of ties.

SOCIAL NETWORK analysts study social structure and its effects by analyzing patterns of relationships.

Although most network analysts study relations among persons or groups, others study relations among units as large as organizations, cities, or nations. This entry discusses the development and basic principles of social network analysis. It describes the nature of personal community networks and shows how such networks are related to the provision of social support.

I. DEVELOPMENT AND PRINCIPLES

Social network analysis conceives of social structure as a network, that is, as a set of nodes and a set of ties connecting these nodes. The network's nodes (or *network members*) can be groups or organizations as well as persons, and the ties are flows of resources that reflect relations of control, dependency, and cooperation. The interconnections of these ties channel resources to specific structural locations in social systems. Thus, social network analysis is more than a set of topics, a bag of methodological tricks, or a new mystifying vocabulary. It is essentially an attempt to take social structure seriously.

Social network analysis has moved in the past two decades from a suggestive metaphor to an analytic approach that is developing into a paradigm. Social scientists have long used network concepts as partial, allusive descriptions of social structures. In the 1950s, British-based anthropologists started developing social network concepts in order to study ties that cut across the boundaries of institutionalized groups or social categories. By the 1970s, this work had co-

Encyclopedia of Mental Health
Volume 3

525

Copyright © 1998 by Academic Press.
All rights of reproduction in any form reserved.

alesced with a parallel American sociological tradition of analyzing patterns of interpersonal and interorganizational relationships. Where early analyses treated social networks as just one among many forms of social organization, analyses now treat all social structures as social networks.

Social network analysts reason from whole to part, from structure to relation to individual, from behavior to attitude. They believe that their social structural explanations have more analytic power than individualistic analyses that ignore linkage patterns and which interpret behavior in terms of the internalized norms of atomized individuals. They treat norms as effects of social structural location and not as initial causes of behavior. They seek explanations in the patterns of how people and collectivities connect and behave rather than in people's normative beliefs about how to behave. They interpret behavior in terms of structural constraints on activity instead of assuming that inner forces (i.e., internalized norms) impel actors toward desired goals. Their work does not deny the existence and force of norms and agency, but works from the premise that norms only operate within the constraints and opportunities that social structures provide for human behavior.

Social network analysts suggest that structures of social relationships are more powerful sources of explanation than personal attributes of individuals. This contrasts with other analyses that treat social structure and process as the sum of such personal attributes as gender or socioeconomic status. In such studies, each person is treated as an independent unit of analysis and taxonomically lumped together into social categories with others possessing similar attributes, without regard for the structure of relationships in which these persons are embedded.

Instead of such an aggregative approach, network analysts directly study relations between social system members. They use ethnographic and statistical methods to analyze patterned differences in how people are linked to different kinds and amounts of resources. Analysts often use clustering techniques to find patterns of connectivity and cleavage, block modeling to identify actors in similar structural positions, and simulations to model structural dynamics.

Many social scientists treat personal relationships as the basic unit of analysis, disregarding the structure of relationships within which these two-person ties (or dyads) are embedded. Thus, many studies of social support view interpersonal help as emerging from multiple duets with separate others. Yet, social network analysts point out that social structural features affect the milieus within which personal relationships operate. For example, social structures create relatively homogeneous social contexts—kinship groups, cafes, workplaces, neighborhoods, and so on—within which most people obtain their relational partners.

Not only does network structure affect personal relationships, the network itself can be the focus of analytic attention. For example, people use a variety of direct and indirect ties in their networks to search for resources. Indirect ties concatenate into compound relationships (e.g., friends of friends) that fit network members into large social systems by transmitting and allocating scarce resources. For example, interpersonal networks efficiently transmit information about available jobs, housing, and mates, although if the network members are not well-positioned, they may direct people to undesirable locations.

Social network analysts try to avoid imposing prior assumptions about the boundaries of aggregates. They caution that focusing on bounded groups produces oversimplified descriptions of complex social structures, when it is the network members' crosscutting memberships in multiple social circles that interweave social systems. They point out that shifts in analysis from small-scale to large-scale systems can be aided by considering large-scale systems as "network of networks" in which clusters of members of small-scale (interpersonal) networks are treated as single members of large-scale (interinstitutional) networks. The network-of-networks approach also permits the discovery of complex hierarchies rather than assuming that all hierarchies are simple trees.

Many analysts study social networks much as contemporary astronomers study a galaxy: as observers from outside seeking to map the relationships linking all of the members of a population. Such *whole network* studies describe the overall structure of one or a few specified kinds of relations linking all of the members of a population. Whole network analysis allows a simultaneous view of both a social system as a whole and the parts that make up the system. This helps analysts to trace lateral and vertical flows of resources, identify sources and destinations, discover role relationships, and detect structural constraints operating on the flow of resources. Several studies have examined interorganizational networks of caregiving agencies and interpersonal networks of isolated populations. However, whole network studies are limited to studies of well-defined populations in which all members—and almost all relations between members—are known.

II. PERSONAL COMMUNITY NETWORKS

The open nature of developed Western societies precludes the whole network study of communities because the communities are rarely insular villages, workgroups, or neighborhoods. Therefore, many analysts study *ego-centered* or *personal networks,* whose composition, structure and contents are defined from the standpoint of the *focal persons* at their centers. Such studies present a Ptolemaic view of the network universe as it is uniquely experienced by each participant. Typically, personal network analysts take a sample of people and treat each person as an Ego: the focal center of a network consisting of the ties radiating out from this Ego to other network members plus the ties connecting these network members with each another.

The ego-centered approach leads to viewing community as *personal community:* an individual's (and a household's) set of ties with friends, neighbors, kin, and workmates. Armed with this network approach to defining the intellectual question and gathering data, researchers are no longer restricted to searching for community in the solidarities of neighborhoods and kinship groups. Instead they can study all active community-like relationships, no matter where located, with whom, and how solidary. This approach has shown that community has neither been lost under the impact of contemporary societal transformations nor stayed within village-like neighborhoods. Rather, people form sizable, far-flung networks with kith and kin that supply sociability, support, information, and indirect links to other social milieus.

The reconceptualization of community as social network has helped to document the persistence of communities when neighboring and kinship are weak. It has opened up examination of traditional assumptions that personal communities are socially homogeneous, spatially local, tightly bounded, densely knit, and involuntary. It has encouraged analysts to evaluate different types of ties—kin or friend, intimate or acquaintance, local or distant—in terms of the access

to resources that they provide. It has produced a basis for understanding when kin, neighbors, friends, and workmates are substitutable, complementary, or dispensable.

Researchers typically use survey research to learn about a variety of personal network characteristics that can affect mental health and well-being:

- *Network member composition:* aggregate information about the attributes of network members (e.g., percent women, socioeconomic homogeneity)
- *Relational characteristics:* aggregate information about the dyadic relationships in the network (e.g., mean frequency of contact, percent kin)
- *Structure:* information about the arrangement of ties in each network (e.g., network density, clustering)
- *Contents:* information about the quality and quantity of supportive resources (e.g., volume of emotional aid, prevalence of companionship, percentage of relationships providing informal health care aid)

III. DENSE, BOUNDED, STABLE GROUPS AND SPARSE, LOOSE, CHANGING NETWORKS

The most commonly used measure of network connectivity is *density:* the ratio of the number of ties actually present in a network to the number that theoretically could be present. Social scientists have often depicted ideal communities as densely knit solidarities in which most members are directly linked with each other as kin, neighbors, or co-workers. They see these communities as having tight boundaries with relationships largely confined within communal boundaries. Densely knit and tightly bounded communities make it easy for members to control and coordinate behavior, whether this be aiding the distressed or punishing the errant.

However, contemporary personal communities in developed societies are rarely dense, bounded groups. They are sparsely knit: only a minority of members are directly connected with each other. There is little structural basis for network members to work collectively to enforce norms or to provide social support. The fragmented and specialized nature of these personal communities means that people must actively maintain each relationship and actively seek help for problems from those few community members who will provide them with that type of support. At the same time, these fragmented communities connect people to the diverse information and resources of multiple social arenas, rather than locking them into a single social circle.

Membership in personal communities changes regularly, and even strong ties turn over. Kin are the most stable intimate network members. The composition of the personal communities changes slowly over the life-course with age and rapidly with changes in family status (e.g., marriage, childbirth). That network ties have a kind of half-life and a life-course component introduces a new consideration for evaluating inter-personal support. If personal communities change most dramatically with changes in family status, then secular changes in the age of marriage, divorce, and widowhood carry important implications for assessing emotional and community life. It may be that contemporary personal communities are changing according to three distinct rhythms, analogous to the paleontological concept of "punctuated equilibrium":

1. A relatively stable set of immediate kin, changing principally in response to aging and in demographically predictable ways.
2. A slowly changing set of strong ties with friends, neighbors, co-workers, and other adult kin, altering in response to changes in the community members' situations.
3. Large-scale turnover associated with setting up independent households and predictable with marriage or divorce.

IV. NETWORK SIZE

Social networks have fuzzy boundaries because there is no one answer as to how large they are. Because no clear borders divide members from nonmembers, analysts must develop a sharp picture from an unliminable and dynamic reality. Friends, neighbors, and workmates come and go, and their definition and importance to individuals may vary at any time. Ties to a married couple can function as one relation or two. There is no such thing as *the network*: analysts must specify inclusion criteria. It is likely that networks of people seen frequently—mostly neighbors and work-

mates—have little in common with networks of intimate, supportive ties—mostly immediate kin (parents, adult children and siblings) and close friends.

The broadest possible personal network of direct ties contains the 1500 or so people with whom an individual currently has informal relations. Weak ties of acquaintanceship far outnumber stronger ties of intimacy, support, companionship, or routine contact. These weak ties integrate social systems and speed the diffusion of information. Whereas strong ties link people who travel in the same social circles and who therefore learn similar things, weak ties provide access to more people, a greater variety of people, and are more structurally complex. Instead of being bound up in one densely knit core cluster (as strong ties often are), weak ties complexly link people to networks whose members travel in different social circles and thus hear new things. The larger the network, the more structurally complex.

Neither community network nor social support studies have been financially able to look at many of a person's 1500 or so informal ties. They have looked only at small subsets of personal networks. Researchers have identified a range of 10 to 25 *active* ties, persons who are significant in one's life because of repeated sociable contact, supportiveness, or feelings of connectedness. Active ties give people much of their interpersonal support and companionship.

One rarely finds relations through random encounters. Social and physical *foci* such as kinship groups or neighborhood street corners bring people together under auspices conducive for interaction. Kin are well represented in most active networks, even though they are less than 5% of a person's 1500 ties. The prominent role of kin (and neighbors and co-workers) in active networks suggests that people do not voluntarily choose all of their ties for their utilitarian value. There are higher proportions of kin in rural areas where fewer people with similar interests are available as potential friends and network members.

Not all types of kin are equally represented in personal communities. Most active kin relations come from the small number of available *immediate kin* (parents, adult children, siblings, in-laws). By contrast, only a small minority of available *extended kin* (aunts, cousins, grandparents, etc.) are active network members.

A set of kin usually forms both a densely knit cluster that is part of a broader personal community network. A central *kin-keeper*—usually a mother or daughter—often maintains family ties. The result is that kin are more likely to gather in group contexts such as dinners, holidays, or picnics. By contrast, most friendship ties meet privately as relations between individuals or couples.

Even though marriage brings more kin into networks, it lowers the density of connections in these networks. Furthermore, the number of friends shrinks after marriage, as spouses withdraw inward to contemplate each other and their children.

Most network studies have looked at small subsets of three to seven network members: either frequently seen *interactors* or socially close *intimates*. Only to some extent are the same persons both intimate and frequent interactors. Many of a person's 10 or so frequent interactors are neighbors or workmates who are rarely intimates. Intimate networks often contain equal numbers of kin and friends; neighbors and workmates are rarely intimates. Most intimate kin are immediate kin: usually equal numbers of parents (or adult children, depending on age) and siblings.

A few studies have looked only at tiny sets of socially close *confidants:* the one to three close friends and immediate kin to whom people pour out their hearts. Although most intimate and active network members provide only specialized kinds of support, confidants usually help in many ways.

V. SPATIALLY DISPERSED, SOCIALLY RAMIFIED NETWORKS

Contemporary personal communities are not local groupings of neighbors and kin. North American, European, and Japanese studies have shown that although people know a few neighbors, most members of personal communities live outside the neighborhood but within an hour's drive (or transit ride). A substantial minority live much further, requiring a long drive, train/bus journey, or airplane ride to have face-to-face contact.

With local ties comprising only a small minority of people's active ties, the neighborhood is not the focus of contemporary community life. Communication and transportation facilities have enabled communities to transcend the confines of neighborhood and kinship solidarities. However, some people—usually from ethnic minorities or low socioeconomic circumstances—have large clusters of network members nearby for companionship and support.

As personal community networks are rarely local residential groups, it takes a trip, telephone call, or electronic mail message to keep in touch with most network members. The greater the distance apart, the less network members see each other and the more they telephone each other. The biggest decline in contact and social support occurs when meetings require more than an hour's drive. Kinship ties withstand separation better than friendship ties, although few people have more than one or two kinfolk whom they see daily. The variety of residential distances may help to explain why networks interact in small groups rather than as wholes: it is difficult for many network members to get together at the same time. However, latent ties with distant network members remain in place, to be activated for specialized needs, family gettogethers, or on migration.

Telephone contact is a universal backdrop, enabling network members to keep connected—and supportive—even over large distances. Telephone contact is usually more of a voluntary act than is face-to-face contact, at least on the part of the caller. Thus, frequent telephone contact is significantly correlated with the strength of a relationship as well as with the frequency of face-to-face contact. Telephone and electronic mail do not replace face-to-face contact but are complements to it. They provide companionship and emotional support, and they aid making arrangements for visits and the delivery of material aid.

Does this mean that social network analysts have been mistaken in thinking that much of community is nonlocal? No, no, and yes. *No,* in one respect because neighbors and workmates are only a minority of active ties, and these relationships tend to be weaker than most other active ties. Neighbors and workmates are rarely socially close intimates and they do not give much social support other than small services. *No,* in another respect because local ties usually make up less than 5% of a person's overall network. *Yes,* in one respect because many network members in frequent contact do live or work nearby. Yet contact does not equal intimacy. Although the contact network is often quite different from the intimate network, both can validly and reliably be called social networks, and both are important elements of overall personal communities.

VI. FROM PUBLIC SOCIABILITY TO PRIVATE INTIMACY

Until recently, urban men customarily gathered in communal, quasi-public milieus, such as pubs, cafes, athletic fields, parks, and village greens. Work groups spilled over into pubs after hours, sports teams fostered supportive male friendships, and street corners had their regular crowds of male buddies. Such gathering places have been semipublic settings, drawing their clienteles from fluid networks of regular habitues with similar social backgrounds. These male public communities were both instrumental and sociable. The high density of the urban environment meant that people were likely to find others with whom to talk, form new relationships with the friends of friends, organize collective tasks, accomplish political goals, and deal with larger organizations.

Large-scale social changes have reduced the vitality of public neighborhood communities in three ways:

1. The reorganization of work in the Industrial Revolution has helped move friendships from shops (and nearby pubs) to homes. Zoning segregates workplaces and homes so that workmates now rarely come home with each other to the same neighborhood.

2. Since World War II, communication and transportation facilities have better enabled people to maintain active community ties over long distances. Yet these technologies are essentially privatizing, with telephones and electronic mail principally used between two persons and most automobiles carrying one or two persons on trips between private garages.

3. Larger homes provide more space suitable for private entertainment between community members who already know each other. There are few opportunities to form new relationships. Yet the scale of contemporary cities means that when people go out, they are surrounded by strangers but rarely encounter network members who can introduce them.

Private contact with familiar friends and relatives has replaced public gregariousness. Rather than being accessible to others in public places, people must overcome their isolation by getting together with friends and relatives in private homes and by telephone. Only a minority of relationships operate in the public contexts of the neighborhood, formal organizations, or work. Friends get together voluntarily as small sets of singles or couples, but rarely in communal groups. Personal communities now have high proportions of people who enjoy each other and low proportions of people who interact only because they live in the same neighborhood, work together, or belong to the same kinship group. As community becomes private, people may continue to feel responsible for their "own," but they do not feel as responsible for the many others with whom they rub shoulders but with whom they do not feel attached.

As community has moved from accessible public spaces to private homes, men's networks have become domesticated just as women's usually have been. Women have moved beyond their traditional kinkeeping role to assume the triple load of paid work, domestic work, and net work. They are the ones who keep their households in touch with friends, neighbors, relatives, and in-laws. Consequently, women now have more influence in defining the nature of friendship and other community ties. Concomitantly, personal communities now heavily emphasize sociable companionship and emotional support rather than the mutual exchange of supportive goods and services.

VII. SOCIAL SUPPORT

A large body of social scientific and medical research has investigated the extent to which interpersonal social support affects mental health and well-being. This research has concentrated on documenting health-promoting outcomes: showing that social support helps people to be happier, healthier, and longer-lived. However, the field has often taken the causes of social support for granted. Many support analysts originally believed that social support was a single, generalized interpersonal resource to deal with routine problems, acute crises, and chronic burdens. They assumed that it was supplied by all network members; hence, they confused network ties with supportive ties. They treated social support as a unidimensional, sensitizing metaphor rather than as a variable to be studied.

When one looks only for supportive ties, one finds only supportive ties. This introduces a triple distortion. First, it limits consideration of the content of ties to their supportive elements. Second, it unwarrantedly assumes that social support is always given by an individual provider acting voluntarily and in social isolation. Third, it distorts the structure of social networks by wrenching these ties out of the large networks in which they are embedded and that give them meaning.

Social support does not appear by magic; it is conveyed through personal community networks. The nature and kind of social support are variable phenomena. In addition to analyzing the consequences of social support for health, investigators need to consider its etiology and to understand what kinds of personal relationships and community networks produce which kinds of social support. For analytic purposes, social support should be deconstructed into its constituents, operationalized for measurement, and studied for its functionality. By treating social support as a set of contingencies that might occur, and not as a given, analysts gain more power because they can study the circumstances under which a tie will or will not provide support. They can do a more fine-grained investigation of how the quantity and quality of support conveyed is related to the composition of personal networks, the nature of the relationships, and the ways in which these relationships are structured. This approach keeps social support as the object of study, but uses personal community networks as the subject of study.

Although mental health analysts have used "the social network" as a metaphor since the 1960s, few have embraced the substance, theory, or methods of the social network paradigm. Yet social network analysis offers several leverage points for studying mental health:

1. Its avoidance of the assumption that people necessarily interact in neighborhoods, kin groups or other bounded solidarities facilitates the study of a wide range of relationships wherever located and however structured.
2. Its ability to study links ranging from interpersonal relations to world systems facilitates the analytic connection of everyday lives with large-scale social change.
3. Its ability to disentangle different types of resource flows allows analysts to examine how different types of social support affect mental health and well-being.
4. It has developed a body of techniques, both quali-

tative and quantitative, for discovering and describing the presence, composition, structure, and contents of interpersonal networks.

As theory and research developed in the 1980s, researchers discovered that although most active community members provide support, their support is usually specialized. Different network members often provide emotional aid, financial aid, routine goods and services, material aid in crises, information, and companionship. Thus personal communities often have distinct divisions of labor, with kin, friends, neighbors, and workmates rarely being interchangeable parts. Not only do kin behave differently from friends in the provision of support, parents and their adult children, siblings, and extended kin each exhibit distinct patterns of support. The ties between parents and adult children are the strongest, and provide emotional support along with both small and large services. Siblings behave similarly to friends in providing emotional support, and extended kin are the least likely of all network members to render any kind of support. The dearth of aid from extended kin suggests that the supportive power of kinship rarely extends beyond a small number of immediate kin. Extended kin are network members because of their positions in kinship systems and not because they are supportive or companions. Neighbors provide small services, some companionship, but little else. Despite their frequent exchanges of services, neighbors and co-workers are often not socially close. They help each other out of convenience. There is no association between frequency of face-to-face contact and the strength of the relationship.

Differentiation in the nature and source of social support means that people must work hard to maintain diverse, supportive relations with a variety of network members. They cannot rely on more than one or two network members to provide a wide range of support (typically a parent, adult child, or very close friend). To be able to obtain a variety of resources, they must maintain portfolios of specialized ties. They cannot and do not assume that each or all of their relationships will help them, no matter what the problem is. Yet, taken as a whole, personal community networks provide a broad range of support so that people can count on finding the kind of support they need from somewhere in their network.

Gender is the personal characteristic most clearly related to support, with women providing more emotional aid than men. Mothers, daughters, and sisters have particularly strong ties. More generally, women fix relations and keep households and networks going. Although intimate ties (with men as well as women, friends as well as kin) are more apt to provide companionship and emotional aid, all intimate ties are not especially likely to provide financial aid or crisis intervention. That is the domain of immediate kin, whether or not they are intimate. Yet parents and children are not likely to be companions. That is the domain of friends, siblings, workmates, and for some women, neighbors.

There has been more research into which kinds of ties are supportive than there has been into what kinds of network characteristics are associated with supportive networks: network member composition, relational characteristics, and network structure. The *range* of a network—its *size* and *heterogeneity*—is the set of network characteristics most clearly associated with the provision of support. Not only are large networks likely to provide more support, but there is some evidence that each member of a large network is more apt to be supportive: the quality of relationships is positively associated with the quantity of relationships. Furthermore, socially heterogeneous networks are more apt to provide a range of useful information because they connect with a more socially diverse array of other networks.

The *availability* of a network—frequent contact and physical accessibility—substantially fosters the provision of goods and services. Not only are network members physically able to deliver tangible aid, but frequent contact helps in making the arrangements that are necessary for the provision of such support.

Densely knit networks, with *clusters* of kin (or, more rarely, close friends) usually provide more emotional and material support. The many interpersonal interconnections of densely knit networks aid communication about needs, normative mobilization to deal with problems, and coordination of effective delivery.

The *composition* of networks affects the provision of support. Networks with a higher percentage (or number) of women usually provide more emotional support, and networks with many members of high socioeconomic status can provide more information and more material aid.

Thus, the supportiveness of networks is related to the aggregated characteristics of network members and relationships as well as to the emergent structural properties of networks. Many structural effects cannot be inferred from the aggregated characteristics of ties. When it comes to providing social support, a social network is more than the sum of its ties. [*See* SOCIAL SUPPORT.]

VIII. A COMPARATIVE PERSPECTIVE

Unlike traditional conceptions of community and social support, personal community networks are not merely passive refuges from large-scale social forces. They are active arrangements by which people and households reproduce and engage with the outside world. Most studies of social support and social networks have been conducted in the developed Western world, yet too many researchers have unwarrantedly generalized their findings to other milieus.

The supportive networks of the Western world—with its comparatively high level of general material comfort—differ substantially from those of people in other circumstances. The low importance of work and politics in the networks of affluent members of the Western world differs from the prominence of work and politics in the social networks of people who are less economically or politically secure. Most members of the developed Western world are not coping with shortages in consumer goods or pervasive bureaucratic regulation of their daily lives. They rely on market exchanges for almost all of their production and for much of their consumption. Despite some variation, many institutional benefits such as schooling and medical care are available to Westerners as citizenship rights. Hence, materially comfortable Westerners do not pay as much attention as do members of subsistence or central-bureaucratic societies to having network connections with persons skilled in making and fixing things or with strong links to influential bureaucratic circles. Having no urgent cares about daily survival, Westerners can manage domestic resources with less apprehension than those living on the margins.

The social networks of Westerners are built around providing companionship, calming domestic stresses, and obtaining reliable, flexible, low-cost domestic services. These are not trivial pursuits, as few people want to place themselves at the mercy of markets and institutions when they need to deal with their needs. Although analysts are just starting to calculate the costs and benefits of transactions in personal networks, such networks clearly contribute important and central resources that enable people to go about their daily lives, handle chronic stresses, and cope with acute crises.

These are networks that primarily support reproduction, and not production. They center primarily on the household, secondarily on the neighborhood and active community ties, and rarely with earning a living. These personal networks provide havens: a sense of belonging and being helped. They provide bandages for routine emotional support and services to help people cope with the stresses and strains of their situations. They provide safety nets that lessen the impact of acute crises and chronic difficulties. These networks are not just passive reactors. They provide people with social capital: to change situations—homes, jobs, spouses—or to change the world through interest group activity. These networks are important to the routine operation of households, crucial for the management of crises, and instrumental in helping people to change their situations.

BIBLIOGRAPHY

Berkowitz, S. D. (1982). *An introduction to structural analysis: The network approach to social research.* Toronto: Butterworth.

Borgatti, S., Everett, M., Freeman, L. C. (1992). *UCINET IV Version 1.0.* Columbia, SC: Analytic Technologies.

Burt, R. S. (1992). *Structural holes: The social structure of competition.* Cambridge, MA: Harvard University Press.

Fischer, C. S. (1983). *To dwell among friends: Personal networks in town and city.* Chicago: University of Chicago Press.

Granovetter, M. (1982). The strength of weak ties: A network theory revisited. In P. Marsden & N. Lin (Eds.), *Social Structure and Network Analysis* (pp. 105–130). Beverly Hills, CA: Sage.

Scott, J. (1992). *Social network analysis.* London: Sage.

Wasserman, S. & Faust, K. (1994). *Social network analysis: Methods and applications.* Cambridge: Cambridge University Press.

Wellman, B. (1988). The community question reevaluated. In M. P. Smith (Ed.), *Power, community and the city* (pp. 81–107). New Brunswick, NJ: Transaction Books.

Wellman, B. (1992). Which types of ties and networks give what kinds of social support? In E. Lawler, B. Markovsky, C. Ridgeway, & H. Walker (Eds.), *Advances in group processes* (Vol. 9). Greenwich, CT: JAI Press.

Wellman, B. & Berkowitz, S. D. (Eds.). (1997). *Social structures: A network approach* (updated ed.). Greenwich, CT: JAI Press.

Social Support

Mario S. Rodriguez

Carnegie Mellon University and University of Pittsburgh

Sheldon Cohen

Carnegie Mellon University

Direct (or Main) Effect Model A theoretical model of social support that suggests that social support enhances health and well-being irrespective of stress exposure.

Functional Support The psychological and material resources available from an individual's interpersonal relationships; types of functional support generally include instrumental (or tangible) support, emotional support, and informational support.

Social Integration A theoretical construct that refers to the extent of participation and involvement (or embeddedness) of a person in his or her social network.

Social Network A system of interpersonal relationships.

Social Support A multidimensional construct that refers to the characteristics and functions of social relationships thought to enhance mental and physical health; also, the psychological and material resources available to individuals through their social networks.

Stress-Buffering Model A theoretical model of social support that proposes that social support protects or buffers individuals from the harmful effects of stress on health and well-being, and that the beneficial effects of social support can only occur when individuals are exposed to stress.

Stressor-Resource Matching Hypothesis Proposes that for social support to have a protective effect against stress, the support resources that are perceived to be available must match the support needs that are elicited by a stressful event.

Structural Support The extent and interconnectedness of an individual's social relationships.

SOCIAL SUPPORT is a multidimensional construct that refers to the psychological and material resources available to individuals through their interpersonal relationships. Social support is thought to have beneficial effects on both mental and physical health. This article presents a discussion of the fundamental concepts and approaches used in the study of social support and its relations to well-being. Representative studies from the social support literature are presented to illustrate key concepts as well as to provide evidence linking social support and health.

I. INTRODUCTION

A substantial body of research has documented relations between the extent and quality of social relationships and better mental and physical health. Early research revealed that individuals who were socially isolated or unmarried were more likely to commit suicide, had higher age-adjusted mortality rates from all causes of death, and higher rates of tuberculosis, accidents, and psychiatric disorders than their more socially connected and married counterparts. Having social relationships can also have negative effects on well-being, particularly when relationships become a source of stress, for example, enduring conflicts with a spouse or excessive demands and criticism from an employer. Notwithstanding the potential adverse effects of social relationships, research in the last two decades has focused primarily on socially derived health benefits. The term *social support* has been used to refer to the characteristics and functions of social relationships thought to enhance mental and physical health. Psychologists, sociologists, epidemiologists, medical practitioners, and other biomedical and social scientists continue to investigate the ways in which social support affects physical and psychological well-being. What remains unclear is which characteristics and functions of social support are most important for better health and well-being, and what the mechanisms are through which they operate.

The purpose of this article is to briefly review the psychosocial and biomedical literature that helps explain how the social environment can positively affect health and well-being. We begin by clarifying the ways that social support has been conceptualized and the basic measurement approaches used to study it. We review the prevalent theoretical models and key concepts that have guided research in this area. Findings from representative studies demonstrating ways the social environment can improve psychological and physical health are presented. Lastly, we discuss the various types of support interventions with an emphasis on support groups, citing examples from the research literature.

II. DIMENSIONS OF SOCIAL SUPPORT

Social support is a theoretically complex, multidimensional construct that has been conceptualized and measured in a variety of ways. Despite the diversity of conceptualizations and measurement strategies, the evidence that social ties have a beneficial effect on both mental and physical health is impressive. This diversity in the support literature reflects the lack of consensus within the scientific community as to a precise definition of social support. Nevertheless, the term social support generally refers to the process by which individuals manage the psychological and material resources available through their social networks to enhance their coping with stressful events, meet their

social needs, and achieve their goals. Efforts to better define social support have led to the development of several typologies of social environmental measures. The most basic of these distinguishes between measures that assess the structural characteristics of social networks (structural support) and those that assess the resources that networks provide (functional support).

Structural support measures assess the extent and interconnectedness of one's social relationships. Typical measures include marital status, the existence of friends and relatives, and membership in groups and religious organizations. The number of family members, friends, coworkers, and so on, with whom there is regular social contact is referred to as network size. Another frequently used measure of structural support, social integration, is a global index of the extent of one's social connections or embeddedness in a social network. A prototypic measure of social integration is an index that includes marital status, the number and frequency of contacts with close family and friends, participation in group activities, and church/religious affiliations. While structural support measures provide only an indirect index of the resources potentially available from one's interpersonal relationships, the structure of individuals' social networks can have important implications for the provision of support. [*See* SOCIAL NETWORKS.]

Functional support measures assess the availability of psychological and material resources from one's interpersonal relationships. Resources are usually differentiated in terms of three types of support: instrumental, informational, and emotional. Instrumental support involves the provision of material aid, for example, financial assistance or help with daily tasks. Informational support refers to the provision of relevant information intended to help the individual cope with current difficulties and typically takes the form of advice or guidance in dealing with one's problems. Emotional support involves the expression of empathy, caring, reassurance, and trust, and provides opportunities for emotional expression and venting.

In addition to the basic distinction between structural and functional support, other conceptual issues influence the ways in which social support is measured and understood. One issue is whether support must actually be received to be beneficial or if simply perceiving that support is available is sufficient to gain psychological and physical health benefits. It has been shown that perceived support and received support are not strongly related and that perceived support is associated with improved emotional adjustment to stressful life experiences, while received support often is not. Because personality traits (e.g., neuroticism, extraversion, social competence) can influence perceptions of support, it is an open question as to whether it is the actual support, the personality of persons who report greater levels of support, or both that are responsible for the benefits accrued by those reporting higher levels of available support.

There are a number of other factors thought to contribute to the relation between social support and health outcomes. These include individual differences in the need or desire for support; individual characteristics of the support recipient and provider; the nature of their relationship; circumstances surrounding the support transaction (e.g., timing of support, duration of stressful event, costs of giving and receiving support); and the match between support needs and available resources. The relative importance of these and other issues in understanding the complex processes that link social support to health and well-being are yet to be fully elucidated.

III. CONCEPTUAL MODELS OF SOCIAL SUPPORT

Two alternative conceptual models explaining how social support may affect physical and psychological health have been proposed. The first model posits that support is related to well-being only (or primarily) when people are dealing with stressful events in their lives. This model is termed the *stress-buffering* model because it suggests that support "buffers" or protects people from the potentially deleterious effects of stress on mental and physical health. Statistical tests of this model are supported by an interaction between stress and support, in which support attenuates the impact of stress on health outcomes but has no effect on health in the absence of stress. The second model proposes that social support enhances well-being irrespective of peoples' stress levels. This model is referred to as the *direct effect* (or main effect) model because it is supported by a statistical main effect of support on well-being and the absence of a stress by support interaction. Although evidence supporting both the direct effect and stress-buffering models has been reported,

these two support processes are frequently associated with different types of measures of social support. Specifically, direct effects of support are generally found when structural support measures are used, particularly social integration, whereas stress-buffering effects are more common when functional support measures are used, particularly perceived support.

The stress-buffering and direct effects models and the significance of the particular support measures most frequently associated with them are discussed in the sections that follow. We illustrate some of the conceptual issues related to each model with examples from the research literature.

A. Stress-Buffering Model

Recall that the stress-buffering model argues that social support exerts its beneficial effects in the presence of stressful events, as this is when support is needed. In this model, social support can buffer against the negative impact of stressful events in two ways. First, perceived support can intervene between the occurrence of a potentially stressful event and the experience of a psychological and physiological stress reaction by influencing appraisals of how stressful the events are. Here, perceived support may enhance individuals' perceptions about their ability to cope with the demands imposed by an event and as such a negative event may be seen as less stressful and less potentially harmful. Second, perceived support may intervene between the experience of a stress reaction following an event and the onset of a pathological process (psychological and/or physiological) by reducing or eliminating the stress reaction. At this point, support may reduce the stress response by enhancing coping efforts to deal with both the practical and emotional consequences of the event and reducing its perceived importance. Thus, social support may protect against the potentially injurious effects of stress at different times by positively influencing individuals' appraisals of both stressful events (i.e., as less threatening and harmful) and their ability to cope (i.e., as sufficient and effective, particularly with the help of others if needed).

In 1984, Sheldon Cohen and Garth McKay suggested that for support to lessen the adverse effects of stress on well-being, the resources that are perceived to be available must match the needs elicited by the stressful event. This prediction, known as the stressor-resource matching hypothesis, reflects the view of stressors as events that create deficits or losses and that the nature of the loss determines the nature of the resources needed to replace that which was lost. For example, financial loss associated with involuntary unemployment would presumably elicit needs for tangible support such as financial assistance from family and friends, whereas emotional and psychological loss associated with the death of a friend would presumably elicit needs for emotional support.

In 1990, Carolyn Cutrona and Dan Russell argued that the perceived controllability of stressful events is a critical factor in matching support resources to support needs. Specifically, stressful events that are potentially controllable are thought to elicit needs for support resources that enhance the individual's ability to actively cope (for example, by problem solving or planning) with the demands imposed by the stressor. These support resources (informational and tangible support) may in turn help individuals to cope more effectively with the consequences of an event or even prevent the event from occurring. Conversely, uncontrollable events are presumed to elicit needs for resources that facilitate the emotional processing of the negative psychological impact of the stressor. In this case, support resources (emotional support) serve to facilitate the processing of negative emotions elicited by uncontrollable events, thereby helping individuals to recover from the emotional impact of such events.

Although buffering effects generally occur when the kinds of available support match the needs elicited by a stressful event, other factors such as stressors that elicit multiple needs, needs that shift over time, and the meaning of the loss created by the stressful event complicate the application of resource-matching models to real world situations. Moreover, some stressful events may elicit needs other than those for informational, emotional, and tangible resources. A special case of a stress-induced loss that creates other needs is the loss of an intimate relationship, such as the death of a spouse. Wolfgang and Margaret Stroebe have recently argued that the loss of a spouse represents not only the loss of the support they provided, but also the loss of a significant social role that comprised the individual's sense of identity, self-esteem, and self-worth. Consequently, replacing the resources traditionally thought to be depleted by stressful events (instrumental, emotional, and esteem support) may not be sufficient to buffer the effects of losing an intimate network member. This is exemplified in a recent longitudinal study of 60 widowed men and women that found that the support of friends and family could not compensate for the loss of a spouse.

Many studies have documented evidence supporting the stress-buffering model in relation to mental health outcomes. Early research in this area demonstrated buffering effects of perceived emotional support on suicide attempts in bereaved persons, psychological distress in single parents, adjustment in students returning to school, and depression in the recently unemployed, pregnant teenagers, and widows. In a review of the research on the effects of social support on mental health in community samples, four of five studies that examined interactions between perceived support and stressful life events found significant stress-buffering effects of support. For example, in a study of 320 community-dwelling adults, those with more stressful life events reported greater psychological distress. However, the relation between stressful events and distress was attenuated among those with the most potential supporters. A stress-buffering effect was also found in a study of 1809 men working in a manufacturing plant. Although higher levels of job stress were associated with greater psychological distress, this association was attenuated among men with more emotional support from spouses and coworkers (but not from supervisors and other family members). A study of 636 adults employed in a variety of occupations found similar stress-buffering effects of emotional, tangible, and informational support. Although greater job stress was associated with work related strains such as job dissatisfaction and boredom, support from family, coworkers, or friends greatly attenuated this relation. Finally, in a study of 1026 married community residents, perceived support (emotional, tangible, and informational) was found to buffer against the effects of undesirable life events on depressive symptoms among homemakers (but not among men or women in the labor force).

Other studies have examined the role of perceived support on stress-induced physical health outcomes. Most of this research has focused on the role of support for chronically ill (and therefore high stress) patients and do not include low-stress comparison groups. Outcome measures have included self-reported somatic symptoms; biologically verifiable markers of disease, such as cardiovascular events, cancer survival, pregnancy outcomes, and neuroendocrine and immune function; health behaviors, such as tobacco use, exercise, diet, and adherence to prescribed medical treatments; and health care utilization, such as emergency room visits, number of postsurgical hospital days, and health care costs. These types of studies have documented enhanced recovery, longer survival, increased compliance, and better psychosocial adjustment in patients reporting higher levels of support (including perceived availability of emotional, instrumental, and informational support as well as membership in affiliative networks) across a range of medical populations. For example, response to rehabilitation following stroke, orthopedic disability, and myocardial infarction has been associated with greater perceived emotional and instrumental support.

Other studies have included low-stress comparison groups and hence can be used to distinguish stress-buffering from direct effects of perceived support. For example, women who reported high numbers of stressful life events before and during pregnancy experienced more pregnancy complications. However, this association was attenuated among those with social resources provided by spouse, extended family, and friends. In another study, asthmatic adults who reported high numbers of stressful life events took more asthma medication, but those reporting greater availability of social support resources were protected from stress-induced increases in medication use. Finally, in a study of recently unemployed males, perceived emotional support (from spouse, friends, and relatives) was found to buffer against the effects of unemployment-related stress on self-reported physical symptoms and on a biological measure associated with risk of coronary heart disease—serum cholesterol level. Specifically, unemployed males with low emotional support had higher serum cholesterol and more physical symptoms than those with high emotional support or those who were promptly reemployed (low stress).

A recent study examined the somatic and psychological effects of common everyday stress (or hassles) and the roles of perceived emotional support in the stress process. Seventy-five married couples completed a battery of questionnaires and were interviewed once a month for 6 months. Participants also provided daily reports (for a total of 20 days) of stress, physical health, and psychological well-being. Perceived emotional support (from spouse, close family and friends, and work supervisor combined) buffered against the negative effects of daily stress on same-day mood as well as on physical symptom reports on the day following a high stress day.

The studies just described all report findings of an interaction of social support with stress that resulted in an attenuation of the impact of stress on some health outcome. As such, these studies provide evidence consistent with the beneficial buffering effect of perceived support on health in persons experiencing increased levels of stress. Although these studies all showed stress-buffering effects of perceived support on physical well-being, the literature also includes evidence consistent with main effects of perceived support on health, although main effects are more often found when support is indexed using measures of social integration. [*See* COPING WITH STRESS; STRESS.]

B. Direct Effect Model

Recall that the direct effect model proposes that having social relationships has an overall beneficial effect on individuals' health and well-being regardless of the occurrence of stressful events. In addition, direct effects are most frequently observed when structural support measures are used, particularly social integration. Direct benefits of social integration could occur because diverse social networks provide individuals with sets of stable, socially rewarded roles in the community, and regular positive interpersonal experiences. In addition, socially integrated individuals may be more likely to receive feedback from others that helps them to form their self-identities and promotes feelings of self-worth, predictability, stability, and control in their lives. Finally, direct benefits of social integration may also reflect the effect of extreme isolation for those with very few social connections.

Several epidemiological studies of community residents have reported evidence supporting direct effects of social integration on mental health. For example, in a longitudinal study of 2234 health insurance subscribers, socially integrated persons were found to have less anxiety, less depression, and greater positive well-being over a 1-year period regardless of their level of stressful life events. In a cross-sectional study examining negative life events and chronic strains (financial, marital, and work-related) in 1003 adults residing in Los Angeles, a single-item measure of the total number of close relatives and friends was also found to have a direct effect on reports of depressive symptoms. Finally, in a study of 170 Chinese American adults residing in Washington, D.C., higher scores on a social network index measure (including marital status, number of friends and relatives, membership in clubs and church, and frequency of social interactions) were associated with less psychological distress irrespective of individuals' scores on a weighted life events inventory. The evidence provided by these and other studies suggest that being embedded in a diverse social network is directly associated with better mental health.

Although direct effects of support on health and well-being are typically found for social integration, direct effects of perceived support has also been documented. In a recent study of 1174 elderly men and women (age >50), three types of stressors (physical disability, financial strain, and undesirable life events) were included to investigate the possible buffering effects of perceived emotional support from specific sources on depressive symptoms. Although increases in all three types of stress were associated with greater depressive symptoms and greater perceived emotional support with fewer symptoms, no statistical interactions between stressors and support were found. It is possible that buffering effects were not found in this case because the measure of support tapped unspecific emotional support but did not assess support associated with a specific stressful event.

The most provocative evidence linking social integration to physical health is provided by epidemiological studies of all-cause mortality. Studies of community residents followed over an extended period of time (30 months to 12 years) have shown that initially healthy people with relatively lower levels of social integration have higher mortality rates from all causes, even after controlling for traditional risk factors such as blood pressure, cigarette smoking, and serum cholesterol. One such study followed a sample of 4775 healthy residents of Alameda County, California, for 9 years beginning in 1965. A social network index comprised of marriage, contacts with family and friends, church membership, and other group affiliations predicted mortality such that persons with fewer types of relationships were twice as likely to die as persons with more, even after statistically controlling for physical health at study onset, socioeconomic status, smoking, alcohol consumption, physical activity, obesity, race, life satisfaction, and use of preventive health services. In another study of 2059 adults in Evans County, Georgia, a similar social network index predicted mortality for an 11-to-13 year follow-up period, after statistically controlling for age and baseline measures of biomedical as well as self-reported risk factors for mortality. The relation between social integration and mortality is generally weaker for women and non-Whites than for White men, although the data on gender differences is somewhat mixed.

Evidence that social integration predicts mortality in initially unhealthy persons also exists. For example, in a study of male survivors of acute myocardial infarction (MI) those who were less socially integrated during the 1-to-3 year post-MI follow-up period were found to have more total deaths and more sudden cardiac deaths than their more integrated counterparts. Several studies have also reported prospective associations between social integration and increased survival in patients with cancer. In one study of 118 women with breast cancer (any stage) social integration measured at study onset was related to a greater likelihood of survival over 1 to 4 years. In a study of 208 women with local and regional breast cancer, social integration measured at study onset was associated with longer survival over a 20 year follow-up period, even after controlling for stage at diagnosis, past health status, and socioeconomic status.

It is thought that persons who are embedded in a social network may benefit from a set of stable, socially rewarded roles that provide regular social interactions, a sense of predictability and stability in one's life, a source of self-esteem and self-worth, and that may help maintain positive affect. This kind of support may in turn be related to better physical health outcomes through effects on neuroendocrine or immune system functioning or on health-related behavioral patterns, such as reduced smoking and alcohol consumption, or promoting medical help seeking. Alternatively, feeling that one is valued and held in high esteem by others may influence motivation to get well and consequently increase adherence to medical regimens and improve performance of health care behaviors. [See SELF-ESTEEM.]

Although associated with survival among persons suffering from life-threatening chronic illnesses, existing studies provide little support for relations between social integration and the *onset* of specific diseases that may contribute to mortality. Only one of two studies (both of Japanese American men) found social integration associated with the onset of coronary artery disease. Neither of two studies that examined the effects of social integration on the onset of cancer found a relation. One of these studies followed 2603 men and women over 15 years. The other followed 6848 men and women over 17 years. Thus, while considerable evidence exists for an association between social integration and total mortality, and between social integration and recovery from chronic illness, there is currently little evidence for a similar effect of social integration on the onset of physical disease.

IV. SOCIAL SUPPORT INTERVENTIONS

The purpose of support interventions is to increase the quality and/or quantity of socially derived resources. In general, support interventions attempt to create new social networks or enhance interactions with existing network members so as to optimize the match between an individual's psychosocial needs and the provision of support resources. In this section, we briefly describe the basic types of support interventions and focus on the most common among them, namely support groups. We then present several examples of intervention studies drawn from the research literature and discuss some of the factors that can influence the effectiveness of support interventions.

In theory, there are several different types of interventions that could increase the availability of social support in the face of stressful events. For example, one could train individuals to develop, maintain, and mobilize their natural support networks, or train existing network members to recognize and effectively respond to the needs of the person or persons facing a stressful challenge. However, in practice, most social support interventions have attempted to supplement existing networks by creating new networks made up of people experiencing the same stressful event, e.g., fellow cancer patients, divorcees, or widows. These "support groups" are intended to provide a level of empathy and understanding not available from others who have not experienced the same traumatic event.

Support group interventions are the most widely used and most widely studied type of social support intervention. They involve the creation of social aggregates composed of similar peers experiencing or anticipating the same or similar stressful life events or transitions. Essentially, support groups supplement or substitute for the network of ongoing social contracts that people maintain in their daily life, thereby increasing their access to support provisions. Support group interventions are based on the assumption that social comparison among similar peers can improve coping and foster adaptation. Specifically, the social comparison process facilitates the expression of nega-

tive affect, offers validation for new social identities and roles, and reduces threatening appraisals of both current and future stressors. It has been suggested that this process of social comparison is central to social support's stress-buffering role, and is in large part responsible for producing its beneficial effects on cognitive, affective, behavioral, and physiological functioning. Lastly, support group interventions typically include several steps: creating interpersonal conditions that are conducive to the expression of support needs; teaching group members how to recognize and respond to requests for support; promoting the responsive provision of support, and assessing the impact of support transactions.

There is considerable evidence to suggest that support groups can be associated with better psychosocial adjustment to stressful life changes and better health outcomes in persons with a variety of physical illnesses. Support group interventions have been applied to a variety of populations, including the bereaved, recently separated or divorced persons, children coping with parental separation, individuals with serious chronic or life-threatening illnesses (such as rheumatoid arthritis, CHD, and cancer), and persons attempting behavioral life-style changes that impact on their health, including smoking cessation, weight reduction, and abstinence from drugs and alcohol.

One reason for the ubiquity of the support group format is that it is cost-effective. This is primarily because many individuals can gain psychosocial benefits simultaneously. However, it is also because many types of support groups do not necessarily require highly trained mental health professionals to lead or facilitate them. Although many types of support groups can be led effectively by nonprofessionals, professional consultation is needed to develop group intervention protocols, screen and identify appropriate group members, and train nonprofessional group leaders to manage group processes and facilitate therapeutic communication between group members. Poorly designed and managed groups have a tremendous potential for harming the well-being of group members, and the formation of such groups should not be taken lightly or without experienced professional consultation.

Support group interventions can offer several advantages over individual (one-on-one) support interventions. These advantages include role modeling by group members for one another, learning new solutions to commonly shared problems, thereby increasing members' repertoires of effective coping skills, enhanced self-esteem and self-efficacy gained through helping others, and a sense of community and belonging not available in traditional, individual intervention approaches. Conversely, participation in a support group may also expose individuals to group members who are unable to cope effectively with their stressful life circumstances and who consequently experience significant hardship and distress. This kind of exposure can precipitate negative emotional reactions among group members that can result in negative appraisals of their own coping abilities, reduced expectations about potential outcomes, and even withdrawal from the group resulting in a reduction in support. Thus, while support groups can provide emotional, informational, and esteem support, reduce feelings of isolation, enhance participants' repertoire of coping strategies, and are cost-effective, they can also have the paradoxical effect of increasing negative affect. Negative emotional reactions, including feelings of helplessness, hopelessness, and decreased feelings of control and self-esteem, are more likely to occur if there is a poor match between the individual's needs and the resources available from a support group. Negative emotional reactions can also occur if group processes and interpersonal interactions are left unchecked and allowed to create an overly critical and defensive atmosphere rather than one of mutual support and acceptance.

In addition to the careful selection of group members, the effective management of group dynamics, and the monitoring of interpersonal interactions to ensure group cohesion, the timing and duration of support group interventions have also been shown to be important factors in determining their success. The optimal timing and duration of support group interventions depends on the nature of the stressful life events or transitions that group members share. For example, some stressful life events, such as school entrance, job change, or new parenthood, are clearly time-limited and characterized by an intensive period of adjustment. Support groups for individuals facing such events should be offered at a time that coincides with the intensive period of adjustment that is required. These groups can be time-limited so as to maximize the provision of support resources when they are needed most. Other life changes and stressful experiences, such as caregiving to a relative with Alzheimer's disease or parenting a child with a physical

or mental disability, engender chronic burdens that continuously tax the adaptive resources of the affected individual. The support needs of individuals facing these types of stressors may best be met by support groups that are open-ended (not time-limited and able to accept new members at any time) and therefore able to provide ongoing support for extended periods of time.

Evidence that support groups can facilitate the process of adjustment following stressful life events has been reported in the literature. For example, one study randomized 16 couples who were parents of premature infants to either a support group or a no treatment control condition. The support groups met for 1.5 to 2 hours weekly for 7 to 12 weeks. A nurse-counselor and a veteran mother of a premature infant facilitated the support groups. The support group focused on enhancing parenting competence, the quality of mother–infant interactions, and parents' attitudes towards hospital personnel and practices. Mothers who attended the support groups touched their babies more, looked at the faces of and spoke to their infants more frequently, and visited them more often in the hospital than did mothers in the control groups. Because this intervention study included an educational component aimed at increasing parenting competence, it is unclear to what extent the results can be attributed solely to the effects of emotional support versus those of informational (education) support.

Studies have also shown benefits of group approaches to the provision of social support for patients with chronic and/or life threatening illnesses. For example, support group interventions for cancer patients have not only shown improvements in mood, psychosocial adjustment, and pain, but also in survival. One such study found that women with metastatic breast cancer who were randomly assigned to participate in a psychosocial support group lived on average 18 months longer than did those in the control group. The support groups, which met once a week for 12 months and were led by mental health professionals, focused on participants' coping efforts in dealing with cancer, their feelings about the illness, its effect on their lives, death and dying, and the development of strong supportive relationships between group members. Although this and other support intervention studies with cancer patients have shown psychological and physical health benefits, the studies are few in number and involve different intervention protocols and interventions involving multiple types of support making it difficult to identify the specific support components driving the effects. [See Cancer.]

Some studies evaluating the impact of support groups on mental and physical health outcomes fail to demonstrate beneficial effects. In a recent review of support interventions for rheumatoid arthritis patients, several studies showed no effects of support group participation on psychological or physical functioning. One of these studies compared mutual support, stress management (10 sessions each), and no-treatment control groups, and found no differences in life satisfaction, depression, or health status measures (such as joint tenderness and pain) at postintervention or 8 month follow-up assessments.

In addition to support groups, other types of support interventions have been used to enhance the provision of direct support aimed at improving health outcomes. One alternative intervention approach attempts to modify the quality of the support offered by select members of an individual's social network. Such an approach was used in a study designed to help individuals quit smoking cigarettes. The results of the study showed that married persons (or those living with a partner) enrolled in a 6-week smoking cessation program were more likely to quit smoking at the end of treatment if their partners had received minimal training on how to help them quit. Two other studies have also found evidence for the beneficial role of a partner's direct support for quitting in both cessation and short-term maintenance of smoking abstinence.

In another study, a program of education and support was designed to focus on shifting families toward a calmer, more accepting, and tolerant style of interacting with a schizophrenic family member. This intervention was based on evidence that schizophrenics are more likely to experience psychotic relapses following periods of frequent contact with close relatives who express highly critical or emotionally overinvolved attitudes towards them. These investigators found that more patients from the experimental group remained free of psychotic relapse at follow-up and more of their relatives shifted from high to low levels of expressed emotion than did families in the control group.

The studies presented in the preceding paragraphs all attempted to enhance both the quantity and quality of direct support provided by the members of individuals' social networks (either preexisting or newly created), thereby improving the match between individuals' support needs and available support resources. Many of these studies have found beneficial effects of various types of support interventions on psychosocial and health outcomes, including the quality of mother–infant interactions, psychosocial adjustment and survival in women with breast cancer, smoking cessation, and lower rates of psychotic relapse in schizophrenic patients. However, most intervention studies fail to measure perceived support, making it difficult to know whether they actually succeeded in enhancing support or if observed effects are due to other factors. In addition, relatively little thinking has been done about the potential negative consequences of support interventions. Indeed, research into self-help groups suggests that at certain times and for certain people, social comparisons with others who are better or worse off may actually impede psychosocial adjustment. Finally, while emotional support is thought to be of primary importance in explaining the beneficial effects of support interventions, many of them include strong educational components, making it difficult to know which components are most responsible for the observed effects. Future research should seek to develop theoretically based interventions that permit the differentiation of the effects of specific intervention components on mental and physical health outcomes.

V. CONCLUSION

Social support is a theoretically complex, multidimensional construct that has been conceptualized and measured in a variety of ways. Despite the diversity of conceptualizations and measurement strategies, the evidence that social ties have a beneficial effect on both mental and physical health continues to grow. There is considerable evidence for both the stress-buffering and main effects of support on health and well-being. Moreover, it is clear that having diverse social ties and perceiving that support resources are available are often health enhancing. Even though there is considerable evidence for the potentially positive effects of social support, we still lack an integrated coherent theory of how such support operates in the context of complex real-life situations. As a result, our attempts at providing support through intervention programs have been limited and although promising, only partly successful. Translating theory to intervention is often cumbersome, and efficient and effective ways of intervening in the networks of persons confronting traumatic life events are still only partially fulfilled promises.

BIBLIOGRAPHY

Cohen, S. (1988). Psychosocial models of social support in the etiology of physical disease. *Health Psychology, 7,* 269–297.

Cohen, S., & Syme, S. L. (Eds.). (1985). *Social support and health.* Orlando, FL: Academic Press.

Gottlieb, B. H. (Ed.). (1988). *Marshalling social support: Formats, processes, and effects.* New York: Sage Publications.

Sarason, B. R., Sarason, I. G., & Pierce, G. R. (Eds.). (1990). *Social support: An interactional view.* New York: John Wiley and Sons.

Veiel, H. O. F., & Baumann, U. (Eds.). (1992). *The meaning and measurement of social support.* New York: Hemisphere Publishing.

Societal Influences on Mental Health

David Pilgrim

*CommuniCare NHS Trust
Blackburn, United Kingdom*

Anne Rogers

*National Primary Care Research
and Development Centre,
University of Manchester, United Kingdom*

I. Introduction
II. The Three Perspectives on the Social
III. Mental Health in Society

Biodeterminism/Biological Determinism   The view that mental health problems result from biological abnormalities inside individuals.
Deconstruction   The critical reading of texts or practices to study of how reality is socially constructed.
Deviance (Primary)   This refers to rule breaking in society, which can arise from biological, psychological or social causes.
Deviance (Secondary)   This refers to the maintenance and amplification of primary deviance by the reactions of others.
Labeling (or Societal Reaction) Theory   The study of the interaction between deviants and non-deviants to establish the processes of transition from primary to secondary deviance.
Social Causationism   The view that mental health problems are caused by stressors impinging upon individuals in their social context.
Social Constructionism   The view that all human knowledge is a product of communal exchange and that reality cannot be understood without reference to the representations created by this exchange.

This topic will be discussed in two main sections. The first refers to the competing views that exist about the conceptual and causal links existing between SOCIETY AND MENTAL HEALTH. The second will offer a wider discussion of mental health in society.

I. INTRODUCTION

The relationship between society and mental health can be broadly understood in four ways:

1. The mental health of people is biologically determined and so society is irrelevant as a causal influence, even if mental health problems have social consequences (biological determinism or bio-determinism).
2. The mental health of people is partially or wholly *caused* by societal influences (social causationism).
3. The mental health of people is a socially *negotiated* (societal reaction or labeling theory).
4. Notions of mental health and ill health are socially *constructed* (social constructionism).

Professional views in the first item on this list emphasize that social context is irrelevant because our mental health or ill health is a product of our genetic make up and brain functioning. The rest of the items on the list are summaries of professional views that, in differing ways, emphasize "the social." Each of the three will be described now in a little more detail. After that, a discussion will be provided about mental health in society.

Encyclopedia of Mental Health
Volume 3

II. THE THREE PERSPECTIVES ON THE SOCIAL

Social causationists emphasize that our mental health is a direct product of various forms of social stress, pressure, or trauma. This position does not usually problematize the diagnostic descriptions arising from this external stress. Diagnoses such as "schizophrenia" or "depression" are accepted as being valid. The social causationist is interested in accounting for these states by tracing the antecedent social conditions that increase the probability of the occurrence of various forms of mental ill health. They are also interested in the reverse of this—which social conditions protect, enhance, or maintain positive mental health. The method associated with social causationism is some version of psychiatric epidemiology. Populations or subpopulations (social groups) are studied in order to discover the distribution of first cases of mental ill health (incidence) and the aggregate of all diagnosed cases at a point in time (prevalence). In addition, the causal factors involved in variations in incidence or prevalence are proffered by researchers using this perspective.

According to those emphasizing societal reaction (labeling theorists) mental health can have a variety of causes, including biological, psychological, and social factors. However, what labeling theorists are then keen to emphasize is that in certain situations (contingencies) rule breaking is accepted, ignored, or "normalized," whereas at other times it is labeled as deviant. Once action is taken in the wake of this labeling it sets in chain a process of negotiation about a deviant role. Under these circumstances, the labeled person starts to take on the role of being a mentally ill person. This role is maintained by the views of others and the new identity that the mentally ill person ascribes to herself. The main interest of labeling theorists is *secondary deviance*. They are less interested in what caused people to act oddly in the first place (*primary deviance*). The methodological emphasis of labeling theorists, as their name implies, is on investigating the process and consequences of labeling.

The social constructionist position about mental health goes further than that put forward by the labeling theorists. Social constructionists are interested in the categories used to describe or account for primary deviance. They are concerned with understanding the ways in which concepts, constructs, or representations about mental health emerge as products of communal exchange between social groups. There is a particular emphasis within this approach on analyzing dominant professional representations and the interests that are served by them. Thus the method of investigation associated with social constructionism is *deconstruction* or *discourse analysis*. Accordingly, social constructionists emphasize that reality (about mental health or anything else) is socially constructed and thus bound up with the material and cognitive interests of social groups. This contrasts with the position of social causationists, which is that there is a stable reality that exists independently of the investigator (*realism* or *positivism*). The social constructionist is interested in examining how variations in human experience and conduct come to be represented as illness categories and how diagnoses *inscribe* a version of reality on some people but not others. [*See* MYTH OF MENTAL ILLNESS.]

Having outlined the three main social perspectives on mental health, some examples will be given of research in each.

A. Some Examples from Social Causationism

There is a large body of knowledge about the various ways in which membership of particular social groups makes people vulnerable to mental health problems. Put differently, mental health is *socially patterned*. Some examples can be summarized here:

- *Social class.* Mental health is positively correlated with social class. The poorer people are, the greater the chances that they will be diagnosed as being mentally ill. This is not to argue that rich people do not suffer mental ill health, of all degrees. The correlation indicates *the increased probability* of mental health problems with decreasing socioeconomic status.

  The direction of causality is a particular controversy that has emerged about this association between poverty and severe mental health problems. Social causationists argue that the stress of poverty increases the incidence of depression and increases the prevalence of schizophrenia (by inducing recurring relapse). By contrast, biological determinists argue that mentally ill people drift into poverty because their illness makes them socially incompetent. [*See* SOCIOECONOMIC STATUS.]

- *Gender.* Women are diagnosed as suffering from mental illness more often than are men. Most of this difference is accounted for by the diagnosis of depression. There are no gender differences in the diagnosis of the main types of psychosis (such as manic-depression or schizophrenia). The exception in this regard is the incidence of puerperal psychosis in women in the wake of childbirth, which has no male equivalent. In later life, women are more likely to develop dementia than men. This is accounted for by the slightly longer average female life span. Men are more likely than women to abuse alcohol and use illicit drugs (and thus suffer the psychological consequences of this abuse.) Men are also more likely than women to be managed in secure mental health facilities and to be treated coercively with medication. [*See* GENDER DIFFERENCES IN MENTAL HEALTH.]

- *Race.* Mental health is racially patterned. Generally, this reflects continuing disadvantages that were rooted in slavery, enforced migration, colonialism, and racial discrimination. For example, in Australia aboriginal people are overrepresented in psychiatric populations. In the United States Black, Hispanic and "Indian" groups are overrepresented. In England, Irish and Afro-Caribbean people are more likely to have mental health problems than are indigenous Whites. [*See* ETHNICITY AND MENTAL HEALTH.]

- *Age.* Certain problems emerge at different points in the life span. In old age, dementia increases in probability over time. A greater problem though is depression. Twice as many old people are depressed than they are dementing. The raised incidence of dementia is generally deemed to be an amplification of neurological deterioration that occurs with the aging process. However, social factors are also implicated. The severity of symptoms in dementia is correlated with both social stimulation and with earlier educational experience. With regard to depression in old age, this has been accounted for by one or more combination of the following stressors: poverty; the distress of multiple physical illness; aggregating grief as peers die

around survivors; understimulating living conditions; and loss of control of the latter with enforced moves to hospitals, nursing homes, or residential facilities. Severe mental health problems are also more likely to occur in young adulthood and late adolescence than in childhood and middle and later adulthood. [*See* AGING AND MENTAL HEALTH.]

- *Victims of trauma.* People who have been sexually abused (in either childhood or later years) are more likely to develop mental health problems than those who are not sexually assaulted. Problems can emerge both in the immediate wake of the abuse and many years later. The correlation with diagnosis is important to note here. The overrepresentation of survivors of sexual abuse in a psychiatric population is accounted for by all diagnoses except schizophrenia, manic-depression, and obsessive compulsive disorder. Other sources of trauma that increase the probability of suffering from mental health problems include warfare, domestic violence, being a victim of urban crime, physical injury from accidents, and bereavement. [*See* CHILD SEXUAL ABUSE.]

Because the above list of social groupings is not mutually exclusive (for example an older poor Black woman may become the victim of violent crime) the social causationist position inevitably leads to complex, multifactorial models of causation. A good example of such a complex model within a social causationist framework is provided by Brown and Harris in their study of depression in working class women in the community.

The social causationist position provides a framework for understanding the promotion of mental health in society. Among other things it would imply that the mental health of individuals and groups would be facilitated and maintained by interpersonal support throughout the life span and the avoidance of stressors such as poverty, sexism, and racism.

Critics of the social causationist position come on the one side from biodeterminists and on the other from labeling theorists and social constructionists. Biodeterminists privilege biological over social causes. Labeling theorists and social constructionists emphasize that mental health is negotiated and thus cannot be understood simply in terms of cause and effect relationships.

B. Some Examples from Labeling Theory

Labeling theorists have pointed out that a deviant role can emerge either rapidly or following a lengthy period when oddity is present but a problem is denied. For example, in one study it was found that the partners of men eventually diagnosed as schizophrenic ignored or rationalized symptoms for varying periods of time before they sought professional help. Similar denials can be found for long periods of time in the relatives of people with severe alcohol problems. This picture about prediagnosed events is consistent with the finding of community surveys that the incidence of symptoms exceeds the incidence of formal diagnosis. This has been described as the "clinical iceberg" phenomenon. More recently, there is evidence that hearing voices (auditory hallucinations) is widespread in community samples, and that voice hearers who have not been diagnosed as suffering from schizophrenia have various ways of living with the experience. This prediagnosed abnormality is termed "primary deviance" within a labeling theory framework.

Of greater interest to labeling theorists is the development of *secondary deviance*. In particular, there is an interest in the circumstances under which primary deviance is confirmed and amplified by contact with professionals. The first part of this is that in the lay area, relatives or other "significant others" change from tolerating, denying, or ignoring problem behavior and begin to acknowledge its existence. Mental illness is recognized in families before professionals are invited to rubber stamp this lay decision making. Labeling theorists then point out that the combined forces of labeling from professionals and significant others defines the deviant person in a new role (of psychiatric patient). The final phase of the process entails the labeled person accepting or internalizing the ascribed deviant identity. Mental hospitalization strips them of their old identity in what Goffman calls a "status degradation ceremony" and is replaced by a new identity and social role. Being a patient can then become a "career."

While generally a deviant role takes a while to emerge and to be confirmed and internalized, there has been some experimental evidence that it can occur very rapidly. For example, in one study, confederate "pseudopatients" were admitted to psychiatric facilities by presenting with isolated auditory hallucinations. In all other respects the confederates did not act

oddly once admitted. Despite this, the psychiatric staff treated them as if they were mentally ill and reframed their actions in this light. For example, when the confederates were seen keeping field notes, their actions were recorded as "indulges in writing behavior."

The popularity of labeling theory declined in part because supporting empirical evidence was weak or ambiguous. There is certainly strong evidence that being in an institutional setting both induces oddity and socially disables residents. Also, the ascription of psychiatric deviance is commoner in social groups that are relatively powerless. For example, women are more likely to labeled mentally ill than are men in lay networks. However, these findings need to be set against others. If lay people are so important in shaping the labeling process, we would expect their stereotypes of mental illness to mirror the patterning of psychiatric diagnosis in society. However, this is not the case. Lay people emphasize florid psychotic symptoms in their stereotypes and fail to describe depression. The latter is the commonest of all psychiatric diagnoses. Similarly, psychiatrists do not always concur with the ascriptions of deviance made by family members. Moreover, the confederates in the experiment noted above did not, once the study was over, continue to act oddly because they had taken on the role of a psychiatric patient and been confirmed in this role by the staff.

C. Some Examples from Social Constructionism

Social constructionists who have researched mental health have made two main critical points. The first is that concepts (or constructs) that are fragile, incoherent, illogical, or invalid may still survive or may even be actively promoted in society. The second point they make is that constructs serve the interests of the social groups associated with discourses utilizing them (e.g., mental health professionals, relatives of identified patients, drug companies). Here are some examples from the field of mental health:

1. Schizophrenia has the status of an illness and yet the diagnosis lacks both conceptual validity and reliability. Two people with no symptoms in common can both be diagnosed as schizophrenic—it is a disjunctive construct. Despite vast amounts of research funding over the past 100 years for investigations that

have tested a variety of environmental and biological hypotheses the etiology of the disease remains unknown. There is no biological marker (analogous to a blood test to diagnose diabetes) for schizophrenia. One possible explanation for the continuation of a weak construct is the role it plays in supporting the mandate of psychiatry in society and the comfort it gives to the relatives of mad people. [*See* SCHIZOPHRENIA.]

2. Agoraphobia emerged at a time in society when the social emancipation of women became a possibility. For this reason, the meaning of the condition can be understood as part of a context that problematized the use of public space, not just as a set of symptoms within its individual sufferers. [*See* PHOBIAS.]

3. Like schizophrenia, the concept of psychopathy is incoherent because it covers so many people who have different symptoms but can share the same label and has no biological marker. The definition is inevitably circular. People are deemed to be psychopathic because of their antisocial acts and their antisocial acts are explained by the actor's psychopathy. As a consequence, there is no independent way of validating the diagnosis. It has the same explanatory value as the notion of evil. Given that evil has been medicalized, the deconstructionist would be interested in the social history of this professional interest in certain types of antisocial action.

4. Depression seems to be a straightforward description of depressed mood. However, ascriptions of helplessness, powerlessness, and worthlessness can only be made in relation to interpersonal processes. Thus depression cannot be understood simply as a set of affective and cognitive characteristics of suffering individuals—it is defined and constituted by social processes. [*See* DEPRESSION.]

These are some specific examples of how psychiatric diagnoses might be understood within a social constructionist framework. Some deconstructionists, like Szasz, have argued that the whole body of knowledge that follows from a commitment to the notion of mental illness has arisen in order to ensure the individual and collective advancement of psychiatric professionals and to protect the social order. In this way, he argues, professional knowledge, professional advancement, and social control are intimately entwined. Other deconstructionists such as Rose, extending the work of Foucault, go farther and argue that voluntary

therapies that are anxiously sought and gratefully received by clients also contribute to social order via self-surveillance and the individualization of distress.

III. MENTAL HEALTH IN SOCIETY

Having outlined the three main perspectives on the social in discussions about mental health, we will now discuss some wider issues about mental health in society.

A. Mental Health or Mental Illness?

Both professionals and lay people have a disproportionate interest in mental abnormality or illness. This in itself is a social phenomenon. The term "mental health" in recent years has come to be used throughout Western societies as a substitute for its opposite (mental illness). For example, it is commonplace now to hear terms such as ""mental health policy" or "mental health facilities," which are actually euphemisms that refer to the management of mental abnormality in society.

Neither professionals nor lay people have a well-proved facility for discussing mental health. For example, all of the approaches described above refer to perspectives on mental abnormality—how it is determined, negotiated, or constructed. There has been comparatively little professional interest in positive notions of mental health. Moreover, much of this minority interest has been defined in relation to *preventing* mental illness. This lopsided interest in illness or abnormality reflects social processes that are common to professionals and lay people alike. Sociologists of talk point out that we are generally asked to produce accounts for others when things go wrong. For example, if a rule is broken, a convention breaks down, or a person acts out of character or out of role, explanations are expected. These explanations may be invited from the people acting in a deviant way, those who witness the events or those who are responsible for formally recognizing and managing their consequences. By contrast, when life goes smoothly with no rule infraction and people acting in the way they expect of others and themselves, there are few calls for explanation. As a consequence of this difference between the two conditions, we become much more skilled at articulating reasons for abnormal than for normal phenomena in everyday life.

B. Professionals and Mental Health

Mental health professionals hold a wide variety of views about the focus of their expertise. The social constructionist perspective noted above would suggest that mental health has been the subject of diverse or fragmented discourses. Professionals are noted more for their disagreement about mental health rather than for their consensus. The only clear point of agreement (note the previous section) is the emphasis on *mental abnormality*, not *mental health*. The discourse on mental health is noteworthy for its minority status. The following criteria have been put forward for positive mental health that reflects a combination of psychoanalysis, humanistic psychology, and everyday notions of normality.

1. Balance of psychic forces;
2. Self-actualization;
3. Resistance to stress;
4. Autonomy;
5. Competence;
6. Perception of reality.

All of these criteria can be rendered problematic if understood in their social context. The first two are only meaningful to people in cultures that contain and appreciate psychoanalysis or humanistic psychology. Resistance to stress is superficially appealing but what of those people who are unperturbed by stress? Many psychiatrists would describe these as "primary psychopaths." As for autonomy, what of people who are compulsively independent and avoid social relationships? Competence is not an invariant capacity but relies for its definition on value judgments made in a specific social setting about conformity to expectations of roles and rules. The social context also determines whose judgment prevails about the competence of others. Finally, judgments about accurate perception of reality are social judgments. Hearing voices, or seeing things others cannot, may be judged as signs of mystical powers in one culture or they may be deemed to be symptomatic of schizophrenia in another.

Notwithstanding these difficulties with conceptualizing positive mental health, the main point here is that such a positive view is rare in comparison to a variable Western professional discourse about abnor-mality. Below we list some competing perspectives within this professional field:

1. Biodeterminism;
2. Social causationism;
3. Psychoanalysis;
4. Behavioral psychology;
5. Humanistic psychology;
6. Legalism.

Biodeterminism was mentioned at the start of this entry. Mental illness is deemed to be a nonproblematic fact and a direct result of biological abnormalities. Although some version of biodeterminism has been central to the development of psychiatry as a branch of medicine, it has attracted recurrent criticism. The latter mainly centers on the illogicality of asserting biological causation in the absence of empirical evidence. As confirmation of the dominant role of biological reasoning within psychiatry, these critics are labeled as "antipsychiatrists." In other words, to challenge biology is to challenge psychiatry as a profession.

Some psychiatrists are *social causationists*. They accept the legitimacy of mental illness but they explain the occurrence of symptoms in people who are either genetically vulnerable to social stress or who are traumatized or emotionally distressed by external stressors. This position is also shared by some collaborators with social psychiatrists. (Sometimes the term "social psychiatry" is used generically to denote a multidisciplinary commitment to the study of the social antecedents of mental illness.) Sociologists and psychiatrists have cooperated with psychiatrists in developing psychiatric epidemiology and clinical psychologists have collaborated with psychiatrists to investigate stressors, such as the research on relapse in schizophrenia.

Psychoanalysis is a paradoxical body of knowledge. On the one hand it is sometimes practiced by people other than medical practitioners (although they are still called "lay analysts") and it is committed to an interpretive *psychological* approach. On the other hand, the terminology it deploys indicates a medical framework. Clients are called "patients." Inner life is called "psychopathology." Mental processes and personality described using the terminology of illness (e.g., "paranoid defenses," "schizoid personality," "psychoneuroses," etc.). Thus the discourse of psychoanalysis has both a medical and a psychological dimension. Although psychoanalysis is associated with a group of specially trained mental health workers, its social relevance goes beyond this limited clinical culture. Psychoanalytical ideas have been influential in forms of psychotherapy practiced across a variety of professions, including psychiatry, clinical psychology, social work, and mental health nursing. Psychoanalysis has also been a focus of opposition or reaction for both behavioral psychology and humanistic psychology. It has a further relevance in the widespread cultural association with psychiatry and psychology. Lay people may assume, stereotypically, that practitioners in these occupational groups are psychoanalysts. [*See* PSYCHOANALYSIS.]

Behavioral psychology is an environmentalist body of knowledge, but its focus of analysis is the behavior of individuals (humans or other species). As a consequence, it tends to leave social values and norms implicit. For example, its terminology includes notions of "maladaptive" or "unwanted" behavior without reference to who has the power to define these conditions in particular situations. The focus on the scientific study of behavior (as opposed to experience and ideas) was associated at the start of the twentieth century with the professional differentiation of psychology from philosophy. Thus behaviorism emerged as part of a strategy of professionalization for psychology as a new applied and academic discipline in the twentieth century.

Humanistic psychology stands separately from both psychoanalysis and behavioral psychology, although its emergence could be understood as a reaction against both of these theoretical positions. Its emphasis is upon the potential from psychological growth inherent in the human condition. Choice and human agency are given a central role, distinguishing this position from the determinism associated with both the unconscious of depth psychology and the conditioning of behavioral psychology.

Legalism stands somewhere between a professional and a lay contribution to the discourse on mental health. Judgments in court about mental abnormality are generally made on the basis of professional reports (from psychiatrists and clinical psychologists) about a person's mental state. Thus legal judgments are parasitical upon those of mental health professionals. There is not a neat conflation of legal and professional judgments. If in doubt, courts will fall back on ordinary common-sense definitions. This is sometimes called "the-man-must-be-mad test." It is captured by

this comment from a British judge when considering an offender's sanity: "I ask myself what would the ordinary sensible person have said about the patient's condition in this case if he had been informed of his behavior? In my judgment such a person would have said 'Well the fellow is obviously mentally ill.'" The tension between a lay and professional view about mental abnormality is also highlighted at times in a legal arena, for example, when juries do not accept the view from expert witnesses that the accused is mentally disordered.

C. Lay People and Mental Health

Lay people are relevant to the construction of mental health in society in a number of ways:

1. They may support and extend the professional discourse on mental health.
2. They may be called upon to adjudicate on the existence of sanity or insanity in relation to offenders in the criminal justice system.
3. They may challenge professional views about mental health.
4. Their views may influence the development of social policy about mental health services.
5. Lay epidemiology is a model for mental health promotion.

Expanding a little on each of these:

1. *Supporting the professional discourse.* Lay people may learn about and internalize professional perspectives on mental health. This process has been dubbed "protoprofessionalization." Exposure to professional views in the media via both documentary and fictionalized accounts of mental health work encourages the process, as does personal contact with mental health workers. In addition to protoprofessionalization, some lay people simply unconditionally accept expert knowledge.

2. *Adjudicating on the professional discourse.* We noted above that juries may be asked to confirm or reject the views of expert psychiatric witnesses about the presence of mental disorder in criminal proceedings. For example, during the 1980s in Britain a famous case illustrated the resistance jurors can have to psychiatric attributions about criminal motivation. Peter Sutcliffe, the so-called "Yorkshire Ripper," murdered several women on the pretext of being on a mis-

sion from God. Expert witnesses called for *both* the defense and prosecution were of the view that the defendant was a paranoid schizophrenic. However, the jury rejected this opinion, considered him sane, and found him guilty of acting with malice aforethought.

3. *Resisting the professional discourse.* Some lay people resist the professional discourse. For example, one study found that only 10% of psychiatric patients described their difficulties in terms of suffering from mental illness (even though all of them had a psychiatric diagnosis). The rest considered their problems to be a function of various forms of stress or trauma such as sexual abuse, work pressure, unemployment or anxiety about studying. Most of the organized resistance to psychiatry by its recipients has rejected psychiatric diagnosis as being unhelpful and stigmatizing.

4. *Influencing mental health service policy.* Politicians are sensitive to views in the population. The majority of people are not psychiatric patients and in many countries the latter are debarred from voting in elections. The history of social policy about mental health has involved reassuring a voting public that the sane will be left alone and that the insane will be controlled humanely. Thus, while professionals may have dominated and shaped the type of mental health services available, trends about such provision have been influenced by legislators sensitive to public opinion about wrongful detention and the social control of madness.

5. *Providing a basis for mental health promotion.* Traditional psychiatric epidemiology has been joined recently by research on lay epidemiology. The traditional approach has been only partially adequate for planners interested in the primary prevention of mental illness (i.e., mental health promotion). Psychiatric diagnosis is contested both in principle and in relation to specific labels. This inspires less confidence in psychiatric knowledge than in other medical specialties. Also, in physical medicine, epidemiology has entailed studying not only the distribution of diagnosis cases in a population but also the distribution of their *causes*. In psychiatric epidemiology the causes of mental illness remain unknown or disputed and therefore it is an incomplete version of general epidemiology. This weakens the case for mental health promotion being based upon psychiatric epidemiology and creates an opportunity for lay people to influence legislators and health promoters. The latter are sensitive to the receptivity of lay people to health promotion messages and are interested in understanding ordinary views about mental health.

The variable relationship between lay and professional accounts of mental normality and abnormality described above begs a question. Are mental health and mental illness mere by-products of professional discourse? It is certainly true that specific professional representations, such a schizophrenia, are the (dubious) inventions of medicine. However, does this mean that if psychiatry did not exist that mental illness would not? The cross-cultural and historical evidence suggests that mental illness may be cultural artifact produced by psychiatry, but mental distress and madness are not. The following points can be made to support this conclusion:

1. In the prepsychiatric times of Ancient Rome and Athens, madness was documented as being associated with aimless wandering and violence.
2. In more recent times, people living in societies such as Laos, which had neither mental hospitals nor psychiatric professionals, still provided accounts of madness.
3. In localities without mental institutions, very clear conceptual distinctions are made by lay people about sanity and insanity.
4. Whereas there are differences between cultures about how sadness, fear, and madness are represented and explained, all societies, now and in the past, have provided descriptions of these emotional and behavioral phenomena. Put differently, anxiety, depression, and psychosis may be products of modern Western psychiatry, but fear, sadness, and madness are not.

D. Mental Health Services in Their Social Context

The discussion above has mainly focused on the relationship between society and forms of knowledge about mental health. Societal influences are also relevant when we come to understand the provision of mental health services. The notion of "mental health services" is actually quite recent. Up until the first part of the twentieth century there were only hospitals, clinics, and asylums. The notion of "services" has replaced these individual descriptions of facilities in the last 50 years.

During the nineteenth century in Western Europe and North America most countries developed centrally regulated asylum systems. The emergence of large asylums in most localities was associated with the need to control nonproductive deviance in increasingly urbanized and complex capitalist societies. In other words, economic life was disrupted or impaired by madness ("lunatics" or "dements") and by those with learning difficulties ("aments"). Both of these groups were "warehoused" in asylums to remove their negative impact on socioeconomic order and efficiency just as orphans, the physically sick, and the elderly were placed in poorhouses. Professionals at that time took little or no interest in sane people who were frightened or sad (the neuroses). This changed after the First World War, when the "shell shock" problem altered the focus of professional interest. Warfare ensured that stress induced problems, later to be called "battle neurosis" or "posttraumatic stress disorder," recurrently shifted professional attention away from madness and toward neurosis during the twentieth century. This also expanded the range of interventions offered or preferred by professionals to include talking treatments. As a result, psychiatric treatment became more eclectic, although it remained dominated by biomedical interventions.

During periods of peacetime, the focus on madness returned, along with biological treatments in institutional settings. After the Second World War, the old asylum system came into crisis for a number of reasons:

1. The expanded remit of psychiatry and its associated professions, to including talking treatments with neurotic patients in community settings, increased expectations that mental health services should shift away from biomedical treatments inside institutions.

2. In the wake of the widespread cultural shock of the Nazi concentration camps, Western liberal democracies witnessed a popular disquiet about segregation. Also, lessons about the disabling impact of institutionalization ("institutional neurosis") were drawn from observations in the camps of ritualized, rigid, and stereotyped behavior of their inmates.

3. Large institutions were expensive and placed a large fiscal burden upon government budgets. Deinstitutionization offered itself as a cost-cutting exercise.

4. Doubts about institutional life were reinforced by research on its negative impact from social psychiatry, sociology, and from dissent within clinical psychiatry ("antipsychiatry").

5. A new social movement of mental health service users that was critical of hospital-based biomedical regimes emerged internationally.

The above list does not contain any allusion to the so-called "pharmacological revolution." It is a commonly reported misconception that the increasing use of neuroleptic drugs (major tranquilizers) during the 1950s led to a process of deinstitutionalization. In some countries, bed numbers began to drop before the introduction of the drugs. In others, bed numbers actually increased despite this introduction. The drugs also have been used on a variety of populations that were not deemed to be mentally ill (such as people with learning difficulties and older people). The drugs were only relevant in giving psychiatric staff more confidence in dealing with community-based patients; they do not explain the policy of deinstitutionalization.

At the end of the twentieth century deinstitutionalization has become a dominant mental health policy goal in most Western democracies. However, this formal goal has become clouded by evidence that the gradual reduction of large institutions has been replaced by a scattering of smaller ones "in the community." Also, most countries still have legal statutes to coercively remove madness from community settings. The extent of this continued coercive control varies from one country to another. For example, more conformist or authoritarian cultures such as Japan or Russia have higher rates of involuntary detention in psychiatric facilities. What is clear at the time of writing is that a policy of deinstitutionalization and one of genuine community care are not the same. Currently, it may be more accurate to talk of "reinstitutionalization" as the actual outcome of large hospital closures rather than "community care." [See MENTAL HOSPITALS AND DEINSTITUTIONALIZATION.]

BIBLIOGRAPHY

Boyle, M. (1991). *Schizophrenia: A scientific delusion?* London: Routledge.

Brown, G., & Harris, T. (1978). *The social origins of depression.* London: Tavistock.

de Swann, A. (1990). *The management of normality.* London: Routledge.

Foucault, M. (1971). *Madness and civilisation.* London: Tavistock.

Horwitz, A. (1983). *The social control of mental illness.* New York: Academic Press.

Ingleby, D. (Ed.). (1981). *Critical psychiatry.* Harmondsworth: Penguin.

Parker, I., Georgaca, E., Harper, T., & Stowell-Smith, M. (1995). *Deconstructing psychopathology.* London: Sage.

Pilgrim, D., & Rogers, A. (1993). *A Sociology of Mental Health and Illness.* Buckingham: Open University Press.

Rose, N. (1990). *Governing the soul.* London: Routledge.

Szasz, T. (1970). *The manufacture of madness.* New York: Harper Row.

Socioeconomic Status

Halle D. Brown and Nancy E. Adler

University of California, San Francisco

Coping Resources Psychological and economic factors that can be readily made available in the face of a stressful event, which act to reduce adverse effects of that event; includes social support and resilient personality characteristics.

Education Intellectual accomplishment, defined in terms of years of formal schooling, with especially important benchmarks such as graduation from high school or college.

Income The amount of money earned by an individual, family, or household, bearing in mind the number of people supported by that income: household wealth.

Occupational Prestige Rating of one's occupation, typically measured by Duncan's Socioeconomic Index, in which 45 of the most common occupations are rated in terms of perceived prestige.

Social Causation The theory that the relationship between SES and mental illness is due to factors associated with lower social status.

Social Selection The theory that individuals with predispositions for mental illness drift down to or fail to rise out of lower social strata.

Social Stress The appraisal of events as taxing or exceeding one's available coping resources, generated primarily by events that are appraised as threatening, harmful, or challenging.

Social Support Contact with and feedback from a network of friends, family, and peers in which each member is mutually obligated to provide information that the others are cared for and valued. Support can be actual or perceived.

Socioeconomic Status (SES) Social status, or position in the social hierarchy, as typically determined by income, occupational prestige, and/or education.

Upward Mobility Movement out of a lower level of SES into a higher level, either by entering a more prestigious and/or higher paying occupation, or by completing more years of education than one's parents.

SOCIOECONOMIC STATUS (SES) is a fundamental risk factor for both mental and physical illness. In general, the higher the SES, the lower the prevalence of psychiatric disorders and psychological distress. In this article, we describe evidence for this inverse relationship between mental illness and SES, and review existing theories for why this association occurs.

I. WHAT IS SOCIOECONOMIC STATUS?

A. Traditional Indicators

Socioeconomic status (SES) is not a single variable. It can be defined on either the individual level or on the neighborhood level; each type of measure gives a different picture of the social and economic conditions in which an individual lives. Individuals' SES is a reflection of their standing in relation to others on several dimensions. Traditionally, education, occupation, and gross income have been used as individual-level indicators of SES. Education is assessed not only in terms of the number of years of education, but also the highest degree achieved. More years of education presumably provide individuals with greater intellectual resources. In addition, achieving benchmarks such as college graduation or a professional degree has implications for occupational attainment. These benchmarks also have social significance as status indicators. The social meaning of educational attainment has changed over the years as more individuals have obtained higher education. In earlier generations, relatively few individuals graduated from college, and a high school diploma was sufficient for many jobs. In recent years, a college degree has become both more common and more critical for employment. Because of this, the significance of a given educational level may differ for different age cohorts.

Occupation is assessed in terms of occupational prestige. A commonly used scale of occupational prestige is Duncan's Socioeconomic Index. This scale was developed in the 1960s by having individuals rate the relative prestige of 45 occupations, based on a scale of 0, the lowest prestige, to 99, the highest prestige. For the occupations that were not rated, scores were estimated from the mean levels of income and education of the males in that occupation. Newer scales are now available that are based on more current ratings, although problems remain about classifying women, retired people, and those who work part-time.

Gross income is assessed in terms of yearly or average monthly income from salaries and other sources. Income can be assessed in terms of an individual's own income or in terms of a household's income. If the latter is used, it is important to take into account the number of individuals in the household. Given the sensitivity that many individuals have about reporting their personal finances, income is typically assessed in broad categories. Although most studies of SES and health have made comparisons between those below the level of poverty and those above, the evidence (as discussed later) is that the relationship between SES and health is linear, with incremental improvements in health corresponding to elevations in SES throughout the range of SES levels. This suggests the importance of assessing differences in income at the middle and upper end and not simply cutting at the poverty line.

Although education, occupation, and income are related (e.g., individuals who are more educated generally obtain more prestigious jobs and earn more money), they are not highly correlated. The strongest relationship among pairs of indicators is between occupation and education. There are only moderate relationships between income and occupational prestige and between education and income, and these associations are generally weaker for women than for men. Although two or more of the indicators are sometimes combined to provide a global measure of SES, it may not be advisable to do so as one may want to determine the specific contribution of each component.

It is interesting to note that the association of SES and health emerges no matter which SES indicator is used. This suggests that in addition to the particular resources and buffers provided by each component of SES, a more general effect of social ordering may be operating. It may not be the absolute level an individual occupies, but one's relative standing on these indicators that is most powerful. This is also consistent with the fact that the association of SES and health holds much more strongly within countries than across countries, suggesting that it is relative and not absolute deprivation that is having the effect. A number of studies of hierarchies in human and nonhuman primate groups have shown that occupying a lower position in a social hierarchy is associated with stress, which can adversely affect physical and mental health over time.

Beyond the three indicators of individual SES, neighborhood-level SES may also influence risk for mental disorders. One source for determining SES on this level is census block data, which can be derived by knowing an individual's zip code. Neighborhoods can be characterized in terms of the individuals who reside there (e.g., percentage of neighborhood residents who have graduated from high school or from college; percentage of residents who fall below the poverty line). Other data on neighborhood characteristics (e.g., crime rates, housing conditions, unemployment rates) provide complementary information on the social and economic conditions in which individuals are living. Block group measures based on smaller geographic regions that are more homogeneous than zip codes can also be used. Neighborhood-level measures of SES have been examined in relation to physical health outcomes, and it has been shown that these characteristics contribute to health status above and beyond the contribution of an individual's own socio-economic status.

An individual's SES is not always static and can change over time. Both upward and downward mobility are possible. Some individuals exceed the SES level of the families in which they were raised. In recent years, because of changes in economic and demographic factors, a growing number of individuals have experienced a lower socioeconomic position in adulthood than that of their parents. Income, in particular, can fluctuate over time. Many individuals experience sharp drops in income; a smaller number benefit from significant increases.

In understanding the role that SES plays in mental health, it is important to consider an individual's current level of SES as well as their history. In particular, the socioeconomic level of one's parents may determine trajectories that influence later development. Child-rearing patterns and childhood socialization differ between parents with more and less education and income. The experiences in childhood associated with SES differences may affect an individual's resilience in the face of adversity and their subsequent vulnerability to mental illness.

B. Interaction with Race and Ethnicity

In some epidemiologic studies, race is used as an SES indicator because minority groups, particularly African-Americans, on average have lower socioeconomic status. However, race or ethnicity is not sufficient to account for SES-related variability in mental illness, and many studies have found no race differences in rates of mental illness once SES is accounted for. Moreover, unlike physical health problems such as cardiovascular disease or diabetes, for which African Americans, as well as those lower in the SES hierarchy, show higher incidence and prevalence, mental health problems are not necessarily higher among African Americans. In fact, a recently conducted national study of the prevalence of psychiatric disorders found an equal or lower prevalence of disorders among African Americans than among white Americans. Another study, which compared the incidence of mental disorders of African American and white males found that incidence was higher among lower SES men in both ethnic groups, but when comparing incidence rates between these groups, incidence was lower

among African American than white males. [*See* ETH-NICITY AND MENTAL HEALTH.]

II. SES AND MAJOR PSYCHIATRIC DIAGNOSES: EVIDENCE FOR ASSOCIATIONS

A recent review of epidemiologic studies of variations in rates of psychiatric disorder according to SES revealed that more than 80% of all studies in the United States, and more than 60% of non-U.S. studies, found the highest rates of disorder in the lowest SES categories. Overall, rates of psychiatric disorder were 2 to 3 times higher among those in the lowest SES categories than in the highest SES categories. Although, in general, rates of psychiatric disorders decline as SES increases, in some studies the association between SES and mental health is not uniformly linear as one goes up the SES hierarchy. Rather, the greatest proportion of mental illness in some studies has been found in the lowest SES category, with smaller decreases in rates of disorders at higher levels of SES. [*See* EPIDEMIOLOGY: PSYCHIATRIC.]

Socioeconomic status is among the most significant correlates of the prevalence of mental illness, but the question of how SES exerts an effect on mental health remains unanswered. A number of moderating factors have been identified, such as gender, age, and marital status, as well as living in urban versus rural communities. There are gender differences in rates of specific mental disorders as well as in the relative impact of SES on prevalence for men and for women. Men have higher rates of substance use disorders, schizophrenia, and personality disorders, whereas women have higher rates of affective disorders and anxiety disorders, and these disorders, in turn, vary in their frequency at different levels of SES. The negative impact of lower SES on mental health is greater for men than for women. Rates of current mental disorders generally decline with age, but often the highest incidence is in the young-to-middle adulthood category, ages 25 to 44. The relative impact of SES at different ages is not known for mental illness; for physical illness, the association is strongest in middle and late adulthood and declines after age 65. The SES–mental illness relationship is generally more pronounced in urban dwellers than in those living in more rural settings. [*See* AG-

ING AND MENTAL HEALTH; GENDER DIFFERENCES IN MENTAL HEALTH.]

The documentation of a relationship between social class and mental illness has a long history, dating back to a report in 1855 by Edward Jarvis, a Massachusetts epidemiologist. Jarvis reported rates of insanity 64 times higher in the "pauper" class than in the "independent" class. In general, the relationship of SES and mental disorder has held, even as methods of measuring SES and classifying mental disorders have changed. Studies that use the most recent diagnostic systems, such as the Research Diagnostic Criteria (RDC), the National Institute of Mental Health Diagnostic Interview Schedule (DIS), and the *DSM* (although few epidemiologic studies to date have used the most recent *DSM-III-R* and *DSM-IV* criteria) have found that SES is associated with the prevalence of most mental disorders. However, the strength of the relationship between prevalence and SES is not uniform across types of mental disorders, and is stronger for some disorders than for others.

The strongest relationship of mental disorder with SES is generally found for the diagnosis of schizophrenia, with the odds for having this disorder much greater for the lowest SES category than for the highest SES category. Inverse relationships with SES are also strong for substance use disorders, anxiety disorders, and antisocial personality disorder. SES is related to the prevalence of depression, but the relationship is not as strong as for the disorders just described. For depressive disorders, rates are generally greater in the lowest SES category than in the highest SES category, but at least one study did not find a gradient between SES and depressive disorders. In contrast to other disorders, bipolar disorder is generally more likely to occur in higher SES individuals than in lower SES individuals. In addition to these associations with psychiatric disorders, SES is also inversely related to mental distress in studies with nondiagnostic symptom scales that measure nonspecific distress. [*See* ANXIETY; DEPRESSION; SCHIZOPHRENIA; SUBSTANCE ABUSE.]

There are at least three recent large-scale epidemiologic studies, two in the United States and one in Israel, that provide information on the prevalence of mental disorders by SES. A study of almost 5000 Israeli adults used RDC criteria for diagnosis and compared the incidence of schizophrenia, major depression, antisocial personality, and substance use dis-

orders by SES. Rates for each of these disorders decreased as SES increased. In this study, as in past research, base rates of major depression were higher in women and base rates of antisocial personality and substance use disorders were higher in men.

A study of 1-month prevalences of mental disorders in the United States, using DIS criteria and data obtained from all five sites in the Epidemiologic Catchment Area study, measured a wide variety of disorders and permitted direct comparisons of the SES–mental illness relationship across these disorders. The largest difference in prevalence rates between the lowest and highest SES was found for schizophrenia, panic disorder, and severe cognitive impairment. Rates of anxiety disorders, and also substance-related disorders and antisocial personality disorder, decreased as SES increased, with a significant difference in rates between the highest and lowest SES. The discrepancy between the lowest and highest SES was smallest for diagnoses of depressive disorders. Similar findings emerged in a national sample of noninstitutionalized individuals in the National Comorbidity Survey, which examined both lifetime prevalence and current prevalence of disorders. There was a linear relationship of income and education with the prevalence rates of many disorders. The associations were stronger for anxiety disorders (including phobias, panic disorder, and generalized anxiety disorder) than for affective disorders (including major depression, mania, and dysthymia). In this study, however, patterns of substance use differed from the other disorders, with higher lifetime prevalence of substance use disorders in the middle education group than in groups with either more or less education. [*See* PANIC ATTACKS; PHOBIAS.]

III. SES AND MENTAL HEALTH: SOCIAL SELECTION VERSUS SOCIAL CAUSATION

The causal direction of the SES–mental illness association has not been definitively established. More low-SES individuals may develop mental illness because of their low social status or as a result of other factors associated with low SES. Alternatively, individuals prone to mental illness may be less likely to attain higher education, obtain prestigious jobs, and earn higher incomes. Such individuals would end up in lower SES categories because of their mental illness, not the reverse. The former causal path, that SES leads to mental illness, is known as the social causation hypothesis. It posits that variation in environmental factors associated with SES, such as stress, coping resources, and childhood socialization practices, lead to higher rates of psychiatric disorders in lower status individuals. The alternative causal path, from mental illness to SES, is known as the social selection hypothesis. It posits that individuals become sorted into different levels of status based in part on their mental health and level of competence. A variant of this hypothesis, termed social drift, suggests that individuals with mental (or physical) disorders drift downward in the social hierarchy. These hypotheses have been difficult to investigate; retrospective studies of social mobility have been inconclusive and prospective longitudinal studies are impractical.

One method of evaluating the social causation versus social selection hypotheses is to examine patterns of associations of various SES indicators that have varying degrees of sensitivity to the effects of mental disorder. For example, current occupation and income are likely to reflect current and past mental health and illness; individuals with serious mental disorders may be less able to obtain and keep a high-paying position in a high-prestige occupation than those who are free of mental illness. In contrast, education is obtained earlier in life and should be less affected by mental illness that has its onset in adulthood. A stronger association of mental disorders with income and occupation than with education suggests that mental illness affects SES and provides backing for social selection or drift. Because education represents achievement earlier in life, it will not be affected by adult experiences of mental disorders, although it may reflect childhood-onset mental disorders. Relatively stronger associations of mental disorders with education than with income or occupation suggests that SES affects mental health and provides evidence for social causation. Another method for comparing the social causation versus social selection hypotheses has been to correlate different types of risk factors with incidence of mental disorder and with SES. Support for the social causation hypothesis is demonstrated by showing that risk factors such as exposure to stress, impact of stress, and effectiveness of coping strategies are related to both SES and mental disorders; alternatively, support for the social selection hypothesis is found

when genetic factors or early environmental risk factors (with parental SES held constant) are significantly related to both SES and mental disorders.

By these methods, social causation factors have prevailed in accounting for the relationship between SES and several mental disorders. Depression and anxiety have been strongly linked to SES-related stress exposure. The social selection hypothesis has been more strongly favored for schizophrenia, but the evidence has been mixed. At least one study has found evidence for a role of stress associated with low-status occupations in the development of schizophrenia, in support of the social causation hypothesis. For other psychiatric disorders, such as personality disorder and substance use disorders, roles for both causation and selection have been identified. At present, the precise causal nature of the SES–mental health relationship remains unresolved.

A. Social Stress

One pathway by which SES may influence risk for mental disorders is through differential exposure to stressors, coupled with varying levels of resources to cope with these stressors. Greater exposure to social stress has repeatedly been shown to be associated with increased psychological distress, as well as with poorer mental and physical health. Several studies have shown that lower SES individuals experience greater exposure to stress, but few studies have included mental health outcomes. In one recent study, social stress was measured broadly in terms of a negative life-events checklist, an inventory of chronic stressors (in the areas of financial issues, general or ambient problems, work, marriage/relationship, parental, family, social life, residence, and health), and an assessment of major lifetime traumas. The lower the SES, the higher the exposure to stress and the higher the psychological distress. [See STRESS.]

B. Psychological Resources for Coping

In addition to a higher rate of exposure to stress, lower SES individuals may also be more vulnerable to experiencing adverse effects on mental health of exposure to stress. Research has shown that not only do lower SES individuals face more stressors, but they are also more likely to be negatively affected by stressors.

Greater vulnerability among lower SES individuals may result from a lack of adequate resources for coping with stressors, including psychological and social resources for coping. Each aspect of SES has different implications for the availability of coping resources and provides a pathway by which SES can affect mental health. For example, in relation to income, lower SES is associated with both more financial stressors and less financial resources for coping with such events as job loss or foreclosure, or even a health problem. In contrast, education may affect psychological distress indirectly by having an impact on psychological coping resources such as social support, including the perception of being integrated into society, and resilient personality characteristics, including feelings of mastery. Individuals who are socialized by parents with more education and who themselves have more education may have a greater range of psychological resources and coping skills to deal with stressors and will be able to deal more effectively with exposure to stressful events. [*See* COPING WITH STRESS; SOCIAL SUPPORT.]

The means by which SES influences psychological coping resources is not known. Some studies have shown that feelings of powerlessness or loss of control constrain coping attempts. Individuals lower in the SES hierarchy are, in fact, in less control of their environments and have relatively less power; not surprisingly, they are more likely to experience feelings of powerlessness and lack of control, which, in turn, may hinder coping efforts. Similarly, having greater social support is known to facilitate coping with stress, and individuals of lower SES report having less social support than do higher SES individuals.

In addition to having fewer coping resources, lower SES individuals may use coping strategies that are less adaptive. Lower SES individuals have been found to use more avoidant coping strategies, whereas higher SES individuals use more problem-oriented coping strategies. Coping with a potentially changeable stressful event by attempting to avoid it is considered less adaptive than actively approaching the stressful event as a problem to solve and has been associated with poor adjustment.

C. Childhood Socialization

Differences related to SES in vulnerability to stress and availability of psychological coping resources may par-

tially arise from early socialization experiences. Some response styles that individuals begin to develop early in life are more conducive to coping with stressful situations than are others. In addition, high levels of stress and/or ineffectual coping resources associated with growing up in lower SES environments may be related to engaging in risk behaviors or to other behavioral problems during childhood. Lower family SES is a risk factor for depression and also for suicidal ideation in children; in turn, self-reported depressed mood in children (linked to SES) correlates with acts of delinquency.

In one recent study, a number of socialization factors were found to be related to both SES and childhood behavior problems. Children from lower SES families were more likely to experience each of eight potentially problematic socialization experiences: harsh disciplinary practices by parents, lack of warmth toward the child, observation of violence, endorsement of aggressive values by the mother, unstable peer groups, lack of cognitive stimulation, stressful life events, and lack of social support. Not only was SES significantly negatively correlated with all eight of these factors, but taken together, these factors accounted for a part, though not all, of the relationship between SES and aggressive behavior in the children in this study.

D. Implications for Improving Mental Health

Finding an inverse relationship between SES and mental disorders does not tell us whether it is low social status that makes an individual vulnerable to mental illness or high social status that provides protection against it. The finding that SES shows a stronger association with anxiety disorders than with depression has been attributed to the fact that higher SES is more protective against threat and worry than against loss and sadness. This makes intuitive sense as some losses are inevitable and may not be buffered by social resources.

Experiences of low SES do not inevitably result in mental distress; there are many resilient individuals who do not experience mental disorders despite exposure to adverse early environments, few economic resources, or engagement in low-paying or low-prestige occupations. Having close supporting relationships and being involved in social organizations appear to be helpful in offsetting early adversity as well as difficulties in adulthood. It is important to determine which aspects of SES may be toxic to individuals in terms of their mental health and/or which provide a buffer against mental distress. It is equally important to recognize the substantial individual variability in mental health at all levels of SES. Thus, we need to identify the factors that vary across SES levels and that affect risk or protection against mental disease, as well as determine whether these same factors or different ones affect individual variability within SES strata. [See PROTECTIVE FACTORS IN DEVELOPMENT OF PSYCHOPATHOLOGY.]

Although further research on the causal nature of the SES–mental illness relationship is needed, it is clear that improvement in economic conditions, as well as in educational and occupational opportunities, for lower SES individuals is likely to foster better mental health. Increasing opportunities for upward mobility is one possible avenue to improvement in mental health. Although upward mobility can create its own stress because of inconsistencies between the culture in which one is reared and the culture to which one ascends, at least one study has shown that individuals with higher occupational than educational status did not experience more psychological distress than non-upwardly mobile individuals.

In the realm of physical health, recent data have shown that it is not absolute levels of economic resources that influence health outcomes as much as relative inequalities in the distribution of resources. This suggests that decreasing social inequalities in society may have the benefit of improved mental as well as physical health.

ACKNOWLEDGMENT

Preparation of this manuscript was supported by the John D. and Catherine T. MacArthur Foundation Research Network on Socioeconomic Status and Health.

BIBLIOGRAPHY

Dodge, K. A., Pettit, G. S., & Bates, J. E. (1994). Socialization mediators of the relation between socioeconomic status and child conduct problems. *Child Development, 65,* 649–665.

Dohrenwend, B. P. (1990). Socioeconomic status (SES) and psychiatric disorders: Are the issues still compelling? *Social Psychiatry and Psychiatric Epidemiology, 25,* 41–47.

Dohrenwend, B. P., Levav, I., & Shrout, P. E. et al. (1992). Socioeconomic status and psychiatric disorders: The causation–selection issue. *Science, 255,* 946–952.

Hudson, C. G. (1988). The social class and mental illness correlation: Implications of the research for policy and practice. *Journal of Sociology and Social Welfare, 15,* 27–54.

Kessler, R. C., McGonagle, K. A., Zhao, S., Nelson, C. B., Hughes, M., Eshleman, S., Wittchen, H. U., & Kendler, K. S. (1994). Lifetime and 12-month prevalence of *DSM-III-R* psychiatric disorders in the United States: Results from the National Comorbidity Survey. *Archives of General Psychiatry, 51,* 8–19.

McLeod, J. D., & Kessler, R. C. (1990). Socioeconomic status differences in vulnerability to undesirable life events. *Journal of Health and Social Behavior, 31,* 162–172.

Ortega, S. T., & Rushing, W. A. (1983). Interpretation of the relationship between socioeconomic status and mental disorder: A question of the measure of mental disorder and a question of the measure of SES. *Research in Community and Mental Health, 3,* 141–161.

Regier, D. A., Farmer, M. E., Rae, D. S., Myers, J. K., Kramer, M., Robins, L. N., George, L., Karno, M., & Locke, B. Z. (1993). One-month prevalence of mental disorders in the United States and sociodemographic characteristics: The Epidemiologic Catchment Area study. *Acta Psychiatrica Scandinavica, 88,* 35–47.

Turner, R. J., Wheaton, B., & Lloyd, D. A. (1995). The epidemiology of social stress. *American Sociological Review, 60,* 104–125.

Solitude

Jerry M. Burger

Santa Clara University

Experience Sampling Method An experimental procedure in which participants carry electronic pagers and are contacted at random intervals. Participants report on their immediate behavior and experiences whenever paged.

Loneliness An unpleasant emotional experience accompanying the perception that the quantity and quality of one's social interactions and relationships fall below the level one desires.

Solitude The experience of being removed from the immediate expectations and demands of social interactions.

Experiences with **SOLITUDE** often are unpleasant and may even contribute to or be a sign of psychological problems; however a small but growing amount of research now indicates that this is not always the case. Short periodic breaks from social contact sometimes contribute to well-being. Moreover, many people benefit from extended periods of time alone. Preliminary research has identified several variables that help explain when solitude contributes to well-being and when it is undesirable.

I. SOLITUDE

Research on how people restrict their contact with others has been identified with a variety of terms. For example, psychologists have written about *privacy, privacy regulation,* and a *need for privacy* when referring to such varied phenomena as how people restrict intimate information to select individuals, how people use and protect their personal space, and how physically isolated people are from others. In response to this confusion, many psychologists have begun to use the term *solitude* to refer to a more narrowly defined kind of privacy. People are said to experience solitude when the immediate demands of social interaction are absent. Usually this means that people are physically isolated from others, such as when alone at home or when taking a walk in a secluded location. However, people also can experience solitude in a public setting, such as when sitting by oneself in a park even though other people are around. The defining characteristic of solitude is the absence of the immediate expectations that govern our social interactions. That is, social rules require that we attend to the people we interact with and that we consider how our behavior is seen by the other person. Although someone experiencing solitude probably will not scream out loud or babble incoherently if others are nearby, that person is free to focus attention on his or her own thoughts and feelings in a way that is not possible when actively engaged in a social encounter or when the possibility of a social encounter is imminent (for example, when in a business meeting attended by a dozen other people).

Within this definition, studies find that the typical

American spends a great of his or her time in solitude. To determine the extent of this solitude, Reed Larson and his colleagues conducted a series of investigations with a procedure known as the Experience Sampling Method. Participants in these studies carry electronic pagers and are contacted at random times throughout the day for the duration of the investigation. When contacted, participants quickly complete measures to record what they are doing and how they are feeling. The results from these investigations find that the percentage of time spent in solitude varies as a function of age. Elementary school children spent approximately 17% of their time alone. High school students were found to spend about 26% of their day in solitude. Adults spent an average of 29% of their time alone, and elderly adults typically spent 48% of their day in solitude. The most common place for solitude was in one's own home. Interestingly, men and women tend to spend an equal amount of time in solitude. Although there is no direct evidence that people spend more time in solitude today than in the past, a recent report found that more American adults live by themselves than ever before. The number of people who live alone rose from 8% of the population in 1940 to 25% in 1995. Finally, it should be noted that data on the amount of time people spend by themselves has been limited almost exclusively to American samples. Moreover, virtually all of the research on the effects of solitude has been conducted with people from Western societies. Consequently, it is not clear how well the findings discussed here will generalize to people living in other cultures.

II. NEGATIVE REACTIONS TO SOLITUDE

A great deal of research has demonstrated the psychological benefits of intimate social relationships and social support. When people are asked to list the things that make them happy, their relationships with family members and friends inevitably are near or at the top of the list. Consequently, it often is assumed that the absence of social interaction must therefore have a negative impact on well-being. Commonly held stereotypes of people who spend a great deal of time by themselves reinforce this perception. These people are seen as shy, strange, withdrawn, lonely, and unattractive. The assumed preference for social contact over solitude is so widespread that parents, teachers, and

prison officials often use isolation from others as a form of punishment. [See SOCIAL SUPPORT.]

Consistent with these negative images of solitude, researchers find that people typically enjoy the time they spend with others more than the time they spend alone. Moreover, for many people solitude tends to be unpleasant. The most common complaints about time spent by oneself are feelings of boredom and loneliness. Researchers using the Experience Sampling Method typically find decreases in positive emotions when people move from social encounters to solitude. Participants in these studies often report feeling less cheerful, less happy, and less active when by themselves. A great deal of research suggests that loneliness is a common problem among all age groups, beginning with adolescence. Studies with college students find that as many as 70% suffer from occasional loneliness during their first year at a new school. Thus, it seems that solitude is unpleasant and unproductive for many, if not most, people. [See LONELINESS.]

Researchers also find that people who spend a large amount of time by themselves tend to score lower on measures of well-being than those who spend a moderate amount or relatively little time in solitude. However, this research does not tell us the causal direction of this association. That is, it is possible that spending an excessive amount of time by oneself causes a reduction in well-being. Consistent with this interpretation, there is evidence that excessive solitude contributes to feelings of loneliness and sadness. Moreover, the attributions people make about the reasons for their lack of social activity may lead to unflattering self-appraisals. Finding oneself without someone to talk with might lead people to see themselves as undesirable and unworthy of friends. Another possible explanation for lower well-being scores among those who spend a great deal of time in solitude is that these people may not spend enough time with others to obtain the benefits of social contact. The boost to well-being that comes from satisfying intimate relationships and the stress-buffer effect of social support might not be available to people who spend the majority of their time by themselves. Finally, spending a large amount of time alone may be a sign or symptom of poor adjustment or of deeper psychological problems. That is, a low sense of well-being may cause people to shy away from social relationships and thus spend an excessive amount of time alone. It also is possible that a reduction in social contact is the result of a psychological disorder. Most notably, social withdrawal is a well-documented characteristic of people suffering from depression. Each of these possible causal connections may be correct, depending on the individual. Moreover, it is possible for people to fall into a spiraling situation in which their lack of social contact contributes to their low sense of well-being, and their low sense of well-being prevents them from developing and maintaining significant social relationships.

Finally, there is some evidence that solitude may exacerbate existing psychological disorders. In particular, Larson and his colleagues compared reactions to solitude between a sample of bulimic patients and a matched control group. They found the bulimics had a particularly strong emotional reaction to the time they spent alone at home. Compared to the time they spent with other people, these participants reported that they were more irritable, sad, lonely, vulnerable, and guilty when home alone. Moreover, the bulimics who felt the worst during solitude were the most likely to engage in binging and purging. The researchers speculate that the bulimic behavior may be triggered by the negative emotions and may represent an attempt by the bulimics to cope with their feelings. [See ANOREXIA NERVOSA AND BULIMIA NERVOSA.]

III. THE BENEFITS OF SOLITUDE

As described above, there is ample evidence that solitude can be an unpleasant and unwelcome experience and that spending time by oneself may have a negative impact on a person's well-being. However, other research suggests that this negative portrayal of solitude may be only half of the picture. Although less compelling than the case against solitude, a growing number of studies find spending time by oneself also has the potential to contribute to one's self of well-being. The benefits that come from spending time alone can be categorized according to the length of time people spend in solitude. Specifically, we can look at the benefits that come from three different kinds of solitude: short periods of solitude during the day, extended periods of time alone, and lengthy periods of isolation from others.

The most well-documented benefits of solitude come from research on the short breaks people often take to get away from social activity. That is, many people find it beneficial to take a few minutes out of their busy days to be by themselves. Typically these breaks last a matter of minutes, but can extend to an hour or more. Many people seek out these short periods of solitude by retreating to a selected quiet place, such as a garden or a quiet room. Others take walks or engage in some other solitary physical activity. Millions of people worldwide meditate, an activity that may provide benefits beyond those that come from simply removing oneself from others. [See MEDITATION AND THE RELAXATION RESPONSE.]

These short bouts of solitude appear to serve a number of functions. Perhaps foremost among these is the opportunity to escape from the stress that often accompanies social activity. Although most social encounters are pleasant, interacting with others also demands a great deal of attention and energy. Social psychologists have demonstrated that people typically engage in impression management or self-presentation strategies when interacting with others. That is, when interacting, we think about the kind of impressions we are making and constantly monitor the reactions of the other person. Because this self-monitoring process can be emotionally draining, constant social interaction can be stressful. Stepping away from this ongoing effort for a few minutes allows people to relax, to "lower their guard," and to prepare themselves for upcoming social encounters.

Consistent with these descriptions, studies using the Experience Sampling Method find that both adults and adolescents report feeling less self-conscious when alone than when in a social situation. These people also report higher levels of concentration when alone. Other studies find that people often identify a "lack of privacy" as a source of stress in their lives. A survey of New Zealand residents found that self-reported stress was highly correlated with complaints of too little privacy and too little time spent by oneself. This association was particularly strong for the females in the sample. [See STRESS.]

Thus, occasional short bouts of solitude during a busy day can provide a release from stress. This may be particularly the case when the social contact either requires a great deal of self-monitoring or is especially anxiety-provoking. For example, a few breaks built into a series of important meetings or during a lengthy job interview might provide a welcomed relief from accumulated stress. Some psychologists have described this benefit of solitude as a kind of stress buffer, similar to the stress-buffering effects demonstrated in research on social support.

Short breaks from social contact also appear to serve a kind of "self-restoration" function. That is, by removing oneself from the immediate demands inherent in most social situations, people are able to reflect on how the day's events are going and even on their ability to deal with the stresses they have encountered. In a sense, these short experiences with solitude allow one to emotionally catch one's breath. As a result of this emotional restoration, people return to their social worlds better to deal with the demands and stresses of social activity.

Consistent with this description, Larson and his colleagues found that solitude had a renewing effect on people's moods. People who returned to social situations after spending some time in solitude reported that they were more cheerful, more alert, and felt stronger than they had been before experiencing solitude. These positive reactions to solitude appeared in both adult and adolescent samples and were found even when participants experienced loneliness and boredom during their time alone.

In addition to small breaks from social activity during the day, some research indicates that people also can benefit from spending longer periods of time alone. These episodes of isolation, perhaps lasting a few hours at a time, occur less frequently than the shorter breaks described above. They are also more likely to be planned time alone, just as one might plan time to work on a specific task. Thus, people often set aside an afternoon or a weekend day to be by themselves. These extended periods of solitude appear to serve different needs than the shorter, restorative breaks. Prolonged experience with solitude allows people to reflect on topics and concerns that require an extended amount of time for adequate consideration. Spending occasional blocks of time alone may be particularly beneficial when people have important decisions they need to make and important issues they need to address. Questions about careers, relationships, personal problems, and so on probably require extended periods of time to ponder. A few hours alone may be required for people to contemplate and sort out their thoughts on such matters. Of course, discussing these concerns with family members, friends, or a professional counselor can be beneficial. But it also may be the case that a certain amount of quiet contemplation is needed for successful resolution of many personal issues.

Some research suggests that extended periods of solitude may be particularly valuable for adolescents. Many teenagers wrestle with decisions surrounding academic choices and romantic relationships. Adolescence also is a time for developing values, establishing personal goals, and addressing religious questions. In particular, adolescents face the formidable task of developing a personal identity. Larson and his colleagues found that adolescents who spent a moderate amount of time in solitude (about 30% of their day) were more well-adjusted than those who spent relatively little time alone or those who spent a great deal of time by themselves. The researchers argue that too little solitude may deprive teenagers of the opportunity to work on the personal issues that adolescents must resolve. However, too much time alone may mean the adolescent does not spend enough time in social activities, thus failing to obtain the benefits social interactions provide.

Some therapists have incorporated periodic experiences with solitude as part of their treatment program. In particular, Peter Suedfeld has developed Restricted Environment Stimulation Therapy (REST). Clients participating in these programs spend an extended amount of time, up to 24 hours, in social isolation. Typically the setting for this solitude is a quiet and dark room in which the client lies on a bed. Although a convincing body of evidence for the effectiveness of the procedure is still forthcoming, Suedfeld points to a series of studies in which the REST procedure has proven therapeutic for clients with a wide variety of needs. It is important to note that participants in REST programs are volunteers. Thus, it is not clear if the benefits ascribed to this treatment also would be found for the typical psychotherapy client.

Finally, there is some evidence that people also benefit from very extensive periods of solitude. Although most of this evidence is based on individual case studies, investigators have identified a large number of people for whom extensive solitude appears to have been especially beneficial. In particular, Anthony Storr, Suedfeld, and others have examined the reactions of people who by choice or involuntarily have spent several days or the greater part of years by themselves. These authors point to religious leaders, such as Buddha and Jesus, writers and artists, such as Beatrix Potter and Rudyard Kipling, and great thinkers, such as Carl Jung, who gained personal insights during their extended isolation from other people. According to Storr, this extended time away from other people frees the person to think in novel and unconventional ways. Extended experience with solitude thus leads to creative insights and new ways of thinking about old problems and issues. [See CREATIVITY AND GENIUS.]

These long periods of solitude also can be therapeutic. The opportunity for introspection and reappraisal provided by the extended time alone may lead to improved self-understanding and personal growth. Suedfeld points out that throughout history and within many different cultures we find groups that encourage or require long periods of isolation as a step in the individual's personal development. For example, many religious traditions include extended time for quiet contemplation and many cultures have incorporated long periods of solitude as a step in the transition from adolescence to adulthood. A few individuals, like Carl Jung, have voluntarily separated themselves from others for extended periods of time as part of a personal quest for insight and growth. Individual reports by those going through lengthy periods of solitude suggest that the isolated individuals benefitted from the experience. However, whether these extensive periods of solitude actually provide the benefits some of the practitioners claim has yet to be demonstrated empirically.

IV. VARIABLES AFFECTING REACTIONS TO SOLITUDE

The key question that surfaces when reviewing the different reactions people have to solitude is how to distinguish episodes of solitude that lead to increased well-being from those that result in negative psychological reactions. At least four variables need to be considered when answering this question. These four are choice, balance with social contact, age, and individual personality differences. Solitude is more likely to be beneficial when it is voluntary, is in balance with the amount of social contact, occurs at an appropriate age level, and is consistent with the person's individual needs and preferences.

First, solitude is more likely to be beneficial when entered into voluntarily. People who choose to spend time by themselves occasionally complain about boredom and loneliness. However, negative reactions to solitude are far more common when people find themselves alone because of life circumstances rather than

by choice. Consequently, people who move to a new community, students enrolling at a new school, and recently widowed elderly people may find the time they spend alone particularly difficult to manage.

Second, we need to examine the balance between solitude and social contact. For adolescents and adults, there may be an optimal balance between the amount of social interaction and the amount of time spent by oneself. Studies find that people typically regulate their amount of social contact. That is, after an extended period of social isolation, most people are eager to seek out social interactions. On the other hand, after a lot of social contact, people often seek out time by themselves. Thus, most people work to maintain an appropriate balance between their amount of social interaction and their amount of solitude.

Research suggests that a good balance between one's social and solitary experiences may allow people to reap the benefits from both worlds. Many studies have demonstrated the mental health benefits that come from social contact and social relationships. Not enough social activity may take away from these social benefits. In addition, whereas a moderate amount of solitude can be pleasant and contribute to well-being, the experience can turn to boredom and loneliness if it goes on too long or occurs too frequently.

Age also appears to play a role in how people respond to time alone. Children usually find solitude unpleasant and typically choose to spend time with others whenever possible. One longitudinal study found that the amount of time early elementary school children spend away from others is related to adjustment problems a few years later. The children who spent a large amount of time by themselves were more likely than other children to show evidence of adjustment problems when they reached the fourth and fifth grade. However, studies also find the amount of time boys and girls choose to spend in solitude increases as they enter adolescence. This shift occurs at the same time children begin to address questions about their personal identity as separate from their identity with the family. Consequently, as described earlier, there is evidence that some adolescents take advantage of their experiences with solitude to work through the personal tasks and decisions they confront at this age.

Studies find that elderly people spend a large amount of their lives in solitude, particularly those who are unmarried and living alone. However, it is not clear that this time alone is necessarily unpleasant or unwelcomed. Some research indicates that elderly people in general are less likely to complain of loneliness than are people in other age groups, all of whom spend more time socializing with others. Like people of all ages, the well-being of elderly people is strengthened by contact with intimate and supportive companions. However, other studies find little relation between the *amount* of time the elderly spend socializing and their sense of well-being.

Research by Larson and his colleagues helps to explain this apparent inconsistency. The researchers found that married elderly people, who presumably had access to the benefits that come from intimate companionship, also tended to enjoy the time they spent by themselves. These people reported higher levels of energy, better concentration, and a greater sense of challenge when alone than when interacting with others. The married elderly people apparently had learned how to use their time alone in a way that allowed them to focus their attention and engage in tasks they found pleasant and challenging. However, a different pattern was found for the elderly participants who were unmarried and living alone. These people spent more of their typical day by themselves, and found this time more unpleasant and unproductive than when they were interacting with others. Common complaints included increased feelings of boredom and sadness, and a decrease in energy and motivation when alone. In short, it appears that many elderly people have learned how to enjoy the time they spend alone. However, consistent with the points made earlier, elderly people typically do not enjoy solitude when it is extensive and when it is cast upon them by life circumstances rather than by choice.

Finally, there appear to be individual differences in the extent to which people seek out solitude and are able to benefit from the time they spend by themselves. That is, some people have a higher need or preference for spending time by themselves than others. Whereas one person may find a few hours of solitude pleasant and invigorating, another person might become overwhelmed with loneliness if left alone for this same amount of time. Some psychologists have suggested that a preference for solitude may be both a cause and a result of well-being. For example, Abraham Maslow identified a desire to spend time alone as a characteristic of psychologically healthy (self-actualized) people. That is, he suggested that it was because these people were psychologically healthy that they had come to see the value of solitude.

Several researchers have examined individual differences in how people approach and react to solitude. Reed Larson, Darhl Pedersen, Nancy Marshall, and Jerry Burger each have developed self-report inventories to measure the extent to which people prefer and benefit from spending time by themselves. Larson's measure provides two subscale scores. One of these identifies the extent to which people find solitude an effective means of handling stress, the other measures the test taker's emotional comfort or discomfort with solitude. Pedersen's scale provides scores for six different domains within which people might prefer privacy. Of particular interest here is the solitude subscale examining efforts to be by oneself. Marshall's measure also provides six subscale scores. However, none of these appears to assess solitude as the concept is defined here. Finally, Burger's Preference for Solitude Scale identifies the extent to which people prefer solitude when faced with a choice between solitude and social interaction.

It is important to distinguish between the constructs these scales are designed to measure and other personality variables. In particular, comfort with solitude or a preference for solitude is not the same as social anxiety or shyness. People who are high in social anxiety are very concerned about negative evaluation from others and thus tend to find social interactions stressful and unpleasant. Highly socially anxious people seek out solitude, but do so more to escape from social contact rather than to obtain the benefits that come from time alone. Similarly, preference for solitude is not synonymous with introversion. Introverts are said to seek time by themselves in an effort to lower arousal or stimulation levels that exceed the introvert's personal threshold. Although these people may be comfortable with their time alone, they do not necessarily find solitude an emotionally satisfying or productive experience. [*See* SHYNESS.]

Although to date only a handful of studies has been conducted with these personality measures, some promising findings have been uncovered. For example, Larson found that people who are comfortable with solitude are less likely to become depressed than those who score low on his measure. Other studies find that people who report a strong need to spend time by themselves actually prefer to spend most of their free time with others. These people also report that they typically enjoy these social interactions. Thus, it would be incorrect to assume that people prefer either social contact or social isolation. Rather, it appears that some people who enjoy their social relationships also have a desire to get away by themselves on occasion and that these people find this time alone pleasant and beneficial.

Research on loneliness points to a similar individual difference component. Loneliness occurs when the quality and amount of social interactions fall short of the individual's desired levels. However, studies find that people differ greatly in the extent to which they desire social contact. Whereas one person might require several deep, personal relationships and constant social contact to avoid feelings of loneliness, others are satisfied with a few close friends and occasional social interactions.

The results from these investigations suggest that there is no optimal amount of social activity or solitude that we can apply to all individuals. Rather, whether an increased or a decreased amount of solitude is best for the person's well-being is partly a function of the individual's needs and preferences.

V. CONCLUSIONS

Although solitude is often seen as detrimental to mental health, there is evidence that some experiences with solitude have a positive effect on well-being. The benefits of solitude can be found in short breaks from social interactions during the day and from more extended periods of time alone. There is some evidence that people also may benefit from very prolonged isolation from others. Several variables need to be considered when assessing the effects of solitude on well-being, and much more research is needed to understand when solitude is beneficial and when it is undesirable. Nonetheless, it is clear that we should not automatically assume that the time an adolescent boy spends alone in his room or the many afternoons an elderly woman spends by herself are problems that need correcting. Rather, it is possible these experiences with solitude are contributing in important ways to the boy's personal growth and the woman's sense of well-being.

BIBLIOGRAPHY

Burger, J. M. (1995). Individual differences in preference for solitude. *Journal of Research in Personality, 29,* 85–108.

Larson, R. (1990). The solitary side of life: An examination of time people spend alone from childhood to old age. *Developmental Review, 10,* 155–183.

Storr, A. (1988). *Solitude: A return to the self.* New York: Free Press.

Suedfeld, P. (1982). Aloneness as a healing experience. In L. A. Peplau & D. Perlman (Eds.), *Loneliness: A sourcebook of current theory, research and therapy* (pp. 54–67). New York: Wiley.

Somatization and Hypochondriasis

Javier I. Escobar

UMDNJ-Robert Wood Johnson Medical School

Michael A. Gara

UMDNJ-Robert Wood Johnson Medical School
UMDNJ-University Behavioral HealthCare

I. Introduction
II. Systems of Classification
III. Pathogenesis
IV. Detection, Recognition, Diagnosis
V. Cross-Cultural Issues
VI. Clinical Management

Abridged Somatization Construct A method for classifying somatization disorder and subsyndromal somatization using a simple series of interview probes and the somatic symptom index (see below).

Hypochondriasis A preoccupation with fears of having a serious, often life-threatening disease, despite overwhelming medical evidence to the contrary.

Somatic Symptom Index A count of the number of unexplained physical symptoms. The presence of four unexplained symptoms in males, and six in females, suggests somatization.

Somatization As a broad notion, the presentation of somatic complaints not explained by any known general medical condition or substance abuse, and that may represent a psychopathological state.

Somatoform A label used to group clinical syndromes in which the patient presents with multiple physical symptoms that have no clear medical explanation.

SOMATIZATION refers to multiple physical complaints for which there are no medical explanations, and that may be related to coping mechanisms or psychopathological states. This article will discuss the links of somatization and other somatoform disorders

(e.g., hypochondriasis) to common psychiatric disorders, such as depression and anxiety. There will also be a focus on systems of classifying somatoform disorders, as well as the epidemiology, pathogenesis, diagnosis, cross-cultural, and clinical management of somatoform disorders.

I. INTRODUCTION

A general conception in psychology and psychiatry that has been held for more than a century is that somatization represents negative emotions and/or rather intense psychological conflicts that have been unconsciously converted into physical symptoms or somatic sensations. The exact mechanism mediating this conversion process is unknown, although there is extensive speculation about its psychological, social, and biological underpinnings. Nonetheless, the subjective experience of having a physical illness is a compelling reality for the somatizing patient, which tends to persist despite reassurance from physicians that no medical explanation can be proffered for the patient's complaints. The somatizer vigorously resists any efforts that are made to reframe his or her distress as a consequence of psychiatric disorder, (i.e., depression, anxiety) or even psychosocial stressors. [*See* STRESS.]

A conceptual difficulty in advancing the fields is the fact that somatization is a diagnosis always made by exclusion. Hence, there is always a chance that a heretofore undetected or yet-to-be discovered underlying physical disorder may account for the complaints. Medical disorders that pose the greatest difficulty for differential diagnosis obviously are those with multiple ambiguous symptoms (for example, lupus erythematosus or multiple sclerosis).

In order to reduce the rate of "false positive" diagnoses of somatization, diagnostic criteria for somatization have emphasized issues of severity, a polysymptomatic presentation, and the absence of positive physical findings as key elements for the diagnosis. When presenting symptoms cut across many organs/biological systems, the likelihood of a somatization diagnosis is much higher.

II. SYSTEMS OF CLASSIFICATION

In the most recent psychiatric nosologies, the American Psychiatric Association's *Diagnostic and Statistical Manual,* 4th Edition (*DSM-IV*), and the *International Classification of Diseases,* 10th Edition (*ICD-10*), the label "somatoform" is used to group clinical syndromes whose most distinguishing feature is the presentation of and preoccupation with physical symptoms or somatic sensations that remain without a clear medical explanation.

The syndromes that have been grouped under the rubric "somatoform" in *DSM-IV* are somatization disorder, hypochondriasis, conversion disorder, body dysmorphic disorder, pain disorder and undifferentiated/not otherwise specified somatoform disorder.

Somatization disorder is an entity that can be traced to older concepts in psychiatry, such as hysteria or Briquet's syndrome. The criteria for this disorder are fairly stringent, such as age of onset before 30, several years of unsuccessful medical treatment with significant loss of functioning in one or more domains (e.g., occupational), many unexplained symptoms (in *DSM-IV* at least eight unexplained symptoms are required) spread across different physical sites or systems. This diagnosis has high validity and reliability indexes and generally leads to poor outcomes.

The other somatoform disorders in the *DSM-IV* have much less stringent criteria than does full-blown somatization disorder and their validity seems less clear. Undifferentiated somatoform disorder requires that the patient present with at least one unexplained symptom that persists beyond 6 months and causes significant functional impairment.

Hypochondriasis requires that the patient be preoccupied with having a serious disease, such as cancer, for at least 6 months, which persists despite medical

reassurance. Body dysmorphic disorder is defined by a preoccupation with an imagined deficit in appearance, which at times may reach psychotic proportions.

Table I compares the taxonomy of somatoform disorders that exists within *DSM-IV* with those in *ICD-10*. Although *DSM-IV* and *ICD-10* resemble each other more than did any of their predecessors, there are still significant differences between the two taxonomies in the case of several diagnostic categories, including dissociative and somatoform disorders. For example, the most pressing reason for mentioning "dissociation" in this article is the inclusion of "conversion disorders" under a superordinate dissociative class (F44) in the *ICD-10*. In contrast, "conversion disorders" are subsumed under somatoform disorders in *DSM-IV*. One additional reason to mention somatization/conversion in the context of dissociation acknowledges the historical cogenesis of dissociative and hysterical phenomena in nineteenth-century French psychiatry. In addition, *DSM-IV* highlights psychological elements thought to be at work in conversion disorder (e.g., temporal onset of conversion symptoms immediately after psychological trauma), whereas *ICD-10* tends to elaborate the physical aspects of conversion symptoms.

Because of the limitations of current diagnostic classifications, a number of proposals have been made to reframe somatoform syndromes in simpler, more practical ways. These proposals suggest a somewhat different taxonomy than that appearing in the *DCM* or *ICD* systems, albeit with discernable areas of overlap, at least for the symptoms more commonly seen in primary care settings. For example, in 1991 Kirmayer and Robbins at McGill University proposed three forms of somatization in primary care. These are (1) high levels of functional somatic distress measured by the somatic symptom index of Escobar; (2) hypochondriasis, measured by high scores in an "illness worry" scale; and (3) somatic manifestation seen exclusively in patients with current depression or anxiety. Over 25% of patients attending a family medicine clinic met criteria for one or more of these forms of somatization. Interestingly, these forms were only mildly overlapping.

G. Richard Smith's (1994) review of the literature on the course of somatization and other aspects of the disorder, proposes four categories in his classification: (1) clear somatization disorder or SD (essentially the same entity as in *DSM-IV*); (2) subthreshold somatiza-

Table I *ICD-10* and *DSM-IV* Nosologies

ICD-10 **Diagnostic Criteria for Research (DCR)**

F 44—Dissociative and Conversion Disorders
(Primary symptom = "Physical"/Includes "stress" component)

  F 44.0 Dissociative amnesia
  F 44.1 Dissociative fugue
  F 44.2 Dissociative stupor
  F 44.3 Trance and possession disorders
  F 44.4 Dissociative motor disorders
  F 44.5 Dissociative convulsions
  F 44.6 Dissociative anesthesia, sensory loss
  F 44.7 Mixed dissociative/conversion disorder
  F 44.8 Other dissociative disorders (Ganser, multiple personality disorder, and so on)

F 45—Somatoform Disorders
  F 45.0 Somatization disorder (Criteria = 6 or more symptoms from a list of 14, that includes 6 gastrointestinal, 2 cardiovascular, 3 genitourinary and 3 skin and pain symptoms)
  F 45.1 Undifferentiated somatoform disorder
  F 45.2 Hypochondriacal disorder
  F 45.3 Somatoform autonomic dysfunction
  F 45.4 Persistent somatoform pain disorder
  F 45.8 & 45.9 Other/unspecified somatoform disorders
  F 48.0 Neurasthenia (listed under F48 "Other neurotic disorders")

DSM-IV **Criteria**

Dissociative Disorders
  (Primary symptoms = "Psychological"; "Disturbance of normal integration functions of identity, memory or consciousness")
  Dissociative amnesia
  Dissociative fugue
  Dissociative identity disorder (multiple personality)
  Depersonalization disorder
  Dissociative disorder not otherwise specified

Somatoform Disorders
  Somatization disorder (8 symptoms = 4 pain, 2 gastrointestinal, 1 sexual, 1 pseudoneurologic, down from 13 in *DSM-III-R*)
  Hypochondriasis
  Conversion disorder (either "motor deficit," "seizure," "sensory deficit," or "mixed")
  Body dysmorphic disorder
  Pain disorder
  Undifferentiated/not otherwise specified

tion (for patients with unexplained physical symptoms who do not meet all criteria for SD); (3) somatization with comorbid physical illness; and (4) somatization with comorbid psychiatric illness.

Smith's review suggests that patients with full-blown SD perceive themselves as "sicker than very sick," spending, on average, 1 week per month in bed. In addition, these patients, relative to medical controls, present with a greater number and intensity of psychological symptoms (depression, panic) and greater work and social disability. Interestingly, the strong belief held by SD patients that their health is "extremely poor" is not corroborated by research evidence. For example, Smith cites the mortality rate of SD as being equal to that of patients in the general population and significantly lower than that found in major depression. Perhaps most telling of all statistics cited by Smith is the fact that SD patients evince health care utilization costs at nine times the U.S. per capita average.

According to Escobar, parallel to patients with SD, those with subsyndromal SD also report increased sick leave, restricted activities, and avid use of nonpsychiatric medical services compared with the general population. Moreover, when somatization coexists with either physical or psychiatric illness (Categories 3 and 4 in Smith's taxonomy), there is a significant amplification of the discomfort and disability typically associated with either class of illness when occurring in isolation. Smith notes that it has also been established that high levels of psychiatric comorbidity are much higher for somatizing patients than for nonsomatizing controls, particularly with respect to major depression, generalized anxiety, phobia, and some Axis II personality disorders, such as avoidant, paranoid, and self-defeating disorders.

A. Escobar's Abridged Construct of Somatization

Because more than one-fourth of all patients seeking primary care services are somatizers and many of these would not be captured by the SD diagnosis in current nosologies, the first author (JIE) and his colleagues sought to develop methods of identifying and classifying SD and subsyndromal somatization phenomena that would be feasible for use by primary care providers. In this context Escobar proposed an "abridged" somatization construct, along with a relatively simple series of interview probes to be used by the physician or lay interviewer. Figure 1 is a flowchart that provides a practical example of the probing logic for chest pain, a common symptom in a primary care setting. Essentially, male patients satisfy criteria for Escobar's "abridged" somatization if they present with four or more unexplained physical symptoms that impair

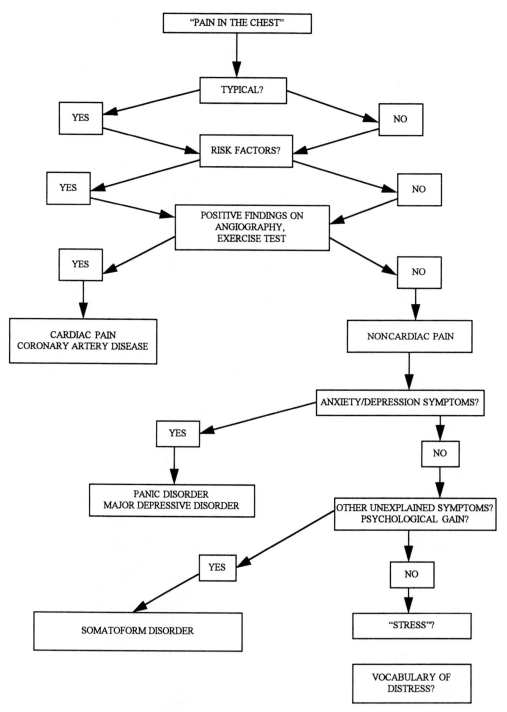

Figure 1 Probing logic for chest pain.

some aspect of functioning and daily living, whereas females satisfy criteria with six or more unexplained symptoms. More recently, the WHO-sponsored international classification (*ICD-10*) drafted a "primary care version" of the diagnostic criteria for SD and subsyndromal somatization that uses this more generic definition of somatizing patients as those "presenting with many unexplained somatic complaints."

According to Escobar, a somatization symptom should be coded individually on the basis of its severity, frequency, and the degree of functional interference and disability it conveys. A rigorous system of probes should be used to rule out alternative explanations for a given symptom, such as the use of medications, drugs, or alcohol, or the presence of a physical illness or injury. High levels of unexplained symptoms elicited in this manner (e.g., more than four lifetime symptoms for males) imply "somatization." Escobar's extensive program of research on both general populations and primary care samples has validated his method of identifying the disorder by showing that patients who satisfy these abridged criteria independently evidence elevated scores on standardized measures of psychopathology, show high levels of utilization of inpatient and outpatient medical services, and present with greater disability in work, family, and social domains. Put another way, the validity coefficients (correlates) of Escobar's abridged somatization construct have been observed to be similar both in direction and magnitude to the correlates of "full-blown" SD. These results are consistent with but do not prove a "dimensional" as opposed to a "discrete" view of the somatization phenomena. Interestingly, although the threshold for "full" somatization disorder required 13 or more unexplained symptoms in *DSM-III-R*, the threshold has been moved closer to that of Escobar's in *ICD-10* and *DSM-IV* (Table 1). Thus, in the Diagnostic Criteria for Research in *ICD-10* only six symptoms are required, while in *DSM-IV* only eight symptoms are now required, with the caveat that at least two of these must be pseudoneurological (e.g., numbness, blindness, seizures).

B. Are "Medically Unexplained Somatic Symptoms" Always Psychiatric Symptoms?

There seems to be some consensus, based on the reviews by Escobar, Noyes, Holt and Kathol, and Smith that prior to assuming that a somatic symptom that remains medically unexplained has a psychiatric basis, the symptom should have the following characteristics:

1a. The symptom is associated with a "primary" psychiatric disorder (e.g., major depression or panic disorder).

1b. The symptom appears in close temporal proximity with certain life events such as overwhelming trauma or other severe stressors.

2. The symptom provides some sort of psychological "gratification" to the individual (e.g., "secondary gain" such as decreased work or family responsibilities) or represents a less-stigmatized (than mental illness) mode of expressing underlying chronic unhappiness (as in the personality "trait" of neuroticism).

3. The symptom becomes persistent, joins a conglomerate of other unexplained physical symptoms, setting in motion extensive use of health services and chronic dissatisfaction with medical care.

III. PATHOGENESIS

The pathogenesis of somatization is unknown. A number of factors is thought to act in concert to produce somatization. One sociological explanation is that adoption of a "sick role" provides secondary gains to the person who adopts it (lowering of work responsibilities) while simultaneously shielding the individual from the stigma associated with mental illness. The "primary gain" associated with somatization, according to psychoanalytic theory, is the amelioration of intrapsychic conflict. There are also many other plausible psychological and biological explanations, some of which have been summarized by Noyes, Holt and Kathol.

> One of these factors is autonomic arousal. Under the influence of stress or anxiety, patients experience heightened arousal and, with it, a host of mediated symptoms. Palpitations, shortness of breath, dizziness, sweating and other symptoms may all become a focus of health concern. Excessive worry about health, regardless of its source, may be another factor. Worried persons are vigilant and scan their bodies for sensations that then become an object of worried concern. By focusing narrowly on a body part, a person may intensify sensations arising from it, sensations that may grow distressing or even painful. Still another factor has to do with communication of distress. Some somatizers are unable to distinguish between emotions and bodily sensations and have difficulty communicating feelings (p. 741).

Somatizers may also have lower thresholds and tolerance for physical discomfort. For example, in experimental situations, the same stimulus that elicits a simple sensation of "pressure" in the nonsomatizer can elicit "pain" in the somatizer. There is speculation that this lower threshold is constitutional in nature. [*See* PAIN.]

The prevalence of SD or subsyndromal somatization in general medical practice has risen over the last half century. This rise seems less attributable to an actual increase in mild, self-limiting physical symptoms (such as fatigue, headaches, and upper respiratory distress) than to a societal tendency to reclassify mild and benign bodily discomfort as symptoms of medical disease. In line with increased "medicalization" of benign transient symptoms is a growing list of "functional somatic syndromes" whose scientific status and medical basis remain unclear. These include chronic fatigue syndrome, total allergy syndrome, food hypersensitivity, reactive hypoglycemia, systemic yeast infection (*Candida* hypersensitivity syndrome), Gulf War syndrome, fibromyalgia, sick building syndrome, and mitral valve prolapse.

A. FROM "DISTRESS" TO "PSYCHOPATHOLOGY": IS THERE A "BRIDGE"?

Theoretical formulations within a variety of social and behavioral science disciplines, such as sociology, anthropology, and psychology, invariably link psychiatric disorders with "stress." Because "distress," regardless of its source, commonly is expressed in psychological or behavioral terms (e.g., "demoralization," "anxiety," "depression"), these formulations continue to hold significant influence on the mental health field. However, a distinction must be made between expressions of "distress" (or "stress-induced" states) and formal "psychopathologic" states. Psychiatric diagnoses that are distinct, reliably made, and predictable, such as endogenous/melancholic depression, do not seem to fit well the theoretical framework of the "stress spectrum disorder." Quite naturally, the theorizing that linked "distress" to psychiatric disorder was transported to the field of psychiatric epidemiology, and therefore, instruments used in these surveys tend to be simple self-report measures of "distress." In this zeitgeist, even a formal diagnostic system such as *DSM-IV* can be truncated to a mere symptom checklist, used by clinicians simply to elicit symptoms one by one. In the opinion of the authors, key elements in generating valid psychiatric diagnosis should in-

clude not only each reported symptom but also its intensity or severity, and the way in which it clusters with others symptoms and psychosocial attributes.

Somatization may be an interesting exception to the trend of reducing psychiatric diagnostic process to symptom inventories, at least in *DSM-IV*. Since it rules that in order to score a physical complaint as a psychiatric symptom the probing needs to scrutinize severity issues in addition to documenting medical visits and lack of clear medical explanations for the symptom. In our opinion, high levels of somatic symptoms represent a reliable entity, akin to the sturdier disorders in psychiatry such as melancholia. As such, somatization may be much more accessible to empirical scrutiny than most other symptomatic constructs in psychiatry.

IV. DETECTION, RECOGNITION, DIAGNOSIS

Somatization and its various syndromes, although well documented throughout the years, have baffled medical practitioners with their tendency to metamorphism as part of cultural evolution and the changing perspectives of the medical paradigms. For example, Barsky and Borus have argued that somatization is on the rise because "sociocultural currents reduce the public's tolerance of mild symptoms and benign infirmities and lower the threshold for seeking medical *but not psychiatric* (italics ours) attention for such complaints. These trends coincide with a progressive medicalization of physical distress in which uncomfortable bodily states and isolated symptoms are reclassified as diseases for which medical treatment is sought" (p. 1931). In clinical settings as well as in common parlance, somatizers tend to be labeled in a derogatory manner. Curiously, however, these vernacular terms (such as "hysterics," "Gomers" [acronym for **G**o **O**ut of **M**y **E**mergency **R**oom], "turkeys," "hypochondriacs," and many others) seem to have more currency in describing the experience of dealing with these patients than do the more refined and euphemistic diagnostic labels.

The fact that somatoform disorders lag far behind other psychiatric diagnoses in terms of their proper recognition and visible research activity may be explained by their rather ambiguous nosological status. Problems in classifying these syndromes include issues of diagnostic validity and the excessive comorbidity that exists with other types of psychopathology. Also, since patients affected by these disorders believe their illness is "physical," they reject psychological labeling or referral and are rarely seen in psychiatric settings. Moreover, they are unlikely to form "advocacy groups" such as those seen in the case of people with anxiety or mood disorders. It is likely, however, that many somatizing patients readily joint patient groups with more "medicalized" labels such as functional somatic syndromes like "chronic fatigue," "TMJ," "Fibromyositis," "Multiple Chemical Sensitivity," among numerous others.

The current age of cost containment has brought new awareness about these patients, since they are avid consumers of services and technologies, thus taxing health care systems excessively. Following suit with tradition, newly found characterizations of these somatizing patients prove colorful though still highly pejorative. Thus, the traditional "hysterics" or "hypochondriacs" at the medical clinics are becoming the "frequent flyers" at the corporate health headquarters.

Because of the ambiguity of their symptoms, treatment refractoriness and lack of psychological mindedness, somatizing patients use health services excessively, in pursuit of diagnostic confirmation or reassurance. This leads to heavy utilization of expensive technologies and often may result in unnecessary procedures being performed. It is as if medical care became an essential social support network and the patient role part of personal identity for these patients. Paradoxically, these patients also display chronic dissatisfaction with the care received, and may often seek financial compensation for their symptoms and "mishaps." This latter factor, when added to avid service use and disability inherent in the disorder, makes somatizing syndromes some of the most expensive entities in medicine. Indeed, somatization is on a collision course with cost-containing trends in managed care.

A. Somatizers and Hypochondriacs: A Profile

Individuals affected with these traits, generally display a tendency to amplify physical symptoms and sensations. They also tend to endorse multiple physical symptoms involving various body areas. My impression (JIE) in working with many of these patients, is that there is a tendency to "overreport" not only physical symptoms, but also psychiatric ones, hence the high levels of psychiatric comorbidity that are well

documented in the literature. In addition to over reporting physical symptoms, these patients also tend to overreport negative "experiences" (e.g., trauma, instances of being victimized, sexual abuse), relative to other clinical populations.

Contrary to much theorizing, "somatizers" are not a good model for "masked" psychiatric disturbances since they report very high levels of psychological distress. High levels of these unexplained physical symptoms seem to be a good marker for affective and anxiety syndromes, and possibly several other psychiatric disorders. Anxiety syndromes would primarily imply unexplained cardiopulmonary symptoms, while depressive syndromes would coexist with unexplained somatic pain in many sites, muscular-skeletal weakness, and pseudoneurological symptoms (e.g., numbness, amnesia). In advancing the specificity of somatization indexes, the authors are currently exploring clustering of somatic symptoms for the various disorders. [*See* ANXIETY; DEPRESSION.]

B. Problems with the New Classifications

A glance at some *DSM-IV* and *ICD-10* categories leaves one with the impression that in trying to make larger numbers of individuals fit the criteria, the "net" has become much less discriminating, and the "catch" much less specific. In the hands of less experienced clinicians, many of these nosologic categories end up as mere "symptom checklists," simply eliciting symptoms as present or absent regardless of their severity or clustering attributes. Although this may be a convenient feature in the age of managed care, it flies in the face of traditional psychopathology that has relied on detailed anamnesis, natural course of illness, and precise dissection of symptom phenomenology in the creation of "valid" diagnoses. To counter the lack of specificity of many psychiatric syndromes, it is important to restore the Kraepelinian tenet, that the intensity or severity of the symptom, its temporal evolution, and its clustering, rather than the symptom per se, should remain the key elements in psychiatric diagnosis. Fortunately, in eliciting somatization symptoms, *DSM-III-R* and *DSM-IV* have drafted unambiguous rules. For example, the "probing" is expected to scrutinize severity issues in addition to documenting medical visits and lack of clear medical explanations for the symptom prior to scoring it as present. Thus, when elicited in this manner, high levels of medically unexplained somatic symptoms may represent more valid and reliable indexes than other symptom clusters. Besides, a medically unexplained symptom is more objective, more accessible to scrutiny, and, also, it may prove less intrusive, eliciting far less resistance from the individual affected than other psychopathologic concepts.

V. CROSS-CULTURAL ISSUES

It is generally accepted that cultural influences may color the expression of somatization and hypochondriasis. Although it is often difficult to disentangle the contribution of ethnicity from other demographic factors (e.g., socioeconomic status: patients of lower socioeconomic status tend to somatize more than those of higher status), most studies reinforce the view that culture exerts a powerful influence in shaping symptom presentation and determining health-related attitudes. For example, in the United States the prevalence of somatization, based on counts of unexplained physical symptoms, is higher for some ethnic groups (e.g., Jewish and Italian Americans) than for others (e.g., Irish Americans). Also, relatively high levels of unexplained physical symptoms in the United States have been reported in the case of Middle Eastern, Southeast Asian, and Latino patients. However, there is also significant within-group variation among the different Southeast Asian ethnic groups and also among such Latino subgroups as Mexican American, Puerto Rican Americans and Cuban Americans.

It is conceivable that the type of symptoms presented by "somatizing" patients may differ in various cultural settings. International research reports reveal rather pathognomonic symptom presentations for patients with somatoform disorders in various cultures. For example, in Africa (Nigeria), "feeling of heat," "peppery and crawling sensations," and "numbness"; in India, "burning hands and feet," "hot, peppery sensations in head"; and in Puerto Rico, headache, trembling, stomach disturbances, palpitations, and dissociative symptoms, all components of a syndrome called "ataque de nervios."

Moreover, even within similar countries, such as European and North American, there are unique differences. For example, in North America there is an emphasis on immunologically based symptoms.

VI. CLINICAL MANAGEMENT

The clinical management of somatizing syndromes continues to be an area of active debate and improvisation. These disorders confront us both with diagnosis and therapeutic challenges because of their polysymptomatic (multiorgan) and polysyndromic (comorbid) features, their persistence, and their refractoriness to traditional interventions. The lack of psychological "mindedness" in somatizers poses serious hurdles to psychotherapeutic management and negatively affects adherence to psychiatric interventions. Because of the diagnostic dilemmas often faced, and possibly because these patients rarely present to mental health treatment settings, very few scientific data are available on how the various therapeutic interventions affect the most salient outcomes.

One of the few exceptions is the study by Smith, Rost, and Kashner on the effects of a brief intervention on costs of care, level of functioning, and clinical outcome. The intervention was followed by primary physicians and had several distinct features. These included the adoption of an understanding and reassuring attitude, taking the patient's complaints seriously, performing a brief physical assessment during regularly scheduled visits, and an active avoidance of procedures and medications. The latter strategy prevents iatrogenic complications that often result from unnecessary medical and therapeutic interventions performed on these patients. It was found that when these procedures were followed, physical functioning improved and costs of care went down.

Noyes, Holt, and Kathol also emphasize the importance of regularly scheduled visits in order to reassure the somatizing patient that the physician is concerned about his or her well-being. At the same time, unscheduled visits are actively discouraged, since these tend to reinforce the patient's well-honed tendency to amplify existing symptoms or to generate new ones.

Physicians themselves may need the support of colleagues or consultants in order to deal with negative emotions that arise when treating somatizers. Common emotions experienced by treating physicians are guilt and anger. Guilt may accompany the clinician's attempt to set limits on frequent phone calls or unscheduled visits from demanding patients. It is not uncommon to experience anger when treating a particularly demanding and resentful patient, especially when he or she begins to test already established limits, and the provider may need a means to vent this anger or talk to a colleague so as not to direct the anger at the patient.

Regarding pharmacotherapy, the use of antidepressants has been proposed for a number of the somatizing syndromes including chronic pain, chronic fatigue, somatization, and hypochondriasis, whereas neuroleptic agents such as pimozide are advocated for delusional syndromes such as delusions of infestation and severe cases of dysmorphophobia. With very few exceptions, however, most of these claims are based on anecdotal reports. The first author (Escobar) is aware of two currently ongoing double-blind trials in this area, one on hypochondriasis and the other on dysmorphophobia. Results of these important studies were not available as of September 1997 (JIE). [*See* Psychopharmacology.]

Secondary syndromes, such as the somatic equivalents of anxiety and depression, would be expected to respond to traditional treatments such as antianxiety and antidepressant agents such as selective serotonin reuptake inhibitors. Few systematic data, however, are currently available.

Psychological treatments, such as cognitive-behavioral treatments aimed at enhancing emotional expression and correcting dysfunctional attitudes towards illness and patient roles have also received some empirical support of efficacy. Treatments based on the behavioral paradigm of exposure-response prevention have also been developed. These psychological treatments, while promising, are in need of further research and development. [*See* Behavior Therapy; Cognitive Therapy.]

Finally, on the basis of clinical experience and the studies described in a previous section, one would strongly predict the relevance of ethnic background to the processes of treatment seeking, adherence, and response of somatizing patients. Once again, however, there are no scientific data to provide guidance in this regard. This should become an important priority for future studies.

BIBLIOGRAPHY

American Psychiatric Association. (1994). *Diagnostic and statistical manual of mental disorders* (4th ed.). Washington, DC: Author.

Barsky, A. J., & Borus, J. F. (1995). Somatization and medicalization in the era of managed care. *J. Amer. Med. Assoc., 274,* 1931–1934.

Castillo, R., Waitzkin, H., Ramirez, Y., & Escobar, J. I. (1995). Somatization in primary care, with a focus on immigrants and refugees. *Arch. Fam. Med., 4,* 637–646.

Escobar, J. I. (1995). Transcultural aspects of dissociative and somatoform disorders. *The Psychiatric Clinics of North America, 18,* 555–569.

Kirmayer, L. J., & Robbins, J. M. (1991). Three forms of somatization in primary care: prevalence, co-occurrence, and sociodemographic characteristics. *J. Nerv. Ment. Dis., 179,* 647–655.

Noyes, R., Holt, C. S., & Kathol, R. G. (1995). Somatization: Diagnosis and Management, *Arch. Fam. Med., 4,* 790–795.

Smith, G. Richard, Rost, K., & Kashner, T. M., (1995). A trial of the effect of a standard psychiatric consultation on health outcomes and costs in somatizing patients. *Arch. Gen. Psychiatry, 52,* 238–243.

Smith, G. Richard. (1994). The course of somatization and its effects on utilization of health care resources. *Psychosomatics, 35,* 263–267.

Sport and Mental Status

Judy L. Van Raalte and Britton W. Brewer

Springfield College

Anxiety A negatively charged emotional state that is characterized by internal discomfort and a feeling of nervousness, dread or worry.
Imagery The process of mentally creating or recreating an experience, which has also been termed mental practice, mental rehearsal, and visualization.
National Governing Body An organization that administers elite amateur sport (e.g., United States Skiing).
Optimal Performance State The ideal physical and mental state during which extraordinary sport performances occur; this has also been termed flow state, peak performance, and the zone.
Staleness An overall physical and emotional state in which performance declines and symptoms mimicking those of depressive disorders and chronic fatigue syndrome may emerge.

SPORT has no universally agreed upon definition. However, sport is generally described as a competitive athletic activity that requires skill or physical prowess (e.g., tennis, football, cycling). Sport typically includes recreational activities that provide diversion for participants and spectators, such as participation in youth soccer, high school basketball, college swimming, professional golf, elite amateur gymnastics, recreational

softball, and masters track and field. Some sports are contested on an individual basis (e.g., racquetball singles, skiing, swimming), whereas other sports involve team play (e.g., hockey, rugby, volleyball).

I. INTRODUCTION

For many people, sport and mental health are inextricably intertwined throughout the life span. This article uses a developmental perspective to highlight psychological factors in sport performance. Performance problems, psychopathology, and the treatment of mental disorders in sport are also discussed.

II. PSYCHOLOGICAL FACTORS IN SPORT PERFORMANCE

Sport performance is dependent on both physical and psychological factors. Physical talent and training undoubtedly contribute to sport performance, and there is evidence that personality characteristics, use of cognitive strategies (e.g., self-talk, imagery, goal setting), the ability to reach optimal performance states (i.e., "the zone"), and the management of arousal and anxiety may all influence sport outcomes.

A. Personality Characteristics

Personality is described as a group of core traits, typical response patterns, and role-related behaviors that are affected by the social environment. Despite the widespread belief that certain personality characteristics or traits are optimal for sport performance, no identifiable "sport personality" has been shown to exist. However, sport success has been associated with positive mental health and positive self-perceptions.

Researchers have used general personality tests, situation-specific questionnaires, and sport-specific personality inventories in an attempt to identify the psychological characteristics that distinguish subgroups of athletes (e.g., contact versus noncontact sport participants, team versus individual sport participants) and successful athletes from less successful athletes. No consistent personality differences have been documented between athletes in contact versus noncontact sports and team versus individual sports. In comparing successful and less successful athletes, it has been found that successful athletes report more vigor and less tension, depression, anger, fatigue, and confusion on the Profile of Mood States (POMS) than do less successful athletes. [*See* PERSONALITY.]

Athletes' responses on the Test of Attentional Interpersonal Style (TAIS) (measures athletes' attention-focusing style), the Psychological Skills Inventory for Sports (PSIS) (assesses athletes' psychological strengths in sport), and the Athletic Motivation Inventory (AMI) (developed to distinguish athletes expected to be more successful and those expected to be less successful) have failed to consistently distinguish between more and less successful athletes. Failure to find differences between more and less successful athletes may be due in part to the relatively low reliability and validity of sport personality measures. Currently, no personality test has been developed that is sufficiently valid to be used for athlete selection purposes.

B. Cognitive Behavioral Attributes

Conventional wisdom suggests that if athletes want to improve in their sport, then they should practice more. Often, however, what is lacking is not athletes' physical training, but rather their mental skills. Research has indicated that successful athletes use a variety of cognitive strategies (e.g., self-talk, imagery, goal setting) more than do less successful athletes.

I. Self-Talk

Self-talk, the things that athletes think or say to themselves, can be modified through training to correct errors, focus attention, moderate activation levels, and maintain self-confidence. Research has shown that self-talk is related to sport performance. In general, it has been suggested that positive self-talk (e.g., "I can do it") or instructional self-talk (e.g., "bend your knees and follow through") can be useful in enhancing performance. Negative self-talk (e.g., "I can't hit anything") may serve a motivating function, but should be used sparingly because it has been associated with poor sport performances. The specific mechanisms by which self-talk affects performance have not been determined.

2. Imagery

Imagery involves using stored sensory experiences that are internally recalled and performed. When using imagery, athletes may adopt an internal perspective that involves imagining from their own vantage point (i.e., as if they are competing) or an external perspective that involves imagining from the vantage point of an external observer (i.e., as if they are watching themselves on video). Imagery can be used to practice specific skills, build confidence, improve concentration, control emotional reactions, practice strategy, analyze errors, and cope with pain and injury. Most applications of imagery encourage athletes to image positive sport outcomes and to use all the senses, including the kinesthetic (movement) sense in the images. Although many practitioners suggest that imagery can be combined with relaxation for maximal effect, no added benefit has been found for using relaxation in combination with imagery.

Researchers have explored the effects of imagery on performance by comparing use of imagery (i.e., mental practice) to physical practice and to a combination of physical practice and imagery. Research has indicated that a combination of physical practice and imagery is generally superior to physical practice or imagery alone. However, it has also been suggested that the effectiveness of imagery in enhancing performance in any particular situation may depend on the task and the personality and skills of the individual involved. As with physical skills, it has been suggested that imagery effectiveness is enhanced by practice.

Several theories (e.g., symbolic learning theory, psychoneuromuscular theory) have been proposed to explain the mechanisms by which imagery works. Current approaches support the idea that imagery facilitates performance by providing additional opportunities for athletes to develop symbolic elements of motor tasks.

3. Goal Setting

Goals are objectives or aims of an action. In sport, goal setting works by directing athletes' attention to important elements of the task being performed, mobilizing effort, prolonging persistence, and encouraging the development of new learning strategies. A consistent body of research has demonstrated that specific and challenging goals result in better performances than having no goals, easy goals, or vague "do your best" goals. Other goal setting strategies that have been suggested to enhance performance include setting both long- and short-term goals, setting goals for both practice and competitions, setting individual and team goals, developing goal achievement strategies, making goals public, providing support for goals, and evaluating goals.

A number of factors that inhibit the effective implementation of goal-setting strategies have been identified. Common goal setting problems include: setting too many goals at the beginning; failing to set specific, measurable goals; and failing to monitor and readjust goals. [*See* Intrinsic Motivation and Goals.]

C. Optimal Performance States

Athletes sometimes describe themselves as having had a "peak performance" or of having been "in the zone." These sport experiences involve performances that transcend the ordinary and stand out as being exceptional. Often they are similar to the "flow experience," in which a person acts with total involvement in the moment. Due to the elusive nature of optimal performance states, a precise definition has not been developed. Five of the most common characteristics of peak performances described by athletes are: (a) clearly focused attention; (b) lack of concern with outcome; (c) effortless performance; (d) perceptions of time slowing; and (e) feelings of supreme confidence. Many sport psychology interventions are designed to help athletes improve particular psychological skills with the ultimate goal of helping athletes to achieve optimal performance states more frequently.

D. Arousal/Anxiety and Performance

People who are anxious in many situations are said to have high trait anxiety. The temporary anxiety that athletes experience that centers on sport-related situations has been called competitive state anxiety and has been further described as having cognitive (e.g., worry, emotional distress) and somatic (e.g., rapid heart rate, sweaty hands) components. Although some level of physiological arousal is essential for sport performance, excessive anxiety has been associated with poor sport performances. [*See* Anxiety.]

Four theories (i.e., inverted-u theory, drive theory, zone of optimal functioning, and catastrophe theory) serve as the primary explanations for the relationship between arousal or anxiety and performance. All four theories note that a minimum level of arousal is necessary for sport performance and that individuals and sport task demands differ in the level of arousal required for maximal performance. With the exception of drive theory (which posits that arousal is positively associated with performance), the theories hold that overarousal and underarousal are both associated with decrements in sport performance.

A number of strategies have been proposed to help athletes achieve their ideal level of arousal. Cognitive reappraisal approaches operate on the assumption that arousal is caused by thought patterns. Changing negative cognitions or the situations that cause such cognitions can help adjust arousal levels and enhance performance. Physiological interventions work by affecting physical parameters. For example, it has been demonstrated that physiological arousal can be reduced through the use of techniques such as diaphragmatic breathing and progressive relaxation. Hypnosis has also been found useful in regulating arousal and performance levels. [*See* Hypnosis and the Psychological Unconscious.]

III. DEVELOPMENTAL ISSUES

A. Sport as a Life-Span Activity

Physical abilities related to sport performance develop throughout childhood and peak in early adulthood. Once thought to be only the preserve of the young, more adults have become involved or continued their involvement in competitive sport well into middle age and beyond. Sport is now an activity that people can participate in throughout their life spans.

1. Youth

Youth sport has been heralded as a character-building activity that enhances physical and psychological development. It has also been criticized as overly stressful, causing undue anxiety and possible harm for young participants. Research has shown that when sport settings are designed to foster psychological growth, positive character development is more likely to occur.

Children participate in sport for a variety of reasons. The main reason that children in the United States report that they participate in sport is to have fun. Children also like to improve their skills, stay in shape, do something at which they are good, get exercise, learn new skills, and compete. In other cultures, children have reported that they are involved in sport because it provides opportunities for independence, taking responsibility, and making decisions.

There are numerous opportunities for children to be involved in sport. A large number of children, however, drop out of competitive sport programs each year. Children's sport involvement steadily declines from the age of 13 to the age of 18. Children drop out of organized sport for a number of reasons, including: having other things to do, changing interests, not being as good at the sport as they had wanted to be, not having enough fun, being bored, disliking the pressure, disliking the coach, and finding the training too hard. Research has indicated, however, that high levels of stress are not the main reason that young athletes drop out of sport. Most young athletes do not experience significantly more anxiety than children who are involved in other activities.

Youth sport researchers have concluded that sport involvement is most likely to produce positive experiences for young athletes when the sport environment is designed to foster development of self-esteem. Evaluation of Coach Effectiveness Training, one of several coach training programs, has demonstrated that an encouraging and technically instructive approach to coaching helps children to develop self-esteem and makes them less likely to drop out of sport.

2. College

Students participate in intercollegiate athletics for a variety of reasons, including love of the sport, financial need for an athletic scholarship, and a desire to have their talent showcased for professional sport teams. College student-athletes encounter the same developmental pressures (e.g., transitions, substance use, peer pressure) that other college students experience as well as the specific demands of the sport environment (e.g., training, competition, travel). Factors such as divisional and scholarship status can shape student-athletes' college sport experiences.

Student-athletes attending National Collegiate Athletic Association (NCAA) Division I and II colleges and universities may receive full or partial athletic scholarships. Athletes in these high profile programs often worry about athletic scholarships, feel pressure from their coaches, have concerns about athletic injury, and are under the scrutiny of the media. Many student-athletes attending junior colleges have the added burden of transferring to 4-year schools to complete their educations. Sport involvement can enhance student-athletes' college experience by providing opportunities to improve in sport, compete, and have fun, but sport can also be an additional pressure due to travel, fatigue, and competitive stress.

3. Professional and Elite Amateur

The professional and elite amateur (e.g., Olympic) levels of sport require athletes to demonstrate considerable skills and abilities. Competing at these levels also generally requires athletes to devote maximal physical and emotional resources to sport. Competitive stress, life on the road, concerns with injuries, dealing with the media, competitive pressure, and training demands can all add to the challenges experienced.

4. Recreational

Recreational athletes are the largest group of athletes in the United States. People report involvement in recreational sport activities for reasons of enjoyment, competition, and recognition of the benefits of exercise such as increased confidence and well-being and decreased anxiety, depression, anger, and hostility. Other reasons for recreational sport involvement include establishing a social support network, managing stress, controlling body weight, and combatting the aging process.

5. Senior

Sport involvement can continue throughout the life span. In many sports (e.g., bowling, triathalon, running, swimming, tennis) adult or age group competitions exist at the local, national, and international level. Senior athletes compete in sport for reasons that are similar to those of other athletes. Unlike some other athlete groups, who can focus primarily on their sport, senior athletes often have significant family, career, and social demands in addition to the physical and emotional demands of their sports. Although managing conflicting demands can be challenging, many senior athletes report that the benefits of sport involvement outweigh the costs.

B. Developmental Parameters Affected by Sport Involvement

Involvement in sport clearly influences physical development. Sport involvement also affects other areas of human development including moral development, social development, and career development.

1. Moral Development

It is often assumed that involvement in sport activities builds character (e.g., compassion, fairness, sportspersonship, and integrity). Media coverage of sport, however, suggests that sport promotes violence among players, use of illegal drugs, and ridiculing of opponents. Although it cannot be concluded that sport impedes moral development, it is likely that sport reflects the values and moral strengths and failings that affect society as a whole.

The sport arena has been described as a microcosm of society in which athletes are challenged to deal with the conflict between the desire to win and the norms of fair play. Research with competitive athletes has demonstrated that they are more aggressive and, in some cases, less sophisticated in moral reasoning than nonathletes. Research has also shown that sport is effective in enhancing moral development when sport programs are specifically designed to include a moral development component.

2. Social Development

Involvement in sport affects a number of important social outcomes. Sport participants are less likely than nonparticipants to drop out of school, use drugs, become teenaged parents, smoke cigarettes, and be arrested. Retrospective reports have suggested that sport participants also have fewer unexcused absences from school, earn better grades, and have fewer behavior problems outside the classroom.

Much research has focused on the ways that social evaluation in sport affects the development of self-concept. Three social evaluation processes provide information to the athlete that is incorporated into the self-concept. First, comparative appraisal occurs when athletes compare their abilities to peers. Comparative appraisal gives athletes important information about their relative skills. Second, reflected appraisal occurs when athletes make inferences about themselves based on what they infer from the reactions of others. Third, direct feedback occurs when athletes are given feedback by others (e.g., coaches, parents). Sport ability is an important determinant of peer acceptance. The information that athletes receive via comparative appraisal, reflected appraisal, and direct feedback can contribute in a positive or negative way to their social development and self-concept.

3. Career Development

The various demands of sport can reduce opportunities for career exploration. Some athletes are so involved in their sport that they do not have time for or interest in career development. Other athletes, hoping that they will be selected to the professional sport ranks, have foreclosed their identities as athletes and failed to engage in broader career exploration. Lack of career exploration can leave athletes at a disadvantage relative to their nonathlete peers when their sport careers end.

Sport careers can end when athletes choose to retire, but they also can end unexpectedly due to injury, deselection, and forced retirement. When sport careers end "off-time" (i.e., out of the typical developmental sequence), athletes may not have the informal and formal support networks that they need to ease the transition. Because many athletes are not prepared for the end of their sport careers, programs have been developed to help athletes with career development. For example, the United States Olympic Committee developed the Career Assistance Program for Athletes (CAPA) to help athletes: (a) assess their needs, interests, and skills; (b) develop a life-work plan; and (c) build confidence in career issues. CAPA helps athletes to understand that the skills they have developed in sport (e.g., ability to perform under pressure, organizational skills, patience, flexibility, risk taking, self-control, ability to accept criticism and feedback, ability to set and meet goals, ability to communicate with others) can be used in other nonsport domains. Research has shown, however, that for these skills to transfer to other careers, athletes must be aware of their various skills, should know how the skills were acquired, should believe that these skills can transfer to other settings, should seek social support, and should have the ability to adjust to initial failures and setbacks.

IV. PSYCHOPATHOLOGY

A. Prevalence in Sport Populations

Although the beneficial effects of *exercise* on psychological functioning are well documented and there is evidence that positive mental health is an asset to sport performers, there are few experimental or epidemiological data suggesting that mental health benefits accompany *sport* participation. It is safe to assume that severe psychopathology (e.g., psychosis) is rare among athletes. Nevertheless, athletes are susceptible to psychological problems. There is anecdotal evidence of various psychological disorders (e.g., bipolar disorder, obsessive-compulsive disorder, panic disorder, Tourette's syndrome) among successful professional and elite amateur competitors. The unique demands of competitive sport involvement may even contribute to the development of certain forms of psychopathology. [*See* EXERCISE AND MENTAL HEALTH; PHYSICAL ACTIVITY AND MENTAL HEALTH.]

B. Disorders for Which Athletes Are at Higher Risk

Although prevalence rates have varied extensively across studies, research has consistently shown that athletes are at increased risk for eating disorders (i.e., anorexia nervosa, bulimia nervosa). Sport-specific contributors to disordered eating are thought to include involvement in sports with competitive weight restrictions (e.g., wrestling), pressure from coaches to lose weight, and participation in sports where physical appearance is important (e.g., gymnastics, figure skating).

Substance-related disorders have also been well-documented in sport populations. Research has indicated that high school and college athletes use recreational drugs (e.g., alcohol, marijuana) to the same extent as their nonathlete peers, although they may restrict use of recreational drugs during the competitive season. Some athletes use drugs for performance enhancement purposes, such as increasing muscular size and strength, reducing pain, increasing energy and arousal, promoting relaxation, and controlling weight. [*See* SUBSTANCE ABUSE.]

Athletes may experience affective disturbances when engaging in heavy training or while adjusting to injury. Competitors who train at high volume are at risk for developing staleness, a condition in which performance declines and symptoms mimicking those of depressive disorders and chronic fatigue syndrome may emerge. Approximately 5 to 13% of injured athletes experience clinically meaningful levels of psychological distress.

V. TREATMENT

A. Athletes and Mental Health Services

Historically, athletes have underutilized mental health services. This reluctance to seek psychological assistance may, in part, be attributable to the stigma of seeing a psychologist and a realistic fear of derogation from teammates, coaches, and others. Providing evidence of increased acceptance of the field of sport psychology, recent research has shown that athletes may be more receptive to consulting a sport psychologist than a traditional mental health professional (e.g., psychotherapist) for performance enhancement reasons.

B. Consulting with Sport Psychologists

Sport psychology consultants are the primary providers of psychological services to athletes. Sport psychology is an interdisciplinary field and, as such, has practitioners trained in psychology and the sport sciences. The Association for the Advancement of Applied Sport Psychology provides certification for professionals with specialized training and applied experience in sport psychology. The United States Olympic Committee maintains a registry of sport psychology consultants for distribution to the National Governing Bodies of various sports.

C. Performance Enhancement Interventions

Unlike many other areas of mental health practice, applied sport psychology has a primary focus on enhancing performance rather than treating pathology. Sport psychology consultants use a variety of intervention strategies to help athletes improve their performance. Typical psychological interventions for sport performance enhancement have a strong foundation in cognitive behavioral therapy. Common components of performance enhancement interventions are goal setting, imagery, relaxation training, cognitive self-regulation, and modeling. Treatment packages in which two or more of these techniques are combined are often used. Meta-analytic reviews of the literature have shown that psychological interventions can enhance sport performance. [*See* BEHAVIOR THERAPY; COGNITIVE THERAPY.]

VI. SUMMARY

As an area of human performance, sport participation is entwined with mental health. Across the life span, general psychological factors (e.g., personality, cognitive behavioral attributes) affect sport performance. Sport involvement also affects human development. For example, although psychopathology may occur infrequently in athletes, sport involvement may contribute to the development of certain disorders. Athletes may seek assistance for psychological or performance problems from sport psychologists. A number of techniques (e.g., imagery, goal setting) have been used by athletes to enhance their sport performances.

BIBLIOGRAPHY

Horn, T. S. (Ed.). (1992). *Advances in sport psychology.* Champaign, IL: Human Kinetics.

Meyers, A. W., Whelan, J. P., & Murphy, S. M. (1996). Cognitive behavioral strategies in athletic performance enhancement. In M. Hersen, R. M. Eisler, & P. M. Miller (Eds.), *Progress in behavior modification, Volume 30* (pp. 137–164). Pacific Grove, CA: Brooks/Cole.

Murphy, S. E. (1995). *Sport psychology interventions.* Champaign, IL: Human Kinetics.

Shields, D. L. L., & Bredemeier, B. J. L. (1995). *Character development and physical activity.* Champaign, IL: Human Kinetics.

Van Raalte, J. L., & Brewer, B. W. (Eds.). (1996). *Exploring sport and exercise psychology.* Washington, DC: American Psychological Association.

Weinberg, R. S., & Gould, D. (1995). *Foundations of sport and exercise psychology.* Champaign, IL: Human Kinetics.

Williams, J. M. (Ed.). (1993). *Applied sport psychology: Personal growth to peak performance* (2nd ed.). Mountain View, CA: Mayfield.

Standards for Psychotherapy

Robyn M. Dawes

Carnegie Mellon University

Hortatory Rules Those that mandate what should be done.

Meta-Analysis A statistical technique for combining studies with different outcome measures in order to test the generality of their results.

Minatory Rules Those that mandate what should not be done.

Psychotherapy The attempt to use psychology— through some form of conversation—to alleviate distressing or debilitating symptoms or hypothesized conditions leading to them.

Randomized Trials Experiments Investigations in which subjects are randomly assigned to an experimental versus a control group, as in evaluating vaccines.

Regression Effects The statistical fact that when two variables are not perfectly correlated, the standardized value of the one predicted will on the average be closer to its standardized mean than is the standardized value of the one from which the prediction is made.

STANDARDS OF PSYCHOTHERAPY practice refer to what psychotherapists actually do, not to their education or their credentials or experience—although these factors might be precursors for practicing in a way that meets standard of ethics and efficacy. To understand these standards, it is first necessary to know what has been established about the effectiveness of psychotherapy. Randomized control studies indicate the existence of particular "protocol" therapies that are effective for specific conditions, and otherwise all types of therapies appear to work equally well (the "Dodo Bird" finding), perhaps due to the quality of the "therapeutic alliance." It follows that standard dictate what should be done ("hortatory rules") when conducting a protocol therapy, but do not provide explicit rules about what to do in other types of therapies, which constitute the vast majority. Instead, the standards for these require that therapists not behave in ways inconsistent with what is known from scientific research, or at least what is believed to be known on the basis of empirical investigations interpreted in a rational manner. Thus, standards are minatory ones that prohibit "out of bounds" behavior. Such behavior occurs, often justified on the grounds that "we do not know," or that something might or could be true (e.g., recovered repressed memories), or may be shown in the future to be true to at least some extent or other. Standards of practice require, however, behavior consistent with what is currently known.

I. INTRODUCTION

Standards of practice refer to principles governing effective and ethical practice of psychology—whether in a private setting, clinic, or a nonprofit institution. The standards refer to the actual behavior of the individual alleging to apply psychological principles, or

589

experience, or even "intuition" for the purpose of helping other individuals or groups or organizations, most usually for monetary remuneration. The standards refer to what people do—or should do—not to their training, or knowledge, or "consideration" prior to acting. There are also standards of training (often assessed by educational record) and knowledge (often assessed by testing), but they are secondary to practice standards. First, meeting these standards in no way guarantees meeting standards of practice; second, the very existence of these secondary requirements is based on the belief that satisfying them will enhance the probability of high quality and ethical practice. These secondary standards (e.g., "credentialing") can not substitute for standards of practice.

In order to justify these standards of actual practice, it is first necessary to understand what we know about the practices of psychology. Here, I will concentrate on what we know about psychotherapy for mental health problems. Moreover, I will concentrate on knowledge that can be justified by current empirical evidence assessed in a rational manner. A particular practitioner, for example, may have some ideas about psychotherapy and mental health that under later close examination turn out to be valid, or at least useful. If, however, there is no systematic evidence at the time the practitioner applies these ideas, then they cannot be categorized and part of "what is known" in the area of mental health. As will be argued later, the fact that these ideas are not yet validated (and might never be) may not *prohibit* their use, although it may. The conditions of such potential prohibition will be considered later. What is important at this point is to understand that practice standards must be based on current knowledge, which can be equated with current belief justified on an empirical and rational basis—even though some later time such belief may turn out to be incomplete, flawed, or even downright wrong. People claiming to apply psychological knowledge, however much individual skill may be involved in the application, are bound by the nature of the knowledge at the time they apply it.

II. FINDINGS ON PSYCHOTHERAPY EFFECTIVENESS

A. Standard Randomized Trials

There are two basic findings in the area of psychotherapy, the subject of this article. Both of these findings are based on standard randomized trials investigations, where subjects are randomly assigned to experimental group versus comparison group and outcomes are assessed using as "blind" a method as possible. The comparison group can consist of a no-treatment control group, of a wait list control group, or of a commonly accepted treatment to which the experimental one is to be compared. The reason for random assignment is that the *expectation* of the effect of variables not manipulated by the assignment itself is the same for both groups (or for all groups in multiple assessments), and we have greater reason to believe that this expectation will approach reality the larger the sample. The mathematical result is that (critics might argue somewhat circularly) the expectation of deviations from these expectations becomes smaller the larger the sample, so that we can have greater and greater confidence with larger samples that "nuisance" and "confounding" variables do not affect the outcome of the investigation.

B. Quasi Experiments

The alternatives to standard randomized trials often involve matching or some type of quasi-experiment that can lead to plausible but not "highly justifiable" results. Consider, for example, a study using a matching strategy to attempt to assess the effect of having an abortion. We might have two groups of women experiencing unwanted pregnancy who are alike in many of the respects we think may be relevant to how an abortion will affect them (e.g., religion, social class, education, political orientation) and observe how the women in these two groups are different some years later—after most in one group have freely chosen to get an abortion and in the other group have freely chosen not to do so. The problem, however, is that there must be *some* variable or variables on which the women in these two groups are radically different, given that they made different choices. In fact, this variable or variables must be very powerful given that we have "controlled" for the important variables that we believe are relevant to the choice and its effects. This "unobserved variable problem" is an extremely important one that makes matching studies suspect.

In contrast, true quasi-experiments tend to be valid to the degree in which they approach true randomized ones. For example, consider the "interrupted time series" assessment of providing a psychoactive drug. Individual or individuals are assessed prior to the time the drug is administered on a regular basis and then assessed afterwards. But in the actual clinic setting, the introduction of the drug is often in response to some particular problem or problems that lead the clinician to believe that drug treatment is desirable or necessary. For example, a woman who is raped at a halfway house by a counselor may enter an inpatient treatment facility and—due to her condition—be immediately given Prozac. Now she is calmer. Is this calmness the effect of getting away from the halfway house? Due to the more relaxed inpatient environment itself (which people do not learn to hate immediately)? Due to the Prozac?

C. Regression Effects

A *regression* effect refers to the fact that if two variables are not perfectly correlated, the one we predict will on the average be closer to its standardized mean than the one from which we make the prediction. (In the linear prediction equation for standard scores, the predicted value of y is equal to r times actual value of $x,$ and conversely the predicted value of x is equal to r times the actual value of $y.$) Moreover, we have no way of assessing regression independent of other factors, because regression *includes* "real world" variables responsible for the lack of a perfect correlation. Now if instead the drug is introduced at a randomly determined time, we do not have to worry about such systematic regression effects or confounds. (But we may be justified in worrying about unsystematic ones.) What we are doing when we introduce the manipulation at a randomly determined time, however, is to approximate a truly randomized experiment.

D. Rationale for Randomization

The basic rationale for randomization is that we ideally want to know what *would* have happened to subjects had they not been assigned to the experimental treatment, a hypothetical counterfactual. Of course, because we cannot both assign and not assign at the same time, a direct assessment of this counterfactual is impossible. Randomly assigning people so that the expectation is that they are equivalent on variables that might affect outcome but in which we are not interested is the best justified substitute for actual knowledge of the hypothetical counterfactual. There are, of course, problems, particularly in the psychotherapy area. For example, it is impossible for the subject to

be "blind" to receiving therapy, and often it is impossible for those evaluating its effects to be blind as well. Experiments in this area contrast quite sharply with many experiments in medicine, where subjects are given placebos without being told if they are given the actual drug or placebos (or one of two drugs) and those evaluating their status are also ignorant of the assignment. Another problem is that randomized control experimentation can (should) be conducted only with subjects who agree to be randomly assigned. Perhaps such subjects—or even those who agree to be evaluated in a setting that does not use random assignment—are different from those who will receive or not receive the treatments evaluated. But that problem arises in any evaluation, not just random ones. (While there is the possibility of using "phony" therapy as a "placebo control," such a procedure raises severe ethical problems.) Thus, not because it is perfect, but because it yields the best knowledge available, we must turn to randomized trials to understand psychotherapy. As the eminent statistician Frederick Mosteller vigorously argued in 1981, while we should strive to appreciate the strengths and weaknesses of different approaches instead of being dogmatic about statistical purity, we must be aware that "the alternative to randomized controlled experiments is fooling around with peoples' lives."

E. Conclusion of Randomized Trials

Randomized trials of psychotherapy effectiveness yield two rather simple conclusions. The first is that there exists a set of problems for which carefully constructed ("protocol") therapies are effective—according to the criteria that at least one randomized trials study has "validated" these forms of psychotherapy. These therapies are listed in a 1995 report from the Task Force on Promotion and Dissemination of Psychological Procedures, division of clinical psychology, American Psychological Association. As the critic Garfield pointed out that same year, these results could not be used as a basis for justifying all—or even most—psychotherapy, or for setting standards. First, the number of conditions and the number of therapies is quite limited, hardly representative of the practice of "psychotherapy." In fact, the task force itself noted that these types of validated therapies are often not even taught in programs that are listed as good ones in various sources for training graduate students in clinical psychology. The constrained nature of the types of therapy provided overlooks, to quote Garfield (pg. 218): "the importance of client and therapist variability, the role of the common factors in psychotherapy, and the need to adapt therapeutic procedures for the problems of the individual client or patient." In a highly influential report of a Consumers' Union study he published that same year of 1995, Seligman refers to such studies as "efficacy" ones. He writes (pp. 965–966) "In spite of how expensive and time-consuming they are, hundreds of efficacy studies of both psychotherapy and drugs now exist—many of them well done. These studies show, among many other things, that cognitive therapy, interpersonal therapy, and medications all provide moderate relief from unipolar depressive disorder; that exposure and clomipramine both relieve the symptoms of obsessive-compulsive disorder moderately well, but that exposure has more lasting benefits; that cognitive therapy works very well in panic disorders; that systematic desensitization relieves specific phobias; that "applied tension" virtually cures blood and injury phobia, that transcendental meditation relieves anxiety; that aversion therapy produces only marginal improvement with sexual offenders; that disulfram (Antabuse) does not provide lasting relief from alcoholism; that flooding plus medication does better in the treatment of agoraphobia than either alone; and that cognitive therapy provides significant relief of bulimia, outperforming medications alone." [*See* COGNITIVE THERAPY; DEPRESSION; OBSESSIVE–COMPULSIVE DISORDERS; PANIC ATTACKS; PHOBIAS; PSYCHOPHARMACOLOGY; SUBSTANCE ABUSE.]

But then Seligman compares such studies to what he terms "effectiveness" studies, that is, those of "how patients fare under the actual conditions of treatment in the field" (p. 966)—and finally reaches a conclusion with which few of his critics agree: "The upshot of this is that random assignment, the prettiest of the methodological niceties in efficacy studies, may turn out to be worse than useless for the investigation of the actual treatment of mental illnesses in the field" (p. 974).

F. SUMMARIES AND META ANALYSES

There are, despite the claims of Seligman, a multitude of studies involving random assignment that attempt to assess what is actually done in the field—without limiting the practitioner to following a carefully crafted protocol. See, for example, the article of Laneman and Dawes—discussed in greater detail later—for a description of the diversity of the studies involving random assignment.

These diverse studies have been either summarized qualitatively, analyzed by "vote counts" based on their outcomes, or subjected to meta-analysis to reach general conclusions, because each in fact concerns one type of distress in one setting, often with a single or only a few therapists implementing the procedure under investigation. (Note that the same limitation applies to the "validated efficacy studies" as well.) Most summaries and meta-analyses consider reductions in symptoms that the people entering therapy find distressing or debilitating. Some measure of these symptoms' severity is then obtained after the random assignment to treatment versus control, and the degree to which the people in the randomly assigned experimental group differ from those in the control group on the symptoms is assessed, and averaged across studies. (Occasionally, difference scores are assessed as well.) The summaries and meta-analyses concentrates on symptoms, which can be justified because it is the symptoms that lead people to come to psychotherapists. The summaries and meta-analyses involves "combining applies and oranges," which can be justified by the fact that the types of nonprotocol therapies are extraordinary diverse (fruits). For example, simply providing information on a random basis to heart attack victims in an intensive care unit can be considered to be psychotherapy.

The "classic" meta-analysis of psychotherapy outcomes was published by Smith and Glass in 1977, and there has been little reason since that time to modify its conclusions. In general, psychotherapy is effective in reducing symptoms—to the point that the average severity of symptoms experienced by the people in the experimental group after completion of therapy is at the 25th percentile of the control group (i.e. less severe than the symptoms experienced by 75% of the people in the control group after the same period of time). That translates *roughly* (assuming normality and equal variance of the two groups) into the statement that if we chose a person at random from the experimental group and one at random from the control group, the one from the experimental group has a .67 probability of having less severe symptoms than the one from the control group. The other major conclusions were that the type of therapy did not seem to make a difference overall, the type of therapist did not seem to make a difference, and even the length of psychotherapy did not seem to make a difference. These conclusions are based both on evaluating the consistency of results and evaluating their average effect sizes. These conclusions have survived two main challenges.

The first is that while Smith and Glass included an overall evaluation of the "quality" of the study, they did not specifically look at whether the assignment was *really* random. To address that problem, Landman and Dawes published a paper in 1982 reporting an examination of every fifth study selected from the Smith and Glass list (which had increased to 435 studies by the time it was given to Landman and Dawes); these researchers concluded—with a very high degree of inter-rater reliability based on independent judgments—that fully a third of the studies did not involve true random assignment. A particularly egregious example involved recruiting students in a psychology department with posters urging group psychotherapy to address underachievement; the authors then compared the students who self-selected for this treatment with some students with similar GPAs "randomly" chosen from the registrar's list, who for all the experimenters knew have given up and left town. A more subtle example may be found in comparing people who persist in group psychotherapy with people in an *entire* randomly selected control group. Yes, the two groups were originally randomly constructed, but the problem is that we do not know which people in the control group *would* have stayed with the group psychotherapy *had* they been assigned the experimental group—thereby invalidating the control group as a comparison to the experimental one. While it is possible to maintain that it seems bizarre to include in an evaluation of group psychotherapy those who did not actually participate in the groups, if there is really an effect of a particular treatment and assignment is random, then it will exist—albeit in attenuated form—when the *entire* experimental group is compared to the control group. (A mixture of salt and fresh water is still salt water.) The way to deal with selective completion is to study enough subjects to have a study powerful enough to test the effects based on "subsets" of the people's assigned to experimental manipulation (e.g., those who completed). Landman and Dawes deleted the 35% of their studies that they believed not to

be truly random ones from their meta-analysis, and reached exactly the same conclusion Smith and Glass had earlier.

A second problem is the "file-drawer" one. Perhaps there are a number of studies showing that psychotherapy does not work, or even having results that indicated that it might be harmful, which simply are not published in standard journals—either because their results do not reach standard results of "statistical significance" or because flaws are noted as a result of their unpopular conclusions that might be (often unconsciously) overlooked had the conclusions been more popular. The problem has been addressed in two ways. First, the number of such studies would have to be so large that it appears to be unreasonable to hypothesize their existence in such file drawers. Second, it is possible to develop a distribution of the statistics of statistical significance actually presented in the literature and show that their values exceed (actually quite radically) those that would be predicted from randomly sampling above some criterion level that leads to publication of the results.

Another problem concerns the identity of the psychotherapists. Here, there is some ambiguity, because the studies attempting to "refute" the conclusion of Smith and Glass are generally conceived poorly, in that the psychotherapy subject rather than the psychotherapists themselves are sampled and used as the unit of measurement—especially for statistical test. But if we want to generalize about psychotherapists, then it is necessary to sample psychotherapists. For example, if a standard analysis of variance design is used where therapists are the "treatment" effect, then generalization to therapists—or to various types of therapists—requires a "random effects" analysis rather than a "fixed effects" one. One study did in fact follow this prescription, but then concluded on the basis of a post hoc analysis how more successful therapists were different from less successful ones after finding no evidence for a therapist effect overall!

The results of studies treating each psychotherapist as a separate sample observation generally conclude that beyond a very rudimentary level of training, credentials and experience do not correlate (positively) with efficacy, as summarized by Dawes in his 1994 book, Chapter 4. There is some slight evidence that people who are considered "empathetic" tend to achieve better outcomes (where this characteristic is assessed by colleagues—not in a circular manner by clients who themselves improve); also there is some evidence that when therapists agree to engage in different types of therapy, they do best applying ones in which they have the greatest belief. (It is possible to question the importance of the latter finding, given that outside of randomized control studies, therapists tend to provide only the type of psychotherapy that they believe to be the most helpful to their clients.)

III. WHAT FINDINGS IMPLY ABOUT STANDARDS

The overall conclusion supports the importance of "nonspecific" factors in therapeutic effectiveness. This general result about the quality of the "therapeutic alliance" as opposed to the specific type of therapy has been somewhat derogatorily referred to as the "Dodo bird finding" in that "all win and all must have prizes." (For the latest explication see the 1994 paper of Stubbs and Bozarth.) The problem is that findings hypothesizing the "quality of relationship" generally lack independent definitions of "quality" or evaluation of exactly *which* nonspecific factors are responsible for success or failure.

Now let us consider what these two findings—about specific protocol therapies and about nonspecific factors—imply about standards. In a 1996 report from the Hasting Center entitled "The Goals of Medicine," a panel of international group leaders sponsored by the Institute wrote: "On necessity, good caring demands technical excellence as a crucial ingredient" (p. s12). The protocol therapies clearly demand technically correct implementation as a crucial ingredient; failing to be technically correct completely violates standards of practice.

But what about the other types of therapies? It is very difficult to require technical excellence of "relationship" therapies—which, again, constitute the majority.

What then can be demanded as a standard? Therapists often point out that the research in psychology does not imply exactly what they should do. True, except for the protocol therapies. Conversely, however, research does imply what should *not be done*, what is "out of bounds." Thus, research in psychology and related areas implies minatory ("thou shalt not") as oppose to hortatory ("thou shalt") directives and standards for much of therapy. Of course, it is possible to rephrase minatory statements to become hortatory

(e.g., "thou shalt avoid doing this thing," such as committing murder), but most people recognize the distinction between two types of statements. For example, laws are based on violation of minatory rules, not hortatory ones, and even outside of the legal context we often make the distinction between the morality of simply not breaking rules versus that of doing something positive for our fellow humans. Moreover, people are often willing to engage in compensation between differing hortatory goals, but not "weight" various violations of minatory rules, unless explicitly decided in advance—such as killing in wartime or lying when a spy or carrying messages for Refusniks. We do not, however, talk about "trade-offs" between murder versus achieving some valuable goal (for example, saving the lives of 10 people by slaughtering a homeless man whose body can provide 10 organs to be transplanted in these people who would otherwise die).

Of course, when the boundaries of "thou shalt not" are sufficiently narrow, then minatory directives can become hortatory ones, but that is not common in psychological practice. We find, for example, a positive correlation between *peer* evaluations of therapist empathy and therapist effectiveness—as mentioned earlier—but we cannot demand a therapist be empathetic all the time: in particular, not that therapists be empathetic "types" of people, which are what their peers are evaluating.

IV. SPECIFYING UNACCEPTABLE BEHAVIOR

Is there really the possibility of specifying such "out of bounds" behavior? Does it occur? Or does "anything go?" There is a possibility, it does occur, and anything does not go. Such behavior clearly violates standards of psychotherapy—whether the standards are based on our views of ethics or of effectiveness. For example, psychology research shows memory to be "reconstructive" and hence prone to errors that "make sense" of what happened, considered either by itself or in broader contexts such as one's "life story." Further, there has never been any research evidence for the concept of "repression." That absence does not mean it is impossible for someone to "recover a repressed memory," or that such reconstructed memories are necessarily historically inaccurate. What it does mean is that as *professionals* practicing their trade—which means applying psychological knowledge as we now know it—therapists should not be involved in attempting to do something that current research evidence indicates can easily create illusion, and needless suffering.

Nevertheless some are. For example, in a survey of licensed U.S. doctoral-level psychologists randomly sampled from the *National Register of Health Service Providers in Psychology* by Poole, Lindsay, Memon, and Bull in 1995, 70% indicated that they used various techniques (e.g., hypnosis, interpretation of dreams) to "help" clients recover memories of child sexual abuse; moreover, combining the sample from the register with a British sample from the *Register of Chartered Clinical Psychologist*, the authors conclude: "Across samples, 25% of the respondents reported a constellation of beliefs and practices suggestive of focus on memory recovery, and these psychologists reported relatively high rates of memory recovery in their clients" (pg. 426). The study asked about the use of eight techniques that cognitive psychologists have found to involve bias and create errors. Hypnosis, age regression, dream interpretation, guided imagery related to abuse situations, instructions to give free reign to the imagination, use of family photographs as memory cues, instructions for remembering/journaling, and interpreting physical symptoms. Remarkably, with the exception of the last three techniques, the proportion of survey respondents who reported using them was overshadowed by similar or higher proportions of respondents who "disapproved" of using them.

In addition, failure to disapprove of interpreting physical symptoms as evidence of unusual events can be traced to a failure to understand the base rate problem in interpreting diagnostic signs—a failure that has been decried ever since Meehl and Rosen first discussed it in detail in 1955, but which is remarkably robust—as experimental studies in the area of behavioral decision making indicate that people equate inverse probabilities without equating simple ones, even in the face of evidence that these simple probabilities are quite discrepant. It takes one step to move from the definition of a conditional probability to the ratio rule, which states that $P(a$ given $b)/P(b$ given $a)$ $= P(a)/P(b)$. For example, the probability of being a hard drug user given one smokes pot divided by the probability of smoking pot given one is a hard drug user is exactly equal to the simple probability of being a hard drug user divided by the probability of smoking pot. Exactly. To maintain that because (it is believed that) a very low base rate event (e.g., being brought up in a satanic cult, an event that may have probability zero) can imply high base rate distress (e.g., poor self-image and an eating disorder) it therefore follows that the distress implies the event is just flat-out irrational. Doing so violates the standard of practice proposed, which is that it be based on empirical knowledge interpreted in a rational manner.

Unfortunately, however, the debate about recovered repressed memories has degenerated into claims and counter claims about whether they *can* exist, or the—totally unknown—frequency with which they are accurate or invented, rather than around the question of whether attempting to recover them is justified by what is known. In fact it is not; the real question is whether doing so is "out of bounds" behavior, and given we do know a lot about the reconstructive nature of memory, but very little about whether memory of trauma differs from other memories—and if so in exactly what way—such recovery must be categorized as out of bounds, that is, practice that violates standards.

V. PURPOSE OF STANDARDS

The purpose of standards of psychological practice is to aid the client with knowledge-based skills; ignoring knowledge is no more appropriate than having sexual contact with a client. Standards must be extended in a minatory way to prohibit application of ignorance, just as there are minatory standards about the behavior of the therapist that may both harm the client and degrade the profession (e.g., sexual contact). Moreover, a minatory standard can be enforced, and in the current author's experience on the American Psychological Association Ethics Committee, such standards were indeed the ones enforced. People were kicked out of the American Psychological Association or lost their license to practice (in one order or another) primarily on the basis of sexual contact with the clients, on the basis of having been found guilty of a felony involved in their practice (e.g., cheating on insurance), or on the basis of practicing beyond their area of competence.

VI. CHANGING DEFINITION OF COMPETENCE

The last reason for kicking people out of the association brings up a specific distinction between the standards proposed in the current chapter versus those proposed by the American Psychological Association. (See its Ethics Code published in 1992.) The latter *defines* "competence" in terms of education, training, or experience. Specifically, principle 1.04 (a) reads that: "psychologists provide services, teach, and conduct research only within the boundary of their competence, *based on their education, training, supervised experience, or appropriate professional experience*" (italics added). The problem with this definition of competence is that it does not indicate that training must be in something for which there is some scientific knowledge. For example, training in the alleviation of posttraumatic stress disorder (PTSD) could involve people whose trauma was supposedly that of being kidnapped by aliens. In fact, (see Dawes, 1994, Chapter 5) there is a set of psychotherapists who have exactly this specialty, and one of them mentions the others in the back of her book, others who are licensed and can receive third-party payment for treatment of this type of PTSD. [*See* Posttraumatic Stress.]

The other problem with this definition is that it allows a very specific characterization of what is relevant "training," a characterization that could even *exclude* generalizations based on scientific studies. For example, Courtois criticized in 1995 those who criticize recovered repressed memory psychotherapists, on the grounds that these critics themselves have not been involved with recovering repressed memory. She writes: "Unfortunately, a number of memory researchers are erring in the same way that they allege therapists to be erring; they are practicing outside of their areas of competence and/or applying findings from memory analogues without regard to the ecological validity and making misrepresentations, overgeneralizations, and unsubstantiated claims regarding therapeutic practice" (p. 297). The criticized claims are, of course generalizations that are based on what is known about *memory in general,* and the claim that a specific type of memory is inadequately or incorrectly characterized by such generalizations requires assuming a "burden of proof." Exceptions to rules require evidence that they are indeed exceptions. No evidence is presented. Instead, a statement is made that people who based generalizations on well-established principles derived from empirical research are themselves behaving unethically because they have not been immersed in the context in which these exceptions are *claimed* to occur. It is a circular argument that can equally well be made against those of us who believe

that PTSD researchers who help people recover the memory of being kidnapped by aliens should not be reimbursed from government or insurance funds. Since we ourselves would not even think of conducting such therapy, how can we evaluate it?

The Ethics Code of the American Psychological Association also emphasizes "consideration of" what is known, but it does not mandate applying it. More specifically, for the type of relationship therapy, it does not mandate that psychotherapists should definitely not do what careful consideration indicates they should not. Certainly, training and consideration are precursors to practicing well and ethically, but as pointed out earlier, they cannot be substitutes. The reason that they cannot be substitutes is that the training must be training in that which works, which is then applied. "Consideration" must be consideration of valid knowledge, which is then applied. Again, I'm not claiming that knowledge will not change in the future, or that everything psychologists currently believe to be true is necessarily true. The point is that good practice must be based on the best available knowledge and evidence—not on what *might* be, *could* be, or what *may* turn out to be true after years of subsequent investigation. Moreover, what is believed to be true *does* provide bounds—minatory standards.

The philosophy espoused in this standards of practice chapter is close to that of the National Association for Consumer Protection in Mental Health Practices. (See its goals as enunciated in 1996 by its President Christopher Barden.) The major difference, if there is one, involves how much emphasis is placed on the clients' explicit recognition that when the type of therapy is a "relationship" one, there is really no hard evidence that the *particular* type offered works better than any other. Relationship therapies do work overall, and it is very tricky to obtain "informed consent" about a whole huge category of therapy, while at the same time indicating that particular members of it may not have empirical justification. The additional problem is that by emphasizing that lack for particular members, whatever placebo effects can account for the efficacy of the entire class may be diminished. Avoiding such emphasis in obtaining informed consent is clearly self-serving for the psychotherapist. The question is whether it also serves the client. Rather than just assuming that it does, we could put this question to an empirical test—through randomized trials.

VII. CONCLUSION

The final point of this article is part minatory, part hortatory. The purpose of psychological practice is to provide *incremental validity,* that is, to help in ways that the clients could not help themselves (at least to increase the probability of such help). The fact, for example, that a flashbulb memory may be corroborated by others does not imply that the practitioner should encourage or interpret such memory, because corroboration by others involves historical accuracy, and the psychologist provides no incremental validity about how such corroboration may be obtained, or what sort of corroboration may validate or invalidate the conclusion that the memory is historically accurate. Incremental validity, however, is both desirable and required, especially in a society that demands "truth in advertising."

A note at the end. This article has been devoted to the questions of standards of practice in psychotherapy. It has not dealt with forensic psychology and the subsequent standards of expert testimony in courts and other legal settings. Everything argued here applies to such settings. Because testimony in courts can result in loss of freedom, it is urgent that psychotherapists who do testify meet the standards enunciated in this article.

BIBLIOGRAPHY

American Psychological Association. (1992). Ethical principles of psychologist and code of conduct. *American Psychologist, 47,* 1597–1611.

Barden, R. C. (1996). The National Associations for Consumer Protection in Mental Health Practices: Office of the President. Plymouth, MN: Copies available from R. Christopher Barden, PhD., J.D. 4025 Quaker Lane North, Plymouth, MN 55441.

Courtois, C. A. (1995). Scientist-practitioners and the delayed memory controversy: Scientific standards and the need for collaboration. *The Consulting Psychologist, 23,* 294–299.

Dawes, R. M. (1994). *House of cards: Psychology and psychotherapy built on myth.* New York: The Free Press.

Garfield, S. A. (1996). Some problems associated with "validated" forms of psychotherapy. *Clinical Psychology: Science and Practice, 3,* 218–229.

The Hasting Center. (1996). The goals of medicine: setting new priority. Briarcliff Manor, NY: Publication Department, The Hasting Center.

Landman, J. T., & Dawes, R. M. (1982). Psychotherapy outcome: Smith and Glass' conclusions stand up under scrutiny. *American Psychologist, 37,* 504–516.

Meehl, P. E., Rosen, A. (1955). Antecedent probability and the efficiency of psychometric signs, patterns, or cutting score. *Psychological Bulletin, 52,* 194–216.

Mosteller, F. (1981). Innovation and evaluation. *Science, 211,* 881–886.

Poole, D. A., Lindsay, D. S., Memon, A., & Bull, R. (1995). Psychotherapy and the recovery of memories of childhood sexual abuse, U.S. and British practitioners' opinions, practices, and experiences. *Journal of Consulting and Clinical Psychology, 63,* 426–437.

Seligman, M. E. P. (1995). The effectiveness of psychotherapy: The consumer reports study. *American Psychologist, 50,* 965–974.

Smith, M. L., & Glass, G. V. (1977). Meta-analysis of psychotherapy outcome studies. *American Psychologist, 32,* 752–760.

Stubbs, J. T., & Bozarth, J. D. (1994). The Dodo bird revisited: a qualitative study of psychotherapy efficacy research. *Applied and Preventative Psychology, 3,* 109–120.

Task Force on Promotion and Dissemination of Psychological Procedures. Division of Clinical Psychology, American Psychological Association (1995). Training in and dissemination of empirically-validated psychological treatments. Report and recommendations. *The Clinical Psychologist, 48,* 3–23.

Stress

Angela Liegey Dougall and Andrew Baum

University of Pittsburgh

Alarm Reaction The first stage of the General Adaptation Syndrome characterized by a mobilization of resources, especially corticosteroid release.

Diseases of Adaptation Diseases that appear to be determined, in part, by a failure to adapt to stress.

Exhaustion The third stage of the General Adaptation Syndrome characterized by a depletion of resources necessary for resistance, failure to adapt, and disease.

Fight or Flight Response Response of generalized activation during stress that prepares an organism to either conquer the threat or flee.

General Adaptation Syndrome A model of stress in which stress follows a course of three stages: Alarm Reaction, Resistance, and Exhaustion.

Posttraumatic Stress Disorder An extreme reaction to severe trauma that is characterized by continual reliving of the trauma. Hallmark symptoms include recurring intrusive thoughts and nightmares about the trauma, emotional blunting, exaggerated startle response, and heightened responding to reminiscent stimuli.

Primary Appraisal The appraisal of a situation as either irrelevant, benign/positive, or stressful.

Resistance The second stage of the General Adaptation Syndrome characterized by responses aimed at

dealing with the stressor and ultimately producing adaptation.

Secondary Appraisal Evaluation of a stressful situation and the resources available to the individual to determine what can be done to handle the situation.

STRESS is a psychobiological process that is characterized by alterations in psychological, behavioral, and physiological response systems that are directed toward adaptation. It is initiated by stressors, events, or thoughts that threaten, harm, or challenge the organism or that exceed available coping resources. While stress can facilitate adaptation to a range of situations, prolonged or extreme episodes of stress may have negative effects on physical and mental health. Factors affecting appraisal of stressors or coping can moderate these negative effects and promote successful adaptation and are the focus of many treatment strategies aimed at preventing or alleviating symptoms caused by stress.

I. THE STRESS CONCEPT

While almost everyone knows what stress is and that it affects health, there is no universally accepted definition of stress in the literature. Early scientists focused their research on specific physiological responses, resulting in several different theories of stress. Increasingly, stress has been viewed as a process that links environmental threats and change to people's responses and adaptation to them. Responses and coping strategies used to deal with each situation vary, depending

Encyclopedia of Mental Health
Volume 3

599

on the type of stressor presented and on characteristics of each individual. The bases of this process are both biological and behavioral, acting to modify the organism to allow optimal responses. Historically, physiological and psychological models of stress developed independently.

A. Biological Models of Stress

One of the first scientists to use the term *stress* in describing the behavior of living organisms was Hans Selye. He borrowed the term from the field of physics where it referred to a driving force acting against a resistance. Based on controlled laboratory studies with animals, Selye defined stress as a stereotypic response syndrome that was nonspecifically induced. All stressors or noxious stimuli caused a universal triad of physiological consequences. Regardless of the stressor, the reaction to it was always the same and followed the same three stages of the *General Adaptation Syndrome* (GAS). In study after study involving stressors as diverse as injection of hormonal extracts and chronic skin irritation or irradiation, animals exhibited enlargement of the adrenal glands, atrophy or shrinkage of structures in the lymphatic system (i.e., thymus, spleen, and lymph nodes), and ulceration and bleeding in the gastrointestinal system.

The hypertrophy of the adrenals suggested increased activity in the Hypothalamic-Pituitary-Adrenal Cortical (HPA) Axis resulting in elevation of corticosteroid levels. Selye based the GAS on this system and described three specific stages. The first stage was called *Alarm Reaction* and was characterized by dramatic increases in corticosteroid release. It occurred immediately and constituted mobilization of resources. Once this mobilization was complete, response proceeded to a second stage, *Resistance*. This stage was characterized by restoration of resources (e.g., replenishing corticosteroids in the adrenal cortex) and yielded a different pattern of responses. Typically, adaptation was achieved during this resistance phase. In cases of continued or extreme exposure, adaptation was not possible and a stage of *Exhaustion* was reached in which resources necessary for resistance were no longer available. The manifestations of exhaustion resembled those seen in alarm but the end result was more likely death or chronic debilitating disease.

Selye proposed that disease states occurred when adaptation was not successful, the result of overactivation or underactivation of cortical response systems. He referred to diseases such as hypertension, arthritis, cancer, and psychiatric morbidity as *Diseases of Adaptation*. He believed that identification of the mechanisms through which nonspecific activation of the HPA occurred would allow development of more comprehensive treatment strategies targeted at both the specific and nonspecific aspects of disease.

Selye's depiction of stress was a departure from Cannon's earlier work on emotional stress and the *fight or flight* response. Cannon viewed stress as the result of disturbances in homeostasis or physiological equilibrium, suggesting that every physiological variable had a homeostatic range and that when balance was disturbed or threatened the organism had to respond to restore homeostasis. He believed that stressors were usually acute in duration and elicited negative emotions such as fear and anger. These emotions were associated with activation of the sympathetic nervous system (SNS) and release of sympathetic adrenal hormones (i.e., epinephrine, norepinephrine). Release of these catecholamines facilitated responses directed at remedying disturbances in homeostasis. The adaptive function of the fight or flight response was generalized activation that prepared the individual to deal with the threat by either conquering it or fleeing. In addition to immediate behavioral and physiological reactions, anticipatory reactions could also be triggered to prepare the individual for future challenges and dangers.

These views were the dominant views of stress for the first two-thirds of this century, but were not without critics. Opposing Selye's notion of nonspecific stress and his narrow focus on the HPA, Mason argued that reactions to different stressors vary and that stress is manifest in many biological systems. His work began at around the same time as work on psychological stress and reflected greater interest in psychological and central nervous system integration of stress and physiological responses to danger. Through careful studies of a number of hormones, including epinephrine, norepinephrine, corticosteroids, estrogen, insulin, glucose, and growth hormone, he concluded that stress is a unified catabolic response driven by both sympathetic and HPA activation. Its function, he argued, was to maintain high levels of circulating glucose to sustain prolonged resistance. Mason also proposed that the generalized response pattern Selye observed was actually a general response characteristic of emotional distress, that psychological, behavioral, and some physiological responses were specific to the stressor, and that neuroendocrine response patterns unfolded over time. [*See* PSYCHONEUROIMMUNOLOGY.]

These observations led Mason to conclude that the stress response was specific to the stimulus and the individual instead of the nonspecific GAS proposed by Selye. Furthermore, Mason believed that the nonspecific emotional reactions (e.g., fear, pain, discomfort) elicited by the situation mediated the responses that were seen. He viewed stress as a pathogen: It had the potential to promote disease, but did or did not do so depending on individual and situational factors. This conceptualization allowed for individual variation but made specific predictions more difficult.

B. Psychological Stress

Parallel to these developments in the physiology of stress were important but separate theories in psychology. Richard Lazarus proposed that it was not the event alone that induced a stress response but rather the individual's appraisal of the event as threatening or harmful. This interaction between person and environment emphasized individual differences in stress and suggested a complex process that could be altered at many points.

Lazarus argued that people engage in two types of appraisal processes that determine their perceptions of threat and their ability to cope or handle the situation. Primary appraisal was the process by which individuals determined whether they were facing a stressful situation (i.e., either a threat, a challenge, or actual harm or loss) or an irrelevant or benign/positive situation that required no further response. Appraisals of stress elicited emotional responses, but unlike more biological models, Lazarus suggested that it was not the emotions but rather the appraisal that determined subsequent physiological and behavioral responses. Following initial appraisal, secondary appraisals described how people determine what available coping strategies could be used to deal with the situation and whether to attack the problem or accommodate it. Be-

cause stress was viewed as a dynamic process, individuals were constantly engaged in reappraisal of the situation as new information was obtained. Therefore, cognitive appraisal and coping mediated the process and determined stress-related outcomes.

Like Mason, Lazarus contends that individual differences play a prominent role in susceptibility to stress and its deleterious effects. He believed that stress was most likely to occur when the individual lacked certain social and/or physical resources that would normally be protective. He referred to this state as vulnerability. Most researchers now use some version of the basic model of stress proposed by Lazarus when they refer to stress and its consequences. [*See* PROTECTIVE FACTORS IN DEVELOPMENT OF PSYCHOPATHOLOGY.]

A number of derivations and developments in this general model of stress have been made, including revision and augmentation by Lazarus and Folkman in 1984. Other versions of this approach have also been proposed. Some have sought to integrate psychological and biological models, such as the depiction of stress by Baum in 1990. This model draws heavily from Lazarus' conceptualization of stress and from some of the other theories already discussed. Stress is defined as a negative emotional state that is characterized by physiological and behavioral changes. It is part of an adaptive process aimed at either altering a stressful situation or accommodating its effects. It can be described by the interactions among the duration of the event itself, the duration of the perceived threat, and the duration of the psychological, physiological, or behavioral responses. When stressors evoke stressful experiences, the whole body responds in ways consistent with a catabolic fight or flight reaction. The inappropriateness of these emergency responses to more modern stressors appears to be one source of the negative effects of stress on health. This highlights the variability in exposure to stress and the many mental and physical variables that can alter the effects of stress on health at any stage of the process.

This model is summarized in Figure 1. The box on the left represents characteristics of the situation and

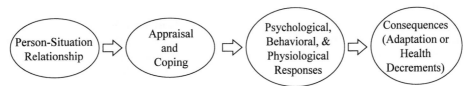

Figure 1 Conceptual model of the stress process.

the individual that provide context and interact to determine whether a situation is appraised as stressful and what coping strategies will be used to deal with the situation. These responses determine whether stress is experienced, how we respond, and what consequences are seen. Immediate physiological, psychological, and behavioral responses are adaptive, preparing the individual to act (e.g., increases in emotional and physiological arousal, increased alertness, diversion of blood flow from digestive processes to systems involved in movement). However, if there is extreme or prolonged activation of the response pathways, adaptation may be hindered and consequences for physical and mental health may be seen.

C. Response Patterns

A large body of research has focused on characterizing the typical alterations seen in cognitive, behavioral, and physiological response systems during stress. Examples of physiological changes include increases in resting heart rate and blood pressure as well as increases in the release of neuroendocrine factors such as epinephrine, norepinephrine, adrenocorticotropic hormone (ACTH), glucocorticoids, and prolactin. Additionally, decreases in immune cell numbers and function are often present. Emotional changes are consistent with negative emotions, typified by increases in negative affect such as depression, anxiety, anger, and fear, and general increases in symptom reporting. Unwanted and uncontrollable thoughts and memories about the event are also likely to occur. Attention deficits are manifested in behavioral alterations in task performance as people narrow their attention and focus more exclusively on the sources of stress. Individuals given a task to perform either during exposure to stress or after it tend to perform more poorly. Even though adaptation to acute stress is rapid, aftereffects, occurring after the stressor has passed, appear to be substantial. Deterioration of sleep quality and quantity, increases in aggressive behaviors, and modification of many appetitive behaviors (e.g., eating, drinking, and smoking) have also been observed.

As suggested by the wide variety of responses listed, stress is a multifaceted process that draws on the entire organism rather than on a single system. Together these responses help the individual adapt either by altering the situation or by accommodating its effects. However, extreme or prolonged activation of these response systems can lead to health problems rather than adaptation.

II. STRESS, MENTAL HEALTH, AND DISEASE

It is important to note that each stage of stress affects the individual (see Fig. 1). As a result each stage can influence the maintenance of health and progression of disease. One way to view health is as an optimal balance of psychological and biological activity. If optimal immune activity is maintained, defense against infectious agents will be maximized. If this system or any other system that affects it is disturbed, the resulting decrease in activity may permit illness processes to develop. Adaptation can be prevented by continued presence of the stressful situation, inaccurate stress appraisals, choice of inappropriate coping strategies, and/or extreme activation of response systems. Stress can render organisms more prone to physical and mental disease states. However, stress acts not only on the onset of disease but can also act to promote disease progression, interfere with disease treatment, or trigger critical events. In addition, exposure to stress following extremely threatening stressors can result in profound dysfunction, illustrated by Posttraumatic Stress Disorder (PTSD). [See POSTTRAUMATIC STRESS.]

A. Stress and Health

The relationship between stress and health is complex. An exhaustive summary of these links is beyond the scope of this article. Instead, we provide a brief overview of some of the ways stress may affect health. In general, stress can affect health in three basic ways, as direct physiological effects (e.g., wear and tear on blood vessels, immunosuppression), as behavioral changes that convey physiological changes (e.g., smoking, drug use), or as behavioral changes that affect one's treatment once he or she is ill (e.g., adherence with prescriptions, seeking medical help). These levels of influence, in turn, affect a broad scope of disease processes.

I. Onset of Disease

Although often difficult to measure, stress appears to affect pathophysiological processes that contribute to disease. One of the most salient mechanisms through which stress may act is through prolonged continuation of normal stress responses. For instance, chronic feelings of anxiety, depression, or fear may develop into clinically relevant psychiatric diagnoses that can interfere with normal functioning. Prolonged self-medication or continued use of licit or illicit substances may lead to addiction, and extreme alterations in eating patterns may develop into eating disorders. Sustained physiological arousal may also promote disease states. For instance, continued stress-related elevations in blood pressure appear to result in permanent elevations and may contribute to hypertension. Sustained or repeated increases in stress hormones appear to contribute to atherosclerosis, and chronic immunosuppression may interfere with our ability to ward off foreign pathogens. Chronic immune system suppression also appears to heighten susceptibility to viral and infectious diseases such as colds and flu as well as to cancer and the Human Immunodeficiency Virus (HIV) disease. With the exception of cardiovascular disease, where several mechanisms have been mapped and the importance of stress in the slow degeneration of the cardiovascular system is clear, these relationships are suggestive and need more attention. Recent studies of controlled viral challenge or wound healing offer new support for this clinically relevant stress impact.

Finally, behavioral and cognitive deficits seen during stress may increase one's risks for damaging or fatal accidents. Decrements in performance could result in injury or death if they affect activities such as driving a car or operating heavy machinery, situations in which concentration and attention to detail are important.

2. Progression and Treatment of Disease

Once a disease state is established, stress may act to promote this state or to interfere with its treatment. Some of the mechanisms by which disease course is affected are similar to those noted above. New feelings of depression or anxiety often associated with stress may set back treatment for pre-existing disorders and can make disease events such as a heart attack more likely. Individuals in treatment for substance abuse or who seek to quit smoking may relapse and return to abuse of one or more drugs, and recurrence of cancer may also be linked to stress. Buildup of vascular plaque and increases in blood pressure in an individual with cardiovascular disease may heighten the likelihood that acute events or triggers cause myocardial ischemia and myocardial infarction. Immunosuppression in individuals with latent viruses in their bodies may experience reactivation and disease symptoms. Additionally, stress may affect progression of HIV disease and cancer metastasis.

Stress can also affect treatment of a disease. Successful treatment, for example, requires that patients comply with instructions, prescriptions, and suggestions offered by their physicians and medical team. Stress may reduce this adherence. Patients may forget to take their medications on time or they may feel that they do not have enough time to keep treatment appointments. In addition, certain coping behaviors such as substance use, smoking, and eating may interfere with treatment regimens. Interventions to reduce stress, either by providing support or enhancing coping and problem-solving capabilities, can enhance quality of life as well as slow progression of life-threatening diseases.

B. Posttraumatic Stress Disorder

One should expect that most people who experience extreme stress should be affected acutely but that most will recover readily. However, following cataclysmic events such as war, rape, disasters, or motor vehicle accidents, a significant percentage of victims continue to experience stress long after the event has passed. Posttraumatic stress disorder is an extreme form of chronic stress responding and can result in severe psychophysiological disability. It is characterized by a chronic reliving of the trauma. Instead of habituating to the stressor individuals become sensitized, reacting strongly to any reminiscent stimuli. This disorder may persist indefinitely and is characterized, in part, by exaggerated and unusually prolonged symptoms of stress.

PTSD is characterized by several essential hallmark symptoms, including but not limited to recurrent dreams and intrusive thoughts about the event, sleep disturbances, withdrawal, numbing, anxiety, dissociation, aggressiveness, hyperarousal, and an exaggerated startle response. It is also characterized by specific physiological response profiles including heightened reactivity to reminiscent stimuli. When victims hear or see reminders of an event, they exhibit cardiovascular, respiratory, and galvanic skin reactivity and distress. Alterations in the regulation of noradrenergic systems and the HPA axis are also seen. Individuals with PTSD exhibit elevated levels of epinephrine, norepinephrine, and their metabolites. Chronic adrenergic activation is associated with downregulation of noradrenergic receptors, possibly sustaining increases in output.

In contrast to elevated catecholamine release, resting levels of glucocorticoids can be decreased. This appears to be due to a dysregulation in the HPA axis. Normally the hypothalamus releases corticotropin releasing factor (CRF), which acts on the pituitary to release ACTH among other hormones. ACTH then travels to the adrenal cortex where it stimulates release of corticosteroids such as cortisol in humans. However, in individuals with PTSD, the pituitary exhibits a blunted ACTH response to CRF challenge. Therefore, less cortisol is excreted. Additionally, there is an upregulation of glucocorticoid receptors on lymphocytes possibly due to low circulating levels of cortisol.

These psychobiological alterations can affect physical and mental functioning in the same ways mentioned above (see Stress and Health). Several vulnerability factors have been proposed that may make an individual more susceptible to symptoms of PTSD. Increased risk is associated with a genetic predisposition to heightened autonomic arousal as well as an interaction between extent of exposure and familial history of psychopathology. Additionally, the same factors that are important in determining normal stress responses (e.g., social support and perceived control), may also influence the development of PTSD.

III. MODERATORS OF STRESS

Successful adaptation and well-being can be affected by several psychosocial factors that influence appraisal and use of coping strategies. These factors can be related to the event or to the individual. Four of the most widely studied factors are predictability, controllability, expectations about the future, and social support.

A. Predictability

Predictability of an event refers to the extent to which an individual can anticipate the nature of the event and its consequences, the extent to which one knows what is going to happen. When individuals believe that they can predict what will happen, they typically experience less stress when stressors occur. Two hypotheses have been proposed to explain why predictability is beneficial. The first centers on the idea that advance warning allows one to better prepare. Predictability defines a time period during which individuals can initiate coping behaviors to fortify against danger or threat. The second hypothesis is that when an event is signaled, a period of safety or absence of the event is also signaled. This safety period may allow the individual to rest and relax as well as prepare.

B. Control

Better health and less stress are also associated with perception of control, whether it refers to the situation or to interpersonal factors such as self-efficacy. The extent to which a situation or event can be altered or controlled can affect one's appraisal of stress and the coping strategies one uses (e.g., increased use of problem-solving coping). However, perceptions of control may be more important than actual control. In general, it is beneficial if an individual believes something can be done either to alter the situation or to help accommodate its effects.

Feelings of control that generalize across situations or represent broad expectations about self-efficacy may be more beneficial in situations that are new or ambiguous, possibly allowing the person to appraise the situation as more of a challenge than as a threat. These expectations can also affect coping. In contrast, perceptions of control that are specific to the situation may be more beneficial in situations that are less ambiguous. Although perceptions of control for the most part are thought to alleviate stress, there are instances when controllability may heighten stress, as when it conflicts with particular coping styles or with other beliefs such as expectations and predictability.

C. Expectations

Similarly to perceptions of predictability and control, expectations about what the future holds also influence appraisal and coping. Those individuals who believe that every situation results in something good are often referred to as optimists and typically they experience less stress and better health outcomes than individuals who expect negative outcomes.

Good versus bad expectations also predict use of coping. Optimists use active coping (e.g., problem-focused coping and seeking social support), whereas pessimists use more palliative coping (e.g., denial and avoidance). These divergent coping strategies can explain the relationship between optimism and the experience of stress. Recent research has identified availability of social support as another important mediator of optimism's effects on the experience of stress, accounting for coping strategies used as well as symptom distress and physiological arousal.

D. Social Support

One's social context has broad effects on how an individual perceives an event and what that individual decides to do. Sources of support within an individual's environment, and the benefits they convey (e.g., information, tangible help, emotional support) are key factors in this relationship and can influence the stress process at any stage. High levels of social resources may help to alleviate uncertainty and worry by allowing the individual to gather more information or share their concerns with others. They may influence coping strategies by offering reassurance, confirming perceptions and choice of action, and supplying additional information. Additionally, they may increase adherence to treatment regimens. However, these same characteristics may heighten stress if the wrong information is provided or if sources of support consistently disapprove or disagree with an individual's appraisals and plans of action.

It is not clear whether social support has direct effects on health and well-being or is only beneficial under times of stress. However, for the most part, high levels of social support are beneficial. One aim of many treatment strategies is to bolster social support either by enhancing existing social support networks or by creating new ones. Enhancement of social support has been shown to alleviate stress and help combat negative health effects. [*See* SOCIAL SUPPORT.]

IV. COPING WITH STRESS

There are two primary forms of coping, active coping and palliative or emotion-focused coping. Active coping strategies, as the name suggests, are directed at altering the situation to reduce or eliminate threat or danger. Both problem-solving behavior and use of social support networks give individuals avenues for doing something about their situation, whether it is gathering information or physically removing the stressor. Generally thought of as problem-focused coping, this response can be very effective when sources of stress are modifiable or situational stressors can be eliminated.

Palliative coping strategies entail a much larger group of responses and are directed at regulating one's emotional experience of stress. As noted earlier, stress is usually an aversive experience, and strategies used to decrease negative affect include the use of denial, avoidance, minimization, positive reinterpretation, and distancing. Assuming responsibility or blame appears to be a counterintuitive coping strategy used to increase perceived control. Other emotion-focused strategies may be aimed at altering one's perceptions of an event or situation. Individuals use cognitive reappraisal to change their assessment of the situation from stressful to benign/positive or irrelevant.

While some researchers believe that problem-focused coping styles are better than palliative ones, it is not the type of coping strategy used *per se* but whether or not the coping strategy fits the situation at hand. For instance if a busy executive notices recurrent chest pains, a direct response (i.e., go to the hospital, call the doctor) is probably more adaptive than a palliative coping style (i.e., denying the occurrence of the pain, having a drink to calm down). The latter strategy may result in a cardiac event and/or death because the individual did not seek treatment and may have exacerbated an underlying condition by self-medicating. Likewise, in some situations the use of denial or avoidance may be more adaptive than using resources to try to alter a situation that cannot be changed. Patients with terminal illness may experience less stress and better quality of life if they accept or deny that they are going to die than if they continued to battle an uncontrollable disease. Additionally, a mixture of the two types of coping strategies may be appropriate. Researchers report that use of denial and avoidance soon after an event may in fact lessen the degree of stress experienced in the short term. This reduction in arousal may allow more problem-focused coping to emerge and be more effective.

One focus of coping research has been to try to identify which individuals use particular coping strategies. Numerous coping styles and traits have been proposed, such as repression-sensitization, coping-avoiding, monitoring-blunting, and anger-in and anger-out. While taxonomies such as these may help to systemize research on the relationship between coping and adaptation, these classification schemes do not entirely predict use of coping strategies in specific situations. However, most are unidimensional in nature and do not adequately reflect the multidimensional process of coping or the assumption that successful adaptation requires matching coping styles to the situation. [*See* COPING WITH STRESS.]

V. STRESS MANAGEMENT

The impact of stress on health and disease can be managed in a variety of ways and at every stage of the stress process (see Fig. 1). Previously, we suggested that every stage of the stress process has important implications for health and disease progression. Interventions targeted at each stage can also serve to alleviate or buffer the effects of stress and can affect health systematically.

Probably the simplest way to interrupt the stress process is to remove the stimulus. If your furnace starts making a lot of noise, interrupting your sleep at night, you can either fix the furnace or get a new one. However, many situations are not easily altered, especially in cases of sudden, acute stressors like assault. One can never go back and undo a traumatic event like rape. Preventive strategies may focus on the coping resources the individual brings into the situation with them, such as social support networks, perceptions of control over the environment, and future expectations. However, this coping can only affect stressful situations in the future.

Given that direct action is not always feasible or likely to be successful, formal intervention programs focus on two types of distress management involving cognitive techniques and somatic techniques. Cognitive techniques are designed to alter appraisal of the situation and the choice of coping strategies. Many focus on the types of appraisals made and the choice of coping strategies. One of the goals is to reduce or eliminate perceptions of stress (harm/loss, threat, or challenge). This may be accomplished by enhancing perceptions of control, predictability, and social support as discussed above. Another goal of cognitive techniques is to teach individuals how to match their coping strategies to the situation. [*See* COGNITIVE THERAPY.]

In contrast, somatic techniques alleviate physiological arousal through the use of behavioral strategies such as relaxation training, meditation, biofeedback, and exercise. It is believed that when physiological arousal is reduced or made more controllable, emotional and behavioral responses will follow.

Package approaches that use both cognitive and somatic techniques are usually the most effective stress-management programs. In part, this is due to the clear linkages between psychological and biological aspects of stress. Decreases in physiological arousal may enhance effectiveness of cognitive strategies, and alterations of cognitive appraisals can affect arousal. Regardless of the intervention used, the more often stress management is practiced the greater the reduction in stress or disease markers.

VI. CONCLUSION

Stress is a ubiquitous phenomenon that has provided survival advantage to humans and other species by facilitating adaptation to threatening or harmful conditions. Under acute stress conditions, the biobehavioral changes that occur during stress have great value in alerting, strengthening, and motivating the individual to act to reduce sources of danger or otherwise reduce its effects. Frequent repetition of stressors, or instances in which stress persists for an unusually long time, may also be more readily overcome by virtue of these emergency responses. However, frequent elicitation of stress responses or chronic, unyielding exposure to danger or threat appear to have consequences for mood, behavior, and health. Biological changes during stress, when unusually severe or prolonged, can affect bodily systems and contribute to ill health, while behavioral changes may cause additional biological changes or affect the quality of one's interactions with the environment. Additionally, the byproducts of coping with stress may convey substantial risks for health and illness.

BIBLIOGRAPHY

Avison, W. R., & Gotlib, I. H. (Eds.). (1994). *Stress and mental health: Contemporary issues and prospects for the future.* New York: Plenum Press.

Baum, A. (1990). Stress, intrusive imagery, and chronic distress. *Health Psychology, 9,* 653–675.

Glaser, R., & Kiecolt-Glaser, J. K. (Eds.). (1994). *Handbook of human stress and immunity.* San Diego: Academic Press.

Lazarus, R. S., & Folkman, S. (1984). *Stress, appraisal, and coping.* New York: Springer Publishing.

Weiner, H. (1992). *Perturbing the organism: The biology of stressful experience.* Chicago: The University of Chicago Press.

Substance Abuse

Thomas Ashby Wills

Albert Einstein College of Medicine

Buffering Effect A process in which a protective factor reduces the adverse impact of a risk factor; also termed resiliency effect.

Chronicity The extent to which the disorder continues to affect the person over an extended period of time.

Comorbidity A phenomenon in which having one disorder increases the likelihood that the person will have one or more other disorders.

Executive Functions A set of interrelated abilities that involve planning and organization, sequencing of activity, and monitoring of ongoing behavior.

Population Prevalence The proportion of the population that has a given mental disorder. This is subdivided into two types of prevalence. Lifetime prevalence is the proportion of the population that has had the disorder at some time in their life; current prevalence, also point prevalence, is the proportion that has the disorder within a defined recent time interval (e.g., past 6 to 12 months).

Protective Factor An environmental, social, or personal variable that is related to a lower rate of substance abuse; a protective factor at one point in time indicates a lower likelihood that a person will be a substance abuser at a later point in time.

Risk Factor An environmental, social, or personal variable that is related to a higher rate of substance abuse; a risk factor at one point in time indicates a

greater likelihood that a person will be a substance abuser at a later point in time.

Substance Abuse A condition where the level of substance use causes significant problems for the individual in important life domains such as work performance or social relationships with significant others.

Substance Dependence A condition where the individual uses a substance in increasingly larger amounts, spends much time getting it and using it, and experiences negative physiological or psychological states when the substance is reduced or withdrawn.

SUBSTANCE ABUSE is construed here as the use of one or more substances which may include tobacco, alcohol, and illicit drugs (marijuana, cocaine, or heroin). This entry addresses substance abuse and related life problems. The generic definition of substance abuse is based on several concepts. First is level of use: an individual uses the substance frequently. Second is the concept of abuse: using the substance causes significant problems for the individual in important life domains such as work performance or social relationships with significant others. Third is the concept of dependence: the individual may use the substance in increasingly larger amounts, spend much time getting it and using it, and experience negative physiological or psychological states when the substance is reduced or withdrawn. Although the application of these criteria varies somewhat for different life stages (e.g., adolescence vs. adulthood) and for different drugs of abuse, when all of the defining conditions are met, then the individual can be diagnosed as having the disorder of substance abuse or substance dependence. It is recognized that there is heterogeneity within a group of persons who all meet sufficient diagnostic criteria for a substance abuse disorder, and for some disorders (particularly alcohol abuse), evidence for subtypes has been reported. However, in the *Diagnostic and Statistical Manual of the American Psychiatric Association (DSM-IV)*, the core conditions are similar across diagnoses for all drugs of abuse, and the only diagnostic distinction allowed is between substance dependence and substance abuse. This entry examines epidemiologic findings on the prevalence of substance use and current knowledge about protective and risk factors for substance abuse.

I. INTRODUCTION

Within the general population there are many persons who have tried cigarettes, alcohol, or marijuana at some time in their lives. There is a substantial proportion of persons who use substances in a consistent but infrequent pattern, such as persons who occasionally have a glass of wine with meals or who drink beer on social occasions. The number of persons who exhibit frequent, high-intensity substance use, however, is a smaller proportion of the population. For example, if the overall amount of alcohol use in the population is broken down, it is evident that a large part of total consumption is attributable to a small part of the population; these are the persons who would be characterized as heavy users. From the group of heavy users, some persons who meet the necessary defining conditions would be described as affected by diagnosable alcohol abuse or (if more severe) alcohol dependence. The prevalence of persons who have tried a substance, and the relative proportions of occasional users, heavy users, and abusers, differ considerably across drugs of abuse. For example, the proportion of the population who have tried cocaine is relatively small, but cocaine (particularly smokable or "crack" cocaine) is sufficiently addictive that a large proportion of triers move rapidly to abuse–dependence status.

Several themes about substance abuse emerge in this entry. First is the concept of multiple risk factors. One way to approach substance abuse is to think about finding the particular factor that is responsible, for example, having an "alcoholic gene," or being the child of a substance-abusing parent, or living in a

poor inner-city area. Although each of these factors has some relevance for predicting substance abuse, research does not support the notion that there is one single cause of substance abuse; for example, although having an alcoholic parent increases children's risk for alcoholism, the majority of adult alcoholics do not have a family history of alcoholism. Instead of indicating a single cause, research indicates that it is a combination of environmental, personal, and social factors that puts some persons on a trajectory of life experiences that ultimately involves an extent and type of use that are indicative of substance abuse disorder. To understand and predict substance abuse, it is essential to consider information about the total number of environmental, personal, and social risk factors and protective factors that impinge on an individual.

A second theme is multiple use. It is possible to find individuals who show only a high level of cigarette smoking, or only a high level of alcohol use, or only the use of an illicit drug (e.g., heroin or cocaine) with nothing else. However, such individuals are statistically rare in the population. Instead, it is more common to find that an individual with a high level of one type of substance use also shows high levels of other types of substance use. Although people have a clear stereotypic picture for the kind of person labeled "alcoholic," they often miss the fact that persons diagnosed with alcohol abuse also tend to be cigarette smokers; correspondingly, the kinds of persons labeled as "drug abusers," because they inject heroin, also tend to have high rates of alcohol, cocaine, and other drug use. The phenomenon of multiple use has been identified consistently in both adolescent samples and adult samples. However, the causal basis for the co-occurrence of tobacco, alcohol, and illicit drug use has not been definitively established at this time.

The third theme is comorbidity. Recent research with general population samples has found that individuals with a substance abuse disorder have elevated rates for other mental health disorders, including anxiety or depressive disorders. Demonstration of substantial comorbidity of substance abuse with mental health disorders is a relatively recent development. The reasons for the comorbidities are not completely understood, but the phenomenon is believed to have significant implications for treatment of substance abusers.

In the context of these themes, this entry summarizes current knowledge about substance abuse from the perspective of epidemiologic research, with epidemiologic data on the prevalence of substance abuse and the comorbidity of substance abuse with other disorders. Risk factors and protective factors, conditions that increase or decrease the likelihood that an individual will be affected by substance abuse, are explored because recent work has shown that it is the *balance* between risk and protective factors that may be crucial for helping to steer an individual toward or away from substance abuse. Risk and protective factors have been studied in both adolescent and adult populations, so findings from both types of research are considered.

II. EPIDEMIOLOGIC FINDINGS ON SUBSTANCE USE AND ABUSE

A. Prevalence of Substance Use and Multiple Use

What proportion of the population engages in substance use? This question is addressed by studies that inquire about whether a person has ever used, or currently uses, a given substance (population prevalence). Surveys administered to samples of adolescents or adults include questions about the extent to which the person has used the substance, for example, Have you ever smoked marijuana? or Have you smoked marijuana in the past 30 days? Additional questions may establish whether the adolescent is a regular user (e.g., smokes every day or usually drinks alcohol several times a month). For adolescents, detailed information on substance use prevalence is available from household surveys and studies of school students. A large study of high school seniors, Monitoring the Future (MF), conducts repeated annual surveys to track current trends in adolescent substance use.

In thinking about substance abuse, it is important to note that substance use typically begins in adolescence. Around age 12 years, prevalence rates for regular tobacco and alcohol use are low, single-digit figures, but these rates increase steadily over adolescence; by age 18, rates of regular use for tobacco, alcohol, and marijuana range from 15 to 30% of the adolescent population. Use of illicit drugs (e.g., heroin and cocaine) is relatively infrequent in the general population of adolescents, but increases markedly during young adulthood (ages 18 to 25 years), with declines thereafter.

However, users of illicit drugs in adulthood typically have a history of prior substance use in adolescence.

Adolescent data show variation for rates of use across different substances. Survey data for high school seniors from 1994 show that for cigarette smoking, 62% have smoked a cigarette at some time in their lives and 19% are current daily smokers. For alcohol, 80% have tried alcohol at some time, 50% had alcohol in the past month, and 28% engaged in what is defined as heavy drinking (five or more drinks on one occasion) during the past 2 weeks. Rates of use of illicit substances are lower but not negligible. Among high school seniors, 38% have tried marijuana at some time in their lives and 19% have used it recently (past 30 days); 16% have tried amphetamines without a medical prescription and 4% have used them recently; 6% have tried cocaine and 2% have used it recently; 1% have tried heroin and 0.3% have used it recently.

Data from samples of the adult general population (ages 18 to 65) in some ways mirror the relative rates of use found in adolescence, with alcohol use fairly prevalent, cigarette smoking intermediate, and rates of illicit drug use relatively low in comparison. The 1995 National Household Survey (NHS) indicated that 29% of U.S. adults are regular smokers. For alcohol use, data from the Epidemiologic Catchment Area Study (ECA) showed that 12% of U.S. adults are total abstainers, 60% engage in social drinking, and 14% can be characterized as heavy drinkers (seven or more drinks at least one evening a week for several months), but are not diagnosable as alcohol abusers. For the illegal substances, 5% of adults are characterized in NHS data as marijuana users (used in past month), 1% as heroin users, and 0.7% as cocaine users. Other research, discussed subsequently, indicates that rates of substance use vary considerably across particular subgroups of the population.

The phenomenon of multiple substance use begins in adolescence. Studies of adolescent samples show substantial interrelationships for tobacco, alcohol, and marijuana use from early ages. The correlation between continuous scores for involvement in various types of substance use is around $r = .35$ in early adolescence (age 12 years), and the magnitude of the correlations increases with age to $r = .60$ or more in later adolescence (age 16 years). These data indicate that the great majority of adolescents who use one substance also use others regularly.

This pattern of multiple use continues into adulthood. In general population samples of adults there are substantial correlations among tobacco, alcohol, and caffeine use. The recent NHS data indicated similar findings, showing that persons who smoked cigarettes were more likely to use alcohol and illicit drugs (marijuana and cocaine). Alcohol use, particularly heavy use, was also correlated with several types of illicit drug use.

The evidence on multiple use has important implications for treatment programs. Many substance abuse treatment programs are specifically focused on one substance (e.g., alcoholism treatment) and may not provide mechanisms for dealing with other types of substance use. In addition, there are significant clinical questions as to whether the therapist and client should try to address different issues in treatment (e.g., simultaneous alcohol abuse treatment and smoking cessation) versus whether treatment should focus on only one addiction problem and how that problem should be selected, that is, which problem should be dealt with first. These questions are beginning to be addressed in clinical research.

B. Prevalence of Substance Abuse

What part of the population can be characterized as affected by substance abuse? This question has been addressed by several recent studies conducted in the United States. Researchers conducted interviews in homes with a large sample of persons who were selected randomly so that they are representative of the U.S. population. The respondents were given a lengthy interview that asked detailed questions about whether they recently experienced signs and symptoms relevant for diagnosis of various mental disorders. An individual's responses were combined to determine whether he or she met the diagnostic criteria for a given disorder, either at some time in his or her life (lifetime prevalence) or in the past 6 to 12 months (current prevalence).

General population research indicates that substance abuse affects a significant proportion of the adult population. The most recent U.S. study, the National Comorbidity Survey (NCS), showed that one in four persons in the population will experience a substance abuse disorder at some time in his or her life. Data from the ECA and NCS studies, which used somewhat different interviews, indicate that 17 to 27%

of the population met the criteria for having a substance abuse disorder at some time in their life, and 6 to 11% evidenced a substance abuse disorder within the past 6 months to 1 year. Thus, even with stringent diagnostic criteria, substance abuse is not a rare disorder. [See EPIDEMIOLOGY: PSYCHIATRIC.]

In relative terms, substance abuse has a prevalence comparable to other disorders. For example, NCS data showed that 19% of the population have had an affective disorder at some time in their life, and 25% have had an anxiety disorder at some time; this compares with a lifetime prevalence of 27% for substance abuse. Considering only episodes within the last year, 11% of the population experienced a depressive disorder, 17% experienced an anxiety disorder, and 11% experienced a substance abuse disorder. Thus substance abuse represents a significant part of the mental health burden in the population. [See ANXIETY; DEPRESSION; MOOD DISORDERS.]

Within the several types of substance abuse disorders, alcohol abuse is the most frequent. The NCS showed a lifetime prevalence of 14% for alcohol dependence and a lifetime prevalence of other substance dependence for 8% of the population. Data on specific dependence–abuse diagnoses from the ECA study showed lifetime prevalences of 4.3% for marijuana, 1.7% for amphetamines, 0.7% for opiates, and 0.2% for cocaine. These studies did not report data for tobacco dependence, a recently added diagnostic category, so the relative prevalence for this substance is currently unclear. [See ALCOHOL PROBLEMS; SMOKING.]

A noteworthy aspect of substance abuse is that it is episodic. The few studies that have made repeated observations of adult substance abusers (e.g., alcoholics) show that rates of use vary widely over time, including many periods of minimal use together with some episodes of heavy or "binge" drinking. This aspect is mirrored in findings from the prevalence studies, which show that many more persons have had a substance abuse disorder *sometime* in their lives compared with the number who have a *current* disorder. One may speculate that together these findings suggest that rates of substance use are partly responsive to environmental conditions that are relatively short-term (e.g., argument with a significant other) or longer term (e.g., unemployment). However, there has been little research involving longitudinal observations of substance abuse episodes, and interpretation of the available findings is somewhat inferential at this time.

C. Temporal Trends

Is the prevalence of substance abuse increasing or decreasing in the population? Data from the NHS on prevalence of substance use have shown a steady decline in cigarette smoking among U.S. adults, from a prevalence around 44% in 1975 to a prevalence of around 29% in 1995. This was accompanied with substantial decreases in marijuana use (compared with a peak in the mid 1970s) and cocaine use (from a peak in the late 1980s) and a modest decline in current alcohol use. In contrast to population trends in overall use, however, is evidence from the recent ECA and NCS studies that concur in finding rates of mental health disorders to be elevated among persons born in more recent years. This has been interpreted as indicating that the prevalence of psychopathology is increasing in the general population.

Regular studies of adolescents provide a more precise picture of how the frequency of particular types of substance use is changing over time. Although this research does not provide diagnostic indices, it does provide yearly standardized data on the prevalence of substance use among adolescents (which has implications for their use as adults). Cigarette smoking among high school seniors has steadily declined since 1975, paralleling the decline in smoking among adults, whereas rates of overall alcohol use have not shown large changes. Rates of adolescents' marijuana use were declining during the 1980s, but began to increase around 1992. This increase in marijuana use has been paralleled by increases in cigarette smoking among younger adolescents (age 13 years). This worrisome trend is currently the subject of considerable attention and public policy debate.

D. Variation by Gender, Socioeconomic Status, and Ethnicity

Substance abuse is not randomly distributed in the population, and attention to how the prevalence of substance abuse differs across demographic subgroups of the population provides a valuable perspective on the nature of these disorders. The nature of the demographic differences, however, depends on the type of substance involved. With regard to gender, adult alcohol abuse is more common among males. For example, NCS data showed the lifetime prevalence of alcohol dependence was 20% for males and 8% for females; and although the rate of the disorder among females is not trivial, the disorder is 2.5 times more frequent among males. Similar findings are usually noted for substance abuse other than alcoholism; for example, in NCS data, the prevalence of other drug dependence was 9% for males and 6% for females. The only type of substance use consistently found greater for women is tranquilizer use, consistent with the female differential found for anxiety disorders. Even this picture is unclear, because much of the total consumption of anxiolytic drugs is from medical prescription; when studies distinguish between prescribed and nonprescribed tranquilizer use, males have higher rates of nonprescribed tranquilizer use (which often goes along with illicit drug use). [*See* GENDER DIFFERENCES IN MENTAL HEALTH.]

It is difficult to know which aspect of these findings deserves more emphasis. On the one hand, the prevalence of alcohol abuse among males is substantial, and it can be anticipated that a considerable proportion of males will experience diagnosable alcohol abuse at some time in their lives. On the other hand, the rate of substance abuse among women is not zero, and considering the broad-band diagnosis of any substance abuse/dependence, NCS data showed that 18% of women will have a substance abuse disorder at some time in their lives, compared with 35% for males. Thus the risk for women is lower, but not negligible.

Drug abuse is more prevalent among persons of lower socioeconomic status. The results of several large-scale studies show diagnoses of substance abuse to be more frequent among persons with lower income and education. This does not, of course, mean that substance abuse is absent among persons with high socioeconomic status, as shown, for example, in media portrayals of highly paid athletes and entertainment personalities who have used cocaine and other drugs. However, the greatest risk of substance abuse is at the lowest rungs of the socioeconomic ladder. Studies also indicate that the chronicity of substance abuse and other mental health disorders is greater for persons with low socioeconomic status, and that comorbid disorders are markedly more frequent for persons of low socioeconomic status. Thus, the burden of disorder is substantially greater for this part of the population. The picture is complicated a little by alcohol statistics; moderate drinking tends to be more frequent among persons of middle or higher education, but alcohol abuse is elevated for persons with lower income and occupational status. [*See* Socio-economic Status.]

Current findings on ethnicity and substance abuse are consistent in showing a lower prevalence among African Americans for most types of substance abuse. Data from the NCS indicate that African American adults have a lower rate of any substance abuse disorder compared with whites. This finding is comparable to ECA data, which showed lower rates of substance and alcohol abuse dependence among young African Americans than among whites. In these studies, Hispanics approach non-Hispanic whites in rates of disorder but generally are not higher. These findings are parallel to findings from studies of adolescents' substance use, which consistently show African American adolescents as having the lowest rates of tobacco and alcohol use, Hispanic adolescents intermediate, and whites highest. These observations are balanced by studies of ethnic differentials in morbidity and mortality that show that adult African Americans are more affected by chronic disease, some of it substance-related. These findings have been interpreted as reflecting a greater impact of health risk factors in minority populations because of greater environmental stressors and reduced access to screening programs and medical care. [*See* Ethnicity and Mental Health.]

E. Comorbidity of Substance Abuse and Mental Disorder

The issue of comorbidity involves the following question: If a person has a substance abuse disorder, is he or she more likely also to have one or more other diagnoses of mental disorder compared with the base rate in the population? Recent epidemiologic studies have provided an answer to the question by studying the co-occurrence of diagnoses among persons in representative community samples. Results have shown that there is extensive comorbidity. For example, ECA data showed persons with alcohol abuse had twice the risk for mental disorder (compared with the population base rate), and persons with other drug abuse disorders showed a fourfold increase in risk for mental disorder. Among persons with alcohol abuse, the risk for other drug abuse disorder was 7 times greater, and there is also a high co-occurrence of substance abuse and antisocial personality. In other words, abuse of one substance increases by 7 times the risk of abusing another substance, and a person with alcohol or substance abuse has 2 to 4 times the risk of a mental disorder.

Comorbidity with alcohol or other substance abuse was found for affective disorders (particularly bipolar depression), anxiety disorders (particularly panic and obsessive–compulsive disorder), and schizophrenia. The NCS data showed that of persons with any lifetime disorder, only one-fifth (21%) had one disorder; the rest had two or three disorders. This indicates that the great majority of mental disorder is comorbid disorder. Moreover, comorbidity was related to chronicity: persons with a comorbid disorder were more likely to have had a recent experience of disorder and to have had more severe disorder. The degree of comorbidity was high among both treated and untreated parts of the population, but was found to be even greater among persons who had sought treatment.

The high degree of comorbidity found in these studies has major implications for treatment professionals. One implication is that clinicians who focus on treatment of mental health problems will actually be encountering a substantial number of persons with a co-occurring substance abuse problem. Another implication is that the high degree of comorbid mental disorders among substance abusers probably presents a significant impediment to treatment for this population. A number of clinical research studies are currently underway to investigate how the effectiveness of substance abuse treatment programs may be enhanced through recognition and treatment of other disorders.

F. Treatment Rate

One of the contributions of psychiatric epidemiology has been to determine what proportion of persons with mental illness receive professional treatment (the treatment rate). After determining whether a person has had a mental health disorder, researchers can then determine whether the person has received treatment at some time from a mental health professional (psychologist or psychiatrist), from other medical personnel (e.g., primary care physician), or from community agents who provide counseling and guidance (e.g., clergy).

Data on persons with affective disorders have indicated that only a minority receive professional treatment. The figure is usually around 25% for persons with depressive or anxiety disorder. The remainder of persons with clinical depression or anxiety either receive brief contact with a primary care physician or receive no professional treatment at all. The experience of persons with substance abuse disorders appears to be even worse. For example, of persons who had a substance abuse disorder within the past year, only 4% received treatment in any kind of substance abuse facility (either inpatient hospitalization, outpatient treatment, or a drop-in program). This low treatment rate may be the result of a range of factors, including limited availability of treatment, restrictions on insurance coverage for treatment of substance abuse, or personality characteristics associated with substance abuse (e.g., alienation and antisocial behavior) that discourage drug abusers from becoming involved with any kind of professional agency, but the evidence shows that only a small proportion of affected persons receives professional treatment. What encourages persons with substance abuse to seek treatment is an important question that has received relatively little attention.

The ECA study, which showed that primary-care physicians are a major source of treatment for mental disorders, included questions on whether a person had ever talked with their physician about an emotional problem or about substance abuse. Results showed that persons with any kind of emotional problem were unlikely to talk about it with the physician, and persons with substance abuse problems were particularly unlikely to do so. These findings suggest that health care providers encounter a substantial number of persons who are experiencing substance abuse, but frequently do not learn of this from their patients. This indicates that studying ways to increase recognition of substance abuse in treatment settings could be an avenue to opening treatment accessibility.

Given the evidence about the episodic nature of substance abuse and the relatively low utilization of professional treatment programs, a significant question has arisen: How do persons who are affected by alcohol or other substance abuse, but who do not receive formal treatment, deal with their problem? One possible answer to the question is that many persons draw on social support from significant others and learn to control the substance abuse problem on their own, either by reducing their use to a level where it is no longer problematic to themselves or others, or by ceasing it entirely. Another possible answer is that persons participate in informal self-help groups such as Alcoholics Anonymous, a widely available resource

that promotes abstinence as the route to recovery. Although there is some evidence for both avenues of coping with substance abuse, this issue has been controversial because of evidence from studies of self-quitters suggesting that some persons may recover from alcohol abuse by learning self-control skills to reduce their use to low levels (controlled drinking). Research has explored the extent of recovery in untreated samples and has followed alcoholics in formal treatment programs to determine their subsequent experiences with abstinence, controlled drinking, or relapse. The present evidence indicates that recovery through controlled drinking occurs for only a small proportion of serious alcohol abusers. However, research on the comparative efficacy of self-change and formal inpatient or outpatient treatment is continuing. This remains an area where well-designed scientific research is needed to obtain more definitive answers.

III. PROTECTIVE AND RISK FACTORS

A. Definitions

The concept of protective factors and risk factors for substance abuse requires some discussion. A *protective factor* is an environmental, personal, or social variable that is related to a lower rate of substance abuse, either at the same point in time or over time. Such a factor could deter a person from becoming involved in substance use in the first place, or prevent a person from progressing to a high frequency and intensity of use. A *risk factor* is an environmental, personal, or social variable that is related to a higher rate of substance use or abuse; in the context of longitudinal research, the level of a risk factor at one point in time would predict the likelihood that a person will be a substance abuser at a later point in time. The concepts are linked in the sense that the level of protective factors may be particularly relevant for individuals with a high level of risk factors, so that substance use could be greatly reduced among persons who had a high level of risk factors but also had a high level of protective factors. Overall levels of protective factors and risk factors are not highly correlated, and protective factors may reduce the potentially adverse effect of risk factors. This is alternately called a *buffering effect*, in the sense that protective factors buffer a person from the impact of risk factors, or a *resiliency effect*, in the sense that protective factors enable persons to be resilient in the face of pressures that otherwise would operate to encourage substance use or abuse. [*See* Protective Factors in Development of Psychopathology.]

The ideal study of risk for substance abuse would use a wide range of biochemical, neurological, and psychological measures; obtain such measures from a large and representative sample; collect data on a range of outcomes, including psychiatric diagnosis, work performance, and social relationships; and follow the respondents from infancy through age 35. No single study exists that has all of these characteristics. Accordingly, current knowledge about protective and risk factors is derived from a variety of studies that were designed at different times over the past 40 years. They were conducted for differing periods with samples that span the range somewhere between childhood to young adulthood, and used a wide variety of measures. The discussion here is based on a composite of findings from studies of children, adolescents, and adults which have examined different aspects of risk for substance abuse.

Researchers have generally given more weight to knowledge derived from variables obtained at earlier measurement time points as predictors of adult substance abuse. The reason is that results may be ambiguous when study variables are measured at the same point in time as substance abuse in adulthood. For example, the finding of a correlation between depression and substance abuse is ambiguous because the depression may be a result of adverse consequences caused by the abuse, not a predictor. Although it may sound paradoxical to discuss variables measured at age 12, when there is virtually no cocaine use, in relation to cocaine use at age 25, such findings have significant interest because they precede the onset of the substance abuse. In addition, it is common to find drug abuse occurring in a context of multiple substance use and a history of prior substance use. Although many persons who experiment with substances in adolescence reduce or cease their use as they move into adulthood (a phenomenon called "maturing out"), there is evidence for stability of heavy use over time and this is a primary risk factor for substance abuse in adulthood.

B. Protective Factors

The following section presents a summary of knowledge about protective factors. The distinction be-

tween protective and risk factors can sometimes be arbitrary; for example, one could plausibly argue that high academic achievement is a protective factor or that low academic achievement is a risk factor. The discussion tries to classify factors according to observed main effects and buffering effects.

1. Gender

Gender could be characterized as a protective factor in the sense that girls have lower rates of substance use throughout adolescence and women have a lower prevalence of alcohol and other substance abuse disorder in adulthood. In addition, effects of adverse early environments (e.g., parental poverty and alcoholism) on substance use appear to be less for girls than for boys.

2. Temperament

Two dimensions of temperament—precursors of adult personality characteristics that are observable in childhood and adolescence—have been related to substance abuse liability. *Attentional orientation,* the ability to focus attention and concentrate on tasks, is greater among persons with low levels of substance use. *Positive emotionality,* the tendency to be generally cheerful and happy, is also a protective factor and has been shown to buffer the impact of risk factors. [*See* Personality.]

3. Intelligence and Verbal Skills

Although one might expect intelligence to be a protective factor, evidence on overall IQ is actually quite mixed. Rather, it is an advantage specifically on verbal ability in IQ tests that is consistently noted to be a protective factor. Whether verbal skills are protective because they facilitate the development of problem-solving ability or because they contribute to better interpersonal relationships with parents and peers is not currently known; it is recognized that both mechanisms are possible. [*See* Intelligence and Mental Health.]

4. Executive Functions and Problem Solving

This concept refers to a set of interrelated abilities measured at the neuropsychological level as functions for planning, organization, and sequencing of activity, and measured at the behavioral level as dealing with problem situations by getting information, considering alternative courses of action, and thoughtfully selecting an alternative before acting. Higher levels of these abilities are present in children and adolescents who do not use substances, and the abilities protect against escalation and multiple use that occur for some individuals who are low on these functions. Executive functions are not strongly correlated with full-scale IQ and this domain of cognitive functioning is not merely a proxy for general intelligence.

5. Family Support and Relationships with Significant Others

A strong protective factor among adolescents is positive relationships with parents and other family members. The construct of family support includes feeling accepted and valued, and feeling that emotional support is available because one can talk to a parent when one has a problem and that one can receive advice and assistance from a parent for instrumental needs. To some extent this is independent of the number of parents in the home; although a single-parent household is a risk factor for substance use, the level of support in the household appears to be a more important factor. In adulthood, marriage is a protective factor with regard to substance abuse, and a supportive relationship (involving emotional and instrumental support) with a significant other is a protective factor—as long as the significant other is not a drug user. [See SOCIAL SUPPORT.]

6. Academic Achievement

This is a simple term for a complex construct. The basic finding is that adolescents who get good grades in school are less likely to be substance abusers as adults, hence academic achievement is a protective factor. This probably involves a constellation of characteristics, with higher-achieving individuals having positive attitudes toward school and valuing conventional achievement as a goal; getting support and assistance from parents for doing well; performing better in task situations and organizing behavior to meet requirements (e.g., completing homework on time); and behaving appropriately to meet the demands of the setting (e.g., sitting still in class and not "talking back" to teachers).

7. Religiosity

Substance use is lower among persons who hold religious beliefs. This construct is sometimes measured by asking respondents whether they belong to a church, temple, or other religious institution, and, if so, how often they attend; sometimes by asking whether they hold religious beliefs; and sometimes by asking whether they engage in prayer or meditation. Findings are generally robust across different measures of the construct of religiosity. Moreover, the protective effect is generally found across a number of different religious denominations. Some theorists have suggested that the effect of religiosity is mediated through an individual's identification with conventional social values, but there have been few explicit tests of this proposition. [See RELIGION AND MENTAL HEALTH.]

8. Perceived Harmfulness of Drugs

Persons who perceive substances to have adverse consequences (for health, social acceptance, or interpersonal relationships) are less likely to be substance users. This has been shown, in data from the MF study, to account for long-term trends in adolescent substance use. Where these attitudes come from has not been completely established, but research suggests some combination of communications from parents, personal observation, and exposure to educational programs.

9. Perceived Disapproval for Use

The perception that significant others (parents, friends, or spouse) disapprove of substance use is a deterrent to substance abuse. To some extent this may be a self-guided effect, because persons with relatively positive attitudes toward drugs will tend to gravitate toward persons who are drug users and who have favorable attitudes themselves; conversely, individuals who hold negative attitudes toward drugs will tend to select friends with similar views. However, the perceived attitudinal climate has been shown in longitudinal studies to be a deterrent to involvement in substance use.

C. Risk Factors

Risk factors for substance abuse make up what seems like a longer list. This may to some extent reflect an imbalance in the literature, with researchers tending to concentrate on finding variables that predict bad outcomes rather than protective variables that are related to good outcomes. It may partially reflect the nature of substance use, if there are many different types of factors that produce escalation of substance use among individuals who have experimented. In the listing that follows, it should be recognized that several of the risk factors are correlated. For example, parental alcohol abuse is typically related to discord and conflict between parents and children. The nature and reasons for correlations among risk factors is not well understood and is the subject of ongoing investigation, but the reader should keep in mind that the risk factors discussed here are not necessarily independent. In the following section, little attention is given to cultural issues. This is not because these issues are unimportant; cross-cultural work suggests that drug use rates, preferences, and practices vary widely across cultures. However, the epidemiologic studies have mostly been conducted in North American samples and the discussion is focused on this type of evidence.

1. Gender

Male gender may be construed as a risk factor for substance abuse. Not only are rates of alcohol and illicit drug use higher among male adolescents, but the differential increases with age. In adulthood, the prevalence of alcohol and other substance abuse disorders is consistently greater among men compared with women.

2. White Ethnicity

The prevalence of substance use and abuse is greater among whites, and the strength of relationships between predictive factors and substance use outcomes is consistently found to be greater among whites compared with African Americans. This does not necessarily mean that the predictors of drug abuse are different for whites and for members of ethnic groups, as predictive relationships for a given variable are often found to be significant in all ethnic groups, but predictive effects are typically greater for whites.

3. Lower Socioeconomic Status

The risk of substance use or abuse is greater for persons with lower socioeconomic status. This effect is observable beginning in adolescence for teenagers from families with lower education, hence this is a true predictive relationship. There is evidence that persons with substance abuse problems beginning in later adolescence or early adulthood may experience downward mobility, but this does not contradict the risk status that occurs early on. Studies conducted in adolescence have also shown the impact of risk factors on substance use to be greater among adolescents from lower-income families.

4. Family History of Substance Abuse

Persons with a history of alcoholism among parents and/or grandparents are at increased risk for alcohol-

ism as adults. Evidence that this is attributable to genetic transmission has been shown by studies of twins and studies of adopted children, each type of research indicating a heritable basis for substance abuse liability. History of paternal alcoholism provides about a fourfold increase in children's risk; for example, a study in Sweden showed that 18% of male children of alcoholic fathers became alcoholic as adults, compared with a rate of 4% for children of nonalcoholic fathers in the population studied. At the same time, it should be noted that the majority of children of alcoholic parents (over 80%) did not become alcoholic themselves, so the data indicate there may be many factors beside family history that contribute to influencing substance abuse.

5. Temperament

Two dimensions of temperament have been linked to greater liability for substance abuse. One is physical *activity level,* the tendency to be physically active and to be unable to sit still for long. The second is *negative emotionality,* the tendency to be easily frustrated, irritated, and angered. These characteristics are related to substance use at early ages and are found to be more prevalent in the histories of adult substance abusers. Negative emotionality and high activity level are also more common among children of substance abusers, and current research is exploring the possibility that effects of family history are partly transmitted by influencing the development of these temperament dimensions.

6. Poor Parental Relationship and Supervision

Discordant relationships between parents and children, with frequent arguments and conflict, predict adolescent substance use and are found to be more common in the life history of adult substance abusers. Accompanying family discord is poor parental monitoring and supervision of children, so that parents frequently do not know where the children are (when they are out of the home) or who they are with. A combination of poor relationship with parents and lax supervision may encourage a child to begin affiliating with deviance-prone peers who can introduce him or her to substances and encourage their use.

7. Early Onset

The age at which a person begins using substances predicts future substance abuse risk. Retrospective studies have shown that individuals who began using illicit substances before age 15 are more likely to be affected by substance abuse as adults, whereas persons who began substance use later in adolescence do not show this degree of risk. Although a considerable proportion of teenagers engage in minimal experimentation with tobacco and alcohol, it is the smaller proportion of individuals who engage in early, persistent substance use, including illicit drugs, who are at greatly increased risk.

8. Poor Self-Control

Lower ability for self-regulation of emotions and behavior is a risk factor for substance use and has been demonstrated among both adolescents and adults. The construct of poor self-control is a generalized one involving areas such as poor control of behavior in everyday situations (e.g., cutting in line), impatience in social interactions, low dependability in meeting responsibilities, acting without thinking, and less ability to calm down when upset and recover from irritations or embarrassments. Alternate labels given for this construct in the literature are impulsivity, disinhibition, or behavioral undercontrol. Although many persons will display one or two of these behaviors at some time, it is a high level of poor self-control across many situations that is indicated as a risk factor. It is important to note that poor self-control is not simply the absence of good self-control. Although these two dimensions are inversely related, they are not redundant and appear to derive from two different developmental systems. Good self-control has been shown to buffer the impact of poor self-control on substance use. [*See* IMPULSE CONTROL.]

9. Novelty Seeking and Risk Taking

A personality constellation has been identified that involves constantly seeking novel experiences, trying new things for fun and thrills, becoming easily bored, and liking to be involved in risky or dangerous situations. This construct of *novelty seeking* (sometimes called sensation seeking or risk taking) has been linked to substance abuse liability in animal research and in human studies, with individuals who score high on novelty seeking shown to be at increased risk. There is evidence that this dimension has substantial heritability, and recent research with humans has suggested a linkage with dopamine, a neurotransmitter that is central for brain reward mechanisms. Thus, a psychobiological basis for the novelty-seeking dimension is credible at this time.

10. Anger, Hostility, and Aggression

This set of interrelated attributes involves feelings of alienation from others, cynical perceptions of hostile intent and distrust of others' motives, and overt aggression toward others including verbal aggression such as teasing, blaming, and criticizing, and physical aggression such as damaging objects or hitting persons. Measures of anger are one of the strongest predictors of substance use in adolescence, and the temperament dimension of negative emotionality appears to be a precursor of this attribute. Irritability and anger are quite stable in childhood and adolescence, and these constructs have been shown to predict substance abuse liability over long time periods. [*See* AGGRESSION; ANGER.]

11. Avoidant and Helplessness Coping

In contrast to active types of coping, some persons may cope with problems by trying in various ways to avoid dealing with the problem or by disengaging from coping efforts entirely and taking the view that there is nothing they can do to cope. Measures of coping through avoidance and helplessness are related to increased risk for substance use and abuse over a wide range of ages, from early adolescence through later adult years; more traitlike measures, indexing perceived lack of control over the important things in one's life, have also been related to substance use risk in prospective investigations. It is possible that avoidance and helplessness may be a consequence of poor self-control and low actual competence in domains such as academic or work performance; interrelations among these constructs are currently being investigated. [*See* COPING WITH STRESS.]

12. Tolerance for Deviance

This attitudinal dimension represents devaluation of conventional values and routes to accomplishment; for example, the belief that school (for adolescents) or work (for young adults) is boring and irrelevant together with endorsement of the attitude that behaviors such as lying, stealing, or fighting are not really so bad and that rule-breaking behavior is all right if one can get away with it. This attitudinal dimension may not be independent of other risk factors; adolescents who are doing poorly in school and who feel angry and alienated from their parents and community might tend to endorse these kinds of attitudes. However, it has been shown that this attitudinal dimension contributes to escalating involvement in substance use.

13. Conduct Disorder and Antisocial Personality Disorder

Substance use is found empirically to co-occur with conduct disorder in adolescence and with antisocial personality (ASP) in adulthood; in the latter case, substance use is one of the diagnostic criteria for ASP because it is highly associated with fighting, stealing, and involvement in other illegal behaviors. Substance use in adolescence is also found to co-occur with other adolescent problem behaviors, such as drunk driving and precocious, frequent sexual relations. The extent to which the diagnostic label is merely a convenient summary for dimensions such as poor self-control, anger, and risk-taking orientation is not known at present because studies have approached the question from such different perspectives. A recent retrospective study by Robins and McEvoy in 1990, using ECA data, did show that adult substance abuse disorder was best predicted by the total number of behavior problems in childhood; the presence of a conduct disorder diagnosis did not add additional ability for prediction of substance abuse. [See CONDUCT DISORDER.]

14. Negative Life Events

Negative life events have been shown to precede the onset and escalation of substance use. In adolescent samples, it has been shown that both events occurring to family members (e.g., illness, unemployment) and events occurring directly to children (e.g., serious accidents) predict substance use, and statistical analyses have shown that negative life events are not simply a proxy for demographic factors. Research has indicated that negative events can be a consequence of other variables, such as poor self-control and tolerance for deviance, and can also be a predictor of other variables, such as deviant peer affiliations. The mechanism through which negative events influence substance use has not been completely established. Emotional distress evoked by negative events may be a predisposing factor for high-intensity substance use motivated by self-regulation of negative emotions. It is also possible that feelings of helplessness evoked by negative life experiences make individuals disengage from active modes of coping and seek out deviant companions who can provide hedonistic activities that help dampen the impact of negative experiences in other areas. Some evidence is available for both mechanisms.

15. Affiliation with Peer Users

Having friends who smoke, who engage in heavy drinking, and/or who use illicit drugs is generally indicated as being the final common pathway to substance use, predicted by many other risk factors and strongly related to an individual's level of substance use. "Hanging out" with peer smokers and drinkers in early adolescence predicts subsequent escalation to high-intensity substance use, and studies of adult drug abusers show heavy use encouraged by involvement in a drug subculture that features a group of drinking companions or "shooting buddies." It is unlikely that the operation of peer affiliations involves just overt social pressure; although this element is not absent in any group situation, the available evidence suggests that vulnerable persons experimenting with substances seek out affiliation with groups of known users and thereby involve themselves in a cyclical process that promotes higher levels of use and increasing identification with users over time.

IV. SUMMARY

The statistics on the prevalence of substance abuse show that alcohol or other substance abuse occurs for a significant part of the population, often comorbid with other mental disorders. Whether substance abuse disorders are decreasing or increasing in the general population is not yet clear. Some evidence can be noted for promising trends, such as declines in tobacco and cocaine use, but this may be offset by other trends such as increases in marijuana use. The one clear conclusion from the current prevalence studies is that substance abuse is not going to go away soon, and continued prevention and treatment efforts are necessary and valuable for the health of the population.

Development of substance abuse is a complex process that is rooted in many factors. Having a single risk factor does not indicate that a person is likely to develop substance abuse. It is only when multiple risk factors are present that an individual has a substantial increase in risk. These factors span a wide range of areas including socioeconomic status, family history of substance abuse, patterns of temperament and personality, the individual's own early history of use, patterns of stress and coping, attitudes about deviant behavior in general and substance use in particular, and choices of mates and companions. An individual's profile on all of these attributes produces a trajectory that over time may steer the individual toward or away from the rocky shore of substance abuse; but as the number of risk factors one has increases, the probability of substance abuse increases.

Although substance abuse is expressed in adulthood, research suggests that liability is contributed by factors that are observable at early ages. Diagnosing an individual as alcoholic at age 30 does not explain how he or she ended up in that condition, and research conducted at younger ages indicates that dispositional attributes, learned ways of coping with situations and feelings, and relationships with parents and peers all are acting to influence an individual's likelihood of substance use. Thus the study of substance abuse has much to gain from studying individual trajectories of use or nonuse over time, identifying early factors that make a minority of persons particularly vulnerable when pressures accumulate in adulthood. All the evidence suggests that prevention programs should begin early, and research has shown a number of modifiable factors that can reduce the likelihood of substance abuse.

Many persons with risk factors do not develop substance abuse. Protective factors such as supportive family relationships, self-regulation skills, and developed competencies (e.g., academic performance) serve to blunt the impact of adverse conditions. Again, the existence of a single factor does not guarantee a positive outcome, but persons whose environments contain several protective factors may be buffered against risk to a considerable extent. Research indicates it is the balance of protective and risk factors that is most important for understanding vulnerability versus resilience.

ACKNOWLEDGMENTS

Preparation of this article was supported by Research Scientist Development Award K02-DA00252 from the National Institute on Drug Abuse. The author thanks Sean Cleary, Marnie Filer, and Ori Shinar for assistance.

BIBLIOGRAPHY

American Psychiatric Association (1994). *Diagnostic and statistical manual of mental disorders* (4th ed.). Washington, DC: Author.

Baer, J. S., Marlatt, G. A., & McMahon, R. J. (Eds.). (1993). *Addictive behaviors across the life span: Prevention, treatment, and policy issues.* Newbury Park, CA: Sage.

Bukstein, O. G. (1995). *Adolescent substance abuse: Assessment, prevention, and treatment.* New York: Wiley.

Fertig, J. P., & Allen, J. P. (Eds.). (1995). *Alcohol and tobacco: From basic science to clinical practice.* Bethesda, MD: National Institute on Alcohol Abuse and Alcoholism.

Galizio, M., & Maisto, S. A. (Eds.). (1985). *Determinants of substance abuse: Biological, psychological, and environmental factors.* New York: Plenum.

Glantz, M., & Pickens, R. (Eds.). (1992). *Vulnerability to drug abuse.* Washington, DC: American Psychological Association.

Hawkins, J. D., Catalano, R. F., & Miller, J. Y. (1992). Risk and protective factors for alcohol and other drug problems in adolescence and early adulthood. *Psychological Bulletin, 112,* 64–105.

Johnston, L. D., O'Malley, P. M., & Bachman, J. G. (1995). *National survey results on drug use from the Monitoring the Future study, 1975–1994* (2 vols.). Rockville, MD: National Institute on Drug Abuse.

Littrell, J. (1991). *Understanding and treating alcoholism: An empirically based clinician's handbook* (Vol. 1). Hillsdale, NJ: Erlbaum.

Lowinson, J. H., Ruiz, P., & Millman, R. B. (Eds.). (1992). *Substance abuse: A comprehensive textbook* (2nd ed.). Baltimore: Williams & Wilkins.

Robins, L. N., & Regier, D. A. (Eds.). (1991). *Psychiatric disorders in America: The Epidemiologic Catchment Area Study.* New York: Free Press.

Rouse, B. A. (1995). *Substance abuse and mental health statistics sourcebook.* Washington, DC: Substance Abuse and Mental Health Services Administration.

Sobell, M., & Sobell, L. (1995). Controlled drinking after 25 years: How important was the great debate? *Addiction, 90,* 1149–1153.

Sussman, S., & Johnson, C. A. (Eds.). (1996). Drug abuse prevention: Programming and research recommendations. *American Behavioral Scientist, 39,* 787–942.

Tarter, R. E., Moss, H. B., & Vanyukov, M. M. (1995). Behavior genetic perspective of alcoholism etiology. In H. Begleiter & B. Kissin (Eds.). *The Genetics of Alcoholism* (Vol. 1, pp. 294–326). New York: Oxford University Press.

Warner, L. A., Kessler, R. C., Hughes, M., Anthony, J. C., & Nelson, C. B. (1995). Prevalence and correlates of drug use and dependence in the United States: Results from the National Comorbidity Survey. *Archives of General Psychiatry, 52,* 219–229.

Wills, T. A., McNamara, G., Vaccaro, D., & Hirky, A. E. (1996). Escalated substance use: A longitudinal grouping analysis from early to middle adolescence. *Journal of Abnormal Psychology, 105,* 166–180.

Zucker, R. A., Boyd, G. & Howard, J., (Eds.). (1994). *The development of alcohol problems: Exploring the biophyschosocial matrix of risk.* Rockville, MD: National Institute on Alcohol Abuse and Alcoholism.

Suicide

Ronald W. Maris

University of South Carolina Suicide Center

Biological Fitness Being capable of reproducing and propagating one's own genes.

Developmental Stagnation Inability to mature normally or the failure to acquire behavioral skills appropriate to chronological human life stages.

Dexamethasone Suppression Test Relatively cheap, simple, and safe biological measure of depression that assesses the hypersection of cortisol.

Hopelessness Despair over a future tolerable existence related to vulnerability, deprivation, cognitive constriction, and repeated stress and depression.

Interdisciplinary Etiology Complex and interrelated mix of biological, psychological, social, anthropological, and economic factors in the production of a behavioral outcome, such as suicide.

Serotonin Hypothesis Prediction that low levels of hydroxyindoleacetic acid (5-HIAA), a metabolite of serotonin (5-HT), is causative of suicide—especially of violent suicides.

Minimally, **"SUICIDE"** is intentional self-murder. The concept derives from the Latin *sui* ("of oneself") and *cide* ("a killing"). In German, suicide is literally self-murder (*selbstmord*). Suicide is usually distinguished from homicide (which is contraintentioned), natural death (which is unintentioned) and accident (which

may be subintentioned), making up the so-called "NASH" classification of manners of death on death certificates (sometimes a fifth manner of "undetermined" or "pending" death is added).

A more elaborate definition of suicide by the French Sociologist Emile Dirkheim is *any death that is the direct or indirect result of a positive or negative act accomplished by the victim him(her) self, which he(she) knows or believes will produce this result*. Several important consequences follow from this definition. First, suicide must be a *death*. Nonfatal suicide attempts, self-destructive thoughts or gestures, partial suicides, and so on, strictly speaking are not suicides. Second, suicides must be *self-inflicted*. The agent ("efficient" or "proximate" cause) must not be another person (murder), atrophy or disease of the human body (natural death), or an external, impersonal agent encountered capriciously (accidental death). Third, *risk-taking* that leads to death, if the indirect causal sequence can be specified and was intentional, is suicide. Indirect suicide is a common but neglected form of suicide.

Fourth, *not doing something*, as well as positive action, can be suicidal. Obvious examples include not taking life-preserving medication or not moving from the path of an approaching vehicle (*ceteris paribus*). Fifth, suicide is an *intentional* death. If someone swallows fifty Seconal capsules and dies, but did not believe or know (e.g., was a child) they were lethal enough to kill, then the death was an accident. Problems of measurement of intentionality (especially after death) have led some investigators to focus on lethal behaviors and to ignore intentionality altogether. This approach is unacceptable, since many lethal behaviors result in accidental deaths or even in murders. Finally, death must be *certain* or thought to be certain. The essential point here is negative. If someone does something (e.g., jumps out of a second-story apartment window) and does not believe that it will kill, but it does, then the outcome is an accidental death. In 1995 the National Institute of Mental Health held a conference to address issues of suicide nomenclature, which resulted in a publication entitled "Beyond the Tower of Babel—A Nomenclature for Suicidology."

Suicide can be thought of as resulting from the inability or refusal to accept the terms of the human condition. As such, suicide is problem-solving behavior. In fact, suicide is a drastic solution to the problem of life itself, as well as to many other specific life problems. Edwin Shneidman describes suicide as "a conscious act of self-induced annihilation, best understood as a multidimensional malaise in a needful individual who defines an issue for which suicide is perceived as the best solution." Of course, suicide is often, even usually, not the preferred resolution to one's life problems.

"Rational" suicides are usually committed by older adults, who are nonpsychotic, who wait until their depression remits, have a consistent wish-to-die over time, consider deleterious consequences for significant others (even involve them in the decision, particularly their children), explore nonsuicidal alternatives thoroughly, are often in hopeless, irreversible physical conditions, sometimes with unrelenting pain or discomfort, and have made all necessary preparations for death. Under these conditions and perhaps a few others, some (not many) suicides can be said to be rational. One of the problems with the spate of assisted suicides by Dr. Jack Kevorkian is that it is not clear that his clients were assessed or treated first for clinical depression.

Although the types of suicides vary, there probably are some common traits of most suicides. In addition to being seen as problem-solving, according to Shneidman, many suicides:

- wish to produce cessation of consciousness;
- wish to reduce intolerable psychological pain;
- have frustrated psychological needs;
- feel helpless and/or hopeless;
- are ambivalent about dying;
- are perceptually constricted;

- feel a need for egression or fugue;
- interpersonally communicate their suicide ideas;
- use self-destruction as life-long coping.

The concept of suicide also needs to be differentiated carefully from attempted suicide. "Attempted suicide" usually implies a conscious intent to kill oneself. However, most suicide attempters never die suicidal deaths (perhaps 85 to 90% die nonsuicidal deaths) and some of them also wish to live (i.e., they are ambivalent). This fact seems to escape many physicians, clinical psychologists, and research psychiatrists who claim they are studying suicide but whose only samples are patients who have made nonfatal suicide attempts. To help resolve such conceptual problems Norman Kreitman recommends the term "parasuicide," that is, nonfatal acts of deliberate self-injury (ignoring one's intent to die). As Figs. 1 and 2 suggest, the concept of suicide is actually a continuum of related overlapping behaviors and attitudes, including attempts, plans, risk-taking, gestures, and ideas.

Probably the most numerous of all self-destructive behaviors are those that are indirect. It will be recalled from Durkheim's definition that under carefully speci-

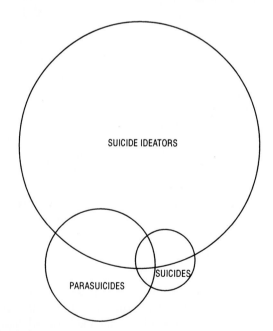

Figure 1 Linehan's overlapping populations model of suicide. [From M. M. Linehan (1986). Suicidal people: One population or two? *In* "Psychobiology of Suicidal Behavior" (J. J. Mann and M. Stanley, eds.), p. 21. New York Academy of Sciences, New York.]

Totally Nonsuicidal

Suicide Ideation (fleeting)

Suicide Ideation (chronic)

Suicidelike Gesture

Diffuse Risky Lifestyle

Suicide Plan (vague, nonlethal)

Suicide Plan (specific, lethal)

Nonserious Suicide Attempt

Serious Suicide Attempt

Completed Suicide

Lowest

Highest

−

+

Figure 2 A continuum of suicidality.

fied conditions indirect self-destructive behaviors are in fact suicides. Since the 1930s and the work of Karl Menninger, the following behaviors have sometimes been regarded as partially or chronically suicidal:

- alcoholism and drug abuse;
- chronic overeating and obesity;
- smoking to excess;
- reckless driving and accident proneness;
- sexual promiscuity and prostitution;
- ignoring needed medications (like insulin);
- gambling;
- risky sports;
- certain crimes.

(See part V in Table I.)

Of course, not all behaviors that are self-destructive are suicidal. Some partial self-destruction is absolutely necessary for growth to occur. In fact the educational process itself requires giving up prior ideas and conditioning in the interest of intellectual growth. The word "pseudocide" could be coined to describe adaptive behaviors that are partially self-destructive. It has long been recognized that many nonfatal suicide attempts are cries for help or appeal behaviors. Some parasuicidal behaviors are attempts at self-transformation and not at all intended to end one's life.

It must also be noted that not all suicides are *individual* suicides, nor do all individual suicides have purely individual causes. In 1978, 911 fundamentalist followers of Jim Jones committed suicide (some were murdered) in Guyana. In AD 72–73, 960 Jews sui-

cided at Masada, rather than become captives of the Romans. More recently, there were 48 Swiss suicides/murders of the Order of the Solar Tradition (October 1994) and 39 suicides by members of the "Heaven's Gate" cult in California (March, 1997). It is not too far-fetched to consider even industrial pollution or nuclear war as social suicides. There are clearly social-structural factors in what seem to be only personal motivations. One thinks of the economic *anomie* of the stock market crash in 1929 in the United States or the role of competition in some Japanese suicides. There can be mixtures of suicide and nonsuicides as well, such as mass murder followed by suicide.

The concept of suicide is not new. Art and history reveal numerous suicides resulting from defeat in battle, dishonor, shame, social obligation, and depressive illness. Probably the first visual reference to suicide is Ajax falling on his sword in a painting done about 540 BC. We also think of Socrates (399 BC), Samson and Judas in the Judeo-Christian scriptures, Dido, Lucretia, Thomas Chatterton, and more recently Yukio Mishima and Marilyn Monroe. The Asian ritual of *seppuku* and the Indian custom of *suttee* should be noted as well.

I. TYPES OF SUICIDE

Suicide is not one kind of behavior. Thus, the explanation of suicide cannot be by a single factor or the province solely of one professional discipline. Suicid-

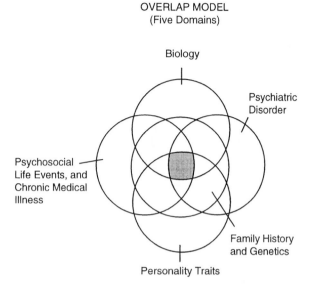

OVERLAP MODEL
(Five Domains)

Biology

Psychiatric
Disorder

Psychosocial
Life Events, and
Chronic Medical
Illness

Family History
and Genetics

Personality Traits

Figure 3 Overlap model for understanding suicidal behavior. [From S. J. Blumethal and D. J. Kupfer (eds.) (1990). "Suicide over the Life-Cycle" p. 693. American Psychiatric Press, Washington, D.C.]

ology cannot be reduced to biology, genetics, psychology, or sociology (Fig. 3). Suicidology is doomed to be an inexact science unless it carefully specifies and delineates its dependent variable. Predictor variables must be tailored to the type of suicide to be investigated, understood, and controlled. For example, some suicides have clear biological markers (especially low brain serotonin levels), whereas other suicides have few or none. Some suicides are interpersonal, but some others are largely intrapersonal. Every individual suicide or type of suicide shares some common predictors with most other suicides, but also has some relatively unique predictors of its own.

Theoretically there can be as many or as few types of suicide as one wishes to specify. Most suicidologists define three or four basic suicide types and one to three subtypes for each basic type. When a suicide researcher goes beyond four to twelve suicide types, he or she runs the risk of having too small a sample to analyze meaningfully (which includes the statistical problem of low power), since suicide is a rare behavior (namely, 1 to 3 per 10,000 in the general U.S. population). For present purposes, the suicidal typologies of Durkheim, Freud and Menninger, Baechler, and Maris will be reviewed briefly. Biological types are sufficiently important to be examined separately (see

Section IV). It should be remembered that here we are focusing on *completed* suicides. Another important continuum of self-destructive types is suicide ideas, gestures, nonfatal suicide attempts, and suicide completions (see Fig. 2).

Emile Durkheim was one of the founders of the scientific study of suicide and published a hallmark study in 1897. Durkheim believed that there were four basic types of suicidal behavior (with seven subtypes and six mixed types). The four basic (pure or ideal) types of suicide are:

1. egoistic
2. altruistic
3. anomic
4. fatalistic.

Egoistic and altruistic suicides are polar types, as are anomic and fatalistic suicides. It must be remembered that Durkheim was interested in broad *social* conditions of suicide, not in the attributes of individual suicides, and that his pure types of suicide are in fact mixed in real life.

Durkheim argued that suicide rates varied inversely with the degree of integration of the social groups of which the individual forms a part. For example, *egoistic* suicide results from excessive individuation or lack of social integration. Other things being equal, Protestants (who tend to advocate a "priesthood of all believers") should have higher suicide rates than Catholics or Jews (who are more socially homogeneous and bound by tradition, catechisms, the Torah, etc.). On an individual level, male skid-row outcasts would be close to the egoistic suicide type. Apathy characterizes egoistic suicides.

Altruistic suicide, on the other hand, results from *insufficient* individuation and is characterized by energy or activity, rather than apathy. The altruistic suicide type typically finds the basis for existence beyond earthly life, as with religious martyrs (like the Jonestown, Waco, and Swiss cults), soldiers who die for their country (like the Japanese *kamikaze* pilots in World War II), or Indian widows who were sacrificed on their husband's funeral pyre (*suttee*).

If egoistic and altruistic suicides refer to social participation or involvement, anomic and fatalistic suicides concern social deregulation or hyperregulation. In a sense then, ego-altruistic suicides operate on the level of horizontal or social restraint, whereas anomic-fatalistic suicides result from vertical or normative restraint. In French, *anomie* literally means without norms and *anomic* suicide results from a temporary but abrupt disruption of normative restraint. Suicides following stock market crashes or high rates of divorce could be considered anomic.

Fatalistic suicide (which Durkheim considers only in a footnote) refers to suicides generated by excessive regulation. One thinks of jail or prison suicides or suicides of very young married couples. Most real-world suicides have both anomic and egoistic traits (and to a lesser degree altruistic and fatalistic traits). Note, too, that suicide varies only negatively with social integration, if the society's or group's norms are against suicide. For example, in Jonestown, Guyana, or the Heaven's Gate cult suicide and social integration were *positively* related. Durkheim maintained that altruistic and fatalistic suicidal types were relatively rare.

Psychiatric and psychological types of suicides were developed by the celebrated Viennese physician Sigmund Freud and the American psychiatrist Karl Menninger. For Freud and Menninger, suicides had three fundamental dimensions, namely, hate, depression (melancholia), and guilt. It followed that all suicides were of three interrelated types:

1. revenge (a "wish-to-kill")
2. depressed (a "wish-to-die")
3. guilty (a "wish-to-be-killed").

Freud thought that the loss of an important love object(s) (such as the death of one's father; see the example of American poet Sylvia Plath) who had been internalized as part of one's own ego ("introjection") often resulted in adult melancholia (depression). Freud claimed that all suicides concerned hostility or a death wish originally directed at an external object (father, lover, etc.). Accordingly, one component of (and one type of) suicide comprised anger, rage, hatred, revenge, or a "wish-to-kill." Menninger called such suicide "murder-in-the-180th degree" or retroflexed anger.

Psychologically trying to kill an introjected object results in ego-splitting and regression. The suicide also feels guilty for harboring murderous wishes toward love objects. Thus, suicides are not only a "wish-to-kill" but also a "wish-to-be-killed" or punished for one's murderous feelings. Finally, suicides are depressed, hopeless, and cognitively constricted. As one's ego is destroyed by self-hatred and guilt, a "wish-to-die" arises. Freud further thought that pro-

cesses of civilization required collected repression of sexuality and aggression, which in turn were channeled into a group superego, fragmenting and diminishing healthy egos even more. In a sense, higher suicide rates were one cost of civilization.

In an interdisciplinary synthesis published in 1979, French social philosopher Jean Baechler contended that there were eleven types of suicide (including non-fatal suicide attempts) fitting into four broad categories:

1. escape
2. aggressive
3. oblative
4. ludic.

With all *escape* suicides the central meaning is to take flight. There are three subtypes: *flight* (to avoid an intolerable situation), *grief* (to deal with a loss), and *punishment* (to atone for a fault). *Aggressive* suicides are directed against another person or persons and consist of four subtypes: *vengeance* (revenge suicides), *crime* (murder-suicides), *blackmail* (putting pressure on another person), and *appeal* (a cry for help or alarm signal).

Oblative suicides are reminiscent of Durkheim's altruistic suicides. There are two subtypes: *sacrificial* (to gain a value greater than one's own life) or *transfiguration* (to obtain a state, like religious martyrdom). Finally, *ludic* suicides are either of the *ordeal* type (to prove something) or the *game* type (to play with or risk one's life). Except for the ludic suicidal types, Baechler's types are mainly an amalgam of Durkheim and Freud's types. It is a conceptual flaw that Baechler includes nonfatal suicide attempters in his typology of suicides.

In my own view, most suicides (about 75%) are of the *escape* or fugue variety. Usually suicides are trying to escape from pain, aging, shame, unhappiness, failure, loneliness, or fatigue. As such, suicide is problem-solving behavior. As much as we do not like to admit it, the only real solution to some life problems is to die. Hopelessness and repeated depressive illness figure prominently into escape suicides. Most other suicides (roughly 20% of all suicides and many nonfatal suicide attempts) are *revenge* or aggressive suicides. Such suicides have strong interpersonal components and include motivations of anger, retribution, or manipulation. A few suicides are *self-sacrificing* or self changing. Such suicides typically give their lives for

Table I A Multiaxial Classification of Suicidal Behaviors and Ideation[a,b]

Suicidal behaviors/ideas	Check (√)	1. Primary type	2. Cer-tainty	3. Lethal-ity	4. Intent	5. Circum-stances	6. Method	7. Sex	8. Age	9. Race	10. Marital status	11. Occu-pation
I. Completed suicides												
A. Escape, egotic, alone, no hope												
B. Revenge, hate, aggressive												
C. Altruistic, self-sacrificing, transfiguration												
D. Risk-taking, ordeal, game												
E. Mixed												
II. Nonfatal suicide attempts												
A. Escape, catharsis, tension reduction												
B. Interpersonal, manipulation, revenge												
C. Altruistic												
D. Risk-taking												
E. Mixed												
F. Single vs. multiple												
G. Parasuicide												
III. Suicidal ideation												
A. Escape, etc.												
B. Revenge, interpersonal, etc.												
C. Altruistic, etc.												
D. Risk-taking, etc.												
E. Mixed												
IV. Mixed or uncertain mode												
A. Homicide-suicide												
B. Accident-suicide												
C. Natural-suicide												
D. Undetermined, pending												
E. Other mixed												
V. Indirect self-destructive behavior (not an exclusive category)												
A. Alcoholism												
B. Other drug abuse												
C. Tobacco use												
D. Self-mutilation												
E. Anorexia-bulimia												
F. Over- or underweight												
G. Sexual promiscuity												
H. Health management problem, medications												
I. Risky sports												
J. Stress												
K. Accident-proneness												
L. Other (specify)												

[a] From R. W. Maris *et al.* (eds.) (1992). "Assessment and Prediction of Suicide," p. 82. Guilford, New York.

[b] Certainty: 0–100%.

Lethality (medical danger to life): zero, low, medium, high (O, L, M, H).

Intent: zero, low, medium, high.

Mitigating circumstances (psychotic, impulsive, intoxicated, confused): zero, low, medium, high.

Method: firearm (F); poison (solid and liquid) (P); poison (gas) (PG); hanging (H); cutting or piercing (C); jumping (J); drowning (D); crushing (CR); other (O); none (N).

Sex: male (M) or female (F).

Age: actual age at event.

Race: white (W), black (B), Asian (A), other (O).

Marital status: married (M), single (S), divorced (D), widowed (W), other (O).

Occupation: manager, executive, administration (M); professional (P); technical worker (T); sales worker (S); clerical worker (C); worker in precision production (mechanic, repairer, construction worker) (PP); service worker (SW); operator, laborer (OL); worker in farming, forestry, fishing (F); other (O); none (N).

others or for a higher cause. Lastly, a small number of suicides (and many nonfatal suicide attempters) are *risk-related*. These suicides lose their lives in attempts to live on the edge of life or to enhance the quality of their life. Most risk-taking suicides are willing to die but death is not their primary objective. Of course, there are subtypes to these four basic suicide types and actual suicides are a mixture of these ideal types (see Table I).

II. PREVALENCE AND EPIDEMIOLOGY

Suicide is and always has been a relatively rare behavior. In general population, one to three persons per 10,000 takes their lives each year. In 1991 in the United states (the latest year for which official statistics were available at this printing), there were 30,810 suicides. This amounts to a rate of suicide of 12.2 per 100,000 population (Table II). Suicide is now the ninth leading cause of death in America, ranking ahead of cirrhosis of the liver (tenth) and just behind AIDS

Table II Mortality from 10 Leading Causes of Death: United States, 1994 (Rates per 100,000 Population)[a]

Cause of death and rank order	Rate	Percentage of total deaths
All causes	875.4	100.0
1. Diseases of the heart	281.3	33
2. Malignant neoplasms, including neoplasms of lymphatic and hematopoietic tissues	205.2	24
3. Cerebrovascular diseases	58.9	24
4. Chronic obstructive pulmonary diseases and allied conditions	39.0	5
5. Accidents and adverse effects Motor vehicle accidents		
All other accidents and adverse effects	35.1	4
6. Pneumonia and influenza	31.3	4
7. Diabetes mellitus	21.8	3
8. HIV infection	16.2	2
9. Suicide	**12.0**	**2**
10. Chronic liver disease and cirrhosis	9.8	2
All other causes	164.8	19

[a] From National Center for Health Statistics (1996). "Vital Statistics of the United States, 1994, Vol. II, Mortality, Part A." U.S. Public Health Service, Washington, D.C.

(eighth) and pneumonia-flu (sixth). Among adolescents, suicide is the third leading cause of death after accidents and homicides (of course, most adolescents do not die at all). For the last several years, suicide has accounted for about 1.5% of all deaths in any given year.

National suicide rates tend to drop in war times (especially during major wars) and rise in economic crises (such as the 1929 great depression in the United States). Suicide rates are highest in western mountain states, like Nevada, Arizona, New Mexico, Montana, and Alaska. Although heart diseases and cancers are still the leading causes of death in most age categories, until late middle-age (i.e., 35–44), three of the five leading causes of death are violent. Accidents, suicides, and homicides rank as the third, fourth, and fifth leading causes of death, respectively, among the middle-aged.

Suicide rates also vary considerably by age, sex, race, marital status, and occupation. Generally, suicide rates increase gradually with age until about age 85, after which they drop off slightly. The increase in suicide rates by age is mainly a male trend. Typically, female suicide rates peak in midlife (about ages 45 to 54), then plateau or decline slightly (Table III). Overall, the ratio of male to female suicide *rates* is three or four to one. The highest suicide rates are consistently observed among white males, followed in declining order by black males, white females, and black females. In 1989, 72% of all suicides were by white males and 18% were by white females (note that 90% of all suicides in the United States are committed by whites). It is estimated that there are eight to twenty nonfatal suicide attempts for every completed suicide. Thus, there could be as many as 600,000 suicide attempts in the United States each year (not all attempts, as opposed to the legal requirement to report all deaths, are reported to emergency rooms). The ratio of nonfatal suicide attempts to suicide completion is thought to be especially high among young people. Between 1960 and about 1977 (the peak year for which teen suicide rate increased), the suicide rate among 15- to 24-year-olds (largely males) rose dramatically (roughly 230 to 250%; see Table III).

Typically, marriage (and having children) protects one against suicide, especially among whites. Suicide rates are higher for the widowed, followed by the divorced and the never-married or single. Studies of the relationships of occupations, social class, and suicide

Table III Death Rates for Suicide, According to Sex, Race, and Age: United States, Selected Years 1950–1989[a]

Sex, race, and age	1950[b]	1960[b]	1970	1980	1989
All races					
All ages, age adjusted	11.0	10.6	11.8	11.4	11.3
All ages, crude	11.4	10.6	11.6	11.9	12.2
Under 1 year	—	—	—	—	—
1–4 years	—	—	—	—	—
5–14 years	0.2	0.3	0.3	0.4	0.7
15–24 years	4.5	5.2	8.8	12.3	13.3
25–34 years	9.1	10.0	14.1	16.0	15.0
35–44 years	14.3	14.2	16.9	15.4	14.6
45–54 years	20.9	20.7	20.0	15.9	14.6
55–64 years	27.0	23.7	21.4	15.9	15.5
65–74 years	29.3	23.0	20.8	16.9	18.0
75–84 years	31.1	27.9	21.2	19.1	23.1
85 years and over	28.8	26.0	19.0	19.2	22.8
White male					
All ages, age adjusted	18.1	17.5	18.2	18.9	19.6
All ages, crude	19.0	17.6	18.0	19.9	21.4
Under 1 year	—	—	—	—	—
1–4 years	—	—	—	—	—
5–14 years	0.3	0.5	0.5	0.7	1.0
15–24 years	6.6	8.6	13.9	21.4	23.2
25–34 years	13.8	14.9	19.9	25.6	24.9
35–44 years	22.4	21.9	23.3	23.5	23.8
45–54 years	34.1	33.7	29.5	24.2	24.2
55–64 years	45.9	40.2	35.0	25.8	26.6
65–74 years	53.2	42.0	38.7	32.5	35.1
75–84 years	61.9	55.7	45.5	45.5	55.3
85 years and over	61.9	61.3	45.8	52.8	71.9
Black male					
All ages, age adjusted	7.0	7.8	9.9	11.1	12.5
All ages, crude	6.3	6.4	8.0	10.3	12.2
Under 1 year	—	—	—	—	—
1–4 years	—	—	—	—	—
5–14 years	—[c]	—[c]	—[c]	0.9	0.9
15–24 years	4.9	4.1	10.5	12.3	16.7
25–34 years	9.3	12.4	19.2	21.8	22.0
35–44 years	10.4	12.8	12.6	15.6	18.1
45–54 years	10.4	10.8	13.8	12.0	10.9
55–64 years	16.5	16.2	10.6	11.7	10.4
65–74 years	10.0	11.3	8.7	11.1	15.4
75–84 years	—	6.6	8.9	10.5	14.7
85 years and over	—	6.9	8.7[c]	18.9[c]	22.2[c]
White female					
All ages, age adjusted	5.3	5.3	7.2	5.7	4.8
All ages, crude	5.5	5.3	7.1	5.9	5.2
Under 1 year	—	—	—	—	—
1–4 years	—	—	—	—	—
5–14 years	0.1[c]	0.1[c]	0.1	0.2	0.3
15–24 years	2.7	2.3	4.2	4.6	4.4
25–34 years	5.2	5.8	9.0	7.5	5.9

Table III *Continued*

Sex, race, and age	1950[b]	1960[b]	1970	1980	1989
White female					
35–44 years	8.2	8.1	13.0	9.1	7.1
45–54 years	10.5	10.9	13.5	10.2	8.0
55–64 years	10.7	10.9	12.3	9.1	7.9
65–74 years	10.6	8.8	9.6	7.0	6.4
75–84 years	8.4	9.2	7.2	5.7	6.3
85 years and over	8.9	6.1	5.8	5.8	6.2
Black female					
All ages, age adjusted	1.7	1.9	2.9	2.4	2.4
All ages, crude	1.5	1.6	2.6	2.2	2.4
Under 1 year	—	—	—	—	—
1–4 years	—	—	—	—	—
5–14 years	—[c]	0.0[c]	0.2	0.1[c]	0.3[c]
15–24 years	1.8[c]	1.3[c]	3.8	2.3	2.8
25–34 years	2.6	3.0	5.7	4.1	3.7
35–44 years	2.0	3.0	3.7	4.6	3.9
45–54 years	3.5	3.1	3.7	2.8	3.0
55–64 years	1.1[c]	3.0	2.0[a]	2.3	2.5
65–74 years	1.9[c]	2.3[c]	2.9[c]	1.7[c]	2.1[c]
75–84 years	—	1.3[c]	1.7[c]	1.4[c]	1.7[c]
85 years and over	—	—[c]	2.8[c]	—[c]	0.6[c]

[a]Data are based on the National Vital Statistics program. For data years shown, the code numbers for cause of death are based on the then current International Classification of Diseases which are described in Appendix II, Tables IV and V.

[b]Includes deaths of nonresidents of the United States.

[c]Based on fewer than 20 deaths.

rates have been equivocal. Some (Durkheim) have found suicide rates to be highest in the upper social classes and in the professional and managerial occupations. Others (Warren Breed and Ronald Maris) have found just the opposite. It is now apparent that within each broad census occupational category there are job types with both high and low suicide rates. For example, among physicians, psychiatrists tend to have the highest suicide rates, whereas surgeons and pediatricians typically have low suicide rates. The predominant method of suicide for both males and females is firearms (see Table IV). Suicide rates are slightly higher in the months of March through May and on Mondays. There has been a spate of recent books focusing on suicide and the life span. Suicide varies by each major age or developmental group. Suicide is a special and somewhat different problem for children, adolescents, young adults, the middle-aged, the young-old, and the old-old.

Table IV Percentage of Completed Suicides (1987, 1991) by Method and Gender[a]

	Gender			
	Male (%)		Female (%)	
Method	1987	1991	1987	1991
Firearms (E955.0–955.4)	64.0	65	39.8	40
Drugs/medications (E950.0–950.5)	5.2	—	25.0	—
Hanging (E953.0)	13.5	15[b]	9.4	13[b]
Carbon monoxide (E952.0–952.1)	9.6	—	12.6	—
Jumping from a high place (E957)	1.8	—	3.0	—
Drowning (E954)	1.1	—	2.8	—
Suffocation by plastic bag (E953.1)	0.4	—	1.8	—
Cutting/piercing instruments (E956)	1.3	—	1.4	—
Poisons (E950.6–950.9)	0.6	—	1.0	—
Other[c]	2.5	—	3.2	—
Totals	100.0	—	100.0	—

[a]Data from National Center for Health Statistics (1990) and Statistical Abstract, U.S. (1994).

[b]Includes suffocation.

[c]Other: Includes gases in domestic use (E951), other specified and unspecified gases and vapors (E952.8–952.9), explosives (E955.5), unspecified firearms and explosives (E955.9), and other specified or unspecified means of hanging, strangulation, or suffocation (E953.8–953.9).

III. PREDICTORS

Prediction of suicide is such a complicated process that some scholars believe that accurate identification of suicidal *individuals* before the fact is impossible. As with many rare events, the major problem is one of too many false positives, that is, identifying someone as a suicide when they are in fact a nonsuicide. Correctly identifying true suicides (positive cases) is referred to as "sensitivity" and correctly identifying true nonsuicides (negative cases) is called "specificity." In one study of 4800 psychiatric patients, Alex Pokorny was able to predict 15 of 67 completed suicides. However, he also got 279 false positives.

Ten major sets of predictors of suicide will now be examined. However, the reader should be cautioned that single-variable predictors seldom explain suicides or suicide rates well. Most suicides exhibit *comorbidity* (i.e., have multiple psychiatric diagnoses) or polymorbidity. There are in fact several different key predictors involved in most suicides. Often predictors interact with each other and vary in relative impor-

tance or weight depending on the type of suicide one is attempting to predict. Most prediction of suicide takes the form of specific scales.

A. Depression, Hopelessness, and Mental Disorders

It should be self-evident that very few happy people take their own lives. We now know that about 15% of those with primary depressive illness will eventually suicide, at a rate of roughly 1% per year. Notice, however, that it follows that 85% of depressives will die a nonsuicidal death. There are also many specific types of depressive illnesses (probably the most common suicide-related diagnosis is major depressive episode). George Murphy and Eli Robins state that 47% of completed suicides in their St. Louis sample were manic-depressives. In another study in England, Brian Barraclough found that 64% of completed suicides had a primary depressive illness. Schizophrenics are also overrepresented among suicides, especially among hospital suicides. Still, the suicide rate among schizophrenics is relatively low compared to that of depressives. Ronald Maris found that several specific depression items were particularly related to completed suicide. These predictors included sleep disturbances, feelings of hopelessness, dissatisfaction, wanting to die, and loss of interest in other people. Aaron T. Beck claims that hopelessness is a better predictor of current suicidal intent than depression. [*See* DEPRESSION.]

B. Alcoholism and Drug Abuse

George Murphy and Eli Robins state that 72% of all completed suicides are depressed (47%) and/or alcoholic (25%). No other single variable was present in even 5% of their St. Louis suicide completers. In a thorough review of many research studies on suicide and alcoholism, Alec Roy and Markku Linnoila concluded that, on average, 18% of all alcoholics will eventually die a suicidal death. Curiously, alcohol abuse may actually protect against suicide early on (perhaps in part by transiently raising hydroxyindoleacetic acid levels). Alcoholic suicides tend to be older males who have been alcoholic for 5 years. Some alcoholics may be using alcohol as self-treatment of depressive illness. Alcoholism aggravates other predictors of suicide as well. For example, alcoholism usually leads to loss of important social relationships.

One study of adolescent suicide attempters discovered that 43% had serious drug problems.

C. Age, Sex, and Race

It is important to remember that the typical suicide tends to be an older white male. Some biological researchers have argued that maleness is more lethal than femaleness at all ages (even *in utero*). Males are more likely to die from most causes (except from obvious sex-linked illnesses and injuries, such as reproductive problems) than females are. Males usually make more violent suicide attempt than females. Perhaps part of these differences is related to male hormones and chromosomal differences. Although the patterns of suicide over the life span are changing, it is still true that suicides tend to develop slowly over a period of years. Everywhere in the world the lowest suicide rates are among the young. Suicides have developmental careers that peak around the ages 40 to 50 in most groups.

D. Prior Suicide Attempts, Ideation, and Suicide Talk

Obviously one has to make a suicide attempt in order to complete suicide. Roughly 15% of all nonfatal suicide attempters go on to complete suicide sometime in their lives. However, most (85 to 90%) older males (over 45 years) make *only* one fatal suicide attempt. Thus, a suicide attempt can be used to predict suicide in such cases but not to prevent suicide. Younger women are more likely than other groups to make repeated suicide attempts, but even they seldom make more than five nonfatal attempts before completing suicide. Only about 15 to 25% of suicides leave suicide notes. In the general population (such as random surveys taken in shopping malls), as many as 20% have considered suicide at some time in their lives. Most suicides do talk about suicide and death before their suicides, if you listen carefully. Of course, the trick is to know which of these suicide comments to take seriously. It is very useful to ask directly if an individual is suicidal, although often the individual will deny suicidal intent. If one should get a positive response to such questions, it is wise to follow-up with questions about the individual's specific plan, method, timing, and other detailed preparations for death. A skilled clinician can also consider a patient's dreams and, use projective tests or even hypnosis to get at suicidal ideation.

E. Lethal Methods

Often a life or death outcome in a suicidal crisis is largely predicted by the availability of a lethal method. Indeed, "suicide proofing" in hospitals, jails, and prisons focuses on removing sharp or protruding objects, clothing and bedsheets that could be torn and made into nooses, and large supplies of medicines that could be used to overdose. In Great Britain, toxic gas supplies to homes were a primary method of suicide. When home gas was detoxified, the suicide rate went down. Potential suicides did not just switch to another method, like hanging or shooting themselves. Although in 1970 in the United States, poisons were the leading method for female completed suicides, by 1987 firearms were the single most common suicide method for both men (64–75%) and women (40%). Many observers have concluded that suicide control in effect amounts mainly to gun control. Hanging is the second most common suicide method (14–15%) for males (especially in jails and hospitals) and poisoning is the second most common method for females (25%).

F. Social Isolation and Negative Interaction

Numerous experiments (e.g., with mice or in confined human sea travel) have demonstrated that prolonged social isolation raises levels of irritability, hostility, and aggression. In Ronald Maris's Chicago research about 50% of completed suicides reported having no close friends at all. Whereas 71% of natural deaths had been "very or fairly close" to their parents, only 41% of nonfatal suicide attempters and 29% of suicide completers were close to their parents. Completed suicides were also much more likely than natural deaths (even though the natural deaths on average were 20 years older) to be unemployed at the time of their deaths (33% versus 16%). In another study, 42% of suicidal depressives lived alone compared to only 7% of nonsuicidal depressives. However, social involvement can *increase* suicide potential if one's social relations are negative and disruptive (as in many revenge suicides). How one came to be alone is probably just as important as the simple fact of social isolation.

G. Suicide in Families and Imitation

It is well known that suicides tend to run in families. Maris discovered that 11% of Chicago suicides had other antecedent first-degree relatives who suicided, whereas none of the natural death controls had suicides in their families. This pattern could be the result of genetic factors or of modeling. For example, the *Journal of the American Medical Association* (1985) investigated suicide and manic-depressive illness in Amish families and claimed that both outcomes were related to a defect in a narrow portion of chromosome 11. Contagion influences on suicide seem to be greatest among the young. *The New England Journal of Medicine* reported in 1986 that the adolescent suicide rate rose about 7% in New York City roughly up to a week after the broadcasting of television network films on adolescent suicide. In the same time frame, adult suicide rates rose only 0.5%.

H. Stress and Negative Life Events

Most suicides are chronic and develop over a period of 40 to 50 years, but against this backdrop acute stress or negative life events can "trigger" a suicide. This is especially the case if stressors have been repeated, as in the third or fourth hospitalization for depressive illness. It must be remembered that stress operates in concert with other predictive factors (i.e., there are interactive effects). Shneidman (in reviewing the Stanford Terman data) found that suicide was especially probable if a key supporting person (a "significant other") was lost, such as a midlife male losing a wife through death or divorce. Other acute negative life events that have shown to exacerbate suicide potential include having to go to prison or jail, shame, major financial failure, and terminal or painful irreversible physical illness.

I. Anger, Irritation, and Dissatisfaction

It must never be forgotten that most suicides are violent aggressive acts. Anger and irritation are frequently the catalytic agents that ignite depression and hopelessness into a suicide attempt. Psychiatrists argue that suicide is in many cases thinly disguised murderous rage that gets turned back upon the eventual suicide. Gerald Brown and Frederick Goodman claim that aggression may in fact be a more basic affectual response to frustration than depression is (since aggression clearly occurs in animals, but depression may not). It is interesting to speculate on the role of lithium carbonate in the treatment of suicidal behavior among manic-depressives. For example, does it treat the depression or the libidinal and aggressive energy? Anger is particularly suicidogenic when coupled with conceptual rigidity. Shneidman says the "four letter word" in suicidology is "only," as in "suicide was the only thing I could do." Suicide has a purging or cathartic effect. Survivors of serious suicide attempts often report feeling in effect that a valve has been opened and their anger or pain level has now been reduced to a tolerable level. There is also an element of atonement or expiation in aggressive self-destructive acting out.

J. Physical Illness

Thirty-five to forty percent of all suicides have significant physical illness. Since most suicides are older males, this is not too surprising. Certainly physical illness in and of itself seldom causes suicide. Maris found that his natural death control group had far more physical illness than his Chicago suicides, but of course none of the natural deaths suicided. Most physically ill individuals (even terminal cancer or AIDS patients) do not suicide. Like other single predictors, physical illness has a complicated relationship to suicide outcomes. Having pronounced these caveats, it does seem that some diseases are more related to suicidal outcomes than others. Suicide is more common among individuals suffering from epilepsy, malignancies, gastroenterological problems, and musculoskeletal disorders (like arthritis or chronic lower back pain).

IV. BIOLOGICAL FACTORS

The biology of suicide is primarily a derivative of the phychobiology and psychopharmacology of depression and is clearly still in its infancy, although a promising beginning has been made.

Perhaps the major finding is a disturbance of the metabolism of central monamines in suicides and depressives. Herman Van Praag hypothesizes that disturbances of central serotonergic functions form the root for disturbances of mood and aggressions. Following the work of Marie Asberg *et al.*, van Praag argues that low levels (below 92.5 nmol/liter) of hydroxyindoleacetic acid (5-HIAA; a metabolite of the neurotransmitter serotonin or 5-HT) in cerebrospinal fluid (CSF) are predictive of suicidal acts, especially of violent suicides. The best-fitting *Diagnostic and Statistical Manual of Mental Disorders-IV (DSM-IV)* diagnoses to low levels of 5-HIAA appears to be "major depressive episode" and "dysthymic disorder." The correlation between 5-HIAA and suicidal behavior

occurs primarily in unipolar depressions. Some of the selective serotonin reuptake inhibitors (SSRIs), like fluoxetine hydrochloride (Prozac), have been thought to paradoxically increase suicide ideation and akathisia in some patients (see Fig. 4). The dexamethasone suppression test (DST) is probably the best-known

---

Can Fluoxetine (Prozac) Antidepressant Pharmacology
Cause Suicidal Ideation or Suicidal Behavior?

Yes: Martin H. Teicher, Carol Glod, and Jonathan
Cole. **American Journal of Psychiatry** 147:2,
February, 1990: 207-210.

No: J. John Mann and Shitji Kapur. **Archives of
General Psychiatry** 48, November 1991: 1027-1033.

Issue Summary:
Yes: Five depressed outpatients and one inpatient
(five females and one male 19-62 years of age) developed
intense suicidal thoughts a mean of 26 days (range was 12-
50 days) after the initiation of fluoxetine treatment.
Upon discontinuing fluoxetine the self-destructive
thoughts faded after about 27 days (range 3-49 days).
Four patients were receiving 60-80 mg of fluoxetine each
day and two received 20-40 mg/day. No patient was
actively suicidal at the time fluoxetine treatment began.
Fluoxetine is known to be a potent and selective
serotonergic uptake inhibitor. Serotonin may well be
related to violent suicidal ideation or action and to
obsessional thinking...fluoxetine may exert a paradoxical
response in some patients (e.g., akathisia or motor
restlessness, anxiety, nervousness, and insomnia might be
special problems with fluoxetine treatment of some
patients).
    No: The hypothesized association (of fluoxetine and
suicidal ideation or acts) is surprising because there is
considerable evidence of serotonin deficiency in patients
who attempt or complete suicide and fluoxetine selectively
enhances serotonergic transmission...In cases like
Teicher's the presence of comorbid disorders, previous
suicidal tendencies or attempts, and a highly variable
time interval between the development of suicidal ideation
and the initiation of fluoxetine treatment...make it
difficult to draw any clear conclusions...If suicidal
ideation or behavior emerges with fluoxetine
administration, it is not simply a complication of higher
doses of fluoxetine...One hypothesis is that increased
suicidality is secondary to the disorganization of certain
vulnerable individuals in response to drug-induced
activation and akathisia...the emergence of
intensification of suicidal ideation and behavior...has
not been proven to be associated with any specific type of
antidepressant.

Figure 4 Can Fluoxetine (Prozac) Antidepressant Pharmacology Cause Suicide Ideation or Suicidal Behavior?

biological measure of depression. In nondepressed persons the synthetic steroid dexamethasone will cause suppression of cortisol secretion for about 24 hr, whereas in roughly 50% of primary unipolar depressives the suppression does not occur. This test is most specific for endogenous depression. Typically patients who are depressed hypersecrete cortisol. [*See* DEPRESSION.]

In a related set of studies by Brown and Goodwin it is argued that while it is commonly assumed in human self-injury that thought initiates the act, the order in fact may be reversed, with thought being used to elaborate and transform suicidal behaviors rather than to initiate them. Brown and Goodwin claim that aggression is a more primitive response to the environment than depression, since aggression is found at all ages and in all species, but significant depression and suicide are not.

Another major biological factor in suicide is clearly alcoholism. As mentioned earlier, Roy and Linnoila surveyed follow-up studies of 27,956 alcoholics, and on the average 18% of all alcoholics in these studies died by suicide. Alcoholic suicides are much more likely to be men rather than women: almost 90% of alcoholic suicide victims are men. The mean age of alcoholic suicides is about 47 years old, with a mean duration of alcoholism of about 25 years. J. B. Ballenger *et al.* suggest that alcoholics have preexisting low brain serotonin levels that are transiently raised by alcohol consumption, but that in turn eventually lead to further depletion of brain serotonin levels. This may in part account for the paradoxical relation of alcoholism to suicide. That is, alcohol raises low brain 5-HT levels, but in the long run it lowers them. Of course, development of physical problems like cirrhosis of the liver also takes time.

One of the earliest biological markers of suicide risk was developed by W. F. Bunney and Jan Fawcett. They discovered that 3 of their 36 depressed research subjects who committed suicide had very high levels of urinary 17-OHCS (hydroxycorticosterone), namely, 9+ mg/24 hr for women and 14+ mg/24 hr for men. Subsequent efforts to replicate 17-OHCS findings have been frustrated by the need for recording long-term elevated levels and the difficulty of collecting 24-hr urine samples from confused, uncooperative psychiatric patients. As a result, Krieger recommends measuring a precursor of 17-OHCS, namely, plasma cortisol. In one study, Krieger found that 13 patients who committed suicide had significantly higher serum cortisol levels than did 39 matched patients who did not suicide. In 1983, Agren found that subjects with a history of serious suicide attempts earlier in life had higher plasma cortisol levels.

The sociobiology of suicide suggests that individuals are especially vulnerable to suicide when they experience severe coping impasses related to relationships to the opposite sex, health, and socially productive behavior. These factors are related to diminished capacities to reproduce and/or to produce for the welfare of one's kin (i.e., to being less biologically fit).

Frederick Struve contents that suicide attempts are positively related to paroxysmal electroencephalogram (EEG) dysrhymthmia. Paroxysmal abnormalities are those that occur suddenly and episodically during a tracing. His research shows that both males and females with suicide ideation had more than twice the incidence of paroxysmal EEG dysrhythmias than did control patients, who were free of suicide and assaultive behaviors. The data suggest further that paroxysmal EEGs are associated with suicidal behavior that is impulsive. Cerebral dysrhythmia may impair emotional and behavioral control during periods of high situational stress.

Finally, Bryan Tanney argues that electroconvulsive therapy (ECT) is very effective in the rapid amelioration of depressive disorders of biological origin, especially the delusional depressives or acutely suicidal patients who cannot wait for antidepressant medications to take effect. The side effects and dangers of ECT are minimal. ECT's action to increase 5-HT2 receptor activity offers support for the diminished 5-HT function in those with suicidal predispositions.

This review of the biology of suicide has left some factors out. Little has been said about genetics, drugs used to suicide or treat suicides, hormones, urinary norepinephrine, CSF magnesium, symptomless autoimmune thyroiditis, and newer diagnostic tools like positron emission tomography (PET), nuclear magnetic resonance (NMR), and other brain imaging. In closing, it should be remembered that suicidal behaviors require a complex multidimensional model (like that in Fig. 3). Biological markers are only one part of this complex etiology. They are not yet specific or predictive of just suicidal behaviors. The accuracy of biological predictors of suicide when used alone is quite weak and, as with other single predictors, produces many false positives.

V. CONCLUSION

Suicide is a conscious act of self-induced annihilation, best understood as a multidimensional malaise in a needful individual who defines an issue for which suicide is perceived as the best solution. Suicide is not one behavior but in fact consists of several discrete but overlapping types, each with its own relatively unique etiology and predictors. Some of the basic types of suicide are escape, revenge, altruistic, and risk-taking. These basic types can be further specified by age, sex, race, and a few other variables.

Suicide is a rare behavior, namely, 1 to 3 per 10,000 in the general population. Suicide is a behavior characteristic of older white males, at least in the Western world. Other relevant factors in the prediction of suicide include depressive illness, alcoholism, suicide ideation and nonfatal attempts, lethality of method, social isolation, suicide in the family, stress, anger, and certain types of mental illness (e.g., schizophrenia and borderline personality disorder). The predominant biological market of suicide at this time is low CSF 5-HIAA, a metabolite of serotonin.

This article has been reprinted from the *Encyclopedia of Human Biology, Second Edition, Volume 8.*

BIBLIOGRAPHY

Blumenthal, S. J., & Kupfer, D. J. (Eds.) (1990). "Suicide over the Life-Cycle." American Psychiatric Press, Washington, D.C.

deCatanzaro, D. (1981). "Suicide and Self-Damaging Behavior: A Sociobiological Perspective." Academic Press, New York.

Evans, G., & Farberow, N. L. (1988). "The Encyclopedia of Suicide." Facts on File, New York/Oxford, England.

Jacobs, D., & Brown, H. N. (Eds.) (1989). "Suicide, Understanding and Responding: Harvard Medical School Perspectives." International Universities Press, Madison, Connecticut.

Kushner, H. I. (1989). "Self-Destruction in the Promised Land: A Psychocultural Biology of American Suicide." Rutgers Univ. Press, New Brunswick, New Jersey.

Mann, J. J., & Stanley, M. (Eds.) (1988). Suicide. *In* "Review of Psychiatry," Vol. 7. American Psychiatric Press, Washington, D.C.

Maris, R. W. (1981). "Pathways to Suicide: A Survey of Self-Destructive Behaviors." Johns Hopkins Univ. Press, Baltimore.

Maris. R. W. (Ed.) (1986). "The Biology of Suicide." Guilford, New York/London.

Maris, W., *et al.* (Eds.) (1992). "Assessment and Prediction of Suicide." Guilford, New York/London.

Murphy, G. (1992). "Suicide in Alcoholism." Oxford Univ. Press, New York.

O'Carroll, P., *et al.* (1996). Beyond the tower of Babel—A nomenclature for suicidology. *Suicide and Life-Threatening Behav.* **26**(3).

Pokorny, A. (1993). Suicide prediction revisited. *Suicide and Life-Threatening Behavior* **23**(1) (Spring), 1–10.

Shneidman, E. S. (1985). "Definition of Suicide." Wiley-Interscience, New York

Support Groups

Benjamin H. Gottlieb

University of Guelph

I. Introduction
II. Definition and Overview
III. Rationales for the Implementation
    of Support Groups
IV. Core Characteristics of Support Groups
V. The Impacts of Support Groups
VI. Linking Group Structure, Processes, and Composition to Outcomes
VII. Potential Risks and Shortcomings
    of Support Groups
VIII. Conclusion

Social Comparison The process of comparing one's own actions, beliefs, abilities, feelings, or other personal characteristics to other people's in order to see how well or poorly one is doing.
Social Support A process of interaction in relationships that can improve coping, esteem, belonging, and competence through actual exchanges of practical or psychosocial resources or through their perceived availability.

A SUPPORT GROUP is composed of from 6 to 10 people who share a similar life stressor, transition, affliction, or noxious habit, and who receive expert information and training, and exchange mutual aid for a predetermined period of time in order to foster improved coping and adjustment. This article will present the rationales for and core characteristics of support groups, it will review evidence concerning their impacts on participants, and it will discuss the varied ways in which the groups' structures and formats affect the support process.

I. INTRODUCTION

Jimmy Armstrong's Mom knows that every Tuesday she is to pack a double dessert in Jimmy's lunch pail because that's the day he attends his K.O.P.S. group in Pioneer Elementary School. The acronym stands for Kids of Parental Separation, but none of the eight sixth-grade students who attend this weekly support group would recall that. All they know is that, halfway through the hour, they get to dump the extra desserts in a pile on the table, and then pick numbers from a hat to determine the order of choosing the desserts. On this, the fifth of eight meetings, the hat will do extra duty because each of the children is supposed to deposit a question, an upset, or a happiness in it, and then, one by one, each child will choose a slip of paper, read it aloud, and discuss it with the group. Ms. James, the social worker from the local community mental health center, and Todd Williams, a high school senior whose parents separated when he was in grade six, will help lead the discussion of each note. They have a way of getting the group to talk about the things they feel angry, sad, and glad about without anyone getting too upset. Last Tuesday, when Jimmy's Mom picked him up from school, she was amazed because, for the first time, Jimmy told her how much he missed Dad, but not the fights she and Dad always had after he went to bed.

Carol Swenson, 48-year-old mother of two active teenagers, and daughter of Sylvia, who was recently pronounced to have Alzheimer's Disease, attends a support group called "Coping with Caregiving." So far, the best thing that has happened in the group is that the leader taught the members some very practical techniques of managing their anger toward their relative and of relaxing by using their imagination and their muscle control. The worst thing that has happened is that, 2 weeks ago, one group member's demented relative actually died from the disease. What made the death so hard to understand is that the deceased was only 63 years old and in perfect physical health. Carol knew this because the group members bring pictures of their relatives to each meeting, and this relative's picture displayed a vital gentleman wearing a pair of shorts that showed off his muscular legs. But as Dr. Morton, the group facilitator, pointed out, there was nothing that could have been done to prevent or postpone the death, and it surely was softened by the love and compassion of a dutiful wife. In fact, although frightening, the death seemed to draw the group members closer together, and some members were beginning to call one another and even get together between meetings. It looked like more lasting friendships were being formed.

At 7:30 A.M., in the Hotel Excelsior's fitness center, 10 middle-aged men sit around a treadmill, 8 of them sitting in pairs while pouring over the results of their latest stress tests. One of the men is their physician and another is an occupational therapist. The members of this "Heart Club" have met together on a biweekly basis for the past 6 months. After the first few meetings in the cardiac rehabilitation unit of the hospital, the group's venue changed to the hotel's fitness center because it was located within easy striking distance of each member's workplace. They had also formed a buddy system so that each of them had a partner to call if he wanted to work out with someone or just talk about how to deal with a boss who had forgotten to ease up on the pressure or with a spouse who was afraid of the exertion required by lovemaking and lawn mowing. Today, the topic was called "Stress: Body and Soul." The format was always the same, beginning with a lecturette by the doctor on the body's response to stress, followed by a half hour of experience swapping among the participants. After the hour meeting, the Heart Club adjourned to the bagelry downstairs to enjoy the food and camaraderie.

II. DEFINITION AND OVERVIEW

These are only three examples of a vast and growing number of support groups that have been organized by virtually every health and human service organization in North America. As the examples reveal, support groups have been convened on behalf of people of all ages who face a wide range of adaptive challenges that call for more specialized or intensive support than is naturally available to them. The groups are typically led or co-led by professionals who meet with from 6 to 10 people who are facing similar stressful events, transitions, or circumstances, or who have in common an affliction, disability, noxious habit, or problem in living. Typically, once composed, the support group is closed to new members, and meets on a regularly scheduled basis for a predetermined period of time and number of sessions. Although there are innumerable variations, the standard format involves the transmission of information and skills by one or more professionals, and exchanges of information and mutual aid among the participants. In principle, the combination of expert and experiential knowledge in the context of a supportive peer culture creates optimal conditions for improved coping and adaptation.

This chapter sets out the distinguishing characteristics of support groups, including their basic structural properties and formats. It explains the theoretical justification for this type of psychosocial intervention, and delves into the social influence processes that arise during the course of the intervention. Drawing on recent reviews of support groups for cancer patients and family caregivers of elderly persons, it weighs the empirical evidence concerning the mental health impact of such groups, spotlighting aspects of their design, composition, and process that deserve greater attention in the future.

III. RATIONALES FOR THE IMPLEMENTATION OF SUPPORT GROUPS

The theoretical rationale that usually introduces studies on the use of support groups to maintain and promote mental health is based on the broad fabric of evidence, reviewed by Cohen and Wills in 1985, revealing that the support of one's personal community of associates has health protective effects. They concluded that it is largely perceived support that cushions the impact of a wide range of stressful life events and transitions. In addition, in 1988, House, Landis, and Umberson reviewed a number of epidemiological studies that showed that social integration was prospectively linked to lower morbidity and mortality. That is, the stress moderating function of social support appears to rest on people's belief that they are reliably allied with certain associates who are prepared to provide needed practical assistance and emotional support. From an epidemiological perspective, the advantage that social support confers on health and survival stems from more abundant contact with family members and friends, as well as from participation in voluntary associations. Support groups therefore cannot be justified on the basis of either the stress-related or epidemiological findings. Such groups do not concentrate on conditioning a psychological sense of support, nor do they intensify or enlarge contact with natural network members.

Instead, support groups are artificial and temporary systems of mutual aid. In large part, they involve the disclosure of personal problems, fears, and doubts to a set of strangers, collective problem solving, and the sharing of coping strategies. Yet evidence for the protective effect of actually receiving support is mixed, with null or negative effects resulting from the damaging psychological implications of seeking help from others or from a miscarried support process. In short, the weight of the empirical evidence suggests that the adaptive value of support derives largely from the perception that one has worth and importance to others and can count on them when needed, rather than from actual exchanges of help and support.

This distinction between perceived and received support generally has not been recognized by those who have mounted support groups. Since the stress-buffering effect of social support is mainly predicated on perceived rather than received support, the most appropriate intervention would be to persuade people that they can gain the support they need from others rather than involving them in a process of mutual aid. On the other hand, it is possible that involvement in the process of mutual aid is a precondition of perceived support, giving rise to perceptions of caring and belonging. In fact, whatever beneficial effects of support groups may occur could result from the psychological sense of support that the group instills rather than from its helping processes. This is why it is particularly important to compose the group in a way that will enable the members to perceive one another as similar peers who are "in the same boat" since this will magnify feelings of connection and mutual responsiveness. This may also help to explain why support group members generally agree that the most beneficial aspects of their group experience were that they felt less emotionally alone, and gained comfort from learning that their thoughts, feelings, and behaviors were normal and validated by others.

A second rationale for introducing support groups is based on the supposition that certain stressful events and transitions create rends in the affected parties' natural networks or overtax the resources or tolerance of network members. In circumstances that call for prolonged help from family members and friends, when stigma and embarrassment surround the affected parties, or when the victims of life events express threatening emotions, close associates are often incapable of providing needed support. In addition, there are instances when the stressor is so severe or pervasive that it restricts social participation, such as when family caregivers withdraw from employment and become homebound in order to supervise a demented relative. Similarly, people with certain medical conditions, diseases, or disabilities must often limit or surrender their social activities, with the attendant loss of valued relationships. [See COPING WITH STRESS; STRESS.]

Short of losing touch with their natural network, people may feel that their associates simply do not understand what they are experiencing or that their difficulties are compounded by their associates' own efforts to cope with the difficulty or by their misguided helping efforts. For example, there is evidence that a spiral of conflict can occur when spouses clash with one another in their ways of coping with a shared stressor, such as a child's serious illness. In 1988, Coyne, Wortman, and Lehman identified several other ways in which support can miscarry and undermine close relationships.

Hence, support groups have been introduced to compensate for absent, insufficient, or irrelevant support from the members' natural networks. For example, based on the findings of their survey of 667 cancer patients, Taylor, Falke, Shoptaw, and Lichtman found in 1986 that 55% wished "very much or somewhat" that they could talk more openly to family members, and 50% said the same thing about friends. More than a third agreed with the sentiment that family members did not truly understand their experience of cancer. However, it is important to note that those patients who had participated in a support group did not differ from those who had not with respect to their network's support, suggesting that other factors come into play in spurring support group participation. In fact, Taylor and colleagues discovered that support group users generally disclosed their cancer-related concerns to a larger number of informal and professional resources than the nonusers, and also had a more extensive help-seeking history than the nonusers. Support group users, or perhaps those who benefit most from such groups, may therefore be particularly disposed to cope by seeking information and feedback, a point that is discussed in greater detail later.

Another rationale for introducing support groups has more to do with the transmission of information, education, and skills to the participants than with the emotional support provided by the group. There are several reasons why a support group is a desirable context for learning new information and skills. First, there may be a significant amount of technical information that all participants want and need to know to improve their comprehension and handling of their situations. The sheer volume of information may require it to be divided into consumable chunks that can be disseminated more efficiently en masse than individually. For example, support groups for cancer patients typically cover the following topics: the causes of cancer; explanation of the diagnoses, tests, and prognoses of the various subtypes of the disease; explanation of the various components of the treatment plan, such as surgery and chemotherapy, and their side effects; discussion of the personal and social impacts of treatment, such as changes in body image and sexuality; education about diet, exercise, and any other life-style changes; explanation and demonstration of the use of prostheses; instruction about relaxation and visualizing techniques; and discussion of issues that arise in communicating needs and problems to both health care providers and network members. [See Cancer.]

Second, it is widely understood that discussion facilitates the learning of new information, an advantage that is offered by the group context. Moreover, since the group meets over a period of several weeks, the information can be divided into manageable units and time can be set aside to practice, review, and reinforce any skills that are taught. For example, in 1994, Gallagher-Thompson described two different cognitive-behavioral group programs for the family caregivers of persons with dementia, one focused on

the alleviation of depression and the other on anger management. In each case, she has planned eight sessions plus two additional booster sessions at 3-month intervals, beginning with an overview of the model, progressing to the acquisition and practice of component skills in the group and at home, and culminating with continued implementation and monitoring of outcomes. [See Dementia.]

Third, aside from their cost-effectiveness compared to individual education and skill training, support groups offer other advantages over individual counseling. The group members can serve as role models for each other, sharing methods of solving problems and coping. In these ways, they are at once being helped and helping others, the latter counteracting feelings of helplessness and enhancing feelings of self-worth and usefulness to others. In addition, the support group can lead to the formation of friendships that endure beyond the formal group sessions, helping to populate the participants' natural networks with similar peers.

IV. CORE CHARACTERISTICS OF SUPPORT GROUPS

A support group can be defined as a small group of from 6 to 10 people who are in similar circumstances that pose an adaptive challenge, and who are convened and led by a professional who provides education and/or training over a period of several weeks, and who facilitates a process of mutual aid among the participants for the purpose of fostering their health and well-being. Support groups differ from self-help groups by virtue of three characteristics: the direct involvement of professionals in the group sessions, their time-limited nature, and the tendency of support groups to look inward rather than outward, generally eschewing advocacy and social action. Support groups differ from conventional group therapy as well. In support groups, professionals do not make psychological interpretations or keep case records, and the members come for information, guidance, emotional validation, and skill training, not for psychotherapy.

While acknowledging the differences between support groups and other similar vehicles of social influence, it is also necessary to highlight the similarities. Like self-help groups, support groups aim to animate a process of mutual aid from similar peers and thereby to temporarily enrich and specialize, if not compensate for deficiencies in the support available from the participants' natural networks. Like psychoeducational groups, support groups provide extra information and training that professionals believe will shore up the participants' coping efforts. Like therapy groups, support groups provide a context that promotes emotional catharsis, social comparison, and mutual identification.

The structural properties of support groups are highlighted in Table I. These properties can be altered in accordance with practical or logistical constraints, and to meet the adaptive challenges faced by the group members. More important, since the support process is likely to be affected by the ways in which the group is structured, practitioners should consider these properties carefully when they design the group. For example, in planning the group's membership (see criteria for matching in Table I), they must consider how the support process would be affected by including spouses in a group for men who are recovering from heart attacks. Would their inclusion preclude discussion of interspousal conflict about the timing of the husbands' return to work? Would the wives express emotions that might threaten the men? Similarly, in designing the individual sessions (see format in Table I), would it be better to adopt a fixed format involving a predetermined series of didactic presentations during the first half of each meeting, followed by experience swapping on any topics during the second half? Or would the members' needs be served better by opening each session with a free-floating discussion and introducing the educational or skill-training component only if and when its subject matter is raised by the group members?

The group's composition should be of paramount importance to those planning support groups since members have to be chosen in a way that will optimize their identification with one another and their participation in the group process. If they do not perceive one another as similar along certain valued dimensions, and if they do not have a common basis for comparing the feelings, actions, and thoughts that arise out of their circumstances, then the group will have little appeal to them and could actually intensify the stress they experience. For example, in composing a support group for the family caregivers of persons with dementia, practitioners must carefully weigh the importance of similarity with respect to the stage and

Table I The Design and Processes of Support Groups

Design Features: The Structural Properties of the Support Group

Venue or setting
- Geographic proximity to participants
- Informal or agency/institutional setting
- Total number, length, and duration of sessions
- Interval between sessions

Leadership and facilitation
- One or more professionals only
- Co-led by a participant and a professional
- Rotating professional leaders

Composition
- Number of participants
- Open or closed membership
- Geographic proximity of participants to one another

Criteria for matching, including
- Gender, age, socioeconomic, ethnic, racial, and verbal skill factors
- Severity of the stressor
- Stage of coping with stressor
- Intensity of distress and emotional expression
- Extent of mobilization of personal coping skills

Format
- Structured vs. unstructured agenda and allocation of time
- Balance between expert input and experience swapping
- Rotating or continuous leadership
- Use of contracts vs. no contract
- Homework assignments (e.g., skill practice) vs. none
- Prescribed extra-group contacts among participants or not
- Instructions regarding extra-group exchanges of support or not
- Occasional participation of network associates or not

Mechanisms of Action: Processes Linking Support to Outcomes
- Catharsis: emotional ventilation
- Normalization of emotions
- Validation: affirmation of valued role and identity
- Helper-therapy: helping others helps oneself
- Reduction of uncertainty in novel circumstances
- Modeling of coping strategies
- Hope and a positive outlook
- Making meaning of the adversity and consolidating a new or changed identity
- Predictability and anticipatory coping
- Social comparisons

severity of the disease (e.g., early- versus late-stage Alzheimer's), the relationship between the caregiver and relative (e.g., spouses versus daughters and daughters-in-law), and the two parties' living arrangement (e.g., living in the same or different households). Other stressor related, demographic, and contextual variables may also affect the members' rapport and ease of communication, such as their education, ethnicity, income, and gender, their family and occupational contexts, and their level of physical and emotional functioning at the time they join the group.

To date, there has been little experimentation with alternative ways of composing groups and virtually no follow-ups of people who have dropped out of groups in order to determine the social dimensions that impede and facilitate communication and exchanges of information and support. Nor have prospective group members been canvassed about who they would and would not prefer to meet with. Consequently, there is no empirical basis for deciding how to compose a support group to optimize members' attraction, active participation, and social learning and support.

As for a theoretical rationale for the group's composition, social comparison theory offers abundant but inconsistent predictions about the benefits and risks of both downward and upward comparison processes, leaving considerable ambiguity about how to engineer a social milieu that will lower distress, and maintain or increase self-esteem as well as other bases of self-evaluation. Specifically, as Gibbons and Gerrard pointed out in 1991, there is a vast literature testifying to the esteem-enhancing functions of downward social comparison or comparisons to people or even imaginary targets perceived to be worse off than oneself on certain dimensions. There is also an extensive list of papers documenting that self-esteem is bolstered when people assimilate their status to that of upward targets, and that they gain useful information from their observations of superior others. As Collins observed on the basis of her 1996 review of the social comparison literature, "Ultimately, positive self-regard depends on striking the proper balance between the number of people who are better than oneself and the number who are worse" (p. 65). Unfortunately, her conclusion provides little guidance regarding the optimal composition of a support group.

Even if the literature yielded more consistent propositions about the dimensions of comparison that enhance self-appraisals and mood, it contains no information about how the social comparison process might affect group cohesion and the exchange of support. For example, it is conceivable that exposure to a target who is perceived to be coping less effectively than oneself might raise one's self-esteem, but it may also result in rejection of the target due to the distressing affect that he or she is displaying. Indeed, most people who refuse invitations to join a support group

or who drop out explain that they do not want to expose themselves to others' distress and complaints.

A second factor that militates against systematic experimentation with group composition is logistical. Those who convene support groups usually do not have the luxury of selecting the optimal membership because there are too few candidates for the groups to match people on the relevant dimensions, and most agencies do not have the resources or know-how to screen prospective participants in advance. For example, if the local chapter of the Alzheimer Disease Association attracts only 10 caregivers who are interested in attending a support group, half of whom are elderly spouses and half middle-aged daughters, and their demented relatives range from mild to severe cases, then the organization is ethically bound to offer them a group despite these apparent differences. Moreover, even when a large number of prospective group participants is available for group assignment, if a formal evaluation is in the offing, then random allocation of participants to experimental and control or comparison conditions may preclude appropriate matching within groups.

In sum, although there is little doubt that the social comparisons that occur both overtly through discussion and covertly through observation constitute a fundamental process whereby support groups influence adaptation, there exist no guidelines regarding ways of structuring the group's membership to optimize the support process and beneficial outcomes arising from it. Short of exploring how the support process and its outcomes are affected by systematically varying certain dimensions of comparison, such as the stage and severity of the members' stressful experience or their apparent mastery of their circumstances, researchers can gather information directly from members about their preferences for and reactions to their fellow sufferers. If an individual with a mild case of Multiple Sclerosis does not wish to see and hear from someone who is confined to a wheelchair due to the disease's progression, then they can report this before or after their first group session. Similarly, if a teenager who is acutely distressed by his parents' recent separation finds it reassuring to talk to youths who are calmer now that their parents have concluded the divorce and each has established a new household, then they can report this. Such information can be immensely helpful to other practitioners by informing their decisions about the composition of subsequent support groups, and it can enrich social comparison theory by adding knowledge based on intervention.

V. THE IMPACTS OF SUPPORT GROUPS

To properly assess the impacts of support groups, it is necessary to adhere to the requisites of a scientific evaluation. This means that ideally, a reasonably large number of participants should be randomly assigned to support and control or comparison groups, and outcomes should be standardized and examined well after the formal intervention concludes. In addition, it is desirable to carefully document the actual substance of the intervention so that any observed effects can be appropriately attributed to the intervention maneuvers. For example, if the process of experience swapping consumes virtually all the group's time, then any effects can be reliably attributed to this component of the intervention. However, few investigators have been able to devote the resources and develop the tools needed to gauge the differential impact of the several components that typically comprise support groups. These components may include educational input from expert sources, skill training, supportive contact among members within and between group sessions, homework assignments, and more general group discussion and problem solving. Hence, to date, evaluations of this multifaceted social intervention have not isolated the effects of its components.

As one might expect, it is impossible to offer any general conclusions about the mental health impact of support groups because of the sheer volume of studies that have been completed and the many differences in the characteristics of the participants and their stressful predicaments, the structure, format, and content of the group sessions, the "dosage" (number, length, and duration of the group sessions), as well as the measures used to tap outcomes. Although there are many individual reports of support groups that have had impressive and relatively lasting desirable mental health effects, there are also many articles reporting marginal or null effects.

There have been three critical reviews of the literature on the effects of support groups for family caregivers of elderly relatives (Bourgeois, Schulz, and Burgio in 1996, Lavoie in 1995, and Toseland and Rossiter in 1989), and two concerning their effects on

cancer patients (Fawzy, Fawzy, Arndt, and Pasnau in 1995, and Helgeson and Cohen in 1996). Generally, the evidence strongly suggests that the typical, short-term support group that meets on a weekly basis for 6 to 10 sessions does not have a comparative edge in terms of its mental health effects. The impact of longer term groups, specifically, groups that meet for at least 6 months, shows more promise. However, as discussed later, the group's duration is not the only factor that affects its success.

A. Support Groups for Caregivers of Elderly Relatives

Although the evidence is mixed, the general consensus is that groups for the caregivers of elderly family members have a negligible impact on mental health outcomes, measured by widely accepted psychiatric symptom, general distress, and burden scales, and by indices of socioemotional functioning. Toseland and Rossiter's careful review of this literature led them to conclude that the groups should be composed of more homogeneous subgroups of caregivers, such as separate groups for spouses and adult children, and that they should last longer, gauge more specific behavioral changes, and experiment with alternative formats and curricula. Finally, both Lavoie and Bourgeois, Schulz, and Burgio suggest that support groups may not address the unique circumstances and needs of individual caregivers, and therefore in many cases the outcomes that are measured are not relevant.

Generally, family caregivers report high levels of satisfaction with their group experience, and deeply regret the fact that the group must terminate after the prescribed number of sessions. This suggests that a short-term model of practice is inappropriate for a population that is dealing with a host of chronically stressful demands that change over time. Most family caregivers require continuing support, training, and guidance, in addition to a range of community services that can alleviate the objective burdens they shoulder. As Lavoie observed in 1995, "To expect to change well-established behaviors such as personal coping styles, or deep-seated dynamics such as anxiety or depression over the illness of a loved one and the need to care for that person, by means of a limited number of group meetings with peers could seem like wishful thinking" (p. 589).

Even more fundamental questions can be raised

about the nature and meaningfulness of the mental health outcomes that have been gauged. Is it appropriate to reduce feelings of sadness and loss when such feelings are to be expected under the harsh circumstances imposed by dementia? Should a statistically significant reduction in anxiety or depressive affect be considered meaningful apart from its clinical significance? Are there other mental-health-related variables that may be more important to the subjective well-being of family caregivers, and more amenable to the influence of a support group? For example, through group discussion and social comparisons, the members may come to adopt a more sanguine perspective on their situation, normalize their feelings of frustration and loss, and even rid themselves of the guilt they anticipate experiencing if they were to avail themselves of respite programs and solicit more help from other family members. These are important potential contributions of the support group, yet they have not been systematically addressed in evaluations of its effects.

B. Support Groups for Cancer Patients

Reviews of the mental health effects of support groups for cancer patients have also yielded mixed results. In 1995, Fawzy, Fawzy, Arndt, and Pasnau identified 15 "group interventions" for cancer patients, the majority of whom were women who participated in heterogeneous groups composed of patients with mixed diagnoses and with both initial and recurrent/metasticized disease. With one exception, the groups met from 4 to 11 times over a period of from 2 to 8 weeks, and typically included education, stress management (coping; relaxation) training, and mutual aid. In 1996, Helgeson and Cohen identified seven evaluations of support groups that involved various degrees of peer discussion and education from expert leaders, as well as four studies that compared the effects of group discussion only to the effects of education only or combined education and group discussion. Both reviews underscore the fact that many of the studies did not meet the requirements of a formal randomized controlled trial (RCT).

Fawzy and colleagues concluded that separate support groups should be convened for cancer patients who are newly diagnosed or in the early stage of treatment versus those who have advanced metastatic disease. They suggest that the former population benefits most from a structured, multifaceted, short-term program that combines didactic education, skill training, problem solving, and mutual support, whereas the latter population benefits most from a long-term, weekly support group that concentrates on shoring up the participants' daily coping and pain management skills, while offering the empathic understanding and emotional validation of peers. Both reviews cite the support groups for metastatic breast cancer patients that Spiegel, Bloom, and Yalom organized in 1981, as exemplary of the kind of long-term program of support that appears to be needed by and of benefit to patients with advanced disease. It consisted of weekly, 90-minute sessions that lasted for 1 year and focused on ". . . the problems of terminal illness, including improving relationships with family, friends, and physicians and living as fully as possible in the face of death" (p. 527). Each of the three groups they organized was co-led by a psychiatrist or a social worker and a counselor whose breast cancer was in remission. The group's main emphasis was on the development of an emotionally sustaining culture, not on educational material supplied by the leaders. Finally, participants also had supportive contact with one another outside the formal group sessions, and after the 1-year mark of data collection, the survivors continued to meet as a group for a second year and informally thereafter.

The findings of this RCT underscore the importance of offering a relatively long-term program of support, and of measuring various intervention effects at several points in time. Specifically, compared to the control group, those in the three support groups reported better adjustment after a year but not at the 4-month or 8-month time points. That is, the effects of the intervention on total mood disturbance, and on the subscales of tension-anxiety, vigor, fatigue, and confusion appear to have been cumulative in nature. Moreover, in 1989, Spiegel, Bloom, Kraemer, and Gottheil presented a 10-year follow-up of the study participants that revealed that the intervention increased survival by 18 months.

In comparing the effects of short-term groups that concentrate on discussion and support with the effects of groups that concentrate on education, Helgeson and Cohen tentatively conclude that the latter demonstrate superior adjustment benefits. This is not to say that the support and discussion component is superfluous, but that the education component is necessary to achieve desired effects. It may be that people who have been diagnosed with cancer need the technical information that professionals provide, and gain a stronger sense of security from the professional's presence and special interest in the group members. It is also possible that feelings of control and predictability are uniquely predicated on the authoritative information and skill training professionals provide. In contrast, Helgeson and Cohen suggest that groups that concentrate strictly on peer support may undermine feelings of control if they disrupt denial or other emotionally avoidant modes of coping. In addition, they may adversely affect participants' reactions to their illness by exposing them to peers who are losing their battle with cancer, or who raise frightening topics that are not worked through with professional guidance, or whose cancer site and stage are so different that they cannot validate one another's emotional experience. In the future, more careful measurement will be needed to identify these and other potential mediating processes associated with the peer and professional sources of influence in the group.

VI. LINKING GROUP STRUCTURE, PROCESSES, AND COMPOSITION TO OUTCOMES

There is a tight interdependence among the structure, composition, and process of support groups. Leaders can place varying emphases on the experience-swapping, behavioral-training, and information-dissemination functions of the group, thereby affecting the group's cohesion, intimacy, and overall social climate. Leaders can concentrate on either the emotional or the instrumental coping assistance offered by the group, and establish norms governing the extent and style of disclosure, confrontation, and affective release. There are also vast differences in the training and orientation of leaders themselves, a factor that is rarely taken into account in interpreting and comparing the effects of the groups. Moreover, the credentials and style of the leaders can play a critical role in recruiting and retaining group participants. For example, experience shows that support groups for male cardiac patients are more successful when the leader is a staff member with medical training in heart disease, the group is introduced as a routine aspect of medical care, and is called a rehabilitation group rather than

a support or therapy group, and when wives are not included in the same group because they would interfere with their husbands' tendency to resist discussing their feelings about the threatening aspects of their condition. Hence, the group's composition can powerfully affect its process.

A. Documenting Support Group Processes

There is no dearth of hypotheses about the mediating processes or mechanisms at work in support groups. Biological pathways include alterations in immune system function, blood pressure, and urinary cortisol, whereas behavioral changes range from improved adherence to recommended dietary and drug regimens to changes in modes of coping, including the use of community services. The psychological factors that have been cited most frequently as potential mediators include the 10 listed at the bottom of Table I. At present, little is understood about the complex ways in which psychological, biological, and behavioral changes interact to produce durable and important outcomes such as the improvements in mood and survival of the cancer patients who were involved in the support groups organized by Spiegel, Bloom, Kraemer, and Gottheil in 1989.

It is therefore necessary to begin documenting aspects of the process of support groups, and systematically varying their structure and emphasis to determine how the process is altered and how it affects the observed outcomes. In addition to varying the proportion of time that is devoted to education and peer discussion, group planners can vary the emphasis they place on various goals. For example, Lavoie maintains that those who have organized support groups for family caregivers have aimed to reduce the participants' stress, whereas the participants themselves have typically aimed to improve and gain confidence in their caregiving skills. Obviously, some attention should be paid to participants' goals at the outset of the intervention, and different groups can be formed to address different goals. Even when support groups are designed to blanket all the principal sources of stress and to foster improved coping, as is the case in groups for children whose parents are divorcing or for recently bereaved people, large differences among individuals in the salience of certain stressors and in their need for supplemental coping resources may call for more specialized groups. It is also important to acknowledge that even when groups are initially structured along the same lines, each will develop its own culture and participants who are in the same group will experience the support process differently (J.-P. Lavoie, personal communication, August 19, 1996).

In addition, as Lavoie and Bourgeois, Schulz, and Burgio observe, implementation evaluation that involves assessment of the intervention process and structure is so rare that the details regarding the psychoeducational maneuvers, the leadership, the balance between mutual aid, skill training, and education, and the group's composition are not available for the purpose of replication or verification that the intervention is faithful to its blueprint. Without knowing what actually transpired over the life of the group, it is impossible to determine whether the process accurately reflected the theory that links the intervention's content to its intended outcomes. For example, if support groups for the family caregivers of persons with dementia concentrate on the acquisition of anger management skills, then it is necessary to adopt outcome criteria that reflect this specific goal, and to ensure that the requisite amount of time is spent on effectively teaching these skills and proficiently applying them at home. Similarly, if the intervention aims mainly to decrease stress and uncertainty by disseminating authoritative information about the nature and typical course of dementia, and by introducing the specialized support of similar peers, then measures of knowledge and of global stress or subjective burden should be adopted as outcomes, and members' perceptions of their similarity, the support they exchange, and the information they receive should be tapped through formative evaluation.

B. Support as a Means or as an End

When program planners consider participants' needs for supplemental coping resources, they must assess not only the kind of resources that are needed, but also how long they will be needed. Earlier, evidence was presented in favor of the efficacy of longer term groups for patients with advanced cancer and for family caregivers. It stands to reason that the duration of the support group should be matched to the duration of the adjustment demands faced by the participants. Chronic disorders, disease, and life difficulties may require ongoing or prolonged support, whereas time-

limited acute life events and transitions may be addressed through a short-term group. Moreover, those designing support groups may wish to use the group as a way of permanently adding similar peers to people's natural social networks. This may be called for when existing network members are unable or unwilling to extend the kinds of practical help and emotional support that are needed because they feel helpless, drained or threatened, or because they have become critical, emotionally overinvolved, or overprotective. Among the techniques that can be used to accomplish this is to explicitly state this goal at the outset of the group, informing members that they can choose to continue to meet on their own following the final formal group meeting, and that a resource person can be made available to them when needed. In addition, members can be encouraged to have contact with one another between the group sessions, either informally or by setting up a rotating or permanent buddy system with or without a specific agenda. For example, buddies can be encouraged to simply call one another when they need extra support and dialogue, or to practice together the skills they have learned in the group. Naturally, to examine the impact of such supplemental support, records must be kept of the kind and amount of extra-group contact. Evaluation researchers should also keep in mind that social support may be an end in itself, rather than a means to an end. That is, the goal of some groups may be to combat social isolation by establishing durable and intimate dyadic or group ties among the members, as in the case of support groups for chronically mentally ill persons or teenaged, sole-support parents. Other groups may concentrate on mobilizing support as a resource for resisting stress-induced disease, illness, or maladjustment, or for promoting more positive functioning.

C. Group Composition and the Bases of Similarity

As discussed earlier, as long as the members perceive one another as similar peers, social comparison will be an ongoing covert process throughout the course of the group. Ideally, in composing the group, some thought should go into ways of exploiting this psychological process to the best advantage of the participants. For example, in most self-help groups there is a "veteran sufferer" who serves as a model of effective coping and thereby instills hope and motivation to comply with the group's behavioral prescriptions. Social comparison theory also postulates that, to accomplish its stress-reducing effect, the companions must be perceived to be reacting relatively calmly to their situation, suggesting that support groups are not appropriate during periods when people are feeling emotionally overwhelmed. It is therefore advisable to recruit participants only after they have recovered from the initial shock of a crisis, and are ready to commence a structured and paced social support program.

Once it is conceded that experiential similarity serves as a stronger basis for mutual identification and empathic understanding than structural similarity based on age or marital status, for example, questions arise concerning how similar the common experience must be in order for the participants to attend and compare themselves to one another, and to develop bonds of affection and belonging. For example, for a group of recent widows, their bereavement is probably not sufficient to level differences based on the cause and age of their partner's death. It is unlikely that widows whose husbands had died of heart attacks would perceive themselves to be "in the same boat" as widows whose husbands had been murdered or killed in a traffic accident or who had died in the line of wartime fire or by taking their own lives. The same careful consideration of the bases of similarity is warranted in planning the composition of virtually every group for people who have undergone stressful life events and transitions, such as parental death or divorce, retirement, new parenthood, job loss, serious accidents, and illness diagnoses. Three factors in particular warrant consideration: (1) the contextual or situational parameters that are likely to be most salient to the participants; (2) factors that are known to affect people's risk status; and (3) the probable trajectory the participants will experience. For example, in composing support groups for the family caregivers of elderly relatives, program planners should recognize that caring for a relative afflicted with dementia poses greater risk to the mental health of the caregiver than caring for a frail but cognitively intact relative, and that the future course of dementia is distinctly different from other disabilities and conditions. Hence, it would not be advisable to compose a group that combines caregivers in these contrasting situations. Of course, if the prospective participants are children or youth, it is necessary to ensure that the group content and composition is developmentally appropriate.

Finally, the similarity of the participants not only bears on their ability to relate and compare themselves to one another, but it also affects the substantive content of the educational component and ultimately, the impact of the intervention. As noted earlier, reviews of the support group literature have been consistent in their criticism of the heterogeneity of groups, arguing that interventions will impact differently on various subgroups of participants and suggesting that null results may mask differential effectiveness for such subgroups. In addition to structural and experiential differences among participants, they may also differ on the basis of the stage of the condition or problem they face, their use of both informal and formal supports in the community, and a number of personality and coping factors that affect their receptiveness to and benefit from this type of intervention.

D. Adapting the Group to Personal Coping Styles

This brings us to the larger question concerning the personal characteristics that distinguish those who gravitate toward support groups from those who decline participation, and those who are most likely to benefit from those who do not benefit or who may be adversely affected by joining such a group. Although only rarely reported, refusal rates for support groups are quite high, and to a lesser extent, attrition is a problem as well. Aside from the standard psychological (e.g., stigma and fear of disapproval or rejection) and logistical (e.g., access, scheduling, and coverage of competing demands such as childcare) impediments to participation in any social program, support groups pose some unique threats and offer a particular way of coping with one's difficulties that does not have universal appeal or benefit.

The threats posed by support groups include a fear of becoming overwhelmed by attending to and disclosing one's difficulties, and by exposing oneself to the more severe difficulties faced by other group members, especially if those difficulties preview one's own possible fate. Although some members may benefit from this because of the anticipatory coping and sense of control such advance information may promote, others may cope most effectively by keeping such information out of conscious awareness. In short, differences in people's coping styles may powerfully affect their interest in and the value they gain from participating in support groups. Specifically, differences in information and help seeking, and more generally, avoidant versus approach-oriented coping styles under threat, may distinguish between those who are attracted to and make good use of the group experience and those who do not. In plain language, some people deal with threat by seeking as much information about it as they can and by venting their fears and emotional distress, whereas others maintain their equilibrium best by avoiding threatening information and blunting their emotions. In their 1996 review of psychosocial interventions for patients with chronic physical illnesses, Devins and Binik cite numerous studies revealing that social programs that concentrate on imparting information are more effective when they are matched to the participants' information processing style. Hence, "blunters" may fare better with more structured, task-centered, behavioral intervention protocols, whereas "monitors" may respond best to formats that provide plentiful details about the stressful context, and that allow them to discuss their feelings and experiences, and to ask questions.

Depending on how they are marketed and actually run, support groups may be more or less threatening or attractive to people with contrasting information- and support-seeking coping styles. As noted earlier, if they smack of group therapy with all of its emotional trappings and disclosure requirements, or if their advertisements promise to deliver detailed information about the more threatening aspects of the present and future, then they are likely to be shunned by and maladaptive for those who tend to regulate their emotions by avoidance and distraction. Indeed, the combination of unbridled emotional expression among peers and abundant information from experts is likely to drive the blunters away, while appealing to the monitors whose emotional self-regulation and sense of control are augmented by these two components. It follows that, in both advertising and implementing groups, the format, emotional climate, and type of information supplied should be pitched differently, depending on the prospective participants' coping styles. Where feasible, a measure of their information-processing style can be used as a screening and group placement tool. If this is not possible and people with different styles are assigned to the same group, then potential moderating effects of these coping styles can be tested to determine whether they have influenced intervention outcomes.

VII. POTENTIAL RISKS AND SHORTCOMINGS OF SUPPORT GROUPS

If prospective participants are geographically dispersed, as is the case for people who reside in rural areas, then logistical difficulties may prevent them from attending a support group. Alternatives that have recently been initiated are to create telephone and electronic mail support groups. By means of teleconferencing and occasional face-to-face visits, much of the experiential knowledge and a substantial amount of emotional and esteem-relevant support can still be exchanged in such groups. A second shortcoming is that support groups do not allow for the individualization of helping. Thus, what is gained in cost efficiency through the group format is lost in personalized attention. However, in many instances, support groups are designed to supplement rather than to substitute for the individual counseling or treatment offered by mental health or medical practitioners, and so members' unique needs are addressed. Moreover, when individual counseling precedes support group participation, the counselor may be able to make more judicious judgments about group assignments. As Gottlieb pointed out in 1988, there are also several types of one-to-one formats for marshaling support that may be better suited to people's needs and preferences than a group intervention. Hence, practitioners should consider and even compare the effectiveness of alternative support strategies.

Third, support groups can have adverse social repercussions. They can threaten natural network members who perceive the group as an affront to the support they offer instead of recognizing that the support of similarly stressed peers is a vital complementary coping resource. The group leaders can guard against such resentment, injury, or backlash from the participants' network members by not only advising the participants to explain the special value of the support group, but also by inviting key network members to attend a meeting of their own in which they can ask questions, air their concerns, and learn how they can optimize the group's impact on their associate. A related social and ethical concern that has not received sufficient attention from group planners is the potential negative effect of withdrawing the peer support when the final group session has ended. In virtually every published report of support groups, the members lament the group's termination. This suggests that many groups do, in fact, terminate prematurely and ought to have a longer course or at least offer the members the option of continuing to meet on their own as a mutual aid group or at least to socialize with one another. Naturally, this will not be possible if the participants are minors or if they are dealing with such sensitive or technical matters that they require professional guidance. In any case, it behooves the group leaders to carefully plan for the group's termination, and to monitor any rebound effects that may result therefrom.

Finally, as is the case for all group interventions, there is the possibility that a negative emotional contagion will spread through the group, especially if the members face circumstances that are known to deteriorate over time or suffer from a condition that has a poor prognosis. Many practitioners question the wisdom of bringing together people with terminal diseases such as cancer because they fear that they will only exacerbate their distress and further demoralize them. Although this adverse development is certainly possible, its likelihood can be minimized by leaders who carefully monitor and control the group's affective tone. Moreover, those who clinicians worry about most are usually people who suffer from both social and emotional isolation, and who therefore are most likely to benefit from the empathic understanding, companionship, and solidarity that a support group can offer. It is also important to keep in mind that people want to be well and that the support group can teach participants how to reinforce one another's wellness rather than their distress.

VIII. CONCLUSION

If there is a single message that deserves emphasis it is that practitioners need to attend more closely to the composition and duration of support groups, and apportion the time allotted to expert information and peer interaction in a way that suits the participants' needs and coping styles. Where possible, the group's composition should be determined by taking into account at least three sets of similarity factors, namely, experiential similarity, structural similarity, and similarity in the members' information-processing style of coping. Sustained rather than brief groups are called

for and have proved more effective for chronic life difficulties, role strain, and other circumstances of unremitting demand, whereas short-term groups are called for during periods of crisis and transition.

Support groups have broad, although not universal, appeal. For people who tend to cope by seeking information and affiliation with similar peers, such groups can reduce distress and promote adjustment. Yet the processes implicated in the group's ameliorative psychosocial impact are not well understood. For this reason, more careful documentation is needed of the physiological, behavioral, and psychological mechanisms that underlie this mode of intervention. In addition, there is a need for comparative studies that systematically vary the group's structure, composition, and emphases, in order to discern how the process and outcomes are affected. Although mental health ranks among the most important of these outcomes, the support group may also give the participants a sense of reliable alliance and belonging that can dispel their feelings of emotional isolation. At bottom, the support group is a highly specialized personal community that gives full expression to the human impulse to care for others and to be cared for by them.

BIBLIOGRAPHY

Bourgeois, M. S., Schulz, R., & Burgio, L. (1996). Interventions for caregivers of patients with Alzheimer's Disease: A review and analysis of content, process, and outcomes. *International Journal of Aging and Human Development, 43,* 35–92.

Cohen, S., & Wills, T. A. (1985). Stress, social support, and the buffering hypothesis. *Psychological Bulletin, 98,* 310–357.

Collins. R. L. (1996). For better or worse: The impact of upward social comparison on self-evaluations. *Psychological Bulletin, 119,* 51–69.

Coyne, J. C., Wortman, C.B., & Lehman, D. R. (1988). The other side of support: Emotional overinvolvement and miscarried helping. In B. H. Gottlieb (Ed.), *Marshaling social support* (pp. 305–330).

Devins, G. M., & Binik, Y. M. (1996). Facilitating coping with chronic physical illness. In M. Zeidner & N. Endler (Eds.), *Handbook of coping* (pp. 640–696). New York: John Wiley & Sons.

Fawzy, F. I., Fawzy, N. W., Arndt, L. A., & Pasnau, R. O. (1995). Critical review of psychosocial interventions in cancer care. *Archives of General Psychiatry, 52,* 100–113.

Gallagher-Thompson, D. (1994). Clinical intervention strategies for distressed caregivers: Rationale and development of psychoeducational approaches. In E. Light, G. Niederehe, & B. D.

Lebowitz (Eds.), *Stress effects on family caregivers of Alzheimer's patients* (pp. 260–277). New York: Springer.

Gibbons, F. X., & Gerrard, M. (1991). Downward comparison and coping with threat. In J. Suls and T. Wills (Eds.), *Social comparison: Contemporary theory and research* (pp. 317–346). Hillsdale, NJ: Erlbaum.

Gottlieb, B. H. (1988). Support interventions: A typology and agenda for research. In S. Duck (Ed.), *Handbook of personal relationships: Theory, research and interventions* (pp. 519–542). Chichester, England: John Wiley & Sons.

Helgeson, V. S., & Cohen, S. (1996). Social support and adjustment to cancer: Reconciling descriptive, correlational, and intervention research. *Health Psychology, 15,* 135–148.

House, J. S., Landis, K. R., & Umberson, D. (1988). Social relationships and health. *Science, 241,* 540–545.

Lavoie, J.-P. (1995). Support groups for informal caregivers don't work! Refocus the groups or the evaluations? *Canadian Journal on Aging, 14,* 580–595.

Spiegel, D., Bloom, J., & Yalom, I. D. (1981). Group support for patients with metastatic breast cancer. *Archives of General Psychiatry, 38,* 527–533.

Spiegel, D., Bloom, J., Kraemer, H. C., & Gottheil, E. (1989, October 14). Effect of psychosocial treatment on survival of patients with metastatic breast cancer. *Lancet,* pp. 888–891.

Taylor, S. E., Falke, R. L., Shoptaw, S. J., & Lichtman, P. R. (1986). Social support, support groups, and the cancer patient. *Journal of Consulting and Clinical Psychology, 54,* 608–615.

Toseland, R. W., & Rossiter, C. M. (1989). Group interventions to support family caregivers: A review and analysis. *The Gerontologist, 29*(4), 438–448.

T

Television Viewing

Dorothy G. Singer and Jerome L. Singer

Yale University

Aggression The delivery of a harmful stimulus to a person or to property. In television research with young children it may involve uncalled for kicking, hitting, snatching of others' toys or possessions, or tearing posters off school walls. For adolescents and adults it may include serious violence, including the use of weapons. It should be differentiated from *assertiveness,* which refers to a clear assertion of one's rights or of others' obligations or the taking of a firm stand on issues without actual physical action.

Catharsis A Greek term meaning expurgation of feelings introduced by Aristotle to explain the intensity of emotion experienced by the audience witnessing a powerful scene in a play. As used in psychoanalysis the concept took on the meaning that important drives such as sex or aggression could be at least partially reduced through watching such sports as boxing or wrestling or through viewing aggressive or sexual material in film or television. Practically all available research suggests that the above catharsis theory is *incorrect* and that people are more likely to be aggressive after viewing violent stories.

Cognitive Processing The discrimination, identification, verbal labeling and storage of new information

in memory for later retrieval as needed in confronting the novelties and ambiguities of our physical and social environments.

Correlation An important statistic designed to show that two variables are linked together at a magnitude between -1.0 to $+1.0$ at a probability well above sheer chance. It is used, for example, to show that scores on hours of television viewing per week for children are consistently associated with scores of their aggressive behavior in school. A correlation in itself does not mean that one of the variables *caused* another but if a linkage is found further methods can demonstrate a causal connection.

Desensitization Frequent exposure to particular events, for example, violence in TV programming or in movies, may lead to viewers becoming less shocked or distressed and may subsequently lead to their tendency to accept or ignore comparable scenes on the screen and even in real life.

Modeling Behavior Much human learning involves imitation of behavior demonstrated by parents, older siblings or respected figures in television or film.

Schema An organized mental structure through which we identify information, store it for later retrieval, and anticipate what to expect in novel situations as well as to help in interpreting new stimuli. A script is a form of schema that helps us anticipate the action sequences in a given situation, for example, what to expect when entering a barber shop or a restaurant, or when watching a new television show.

Social Reality As children grow they must form schemas and scripts not only about their physical environment but also about their social settings, for example, their relations to parents, siblings, friends, their school, their church, their nation. One feature of social reality deals with expectations of trust in others, of dangers and risks, or of friendships. Much of our modern social reality is shaped by media such as movies, books, newspapers, and television. Because television images are so vivid and because we watch so many stories (fictional or news) there is reason to believe that many of the schemas or scripts we form may depend on the largely fictional world of television rather than on our own direct experience.

Stereotypes   Stereotypes are forms of schemas that classify groups of people or events on the basis of widely accepted surface characteristics that may not necessarily apply to a given individual person or occurrence. Thus, a person with red hair may be stereotyped as outgoing and pugnacious, a member of an ethnic or racial group may be stereotyped as miserly, dull witted, or shrewd. Television, by repeatedly showing women in commercials as mainly housecleaners, may be helping viewers form a stereotype that can be seriously misleading as part of one's social reality or may become the basis for prejudice.

TELEVISION has become a "member of the family" since the 1950s, when it entered a vast number of American households. More young people are receiving messages from this electronic box then they do from parents and teachers. There is no evidence that sheer viewing is hazardous in terms of radiation or optical effects. There has been, however, considerable concern over whether the *format* of the television medium with its rapid shifts of scene, frequent interruptions for commercials, loud music, and related features of the American industry's presentation may be influencing the cognitive processes of children. In addition, the *content* of television programming, most of it oriented toward adult viewers, has been even more problematic because of the well-documented high frequency of violent or sexually provocative images presented both in fictional shows and in news or documentary shows. This article presents both sides of the television controversy, the negative effects of heavy and indiscriminate viewing, and the potentially positive results when parents and educators take a more active role in helping young people watch TV in an intelligent and critical manner.

I. HISTORICAL OVERVIEW

Most behavioral scientists and intellectuals in our society have been peculiarly indifferent to the psychological and social implications of the television sets ensconced in almost every home in the United States. The electronic screen has proved to be a convenient place before which we settle the children on a Saturday morning or else on an evening when one has printouts to review or scholarly work to perform without interference by little voices.

Until the 1970s the small amount of research by behavioral scientists bearing on the significance of television for child development focused chiefly on possible influences on aggressive behavior. Despite some modest proliferation of research in the decade following the Surgeon General's Report on Television and Social Behavior published in 1972 and culminating in another government report edited by Pearl, Bouthilet and Lazar in 1982, child development journals and textbooks on cognitive and emotional development of children have rarely mentioned television. Perhaps this indifference by social scientists reflects a massive blind spot that is only recently being corrected. We may have hoped that by ignoring it, what intellectuals still call the "idiot box" would go away.

We can recognize the political ramifications of the medium simply from the millions of dollars political candidates are prepared to spend for advertising during election campaigns. Is it possible that our daily reliance on the television medium (which is essentially a picture story-telling system) has led to a change in how we think, what we think about, and how hard we are willing to work to extract information from other communication media? Is television implicated in the fact that magazines such as *Newsweek* and *Time* now include many more pictures, shorter paragraphs, and a vast increase in articles that deal with celebrities whose fame chiefly resides in their appearances on television? Compare psychology textbooks of a few decades past with those of today and note the reduction in sheet textual content relative to "boxes," pictures, and other visually attractive rather than semantically complex features. Did human beings always have so short an attention span or have we all been transmogrified by watching the rapid pace, quick cuts to unrelated material, and pixillation that characterized *Sesame Street* and still prevail on commercial television, where tragic death scenes or desperate car chases are interrupted by deodorant or beer commercials?

A. Brief History of Legislation

The Radio Act of 1927 established the legal framework for broadcasting while the communications industry was in its infancy. The airwaves were declared to be the property of the people. The Communications Act of 1934 regulated station licensing to provide maximum opportunity for all communities to obtain strong broadcast signals. Under this act, the Federal Communications Commission (FCC) was created and given the power to renew or revoke a station's license based on the station's actual performance in comparison to original intentions. The Commission currently consists of five presidential appointees. Under Section 326 of the act, the FCC is forbidden to censor programming. In addition, the FCC initiated the Fairness Doctrine requiring that discussion of public issues be presented on broadcast stations and that each side of these issues be given fair coverage.

Several more recent laws deal primarily with children. The Children's Television Act of 1990 requested an increase in the amount of educational and informational shows broadcast to children. Two laws emanating from the 1990 act may affect children's readiness for school learning:

1. The Public Telecommunications Act of 1992
2. The Ready to Learn Act of 1992.

The Public Telecommunications Act authorized appropriations for the Corporation for Public Broadcasting to grant funds for children's programming. The Ready to Learn Act called for the expansion and distribution of educational and instructional video programming and supporting educational materials. The aim is to improve school readiness for preschool and elementary school children, to distribute support materials to parents and child care providers, and to expand Head Start services.

The Telecommunications Act of 1996 mandated a V-chip to be implanted in every new TV set. The V-chip is a technology designed primarily to permit parents to restrict children's viewing of violent television programs. Educators and researchers are suggesting coding systems to help parents to determine which programs are suitable for children to watch whether

or not a V-chip is used. The Entertainment Software Review Board and the Recreational Software Advisory Committee have established rating systems for video games and for packaged computer programs. Currently, a coalition of telecommunications hardware, software, and on-line companies and organizations are collaborating on a flexible system for guiding and restricting internet access.

Finally, the FCC's 1996 rules specified that local television stations must broadcast three hours per week of programming that is specifically designed to serve the educational and informational needs of children aged 16 and under. The programs must be of 30 minutes in length and be broadcast between 7 a.m. and 10 p.m. on a regular weekly schedule. Each program must have an educational and informational objective and the station must specify the age group of the target child audience in writing. Failure to comply with these regulations could lead to refusal of license renewal.

B. Patterns of Viewing

Since television was introduced in 1939 at the World's Fair in New York City, its growth has been phenomenal. In 1945, for example, there were around 10,000 sets in use compared to the many millions in use today. Over 98% of American households own at least one TV set (60% of American families have cable), and multiple ownership of TV sets in growing as are cable hookups. In homes with teenagers, 87% have multiple sets, and 50% of children with their own rooms have a set in it. According to a Nielsen Media Research report in 1993, males and females ages 12 to 17 are watching about 22 hours of television per week. Children ages 6 to 11 watch about 20 hours and 49 minutes per week, while children ages 2 to 5 watch the most, 23 hours and 31 minutes per week. The average American family has the TV set on about 7 hours and 51 minutes per day. By the time children reach the age of 18, they will have watched more than 20,000 hours of television, while they will have spent less than 13,000 hours in the classroom.

Despite the fact that our youth are watching a good deal of television, the educational and informational programming produced by the networks and directed to children has declined since 1975 from 9.75 hours per week to 1.75 hours in 1996; this has remained relatively stable since then. In 1992 there was a slight increase to 3.4 hours per week. Some broadcasters, trying to keep their licenses, have listed such entertainment programs as *G.I. Joe* and *The Jetsons* as "educational" fare and have even included *Yogi Bear, Power Rangers* and *America's Funniest Home Videos* in that category.

The Children's Television Act of 1990 and the FCC Rule of 1996 mentioned above require that TV stations must serve the educational and informational needs of children through its overall programming, including content specifically designed to serve such needs. The law does not apply to cable television. In reviewing license renewal applications, the Federal Communications Commission considers whether TV stations do indeed offer programs that further the positive development of the child, including cognitive/intellectual or emotional/social needs.

The law also posited some limits on commercials. The number of commercials in children's programming may not exceed 10.5 minutes an hour on weekends and 12 minutes an hour on weekdays. The commercial limitations apply to both broadcasters and cable operators and deals with programs aimed at children 12 years and under. Records must be kept by companies demonstrating their compliance with both commercial and programming requirements. Unfortunately, the FCC has limited power of enforcement. In the history of television, the FCC has very rarely denied renewal applications.

Given the fact that children and adults watch a considerable amount of television, the question arises: Does television have any effects on the mental health of our population? Psychologists such as David Walsh and Leonard Eron believe that television contributes to the violent acts in our society. The average child will witness more than 2000 acts of violence on TV by the time he or she is 18 years old. About 45,000 messages about sex are received by the average child during the formative years, with many references to sexual activity among unmarried people. Drug- and alcohol-implicit messages suggesting use are more in evidence than are reflections of the government campaign to "just say no." Figures in 1996 from the Institute for Social Research at the University of Michigan indicate that alcohol was the most commonly used drug among high school seniors, with 51% stating they had used alcohol within the past month. Other researchers are concerned about negative values portrayed on TV

such as disrespect, selfishness, emphasis on money and rewards without work, and a lack of moral judgment.

C. Family Interaction

Considering the number of hours that television is on during the day, is it possible that parents and children are coviewing programs and discussing them with the goals of understanding and making sense of the numerous pro- and antisocial messages? It is difficult to study the families' use and interaction vis-à-vis television. Work by Leichter and colleagues in 1985 examined how family members view and use television. Data suggest that some families do modify and mediate the experience of viewing television. It is used as an educational strategy in family life and that spatial, temporal, and interpersonal relationships surrounding television are significant variables in understanding the degree of influence on a family and fundamental to the overall organization of the family system.

II. COGNITIVE EFFECTS OF TELEVISION

A special property of American television certainly, and perhaps increasingly of television production in other nations, is the rapid pace of presentation of material with constant intercutting, interruption, and shifts in sound levels. Our commercial television is primarily designed to keep the viewers' attention on the screen. This is accomplished quite skillfully by producers who know to shift sequences rapidly, zoom in and zoom out, and suddenly introduce new settings, loud music, new characters, and a variety of special effects. Foreigners not used to American television, watching the brief segments, the constant interruptions by brief rapid-fire commercials, and the quick changes of pace even within plot sequences, as well as the heavy emphasis on physical action, report that it is disorganizing and often arouses anger or almost physical distress. But American children have grown up with this pattern of quick-paced stimulus presentation, and this must indeed be a new kind of experience never before a part of the perceptual environment of the child in civilization.

Here, then, we confront the major question about this medium. A cognitive analysis suggests that because cognitive processing takes place over time, effective learning and storage of material presented requires some mental replaying and rehearsal with an occasional opportunity to shift one's attention away from the television set and to reflect on what was seen. If new material is piled on top of other material, particularly irrelevant contents, can one really intelligently sift and reexamine information?

To what extent does the sheer proliferation of information provided on the television set interfere with some of the reflective thought that is necessary for the development of longer term intentions and action sequences? It may be that the very rapid form of presentation on American television, in which novelty piles upon novelty in short sequences, may be counterproductive to organized and effective learning sequences. In one of the earlier reviews of television and cognition, W. Andrew Collins noted that three cognitive tasks are involved in comprehending materials on television: (1) selective attention to events that are central to a program; (2) the orderly organization of these events; and (3) formation of inferences about implicit relations among explicit scenes (imputing a causal relationship between two scenes although the causal relationship is not depicted explicitly). Collins reported that there are substantial variations in comprehension that occur with age, general experience, and knowledge of the television medium. Memory for depicted actions and for commercial messages on television thus increases from elementary to high school age range for central content of programs as well as for incidental or nonessential content.

Most of the studies on cognition and television have been carried out with young children. The work of Gavriel Salomon is particularly important because of the clever experiments concentrating on AIME or the *Amount of Invested Mental Effort* an individual brings to a particular television program. Children in high-demand conditions (told "to learn" rather than to watch "for fun") learned a great deal more from TV than children in the low-demand condition. Other researchers have found that younger children mention primarily common knowledge content. These are the bits of information a child brings to a TV program such as police officers wear uniforms or people eat in restaurants. Older children can be more program specific (certain police officers are out of uniform). Older students also notice some events that deviate from expectation, while younger children fill in story lines with stereotypical responses.

Television does seem to have some limited effect on acquisition of vocabulary. Researchers have found that children do learn words from television if parents coview and mediate or explain the words. Mabel Rice and her collaborators in 1990 indicated that educational programming can have an effect on a child's vocabulary development at a later time in their development while the viewing of animated cartoons does not. Our own research has shown that programs carefully designed for children such as *Barney & Friends* can lead to an enriched vocabulary especially when reinforcement by adults occurs.

When television's effects on the cognitive development of adolescents were examined, heavy television viewing (more than 6 hours per day) was associated with poorer reading achievement. In 1986, Michael Morgan studied 200 males and females and found that heavy television viewers preferred stories that reflect common TV programming such as plots involving love and families, teenage stories, and stories about celebrities significantly more than did light viewers. Light TV viewers chose science fiction mysteries and general nonfiction stories. Poor reading skills along with greater television viewing and less reading have been observed among high school students from poor economic backgrounds.

When adults' cognitive skills are examined in relation to television viewing, research evidence mainly comes from responses to news and public affairs programs. National opinion polls have suggested that television is the major source of news information about the world, and that if there is a conflicting story between a newspaper report and television, the majority of Americans accept the television version. Barrie Gunter reviewed the data on adults' ability to remember news from print, radio, and television. Variables such as education, socioeconomic status, motivational and interest factors, and time of day news is presented were examined. Unfortunately, most of the studies Gunter cited in a 1991 publication were carried out in the early 1970s and 1980s, but some of the findings are noteworthy. As arousal increases during the day, the processing of new information becomes less efficient. Memory performance appears to be best in the morning and worst in the evening. An exception is violent news, which is recalled better than nonviolent information regardless of the time of day it is presented.

If we accept the theoretical construct developed in cognitive psychology of the schema as a network of interrelated elements that help an individual define a concept, individuals then can begin to understand how viewers' schemas correspond to the different television formats. Even if we miss part of a situation comedy, we automatically fill in the gaps based on our preexisting schemas or mental scripts of how the typical plot will develop. We also automatically process the formal conventions of television, light, music, sound effects, and special camera effects. These conventions are associated with particular actions and emotions. An individual thus could engage in mindless activity while watching TV unless the content is so different from a previous existing schema that intentional processing will occur. In 1989 Thorson presented a theoretical cognitive communication model consisting of (1) primary and higher order cognitive processes (conscious attention, working memory); (2) structural storage areas (grammar analyzer, semantic dictionary); (3) two levels of awareness of processing (processes unavailable to consciousness and processes available to consciousness); (4) the role of emotion in processing commercials; (5) the role of environmental and programmatic distractions; and 6) the role of program context.

An example of a failure to process information, although the words are heard, comes from the research on Music Television (MTV). Several researchers found that teenage rock listeners are attracted to the sounds and visual aspects of the videos and do not process the words. The lyrics must be extracted by a special effort or intentional processing. In addition to a lack of comprehension or misunderstandings of lyrics, researchers also indicated that interpretation of lyrics depends on teenagers' prior experiences with the themes expressed in the song. Girls, for example, who reported prior pregnancy experiences, either their own or friends, were more likely to connect *music videos* to their own lives, both in terms of amount of effort expended and sheer number of connections they made.

III. TELEVISION AND PERSONALITY DEVELOPMENT

A. Perceptions, Beliefs, Social Cognition

In an important 1986 study by Mullen dealing with the effects of newscasters' facial expression and voting

behavior of viewers, the researchers found that a particular newscaster, Peter Jennings, unwittingly used more positive facial expressions while commenting on Ronald Reagan. This significantly influenced the voting behavior of the television viewers in the direction of Reagan. The other two network "anchor" newscasters did not exhibit any noticeable facial bias. Perceptions of a presidential candidate's fitness were influenced by a smile rather than by the content of the news coverage relating to him. Jennings exhibited no verbal bias for Reagan, but the repeated exposure to a conditional stimulus (the word, Ronald Reagan) and a conditioned response (the smile) may have resulted in a vicariously conditioned positive response to that candidate.

Another example of how perceptions are influenced by television comes from the work of George Gerbner. Using a "scary world" test, Gerbner examined the degree of fear about environmental violence of a sample of TV viewers. Regardless of age, socioeconomic condition, education, sex, and ethnicity, a significant positive relationship was found between heavy viewers of television and a view of the world as a scary place. Similarly, Singer, Singer, and Rapaczynski in 1984 found that parents and children who were heavy TV viewers also were more apt to view their neighborhoods as more scary than a sample of light television viewers. This was attributed to the heavy doses of violence and danger in fictional TV shows as well as in the news.

Most studies demonstrate a relationship between television viewing and social reality. Hawkins and Pingree in 1982 examined over 60 studies with samples ranging in size from 57 to 4254 and over many geographical areas. Although there seems to be a relationship between social reality and television, they caution that the research is only partially true for fear of victimization and for alienation. Certain conditions other than television viewing may also account for these perceptions of a dangerous world. Still, heavy viewers, especially those who fall into categories most likely to be "victims" in fictional shows or in the news, are most likely to adopt television's "violent" representation of social reality.

People need to maintain some control and order over their lives. Perhaps this is why TV viewers feel more comfortable with commercial television than with public television. People who were interviewed by the Corporation for Public Broadcasting in 1978 enjoyed seeing familiar actors and episodes of programs they had viewed previously and were disappointed and angry if their expectations were not met by the programs they viewed regularly. Comedies, for example, need to remain with their tradition of amusement and escape. As researchers Robert Kubey and Mihalyi Csikszentmihalyi have pointed out, television needs to perform "some of the reality-maintenance functions of conversation, but also those of a much repeated fairy tale; it is familiar and predictable." In terms "of imaginal styles," TV contents such as drama/comedy series, classic comedies, and music/entertainment are associated with positive-constructive daydreaming among college students. Here again, the comedies play a positive role in the inner life of these viewers, while violent programming was linked to depressed or angry thoughts.

B. Role Models

Children in prime time television are presented in limiting roles that often serve to build up the adults in the program. Children are often victimized and portrayed in poor health. Children fare better in programs designed to be viewed by younger audiences. Preschool children, for example, do identify with characters on *Sesame Street, Barney & Friends,* and *Shining Time Station.* The children on these shows model socially appropriate behaviors. In addition there are storylines that emphasize various occupations and roles in society. Children, ages 9 to 13, who are the heaviest TV watchers, may be influenced by the medium concerning beliefs and attitudes about gender and occupational roles. Some researchers have found correlations between general sex-typed attitudes and television viewing. One of the most extensive reports carried out by Williams, LaRose, and Frost in the late 1970s found that children exposed to *Freestyle,* a program showing girls in nontraditional roles, did change the attitudes of viewers to expand the number of jobs they would consider. The positive changes in attitude lasted 9 months after posttesting.

Research on adolescents demonstrates that heavy TV viewers are more likely to express attitudes that reflect traditional sex-role stereotypes. Adolescents also learn a considerable amount about occupations from television even when they are not likely to have personal contact with members of these occupations in their daily living. Research also finds that girls are generally more open to aspiring to masculine television occupations and prefer them than feminine real-life occupations. Boys tend to be biased against counterstereotyped participation.

Adults also are influenced by role models on television. The soaps especially affect the attitudes of their daytime, largely female viewers. Talk shows with their large audiences are another influence on American attitudes. The clothing, hair styles, and language of popular stars on situation comedies and serial dramas do influence the audience as well. *Dynasty* products were a sellout when introduced to department stores several years ago. The most dramatic evidence of TV's constructive influence was the rush for library cards by children and even adults after a charismatic character, Fonz, on a popular television series, *Happy Days,* joined his local library.

Role models can influence children in negative ways if shown smoking, drinking, or using drugs. Although cigarette and hard liquor commercials are banned from television, characters do smoke and drink, and in some cases are involved with drugs. Some of these characters are admired by children. A public television program, *Degrassi Junior High,* and network afternoon specials did much to promote an anti-smoking, drinking, and drug use message. Too many of the programs geared to adults, but watched by children, still are counterproductive with numerous portrayals of smoking and drinking. [*See* Smoking.]

C. Stereotypes

Men outnumber women by two to three to one in prime time dramatic programming according to Signorielli's 1993 report. Women are portrayed as younger than men, and cast in more traditional roles such as nurses, secretaries, homemakers, and are primarily involved in nurturing, romance, and family. The victim in a dramatic or action-adventure program is usually a young, attractive woman. While men can be involved in numerous occupations and are seen as powerful and in prestigious roles, women are portrayed as thin, usually with blond or red/auburn hair, rarely employed outside the home, more likely than men to be married, and less likely to be decision makers. The employment of women on television is at odds with the actual status of women today. While one-half of all married women are employed in the United States, 3 out of 10 married characters are employed on television. Young women do not see enough characters on TV who successfully combine a career with marriage and raising a family. The woman who remains at home is given lower status than the unmarried career woman in numerous shows. The 1997 season of TV programs presenting single young people in a glamorous way of living offers a message to the viewers that living alone or with a group of friends is sophisticated and fun, but there is a continuous struggle to find a compatible mate.

Minority groups, as described in a book edited by Gordon L. Berry and Joy K. Asamen, are underrepresented on American television. African Americans, for example, are segregated in specific types of program content. We see them in all-minority situation comedies, or if they are in dramatic shows, they are often associated with violent acts or abuse of drugs. They tend to play roles where they are younger than European Americans and are seldom involved in cross-ethnic interactions.

As is the case with African Americans, Hispanics are rarely seen on the three major networks, but there are three Hispanic-oriented networks in the United States. Although there is a tremendous growth of the Hispanic population in the States, the American-oriented networks lag behind in their attempts to include Hispanics as major characters in both children's and adult programs. When Hispanics do appear, they are portrayed in a stereotyped fashion with relatively minor contributions to the story lines. Public television and Nickelodeon utilize Hispanics, African Americans and other minorities in substantive roles, but unfortunately, the audience for such television programs is relatively small compared to the network's number of viewers.

Asian Americans fare no better than the above minorities. About 2.5% Asian characters were on television in the early 1970s with little change in their representation in the 1980s and early 1990s. When Asians are seen on television, they are in the news, or in some cities they are news anchorpersons. In prime time, Asians are connected with police departments in assistant roles, or in action-adventure programs, but rarely as starring figures. A situation comedy featuring an Asian family existed on a major network for a brief period and, although considered a breakthrough, is no longer available.

The stereotypical portrayals of minorities and the paucity of positive minority role models help to create a society that maintains separatist views and distortions about these groups. Such portrayals discourage relationships among various ethnic groups and in many cases perpetuates prejudice and bigotry. The self-esteem of minority groups is affected when they see themselves excluded for the most part on television despite the fact that they are consumers of the many products advertised on the networks and that sponsor the programs that underrepresent them.

IV. EFFECTS OF TELEVISION VIOLENCE

A. Theories of Aggression

1. Modeling

The theory that people may acquire aggressive responses as a result of observing such behavior was proposed by Albert Bandura in the early 1960s. Experiments employing this technique depended on the fact that child subjects were not aggressive at the time they saw aggressive acts being carried out. Modeling provides certain cognitive representations of novel aggression that can become part of a child's overall cognitive structure. Aggressive behaviors viewed in the media by the audience activate ideas, emotions, and implicit behavior associated with them. If a viewer sees people fighting on TV, thoughts of other aggressive acts may be revived and feelings such as rage or anger may be associated with these scenes, creating a behavioral readiness to act in an aggressive manner with whatever means are available. Weapons, for example, shown in pictures or physically present in controlled studies have been shown to elicit aggression according to cognitive-associationist analyses. Current information-processing theories suggest the importance of schemas, that is, organized mental structures that govern an individual's attention and retrieval of information as key features of subsequent action patterns. These schemas are derived not only from direct social experience but also vicariously through observing television. Heavy viewing of violence may lead to sets of expectations that aggressive behaviors are appropriate methods for dealing with frustrations or social conflicts. [See AGGRESSION.]

Two cases that received much national publicity claimed that behavior modeled on television was a contributing factor in both crimes. Ronald Zamora, a disturbed teenager, killed an elderly woman after burglarizing her home. Zamora identified with cops-and-robbers programs, believing that one had to kill the victim lest he or she could later identify him. Olivia Niemi, a 9-year-old, was attacked by three girls and a boy on a beach, in the process of which she was artificially raped with a bottle. The attackers admitted that they had been influenced by a scene in a TV movie, *Born Innocent,* where a girl was raped with a plunger.

On August 1, 1981, Warner Amex Satellite Entertainment launched Music Television (MTV). In 1993, 57.3 million households subscribed to MTV, and of these, about 8.4 million had young people ages 12 to 17 years who watched weekly. Unfortunately, children are also MTV viewers, and recently a 5-year-old in Ohio set his family's mobile home on fire, killing his baby sister. The mother publically blamed "Beevis and Butthead," MTV's highest rated show, stating that the child imitated behavior seen on the show. In response to this, the segment was moved to a later time slot than its original 7 P.M. hour.

The study of suicide and its link to television and modeling behavior has been of concern to health workers. Using data from 1973 to 1984 Kessler and colleagues examined the relationship between network TV news stories and subsequent U.S. suicides. Although there was no reliable association between network news stories and suicide among adults, through 1980 a significant association existed among teenagers and was more pronounced among girls than boys. The risk ratio reversed consistently from 1981 through 1984, suggesting that public sensitivity to teenage suicide may have created a context in which teenagers were more resistant to television's influence. [*See* SUICIDE.]

Phillips in 1982 also reported similar results examining the rate of suicide among U.S. teenagers before and after televised new stories about suicide. After the broadcasts, the number of suicides increased significantly more than the expected number. Even after correction was made for the effects of the days of the week, the month, holidays, and yearly trends, the findings persisted. Suicides increased as much after general-information or feature stories about suicide as after news stories about a particular suicide. Similar findings were reported by Stack in 1989 in his study of TV news stories and their effect on suicide rates. Phillips has also examined the relationship between suicides on "soaps" and actual suicides. He

found that the nation's suicide rate rises significantly after a soap character attempts or commits a fictional suicide.

Phillips explains his results in part by the imitation hypothesis. Similarly, Gould and Shaffer in 1986 found that in the greater New York area, suicides increased significantly after four fictional films were broadcast on television. The number of suicides were compared 2 weeks before and 2 weeks after the films were shown. Results are consistent with the imitation hypothesis. Alternative explanations such as increased referrals to hospitals or increased sensitivity to adolescent suicidal behavior on the part of the hospital personnel did not account for the increase of attempted and completed suicides.

A replication of this study by Phillips and Paight in 1987, however, in California and Pennsylvania before and after the showing of three of the four fictional films, found no evidence of increased teenage suicides after the films were shown. There may have been differences in the kinds of teenagers who viewed the films to account for the discrepancy in the results. On the other hand, research by Ostroff and Boyd in 1987 found that data gleaned from suicide reports at a hospital in Connecticut supported the association between viewing and subsequent teenage suicides found in New York.

Interestingly, research in Germany examined the effects of a six-part German TV series that was telecast twice in a 17-month period. The story portrayed the fictional railroad suicide of a 19-year-old student. A rash of imitative suicides occurred among young people (15–19 years) near the age of the hero. The suicides occurred during the interval between the two telecasts and after the second one at a rate of 175% for males and 167% for females compared with lower rates during previous time periods of the same duration. The telecast had no significant impact on women over 30 years of age or men over 40 years of age. The authors stated that the people affected were suicide-predisposed, suggesting that they already had some psychological problems.

2. Arousal and Desensitization

Dolf Zillman has reviewed the literature on arousal extensively in his chapter in his edited book, *Responding to the Screen.* The notion that moderate increases in arousal such as presented by television are pleasurable, whereas extreme increases are aversive is discussed at length by him. He offers two suggestions: (1) persons who experience how levels of arousal may respond more intensely to affect-inducing stimuli. These persons may expect great pleasure from watching TV. (2) As the experience of great pleasure is repeated, there will be a tendency to seek out this pleasure and be drawn to the TV set. Experiments have demonstrated that images of sex and violence are arousal inducing, and arousal reactions appear to increase with the degree of reality in the portrayal of violence. Some research also indicates that exposure to violent programming makes individuals more tolerant and accepting of violence among others. These studies have generally been correlational and do not permit causal inferences.

3. Catharsis versus Social Learning

Most researchers reject the idea that watching violent television leads to a draining off or catharsis of hostility. It is more widely accepted among social-learning theorists that watching violent television leads to an increase in aggressive behavior. Learning is divided into (1) acquisition and encoding, in which the script for guiding behavior is first acquired and internalized; (2) maintenance phase, where the internal representation of the script is strenthened; and (3) retrieval and emission whereby the internal representation manifests itself through overt action.

B. Research

1. Laboratory Studies

Numerous studies conducted in laboratories follow a similar model. Subjects are arbitrarily provoked by an experimental confederate before subjects view a violent film or are permitted to confront their former tormenters. Expectation is that subjects will become more aggressive to the tormenter than subjects who were not exposed to a violent film. The subjects' identification with the characters in the film plays an important part in the acting out of aggression. If a character is punished, viewers should be less aggressive than viewers who identify with characters who receive reinforcement for their aggressive acts. Other variables, of course, must be taken into consideration, such as amount of previous TV viewing, employment status, marital satisfaction, or familial stress. For children one must consider factors such as academic achievement, parental control over TV, and kinds of parental discipline, as well as programs typically viewed.

Limitations of laboratory experiments include the artificial circumstances of the studies, the absence of possible retaliation by the victim, brevity of the television exposure (usually one or two programs), and the immediacy of the measurement of effect. They do, however, permit causal inferences. Results of most of the laboratory studies indicate that viewing violent television leads to later aggression. One review in 1984 by Friedman challenged the major studies on the grounds that the correlations between viewing television violence and aggressiveness are small, and that the data from laboratory experiments cannot be carried over into real-life situations. A statistical approach called meta-analysis, however, carried out by Paik and Comstock in 1994 examined 217 studies, including laboratory research, field experiments, time series, and surveys. Laboratory experiments produced the strongest magnitude of effect. The researchers found a consistent positive and significant correlation between television violence and aggressive behavior across almost all the studies.

2. Time-Series Experiments

These studies focus on the impact of such events as publicized homicides, prize fights, and criminal execution on later homicide rates. Researchers focus on the month-to-month changes in violent crimes such as homicide, rape, robbery, and aggravated assaults in cities across the country. Rates are measured before and after a much-publicized crime. A time-series statistical measure is used permitting researchers to determine increases and decreases of specific crimes that could be attributed to a specific criminal act. Findings suggest that highly publicized crimes can have both an inhibiting and instigatory effect on behavior. Many of the suicide studies used the time-series approach.

An important study published in 1989 by Brandon Centerwall is an example of a time-series study. He examined the homicide rates in South Africa, Canada and the United States comparing only Whites in each country. Television was not permitted in South Africa prior to 1975. Thus, Centerwall was able examine data from 1945 to 1975. Following the introduction of television into the United States, the White homicide rate increased 93% from 3.0 homicides per 100,000 White population in 1945 to 5.8 per 100,000 in 1974. In South Africa, with no television the White homicide rate decreased by 7% from 2.7 homicides per 100,000 White population in 1943 to 2.5 per 100,000 in 1974. In Canada, following the introduction of television, the homicide rate increased by 92% from 1.3 homicides per 100,000 in 1945 to 2.5 per 100,000 in 1974. The researcher isolated the effect of television from other media influences and examined such variables as age, urbanization, economic conditions, alcoholic consumption, capital punishment, unrest, and availability of firearms. None of these variables offered a satisfactory alternative explanation to the influence of television.

Phillips and Hensley in 1984 examined the potential influences of judicial decisions relating to punishment and prizefight events on homicide rates in the United States from 1973 to 1974. Results indicate that following publicized events such as a prizefight a significant increase in homicides occurred on the third day after a fight. After a highly publicized punishment took place, the number of White murder victims decreased significantly on the fourth day after the event. These data are consistent with laboratory research indicating more aggression takes place if subjects believe violence on the media was real rather than fictionalized.

3. Field Studies—Longitudinal Research

One way to examine the link between television viewing and behavior is to carry out extensive field observations over time. Data are collected from parents, teachers, peers, observations, and through more formal testing. In a 5-year study, beginning in 1977 and ending in 1982, Singer and Singer demonstrated that a heavy diet of television violence is associated with a decrease in self-restraint, an increase in aggression, a lowering in reading scores, a decrease in imagination, and a more scary view of the world for these children. Parents' emphasis on physical punishment was a contributing factor to the aggressive behavior.

In the longest study of television and aggression, Leonard Eron and Rowell Huesmann, who began their work in 1963 in a small upstate New York town, followed a group of children aged 8 for more than 20 years. Children who were rated as more aggressive by their peers at age 8 were more likely to be convicted of crimes by age 30. They also were more likely to physically abuse their spouses and children, and they were more likely to have been convicted of moving traffic violations, including drunk driving. These

adults were the ones who watched the most violent television at age 8. Those children exposed to violence maintained cognitive scripts emphasizing aggressive solutions to social problems. The violent television may also have stimulated aggressive fantasies in which the scripts were rehearsed enabling them to be recalled and utilized in the future.

A study commissioned by the National Broadcasting Company examined the effects of television violence on the aggressive behavior of more than 3000 youths aged 7 to 19. J. Ronald Milavsky studied the children from 1970–1973 concluding that there was no evidence of any consistent effects of television violence on the aggressive behavior of the boys and girls aged 7 to 12 or on teenage boys. These data appear to be at odds with the numerous studies suggesting that violent television does have an effect on children's aggressive behavior. Subsequent reanalysis of the data from this study has shown that the linkage of television and aggression does occur here too.

The accumulating data of several hundred studies from surveys, field observations, and laboratory experiments are almost unanimously positive in showing a linkage between heavy television viewing (especially of violent programming) with antisocial or overt aggressive behavior. Some critics have questioned whether the modest size of the relationships found, even if statistically reliable, has any practical importance. A series of highly sophisticated statistical analyses by Robert Rosenthal and various colleagues at Harvard University have demonstrated that the so-called "effect-sizes" in these studies are sufficiently powerful to be of considerable significance for social policy. According to these analyses, the social consequences of neglecting the findings would be akin to government agencies or families neglecting or ignoring important evidence of the causes of diseases or the bases of crime. Where specific efforts are made to mitigate the effects of television viewing upon aggressive behavior, as in a study by Rowell Huesmann and Leonard Eron, the result yielded a reduction in aggression by children from 62% to 38%, an effect of major mental health importance.

V. EFFECTS OF SEXUAL CONTENT

Television rather than home or school appears to be the leading source of sex education in the United States.

Each year American youths can view 14,000 sexual references, innuendos, and behaviors on television. Unfortunately, there are few references to birth control devices, self-control, abstinence, consequences of sexual acts, or responsibility. Bradley Greenberg summarized the data in his chapter "Content Trends in Media Sex" in the book *Media Children and the Family*. Victor Strasburger devoted an entire book published in 1995 to adolescents and the media, with a chapter about adolescent sexuality and the media. Excellent research by Neil Malamuth and Edward Donnerstein substantiated the findings that considerable sexual activity is available on television and that exposure to media sexual aggression may adversely affect some men's thought patterns in the direction of tolerating or even contemplating brutal sex acts.

In recent years there is more sex on a regular basis on the soaps than during preferred prime-time series. There is more varied sexual activity within prime time such as homosexuality, unmarried intercourse, and prostitution, while soaps maximize intercourse and long kisses. Extramarital intercourse is more prevalent on the soaps, while premarital intercourse has more participants in prime-time series. Fantasizing or daydreaming about sexual activities is unique to the soaps. Music Television (MTV) averages about six sexual activities per video. Content consists of intimate touching, kissing, hugging, and flirting, with most of the activity primarily heterosexual and about one-quarter of the exchanges homosexual.

Greenberg presents seven propositions based on his content analyses of the media that he suggests are open to further research: (1) more regular viewers of media that feature sexual incidents are more likely to be preoccupied with sex; (2) heavy users have stronger beliefs that sex is a more regular and popular activity among younger people; (3) more regular users are more likely to believe that sex in various forms happens more frequently (more premarital, more extramarital, more postmarital, more rape, more prostitution); (4) more regular viewers believe they know more about sex and can counsel others about sex; (5) more regular viewers are more likely to be sanguine about the sacredness of marriage; (6) participants in sexual activities are not negative about encounters and are less concerned about contraception or negative consequences; and (7) the combination of music and sexual activity raises questions about the meaning of that combination. In addition, a person who experiences sexual encounters in his own life may have his or her self-esteem and perception adversely affected if the encounters are not as exciting as those portrayed on television.

VI. COPING WITH TELEVISION

Three forces interact to determine the possible influence of television viewing on children's or adults' mental health and cognitive functioning. They are the industry itself (broadcasters, writers, and producers of programs who determine content and format of presentation); policymakers/educators; and of course, parents. In addition, a significant role in helping to control violent and sexually provocative program content is played by the sponsors of commercial programs. Their reluctance or refusal to pay for advertising that accompanies offensive programming could force the networks and cable companies to self-monitor and to be more concerned with their offerings.

A. The Industry

Two major reports, one issued by the UCLA Center for Communications Policy in 1995, and one issued in 1994–1995 by four universities (University of California, Santa Barbara, University of North Carolina, Chapel Hill, University of Texas, Austin, and the University of Wisconsin, Madison) indicate that there are substantial risks of harmful effects from viewing violence on television that coincide with the data reported above. Very few of the programs monitored employed a strong antiviolence theme, nor were many of the perpetrators of violence in TV stories punished or (as in the case of police) held accountable for their actions.

Both reports recommend a need for the networks to work with the creative community to produce less violent programs, and when violence does occur, to show more negative consequences and alternatives to solving problems. In addition, recommendations were made to schedule programs that do have violent themes in late evening slots when the younger audience is less likely to be viewing TV. The industry has set up coding or rating systems and program advisories so that parents may be alerted to violent content.

The Standards and Practices departments of the major networks set the rules that are supposed to govern television definitions of violence, sexuality and language. Unfortunately, these rules are not always followed or enforced because of the desire to get large audiences who seem, according to the networks, to favor violent, exciting, or sexually provocative programs.

The Entertainment Industry Task Force on AIDS has presented guidelines concerning sexual presentations emphasizing discussion of sex as a natural, healthy part of life; a respect for abstinence; use of condoms; and consequences of unprotected sex. If one monitors the soaps or prime time dramatic programs, it appears that these guidelines are ignored.

The Caucus for Producers, Writers and Directors has prepared guidelines for alcohol use on television such as trying not to show excessive drinking, avoiding glamorization of drinking, and allowing characters to refuse a drink or have nonalcoholic beverages as alternatives to the liquor that is available. These suggestions, however, appear not to be followed stringently by the networks. Numerous research articles found that a relationship between at-risk preadolescents' decisions about alcohol use were predicted in part by the television characters they viewed, and by their expectancies that drinking brings rewards. Slightly older children were found in another study to be influenced by TV beer advertising. They had more favorable beliefs about drinking, greater knowledge of beer slogans and brands, and increased intentions to drink as an adult. Most of the research reports in this area indicate that the effects of alcohol advertising may indeed predispose youths toward drinking.

B. Policymakers/Educators

Approaches to the violence issue have included a recommendation by the government in the Telecommunication Act of 1996 to install a V-chip in every new television set. This would have the capability of blocking-out offensive programming. A "safe-harbor" approach has also been suggested that would mean that television stations would schedule programs deemed violent during special hours. Monitoring programs by organizations such as the Center for Media Education and the Parent Teachers Association followed by publishing "report cards" to potential sponsors also could be effective in curbing violence. A minimum of 3 hours per week of quality children's program, an idea set forth by the FCC in 1990 and passed by Congress in 1996, is a start toward more educational TV fare for children.

Educators in charge of teacher-training institutions need to become more informed about the new technology, and they need to implement methodology courses geared to the new approaches to learning: long distance learning; interactive learning; the use of the Internet; and the use of CD-ROM in the classroom.

There has been a widespread movement to teach media literacy in the classrooms. Such curricula seek to train "critical viewing" skills such as how to watch television in an intelligent, analytic manner. Currently, there are numerous organizations and schools that have developed media literacy curricula for kindergarten through high school and some are even used in colleges. Kidsnet, located in Washington, D.C., is a clearing house for information about materials and programming in all media including print, television, and radio. Magazines such as *Better Viewing* and *Wired* address issues dealing with telecommunications and the information superhighway.

C. Parents

Parents are perhaps the most important force we have in controlling their children's viewing habits, and in changing their own television usage. Parents can set rules regarding the number of hours their children can watch TV. With the help of a guide in the newspaper or in the various television publications, they can, with their children, select appropriate programs to view. Parents should try and preview certain programs or videotape them if they have any doubt about their content before exposing their children to them. Parents or other caregivers should talk with children about program content, explaining how certain TV effects are produced. They should point out offensive material, deal with stereotypes, moral issues, and violent themes. Such discussion can help children gain some perspective about the fictional, entertainment world of television. [See PARENTING.]

Family intervention, especially in the area of violent programming, can help a child see that aggressive acts on TV are carefully staged and that in real life a victim suffers, he may die, a family mourns, and usually society will punish the perpetrator of the crime.

When a parent is in doubt about the suitability of a program for a child, the program can be turned off.

The videocassette recorder plays an important role in how the family uses television. Prerecorded videos attract a larger family audience than prime-time television, with nearly three persons watching together per household versus 1.7 for prime-time television. Television as a whole provides an opportunity to be together, but places few demands on the quality of that togetherness. Brody, Stoneman, and Sandus in 1980 found that preschoolers who viewed with their parents talked less, they paid less attention to their parents, but affectionate touching between parents and child was greater when watching television. The advantage of VCR usage for parents is that they can choose wholesome and educational programming without television's fast pace and commercial interruptions. They can talk with children about the story being watched.

Parents can find alternatives to TV viewing for their children and for themselves such as reading, attendance at cultural exhibits, sports, hobbies, music, and socialization with peers. In addition, parents can guide children to carefully selected and controlled TV viewing. When parents do select educational programs on television for their children, and they also explain or mediate the content, children do learn more from the programs and can perform better in schools as studies about *Barney & Friends* and *Sesame Street* have recently indicated. Singer and Singer's report in 1994 and 1995 and Wright and Huston's report in 1995 attest to the value of public television and the carefully thought-out children's programs featured on this network.

VII. CONCLUSIONS

Television and related newer technologies such as videocassettes for home use or CD-ROMs for use with a computer have special features beyond books and related written materials, which for thousands of years have served as repositories and communicators of human knowledge. Because it provides vivid, active visual materials, television is instantly accessible and has become an ingrained feature of the household in almost every culture of the modern world. Delivery systems will become more extensive through cable, home satellite receivers, or telephone wiring with the

further likelihood that some form of integration of the TV set with the interactive features of the computer is in the offing.

A substantial body of social science research has now accumulated in these first 50 years since the introduction of the medium. It is clear that the powerful attraction of this medium has introduced certain hazards for mental health into the home but that as a remarkable communications technology television has many potentially useful possibilities as well.

A. Hazards

We have no evidence that the sheer watching of television offers substantial physical risks either to the eyes or from supposed radiation effects. No knowledgeable person would attribute most human violence, fears, or prejudices with their long pretelevision histories to the viewing of this new medium. Nor is there at this time any significant body of evidence that can attribute the regular occurrence of specific, diagnosable mental illnesses to individuals' viewing of television.

What is clear from the research literature reviewed above is that heavy viewing by children may put them at risk for certain cognitive, attitudinal, and behavioral problems. Children who watch a great deal of television from earliest ages may fail to practice autonomous play skills or engage in other book-related activities that are important to the development of reading and writing skills. Such skills are advantageous for later employment. If the child has not mastered moderate literacy in the first 5 years of school the whole system of compulsory attendance at school becomes a burden. Illiterate or semiliterate children often form peer groups built around drug use, truancy, and various other forms of delinquency that have long-term mental health implications.

At the attitudinal level the research data strongly suggest that heavy television viewing, especially because of the widespread violent content on fictional and news programming, may lead to an excessive fearfulness about daily life dangers. The often stereotyped nature of representations of gender or of ethnic groups may foster certain prejudices or may even sustain negative self-beliefs in these often misrepresented groups. The heavy exposure to commercials may also create an atmosphere for susceptible children and adults that fosters an almost desperate need for material products well beyond one's means. Finally, the high degree of sexual innuendo may create mistaken emphases in children and adults on the importance of certain body types and physically attractive features and may also desensitize males to the seriousness of sexual assault.

At the behavioral level heavy viewing, especially on violent-content programming, seems consistently associated with the greater likelihood of overt unwarranted physically aggressive behavior in children and adolescents. Such behavior puts youth at considerable mental health as well as legal risk. It adds to the more general public health problem occasioned by overt violence.

B. Constructive Potential of the Medium

Available research evidence suggests that when used with discrimination and with carefully selected child-oriented programming television can foster emotionally healthy and socially adaptive attitudes and skills. Particular programs can foster openness to reading or can encourage other cognitive skills while also providing important basic information that supplements formal education. The attractiveness of well-designed children's programming when supplemented by teacher or parental comments, discussion, and follow-up can be critical in fostering imagination, a clearer sense of reality, constructive social skills, and public civility, all critical features of mental health. More of such constructive age-specific programming is urgently needed and more focused efforts by teachers and parents in fostering media literacy can counteract the hazards of this medium.

Our examination of television and its impact on the lives of American families leads to a full range of psychological challenges. The omnipresence of television has affected our cognitive functioning, our perception of the outside world, and the behaviors of youth and adults in terms of violence, sexuality, and suicide. Health issues in regard to alcoholism are a serious concern because of the numerous commercials promoting beer, and the glamorization of alcohol on soaps and prime-time dramas.

The federal government has now taken a stand on violence by mandating a V-chip, a method by which parents can block out offensive programs on all new television sets. Much more needs to be done concerning program coding or rating systems. Media literacy curricula are proliferating, but new challenges await us as users of the Internet increase, and computer systems become more sophisticated. Given this reality, mental health professionals are going to have to make more serious attempts to not only study the effects of the various types of programming, but to become more active in social policy commissions and groups as advocates using their collective research findings to take a stand for constructive, quality programming as a balance for much material that is now available.

BIBLIOGRAPHY

Berry, G. L., & Asamen, J. K. (Eds.) (1993). *Children and television.* Newbury Park, CA: Sage Publications.

Bryant, J. (Ed.). (1990). *Television and the American family.* Hillsdale, NJ: Lawrence Erlbaum Associates Publishers.

Comstock, G., & Paik, H. (1991). *Television and the American child.* New York: Academic Press.

Huesmann, L. R., & Malamuth, N. M. (Eds.). (1986). Media violence and antisocial behavior. *Journal of Social Issues, 42,* 3.

Kubey, R., & Csikszentmihalyi, M. (1990). *Television and the quality of life.* Hillsdale, NJ: Lawrence Erlbaum Associates Publishers.

Liebert, R. M., & Sprafkin, J. (Eds.). (1988). *The early window* (3rd ed.). New York: Pergamon Press.

Paik, H., & Comstock, G. (1994). The effects of television violence on antisocial behavior: A meta-analysis. *Communication Research 21,* 4, 516–546.

Singer, D. G., Singer, J. L., & Zuckerman, D. M. (1995). *The parents' guide: Use TV to your child's advantage.* Sarasota, FL: Acropolis South.

Strasburger, V. C. (1995). *Adolescents and the media.* Thousand Oaks, CA: Sage Publications.

Walsh, D. (1995). *Selling Out America's Children.* Minneapolis: Fairview Press.

Zillman, D., Bryant, J., & Huston, A. C. (Eds.). (1994). *Media, children and the family.* Hillsdale, NJ: Lawrence Erlbaum Associates Publishers.

Zillman, D., & Bryant, B. (Eds.). (1991). *Responding to the screen.* Hillsdale, NJ: Lawrence Erlbaum Associates Publishers.

Type A–Type B Personalities

Jerry Suls and Annette Swain

University of Iowa

Coronary Heart Disease Cardiovascular pathology characterized by an inadequate supply of oxygen to the heart. Major forms include myocardial infarction, or heart attack, and angina, severe chest pain.
Hyperreactivity Excessive cardiovascular, neuroendocrine, or other physiologic responsiveness to environmental stressors.
Potential for Hostility Predisposition to react to aggravating circumstances with displays of anger, antagonism, rudeness, resentment, etc.

TYPE A behavior pattern (TA), or personality, is defined as an action-emotion complex manifesting extreme competitiveness, achievement-striving, hostility, aggressiveness, and a sense of time urgency evidenced by emphatic speech and psychomotor mannerisms. The absence of these features describes the **TYPE B** pattern. Early psychosomatic describes the Type B pattern. Early psychosomatic theorists had proposed that hostile, overambitious individuals are at increased risk for coronary heart disease (CHD). In the 1950s, two pioneering cardiologists, Meyer Friedman and Ray Rosenman, formally introduced the constellation of behaviors described above as "Type A" as a risk factor for CHD. Epidemiological studies conducted during the late 1950–1960s, using special measures to assess this complex of competitive, aggressive, and impatient behaviors, indicated that Type A's were at a twofold greater risk of incurring coronary heart disease than their Type B counterparts. These findings were considered important because of the prospect that Type A would improve outcome prediction and identify high-risk individuals for treatment programs beyond that afforded by status on traditional risk factors such as serum cholesterol, hypertension, and smoking. Early findings concerning Type A and CHD encouraged the further development of behavioral medicine and health psychology. TA has been controversial in psychological and medical circles, however, almost from its inception. Some researchers and practitioners have embraced the concept noncritically while others have dismissed it out of hand. The present authors believe the validity and usefulness of TA falls somewhere between these extreme positions.

I. ASSESSMENT OF TYPE A

Friedman and Rosenman initially developed the Type A concept from observations of their own cardiac patients. Six features of the patient's conduct appeared relevant: (1) a strong drive to accomplish multiple poorly defined goals; (2) a propensity to compete (3) an intense need for recognition and advancement; (4) habitual time-urgent actions; (5) extraordinary acceleration of physical and mental activity; and (6) intense concentration and alertness. Friedman and Rosenman conceived of Type A as a behavioral style resulting from the interaction between a specific set of predispositions and eliciting situations, rather than as a personality trait, to avoid identification with the traditional psychosomatic approach which emphasized case studies and psychoanalytic theorizing about personality and heart disease.

Despite Friedman and Rosenman's emphasis on TA as a behavior pattern, the construct as a whole differs little from those derived from personality theory. The expression of stable attributes similarly requires eliciting circumstances. Conceptualized in trait terms, Type A-B is probably best considered not as a single dimension, but as a composite of facets or subcomponents of several personality dimensions.

Because of Friedman and Rosenman's emphasis on observable activity, in addition to their belief that TA's were either unreflective or consciously defensive, a behavior-based interview was developed to assess the presence of Type A. The "Structured Interview" (SI) consists of approximately 25 questions regarding the individual's typical response to various potentially hostile, competitive, or otherwise stressful circumstances. Type A scoring is based partially upon the content of the interviewee's answers, but more weight is given to both the style of his or her responses (e.g., loud explosive speech) and accompanying behavior (e.g., speech hurrying and anticipation of questions). The interviewer deliberately creates a moderately challenging situation by probing some of the interviewee's answers in a semi-accusatory manner to assess aggressive tendencies and by asking very predictable questions quite slowly to assess impatience. Based on the audiotaped responses, subjects are classified as extreme Type A1, incompletely developed A2, or the converse, Types B3 and B4. The label X is reserved for a small percentage of subjects who exhibit equal amounts of Type A and B behaviors.

Both Friedman and Rosenman's classification system and the use of the term "Type" give the impression that TA is a typology; however, subsequent researchers often treat the construct as a continuous dimension. The validity and relative merits of dimensional versus typological systems is, unfortunately, beyond the scope of this essay. TA is defined by a complex of presumably co-occurring attributes. Confusion is possible, however, because individuals may be grouped within the same category even if they differ in their possession of specific Type A behaviors. For example, some persons may be designated as Type A who are extremely time urgent and explosive in their speech, but only moderate in hostility and achievement-striving, while others might be labeled Type A on the basis of an extreme standing on hostility and achievement-striving. This lack of specificity allows for a diverse population to be categorized as Type A/B and thus may increase the false-positive rate when TA status is used as a predictor of CHD.

Published reports of inter-rater and test-retest reliabilities for the SI are consistent and acceptable, between 79 and 84% agreement for the former and approximately 80% agreement for the latter with an interval of 12–20 months. Although these psychometric properties of the SI are satisfactory, global Type A/B ratings do not reflect or assess all of the central components included in the original conceptual definition (e.g., dissatisfaction with life, worthiness of one's activities). The present version of the SI represents a combination of objective and subjective aspects of measurement. An additional complication is that interviewee's responses, and hence their classification, may be influenced by interviewer characteristics and style.

Construct validity studies of the SI have found that Type A's work longer hours, work more overtime, and travel more on the job. SI-assessed Type A's do not appear to report more psychological strain than their Type B counterparts, either because multiple tasks and time pressure do not bother Type A's or because they are reluctant to acknowledge their distress. Most of these findings are limited, however, by reliance on global self-reports rather than on extensive daily measurements.

An issue related to the reliability, validity, and continued applicability of the SI concerns its vulnerability to change over time. In recent years, interviewers have been trained somewhat differently than those who were employed in the original epidemiological studies of Type A. Although the question content is basically the same, the number of questions has been reduced, and the interview style has been modified. For instance, in comparison to examiners for the first large-scale epidemiologic study of TA and CHD, who were taught to be more gentle and not necessarily hostile, those employed in the later Multiple Risk Factor Intervention Trial (MRFIT) were trained to be more aggressive, rudely interruptive, and confrontational. Friedman also altered the administration procedures for the SI in his Recurrent Coronary Prevention Project (RCPP), under the assumption that the original SI lacked sufficient sensitivity. For the RCPP, videotaping was added to allow visual cues to be incorporated into the assessment process. Although these changes permit the analysis of a greater number of Type A indicators, the revisions make the RCPP interview noncomparable to prior administrations and pose problems for generalizability.

A number of standardized paper and pencil questionnaires have been developed in an attempt to duplicate the evaluation achieved with the SI. The Jenkins Activity Survey (JAS), which is the most popular, uses many of the same questions as the SI, but its validity depends upon the insight and candor of the test taker. This is at odds, however, with Friedman and Rosenman's original belief that Type A's are either too unreflective or too defensive for a self-report questionnaire to adequately assess the presence of TA. Unsurprisingly, the JAS does not correlate with SI assessments of TA at levels significantly above chance even though the JAS attempts to assess similar content. The JAS also has no predictive validity for CHD incidence or mortality after adjusting for traditional risk factors.

The Framingham Type A scale (FTAS) is another popular measure of TA. This 10-item inventory was derived from a pool of 300 questions administered to the participants of the Framingham Heart Study. The FTAS also lacks significant agreement with SI classifications. Its predictive ability is limited solely to the study from which it was derived. Finally, there are no normative data for FTAS, a necessity for the integrity of any psychometric measure.

Given their limited predictive validity, it is somewhat ironic that the construct validity of self-report Type A measures has been studied extensively. This research confirms that persons scoring in the Type A direction prefer higher levels of task difficulty, carry more demanding academic loads, view opponents as more competitive, and attempt to complete tasks as quickly as possible. These results bear on the achievement-striving and job-involvement aspects of TA, but appear uncorrelated with other aspects, such as hostility or nonverbal stylistics, which are assessed by the SI.

Researchers recognized by the late 1970s that only some of the dimensions of TA may represent coronary-prone tendencies. Although attention to particular subcomponents was largely based on serendipitous results, psychosomatic theorists have long advocated a critical role for hostility in the etiology of cardiovascular disease.

In 1977, Matthews and her colleagues examined elements of the SI including anger expressed outward, competitiveness, explosiveness of speech, etc. A more focused component scoring system, emphasizing the anger/hostility aspects of the pattern, was developed by Dembroski soon afterward. Three factors were considered: (1) hostile content—reported frequency of experienced anger and irritation; (2) response intensity—use of emotion-laden, profane, emphatic expressions; and (3) antagonistic interpersonal style—displays of rudeness, condescension, and contempt toward the interviewer. After listening to the taped interview the auditor rates each dimension separately on a 5-point scale. These values are then aggregated (or averaged) to obtain an overall potential for hostility (PH) score. The three sub-component measures have also been used on occasion to predict CHD. Hecker and Chesney at Stanford Research Institute and Barefoot et al. at Duke University Medical Center have recently developed even more elaborate subcomponent scoring systems for the SI which code subject responses question-by-question. The inter-rater reliability of the Dembroski component scoring system falls between .70 and .85, while test-retest reliability has been estimated at .55. Consistency studies for the other systems are still under way, but appear to be in the same range. Evidence for the construct validity of PH is limited, however.

Scores of the Cook-Medley hostility scale (HO), a measure derived from the Minnesota Multiphasic Personality Inventory (MMPI), have also predicted, though less consistently, overall and CHD-related mortality. This standardized inventory appears to measure particular covert facets of hostility, namely, cynicism, suspiciousness, distrust, and resentment. The correlation between PH and HO scores is modest (.29–.37). Careful inspection of the Cook-Medley items indicate that most tap subjective aspects of the construct, sometimes referred to as "neurotic" or "experiential hostility." A smaller set of items measures tendencies to express ill will and negativism through verbal or physical aggression, often described as "antagonistic" or "expressive hostility." The latter dimension is more highly correlated with PH, particularly the interpersonal subcomponent. Evidence to be discussed below indicates that the antagonistic style aspect of hostility may be the toxic element involved in the pathogenesis of CHD.

The hostility construct shares the same multidimensionality problems alluded to earlier with respect to global Type A. Separate facets measured with multiple inventories vary in terms of their affective intensity, expression, and direction. Furthermore, the extent to which these negative tendencies are situation-specific is unknown.

II. PERSONALITY CORRELATES OF TYPE A

Conceptualizing TA as a behavior had benefits, but also tended to divorce it from advances in the study of personality and individual differences. The theoretical investigation of TA as a trait was also impeded by past emphasis upon its potential practical uses in identification, treatment, and prevention in medicine. Researchers have only recently begun to examine how TA is related to underlying personality dimensions.

One advance has come from researchers employing an interactionist approach, which proposes that particular environmental stimuli may not be necessary to elicit Type A reactions from predisposed individuals. Rather, these people may actually create a personal environment that is physically and psychologically taxing. Their competitive and aggressive demeanor may elicit reactions from others that serve as stimuli for continued Type A behavior. They may also subjectively evaluate situations as being more challenging and stressful. These ideas characterize Type A from a broader, less behaviorist perspective and view Type A as more than simply a response pattern.

Especially relevant is the five-factor model of personality, consisting of the major dimensions of neuroticism, extraversion, agreeableness, openness to experience, and conscientiousness. Within this scheme, TA individuals may be seen as high in conscientiousness and extroversion, and low on agreeableness. These ideas are compatible with results of recent studies examining the dispositional correlates of SI Type A, which indicate modest associations with extroversion, need for power, and achievement, but no relationship with neuroticism. Whether openness to experience is relevant to TA is unclear, though a case might be made that Type A's have a narrow range of feelings and are relatively insensitive to their surroundings (i.e., low in the "feelings" facet of openness). Although Type A measured with the SI is not associated with the general dimension of neuroticism, may characterize Type A's. Otherwise, the extreme need to succeed and heightened tendency to become impatient and openly hostile when threatened or frustrated are without obvious explanation. Since feelings of self-doubt are only one as-

pect of the basic dimension of neuroticism (which also includes other elements such as tenseness, fearfulness, and impulsivity, that have no obvious connection to TA), SI Type A-B may be uncorrelated with the general dimension of neuroticism. Still another possibility is that Type A's conceal or deny their underlying neurotic concerns. Defensiveness or denial, coupled with insecurity, may be important elements of the behavior pattern. [See PERSONALITY.]

JAS and FTAS Type A are strongly associated with neuroticism and nonpathological, chronic dysphoria, still another indication that the SI taps a different constellation of dispositions. The overlap with neuroticism might lead to the inference that these self-report measures of Type A are predictive of physical disease. Interestingly, contrary to early psychosomatic theorizing, neuroticism is unrelated to morbidity or mortality from physical disease. On the other hand, persons high on this factor report more bodily complaints, apparently because they are somatically overconcerned and frequently label benign physical changes as signs of illness.

Recently, attention has been devoted to the personality correlates of the hostility complex. The overtly aggressive interpersonal style reflected in PH ratings maps well onto the negative pole of the agreeableness continuum (antagonism) and, as noted earlier, is proposed to be the "toxic" component of hostility and global Type A. The items of HO scale that tap experiential hostility demonstrate its similarity to neuroticism. Questions that measure expressive hostility are associated with antagonism.

III. EPIDEMIOLOGICAL FINDINGS FOR TYPE A BEHAVIOR

A. Prospective Studies

The first prospective study of the Type A–CHD relationship and a major impetus for subsequent research was the Western Collaborative Group Study (WCGS). Led by the originators of TA, this investigation followed approximately 3200 middle-aged, white-collar men who were initially free of CHD. After 8.5 years, those men classified as Type A by the SI were twice as likely to develop CHD compared to their Type B counterparts, even after statistical adjustment for the traditional CHD risk factors. Actual CHD mortality, however, was not an outcome measure.

The JAS was also administered to a subset of the WCGS study population. After four years, a comparison of new CHD cases (again, morbidity and not necessarily fatalities—though these were included) with matched controls revealed JAS Type A individuals to be nearly twice as likely to develop CHD. When simultaneous adjustments for other risk factors were performed, however, the JAS ceased to be a significant predictor.

The next major prospective research on the Type A–CHD relationship was the Framingham Heart Study. Unlike the WCGS, this investigation followed a population of both men and women from both white-collar and blue-collar jobs, all diagnosed as CHD-free upon study entry. Type A/B classification, using the Framingham Type A scale, was determined with a median split within sex and age to form the respective groups. Multivariate analyses at 8-year follow-up found Type A to be a significant, independent predictor of total CHD incidence, myocardial infarction (MI), and angina in white-collar men and total CHD and angina in women. However, TA predicted only differential rates of angina after 10 years.

Enthusiasm for the Type A construct reached its peak in 1978 when a distinguished review panel sponsored by the National Heart, Lung, and Blood Institute concluded that Type A was a significant risk factor for the development of CHD, independent of and comparable in magnitude to standard risk factors. The strength and credibility of the Type A–CHD association began to decline in the 1980s, however, following the publication of negative findings.

Outcomes from the Multiple Risk Factor Intervention Trial (MRFIT) provided much of the initial damage to the predictive validity of the Type A construct. Participants of this study were middle-aged males, chosen on the basis of their high-risk status with respect to blood pressure levels, serum cholesterol, and cigarette smoking who were CHD-free at study entry. These individuals were randomly assigned into either a usual care or a special care group, with the latter group exposed to a variety of interventions designed to reduce their high-risk factor status. After being followed an average of 7 years, results indicated that TA classification, assessed either by the SI or by the JAS, did not predict either total mortality or mortality specifically from CHD.

At approximately the same time as the MRFIT investigation was conducted, survivors of acute MI were being followed in the Multicenter Postinfarction Program. The JAS Type A failed to predict mortality at 1- and 3-year follow-up. This analysis was flawed, however, because the sample comprised patients with relatively mild disease. Individuals in the same program who could not be included in the analysis due to loss of their original Type A assessments had more severe cardiac disease and a higher mortality rate.

After publication of these negative results, there was skepticism about the predictive validity of global Type A. This skepticism was increased by the report of the 22-year follow-up of the original WCGS sample by Ragland and Brand, who failed to find a significant association between Type A/B classification and CHD mortality rates while traditional risk factors continued to be significant predictors of CHD. Also, analyses of the subset of 257 WCGS participants diagnosed as suffering from CHD during the 8.5-year follow-up showed that Type B's actually had a significantly higher reinfarction rate. One possible explanation for the discrepancy between the original WCGS findings and later follow-up is that the outcome measure taken at longer intervals was CHD mortality rather than CHD incidence. Hence, Type A may be related to CHD morbidity, but not to CHD fatality. Ragland and Brand also failed to mention the complicating factor that several of the participants who had developed CHD in the 8.5-year follow-up had been simultaneously receiving Type A behavioral counseling in the Recurrent Coronary Prevention Project.

B. Angiography Studies

The development of precise measures of coronary artery stenosis using angiographic imaging provided new means for studying the relationship between the Type A construct and the extent of coronary artery disease. Numerous trials of individuals referred for angiography were conducted, which assessed TA using the JAS. The few investigations employing the SI yielded an overall positive relationship between Type A and the extent of CAD. Those using self-report techniques, however, did not find significant associations.

C. Meta-Analytic Studies of Global Type A

By the late 1980s a number of researchers began using quantitative, meta-analytic review methods to aggregate the many studies exploring the Type A–CHD relationship. Results from these reviews indicate a significant, though modest, association between TA, as assessed by the SI, and CHD incidence. Self-report measures, on the other hand, were neither reliable nor valid predictors. These meta-analyses also revealed a trend during recent years toward null findings, possibly due to such factors as insufficient sample size, inadequate disease criteria, the dependence upon questionnaires to determine Type A status, and disease-based spectrum (DBS) bias. This final explanation refers to a type of range restriction problem in studies that employ only high-risk or diseased participants. When the subject sample is limited to such a select group of individuals, the range of disease severity is likewise limited, creating a range attenuation effect and thereby possibly decreasing the magnitude of the relationship between Type A and CHD.

In sum, prospective and cross-sectional investigations have found a significant association between TA and the pathogenesis of CHD, though it is small and is observed only for SI-assessed Type A. This relationship applies to CHD incidence, but not CHD mortality, and is weaker than that of standard risk factors. Finally, the association tends to be restricted to general population studies.

D. Hostility Studies

The hostility complex has emerged as a predictor of CHD, even in those studies such as MRFIT, which failed to show a global Type A–CHD relationship. An assessment of hostility made using standardized measures such as the HO Scale or the SI-based PH suggest that a cynical, mistrusting attitude, evidenced by anger, contempt, and aggression, is a predictor of clinical end points.

The first study that examined the relative importance of the SI subcomponents of Type A compared new CHD cases of WCGS participants with matched controls. Potential for Hostility scores best discriminated cases from controls. This was followed by overt anger, competitiveness, experiencing anger more than once a week, vigorousness of response, irritation at waiting in lines, and explosiveness of speech. Analyses of all available cases from the 8.5-year follow-up of WCGS participants also illustrated that PH (using the Hecker and Chesney coding system) best discriminated cases from controls, independent of traditional risk factors.

Recent research has demonstrated that PH and the HO scale significantly predict angiographically docu-

mented CAD severity, even after statistically controlling for age, sex, and traditional risk factors. Prospective studies employing the HO scale have produced inconsistent outcomes. Results from a 20-year follow-up of 1877 males who completed the MMPI in the Western Electric Study demonstrated a significant increase in 10-year CHD incidence in those participants with higher HO scores. A 25-year follow-up of 255 physicians also yielded a four- to five-fold incidence rate among those with an elevated HO scale. However, another study, using a similar methodology, which followed 478 doctors after 25 years failed to replicate these findings. The inconsistent outcomes may be related to the differing circumstances under which the inventory was administered or to the fact that the HO represents a mix of experienced and expressed hostility items.

Accumulated evidence suggests that both global TA and the hostility complex are modestly associated only with CHD morbidity. Although these predispositions predict disease, their predictive utility is modest, and the majority of new CHD cases still cannot be predicted by the best combination of traditional and psychological risk factors. Some researchers have suggested that hostility and Type A are also risk factors for general illness susceptibility, but relevant evidence is scarce.

IV. EXPLANATIONS FOR THE TYPE A–CHD RISK

The hyperreactivity hypothesis is the most popular explanation for the association between TA (or hostility) and CHD. The theory proposes that persons high in TA or hostility exhibit excessive elevations in cardiovascular and neuroendocrine arousal in response to particular environmental situations, and thereby accelerate the atherosclerotic process and increase the incidence of life-threatening cardiac arrhythmias. This hypothesis assumes that a predisposition to hyperresponsivity creates physiologic changes that eventuate in disease. There is some evidence that sympathetic nervous system (SNS) arousal alters metabolic function in myocardial cells, increases the deposition and incorporation of coronary artery plaques, and may facilitate their rupture. These changes can produce coronary artery thrombosis and myocardial infarction. Catecholamines may also interact with existing atherosclerosis to generate cardiac arrhythmias. The pituitary-adrenocortical system may additionally be implicated in the pathogenesis of CHD. Chronic elevations in cortico-steroids have been linked to elevations in serum lipids, increased atherosclerosis in animals, and higher proportions of dead or injured endothelial cells. Studies using coronary angiography have also found positive correlations between elevated plasma cortisol and early atherosclerosis. Exaggerated physiological responses may also compromise the immune system, thus increasing susceptibility to other illness in addition to CHD. Although chronic elevations in these physiologic systems have been alleged as possible mechanisms for CHD development, definitive evidence indicating the degree of risk associated with a given magnitude of reactivity is lacking.

A large number of laboratory-based studies have documented that SI-assessed Type A males manifest larger increases in systolic blood pressure, diastolic blood pressure, and heart rate in response to stressors than do male Type B's. These differences are particularly evident in response to moderately stressful or challenging cognitive tasks. Type B males actually demonstrate higher arousal, however, in situations that are ambiguous or involve role-conflict. Physical stressors have not consistently elicited differences, unless an incentive has been simultaneously provided. There are relatively few studies involving Type A/B females and those available are inconclusive. The failure to produce differential reactivity in Type A/B women may be due to sex-role expectations, inappropriate stimuli, or because of the inapplicability of the global Type A construct to females.

Trait anger and hostility as measures by PH also appear modestly, though less consistently, related to blood pressure responses to anger-eliciting tasks. HO scores are somewhat more consistently related to heightened pressor changes, especially in response to interpersonal stressors. Support for the reactivity model for hostility appears to be dependent upon the assessment measure employed.

The magnitude of physiological responsivity differences between high TA vs low TA (or hostile) persons is modest, raising the question of whether such differences could produce cardiovascular pathology. Whether exaggerated reactivity to laboratory stimuli possesses external validity is still unclear. Research using ambulatory monitors of cardiovascular functioning is, unfortunately, still in its early stages.

The bulk of laboratory research has focused primarily on heart rate and blood pressure changes, indices of SNS arousal. There is some, albeit sparse, evidence to suggest that excessive pituitary-adreno-cortical responses may be implicated in the etiology of CHD in Type A's. One problem or ambiguity, however, is that elevated physiological measures may simply be indicative of increased effort to cope with challenges by Type A individuals as opposed to a predisposition or pathogenic mechanism. Human psychophysiological investigations indicate that exaggerated reactivity may be shown using either positively or negatively valenced stimuli (i.e., challenges and threats).

Although most Type A researchers have appropriately assumed that challenging or stressful situations elicit both stereotypical Type A reactions and hyperresponsivity in particular individuals, an equally plausible explanation is that these persons have an underlying diathesis, or physiological responsiveness, which is reflected not only in their reactivity to experimental tasks but also in their Type A personality. A constitutional predisposition for exaggerated responses could be the course of TA itself.

A critical question concerns why TA relates to CHD incidence, but not to CHD mortality. One suggestion is that coronary-prone behavior may be more strongly related to acute precipitating factors (e.g., cardiac arrhythmias, vessel spasm) than to atherosclerosis. Consequently, Type A's may be more likely to experience cardiac events, but are not necessarily destined to die prematurely.

An additional explanation for TA or hostility as risk factors is that coronary-prone persons act in ways, or have health habits, that encourage the disease process. For example, TA's may ignore early cardiac symptoms or create frequent stressful episodes for themselves. Perhaps the difference in arousal between persons high vs low in coronary-proneness is not crucial, but rather the frequency with which such episodes occur. Type A's and hostile persons may also suffer from other inborn physiological weaknesses or liabilities that predispose them to CHD (e.g., greater clotting). Finally, persons presumed to exhibit a high number of coronary-prone behaviors may be vulnerable because they are also high on traditional risk factors. This possibility has been given little consideration because it has been claimed that Type A predicted CHD independent of traditional risk factors. However, epidemiologic studies assess many traditional risk factors in simple ways that may overlook important subtleties in smoking patterns, eating patterns, etc. A recent investigation using improved procedures (e.g., ambulatory blood pressure measurement) showed that Type A's are more likely to be hypertensive, even though TA had been previously assumed to be unrelated to chronically elevated blood pressure. [*See* HEART DISEASE: PSYCHOLOGICAL PREDICTORS.]

V. THEORIES OF THE ORIGINS OF TYPE A BEHAVIOR

The search for the origins of TA is dependent upon the researchers' theoretical position on the Type A–CHD relationship. Cognitive-social learning theory is a popular perspective, but others have argued for a genetic or constitutional basis. Evidence is available for both views.

The psychobiological, or constitutional predisposition, perspective elaborated upon in the previous section is compatible with a genetic basis for the TA construct. Twin studies of the heritability of cardiovascular reactivity have, unfortunately, been methodologically inadequate (e.g., failing to adjust for twin resemblance in baseline blood pressure) and, hence, inconclusive. Research with twins and families has also examined the heritability of Type A and its components. Analysis of the single investigation using SI-assessed twins did not detect a genetic component of global Type A, but did find hostility to be modestly heritable. The inconsistent findings may be due to different evaluation procedures or the possibility of polygenetic influences in TA development.

Social learning theorists emphasize the role of parenting behaviors in the evolution of Type A personality. Parents of Type A's tend to be more critical of their children, but they also provide higher and more ambiguous performance standards in comparison to the parents of Type B children. Such behaviors may foster TA in children to the extent that the children are repeatedly urged to try harder and perform better, yet are not given precise standards with which to gauge their performance. An important point of confusion lies in the direction of effect. Although Type A may be the result of particular environmental elicitors, such as parenting styles, Type A/B children may also evoke differential parenting styles from their caregivers. The latter hypothesis is compatible with the genetic argument. A transactional approach, which assumes that both parenting behaviors and inborn temperament act reciprocally to make significant contributions to the growth of TA, is also compatible with existing evidence.

Cognitions, more specifically personal beliefs, may foster and promote TA. Type A's may equate personal worth with their achievements, believe that there are no universal moral principles, and believe that resources are scarce (thereby justifying hostile, competitive behavior). The Type A personality would then evolve as a coping strategy to deal with these thoughts and fears. Empirical evidence for this view is unavailable. Also, there is no evidence that these kinds of cognitive beliefs are associated with exaggerated physiological responses, poor health habits, or constitutional predisposition. In a parallel literature, hostile persons tend to perceive that they have been treated unjustly and that aggressive behavior may be necessary to maintain their integrity, but there has been no systematic study of how these beliefs relate directly to cardiopathogenic processes.

VI. ISSUES CONCERNING INTERVENTION

Type A has also been the target of intervention measures to improve prevention efforts and prognosis for CHD. Enthusiasm about altering TA pattern has been tempered, however, by ongoing controversy about the nature of Type A, which components of TA are coronary-prone, how accurately TA is measured, and how changes in TA as a result of treatment can be documented.

Clinical research has demonstrated that personality traits are very difficult to change and efforts to do so are generally met with resistance. A number of studies investigating the effectiveness and feasibility of modifying Type A personalities have nevertheless been undertaken. The most impressive of these endeavors is the Recurrent Coronary Prevention Project (RCPP) which randomized 862 post-MI patients into either a control treatment group or Type A counseling group. Controls were counseled to improve their diets, exercise patterns, and medication compliance. In addition to these recommendations, participants in the experimental group were exposed to a variety of cognitive-behavioral techniques (e.g., time management, relaxation) designed to modify daily Type A behaviors. At a 4.5-year follow-up, Type A modification procedures significantly lowered the CHD recurrence rate, although no differences in cardiac mortality rates were found.

With the exception of the RCPP, treatment studies have found little evidence of disease reduction, although a number of investigations have documented significant behavior modifications in Type A participants. Focused approaches using subcomponent models of coronary-prone behavior (e.g., hostility) have also been effective in producing behavior change. None of these studies have demonstrated significant reductions in CHD incidence, recurrence, or mortality rates, however. This may be partially due to the short-term nature of most of the interventions and reliance on healthy samples.

The practicality and feasibility of employing Type A modification procedures to reduce CHD risk needs to be carefully considered. As a CHD-prevention tool for the general population such treatment would be extremely costly in terms of money, labor, and time. Given the small number of actual CHD cases that TA can identify in advance, the benefits would be relatively small. Although TA's may have double the CHD incidence of Type B's, the number of false-positives (i.e., TA's who do not develop CHD) is many times the number of true-positives (i.e., TA's who do develop CHD). (Traditional risk factors also possess this predictive problem, though not as severely.) For high-risk individuals or those who have survived an MI, the potential benefits of intervention may be more substantial.

VII. UNRESOLVED QUESTIONS AND FUTURE DIRECTIONS

The introduction of the Type A construct was a milestone in the study of behavioral factors in disease and in the general development of behavioral medicine. Yet, over 30 years after its formulation, controversy and criticism still surround the relationship between Type A and CHD. Much of this stems from a number of unresolved questions, most of which have already been raised in this article and thus need only brief explication here.

First, the relationship between Type A and the more general theory and measurement of personality needs further examination. The original "behavioral" emphasis had the advantage of avoiding the excesses of psychoanalytic speculation, but also isolated Type A

from advances in the study of personality. The Five-Factor Model is relevant to TA, but more research and theorizing are needed. A clearer conception of the attributes underlying Type A may lead to the creation of instruments, or the use of conventional personality measures, which are more objective, convenient, and less costly to both subjects and researchers than the SI.

The relationship between Type A and conventional dimensions of personality also raises concerns about how TA individuals actually behave in their daily life. Researchers of coronary-prone behavior have relied almost exclusively upon global self-reports. Naturalistic observation using state-of-the-art experience sampling and ambulatory monitoring would provide valuable information about whether TA behavior in daily life is similar to responses to the SI, and to Friedman and Rosenman's original conceptions. Such research may also provide opportunities for the design of an accurate, reliable, and more predictive assessment instrument.

Another set of unresolved matters concern the actual size of the relationship between TA and CHD. Meta-analytic surveys indicate that the magnitude of risk associated with the Type A personality is statistically significant, but how clinically meaningful it is remains unclear. Why TA relates to higher morbidity, but not to mortality is an especially puzzling and important question. Perhaps TA is associated only with acute precipitating events, but not atherosclerosis. There may even be protective factors associated with global Type A that allow the individual who experiences a cardiac event to recover.

Similar questions may be raised about the hostility complex. Again, the size of the relationship with CHD is modest at best. Unresolved questions include which components of hostility are general disease factors and which, if any, are CHD-specific. Rosenman and Friedman originally conceptualized Type A as consisting of two components—impatience and hostility—but some research indicates that global Type A and hostility are independent risk factors for CHD.

The developmental origins of TA are also unclear. Type A as a personality construct implies a constitutional, biological temperament as its base, but many researchers subscribe to a social learning model and minimize the role of heredity. More research into genetic factors and mechanisms underlying the temperament of TA is needed.

The mediators linking Type A personality and CHD

incidence are currently under investigation. Although chronic sympathetic arousal is a popular explanation for the association, results are inconclusive. Hyperreactivity, by itself, seems unlikely to furnish a complete explanation for the CHD risk conferred by TA or hostility.

Finally, the feasibility, practicality, and necessity of intervention procedures to reduce TA behavior in healthy populations need further attention. If TA modification is promoted, whom should be targeted, what procedures should it include, and how will it be made cost-effective? At this stage, high-risk individuals and persons with existing CHD seem to be the most appropriate candidates for behavioral treatment.

These unresolved and somewhat daunting questions may discourage the prospects of success in understanding how dispositional factors influence disease and the application of this knowledge for medical practice. There are clearly some difficult issues to be faced. Future research should concentrate upon a clearer conceptualization of TA and hostility by drawing upon theoretical advances in the relevant areas of personality and temperament and upon methodological advances in the study of everyday behavior. The recognition that TA is related, albeit modestly, to morbidity, but not to mortality, should also promote research to go beyond a simplistic hyperreactivity explanation for the TA–CHD association. The Type A personality is not a dead issue, as some might suggest; however, some major rejuvenation is in order.

This article has been reprinted from the *Encyclopedia of Human Behavior, Volume 4.*

BIBLIOGRAPHY

Chesney, M. A. (Ed.) (1988). Area review. Coronary-prone behavior: Continuing evolution of the concept [Special Issue]. *Ann. Behav. Med.* 10(2).

Houston, B. K., & Snyder, C. R. (Eds.) (1988). "Type A Behavior Pattern." Wiley, New York.

Miller, T. Q., Turner, C. W., Tindale, R. S., Posavac, E. J., & Dugoni, B. L. (1991). Reasons for the trend toward null findings in research on Type A behavior. *Psychol. Bull.* 110, 469–485.

Smith, T. W. (1992). Hostility and health: Current status of a psychosomatic hypothesis. *Health Psychol.* 11, 139–150.

Strube, M. (1991). "Type A Behavior." Sage, Newbury Park, CA.

Suls, J., & Sanders, G. (1989). Why do some behavioral styles place people at coronary risk? In "In Search of Coronary-Prone Behavior" (A. W. Siegman and T. M. Dembroski, Eds.), pp. 1–20. Erlbaum, Hillsdale, NJ.

Unemployment and Mental Health

Samuel H. Osipow

The Ohio State University

Career An individual's lifelong sequence of work activities.
De-skillinization A decline of job skills through disuse and obsolescence.
Job A set of specific work tasks.
Moderator Variable A variable that operates indirectly on the relationship between two other variables.
Outplacement Counseling Assistance given by organizations to former employees who have lost their jobs.
Position Several jobs that have similarities across organizations.
Vocation The positions occupied by an individual over a period of time.

UNEMPLOYMENT has long been a problem in industrial countries. Periods of high employment usually reflect strong and robust economies during which times most workers find employment relatively easily. When the strength of the economy falters, as it inevitably seems to do, workers are typically laid off, sometimes temporarily, sometimes permanently, when their particular industry suffers a permanent down-

turn. Such permanent changes occur when an industry is replaced by a newer one that uses a new technology. While some employees can make the transition to the newer methods with relatively little retraining, often employers prefer to hire new people trained in the technology because they are seen to be more current with the methods and also because they are likely to be young and, thus, less expensive to hire than older workers familiar with the older methods.

I. INTRODUCTION

The cyclical nature of these employment patterns is troublesome, and contributes to employee uncertainty and anxiety about job stability. In a former time, workers had the expectation (realistic or not) that employers expected their loyalty and, in return, would be loyal to the workers in times of economic contraction by trying to keep them employed during downturns. In the modern era, however, that expectation no longer exists. Workers often feel like dispensable components of their organization, and are led to believe, realistically, that they are likely to change jobs, and even careers, a number of times during their work life. This attitude of temporariness exerts a price on the well-being of workers. For example, studies have shown that variations in the strength of the economy can predict rates of hospital admissions, along with a variety of other indicators, such as rises in infant mortality rates and the demand for and costs associated with social services. [*See* ANXIETY.]

As a consequence of the change in attitude, industrialized countries have developed institutions to aid people during their involuntary job transitions. These institutions involve government- and employee-sponsored financial benefits, as well as some (mostly minimal) government assistance in providing job leads and job seeking. Most recently, some large employers who are terminating the employment of large numbers of workers (downsizing) sometimes provide what is called "outplacement" counseling. This outplacement counseling is designed to help the employee find another job, or a training program, and often includes temporary clerical and office facilities for the employees to use in their search. Because of the widespread nature of unemployment, volunteer social support networks have also sprung up, such as "Forty Plus," which provides help in job search, resume preparation, and psychological support from others in the same position. [*See* SOCIAL SUPPORT.]

In considering the mental health implications of unemployment, it is important to recognize that many idiosyncratic factors influence how stressful unemployment may be to an individual. A major factor would be whether or not the loss of the job was voluntary or involuntary, and, if involuntary, whether it affected only the individual employee (fired for "cause") or others in the organization (terminated for economic reasons). It is also important to consider variables such as sex, age, and occupational level in trying to understand the effects of unemployment on individuals.

II. EFFECTS OF UNEMPLOYMENT ON MENTAL HEALTH BY AGE AND SEX

A complicated relationship between mental health and unemployment exists, differing for men and women and with an interaction by age as well. Research results found by Warr and his associates indicate that the group most seriously impaired by unemployment is middle-aged men, whose work life seems intimately associated with their sense of self worth and the fulfillment of their life role. In addition, men in this age group are often under heavy financial strain, supporting children in college, as well as helping older parents. When such men become unemployed and do not find jobs relatively quickly, they lose hope and often suffer noticeable depressions. The mental health of men who had good jobs and more attachment to their job before unemployment is more negatively affected by unemployment than for men who had poor jobs. [*See* DEPRESSION.]

However, in somewhat older men, that is, those approaching retirement, there is a somewhat different effect. Many of these men have been looking forward to leaving the work force, and, at least psychologically, can often rationalize the job loss to be early retirement. Although they may experience many serious financial problems, psychologically, the impact of their unemployment does not seem to be as devastating as that experienced by men in the middle-age category. For example, in general, loss of hope is not a significant feature seen in the older group. Their concerns may be mostly financial along with a sense of "betrayal" by an employer. [*See* HOPE; RETIREMENT.]

For younger men, those in their 20s and early 30s, unemployment seems to have serious effects, but not as bad as for the middle-aged men. The younger men realistically seem to understand that they still have time to make major career changes and recover financially and psychologically from a period of unemployment. With the prospect for recovery of self-esteem and income relatively good, unemployment has less negative effect on mental health. Men in their 20s and 30s can also realistically expect to find employment more easily than men in their late 40s and 50s.

For some of these younger men, in fact, unemployment can sometimes even provide a socially acceptable escape from an unsatisfactory job or career and enable the worker to get retraining or seek work in a field potentially more satisfying. These men, even if they have started a family, are usually not experiencing the major financial responsibilities of the middle-aged group. Nonetheless, young men unemployed for at least 3 months or more often turn to their parents for help, and in many ways, deal with the situation as if they were adolescents rather than young adults.

Next, consider the impact of unemployment on adolescent males. The psychological effects on this group are minimal. The explanation lies in several factors: work has not yet begun to define their identity; they have few significant financial responsibilities; and their life stage requires the mastery of other developmental tasks with which they can occupy their attention. However, there are data that suggest a lingering effect of unemployment for many late adolescents and early/young adults.

The impact of unemployment on women is even more complex than it is for men, as is often the case with respect to women's careers. At first, findings of research seemed to indicate that unemployment had relatively little effect on the mental health of women. These results probably grew out of the belief that men and women differ with respect to the salience and centrality of work in their lives. Since work salience seems to be negatively correlated with the level of distress when unemployed, and since work is seen to have less importance in the lives of women, it would stand to reason that unemployment might have relatively little effect on women.

However, it proves to be an error to consider all women as a single group. For career-oriented women, the impact of unemployment on mental health was found to be similar to that of men. However, for women who were working but for whom their jobs were not "careers," the impact was much less severe. Marginally employed women suffered less impairment to their mental health when unemployed than women whose jobs were better and more career oriented. It should be remembered that many women often occupy short-term jobs, and may view unemployment as a natural event, and expect to experience periods of unemployment, both planned and unplanned. For example, they may leave work for a period after childbirth or at other important junctures in their lives, and can accept periods of unemployment with more equanimity than do most men. This situation may be changing, as a result of the explosive growth of two-earner and even two-career families, in which the income of both partners is essential to the maintenance of the standard of living sought. Thus, the question of the impact of unemployment on the mental health of marginally or non-career-oriented women deserves reexamination, since increasing numbers of women in the labor force view their jobs as financially and psychologically necessary in a manner similar to that of men.

III. SOME OUTCOMES OF UNEMPLOYMENT ON MENTAL HEALTH

One of the first variables examined associated with mental health and unemployment has been the duration of unemployment. There have been a number of investigations of the correlation of the two variables. One finding is that prolonged unemployment has a serious negative impact on health in general and on the quality of an individual's life. Lengthy periods of unemployment seem to exacerbate existing health problems, both chronic and latent in nature, as well as to interfere with desirable health-seeking behaviors.

Certainly, in the United States, with health insurance intimately tied to employment, former workers will have seriously reduced access to medical care even if they have major medical problems and desire treatment. Thus, there is an additional and obvious relationship between unemployment and economic decline which adds to the reduced availability of health care.

For example, we find high rates of both physical and mental disorder among the urban poor, Although there might be a "chicken and egg" phenomenon involved—that is, do physical and mental problems contribute to unemployment or are they the result of unemployment?—the correlation between the two is evident. It is well known that unemployment rates vary for different cultural, racial, and ethnic groups in the United States. For example the rate of unemployment of African Americans has been more than 11% since 1978, 2.5 times greater than that for Whites, with an even greater difference when looking at inner-city unemployment

Overall, it seems clear that there are indirect effects of the reduced income of prolonged unemployment on psychological well-being, transmitted via the perceived (if not actual) financial strain that results from unemployment.

In addition, studies have found that unemployment is associated with rises in infant mortality, increased deaths from cardiovascular disease and alcohol-related disorders, increases in suicide rates, and problems in family relations. It has been speculated that early family experiences may be related to work dysfunction, which interacts with stress, exacerbating the problems that may contribute to an individual's unemployment. If this is so, it is possible that the unemployment of one generation can lead to dysfunctional family experiences, which, in turn, can contribute to the unemployment of the next generation. [*See* ALCOHOL PROBLEMS; FAMILY SYSTEMS; SUICIDE.]

One unmeasured impact of unemployment is the degree to which it impairs the mental health of family members other than the unemployed individual. Unemployed workers experience family tension, loss of self-respect, and emotional disturbance. Some also project their loss of self-respect to other family members, assuming that they are no longer valued by spouse and children. However, the families of the unemployed also experience tension that may result from discomfort in interacting with the unemployed member. Families also experience anxiety about their well-being since they are concerned about economic resources. Since financial conflicts are frequently the major cause of marital breakups, one would also expect the divorce rate to rise during periods of widespread unemployment. [See DIVORCE.]

Self-esteem seems to serve as a moderator variable between unemployment and psychological well-being. People who are low in self-esteem before they are unemployed are more sensitive to their employment status and more flexible regarding job offers than individuals high in self-esteem before unemployment. Anxiety, loss of self-esteem, and loss of self-confidence seem to be especially noticeable for people who had been at lower socioeconomic levels prior to unemployment. Another undesirable impact of unemployment is seen in the erosion of the former worker's sense of skill. There is a process called "de-skillinization" that can occur over time in ex-workers, a process that leads to self-doubt as well as doubt by others that the individual can make a contribution to an organization. This process contributes to the downward spiral of the mental health of the unemployed worker. [See SELF-ESTEEM.]

Work identity seems to be an integral part of the self-concept. Work identity is thought to evolve, at least partly, through vocational role playing in which individuals learn to gravitate toward work that is perceived to be congruent with individual needs, abilities, values, and interests.

It has also been found that unemployed workers seem to lose an accurate sense of time. The loss of a regular daily schedule, to which most individuals have become accustomed, can lead to added feelings of depression and anxiety. It has been found that the purposeful use of the spare time made available by unemployment can serve to buffer stress resulting from unemployment.

Studies conducted that examined health rates during the great economic depression of the 1930s found that the rate of recovery from schizophrenia declined during that period, but appeared to improve with counseling, rehabilitation, training, and, of course, the availability of employment. In this connection, it is important to underscore the long-term impact of mental

disorder on a return to work. Studies have shown that only 29% of people with mental illness are seen to be viable candidates for hiring by employers, and the more severe the disorder, the worse the chances of getting hired. Thus, the social stigma of mental disorder further reinforces the problems of unemployment for individuals whose mental disorder has abated, and could conceivably become a stressor leading to a mental health relapse. [See SCHIZOPHRENIA.]

An unseen negative mental health outcome of unemployment lies in work settings themselves. Uncertainty and ambiguity in the workplace are potential stressors. Among those factors contributing to uncertainty and ambiguity is job insecurity. Job insecurity has been found to predict changes over time reflecting reduced job satisfaction and physical symptoms. In addition, job strain often fosters increased worries about health; thus, it is not even necessary to be unemployed for its negative effects on mental health to be experienced, merely the "threat" can be a negative factor on mental health.

Finally, it has been proposed that the unemployed experience emotions similar to those a grieving person experiences in association with the loss of a loved one, for example, anger, bargaining, depression, and finally, acceptance. Significantly, anticipated job loss has similar effects on people. With respect to reducing the negative effects of anticipated job loss, the major treatments are prevention and increasing the sense of competency in the worker.

There seems to be a relatively well-documented connection between alcohol abuse and unemployment. This link has been demonstrated in at least one study.

IV. FACTORS IN MENTAL HEALTH INTERVENTION IN UNEMPLOYED WORKERS

Career development theory suggests certain concepts that can be helpful in dealing with the negative mental health effects of unemployment. For example, theory suggests that there is an interaction between one's interests and personality and the variables in the work setting (e.g., stress) which can "cause" mental health problems in certain kinds of individuals.

It has usually been assumed that career counseling should occur only after an individual's mental health has been established. Recent findings have demonstrated impressively that career problems and mental health problems interact, and that sometimes starting to treat both issues at the same time can be more effective than approaching them sequentially. Thus, some current writers have proposed that since there is a powerful interaction between career adjustment and mental health, both should be simultaneously emphasized in counseling.

In order to accomplish this, however, a somewhat differently trained provider than the typical clinician is needed. The task requires someone who is familiar with both psychopathology and psychological processes as well as with career theory, issues, and career counseling techniques. Ordinarily, counseling psychologists have such training and experience and are likely to be uniquely qualified to provide such interventions. Counselors sophisticated about career processes might be helpful to workers in becoming realistic in their career aspirations and also in the identification of educational interventions that might be helpful in a return to work.

The merger of treating pathological and normal processes has important implications for counseling interventions. Instead of disjointed attempts to deal first with mental health problems and then with their career implications, by dealing with the two together the length of time to a desirable outcome can be decreased.

This approach can be especially important given the often-repeated finding that the longer the wait to offer a mental health intervention to an unemployed worker, the more emotional deterioration will occur, making it more difficult for the counseling to be effective. In addition, the more time that goes by, the greater is the deterioration in family relations, ex-worker self-esteem, and financial resources, all of which probably contribute to the poorer prognosis over time. Some evidence exists that mental health interventions are best begun within 3 months of unemployment.

V. SOCIAL IMPLICATIONS

The question remains of who shall provide mental health services to unemployed or about-to-be-unemployed workers. State employment services are usually well equipped to aid in the job search but not with the impact of unemployment on the person. This lack is made even worse by the erosion of institutional support for unemployed workers, for example, less power for government agencies such as the National Labor Relations Board and labor unions. In fact, one would think the task of helping unemployed workers regain their mental equilibrium would be a high priority item for labor unions, but it is not. There are no organizational sources for such assistance.

BIBLIOGRAPHY

Adams, A. V. & Mangum, G. (1978). *The lingering crisis of youth unemployment.* Kalamazoo, MI: Upjohn Institute for Employment Records.

Borgen, W. A., & Amundsen, N. E. (1987). The dynamics of unemployment. *Journal of Counseling and Development, 66,* 180–184.

Borman, T. (1991). *The first "real" job: A study of young workers.* Albany, NY: The State University of New York Press.

Crites, J. O. (1981). *Career counseling. Models, methods, and materials.* New York: McGraw-Hill.

Feather, N. T., & O'Brien, G. E. (1986). A longitudinal study of the effects of employment and unemployment on school leavers. *Journal of Occupational Psychology, 59,* 121–144.

Heany, C. A., Israel, B. A., & House, J. A. (1994). Chronic job insecurity among automobile workers: effects on job satisfaction and health. *Social Science Medicine, 38,* 1431–1437.

Herr, E. (1989). Career Development and mental health. *Journal of Career Development, 16,* 5–18.

Latack, J. C., & Dozier, J. B. (1986). After the ax falls: job loss as a career transition. *Academy of Management Review, 11,* 375–392.

Osipow, S. H. & Fitzgerald, L. F. (1993). Unemployment and mental health: a neglected relationship. *Applied and Preventive Psychology, 2,* 59–63.

Swinton, D. H. (1992) The economic status of African Americans. In B. J. Tidwell, (Editor). *The state of Black America* (pages 61–117). New York: Urban League.

Warr, P. (1987). *Work, unemployment, and mental health.* Oxford, England: Clarendon.

Warr, P., & Jackson, P. (1982). Factors influencing the psychological impact of prolonged unemployment and of re-employment. *Psychological Medicine, 15,* 795–807.

Urban Life and Mental Well-Being

Maureen M. Black

University of Maryland School of Medicine

Indicated Prevention/Intervention Intervention directed to individuals or groups of individuals who are experiencing a problem.

Prevention Science Programs to prevent or to moderate major human dysfunction by eliminating the causes of the disorder before the problem is manifested.

Selected Prevention/Intervention Intervention directed to individuals or groups of individuals who are at increased risk for a problem.

Universal Prevention/Intervention Intervention directed to an entire group or population before a problem exists.

Urbanization Concentration of citizens in an area defined by political and/or geographical boundaries.

URBANIZATION occurs as citizens migrate to urban areas, often in search of increased opportunities for education, employment, housing, or recreation. Yet the population density, limited resources, and rigid infrastructure inherent in cities often present challenges to urban dwellers that undermine their mental health and well-being. This article will discuss the problems of urbanization related to mental health and intervention strategies to promote mental well-being.

I. URBANIZATION

Urbanization is occurring at alarming rates throughout the world as people migrate into urban areas in search of jobs, education, and health and social services. In the United States and Canada approximately three quarters of the population lives in urban communities (76% and 78%, respectively), and by 2000, it is expected that half the people in the world will live in cities. Urban areas offer a vast array of excellent opportunities for recreation, services, and housing. However, urban areas also include serious challenges often associated with poverty, including failed housing projects, boarded up houses, crowding, and inhumane living conditions.

Although most depictions of urbanization include buildings and structures, the primary aspect of urbanization is people. Urbanization brings people together into densely populated areas. In many cities middle-class families migrate to the suburban areas, leaving the cities to two divergent groups of people: (1) upper class families who can afford to insulate themselves from the negative aspects of urban life and (2) lower class families who have few economic resources. Commercialism and the increasing disparity between the upper and lower classes often lead to frustration among families living in poverty.

When living and working conditions become too confined, they breed stress, including decreased support for prosocial behavior, disintegration of extended families, and tolerance for deviance. These problems, in turn, increase the risk for mental health problems in both adults and children, including depression, substance use, delinquency, violence, and post traumatic stress disorder. In addition, the low socioeconomic status that often occurs among urban families increases their vulnerability to negative health outcome. Much attention has been focused on the relationship between urbanization and mental health. [*See* AGGRESSION; DEPRESSION; POSTTRAUMATIC STRESS; SOCIOECONOMIC STATUS; STRESS.]

William Julius Wilson has studied and described the challenges that urbanization brings to low income citizens, particularly those from ethnic minorities. Limited opportunities for social and economic mobility contribute to feelings of helplessness, hopelessness, and despair. These negative attitudes undermine the social fabric of the community and challenge basic values such as personal commitment, interpersonal respect, and family relationships. It is no surprise that the impoverished areas of our cities are overcome by high rates of single parenthood, substance abuse, and violence.

II. URBAN PROBLEMS WORLDWIDE

In developing countries, people living in crowded urban slums are threatened by infectious diseases and nutritional problems. Children are particularly vulnerable with rates of undernutrition among young children approaching 50% in many countries of Asia and sub-Saharan Africa, leaving them with little resistance when they are threatened by infectious diseases. Although undernutrition and infectious diseases continue to be major problems in developing countries, thanks to vaccine development and other public health measures, significant progress has been made in reducing malnutrition and the threat from infectious diseases such as small pox, measles, and polio. Yet UNICEF claims that the physical and mental health of millions of children and adults in developing countries continues to be challenged by urban forces that have no biomedical or technical solutions. Problems associated with poverty, population, and environmental stress are exacerbated in urban areas. With few options to effect change, urban dwellers are often left with a sense of isolation and futility that can lead to mental health problems and a negative cycle whereby those most at risk for health and mental

health problems are further traumatized. The forecast is of major concern because the vast majority of the world's largest cities are in developing countries where the disparity between social classes is often overwhelming. Social and behavioral interventions are necessary to address these issues and to prevent the problems from overtaking the benefits associated with urbanization.

Industrialized countries are often heavily urbanized. Rates of undernutrition are very low, largely due to economic development, availability of food, and social and educational programs. Ten years ago, we may have said that effective public health programs had virtually eliminated the threats from infectious diseases in industrialized countries. However, an infectious disease (acquired immune deficiency syndrome—AIDS) is now the leading cause of death among males and females between the ages of 15 and 44 in the United States. The virus that causes AIDS (human immunodeficiency virus—HIV) is spread through the transfer of bodily fluids and prevalence rates are highest in urban centers. With no cure and no effective vaccine to prevent HIV infection, we are completely dependent upon behavioral interventions to prevent the spread of this deadly disease. [*See* HIV/AIDS.]

The problems of poverty, population, and environmental stress, identified by UNICEF as challenging citizens in developing countries are all too familiar in industrialized cities and may be particularly challenging to specialized groups of citizens, such as children, elderly, disabled, and ethnic minorities. For example, epidemiological studies from both industrialized and developing countries suggest that in comparison with children in rural areas, urban children have elevated rates of delinquency, psychological disturbance, and behavior problems. The poverty, population density, and environmental stress that characterize many urban environments undermine healthy child development.

In this era of fiscal conservatism, much attention has been directed to the need for outcome studies that are focused on reducing public health problems and improving the lives of urban citizens. Evaluations of interventions that are limited to process measures (e.g., number of people served, number of sessions conducted) are no longer adequate. Funders want to examine changes in behavior; even changes in attitude are often insufficient. Yet, solutions to these global problems are neither simple nor straightforward. Multifactorial strategies that address interventions at the level of communities, families, parents, and children are needed to solve these problems and to secure health and dignity for urban citizens of the future.

III. INTERVENTIONS

There is widespread recognition that interventions conducted by psychologists and other social scientists can be effective in changing behavior and are essential to overcome some of the most severe challenges facing urban citizens, including HIV infection and violence. However, most of the emphasis in psychological interventions has been placed on implementation and evaluation of intervention strategies with individuals who are experiencing a problem. Less focus has been placed on interventions with *groups* of individuals or on interventions that *prevent* problems before they occur. As policymakers recognize that preventing problems associated with urban living is a responsible fiscal policy, they need guidelines to inform them on social policy recommendations regarding the mental health and well-being of urban dwellers.

In the past many interventions were based on elimination or reduction of risk factors with little attention to theory. However, the link between risk factors and behavior is often indirect and influenced by social–psychological factors. When interventions are based on theories of behavioral or developmental change, investigators are protected against missing critical variables and are more able to interpret their findings. Without knowing how and why interventions work (or do not work), planners and policymakers have difficulty replicating successful interventions and avoiding the pitfalls of unsuccessful ones.

The principles of prevention science, articulated by Coie and colleagues, can be applied to urban issues. Prevention science attempts to prevent human dysfunction by eliminating the cause before the dysfunction actually occurs. By counteracting risk factors with protective factors, prevention scientists strive for a balance that enables individuals to avoid disorders, such as mental illness. Risk factors for mental illness may include a family history of mental illness, a stressful environment, and ineffective coping strategies. In contrast, protective factors may include individual characteristics, such as an adaptable temperament or cognitive skills, or environmental characteristics, such as a supportive family or school. Although protective factors may ameliorate the problem directly, they often work by moderating the potentially negative consequences associated with risk factors. Therefore, prevention scientists emphasize the importance of conceptualizing investigations of urbanization and mental health from an ecological perspective that includes cultural and social factors, as well as individual factors. [*See* PROTECTIVE FACTORS IN DEVELOPMENT OF PSYCHOPATHOLOGY.]

Just as individuals vary in their response to specific risk factors, they also vary in their response to interventions and to protective factors. For example, developmental models are necessary to understand how the role of aggressive behavior varies depending on individual factors such as age and gender, and on contextual factors, such as peer group behavior and expectations. Similarly, interventions that are effective in alleviating aggression among preschoolers may differ from those that are effective with older children. Given the pervasive influence of environmental factors associated with urbanization on individual well-being, prospective longitudinal designs are often necessary to understand how resilient citizens are able to mobilize protective factors and thrive, despite the presence of individual and environmental risk factors in an urban environment.

Urban policymakers are looking for credible evidence regarding the impact interventions have on the behavior of urban dwellers. Emotional appeals are no longer effective. The optimal design for evaluating an intervention is a randomized clinical trial in which a randomization procedure is used to assign participants to an intervention or a control group. However, in many urban situations it is not possible, or desirable, to randomize services. If randomization is not feasible, there are quasi-experimental procedures to reduce bias and ensure validity. Regardless of the overall design, the intervention or service should be clearly defined and applied, and the sample should be described clearly so others can make informed decisions about replication and generalizability. Methodological problems such as small sample sizes, lack of group equivalence, unblinded evaluators, lack of objective outcome measures, few process measures, and lack of follow-up can undermine the evaluation and cast doubt on the usefulness of the entire intervention.

Evaluations of urban programs have focused not only on whether interventions work, but why they work and for whom. Long-term evaluations of urban educational programs have shown that the effects of early intervention may be apparent in the academic achievements of school-age children and the social competence (including avoiding delinquency) of adolescents. However, in keeping with the complex relationships between contextual variables and development, interventions do not necessarily have universal effects on participants. For example, in a recent follow-up of a home intervention program for pregnant women, Olds and colleagues found that the effects of the intervention were potentiated among the highest risk group of women (low income, unmarried, teenagers).

A. Level of Intervention/Prevention

The terms primary, secondary, and tertiary are often used to define levels of prevention from a medical or health perspective. Primary prevention occurs before the problem exists. For example, vaccines are given to children to prevent infectious diseases, such as measles or polio. Secondary prevention occurs when the individual or group is at very high risk to experience the problem. For example, flu shots are given to individuals who are vulnerable (e.g., elderly) or would have difficulty recovering from the flu. Tertiary prevention occurs after the problem exists and the goal is to prevent or reduce further debilitation. Providers of mental health services are often part of the tertiary system because many of their services are delivered to individuals with a recognized problem who are referred by primary providers.

A recent report from the Institute of Medicine by Mrazek and Haggerty in 1994 includes a similar categorization that can be applied to the prevention of urban problems. *Universal* or population-based interventions attempt to prevent urban problems and to promote mental health among an entire population. They may include mass media campaigns, public service announcements, or universal policies such as limited access to firearms. Universal interventions directed toward youth are often implemented in schools or other centers that attract youths. An important advantage of population-based interventions is that they are available to all, rather than possibly stigmatizing youth who are identified as high risk. However, by definition most universal interventions are not indi-

vidually tailored. They usually consist of a set curriculum with broad and diffuse applications.

One excellent example of a universal program to prevention violence and chronic drug use among urban middle school youth is a 2-year classroom-based intervention introduced among first- and second-grade students in inner-city Baltimore schools by Kellam and colleagues. The program, a collaborative effort between the Baltimore City Public School and The Johns Hopkins School of Public Health, illustrates how early intervention aimed at reducing aggressive behavior during elementary school can contribute to increased social adaptation and less violent and drug behavior during pre-adolescence. Solutions to complex urban problems, such as youth violence, often require interventions that are developmentally oriented and address the origins of the problem, rather than merely trying to eliminate the symptoms.

Advocates of violence prevention programs for urban youth recommend that intervention begin prior to middle school because the patterns of problem behavior among younger children differ from those of older adolescents and may be more amenable to intervention. Studies of long-term outcomes of early intervention programs that have examined patterns of adolescent delinquency, including violence, have shown the effectiveness of prevention programs initiated among preschool children in demonstration Head Start programs, such as the Perry High Scope Project. Presumably, early intervention enabled young children to gain skills that protected them from engaging in violence in their schools and communities. These findings are consistent with recommendations from prevention science that interventions should be introduced early before the problem has taken hold.

There are also examples of environmental interventions designed to reduce opportunities for urban violence (e.g., guards, increased lighting, metal detectors, etc.). The Safe Kids/Healthy Neighborhoods Injury Prevention Program in Harlem, which was evaluated using public health data, demonstrated that safe playground equipment was associated with reductions in injuries. Unfortunately, most other universal urban violence prevention programs have not been systematically evaluated, so little is known about the impact of universal prevention on urban violence.

Selective interventions are directed toward individuals or groups of individuals who are at increased risk of experiencing a negative outcome. For example, selective interventions have been designed to reduce the likelihood of violent behavior among urban youth who are at increased risk for violent behavior. Unlike universal interventions, selective interventions are targeted to specific youth and are often individually tailored. For example, PACT (Positive Adolescent Choices Training) is a culturally relevant intervention that focuses on violence education, anger management, and prosocial skills training to help youth learn to negotiate though potentially conflictual situations. The program is centered around three instructional videotapes that incorporate African American youth, street language, and familiar conflict situations (Dealing with Anger: Givin' It, Takin' It, and Workin' It Out). Hammond and Yung report that participation in the intervention resulted in fewer referrals to juvenile court and less likelihood of violent offenses among youth with prior juvenile involvement.

Indicated interventions are directed toward those who are experiencing negative consequences associated with urbanization. Mental health providers usually direct their attention toward *indicated* interventions—individuals with a problem to be solved or reduced—and there are many examples of successful interventions. For example, the multisystematic model of treatment (MST) developed by Henggler and Borduin is an intensive, home-based strategy used to prevent violence among juvenile offenders. Based on ecological theory, MST views families as partners and as active team members, rather than as recipients of services. MST extends from a focus on individually oriented attitudes and skills to family organization and communication patterns. Randomized clinical trials with juvenile offenders have shown that youth in the MST condition had less criminal activity and were less likely to be rearrested or incarcerated more than 2 years after the intervention.

B. Link between Urban Intervention Research and Policy

Interventions can be classified into three categories based on their purpose and design: efficacy, effectiveness, and efficiency. These categories are critical in the link from research to policy. Efficacy studies are the first stage and they are conducted to determine if the intervention works under optimal or ideal conditions. Demonstration projects that include funds for implementation and evaluation or university-based intervention trials with highly trained personnel, such as the Infant Health and Development Project, are ex-

amples of efficacy studies. Efficacy trials are highly informative, but they do not examine whether the intervention can be applied in naturalistic settings without external controls. In contrast, effectiveness trials assess whether an intervention works in the field and can be integrated into existing systems. For example, Project ALERT is an urban, school-based intervention to prevent drug use that has been implemented and evaluated in the Philadelphia public school system. Finally, efficiency refers to an analysis of the costs and the benefits of the intervention. Investigators who conduct effectiveness trials in schools or other community settings and include an efficiency analysis can be convincing when they advocate the transition from research to policy because they can address the implementation and economic questions often posed by policymakers. An excellent example of longitudinal intervention research that is relevant to urban policy and includes efficacy, effectiveness and efficiency analyses is the High/Scope Perry Preschool Program. Data from early efficacy trials, together with comprehensive efficiency analyses conducted over 20 years, served as a basis for the expansion of Head Start programs for low income children.

C. Partnerships with Urban Communities

Programs to prevent the negative consequences of poverty, population, and environmental stress associated with urbanization are complex and require hierarchial interventions developed in collaboration with communities, families, parents, and individual children. Evaluators have found that projects are most successful when they are decentralized, limited in scale, well-planned, carefully timed, and involve equitable representation from the community, including having recipients of services in decision-making roles.

Community-based models for health promotion are often conceptualized as empowering processes whereby health care providers serve as consultants to community members and enable them to define their priorities and solutions. If urban intervention and prevention programs are going to be sustained, they must be incorporated into existing community services so community members feel both pride and responsibility.

Urban leaders, such as Andrew Young, call for a reinvestment in cities and in urban citizens. He advocates community cohesion and a social and economic infrastructure that emphasizes high expectations and provides opportunities that enable youths to succeed in school and citizens to occupy meaningful places in the workforce. Punitive measures of dealing with urban problems, such as restricting resources to schools, libraries, and youth centers, and relying on the judicial system to solve urban problems are unlikely to produce responsible, healthy, productive citizens. The focus on social and financial capital emphasizes the importance of relationships within families and within communities, together with available, accessible economic resources. Community pride and positive activism enable citizens to work within existing institutions and should counteract the feelings of helplessness and hopelessness that often characterize low-income, urban dwellers.

Although community-level programs are a critical component in the prevention and remediation of urban problems, families make many decisions at the household level that impact the well-being of family members. In order to understand why intervention strategies lead (or do not lead) to better mental health outcomes, it is necessary to consider intervening variables, such as time constraints, economic demands, or personal perceptions and understanding regarding recommended interventions. For example, a recent survey among parents of urban youth and providers from a mental health clinic indicated that parents and providers did not share the same concerns. Parents were concerned about their children's school performance and providers were concerned about children's depression. Compliance and success are likely to be difficult if providers, families, and communities do not share similar views of the problems and plans for intervention.

D. Accessibility of Urban Programs

Over the past few years many social scientists have moved from tertiary or indicated interventions delivered in clinics or offices to secondary or selected interventions delivered in homes, schools, and communities. Black and colleagues have conducted two randomized clinical trials of home visiting programs with low-income families of young children residing in urban Baltimore. In both programs the interventions were designed to provide maternal support and to promote parenting, child development, utilization of informal and formal resources, and parent advocacy.

One involved drug-abusing women (cocaine and/ or heroin users), most of whom were single, African American, multiparous, non-high school graduates from low-income families with a history of incarceration. The women in the intervention group received biweekly home visits beginning prior to delivery and extending through the first 18 months of their child's life. Findings suggested that women in the intervention group were somewhat more likely to report being drug-free, to comply with primary care appointments for their children, to respond to their children, and to provide opportunities for stimulation.

A second home intervention program involved children with nonorganic failure to thrive (NOFTT) recruited from urban pediatric primary care clinics serving low-income families. All children had been healthy and full term at birth, but experienced growth faltering (weight-for-age under the 5th percentile) during the first 2 years of life, with no identified medical explanation. Most children were raised by single, African American mothers who received public assistance. All children received services in a multidisciplinary Growth and Nutrition Clinic and half the children also received weekly home intervention visits for 1 year. Children's growth parameters improved significantly over the 12-month study period, regardless of intervention status. Children who received home intervention had better receptive language over time and more child-oriented home environments and the infants had better cognitive development. Follow-up was conducted when the children were 4 years of age. Children's developmental scores and behavioral performance varied as a function of their intervention status and their mother's mental health. Specifically, children who received the home intervention and had mothers with low scores on negative affectivity had higher scores on cognitive development (M = 87), than children in the other three groups (home intervention, high scores on negative affectivity, M = 81) (clinic intervention, regardless of negative affectivity, M = 80, 81). Similar patterns occurred on task engagement, negativity, and motor development. [See COGNITIVE DEVELOPMENT.]

These studies reveal several important lessons about the health and development of urban mothers and children. First, interventions directed toward low-income, urban families who are at risk either because the mother is a drug-abuser or the child has not grown adequately, can be effective in promoting parenting and child development. Second, even with early intervention, children raised in low-income urban families that are further challenged by either prenatal drug exposure or failure to thrive are at risk for developmental delays. Third, the impact of early intervention on the development and interactive behavior of vulnerable children may be moderated by maternal mental health. Among low-income, urban families home intervention may be most useful when mothers are not besieged by their own mental health problems, such as negative affectivity (a combination of depression, anxiety, and hostility). These findings highlight the importance of considering universal strategies to promote the development of children living in low-income, urban families; of incorporating contextual factors, such as maternal psychological functioning, into the development of early intervention services; and of conducting follow-up assessments to examine the carryover from early intervention services. They also suggest that mental health services should be integrated into early intervention services to create a family-focused home intervention among extremely high-risk women and children in urban communities, particularly when mothers report high rates of negative affectivity.

There has also been enthusiastic support for *school-based* interventions to promote the health of urban youth, partially because schools are an excellent venue for universal interventions. School-based health centers provide access to preventive health services, while educating youth about the roles of health care providers. School-based services also provide opportunities for interdisciplinary collaboration and training. For example, psychologists have trained school personnel to provide crisis counseling. Thus more urban children receive the benefit of crisis counseling and psychologists can serve as consultants or intervene directly with those most in need of services. Although school-based services may not address the needs of the most at-risk group of youth (those who are chronically truant or have dropped out of school), they are a valuable resource and should include universal, selected, and indicated interventions directed toward issues such as life planning, career orientation, and community empowerment.

E. Interdisciplinary Urban Programs

Intervention programs are unlikely to be sustainable unless they are integrated into existing urban service systems. Interdisciplinary collaboration among psychologists, social workers, physicians, urban planners, economists, epidemiologists, police officers, and citizens is often necessary to build effective service systems to address urban issues. For example, the Child Development Community Policing Program is a collaboration between psychologists and an urban police department that is directed toward youths who have been involved with violence as victims or perpetrators. The program mobilizes treatment quickly, ensures that providers know the real challenges facing youth, helps police focus on prevention, and evaluates program services.

These interdisciplinary collaborations must also be sensitive to the cultural needs of the community. Innovative, culturally and developmentally sensitive intervention strategies are often necessary to reach low-income, urban adolescents who may question the usefulness of traditional educational methods and may not visit physicians or other traditional health care providers. Videotapes have been used effectively with parents to increase knowledge and problem-solving skills regarding AIDS and with adolescents to promote parenting. For example, urban adolescent mothers who viewed a culturally sensitive videotape about reciprocal communication between mothers and babies that had been made by other teenage mothers, were more likely to talk to their babies during a feeding observation and to endorse the importance of communication than mothers who did not have access to the videotape. Process evaluations indicate that the youths like the videotapes, show them to others, and remember aspects about the videotapes. The effectiveness of videotapes may be explained by social learning theory, which relies on altering behavior through modeling and may be a particularly effective strategy for urban adolescents who are often influenced by the behavior of peers. Videotapes that can be shown at home have multiple advantages: (1) they can reflect the cultural and developmental orientation of the target recipients; (2) they can reach family members who might be disinclined to attend a group session; (3) they can reach friends and other influential members of an adolescent's social network; and (4) they can be shown multiple times.

IV. CONCLUSION

The solution to urban challenges should be broadened beyond tertiary or indicated care directed to individuals with mental health problems to include universal and selected interventions to prevent mental health problems and to promote the well-being of urban families. The challenge is to move beyond efficacy studies to examine the effectiveness and efficiency of interventions to promote healthy behavior in real-world settings. Armed with this information, social scientists can work with urban citizens and social policymakers to promote sustainable services to prevent urban problems. The resolution of many of the urban challenges and the promotion of the mental health and well-being of urban citizens require collaboration among community organizations, families, and health and mental health care providers in the planning, implementation, and evaluation of interventions directed toward individuals and groups. Through our collaborative efforts the goals stated by UNICEF in *The Progress of Nations* can be realized. "The day will come when the progress of nations will be judged not by their military or economic strength, nor by the splendor of their capital cities and public buildings, but by the well-being of their people."

BIBLIOGRAPHY

Coie, J. D., Watt, N. F., West, S. G., Hawkins, J. D., Asarnow, J. R., Markman, H. J., Ramey, S. L., Shure, M. B., & Long, B. (1993). The science of prevention: A conceptual framework and some directions for a national research program. *American Psychologist, 48,* 1013–1022.

Harpham, T. (1994). Urbanization and mental health in developing countries: A research role for social scientists, public health professionals, and social psychiatrists. *Social Science and Medicine, 39,* 233–245.

Marsella, A. J. (1991). *Urbanization and mental disorder: An overview of conceptual and methodological research issues and findings.* Report prepared for The Urbanization Panel of World Health Organization Commission on Health and the Environment. Geneva: World Health Organization.

Mrazek, P. J., & Haggerty, R. J. (1994). *Reducing risks for mental disorders: Frontiers for preventive intervention research.* Washington, DC: National Academy Press.

Parry-Jones, W. L. (1991). Mental health and development of children and adolescents in cities. In W. L. Parry-Jones & N. Queloz (Eds.), *Mental health and deviance in inner cities.* Geneva: World Health Organization.

Queloz, N. (1991). Urban process and its role in strengthening social disadvantages, inequalities and exclusion. In W. L. Parry-Jones & N. Queloz (Eds.), *Mental health and deviance in inner cities.* Geneva: World Health Organization.

Rossi-Espagnet, A., Goldstein, G., & Tabibzadeh, I. (1991). Urbanization and health in developing countries: A challenge for all. *World Health Statistics Quarterly, 44,* 187–244.

Rutter, M. (1981). The city and the child. *American Journal of Orthopsychiatry, 51,* 610–625.

UNICEF (1996). *The progress of nations.* New York: Oxford University Press.

Wilson, W. J. (1987). *The truly disadvantaged: The inner city, the underclass, and public policy.* New York: Alfred A. Knopf.

Wilson, W. J. (1996). *When work disappears: The world of the new urban poor.* New York: Alfred A. Knopf.

Wellness in Children

Emory L. Cowen

University of Rochester

Attachment Relationship Relationship formed between caregiver and infant that significantly shapes the child's emergent senses of security, worth, and belongingness.

Meta-Analysis A technology for studying the overall efficacy of a given approach, based on many individual outcome studies of programs exemplifying the approach.

Nosological Framework Network of diagnostic categories.

Paradigm Shift A new, qualitatively different way of addressing problems that an existing system cannot resolve.

Pathogenesis Processes that lead up to, and eventuate in, disordered behavior.

Protective Factors Variables or conditions that reduce the effects of factors that otherwise predispose maladaptive outcomes.

Psychopathology Collective term used to describe many different disordered psychological outcomes, and their study.

Risk Factors Variables, conditions, or factors that increase the likelihood of a person's developing a psychological disorder.

Salutogenesis Processes that lead up to, and eventuate in, healthy psychological adaptation.

Stren An event or experience that helps to strengthen one's adaptation or personality.

Born of concerns about mental health's past limitations and failures, there is now an emphasis on prevention and the enhancement of **WELLNESS IN CHILDREN** from the start, as opposed to striving to repair longstanding deficits in wellness. To the extent that wellness enhancement is the goal, children and youth, and the prime settings that shape their development, are focal targets. Examples of effective programs in wellness enhancement are cited and the case is made that these emergent approaches merit stronger emphasis and greater allocation of resources in future mental health portfolios.

I. INTRODUCTION AND FORMULATION OF ISSUES

The mental health fields have always focused unswervingly on things that go wrong psychologically in people (i.e., on psychopathology). Their defining mandates have been to: (a) understand processes that lead up to major psychological dysfunction (i.e., pathogenesis); (b) establish sensitive frameworks for identifying and classifying such conditions (i.e., diagnosis); and (c) develop effective ways to repair, or at least contain, them (e.g., psychotherapy).

Although this way of viewing and engaging psychological problems has remained constant over the centuries, several factors have led to changes in mental health's scope and literal practices. One is an ever-broadening view of what a psychological problem *is*, with parallel changes in people's views of the nature of appropriate mental health activities. Thus, whereas mental health's earliest focus was limited to florid, indisputable disorders reflecting gross departures from reality, the field's more elasticized mandate today encompasses many different, and more subtle, forms of human dysfunction (e.g., unhappiness and ineffectuality). This trend has had several consequences. First, it has increased demand for mental health services. Moreover, this broadened view of scope, along with greater public awareness of the nature of psychological problems and their potentially adverse effects on many aspects of human functioning, has led to the hiring of mental health professionals to work in many different community settings (e.g., schools, businesses, the legal and enforcement systems, the military). Their roles in these settings differ appreciably from the stereotypic mental health roles of yesteryear in clinics, hospitals, and the consulting room.

A second important evolutionary trend has been an on-going process of diversification and refinement of the "tools of the trade" (i.e., diagnosis and treatment) that have centrally defined mental health's modus operandi. Mental health professionals today: (a) are more skillful than their predecessors were in identifying, and distinguishing among, different forms of psychological dysfunction; (b) use more intricate, precisely articulated, nosological frameworks; and (c) have more technologies available in seeking to remediate psychological problems. In sum, the mental health delivery system has continued to become more sophisticated, sensitive, and effective in doing the things that have defined its historical mandate.

Although the system that evolved has, unquestionably, brought help to many individuals, there is need to distinguish between success at the individual level versus systemic, or societal, success. At the latter level, awareness has continued to grow of the significant problems that the existing mental health order has *not* been able to resolve. Principally, those are problems of efficacy and reach. The former include the system's failure to address (i.e., to deal effectively with) major clusters of serious mental disorders such as schizophrenia, and the fact that even using its best developed and most finely honed technologies, many of the problems it does engage are not satisfactorily resolved. The latter failures reflect the fact that most of the system's efforts have been targeted to people with

serious, longstanding problems—precisely those that most resist change. [*See* SCHIZOPHRENIA.]

The system has also had vexing problems of reach. Given its predominant focus on difficult, often deeply rooted, problems, and the costly, time-consuming nature of its repair efforts, mental health's limited services have been allocated unevenly in ways that favor people who are both comfortable with its typical operating ways, and can best afford its costs. This bias in targeting was once described with the tongue-in-cheek acronym "YAVIS-syndrome," (i.e., *y*oung, *a*ttractive, *v*erbal, *i*ntelligent, and *s*uccessful). The irony implied in that term is that the de facto allocation of limited mental health resources follows the rule that help is least available where it is most needed. As stressed in the Report of the Joint Commission on Mental Health in 1961, among the groups that historically have been short-changed in terms of access to the mental health system, are the poor, the elderly, and, importantly for this essay, children and youth. Indeed, over the years it is clear that the lion's share of mental health's finite resources has gone to troubled adults.

The problems noted above are considerable. In the aggregate, they suggest that the existing mental health system cannot adequately deal with society's mental health problems. It is a system that: (a) offers too little, too late; (b) entails ever spiraling costs; and (c) leaves massive residues of misery, ineffectuality and wasted human potential. These stark realities push for consideration of a paradigm shift, that is, qualitatively different ways of approaching the major problems that the system has not been able to resolve.

One seemingly sensible path to follow in any such search is that of prevention. This means, among other things, actively pursuing before-the-fact efforts to enhance wellness as opposed to struggling, however valiantly, to undo or repair established dysfunction in adults. Meaningful pursuit of a prevention course necessarily directs attention to young children and their formation, including the settings (i.e., families and schools) in which such formative processes unfold. A prime focus on young children is further justified by their flexibility and malleability. Otherwise put, because early problems tend to be more circumscribed and less debilitating, they can, in principle, be addressed in more humane, cost-effective ways.

The conceptually appealing alternative of wellness enhancement in children has attracted increasing recent interest and exploration, with promising yields. This article describes that emerging development briefly. It first considers the nature and rationale of a wellness enhancement strategy, and identifies several different ways in which such a strategy can be implemented. Within that framework, it next gives examples of effective programs reflecting different aspects of a wellness approach. Finally, it identifies needed further steps in pursuing a wellness enhancement approach, and the potential rewards that can accrue from such efforts.

II. PSYCHOLOGICAL WELLNESS: THE NATURE AND UTILITY OF THE CONCEPT

Although the concept of psychological wellness is not a new discovery, it has not, viewed historically, been especially influential. In fact, for most people, it has been at best a minimally visible, rather fuzzy notion. This point can be illustrated by several examples reflecting standard mental health vocabulary. The word *trauma,* well known both in medical and lay circles, has been widely used to describe severe damage to the body or a serious blow to the personality. Notwithstanding this widespread popular usage, the English language lacks a word to describe the opposite process, that is, an experience that strengthens personality. In seeking to fill that void, the psychiatrist Hollister proposed the term "stren." Similarly, the sociologist Antonovsky observed that although the English language contained a frequently used word to describe the processes by which diseases unfold (i.e., pathogenesis), it did not have a parallel word to describe processes that promote healthy outcomes. To fill that void, he proposed the word "salutogenesis"— a term intended both to describe health-promoting processes and to direct attention to the ideal of promoting wellness. It is ironic that our society has always had a far clearer view of, and a stronger focus on, failures in wellness than it has had on wellness and its promotion, and that the former orientation and viewing lens has so long, and overwhelmingly, shaped the focus and practices of the mental health fields.

The term wellness is not automatically self-defining. Like the term sickness, it implicates value judgments that may differ across cultures and groups. Even so, because the concept offers a much needed contrast to mental health's longstanding, near exclusive focus on pathology, it may be useful to highlight several of its

defining attributes that most people in our society would see as positive. These include basic behavioral indicators such as being able to eat, sleep, and work well, and psychological indicators such as having a sense of purpose, belongingness, efficacy, being in control of one's fate, and feeling satisfied with oneself and one's existence. The qualities cited are simply to suggest, in an approximate way, how the concept is being used here. Other writers reflecting a wellness orientation have used kindred terms such as life satisfaction and gratification in living.

Several related definitional issues bear mention. First, the term wellness in this essay, is used in a more or less, rather than absolute, sense, with wellness anchoring one end of an adaptive continuum and sickness (or psychopathology) the other. We also use the term to mean something other than just the absence of disease; rather, it is centrally defined by the presence of the marker qualities noted above—characteristics that make for wholesome adaptation. Thus, among the many people in society who do not "classify" as sick or as psychological casualties in any formal diagnostic sense, large numbers may also fail to approach the ideal of psychological wellness. The preceding formulation is to suggest that the goals of wellness enhancement rightfully pertain to all people, and must be pursued actively and systematically across the life span in ways that differ qualitatively from the past-defining strategies of the mental health fields.

Wellness enhancement is building, not undoing. Its closest kindred concept in mental health's existing vocabulary is primary prevention. Those two concepts, however, are neither identical nor transitive. Increasingly, the more popular term primary prevention has come to be used to refer to specific efforts, built around the concepts of risk and protective factors, to reduce the occurrence of major mental disorders. This usage is well reflected in the recent, groundbreaking report to the Institute of Medicine, entitled: *Reducing Risks for Mental Disorders: Frontiers for Preventive Intervention Research.* Wellness enhancement is a broader, population-oriented, superordinate notion that includes the preceding risk-driven, disorder-reduction concept of primary prevention as only *one* of its components. Although this distinction is important to keep in mind, it is still the case that many primary prevention activities with children are built around wellness enhancement objectives.

The view that wellness enhancement is a lifetime challenge implies that diverse strategies—differentially relevant to different situations, and at different points in the life span—are needed to pursue that objective. At least five such families of strategies have been considered, and work undertaken to probe their utility. These include: (a) promoting the formation of wholesome caregiver–child attachment relationships; (b) facilitating children's acquisition of stage-salient competencies; (c) engineering settings that favor adaptive outcomes for their inhabitants; (d) fostering a sense of empowerment, (i.e., being in basic control of one's destiny) in people; and e) promoting the development of skills needed to cope effectively with stressful life situations. [*See* ATTACHMENT; COPING WITH STRESS; HEALTHY ENVIRONMENTS.]

Describing these approaches as a *family* of wellness enhancement strategies is intended to suggest that: (a) they are mutually supportive and enhancing; and (b) collectively, they comprise a population-oriented framework for a wellness enhancement approach across the life span. The sections that follow clarify the place of these strategies within an overall wellness enhancement framework, and cite examples of their effective application. Consistent with the main focus of this essay, wellness enhancement strategies for children and youth are emphasized.

III. PATHWAYS TO WELLNESS

An aphorism that comes to mind in starting this discussion is: "As the twig is bent, so grows the bough!" One attribute that distinguishes the human infant from most other forms of animal life, is the lengthy period of its dependence on adult caregivers for survival. In humans, this long dependency period unfolds within a family structure and a particular type of infant–caregiver attachment relationship. Such attachment relationships, which range from warm, loving, and caring at one end of a continuum, to cold, distant, and rejecting at the other, have markedly different consequences for the child's formation and subsequent development.

A warm, secure attachment relationship is a first vital step (process) toward enhancing the psychological wellness of the young child. Such a relationship helps the child to feel safe, secure, loved, and worthwhile and, on that base, to form a worldview that centrally reflects such self-perceptions. Thus, an enduring, secure attachment relationship is an important step to-

ward wellness both in its own right and in terms of the solid base it establishes for later wellness-enhancing steps. By contrast, an inadequate or disturbed attachment relationship creates a porous base, often permanently so, that can greatly restrict later essential, wellness enhancement steps. Although the parent–child attachment relationship continues to be a vital force in wellness formation throughout childhood and adolescence, its form of manifestation must change as the child develops. Illustratively, the caregiver's role as protector must inexorably yield place to one of facilitating age-appropriate autonomy and independence in the developing child. Failures in that important transition processes are also likely to limit the child's wellness development.

A good deal is known about factors that shape the formation of wholesome, and less than optimal, parent–child attachment relationships. These sources of influences include: (a) *caregiver variables* such as the caregiver's life history and current adjustment; her readiness for a child and her child-focus; her sensitivity to the child's needs, and her sense of well-being and efficacy as a parent; (b) *family milieu variables* such as the soundness of the partner relationship and a familial climate of mutual respect and support, as viewed by the caregiver; (c) *environment variables* such as harsh living conditions, exposure to chronic stress and absence of outside support, again as seen by the caregiver and (d) *child attributes* such as gender, temperament, brightness, attractiveness and outgoingness.

Some of these input sources (e.g., child gender, early temperament, and IQ) are "givens." Others, including environmental conditions such as poverty and violence, while theoretically amenable to future change, remain as omnipresent de facto realities that individual families cannot modify today or tomorrow. Decreasing the burdens that such oppressive realities impose depends heavily on social change and reform that will, at best, unfold only slowly over time. The important point to stress here, however, is that *some* factors that importantly shape early childhood wellness are at least, in principle, modifiable. These factors (e.g., the parent–child attachment relationship, the rooting of essential stage–salient competencies) comprise focal targets for intervention efforts designed to enhance children's wellness. Here-and-now success in such efforts can ultimately help to reduce repetitive, intergenerational scenarios typified by personally, and societally, unfortunate outcomes.

A second important early-life challenge for the child is to acquire age-appropriate cognitive, interpersonal, and readiness skills. Strayhorn's taxonomy of essential early competencies lists 62 such skills, comprising nine major clusters. Many of these skills are formed in infancy and early childhood within the framework of the child's two most important early contexts, the home and school. Their actual formation is shaped by many factors over and beyond the child's natural abilities, including the soundness of the caregiver–child relationship, the caregiver's orientation to learning and having the skills needed to nourish the child's curiosity and interest, and the kinds of modeling experiences that the caregiver provides of the child. Again the key point to emphasize is that promoting the development of stage-salient competencies and readiness skills is among the more addressable early wellness enhancement steps that can be taken in children's behalf.

Thus, the formation and maintenance of a sound parent–child attachment relationship, and the child's acquisition of age-appropriate skills and competencies are essential, early-life steps toward wellness. Wholesome starts in these two directions depend squarely on the flow of nutrients from the child's early home and school environments, and the positive worldviews and solid competence bases that such inputs can potentially shape. Otherwise put, to the extent that psychological wellness is seen as the overarching goal, the contexts of childrearing and education within which the young child develops harbor the essential formative ingredients needed to advance this outcome. Although the formation of a wholesome early parent–child attachment relationship and the acquisition of stage-salient early competencies do not guarantee later wellness, they provide a powerful start in that direction. And, on the flip side of the coin, it is difficult to imagine how wellness can come about in a child in the absence of these two essential sets of inputs.

The key question highlighted by this analysis is: "What can be done to maximize the likelihood that these first crucial, wellness-enhancing processes will unfold positively?" Answers to that question are not at all simple. Indeed, as suggested above crucial input strands are likely to reflect diverse sources ranging from qualities of the caregiver, and the caregiver–child attachment relationship, at one extreme, to the nature of the environment (and its stressors), in which the child is born and reared. The diversity of these shaping strands highlights the fact that systematic en-hancement of children's wellness is likely to depend on coordinated, mutually supportive approaches, ranging from social reform to specific programs designed to fortify essential elements in the caregiver formula (e.g., a sound attachment relationship, and enhancing teaching skills and the child's school preparedness).

The two early routes thus far considered lay down a vital formative base for wellness outcomes. Other input strands take on greater significance in later childhood and adolescence, and are important elements in a life-span approach to wellness enhancement. This is necessarily the case both because: (a) people experience new challenges to wellness, and new wellness enhancement opportunities, as part of the normal process of growing up (e.g., as in developmental transitions); and (b) life situations and sources of stress often change unpredictably over time.

One important later wellness force, pro or con, is the shaping potential of high-impact social environments in which people interact over long time periods. Although most of the child's early formative experiences unfold in home and school, later on other environments such as churches, work sites, and community settings and agencies become increasingly influential as wellness-shaping forces. Such environments are rarely neutral in their impact; more often they act either to enhance and impede wellness. In this context, it should be noted that social environments exert influence in two very different ways. The more obvious one is an environment's success in discharging its stated mandate, (e.g., a school's success in imparting essential bodies of knowledge to children). A second vital, but more subtle, source of environmental influence, is *how,* among many potential alternative ways, a setting goes about discharging its mandate. Such "structural ways" can, however unostentatiously, advance or restrict outcomes such as the development of autonomy, and mutual help and affiliative behaviors. We tend to pay much more attention to a system's success or failure in discharging its formal mandate, than to how it goes about doing so, when, in fact, such process factors may have as much or more, wellness-shaping potential. In the school context, for example, it has been suggested that even if these unobtrusive "operating-style" elements do not affect children's grades or achievement test scores, they may importantly shape such wellness-related outcomes as friendship formation, cooperative behavior, and conflict resolution skills.

Thus, high-impact settings can discharge their

mandates in different structural ways that either promote or hinder children's wellness outcomes. There is a need to learn more about relationships between these structural variations in *how* a system goes about conducting its business, and outcomes that reflect both the system's mandate and the personal wellness of its inhabitants. Knowing that particular ways of system operation both meet a system's most important mandated goals and also strengthen wellness outcomes helps to identify system modification steps that can be taken to enhance wellness outcomes.

Several other routes to wellness also become more important as children grow up. One, mentioned increasingly in a wellness context, is empowerment, that is, gaining control over and being able to make decisions that shape important areas of one's life. The appeal of the empowerment concept stems from omnipresent and evident connections between *dis*empowerment and significant problems of living, for many people in modern society (e.g., children, disabled people, minority group members, poor people), and the related conclusion that people benefit psychologically when they gain control over their lives. The notion of empowerment as a gateway to wellness can be applied to many different situations, and many different walks of life, starting with the provision of age-appropriate autonomy support to young children. To date, however the term's most extensive and animated usage has been in the context of addressing oppressive macrosocial realities. In that arena, however, some forms of social disempowerment are so complex and deeply rooted, that they can, at best, change slowly and only with major social reform. Accordingly, societal empowering strategies, as part of a comprehensive wellness enhancement agenda, are likely to be more complex and more difficult to bring off than early attachment and competence-building approaches.

A fifth, important wellness-building route, pertinent to all people at all developmental stages, and in all walks of life, is the acquisition of skills needed to cope effectively with life stress. All people are susceptible to significant stress at some time in their lives. For children, such stressors include both powerful, often unanticipable, events such as death of a close family member or parental divorce, and less dramatically, although often more corrosively, exposure to chronic, pervasive stressors, that centrally define the very fabric of growing up for many children in modern society. [*See* STRESS.]

People, including young children, vary markedly in how they adapt to major life stress. Whereas many are badly, indeed sometimes irreparably, scarred by such exposure, some fraction of exposed children somehow come to cope and adapt very well, even in the face of the most dire stress. These children are called resilient. They have become the object of careful, intensive study, both as "the keepers of a dream," and because an understanding of the mechanisms and processes that move them to wholesome adaptation, in spite of the heavy odds against them, harbors much potential knowledge for advancing a psychology of wellness.

The five pathways to wellness described, it should be stressed, do not compete with each other. Rather, they are mutually enhancing and supportive, notwithstanding important differences among them in defining substance and methodologies, and in terms of the age ranges, groups, and life situations for which they have prime relevance. Collectively, however, they comprise a coordinated, health-oriented, building framework, that offers a clear contrast to: (a) mental health's classic disease-undoing stance; and to a lesser extent, even to (b) primary prevention approaches specifically to preventing seriously dysfunctional psychological outcomes.

Thus, a wellness enhancement framework is broad enough to incorporate more narrowly defined primary prevention built around the concepts of risk and disease prevention. Indeed, integral to a wellness enhancement view is the belief that in mental health, a good offense (i.e., health building that focuses on young children) may be the best of all defenses, perhaps even more promising for disease prevention than later, targeted interventions that seek specifically to prevent serious maladaptive outcomes (e.g., substance abuse, delinquency, and criminal behaviors). The next section briefly described several effective wellness enhancement programs and overviews emergent research findings that form a substantial, and expanding base of justification for this type of programming.

IV. ILLUSTRATIVE PROGRAMS AND EMERGENT FINDINGS

The preceding section identified five different approaches to wellness enhancement. Notwithstanding major differences in their literal ways of operation these approaches share several important common features. In contrast to classic mental health approaches, they are *not* targeted to already sick people; in fact they are not targeted to individuals at all. Rather, whatever their format, they seek to build wellness in the many, in before-the-fact ways. Although we have spoken of these programs as if they fell neatly into discrete strategic categories, in real life they are not always independent of each other. To the contrary, *some* wellness-targeted programs clearly incorporate multiple health-building strategies. It is also the case that the five wellness enhancement strategies described are interdependent, indeed mutually supportive. It is, for example, very likely that early failure to promote wellness outcomes will seriously limit what later wellness-enhancing steps can hope to accomplish.

This section describes several promising examples of a wellness-building approach for children. These examples, it will be noted, differ importantly in substance, timing, targeting, and defining mechanisms. The intent here is to illustrate, not exhaust, the category of effective wellness enhancement approaches. A recent chapter by Weissberg and Greenberg offers a current, more comprehensive, overview of emergent programs in the prevention, wellness enhancement arena, for children and youth from birth to age 18.

The Perry Preschool Project is among the best known projects of this type, both because of its longevity (nearly 3 decades), and the fact that its outcomes have been carefully tracked over that entire time-period. This early, comprehensive, two-pronged program was targeted to poor, primarily Black, inner-city families, with 3- to 4-year-old children. The program sought to advance two primary, interconnected, early wellness enhancement goals, i.e., strengthening the parent–child attachment relationship, and enhancing the early development of child competencies and school preparedness skills. Its two main components were: (a) an enriched preschool experience for the targeted children, i.e., those at high risk for many different adverse outcomes; and (b) weekly, 1.5-hour home visits, intended both to stimulate children's learning and to promote wholesome attachment relationships and child-rearing milieus.

Not surprisingly, the earliest program benefits noted came in the areas of children's improved preparedness for, attitudes toward, and actual performance in, school. These early accomplishments paved the way for an escalating cycle of gain, that touched in-

creasingly on bellwether domains of major importance both to children and to society at large. When program participants were last studied systematically, at age 27, powerful long-term benefits were found in domains that "really count," including: (a) improved literacy rates, intellectual performance, and attaining more schooling; (b) higher employment rates and average earnings, as well as larger numbers of homeowners; (c) lower arrest rates, including drug-related arrests; and (d) reduced use of welfare and social services. Clearly, these outcomes reflect great benefit to people's happiness and the efficacy of their lives. Moreover, a cost-benefit analysis conducted by an economist demonstrated that ultimate savings to society (as in later costs associated with delinquency, criminality and unemployment) from this enriched preschool and family experience, came to approximately $7 saved for each dollar invested in the program. This project—indeed the thrust of the broader Headstart movement that it reflects—offers strong support for the promise of early, proactive, wellness enhancement programs in preventing diverse, costly, and unfortunate outcomes.

Within a wellness framework, the optimization of age-appropriate competencies in children and youth is an ongoing challenge, not just a task for the early years. Programs reflecting this belief, most school based, have increased steadily in number and complexity. Early versions of such programs, as, for example, ones designed to train children in interpersonal, or social, problem-solving skills (e.g., generating alternative solutions to problems, evaluating the consequences of those alternatives) were relatively narrow in focus and time limited. Moreover, their seemingly useful, heuristic initial findings proved to be less robust or enduring than originally hoped. As that limitation became more apparent, several program-related realities began to fall more clearly in place, including the realizations that: (a) a maximally fruitful notion of social competence in children and youth had to be broader than *just* social problem solving skills, that is, it had to embrace several different, major families of social competencies that cannot be taught, in depth, in a single, unidimensional short-term programs; (b) a circumscribed, time-limited program experience is not sufficient to produce meaningful, enduring skill acquisition; and (c) training programs must be responsive to the fact different skills and social competencies phase in at different developmental stages.

These awarenesses powered significant, second generation transformations (evolutionary steps) in the social competence training approach to wellness enhancement. Greater breadth, depth, and continuity of training are at the core of these changes. Programs that have evolved in this tradition thus seek to teach multiple sets of skills and competencies, often including ones that relate to physical, as well as psychological, wellness. Such training extends over a number of years; uses developmentally appropriate entry points to introduce relevant new families of competencies; provides refreshers, and "booster shots" for core skills taught earlier in simpler forms; and strives to establish class and school climates that support permanent rooting, and constructive application, of seminal program learnings.

We have now reached a point where carefully staged, sequential, curricula in social competence training have been developed, that start at kindergarten and continue each year through 12th grade. Programs of this type have been shown to yield a range of positive child outcomes including enhanced self-control; improved interpersonal problem-solving, decision-making, and conflict resolution skills; and reduced susceptibility to such negative outcomes as anxiety, poor school attendance and performance, and (later), alcohol and substance use. Comprehensive, mass-oriented, before-the-fact programs of this nature well exemplify a proactive wellness-building approach for children and youth that can be neatly, sensibly, and unobtrusively incorporated in the everyday educational experience.

A final wellness-targeted program example is the school-based Child Development Project (CDP), a comprehensive program with core components that reflect competence enhancement, environment modification, and empowerment strategies. CDP's underlying goal is to create a caring school community that enhances children's senses of autonomy, belongingness, and competence. Schoolwide formats are used consistently from kindergarten through 6th grade to advance those goals. Those strategies include: (a) having students set and uphold classroom rules hopefully, to strengthen their sense of autonomy; (b) using both cooperative learning formats and a Buddies' program pairing older and younger children, to enhance children's sense of relatedness; and (c) selecting curricular materials to help children better understand themselves, others, and prosocial values. The central notions that fuel the CDP approach are that children can

profit more from the school experience if they have a genuine stake (ownership) in what they do, and if the educational experience is interesting to, and rewarding for, them.

Classroom observations confirmed that the program had been implemented as intended. Thus, CDP classes exceeded comparison classes in such program defining qualities as: (a) opportunities provided for pupil input and autonomy; (b) actual use of cooperative learning formats; (c) judged presence of mutual help, warmth, and supportiveness in the classroom; (d) highlighting of prosocial values; and (e) use of discipline styles that promote responsible behavior.

Program outcome studies demonstrated that CDP's goal of enhancing children's wellness was well met. Program children exceeded comparison children in terms of judged cooperativeness, and the abilities to defend their views and deal effectively with conflict situations. They also had more friends, felt better accepted by peers and more competent socially, and evidenced a more sensitive understanding of others. Moreover, they exceeded comparison children in self-esteem, empathy, and in the sense of community. These systematic wellness gains came about without academic slippage. To the contrary, program children did every bit as well as comparison children; indeed, they were somewhat better in some areas such as reading comprehension.

The several program examples cited are intended only to illustrate the potential of different approaches to enhancing children's psychological wellness. Programs of this nature, resting on qualitatively different assumptions and practices than those at the defining core of traditional mental health approaches, have been on the rise in the past several decades, prompted in good measure by insufficiencies in the scope and efficacy of past approaches.

V. OVERVIEW AND CONCLUSIONS

The three programs described were selected as outstanding examples of a wellness enhancement approach. However appealing those programs seem to be, the central issue at stake involves the more general question of the *overall* efficacy of the primary prevention/wellness movement. Answering that question requires consideration of many more programs, reflecting the categories of interest, than the three exemplary ones spotlighted here. Two major, independent research overviews have recently sought to evaluate the *overall* efficacy of primary prevention and wellness enhancement programs.

The first is the recent, comprehensive report to the Institute of Medicine (cf. above). Among other things, this thoughtful, detailed document included a review of several hundred studies of the efficacy of primary prevention programs, selected as outstanding examples of the approach. The second was a meta-analysis (i.e., simultaneous, overall evaluation of an approach based on multiple exemplars) of 177 primary prevention program evaluation studies, also selected as outstanding examples on the basis of the rigor of the methodologies and designs they used. Although the two reviews shared a prime focus on sound research studies, they differed in other ways. For examples, whereas Durlak & Wells' meta-analysis was limited to studies with children and youth, the IOM report, in principle, covered the full life span. In practice, however, 70% of the studies it included involved children and youth. A second difference between the two reports was more substantial. Whereas the studies reviewed in the IOM report focused almost exclusively on primary prevention programs that sought to reduce the occurrence of serious (diagnosable) psychological disorders, Durlak and Wells' meta-analysis included studies with primary health promotion, or wellness enhancement goals.

The point to stress, however, is that both reviews included large numbers of programs reflecting the categories of disorder prevention and/or wellness promotion and, in that sense, provide a more sensitive, stable index of the efficacy of a generalized approach. Hence, their conclusions carry more weight than the three specific examples cited above. The IOM Report's main conclusion highlighted "encouraging progress" in preventive intervention the past decade. In its words: "At present, there are many intervention programs that rest on sound conceptual and empirical foundations and a substantial number are rigorously designed and evaluated" (IOM Report, p. 215). In parallel, working with different data input sources, that nevertheless also reflected a strong primary prevention thrust, Durlak and Wells concluded that "Outcome data indicate that most categories of primary prevention programs for children and adolescents produce significant effects. These findings provide empirical support for further research and practice in primary prevention" (p. 142).

The importance of the findings reported by these two independent sources stems from the fact that they both reflect many (and diverse types of) studies, conducted over substantial time periods. Their conclusions converge to identify an important evolving trend in the mental health fields (i.e., the emergence of primary prevention and wellness enhancement approaches), and document the efficacy of those approaches. Thus, from the position of having been, so to speak, easily ignored "new young kids on the block," less than 2 decades ago, primary prevention and wellness enhancement approaches with children have come increasingly, and impressively, to be seen as effective and useful. As such, these approaches have taken on the status of important tools in a modified, more proactively oriented, mental health armamentarium.

One critical cornerstone of these approaches is their central focus on enhancing the wellness of children and youth, that is to say, on before-the-fact-prevention as opposed to the difficult, often impossible, task of trying to undo rooted damage. This new direction is powered by the hope that systematic, effective early wellness building in children and youth, may be an essential step in any serious campaign to reduce the heavy individual and societal tolls that diverse forms of major mental dysfunction exact. Because history suggests that there is more reason to be hopeful about building than undoing, and given the demonstrated effectiveness of wellness-building approaches for children, it is to be hoped that future mental health portfolios will increasingly reflect investments and resource allocation in that mode.

BIBLIOGRAPHY

Battistich, V., Solomon, D., Kim, D., Watson, M., & Schaps, E. (1995). Schools as communities, poverty levels of student populations, and students' attitudes, motives and performance: A multilevel analysis. *American Educational Research Journal, 32,* 627–658.

Carnegie Foundation Report (1996). *Carnegie Task Force on Learning in the Primary Grades.* New York: Carnegie Foundation.

Consortium on the School-Based Promotion of Social Competence (1994). The school based promotion of social competence: Theory, research, practice and policy. In R. J. Haggerty, L. R. Sherrod, N. Garmezy, & M. Rutter (Eds.), *Stress, risk, and resilience in children and adolescents: Processes, mechanisms and interventions* (pp. 268–316). New York: Cambridge University Press.

Cowen, E. L. (1994). The enhancement of psychological wellness: Challenges and opportunities. *American Journal of Community Psychology, 22,* 149–179.

Cowen, E. L., Hightower, A. D., Pedro-Carroll, J. L., Work, W. C.,

Wyman, P. A., & Haffey, W. G. (1996). *School-based prevention for children at risk: The Primary Mental Health Project*. Washington, DC: American Psychological Association.

Dryfoos, J. G. (1994). *Full service schools: A revolution in health and social services for children, youth and families*. San Francisco: Jossey-Bass.

Durlak, J. A. (1995). *School-based prevention programs for children and adolescents*. Thousand Oaks, CA: Sage Publications.

Durlak, J. A. & Wells, A. M. (1997). Primary prevention mental health programs for children and adolescents; A meta-analytic review. *American Journal of Community Psychology, 25,* 115–152.

Joint Commission on Mental Illness and Health. (1961). *Action for mental health*. New York: Basic Books.

Mrazek, P. J., & Haggerty, R. J. (Eds.). (1994). *Reducing risks for mental disorders: Frontiers for preventive intervention research*. Washington, DC: National Academy Press.

Schweinhart, L. J., Barnes, H. V., & Weikart, D. P. (with Barnett, W. S., & Epstein, A. S.). (1993). *Significant benefits: The High/Scope Perry Preschool study through age 27*. Ypsilanti, MI: High/Scope Press.

Strayhorn, J. M. (1988). *The competent child: An approach to psychotherapy and preventive mental health*. New York: The Guilford Press.

Weissberg, R. P., & Greenberg, M. T. (1997). School and community competence-enhancement and prevention programs. In W. Damon (Series Ed.) & I. E. Siegel & K. Renninger (Vol. Eds.): *Handbook of child psychology, Vol. 5: Child psychology in practice* (5th Ed.), (pp. 1–125), New York: John Wiley & Sons.

Werner, E. E. & Smith, R. S. (1992). *Overcoming the odds: High risk children from birth to adulthood*. Ithaca, NY: Cornell University Press.

Yoshikawa, H. (1995). Long-term effects of early childhood programs on social outcomes and delinquency. *The Future of Children, 5,* 51–75.

Wisdom

Paul B. Baltes and Ursula M. Staudinger

Max Planck Institute for Human Development

Life-Span Theory A metatheoretical approach encompassing a family of perspectives (e.g., dynamic between biology and culture, gain/loss dynamic, allocation of resources) characterizing psychosocial and behavioral development across the whole life span.

Personality–Intelligence Interface Wisdom-related performance has been shown to be more strongly related to measures designed to assess a combination of personality and intellectual functioning, such as creativity, social intelligence or cognitive style, than to "pure" personality or intelligence measures.

Psychological Maturity In theories of personality development, maturity has often been specified as the ideal end point and has also been used synonymously with wisdom.

Successful (Positive) Aging Theories of successful aging help to elucidate the potential of aging. The dynamic between developmental gains and losses can be optimized by processes like selection, optimization, and compensation.

Wisdom A complex and content-rich phenomenon used to describe the ideal of human insight and character.

WISDOM is a phenomenon characterized by a rich cultural history and complex associations. Across cultures and history, wisdom has been discussed as the ideal of human knowledge and character. Starting from the dictionary definition of wisdom as "good judgment and advice in difficult and uncertain matters of life," psychologists have described wisdom as the search for the moderate course between extremes, a dynamic between knowledge and doubt, a sufficient detachment from the problem at hand, and a well-balanced coordination of emotion, motivation, and thought. Within psychological research on wisdom, two kinds of approaches can be distinguished. One is the study of lay conceptions of wisdom and the other is the attempt to measure behavioral expressions of wisdom. Such behavioral expressions are either subsumed under personality characteristics, postformal kinds of thinking, or expertise in the fundamental pragmatics of life.

I. A SHORT HISTORICAL ACCOUNT OF WISDOM

For millennia, wisdom and related constructs have been believed to be the ideal of knowledge and personal functioning. Indeed, the idea of wisdom as one of the highest forms of knowledge and skill is evident in the very definition of the historical grand master of all scholarship, philosophy (philosophia): "The love or pursuit of wisdom." Historically, wisdom was defined in terms of a state of idealized being (such as Lady Wisdom), as a process of perfect knowing and judgment, as in King Solomon's judgments, or as an oral or written product, such as wisdom-related proverbs and the so-called wisdom literature.

It is important to recognize that the identification of wisdom with individuals (such as wise persons), the predominant approach in psychology, is but one of the ways by which wisdom is instantiated. In fact, in the general historical literature on wisdom, the identification of wisdom with the mind and character of individuals is not the preferred mode of analysis. Wisdom is considered an ideal that is hardly ever fully realized in the isolated individual.

Throughout history, interest in the topic of wisdom has waxed and waned. In general, two main lines of argument have been in the center of the historical evolution of the concept of wisdom. First is the distinction between philosophical and practical wisdom, often attributed to Aristotle's differentiation between sophia and phronesis. Second is the question of whether wisdom is divine or human.

In the Western world, these two issues (philosophical vs. practical, divine vs. human) were at the center of heated discourse during the Renaissance, with many important works written on these wisdom topics during the fifteenth through seventeenth centuries. An initial conclusion of this discourse was reached during the later phases of the Enlightenment. Wisdom was still critical, for instance, to the thinking of Kant and Hegel. Both understood wisdom as being based on the coordination of the world of science and the practical world of humankind. However, the eighteenth century French Encyclopedia of Diderot (and others), despite its more than 50 volumes, barely mentioned the topic. During the Enlightenment and the process of secularization, wisdom lost its salience as one of the fundamental categories guiding human thought and conduct.

Nevertheless, from time to time, scholars in such fields as philosophy, political science, theology, and cultural anthropology continue to attend to wisdom, although in our view, less in a cumulative sense of theory building than in rejuvenating and revisiting its meaning, historical roots, and implications for raising human awareness about the complexities and uncertainties of life. During the last decade, for example, some philosophers have struggled with the definition of wisdom, including the polarization between practical and philosophical wisdom, the integration of different forms of knowledge into one overarching whole, and the search for orientation in life. In Germany, the latter issue has gained special importance in relation to the advent of postmodernity.

Finally, there is the archeological–cultural work dealing with the origins of religions and secular bodies of wisdom-related texts in China, India, Egypt, Old Mesopotamia, and other sites of ancient civilizations. The cultural–historical scholarship is important as we try to understand the cultural evolution and foundation of wisdom-related thought. Proverbs, maxims, and fairy tales constitute a great part of the materials underlying such efforts. It is impressive to realize how wisdom-related proverbs and tales evince a high degree of cultural and historical invariance. This relative invariance gives rise to the assumption that concepts such as wisdom, with its related body of knowledge and skills, have been culturally selected because of their adaptive value for humankind.

II. PSYCHOLOGICAL DEFINITION OF WISDOM

A first approach to the psychological definition of wisdom is its treatment in encyclopedias and dictionaries. The major German historical dictionary, edited by the brothers Grimm, for instance, defined wisdom as "insight and knowledge about oneself and the world . . . and sound judgment in the case of difficult life problems." Similarly, the *Oxford Dictionary* includes in its definition of wisdom: "Good judgment and advice in difficult and uncertain matters of life."

When psychologists approach the definition of wisdom, they like philosophers are confronted with the need to specify the content and formal properties of wisdom-related thought, judgment, and advice in terms of psychological categories, and also to describe the characteristics of persons who have approached a state of wisdom and who are capable of transmitting wisdom to others. These initial efforts by psychologists for the most part were theoretical and speculative. In his pioneering piece on senescence, G. Stanley Hall (1922), for example, associated wisdom with the emergence of a meditative attitude, philosophic calmness, impartiality, and the desire to draw moral lessons that emerge in later adulthood. Furthermore, other writers have emphasized that wisdom is the search for the moderate course between extremes, a dynamic between knowledge and doubt, a sufficient detachment from the problem at hand, and a well-balanced coordination of emotion, motivation, and thought. In line with dictionary definitions, such writings by psychologists typically include varied statements that wisdom is knowledge about the human condition at its frontier, knowledge about the most difficult questions of the meaning and conduct of life, and knowledge about the uncertainties of life, about what cannot be known, and how to deal with that limited knowledge.

III. IMPLICIT (SUBJECTIVE) THEORIES ABOUT WISDOM

Most empirical research on wisdom in psychology so far has focused on further elaboration of the definition of wisdom. Moving beyond the dictionary definitions of wisdom, some research has explored the nature of everyday beliefs, folk conceptions, and implicit (subjective) theories of wisdom. The pursuit of answers to questions such as What is wisdom? How is wisdom different from other forms of intelligence? Which situations require wisdom? and What are the characteristics of wise people? was at the center of psychological wisdom research throughout the 1980s.

These studies, in principle, build on research initiated by Clayton in 1976 (see Sternberg, 1990). In her work, these dimensions are typical of wise people: (1) affective characteristics such as empathy and compassion, (2) reflective processes such as intuition and introspection, and (3) cognitive capacities such as experience and intelligence (see also Table I).

The focus of a study conducted in 1986 by Sternberg, which investigated implicit theories, was the location of wisdom in the semantic space marked by other constructs such as creativity and intelligence. Within that frame of reference, Sternberg found wisdom described by six dimensions: reasoning ability, sagacity, learning from ideas and environment, judgment, expeditious use of information, and perspicacity. When asking people about their views on wisdom, the greatest overlap was found between intelligence and wisdom. The sagacity dimension, however, was specific to wisdom. Sagacity seems to build in Clayton's affective and reflective dimensions and includes such behavioral expressions as displaying concern for others or considering advice. In later theoretical work, Sternberg used these results and others to specify six

Table I   Implicit Theories of Wisdom: A Comparison of Findings from Three Studies with Sample Items[a]

Clayton (1976)	Sternberg (1986)	Holliday & Chandler (1986)
Affective (1) Empathy Compassion	Sagacity (2) Concern for others Considers advice	Interpersonal skills (4) Sensitive Sociable
	Perspicacity (6) Intuition Offers right and true solutions	Judgment and communication skills (2) Is a good source of advice Understands life
Reflective (2) Intuition Introspection	Judgment (4) Acts within own limitations Is sensible	Social unobtrusiveness (5) Discreet Nonjudgmental
	Learning from ideas and environment (3) Perceptive Learns from mistakes	Exceptional understanding as based on ordinary experience (1) Has learned from experience Sees things in a larger context
Cognitive (3) Experience Intelligence	Reasoning ability (1) Good problem-solving ability Logical mind	General competence (3) Intelligent Educated
	Expeditious use of information (5) Experienced Seeks out information	

Note. Sequence of factors or dimensions obtained in original research is given in parentheses. Studies are based on different methodologies (factor analysis, multidimensional scaling).

[a] After Staudinger and Baltes, 1994.

domains which lead people to label a person as wise: (1) understanding of presuppositions, meaning, and limits (knowledge); (2) resisting automization of one's own thought but seeking to understand it in others (process); (3) judiciousness (primary intellectual style); (4) understanding of ambiguity and obstacles (personality); (5) desire to understand what is known and what it means (motivation); and (6) depth of understanding, needing to find appreciation in context (environmental context).

Another major study on subjective theories of wisdom was conducted by Holliday and Chandler also in 1986 (see Sternberg, 1990). Their work included an analysis of the words people use to describe wisdom and wise persons and the attributes judged to be the most typical indicators of these concepts. A summary of their outcomes and also the results of Clayton and Sternberg is presented in Table I.

A factor analysis of the attributes judged to be "most prototypical" of a wise person and wise behavior revealed two factors. Holliday and Chandler labeled one dimension the "exceptional understanding of ordinary experience." This dimension combines qualities of the mind with practical virtues of leading a good life. They labeled the second factor "judgment and communication skills." This factor referred to qualities such as comprehending, weighing consequences, and giving good advice. Combining these results with notions from Habermas lead Chandler and Holliday to emphasize the importance of a multidimensional account of wisdom, comprising technical, practical, and emancipatory forms of knowledge.

Two studies in the tradition of implicit-theory research asked subjects to nominate wise people and subsequently to characterize the nominees. Two reported findings were of special importance. First, it seemed that the characterization of wisdom and wise persons was a task readily performed by elderly research participants. Second, subjects emphasized the notion that the persons they had nominated as wise displayed "excellent character." Wisdom nominees tended to be middle-aged to old, male rather than female, and more highly educated. However, none of these studies used heterogeneous, representative samples. Therefore, it may very well be that as such research is applied systematically to nominators from various cultural subgroups, new constellations of person characteristics, including different gender and age distributions, would emerge.

From this research on implicit theories of wisdom and wise persons, it is evident that people in Western samples hold fairly clear-cut images of the nature of wisdom. Four findings are especially noteworthy. First, in the minds of people, wisdom seems to be closely related to wise persons as "carriers" of wisdom. Second, wise people are expected to combine features of intellect and character. Third, wisdom carries a very strong interpersonal and social aspect with regard to both its application (advice) and the consensual recognition of its occurrence. Fourth, wisdom exhibits overlap with other related concepts such as intelligence, but in aspects of sagacity, prudence, and the integration of cognition, emotion, and motivation, it also carries unique variance.

IV. EXPLICIT THEORIES AND ASSESSMENT OF WISDOM

A more recent line of empirical psychological inquiry on wisdom addresses the question of how to measure behavioral expression of wisdom. Within this tradition, three lines of work can be identified: (1) assessment of wisdom as a personality characteristic, (2) assessment of wisdom in the Piagetian tradition of postformal thought, and (3) assessment of wisdom as an individual's problem-solving performance with regard to difficult problems in the interpretation, conduct, and management of life.

Within personality theories, wisdom is usually conceptualized as an advanced, if not the final, stage of personality development. Wisdom in this context is comparable to "optimal maturity." A wise person is characterized, for instance, as integrating rather than ignoring or repressing self-related information, by having coordinated opposites, and by having transcended personal agendas and turned to collective or universal issues. Ryff and Whitbourne, for example, have undertaken the effort to develop self-report questionnaires based on the Eriksonian notions of personality development, especially the traits of integrity and wisdom. In a study of people who had been nominated as "wise," according to subjective beliefs about wisdom, wise nominees were characterized by high scores on Eriksonian measures of ego integrity and showed a greater concern for the world state or humanity as a whole than the comparison group. By means of her widely used sentence completion technique, Loevinger developed a measure of her theoretically postulated stages of ego development. Loevinger's last stage, labeled "ego integrity," has been found to be related to other personality dimensions, such as competence from the California Personality Inventory or openness to experience from the Neuroticism-Extraversion-Openness-Personality Inventory.

Central to neo-Piagetian theories of adult thought is the transcendence of the universal truth criterion that characterizes formal logic. This transcendence is common to conceptions such as dialectical, complementary, and relativistic thinking. The tolerance of multiple truths, that is, of ambiguity, has also been mentioned as a crucial feature of wisdom. Empirical studies in this tradition have found that at least up to middle adulthood, performances on such measures of adult thought evince increases.

Besides the measures of wisdom as a personality characteristic and as a feature of mature thought, there is also work that attempts to assess wisdom-related performance in tasks dealing with the interpretation, conduct, and management of life. The conceptual approach taken by the Berlin Max Planck Institute group is based on life-span theory, the developmental study of the aging mind and aging personality, research on expert systems, and cultural–historical definitions of wisdom (Baltes, Smith, & Staudinger, 1992). By integrating these perspectives, wisdom is defined as "an expert knowledge system in the fundamental pragmatics of life permitting exceptional insight, judgment, and advice involving complex and uncertain matters of the human condition."

The body of knowledge and skills associated with wisdom as an expertise in the fundamental pragmatics of life contains insights into the quintessential aspects of the human condition, including its biological finitude and cultural conditioning. At the center are questions about the conduct, interpretation, and meaning of life. Furthermore, wisdom includes a fine-tuned coordination of cognition, motivation, and emotion. More specifically, wisdom-related knowledge and skills, shown in Table II, can be characterized by a family of five criteria.

To elicit and measure wisdom-related knowledge and skills, the Berlin group of wisdom researchers presented subjects with difficult life dilemmas such as the following: "Imagine a good friend of yours calls you up and tells you that she can't go on anymore and has decided to commit suicide. What would you be thinking about, how would you deal with this situation?." Participants are then asked to "think aloud" about such dilemmas. The five wisdom-related criteria introduced in Table II are used to evaluate these protocols. The obtained scores are reliable and provide an approximation of the quantity and quality of wisdom-related knowledge and skills of a given person. When using this wisdom paradigm to study people who were nominated as wise according to nominators' subjective beliefs about wisdom, wisdom nominees received higher wisdom scores than comparable con-

Table II A Family of Five Criteria Characterizing Wisdom and Wisdom-Related Products

Criteria	Description
Basic criteria	
Factual knowledge	To what extent does this product show general (conditio humana) and specific (e.g., life events, institutions) knowledge about life matters and the human condition, as well as demonstrate scope and depth in the coverage of issues?
Procedural knowledge	To what extent does this product consider decision strategies, how to define goals and identify the appropriate means, with whom to consult, and consider strategies of advice giving?
Metalevel criteria	
Life-span contextualism	To what extent does this product consider the past, current, and possible future contexts of life and the many circumstances in which a life is embedded?
Value relativism	To what extent does this product consider variations in values and life priorities and the importance of viewing each person within his or her own framework despite a small set of universal values?
Awareness and management of uncertainty	To what extent does this product consider the inherent uncertainty of life (in terms of interpreting the past and predicting the future) and effective strategies for dealing with uncertainty?

Note. For further detail, see Baltes, Smith and Staudinger, 1992.

trol samples of various ages and professional backgrounds (Baltes & Staudinger, 1993).

Researchers of wisdom are usually quite aware that it is a courageous undertaking to try to study wisdom empirically. Wisdom is a complex and content-rich phenomenon, and, as many scholars have claimed, it defies attempts at scientific identification. However, research on explicit theories of wisdom has shown that it is possible to measure wisdom in terms of personality characteristics (standardized or open-ended), characteristics of adult thought, and performance (judgment, advice) on difficult life tasks.

V. WISDOM AND MENTAL HEALTH

In almost any of the many different conceptions of mental health that also encompass positive features, there is one component that relates to ideals of positive functioning. Jahoda's conception, which exclusively focuses on the positive pole of mental health, even lists characteristics such as growth and self-actualization, or integration of personality. Therefore, when exploring links between the constructs of wisdom and mental health, historically and theoretically, the work of Erikson and also of Jung are critical.

Erikson, in his epigenetic theory of personality development, identified the achievement of integrity and wisdom as the last and highest form of personality functioning. Achieving this last stage requires, on the one hand, successful mastery of the previous life tasks and, on the other hand, accelerative and supportive conditions associated with the social environment. Wisdom, in the Eriksonian sense, necessitates the full expression of mature identity, including the transcendence of personal interests, mastering one's own finitude, and the attention to collective and universal issues.

Empirical research on these Eriksonian notions, in the narrow sense, is scarce. However, as alluded to earlier, a few studies derived from theories of the life-span development of personality and based largely on Eriksonian ideas have appeared in the literature in recent years. Ryff and Heincke, in 1983, compared people of different ages on self-report measures based on the Eriksonian notions of personality development. The oldest group (average age: 70 years) reported higher levels of integrity than the middle-aged and young participants. In a longitudinal study with a sample of young and middle-aged adults, in 1992 Whitbourne,

Zuschlag, Elliot, and Waterman also found evidence for integrity in the manner of Erikson. At the same time, however, there was a historical trend toward declining levels of integrity in the population. The authors related this finding to the increasing materialism and individualism in Western societies which, in their view, was characteristic of the 1980s.

Wisdom, in the sense of a personality characteristic, has been defined as the ideal end point of personality development. When it comes to wisdom in the sense of export-level knowledge and judgment about difficult and uncertain life problems, mental health has been defined as one precondition for the development of this expertise. Within the Berlin wisdom paradigm, we have developed a general framework outlining the conditions for the development of wisdom as expert-level judgment and knowledge in the fundamental pragmatics of life. The model (see Figure 1) presents a set of factors and processes that need to "cooperate" for wisdom to develop. We postulate certain cognitive and emotional–motivational processes, as well as certain experiential factors associated with the interpretation, conduct, and management of life, to be important antecedents of wisdom.

First, as shown on the left-hand side of Figure 1, there are general individual characteristics related to adaptive human functioning such as intelligence and personality. Mental health or level of ego development is listed under this category as well. Second, the model presumes that the development of wisdom is advanced by certain expertise-specific factors, such as practice and being guided by a mentor. Third, the model implies the operation of macro-level, facilitative experiential contexts. For instance, certain professions and historical periods are more facilitative than others. In the center of Figure 1, some of the organizing processes (life planning, life management, and life review) that may be critical for the development of wisdom-related knowledge are identified. Finally, on the right-hand side, certain theoretical assumptions about where the five criteria fall in the course of the development of wisdom are depicted. [See INTELLIGENCE AND MENTAL HEALTH.]

The empirical work based on this ontogenetic model and the measurement paradigm presented here produced outcomes consistent with expectations. For instance, contrary to work on the fluid mechanics of cognitive aging, older adults performed as well as young adults. Furthermore, when age was combined with wisdom-related experiential contexts, such as

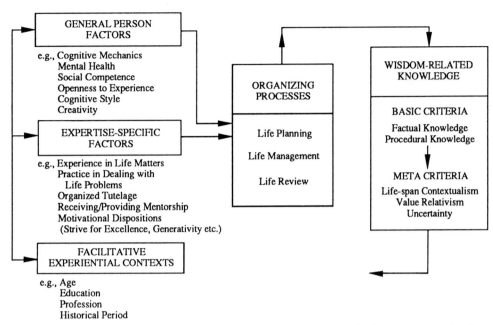

Figure 1 A research framework describing factors and mediating processes for the acquisition and maintenance of wisdom-related knowledge and skills across the life span.

professional specializations that specifically involve training and experience in matters of life (e.g., clinical psychology), even higher levels of performance were observed. Explorations into the location of wisdom-related performance in the psychometric space between intelligence, personality, and the intelligence–personality interface suggested that neither personality nor intelligence measures by themselves predicted as much variance as did measures of the personality–intelligence interface such as creativity and cognitive style. In addition, our measure of wisdom-related performance retained a sizable amount of uniqueness when projected into a measurement space defined by 30 indicators of personality and intellectual functioning.

VI. SUMMARY AND FUTURE DIRECTIONS

The concept of wisdom represents a fruitful topic for psychological research and specifically for research on mental health in various respects: (1) the study of wisdom emphasizes the search for continued optimization and the further evolution of the human conditions, and (2) in a prototypical manner, it allows for the study of collaboration of cognitive, emotional,

and motivational processes. We expect that future research on wisdom will be expanded in at least four ways: (1) the use of social-interactive or communicative paradigms to make more explicit the social nature of wisdom, (2) the further identification of social and personality factors and life processes that are relevant for the ontogeny of wisdom, (3) the delineation of commonalities and differences of wisdom-related processes in the larger framework of research on intelligence and personality, and (4) the comparison of wisdom as it applies to oneself and wisdom as it is used for judgment and advice on life problems in general.

BIBLIOGRAPHY

Assmann, A. (1994). Wholesome knowledge: Concepts of wisdom in a historical and cross-cultural perspective. In D. L. Featherman, R. M. Lerner, & M. Perlmutter (Eds.), *Life-span development and behavior* (pp. 187–224). Hillsdale, NJ: Lawrence Erlbaum.

Baltes, P. B., & Staudinger, U. M. (1993). The search for a psychology of wisdom. *Current Directions in Psychological Science, 2,* 1–6.

Baltes, P. B., Smith, J., & Staudinger, U. M. (1992). Wisdom and successful aging. *Nebraska Symposium on Motivation, 39,* 123–167.

Dittmann-Kohli, F., & Baltes, P. B. (1990). Toward a neofunction-alist conception of adult intellectual development: Wisdom as a prototypical case of intellectual growth. In C. Alexander & E. Langer (Eds.), *Higher stages of human development* (pp. 54–78). New York: Oxford University Press.

Kekes, J. (1983). Wisdom. *American Philosophical Quarterly, 20,* 227–286.

Oelmüller, W. (Ed.). (1989). *Philosophie und Weisheit.* Paderborn: Schöningh.

Rudolph, K. (1987). Wisdom. In M. Eliade (Ed.), *Encyclopedia of religion: Wisdom* (Vol. 15, pp. 393–401). New York: MacMillan.

Staudinger, U. M., & Baltes, P. B. (1994). The psychology of Wisdom. In R. J. Sternberg (Ed.), *Encyclopedia of intelligence* (pp. 1143–1152). New York: Cambridge University Press.

Staudinger, U. M., & Baltes, P. B. (1996). Interactive minds: A facilitative setting for wisdom-related performance? *Journal of Personality and Social Psychology, 71,* 746–762.

Staudinger, U. M., Lopez, D. F., & Baltes, P. B. (1997). The psychometric location of wisdom-related performance: Intelligence, personality, and more? *Personality and Social Psychology Bulletin, 23,* 1200–1214.

Sternberg, R. J. (Ed.). (1990). *Wisdom: Its origins and development.* New York: Cambridge University Press.

Women's Health

Tracey A. Revenson and Tracy A. McFarlane

The Graduate School of the City University of New York

Autoimmune Disorders The failure of the immune system to distinguish between the body and foreign antigens, thus attacking the body's own cells.

Biopsychosocial Model An approach used to study health and disease that addresses the relationships between biomedical, psychological, and sociocultural factors.

Coping A psychological mechanism for managing stress, involving thoughts, behaviors, and feelings.

Mammography An X-ray examination of breast tissue to detect abnormalities and possible cancer.

Morbidity Rate The number of cases of a disease or other disorder per unit of population in a given period of time.

Mortality Rate The number of deaths per unit of population in a specific time period.

Resilience The ability to recover and experience growth from disadvantage or adversity.

Stress A negative experience accompanied by predictable biochemical, physiological, cognitive, and behavioral changes that are directed either toward altering an event perceived as stressful or accommodating its effects.

WOMEN'S HEALTH research examines behavioral and psychosocial factors affecting women's physical and psychological well-being. Women's health encompasses health issues that are unique to women, diseases that are experienced to a greater extent by women, diseases that are experienced by particular subgroups of women, and risk factors that are unique to women. This article provides statistics on sex differences in morbidity and mortality, delineates cross-cutting themes, and illustrates these by focusing on seven exemplars of current research. Finally, the notion of resilience is introduced as a new approach for women's health.

I. INTRODUCTION

We begin with the most obvious, yet most difficult question: What do we mean by women's health? We can place the emphasis on the first word, *women*. By doing that we can argue that our goal is to describe current theories and research on the health of a particular biological/demographic group, *females*. We can present information concerning all women, on particular cultural or medical subgroups of women, on health issues that are unique to women (e.g., childbirth, menopause), on diseases that are experienced to a greater extent by women (e.g., breast cancer, osteoporosis, eating disorders), on risk and protective factors that are unique to women (e.g., [failure to] obtain regular mammograms), or on those that predispose women more than men to particular illnesses.

Or, we could place the emphasis on the second word, *health*. The World Health Organization's (WHO) definition of health includes not only physical health but also mental, social, functional, and spiritual health, as well as the utilization of health care services and the development of health policy. Thus, we need to address the prevention of disease and promotion of health as well as the treatment of illness, the interaction between patients and providers, and cultural definitions of health and illness.

Both emphases are much too broad to cover here and would result in a superficial presentation of knowledge. Instead, we will provide some epidemiological data to indicate why it is so important to study issues in women's health as we near the dawn of the twenty-first century and to provide some indication of the gender differences in health that have been found. We present three overarching themes that are particularly important to guide women's health research (but also may be relevant to men's health) and provide several illustrative examples of current research in women's health. We conclude with the idea for a new paradigm in women's health: one that focuses on resilience and strength, as opposed to pathology and maladaption.

II. A RESEARCH AREA WHOSE TIME HAS COME

The study of women's health as its own "specialty" is a recent development, although an awareness that inequities existed in women's health care has been growing for a long time. For many years, inattention to women's issues could be found in the conduct of research and the clinical practice of medicine: The historical exclusion of women and members of racial/ethnic minorities from clinical trials and major studies of medical conditions affecting men *and* women limits our ability to understand fully many issues in women's health. A 5-year study of 22,000 male physicians that examined the benefits of taking a daily aspirin to prevent heart attacks brought the issue to national attention. No women were included in the study; but more importantly, the conclusions based on a male sample were being generalized to women. This was a galvanizing factor in the creation of the Office on Women's Health within the Department of Health and Human Services in 1990. Along with federal regulations requiring the inclusion of women (and ethnic minorities) in government-supported research, there is both a growing interest in women's health and more scientific legitimacy to study it.

Many studies examine the linkages between women's behavior and their health outcomes. This is part of a move within medicine and the behavioral sciences toward use of a comprehensive biopsychosocial model to study health and health care. Behavioral and psychosocial factors are pivotal in the development of many diseases, particularly chronic diseases, and in the practice of health habits. Thus, these factors have potential to help prevent illness and improve quality of life. When people become ill, psychosocial factors influence adjustment to the illness and may affect the course of the illness (indirectly) by influencing compliance with treatment or the immune system response.

III. CROSS-CUTTING THEMES IN WOMEN'S HEALTH

There are a number of overarching themes that are important to the study of women's health. First is the need to recognize the interdependence of physical and mental health. Physical health affects mental health, and, at the same time, mental health affects physical health. For example, the onset of a chronic illness and its treatment regimen may result in increased depressive symptoms, and depression may inhibit the use of effective coping strategies, including adherence to treatment, which could cause greater health declines. As will become apparent in the examplars presented later, it serves no purpose to separate physical and mental health—they are braided together.

The second theme is the fact that women's health must be studied within its social and cultural context.

There is an unstated assumption in the social and medical sciences that women are a homogenous group, particularly in studies in which women are compared with men. However, there is probably as much variation *among* women as there is *between* women and men. Sociodemographic factors such as age, race/ethnicity, social class, and poverty influence health status and health behaviors in their own right, but also interact with gender. Despite the social, economic, and cultural diversity among minority women, as a group, they disproportionately experience disease, disability, and premature death. For example, although the incidence rate of breast cancer is lower among Black women than White women, the death rate for Black women due to that disease is higher. Poverty appears to contribute to the greater morbidity and mortality among minority women, in large part because of their limited access to quality health care, particularly preventive care, and their greater likelihood of being uninsured or underinsured.

It is also important to examine health and behavior processes among women of different sexual orientations, though this is a very recent focus. For example, current research on HIV/AIDS has examined behavioral transmission among women who have sex with women and the "minority" stress that lesbians experience. National surveys indicate underutilization of routine preventive care by lesbians, perhaps because of stigmatization by health professionals.

The third theme is that the behavioral and psychosocial aspects of women's health must be studied within women's lived experience. This means that there is a need for naturalistic studies, framed within the context of women's lives. Research needs to consider women's roles as wives, mothers, and caregivers of others as it considers how they cope with their own or a family member's illness, adhere to prescribed treatment, or find the time to seek and practice preventive care, such as breast self-examination. For example, in reporting the occurrence of stressful life events, women tend to include events that happen to family members and friends as their own to a greater degree than do men, suggesting that their experience of stress is qualitatively different. It is also critical to include a life-span developmental perspective in women's health research. A women's age reflects not only her reproductive cycle and the normative biological changes occurring in her body, but also the social and developmental tasks appropriate for her life stage.

IV. SEX DIFFERENCES IN HEALTH STATUS

There is much research evidence indicating that differences in health status between men and women do exist. When the biological evidence is considered, women may be regarded as having health advantages over men; however, these differences become further complicated when one considers mortality versus morbidity. The odds of being born male are 1.25 times greater than being born female, but 27% more boys than girls die in the first year of life. In fact, mortality rates are higher for men than for women in all age groups across the life span, and for almost every cause of death. Females have greater life expectancies than males across all racial/ethnic groups (although White females have greater life expectancies than females of other ethnicities).

Longitudinal data show that this sex differential gradually increased until 1970, when the rate of increase slowed, resulting in less marked differences in women's longevity advantage. This change may be attributed, in part, to changes in the epidemiology of major diseases. Rates of heart disease in women have increased while they stayed about the same for men. Heart disease is now the leading cause of death among American women (as well as for men). Cancer rates rose more rapidly for women than men prior to 1979, when they started to decline more rapidly for men.

Despite living approximately 7 years longer than men, women report poorer health than do men. Women have a greater incidence of morbidity—that is, they experience more symptoms, acute health conditions, greater disability from disease, and poorer health outcomes than men. Black women report more ill health than White women, and women who live in poverty have shorter life spans, higher rates of illness, and more limited access to medical care. Women also experience more acute conditions than men do. This is consistent for all categories except for injuries, where men show higher rates than women. Thus, in part because they live longer than men, older women are more likely to live in poverty and to be affected by chronic disabling conditions, such as osteoporosis, osteoarthritis, urinary incontinence, and Alzheimer's disease.

Rates of health care utilization are also an important indicator of sex differences in health status. Thirteen percent of women did not get the medical care they needed in 1992, compared with 9% of men. That number is much greater among uninsured women:

30% of uninsured women did not get the care they needed. Of those women who do have access to health care, many are dissatisfied with the care provided or with the communication between themselves and their doctors. More women (over 40%) changed physicians at some point because they were unhappy with the care being provided than did men (27%).

Weaving these three cross-cutting themes through our writing, we briefly review seven issues that highlight behavioral and psychosocial issues in women's health. These issues were chosen because they represent salient or emergent health issues for women at different stages of the health–disease continuum (i.e., prevention through treatment) and at different life stages.

V. BREAST CANCER PREVENTION: MAMMOGRAPHY SCREENING

Cancer is a major source of mortality and a serious health problem for women in the United States. It is estimated that breast cancer will account for 30% of all new cases of cancer incidence in women in the United States in 1997, and, second only to lung cancer, will be the cause of 16.5% of deaths due to cancer during that year. Breast cancer is the leading cause of death for women aged 40 to 44, and the second leading cause of death (after cardiovascular disease) for women over 50.

Psychosocial, biological, and behavioral factors have been identified as risk factors for breast cancer. Age, race/ethnicity, and income have all been associated with variations in risk. The *lifetime* risk for all women is 1 in 8, but the likelihood of developing breast cancer increases with age: 1 in 622 women at age 35 versus 1 in 9 by age 85. Although the incidence of breast cancer among White women is higher than for Black women, the 5-year survival rate is significantly lower for Black women. Recent data indicate, however, that for the first time, mortality rates are declining in younger African American women, perhaps because of earlier detection and improved treatment. Minority, low-income women are less likely to recognize risk factors. Women with low income and education are less likely to be screened for breast cancer, delay seeking treatment in the presence of symptoms, and are diagnosed at a later stage of the disease.

Heredity is a strong factor in breast cancer risk:

Women who are first-degree relatives (daughters, sisters, or mothers) of breast cancer victims have 3 times higher risk than those who are not. Recently, two breast cancer susceptibility genes, BRCA-1 and BRCA-2, have been discovered. Inheritance of abnormality in these genes accounts for about 25% of breast cancers in women below age 30. Nulliparity (never having given birth) or having a first child after the age of 30 increases risk. Other risk factors include estrogen replacement therapy, alcohol consumption, and some forms of fibrocystic disease. Women who have fibrocystic disease of the breast have a 2 to 5 times greater risk of developing breast cancer.

Objective risk is not the same as subjective or perceived risk. Although most women are aware of the risk due to family history, many fewer women are aware of the risk from advancing age. Women also hold misconceptions about breast cancer risk, believing that breast injury, breast-feeding, stress, or caffeine consumption play a causal role. In general, women underestimate their own risk of breast cancer relative to women of their age, although women who have a family history of breast cancer typically overestimate their risk. In explaining risk perceptions, one study found that women associated their healthy lifestyle behaviors and having no family history of breast cancer with decreased risk, and associated a family history of breast cancer and the presence of biological factors such as fibrocystic breast disease or having had children at a late age with increased risk. Greater risk perceptions were related to taking preventive actions (performing regular breast self-examination or obtaining mammograms) but family history was not.

Screening and early detection can identify breast abnormalities that may be cancer before physical symptoms develop and reduce the number of women who die from this disease. Today, 65% of women diagnosed with breast cancer survive 10 years, and 56% survive 15 years. The 5-year relative survival rate for localized breast cancer is 97%; if the cancer has spread regionally the rate drops to 76%, and for women with distant metastases the rate is 20%. Medical system barriers such as cost and access to health care, and psychological barriers such as ineffectiveness of physician's communication, inconvenience, or anxiety about receiving positive results may deter women from obtaining screening mammograms at the recommended intervals. Discussions with health care professions about family history and other risk factors can lead to more accurate risk perceptions and individualized screening schedules. Current recommendations are that asymptomatic women aged 20 to 39 should perform breast self-examination every month and have a physical breast examination performed by a health care professional every 3 years.

There is debate over the efficacy of mammography screening among healthy (asymptomatic) women aged 40 to 49. More than 22% of all cases of breast cancer are diagnosed in women under 50. When women who are 50 or older have screening mammograms ever 1 to 2 years, they reduce their chances of dying from breast cancer by about 30%. Whether or not women under 50 benefit from similar screening is uncertain. Five of eight large randomized clinical trials have shown a reduction in mortality for women aged 40 to 49 who were screened; however, when a statistic known as meta-analysis is used to compare these trials, the benefits are not as apparent. Because of their denser breast tissue, mammography is less sensitive in younger women and some tumors may go undetected. Recent findings indicate a 24% mortality reduction from breast cancer among women in their 40s who were screened. The results of a 1997 National Institutes of Health (NIH) Consensus Development Panel concluded that there was not enough scientific evidence that women in their 40s would benefit from annual mammography screening for the panel to recommend its use. However, other experts, such as the American Cancer Society and the National Cancer Institute *do* recommend annual screening for women in their 40s. This may be even more important for African American women who, on average, are 7 years younger than White women when diagnosed. Women should consult their health care providers to determine the frequency of mammography screening that is best for them. However, these recommendations for breast cancer screening are intended to apply to women with no symptoms. If women have any hint of a symptom, they should see a clinician who may suggest mammography for diagnosis.

Many women do not comply with the recommended guidelines for obtaining screening mammograms, clinical breast examinations, or practicing monthly breast self-examination. Women with higher educations and incomes are more likely to take such actions, and it is these factors, and not simply ethnicity, that may explain why older Hispanic, White, and Black women have lower screening rates. Behavioral

interventions to encourage women to have screening mammograms have proven effective. As one example, an educational program designed to increase women's perception of their susceptibility to breast cancer, of the severity of breast cancer, and of the benefits of mammography was successful in influencing women who had never had mammograms to have them, and in encouraging repeated mammograms in women who had previously had a mammogram. [*See* CANCER.]

VI. WOMEN AND HIV: BEHAVIORAL RISK AND PROTECTIVE FACTORS

Over the last decade, women have accounted for an increasing percentage of people with HIV/AIDS in the United States. The number of women infected with HIV is doubling every 1 to 2 years, rising from 6.6% in 1985 to 18% in 1994. Although women remain among the minority of AIDS cases in the United States (19% in 1995), women currently represent 50% of the reported nonpediatric cases of AIDS throughout the world.

HIV infection in the United States has advanced from being the fifth leading cause of death among women aged 25 to 44 years in 1991 to being the third leading cause of death among women in that age group in 1996. Data from the Centers for Disease Control and Prevention indicate that as many as 80,000 women of reproductive age could be infected with HIV, creating additional risks to their health during pregnancy and to the health of their children. Because the rate of transmission from an infected woman to her fetus is about 30%, about 1 in every 2200 infants born in the United States may be infected with HIV through perinatal transmission.

Infection patterns among women reveal that minority women are disproportionately represented among women with AIDS. The incidence of AIDS cases per 100,000 among African American women is more than 15 times that of White women, and among Latina women, more than 6 times the rate of White women. Of the total number of women diagnosed with AIDS, the majority are poor. More than half are African American, one-fifth Hispanic. It is essential to understand the social context in which these women live. The higher prevalence of poverty and drug use in minority communities, and cultural factors such as negative attitudes toward condom use, undermine prevention strategies. Poor, ethnic minority women who are primarily concerned with providing food and shelter for themselves and their children may consider their HIV/AIDS risk to be a less important consideration.

Heterosexual transmission and intravenous drug use have been identified as the two primary routes of transmission for both heterosexual women and women who have sex with women. Recent evidence suggests that certain populations of women who have sex with women (including self-identified lesbian and bisexual women) are at greater risk for HIV/AIDS than was previously thought. Many women are at risk because of sharing drug injection equipment with a sex partner. Although having multiple partners is a risk factor for women, having only one partner who engages in risky behavior, such as intravenous drug use, places women at increased risk.

As HIV is transmitted behaviorally, most intervention efforts to control the AIDS epidemic have focused on using education and behavior modification to increase a sense of (perceived) risk and consequently change individual behavior. Although seemingly the gold standard, these programs have had limited success, in part because they focus on increasing condom use, a male-controlled behavior, and also because they have not been culturally sensitive—that is, they have not taken into consideration the cultural beliefs and constraints of specific risk populations.

Current research findings indicate that community-based needle exchange and drug treatment programs are potentially effective strategies for reducing HIV transmission. However, barriers to participation in these programs have restricted their effectiveness among women. For example, women report that fear of arrest or harassment by police and the stigma of being identified as intravenous drug users are deterrents for participating. Many drug treatment programs do not accept women, and few offer accommodations for children or are willing to assume medical responsibility for pregnant women.

The demands of the HIV epidemic exceed traditional models that focus simply on changing individual perceptions. Clearly, interventions that do not consider the multiple contexts of sexual behavior when attempting to deal with HIV have limited usefulness in controlling this disease. New data indicate that interventions that teach women to negotiate condom use with their partners (particularly when taught in groups consisting solely of women) are effective.

Efforts to reduce risky behaviors among women have resulted in very modest gains in the fight against the spread of this epidemic. Research has identified some psychosocial factors that influence rates of HIV transmission among women. Future efforts to increase HIV-related knowledge, identify and reduce barriers to participation in intervention programs, and address sociocultural factors that influence sexual behaviors (e.g., the decision to use condoms) are crucial for arresting the increasingly rapid rate at which HIV affects women. [*See* HIV/AIDS.]

VII. WOMEN AND STRESS: THE IMPACT OF GENDER ROLES

Stress has emerged as a significant factor in health for both men and women, and may be a critical concept for explaining gender differences in morbidity and mortality. Considerations of the biological and psychological impact of stress have expanded beyond simply noting the extent of exposure to major life events, such as divorce or unemployment, to the recognition that the daily stressors or hassles in one's life have even more potent health effects. Moreover, the health effects of stressors are largely determined by appraisals or perceptions of the severity of those stressors and the relevance for one's life. Hence, women may not only differ from men in the number and types of stressors that they experience, but may also differ in the way they appraise stressful events and may employ different approaches to coping with stress.

Shifts in work and family patterns have resulted in changes in the definitions of marital and parental roles for women. The stress created as a result of these new roles is changing character, as increased employment opportunities and reduced household responsibilities allow many women to be less economically dependent on men. On the other hand, these gains introduce new stresses for women as it becomes necessary to define and seek equity in other traditionally gender-defined domains, such as the workplace and participation in child-rearing. Recent studies have disputed previous notions that multiple roles for women result in increased physical and psychological distress. Instead, multiple role involvement enhances physical health, increases life satisfaction, and lowers depression.

Research has revealed the importance of recognizing distinctions in the types of roles that women occupy when considering their effects on health. Family roles, such as those of wife and mother, may be a source of fulfillment for some women but may be a source of distress for others, depending on the number of children and their ages, the mother's marital status, and the availability of financial resources. In contrast, paid employment offers significant health benefits for women. These mental and physical health benefits are most notable for women in high-status positions, but are also evident among women in low-status jobs.

There is also substantial evidence that the effect of psychological stress is reflected in biological systems. Observations of biological responses to stress indicate that women and men differ in their vulnerability to stress. For example, in studies of cardiovascular reactions, men show higher systolic blood pressure reactions to a stressor, whereas women tend to show greater heart rate increases. Similarly, studies have shown that women's and men's immune systems react differently to stressors. One study of 20- to 37-year-old, predominantly White newlyweds showed that the immune systems and endocrine functioning of both spouses were adversely affected by hostile or negative behavior during a 30-minute discussion. However, wives became more physically aroused, with greater changes in endocrine and immune function that were more closely related to the negative behaviors during the social interaction. (Similar findings have been observed in studies of hostility and cardiovascular functioning.) Because women are more frequently affected by autoimmune disorders, it is important to continue to study the relationships between gender, stress, and immune function. [*See* COPING WITH STRESS; STRESS.]

VIII. ARTHRITIS: A LINK BETWEEN CHRONIC ILLNESS AND DEPRESSION

Arthritis and musculoskeletal disorders are the most common self-reported chronic conditions affecting women. Many of the more common and more serious forms of arthritis affect 2 to 5 times more females than males. Thus, arthritis represents a significant health problem for women. Despite its prevalence, arthritis is overlooked because of the tendency of biomedical research to focus on fatal conditions, even though America's health future will be dominated by chronic, nonfatal health conditions.

Rheumatoid arthritis (RA) is an autoimmune dis-

ease of unknown cause. Major features including inflammation of the area around the joints, often leading to progressive joint destruction. Between 1 and 2% of the adult population have rheumatoid arthritis. Its prevalence increases with increasing age, and, overall, at different points in the life span 2 to 6 times as many women have it as men. Systemic lupus erythematosus (SLE) is also an autoimmune disease which can involve multiple systems of the body. Symptoms may include malaise, fever and weight loss, joint pain, renal, cardiac, neurological, and liver problems, and skin and mucous membrane problems. The peak incidence of SLE is between ages 15 and 40, almost 90% of cases are female, and its prevalence is significantly higher among African American women. Osteoarthritis (OA) is the most common form of arthritis, marked by pain in an involved joint (or joints) that worsens with activity, joint stiffness and enlargement, and functional impairment. The prevalence of OA increases with age for both men and women, but after age 50, women have higher prevalence and greater incidence of OA than men. Women are twice as likely as men to have OA of the knee, which is more likely to result in disability more than OA at any other site, and Black women are twice as likely as White women to have OA of the knee.

Arthritis and musculoskeletal diseases pose common psychosocial and behavioral challenges, including recurrent and severe joint pain, potential disability and loss of role functioning, increased risk for developing depression, and frequent interaction with health care providers. Treatment regimens, especially for RA and SLE, can involve medications with unpleasant side effects. Most forms of arthritis pose no immediate life threat, but symptoms, disease course, and prognosis are unpredictable. Therefore, the need to tolerate and cope with uncertainty is an ever-present stressor for women with arthritis.

In a study of gender differences in symptom reporting among people with RA, women reported more symptoms than men. When disease severity was taken into account, however, women had *fewer* symptoms than men. This finding suggests that women do not overreport symptoms and may, in fact, report RA symptoms more conservatively than men.

The symptoms associated with arthritis often lead to functional limitations. Data from the National Health Interview Study indicate that among women aged 15 and over, arthritis is the most frequently cited reason for activity limitations. As a result, women with arthritis have lower participation in the labor force; the economic impact of women's work disability is underestimated because women's nurturant, teaching, and housekeeping work in the paid labor market is economically undervalued, as is the work that women do at home without pay.

Functional limitations impact quality of life in other ways as well. In one study of women with rheumatoid arthritis, approximately 40% of the women studied reported limitations in such important role activities as making arrangements for others and taking them places, maintaining social ties by writing or calling, and visiting or taking care of sick people. In addition, women who experienced these types of limitations were less satisfied with their ability to be a nurturant support provider compared with unimpaired women. Thus, nurturant functions appear to be an important part of the homemaker role that have been neglected in most past research.

The presence of chronic disease is a risk factor for depression when it involves the loss of the ability to perform valued social roles. Again, this suggests that to understand the impact of chronic disabling illness, we must examine not just physical limitations but women's psychological interpretations of those limitations.

The most frequently studied effect of arthritis on psychological functioning has been its impact on depression and depressive symptoms. A conclusion from two recent reviews on depression in rheumatic diseases is that depressive disorders and depressive symptoms are more prevalent in people with rheumatic diseases compared with people without any serious, chronic illness. Depression alone is a devastating condition: People with symptoms of depression, in the absence of any other health problems, have worse functioning and well-being than people with arthritis, angina, hypertension, diabetes, gastrointestinal problems, lung problems, or back problems. More importantly, when depressive symptoms occur in combination with any of those other diseases, declines in functioning are additive.

Depression is more prevalent among women than men, with the average female-to-male ratios close to 2:1. Thus, women are not only at greater risk than men for some of the more common and serious rheumatic diseases, but also are at greater risk for depression. Therefore, health practitioners need to be es-

pecially alert for depression in female patients with rheumatic diseases so that both the depression and the rheumatic disease are recognized and treated. If depression in women with rheumatic diseases is overlooked, then declines in functioning caused by depression could be mistakenly attributed to the rheumatic disease and result in overtreatment. Alternatively, if symptoms of depression are mistakenly assumed to be a natural part of a rheumatic disease process that does not warrant treatment, women may suffer needlessly given the presence of efficacious treatments for depression. [*See* DEPRESSION.]

Given the stress of living with a chronic condition such as arthritis, what coping strategies seem to work? Coping has been defined as a person's cognitive and behavioral efforts to manage specific external and/or internal demands that are appraised as taxing or exceeding the person's resources. Coping efforts can be directed toward dealing with the stressful situation itself (problem-focused coping) or toward managing psychological distress aroused by the situation (emotion-focused coping). Most stressful situations evoke both types of coping efforts.

Research with arthritis patients, mostly women, has found that wishful thinking, self-blame, and other avoidant and passive coping strategies are associated with poorer psychological functioning. This research includes longitudinal investigations, which provide stronger evidence that using these coping strategies increases psychological distress. Research also suggests that active coping strategies such as seeking information and reframing the problem are associated with better psychological functioning.

Only a few studies have examined gender differences in coping. The most often cited finding is that men use more instrumental or problem-focused strategies, whereas women use more emotion-focused strategies and seek social support to a greater degree. However, gender differences in coping often fail to emerge in studies of serious illness, perhaps because situational factors such as the medical controllability of the illness and the level of disability shape the choice of coping strategies. In a study of daily processes in which RA patients were studied over 75 consecutive days, women and men differed in the use of only one of seven coping strategies: women tended to seek social support to a greater degree. Nonetheless, women made a greater number of coping effects overall and used a greater number of coping strategies than men.

One interpretation is that women may be more flexible than men in their coping efforts.

IX. ASSISTED REPRODUCTIVE TECHNOLOGIES: A RESEARCH AREA FOR THE FUTURE

Over the past decade we have witnessed the advent of assisted reproductive technologies (ARTs) which provide new avenues to biological motherhood, such as in vitro fertilization (IVF), zygote intrafallopian transfer (ZIFT), gamete intrafallopian transfer (GIFT), intracytoplasmic sperm injection (ICSI), egg donation, and surrogate motherhood. These reproductive technologies have stimulated considerable public interest and debate, but far less research attention or critical analysis. Reproductive technologies arouse both marvel and concern: Marvel because they are viewed by many infertile people and by physicians as a "last chance solution" at biological reproduction; concerns because of the ethical, social, and legal issues they raise, as well as the fact that they question our social construction of motherhood and of women's role in society.

In vitro fertilization, or IVF, is a medical procedure that combines sperm and egg outside the body. Hormones are injected to overstimulate a woman's ovaries to provide multiple eggs in one cycle, which are then removed surgically and mixed in a laboratory dish with the husband's or donor's sperm. If fertilization is successful, the embryo or embryos are implanted in the uterus, in a procedure known as embryo transfer. The IVF procedure was developed originally for women with missing or damaged fallopian tubes, as the procedure bypasses the tubes to achieve conception. In actuality, IVF is used to treat infertility related to other female reproductive disorders, such as: endometriosis or ovulation disorders; immunologic problems; unexplained infertility; and male subfertility, involving the sperm's inability to navigate the vaginal canal or cervical mucus, or penetrate the egg membrane.

Thus, even when the physiological problem is determined to be the man's, often the woman is treated. Women seek infertility treatment more often and with greater frequency than their partners, and their treatment is more invasive and more costly than treatment for male infertility. More distressing are data that sug-

gest that IVF is less "successful" in cases of male infertility. For women under 40, there were 15.3 babies born per egg retrieval in cases of male factor infertility compared with 19.8 when there was no male factor; for women over 40, the rates were 4.9 and 7.2, respectively.

Current estimates for the success of any one IVF treatment cycle are about 7% and 13% across several cycles. These statistics represent what has been called the "take-home baby rate." However, a treatment cycle can be halted at any number of points, such as when the follicles do not mature sufficiently. Because of this, most women endure multiple cycles of treatment. There is a lot of information in the popular press about the psychological consequences of infertility and the psychological aspects of undergoing treatment, but little systematic research.

The research that has been done falls into essentially three categories. The first group of studies presents the psychological profiles of infertile women before they started infertility treatment. For the most part, these are descriptive studies of the characteristics of infertile women who are entering or thinking about entering an IVF program, or their expectations for treatment. Several studies use standardized personality scales or measures of psychopathology to compare infertile women to normative data for healthy women. They find that infertile women (before treatment) score within normal limits on measures of preexisting pathology, although they are (understandably) anxious about the medical procedures they are about to undergo and the outcome of treatment. A number of studies focus on cognitive processes, examining the reasons for women's optimistic bias about their own chances for treatment success (i.e., women know the low probability of conceiving a child, but believe they will be the exception) and how this bias affects treatment decisions.

A second group of studies examines the experience of IVF treatment from the patient's perspective. These articles, largely descriptive in nature, delineate the stressful aspects of treatment and women's emotional lives during the treatment process. They describe, in the women's own words, their feelings of stigma and abnormality, of not being complete, of causing their husbands and families emotional pain, and of suffering in silence. They address the woman's relationship with her partners, and with the medical professionals administering the treatment. However, as most studies focus on the stressfulness of those living with infertility and/or the treatment procedures, questions about the positive aspects of the experience (e.g., increased closeness in the marriage) are seldom part of the inquiry; thus, we cannot make conclusions about the full impact of IVF on women's lives.

The final and smallest group of studies examines the effects of IVF treatment on women's mental health. The majority of the articles in this third category focus on women after an unsuccessful treatment cycle, which, in fact, characterizes the majority of women undergoing IVF. Thus, with a few exceptions, the psychosocial literature on ARTs seems to be narrowly focused, emanating from a clinical–pathological perspective, with infertility and its treatment seen though a biomedical lens. Largely missing is any approach that incorporates feminist principles or a consideration of the family context. As conceptualized in these studies, IVF reinforces a definition of motherhood as a biological rather than a social relationship, and the research approach curtails any potential for the redefinition of parenthood by focusing exclusively on biological reproduction.

Currently ARTs are not easily available to poor women, to ethnic minorities, or to lesbians. The costs of ARTs are prohibitive to all but the wealthy, as medical insurance coverage is meager and not uniform across different U.S. states. It is also unknown whether ARTs would be acceptable in particular religious, ethnic, or moral communities.

In vitro fertilization appears to be a meaningfully different experience for women and men. Women undergo more hormonal tests and treatments, experience side effects of ovulation drugs, and endure uncomfortable and potentially humiliating medical procedures; many men report the urgent donation of sperm to fertilize eggs as soon as they have been obtained during surgery to be stressful and emasculating. Wives and husbands share some of the same stressors but from different perspectives—for example, although women suffer the ill effects of large doses of hormones, many husbands administer the daily injections of ovarian stimulation hormones to their wives and are extremely anxious about hurting their partner or not doing it right, thus causing a failed cycle. It is important to study IVF from the woman's, the man's, *and* the couple's experience.

It is also important to consider where in a woman's "infertility career" she is at the time of treatment. In one study, women undergoing IVF for the first time were more distressed than those undergoing later cycles; other research describes the second cycle as the most stressful, as couples look at the first cycle as a test-run. Still other researchers describe the last cycle as the most stressful because it signals the end of hope. And, in a study of couples after a failed IVF attempt, equal numbers of women described their subsequent attempts as more or less stressful than the first attempt. Similarly, some studies find that psychological distress increases over the IVF cycle, whereas others have found that the greatest distress occurs during the first screening visit. Other studies have reported that the first half of the cycle with all of its medical monitoring is the most difficult, whereas a number of studies have found the most stressful times to occur during the second half of the cycle, when women are waiting to hear whether they are pregnant. Thus, IVF needs to be studied as a psychological process, as different points within the treatment process have different personal meanings and different implications for coping.

X. VIOLENCE AGAINST WOMEN: A SOCIAL PROBLEM THAT BECOMES A HEALTH PROBLEM

In the United States, a woman is battered about every 18 seconds. As a result, 4 to 6 million women sustain injuries each year. As many as 30% of emergency room visits by women each year are the result of injuries from domestic violence (also referred to as spousal or wife abuse). Not only is violence that occurs within marriage or domestic partnerships the leading cause of injuries to women between the ages of 15 and 44, but uxoricides (wife killings) accounted for 52% of the women murdered during the 1980s. It is estimated that 37% of women are physically or sexually abused before the age of 21.

Physical and sexual violence against women has become a major public health issue, the effects of which clearly illustrate the relationship between physical and mental health. Physical injuries (e.g., head injuries) place women at increased risk for depression and related disorders. Female victims of violence are more susceptible to sleep disorder, posttraumatic stress disorder (PTSD), alcohol and drug dependence, and obsessive–compulsive disorder.

Although male violence against women is now included in the research agenda for psychosocial and behavioral factors in women's health, there remains evidence of the need for a more inclusive approach to the problem. For example, a recent article that analyzed uxoricides from an evolutionary perspective argued that male violence toward women is contingent on ecologically valid threats to a sexually exclusive relationship. This perspective focuses entirely on a male-centered explanation for male violence, and completely disregards women's needs, or their rights to autonomy and respect.

Physical and sexual abuse of women is relatively new to academic discourse, and was only recognized as a priority by the international women's community as recently as 1980. Family violence was "discovered" in the 1870s as an offshoot of identifying child abuse as a problem, which opened the home to public scrutiny. Even then, discussion focused on the effects of excessive drinking among men, feminist campaigns for divorce, and desirable environments for child-raising. Women's rights in relation to their husbands were not addressed, nor were their rights to freedom from violence. Today, women's rights are being more widely acknowledged and advanced in the domestic violence literature. Similarly, acts of resistance and ways of fostering resilience and thriving among those who are physically abused are being examined.

Federal and state funded options for women who seek to escape abusive unions are disappearing, as recent federal cutbacks on funds for social services have forced many shelters to reduce their services or close their doors. Seventy-six percent of the nation's domestic violence programs have reduced their services, and 79% are not able to meet the needs of the battered women in their communities. This intensifies an already monumental difficulty: Even more women will suffer in silence as their options for leaving disappear.

One important goal for the twenty-first century is to educate health care professionals about the social and cultural contexts of abuse and the importance of developing creative methods of intervention. Most health-care professionals argue that it is not always clear when it is appropriate to take action; many also reveal they have had limited training for handling such problems. Similarly, researchers who study the effects of violence often focus on physical indicators of abuse. For some women, violence is more than a discrete event; it is an enduring presence in their lives. They propose an alternate conceptualization that em-

phasizes the meanings women attach to their experiences, as well as the consequences and social context of violent behavior. This new approach is an important first step toward adopting more comprehensive strategies for addressing the physical and psychological consequences of violence against women. [*See* DOMESTIC VIOLENCE INTERVENTION.]

XI. PATIENT–PROVIDER RELATIONSHIPS: WOMEN AS PATIENTS *AND* PHYSICIANS

In most studies of doctor–patient relationships, the gender of the physician, and often of the patient as well, is ignored. The unstated assumption is that the gender of the patient and physician does not influence their interaction. Indeed, in Western medicine, most physicians *have* been men. But as more women enter medicine, the gender of the physician becomes a salient factor in evaluating the quality of the physician–patient relationship and patient satisfaction, particularly along the affective dimensions of care. Gender may affect the nature and quality of medical treatment for a variety of diseases. Recent evidence has been presented showing that the aggressiveness and type of treatment for coronary heart disease differs for women and men, and that men receive more expensive medical work-ups than women. The use of gender stereotypes by health care providers may affect definitions of mental health and treatment decisions for psychological problems. Physicians tend to see female patients as more emotional and making excessive demands, to take women's medical complaints less seriously, and to classify their conditions as less serious, frequently attributing them to psychosomatic causes.

The increase in the number of women physicians in the past 20 years raises the question of whether women physicians relate differently to patients, and whether these differences affect medical care. The general belief is that female physicians are more humanistic and empathic than their male colleagues as a result of their socialization. This may affect attitudes and expectations toward patients, communication style, and the affective tone of the encounter, which all have been associated with greater patient satisfaction and adherence to treatment. Gender also may have an effect on the power differentials between patient and physician, with female physicians being perceived as less powerful.

Overall, studies have failed to uncover gender differences in technical or diagnostic skills, or general attitudes toward patient care. For example, there is little evidence that women medical students are more nurturing than men or have more patient-oriented attitudes or that women and men internists hold different attitudes toward patients. A number of studies, however, show strong gender differences in communication and practice styles. Women doctors spend more time with patients than do men, and engage in more conversation during a medical visit. Specifically, they engage in more positive talk, partnership building, and question asking, and provide more medical and psychosocial information. In one observational study of doctor–patient interaction, women physicians in general practice outperformed males in areas such as responding to patients' nonverbal cues, requesting psychosocial information from patients, consulting with others, looking up information, and discussing the psychosocial impact of the disease on patient and family.

These studies do suggest that women doctors may be more skillful at communicating with patients and in developing rapport, and pay more attention to psychosocial concerns. Consequently, they may be better able to listen and elicit salient information than male doctors. Female physicians also may be more willing than male physicians to form egalitarian relationships with patients. This is especially true for women doctors treating women: Women doctors, who have broken sex-role stereotypes themselves, may be less likely to assume that women are passive by nature and need decisions to be made for them.

XII. RESILIENCE: A NEW PARADIGM FOR WOMEN'S HEALTH

The concepts of resilience and thriving have been suggested recently by O'Leary and Ickovics as a paradigm shift—a new way to look at health outcomes in response to major stressors. This new formulation of resilience refers to the ability not only to maintain strength in the face of severe or prolonged adversity, but also to experience personal growth and change in response to challenge. Resilience has the characteristics of a personality attribute, a process, *and* a health outcome, making it difficult to study. Some argue that resilient individuals have a definable set of characteristics that enable them to adapt successfully to stress-

ful circumstances. Others suggest that resilience may be the (coping) process of fending off maladaptive responses to risk and their potentially negative consequences. Resilience can also be thought of as a health outcome—successful adaptation to a severe stressor or challenge. In all of these cases, the focus in resilience shifts from the absence of pathology or maladaptation to the concept of positive mental health.

Most theories define successful adaptation as the individual's return to a baseline level of functioning after experiencing a major life threat or stressor. That is, if an individual can return to her previous level of psychological functioning and stave off long-term depression, she has adapted successfully to her life circumstances. In contrast, resilience involves new personal growth as a result of having "come through the storm": An individual goes beyond survival and recovery to thrive. As a result, thriving does not depend solely on physical health outcomes, but includes psychological, social, and spiritual growth. More to the point, thriving may be possible in the absence of physical recovery from disease, as in the case of an individual fighting an illness such as ovarian cancer or HIV/AIDS.

O'Leary and Ickovics have suggested that resilience offers a new paradigm in women's health because it moves beyond viewing health issues solely in terms of vulnerability, deficits, or risk factors, and refocuses on women's strengths and capabilities. Although women do experience greater degrees and different types of stress than men, they also have the advantage of stress-resistance resources. On the biological level, hormones provide a protective health advantage to women, at least until menopause, reducing the risk of cardiovascular disease and osteoporosis, for example. On the psychosocial level, social relationships may be a key to women's resilience. Research has found that women have stronger support networks and are able to mobilize help in a crisis more easily than men, both of which have been linked to better adaptation. Moreover, there is recent evidence that the expression of emotions, long considered a coping strategy that is linked to depression, may be an adaptive strategy for women and not for men.

XIII. CONCLUSION

There are issues in women's health that we have not discussed in this brief article that are central to improving women's health care in the twenty-first century. These topics include risk and protective factors in cardiovascular disease, the link between reproductive processes (menstruation, infertility, childbirth, menopause) and depression, and the role of stress in the development of disease.

In all of this research, we need gender-sensitive measures, not simply defining phenomena as they relate to a male norm but as they vary within a heterogenous population of women. For example, "successful" coping with stress is often defined as an instrumental or problem-focused activity; coping by processing or expressing emotions has been viewed as leading to worse outcomes. However, recent research suggests that emotion-focused coping may be effective in managing stress for women. Current measures ignore fundamental differences in the ways in which men and women interact with others when coping with a serious stressor. We also need to develop gender-sensitive behavioral interventions that target different risk factors in different ways. Already we know that smoking cessation and HIV/AIDS interventions tailored for women are more effective for women than are more generic ones, or interventions that are tested only with samples of men.

Broad-based support for research on women's health—from both the scientific and policy-making communities—is fairly new. The Women's Health Initiative, a national $625 million, 15-year study of medical, physiological, and behavioral factors affecting the three leading causes of death and disability among women—heart disease, cancer, and osteoporosis—is underway. The largest study of its kind in the United States, it may provide answers to questions that have not been studied until now.

BIBLIOGRAPHY

Adesso, V. J., Reddy, D. M., & Fleming, R. (Eds.). (1994). *Psychological perspectives on women's health.* Washington, DC: Taylor & Francis.

Barnett, R. C., Biener, L., & Baruch, G. K. (Eds.). (1987). *Gender and stress.* New York: Free Press.

Chesney, M. A., & Ozer, E. M. (1995). Women and health: In search of a paradigm. *Women's Health: Research on Gender, Behavior and Policy, 1,* 3–26.

DeVellis, B. M., Revenson, T. A., & Blalock, S. (1997). Rheumatic disease and women's health. In S. Gallant, G. P. Keita, & Royak-Schaler, R. (Eds.), *Health care for women: Psychological, social and behavioral influences* (pp. 333–347). Washington, DC: American Psychological Association.

Horton, J. A. (Eds.). (1995). *The women's health data book: A profile of women's health in the United States* (2nd ed.). Washington, DC: The Jacobs Institute of Women's Health.

Koss, M., Goodman, L., Fitzgerald, L., Russo, N. F., Keita, G. P., & Browne, A. (1995). *No safe haven: Male violence against women at home, at work, and in the community.* Washington, DC: American Psychological Association.

O'Leary, V. E., & Ickovics, J. R. (1995). Resilience and thriving in response to challenge: An opportunity for a paradigm shift in women's health. *Women's health: Research on gender, behavior and policy, 1,* 121–142.

Rodin, J., & Ickovics, J. R. (1990). Women's health: Review and research agenda as we approach the 21st century. *American Psychologist, 45,* 1018–1034.

Stanton, A., & Gallant, S. (Eds.). (1995). *The psychology of women's health: Progress and challenges in research and application.* Washington, DC: American Psychological Association.

Travis, C. B. (1988). *Women and health psychology: Mental health issues.* Hillsdale, NJ: Lawrence Erlbaum.

Contributors

Jennifer Abe-Kim
Ethnicity and Mental Health
   Loyola Marymount University
   Los Angeles, California 90045

Robert Ader
Psychoneuroimmunology
   Department of Psychology
   University of Rochester School of Medicine and
      Dentistry
   Rochester, New York 14642

Nancy E. Adler
Socioeconomic Status
   Graduate Program in Health Psychology
   Center for Social, Behavioral, and Policy Sciences
   University of California, San Francisco
   San Francisco, California 94143

Salman Akhtar
Narcissistic Personality Disorder
   Department of Adult Outpatient Psychiatry
   Jefferson Medical College
   Philadelphia, Pennsylvania 19107

Carolyn M. Aldwin
Assessment of Mental Health in Older Adults
   Department of Human and Community
      Development
   University of California, Davis
   Davis, California 95616

John J. B. Allen
DSM-IV
   Department of Psychology
   University of Arizona
   Tucson, Arizona 85721

Virginia D. Allhusen
Day Care
   Department of Social Ecology
   University of California, Irvine
   Irvine, California 92717

Nalini Ambady
Nonverbal Communication
   Department of Psychology
   Harvard University
   Cambridge, Massachusetts 02138

Nader Amir
Anxiety
   Department of Psychiatry
   Allegheny University of the Health Sciences
   Philadelphia, Pennsylvania 19129

Barbara L. Andersen
Cancer
   Department of Psychology
   Ohio State University
   Columbus, Ohio 43210

Dick Anthony
Brainwashing and Totalitarian Influence
   Private practice in forensic psychology in
      Richmond, California 94804

Toni C. Antonucci
Extended Family Relationships
   Institute of Social Research
   University of Michigan, Ann Arbor
   Ann Arbor, Michigan 48109

John S. Antrobus
Dreaming
   Department of Psychology
   City College of the City University of New York
   New York, New York 10031

V. Bessie Aramakis
Brain Development and Plasticity
   Department of Psychology
   University of California, Riverside
   Riverside, California 92521

Roseanne Armitage
Sleep
   Department of Psychiatry
   University of Texas Southwestern
      Medical Center, Dallas
   Dallas, Texas 75235

John H. Ashe
Brain Development and Plasticity
   Departments of Neuroscience and Psychology
   University of California, Riverside
   Riverside, California 92521

Alice M. Atkinson
Child Care Providers
   Division of Curriculum and Instruction
   University of Iowa
   Iowa City, Iowa 52242

James R. Averill
Emotion and Cognition
   University of Massachusetts, Amherst
   Amherst, Massachusetts 01003

Janice I. Baldwin
Sexual Behavior
   Department of Psychology
   University of California, Santa Barbara
   Santa Barbara, California 93106

John D. Baldwin
Sexual Behavior
   Department of Psychology
   University of California, Santa Barbara
   Santa Barbara, California 93106

Margret M. Baltes
Aging and Mental Health
   Free University of Berlin
   14050 Berlin, Germany

Paul B. Baltes
Wisdom
   Max Planck Institute for Human Development
   14195 Berlin, Germany

Albert Bandura
Self-Efficacy
   Department of Psychology
   Stanford University
   Stanford, California 94305

Philip Barker
Family Therapy
   Departments of Pediatrics and Medicine
   University of Calgary Mental Health Program
   and Alberta Children's Hospital
   Calgary, Alberta, Canada T2T 5C7

Russell A. Barkley
Attention Deficit/Hyperactivity Disorder (ADHD)
   Department of Psychiatry
   University of Massachusetts Medical Center
   Worcester, Massachusetts 01581

Patricia A. Barnes
Individual Differences in Mental Health
   Department of Psychiatry
   Louisiana State University School of Medicine
   New Orleans, Louisiana 70112

Andrea Marie Bastiani
Poverty and Mental Health
   Teachers College
   Columbia University
   New York, New York 10027

Andrew Baum
Stress
   Division of Behavioral Medicine and Oncology
   University of Pittsburgh Cancer Institute
   Pittsburgh, Pennsylvania 15213

Roy F. Baumeister
Impulse Control
Department of Psychology
Case Western Reserve University
Cleveland, Ohio 44106

Melanie E. Bennett
Alcohol Problems
Department of Psychology
University of New Mexico
Albuquerque, New Mexico 87131

Herbert Benson
Meditation and the Relaxation Response
Mind/Body Medical Institute
Harvard Medical School
Beth Israel Deaconess Medical Center
Boston, Massachusetts 02215

Dinesh Bhugra
Sexual Dysfunction Therapy
Institute of Psychiatry
London SE5 8AF, United Kingdom

Maureen M. Black
Urban Life and Mental Well-Being
Department of Pediatrics
University of Maryland School of Medicine
Baltimore, Maryland 21201

Jim Blascovich
Reactivity
Department of Psychology
University of California, Santa Barbara
Santa Barbara, California 93106

Joseph P. Blount
Caffeine: Psychosocial Effects
Widener University
Social Science Division
Chester, Pennsylvania 19013

Kathrin Boerner
Grief and Loss
Department of Psychiatry
Massachusetts General Hospital
Harvard Medical School
Cambridge, Massachusetts 02138
and Department of Psychology
Free University Berlin
14195 Berlin, Germany

Laura Boeschen
Rape
Department of Psychology
University of Arizona
Tucson, Arizona 85719

Mark W. Bondi
Alzheimer's Disease
Department of Psychology
California State University, San Marcos
San Marcos, California 92096

Marc H. Bornstein
Parenting
Child and Family Research
National Institute of Child Health and Human
    Development
Bethesda, Maryland 20892

Robert F. Bornstein
Dependent Personality
Department of Psychology
Gettysburg College
Gettysburg, Pennsylvania 17325

Sharon A. Borthwick-Duffy
Mental Retardation and Mental Health
School of Education
University of California, Riverside
Riverside, California 92521

Thomas N. Bradbury
Divorce
Department of Psychology
University of California, Los Angeles
Los Angeles, California 90095

Britton W. Brewer
Sport and Mental Status
Department of Psychology
Springfield College
Springfield, Massachusetts 01109

Jeanne Brooks-Gunn
Poverty and Mental Health
Teachers College
Columbia University
New York, New York 10027

Halle D. Brown
Socioeconomic Status
EEG System Laboratory
San Francisco, California 94105

Kelly J. Brown
Psychopharmacology
  Portland V.A. Medical Center
  Portland, Oregon 97201

Kelly D. Brownell
Obesity
  Department of Psychology
  Yale University
  New Haven, Connecticut 06520

Henry A. Buchtel
Epilepsy
  Psychology Service of the Veteran's Administration
    Medical Center
  and Departments of Psychiatry and Psychology
  University of Michigan, Ann Arbor
  Ann Arbor, Michigan 48105

Jerry M. Burger
Solitude
  Department of Psychology
  Santa Clara University
  Santa Clara, California 95053

Gustavo Carlo
Cooperation, Competition, and Individualism
  Department of Psychology
  University of Nebraska, Lincoln
  Lincoln, Nebraska 68583

Douglas Carroll
Gambling
  School of Sport and Exercise Sciences
  The University of Birmingham
  Edgbaston, Birmingham B15 2TT
  United Kingdom

Laura L. Carstensen
Emotion and Aging
  Department of Psychology
  Stanford University
  Stanford, California 94305

Charles S. Carver
Optimism, Motivation, and
  Mental Health
  Department of Psychology
  University of Miami
  Coral Gables, Florida 33146

Doris Chang
Ethnicity and Mental Health
  Department of Psychology
  University of California, Los Angeles
  Los Angeles, California 90095

Andrew Christensen
Couples Therapy
  Department of Psychology
  University of California, Los Angeles
  Los Angeles, California 90095

Jan Cioe
Brain
  Department of Psychology
  Okanagan University-College
  Kelowna, British Columbia, Canada V1Y 4T4

Cindy Dell Clark
Play
  DePaul University
  Chicago, Illinois 60604

K. Alison Clarke-Stewart
Day Care
  Department of Social Ecology
  University of California, Irvine
  Irvine, California 92717

George A. Clum
Phobias
  Department of Psychology
  Virginia Polytechnic Institute and State University
  Blacksburg, Virginia 24061

Nicholas Cohen
Psychoneuroimmunology
  Department of Microbiology and Immunology
  University of Rochester School of Medicine and
    Dentistry
  Rochester, New York 14642

Sheldon Cohen
Social Support
  Department of Psychology
  Carnegie Mellon University
  Pittsburgh, Pennsylvania 15213

Lee Combrinck-Graham
Family Systems
  Private practice in Stamford, Connecticut 06902

Patrick W. Corrigan
Information Processing and
  Clinical Psychology
  Center for Psychiatric Rehabilitation
  University of Chicago
  Tinley Park, Illinois 60477

Paul T. Costa, Jr.
Personality Assessment
  Laboratory of Personality and Cognition
  Gerontology Research Center
  National Institute on Aging
  National Institutes of Health
  Bethesda, Maryland 21224

Emory L. Cowen
Wellness in Children
  Center for Community Study
  University of Rochester
  Rochester, New York 14620

W. Miles Cox
Caffeine: Psychosocial Effects
  North Chicago Veterans Affairs Medical Center
  Chicago Medical School
  North Chicago, Illinois 60064

Phebe Cramer
Defense Mechanisms
  Department of Psychology
  Williams College
  Williamstown, Massachusetts 01267

Katharina Dalton
Premenstrual Syndrome (PMS)
  PMS Clinic
  University College Hospital
  London W1M 7TD
  United Kingdom

Jorge H. Daruna
Individual Differences in Mental Health
  Department of Psychiatry and Neurology
  Tulane University School of Medicine
  New Orleans, Louisiana 70112

Roger D. Davis
Personality
  Institute for Advanced Studies in Personology and
    Psychopathology
  Coral Gables, Florida 33156

Robyn M. Dawes
Standards for Psychotherapy
  Department of Social and Decision Sciences
  Carnegie Mellon University
  Pittsburgh, Pennsylvania 15213

Charles DeBattista
Mood Disorders
  Department of Psychiatry and Behavioral Sciences
  Stanford University School of Medicine
  Stanford, California 94305

Sarah E. Deitsch
Antisocial Personality Disorder
  Department of Psychology
  University of Kentucky
  Lexington, Kentucky 40506

Anita DeLongis
Coping with Stress
  Department of Psychology
  University of British Columbia
  Vancouver, British Columbia, Canada V6T 1Z4

Bella M. DePaulo
Deception
  Department of Psychology
  University of Virginia
  Charlottesville, Virginia 22903

Padmal de Silva
Sexual Dysfunction Therapy
  Department of Psychology
  Institute of Psychiatry
  London SE5 8AF, United Kingdom

Ed Diener
Happiness: Subjective Well-Being
  Department of Psychology
  University of Illinois
  Champaign, Illinois 61820

Mary Beth Diener
Happiness: Subjective Well-Being
  University of Kentucky
  Lexington, Kentucky 40502

David L. DiLalla
Genetic Contributors to Mental Health
  Department of Psychology
  Southern Illinois University, Carbondale
  Carbondale, Illinois 62901

M. Robin DiMatteo
Health Beliefs and Patient Adherence to Treatment
Department of Psychology
University of California, Riverside
Riverside, California 92521

Beth L. Dinoff
Infertility
Department of Psychology
University of Kansas
Lawrence, Kansas 66045

Rod K. Dishman
Physical Activity and Mental Health
Department of Exercise Science
School of Health and Human Performance
University of Georgia
Athens, Georgia 30602

Keith S. Dobson
Psychopathology
Department of Psychology
University of Calgary
Calgary, Alberta, Canada T2N 1N4

Ronald M. Doctor
Sexual Disorders
Department of Psychology
California State University, Northridge
Northridge, California 91331

Angela Liegey Dougall
Stress
Division of Behavioral Medicine and Oncology
University of Pittsburgh Cancer Institute
Pittsburgh, Pennsylvania 15213

Gwenyth H. Edwards
Attention Deficit/Hyperactivity Disorder (ADHD)
Department of Psychiatry
University of Massachusetts Medical Center
Worcester, Massachusetts 01581

Nancy Eisenberg
Emotional Regulation
Department of Psychology
Arizona State University
Tempe, Arizona 85287

Robert E. Emery
Custody (Child)
Department of Psychology
University of Virginia
Charlottesville, Virginia 22903

Javier I. Escobar
Somatization and Hypochondriasis
Department of Psychiatry
Robert Wood Johnson
Medical School
University of Medicine and Dentistry of New Jersey
Piscataway, New Jersey 08854

Frank F. Eves
Gambling
School of Sport and Exercise Sciences
The University of Birmingham
Edgbaston, Birmingham B15 2TT
United Kingdom

Beverly Fagot
Gender Identity
Department of Psychology
University of Oregon
and Oregon Social Learning Center
Eugene, Oregon 97403

Kathleen Coulborn Faller
Child Sexual Abuse
University of Michigan School of Social Work
Ann Arbor, Michigan 48104

Greg A.R. Febbraro
Phobias
Medical University of South Carolina
Charleston, South Carolina 29425

Deborah Fein
Autism and Pervasive Developmental Disorders
Department of Psychology
University of Connecticut
Storrs, Connecticut 06269

Allan Fenigstein
Paranoia
Department of Psychology
Kenyon College
Gambier, Ohio 43022

Joseph R. Ferrari
Procrastination
    Department of Psychology
    DePaul University
    Chicago, Illinois 60614

Frank D. Fincham
Marital Health
    Department of Psychology
    University of Wales
    Cardiff CF1 3YG, United Kingdom

Susan T. Fiske
Control
    Department of Psychology
    University of Massachusetts, Amherst
    Amherst, Massachusetts 01003

Jose C. Florez
Body Rhythms/Body Clocks
    Department of Medicine
    Massachusetts General Hospital
    Boston, Massachusetts 02114

Bonnie Floyd
Childhood Stress
    Behavioral Medicine and Anxiety Clinic
    Albert Einstein College of Medicine
    and Ferkauf Graduate School of Psychology
    Yeshiva University
    Bronx, New York 10461

Edna B. Foa
Posttraumatic Stress
    Department of Psychiatry
    Allegheny University of the Health Sciences
    Philadelphia, Pennsylvania 19129

Hugh Freeman
Healthy Environments
    Green College
    Oxford
    London W1H 1RE, United Kingdom

Sabine Elizabeth French
Community Mental Health
    Department of Psychology
    New York University
    New York, New York 10003

Arnold J. Friedhoff
Catecholamines and Behavior
    Millhauser Laboratories
    New York University Medical Center
    New York, New York 10016

Howard S. Friedman
Heart Disease: Psychological Predictors
Self-Healing Personalities
    Department of Psychology
    University of California, Riverside
    Riverside, California 92521

Michael A. Friedman
Obesity
    Department of Psychology
    Yale University
    New Haven, Connecticut 06520

Rhonda B. Friedman
Aphasia, Alexia, and Agraphia
    Department of Neurology and Georgetown Institute for Cognitive and Computational Science
    Georgetown University Medical Center
    Washington, District of Columbia 20007

Richard Friedman
Meditation and the Relaxation Response
    Mind/Body Medical Institute
    Harvard Medical School
    Beth Israel Deaconess Medical Center
    Boston, Massachusetts 02215

Ronald Friend
Chronic Illness
    Department of Psychology
    State University of New York, Stony Brook
    Stony Brook, New York 11794

Randy O. Frost
Obsessive–Compulsive Disorder
    Department of Psychology
    Clark Science Center
    Smith College
    Northampton, Massachusetts 01063

Eileen Gambrill
Clinical Assessment
    School of Social Welfare
    University of California, Berkeley
    Berkeley, California 94720

Linda Gannon
Menopause
    Department of Psychology
    Southern Illinois University
    Carbondale, Illinois 62901

Michael A. Gara
Somatization and Hypochondriasis
    Department of Psychiatry
    Robert Wood Johnson Medical School
    and University of Behavioral Health Care
    University of Medicine and Dentistry of New
        Jersey
    Piscataway, New Jersey 08854

Rochel Gelman
Cognitive Development
    Department of Psychology
    University of California, Los Angeles
    Los Angeles, California 90095

Elizabeth R. Gillard
Eating and Body Weight: Physiological Controls
    Departments of Psychology and Neuroscience
    University of California, Riverside
    Riverside, California 92521

Elizabeth L. Glisky
Amnesia
    University of Arizona
    Tucson, Arizona 85721

Guila Glosser
Aphasia, Alexia, and Agraphia
    Department of Neurology
    University of Pennsylvania
    Philadelphia, Pennsylvania 19104

Benjamin H. Gottlieb
Support Groups
    Department of Psychology
    University of Guelph
    Guelph, Ontario, Canada N1G 2W1

Sandra A. Graham-Bermann
Domestic Violence Intervention
    Department of Psychology
    University of Michigan, Ann Arbor
    Ann Arbor, Michigan 48109

LeeAnne Green
Autism and Pervasive Developmental Disorders
    Department of Psychology
    University of Connecticut
    Storrs, Connecticut 06269

Esther R. Greenglass
Gender Differences in Mental Health
    Department of Psychology
    York University
    North York, Ontario
    Canada M3J 1P3

Leonard Greenhalgh
Negotiation and Conflict Resolution
    Amos Tuck School
    Dartmouth College
    Hanover, New Hampshire 03755

Natalie Grizenko
*Protective Factors in Development of
    Psychopathology*
    Department of Psychiatry, McGill University
    Montreal, Quebec, Canada H3A 2T5
    and Lyall Preadolescent Day Treatment Program
    Douglas Hospital
    Verdun, Quebec, Canada H4H 1R3

Neil E. Grunberg
Psychopharmacology
    Medical and Clinical Psychology
    Uniformed Services University of the Health
        Sciences
    Bethesda, Maryland 20814

Richard J. Haier
Brain Scanning/Neuroimaging
    Department of Pediatrics
    University of California, Irvine, Medical School
    Irvine, California 92717

Judith M. Harackiewicz
Intrinsic Motivation and Goals
    Department of Psychology
    University of Wisconsin, Madison
    Madison, Wisconsin 53706

Elaine Hatfield
Love and Intimacy
Department of Psychology
University of Hawaii, Manoa
Honolulu, Hawaii 96822

Todd F. Heatherton
Body Image
Department of Psychology
Dartmouth College
Hanover, New Hampshire 03755

Michelle R. Hebl
Body Image
Department of Psychology
Dartmouth College
Hanover, New Hampshire 03755

Lynne Henderson
Shyness
The Shyness Institute
Shyness Center
Portola Valley, California 94028

C. Peter Herman
Dieting
Department of Psychology
University of Toronto
Toronto, Ontario, Canada M5S 1A1

Scott L. Hershberger
Homosexuality
University of Kansas
Lawrence, Kansas 66045

Michael A. Hoge
Managed Care
Department of Psychiatry
Yale University School of Medicine
New Haven, Connecticut 06519

Grayson N. Holmbeck
Adolescence
Department of Psychology
Loyola University Chicago
Chicago, Illinois 60626

Kim Hopper
Homelessness
Nathan Kline Institute
Orangeburg, New York 10962

Ann L. Horgas
Aging and Mental Health
Wayne State University
Detroit, Michigan 48202

Mardi J. Horowitz
Psychoanalysis
Department of Psychiatry
University of California, San Francisco
San Francisco, California 94143

Rick E. Ingram
Depression
Department of Psychology
San Diego State University
San Diego, California 92120

Carroll E. Izard
Emotions and Mental Health
Department of Psychology
University of Delaware
Newark, Delaware 19716

Lisa H. Jaycox
Posttraumatic Stress
RAND Corporation
Santa Monica, California 90401

Matthew D. Johnson
Divorce
Department of Psychology
University of California, Los Angeles
Los Angeles, California 90095

Rhawn Joseph
Limbic System
Brain Research Laboratory
San Jose, California 95126

Bonnie J. Kaplan
Food, Nutrition, and Mental Health
Department of Pediatrics
University of Calgary
and Behavioural Research Unit
Alberta Children's Hospital
Calgary, Alberta, Canada T2T 5C7

Jonathan S. Kaplan
Ethnicity and Mental Health
Department of Psychology
University of California, Los Angeles
Los Angeles, California 90095

Robert M. Kaplan
Behavioral Medicine
University of California, San Diego, School of
Medicine
La Jolla, California 92093

Robert Kastenbaum
Dying
Department of Communication
Arizona State University
Tempe, Arizona 85287

Alan E. Kazdin
Conduct Disorder
Department of Psychology
Yale University
New Haven, Connecticut 06520

Ernest Keen
*Classifying Mental Disorders: Nontraditional
Approaches*
Bucknell University
Lewisburg, Pennsylvania 17837

Adrian B. Kelly
Marital Health
Department of Psychology
University of Wales
Cardiff CF1 3YG, United Kingdom

David N. Kerner
Behavioral Medicine
University of California, San Diego, School of
Medicine
La Jolla, California 92093

Ronald C. Kessler
Epidemiology: Psychiatric
Department of Health Care Policy
Harvard Medical School
Boston, Massachusetts 02115

Arshad M. Khan
Eating and Body Weight: Physiological Controls
Division of Biomedical Sciences and Department
of Neuroscience
University of California, Riverside
Riverside, California 92521

John F. Kihlstrom
Amnesia
Hypnosis and the Psychological Unconscious
Department of Psychology
University of California, Berkeley
Berkeley, California 94720

Lucy Canter Kihlstrom
Mental Health Services Research
Institute of Personality and Social Research
University of California, Berkeley
Berkeley, California 94720

Laura Cousino Klein
Psychopharmacology
Department of Psychology and Social Behavior
School of Social Ecology
University of California, Irvine
Irvine, California 92697

Richard P. Kluft
Dissociative Disorders
Clinical Professor of Psychiatry
Temple University School of Medicine
Philadelphia, Pennsylvania 19122
and in private practice in Bala Cynwyd,
Pennsylvania 19004

George P. Knight
Cooperation, Competition, and Individualism
Department of Psychology
Arizona State University
Tempe, Arizona 85287

Harold G. Koenig
Religion and Mental Health
Duke University Medical Center
Durham, North Carolina 27710

Bryan Kolb
Brain
Department of Psychology
University of Lethbridge
Lethbridge, Alberta, Canada T1K 3M4

Meni Koslowsky
Commuting and Mental Health
  Department of Psychology
  Bar-Ilan University
  Ramat Gan, Israel 52900

Mary P. Koss
Rape
  Arizona Prevention Center
  University of Arizona College of Medicine
  Tucson, Arizona 85719

Michael J. Kozak
Anxiety
  Department of Psychiatry
  Allegheny University of the Health Sciences
  Philadelphia, Pennsylvania 19129

Jerome Kroll
Borderline Personality Disorder
  Department of Psychiatry
  University of Minnesota Medical School
  Minneapolis, Minnesota 55455

Nicholas A. Kuiper
Humor and Mental Health
  Department of Psychology
  University of Western Ontario
  London, Ontario, Canada N6A 5C2

Elise E. Labbé
Biofeedback
  Department of Psychology
  University of South Alabama
  Mobile, Alabama 36688

H. Richard Lamb
Mental Hospitals and Deinstitutionalization
  Department of Psychiatry
  University of Southern California School of
    Medicine
  Los Angeles, California 90033

Kelly L. Lange
Alzheimer's Disease
  San Diego State University/
  University of California, San Diego, Joint
    Doctoral Program in Clinical Psychology
  San Diego, California 92120

Ellen Langer
Mental Control Across the Lifespan
  Department of Psychology
  Harvard University
  Cambridge, Massachusetts 02138

Jennifer E. Lansford
Extended Family Relationships
  Institute of Social Research
  University of Michigan, Ann Arbor
  Ann Arbor, Michigan 48109

David B. Larson
Religion and Mental Health
  National Institute for Health Care Research
  Rockville, Maryland 20852

Robin Leake
Chronic Illness
  Department of Psychology
  State University of New York, Stony Brook
  Stony Brook, New York 11794

Michael P. Leiter
Burnout
  Department of Psychology
  Acadia University
  Wolfville, Nova Scotia, Canada B0P 1X0

Larry M. Leith
Exercise and Mental Health
  Department of Physical Education
  University of Toronto
  Guelph, Ontario, Canada N1G 1A2

Stephen J. Lepore
Crowding: Effects on Health and Behavior
  Department of Psychology
  Carnegie Mellon University
  Pittsburgh, Pennsylvania 15213

Michael R. Levenson
Assessment of Mental Health in Older Adults
  Department of Human and Community
    Development
  University of California, Davis
  Davis, California 95616

Karen L. Levinson
Emotions and Mental Health
Department of Psychology
University of Delaware
Newark, Delaware 19716

Becca Levy
Mental Control Across the Lifespan
Division on Aging and Department of Social
Medicine
Harvard Medical School
Boston, Massachusetts 02115

Marci Lobel
Pregnancy and Mental Health
Department of Psychology
State University of New York, Stony Brook
Stony Brook, New York 11794

Sandra Losoya
Emotional Regulation
Department of Psychology
Arizona State University
Tempe, Arizona 85287

Kevin MacDonald
Personality Development
Department of Psychology
California State University, Long Beach
Long Beach, California 90840

Salvatore R. Maddi
Hardiness in Health and Effectiveness
Department of Psychology and Social Behavior
School of Social Ecology
University of California, Irvine
Irvine, California 92697

James E. Marcia
*Optimal Development from an Eriksonian
Perspective*
Department of Psychology
Simon Fraser University
Burnaby, British Columbia, Canada V5A 1S6

Ronald W. Maris
Suicide
University of South Carolina Suicide Center
Columbia, South Carolina 29208

Etan Markowitz
Mental Institutions: Legal Issues and Commitments
University of Southern California
Los Angeles, California 90033

Christina Maslach
Burnout
University of California, Berkeley
Berkeley, California 94720

Gerald Matthews
Intelligence and Mental Health
Department of Psychology
University of Dundee
Dundee DD14HN, Scotland

Maxie C. Maultsby, Jr.
Behavior Therapy
Department of Psychiatry
Howard University College of Medicine
Washington, District of Columbia 20060

Barbara S. McCann
Hypertension
University of Washington School of Medicine
Harborview Medical Center
Seattle, Washington 98104

Teresita McCarty
Premenstrual Syndrome Treatment Interventions
Department of Psychiatry
University of New Mexico
School of Medicine
Albuquerque, New Mexico 87131

Joan McCord
Criminal Behavior
Department of Criminal Justice
Temple University
Philadelphia, Pennsylvania 19122

Robert R. McCrae
Personality Assessment
Laboratory of Personality and Cognition
Gerontology Research Center
National Institute on Aging
National Institutes of Health
Bethesda, Maryland 21224

Traci McFarlane
Dieting
Department of Psychology
University of Toronto
Toronto, Ontario, Canada M5S 1A1

Tracy A. McFarlane
Women's Health
Psychology Program/Social-Personality
The Graduate School and University Center of the
City University of New York
New York, New York 10036

Michael T. McGuire
Evolution and Mental Health
University of California, Los Angeles
Los Angeles, California 90095

Richard J. McNally
Panic Attacks
Department of Psychology
Harvard University
Cambridge, Massachusetts 02138

Barbara G. Melamed
Childhood Stress
Behavioral Medicine and Anxiety Clinic
Albert Einstein College of Medicine
and Ferkauf Graduate School of Psychology
Yeshiva University
Bronx, New York 10461

Robert G. Meyer
Antisocial Personality Disorder
Personality Disorders
Department of Psychology
University of Louisville
Louisville, Kentucky 40292

Peggy J. Miller
Play
University of Illinois, Urbana–Champaign
Urbana, Illinois 61801

William R. Miller
Alcohol Problems
Department of Psychology
University of New Mexico
Albuquerque, New Mexico 87131

Richard M. Millis
Smoking
Department of Physiology and Biophysics
Howard University College of Medicine
Washington, District of Columbia 20059

Theodore Millon
Personality
Institute for Advanced Studies in Personology and
Psychopathology
Coral Gables, Florida 33156

James E. Mitchell
Anorexia Nervosa and Bulimia Nervosa
University of North Dakota Medical School
Fargo, North Dakota 58102
and Neuropsychiatric Research Institute
Fargo, North Dakota 58103

Phyllis Moen
Retirement
Bronfenbrenner Life Course Center and Depart-
ment of Human Development
Cornell University
Ithaca, New York 14853

Beth A. Morling
Control
Department of Psychology
Union College
Schenectady, New York 12308

Donald L. Mosher
Guilt
Emeritus Professor
University of Connecticut
Storrs, Connecticut 06209

Ricardo F. Muñoz
Depression—Applied Aspects
Department of Psychiatry
San Francisco General Hospital
University of California, San Francisco
San Francisco, California 94110

Carolyn B. Murray
Racism and Mental Health
  Department of Psychology
  University of California, Riverside
  Riverside, California 92521

Melissa Pederson Mussell
Anorexia Nervosa and Bulimia Nervosa
  University of St. Thomas
  St. Paul, Minnesota 55105
  and University of Minnesota Eating Disorders
    Research Program
  Minneapolis, Minnesota 55414

Patricia Myers
Meditation and the Relaxation Response
  Mind/Body Medical Institute
  Harvard Medical School
  Beth Israel Deaconess Medical Center
  Boston, Massachusetts 02215

Craig T. Nagoshi
Behavioral Genetics
  Department of Psychology
  Arizona State University
  Tempe, Arizona 85287

Bryan Neff
Sexual Disorders
  Department of Psychology
  California State University, Northridge
  Northridge, California 91331

Robert A. Neimeyer
Constructivist Psychotherapies
  Department of Psychology
  University of Memphis
  Memphis, Tennessee 38152

Sarah Newth
Coping with Stress
  Department of Psychology
  University of British Columbia
  Vancouver, British Columbia, Canada V6T 1Z4

Raymond W. Novaco
Aggression
  Department of Psychology and Social Behavior
  University of California, Irvine
  Irvine, California 92697

Akiko Okifuji
Pain
  Department of Anesthesiology
  University of Washington School of Medicine
  Seattle, Washington 98195

Roxanne L. Okun
Negotiation and Conflict Resolution
  Personnel Decisions International
  Foster City, California 94404

L. Joan Olinger
Humor and Mental Health
  Private practice in London, Ontario,
  Canada N5X 3R8

Samuel H. Osipow
Unemployment and Mental Health
  Department of Psychology
  Ohio State University
  Columbus, Ohio 43210

Crystal L. Park
Self-Disclosure
  Department of Psychology
  Miami University
  Oxford, Ohio 45056

Monisha Pasupathi
Emotion and Aging
  Center for Lifespan Psychology
  Max Planck Institute for Human Development
  14195 Berlin, Germany

Letitia Anne Peplau
Loneliness
  Department of Psychology
  University of California, Los Angeles
  Los Angeles, California 90095

Daniel Perlman
Loneliness
  School of Family and Nutritional Sciences
  University of British Columbia
  Vancouver, British Columbia, Canada V6T 1Z1

Paula R. Pietromonaco
Attachment
  Department of Psychology
  University of Massachusetts
  Amherst, Massachusetts 01003

David Pilgrim
Societal Influences on Mental Health
Consultant Clinical Psychologist
CommuniCare National Health Service Trust
Queen's Park Hospital
Blackburn, Lancashire BB2 3HH
United Kingdom

Janet Polivy
Dieting
Department of Psychology
University of Toronto
Toronto, Ontario, Canada M5S 1A1

F. Clark Power
Moral Development
Program for Liberal Studies
University of Notre Dame
Notre Dame, Indiana 46556

Dennis Pusch
Psychopathology
Department of Psychology
University of Calgary
Calgary, Alberta, Canada T2N 1N4

Heather E. Quick
Retirement
Department of Human Development
Cornell University
Ithaca, New York 14853

Richard L. Rapson
Love and Intimacy
Department of History
University of Hawaii, Manoa
Honolulu, Hawaii 96822

Tracey A. Revenson
Women's Health
Psychology Program/Social-Personality
The Graduate School and University Center of the
City University of New York
New York, New York 10036

Ruth Richards
Creativity, Everyday
Saybrook Institute, San Francisco
and Department of Psychiatry
University of California, San Francisco
San Francisco, California 94133

Ronald E. Riggio
Charisma
Department of Psychology
Kravis Leadership Institute
Claremont McKenna College
Claremont, California 91711

Thomas Robbins
Brainwashing and Totalitarian Influence
Santa Barbara Center for Humanistic Studies
Santa Barbara, California 93190

Laura Weiss Roberts
Premenstrual Syndrome Treatment Interventions
Department of Psychiatry
University of New Mexico
School of Medicine
Albuquerque, New Mexico 87131

Lucy Robin
Attachment
Department of Psychology
Indiana University
Bloomington, Indiana 47405

Carie Rodgers
Gender Identity
Department of Psychology
University of Oregon
and Oregon Social Learning Center
Eugene, Oregon 97403

Mario S. Rodriguez
Social Support
Department of Medicine
Allegheny University of the Health Sciences
Philadelphia, Pennsylvania 19102

Scott C. Roesch
Cooperation, Competition, and Individualism
Department of Psychology
University of California, Los Angeles
Los Angeles, California 90095

Anne Rogers
Societal Influences on Mental Health
National Primary Care Research and Development Centre
Manchester University
Manchester M13 9PT
United Kingdom

Robert Rosenthal
Nonverbal Communication
Department of Psychology
Harvard University
Cambridge, Massachusetts 02138

Ralph L. Rosnow
Ethics and Mental Health Research
Department of Psychology
Temple University
Philadelphia, Pennsylvania 19122

Carol D. Ryff
Middle Age and Well-Being
Institute on Aging and Adult Life
University of Wisconsin, Madison
Madison, Wisconsin 53706

Donald H. Saklofske
Intelligence and Mental Health
Department of Educational Psychology
University of Saskatchewan
Saskatoon, Saskatchewan, Canada S7N 0W0

Kristen Salomon
Reactivity
University of Pittsburgh
Pittsburgh, Pennsylvania 15260

Theodore R. Sarbin
*Classifying Mental Disorders:
Nontraditional Approaches*
University of California, Santa Cruz
Santa Cruz, California 95064

Alan F. Schatzberg
Mood Disorders
Department of Psychiatry and Behavioral Sciences
Stanford University School of Medicine
Stanford, California 94305

Michael F. Scheier
Optimism, Motivation, and Mental Health
Carnegie Mellon University
Pittsburgh, Pennsylvania 15213

Christine Scher
Depression
San Diego State University/
University of California, San Diego, Joint Doc-
toral Program in Clinical Psychology
San Diego, California 92120

Jason Schiffman
Schizophrenia
Department of Psychology
Emory University
Atlanta, Georgia 30322

David Schultz
Emotions and Mental Health
Department of Psychology
University of Delaware
Newark, Delaware 19716

Miriam W. Schustack
Human–Computer Interaction
Department of Psychology
California State University, San Marcos
San Marcos, California 92096

Henk A. W. Schut
Bereavement
Department of Clinical and Health Psychology
Utrecht University
3508 TC Utrecht, The Netherlands

Anthony Scioli
Emotion and Cognition
Department of Psychology
Keene State College
Keene, New Hampshire 03431

Diane Scott-Jones
Ethics and Mental Health Research
Department of Psychology
Temple University
Philadelphia, Pennsylvania 19122

Edward Seidman
Community Mental Health
Department of Psychology
New York University
New York, New York 10003

Sally K. Severino
Premenstrual Syndrome Treatment Interventions
Department of Psychiatry
University of New Mexico School of Medicine
Albuquerque, New Mexico 87131

Marybeth Shinn
Homelessness
Department of Psychology
New York University
New York, New York 10003

Raul Silva
Catecholamines and Behavior
Millhauser Laboratories
New York University Medical Center
New York, New York 10016

Dean Keith Simonton
Creativity and Genius
Department of Psychology
University of California, Davis
Davis, California 95616

Burton Singer
Middle Age and Well-Being
Office of Population Research
Princeton University
Princeton, New Jersey 08544

Dorothy G. Singer
Television Viewing
Department of Psychology
Yale University
New Haven, Connecticut 06520

Jerome L. Singer
Television Viewing
Department of Psychology
Yale University
New Haven, Connecticut 06520

Judith R. Smith
Poverty and Mental Health
Graduate School of Social Sciences
Fordham University
Bronx, New York 10458

John Snarey
Fathers
Emory University
Atlanta, Georgia 30322

C. R. Snyder
Hope
Department of Psychology
University of Kansas
Lawrence, Kansas 66045

Mark Snyder
Self-Fulfilling Prophecies
University of Minnesota
Minneapolis, Minnesota 55455

Glen D. Solomon
Headache
Department of General Internal Medicine
The Cleveland Clinic Foundation
Cleveland, Ohio 44195

H. Brent Solvason
Mood Disorders
Department of Psychiatry and Behavioral Sciences
Stanford University School of Medicine
Stanford, California 94305

Stacie M. Spencer
Optimism, Motivation, and Mental Health
University of Pittsburgh
Pittsburgh, Pennsylvania 15260

Len Sperry
Organizational and Occupational Psychiatry
Department of Psychiatry and Behavioral
Medicine
Medical College of Wisconsin
Milwaukee, Wisconsin 53226

B. Glenn Stanley
Eating and Body Weight: Physiological Controls
Departments of Psychology and Neuroscience
University of California, Riverside
Riverside, California 92521

Annette L. Stanton
Infertility
Department of Psychology
University of Kansas
Lawrence, Kansas 66045

Raymond H. Starr, Jr.
Child Maltreatment
Department of Psychology
University of Maryland Baltimore County
Baltimore, Maryland 21250

Ursula M. Staudinger
Wisdom
Max Planck Institute for Human Development
14195 Berlin, Germany

Gail Steketee
Obsessive–Compulsive Disorder
Boston University
Boston, Massachusetts 02215

James A. Stephenson
Information Processing and Clinical Psychology
Center for Psychiatric Rehabilitation
University of Chicago
Tinley Park, Illinois 60477

Alan E. Stewart
Constructivist Psychotherapies
Department of Psychology
University of Florida
Gainesville, Florida 32611

William B. Stiles
Self-Disclosure
Department of Psychology
Miami University
Oxford, Ohio 45056

Margaret S. Stroebe
Bereavement
Department of Clinical and Health Psychology
Utrecht University
3508 TC Utrecht, The Netherlands

Wolfgang Stroebe
Bereavement
Department of Clinical and Health Psychology
Utrecht University
3508 TC Utrecht, The Netherlands

Arthur Stukas
Self-Fulfilling Prophecies
University of Pittsburgh Medical Center
Pittsburgh, Pennsylvania 15213

Kieran T. Sullivan
Couples Therapy
Department of Psychology
Santa Clara University
Santa Clara, California 95053

Jerry Suls
Type A–Type B Personalities
Department of Psychology
University of Iowa
Iowa City, Iowa 52242

Annette Swain
Type A–Type B Personalities
Department of Psychology
University of Iowa
Iowa City, Iowa 52242

Thomas S. Szasz
Myth of Mental Illness
Department of Psychiatry
State University of New York Health Science
Center, Syracuse
Syracuse, New York 13210

Joseph S. Takahashi
Body Rhythms/Body Clocks
Department of Neurology and Physiology
NSF Center for Biological Timing
Howard Hughes Medical Institute
Northwestern University
Evanston, Illinois 60208

David Takeuchi
Ethnicity and Mental Health
Department of Psychology
University of California, Los Angeles
Los Angeles, California 90095

Shelley E. Taylor
Positive Illusions
Department of Psychology
University of California, Los Angeles
Los Angeles, California 90095

Lydia R. Temoshok
HIV/AIDS
Division of Mental Health
World Health Organization
CH1211 Geneva 27, Switzerland
and presently with the Department of Psychiatry
and Neurosciences
Uniformed Services University of the Health
Sciences
Bethesda, Maryland 20814

Ross A. Thompson
Legal Dimensions of Mental Health
Department of Psychology
University of Nebraska
Lincoln, Nebraska 68588

Geoffrey L. Thorpe
Agoraphobia
Department of Psychology
University of Maine, Orono
Orono, Maine 04469

Jenny S. Törnqvist
Deception
Department of Psychology
University of Virginia
Charlottesville, Virginia 22903

Alfonso Troisi
Evolution and Mental Health
University of Rome Tor Vergata
00199 Rome, Italy

Jeanne Tsai
Emotion and Aging
University of California, Berkeley
Berkeley, California 94720

Dennis C. Turk
Pain
Department of Anesthesiology
University of Washington School of Medicine
Seattle, Washington 98195

Susan Turk-Charles
Emotion and Aging
University of Southern California
Los Angeles, California 90089

Jan van den Bout
Bereavement
Department of Clinical and Health Psychology
Utrecht University
3508 TC Utrecht, The Netherlands

Elizabeth A. Vandewater
Extended Family Relationships
Institute of Social Research
University of Michigan, Ann Arbor
Ann Arbor, Michigan 48109

Judy L. Van Raalte
Sport and Mental Status
Department of Psychology
Springfield College
Springfield, Massachusetts 01109

Pathik D. Wadhwa
Prenatal Stress and Life-Span Development
Department of Behavioral Science
University of Kentucky College of Medicine
Lexington, Kentucky 40536

Elaine F. Walker
Schizophrenia
Department of Psychology
Emory University
Atlanta, Georgia 30322

Lynn Waterhouse
Autism and Pervasive Developmental Disorders
Child Behavior Studies
The College of New Jersey
Ewing, New Jersey 08628

Linda E. Weinberger
Mental Institutions: Legal Issues and Commitments
University of Southern California
Los Angeles, California 90033

Marjorie E. Weishaar
Cognitive Therapy
Department of Psychiatry and Human Behavior
Brown University School of Medicine
Providence, Rhode Island 02912

Beth C. Weitzman
Homelessness
Department of Psychology
New York University
New York, New York 10003

Barry Wellman
Social Networks
Department of Sociology
University of Toronto
Toronto, Ontario, Canada M5S 2G8

Ian Q. Whishaw
Brain
Department of Psychology
University of Lethbridge
Lethbridge, Alberta, Canada T1K 3M4

Robert A. Wicklund
Self-Esteem
Department of Psychology
University of Bielefeld
33615 Bielefeld, Germany

Thomas Ashby Wills
Substance Abuse
Ferkauf Graduate School of Psychology
and Department of Epidemiology and Social
Medicine
Albert Einstein College of Medicine
Yeshiva University
Bronx, New York 10461

Lisa D. Wilsbacher
Body Rhythms/Body Clocks
Department of Neurology and Physiology
NSF Center for Biological Timing
Howard Hughes Medical Institute
Northwestern University
Evanston, Illinois 60208

Mariusz Wirga
Behavior Therapy
Las Vegas Medical Center
Las Vegas, New Mexico 87701

Daniel Wolverton
Antisocial Personality Disorder
Department of Psychology
University of Louisville
Louisville, Kentucky 40292

John L. Woodard
Dementia
Memory Assessment Clinic and
Alzheimer's Disease Program
Georgia State University
Atlanta, Georgia 30303

Camille B. Wortman
Grief and Loss
Department of Psychology
State University of New York, Stony Brook
Stony Brook, New York 11794

Moshe Zeidner
Intelligence and Mental Health
School of Education
University of Haifa
Mt. Carmel, Haifa 31905, Israel

Shanyang Zhao
Epidemiology: Psychiatric
Department of Sociology
Temple University
Philadelphia, Pennsylvania 19122

Dolf Zillmann
Anger
College of Communication and Psychology
University of Alabama
Tuscaloosa, Alabama 35487

Philip Zimbardo
Shyness
Department of Psychology
Stanford University
Stanford, California 94305

Index

Volume numbers are boldfaced, separated from the first page reference with a colon.
Subsequent references to the same volume are separated by commas.

A

Abnormality
  brain, in schizophrenia, **3**:404
  mental, emphasis of mental health professionals, **3**:550–551
  neuroendocrine, in mood disorders, **2**:727
  personality, evolutionary model, **3**:118–125
Abortion
  adjustment to, optimism effects, **3**:47
  in case of maternal HIV, **2**:390
  correlation with sex guilt, **2**:306
  spontaneous, **3**:266–267
Abortive medication, headache, **2**:348–349
Absent grief, **1**:238
Absorption
  hypnosis correlate, **2**:470
  physiology, **2**:61
  self, psychosocial stage outcome, **3**:37–38
Abuse, *see also* Domestic violence; *specific forms*
  biofeedback, as clinical issue, **1**:253–254
  intergenerational transmission, **1**:425
  woman, **2**:1–16
Abusive exercise, elevated anxiety, **3**:185–186
Academic achievement, protective factor for substance abuse, **3**:615
Academic procrastination, **3**:282
Acceptance
  dying stage, **2**:51
  as hospice code, **2**:57
  realistic, **1**:212; **3**:207–208
Accessibility, *see also* Availability

appropriate care, by ethnic minorities, **2**:170–171
  mental health care, **2**:658
  urban programs, **3**:686–687
Accidents, on-job, and circadian status, **1**:280
Accommodation
  and modification, polarity, **3**:120–122
  phase of grief, **2**:292–293
Accountability, in family systems theory, **2**:207–208
Acculturation, effect on extended family, **2**:199
Acetylcholine, in neurotrophin release, **1**:312–314
Acetylcholine-releasing neurons, **1**:315
ACh, *see* Acetylcholine
Achievement
  academic, protective factor for substance abuse, **3**:615
  changes during adolescence, **1**:7
  motivation
    and gender identity, **2**:272
    managing childhood stress, **1**:417–418
    in relation to intelligence, **2**:524–525
Achievement goals, **2**:539–542
Acquiescence
  vs. irresistible impulses, **2**:484–485
  temporary, in anger control, **1**:107
Acquired immune deficiency syndrome, *see* AIDS
Activation paradox, REM sleep, **2**:20–22
Activation–synthesis model, **2**:21–22
Active consideration, stage in gambling therapy, **2**:255
Active engagement, relationship-focused coping, **1**:592
Active Gene–Environment Correlation, **2**:286
Activities
  in forensic mental institutions, **2**:688
  physical, *see* Physical activity

G

Isolation
    psychosocial stage outcome, 3:37
    social, suicide predictor, 3:630

J

Jackson *vs.* Indiana (1972), 2:682–683
Jarvis study, psychiatric epidemiology, 2:128
Jealousy, delusional, 3:84
Job
    burnout related to, 1:348–351
    insecurity and strain, 3:678
    parenting, 3:102–103
    satisfaction
        family childcare provider, 1:403–404
        hardiness training effect, 2:332–333
    stress related to, 2:437
    traditional indicator of socioeconomic status, 3:556
Jobs Project, primary prevention strategy, 1:516
Joint custody, child, 1:656
    physical and legal, 1:660–661
Judgments, *see also* Value judgments
    body size, 1:258–259
    clinical, bias, 2:164–165
    diagnostic, 3:329
    emotions as, 2:106
    global, subjective well-being, 2:320
    moral
        by child, 2:734–735
        interview, 2:737
        and moral action, 2:740–741
Jurisprudence, therapeutic, 2:553
Just community approach, moral education strategy, 2:742

K

Kant, contribution to constructivism, 1:549
Kappa, in calculation of inter-rater reliability, 2:37–38
Kernberg, structural organization of character types, 3:113–114
Kids' Club, for children of battered women, 2:11–12
Kindling phenomenon, epileptogenic seizure focus, 2:141
Kinship
    as self-disclosure context, 3:413
    and social networks, 3:528–529
    supportive power, 3:531
Kleitman, dream study, 2:19
Knowledge
    associated with wisdom, 3:703–704
    child development, as parenting tool, 3:106

from core to noncore domains, 1:496–497
    developmental norms in adolescence, 1:10
    ethnic, by mental health professionals, 3:353–354
    gathering, behavior motivated by, 3:445–446
    labeling, and children's play behavior, 2:271
Kohlberg's theory
    levels and stages of moral development, 2:737–738
    moral domain, 2:736–737
    moral judgment interview, 2:737
    reliability and validity, 2:738–739
Korsakoff's psychosis, 1:709
Korsakoff's syndrome, experimental study, 1:84
Korzybski, contribution to constructivism, 1:549

L

Labeling theory, and emergence of deviant role, 3:548
Labels
    ADHD, 1:180
    consequences, 2:181
    diagnostic, assigning, 2:30
    gender, learning, 2:270–271
    psychiatric, role in assessment, 1:480–481
    reflecting gender bias in DSM, 2:258
    stereotypical, and self-fulfilling prophecy, 3:447
Laboratory
    biofeedback
        components and establishing, 1:249–250
        safety considerations, 1:250
    emotional responding in, 2:93–94
Laboratory procedures, personality assessment, 3:130
Laboratory studies
    skill at deceiving, 1:682
    television violence, 3:658
Lacunar state, clinical features and treatment, 1:700
Language
    autistic child, 1:186
    barrier to clinical assessment, 2:166
    cerebral organization, 1:303
    and constructivist epistemology, 1:549
    deficit in Alzheimer's disease, 1:76
    developmental effects of day care, 1:670–671
    disturbance, modality-specific, 1:142
    limbic, 2:564–565
    origin of term homosexual, 2:404
    PET studies, 1:326–327
    and reality, 1:551
    representation in brain, 1:139
    sex differences, 2:566
Language disorders, written, 1:142–146
Lateral preference differences, in theory of homosexuality, 2:414

M

P

Validity (*continued*)
    mental health assessment
        instruments, 2:697–698
        in older adults, 1:149–151
    personality assessment methods, 3:130–131
    self-esteem, 3:434–437
    self-report Type A measures, 3:667
Value judgments
    accompanying concept of disease, 1:467–468
    sexual deviation, 3:474–475
Values
    changing, as strategy, 1:471
    connected to extended family, 2:194
    family
        assessing, 2:223
        and women's roles, 2:199–200
    person, destroyed by dying process, 2:48–50
    social, individual and group differences, 1:574–575
    in theory of subjective well-being, 2:317–318
Variability
    behavioral genetic, 1:193–194, 201–202
    individual, and mental health, 2:177–179
    in normal menstrual cycle, 3:253–254
    schizophrenic symptoms among patients, 3:401
Variety, in family systems theory, 2:208
Vascular disease, peripheral, relaxation response training, 2:627
Vascular headache, 2:338
Vasculitis, associated dementia, 1:701
V-chip, installed in televisions after 1996, 3:651, 661
VCR, programming, 2:434
Verbal flow, covert, in anger, 1:96–97
Verbal skills, protective factor for substance abuse, 3:614
Vertical transmission, HIV, 2:382–383
Vicarious learning, 3:161
Victimization, among homosexuals, 2:406–407
Victimless crimes, 1:635–636
Victims, *see also* PLWHA
    child sexual abuse, 1:436
        treatment, 1:442–444
    crime, reports from, 1:639
    rape
        blaming, 3:360
        self-blame, 3:364
        unacknowledged, 3:365
    trauma
        acute reactions, 3:210
        mental health problems, 3:547
Vigilance
    ethological concept, 1:470
    visual and auditory, caffeine effects, 1:363–364
Violence
    averting, 1:108

cultic mass suicides, 1:344–345
domestic, intervention, 2:1–16
in media, limiting, 1:544–545
prone to snowballing, 2:486–487
in psychiatric hospital, 1:25
rape, 3:361, 363–364
television
    research, 3:658–659
    theories of aggression, 3:656–658
urban, intervention and prevention, 3:684–685
against women, as health problem, 3:716–717
Viral infection
    dementia due to, 1:701–703
    in etiology of schizophrenia, 3:406
Visual cortex, neuronal development, 1:310–311
Vitamin B_1 deficiency
    dementia due to, 1:708–709
    and diencephalic amnesia, 1:84
Vitamin B_{12} deficiency, dementia due to, 1:709
Vitamin deficiencies, dementia due to, 1:708–709
Vocabulary, television effects, 3:653
Vocalization, mother–infant, 2:565
Voice
    communication channel, 2:777
    self-healing person, 3:456
    tone, in health care setting, 2:781
Volatility, cult group and members, 1:344–345
Voluntary control, biofeedback theory, 1:249
Voluntary informed consent, 2:155–156
Vomiting, self-induced, 1:115
Voyeurism, psychiatric diagnosis, 3:479
Vulnerability
    homeless, 2:394, 397
    in PTSD, 3:212
    selective temporal, 1:282–284
    special populations, to HIV infection, 2:387–388
    stress in childhood, predicting factors, 1:413–414
Vygotsky
    sociocultural theory of childhood stress, 1:412–413
    theory of play, 2:191

W

Wakefulness, ultradian rhythms, 3:515–516
Watson, radical behaviorism, 1:224–225
Weight, *see also* Birth weight
    cultural pressures, 1:263–264
    false feedback, 1:745
    physiological controls, 2:59–75
    preoccupation, 1:747–748
    reasonable, obesity treatment approach, 3:8

Z